MCSE TestPrep

Core Exams

Que®

MCSE TestPrep: Core Exams

By Jay Adamson, Michael W. Barry, Robert Bogue, Joe Casad, Hilary Contino, Robert J. Cooper III, Emmett Dulaney, Mark D. Hall, Howard F. Hilliker, Brian Komar, William N. Matsoukas, Ron Milione, Robert Oliver, Joseph Phillips, Luther Stanton, Kristin Wahlquist, Christoph Wille, Kevin Wolford, and David Yarashus

Published by:
New Riders Publishing
201 West 103rd Street
Indianapolis, IN 46290 USA

Printed in the United States of America 1 2 3 4 5 6 7 8 9 0

Library of Congress Cataloging-in-Publication Data

CIP data available upon request

ISBN: 1-56205-831-2

Warning and Disclaimer

This book is designed to provide information about the **Windows NT Server 4**, **Windows NT Server 4 Enterprise**, **Windows NT Workstation 4**, and **Networking Essentials** Microsoft Certified Professional Exams. Every effort has been made to make this book as complete and as accurate as possible, but no warranty or fitness is implied.

The information is provided on an "as is" basis. The authors and Que Corporation shall have neither liability nor responsibility to any person or entity with respect to any loss or damages arising from the information contained in this book or from the use of the discs or programs that may accompany it.

Que Corporation is an independent entity from Microsoft Corporation, and not affiliated with Microsoft Corporation in any manner. This publication may be used in assisting students to prepare for a Microsoft Certified Professional Exam. Neither Microsoft Corporation, its designated review company, nor Que Corporation warrants that use of this publication will ensure passing the relevant Exam. Microsoft is either a registered trademark or trademark of Microsoft Corporation in the United States and/or other countries.

Publisher *David Dwyer*
Executive Editor *Mary Foote*
Managing Editor *Sarah Kearns*

Acquisitions Editors
Danielle Bird, Nancy Maragioglio

Development Editors
Danielle Bird, Kezia Endsley

Project Editors
Amy Bezek, Gina Brown,
Tom Dinse, Brad Herriman,
Christopher Morris

Copy Editors
Amy Bezek, Audra McFarland,
Julie McNamee, Tom Stevens,
Molly Warnes

Technical Editors
Dave Bixler, Brian Komar,
Bob Reinsch, Christoph Wille

Team Coordinator
Stacey Beheler

Manufacturing Coordinator
Brook Farling

Book Designer
Glenn Larsen

Cover Designer
Dan Armstrong

Cover Production
Casey Price

Director of Production
Larry Klein

Production Manager
Laurie Casey

Production Team Supervisor
Vic Peterson

Graphics Conversion Technitions
Steve Adams, Sadie Crawford
Wil Cruz, Tammy Graham
Oliver Jackson

Production Analysts
Dan Harris, Erich J. Richter

Production Team
Kim Cofer, Daniela Raderstorf

About the Authors

Jay Adamson is a senior network analyst for a multinational computer consulting firm. He has been teaching in the computer industry for the past eight years, and has been specializing in Microsoft networking for the past four years. His certifications include MCSE for both Windows NT 3.51 and 4.0 and MCT. He greatly appreciates the support and understanding of his wife Sherri and two sons Matthew and Devon. He can be reached at `jaysher@autobahn.mb.ca`.

Michael W. Barry has 16 years of programming experience. Upon receiving a BSEE from the University of Texas at Austin, Mike went to work for Datapoint Corporation where he was involved in networking and desktop video conferencing. Mike holds numerous patents ranging from video teleconferencing to color-image processing to cluster printing. He has been involved in NT Kernel and User mode programming since the Windows NT 3.1 beta and is considered an expert on the Windows NT operating system. Currently, Mike is Vice President of Development at T/R Systems, Inc. (the inventors of cluster printing), where he and his group are pioneering cluster printing systems based on Windows NT.

Mike lives in Atlanta, Georgia, with his wife and two children. In his free time, he enjoys scuba diving, tennis, camping, water skiing, and knee boarding.

Robert L. Bogue, MCSE, CNA, A+, owns Thor Projects, a consulting company located in Indianapolis, IN. He's also a Microsoft Certified Systems Engineer, Novell Certified NetWare administrator, and certified A+ service technician. In his work at Thor Projects he specializes in solving the networking and integration needs of small-to-medium size organizations. Rob has been involved in over 50 book projects on topics ranging from Visual Basic to Windows NT to NetWare to Microsoft Office. He can be reached at `Rob.Bogue@ThorProjects.com` or (317) 844-5310.

Joe Casad is a freelance writer and editor who specializes in programming and networking topics. He was the managing editor of the short-lived but well-received *Network Administrator Magazine*, a journal of practical solutions for network professionals. Casad received a B.S. in engineering from the University of Kansas in 1980 and, before becoming a full-time writer and editor, spent ten years in the computer-intensive areas of the structural engineering profession. He now lives in Lawrence, Kansas, with wife Barb Dineen and a pair of pint-sized hackers named Xander and Mattie. Look for his recently published books, *MCSE Training Guide: Windows NT Server 4* and *MCSE Training Guide: Networking Essentials*, by New Riders Publishing.

Hilary Contino graduated from the University of North Alabama in May of 1991 with a B.S. degree in Computer Information Systems and Marketing. After graduation, she worked for Intergraph Corporation in Huntsville, Alabama as a systems administrator. During her time at Intergraph, she began working with the NT operating system, using versions as far back as the first Beta release. In late 1994, she became an NT LAN Administrator for Prudential HealthCare in Atlanta, GA, where she is currently responsible for NT Administration, Remote LAN Access, and advanced desktop support for approximately 800 users. In June of 1997, she obtained MCSE certification in the NT 3.51 and NT 4.0 tracks.

Robert J. Cooper III is a networking consultant with Interim Technology in Minneapolis, Minnesota. His specialities include network engineering and architecture, including remote, WAN, and Internet connectivity. He started working with PCs and operating systems in the 1980s when, dissatisfied with the configuration of his newly purchased expensive PC, he promptly disassembled and reassembled it more to his liking. He has worked at length with most of the desktop and network operating systems currently available, and now devotes most of his energy to Windows NT, including its versatile Internet connectivity and ability to interconnect with a variety of other operating systems and platforms.

Rob is following in the family footsteps as his father helped build the precursor to today's Internet in the late 1960s. Rob lives in Minneapolis with his wife, two cats, and, of course, a cross-platform interconnected multisegmented and subnetted LAN.

Emmett Dulaney is an MCSE and MCPS, as well as CNE, CNA, and LAN Server Engineer. A trainer for a national training company, Emmett is also a consultant for D S Technical Solutions in Anderson, Indiana. He can be reached at `edulaney@iquest.net`.

Mark Hall is a Novell CNE and a computer consultant with a Masters degree in Computer Science Education. He has co-authored two previous titles, PC Magazine's *Webmasters Ultimate Resource Guide* and New Rider's *Inside Windows NT 4.0 Ras*. He has also performed technical edits on 52 other computer titles in the last 7 years.

Howard F. Hilliker built his first computer in the late 70s. His major source of influence came from his father, whose career in electrical engineering, communications, and defense work challenged his engineering mind. He has been involved in the microcomputer industry since its infancy. He holds over 70 certifications with major vendors including Microsoft, IBM, Hewlett-Packard, Epson, Zenith, NEC, and Okidata, and has been involved as a Microsoft Certified Professional since the program's infancy (LAN Manager 2.0). He has nearly a decade of network and hardware field experience and holds key networking credentials, including Compaq ASE and Hewlett-Packard Network Professional. Howard has done technical editing and illustration work on several occasions in the past. He has taught classes on Microsoft Windows and Microsoft networking products. His experience includes advanced topics such as SNA Server and SQL Server. Howards also enjoys the benefits associated in being an experienced Pascal, C++, and Foxpro developer. He has been involved with several key Microsoft BETA programs. Howard also holds an amateur radio license and is an active member of the Network Professional Association. He lives with his charming wife and two beautiful young daughters.

Brian Komar is a trainer and consultant with Online Business Systems. He holds a Bachelor of Commerce degree and several professional designations, including Microsoft Certified Trainer (MCT), Fellow Life Management Institute (FLMI), and Microsoft Certified Systems Engineer (MCSE). Brian's six years of experience in the Information Technology industry is supported by strong business skills and a background in accounting and actuarial services. Online Business Systems is a consulting firm with offices in Winnipeg, Minneapolis, and Calgary. Online develops complete, practical computer solutions. Brian can be reached by e-mail at `bkomar@online-can.com`.

Bill Matsoukas is a Certified NetWare Engineer, and works as a Senior Consultant for an international firm. Bill makes his home in Colorado with his wife Teri and their three children. Living in Colorado affords Bill and his family to concentrate on the more important things in life: bicycling, hiking, mountain climbing, and hockey.

Ron Milione is Chief of Technology at Integrated Systems Group in Hauppauge, New York. He is a Microsoft Solution Provider Partner and earned his B.S. and M.S. in Electrical Engineering from City College of New York. He holds the following certifications: MCSE, MCT, Master CNE, CNE, CNP (Certified Network Professional), Compaq ASE in Windows NT and Novell NetWare, and a Commerical License (GROL) from the Federal Commications Commission.

Robert Oliver is the head network administrator for the Columbus State University software engineering program in Columbus, Georgia, which won one of five world-wide awards from Microsoft for innovative uses of new technology. He is an MCP in Windows NT Workstation and Server, and a Win32 software engineer focusing on Internet applications using Visual C++. Visual Basic, and Active Server Page development.

Joseph Phillips, an independent Microsoft Certified Trainer, has been teaching computer science for the past five years. He attended the writing program at Columbia College, Chicago where he later taught computer education. Currently, he resides in Indianapolis, Indiana.

Luther E. Stanton, MCPS, is currently employed by Nextel Communications. Additionally, he and his wife own WebWorks Southeast, a Web Presence Provider assisting small- to medium-size businesses in establishing an Internet presence. He holds Microsoft Certified Product Specialist certifications in Windows NT Workstation 4.0 and Windows NT Server 4.0.

Prior to joining Nextel, Mr. Stanton spent four years in the United States Army as a Signal Corp officer, serving in Honduras, Central America, Kuwait and Fort Stewart, Georgia. After leaving the Army, he and his wife Heidi relocated to Locust Grove, Georgia, where he briefly worked for a management-consulting firm before joining Nextel. He has over 10 years of systems and programming experience.

He holds a B.S. in Electrical Engineering from Lehigh University. He can be reached through email at `LStanton@wwse.net`.

Kristin Wahlquist a CNA, MCSE, and MCT has spent close to six years as a senior technical support professional at WordPerfect and Novell. She has consulted and assisted in network and applications installations for various clients throughout the country. Currently Kristin is an instructor with GSE Erudite Software based in Phoenix, Arizona. Kristin teaches core NT and several back office courses on the MSCE track.

Christoph Wille, an MCSE and MCSD, has an extensive background working with OLE, MFC, Microsoft SQL Server, Microsoft operating systems, and Access. He is currently developing web sites with integrated e-commerce as well as working as a consultant for companies that want to connect their private networks to the Internet and who need someone to design their Internet presence.

Kevin B. Wolford is an MCSE, MCT, Master CNE, and CNI. He has had several careers, including technical writer, pension actuary, and trainer. He is the lead Windows NT trainer for GSE Erudite Software in Salt Lake City, Utah. You also can see Kevin in training videos produced by Keystone Learning Systems of Provo, Utah. Kevin enjoys explaining complex, technical things in a simple manner.

David Yarashus is a Senior Network Engineer with TimeBridge Technologies in Landover, Maryland. He specializes in designing, managing, and troubleshooting large, multiprotocol internetworks. Mr. Yarashus has contributed to several books and magazine articles, has been a featured speaker at the Network Analysis Forum's annual meeting, and is a member of Novell's Master CNE Advisory Council. His major industry certifications include Cisco Certified Internetwork Expert (CCIE), Microsoft Certified Systems Engineer (MCSE), Novell Master CNE, and Certified Network Expert (CNX).

About the Technical Editor

Bob Reinsch is an independent contractor, providing services as a Microsoft Certified Systems Engineer and Microsoft Certified Trainer. He has been working on personal computers and networks for almost 20 years, dating back to Commodore Pets with 16 KB of RAM. In his career, he has served as a network administrator on UNIX, Macintosh, Novell, and Windows NT networks. He has been working with Windows NT since 3.1 and has pursued certification since NT 3.5. He has been a trainer since 1994 and has worked with students from Boeing, Chase Manhattan Banks, John Hancock Companies, Cinergy, and the Department of Defense. He has taught classes from Portland, Oregon to Wiesbaden, Germany.

Bob is husband to Dr. Lisa Friis, PhD, and father to Bonnie Reinsch, a beautiful baby girl who learned to whistle when she was eight months old.

Trademark Acknowledgments

Contents at a Glance

Table of Contents

11 Monitoring and Optimization .. 531

Part Three: Windows NT Workstation 4 711

18 Monitoring and Optimization 939

21 Planning 1133

Introduction

The *MCSE TestPrep* series serves as a study aid for people preparing for Microsoft certification exams. The series is intended to help reinforce and clarify information with which the student is already familiar by providing sample questions and tests, as well as summary information relevant to each of the exam objectives. This series is not intended to be the only source for student preparation, but rather a review of information with a set of practice tests—used to increase the student's familiarity with the exam questions and thus increase the student's likelihood of success when taking the exam.

Who Should Read This Book

MCSE TestPrep: Core Exams is specifically intended to help students prepare for Microsoft's core tests in the MCSE program for the Windows NT 4 track. It includes coverage of the Windows NT Server 4.0 Exam (#70-067), the Windows NT Server 4.0 Enterprise Exam (#70-068), the Windows NT Workstation 4.0 Exam (#70-073), and the Networking Essentials Exam (#70-058).

How This Book Helps You

In addition to presenting a summary of information relevant to each of the exam objectives, this book provides a wealth of review questions similar to those you will encounter in the actual exam. This book is designed to help you make the most of your study time by presenting concise summaries of information you need to understand to succeed on the exams. The review questions at the end of each objective help reinforce what you have learned. The final exams at the conclusion of each chapter help you determine if you have mastered the facts. In addition, the book contains two full-length practice exams for each of the four exams.

How to Use This Book

You should use this book to make sure that you are ready to take the exam after you are somewhat familiar with the exam concepts. At that point, take the practice tests at the back of the book and see how well you really know your subject.

After you are doing well on the practice tests, you are ready to schedule your exam. Use this book for a final quick review just before taking any of the tests to make sure that all the important concepts are clear to you. See Appendix B for more information about taking the test.

What the Windows NT Server 4.0 Exam (#70-067) Covers

The Windows NT Server 4.0 Exam focuses on determining your skill in six major categories of implementing and supporting Windows NT Server. These categories (along with the chapters in this book that cover them) follow:

- Planning (Chapter 1)
- Installation and Configuration (Chapter 2)
- Managing Resources (Chapter 3)
- Connectivity (Chapter 4)
- Monitoring and Optimization (Chapter 5)
- Troubleshooting (Chapter 6)

The exam objectives, listed by topic area, are covered in the following sections.

Objectives for Planning

- Plan the disk drive configuration for various requirements. Requirements include choosing a file system and choosing a fault-tolerance method.
- Choose a protocol for various situations. Protocols include TCP/IP, NWLink IPX/SPX Compatible Transport, and NetBEUI.

Objectives for Installation and Configuration

- Install Windows NT Server on Intel-based platforms.
- Install Windows NT Server to perform various server roles. Server roles include primary domain controller (PDC), backup domain controller (BDC), and member server.
- Install Windows NT Server by using various methods. Installation methods include:
  - Using CD-ROM
  - Installing over-the-network
  - Using Network Client Administrator
  - Performing express versus custom
- Configure protocols and protocol bindings. Protocols include TCP/IP, NWLink IPX/SPX Compatible Transport, and NetBEUI.
- Configure network adapters. Considerations include changing IRQ, IO base, and memory addresses as well as configuring multiple adapters.
- Configure Windows NT Server core services. Services include Directory Replicator and License Manager.
- Configure peripherals and devices. Peripherals and devices include:
  - Communication devices
  - SCSI devices

    - Tape device drivers
    - UPS devices and UPS service
    - Mouse drivers, display drivers, and keyboard drivers

- Configure hard disks to meet various requirements. Requirements include:
    - Allocating disk space capacity
    - Providing redundancy
    - Improving performance
    - Providing security
    - Formatting

- Configure printers. Tasks include adding and configuring a printer, implementing a printer pool, and setting print priorities.
- Configure a Windows NT Server computer for various types of client computers. Client computer types include Windows NT Workstation, Windows 95, and MS-DOS-based computers.

Objectives for Managing Resources

- Manage user and group accounts. Considerations include:
    - Managing Windows NT groups
    - Managing Windows NT user rights
    - Administering account policies
    - Auditing changes to the user account database

- Create and manage policies and profiles for various situations. Policies and profiles include local user profiles, roaming user profiles, and system policies.
- Administer remote servers from various types of client computers. Client computer types include Windows 95 and Windows NT Workstation.
- Manage disk resources. Tasks include:
    - Copying and moving files between file systems
    - Creating and sharing resources
    - Implementing permissions and security
    - Establishing file auditing

Objectives for Connectivity

- Configure Windows NT Server for interoperability with NetWare servers by using various tools. Tools include Gateway Service for NetWare and Migration Tool for NetWare.
- Install and configure Remote Access Service (RAS). Configuration options include:
    - Configuring RAS communications
    - Configuring RAS protocols

    - Configuring RAS security
    - Configuring dial-up networking clients

Objectives for Monitoring and Optimization

- Monitor performance of various functions by using Performance Monitor. Functions include processors, memory, disks, and networks.
- Identify performance bottlenecks.

Objectives for Troubleshooting

- Installation failures
- Boot failures
- Configuration errors
- Printer problems
- RAS problems
- Connectivity problems
- Resource access problems and permission problems
- Fault-tolerance failures. Fault-tolerance methods include:
    - Tape backup
    - Mirroring
    - Stripe set with parity
    - Disk duplexing

What the Windows NT Server 4.0 Enterprise Exam (#70-068) Covers

The Windows NT Server 4.0 Enterprise exam covers six main topic areas, arranged in accordance with test objectives. The exam objectives, listed by topic area, are covered in the following sections.

- Planning (Chapter 7)
- Installation and Configuration (Chapter 8)
- Managing Resources (Chapter 9)
- Connectivity (Chapter 10)
- Monitoring and Optimization (Chapter 11)
- Troubleshooting (Chapter 12)

Objectives for Planning

The exam topic areas and their respective objectives include the following:

- Plan the implementation of a directory services architecture. Considerations include:
    - Selecting the appropriate domain model
    - Supporting a single logon account
    - Allowing users to access resources in different domains
- Plan the disk drive configuration for various requirements. Requirements include choosing a fault-tolerance method.
- Choose a protocol for various situations. Protocols include:
    - TCP/IP
    - TCP/IP with DHCP and WINS
    - NWLink IPX/SPX Compatible Transport Protocol
    - Data Link Control (DLC)
    - AppleTalk

Objectives for Installation and Configuration

- Install Windows NT Server to perform various server roles. Server roles include:
    - Primary domain controller
    - Backup domain controller
    - Member server
- Configure protocols and protocol bindings. Protocols include:
    - TCP/IP
    - TCP/IP with DHCP and WINS
    - NWLink IPX/SPX Compatible Transport Protocol
    - DLC
    - AppleTalk
- Configure Windows NT Server core services. Services include:
    - Directory Replicator
    - Computer Browser
- Configure hard disks to meet various requirements. Requirements include:
    - Providing redundancy
    - Improving performance

- Configure printers. Tasks include:
    - Adding and configuring a printer
    - Implementing a printer pool
    - Setting print priorities
- Configure a Windows NT Server computer for various types of client computers. Client computer types include:
    - Windows NT Workstation
    - Windows 95
    - Macintosh

Objectives for Managing Resources

- Manage user and group accounts. Considerations include:
    - Managing Windows NT user accounts
    - Managing Windows NT user rights
    - Managing Windows NT groups
    - Administering account policies
    - Auditing changes to the user account database
- Create and manage policies and profiles for various situations. Policies and profiles include:
    - Local user profiles
    - Roaming user profiles
    - System policies
- Administer remote servers from various types of client computers. Client computer types include:
    - Windows 95
    - Windows NT Workstation
- Manage disk resources. Tasks include:
    - Creating and sharing resources
    - Implementing permissions and security
    - Establishing file auditing

Objectives for Connectivity

- Configure a Windows NT Server for interoperability with NetWare servers by using various tools. Tools include:
    - Gateway Services for NetWare
    - Migration Tool for NetWare

- Install and configure multiprotocol routing to serve various functions. Functions include:
  - Internet router
  - BOOTP/DHCP Relay Agent
  - IPX router
- Install and configure Internet Information Server.
- Install and configure Internet Information services. Services include:
  - World Wide Web
  - DNS
  - Intranet
- Install and configure Remote Access Service (RAS). Configuration options include:
  - Configuring RAS communications
  - Configuring RAS protocols
  - Configuring RAS security

Objectives for Monitoring and Optimization

- Establish a baseline for measuring system performance. Tasks include creating a database of measurement data.
- Monitor performance of various functions by using Performance Monitor. Functions include:
  - Processor
  - Memory
  - Disk
  - Network
- Monitor network traffic by using Network Monitor. Tasks include:
  - Collecting data
  - Presenting data
  - Filtering data
- Identify performance bottlenecks.
- Optimize performance for various results. Results include:
  - Controlling network traffic
  - Controlling server load

Objectives for Troubleshooting

- Choose the appropriate course of action to resolve installation failures.
- Choose the appropriate course of action to resolve boot failures.

- Choose the appropriate course of action to resolve configuration errors. Tasks include:
  - Backing up and restoring the Registry
  - Editing the Registry
- Choose the appropriate course of action to resolve RAS problems.
- Choose the appropriate course of action to resolve connectivity problems.
- Choose the appropriate course of action to resolve resource access and permission problems.
- Choose the appropriate course of action to resolve fault-tolerance failures. Fault-tolerance methods include:
  - Tape backup
  - Mirroring
  - Stripe set with parity
- Perform advanced problem resolution. Tasks include:
  - Diagnosing and interpreting a blue screen
  - Configuring a memory dump
  - Using the Event Log service

What the Windows NT Workstation 4.0 Exam (#70-073) Covers

The Windows NT Workstation 4.0 exam (#70-073) covers seven main topic areas, arranged in accordance with test objectives. The topics include:

- Planning (Chapter 13)
- Installation and Configuration (Chapter 14)
- Managing Resources (Chapter 15)
- Connectivity (Chapter 16)
- Running Applications (Chapter 17)
- Monitoring and Optimization (Chapter 18)
- Troubleshooting (Chapter 19)

The exam objectives, listed by topic area, are covered in the following sections.

Objectives for Planning

- Create unattended installation files.
- Plan strategies for sharing and securing resources.
- Choose the appropriate file systems to use in a given situation:
  - NTFS
  - FAT
  - HPFS

- Security
- Dual-boot systems

Objectives for Installation and Configuration

- Install Windows NT Workstation on an Intel platform in a given situation.
- Set up a dual-boot system in a given situation.
- Remove Windows NT Workstation in a given situation.
- Install, configure, and remove hardware components for a given situation. Hardware components include the following:
  - Network adapter drivers
  - SCSI device drivers
  - Tape device drivers
  - UPS
  - Multimedia devices
  - Display drivers
  - Keyboard drivers
  - Mouse drivers
- Use Control Panel applications to configure a Windows NT Workstation computer in a given situation.
- Upgrade to Windows NT Workstation 4.0 in a given situation.
- Configure server-based installation for wide-scale deployment in a given situation.

Objectives for Managing Resources

- Create and manage local user accounts and local group accounts to meet given requirements.
- Set up and modify user profiles.
- Set up shared folders and permissions.
- Set up permissions on NTFS partitions, folders, and files.
- Install and configure printers in a given environment.

Objectives for Connectivity

- Add and configure the network components of Windows NT Workstation.
- Use various methods of access network resources.
- Implement Windows NT Workstation as a client in a NetWare environment.
- Use various configurations to install Windows NT Workstation as a TCP/IP client.
- Configure and install dial-up networking in a given situation.
- Configure Microsoft Peer Web Services in a given situation.

Objectives for Running Applications

- Start applications on Intel and RISC platforms in various operating system environments.
- Start applications at various priorities.

Objectives for Monitoring and Optimization

- Monitor system performance by using various tools.
- Identify and resolve a given performance problem.
- Optimize system performance in various areas.

Objectives for Troubleshooting

- Choose the appropriate course of action to take when the boot process fails.
- Choose the appropriate course of action to take when a print job fails.
- Choose the appropriate course of action to take when the installation process fails.
- Choose the appropriate course of action to take when an application fails.
- Choose the appropriate course of action to take when a user cannot access a resource.
- Modify the Registry using the appropriate tool in a given situation.
- Implement advanced techniques to resolve various problems.

What the Networking Essentials Exam (#70-058) Covers

The Networking Essentials Exam focuses on determining your skill in four major categories of network-related skills. They are:

- Standards and Terminology (Chapter 20)
- Planning (Chapter 21)
- Implementation (Chapter 22)
- Troubleshooting (Chapter 23)

The specific objectives for these topics are described in the following sections.

Objectives for Standards and Terminology

- Define common networking terms for LANs and WANs.
- Compare a file-and-print server with an application server.
- Compare user-level security with access permissions assigned to a shared directory on a server.
- Compare a client/server network with a peer-to-peer network.
- Compare the implications of using connection-oriented communications with connectionless communications.
- Distinguish whether SLIP or PPP is used as the communications protocol for various situations.
- Define the communication devices that communicate at each level of the OSI model.

- Describe the characteristics and purpose of the media used in IEEE 802.3 and IEEE 802.5 standards.
- Explain the purpose of NDIS and Novell ODI network standards.

Objectives for Planning

- Select the appropriate media for various situations. Media choices include:
    - Coaxial cable
    - Twisted-pair cable
    - Fiber-optic cable
    - Wireless communications
- Select the appropriate topology for various Token Ring and Ethernet networks.
- Select the appropriate network and transport protocols for various Token Ring and Ethernet networks. Protocols include:
    - DLC
    - AppleTalk
    - IPX
    - TCP/IP
    - NFS
    - SMB
- Select the appropriate connectivity devices for various Token Ring and Ethernet networks. Connectivity devices include:
    - Repeaters
    - Bridges
    - Switches
    - Routers
    - Brouters
    - Gateways
- List the characteristics, requirements, and appropriate situations for WAN connection services. WAN connection services include:
    - T1
    - X.25
    - ISDN
    - Frame Relay
    - ATM

Objectives for Implementation

- Choose an administrative plan to meet specified needs, including performance management, account management, and security.
- Choose a disaster recovery plan.
- Given the manufacturer's documentation for the network adapter, install, configure, and resolve hardware conflicts for multiple network adapters in a Token Ring or Ethernet network.
- Implement a NetBIOS naming scheme for all computers on a given network.
- Select the appropriate hardware and software tools to monitor trends in the network.

Objectives for Troubleshooting

- Identify common errors associated with components required for communications.
- Diagnose and resolve common connectivity problems with cards, cables, and related hardware.
- Resolve broadcast storms.
- Identify and resolve network performance problems.

Hardware and Software Recommended for Preparation

MCSE TestPrep: Core Exams is meant to help you review concepts with which you already have training and experience. In order to make the most of the review, you need to have as much background and experience as possible. The best way to do this is to combine studying with working on real networks using the products on which you will be tested. This section gives you a description of the minimum computer requirements you need to build a good practice environment.

The minimum computer requirement to study everything on which you are tested is one or more workstations running Windows 95, Windows NT Workstation, and two or more servers running Windows NT Server—all connected by a network.

Windows 95 and Windows NT Workstations require:

- Computer on the Microsoft Hardware Compatibility List
- 486DX 33 Mhz (Pentium recommended)
- 16 MB of RAM (32 MB recommended)
- 200 MB (or larger) hard disk
- 3.5 inch 1.44 MB floppy drive
- VGA (or Super VGA) video adapter
- VGA (or Super VGA) monitor
- Mouse or equivalent pointing device
- Two-speed (or faster) CD-ROM drive
- Network Interface Card (NIC)
- Presence on an existing network, or use of a hub to create a test network
- Microsoft Windows 95

Windows NT Server requires:

- Two computers on the Microsoft Hardware Compatibility List
- 486DX2 66 Mhz (or better)
- 32 MB of RAM (64 recommended)
- 340 MB (or larger) hard disk
- 3.5 inch 1.44 MB floppy drive
- VGA (or Super VGA) video adapter
- VGA (or Super VGA) monitor
- Mouse or equivalent pointing device
- Two-speed (or faster) CD-ROM drive
- Network Interface Card (NIC)
- Presence on an existing network, or use of a hub to create a test network
- Microsoft Windows NT Server

How to Contact Que Corporation Publishing

The staff of Que is committed to bringing you the very best in computer reference material. Each Que book is the result of months of work by authors and staff who research and refine the information contained within its covers.

As part of this commitment to you, Que invites your input. Please let us know if you enjoy this book, if you have trouble with the information and examples presented, or if you have a suggestion for the next edition.

If you have a question or comment about any Que book, there are several ways to contact Que. We will respond to as many readers as we can. Your name, address, or phone number will never become part of a mailing list or be used for any purpose other than to help us continue to bring you the best books possible.

You can write us at the following address:

Que Corporation Publishing
Attn: Publisher
201 W. 103rd Street
Indianapolis, IN 46290

If you prefer, you can fax Que at:

317-581-4663

You can also send electronic mail to Que at the following Internet address:

`certification@mcp.com`

Que is an imprint of Macmillan Computer Publishing. To obtain a catalog or information, or to purchase any Macmillan Computer Publishing book, call 800-428-5331 or visit our Web site at `http://www.mcp.com`.

Thank you for selecting *MCSE TestPrep: Core Exams*!

Part I

MCSE TestPrep

Windows NT Server 4

CHAPTER 1

Planning

This chapter helps you prepare for the "Planning" section of Microsoft's Exam 70-67, "Implementing and Supporting Microsoft Windows NT Server 4.0." Microsoft provides the following objectives for the "Planning" section:

- Plan the disk drive configuration for various requirements. Requirements include choosing a file system and choosing a fault-tolerance method.
- Choose a protocol for various situations. Protocols include TCP/IP, NWLink IPX/SPX Compatible Transport, NetBEUI.

1.1 Windows NT Among Microsoft Operating Systems

Microsoft has three operating system products now competing in the marketplace:

- Windows 95
- Windows NT Workstation
- Windows NT Server

A. Windows 95

Windows 95 provides a 32-bit platform and is designed to operate with a variety of peripherals. The minimum hardware requirements for Windows 95 are:

- 386DX/20 processor or better
- 4 MB RAM (8 MB is recommended)
- 40 MB of free disk space

Like Windows NT, Windows 95 supports preemptive multitasking, but unlike Windows NT, doesn't support multiple processors. Windows 95 supports plug and play, not to mention a vast number of hardware devices and device drivers (more than Windows NT).

Windows 95 supports 16-bit and 32-bit Windows and MS-DOS applications, including applications that access the hardware directly. Windows 95 runs only on Intel platforms.

Windows 95 uses the File Allocation Table file system, which is less secure than the NTFS file system that Windows NT supports. Windows NT also supports FAT, but NT does not support the FAT32 file system that is supported by recent versions of Windows 95 (OEM Release 2).

You can network a Windows 95 computer in a workgroup, and you can use a Windows 95 computer as a client in a domain-based Windows NT network. However, Windows 95 alone cannot provide a network with centralized authentication and security.

B. Windows NT Workstation

The original Windows NT operating system has evolved into a pair of operating system products—Windows NT Workstation and Windows NT Server. These two products are virtually the same except that they include some different tools and are configured for different roles. NT Server is designed to operate as a network server and domain controller. NT Workstation, like Windows 95, is designed to serve as a network client and desktop operating system.

Windows NT Workstation can serve as a stand-alone operating system, act as a client in a domain-based NT network, or participate in a workgroup. The most striking difference between Windows NT Workstation and Windows 95 is security. Windows NT Workstation is an extremely secure operating system, and for almost every facet of Windows NT administration and configuration, there are security implications. Windows NT provides security for files, directories, printers, and nearly everything else; in fact, a user must be authenticated to even use Windows NT at all.

Windows NT Workstation's minimum hardware requirements are as follows:

- 486DX/33 or better processor
- 12 MB of RAM (16 MB recommended)
- 120 MB of free disk space

Windows NT is designed to provide system stability; each application can run in its own memory address space. Windows NT supports preemptive multiprocessing and as well as true multiprocessing (more than one processor).

Although Windows NT doesn't support the vast array of devices Windows 95 supports, it supports more processor platforms. Because Windows NT is written mostly in C, it can be compiled separately for different processors. In addition to the Intel platform, versions of Windows NT are available for DEC Alpha and others.

Microsoft designed Windows NT for backward-compatibility with MS-DOS 5.0, Windows 3.1x, OS/2 1.x, and lateral-compatibility with POSIX-based applications.

C. Windows NT Server

Windows NT Advanced Server had some clear advantages over NT Workstation 3.1. Unlike Windows NT Workstation 3.1, it supports Macintosh clients, for example, and provides its users with RAID fault tolerance.

With version 4, NT Server and NT Workstation continue to differentiate themselves as they adapt to their respective markets.

1. Features

The following features are available on Windows NT Server but not on Windows NT Workstation:

- Services for Macintosh
- RAID fault tolerance
- Domain logon validation
- Directory replication
- Windows NT Directory Services (NTDS)
- Multiprotocol routing and advanced network services, such as DNS, DHCP, and WINS

2. Capacity

The following facets of Windows NT differ in capacity on Workstation and Server:

- **Concurrent Client Sessions:** Windows NT Server supports an unlimited number of inbound sessions; Windows NT Workstation supports no more than 10 active sessions at once.
- **Remote Access Sessions:** Windows NT Server accommodates an unlimited number of Remote Access connections (although Microsoft only supports up to 256); Windows NT Workstation supports only a single Remote Access connection.
- **Multiprocessors:** Although both Windows NT Workstation and Server can support up to 32 processors in an OEM (Original Equipment Manufacturer) configuration, Windows NT Workstation can support only two processors out-of-the-box, whereas Windows NT Server can support four.
- **Internet Service:** Both NT Workstation and NT Server come with Internet-type server applications, but the NT Server application (Internet Information Server) is more powerful and better suited to the open Internet than is the NT Workstation application (Peer Web Services), which is designed primarily for in-house intranets. (Personal Web server software packages are available for Windows 95 systems.)
- **BackOffice Support:** Both NT Workstation and NT Server provide support for the Microsoft BackOffice family of software products (SQL Server, Systems Management Server, SNA Server, Exchange Server), but NT Server provides a higher level of support for BackOffice products.

3. Performance

Some of the performance differences between Windows NT Workstation and Server are as follows:

- *Windows NT Workstation preloads a Virtual DOS Machine (VDM), the 32-bit MS-DOS emulator that supports legacy applications.*

  Because older applications are more likely to run on a workstation than a server, the preloading of the VDM speeds up the load time of the first DOS or Win16 application at the expense of the RAM used by the VDM, which most likely would need to be loaded anyway.
- *Caching is handled differently on workstations and servers, enabling better network throughput on Windows NT Server and better local disk access time on Windows NT Workstation.*
- *Windows NT Server includes a configurable server service that enables you to tune the server as an application server or as a file/print server.*

  Windows NT Workstation does not provide this feature, because it is limited to 10 inbound sessions.

- *The server files system driver used in both Windows NT Workstation and Server (SRV.SYS) is more subject to paging under Windows NT Workstation than under Windows NT Server.*

  When Windows NT Workstation runs out of physical RAM, it pages the server code out to disk, which means its network sharing performance takes a hit, but local application performance gets a boost. Windows NT Server does not page out much of the server code.

4. Minimum Hardware Requirements

The minimum requirements for NT Server and NT Workstation are roughly the same, but NT Server needs a little more RAM and a little more disk space, namely:

- 486DX/33 processor
- 16 MB of RAM
- 130 MB of disk space

1.1 Practice Problems

1. Which of the following machine configurations meets the minimum hardware requirements for Windows NT Server? Select all that apply:

   A. Pentium 133, 12 MB RAM, 1 GB hard disk space free

   B. 486 DX2/66, 16 MB RAM, 120 MB hard disk space free

   C. Pentium 200, 32 MB RAM, 200 MB hard disk space free

   D. 486 DX33, 16 MB RAM, 150 MB hard disk space free

2. Your department bought six new DEC Alpha workstations. Which of the following operating systems can be installed? Select all that apply:

   A. Windows 3.11a

   B. Windows 95 for Alpha

   C. Windows NT Server

   D. Windows NT Workstation

3. Which of the following services are not available on Windows NT Workstation? Select all that apply:

   A. DNS

   B. Directory Replication

   C. DHCP

   D. WINS

4. Which of the following statements is true? Select the best answer:

   A. Both Windows NT Workstation and NT Server support multiple processors.

   B. Both Windows NT Workstation and NT Server support unlimited number of inbound sessions.

   C. Both Windows NT Workstation and NT Server support RAID fault tolerance.

   D. Both Windows NT Workstation and NT Server support four processors out of the box.

5. Your boss asks you to enable Mac users from the graphics department to share files with PC users. Which operating systems support file shares for both Macintosh and PC users? Select all that apply:

   A. Windows 95

   B. Windows NT Server

   C. Windows NT Workstation

   D. You have to buy MS MacShare for Windows NT Server

6. Dan manages a workgroup for chemistry research in the company MEGACORP. There are currently 14 computers in this workgroup, with a mix of Windows 95, Windows for Workgroups 3.11, and Windows NT Workstation installed on these. There is a share on his NT Workstation computer that needs to be accessed by every user, but not all users can connect. What is the most likely cause? Select the best answer:

   A. He needs to buy additional client licenses because NT Workstation comes only with ten licenses in the box.

   B. If he intends to share resources effectively, he really should upgrade to NT Server.

   C. He has used up all possible inbound sessions; NT Workstation supports only a maximum of ten.

   D. He needs to restart his computer.

7. Which of the following operating systems support fault-tolerant RAID? Select all that apply:

   A. Windows NT Workstation

   B. Windows NT Server

   C. Windows 95

   D. Windows 3.11a

1.1 Answers and Explanations: Practice Problems

1. **C, D** The minimum hardware requirements for NT Server are a 486DX/33 processor, 16 MB of RAM, and 130 MB of disk space.
2. **C, D** Only Windows NT is available as a Windows operating system for Alpha.
3. **A, B, C, D** All of these services are available only on NT Server.
4. **A** Both NT Server and Workstation support multiple processors.
5. **B** NT Server offers Services for Macintosh, which enable file shares for Mac and PC users.
6. **C** NT Workstation is limited to a maximum of 10 inbound connections.
7. **B** Only NT Server supports fault-tolerant RAID levels 1 and 5.

1.1 Key Words

BackOffice Support

DHCP (Dynamic Host Configuration Protocol)

DNS (Domain Name Service)

FAT (File Allocation Table)

FAT32

Hardware requirements

Multiprocessor

NTFS

Operating system

Platform independent

RAID

Remote Access

Services for Macintosh

Windows 95

Windows NT Server

Windows NT Workstation

WINS (Windows Internet Naming Service)

1.2 Workgroups and Domains

Every networked Windows NT-based computer can participate in one of two environments:

- Workgroup
- Domain

The difference between a workgroup and a domain boils down to the question of where the user accounts are stored. Users must—and it should be stressed that this logon process is completely mandatory—log on to Windows NT to use a Windows NT-based computer.

When a user successfully logs on to Windows NT, an access token is generated that contains the user's security identifier and group identifiers, as well as the user rights granted through the User Rights policy in User Manager or User Manager for Domains.

The access token identifies the user and all processes spawned by the user. No action can take place on a Windows NT system without somebody's access token attached to it.

A. Workgroups

A *workgroup* is a collection of computers grouped together for a common purpose, however, each computer in the workgroup has to manage its own user accounts. The security information necessary to verify the user's credentials and generate the access token resides on the local machine. Thus, every Windows NT computer in a workgroup must contain accounts for each person who might need to access the workstation. This involves a great deal of administration in workgroups that consist of more than a few members.

A workgroup is, however, simpler than a domain and easier to install. A workgroup does not require an NT Server machine acting as a domain controller, and the decentralized administration of a workgroup can be an advantage in small networks because it does not depend on the health of a few key server and controller machines.

Unless a Windows NT Server computer is configured as a stand-alone server, it cannot participate in a workgroup. Windows NT Workstation computers, Windows 95 computers, and older networkable Microsoft systems, such as Windows for Workgroups, can participate in workgroups.

B. Domains

In a domain environment, all nodes must authenticate logon requests with a domain controller that contains the central accounts database for the entire domain. A password needs to be changed only one time to be usable on any member computer of the domain. Likewise, a user needs only a single account to access resources anywhere in the domain. Only Windows NT Server machines can serve as domain controllers in a Windows NT network.

1.2 Practice Problems

1. Which statements are true about domains? Select all that apply:

   A. Centralized user management

   B. Decentralized user management

   C. Works best for small groups of users

   D. Works best for large groups of users

2. Which statements are true about workgroups? Select all that apply:

   A. Centralized user management

   B. Decentralized user management

   C. Works best for small groups of users

   D. Works best for large groups of users

3. To create a domain, which type of operating system should you choose? Select the best answer:

   A. Windows NT Workstation

   B. Windows NT Workstation with Domain Extensions

   C. Windows NT Server

   D. Windows NT Server with Domain Extensions

4. Select all operating systems that enable a user to log on to a domain:

   A. Windows 3.11 for Workgroups

   B. Windows 95

   C. Windows NT Workstation

   D. Windows NT Server

5. The chemistry lab is running a workgroup with a mix of Windows 95 and Windows NT Workstations. Three of the Windows NT Workstation computers have file and printer shares that are accessed from all workgroup users. Dan, who administers this workgroup, complains that every time a user joins, he has to change the account database on all three NT Workstation computers to enable the new user to access all resources. What can Dan do? Select the best answer:

   A. This is easy to solve: Set up user account replication between the three computers so that you have to maintain only one computer, and all changes are propagated to the other two.

   B. Dan has to migrate the workgroup to a domain, because only domains allow central user management.

   C. Dan has to download service pack 3, which solves this problem.

   D. One of the NT Workstation computers must be promoted to master browser for this workgroup.

1.2 Answers and Explanations: Practice Problems

1. **A, D** A domain is used for centralized user management for large environments.

2. **B, C** Workgroups are best for decentralized management of small networks.

3. **C** For a domain, a PDC is needed and only NT Server can be installed as a PDC.

4. **A, B, C, D** All these operating systems support domain logon.

5. **B** Centralized user-management is possible only with an NT domain.

1.2 Key Words

Centralized user management

Decentralized user management

Domain

Workgroup

1.3 Plan the Disk Drive Configuration

Microsoft lists the following objective for the Windows NT Server exam:

Plan the disk drive configuration for various requirements. Requirements include choosing a file system and choosing a fault-tolerance method.

The following sections highlight some specific planning issues related to disk configuration under Windows NT, as follows:

- Partitions
- Windows NT file systems
- Windows NT fault-tolerance methods

A. Partitions

A *partition* is a logical organization of a physical disk. An operating system such as Windows NT can subdivide a disk drive into several partitions. Each partition is formatted separately. Windows NT assigns a different drive letter to each of the partitions, and users interact separately with each partition as if each partition were a separate disk drive.

Partitioning is the act of defining a partition and associating that partition with an area (or areas) of free space from a hard disk.

As you plan your Windows NT configuration, you must make some decisions about the arrangement of partitions on your disk drive, as discussed next.

1. Primary and Extended Partitions

Windows NT provides the following two types of partitions:

- **Primary partitions:** A primary partition cannot be subdivided and is capable of supporting a bootable operating system. One hard disk can contain up to four primary partitions.
- **Extended partitions:** An extended partition can be subdivided into smaller logical drives (see fig. 1.3.1). This feature enables you to assign more than four drive letters to the disk. An extended partition does not support a bootable operating system. The system partition therefore cannot reside on an extended partition (see next section). One hard disk can contain only one extended partition.

If you choose to use an extended partition on a hard disk, you are limited to three (rather than four) primary partitions for that disk.

On an Intel-based computer, one primary partition must be marked *active*. The active partition is then used to boot the computer. Because any primary partition of sufficient size can support a bootable operating system, one advantage of using multiple primary partitions is that you can isolate different operating systems on different partitions.

If you install Windows NT on a computer with another operating system in place, the active partition does not change. If you install Windows NT on a new computer, the partition created by Setup becomes the active partition.

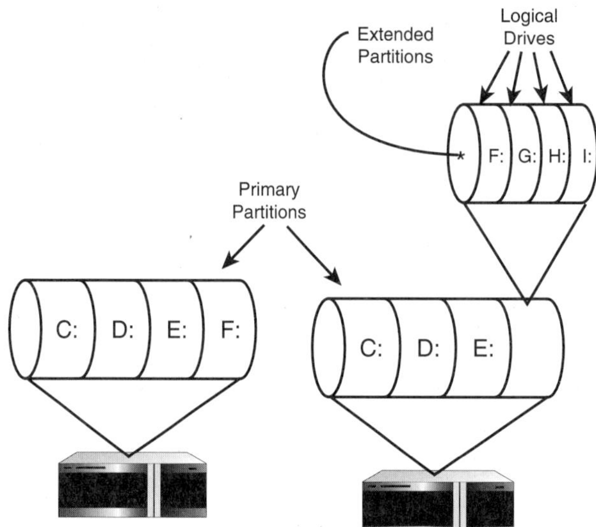

Figure 1.3.1 A physical disk can consist of up to four primary partitions or up to three primary partitions and one extended partition. An extended partition can be subdivided into logical drives.

2. Boot and System Partitions

The *system partition* is the partition that contains the files necessary to boot the operating system. The system partition does not have to be the partition on which Windows NT is installed.

The partition that holds the Windows NT operating system files is called the *boot partition*. If your system boots from drive C, and you install Windows NT on drive D, drive C is your system partition and drive D is your boot partition (see fig. 1.3.2). If you boot from drive C, and Windows NT is installed on drive C, drive C is both the system partition and the boot partition.

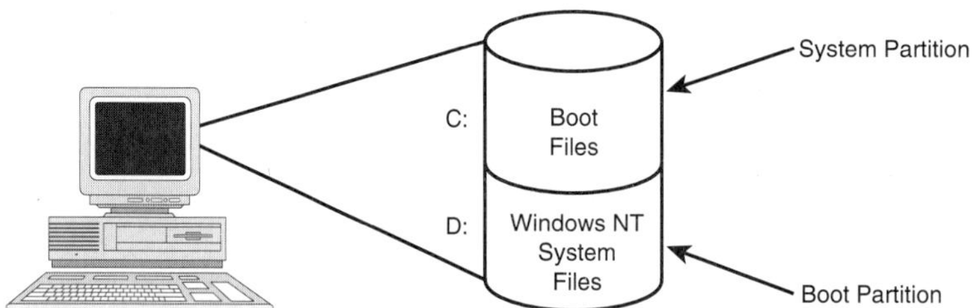

Figure 1.3.2 The partition that boots the computer is the system partition; the partition that holds the Windows NT directory is the boot partition. Note that these names are counterintuitive.

Note that the active partition is the partition used to boot the system. The system partition must therefore be the active partition.

By the way, active partitions are a relevant concept only for Intel-based computers; RISC-based computers use a hardware configuration utility to designate the system partition.

B. Windows NT File Systems

After a partition has been created, it must be formatted with a supported file system. A *file system* is a system for organizing and managing the data on a disk. Windows NT supports three file systems: FAT (File Allocation Table), NTFS (NT File System), and CDFS (Compact Disk File System). CDFS is a read-only file system for CD-ROMs, so you can immediately rule it out for hard disk partitions. Each partition must use either the FAT file system or the NTFS file system.

OS/2's file system HPFS (High Performance File System) is no longer supported by Windows NT 4. You have to convert HPFS-formatted partitions prior to installing NT 4.

1. FAT

The venerable File Allocation Table (FAT) file system was originally invented for MS-DOS. FAT is now supported by Windows NT, Windows 95, and OS/2, making it the most universally accepted and supported file system (see fig. 1.3.3). For this reason alone, you should seriously consider using FAT for your partitions.

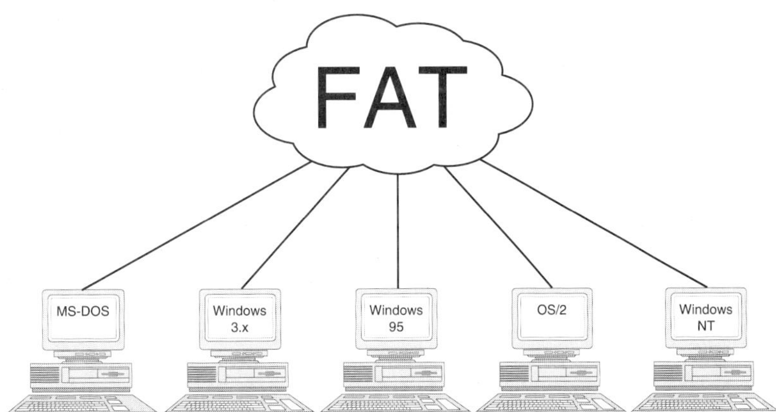

Figure 1.3.3 The FAT file system is accessible from more operating systems than NTFS, but FAT doesn't provide the NTFS advantages.

FAT has a lower overhead than its high-tech counterpart NTFS (less than 1 MB, compared to an average of 5–10 MB for NTFS), and FAT is typically the more efficient file system for small partitions (under 200 MB).

Some of the disadvantages of FAT are as follows:

- FAT is generally slower than NTFS for larger partitions. It takes longer to find and access files. For partitions greater than 200 MB, FAT performance degrades quickly.
- The maximum file, directory, or partition size under FAT is only 4 GB. Also, because Windows NT does not support any FAT compression software, including Microsoft's own DriveSpace and DoubleSpace, you cannot conserve space by compressing files on a FAT partition.
- FAT does not offer the security features offered by NTFS.
- If the power fails during a disk transaction, the FAT file system might be left with cross-linked files or orphan clusters.

You should use the FAT file system if you will be dual-booting your computer with another operating system and you want to access the partition from the other operating system.

If your Windows NT computer is a RISC-based system, your C drive needs to be FAT-formatted with at least 2 MB free space.

2. NTFS

The New Technology File System (NTFS) is designed to fully exploit the features and capabilities of Windows NT. For partitions larger than the range of 200–400 MB, the NTFS file system far outshines the FAT file system. The biggest drawback with using NTFS is that only the Windows NT operating system can access NTFS partitions (see fig. 1.3.4). If you plan to sometimes boot your computer under a different operating system, such as MS-DOS or Windows 95, you should be aware that the other operating system cannot access an NTFS partition.

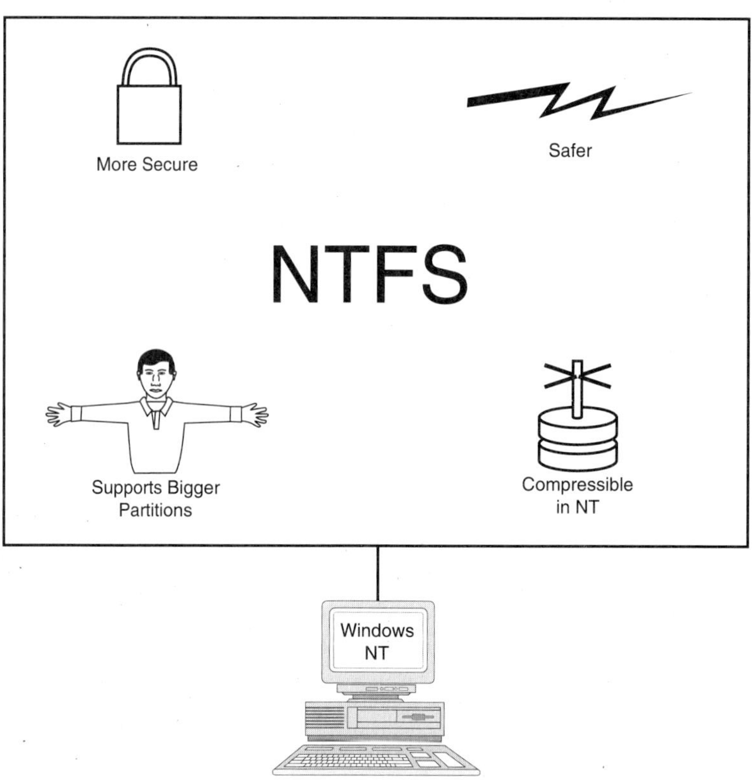

Figure 1.3.4 The NTFS file system is accessible only from Windows NT—it provides a number of advantages for Windows NT users.

When partitions exceed 400 MB (on average), NTFS is your most reasonable choice. Remember that 400 MB is only an average; actual performance owes more to the number of files than to the size of the files.

NTFS is generally faster than FAT, and NTFS supports bigger partitions. (NTFS files and partitions can be up to 16 exabytes—an exabyte is one billion gigabytes, or 2^{64} bytes.)

NTFS is also safer. NTFS supports sector sparing, also known as hot fixing, on SCSI hard drives. If a sector fails on an NTFS partition of a SCSI hard drive, NTFS tries to write the data to a good sector (if the data is still in memory) and map out the bad sector so that it is not reused. NTFS keeps a transaction log while it works. Two other principal advantages of NTFS are as follows:

- **File-level security:** NTFS enables you to assign specific permissions to individual files and directories.
- **File compression:** Windows NT provides the capability to compress NTFS files. Traditional FAT compression utilities, including Microsoft's own DriveSpace and DoubleSpace, don't work under Windows NT.

You should use NTFS if you want to preserve existing permissions when you migrate files and directories from a NetWare server to a Windows NT Server system. Also, if you want to allow Macintosh computers to access files on the partition through Windows NT's Services for Macintosh, you must format the partition for NTFS.

Because NTFS has a higher overhead than FAT, somewhere between 4.5 and 10 MB for the file system itself, you cannot use the NTFS file system for floppy disks.

3. Choosing a File System

Here's a quick summary of the differences between file systems:

Feature	FAT	NTFS
File name length	255	255
8.3 file name compatibility	Yes	Yes
File size	4 GB	16 EB
Partition size	4 GB	16 EB
Directory structure	Linked list	B-tree
Local security	No	Yes
Transaction tracking	No	Yes
Hot fixing	No	Yes
Overhead	1 MB	>2 MB (avg. 4.5–10)
Required for RISC-based computers	Yes	No
Accessible from MS-DOS/Windows 95	Yes	No
Accessible from OS/2	Yes	No
Case-sensitive	No	POSIX only
Case preserving	Yes	Yes
Compression	No	Yes
Efficiency	<200 MB	>400 MB
Windows NT formattable	Yes	Yes
Convertible	To NTFS only	No

Feature	FAT	NTFS
Fragmentation level	High	Low
Floppy disk formattable	Yes	No
Extensible attributes	No	Yes
Creation/modification/access dates	Yes	Yes

Windows NT provides a utility called `Convert.exe` that converts a FAT partition to NTFS. There is no utility for directly converting an NTFS partition to FAT. To change an NTFS partition to FAT, back up all files on the partition, reformat the partition, and then restore the files to the reformatted partition.

C. Fault-Tolerance Methods

Fundamentally, *fault tolerance* is the system's capability to compensate in the event of hardware disaster. The standard for fault tolerance is known as Redundant Array of Inexpensive Disks (RAID). RAID consists of several levels (or categories) of protection that offer a mixture of performance, reliability, and cost. One of the steps in planning your Windows NT system might be to decide on a RAID fault-tolerance method. Windows NT Server offers the following two RAID fault-tolerance methods:

- **Disk mirroring (RAID Level 1):** Windows NT writes the same data to two physical disks. If one disk fails, the data is still available on the other disk.
- **Disk striping with parity (Raid Level 5):** Windows NT writes data across a series of disks (3 to 32). The data is not duplicated on the disks (as it is with disk mirroring), but Windows NT records parity information that it can use to regenerate missing data if a disk should fail.

It is important to note that the fault-tolerance methods available through Windows NT are software-based RAID implementations. Several hardware vendors offer hardware-based RAID solutions. Hardware-based RAID solutions, which can be quite expensive, are beyond the scope of this book and beyond the scope of the Windows NT Server exam.

1. Disk Mirroring (RAID Level 1)

Disk mirroring calls for all data to be written to two physical disks (see fig. 1.3.5). A *mirror* is a redundant copy of a disk partition. You can use any partition, including the boot or system partitions, to establish a mirror.

You can measure the utilization of a fault-tolerance method by the percent of the total disk space devoted to storing the original information. Fifty percent of the data in a disk-mirroring system is redundant data. The percentage utilization is thus also fifty percent, making disk-mirroring less efficient than disk striping with parity. The startup costs for implementing disk mirroring are typically lower, however, because disk mirroring requires only two (rather than 3–32) physical disks.

Disk mirroring slows down write operations slightly (because Windows NT has to write to two disks simultaneously). Read operations are actually slightly faster, because NT can read from both disks simultaneously.

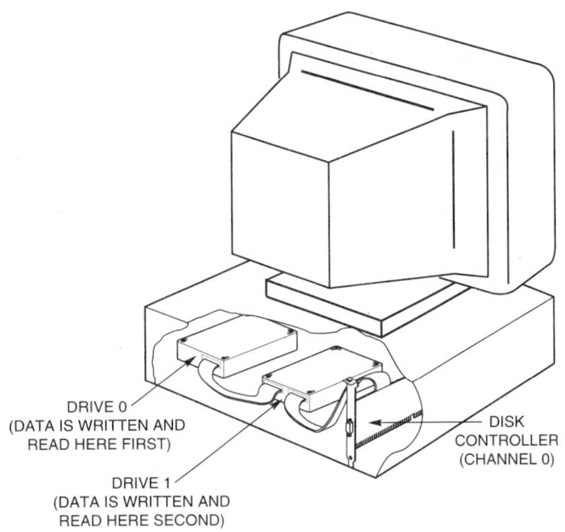

Figure 1.3.5 How disk mirroring works.

In a typical disk mirroring scenario, a single disk controller writes to both members of the mirror set. If a mirrored disk fails, the user can keep working. If the disk controller fails, however, Windows NT cannot access either disk.

Disk duplexing is a special kind of disk mirroring that provides a solution for this potential pitfall. In a disk duplexing system, each of the mirrored disks has its own disk controller. The system can therefore endure either a disk failure or a controller failure. Disk duplexing also has some performance advantages, because the two disk controllers can act independently (see fig. 1.3.6).

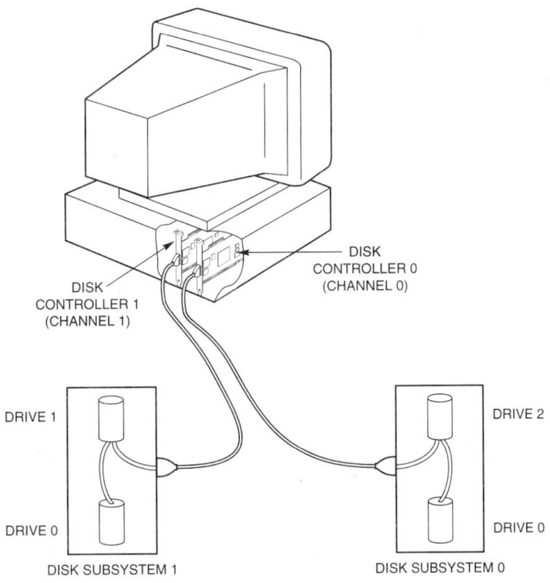

Figure 1.3.6 Disk duplexing.

2. Disk Striping with Parity (RAID Level 5)

A stripe set with parity writes information in *stripes* (or rows) across 3 to 32 disks. For each stripe, there is a parity stripe block on one of the disks. If one of the disks fails, Windows NT can use the parity stripe block to regenerate the missing information. The parity stripe block is the only data that is additional to what the system would need to record the original data without fault tolerance. Disk striping with parity is therefore more efficient than disk mirroring. The percentage of disk space available for storing data is:

```
% Utilization = (no. of disks - 1) / no. of disks x 100%
```

If you have five disks, eighty percent of your disk space is available for storing data. This compares with fifty percent in a disk mirroring system. The more disks you add, the more efficient your fault tolerance becomes. But at the same time, your setup costs also increase as you add more disks.

Windows NT must perform the parity calculations as it writes data to a stripe set with parity. Write operations therefore take three times as much memory if you are using a stripe set with parity.

Any partition except the boot partition and the system partition can be part of a stripe set with parity, provided you have enough other partitions on 3–32 other physical disks.

1.3.1 Exercise: Calculating the Percentage of Available Disk Space when Using Stripe Sets with Parity

The purpose of this exercise is to show you how to calculate how much space (in a percentage) is available for storing data when using RAID level 5, stripe sets with parity.

1. Determine the number of hard disks you want to add to a stripe set. This example assumes that you are adding 10 disks to a stripe set.
2. To calculate the percentage of available hard disk space for data, use the following formula:

```
% Utilization = (no. of disks - 1) / (no. of disks) x 100%
```

3. With 10 disks, you can use ninety percent of the disk space for storing data.

1.3.2 Exercise: Choosing a File System

The purpose of this exercise is to show you how to choose a file system for NT computers.

1. First of all, you must decide whether this computer will be used with NT only or be dual-booted with another operating system like DOS. When you need to dual-boot, you are limited to FAT for the system partition.
2. Decide whether you will be storing sensitive information on this computer. If so, only NTFS enables you to secure the sensitive information. You need to go with NTFS on at least a single partition.
3. If you are expecting high-volume transactions on the file system for this computer, you are also better off with NTFS because of its transaction based file system that can recover in case of unexpected system crash.

1.3 Practice Problems

1. Which of the following statements is true? Select two:

   A. The system partition contains the NT operating system.

   B. The boot partition contains the NT operating system.

   C. The system partition contains the files necessary to load the operating system.

   D. The boot partition contains the files necessary to load the operating system.

2. Which of the following statements is true? Select the best answer:

   A. There can be up to four primary partitions on a disk, or one primary and one extended partition.

   B. There can be one primary partition on a disk, or one primary and one extended partition.

   C. There can be up to four primary partitions on a disk, or three primary partitions and on extended partition.

   D. There can be up to four primary partitions on a disk, or one primary and three extended partitions.

3. Which fault-tolerant RAID levels are supported by Windows NT Server? Select the best answer:

   A. Levels 2 and 5

   B. Levels 0 and 5

   C. Levels 0 and 1

   D. Levels 1 and 5

4. Which of the following file systems are supported by Windows NT? Select all that apply:

   A. FAT

   B. FAT32

   C. HPFS

   D. CDFS

5. Your company is running legacy DOS applications that were tuned heavily and access hardware directly. Because you cannot run these applications from within NT, you have to set up these computers for dual boot. Which of the following statements is true in this situation?

   A. You have to format the system partition with FAT.

   B. You have to format the boot partition with FAT.

   C. You have to format the system partition with NTFS.

   D. You have to format the boot partition with NTFS.

6. You have decided to use NTFS on all computers in your network. Which of the following statements about NTFS are true? Select all that apply:

   A. Required on RISC computers

   B. Low overhead

   C. Accessible from OS/2

   D. Hot fixing implemented

7. What are the advantages of using a stripe set with parity? Select all that apply:

   A. Disk read operations can occur simultaneously.

   B. The boot and the system partition can be part of a stripe set.

   C. Recovery from disk failure is very rapid.

   D. Cost is lower than for a mirror set.

8. What are the advantages of using a mirror set? Select all that apply:

   A. Disk read operations can occur simultaneously.

   B. The boot and the system partition can be part of a mirror set.

   C. Recovery from disk failure is very rapid.

   D. Cost is lower than for a stripe set with parity.

9. Which of the following statements is true about disk duplexing? Select the best answer:

   A. Disk duplexing uses one SCSI controller and two hard disks.

   B. Disk duplexing uses two SCSI controllers and four hard disks.

   C. Disk duplexing uses two SCSI controllers and two hard disks.

   D. Disk duplexing isn't supported by Windows NT.

10. Which of the following statements is true about stripe sets with parity and mirror sets? Select the best answer:

    A. Mirror sets can be created with two disks; a stripe set with parity needs at least five disks.

    B. Mirror sets can be created with two disks; a stripe set with parity needs at least two disks and can employ a maximum of 32 disks.

    C. Mirror sets can be created with two disks; a stripe set with parity needs at least three disks and can employ a maximum of 32 disks.

    D. Mirror sets can be created with up to four disks; a stripe set with parity needs at least three disks and can employ a maximum of 32 disks.

1.3 Answers and Explanations: Practice Problems

1. **B, C** The NT operating system is located on the boot partition and is loaded from the system partition.

2. **C** There can be up to four primary partitions on a disk, or three primary partitions and on extended partition.

3. **D** Only levels 1 and 5 of supported RAID levels are fault tolerant.

4. **A, D** HPFS is no longer supported by NT and FAT32 introduced with Windows 95b isn't supported (yet).

5. **A** To run DOS, you need to format the system partition using FAT.

6. **D** Disk errors can be corrected automatically when using NTFS as your file system.

7. **A, D** Stripe sets with parity allow for simultaneous read operations and are cheaper than mirror sets.

8. **A, B, C** Mirror sets can be used for system and boot partition, recovery is very fast, and read operations can occur simultaneously.

9. **C** Disk duplexing uses two SCSI controllers and two hard disks.

10. **C** Mirror sets can be created with two disks, a stripe set with parity needs at least three disks and can employ a maximum of 32 disks.

1.3 Key Words

Boot partition
CDFS
Compression
Disk duplexing
Disk mirroring
Extended Partition
FAT
Fault tolerance
Hot fixing
HPFS
NTFS
Partition
Primary partition
RAID
Stripe set with parity
System partition

1.4 Choosing a Windows NT Network Protocol

Microsoft lists the following objective for the Windows NT Server exam: Choose a protocol for various situations. Protocols include TCP/IP, NWLink IPX/SPX Compatible Transport, and NetBEUI.

A network protocol is a collection of rules and procedures governing communication among the computers on a network. In a sense, a protocol is a language your computer uses when speaking to other computers. If two computers don't use the same protocols, they cannot communicate.

The three principal Windows NT networking protocols are as follows:

- **TCP/IP:** A widely used, routable protocol that is the basis for communication on the Internet.
- **NWLink IPX/SPX Compatible Transport:** Microsoft's rendition of Novell's proprietary IPX/SPX protocol suite. NWLink is a routable protocol designed to enable Windows NT computers to interoperate with Novell NetWare networks.
- **NetBEUI:** A very fast but non-routable protocol used on Microsoft networks. Because NetBEUI is non-routable, it is suitable only for Local Area Networks (LANs).

You should learn the advantages and disadvantages of each of these protocols and understand when to use each.

A. TCP/IP

Transmission Control Protocol/Internet Protocol (TCP/IP) is the default protocol for the Intel version of Windows NT. TCP/IP is the only protocol supported on the Internet (which is why it is rocketing toward becoming a global standard protocol).

Windows NT's version of the TCP/IP protocol, Microsoft TCP/IP, is a 32-bit native suite of protocols. It requires more configuration than other protocols, but Microsoft also provides some excellent configuration tools. The result is a cross-platform, industry-standard, routable network implementation that you can expect only to grow in popularity.

The important things to remember about TCP/IP are as follows:

- TCP/IP is routable. Because TCP/IP packets can be forwarded through routers, you can use TCP/IP on Wide Area Networks (WANs). (The NetBEUI protocol, by contrast, can only be used on Local Area Networks.)
- TCP/IP is the language of the Internet. If your Windows NT computer will be connected to the Internet, you need to use TCP/IP.
- TCP/IP is a widely accepted standard. You can interconnect with more networks worldwide if you are using TCP/IP.
- TCP/IP accommodates a wide range of network hardware, operating systems, and applications.

You implement TCP/IP on your network with the help of three important services:

- **Dynamic Host Configuration Protocol (DHCP):** Dynamically assign ("lease") IP addresses to DHCP clients.
- **Domain Name System (DNS):** Maps IP addresses to human-readable computer names.
- **Windows Internet Name Service (WINS):** Maps IP addresses to NETBIOS computer names.

The Internet Protocol (the IP in TCP/IP) sends packets using a computer's IP Address—a unique 32-bit binary number that no other computer on the network can possess. (More precisely, it is not every computer, but rather every network adapter card, that requires its own IP Address.)

The 32-bit IP address usually is expressed as four octets, or 8-bit numbers, which then are represented in decimal form. An 8-bit number can have a value of anywhere from 0 to 255, so an IP address consists of four numbers between 0 and 255 separated by decimal points (for example, 111.12.3.141).

Every computer on a TCP/IP network must have an IP address. You can configure a permanent IP address for each computer, or you can configure each computer to receive a dynamically assigned IP address from a Dynamic Host Protocol (DHCP) server. A DHCP server is assigned a range of IP addresses. The DHCP server then "leases" (assigns for a limited duration) these IP addresses to DHCP clients in the subnet.

The Domain Name System (DNS) is a feature of TCP/IP networks that enables you to map an IP address to an alphanumeric name that is theoretically even easier for humans to remember than the decimal octet. (Internet domain names, such as `newriders.mcp.com`, are now easily recognizable in this age of e-mail.) Windows NT Server's Microsoft DNS Server service can map IP addresses to domain names on a TCP/IP network.

Windows NT's WINS service is similar to DNS except that, rather than mapping IP addresses to domain names, WINS maps IP addresses' NetBIOS names. NetBIOS names are used to identify resources on Microsoft networks. NetBIOS names follow the familiar Universal Naming Convention (UNC) format you use to locate resources from the Windows NT command prompt:

```
\\computername\sharename\path
```

The WINS service is also dynamic. Whereas DNS requires a static listing of all domain name-to-IP-address mappings, the WINS service can automatically associate NetBIOS names with IP addresses.

B. NWLink

The primary purpose of Microsoft's NWLink/SPX Compatible Transport protocol is to provide connectivity with the many thousands of Novell NetWare networks. NWLink is, however, a fully functional and fully routable protocol. Because TCP/IP is Internet-ready (and more universally accepted) and NetBEUI is faster and simpler for Microsoft LANs, however, chances are good that if you are using NWLink you will be connecting to NetWare.

NWLink provides compatibility with IPX/SPX-based networks, but NWLink alone does not necessarily enable a Windows NT computer to interact with NetWare networks. Some important points to remember are as follows:

- The NWLink protocol provides compatibility with Novell NetWare IPX/SPX networks.
- A Windows NT Workstation computer running Client Services for NetWare (CSNW) and the NWLink protocol or a Windows NT Server computer running Gateway Services for NetWare (GSNW) and the NWLink protocol can connect file and print services on a NetWare server.
- A Windows NT computer using the NWLink protocol can connect to client/server applications on a NetWare server (without requiring additional NetWare-connectivity services).
- Any Microsoft network client that uses Server Message Block (Windows NT, Windows 95, or Windows for Workgroups) can access NetWare resources through a NetWare gateway on a Windows NT Server computer running Gateway Services for NetWare. The NetWare resources appear to the Microsoft network client as Windows NT resources.

C. NetBEUI

NetBEUI is the fastest protocol that comes with Windows NT, but it cannot be routed. This means that the NetBEUI protocol is generally only useful for what Microsoft calls "department-sized LANs." The recent emphasis on internetworking means that, in all but the smallest and most isolated networks, NetBEUI is usually not the ideal choice for a primary network protocol. That is why NetBEUI has not been a default protocol for Windows NT since version 3.1.

You cannot use NetBEUI with a router, but you can use a bridge to connect LAN segments operating with the NetBEUI protocol.

NetBEUI was designed by IBM in 1985, and one of the advantages of NetBEUI is that it enables Windows NT machines to interact with older Microsoft network machines that use NetBEUI (for instance, Windows for Workgroups 3.1 or Microsoft LAN Manager).

NetBEUI is also extremely easy to implement. It is self-tuning and self-configuring. Because NetBEUI was designed for an earlier generation of lower-performance computers, it also comes with a smaller memory overhead.

The speed and simplicity of NetBEUI comes with a downside, however: NetBEUI relies heavily on network broadcasts, which can degrade performance on large and busy subnets.

D. Planning for Network Clients

The Windows NT CD-ROM includes client software for a number of operating systems that are not as naturally networkable as Windows NT or Windows 95. Some of those client software packages are as follows:

- Microsoft Network 3.0 for MS-DOS
- LAN Manager 2.2c for MS-DOS client
- LAN Manager 2.2c for OS/2 client

Microsoft Network Client 3.0 for MS-DOS enables MS-DOS machines to participate in Windows NT networks. An MS-DOS client using Microsoft Client 3.0 for MS-DOS configured with the full director can perform the following tasks on a Windows NT network:

- Log on to a domain
- Run logon scripts
- Access IPC mechanisms, such as RPCs, named pipes, and WinSock
- Use RAS (version 1.1)

A Microsoft Client 3.0 for MS-DOS client cannot browse the network unless a Windows NT computer or a Windows for Workgroups computer is in the same workgroup.

The Windows NT CD-ROM also includes a pair of network client packages that help connect LAN Manager 2.2c systems with Windows NT. Those client packages are LAN Manager 2.2c for MS-DOS client and LAN Manager 2.2c OS/2 client. The LAN Manager 2.2c for MS-DOS client includes some features not found in the OS/2 version, including support for the Remoteboot service and the capability to connect to a NetWare server.

Table 1.4.1 describes which network protocols and which TCP/IP services each of the client systems supports.

Table 1.4.1 Network Protocol and TCP/IP Service Support for Various Windows NT Client Systems

Network Protocol	TCP/IP Service	IPX-Compatible	IPX/SPX Compatible	NetBEUI	TCP/IP	DLC	DHCP	WINS	DNS
Network Client for MS-DOS	X	X		X	X	X			
LAN MAN 2.2c for MS-DOS	X			X	X	X			
LAN MAN 2.2c for OS/2	X			X					
Windows 95	X		X	X		X	X	X	
Windows NT Workstation	X		X	X	X	X	X	X	

1.4.1 Exercise: Choosing a Network Protocol

The purpose of this exercise is to show uses for the three different network protocols NetBEUI, IPX/SPX, and TCP/IP.

1. If you are running a LAN, need no connectivity to NetWare servers, and have no routers, your best choice is NetBEUI.
2. If your network has NetWare servers and also remote locations connected with routers, IPX/SPX is your best choice when clients connect directly to the NetWare servers. If they use gateway services on a Windows NT Server machine, only this computer must run IPX/SPX additionally, and TCP/IP can be used as primary protocol.
3. If your network is connected to the Internet, there is only one protocol of choice: TCP/IP.

1.4.2 Exercise: Testing Your TCP/IP Setup

This exercise is intended to show you the basics of TCP/IP and how it works with routers and Internet addresses.

1. Make sure TCP/IP is installed on your network.
2. Choose Start, Programs, Command Prompt.
3. From the command prompt, type **IPCONFIG**. The IPCONFIG command tells you the IP address, subnet mask, and default gateway for all network adapters to which TCP/IP is bound.
4. If TCP/IP is working properly on your system, the IPCONFIG utility outputs the IP address, subnet mask, and default gateway for your network adapter(s). If your computer obtains an IP address from a DHCP server that is not working at this time—for instance, if you have a dial-up adapter that you use to access the Internet with an Internet service provider and you are not presently connected—the IP address and subnet mask appears as 0.0.0.0. If you have a duplicated IP address, the address appears, but the subnet mask appears as 0.0.0.0. Write down your IP address.
5. Type **PING 127.0.0.1**. The Ping utility (Packet INternet Groper) tests your TCP/IP connection. You can specify the IP address of another computer with the command, and Ping makes sure your connection with the other computer is working. The format for the Ping command is:

   ```
   ping <IP address>
   ```

   The address you just typed (127.0.0.1) is a special address called the *loopback address*. The loopback address verifies that TCP/IP is working correctly on your system.
6. Ping the IP address of your own computer. This confirms that your IP address is configured correctly and informs you as to whether any duplicate IP addresses are on your network.
7. Ping the address of another computer on your subnet. If a system has a default gateway (see step 4), it is a common practice to ping the default gateway to ensure that your connection to the gateway is working.
8. If you know the IP address of a computer beyond the gateway, ping the IP address of the remote to ensure that you can connect to remote resources.

1.4 Practice Problems

1. Which of the following protocols is mainly used to connect to Novell NetWare servers? Select the best answer:

   A. IPX/SPX

   B. TCP/IP

   C. NetBEUI

   D. AppleTalk

2. Which of the following protocols are routable? Select all that apply:

   A. IPX/SPX

   B. TCP/IP

   C. NetBEUI

   D. NetBIOS

3. For which of the following operating systems are implementations of TCP/IP available? Select all that apply:

   A. MS-DOS

   B. Windows 3.11 for Workgroups

   C. Windows 95

   D. Windows NT

4. Your network is a collection of Windows NT machines, Windows 95 machines, and MS-DOS machines running LAN MAN 2.2c Client for MS-DOS. The network, which uses the NetBEUI protocol, used to perform reasonably well, but you recently added additional nodes and noticed a sharp decline in performance. Now you are planning to add to the network again. Which of the following steps might improve network performance?

   A. Keep NetBEUI, but subdivide the network using a bridge

   B. Switch to NWLink

   C. Switch to TCP/IP

   D. A or C

   E. All of the above

5. Users on your Windows NT network occasionally have to exchange messages with users on a Novell NetWare 4.0 network via the Internet. You must use which protocol?

   A. TCP/IP

   B. NWLink

   C. Both A and B

   D. None of the above

6. Your boss is calling you. She has read about the exciting new features of the Internet, and wants the company connected to it. Which protocol do you need to install in order to make your computers Internet-ready? Select the best answer:

   A. IPX/SPX

   B. TCP/IP

   C. NetBEUI

   D. AppleTalk

7. What are the advantages of NetBEUI? Select all that apply:

   A. It can be used on networks with bridges.

   B. It can be used on networks with routers.

   C. It comes with a small memory overhead.

   D. It relies on network broadcasts.

8. Which of the following services is required for NetBIOS name resolution with TCP/IP? Select the best answer:

   A. DNS

   B. WINS

   C. DHCP

   D. RAS

1.4 Answers and Explanations: Practice Problems

1. **A** IPX/SPX is the primary protocol of NetWare servers.
2. **A, B** Only TCP/IP and IPX/SPX are routable.
3. **A, B, C, D** TCP/IP is available with all.
4. **D** You can switch to TCP/IP or subdivide your network using a bridge.
5. **A** The Internet uses TCP/IP.
6. **B** The Internet uses TCP/IP.
7. **A, C** NetBEUI has small memory overhead and can be used in networks that are connected with bridges.
8. **B** WINS allows for NetBIOS name resolution.

1.4 Key Words

Bridge	CSNW
DNS	DHCP
GSNW	Internet
IPX/SPX	NetBEUI
NetBIOS	Novell NetWare
NWLink	Router
TCP/IP	WINS

Practice Exam: Planning

Use this practice exam to test your mastery of Planning. This practice exam is 13 questions long, so you should try to finish the test within 24 minutes. Keep in mind that the passing Microsoft score is 76.4 percent. There will be two types of questions:

- Multiple Choice—Select the correct answer.
- Multiple Multiple Choice—Select all answers that are correct.

Begin as soon as you are ready. The answers follow the test.

1. Sally needs to enable Mac users from the Sales department to share files with PC users. Which operating systems support file shares for both Macintosh and PC users? Select all that apply:

   A. Windows 95b

   B. Windows NT Server

   C. You have to buy MS MacShare for Windows NT Server

   D. Windows NT Workstation with Macintosh shares

   E. None of the above

2. Which of the following statements is *not* true? Choose all that apply:

   A. NT Server is designed to operate as a network server and domain controller.

   B. NT Workstation, like Windows 95, is designed to serve as a network client and desktop operating system.

   C. Windows NT Workstation can serve as a stand-alone operating system.

   D. The most striking difference between Windows NT Workstation and Windows 95 is Workstation's client capabilities.

   E. All of the above are true.

3. How is NWLink defined? Choose all that apply:

   A. IPX/SPX-compatible transport that provides support for TCP/IP sockets and various APIs.

   B. IPX/SPX-compatible transport that provides support for IPX/SPX Sockets and NetBIOS APIs.

   C. TAPI-compliant protocol that supports Windows Sockets and NetBIOS APIs.

   D. NetBEUI protocol which can be used on networks with bridges.

   E. None of the above.

4. Which of the following statements about workgroups is *not* true?

   A. A Windows NT Server acting as a client can participate in workgroups.

   B. A workgroup is easier to install than a domain.

   C. A workgroup does not require an NT Server machine acting as a domain controller.

   D. A workgroup is simpler than a domain.

5. Which of the following statements about partitions is *not* true? Choose all that apply:

   A. If you choose to use an extended partition on a hard disk, you are limited to three primary partitions for that disk.

   B. A primary partition can be subdivided, as long as one of the divisions is the bootable OS.

C. An extended partition can be subdivided into smaller logical drives.

D. One hard disk can contain four extended partitions.

E. One hard disk can contain up to four primary partitions.

6. With which of the following systems is Windows NT Server compatible? Choose all that apply:

   A. MS-DOS 5.0

   B. Windows 3.1x

   C. OS/2 1.x

   D. POSIX-based applications

7. What are the advantages of NetBEUI? Choose all that apply:

   A. It can be used on networks with bridges.

   B. It comes with a small memory overhead.

   C. It is used on LANs and WANs.

   D. It is easily routable.

8. Which statements are true about TCP/IP?

   A. TCP/IP is routable.

   B. TCP/IP is the language of the Internet.

   C. You can interconnect with more networks if you are using TCP/IP.

   D. TCP/IP accommodates a wide range of network hardware, operating systems, and applications.

   E. All of the above are true.

9. Which of the following statements is/are *not* true about the FAT file system? Choose all that apply:

   A. FAT is typically the more efficient file system for small partitions.

   B. FAT is generally faster than NTFS.

   C. You cannot conserve space by compressing files on a FAT partition.

   D. FAT is more secure than NTFS.

   E. Use the FAT file system if you will be dual-booting your computer with another operating system and you want to access the partition from the other operating system.

10. Which of the following statements is *not* true about the NTFS file system? Choose all that apply:

   A. The biggest drawback with using NTFS is that only the Windows NT operating system can access NTFS partitions.

   B. When partitions are under 400 MB (on average), NTFS is your most reasonable choice.

   C. You cannot conserve space by compressing files on a NTFS partition.

   D. NTFS supports bigger partitions than FAT.

   E. NTFS supports sector sparing, also known as hot fixing, on SCSI hard drives.

11. How is fault tolerance defined?

   A. A system's capability to enable disk mirroring.

   B. A system's capability to duplicate data during backup procedures.

   C. A system's capability to compensate in the event of hardware disaster.

   D. A system's capability to enable disk striping with parity.

12. Which of the following statements about disk mirroring is *not* true?

    A. Disk mirroring is RAID Level 1.

    B. In disk mirroring, Windows NT writes the same data to two physical disks.

    C. In disk mirroring, Windows NT records parity information that it can use to regenerate missing data if a disk should fail.

    D. All of the above are true.

13. Which of the following statements about the performance differences between Windows NT Workstation and Server is/are *not* true? Choose all that apply:

    A. Windows NT Workstation preloads a Virtual DOS Machine (VDM), the 32-bit MS-DOS emulator that supports legacy applications.

    B. Caching is handled differently on workstations and servers, enabling better network throughput on Windows NT Server and better local disk access time on Windows NT Workstation.

    C. Windows NT Workstation includes a configurable server service that enables you to tune the server as an application server or as a file/print server.

    D. The server files system driver used in both Windows NT Workstation and Server (SRV.SYS) is more subject to paging under Windows NT Workstation than under Windows NT Server.

    E. C and D are not true.

Answers and Explanations: Practice Exam

1. **B** NT Server offers Services for Macintosh, which enable file shares for Mac and PC users.
2. **D** The most striking difference between Windows NT Workstation and Windows 95 is security. Windows NT Workstation is an extremely secure operating system.
3. **B** NWLink is defined as the IPX/SPX-compatible transport that provides support for IPX/SPX Sockets and NetBIOS APIs.
4. **A** Unless a Windows NT Server computer is configured as a stand-alone server, it cannot participate in a workgroup.
5. **B, D** Primary partitions cannot be subdivided; one hard disk can contain only one extended partition.
6. **A, B, C, D** Windows NT Server is compatible with all aforementioned systems.
7. **A, B** NetBEUI has small memory overhead and can be used in networks that are connected with bridges.
8. **E** TCP/IP is routable, widely used, flexible, and the Internet-standard protocol.
9. **B, D** FAT is generally slower and significantly less secure than NTFS.
10. **B, C** When partitions are over 400 MB (not under), NTFS is your most reasonable choice. Windows NT provides the capability to compress NTFS files.
11. **C** Fault tolerance is the system's capability to compensate in the event of hardware disaster.
12. **C** In disk striping with parity (not disk mirroring), Windows NT records parity information that it can use to regenerate missing data if a disk should fail.
13. **C** Windows NT Workstation does not provide the configurable server service because it is limited to 10 inbound sessions.

CHAPTER 2

Installation and Configuration

2.1 Installing Windows NT Server on Intel-Based Platforms

The following Microsoft test objectives are covered in this chapter:

- Install Windows NT Server on Intel-based platforms.
- Install Windows NT Server to perform various server roles, including primary domain controller, backup domain controller, and member server.
- Install Windows NT Server by using various methods, including CD-ROM, over the network, Network Client administrator, and express versus custom.
- Install protocols and protocol bindings. Protocols include TCP/IP, NWLink, IPX/SPX compatible transport, NetBEUI.
- Configure network adapters. Considerations include changing IRQ, I/O base, memory address, and configuring multiple adapters.
- Configure Windows NT Server core services, including Directory Replicator, License Manager, and other services.
- Configure peripherals and devices, including communications devices, SCSI devices, tape device drivers, UPS service, mouse drivers, display drivers, and keyboard drivers.
- Configure hard disks to meet various requirements. Requirements include allocating disk space capacity, providing redundancy, improving performance, providing security, and formatting.
- Configure printers. Tasks include adding and configuring a printer, implementing a printer pool, and setting print priorities.
- Configure a Windows NT Server computer for various types of client computers. Client computer types include Windows NT Workstation, Windows 95, and Microsoft MS-DOS-based.

A. Hardware Requirements

Hardware requirements are dependent on the processor type. Intel-based machines have the following requirements:

Intel Processor

80486/33 or higher

16 MB of RAM

125 MB hard disk space

Hard drive may be FAT or NTFS

VGA Display or better

3.5 inch drive required

Note that all hardware must be on a current Hardware Compatibility list (available at www.microsoft.com/ntserver/hcl/hclintro.htm), or the manufacturer must supply an updated driver compatible for NT 4.0. It is possible that a device may be compatible with another driver.

B. Installation Location

Windows NT can be installed alongside other operating systems on the same machine. In this multiboot environment, each OS would be installed in its own subdirectory. The default directory for the system files of NT is WINNT.

Windows NT requires a boot partition, typically the active drive, and a system partition. The boot partition contains information about the platform. The system partition contains the source files for the OS. These can be the same or different partitions.

C. WINNT Switches

The following switches enable you to customize how WINNT.EXE begins the setup process:

/b	No boot floppies
/s	Source file location. Syntax is: WINNT.EXE /s: <path of source files>
/U	Unattended installation
/UDF	Tailored, unattended installation for installation on multiple machines
/T:drive_letter Temporary drive	Tells WINNT or winnt32 to put the installation files on the specified drive
/OX	Creates just the three boot disks
/F	Do not verify files as they are copied to hard disk
/C	Do not check for free space

D. Installation Phases

Microsoft divides the installation into four phases:

Phase 0: Preinstallation

Phase 1: Gathering information about your computer

Phase 2: Installing Networking

Phase 3: Finishing setup

1. Phase 0: Preinstallation

During preinstallation, Setup copies the necessary files to your hard drive and assembles the information it needs for the install based on the hardware detected in your machine. It is during this phase that the three setup disks are created.

- **Setup Disk 1.** When booting from disk 1, the MBR (Master Boot Record) passes control to NTLDR. NTLDR loads the kernel (NTKRNLMP.EXE). Then the HAL (Hardware Abstraction Layer) is loaded.
- **Setup Disk 2.** This disk contains a minimal version of the registry. This simple registry instructs WINNT to load the main installation driver and generic hardware drives for keyboard, floppy, video, and the driver for the FAT file system. In addition, there is provision for SCSI port drivers.
- **Setup Disk 3.** This disk contains additional SCSI drivers, the driver for the NTFS file system, and drivers for various hard disks.

During this process, the setup routine has loaded the minimal drivers for the hardware, and for the file systems. WINNT then begins user interaction by confirming hardware-related information.

a. Mass Storage Devices

Setup asks the user if it should attempt to detect mass storage devices. Upon completion of the detection, a confirmation screen appears with information WINNT has retrieved. The user may press Enter to confirm what Setup has detected or press S to specify additional devices.

b. Hardware and Components

Setup presents a list of detected hardware (mouse, keyboard, and video) and waits for a user confirmation or any changes to the list.

c. Partitions

Setup needs to know where it should install the Windows NT source files. The default directory is WINNT. The user is given the opportunity to change this directory name and to specify in which partition NT should be installed.

Setup also gives the opportunity to create a partition in unpartitioned space.

Setup then presents the following information:

- Format the partition using FAT.
- Format the partition using the NTFS file system.
- Convert the partition to NTFS.
- Leave the current file system intact.

NTFS is designed for NT. It is not accessible from other operating systems including Windows 95 and DOS. If the conversion to NTFS is selected, the conversion does not happen until after setup has been completed. If dual booting is planned for the machine, the active partition must remain as FAT. If it is a RISC-based machine a minimum 2 MB FAT partition is required. This is due to the firmware on RISC-based machines.

Setup examines your hard disk for corruption. Setup allows for an exhaustive examination or a minimal exam. Choose S to skip the exhaustive examination.

Finally, Setup copies the source files to the hard disk; this will take several minutes. When Setup is complete a message appears asking that the floppy be removed and then to press Enter to restart your computer.

2. Phase 1: Gathering Information

After the computer restarts, setup displays the licensing agreement for approval and begins copying files from the CD-ROM or the Network site to the root directory.

The Setup Wizard appears announcing the remaining stages of the setup process:

- Gathering information about your computer
- Installing Windows NT Networking
- Finishing setup
- Name and Company Name

For legal and registration reasons, Setup asks for a name and company name. The Name field must be completed but the Company Name field may be left blank. Setup requires the product ID to continue.

a. Server Licensing Mode

NT Server requires a licensing mode for network connections. There are two types of licensing:

- **Per Server license.** For each per server license you purchase, one concurrent network connection is allowed access to the server. When the maximum specified amount of concurrent connections is reached, NT returns an error to a connecting user and prohibits access. An administrator, however, can still connect to the server to increase the amount of per server licenses.

- **Per Seat license.** Clients are free to connect to any server, and there are unlimited connections to the server. Each client participating in the network must have a per seat license.

Both modes of licenses are on an honor system.

b. Computer Name

Every networked Windows NT–based computer must have a unique NetBIOS computer name. A NetBIOS name may be up to 15 characters. Workgroup and domain names are also NetBIOS names so the computer name must be unique among these as well.

c. Server Type

Windows NT Server is allowed to be a PDC, a BDC, or a Member Server.

d. Administrator Password

Setup asks for an administrator account password. This password is limited to 14 characters and is case-sensitive.

e. Emergency Repair Disk

This is essentially a clone of the information stored in the \REPAIR directory in case of corruption on your hard disk.

f. Optional Components

Setup asks what additional components should be installed for the server.

3. Phase 2: Installing NT Networking

The Wizard announces that it is ready to install the networking portion of the install.

a. Network Participation

The Setup Wizard asks whether this machine will participate on the network. Setup needs to know whether participation will occur via a network card, modem, or both. If No is selected, the Setup Wizard will proceed to Phase 3, "Finishing Setup."

b. Internet/Intranet Service

Windows NT Server 4.0 comes with IIS (Internet Information Server). The Setup wizard will ask if this should be installed. If you choose Yes, the wizard will walk you through the getting started phases of IIS setup. If you choose No, an icon will be displayed on the desktop for future installation.

c. Network Adapter Card

Setup will ask if it should search for a network adapter card. Setup stops after it finds the first adapter card and the Start Search button changes into a Find Next button.

The user may also choose the option to select a network adapter card from a list. The have disk button is used to install a driver provided by an OEM. Setup may display a dialog box asking the user to confirm the network card's settings. Networking services can be installed on top of NT's RAS to use the services via a modem.

d. Network Protocols

Setup gives the user the option to install TCP/IP, NWLink, and NetBEUI. In addition, other protocols such as AppleTalk, DLC, Point to Point Tunneling Protocol, and others may be installed. TCP/IP and NWLINK IPX/SPX protocols are selected by default on Intel-based machines. NT Servers may be clients of DHCP.

e. Network Services

Setup asks what additional services should be installed. If you add to your configuration *after* setup, you may do so through Control Panel, Network.

f. Network Components

Setup completes the networking installation phase by presenting several options, including DHCP participation, IP information, modems installed, and the choice to change any settings created so far.

NT Server must be either a member of a Domain (PDC or BDC) or a member server in a workgroup or a domain. It cannot be a member in both a workgroup and a domain. NT Servers that are joining domains must have a computer account created for them before they join the domain. There are two ways to create a computer account:

- The administrator must manually add the computer account through Server Manager.
- The user adding the workstation must be a member of the Administrators group, or have the user right to "Add workstations to a domain."

4. Phase 3: Finishing Setup

After completing the networking components, setup then finishes its routine with the following steps:

- **Time Zone.** Setup requests the current date and time information during the final phase of setup. NT has an option to account for daylight savings time.
- **Exchange Configuration.** If Microsoft Exchange was selected as an optional component in Phase 1, setup requests information to configure Exchange.
- **Display Settings.** Setup detects the video display adapter.

  If the adapter uses a chipset for which NT includes a driver, it displays that information in the dialog box.

  Setup requires that the settings be tested before installation can continue.
- **Pentium Patch.** If setup detects the presence of the Intel Pentium floating point division error, Setup asks if you want to disable the floating point hardware and enable floating point emulation software.

  Disabling the hardware makes the floating-point calculations much more accurate at the expense of performance.
- **Emergency Repair Disk.** During the final phase, Setup creates a \REPAIR directory in the Windows NT root directory. This directory contains a backup of the current registry in use by NT.

If Setup was told to generate an Emergency Repair Disk, it will request a floppy at this point. Setup will format the floppy and prepare it as an Emergency Repair Disk.

2.1.1 Exercise: Installation Requirements and Procedures

This is a paper-based exercise. The information in this exercise may be applied to an actual install of Windows NT Server 4.0.

Answer the following questions based on your knowledge of the NT Server installation program:

Installation Requirements

Hardware Requirements:

1. What processor type is required?
2. What is the minimum amount of RAM required?
3. What is the minimum amount of hard disk space required?

Installation Procedures:

1. How do you dual boot between 95 and NT?
2. What is the fastest way to install NT?
3. What should you do if you have to install NT many times?
4. How can you avoid using the three setup disks?
5. What does HAL do?
6. How do you specify additional storage devices?
7. Define a Boot partition.
8. Define a System partition.
9. What are two advantages of using NTFS?
10. What are two disadvantages of using NTFS?
11. What is the default root directory of NT?

Gathering Information

1. Why is the Name field required?
2. What does Per server licensing mean?
3. What does Per seat licensing mean?
4. How many characters is the computer name limited to?
5. Why must the computer name be unique?
6. What are the roles the NT Server can play in the domain?
7. How many characters is the administrator password limited to?

Installing NT Networking

1. What does NT need to participate on the network?
2. What can you do to make NT a Web server?
3. How can NT find multiple adapter cards?
4. What is the default protocol for NT Server?

Network Components:

1. What is a domain?
2. In what two network environments will an NT member server take part?
3. What rights do you have to have to join a domain?
4. To join a domain, the computer must:

2.1 Practice Problems

1. Your supervisor would like you to install NT Server on the following machines. Based on your knowledge, which configurations would allow you to install NT Server 4.0?
   - A. 16 MB RAM, 500 MB hard drive, 3.5 inch floppy, CD-ROM, and a Super VGA monitor.
   - B. Pentium 200, 32 MB RAM, 4 GB SCSI hard drive, 3.5 inch floppy, CD-ROM drive, and a VGA monitor.
   - C. 12 MB RAM, 1 GB hard drive, 3.5 inch floppy, and a VGA monitor.
   - D. 32 MB RAM, 500 MB hard drive, 3.5 inch floppy, and a VGA monitor.
2. Your company has purchased new Ethernet network cards that are not on the HCL for NT. You should:
   - A. Contact Microsoft's 800 number for unsupported hardware.
   - B. Visit Microsoft.com and download all Ethernet drivers.
   - C. Contact the OEM and ask for an available drive for the cards.
   - D. Do not install Windows NT Server.
3. You would like to dual boot NT with Windows 95 for testing and evaluating software. You can configure this by (choose the best answer):
   - A. Having two hard drives with NT on disk 0, and having Windows 95 on Disk 1.
   - B. Install NT and 95 on the same hard drive, but in different partitions.
   - C. Install NT and 95 in separate directories.
   - D. This cannot be done.
4. The setup program for installing NT Server 4.0 is called:
   - A. Setup.exe
   - B. WINNT.EXE
   - C. VMM32.exe
   - D. WINCOM
5. Windows NT requires a boot partition. Choose the best description of a boot partition:
   - A. The location of the WINNT directory where all boot and system information is stored.
   - B. The partition that holds the Windows NT operating system files.
   - C. Master Boot Record and NT source files.
   - D. The WINNT directory must be on the active partition.
6. You would like to upgrade your NT Server 3.51 so that you do not lose your current settings. How can you do this? (Choose the best answer.)
   - A. Run WINNT from the run command inside of NT Server 3.51.
   - B. Run WINNT32 from the run command inside of NT Server 3.51.
   - C. Run WINNT.EXE /upgrade at the DOS prompt.
   - D. You must reinstall Windows NT Server 4.0, as there is no upgrade available due to registry difference of NT 3.51 and NT 4.0.
7. You have 100 workstations on which to install Windows NT Workstation 4.0. What is the easiest method to do this? (Choose the best answer.)
   - A. You must visit each workstation and install NT from the CD-ROM.

2

B. You can share out the WINNT directory from another workstation and then connect to this through DOS.

C. You can share out the entire CD-ROM from another workstation and then connect to this through DOS.

D. You can share the entire CD-ROM from an NT Server and then connect to this through DOS.

8. You are installing NT Server 4.0 and do not want the boot diskettes generated by the setup program. How can you disable this portion of the setup program? (Choose the best answer.)

   A. Windows NT Server 4.0 requires the setup disks to install.

   B. Start setup with the following syntax: WINNT.EXE /b.

   C. Start setup with the following syntax: WINNT.EXE /f.

   D. Start setup with the following syntax: WINNT32.EXE.

9. You are installing NT server as a PDC on an Intel-based machine. When you try to designate your password for the administrator's account, you are not allowed to enter the password "Windows NT is Great." Why is this? (Choose the best answer.)

   A. Passwords are limited to 14 characters.

   B. Passwords cannot contain spaces.

   C. Passwords cannot contain the words NT.

   D. Windows NT requires that you enter your password twice to verify all settings. You are probably not typing the password identically in each field.

10. When booting from setup disk 1 during the install phase of NT Server, what role does the HAL play? (Choose the best answer.)

   A. HAL, the Hardware Abstraction Layer, is responsible for hiding the hardware from the operating system. This is what makes NT portable between RISC and Intel-based machines.

   B. HAL, the Hardware Arbitration Layer, is responsible for assigning hardware resources such as IRQs.

   C. HAL passes control to the NTKRNLMP.exe, which allows access to the processor(s).

   D. HAL allows Direct Memory Access for the setup program to access areas of memory directly.

11. Setup Disk 2 instructs the setup program to (choose the best answer):

   A. Scan the hard disk for errors.

   B. Load a minimal file system to begin the file transfer process.

   C. Begin building the registry based on hardware detected.

   D. Load generic drivers for keyboards, floppy, video, and the drivers for the FAT file system.

12. On Setup Disk 2 and Setup Disk 3 there are SCSI port drivers available to setup. Why is this important? (Choose the best answer.)

   A. 16-bit drivers are not compatible with Windows NT.

   B. Setup needs these drivers to compare to any config.sys settings to determine if there are SCSI controllers installed in the machine.

   C. RISC-based systems require a SCSI drive for the hard drive.

   D. Setup might need these drivers to access a SCSI CD-ROM during setup.

13. During NT installation, NT asks you to confirm detected mass storage devices. You discover, however, that setup did not find all of the hard drives in your computer. You should (choose the best answer):

    A. Press escape and then F5 to force setup to look again for mass storage devices.

    B. Simply press F5. This will cause setup to search for mass storage devices.

    C. Press **S** to specify mass storage devices that setup could not recognize.

    D. You need a bus enumerator from the OEM to continue.

14. Setup presents a list of detected hardware including mouse, keyboard, and video settings. If the list is incorrect you should (choose the best answer):

    A. Start setup again using the /m switch for manual detection of devices.

    B. Press F5 to force setup to detect devices again.

    C. Use the arrow keys to select the device that is incorrect and press F8 to see alternatives.

    D. Use the arrow keys to select the device that is incorrect, and press Enter to see alternatives.

15. Setup asks you where it should install Windows NT Server. The default directory is what? (Choose the best answer.)

    A. NTSRV

    B. WINNT

    C. WINNT40

    D. NTSRV40

16. You are installing Windows NT Server 4.0 on a RISC-based machine. You would like to change the partition and the directory in which NT will be installed. (Choose the best answer.)

    A. Change the directory name from NTSRV to whatever you like. Then arrow up or down to choose the correct partition on which the source files should be placed.

    B. Change the directory name from WINNT to whatever you like. Then arrow up or down to choose the correct partition on which the source files should be placed.

    C. Change the directory name from NTSRV40 to whatever you like. Then arrow up or down to choose the correct partition on which the source files should be placed.

    D. This cannot be done because RISC-based machines require that the source files be located on the active partition.

17. You are installing NT Server on an Intel-based machine. During installation, you realize that, although you have a 4GB SCSI drive, you have only partitioned 250 MB of the drive. You would like to dual boot with 95 and NT. What configuration should you choose? (Choose all that would work.)

    A. During setup, choose the option to create a partition in unused space. Create a 2 GB partition, format it with NTFS and install NT onto that partition.

    B. Install NT into the same partition as 95, but in separate directories.

    C. Install NT into the same partition as 95, but in separate directories. Then convert the drive to NTFS.

    D. Exit the setup program, and then use FDISK to create a new partition. Format this new partition, and then run WINNT.EXE again.

18. During setup, you have chosen the option to create a new partition onto which to

install the NT source files. What choices do you have after designating this new partition? (Choose all that apply.)

A. Format the partition as FAT.

B. Format the partition as NTFS.

C. Convert the partition to NTFS.

D. There is no available choice. Setup automatically formats this partition as NTFS.

19. You are installing NT Server and you would like to take advantage of NTFS for security. However, your supervisor is worried about compatibility of NT with other operating systems on the network. Is this a valid concern? (Choose the best answer.)

A. Yes, it is a valid concern because NTFS is not compatible with any other operating system except for NT.

B. No, it is not a valid concern because NTFS is compatible with all operating systems.

C. No, it is not a valid concern because NTFS partitions are not accessible by other operating systems only if those operating systems are on the same machine.

D. Yes, but only because NTFS supports long filename support and other operating systems might not have long filename support.

20. You are installing Windows NT Server onto an Intel-based machine. Currently on this machine you have Windows 95. You would like to dual boot between 95 and NT so you are certain to install NT in a separate directory than 95. Upon completion of NT setup you have no ability to boot into 95. What went wrong? (Choose the best answer.)

A. You must edit the boot.ini to reflect the location of the 95 source files.

B. You told setup to convert the active partition to NTFS.

C. You must add the line to 95's MSDOS.SYS, BootMulit=1 to dual boot with NT.

D. You need to use the Boot Manager in the Administrative Tools folder to setup dual-boot ability with other operating systems.

21. During setup you told NT to format a new partition you created with NTFS. The setup program does this when? (Choose the best answer.)

A. Immediately.

B. After the registry is built.

C. When NT is completely installed and NT reboots for the first time.

D. The first time you open Disk Administrator, a macro runs that performs the conversion.

22. During installation, Setup must examine your hard drives for any corruption. You are confident that your hard drives are okay and would like to skip any exhaustive exams. How can you do this? (Choose the best answer.)

A. Setup requires an exhaustive exam of all media before installation can continue.

B. Press Shift+F8 to skip the exam.

C. Press Escape to skip the exam.

D. Press B to bypass the exam.

23. You are a consultant hired by a company to install NT Server 4. You do not want to put a name in the Name field, as you are not an employee for your client. How can you bypass this field? (Choose the best answer.)

A. Click on the skip button to continue.

B. A value is required to continue.

C. Click on the cancel button to continue.

D. Enter a value now; but later, through Add/remove programs, take out your name.

24. You are a consultant hired by a company to install NT Server. When you get to the product identification field it asks you for a CD Key. Your client tells you this is unavailable. What should you do? (Choose the best answer.)

A. Call Microsoft's support for a CD key.

B. Insert a CD Key from another CD.

C. Stop installation until the original CD key is available.

D. Choose Continue and enter the CD key later, through the registry.

25. You and an associate are installing NT Server and your associate is confused about per server versus per seat licensing agreements. Which would best describe per server? (Choose the best answer.)

A. Per server enables all clients to connect as often as they want.

B. Per server allows for a predetermined amount of concurrent connections.

C. Per server allows for unlimited connections to any server available.

D. Per server allows for a limited number of connections within a 24-hour period.

26. You and an associate are installing NT Server, and your associate is confused about per server versus per seat licensing agreements. Which would best describe per seat? (Choose the best answer.)

A. Per seat allows an unlimited number of concurrent network connections.

B. Per seat allows for a limited number of connections within a 24-hour period.

C. Per seat allows for an unlimited number of concurrent network connections within 30, 60, or 90 day increments.

D. Per seat is only available if you have more than one Domain Controller.

2.1 Answers and Explanations: Practice Problems

1. **A, B, D** The minimum requirements to install NT server on an Intel-based machine are: 80486/33 or higher, 16 MB of RAM, 125 MB hard disk space, VGA or better, and 3.5 inch floppy drive.

2. **C** You should contact the Original Equipment Manufacturer for an updated driver for Windows NT Server. Another possibility is to check whether the network card emulates another card for which there is an NT 4 driver on the NT Server CD.

3. **C** After you have installed Windows 95, followed by Windows NT, you can then choose MS-DOS from the OS Loader menu, or you can edit the boot.ini to create a separate entry for Windows 95.

4. **B** To install Windows NT, run WINNT.exe from a command prompt, or from within Windows for Workgroups. Within previous versions of Windows NT or from within Windows 95, you may run the 32-bit version of the setup program called WINNT32.exe.

5. **B** The partition that holds the Windows NT operating system is called the boot partition. The system partition is the partition that contains the files necessary to boot the operating system. The system partition does not have to be the partition where the operating system is installed.

6. **B** WINNT32.EXE is the command to upgrade from a previous version of NT Server.

7. **D** By sharing out the CD-ROM from a server rather than a workstation, you bypass NT Workstation's limit of 10 concurrent connections. Server connection is limited only by the licensing agreement you have chosen during the install.

8. **B** You should use WINNT /b to disable the generation of floppies during setup. The WINNT /f command is used to disable file verification, as they are copied to the hard disk.

9. **A** Your logon password is limited to 14 characters.

10. **A** The Hardware Abstraction Layer is responsible for hiding the hardware from the OS.

11. **D** These generic drivers are needed so that user interaction can occur throughout the setup phase.

12. **D** Setup will need access to the SCSI CD-ROM drive if one exists so that it can transfer data from the CD-ROM to the hard drive.

13. **C** Press **S** to specify mass storage devices.

14. **D** Use the arrow keys to select the device that is incorrect, and press Enter to see alternatives.

15. **B** During the installation of Windows NT, the setup program recommends that you install Windows NT into the directory called WINNT. You may change this to a new name if you want.

16. **B** You are allowed on Intel or RISC-based computers to rename the directory name and to specify where the directory will be located.

17. **A, B, D** During setup you will have the opportunity to create a new partition. NT and 95 can coexist on the same partition as long as they are in separate directories. You can exit the setup program, create a new partition, and start over with WINNT; but there is no real reason to follow this method because you are able to create partitions from within the text-based setup program.

18. **A, B** During setup you have created a new partition. Because this new partition is unformatted, Setup allows you to format the partition at this time. You can format the partition with FAT or you with NT's filing system, NTFS.

19. **C** NTFS is not accessible by any other operating system that is dual booting on the same machine. Across the network, NT is compatible with most major operating systems.

20. **B** If you told Setup to convert the active partition to NTFS, 95 will be unable to boot because 95 requires a FAT partition.

21. **C** The partition is first formatted with FAT and is marked to be converted to NTFS when NT is rebooted.

22. **C** You are allowed to skip the exhaustive exam.

23. **B** The name field must be completed, the company field may be ignored.

24. **C** The product id is required to continue installation.

25. **B** Per server allows for a limited number of concurrent network connections.

26. **A** Per seat allows for an unlimited number of concurrent network connections.

2.1 Key Words

Protocol

Boot partition

System partition

NTFS

2.2 Windows NT Server 4.0 Server Roles

Windows NT Server plays one of three roles in a network environment:

Role	Characteristics
Primary Domain Controller (PDC)	First server installed in a domain Contains master copy of user database Only one PDC per domain.
Backup Domain Controller (BDC)	Maintains a copy of the domain's user account database Shares logon authentication workload with PDC May be promoted to a PDC should the PDC be taken offline A domain may have more than one BDC.
Member Server	Does not maintain a copy of the user accounts database May serve as a file, print, or application server May be a member of a domain or workgroup Cannot be promoted to domain controller without reinstalling NT server There may be multiple member servers in a domain or workgroup.

A. Domain Attributes

A *domain* is a collection of computer accounts. Only NT Workstations and servers can be true members of a domain.

Windows 95 machines, Windows for Workgroups, and DOS-based machines are not members of a domain, they are clients of the domain. Users are validated by a domain controller through a secure network channel. The NT service responsible for validation is the Netlogon service. The first server online in a domain must be the Primary Domain Controller.

1. Primary Domain Controllers

The PDC maintains a centralized database of all user account information. The PDC is responsible for validating users on the domain.

A PDC may also act as a file, print, or application server. There may be only one PDC in a domain at any given time. The PDC is where all administration of user accounts, and computer accounts should occur. The PDC will synchronize its account database to the Backup Domain Controller.

2. Backup Domain Controllers

The Backup Domain Controllers are responsible for validating user logon requests in conjunction with the PDC. They share the workload of validating user logon requests.

Backup Domain Controllers receive updates of the Domain Account Database in regular intervals, or synchronization sessions from the Primary Domain Controller.

A BDC may also act as a file, print, or application server. There is no limit to how many BDCs are in a domain.

B. Member Servers

Member Servers are NT Servers that act only as a file, print, or application servers. Member Servers may be either a member of a workgroup or a domain. Member servers do not validate user logon requests.

C. Server Maintenance

BDCs may be promoted to a PDC through Server Manager. Only an administrator can perform this function. Promotion is useful if the PDC must be taken down, or goes offline.

Promotion is a manual process; it does not happen automatically. There is no way to promote a Member Server to a Domain Controller without reinstalling NT Server.

Account synchronization may be forced through Server Manager or by typing the command NET ACCOUNTS /SYNC at the command prompt. Accounts can be synchronized throughout the entire domain or through one BDC at a time.

There is no way to move a domain controller from one domain to another without reinstalling NT Server. This is due to the SID of the domains.

There is no way to install a BDC without the presence of a PDC. To join a domain a computer must have a computer account. There are two methods of creating a computer account:

- An administrator adds the computer account through Server Manager before the computer joins the domain.
- If it is NT Server, you may select the option to create a computer account during installation. An Administrators group username and password are required.

It is possible to change the domain name by using the Control Panel network. You can also change the NetBIOS name of the server through this applet. A Domain controller can validate logon requests from any of the following clients:

- Windows NT
- Windows 95
- Windows for Workgroups
- Microsoft LAN Manager
- MS-DOS clients with the enhanced redirector installed

Domain Controller and Member servers have the following features:

- RAS support for up to 256 simultaneous connections
- Fault tolerance
- Internet Information server
- Gateway Services for Netware
- Macintosh file and print services

2.2.1 Exercise: Promoting a BDC to a PDC

This exercise requires two domain controllers. You need to log on to a domain controller with administrative rights.

To promote the BDC to a PDC:

1. Logon as administrator if you have not done so already.
2. Start the Server Manager tool from the Administrative Tools group.
3. Choose the BDC from the list of available computers.
4. What do you notice about the icons of the computers?
5. From the Computer menu, choose Promote to PDC.
6. What does this mean?
7. What messages appear during the promotion?
8. Why would this process be useful?
9. Reverse the roles back to their original setting.

2.2.2 Exercise: Synchronizing the Directory Accounts Database

1. In Server Manager, choose a BDC.
2. From the computer menu, choose Synchronize with the Primary Domain Controller.
3. What does this command mean?
4. Now choose the Primary Domain Controller.
5. From the Computer Menu, choose Synchronize the entire domain.
6. What does this command mean?
7. Exit Server Manager.

2.2 Practice Problems

1. You are the administrator for a network consisting primarily of Windows for Workgroups and Windows 95 clients. You have decided to install Windows NT Server. As you are installing NT Server 4.0, you choose to make this machine a member server because you already have a workgroup in place. With this configuration, what can your clients now do? (Choose all that apply.)

   A. Log onto the domain for centralized security.

   B. Use NT Server as a file, print, and application server.

   C. Store their work on the server for consistent backups.

   D. Your 95 clients can now use user-level security.

2. Your company has three domains: SALES, MARKETING, and ACCOUNTING. You would like to create a new domain for your office in New York to be called NEW YORK. The SALES domain has three BDCs, so you decide to move one BDC to the NEW YORK domain. To make this BDC from SALES a PDC for NEW YORK, what must you do? (Choose the best answer.)

   A. Change the domain name in the Control Panel Network to NEW YORK.

   B. Promote the BDC to a PDC through Server Manager.

   C. Reinstall Windows NT Server 4.0.

   D. Change the domain name in the Network applet to NEW YORK, and change the administrator's password.

3. You are adding a BDC to your current domain. You tell the setup program that this machine should be a BDC in the Domain called CALIFORNIA but it responds with the message, "No domain controller could be found." You verify that the domain name is spelled correctly, that you are connected to the network, and that your PDC is online. What do you suspect is the problem? (Choose all that apply.)

   A. You do not have administrative rights to add a BDC to the domain.

   B. The BDC is not using the same protocol as the PDC.

   C. Your network card has problems.

   D. You are obtaining your IP address via DHCP, and the DHCP server is currently out of IP addresses.

4. You want to create a BDC for your client in Idaho. You decide that you will install NT Server at your office and then ship the finished server to the client. However, when you install NT Server, it will not allow you to create a BDC without the presence of a PDC. Why is this? (Choose the best answer.)

   A. A PDC must establish a secure network channel with the BDC to determine that you are using a legal copy of NT.

   B. A PDC must be present to alert the BDC that a Master Browser is already in place on the network.

   C. The PDC must be available so that the account database can be synchronized to the BDC.

   D. You can make a server a BDC before the PDC. You must, however, start the installation as WINNT.EXE /BDC from a DOS prompt.

5. Your company has just purchased a RISC-based machine that has four processors, 2 4 GB hard drives, 128 MB of RAM, and an external CD-ROM tower. Your domain, MIS, currently has a less attractive NT 3.51 server acting as a

PDC. It is your intention to make your new RISC machine your PDC and demote the 3.51 server to a BDC. What is the correct procedure to do this? (Choose the best answer.)

A. Take the 3.51 server offline, install NT Server 4.0 on the RISC-based machine, and mark it as the PDC. Then bring the 3.51 server back online and demote it through server manager to a BDC.

B. Install NT Server 4.0 as a BDC in your current domain. Then promote the BDC to a PDC in your domain.

C. You must first upgrade the 3.51 server to NT Server 4.0. Install NT Server 4.0 as a BDC in your current domain. Then promote the BDC to a PDC in your domain.

D. This cannot be done without reinstalling NT Server 4.0 on both machines.

6. Your supervisor is concerned about creating a PDC before a BDC. How would you explain the proper order of creating a domain? (Choose the best answer.)

   A. You must have a BDC before a PDC because the backup domain controller is there for backup and safety, in case something happens during the installation of the PDC.

   B. A PDC is always the first server online during the creation of a domain.

   C. A PDC is not required to be the first server online as long as the BDC has the same domain name as the PDC.

   D. The BDC can be installed first as long as the Directory Replicator service has been installed during the initial installation.

7. You are installing NT Server as a PDC for network. You currently have a workgroup called DALLAS. You would like your NT domain to be called TEXAS and your PDC to be called DALLAS. However, when you enter the server name of DALLAS, Setup will not allow you to use that name. Why? (Choose the best answer.)

   A. The server name must be at least 15 characters long.

   B. The server name must contain numbers and letters for security reasons.

   C. The server name must be unique from any other resource on the network.

   D. You must confirm the server name. You are probably not correctly typing in DALLAS in each field.

8. You are installing NT Server as a BDC. You would like to name the domain controller "Backup Domain Controller 101." The setup program will not allow you to use this name. Why? (Choose the best answer.)

   A. You are already using this name somewhere else on the network.

   B. Server names cannot contain spaces.

   C. Server names must have letters and number for security.

   D. Server names are limited to 15 characters.

9. You have accidentally installed NT Server 4.0 as a member server. You were supposed to install NT as a BDC in the domain SALES. How can you change the status of this server? (Choose the best answer.)

   A. Use Server Manager to promote the member server to a BDC.

   B. Run WINNT32.EXE /BDC to promote the server to a BDC.

C. You must reinstall NT Server.

D. Use the Control Panel's network program to change the machine to a BDC.

10. You are the administrator for a 95 workgroup. You have decided to install NT Server as a PDC to move into a domain environment. During install you would like to use the password "AcmeSalesSupport" for the Administrator's account, but the setup program will not allow you to use this password. Why not? (Choose the best answer.)

A. Administrators' passwords must always be alphanumeric.

B. You must confirm your password, as passwords are case-sensitive and you might not be entering the same case each time.

C. Passwords are limited to 14 characters.

D. The administrators' password must match the CD-Key.

11. You are installing NT Server as a BDC. You have a DHCP server located available to this machine. How can you configure this machine to be a client of a DHCP server? (Choose the best answer.)

A. This cannot be done. Domain Controllers must have static IP addresses.

B. You must edit the IPCONFIG.SYS file and add the line of DHCP=1.

C. During IP Configuration, choose to participate in DHCP.

D. After installation, change the DHCP participation option in the Network Applet.

12. You are installing NT server as a BDC in your domain. During installation, Setup will not allow you to create this machine as a BDC in the domain NEW YORK. You confirm that both machines are using the same protocol. The network card and wire is fine, and the name of the server is not in use anywhere else in the domain. What do you suspect is the problem? (Choose the best answer.)

A. You did not select the machine to be a BDC, but a PDC.

B. You are not spelling the Domain name correctly.

C. You do not have a computer account created for the server.

D. You do not have the same version of NT on both the PDC and the BDC.

13. You are about to install NT as a BDC. You know that you must have a computer account for the BDC to join the domain. What are two ways you can create this account? (Choose two.)

A. Use Server Manager on the PDC and add the computer account.

B. Use User Manager for Domains and add the computer account.

C. Add the account during installation of the BDC.

D. Run WINNT.EXE /BDC to add the BDC account to the domain.

14. You are trying to add an additional PDC to the domain called MARKETING. What is the correct procedure to do this? (Choose the best answer.)

A. During setup, make this machine a PDC in the MARKETING domain.

B. Use Server Manager to create a PDC account for the MARKETING domain.

C. You cannot do this.

D. Run WINNT.EXE /pdc2 switch.

15. You and a colleague are adding a BDC to your domain. Your colleague is confused by you needing another domain controller instead of just a member server. You give several reasons for installing a BDC, including which of the following? (Choose all that apply.)

    A. A BDC can be a file, print, and application server.

    B. A BDC can also validate user logon requests

    C. A BDC can be a RAS Server.

    D. A BDC can be a DHCP server.

    E. A BDC can provide backup in case the PDC fails.

16. You have a Windows 95 workgroup called XYZ. You would like to add a server to this workgroup, but your supervisor is uncertain if it should be a PDC or just a member server. You identify several key attributes of a member server, including which of the following? (Choose all that apply.)

    A. A member server can be a file, print, or application server.

    B. A member server can be a member of both a domain and a workgroup at the same time.

    C. A member server can validate logon requests from clients

    D. A member server can be a RAS server.

17. You have a Windows 95 workgroup called XYZ. You would like to add a server to this workgroup, but your supervisor is uncertain if it should be a PDC or just a member server. You identify several key attributes of a PDC, including which of the following? (Choose all that apply.)

    A. A PDC can be a file, print, or application server.

    B. A PDC can validate logon requests from clients.

    C. A PDC can be a RAS Server.

    D. A PDC can be an Internet Information Server.

18. Your domain consists of a PDC, a BDC, and a member server. You want to take the PDC down to add a hard disk, but you are worried about not having a PDC online during the maintenance. What should you do? (Choose the best answer.)

    A. Do nothing. The BDC will promote itself automatically when it detects that the PDC is offline.

    B. Manually promote the BDC to a PDC.

    C. Manually promote the BDC to a PDC, and then promote the member server to a PDC.

    D. There is no real solution. No PDC will be available during maintenance.

19. Your domain consists of a PDC and a member server. As your domain grows, you realize that your PDC is very busy validating user logon requests. To change the member server to a BDC, you do what? (Choose the best answer.)

    A. Promote the member server to a BDC.

    B. Reinstall NT Server on the member server, and tell it to be a BDC during install.

    C. Run WINNT32.EXE.

    D. Use Server Manager to add a BDC computer account to the domain, and give this computer account the same NetBIOS name of the member server.

20. Your supervisor is unclear as to why your Windows 95 machines show up in a workgroup in Network Neighborhood, but your NT Workstations show up in the Domain. You explain that only certain machines are allowed to be domain

members. Choose from the following all that are allowed to be domain members:

A. Windows 95

B. Windows NT Workstations

C. Windows NT BDCs

D. Windows NT member servers

21. A domain controller is responsible for validating user logon requests. The NT Service that is responsible for logon validation is what? (Choose the best answer.)

A. Netlogon service

B. Server service

C. Security Accounts Manager service

D. RPC Mailslots

22. Your domain consists of one PDC and four BDCs. Your domain is still growing, and you would like to add another BDC. However, you are worried about the number of domain controllers a domain can have. What is the best solution? (Choose the best answer.)

A. You are limited to five domain controllers in a domain at a time.

B. There is no limit to the number of PDCs or BDCs a domain may have.

C. A domain may have only one PDC, but may have many BDCs.

D. The number of BDCs allowed depends on the number of user accounts in your domain. You are limited to one domain controller for every 120 user accounts.

23. You are planning on taking your PDC offline to add more memory. You would like to promote the BDC to a PDC through Server Manager. However, when you try to complete this task, you are not allowed to do so. You suspect the problem is what? (Choose the best answer.)

A. You have accidentally selected the PDC in Server Manager.

B. You do not have sufficient privileges to promote or to demote computer accounts.

C. You do not have a BDC, but a member server.

D. You must complete this command at the machine you are promoting.

24. You would like to change the name of your domain from XYZ to SALES. How can you do this? (Choose the best answer.)

A. Server Manager at the PDC

B. Server Manager at the BDC

C. The network applet

D. WINNT.EXE

25. You have successfully changed your domain name from XYZ to SALES, but now none of your 95 clients is able to logon to the domain. You suspect the problem is what? (Choose the best answer.)

A. The Windows 95 clients are still trying to be validated by the old domain name. You must visit each 95 machine and change the NT Domain name there as well.

B. During the domain name change, the Netlogon service has paused. You must restart the PDC to restart the Netlogon service. All clients will need to restart as well.

C. Your PDC needs to synchronize the entire domain. You can force domain synchronization through Server Manager.

D. Your Windows 95 machines must reboot and log on to the domain again.

26. A domain controller can validate user logon requests from any of the following. (Choose all that apply.)

A. Windows NT

B. OS/2 1.x or greater

C. Microsoft LAN Manager

D. MS-DOS Clients with the enhanced redirector installed

E. Windows for Workgroups

27. You are responsible for maintaining two domains. One domain is in California and the other is in New York. These domains are not connected by any means. To make things simpler, you decide to name both domains CORPORATE. The California domain has four BDCs, whereas the New York domain has only two. You decide to move a BDC from California to New York, yet when you add the BDC from California it will not recognize the PDC on the domain. You suspect the problem is what? (Choose the best answer.)

    A. The time difference between New York and California has thrown off the synchronization updates of the BDC and PDC. You must use the net time command.

    B. You cannot move a domain controller from one domain to another.

    C. The IP Address of the BDC is incorrect because it is now in a different subnet.

    D. The BDC does not have a computer account in the domain. You must add the computer account through Server Manager so that the BDC can join the domain.

28. You want to set up a RAS Server for a member server but are uncertain how many connections are allowed via RAS. How many connections are allowed via RAS? (Choose the best answer.)

    A. 1

    B. 250

    C. 256

    D. Unlimited

2.2 Answers and Explanations: Practice Problems

1. **B, C, D** A 95 workgroup would be able to use the NT Member Server as a file, print, and application server; the workgroup would have a network site to store work, and could then use the Member Server to use user-level security.

2. **C** You are not allowed to move a Domain Controller from one domain to another. This is due to uniqueness of the Domain's SID (Security Identifier).

3. **A, B** You must have administrative rights to add a BDC to a domain. If you chose not to use the same protocol as the PDC, there will be no communication between the two machines. Although a network card problem can limit your access to the PDC, you would have received a message stating that the network was unable to start. If you chose to use TCP/IP via DHCP, and there are no IP addresses available, you would have received a message stating that a DHCP server was not attached.

4. **C** If the BDC cannot locate the BDC to synchronize the account database, it will not be able to continue the installation.

5. **B** If you were to take the PDC offline and install NT Server 4.0, you would in effect be creating a new domain. There is no real reason to upgrade the 3.51 server to complete this task.

6. **B** NT requires that a PDC be the first server online during installation. You cannot add a BDC before a PDC.

7. **C** NetBIOS names must be unique from all other resources on the network.

8. **D** Server names are limited by NetBIOS to 15 characters.

9. **C** There is no way to change a member server to a BDC without reinstalling NT.

10. **C** Passwords are limited to 14 characters.

11. **C** All servers may be clients of DHCP.

12. **C** Before an NT machine can join a domain, it must have a computer account created for it.

13. **A, C** You can use Server Manager on the PDC and add the computer account, or you can add the account during installation of the BDC.

14. **C** A domain may have only one PDC at any given time.

15. **A, B, C, D, E** A BDC is capable of serving as a file, print, and application server; it can also validate user logon requests; it can be a RAS Server; it can be a DHCP server; and it can provide backup in case the PDC fails.

16. **A, D** A member server can be a file, print, or application server. A member server can be a RAS Server. A member server cannot validate users. A member server is not allowed to be a member of both a domain and workgroup at the same time.

17. **A, B, C, D** A domain controller may be all of these.

18. **B** You must promote the BDC to a PDC. This will ensure that there is always one PDC available for account maintenance.

19. **B** You must reinstall NT Server and designate during setup that this machine will be a BDC in your domain.

20. **B, C, D** A domain is a collection of computer accounts. Only NT Workstations and Servers are true members of a domain. If you wanted to get the Windows 95 machines to show up in the Domain list in Network Neighborhood, set the Workgroup name to the same as the Domain name.

21. **A** The Netlogon service is responsible for accepting logon validation requests.

22. **C** You are limited to the number of PDCs. BDCs, however, are unlimited.

23. **B** You must belong to the Administrators or Server Operators local groups to promote or demote domain controllers.

24. **C** You can change your domain name through the network applet.

25. **A** If you change the domain name, you must manually change the domain name for your Windows 95 clients as well.

26. **A, C, D, E** Windows NT domain controllers can validate users from NT, LAN Manager clients, MS-DOS, and Windows for Workgroups, as well as Windows 95.

27. **B** You cannot move a domain controller from one domain to another because of the domain SID associated with the domain controller. Even though the names of the domain are the same, it is the SID that differentiates between the two domains. You must reinstall NT Server.

28. **C** 256 simultaneous RAS connections are allowed on NT Server.

2.2 Key Words

Domain

Per Server licensing

Per Seat Licensing

WINNT.exe

WINNT32.exe

Primary Domain Controller (PDC)

Backup Domain Controller (BDC)

Member Server

2.3 NT Server 4.0 Installation Methods

The following are two possible sources of Windows NT 4 installation files:

- The Windows NT Installation CD-ROM (with three setup floppies)
- A network sharepoint (with three setup floppies)

Most installation procedures consist of two distinct phases:

- File copying: This phase takes place under a minimal text-mode version of Windows NT.
- Configuration: This phase runs under the full GUI Windows NT Setup wizard.

A. CD-ROM Installation

Using the Windows NT Installation CD-ROM is the easiest and most common method for installing NT. By booting with the three startup floppy disks that come with Windows NT, you load the necessary drivers for you CD-ROM and can proceed with the installation.

You also can begin the installation by starting the CD-ROM (from within your existing operating system) and double-clicking on Windows NT Setup.

B. Network Installs

A network install is really a CD-ROM install; an initial preinstallation phase is added in which the contents of the CD-ROM are copied across the network from the server to the client computer.

You can use Windows NT's Client Administrator application to create a network installation startup disk that will enable you to boot the client machine and connect to the shared directory with the installation files.

To improve performance, copy the contents of the CD-ROM to the hard drive and share the hard disk's copy rather than the CD's. Hard disks are much faster than CD-ROM drives.

To start an installation across the network, you must first redirect an MS-DOS drive letter to the network sharepoint containing the installation files. Depending on the client you use the following:

- NetWare clients use the MAP command to connect to a Netware server located in the installation directory.
- Windows 95 clients map a drive through the Network Neighborhood.
- MS-DOS clients should use the NET USE command.
- Windows for Workgroups clients use Disk, Connect Network Drive in File Manager.

C. Client Administrator Installation Aids

The Network Client Administrator application, in the Administrative Tools group, lets you configure your Windows NT Server system to assist you with the process of installing client machines on the network. The first two options are designed to help with installing network clients, as follows:

- **Make Network Installation Startup Disk.** Shares the client installation files on the network and creates an installation startup disk you can use to connect to the server from the client machine and to download the installation files.
- **Make Installation Disk Set.** Creates a set of floppies you can use to install network client software on a client computer.

1. Network Installation Startup Disk

The Make Network Installation Startup Disk option in the Network Client Administrator enables you to set up a share containing installation files and then a create a network startup floppy disk that enables you to connect to the installation files from the client machine.

An MS-DOS system disk is required as a startup disk. You can use this option to create a network startup disk for any of the following operating systems:

- Windows NT Server v3.5, 3.51, 4.0
- Windows NT Workstation v3.5, 3.51, 4.0
- Windows 95
- Windows for Workgroups v3.11
- Microsoft Network Client for MS-DOS v3.0

You must purchase a license agreement for each NT, 95, or Windows for Workgroup client you install. The Make Installation Disk Set radio button in the Network Client Administrator dialog box enables you to create a set of floppy installation disks you can use to install the following network client packages:

- Microsoft Network Client 3.0 for MS-DOS and Windows
- Microsoft LAN Manager 2.2c for MS-DOS
- Microsoft LAN Manager 2.2c for OS/2
- Microsoft Remote Access Service Client v1.1 for MS-DOS
- Microsoft TCP/IP for Windows for Workgroups

2. Creating the Startup Disks

Follow these steps:

1. Select the Make Installation Disk Set radio button and click on Continue. The Share Network Client Installation Files dialog box appears.
2. After that, you'll see the Make Installation Disk Set dialog box. Choose the network software you want to install on the client, choose a destination drive, and click on OK.

The floppies used with Network Client Administrator must be formatted before creating the disk set. The Windows NT Server and Workstation startup disks work only for Intel computers.

D. Installation Types

Windows NT Server and Workstation differ in the setup options. NT Server uses the Custom setup option only. The available setup options for Windows NT are:

- **Typical.** Ideal for most installations. Portable installs accessibility options, Accessories, Communication programs, and Multimedia.
- **Portable.** Designed for notebook and other portable computers. Setup installs accessibility options, all Windows NT accessories except for Desktop wallpaper and Mouse Pointers, all communication programs, and all multimedia components supported by the hardware.
- **Compact.** Designed to conserve hard disk space. Only components required by Windows NT are installed.
- **Custom.** Useful when the user installing Windows NT needs to choose individual components that are not available through one of the express setup options.

2.3.1 Exercise: Creating a Network Installation Startup Disk

To create a network installation startup disk:

1. Select the Make Network Installation Startup Disk radio button in the Network Client Administrator dialog box. The Share Network Client Installation Files dialog box appears.
2. You can either copy the files to your hard disk and share them, or share them directly from the Windows NT Server CD-ROM.
3. The Share Files radio button shares the files directly from the CD-ROM, which doesn't require any hard disk space. Choose Copy Files to a New Directory, and then Share radio button to copy the files to your hard disk—you'll need 64 MB of hard disk space.
4. The Use Existing Shared Directory radio button tells Client Administrator to set up the installation disk to use an existing share. You can specify a server name and a share name.
5. When you have configured the location of the installation files, click on OK.
6. The Target Workstation Configuration dialog box appears. Specify the size of the floppy disk, the type of network client software, and a network adapter card for the client machine. Click on OK.
7. The Network Startup Disk Configuration dialog box appears. Specify a computer name, user name, domain, and network protocol for the client machine, plus any TCP/IP settings. The Destination Path is the path to the floppy drive.
8. Insert a formatted, high-density MS-DOS system disk in the destination drive and click on OK.
9. You now can use the network installation startup disk to boot the client machine and connect to the installation files.

2.3.2 Exercise: Creating an Installation Disk Set

The Make Installation Disk Set radio button in the Network Client Administrator dialog box enables you to create a set of floppy disks you can use to install the following network client packages:

- Microsoft Network Client 3.0 for MS-DOS and Windows
- Microsoft LAN Manager 2.2c for MS-DOS
- Microsoft LAN Manager 2.2c for OS/2
- Microsoft Remote Access Service Client v1.1 for MS-DOS
- Microsoft TCP/IP for Windows for Workgroups

To create an installation disk set, follow this procedure:

1. The floppies must be pre-formatted before making the installation disk set. As you select different clients, the dialog box will instruct on the number of floppies required for that client. Select the Make Installation Disk Set radio button and click on Continue. The Share Network Client Installation Files dialog box appears.
2. After that, you'll see the Make Installation Disk Set dialog box. Choose the network software you want to install on the client, choose a destination drive, and click on OK.

2.3 Practice Problems

1. Most installation procedures consists of two distinct phases, which are what? (Choose two answers.)

   A. File copying phase

   B. Registry assembly phase

   C. An .inf file assembly phase

   D. System configuration phase

2. The most practical way of installing NT Server is (choose the best answer):

   A. CD-ROM

   B. Over the network

   C. Floppies

   D. Copy the i386 directory from the CD-ROM to the hard disk and then run WINNT.EXE

3. To start the setup program inside Windows 95, a user can do what? (Choose all that apply.)

   A. Run WINNT.EXE from the Start menu.

   B. If autorun is enabled for the CD-ROM, insert the NT 4.0 CD, and then choose the button for NT setup.

   C. Run WINNT32.EXE from the Start menu.

   D. Map a drive to the network share of NT and double-click on the WINNT.EXE.

4. You would like to do a network install for NT Server 4.0 because the Intel machine you are setting up as a BDC does not have a CD-ROM. You notice, however, that this method takes somewhat longer than when you installed the server locally on your PDC. Why is this? (Choose the best answer.)

   A. BDC must synchronize with the PDC, which takes 20–30 minutes longer.

   B. Setup is doing an exhaustive hardware search looking for a CD-ROM drive on your machine.

   C. Setup must copy the files across the network.

   D. Setup must replicate the account database with the PDC to ensure you have rights to join the domain.

5. What NT tool allows you to create a network installation startup disk? (Choose the best answer.)

   A. NT Disk Administrator

   B. Server Manager

   C. Network Client Administrator

   D. Add/Remove Programs

6. A network client startup disk does what? (Choose the best answer.)

   A. Enables a DOS machine to connect to the server and login as administrator

   B. Enables a RISC-based machine to connect to the server and install the network client software across the network

   C. Enables an Intel-based machine to connect to the server and install the network client software across the network

   D. Enables an Administrator to start an over-the-network installation of a PDC

7. A network client startup disk enables you to do what? (Choose the best answer.)

   A. Connect to a PDC and log on as Administrator.

   B. Connect to an NT Server and start the installation of a network client from a network source file location.

2

C. To have an OS/2 machine join a domain.

D. To have a Windows 95 or Windows NT Workstation client switch between membership in a domain and a workgroup.

8. What must be done to the floppy to be used as the network client startup disk? (Choose all that apply.)

A. It must be formatted in Windows NT.

B. It must be formatted in the same operating from which you will be installing (95, DOS, OS/2).

C. It must be a DOS system disk.

D. It must be an unformatted disk.

9. To improve performance of the network install, you should do what? (Choose the best answer.)

A. Buy a faster CD-ROM drive.

B. Use 3.5-inch floppies rather 5.25-inch floppies.

C. Copy the contents of the CD-ROM to the server rather than sharing out the CD-ROM.

D. Give users full control of the CD-ROM when you share it out at the server.

10. You have shared out the source files for NT Server 4.0. You are ready to begin the network installation of NT Server. To start an installation over the network, you must first do what on the client side? (Choose the best answer.)

A. Confirm that the client is not logged into any domain or workgroup.

B. Map a drive to the shared site on the server.

C. Assign the client an IP address of 127.0.0.1.

D. Assign the client the same IP address of the server.

11. On your BDC called NT4BDC, you have shared out the i386 directory of the CD-ROM as i386 so that you can install NT Server across the network. The machine on which you would like to install NT Server is using DOS 6.22, and you have the full redirector installed. What is the proper command to connect to the server to begin the installation? (Choose the best answer.)

A. net use \\nt4bdc\i386

B. net use W: \\i386\nt4bdc

C. net use W: //nt4bdc/i386

D. net use W: \\nt4bdc\i386

12. You are trying to install NT Server on a Windows 95 machine and would like to map a drive to the shared site on your server. How would you do this? (Choose the best answer.)

A. Restart the machine in DOS and use the NET command.

B. Open a DOS prompt and in Windows 95 and use the NET command.

C. Map a drive through Network Neighborhood.

D. Create a batch file to connect to the share site.

13. The Network Client Administrator enables you to do what? (Choose the best answer.)

A. Add computer accounts to your domain.

B. Add user accounts to your domain.

C. Create a Network Installation Startup Disk.

D. Manage which clients are allowed to connect to resources on your server.

14. The Network Client Administrator enables you to do what? (Choose the best answer.)

    A. Make an Installation Disk Set.

    B. Create shares on other domain controllers.

    C. Stop sharing resources on your servers.

    D. Add computer accounts to your domain.

15. You can use the Network Client Administrator to create a Network Installation Startup Disk for what operating systems? (Choose all that apply.)

    A. NT Server v3.5, 3.51, 4.0

    B. Windows NT Workstation v3.5, 3.51, 4.0

    C. Windows 95

    D. OS/2

16. On the NT Server 4.0, the source files for what clients are included? (Choose all that apply.)

    A. Windows 95

    B. Microsoft Bob

    C. Windows for Workgroups

    D. MS DOS 6.22

17. The Windows NT Server and NT Workstation startup disks will work on RISC-based machines if you (choose the best answer):

    A. Do nothing. They work already on RISC and Intel-based platforms.

    B. These startup disks will not work on RISC-based machines.

    C. Specify in the Network Client Administrator that the target machine is a RISC-based computer.

    D. Format the floppy with NTFS.

18. You are creating a network installation startup disk. You can't decide if you should copy the files to your hard drive and share them out, or share them directly from the CD-ROM. Two factors may affect your decision, they are:

    A. If you copy the files to your hard drive, the access time will be faster than the CD-ROM.

    B. If you copy them to your hard drive, it will use approximately 64-MB hard disk space.

    C. If you copy the files to your hard drive, only an administrator will have rights to them.

    D. If you copy the files to your hard drive, everyone will have full control to the resource.

19. During the creation of a Network Startup Disk, the target workstation dialog box requests three pieces of information. They are:

    A. The size of the floppy disk

    B. The protocol to be used during installation

    C. The type of client software

    D. The network adapter card

20. During the creation of a Network Startup Disk, the Network Startup Disk Configuration dialog box requests specific information to be used during the install. The information requested is what? (Choose all that apply.)

    A. Computer name

    B. User name

    C. Domain name

    D. Network protocol to be used

21. The Network Client Administrator enables you to create an installation disk set to install what network client packages from floppies? (Choose all that apply.)

2

A. Windows 95

B. Network Client 3.0 for DOS

C. Microsoft TCP/IP for Windows for Workgroups

D. Microsoft LAN Manager for OS/2

22. The Network Client 3.0 for DOS and Windows allows a DOS machine to do what? (Choose the best answer.)

A. Participate in server announcements.

B. Receive Exchange email.

C. Map drives to network resources.

D. Participate in domain synchronization.

23. You would like to install NT Workstation on 100 Intel-based computers. You do not want to install from CD-ROM at each machine. What is the best method of installation? (Choose the best answer.)

A. Use the Disk Administrator to create a network startup disk to automatically connect to a server to begin the install.

B. Use Server Manager to create a network startup disk to automatically connect to a server to begin the install.

C. Use the Network Client Administrator to create a network startup disk to automatically connect to a server to begin the install.

D. Map a drive through DOS to the client share site and run WINNT.EXE across the network.

24. You and an assistant are installing NT Workstation. Your assistant is uncertain why you should use the typical install. You identify several key reasons why you are using the Typical install method, including what? (Choose the best answer.)

A. Typical installs accessibility options, Accessories, Communication programs, and Dial Up Networking.

B. Typical installs accessibility options, Accessories, Communication programs, and Multimedia.

C. Typical installs Accessories, Communication programs, and Peer Web Services.

D. Typical installs all Accessories, Communication programs, and Peer Web Services.

25. You and an assistant are installing NT Workstation. You have opted to use the portable option because you are installing NT on a laptop. What features are included with the portable install? (Choose all that apply.)

A. Accessibility options

B. All accessories

C. All accessories except for wallpaper and Mouse Pointers

D. All Communication Programs

E. None of the above

26. You and an assistant are installing NT Workstation. You have opted to use the compact option because you are installing on a computer with very limited hard disk space. Why is this a good solution for your environment? (Choose the best answer.)

A. NT installs all accessories except for games.

B. NT installs only the most common components.

C. Only components required by Windows NT are installed.

D. Only accessories required by NT are installed.

27. You are installing NT Server. What install methods do you have? (Choose all that apply.)

    A. Typical

    B. Portable

    C. Compact

    D. Custom

2.3 Answers and Explanations: Practice Problems

1. **A, D** Windows NT first copies the needed files to a temp directory on your system through a minimal text mode version of Windows NT. Setup then moves into the system configuration phase through the Windows NT Setup Wizard.

2. **A** The CD-ROM method is the most practical way to install NT Server.

3. **A, B, D** Answer C is not acceptable because WINNT32.EXE is for upgrading from a previous version of Windows NT.

4. **C** When installing over the network, Setup adds an additional preinstallation phase of copying the source files across the network.

5. **C** The Network Client Administrator enables you to create a network client startup disk.

6. **C** The Network Client Administrator creates a network startup disk for Intel-based machines only.

7. **B** The Network Client administrator enables you to connect to a shared site on the server and start the installation process of network client software.

8. **C, D** The Network client startup disk must be a bootable disk. It can be formatted using MS-DOS or Windows 95.

9. **C** You will want to copy the contents of the CD-ROM to hard disk space rather than share out the CD-ROM because hard drives are faster than CD-ROM drives.

10. **B** Before you can start the install, you must map a drive to the server's share site.

11. **D** You use the UNC syntax of \\servername\sharename to map a drive to the shared site.

12. **C** By navigating through the Network Neighborhood to the shared sight on your server, you can right-click the share and choose Map Network Drive.

13. **C** The Network Client Administrator enables you to create a Network Startup disk to install client files across the network.

14. **A** The Network Client Administrator enables you to create an Installation Disk Set to install client files through a floppy disk rather than across the network.

15. **A, B, C** You are not allowed to create an startup disk for OS/2 through the Network Client Administrator.

16. **A** Windows for Workgroups is not included with Windows NT 4.0. It was included with Windows NT 3.5x CDs. The Windows 95 client software is included on the CD, but you must purchase a client license for any systems onto which you install Windows 95. DOS 6.22 is not included with Windows NT 4.0. This software must be purchased separately.

17. **B** The Windows NT Server and NT Workstation startup disks will not work on RISC-based computers.

18. **A, B** Hard disks are faster than CD-ROMs. The source files will use 64 MB of hard disk space.

19. **A, C, D** These three pieces of information are required to continue with the network startup disk.

20. **A, B, C, D** The Network Startup Disk Configuration dialog box needs the information to complete the Network Startup Disk.

2

21. **B, C, D** The Network Client Administrator enables you to create an installation disk set to install the Network Client for DOS, TCP/IP for Windows for Workgroups, and LAN Manager for OS/2.
22. **C** The Network Client 3.0 for DOS and Windows will allow a DOS client to have Microsoft networking functions.
23. **C** The Network Client Administrator is used to create a network startup disk to install over the network.
24. **B** Typical is ideal for most scenarios.
25. **A, C, D** Portable install is to be used when you are installing onto a laptop or other mobile type computer.
26. **C** When you are installing the compact method, only the components that NT requires are installed.
27. **D** With NT Server, you can only perform a Custom install.

2.3 Key Words

Network install

Network sharepoint

Disk set

Client Administrator

2.4 Configuring Protocols and Network Bindings

The Control Panel Network application is a central spot for entering and altering network configuration information. The five tabs of the Network application are as follows:

- **Identification.** The Identification tab specifies the computer name for the computer and the domain to which it belongs.
- **Services.** The Services tab lets you add, remove, or configure network services.
- **Protocols.** The Protocols tab lets you add, remove, and configure network protocols.
- **Adapters.** The Adapters tab lets you add, remove, and configure network adapter cards. Click on Add to view a list of available network adapter card drivers. The Properties button lets you configure the IRQ and the Port address for the adapter.
- **Bindings.** Network Bindings are software interfaces between network cards, protocols, and services; the bindings tab enables you to tweak the arrangement of Bindings to increase performance on your NT machine.

A. Installing and Configuring NWLink

NWLink is the Microsoft 32-bit version of IPX/SPX. To connect to NetWare servers, NWLink is required. To install the NWLink protocol, open Control Panel's Network applet, choose the Protocols tab and click on the Add button. From the list of available protocols, choose the NWLink protocol.

NWLink alone will not allow an NT Server to connect to a NetWare Server. IN addition the Gateway Services for NetWare (GSNW) is required. GSNW allows a computer running Windows NT to access file and print resources on a NetWare server.

GSNW also acts as a gateway to the NetWare servers so that the resources on the NetWare server can appear to be shared off of the NT Servers.

GSNW may be installed through Control Panel, Network, Add a Service.

1. Frame Type

If you know which frame type is in use on your network, you can use this dialog box to manually set Windows NT to match it. By default, Windows NT is configured to detect the frame type automatically, which it does by sending out a Routing Information Protocol (RIP) request on all frame types when NWLink is initialized. One of the following scenarios will occur:

- **No response from any of the frame types.** NWLink uses the default frame type, which is 802.2 when Windows NT is first installed.
- **A response from one of the frame types.** NWLink uses this frame type, which also becomes the default protocol the next time autodetection occurs.
- **Multiple responses are received.** NWLink steps through this list (in order) until it finds a frame type that was one of the multiple responses. After it finds a frame type, it stops searching for additional frame types:

- Ethernet 802.2
- Ethernet 802.3
- Ethernet II
- SNAP

NT Workstation and Windows NT Server can be configured for multiple frame types, but you can use Control Panel Network to do so only for Server. If you want Windows NT Workstation to use multiple frame types, you must edit the registry directly with the Registry Editor (RegEdt32.exe).

An incorrect frame type can cause an immense slowdown in network performance. IPXROUTE CONFIG command from the command prompt will generate a report of what frame type is currently in use. The following table shows which frame types particular servers use.

802.2	802.3
Windows NT Workstation 3.5x	Windows NT 3.1
Windows NT Server 3.5x	Windows NT Advanced Server 3.1
NetWare 4.x	NetWare 3.11 and below
NetWare 3.12	Windows for Workgroups 3.x retail
Windows for Workgroups 3.11 from the Windows NT Server CD	
Microsoft Network Client 3.0	

2. Internal Network Number

The Internal Network Number is similar to a subnet address on a TCP/IP network. It determines which servers are considered "local" and which ones are considered "remote."

B. Using TCP/IP

TCP/IP is quickly becoming the industry standard protocol. It is considered an open protocol in that no one company owns the protocol.

1. IP Addresses

The Internet Protocol sends packets using a network interface card's (NIC) IP Address (a unique 32-bit binary number that no other computer on the network can possess). Each NIC requires its own IP address.

An IP Address is a unique 32-bit addressed associate with NIC's Media Access Control (MAC) layer, or serial number of the NIC. No other host on the network can have the same IP address. A typical IP address is 131.107.5.21. Each number separated by a period is called an *octet.*

2. Subnet Mask

Subnet masks are used to mask a portion of the IP address so that the TCP/IP protocol can distinguish the host id from the network id. A Subnet mask is dependent on the class of IP addresses in use on the network. The three classes of IP addresses are:

- **Class A.** The first octet belongs to the net id and the others to the host id. Class A net ids can range from 0 to 127.
- **Class B.** The first two octets define the net id, and the next two octets define the host id.
- **Class C.** The first three octets define the net id, and the last octet is the host id.

Depending on the class of IP address in use, a subnet mask appears as follows:

Class A 255.0.0.0

Class B 255.255.0.0

Class C 255.255.255.0

3. Default Gateway

A default gateway is a *router,* a device that sends packets on to a remote network. A router can be a device created for that purpose, such as Cisco or 3Com makes, or it can be a Windows NT–based computer that has at least two network cards (for spanning two networks) and has IP Routing enabled.

C. TCP/IP Standards

Follow these guidelines for TCP/IP:

- Host ids cannot be set to all zeros or all ones, because 0 refers to the local network, whereas 255 refers to broadcast. An easy rule of thumb is to stay away from 0 and 255 when assigning octets.
- Don't use 127 as a net id. When 127 is used as the first octet of a net id, TCP/IP recognizes the address as a special diagnostic address called the *loopback address*, so called because any message to this address is returned to its sender.
- All net ids on a subnet must match. If an NIC doesn't have the same net id as the rest of the NICs on its subnet, the host can't communicate with the other hosts on the Subnet.
- All NICs must be assigned a unique ID. If two NICs have the same IP Address assigned to them, unpredictable results may happen.

D. Installing TCP/IP

To install TCP/IP, start from the Control Panel Network application. Choose the Protocols tab and click on the Add button. Select TCP/IP Protocol. Choose OK.

You can install TCP/IP in two ways:

- **Installing TCP/IP with DHCP.** When installing TCP/IP setup asks if Dynamic Host Configuration Protocol (DHCP) should be used for dynamically assigning IP addresses. A DHCP server leases addresses to clients when they join the network.
- **Installing and Configuring TCP/IP manually.** To install TCP/IP manually, you must supply the IP address and subnet mask for each NIC in the computer. In addition, the IP addresses of the default gateway, WINS servers, and DNS servers are required if you intend to use these features.

E. Windows Internet Name Service

WINS is a service that runs on NT Server. It is responsible for resolving NetBIOS names to IP addresses. It is similar to the LMHosts file except that it dynamically registers the IP address of hosts and the services that they are providing if they are participating in WINS.

More than WINS server may be added in the TCP/IP properties in the Network Applet. There are three WINS addressing parameters:

- **Enable DNS for Windows Resolution.** Selecting this check box instructs Windows NT to look up NetBIOS names against a Domain Name Server, which is usually a service running on Windows NT Server, or a daemon running on UNIX.
- **Enable LMHOSTS Lookup.** This check box incorporates a text database mapping of NetBIOS names to IP addresses into the name resolution process.
- **Scope ID.** Enables administrators to create logical IP networks that are invisible to each other. Hosts must belong to the same NetBIOS scope before they can communicate.

F. DNS

DNS servers are used to resolve Fully Qualified Domain Names (FQDN) to IP addresses.

To configure DNS, select the DNS tab in the Microsoft TCP/IP Properties dialog box. Enter your domain name. Click on the Add button under the DNS Service Search Order dialog box and enter the addresses of the DNS servers on your network.

G. TCP/IP Diagnostics

A host of TCP/IP utilities are included with Windows NT. Some of the more useful ones are IPCONFIG, PING, and TRACERT.

- **IPCONFIG.** IPCONFIG displays the TCP/IP configuration parameters of the local host. The /ALL switch can be used to display every field, including DHCP and WINS information.
- **PING.** PING is a diagnostic utility used to test the connection between two hosts on an Internetwork. The syntax for ping is as follows:

  ```
  PING 131.107.2.200
  ```

- **TRACERT.** The TRACERT utility traces the hops (number of routers crossed) that packets take on their way from the local host to a remote host.

H. NetBEUI

NetBEUI is a fast non-routable protocol. It is primarily used for small LAN. To install NetBEUI, start from the Control Panel Network application. Choose the Protocols tab and click on the Add button. Select the NetBEUI Protocol. Choose OK.

I. Protocol Bindings

To bind a protocol to a network interface card is to create a direct connection between the hardware and the transport protocol. An administrator can change the bindings for network adapter cards as well as services.

To configure network bindings, choose the Bindings tab on the Network applet in Control Panel. There are several options to adjust on the Bindings tab. The following table list the configuration options.

Option	Action
Show Bindings for	Views bindings for adapters, protocols, and services on the network
Enable	Enables the selected bindings path
Disable bindings	Disables the selected bindings path
Move Up	Moves the selected bindings up
Move Down	Moves the selected bindings down

2.4.1 Exercise: Installing and Configuring TCP/IP

This lab assumes you have an NT Server 4.0 installed. You might need your CD-ROM to install the source files for TCP/IP.

To install TCP/IP:

1. Open Control Network.
2. Choose the protocol tab.
3. Click on the Add button.
4. Choose TCP/IP from the list of available protocols and click on OK.
5. NT will prompt you to use DHCP. Choose No.
6. At this point, NT will ask for the install files for TCP/IP. Map NT to the appropriate location of the i386 directory.

To configure TCP/IP:

1. If you know a valid IP address for your network, enter that IP address. If not, enter the IP address of 131.107.2.200.
2. If you have entered a valid IP address for your network, enter the corresponding subnet mask. If you entered 131.107.2.200, use the subnet mask of 255.255.255.0.
3. If your network has a router and you know the IP address of the router, enter that information now. Otherwise, leave this field blank.
4. Choose the DNS tab.
5. If you have a DNS server, enter that information now. If you are uncertain about this information, leave this field blank.
6. Choose the WINS Address tab.
7. If you have a WINS Server, enter the IP address now. If you are uncertain about the IP address of your WINS server, or you do not have it, leave this information blank.
8. Choose OK to finish the TCP/IP install. NT will need to reboot to configure your TCP/IP bindings.

2.4.2 Exercise: Testing Your IP Address with PING

This exercise assumes you have completed Exercise 2.4.1 or already have an IP address on your NT machine. To test your IP address with PING:

1. Start a DOS prompt.
2. Type in the following command: PING 127.0.0.1.
3. What is the reply you receive?
4. PING the IP address of your machine.
5. What is the reply you receive?
6. If you know the IP address of another NIC on your network, PING that address now.
7. PING an IP address that you know is incorrect. For example, PING 131.107.127.127.
8. What response do you receive?

2.4 Practice Problems

1. The primary location to add or configure network protocols is: (Choose the best answer.)
   A. Control Panel's Protocols applet
   B. Server Manager
   C. Control Panel's Network applet
   D. Network Client Administrator

2. You would like to change the name of your domain from SALES to MARKETING. Where are you allowed to do this? (Choose the best answer.)
   A. The Network Applet's Identification tab.
   B. Server Manager for Domains.
   C. You must use the Registry Editor.
   D. You are not allowed to change domains names due to the SID associated with the domain controllers.

3. You would like to add the Gateway Services for NetWare. Where do you add this service? (Choose the best answer.)
   A. Choose Services for NetWare from the Administrative tools group.
   B. You do not have to add this service. It is installed by default in the Control Panel as GSNW.
   C. Add the service through the Network applet, Services tab.
   D. Add the service through the Control Panel's Add/Remove programs.

4. Your network spans multiple states, and you are primarily using TCP/IP. You have decided that you do not need to use NetBEUI. How do you remove this protocol? (Choose the best answer.)
   A. Choose Network, Protocols, choose NetBEUI and remove.
   B. Choose Network, Protocols, choose remove all inactive transport services.
   C. Use the Add/Remove programs tab.
   D. You cannot remove NetBEUI. NT server requires NetBEUI because of the NetBIOS Name Servers Service.

2

5. Your network is primarily Ethernet, you do however, have a small subnet of Token Ring adapter cards. To provide connectivity for these users, you have added a Token Ring network card to your server. NT, however, has not detected this new hardware at startup time. How can you add the card? (Choose all that apply.)
   A. Using the Add New Hardware in Control Panel.
   B. Using the Network Applet in Control Panel.
   C. Run NTDETECT.COM from a DOS prompt.
   D. Run the NT hardware qualifier from the NT Server CD-ROM.

6. You are responsible for integrating NT Server and your NetWare servers for your company. You have successfully installed NT Server, but NT cannot access any of your NetWare servers. What do you suspect is the problem? (Choose all that apply.)
   A. Your NetWare servers are NetWare 3 servers, which are not compatible with NT Server 4.0.
   B. You need to add the NWLink protocol to your NT servers.
   C. You need to add the Gateway Service for NetWare.
   D. You need to purchase Client 32 for NetWare.

7. You are responsible for integrating NT Server and your NetWare servers for your

company. You have successfully installed NT Server, with the NWLink protocol, but NT cannot access any of your NetWare servers. What do you suspect is the problem? (Choose the best answer.)

A. You need to designate NT to participate in SAP announcements.

B. You need to configure the correct frame type for your NT Server to match the NetWare servers.

C. You need to add the Gateway Service for NetWare.

D. NT cannot participate in RIP, so therefore it cannot access the NetWare servers.

8. You have NetWare 4 servers and NetWare 3 servers that use different frame types. Because NT is using the autodetect method, you are uncertain which frame type NT is using. How can you detect which frame type NT is using? (Choose the best answer.)

A. Use the IPXROUTE CONFIG command from a DOS prompt.

B. Use the IPXROUTE /ALL command from a DOS prompt.

C. Locate the IPFRAME setting in HKEY_LOCAL_MACHINE in the registry. The frame type will be located at this setting.

D. NT defaults to 802.2 if it is using the autodetect frame type.

9. You have NetWare 4 servers and NetWare 3 servers that use different frame types. How can you add additional frame types to your NT server so that it will access both NetWare 4 and NetWare 3 servers? (Choose the best answer.)

A. You are only allowed one frame type per server.

B. You must add an additional network card and assign a frame type to each card.

C. You must edit the registry to add additional frame types.

D. Use the Control Panel Network to add additional frame types.

10. You and an associate are installing NT Server with Gateway Services for Netware and the NWLink protocol so that you can access your NetWare servers. Your associate is confused about how NT can autodetect the frame type. You describe the process by stating what? (Choose the best answer.)

A. NT uses SAP to determine which frame type is in use.

B. NT sends a NetBIOS announcement over IPX/SPX and evaluates the returned packets to determine what frame types are in use.

C. NT uses the Routing Information Protocol (RIP) to determine what frame types are in use.

D. NT simply defaults to 802.2 if autodetect is chosen.

11. Your NT Workstation is currently using the Client Services for Netware and you have NWLink installed so that you can connect to your Netware server's resources. You would like to add additional frame types to your NT Workstation so that it can communicate with multiple servers on your network. How can you do this? (Choose the best answer.)

A. Use the Control Panel Network.

B. Use autodetect for the properties of NWLink.

C. You must edit the registry to add additional frame types.

D. You must add an adapter card for each frame type you would like to use.

12. What protocols ship with Windows NT Server? (Choose all that apply.)

A. NWLink

B. DLC

C. NetBEUI

D. ARCNET v2.x

13. You have installed NT Server as a member server in your NetWare environment. You would like your Windows 95 clients to access resources on your member server. How can this be done? (Choose the best answer.)

    A. Windows 95 can access both an NT member server and a NetWare server through the Microsoft Clients for NetWare and Microsoft Networks available through 95's Network applet.

    B. You need to add the Gateway Services for NetWare.

    C. You need to add the NWLink protocol to your member server.

    D. You need to change your broadcast types from Microsoft browsing to SAP.

14. During installation of NWLink, you access the setting for the internal network number on the properties of NWLink. What does this internal network number do? (Choose the best answer.)

    A. Specifies what frame type will be used with NWLink.

    B. Allows for boot/p to work with NT Server.

    C. Determines which servers are considered local and which are considered remote.

    D. Specifies what version the NetWare server is.

15. Your network consists of NetWare 3.12 servers and NT 4.0 servers, along with Windows 95 clients. You would like your Windows 95 clients to logon to both your NT Domain and your NetWare servers. How can this be done? (Choose the best answer.)

    A. Add the Microsoft Client for Microsoft Networks and the Microsoft Client for NetWare Networks on the 95 machines. Specify what servers they are to log into and what domains they are to log into.

    B. Add NWLink to your 95 and NT Servers.

    C. Add the Client32 from Novell.

    D. This cannot be done. Windows 95 clients are restricted to logging into either Windows 95 machines or NT Servers. They are not allowed to log into both.

16. You would like to add the TCP/IP protocol to your NT server. How can this be done? (Choose the best answer.)

    A. TCP/IP can be installed during setup because it is the default protocol on NT machines.

    B. TCP/IP can be installed in the Control Panel Add/Remove Programs.

    C. Run WINNT32.EXE from a DOS prompt.

    D. Do nothing. TCP/IP is required by NT Server.

17. You would like to add TCP/IP to your NT Domain. Your supervisor is concerned that you will have to purchase IP addresses. He does not want to spend the additional dollars at this time, so he is encouraging you to stay with NetBEUI. Is the supervisor's argument valid? (Choose the best answer.)

    A. Yes. To use TCP/IP you must purchase a class of IP address from the InterNIC.

B. Yes. To use TCP/IP you must purchase IP addresses from the InterNIC, and you have to purchase a router, or default gateway.

C. No. The IP addresses are free of charge; no one company owns the TCP/IP protocol.

D. No. You need to purchase IP addresses from the InterNIC only if your company is planning to have Internet connectivity, such as a Web server. Otherwise, you can create your own IP addresses.

18. You are installing NT Server as a BDC. You have elected to use TCP/IP as this server's only protocol. You decide not to use DHCP, so you manually enter the IP address of this machine. You discover, however, that another computer is currently using the IP address you specified. Why is this a concern? (Choose the best answer.)

    A. It is not a concern because NT Server has precedence over another machine with the same IP address. If the same machine is an NT Server, they will share the IP address.

    B. Because the IP addresses correlate to the MAC layer of the NIC, the IP address may be used by one machine at a time.

    C. IP addresses require a subnet mask. You need to configure a different subnet mask in order to use this IP address.

    D. You need to add the User Datagram Protocol (UDP) through services to allow more than one machine to have the same IP address.

19. You are examining your IP addresses. You realize that IP addresses, such as 131.107.2.21, are broken down by periods. The number between the periods is called what? (Choose the best answer.)

    A. Octave

    B. Octet

    C. Octon

    D. Octove

20. You are installing NT Server as a BDC. Your domain is currently using TCP/IP. You decide to manually configure the IP address of this machine. What components of TCP/IP are mandatory? (Choose all that apply.)

    A. IP Address

    B. Default Gateway

    C. WINS

    D. Subnet Mask

21. You are installing NT Server. You decide to use TCP/IP in your domain. You do have a DHCP server available to you. What does DHCP do? (Choose the best answer.)

    A. DHCP checks for duplicate IP addresses on the subnet to ensure, via ICMP, that no two addresses are the same.

    B. DHCP uses ARP, the address resolution protocol, to associate your IP address with the NIC's MAC layer.

    C. DHCP automatically assigns you an IP address along with any IP information previously established on the DHCP server.

    D. NT Servers cannot be participants of DHCP.

22. You and a colleague are installing NT Server. You are uncertain if you should participate in WINS. What is WINS? (Choose the best answer.)

    A. WINS, the Windows Internet Name Service, maps Fully Qualified Domain Names to IP Addresses. You need this service only if you have also installed IIS and are using it as an Internet server.

B. WINS, the Windows Internet Name Service, maps NetBIOS names to IP addresses. You can use this service to reduce network traffic.

C. WINS, the Windows Internet Name Service, creates http names for your NT Server. You need this service only if you have installed IIS.

D. WINS, the Windows Internet Name Service, maps IP addresses to serial card numbers of NICs.

23. You are installing TCP/IP on your NT Workstation. You are using DHCP, but have been instructed to manually enter the DNS IP addresses manually. What is DNS? (Choose the best answer.)

A. DNS maps FQDN to IP addresses for Internet connectivity.

B. DNS maps NetBIOS names to IP addresses.

C. DNS merges NetWare TCP/IP clients with NT's directory services.

D. DNS generates Domain Names for IIS.

24. You are installing NT Server as a BDC. Your domain is currently using TCP/IP. You decide to manually configure the IP address of this machine, but are uncertain what a subnet mask does. What is a subnet mask? (Choose the best answer.)

A. Subnet masks enable you to segment your DHCP client with scope options set in the DHCP server.

B. Subnet masks are used to mask your NetBIOS name so that your machine can participate in WINS.

C. Subnet masks are used to mask a portion of the IP address so that the transport protocol can differentiate between the host id and the network id.

D. Subnet masks enable an administrator to use an IP address more than once in a domain.

25. You have installed NT Workstation on your computer. Everyone else on the network has access to the Internet, you, however, do not. You verify that your IP address and subnet mask are correct. What do you suspect is the problem? (Choose all that apply.)

A. You have not specified a DNS Server.

B. You have not specified a WINS Server.

C. You have not specified the IP Address of the default gateway.

D. You have not specified the IP address of your domain controller.

26. You have installed NT Workstation and are using TCP/IP. You are obtaining your IP address from a DHCP server. How can you find out what IP address has been assigned to your machine? (Choose the best answer.)

A. Go to the DHCP Server and access the DHCP Manager tool.

B. Go to your WINS Server and access the WINS Manager.

C. Use the IPCONFIG utility.

D. If you are using DHCP, there is no way to determine what IP address has been assigned to your computer.

27. You are troubleshooting an IP address of a user. What tool should you use from your desk to check the status of the user's IP address? (Choose the best answer.)

A. PING

B. IPCONFIG /all

C. TRACERT

D. Network Monitor

28. You have a small workgroup of NT Workstations. What protocol should you use? (Choose the best answer.)

A. NWLink

B. TCP/IP

C. NetBEUI

D. DLC

29. Your domain spans two states. Your supervisor has read about the fast and easy-to-configure protocol NetBEUI. He would like you to use this protocol instead of TCP/IP. What would you tell him? (Choose the best answer.)

A. NetBEUI packets will not pass over routers.

B. NetBEUI will work fine in your environment.

C. NetBEUI is not supported with NT.

D. NetBEUI is very hard to configure and install.

30. What is a protocol binding? (Choose the best answer.)

A. The process of installing a protocol.

B. The process of associating a service or network adapter card with a protocol.

C. The process of adding a third-party protocol.

D. The process of configuring a protocol to ignore network packets from other services on the network.

2.4 Answers and Explanations: Practice Problems

1. **C** All protocol management is done through the Network applet in the Control Panel.

2. **A** You are allowed to change domain names through the Network applet.

3. **C** You add all services through this tab.

4. **A** You can add or remove protocols through this tab.

5. **B** This is the method used to add adapter cards to your network.

6. **B, C** To connect to NetWare, you need to add the NWLink protocol and Gateway Services for NetWare.

7. **C** GSNW is required to access NetWare resources from an NT Server.

8. **A** The IPXROUTE CONFIG command will tell you what frame type NT has detected on the network and is currently using.

9. **D** NT Server enables you add additional frame types through the Control Panel Network. NT Workstation, however, requires that you add additional frame types through the registry.

10. **C** NT takes advantage of RIP to determine what frame type(s) are in use.

11. **C** On Windows NT Workstation, you must edit the registry to add multiple frame types.

12. **A, B, C** NWLink, DLC, and NetBEUI ship with Windows NT Server.

13. **A** Your Windows 95 machines would use the Client for Microsoft Networks and the Client for NetWare networks.

14. **C** The internal network number is similar to TCP/IP's subnet mask.

15. **A** Windows 95 machines are allowed to log on to NetWare servers and Windows NT Servers.

16. **A** TCP/IP is the default protocol for NT servers.
17. **D** You need only purchase IP addresses if your company is planning Internet connectivity. Otherwise, you may follow a set of rules for IP address creation.
18. **B** Only one machine can have a given IP address.
19. **B** The number between the periods is called an octet.
20. **A, D** The IP address, and Subnet masks field must be completed. WINS, the default gateway, and DNS are optional components of TCP/IP.
21. **C** Dynamic Host Configuration Protocol automatically assigns IP Address to computers, including NT Server.
22. **B** WINS maps NetBIOS names to IP addresses.
23. **A** Your DNS servers IP addresses are required so that you can have Internet connectivity using Fully Qualified Domain Names (FQDN) for browsing.
24. **C** Subnet masks are used to mask a portion of the IP address so that the transport protocol can differentiate between the host id from the network id.
25. **A, C** You need the IP address of your DNS server to have access to the Internet. You need the IP address of the default gateway to get access to the Internet.
26. **C** The IPCONFIG command tells you all about your IP address. Answer A and B will work, but they are too impractical.
27. **A** PING is the tool used to test the validity of IP addresses.
28. **C** NetBEUI is the fastest protocol for this environment and requires no configuration after installation. Although TCP/IP or NWLink would work, NetBEUI is the best answer.
29. **A** NetBEUI packets will not pass over routers. TCP/IP was designed for networks that cross routers.
30. **B** Protocol may be bound to network cards or services.

2.4 Key Words

NWLink	NetBEUI
Bindings	DLC
TCP/IP	PING

2.5 Configuring Network Adapters

The Adapters tab of the Control Panel Network application lets you add and configure network adapters for your system. You have several options to install the Network adapters:

- **Installing an adapter after setup.** Open Control Panel Network and click on the Add button. The Select Network Adapter dialog box that appears lets you select an adapter from a list. To install an adapter that isn't on the list, click on Have Disk.
- **Installing Multiple adapters during setup.** During the NT installation, setup can detect your network adapter card. Setup stops after it finds the first card and the Start Search button changes into a Find Next button.
- **Installing Multiple adapters after setup.** Open Control Panel Network and click on the Add button. The Select Network Adapter dialog box that appears lets you select an adapter from a list. To install an adapter that isn't on the list, click on Have Disk.

A. Assigning Resources to Network Adapter Cards

There are three resources to consider for your Network Adapter Card. They are:

- **IRQ.** This is the interrupt request. Interrupts are requests for the CPU to process the data in the NIC before the buffer is cleared by new data from the LAN.

  IRQ are set either by manually assigning the IRQ by setting jumpers on the NIC; running a setup program from the OEM; or by changing the IRQ setting on the properties of NIC in the Control Panel Network.
- **I/O address.** I/O addresses are the electronic location of the Network adapter card in the system. I/O must be unique for each device so instructions sent to the device will be sent to the correct location.

  I/O addresses are set in the properties of the network adapter card in Control Panel Network.
- **Transceiver Type.** The transceiver Type is used to determine what type of cabling you are using on your network.

2.5.1 Exercise: Adding a Network Adapter Card

To add a Network Adapter card, follow these steps:

1. Open the Control Panel Network.
2. Choose the Adapters tab.
3. Click on the Add button one time.
4. The select Network Adapter dialog box appears. Choose the 3COM Etherlink III ISA Adapter.
5. Setup will prompt you for your Windows NT Server CD-ROM.
6. Enter the path to your CD-ROM and to the i386 directory (or to the appropriate RISC directory if you are not on an Intel-based machine).
7. Note the I/O address, the default IRQ, and the Transceiver type.
8. Choose OK.

2.5.2 Exercise: Removing the Network Adapter Card

To remove a Network Adapter card, follow these steps:

1. Open the Control Panel Network if it is not already open.
2. Choose the Etherlink Network Adapter card installed in Exercise 2.5.1.
3. Choose the Remove button.
4. Exit the Control Panel Network.

2.5 Practice Problems

1. You are installing NT Server as PDC on an Intel-based machine. You have two network cards in the machine—an Ethernet card and a Token Ring card. During installation, the Setup program only finds one card. What should you do to make NT find the second card? (Choose the best answer.)
   - A. Setup will automatically stop after finding the first network card. The search button will then change to a Find Next button. You should click on this button.
   - B. You must press Shift+F3 to force setup to detect any additional cards.
   - C. You cannot allow setup to automatically detect the cards. It is only capable of finding one card. You must choose the Specify button and then choose both network cards from the list.
   - D. During setup you can only detect one card. To add additional cards, you must finish setup and use the network applet to add additional cards.
2. You are installing NT on an Intel-based machine. You have a network card that is not on NT's Hardware Compatibility list. You do, however, have the driver on a floppy from the OEM. How can you add the adapter during setup? (Choose the best answer.)
   - A. Copy the contents of the floppy to the active partition before installing NT. This will force NT to discover the card during the network install portion.
   - B. Choose the Have Disk button during the network card installation phase to provide the driver.
   - C. Create a protocol.ini that references the location of the network card driver.
   - D. You must complete setup without the card, and then add it through the Network applet.
3. You would like to check the IRQ of your network adapter card. You can do this using which method(s)? (Choose all that apply.)
   - A. Using the Device Manager
   - B. Using the Control Panel Network and checking the properties on the card on the Adapters tab
   - C. Typing IRQCONFIG at the DOS prompt
   - D. Using the Windows NT Diagnostics utility
4. An IRQ is what? (Choose the best answer.)
   - A. An interrupt of the network card to signify it has received packets.
   - B. An interrupt of the network card to an area of memory so the Virtual Memory will clear address space for the protocol packets.
   - C. An interrupt of the network card to the processor to signify it has data in the buffer. The processor must evaluate the data before the network buffer is flushed for new packets delivered.
   - D. A number assigned to a device to signify what the device is.
5. What is an I/O address? (Choose the best answer.)
   - A. The electronic location of a device in the system
   - B. The number assigned to a device to signify what the device is in the system
   - C. An area of memory used for file I/O

D. A setting used to interrupt the I/O Manager to signify that new data is available to be saved to the hard disk from the device's buffer

2.5 Answers and Explanations: Practice Problems

1. **A** Allow setup to find the next card by clicking the Find Next button.
2. **B** Setup allows for drivers to be added during the detection of network cards.
3. **B, D** You may check the IRQ status of the networks card through Control Panel Network.
4. **C** An interrupt request tells the processor it has information to process now.
5. **A** An I/O address is the electronic location of a device in the system. It allows information sent to the device to be delivered.

2.5 Key Words

Client Services for NetWare

Gateway Services for NetWare

Regedt32.exe	DHCP
IP address	WINS
Subnet mask	IPCONFIG

2.6 Windows NT Core Services

A service is a built-in application that provides support for other applications or other components of the operating system. Examples of Windows NT services include:

- Windows Internet Name Service (WINS), which maps IP addresses to NetBIOS names.
- UPS service, which interacts with an Uninterruptible Power Supply system to prevent your system from abruptly shutting down.
- Server service, which accepts I/O requests from the network and routes the requested resources back to the client.
- Workstation service, which accepts I/O requests from the local system and redirects the requests to the appropriate computer on the network.

Services are background processes that perform specific functions in Windows NT. Typically, services don't interact with the user interface in any way.

A. The Services Application

The Control Panel Services application manages the services on your system. Note that the Services dialog box also includes buttons that stop a service, pause a service, or continue a service that has been paused. Pausing a service causes the service to continue handling the processes it's currently serving, but not take on any new clients.

To enable a service for a given hardware profile, click on the HW Profiles button in the Services dialog box, select a profile, and click on OK. The logon account defines a security context for the service. Because services are Win32 programs, they must run under the aegis of a user account. Here are two options:

- **System Account.** An internal account, called SYSTEM, can be used either by the operating system or by the service. This method isn't recommended, however, because you can't fine-tune rights and permissions without possibly affecting the performance and stability of the operating system and other services that may use this account.
- **This Account.** You may designate any user account from your account database here. You should create a separate account for each service for which you want to configure rights and permissions.

B. Network Services

The Services tab of the Control Panel Network application lets you add, configure, and remove services that support network functions.

Some of the services in the Network Services list are configurable through the Network application and some are not. Select a service and click on the Properties button to open a configuration dialog box for the service.

DHCP, WINS, DNS, RAS, and Gateway Services for NetWare are actually services that, although often configured elsewhere, can still be added, started, stopped, and managed through the Network Services tab and the Control Panel Services application.

C. Directory Replication

Directory Replication is a facility that lets you configure Windows NT Servers to automatically transmit updated versions of important files and directories to other computers on the network.

The purpose of Directory Replication is to simplify the task of distributing updates for logon scripts, system policy files, Help files, phone lists, and other important, generally read-only, files. The network administrator updates the file(s) on a single server (called the *export server*) and the export server automatically distributes the file(s) to other network servers or even to network workstations. The computer receiving the update is called the *import computer*. A Windows NT Server, a Windows NT Workstation, or a LAN Manager OS/2 server can act as an import computer.

The parameters for the Directory Replicator service are found in the Registry key:

```
HKEY_LOCAL_MACHINE\SYSTEM\CurrentControlSet\Services\Replicator\Parameters
```

Most of the parameters in the previous Registry key can be configured within Server Manager. Two important exceptions are:

- **Interval.** A REG_WORD value that defines how often an export server checks for updates. The range is from one to 60 minutes and the default is five minutes.
- **GuardTime.** A REG_WORD value that defines how long a directory must be stable before its files can be replicated. The range is 0 to one half of the Interval value.

The export directory on the export server holds the files and directories are replicated across the network. The default export directory is

```
\<winnt_root>\System32\Repl\Export
```

When the Directory Replicator service starts, NT shares the export directory with the share name Repl$. Each import computer has a directory called the import directory, and the default directory is

```
\<winnt_root>\System32\Repl\Import
```

The Directory Replicator service copies designated directories and their contents from the export server's export directory to the import directories of the import computers. In addition to copying files, the Directory Replicator service automatically creates any necessary subdirectories in the import directory so that after each replication the directory structure of the import directory matches the export directory's directory structure.

The process occurs as follows:

1. The export server periodically checks the export directory for changes and, if changes have occurred, sends update notices to the import computers.
2. The import computer receives the update notices and calls the export computer.
3. The import computer reads the export directory on the export server and copies any new or changed files from the export directory to its own import directory.

1. Troubleshooting Directory Replication

The Status parameter in the Manage Exported Directories and the Manage Imported Directories dialog boxes gives the status of the directory replication for a subdirectory. The possible values are as follows:

- **OK.** The export server is sending regular updates, and the import directory matches the export directory.
- **No Master.** The import computer isn't receiving updates, which means the export server may not be running, or the Directory Replicator service on the export server may not be running.
- **No Sync.** The import directory has received updates, but the data in the updates isn't what it should be, which means there could be an export server malfunction, a communication problem, open files on either the import of the export computer, or a problem with the import computer's access permissions.
- **(Blank).** Replication has never occurred. The cause could be improper configuration on either the import or the export computer.

2. Directory Replication Errors

When the Directory Replication service generates an error, check Event Viewer to learn what you can about the cause. Microsoft recommends the following solutions for some common replication errors:

- **Access Denied.** The Directory Replicator service might not be configured to log on to a specific account.
- **Exporting to Specific Computers.** Designate specific export servers for each import server and specific import computers for each export server.
- **Replication over a WAN link.** When transmitting replication data across a WAN link, specify the computer name rather than just the domain name when you click on the Add button in the Directory Replication dialog box.
- **Logon Scripts for Member Servers and Workstations.** NT Workstations and non-controller NT Servers must use the default logon script directory:

  ```
  C:\<winnt_root>\System32\Repl\Import\Scripts
  ```

D. Windows NT Client Licenses

Microsoft requires that every client accessing a resource on a computer running Windows NT Server have a Client Access License (CAL). Microsoft provides two options for purchasing Client Access Licenses, as follows:

- **Per Server mode.** Client Access Licenses are assigned to each server. A Windows NT Server might be licensed for, say, 10 simultaneous client connections. No more than 10 clients will be able to access the server at one time—additional clients will not be able to connect.
- **Per Seat mode.** Client Access Licenses are assigned to each client machine. You purchase a CAL for every client computer on the network.

Microsoft allows a one-time switch from Per Server to Per Seat licensing mode. If your network has only one server, Microsoft recommends that you choose Per Server licensing mode. If you have more than one server on your network, Microsoft suggests the following formulas:

A=Number of servers

B=number of simultaneous connections to each server

C=total number of seats (clients) accessing computers

If A * B < C use Per Server licensing. Number of CALs=A*B

IF A * B > C use Per Seat licensing. Number of CALs=C

1. The Licensing Application

The Control Panel Licensing application opens the Choose Licensing Mode dialog box. The Choose Licensing Mode dialog box lets you add or remove client licenses or switch from Per Server to Per Seat licensing mode.

License replication is a convenient feature that lets individual servers send their licensing information lists to a master server. The master server creates and updates a database of licensing information for the entire network.

2. License Manager

License Manager, a tool in the Administrative Tools program group, displays licensing information for the network. You can maintain a history of client licenses, examine your network's Per Server and Per Seat licenses by product, and browse for client license information on particular network clients.

You also can use License Manager to add or edit license groups. A license group is a group of users mapped to a group of Per Seat licenses. License groups are a means of tracking per seat license usage in situations where an organization has more users than computers (or in some cases, more computers than users).

E. Computer Browser Service

The Computer Browser service oversees a hierarchy of computers that serve as browsers for the network. A browser is a computer that maintains a central list of network servers.

That list then becomes available to clients who are "browsing" the network looking for remote computers, printers, and other resources. The list that appears when you open the Network Neighborhood application, for instance, comes from a network browser list. In a Windows NT domain, each computer assumes one of five browser roles:

- **Master browser.** Each workgroup or domain subnet must have a master browser. At startup, all computers running the Server service (regardless of whether they have resources available for the network) register themselves with the master browser.
- **Domain master browser.** The domain master browser requests subnet browse lists from the master browsers and merges the subnet browse lists into a master browse list for the entire domain. This computer is always the Primary Domain Controller.
- **Backup browsers.** The backup browser gets a copy of the browse list from the master browser (on the subnet) and distributes the browse list to subnet clients who request it.

- **Potential browser.** A potential browser is a computer that isn't presently acting as a browser but can become a browser at the request of the master browser or as a result of a browser election.
- **Non-browser.** A non-browser is a computer that cannot act as a browser.

The first time a client computer attempts to access the network, it obtains a list of backup browsers for the subnet or workgroup from the master browser. It then asks a backup browser for a copy of the browse list. If a master browser fails, a new master browser is chosen automatically in what is known as a *browser election.* A browser election can occur if a client or backup browser cannot access the master browser. Some of the criteria used in a browser election are as follows:

- **Operating system.** Windows NT Server gets a higher score than Windows NT Workstation, which gets a higher score than Windows 95.
- **Version.** Windows NT Server 4 gets a higher score than Windows NT Server 3.51, and so forth.
- **Present browser role.** A backup browser scores higher than a potential browser.

You can configure a Windows NT computer to always, never, or sometimes participate in browser elections, using the MaintainServerList parameter in the registry key:

```
HKEY_Local_Machine\System\CurrentControlSet\Services\Browsr\Parameters
```

The possible values are as follows:

- **Yes.** Always attempt to become a browser in browser elections (default for Windows NT Server domain controllers).
- **No.** Never attempt to become a browser in browser elections.
- **Auto.** The Auto setting classifies the computer as a potential browser (default for Windows NT Workstations and Windows NT Servers that aren't acting as domain controllers).

2.6.1 Exercise: Configuring Directory Replication

This exercise requires two computers that network together. One computer must be an NT Server and the other can be Windows NT Server or NT Workstation.

To set up the export server for directory replication:

1. Verify that the Registry is okay. Specifically, unless you have added SP1 or SP2, you must manually edit the registry to force Directory Replication to work. The next six steps walk you through the process of correcting the registry entry.
2. Run Regedt32.exe. From the Options menu verify that you are not working in Read Only Mode.
3. Open this key: HKEY_LOCAL_MACHINE\SYSTEM\CurrentControlSet\Control\SecurePipeServers\winreg\AllowedPaths.
4. Double-click on Machine:REG_MULTI_SZ. The Multi-String Editor dialog box opens.
5. In the Data field, add an entry by pressing your arrow key down to clear anything that might be highlighted, and then pressing Enter.
6. Type the following exactly as it appears without the period at the end: System\CurrentControlSet\Services\Replicator.

7. Click on OK, exit the Registry Editor, restart your machine, and then log back on as an administrator.
8. Create a new account for the Directory Replicator service. The Directory Replicator account must be a member of the Backup Operator group and the Replicator group for the domain. When you set up the new account, be sure to enable the Password Never Expires option and disable the User Must Change Password at Next Logon option. Also, make sure the account has logon privileges for all hours.
9. Assign the new account the User Right "Log on as a Service."
10. In the Control Panel, double-click on the Services applet. Select the Directory Replicator Service from the list and click the Startup button. Change the Startup type to Automatic and configure the Log on as section to use the account that you created in step 2 with the password you set.
11. Start the Server Manager application in the Administrative Tools program group. Server Manager is a tool for managing network servers and workstations from a single location.
12. In the Server Manager, double-click on the export server to open the Server Properties dialog box
13. Click on the Replication button to open the Directory Replication dialog box.

A Windows NT Server can serve as an export server, an import computer, or both.

14. In the Directory Replication dialog box, select the Export Directories radio button. The default path to the export directory appears in the From Path box. Click on the Add button to open the Select Domain dialog box. Click on a domain to select it. Double-click on a domain to display the computers within that domain. If you select a whole domain, all import servers in the domain receive the replicated data. If you choose a specific computer, only that computer receives the replicated data. You can choose any combination of domains and specific computers.
15. Click on the Manage button to open the Manage Exported Directories dialog box. Subdirectories within the export directory appear in the Sub-Directory list. You can add or remove subdirectories from the list by clicking on the Add or Remove buttons. By default, the Scripts subdirectory appears.

    Note the check boxes at the bottom of the screen. Enabling the Wait Until Stabilized check box tells the Directory Replicator service to wait at least two minutes after any change to the selected subdirectory tree before exporting. Enabling the Entire Subtree check box tells the Directory Replicator service to export all subdirectories beneath the selected subdirectory. The Add Lock button lets you lock the subdirectory so it can't be exported. More than one user can lock a subdirectory. (Consequently, a subdirectory can have more than one lock.) To remove a lock, click on the Remove Lock button.
16. If you do not see a dialog box stating that the Directory Replicator service is starting, you need to start the Directory Replicator service yourself. In Server Manager, select the Export Computer in the list of computers, and select the Services option from the Computer menu. Select the Directory Replicator service and click on the Start button to start the Directory Replicator service.

2.6.2 Exercise: Configuring the Import Computer

To set up the import computer for directory replication:

1. Verify that Registry is okay. Specifically, unless you have added SP1 or SP2, you must manually edit the registry to force Directory Replication to work. The next six steps will walk you through the process of correcting the registry entry.
2. Run Regedt32.exe. From the Options menu, verify that you are not working in Read Only Mode.
3. Open this key: HKEY_LOCAL_MACHINE\SYSTEM\CurrentControlSet\Control\SecurePipeServers\winreg\AllowedPaths.
4. Double-click on Machine: REG_MULTI_SZ. The Multi-String Editor dialog box opens.
5. In the Data field, add an entry by pressing your down arrow key to clear anything that might be highlighted, and then pressing Enter.
6. Type the following exactly as it appears without the period at the end: System\CurrentControlSet\Services\Replicator.

   Click on OK, exit the Registry Editor, restart your machine, and then log back on as an administrator.
7. Double-click on the Services icon in the Control Panel. Select the Directory Replicator service and click on the Startup button to open the Service dialog box.
8. In the Startup Type frame, select the Automatic radio button. Select the This Account radio button and enter a username and password for the replicator account you created on the export server.
9. Start Server Manager, select the computer you're now configuring, and click on the Replication button in the Properties dialog box. The Directory Replication dialog box appears. This time, you're concerned with the import side (the right side) of the dialog box, but the configuration steps are similar to steps for configuring the export side. The default import directory appears in the To Path box. Click on the Add button to add a domain or a specific export server. Click on the Manage button to open the Manage Imported Directories dialog box, which lets you manage the import directories.
10. In the Manage Imported Directories dialog box, click on Add or Remove to add or remove a subdirectory from the list. Click on Add Lock to add a lock to the subdirectory.
11. If you do not see a dialog box stating that the Directory Replicator service is starting, you need to start the Directory Replicator service yourself. In Server Manager, select the Import Computer in the list of computers, and select the Services option from the Computer menu. Select the Directory Replicator service and click on the Start button to start the Directory Replicator service.

2.6 Practice Problems

1. In Windows NT, a service is what? (Choose the best answer.)
    - A. A network share site
    - B. The component of NT that creates the UNC names
    - C. A built-in application that provides support for other applications
    - D. A component that allows for more than 10 concurrent connections
2. The WINS service does what for Windows NT?
    - A. Allows 16-bit Windows applications to run on NT
    - B. Translates 16-bit calls from a Windows application and converts them into 32-bit calls for NT
    - C. Maps NetBIOS names to IP addresses
    - D. Maps IP addresses to Network card's MAC addresses
3. The DHCP service does what for Windows NT?
    - A. Allows 16-bit Windows applications to run on NT
    - B. Translates 16-bit calls from a Windows application and converts them into 32-bit calls for NT
    - C. Maps NetBIOS names to IP addresses
    - D. Assigns IP addresses to clients automatically
4. Your server shows up in the network neighborhood, and others can connect to your server's shares. However, when you try to connect to another resource on the network you cannot. What do you suspect is the problem? (Choose the best answer.)
    - A. You have a real mode driver for your network card and you need a 32-bit protected mode driver.
    - B. The server service has been paused or stopped.
    - C. The Workstation service has been paused or stopped.
    - D. The Network protocol in use has been disabled.
5. You have an NT Server that is a backup domain controller. You previously had several shares but now all of the sharing symbols in Explorer are gone and no one can connect to your machine. What is the problem?
    - A. The PDC is down.
    - B. You are not logged on as the administrator.
    - C. The server service has been stopped.
    - D. Someone has the same NetBIOS name as your server.
6. Your boss has asked you to pause a service, as she is trying to troubleshoot a problem on your network. You would do this using:
    - A. The Devices Applet in Control Panel
    - B. The Services applet in Control Panel
    - C. The NET STOP command
    - D. The NET PAUSE command
7. Which service is responsible for printing?
    - A. Spooler
    - B. WINS
    - C. SERVER
    - D. PRINT Redirector
8. You would like to enable the Gateway Services for NetWare at different times throughout the day on your test NT server. What are the methods to enable GSNW to start only when you want it to?
    - A. Create a Hardware Profile that matches up with the services you would like to run at startup.

2

B. Configure the Service applet to start only specified services at boot. Then when you need GSNW, start it manually.

C. You cannot do this. GSNW must be running at all times when NT Server is installed on the machine.

D. Create a batch file with NET STOP and NET START commands to stop and start the GSNW service. Then use the AT scheduler to run the batch file at different times throughout the day.

9. You are configuring a service and are uncertain why you need to specify a logon account for the service. The reason is because:

A. No object can access the registry without a logon id.

B. The logon account determines in what security context the service will run.

C. Enables auditing of a service.

D. Services, part of the operating process, will generally run in real time. By specifying the service as a user, the threads will lose thread priority and will be more secure with the system.

10. You are configuring a service to use the SYSTEM account. You have heard that this isn't a wise thing to do. Why not? (Choose the best answer.)

A. The System account may only be used by the Security Accounts manager.

B. The System Account is to be used as a backup administrator account. The password is blank.

C. The System account is a default user account used to validate remote clients.

D. The System account is used by many services and by the Operating System. Any security changes to this account might have detrimental effects on the OS.

11. You and a colleague are installing Windows NT Server 4.0 as a BDC. Your colleague is unclear on why you have decided to use the Directory Replicator service. The primary purpose of the Directory Replicator service is:

A. To automate the installation on NT Server 4.0.

B. To replicate an exact configuration on Widows NT Server 4.0 to another machine.

C. To replicate directories containing logon scripts, system polices, and crucial, read-only information.

D. To allow users to be validated by this BDC. The account database on the server must be replicated to this machine on a regular basis.

12. A computer running this OS can act as an import computer. (Choose all that apply.)

A. Windows NT Server

B. Windows NT Workstation

C. LAN Manager

D. Windows 95

13. You are allowed to edit the parameters for Directory Replication through what? (Choose the best answer:)

A. Control Panel System.

B. Control Panel Devices.

C. The registry editor.

D. You cannot change a value on this service.

14. What is the Interval value and what does it do for Windows NT? (Choose the best answer.)

A. A registry setting that monitors how often NT checks the export directory for changes

B. A registry setting that monitors how often a client checks export directory for changes

C. A service that synchronizes the account database to other domain controllers

D. A service that synchronizes the browse list with other browsers in the network

15. You have configured directory replication on your export server. You decide, however, that you would like to increase the GUARDTIME to ensure stabilization of your directories before they replicate. You can do this by doing what? (Choose the best answer.)

A. Changing the GUARDTIME value in the Server Manager utility.

B. Changing the GUARDTIME value in the Registry.

C. Using the GUARDTIME= command at a DOS prompt.

D. You cannot change the GUARDTIME value anywhere in the system.

16. What is the default directory for exporting data to other computers on your network?

A. \<winnt root>\System32\REPL

B. \<winnt root>\System32\REPL\EXPORT

C. \<winnt root>\System32\REPL\SCRIPTS

D. \<winnt root>\System32\REPL\IMPORT

17. You have configured Directory Replication on your export server and would like to check the status of replication on your import computer. You can do this through which method? (Choose the best answer.)

A. The Registry Editor

B. Server Manager

C. Network Client Administrator

D. The NET=Replication command

18. You have configured Directory replication on your server. However, when you check the status of Directory Replication on the import computer, you receive a message that says "No Master" under the status field. This means what? (Choose the best answer.)

A. There is no Master Domain Controller available.

B. There is no Master Browser.

C. The import computer is not receiving updates from the export server.

D. The import server has not been identified on the export server.

19. You have configured Directory Replication on your server to replicate directories to an NT Server in another domain. However, when you check the status of the directories in the other domain, you receive a "No Master" message. Why is this happening? (Choose all that apply.)

A. You must specify the computer name instead of the domain name when replicating between domains in a trust relationship.

B. You must first create a trust relationship between the domains to establish directory replication between the two domains.

C. Your REPL account must have the same username and password in both domains.

D. You must add the REPL user to the Domain Admins group in both domains.

20. You are about to create a single-server domain and your supervisor asks you why you have chosen to use per server instead of per seat licensing. You would respond with what? (Choose the best answer.)

    A. Per server licensing is needed because you do not have enough clients to justify the cost of buying per seat.

    B. Per server licensing is needed because you have only one domain controller at this time.

    C. Per server licensing is needed because you are integrating with NetWare servers.

    D. Per server licensing is needed because Microsoft requires you to purchase per server when you first install NT Server.

21. You have installed NT Server as a PDC with 25 Client Access Licenses. Your company has hired 20 additional users that need access to your server. To allow these clients access to your server, you must do what? (Choose the best answer.)

    A. Reinstall NT and specify the additional 20 users.

    B. Purchase per seat licenses and use the Control Panel Licensing application.

    C. Purchase additional per server Client Access Licenses and add the additional licenses through the Admin Tools.

    D. Purchase additional per server Client Access Licenses and add the additional licenses through the Control Licensing application.

22. You have a Windows NT Server that is a member server. You would like to configure this machine so that it is never a browser in your domain. You can do this how? (Choose the best answer.)

    A. Through the Control Panel to Network, set the Browsing parameter under services to No.

    B. Through the Control Panel to services. Choose Configure on the Browser service and set the value to No.

    C. Through the Control Panel to services. Stop the browser service.

    D. By editing the registry to change the role of a browser on NT Server.

    E. You cannot do this after the initial server installation.

23. Your NT Domain is segmented into three subnets. You have a backup domain controller on two subnets and a PDC on one subnet. The roles these machines play in browsing are what? (Choose the best answer.)

    A. The PDC is the Domain Master Browser. The two BDCs are clients of the Domain Master Browser.

    B. The PDC is the Domain Master Browser. The two BDCs have no role in browsing.

    C. The PDC and the two BDCs act as backup Master Browsers because the network is segmented.

    D. The PDC is the Domain Master Browser and the BDCs are Master browsers because the network is segmented.

24. You are testing a PDC. During the testing phase you have to reboot the machine several times. Each time you check the Event Viewer and you notice that the Browser service has forced an election. Why is this happening? (Choose the best answer.)

    A. If you have the Browser Service enabled, all NT machines will force an election to determine who is the Browser.

B. Browser elections happen each time a server comes onto the network.

C. Browser elections are forced each time the Primary Domain Controller reboots because the PDC must be the Domain Master Browser.

D. Browser election happen every fifteen minutes on an NT Domain.

25. Based on the previous question, how could you stop these elections from happening each time you reboot the machine? (Choose the best answer.)

A. You cannot stop the elections from happening.

B. You must disable the server service.

C. You must edit the registry and configure the PDC not to maintain a Server List.

D. You must edit the properties of the Browser service through Control Panel Services.

26. You have a Windows NT Server that you are testing as a PDC. You are rebooting this machine every 30 minutes or so due to tests on your system. You notice that after each boot, the Event Viewer has a message that states it is initializing a browser election on your network. Why is this so? (Choose the best answer.)

A. Browser elections happen every 28 minutes regardless of whether they are needed.

B. Browser elections happen every 30 minutes regardless of whether they are needed.

C. The PDC is required, by default, to be the Domain Master Browser. By rebooting, you are forcing a browser election in your domain.

D. The Browser election is a default entry in Event Viewer. No election is actually happening on your network.

2.6 Answers and Explanations: Practice Problems

1. **C** In Windows NT, a service provides support for other applications and components of the operating system.

2 **C** The WINS service maps NetBIOS names to IP address.

3. **D** The DHCP service assigns IP addresses to clients automatically.

4. **C** The Workstation service has been paused or stopped.

5. **C** If the server service is stopped, shares are not available to anyone.

6. **B** Pause the DHCP service using the Control Panel, Services applet.

7. **D** Pausing a service keeps all current connections but does not add any additional clients.

8. **A, D** A hardware profile enables you to configure a service at startup as would using a batch file in conjunction with the AT scheduler.

9. **B** The logon account provides the security context for the service.

10. **D** The System account is used by many services and by the operating system. Any security changes to this account could have detrimental effects on the OS. Instead, you should configure a service to use an account created and configured specifically for that service.

11. **C** The primary purpose of the Directory Replicator service is to replicate directories containing logon scripts, system polices, and crucial, read-only, information.

12. **A, B, C** Windows 95 cannot act as an import computer.

13. **B** You edit the parameters for Directory Replication through the Registry editor. The key for the service is: HKEY-LOCAL MACHINE\SYSTEM\Current ControlSet\Services\Replicator\Paramters.

14. **A** The Interval value is a registry setting that monitors how often NT checks the export directory for changes.

15. **B** You can change the GUARDTIME value only in the Registry editor.

16. **B** The \<winnt root>\System32\REPL\EXPORT directory is the default directory for exporting data to other computers on your network.

17. **B** To check Directory Replication status, use the Server Manger, Directory Replication command.

18. **C** The import computer is not receiving updates from the export server.

19. **A, C** To replicate directories to an NT Server in another domain, you must specify the computer name in addition to the domain name when replicating over a WAN link.

20. **A** Per server licensing is needed because you have only one server in small domain. As your domain grows, you are allowed a one-time conversion of per server to per seat.

21. **D** To allow 20 additional clients access to your server, you must purchase additional per server Client Access Licenses and add the additional licenses through the Control Licensing application.

22. **D** You must edit the Registry to change the role of a browser on NT Server.

23. **D** Each subnet must have a Master Browser; the PDC is always the Domain Master Browser.

24. **C** The PDC is always the Domain Master Browser. Because the machine is being rebooted often, it is announcing its presence to the network.

25. **C** To stop the elections from happening each time you reboot the machine, you have to edit the registry and change the value of the PDC to non-browser.

26. **C** The NT Server PDC is required, by default, to be a browser server. By rebooting, you are forcing an election in your domain for your NT Server.

2.6 Key Words

Directory Replication

Per Server licensing

Per Seat license

Domain master browser

Backup browsers

AT.EXE

Hardware Profile

GuardTime

Interval

2.7 Configuring Peripherals and Devices

Control Panel includes several applications that help you install and configure peripherals and devices.

A. Devices

The Devices application (SRVMGR.CPL) writes to

```
HKEY_LOCAL_MACHINE\SYSTEM\CurrentControlSet\Services.
```

You can start, stop, or disable device drivers in this Control Panel applet. The three columns in the Control Panel Devices main display area are labeled Device, Status, and Startup. The Device column identifies the name of the device driver as it appears in the Registry; the Status column reads "Started" if the driver is active, and otherwise appears blank; the Startup column denotes when each driver is configured to initialize.

Choose one of the following Startup types:

- **Boot.** These devices start first, as soon as the kernel is loaded and initialized
- **System.** These devices start after the boot devices and after the HKEY_LOCAL_MACHINE subtree has begun to be built.
- **Automatic.** These devices start late in the boot process, after the Registry is almost entirely built, just before the Winlogon screen appears.
- **Manual.** These devices are never started without administrator intervention.
- **Disabled.** These devices cannot be started at all unless their startup types is changed to something other than Disabled.

To start a device that isn't active, select the device and choose the Start button. To stop a device that's active, select the device and choose the Stop button. To enable or disable a device for a given hardware profile, select the device, click on HW Profiles, select enable or disable to change to the desired status, and click on OK.

B. Multimedia

The Multimedia application (MMSYS.CPL) writes to

```
HKEY_LOCAL_MACHINE\SYSTEM\CurrentControlSet\Services.
```

Multimedia device drivers are added and configured from this Control Panel applet.

C. Ports

The Ports application (PORTS.CPL) writes directly to the following key:

```
HKEY_LOCAL_MACHINE\SYSTEM\CurrentControlSet\Services\Serial
```

This Control Panel interface lists only the serial ports that are available but not in use as serial ports.

If you need an additional port for use under Windows NT, choose the Add button. You may assign a different COM port number, base I/O port address or IRQ, or enable a First In-First Out (FIFO) buffer for that port.

2

1. UPS

The UPS application (UPS.CPL) writes to the following key:

```
HKEY_LOCAL_MACHINE\SYSTEM\CurrentControlSet\Services\UPS
```

If your computer is equipped with a Uninterruptible Power Supply (UPS), Windows NT can be configured to communicate with it. Armed with the correct information, Windows NT can recognize the following:

- **Power failure signal.** The point when an event is logged and the Server service paused. No new connections to this server can be made, but existing connections still function.
- **Low battery signal at least two minutes before shutdown.** As the name implies, Windows NT recognizes when the UPS battery is about to be exhausted.
- **Remote UPS Shutdown.** Signals Windows NT that the UPS is shutting down.

The Execute Command File option enables an administrator to specify a batch or executable file that runs immediately preceding a shutdown.

If no Low Battery Signal is configured, the administrator can enter the Expected Battery Life and the Battery Recharge Time Per Minute of Run Time in the lower-left corner of the dialog box.

After the initial PowerOut alert is raised (the power failure signal has been received), Windows NT waits until the Time Between Power Failure and Initial Warning Message has elapsed, and then sends an alert to all interactive and connected users.

2. SCSI Adapters

This application is one of the great misunderstandings in Windows NT. As it suggests, this application opens the SCSI Adapters dialog box, which is used to install SCSI adapter drivers. However, this dialog box also is used to install and remove IDE CD-ROM drivers as well as drivers for CD-ROM drives that use proprietary interfaces, such as Mitsumi or Panasonic drives.

IDE drivers are added through this applet because they are ATAPI drivers, which are a subset of the SCSI drivers. To add a SCSI adapter or CD-ROM device driver, follow these procedures:

1. Double-click the SCSI Adapters application in the Control Panel.
2. In the SCSI Adapters dialog box, choose the Drivers tab and click on the Add button.
3. Select the driver from the list of available drivers in the Install Driver dialog box. If your driver isn't listed but you have a disk from the manufacturer with a Windows NT driver, click on the Have Disk button.
4. Choose OK. You must point Windows NT toward the original installation files (or the disk that contains the driver) and restart the computer in order for the new driver to initialize.

To remove a SCSI adapter or CD-ROM device driver, perform these instructions:

1. Select the Drivers tab in the SCSI Adapters dialog box.
2. Select the driver you want to remove.
3. Choose the Remove button.

3. Tape Devices

To add a tape drive device driver, follow these steps:

1. Double-click on the Tape Devices icon in Control Panel.
2. Select the Drivers tab.
3. Click on the Add button.
4. Select the driver from the list of available drivers. If your driver isn't listed but you have a disk from the manufacturer with a Windows NT Driver, click on the Have Disk button.
5. Choose OK. You must point Windows NT toward the original installation files (or the disk that contains the driver) and restart the computer in order for the new driver to initialize.

To remove a tape drive device driver, follow these steps:

1. Select the driver from the list of installed drivers in the Tape Devices dialog box of the Drivers tab.
2. Choose the Remove button.

4. PC Card (PCMCIA)

The PC Card application helps you install and configure PCMCIA device drivers. A red X next to a device in the PC card list indicates that NT doesn't support the device.

5. Modems

The Modems application enables you to add or remove a modem. To add a modem:

1. Double-click on the Modems application in the Control Panel.
2. Click on Add in the Modem Properties dialog box.
3. In the Install New Modem dialog box, click on Next if you want NT to try to detect your modem. If you want to select your modem from the list, or if you're providing software for a modem not listed, enable the check box and then click on Next
4. Select a manufacturer and a model, and click on Next. Or click on the Have Disk button if you're installing software for a modem not shown on the list.
5. Select a port for the modem, or select All ports. Click on Next.

Select a modem in the Modems list and click on Properties to change the parameters for that modem. The Telephony Modem dialog box opens, with two tabs, General and Connection. The General tab enables you to set the port number and the maximum speed.

The Dialing Properties button in the Modem Properties dialog box calls up the My Location tab, which is also in the Telephony application. The My Locations tab enables you to set the dialing characteristics for the modem. To add a new location, follow these steps:

1. Click on the New button at the top of the My Locations tab. (NT announces that a new location has been created.)
2. The new location has the name New Location (followed by a number if you already have a location called New Location). Click on the name and change it if you want to give your location a different

name. (NT might not let you erase the old name completely until you add your new name. Add the new name and then backspace over the old text if necessary.)

3. Change any dialing properties. The new properties will apply to your new location.

6. Keyboard

The Keyboard application opens the Keyboard Properties dialog box, which enables the user to set the keyboard repeat rate, the repeat delay, the cursor blink rate, and the keyboard layout properties.

7. Mouse

The values for this key control the mouse speed, sensitivity, and left- or right-handedness. The one new setting added to this dialog box's Win3.x predecessor is the Snap to Default option in the Motion tab, which instantly positions the pointer over the default button in the active dialog box.

8. Display

The Display application configures the values in the following key, including the video driver, screen resolution, color depth, and refresh rate:

```
HKEY_LOCAL_MACHINE\SYSTEM\CurrentControlSet\Services\<video_driver>\Device0\
```

The five tabs of the Display Properties dialog box are as follows:

- **Background.** Defines the wallpaper for the Desktop.
- **Screen Saver.** Defines the screen saver for the Desktop.
- **Appearance.** Defines window properties.
- **Plus!.** The Visual Enhancements tab from the Microsoft Plus! package for Windows 95 lets you configure the desktop to use custom desktop icons or stretch the wallpaper to fit the screen.
- **Settings.** Defines desktop colors, refresh frequency, and other screen-related settings.

You should always test new display settings before making changes permanent. Although Windows NT can detect the capabilities of your video card, it can't do the same with your monitor.

Windows NT can change video resolution on the fly as long as the color depth does not change. To change the video display adapter:

1. Start the Control Panel Display application and click on the Settings tab.
2. Click on the Display Type button. The Display Type dialog box appears.
3. Click on the Change tab in the Adapter Type frame. The Change Display dialog box appears. Select an adapter from the list and click on OK. Or, if you have a manufacturer's installation disk, click on Have Disk.

2.7 Practice Problems

1. You have opened the Control Panel, Ports to see what ports are on your NT computer. However, Com1 does not appear in the list of ports. Why is this?

   A. Com1 never appears in the list of Ports because it is reserved for the OS.

   B. Com1 is not supported under Windows NT 4 due to the HAL limitations on some computers.

   C. Com1 is in use.

   D. You need to press the refresh button to see the available ports.

2. You have added a UPS to your NT server. The UPS initiates a power failure signal, yet all users stay connected to their home directories on the server. Why is this?

   A. The UPS saves power by disconnecting users that are inactive. All users are currently active on the server.

   B. The UPS saves power by disconnecting users that are active. All users are currently inactive on the server.

   C. The UPS cannot disconnect users to the server, because it would interfere with the NT security model.

   D. Current users will stay connected; however, any new users will not be allowed to connect.

3. You would like to add an IDE CD-ROM device to your NT server. You cannot find an appropriate setting to add this device. Where do you add the IDE CD-ROM driver?

   A. Add the Hardware. NTDETECT.Com will find the device and request the driver from you.

   B. Add the Hardware. NTDETECT.com will automatically pull the driver from its library of IDE devices.

   C. Add the Hardware. Then use the IDE Hardware applet in Control Panel.

   D. Add the Hardware. Then use the SCSI applet in Control Panel.

4. What can you configure in the Keyboard applet? (Choose all that apply.)

   A. Repeat rate

   B. Function key settings

   C. Cursor blink rate

   D. Num lock on or off at startup

5. You have just changed the resolution from 640×480 to 800×600 on your NT machine. Now you must do what to put the settings into effect?

   A. Reboot.

   B. Reboot and choose VGA mode and the reboot as normal.

   C. Press F5 to refresh the screen.

   D. Test your settings and then exit Display.

6. In Control Panel, Devices you have what choices to configure startup for system devices? (Choose all the apply.)

   A. Boot

   B. System

   C. Automatic

   D. Manual

7. The Control Panel, Multimedia enables you to do what?

   A. Adjust system sound

   B. Add video cards

   C. Change video resolution

   D. Add device drivers

   E. All of the above

2

8. You have added a UPS to your NT Server. The Remote UPS Shutdown does what to Windows NT?

   A. Tells Windows NT Clients that the server will be shutting down

   B. Receives a command from Windows NT that the server has been properly shutdown

   C. Receives a command from Windows NT that the server has been improperly shutdown

   D. Tells Windows NT that the UPS will be shutting down

9. You have added a UPS to your NT Server. The power failure signal affects Windows NT Server in what way?

   A. Tells Windows NT that there has been a power surge

   B. Tells Windows NT that there has been no interrupt in power as the power signal has been constant to NT in 30-second pulses

   C. The point where the server service is paused and an event is logged

   D. Emits a whistle through NT's sound system to alert the administrator that there has been an error on the system

10. You would like to schedule a .bat file to run before NT is shut down by the UPS. How can you do this?

    A. You must use the AT scheduler command.

    B. You must use the NET start /interactive command.

    C. You must create a Hardware Profile that specifies the .bat file to run before shutdown.

    D. You must supply the path to the file in the Execute Command File option in the UPS dialog box.

11. You have installed a UPS on your server. During a power failure, when does NT send an alert to all connected users?

    A. After the initial PowerOut message has been received by the server, NT waits until the time between power failure and the initial warning message has elapsed before sending a message.

    B. After the second PowerOut message has been received by the server, NT waits until the time between power failure and the initial warning message has elapsed before sending a message.

    C. After the initial PowerOut message has been received by the server, NT sends a message to all connected users.

    D. Two minutes before remote shutdown of the UPS.

12. You would like to add an IDE CD-ROM drive to your NT Server configuration. How can you do this?

    A. Add the hardware and reboot. NTDETECT.COM will find the hardware and install the necessary drivers.

    B. Use the Controllers applet in Control Panel.

    C. Use the SCSI applet in Control Panel.

    D. Use the Add New Hardware Wizard in Admin Tools.

13. You have received an updated driver for your SCSI controller for NT server 4.0. Where do you add this new driver?

    A. Control Panel, Add new Programs, use Windows NT setup.

    B. Control Panel, System, Device Manager.

    C. Run Setup from the floppy or CD-ROM.

D. Use the Control Panel, SCSI to update the drivers.

14. You have added a tape device to your system; however, it does not show up as a drive letter in Explorer. How do you configure and manage this tape drive?

    A. You have incorrectly installed the tape drive. Tape drives always show up as a drive in Explorer.

    B. You must use the Control Panel, Backup to configure the device.

    C. You must use the Control Panel, Tape Drive to configure the device.

    D. You must use the Control Panel, SCSI to configure the device.

15. You have installed an internal modem in your system, but you are uncertain as to where you should configure this device. How can you configure the modem?

    A. Use the RAS server service in Control Panel services.

    B. Use the RAS Admin tool in the Admin tools folder.

    C. Use the modem applet in Control Panel.

    D. Use the Dial-up Networking applet in Control Panel.

16. You have installed Windows NT Server 4.0 on your Intel-based machine. You would like to check the configuration of current ports installed on your service. You must use what to determine the ports available on your server?

    A. Locate the HKEY LOCAL MACHINE\SYSTEM \CurrentControlSet\Services\Ports in the registry.

    B. Use the Device applet in Control Panel.

    C. Use the Ports applet in Control Panel.

    D. Use the Ports /* command from the DOS prompt.

17. You decide to check the status of your ports by using the Control Panel, Ports applet. When you open the application, you discover that COM1 is missing from the list of installed ports. Why is this?

    A. COM1 is reserved for NT under Windows NT Server4.0.

    B. COM1 is currently in use by a hardware device.

    C. Your registry has become corrupt and you must use the ERD to restore it.

    D. None of the above.

18. You would like to add an additional port to your computer. How can you change the IRQ of this port?

    A. You must use the setup program that came with the new hardware.

    B. You can use the Ports applet in Control Panel.

    C. You must use the Device Manager.

    D. You can edit the registry entry of HKEY LOCAL MACHINE\HARDWARE|PORTS.

2.7 Answers and Explanations: Practice Problems

1. **C** The port application will show only the ports that are available, and Com1 is not available.

2. **D** During a power failure signal, current users stay connected; any new users, however, cannot connect.

3. **D** In addition to adding SCSI devices with the SCSI applet in the Control Panel, you also can add and remove IDE CD-ROM drivers with this applet.

4. **A, C** From the Keyboard applet, you can configure repeat rate and cursor blink rate. You cannot configure Function key settings and Num lock on or off at startup because these options do not exist in this applet.

5. **D** After changing the resolution, you should test your settings and then exit Display.

6. **A, B, C, D** Choosing Control Panel, Devices enables you to choose from all these choices.

7. **D** You can add device drivers from Control Panel, Multimedia.

8. **D** The remote UPS Shutdown tells Windows NT that the UPS will be shutting down.

9. **C** The power failure signal affects Windows NT Server to the point where the server service is paused and an event is logged.

10. **D** To schedule a .bat file to run before NT is shut down by the UPS, supply the path to the file in the Execute Command File option in the UPS dialog box.

11. **A** NT sends an UPS alert to all connected users after the initial PowerOut message has been received by the server. NT then waits until the time between power failure and the initial warning message has elapsed before sending a message.

12. **C** Use the SCSI applet in Control Panel to add an IDE CD-ROM drive to your NT Server configuration.

13. **D** Use the Control Panel, SCSI to update all drivers.

14. **C** You must use the Control Panel, Tape Drive to configure the tape drive.

15. **C** Use the modem applet in Control Panel to configure your internal modem.

16. **C** You can check all available ports in the Control Panel, Ports applet.

17. **B** COM1 is currently in use by a hardware device. The Ports applet shows you only the available ports in your computer.

18. **B** You can use the Ports applet in Control Panel to change the IRQ of a port.

2.7 Key Words

Devices

Multimedia

Ports

UPS

SCSI adapters

PC Cards

Modems

2.8 Configuring Hard Disks with Disk Administrator

Disk Administrator is Windows NT's disk utility. To access Disk Administrator, you must be using an administrator account. To start the Disk Administrator, choose Start, Programs, Administrative Tools (common), Disk Administrator.

When using the Disk Administrator for the first time, a message box appears, telling you the following:

```
No signature found on Disk 0. Writing a signature is a safe operation and
will not affect your ability to access this drive from other operating
systems, such as DOS.
If you choose not to write a signature, the disk will be marked OFF-LINE and
will be inaccessible to the Windows NT Disk Administrator program.
Do you want to write a signature on Disk 0 so that Disk Administrator can
access the drive?
```

If you choose not to write a signature, the disk will be inaccessible to the Windows NT Disk Administrator program. Do you want to write a signature on Disk 0 so that the Disk Administrator can access the drive?

Choosing Yes creates a 32-bit signature that uniquely identifies the disk written to the primary partition. This function makes possible recognition of the disk as the original, even if it is has been used with a different controller or its identification has changed.

A. Customizing the Display

The status bar at the bottom of the Disk Administrator's main window displays basic disk information. Along with the status bar, a color-coded legend displays the different representations for partition colors and patterns.

You also can set different colors and patterns to distinguish between different disks and disk characteristics for the primary partition, logical drive, mirror set, and volume set.

Initially, each disk represented in the display window is sized proportionately. By choosing Options, Region Display, you get several choices in the Region Display Options dialog box for customizing the appearance of each region.

B. Partitioning

Partitioning refers to the method in which hard disks are made usable. To create primary partitions using the Disk Administrator, follow these steps:

1. Select an area of free space on a disk.
2. Choose Partition, Create.

   A message box appears indicating the possible minimum and maximum sizes for a new primary partition.
3. In the Create Primary Partition dialog box, enter the size of the partition you want to create and choose OK.

To create an extended partition using the Disk Administrator, follow these steps:

1. Select an area of free space on a disk.
2. Choose Partition, Create Extended.

   A message box appears indicating the possible minimum and maximum sizes for a new extended partition.
3. In the Create Extended dialog box, enter the size of the extended partition you want to create and choose OK.

To create a logical drive within an extended partition, select the extended partition and choose Partition, Create.

To create a volume set using the Disk Administrator, follow these steps:

1. Select the areas of free space you want to include with a volume set.
2. Choose Partition, Create Volume Set.

   A message box appears indicating the possible minimum and maximum sizes for a new extended partition.
3. In the Create Volume Set dialog box, enter the size of the volume set you want to create and choose OK.

After you create a volume set, you must format it before you can use it (NTFS and FAT are both supported). To format the new volume, you must save the changes by choosing Partition menu, Commit Changes Now, or by responding to the prompts when exiting the Disk Administrator. The only differences between configuring volume sets and ordinary partitions are as follows:

- The system and boot partitions cannot be part of a volume set.
- You can extend an NTFS volume set (but not a FAT volume set) by selecting the volume set in Disk Administrator and simultaneously selecting at least one area of free space (hold down the Ctrl key to select more than one area at a time). Choose the Partition, Extend Volume Set to get a chance to enter a new size for the volume set.
- A volume set can be made up of two to 32 areas of disk space. More than one area can be used on a physical disk.
- You can never shrink a volume set; after creating or extending it, it's set in stone. You can delete the entire volume set, but not any individual area within it.

If you choose to implement a volume set, be aware of the following drawbacks and dangers:

- Only Windows NT supports volume sets; if you're booting between Windows NT and Windows 95, MS-DOS, or another operating system, your volume set is inaccessible if Windows NT isn't active.
- Your volume set will break because all drives fail sooner or later, and combining free space from multiple drives increases the chances of a disaster.

To extend a volume set, both the existing set and the volume you're adding must be formatted with NTFS. To extend a volume set using the Disk Administrator, follow these steps:

1. Select an NTFS volume, and then select the area(s) of free space you want to add. (Hold down the Ctrl key while you select the areas of free space.)
2. Choose Partition, Extend Volume Set.

   A dialog box appears indicating the possible minimum and maximum sizes for the creation of an extended partition.
3. In the Create Extended Volume Set dialog box, enter the total size for the volume and choose OK.

C. Creating Stripe Sets

Stripe sets differ from volume sets in that the free space areas must all be equally sized areas from 2 to 32 physical disks.

Data is read from and written to the stripe set in 64 KB blocks, disk by disk, row by row. If multiple controllers service your stripe set, or if your single controller can perform concurrent I/O requests, you can improve performance dramatically because you can then use multiple drives simultaneously. Be careful, however—not only do the same dangers apply to stripe sets as apply to volume sets, the potential disaster is even more dire. If any single member of a stripe set fails, the entire volume becomes inaccessible to the point that—because your data is contiguous only for 64 KB at a time—not even a disk editor can help you. Windows NT Server has a more robust method of improving performance while maintaining fault tolerance, called stripe sets with parity. Use a stripe set with parity if you really want the performance boost from striping.

If you're using Windows NT Workstation rather than Server, you don't have that option, but you can go with a hardware implementation of striping that offers some method of parity maintenance. This fault tolerant technology is called Redundant Array of Inexpensive Disks (RAID).

The same rules apply for both stripe sets and volume sets—no limits on drive types, no limit for the file system, and no system and boot partitions. You cannot extend a stripe set the way you can volume sets, however, and you cannot shrink one either.

A stripe set can support IDE, EIDE, and SCSI drive types.

When creating a stripe set, the space on each disk must be the same size. To create a stripe set using the Disk Administrator, follow these steps:

1. Select at least two areas of free space on different hard drives.
2. Choose Partition, Create Stripe Set.

   A dialog box appears indicating the possible minimum and maximum sizes for the creation of an extended partition.
3. In the Create Stripe Set dialog box, enter the total size of the stripe set you want to create and choose OK.

As with a volume set, you must format the stripe set before you can use it.

D. Marking Partitions as Active

On a disk(s) using a Windows NT computer, the areas that contain the startup files are called the system and boot partitions.

The system partition contains the boot files, and the boot partition contains the system and support files. These notations appear backwards by conventional terminology, but they accurately describe Windows NT.

With an I386 computer, the system partition is located on the first disk, is marked active, and is designated as the primary partition. You can have only one active partition at a time. To boot between multiple operating systems, you must set the partition as active before restarting the computer.

On RISC-based systems, hard disks aren't marked as active; rather, a manufacturer-supplied hardware configuration utility controls them. To mark a partition as active using the Disk Administrator, follow these steps:

1. Select a primary partition that contains startup files for a particular OS you want to make active.
2. Choose Partition, Mark Active.

   A dialog box appears indicating that the new partition is active and will be used on startup.
3. Choose OK in the Disk Administrator dialog box.

Notice the asterisk that now appears in the color bar of the new active partition.

E. Committing Changes

After you create a partition, you may format it from within Disk Administrator, but only if you choose Partition, Commit Changes Now. Until you commit changes, your commands aren't actually carried out, so you can change your mind if necessary.

F. Deleting Partitions

You can delete any partition except for the system and boot partitions (and you can't delete those because Windows NT is using them) from Disk Administrator. Simply select the partition you want to delete, then choose Partition, Delete. Confirm your action to officially remove the partition from the interface. Again, until you commit changes, nothing officially happens.

G. Saving and Restoring Configuration Information

The Configuration command on Disk Administrator's Partition menu enables you to save or restore a disk configuration using a floppy disk. You can save the disk configuration to a blank floppy, a floppy with a previous disk configuration, or an emergency repair disk.

Microsoft recommends that you save a copy of your disk configuration before upgrading Windows NT. The Configuration Restore option restores a saved disk configuration from a floppy.

Both the Restore and Search options come with a warning that you are about to overwrite your disk configuration. The Restore and Search operations don't create or delete partitions, but they do affect drive letters, volume sets, stripe sets, parity stripes, and mirrors.

H. Using Other Disk Administrator Options

The Disk Administrator Tools menu provides some options for further defining and protecting hard disks.

1. Format

A hard disk is divided into logical sections that enable a disk to locate data in a systematic fashion. This process is called formatting. To format a partition using the Disk Administrator, follow these steps:

1. Select the newly created partition you want to format.
2. Choose Partition, Commit Changes Now. Click on Yes to save the changes.
3. Choose Tools, Format.
4. In the Format dialog box, enter the volume label to identify the partition.
5. Select the type of file system to use, and then choose OK.

   If you enable the Quick Format check box, the Disk Administrator doesn't scan for bad sectors during the format process. This option isn't available when you format mirror sets or stripe sets with parity.
6. Choose Yes from the Confirmation dialog box to begin the process.

You also can format partitions from the command prompt using this syntax:

```
FORMAT <drive_letter>: /FS:FAT[vb]NTFS
```

2. Assigning a Drive Letter

Normally, Windows NT assigns drive letters starting with the first primary partition on the first physical drive, followed by the logical drives, and finally the remaining primary partitions. After Disk 0 is complete, Windows NT begins assigning drive letters to the partitions on the next physical drive in the same fashion.

If you want to override the normal drive-naming algorithm, choose Tools, Assign Drive Letter. You may change the drive designation to any other unused letter, or you may simply remove the drive letter altogether. The latter option may seem of dubious value, but it allows an administrator to "hide" a partition and its files by not providing the computer a "handle." To change a drive letter using the Disk Administrator, follow these steps:

1. Select the partition or logical drive that you want to assign a drive letter.
2. Choose Tools, Assign Drive Letter.

   A message box appears indicating the remaining drive letters for assignment.
3. In the Assign Drive Letter dialog box, select the letter to use and choose OK.

3. Properties

If you click on a volume and choose Tools, Properties, the Volume Properties dialog box appears. (The Volume Properties dialog box is the same dialog box that will appear if you right-click on the disk in Explorer and choose Properties.)

To check for disk problems from Disk Administrator, select the partition you want to check, choose Tools, Properties, and select the Tools tab from the Properties dialog box. Click on the Check Now button to open the Check Disk dialog box, which offers the following options:

- Automatically fix file system errors
- Scan for and attempt recovery of bad sectors

Choose either or both options and click on the Start button to begin checking the partition.

I. Fault Tolerance

Fundamentally, fault tolerance is the system's ability to recover in the event of hardware disaster.

The standard for fault tolerance is known as Redundant Array of Inexpensive Disks (RAID). The two RAID fault-tolerance methods available with Windows NT are as follows:

- Disk Mirroring
- Disk Striping with Parity

1. Creating a Mirror

Disk mirroring is a RAID level 1 fault tolerance method. A mirror is a redundant copy of another disk partition, and it uses the same or a different hard disk controller. To create a mirror using the Disk Administrator, follow these steps:

1. Select at least two areas of free space on different hard drives or you may select an existing partition on one physical disk and an area of free space of equal or greater size on another physical disk.
2. Choose Fault Tolerance, Establish Mirror.

The Disk Administrator then creates spaces of equal size on both disks and assigns a drive letter to them.

2. Creating a Stripe Set with Parity

A stripe set with parity is considered RAID 5. A stripe set with parity ensures fault tolerance because the data is written to 2 to 32 physical disks in 64K segments with parity information written to each drive in rotation. The parity information that spans all drives regenerates data if a drive fails.

To create a stripe set with parity, follow these steps:

1. Select between 3 and 32 areas of free disk space on separate physical disks.
2. Choose Fault Tolerance, Create Stripe Set with Parity.

   A dialog box appears indicating the possible minimum and maximum sizes for a new extended partition.
3. In the Create Stripe Set with Parity dialog box, enter the size of the stripe set to create and choose OK.

The Disk Administrator calculates the stripe set with parity's total size, based on the number of disks selected, and creates a space that is equal on each disk.

As you must with other new volumes, you must format the stripe set before it can be used. To format the new volume, save the changes by choosing Partition, Commit Changes Now or answer the prompts when exiting the Disk Administrator. You also must restart the system before formatting.

J. Securing System Partition on RISC Machines

The system partition on a RISC computer must be a FAT partition. Because Windows NT cannot provide the same security for a FAT partition that it provides for an NTFS partition, the RISC version of Windows NT includes a special Secure System Partition command that provides an extra layer of security for RISC-based system partitions.

2.8.1 Exercise: Creating a Partition

This exercise requires free space on a fixed disk. To format a partition using the Disk Administrator, follow these steps:

1. Select the newly created partition you want to format.
2. Choose Partition, Commit Changes Now. Click on Yes to save the changes.
3. Choose Tools, Format.
4. In the Format dialog box, enter the volume label to identify the partition.
5. Select the type of file system to use, then choose OK.

   If you enable the Quick Format check box, the Disk Administrator doesn't scan for bad sectors during the format process. This option isn't available when you format mirror sets or stripe sets with parity.
6. Choose Yes from the Confirmation dialog box to begin the process.

You also can format partitions from the command prompt using this syntax:

```
FORMAT <drive_letter>: /FS:FAT[vb]NTFS
```

2.8 Practice Problems

1. You would like to add a partition to your NT Server. To do this you must use what utility?
   A. FDISK
   B. Server Manager
   C. Disk Administrator
   D. CHECKDISK
2. To add a partition to NT Server you must be logged on as what?
   A. A member of the Power Users Group
   B. A member of the Administrators Group
   C. A member of the server Operators group
   D. A member of the Domain Users group
3. The first time you start Disk Administrator you receive a message telling you that Disk Administrator will be writing a signature to the disk. What does this mean?
   A. This allows NT to access the FAT file system on the active partition.
   B. This allows NT to have complete access beyond any security set on the system.
   C. This writes a 32-bit signature that identifies the disk as the original.
   D. This writes a 16-bit signature that identifies the disk as the original so NT can boot up through real mode phases into protected mode.
4. Which of the following can be created in Disk Administrator for NT Workstation?
   A. Stripe sets
   B. Stripe sets with parity
   C. Fat extended volume sets
   D. Mirror sets
5. Which of the following can be created in Disk Administrator for NT Server? (Choose all that apply.)
   A. Stripe sets
   B. Stripe sets with parity
   C. Fat extended volume sets
   D. Mirror sets
6. How many primary partitions can you create in Windows NT on one physical drive?
   A. 1
   B. 2
   C. 3
   D. 4
7. What types of file systems are you allowed to format with NT 4? (Choose all that apply.)
   A. NTFS
   B. HPFS
   C. FAT
   D. FAT32
8. You have created a new partition in Windows NT but you cannot see the partition when you reboot to DOS. What is the likely cause of the problem?
   A. You have formatted the partition with FAT32.
   B. You have formatted the partition with NTFS.
   C. Your BIOS has 1024 cylinder limit so your drive is not completely accessible through DOS.
   D. You are not logged on as Administrator.
9. You have just created a new partition but the format command is grayed out in Disk Administrator. What must you do to format the drive?

A. Reboot the machine.

B. Use the convert.exe command.

C. Commit changes now.

D. Format the drive from a DOS prompt.

10. You would like to delete a partition, but when you press Delete on the keyboard, nothing happens to the selected partition. How can you remove the partition from your system?

A. The Delete Key does not work on the keyboard; you must use the Delete command from the Partition menu.

B. You are not logged on as administrator. Only an Administrator can delete partitions.

C. You must commit changes first and then delete the partition

D. You must use the DelPart utility.

11. You would like to extend a volume set that you created and formatted. However, the command to extend the volume set is grayed out. Why can't you extend the volume set?

A. You do not have administrative rights.

B. Items on the volume set are currently in use.

C. The volume set must be formatted with NTFS to be extended.

D. You cannot extend any volume set on NT.

12. You would like to create a volume set. What is the minimum areas of free disk space required?

A. 1

B. 2

C. 3

D. 4

13. You would like to create a volume set. What is the maximum areas of free disk space allowed?

A. 4

B. 8

C. 12

D. 32

14. You would like to create a stripe set. What is the minimum number of hard disks required?

A. 1

B. 2

C. 3

D. 4

15. You would like to create a stripe set. What is the maximum number of hard disks allowed?

A. 4

B. 8

C. 12

D. 32

16. How can stripe sets be dangerous to data?

A. Data can become corrupted easier on the drives.

B. The FAT table cannot keep track of data files larger than 1 GB.

C. There is no fault tolerance on the stripe sets.

D. Stripe sets cannot be backed up by most backup software.

17. You have four hard disks that are configured as follows: Disk 0 has 400 MB of free space; Disk 1 has 150 MB of free space; Disk 2 has 500 MB of free space; and Disk 3 has 200 MB of free space. What is the largest stripe set you can create using any combination of hard disks?

A. 600 MB

B. 800 MB

C. 1350 MB

D. You cannot make a stripe set as you need 32 drives to make a stripe set.

18. Data is read and written to the stripe set in what size?

A. 4 KB

B. 16 KB

C. 32 KB

D. 64 KB

19. A colleague is trying to create a stripe set. He is using IDE, SCSI, and SyQuest drives. He is not allowed to create the stripe. Why not?

A. All drives must be SCSI.

B. All drives must be IDE.

C. You cannot include removable media in stripe sets.

D. Your colleague is not an administrator.

20. In Disk Administrator you can tell which partition is currently active in what way?

A. Choosing Partition to Find Active...

B. Choosing Tool to Find Active...

C. Looking for the Asterisk in the title bar of the active partition.

D. Looking for partition that reads 1381 on the title bar.

21. You and a colleague are making several changes to your hard disk configuration. As a safety method, you would like to save your current configuration before you begin. How can you do this?

A. Run the rdisk utility.

B. Save the registry file to floppy.

C. Choose export configuration from the Partition menu.

D. Copy the Clone directory of the registry to a floppy.

22. You would like to change the drive letter of the CD-ROM drive to W. How can you do this in Disk Administrator?

A. Choose Partition, change drive letter.

B. Choose Tools, change drive letter.

C. Choose Partition, Properties, Advanced, change drive letter.

D. You cannot change drive letters in Disk Administrator, they can only be changed through Computer policies.

23. You would like to create a mirror set on NT Workstation. How can this be done with Disk Administrator?

A. Choose Fault Tolerance, create mirror set.

B. Choose Partition, create mirror set.

C. Choose Partition, properties, Advance, mirror set.

D. This cannot be done on Workstation.

24. What is the maximum number of drives that can be in a mirror set?

A. 1

B. 2

C. 3

D. 4

25. Which are attributes of a mirror set? (Choose all the apply.)

A. Areas of two separate drives must be of equal size.

B. You cannot mirror the system or boot partition.

C. You can mirror the system and boot partition.

D. You can create mirror sets only on Disk Administrator.

26. You would like to create a stripe set with parity on your NT Workstation. How can this be done?
    A. Choose Fault Tolerance, create stripe set.
    B. Choose Partition, create stripe set.
    C. Choose Partition, properties, Advance, stripe set.
    D. This cannot be done on Workstation.
27. Your machine is configured as follows: Disk 0 has 150 MB of free space; Disk 1 has 300 MB of free space; Disk 2 has has 500 MB of free space; Disk 3 has 650 MB of free space. What is the largest stripe set with parity you can create using any combination of disks?
    A. 800 MB
    B. 900 MB
    C. 1000 MB
    D. 1,650 MB
28. With the answer from the above question, what is the total area of hard disk space used for parity?
    A. 150 MB
    B. 300 MB
    C. 600 MB
    D. 900 MB
29. How do you mark a partition as Active on a RISC based machine?
    A. Choose Partition, mark as active.
    B. Choose Tools, mark as active.
    C. Choose the partition area, and press Shift+F5.
    D. You do not mark partitions as active on RISC machines.

2.8 Answers and Explanations: Practice Problems

1. **C** Use Disk Administrator to add a partition to your NT Server.
2. **B** To add a partition to NT Server, you must be logged on as a member of the Administrators local Group.
3. **C** The message telling you that Disk Administrator will be writing a signature to the disk means that this writes a 32-bit signature that identifies the disk as the original.
4. **A** Stripe Sets can be created in Disk Administrator for NT Workstation.
5. **A, B, D** Stripe sets, stripe sets with parity, and mirror sets can be created in Disk Administrator for NT Server.
6. **D** You can create four primary partitions in Windows NT on one physical drive.
7. **A, C** NT allows both NTFS and FAT file systems.
8. **B** If you cannot see a newly created partition when you reboot to DOS, you probably have formatted the partition with NTFS. NTFS partitions are not accessible through any OS other than NT.
9. **C** To format a new partition, choose Commit changes now from the Partition menu.
10. **A** To delete a partition, you must use the Delete command from the Partition menu. The Delete key doesn't work.
11. **C** The volume set must be formatted with NTFS to be extended.
12. **B** The minimum areas of free disk space required to create a volume set is two.
13. **D** The maximum areas of free disk space allowed to create a volume set is 32.
14. **B** Two hard disks are required for a stripe set.

15. **D** The maximum number of hard disks allowed to create a stripe set is 32.

16. **C** Stripe sets can be dangerous to data because there is no fault tolerance on them.

17. **B** 800 MB is the largest stripe set you can create. Use the 400 MB on Drive 0, plus 400 from Disk 2.

18. **D** Data is read and written to the stripe set in 64 KB sizes.

19. **C** You cannot include removable media in stripe sets

20. **C** To tell which partition is currently active in Disk Administrator, look for the asterisk in the title bar of the active partition.

21. **C** To save your current hard disk configuration, choose Export Configuration from the Partition menu.

22. **B** Choose Tools, Change Drive Letter to change the drive letter of the CD-ROM drive in Disk Administrator.

23. **D** This cannot be done on Workstation.

24. **B** The maximum number of drives in a mirror set is two.

25. **A, C, D** You can use a mirror set to mirror the system or boot partitions.

26. **D** You cannot create a stripe set with parity on your NT Workstation.

27. **D** 900 MB. Because three drives are required with stripe sets with parity, you can use the 300 MB from Disk 1, 2, 3 for a total of 900 MB.

28 **B** 300 MB, because three drives are the equivalent of one drive and will be devoted to parity information.

29. **D** You do not mark drives as active on RISC based machines.

2.8 Key Words

Partitioning

Disk Administrator

Stripe set

Stripe sets with parity

Mirror sets

Volume sets

RAID

Boot partition

System partition

2.9 Configuring Printing

In Windows NT the term printer refers to the software that controls a specific printing device or devices.

Windows NT uses the term printing device to refer to the hardware that produces the actual output. Windows NT also uses the term print queue, but in NT, a print queue is simply the list (queue) of documents waiting to print.

A. Windows NT Printing Architecture

You should become familiar with the components of the Windows NT printing process for the MCSE exam. The process goes roughly as follows:

1. When an application on an NT client sends a print job, Windows NT checks to see if the version of the printer driver on the client is up-to-date with the version on the print server. If it isn't, Windows NT downloads a new version of the printer driver from the print server to the client.
2. The printer driver sends the data to the client spooler. The client spooler spools the data to a file, and makes a remote procedure call to the server spooler, thus transmitting the data to the server spooler on the print server machine.
3. The server spooler sends the data to the Local Print Provider.
4. The Local Print Provider passes the data to a print processor, where it's rendered into a format legible to the printing device. Then, if necessary, the Local Print Provider sends the data to a separator page processor, where a separator page is added to the beginning of the document. The Local Print Provider lastly passes the rendered data to the print monitor.
5. The print monitor points the rendered data to the appropriate printer port and, therefore, to the appropriate printing device.

1. Printer Drivers

In the first step of the printing process, Windows NT checks to see if the printer driver on the print client is current; if it isn't, Windows NT downloads a new copy of the printer driver from the print server.

When you set up a Windows NT printer, the Setup wizard asks for the operating systems and hardware platforms of all client machines that are going to access the printer. The wizard then places the appropriate printer drivers on the server so they will be available for downloading.

The Windows NT printer driver is implemented as a combination of two dynamic link libraries (or DLLs) and a printer-specific minidriver or configuration file.

Typically, Microsoft supplies the two dynamic link libraries with Windows NT, and the original equipment manufacturer of the printer supplies the minidriver or configuration file. The following list describes these three files:

- The Printer Graphics Driver DLL. This dynamic link library consists of the rendering or managing portion of the driver; it's always called by the Graphics Device Interface.
- The Printer Interface Driver. This dynamic link library consists of the user interface or configuration management portion of the printer driver; it's used by an administrator to configure a printer.

- The Characterization File. This component contains all the printer-specific information, such as memory, page protection, soft fonts, graphics resolution, paper orientation and size, and so on; it's used by the other two dynamic link libraries whenever they need to gather printer-specific information.

These three components of a printer driver (printer graphics driver, printer interface driver, and configuration file) are all located in the following directory, according to their Windows NT platforms (w32x86, w32mips, w32alpha, and w32ppc) and version numbers (0 = version 3.1, 1 = version 3.5x, 2 = version 4.x):

```
winnt_root\system32\spool\drivers.directory
```

The printer driver is specific to both the operating system and the hardware platform.

2. Spooler

The Spooler is a Windows NT service that operates in the background to manage the printing process.

The NT Spooler service must be running on both the client and the print server machines for the printing process to function properly. By default, the spool file folder is the winnt_root\system32\spool\PRINTERS directory. You can change the spool folder by using the Advanced tab of the printer server Properties dialog box.

In the event that a print job gets stuck in the spooler to the point that an administrator or print operator cannot delete or purge it, you can stop the Spooler service and restart it using the Control Panel Service application.

You also can start or stop the Spooler service using the following commands at the command prompt:

```
net start spooler
net stop spooler
```

3. Router

The print router receives the print job from the spooler and routes it to the appropriate print processor.

4. The Print Processor

The process of translating print data into a form that a printing device can read is called rendering. The rendering process begins with the printer driver. The print processor is responsible for completing the rendering process. The tasks performed by the print processor differ depending on the print data's data type. The primary Windows NT print processor is called WINPRINT.DLL, and is located in

```
winnt_root\system32\spool\prtprocs\platform
```

WINPRINT.DLL recognizes the following data types:

- Raw data. Fully rendered data that is ready for the printer.

- Windows NT Enhanced Metafile (EMF). A standard file format that many different printing devices support. Instead of the raw printer data being generated by the printer driver, the Graphical Device Interface generates NT EMF information before spooling. After the NT EMF is created, control returns to the user.
- TEXT. Raw text with minimal formatting. The TEXT data type is designed for printing devices that don't directly accept ASCII text.

5. Print Monitors

Print Monitors control access to a specific device, monitor the status of the device, and communicate this information back to the spooler, which relays the information via the user interface.

To install a new print monitor, click on Add Port in the Ports tab of the printer Properties dialog box. Click on the New Monitor button in the Printer Ports dialog box that appears. In addition, the print monitor has the following duties:

- Detect unsolicited errors (such as Toner Low).
- Handle true end-of-job notification. The print monitor waits until the last page has been printed to notify the spooler that the print job has finished and can be discarded.
- Monitor printer status to detect printing errors. If necessary, the print monitor notifies the spooler so that the job can continue or be restarted.

Windows NT provides some standard print monitors. These include print monitors for the following:

- Local output to LPTx, COMx, remote printer shares and names pipes (\WINNT_ROOT\SYSTEM32\LOCALMON.DLL).
- Output to Hewlett-Packard network interface printing devices (\WINNT_ROOT\SYSTEM32\HPMON.DLL), which can support up to 225 (configured for 64) Hewlett-Packard network interface printing devices. This print monitor requires the DLC protocol.
- Output to Digital network port printers (DECPSMON.DLL), supporting both TCP/IP and DECnet protocols. The DECnet protocol doesn't ship with Windows NT.
- Output to LPR (Line Printer) Ports (LPRMON.DLL), allowing Windows NT to print directly to UNIX LPD print servers or network interface printing devices over the TCP/IP protocol.
- Output to PJL Language printing device (PJLMON.DLL).
- Output to Apple Macintosh postscript printers (SFMMON.DLL), for Windows NT servers with services for the Apple Macintosh installed.

B. Printers Folder

The Printers folder is the Windows NT printing system's primary user interface. From the Printers folder, you install, configure, administer, and remove printers. You also supervise print queues; pause, purge and restart print jobs; share printers; and set printer defaults.

You can install printers on your Windows NT workstation in two ways: install a printer on your own workstation, or connect to a remote printer. From the Printers folder, double-click on the Add Printer icon to open the Add Printer Wizard.

The first screen of the Add Printer Wizard asks if the new printer will be attached to your computer (the My Computer option) or connected to another machine and accessed via the network.

The My Computer option requires Administrator, Print Operator, Server Operator or Power User rights, whereas the Network printer server option does not; you don't have to be an Administrator or a Power User to connect to a shared printer on another machine.

C. Adding a Printer on Your Own Machine

If you select the My Computer option from the Add Printer Wizard screen, and then click on Next, the Wizard asks you what port you want to use. The next screen asks you to specify the manufacturer and model of the new printer.

The next screen asks for a printer name, and whether you want the printer to become the default printer for Windows-based programs. As with all objects in Windows NT, a printer requires a name. The printer name can be as long as 32 characters and doesn't have to reflect the name of the driver in use.

The next screen asks if you want to share the printer. If you want to share the printer with other computers on the network, you must also specify a share name (the default share name is the first eight characters of the printer name specified in the preceding screen). The wizard also asks you to specify the operating systems of all computers that will be sharing the printer. Your only choices are Windows 95 and a number of NT versions and platforms.

The Add Printer Wizard then attempts to install the printer driver. You may be asked to supply the Windows NT installation disk. (If you designate Windows 95 as the operating system of a computer sharing the printer, you may also be prompted to supply the location of the Windows 95 Printer INF files.) The wizard then asks if you want to print a test page.

D. Adding a Network Print Server

If you choose the network printer server option in the first screen of the Add Printer Wizard, the Wizard opens the Connect to Printer dialog which asks for the name of the shared printer to which you want to connect.

The Wizard then asks if you want the printer to serve as a default printer, and completes the installation. If the installation is successful, the icon for the printer appears in the Printers folder.

Almost all the configuration settings for a printer in Windows NT 4 are accessible through following three options of the Printers folder File menu:

- Document Defaults
- Server Properties
- Properties

You also use the Sharing option in the File menu for configuration; specifically, to set up the printer as a shared printer on the network. It's actually just a different path to the Sharing tab of the Properties dialog box.

1. Document Defaults

Choose File, Document Defaults to open the Default Document Properties dialog box. The Default Document Properties dialog box contains document settings for the documents that are to print on the selected printer.

The Page Setup tab defines the Paper Size, Paper Source, and Orientation options for controlling settings for the document you want to print.

2. Server Properties

Choose File, Server Properties to open the Print Server Properties dialog box.

a. Forms

The Forms tab of the Print Server Properties dialog box defines the print forms available on the computer. Think of a print form as a description of a piece of paper that might be in a printer tray. A print form tells NT the size of the paper and where to put the printer margins. You can create your own print forms from within the Forms tab. To create your own form, follow these steps:

1. Click on an existing form in the Forms On list.
2. Select the Create a New Form check box.
3. Change the name of the form, and change the form measurements to the new settings.
4. Click on the Save Form button.

b. Ports

The Ports tab of the Printer Server Properties dialog box maintains a list of available ports. You can add, delete, or configure a port.

c. Advanced

The Advanced tab of the Printer Server Properties dialog box provides the location of the spooler and an assortment of logging and notification options.

3. Properties

You can find most of the printer configuration settings in the printer Properties dialog box. To open the printer Properties dialog box, select a printer in the Printers folder and choose File, Properties, or right-click on the printer and choose Properties.

a. The Printer Properties General Tab

The General tab lets you install a new driver for the printer. The Print Test Page button provides a convenient method for testing whether a printer connection is working.

b. Separator File

By default, Windows NT doesn't separate print jobs with even a blank sheet of paper; to print a separator page between print jobs, you must configure a separator file, of which three are included with Windows NT.

You may use one of these or create your own:

- SYSPRINT.SEP. Prints a separator page for PostScript printers; stored in the \<winnt_root>\SYSTEM32 directory.
- PSCRIPT.SEP. Switches Hewlett-Packard printers to PostScript mode for printers incapable of autoswitching; located in the \<winnt_root>\SYSTEM32 directory.
- PCL.SEP. Switches Hewlett-Packard printers to PCL mode for printers not capable of autoswitching (and prints a separator page before each document); located in the \<winnt_root>\SYSTEM32 directory.

You also may choose to design your own separator page. If so, use a text editor and consult the escape codes listed in table 2.1. The escape codes are special symbols that prompt Windows NT to replace them with specific pieces of data.

Table 2.9.1 Windows NT Printing Escape Codes

Code	Instruction for Windows NT
\<number>	Skip specified number of lines (0–9).
\B\M	Print text in double-width block mode.
\B\S	Print text in single-width block mode.
\D	Print current date using Control Panel International format.
\E	Eject the page.
\F<filename>	Print a file.
\H<code>	Send printer-specific hexadecimal ASCII code.
\I	Print job number.
\L<text>	Print the specified text (use another escape code to end).
\N	Print username of job owner.
\T	Print time the job was printed. Use Control Panel International format.
\U	Turn off block mode (see \B\M and \B\S).
\W<width>	Set width of the page (<=256).

c. Print Processor

The print processor is the component of the printing subsystem that actually performs the rendering. Typically, WINPRINT.DLL performs the print processor functions. If it becomes necessary to replace it, Windows NT does it for you.

WINPRINT.DLL supports the following five data types:

- Raw Fully rendered data ready for printing.
- RAW (FF appended).

- RAW (FF auto).
- NT EMF (enhanced metafile format) A device-independent file format. An EMF file can be spooled directly to the print server and rendered at the server into the correct print format.
- TEXT Raw, unformatted ASCII text ready for printing as is.

d. Printer Properties Ports Tab

The printer Properties Ports tab lets you select a port for the printer, and add or delete a port from the tab. The Configure Port button allows you to specify the Transmission Retry time (the amount of time that must elapse before NT notifies you that the printing device isn't responding). The Transmission Retry setting applies not just to printer you selected but to all printers that use the same driver.

e. Printer Properties Scheduling Tab

The printer Properties Scheduling tab lets you designate when the printer is to be available, and to set the printer priority. It also displays some miscellaneous settings that define how the printer processes print jobs. Table 2.9.2 describes the options in the Printer Properties Scheduling tab.

Table 2.9.2 Options in the Printer Properties Scheduling Tab

Option	Description
Available	The Available setting lets you limit the availability of a printer to a specific period of time.
Priority	The default priority for a printer is 1, but it can be set as high as 99. Changing this setting from its default of 1 is useful in situations in which you have more than one printer printing to the same printing device, in which case the printer with higher priority (99 being the highest) prints before printers of lower priority (1 being the lowest).
Spool Print Documents	If you spool print documents, the computer and the printer don't have to wait for each other.
Hold Mismatched Documents	In other Windows-based operating environments, improperly configured print jobs—a print job, for example, requesting a paper tray that isn't present—can be sent to a printer, which usually causes the printer to hang with an error message. But with the Hold Mismatched Documents option selected, Windows NT examines the configuration of both the print job and printer to make sure that they are in agreement before it sends the job.
Print Spooled Documents First	Ordinarily, Windows NT prints documents on a first-come, first-served basis; the document at the top of the queue prints before the documents below it. If the document at the top of the queue takes a long time to

continues

Table 2.9.2 Continued

Option	Description
	spool, and if the Job Prints While Spooling option isn't selected, you might want to enable the Print Spooled Documents First setting. Windows NT always prints the first available completely spooled print job.
Keep Post-Print Documents	Windows NT cleans up after itself as it finishes printing each job. If you enable the Keep documents after they have printed option, however, Windows NT keeps the print document after it prints.

Under the Spool print documents option, there are two other options:

- **Start printing after the last page is spooled.**
- **Start printing immediately.**

f. The Printer Properties Sharing Tab

The Sharing tab lets you share the printer with other computers on the network. To share a printer, follow these steps:

1. Select Sharing tab in the printer Properties dialog box.
2. Specify a share name (or accept the default, which is the first eight characters of the printer name).
3. Specify what operating systems the other workstations will be using (so NT can automatically download the necessary print drivers to the connecting computers).
4. Click on OK.

You access the Sharing tab directly by clicking on a printer and choosing File, Sharing in the Printers folder, or by right-clicking on a printer and choosing Sharing.

g. The Printer Properties Security Tab

The Security tab lets you configure permissions, auditing, and ownership for the printer

Windows NT printers are Windows NT resources, and Windows NT resources are Windows NT objects. Windows NT objects are protected by the Windows NT security model. To set or change permissions, a user must be the owner, an Administrator, a Power User, a Server Operator, a Print Operator, or a user who has Full Control permissions on the printer's ACL.

The four possible permission levels are as follows:

- No Access. Completely restricts access to the printer.
- Print. Allows a user or group to submit a print job, and to control the settings and print status for that job.

- Manage Documents. Allows a user or group to submit a print job, and to control the settings and print status for all print jobs.
- Full Control. Allows a user to submit a print job, and to control the settings and print status for all documents as well as for the printer itself. In addition, the user or group may share, stop sharing, change permissions for, and even delete the printer.

These permissions affect both local and remote users. By default, permissions on newly created printers comply with the following scheme:

Administrators	Full Control
Creator/Owner	Manage Documents
Everyone	Print
Power Users (workstations only)	Full Control
Print Operators (domain only)	Full Control
Server Operators (domain only)	Full Control

To change the permission level for a group, select the group in the Name list and enter a new permission level in the Type of Access combo box, or open the Type of Access combo box and select a permission level.

h. Printer Properties Device Settings Tab

The printer Properties Device Settings tab maintains settings for the printing device. These settings differ depending on your printing device.

> **As you install a new printer, you can designate as a printer to share over the network.**

E. Setting Up a Printer Pool

A printer pool is essentially a single logical printer that prints to more than one printing device; it prints jobs sent to it to the first available printing device (and therefore provides the throughput of multiple printing devices with the simplicity of a single printer definition).

Printer pools are an extremely efficient way of streamlining the printing process, although they don't necessarily fit every environment. Before your network can use a printer pool, it must meet the following criteria:

- You must have at least two printing devices capable of using the same printer driver because the entire pool is treated as a single logical device, and is managed by a single printer driver.
- The printing devices should be adjacent to each other. Users aren't notified of the actual device that prints their job; users should be able to check all the printing devices rapidly and easily.

To create a printer pool, configure the printer to print to more than one port, and make sure a printing device is attached to each of the ports that the printer is using.

When creating a printer pool, it's essential to choose the ports in order of fastest to slowest speed, as that is the order the print jobs are routed through.

F. Printing from MS-DOS Applications

MS-DOS applications provide their own printer drivers and automatically render printer data to the RAW data type or to straight ASCII text.

The MS-DOS application typically isn't equipped to process UNC names, so if it is printing to a remote printer, you should map a physical port to the remote printer, as follows:

```
net use LPTx: \\pserver\printer_share_name
```

Because the application itself renders the printer data, an MS-DOS application that prints graphics and formatted text must have its own printer driver for the printing device. An MS-DOS application can print ASCII text output without a vendor-supplied printer driver.

2.10 Configuring Windows NT Server for Client Computers

The Windows NT CD-ROM includes client software to assist with networking certain common operating systems with Windows NT. Chapter 1 discusses some of the client software packages included with Windows NT Server. When you are configuring networking protocols on your Windows NT Server system, it is important to remember that all these software packages don't support all the native Windows NT network protocols and network services.

Table 2.10.1 describes which network protocols and which TCP/IP services each of the client systems supports. This table also appears in Chapter 1, in the section entitled "Choosing a Windows NT Network Protocol." You must ensure that the Windows NT configuration provides the appropriate protocols for whatever client systems you'll have running on your network. For more on these client systems, see Chapter 1.

Table 2.10.1 Network Protocol and TCP/IP Service Support for Various Windows NT Client Systems

Network Protocol TCP/IP Service								
	Net-BEUI	**Com-patible**	**Com-patible**	**TCP/IP**	**DLC**	**DHCP**	**WINS**	**DNS**
Network Client for MS-DOS	X	X	IPX	X	X	X		
LAN MAN 2.2c for MS-DOS	X		IPX/SPX	X	X			
Lan MAN 2.2c for OS/2	X			X				
Windows 95	X		X	X		X	X	X
Windows NT Workstation	X		X	X	X	X	X	X

2.9 and 2.10 Practice Problems

1. What is the difference between a printer and a printing device?
   A. A Printer is where the document's final output is.
   B. A Printing device is where the document's final output is.
   C. A Printer refers to a shared queue.
   D. A Printing device refers to a shared queue.
2. What will NT do if you are printing a network printer and the local driver does not match the driver on the server?
   A. NT will generate error 5738—network printing error.
   B. NT will not respond and your job will not print out on the device.
   C. NT will download the driver from the server to the local machine.
   D. Your document will likely be printed as many pages of code.
3. The Windows NT component is largely responsible for printing is what?
   A. GDI
   B. ActiveX
   C. Preemptive threads
   D. I/O Manager
4. What is the spooler's primary job?
   A. To hold the print job until a printer is available
   B. To hold the print job until the application has relinquished control of the data
   C. To receive notifications from the printer that the job has been finished
   D. To transfer the print file from the local machine to a print server
5. What is the print processor's primary function?
   A. To render the job into a language the printing device can understand
   B. To forward jobs from the GDI to the print spooler service
   C. To handle threads from the spooler service
   D. To monitor all aspects of the print process
6. What is the print monitor's primary function?
   A. To allow user management of print job
   B. To point the data to the appropriate port so the job will be printed on the printing device
   C. To manage the flow of data between clients and servers
   D. To manage the creation of the EMF and RAW data during the print process
7. When you install a printer on Windows NT, why does it ask you what other Operating Systems will be connecting to the shared printer?
   A. For security reasons
   B. To create the NetBIOS share name
   C. To enable EMF printing over the network
   D. To install the drivers needed by those Operating Systems so that they can be downloaded from the server
8. What three components constitute a Windows NT print driver?
   A. The Graphics Driver DLL
   B. The Graphics Device Interface
   C. The Printer Interface Driver
   D. The Characterization File

2

9. What does the Graphics Driver DLL do?
   A. It handles all communication between the NT executive services and the hardware.
   B. It is the rendering and managing portion of the driver.
   C. It is the communication and query portion of the driver.
   D. It generates information from the printer device to the NT executive services.
10. What does the printer interface driver do?
   A. Handles all communication between the NT executive services and the hardware
   B. Handles the communication and query portion of the driver
   C. Generates information from the printer device to the NT executive services
   D. Handles the user interface and configuration management portion of the driver
11. What does the Characterization File do?
   A. Contains all printer specific information
   B. Manages all postscript and true type fonts
   C. Handles the processing of converting True Type fonts into bitmap images on the printer
   D. Manages postscript conversion to bitmap images for the printer
12. The spooler service does what?
   A. Sends data across the network to print servers
   B. Receives data from network interface printing devices
   C. Operates in the background to manage the printing process
   D. Receives true end of job notification
13. If a document will not print what can you do to resume printing?
   A. Reinstall the printer.
   B. Choose the stalled document individually and cancel the document.
   C. Choose Purge Print Jobs from the Printer menu.
   D. Restart the server.
14. If you have tried to purge the printer, but the document will not purge, what should you do next?
   A. Restart
   B. Reinstall NT server
   C. Reinstall the printer
   D. Stop and restart the spooler service
15. What two ways can you use to stop the spooler service?
   A. Reboot the server.
   B. Use Control Panel, Services.
   C. Use the net stop spooler command.
   D. Use the net stop services command.
16. The print router does what?
   A. Accepts print jobs and routes them to the appropriate print processor.
   B. Accepts print job from clients across WAN links.
   C. Routes job from a client machine to a network interface printing device.
   D. Routes job from a client machine to a shared printer.
17. The primary Windows NT print processor is called what?
   A. NTPRINT.DLL
   B. WINPRINT.DLL
   C. WINCOM.DLL
   D. NTWIN4.DLL

18. The advantage of using Enhanced Metafile Spooling is what?

    A. Faster printing on the printing device.

    B. Guaranteed updates of print drivers.

    C. Security.

    D. Returns control back to the application faster than RAW.

19. What are functions of a print monitor? (Choose all that apply.)

    A. Detects unsolicited error messages.

    B. Handles true end of job notification.

    C. Handles entries on the Access Control Lists with the Local Security Authority.

    D. Monitors printers for error messages.

20. What can you do from the printers folder in Windows NT?

    A. Install printers

    B. Configure Printers

    C. Administer printers

    D. Delete printers

21. The printer name in Windows NT can be how long?

    A. 255 character

    B. 254 characters

    C. 32 characters

    D. 15 characters

22. You are configuring a network printer. You would like to specify a new form for a printer. The page size is 8 inches by 10 inches. How can you create this in Windows NT?

    A. You must specify this in each application.

    B. You must use the Device Manager.

    C. Use the Forms tab on the Server Properties.

    D. Use the Advanced tab on the Server Properties.

23. Your company recently added an NT Server to your NT Workstation workgroup. During installation, you configured the server to be a Windows NT Server Primary Domain Controller (PDC). After installing the server, your NT Workstations can see the PDC in Network Neighborhood, however, the machines are still logging into a workgroup. What do you suspect is(are) the problem(s)? Choose all that apply:

    A. You have not created user accounts for your domain.

    B. You have not added the correct protocol on your PDC.

    C. You have not added computer accounts for the NT Workstations through Server Manager.

    D. You have not configured the NT Workstations to log into the domain.

24. Your company recently added an NT Server to your NT Workstation workgroup. During installation, you configured the server to be a Windows NT Server Primary Domain Controller (PDC). The protocol used on the server is TCP/IP. You have created all users and computer accounts on the server, however, when attempt to configure the NT Workstations to log into your domain, you are unsuccessful. What do you suspect is the problem? Choose the best answer:

    A. You do not have rights to add a computer to the domain.

    B. You do not have the TCP/IP installed on the workstations.

    C. Your Server needs service pack 3 to continue.

D. Your workstation must be reinstalled and then configured to log onto the domain because workstations are not allowed to migrate from workstations to domains with reinstalling.

25. You would like your Windows 95 users to log into your Windows NT domain. How can this be accomplished?

    A. You cannot do this unless you have administrative rights.

    B. You cannot do this unless you have a computer account created for you in the domain by the administrator.

    C. Through Control Panel's Network applet, and then configure File and Print sharing for Microsoft Networks to log into the domain.

    D. Through Control Panel's Network applet, and then configure the Client for Microsoft Networks to log into the domain.

2.9 and 2.10 Answers and Explanations: Practice Problems

1. **B, A** A printing device is where the document's final output is.
2. **C** NT will download the driver from the server to the local machine.
3. **A** GDI is largely responsible for printing.
4. **D** The spooler's primary job is to transfer the print file from the local machine to a print server.
5. **A** The print processor's primary function is to render the job into a language the printing device can understand.
6. **B** The print monitor's primary function is to point the data to the appropriate port so the job will be printed on the printing device.
7. **D** It asks what other operating systems will be connecting to the shared printer in order to install the drivers needed by those operating systems so that they can be downloaded from the server.
8. **A, C, D** The three components that constitute a Windows NT print driver are the Graphics Driver DLL, the Printer Interface Driver, and the Characterization File.
9. **B** It is the rendering and managing portion of the driver.
10. **D** It is the user interface and configuration management portion of the driver.
11. **A** The Characterization File contains all printer-specific information.
12. **C** The spooler service is a service that operates in the background to manage the printing process.
13. **B** Try to cancel the single document first. If that does not work, then you should try to purge all of the print jobs.
14. **D** Stop and restart the spooler service.
15. **B, C** Using Control Panel, Services and using the net stop spooler command are the two ways can stop the spooler service.
16. **A** The print router accepts print jobs and routes them to the appropriate print processor.
17. **B** The primary Windows NT print processor is called WINPRINT.DLL.
18. **D** Enhanced Metafile Spooling returns control to the application faster than RAW.
19. **A, B, D** The print monitor detects unsolicited error messages, handles true end of job notification, and monitors printers for error messages.
20. **A, B, C, D** You can do all of the above from the printers folder in Windows NT.
21. **C** The printer name in Windows NT can be 32 characters long.

22. **C** To create a new form for a printer, use the Forms tab on the server properties.

23. **A, C, D** You must create user accounts in User Manager for Domains; you must create computer accounts through Server Manager; and you must configure the NT Workstations to log into the domain.

24. **B** Your workstations cannot see the server because they do not have TCP/IP installed, or configured properly.

25. **D** The Client for Microsoft Networks must be configured to log into the domain.

2.9 and 2.10 Key Words

Printer

Printing device

Printer Graphics Driver DLL

Printer Interface Driver

Characterization File

Spooler service

Printer Pool

Print Processor

Print Router

client computer

domain

PDC

Practice Exam: Installation and Configuration

Use this practice exam to test you mastery of "Installation and Configuration." This practice exam is 20 questions long. The passing Microsoft score is 764 out of 1,000. There will be two types of questions:

- Multiple Choice—Select the correct answer.
- Multiple Multiple Choice—Select all answers that are correct.

1. You have installed NT Server and you are using the per seat licensing agreement. You have purchased 50 client access licenses. The server has reached 50 network connections; what will happen when the 51st person tries to connect? (Choose the best answer.)

   A. The person that has been connected the longest will be disconnected so that the new connection can be established.

   B. The person that has been idle the longest will be disconnected so that the new connection can be established.

   C. NT will evaluate users according to their SID to determine their ranking. The person with lowest network ranking will be disconnected so that the new connection can be established.

   D. The 51st user will not be allowed to connect.

2. You have decided to use per server licensing. Where in Server do you enter the registration numbers for the licensing agreements? (Choose the best answer.)

   A. Control Panel to Licensing

   B. Network Client Administrator

   C. Licenser Manager

   D. There is no requirement to add licensing numbers to NT

3. You have successfully installed Windows NT Server. However, when you go to logon as Administrator for the first time, you are not allowed to logon. You entered you password as "Gun-shy" but you still cannot logon. What could be wrong? (Choose the best answer:)

   A. Gun-shy is not a valid password for NT server.

   B. NT did not confirm your password as Gun-shy, so it substituted your password with the default of "password."

   C. Passwords are case-sensitive. Make certain that your caps lock is not on.

   D. You must logon as Admin instead of Administrator. Admin is the initial administrative account. Administrator is a system account reserved for the OS.

4. You have designated NT to create an Emergency Repair Disk during install. What information is copied to this Emergency Repair Disk? (Choose the best answer.)

   A. A compressed version of the setup files.

   B. The contents of \REPAIR directory.

   C. The SID of the Administrative account.

   D. The Registry Editor.

5. Windows NT Server ships with the Internet Information Server. During setup, you choose not to install this component as part of the NT Server install. After setup, you decide that you would like to install IIS. How can you do this? (Choose the best answer.)

   A. Double-click on the Install IIS Icon on the desktop.

B. Run WINNT32 and choose to only install IIS.

C. Use the Add/remove programs applet in Control Panel.

D. Run IISSetup.exe from the NT Server CD ROM.

6. During the final phase of installation, setup asks for the date and time of your location. You realize that your state participates in daylight savings time and the time change will happen in two weeks. You want to save yourself the trouble of having to change the time in two weeks. What should you do? (Choose the best answer.)

   A. Go ahead and change the time to match the daylight savings time in two weeks.

   B. Use the option to account for daylight savings time.

   C. Use the AT command to schedule a time change.

   D. Reset the CMOS to update the time in military standards.

7. You have installed NT Server as a PDC. During installation, you asked that NT create an Emergency Repair Disk. When NT prompted you for a floppy, you inserted a floppy that contained a README.TXT file that you created for future reference. When setup was finished creating the Emergency Repair Disk, you noted that the README.TXT was no longer on the floppy. Why? (Choose the best answer.)

   A. The Emergency Repair Disk deletes all files not marked as read only on the floppy.

   B. No text files are allowed on the Emergency Repair Disk.

   C. Setup formats the floppy before generating the Emergency Repair Disk.

   D. All original files on the floppy are now marked as hidden.

8. Domain Controllers and member servers have the following in common. (Choose all that apply.)

   A. May be RAS servers

   B. May logon users to the domain

   C. May have unlimited network connections

   D. Offer Macintosh file and print services

9. You are the administrator for three domains. Each domain has a PDC, three BDCs, and five member servers. Your TEXAS domain needs another member server, whereas your UTAH domain doesn't really need one of their member servers. To move the member server from the UTAH domain to the TEXAS domain you must do what? (Choose the best answer.)

   A. Reinstall NT Server 4.0

   B. Add a computer account for the member server and tell it to join the TEXAS domain

   C. Run the convert.exe program

   D. Promote the member server to a BDC in the TEXAS domain

10. The install program for Windows NT Server is called WINNT.EXE. Where on the CD-ROM is this executable located? (Choose the best answer.)

   A. At the root directory

   B. In the \Admin\nettools directory

   C. In the \i386 directory

   D. In the \WINNT\setup directory

11. Where do you configure protocol bindings? (Choose the best answer.)

   A. Control Panel, Add New Hardware

   B. Control Panel, Devices

C. Network Protocol tab

D. Network Binding tab

12. You have an NT Workstation that not only shares out resources for TCP/IP clients, but also connects to resources on a NetWare server. What would be the most effective way to configure the bindings on this machine? (Choose the best answer.)

A. Disable the NWLink protocol on the server service, and disable the TCP/IP protocol on the workstation service.

B. Disable the NWLink protocol on the workstation service, and disable the TCP/IP protocol on the server service.

C. Disable the NWLink protocol on the server service only.

D. You cannot disable bindings on Window NT Workstation.

13. You are installing NT Server on an Intel-based machine. What protocol(s) is/are installed by default? (Choose all that apply.)

A. TCP/IP

B. TCP/IP, NetBEUI

C. TCP/IP, IPX/SPX

D. IPX/SPX

E. IPX/SPX, NetBEUI

14. An I/O address is what? (Choose the best answer.)

A. The electronic location of a device in the system.

B. The number assigned to a device to define the device in the system.

C. An area of memory used for file I/O.

D. A setting used to interrupt the I/O Manager to signify new data is available to be saved to the hard disk from the device's buffer.

15. You network is segmented into three parts. How is the list of resources from each segment replicated to all other segments? (Choose the best answer.)

A. Each segment has a master browser. The master browser for each segment sends its browse list to all other segments.

B. Each segment has a master browser. The master browser for each segment sends its browse list to the Domain Master Browser, which merges the list and then sends it to each of the segment master browsers.

C. Being segmented does not affect your browsing scheme. All machines send their resource lists to the Domain Master Browser.

D. You must use directory replication to force synchronization of browsers across WAN links.

16. You have added an UPS to your NT Server system. You would like to configure NT to run a batch file at shutdown. How can you do this?

A. Using the Execute Command File option in the UPS applet.

B. Using the Execute Command File option in the HKEY LOCAL MACHINE\HARDWARE/UPS setting in the registry.

C. Using the AT Scheduler.

D. Creating a UDF file for the UPS warning and identifying this UDF through the registry setting of HKEY LOCAL MACHINE\HARDWARE\UPS.

17. You would like to add an IDE CD-ROM device to your server, but you cannot find a setting to do this anywhere in Control Panel. You can add this device by:

A. Using the Add New Hardware Wizard.

B. Doing nothing. NTDETECT.COM will detect the device upon rebooting the machine.

C. Using the SCSI adapters applet in Control Panel.

D. Using the setup program that came with the new hardware.

18. How does Windows NT separate print jobs by default?

A. With a blank sheet of paper.

B. With a sheet of paper containing the name, date, and current document title.

C. With a sheet of paper containing the name, date, current document title, and number of pages.

D. NT does not separate print jobs.

19. The print processor does what?

A. Handles all threads of the printing process between the application in User mode and the Microkernel in Executive Services

B. Generates all threads of the printing process between the application in User mode and the Microkernel in Executive Services

C. Renders the job for the final destination

D. Handles true end-of-job notification

Answers and Explanations: Practice Exam

1. **D** The 51st user will not be allowed to connect. Administrators, however, will be allowed to override this restriction so that they can increase the number of network connections.

2. **D** All Client Access Licenses are done on the honor system.

3. **C** Passwords are case-sensitive.

4. **B** The contents of \REPAIR directory is copied to the Emergency Repair Disk.

5. **A** If you choose not to install the Internet Information Server during install, the Setup program will add the icon directly to your desktop.

6. **B** NT includes an option to account for daylight savings time.

7. **C** Setup formats the floppy to ensure validity of the floppy, and to make certain enough room is available on the floppy for the required files.

8. **A, C, D** NT Server, domain controllers, or member servers can be RAS servers, have unlimited network connections, and offer services for Macintosh.

9. **B** Member servers are allowed to migrate from domain to domain as long as they have a computer account in the domain to which they are migrating.

10. **C** Each platform, RISC or Intel, has a corresponding directory on the CD-ROM.

11. **D** You configure protocol bindings in the Network Binding tab.

12. **A** By disabling the NWLink protocol on the server service, only TCP/IP will be bound to that service. If you disable the TCP/IP on the workstation service, NWLink will be the only protocol used for that service.

13. **C** TCP/IP and IPX/SPX are the selected protocols by default on an NT server installation.

14. **A** An I/O address is the electronic location of a device in the system. It allows information sent to the device to be delivered.

15. **B** The list of resources from each segment is replicated to all other segments because each segment has a master browser. The master browser for each segment sends its browse list to the Domain Master Browser, which merges the list, and then sends the merged list back to each of the segment master browsers.

16. **A** Use the Execute Command File option in the UPS applet to configure NT to run a batch file at shutdown.

17. **C** Use the SCSI adapters applet in Control Panel to add an IDE CD-ROM device to your server.

18. **D** NT does not separate print jobs.

19. **C** Print Processor renders the job for the final destination.

Chapter 3

Managing Resources

This chapter helps you prepare for the "Managing Resources" section of Microsoft's Exam 70-67, "Implementing and Supporting Microsoft Windows NT Server 4.0." Microsoft provides the following objectives for the "Managing Resources" Section:

- Manage user and group accounts. Considerations include Managing Windows NT groups, managing Windows NT user rights, administering account policies, and auditing changes to the user account database.
- Create and manage policies and profiles for various situations. Policies and profiles include local user profiles, roaming user profiles, and system policies.
- Administer remote servers from various types of client computers. Client computer types include Windows 95 and Windows NT Workstation.
- Manage disk resources. Tasks include copying and moving files between file systems, creating and sharing resources, implementing permissions and security, and establishing file auditing.

3.1 Managing User and Group Accounts

Microsoft lists the following objective for the Windows NT Server exam: Manage user and group accounts.

Considerations include: managing Windows NT groups, managing Windows NT user rights, managing Windows NT account policies, and auditing changes to the user account database.

Windows NT users get their rights and permissions in either of two ways:

- They are explicitly assigned a right or permission through their accounts.
- They are members of a group that has a right or permission.

An administrator creates an account (maybe more than one) for each person who uses the system. When prompted by WinLogon, the user enters the username and password to log on. Windows NT then checks the user's credentials against the list of valid users and groups for each object to which he or she requests access.

A. Users and Groups

Windows NT administrators can create two types of accounts:

User account	Belongs to one person only; rights and permissions assigned to user accounts affect only the person who uses the account to log on.
Group account	A collection of users that holds common rights and permissions by way of its association with the group. The number of people in a group is unlimited, and all members enjoy the rights and permissions assigned to the group.

In practice, a group is a vehicle for assigning rights and permissions to an individual user. If you determine that a certain group of users in your environment requires a specific set of rights and permissions, you can create a group that has those rights and permissions and add the users to the new group. It is important to note that there is no order of precedence among user and group accounts. No one group takes priority over any other group, and groups do not take priority over user accounts (or vice versa).

For management purposes, it is easier to use group accounts when assigning rights and permissions. First, it's cleaner: users can be members of as many groups as desired, and group names can be more descriptive than usernames. Second, it's simpler: if you need to give a user the right to back up files and directories, you can find a built-in group, called Backup Operators, specifically designed for that purpose. In fact, you rarely have to create a new group because Windows NT has built-in groups for almost anything anyone needs to do on the system.

Windows NT has three types of groups:

Local	Used to assign rights and permissions to resources on the local machine. Remember that these resources consist of drive space and printers on that specific computer. That local group exists only on that computer. This changes slightly at the domain level—a local group created on a domain controller (either PDC or BDC) appears on all domain controllers within that domain.
Global	A collection of user accounts within the domain. These global groups have no power by themselves—they must be assigned to local groups to gain access to the local resources. You use a global group as a container of users that you then can add to local groups.
Special	Generally used for internal system access to resources and permissions. Special groups cannot be added or deleted—they contain predefined sets of users.

When a Windows NT workstation becomes part of a domain, the built-in domain global groups (described later in this chapter) join the corresponding local groups in the workstation's local security database. Each user account in the domain database is a member of an appropriate global group. By nesting global groups in the local groups of individual machines, Windows NT provides users with seamless access to resources across the domain.

A global group must be a member of a local group, but a local group cannot be a member of a global group, nor can a global group be a member of another global group. A global group can contain only user accounts. A local group can contain user accounts and global groups, but putting users in local groups is not good domain management.

1. Built-In Local Groups on Domain Controllers

Windows NT domain controllers oversee eight built-in local groups and three built-in global groups. The Windows NT domain local groups are as follows:

- Administrators
- Users
- Guests
- Backup Operators
- Replicator
- Account Operators
- Print Operators
- Server Operators

a. Administrators

Administrators is the most powerful group. Because Administrators has complete control over the entire Windows NT environment, use caution when adding users to this group. If you are the administrator for a Windows NT machine, consider creating an ordinary user account as well for safety reasons. Use administrator-level accounts only when necessary. In the following situations, it is necessary to use administrator-level accounts:

- To create other administrator-level accounts
- To modify or delete users, regardless of who created them
- To manage the membership of built-in groups
- To unlock workstations, regardless of who locked them
- To format a hard disk
- To upgrade the operating system
- To back up or restore files and directories
- To change the security policies
- To connect to administrative shares

b. Users

By default, new accounts become members of the Users group. The Users group provides users everything needed to run applications safely and to manage their local environment—local to the user, that is, not the computer. Users can:

- Run applications
- Manage their own files and directories (but not share them)
- Use printers (but not manage them)
- Connect to other computers' directories and printers
- Save their settings in a personal profile

Assign the Users account unless you need to perform a task that only an administrator or power user has the right to do.

c. Guests

Because Windows NT Workstation requires accounts for anyone who accesses the system, you can use the relatively powerless Guest account (described later in this chapter) to allow limited access to users who don't possess an account on your computer. Because the default Guest account does not require a password, it poses a security risk. The extent of the access provided to the Guests group depends on how you implement it. If you are concerned about security, disable the Guest account.

d. Backup Operators

Members of the Backup Operators group have a singular purpose: to back up files and directories and to restore them later. Although standard users can back up and restore files to which they have been granted permissions, backup operators can override the security on resources, but only when using the NTBackup program.

Backup operators have the following rights:

- Back up and restore files
- Log on locally
- Shut down the server

e. Replicator

The Replicator group is a special group used by the Directory Replication Service. See Chapter 2, "Installation and Configuration," for information.

f. Account Operators

Account Operators group members can create, delete, and modify users, global groups, and local groups. However, they cannot modify the Administrators or Server Operators group.

g. Print Operators

Members of the Print Operators group waive the following rights:

- Create, manage, and delete print shares
- Log on locally
- Shut down the server

h. Server Operators

The Server Operators group has the power to administer primary and backup domain controllers. It can perform the following actions:

- Log on at servers
- Lock and unlock servers
- Backup and restore servers
- Shut down servers
- Manage network shares
- Format the server's hard disk

2. Built-In Global Groups on Domain Controllers

Windows NT domain controllers also oversee the following three global groups:

Domain Admins	Global group of administrator accounts. It is a member of the Administrators local group for the domain, and is, by default, a member of the local group for every computer in the domain running Windows NT Server or NT Workstation. A domain administrator, therefore, can perform administrative functions on local computers.
Domain Users	Global group of user-level accounts. During setup, the domain's Administrator account is part of the Domain Users global group. All new domain accounts are automatically added to the Domain Users group.
Domain Guests	Global group for users with guest-level accounts. The Domain Guest group is automatically a member of the domain's Guests group.

3. Built-In Special Groups on Windows NT Server

Windows NT Server computers have the following built-in special groups:

Creator/Owner	Includes the user account that created or took ownership of a resource.
Everyone	Automatically includes every user who accesses this computer, either locally or remotely.
Interactive	Includes the user who logs on locally to a machine.
Network	Contains all users connected to a shared resource over the network.

4. Built-In Groups on Workstations and Member Servers

Windows NT Server member servers (servers that are not domain controllers) and Windows NT Workstations have the following built-in local groups:

- Administrators
- Backup Operators
- Power Users
- Guests
- Replicator
- Users

The descriptions for these groups are the same as the descriptions for their domain-controller counterparts, except for the Power User group, which is not a built-in group on Windows NT domain controllers.

Power users have considerably more power than ordinary users, but not nearly the amount of control that an administrator has. Take care when using or giving out Power User accounts. They are ideal for the following types of tasks:

- Sharing (and revoking) directories on the network
- Creating, managing, and sharing printers
- Creating accounts (but not administrator-level)
- Modifying and deleting accounts (but only the accounts that the power user has created)
- Setting the date and time on the computer
- Creating common program groups

Power users cannot touch any of the security policies on a Windows NT system, and their powers are limited in scope. Use a Power User account rather than an Administrator account if you can accomplish what you need to as a power user.

Windows NT member servers and workstations don't control any global groups, because global groups can be created and administered only on domain controllers. Global groups nevertheless play an important part in assigning local rights and permissions to server and workstations resources.

5. Member Server and Workstation Accounts

Windows NT Server machines acting as member servers maintain local account databases and manage a set of local accounts and groups independent of any domain affiliations. To access a Windows NT system, a user must provide credentials even if that system is not attached to a domain, or even if it has never been attached to a domain. The local account information controls access to the machine's resources.

Domain users can access resources on server and workstation machines logged into the domain because (by default) each domain user is a member of the global group Domain Users, and the global group Domain Users is a member of the machine's local group Users. In the same way, domain administrators are part of the global group Domain Admins, which is part of the machine's local Administrator's group.

6. Hard-Coded Capabilities

So far, only the hard-coded characteristics (ones which cannot be modified) of the Windows NT built-in groups have been discussed. Users cannot, for example, share directories, and power users cannot be prevented from sharing directories (to which they have access, of course).

You cannot modify hard-coded capabilities, but you can change user rights. An administrator can grant or revoke a user right at any time. Only administrators have the hard-coded capability to manage this policy. At this point, it is important to clearly distinguish between user rights and resource permissions. *User rights* define what a user can and cannot do on the system. *Resource permissions* establish the scope where these rights can be used. In other words, user rights are stuff you can do, and resource permissions control where you can do it.

7. Built-In User Accounts

Groups are the center of power in Windows NT, but groups need members to have any effect at all. At least two accounts are created when you install Windows NT:

- Administrator
- Guest

a. Administrator

The Administrator account, the first account created during an installation, is a member of the Administrators group. The Administrator account is permanent—you cannot disable or delete it, although it might not be a bad idea to rename it for security purposes.

b. Guest

The Guest account is another permanent account. It is a member of the Guests group, but this affiliation can be changed. Like the Administrator account, the Guest account itself has no inherent power or lack thereof; it is the group membership for the account that establishes its scope.

You can disable the Guest account. You might want to disable the account if you are in a secure environment; otherwise, users who don't have an account on your system can log on as guests. At the very least, consider adding a password to the Guest account.

B. User Manager for Domains

Windows NT Server includes this tool, which you can use to administer User and Group accounts. User Manager for Domains is similar to the User Manager tool available with Windows NT Workstation, but, whereas User Manager is primarily designed to oversee local Workstation accounts, User Manager for Domains includes additional features that enable it to manage accounts at the domain level and even interact with other domains.

To reach User Manager for Domains, choose Programs in the Start menu, choose Administrative Tools (Common), and then select User Manager for Domains.

> **User Manager for Domains enables you to administer any domain over which you have administrative rights. The Select Domain option in the User menu enables you to choose a different domain.**

User Manager for Domains enables you to:

- Create new user and group accounts.
- View and configure the properties of user and group accounts.
- Add and remove members.
- View and configure account policy restrictions.
- Add user rights to users and groups.
- Audit account-related events.
- Establish, view, and configure trust relationships.

You can find most administration and configuration options on the User and Options menus.

1. Creating a User

To create a new user account, choose the New User command in the User menu in User Manager for Domains. The New User dialog box opens.

Only two pieces of information are mandatory to create an account:

Username	The username is a short "handle" used to identify the user to the system. The name in the Username field must be unique. The username can be as long as 20 characters and is not case-sensitive—however, you cannot use the following characters: -"/\[]:;|=,+*?<>.
Password	The password is proof that the user account actually belongs to the person attempting to use it. The password entered in the Password field is case-sensitive and cannot exceed 14 characters. The Password field can also be left blank (although not recommended for obvious reasons). The password must be confirmed to make certain that you did not mistype a character.

The other parameters in this dialog box are optional but useful. These parameters are:

- **Full Name field:** The Full Name is a free text field that can be used for the full name, including spaces and initials, for a particular user. Having both a username and a full name enables users to log on quickly (using the username) but still be listed and available by their full name.
- **Description field:** This field is also free text. Use it to track the department to which a user belongs, or maybe a location or project team.
- **User Must Change Password at Next Logon field:** Because a new account has a preset password picked by the administrator, this option forces the user to change the password immediately after logging on the first time after setting this option. When the user attempts to log on, the message `You are required to change your password at first logon` appears. After the user dismisses the message, a Change Password dialog box appears.
- **User Cannot Change Password field:** Enabling this check box prevents users from making any change to their password at any time. You might want to use this for the Guest account and any other account that several people might share.
- **Password Never Expires field:** Enabling the Password Never Expires check box overrides any blanket password expiration date defined in the Account policy. Again, the Guest account is a likely candidate for this option.
- **Account Disabled field:** To turn off a specific account but not to remove it from the database, enable this check box. In general, you should disable rather than remove user accounts. If a person leaves the organization and then later returns, you can reactivate the account. If the user never returns, you can rename the account and reactivate it for the new person replacing the former user. All rights and permissions for the original user are transferred to the new user.

a. Advanced User Properties

Clicking on the six buttons at the bottom of the New User dialog box opens the following corresponding dialog boxes:

Groups	Add and remove group memberships for the account.
Profile	Add a user profile path, a logon script name, and a home directory path to the user's environment profile.
Hours	Define specific times when the users can access the account. (The default is always.)
Logon To	Specify the workstations to which the user can log on. (The default is all workstations.)
Account	Provide an expiration date for the account. (The default is never.) You also can specify the account as global (for regular users in this domain) or local.
Dialin	Specify that the user can access the account via a dial-up connection. You also can assign call back Properties.

Don't confuse a domain local account with a local group membership or a local account on a workstation. A domain local account is designed to enable individual users from untrusted domains to access to this domain. Unless a domain local account is explicitly granted logon permission, the user must log on normally to a workgroup or domain where he or she has a valid account and then connect to the domain controller that is home to the domain local account.

b. User Environment Profiles

The Profile button invokes the User Environment Profile dialog box, where you can specify the following important user settings:

- User profile path
- Logon script name
- Home directory

Figure 3.1.1 shows how the User Environment Profile dialog box for a new user account can be filled in.

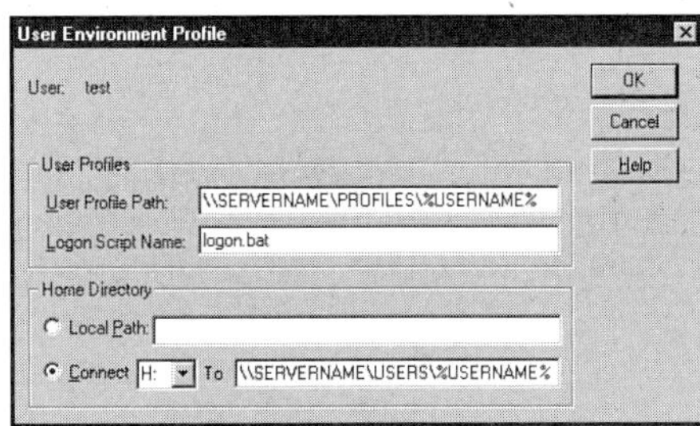

Figure 3.1.1 The User Environment Profile dialog box.

The User Profiles section of the User Environment Profile dialog box enables you to specify the user profile path and the logon script name. The user profile path is for cases in which a roaming or mandatory profile for the user will reside on another computer (as shown for this user in fig. 3.1.1). If the user will log on to both Windows NT 3.x and Windows NT 4 computers, include the user profile file name in the user profile path. If the user will use only a computer running Windows NT 4, the user profile path should point to the user profile directory and should not include the file name. If the directory does not exist, Windows NT creates it when the roaming profile is created, but note that the local machine must have access to the roaming profile directory by way of a network share.

The Logon Script Name text box enables you to specify a logon script for the user. *Logon scripts* are CMD or BAT files that contain a series of valid Windows NT commands. A logon script might re-establish a series of network drive connections or display a welcome message. Notice that the dialog box asks only for the name, not the full path. Windows NT already has a directory for logon scripts, but it is buried pretty deep:

```
<winnt_root>\SYSTEM32\REPL\IMPORT\SCRIPTS
```

The Home Directory section of this dialog box is used whenever a user opens or saves a file in an application, or when the user opens a command prompt window. The default home directory is \USERS\DEFAULT; if a workstation will support more than one user, consider establishing separate home directories for each user. Note that users are not restricted to or from these home directories (unless you establish that security separately); this is just where they start by default when working with documents.

User Manager will create the home directory automatically as long as you have it create a single directory at a time. You might have User Manager create a home directory called c:\ken, for example, but it cannot create c:\ken\home if the \KEN directory did not already exist. That is just a limitation of User Manager.

Click on the Local Path radio button to specify a local path for the home directory. To specify a home directory on the network, click on the Connect radio button, select a drive letter from the drop-down list, and enter the network path in the To box.

Here's a tip for home directory creation: If you would like the home directory name to be the same as the user's username, you can use a special environment variable in this dialog box: %USERNAME% (as shown in fig. 3.1.1). The actual username replaces %USERNAME% after the account is created. This is not really any faster than just typing in the actual username, but it can really save time when copying accounts.

When you use User Manager for Domains to create a user's home directory on an NTFS partition, the default permissions for that directory grant that user Full Control and restrict access to all other users.

2. Creating a Group

You can create new global and local groups by using the New Global Group and New Local Group options on the User Manager for Domains User menu. The following rules apply to global groups and their creation:

- By default, the Administrator account is automatically a member of the new group.
- Only user accounts can be members of a global group.

To add a member to the new global group, select a user in the Not Members list and click on the Add button to add the user to the Members list. Click on the Remove button to remove a user account from the Members list.

The New Local Group dialog box differs slightly from the New Global Group dialog box (fig. 3.1.2 shows the New Local Group dialog box). To add additional members to the new local group, click on the Add button. In contrast to global groups, individual users and global groups both can join a local group.

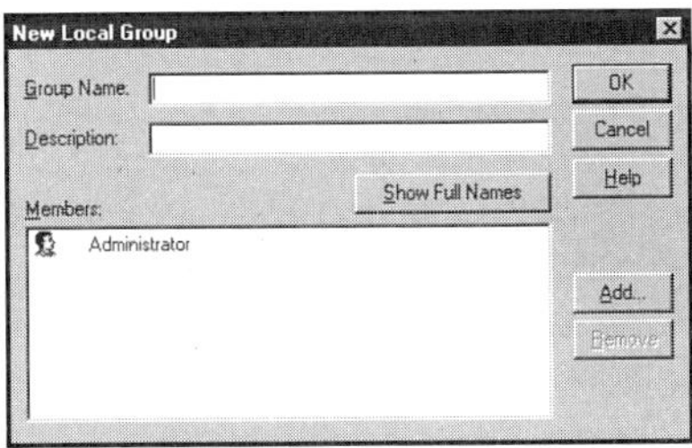

Figure 3.1.2 The New Local Group dialog box.

If you select one or more users in the User Manager for Domains main screen up front creating a new group, those users automatically appear in the membership list for the new local or global group.

After you create your local groups, you can manage them much as you manage your user accounts. You should, however, be aware of the following idiosyncrasies concerning local groups:

- You cannot rename a group after it has been created.
- You cannot disable a group after it has been created.
- If you do want to delete a group, just select the group in User Manager and choose Delete from the User menu. Be aware that you are deleting only the group itself, not the users within the group.
- You can add and/or remove members from the group by selecting the group in User Manager and choosing User, Properties.

3. User and Group Properties

The Properties command on the User menu of the User Manager opens a Properties dialog box for the selected object. The User Properties dialog box resembles the New User dialog box except that all the information is filled in. Use the User Properties dialog box to edit user properties after creating an account.

4. Administering Account Policy

If you need to administer anything related with passwords (expiration, password length, account lockout and more), go to Account in the Policies menu. The Account Policy dialog box opens.

The Account Policy dialog box is pretty busy; the options you can set in this dialog box are described in Table 3.1.1.

Table 3.1.1 Options in the Account Policy Dialog Box

Option	Description
Maximum password age	Setting a maximum password age forces users to choose a new password periodically. Users get a warning 14 days before the password is about to expire.
Minimum password age	The default, Allow Changes Immediately, enables users to change back to a favorite, if overused, password. Allow Changes In *x* forces users to wait anywhere from 1–999 days before making changes.
Minimum password length	Setting a minimum password length forces users to choose longer passwords. Although you can require up to 14 characters, using 6 to 8 usually suffices.
Password uniqueness	This setting tells Windows NT to remember each old password (up to 24). As long as a password is in a user's password history cache, the user cannot reuse it. A Remember setting of 24 combined with a Minimum Password Age of 7 days forces users to wait almost six months before reusing a password.
Account lockout	Windows NT will lock out an account after a certain number of bad logon attempts (that is, an incorrect password for a valid username) within a certain period of time. You can enable this feature by choosing the Account lockout radio button and filling in the appropriate parameters.
Forcibly disconnecting users	To have the system forcibly disconnect users when their logon hours have expired, enable this check box.
Password change policy	When a user's password nears expiration, the user is prompted at each logon to change it. If the user declines and the password age is exceeded, the user cannot log on until the password is changed. If this selection is cleared (the default), the user is presented with the Change Password dialog box and not allowed to proceed until changing the obsolete password.

5. Assigning Rights to Groups

User or group rights cannot be viewed as properties for a user account or group. Instead, you must choose a right from the drop-down list in the User Rights Policy dialog box so that you can view the users assigned to this specific right. You can access this dialog box via the User Rights command on the policies menu.

Whereas a *permission* is targeted at a specific object (such as a directory or file), the term *right* refers to a general right to take a particular action on the system. Some Windows NT rights are as follows:

- Log on locally
- Shut down the system
- Back up files and directories
- Restore files and directories
- Take ownership of files or other objects

The built-in groups described earlier in this chapter are automatically assigned appropriate user rights. Choose Restore files and directories from the Right combo box in the User Rights Policy dialog box. You will see that Administrators, Backup Operators, and Server Operators all have the right to restore files and directories.

6. Auditing Account-Related Events

The Auditing option in the User Manager for Domains Policy menu invokes the Audit Policy dialog box, which enables you to track certain account-related events. You can track either the success or the failure of the following events:

- Logon and Logoff
- File and Object Access
- Use of User Rights
- User and Group Management
- Security Policy Changes
- Restart, Shutdown, and System
- Process Tracking

The event information is stored in the security log. You can view the security log by using Event Viewer.

7. Trust Relationships

The Trust Relationships option on the User Manager for Domains Policy menu enables you to set up and modify trust relationships for the domain.

A trust relationship is a relationship between different domains in which one domain, the *trusting* domain, relinquishes control of its account database to another domain, called the *trusted* domain. Trust relationships are commonly used in Wide Area Network (WAN) situations, and you will get a heavy dose of them if you ever decide to prepare for the Windows NT Server Enterprise exam.

C. Account Administration Tasks

An administrator's job does not end after creating the accounts; in fact, it just begins. Changes and modifications inevitably are necessary in day-to-day operations. You can review the properties of any user account by double-clicking on the username in User Manager for Domains or by selecting the username and choosing User, Properties.

Although you can change most things about a user in the User Properties dialog box, you should be aware of a few separate commands that are available only from the User menu, outlined in Table 3.1.2.

Table 3.1.2 Account Administration Tasks

Option	Description
Copy	If you need to create many users at one time, consider creating a template account and copying it. When you copy an account by choosing User, Copy in the User Manager, you must enter a new username, full name, and password, but the other properties are retained, including the description, group memberships, and profile information. The only exception is the Account Disabled check box, which is cleared automatically.
Delete	Windows NT tracks user accounts internally with a Security Identifier (SID), which is used to track user rights and permissions on resources (the username is never used for this purpose). The SID is unique in the entire system and is never reused again even when the corresponding user has long been deleted.
Rename	The User Properties dialog box shows that although you can change a user's full name at any time, the username is fixed. To change the username (remember, the username is the logon name), you must choose User, Rename in the User Manager for Domains. Remember that the Security Identifier (SID), which, once created, never changes, even if the account is renamed.

3.1.1 Exercise: Adding a New Account Operator User

The purpose of this exercise is to create a new user AccOp that is added to the Account Operators group.

1. Open User Manager for Domains and choose New User in the User menu.
2. The New User dialog box opens. Enter AccOp as the username and a password. All other entries are optional.
3. Click on the Groups button to open the Group Membership dialog box.
4. Select "Account Operators" in the "Not Member of" listbox and click Add to make the new user a member of this group. Click OK when done.
5. Now you can click Add to create the user account.

3.1.2 Exercise: Setting Account Policy

This exercise will give you practice setting account policy. The policy that is set in this example includes setting a maximum password age (25 days), password history (5), and minimum password length (6 characters).

1. Open User Manager for Domains and choose Account in the Policies menu.
2. Enable the Expires In radio button and set Days to 25.
3. Go to Password Uniqueness frame and enable Remember passwords and enter 5.
4. Finally, go to the Minimum Password Length frame and enable the At Least radio button and enter 6 as the minimum password length. Click OK to let your changes take effect.

3.1 Practice Problems

1. You are the administrator of MegaCorp, which is running a Windows NT Domain named MEGANET. You are responsible for all tasks, including user management, but you are short on time. You want to temporarily assign Dan, who is working for finance, the right to administer user accounts. How can you achieve this? Select the best answer:

   A. Assign the right "Administer Accounts" to Dan's account.

   B. Add Dan to the Domain Admins group.

   C. Add Dan to the Account Operators group.

   D. Add Dan to the Power Users Operators group.

2. Dan is now managing user accounts and calls you one day, telling you that he has deleted an account for an employee that had signed off that day, but the employee returned a few days later. Dan tells you that he has created a new account with the same name, but the employee complains that he isn't able to access his files any more. What has happened? Select the best answer:

   A. Someone has taken ownership of the files.

   B. Dan forgot to assign the employee's account to groups that had access permissions.

   C. Accounts are identified by a SID that is unique for every account throughout the system, and simply recreating an account with the same name doesn't bring back the SID.

   D. The employee has entered an incorrect password when he logged on to his workstation.

3. Your account operator, Dan, is facing a new problem: Your company is hiring summer interns that need to have read access to specific resources on your system. How can you achieve maximum security? Select the best answer:

   A. Create a user account for every summer intern, and set the account to expire at the end of summer. Assign the accounts to the project's group in which they are working, giving them full access to all resources.

   B. Create one user account for all summer interns, and set the account to expire at the end of summer. Assign the accounts to the project's group in which they are working, giving them full access to all resources.

   C. Create a user account for every summer intern and set the account to expire at the end of summer. Assign the accounts to a new group, SummerIntern, and grant this group appropriate permissions to the resources they need.

   D. Simply rename a user account of an employee that is currently on vacation and tell the password to the summer interns.

4. You suspect that users are simply recycling their old passwords when the system asks them to change it every 30 days. To prove this, you are running a brute force password cracker program using the Administrator account every 30 days to see which passwords are used throughout the system. You are right, passwords are recycled, some users even use their username as password or simply have a blank password. How can you prevent all of this? Choose the correct answer(s):

   A. Set a minimum password length.

   B. Set the minimum password age.

   C. Keep a password history.

   D. You can't prevent this.

5. You consider the built-in Administrator account a security risk because everyone knows half the information necessary to break into your system. How can you reduce or even eliminate this risk? Select the best answer:

    A. Delete the Administrator account.

    B. Disable the Administrator account.

    C. Choose an impossible-to-guess password for the account.

    D. Rename the Administrator account and assign a hard-to-guess password.

6. The finance division has twenty computers. They have hired two summer interns and want them to be able to use all workstations with exception of the computer named SECUREFIN (running NT Workstation). Both summer interns are using the same account (defined in the domain). How can you achieve this? Select the best answer:

    A. Select the summer interns account, and select "Logon To" and set "Logon to all workstation, except" to SECUREFIN.

    B. Select the summer interns account and select "Logon To," then set "User may logon to these workstations" and enter all other nineteen computers of FINANCE.

    C. You cannot do this.

7. You want to allow members of the finance division to log on to your network only between 8 a.m. and 6 p.m. on workdays. How can you achieve this? Select two:

    A. Specify logon hours for every user.

    B. Enable "Forcibly disconnect remote users from server when logon hours expire."

    C. Enable Auditing of logon and logoff events.

    D. You cannot do this.

8. You suspect that a member of the finance division is working on the weekend using the SECUREFIN computer. How can you prove this? Select the best answer:

    A. Enable auditing for the users of the finance division and check the security log on Monday using Event Viewer to see if someone logged in to the SECUREFIN computer on the weekend.

    B. Enable auditing of logon and logoff events, and check the security log on Monday using Event Viewer to see if someone logged in to the SECUREFIN computer on the weekend.

    C. Audit Process tracking, and check the security log on Monday using Event Viewer to see if someone logged in to the SECUREFIN computer on the weekend.

    D. Enable auditing of logon and logoff events, and check the system log on Monday using Event Viewer to see if someone has logged in to the SECUREFIN computer on the weekend.

9. Which of the following statements is true about security identifiers (SID)? Select the best answer:

    A. A SID is created using a one-time hash function, and thus you can recreate a SID by reentering the same username.

    B. A SID is a unique identifier that is recycled after a certain amount of time, however, you cannot assign a SID to a specific user account.

    C. A SID is a unique identifier for user accounts, it is never recycled and used by Windows NT to track a user internally.

    D. A SID is used to track Windows NT file shares.

10. Which rights do members of the Backup operators group own? Select all that apply:

    A. Back up files.

    B. Restore files.

    C. Log on locally.

    D. Shut down the server.

11. Which of the following groups are available on domain controllers? Select all that apply:

    A. Server Operators.

    B. Power Users.

    C. Domain Admins.

    D. Interactive.

12. A user tells you that he cannot log on to his workstation. After walking to the site and talking to the user, you find out that he changed his password yesterday when he was forced to do so because you set a maximum password age. What can you do to get this user logged on? Select the best answer:

    A. Disable the maximum password age setting, and let the user log on with the old password.

    B. Create a new user account for the user with Password Never Expires enabled, and let the user log on.

    C. In User Manager, assign a new password to the user's account and require "Change Password at next Logon" to be shown at logon. Tell the user to log on with the new password and this time, and to remember the password.

    D. Tell the user to log on as Administrator using his old password.

13. A new department with 120 workers is added to your network. You need to set up 120 identical accounts with home directories for each. How can you achieve this most effectively? Select the best answer:

    A. Create a single user account, assign it to all appropriate groups and assign the home directory to \\MEGASERVER\USERHOME\Template. Copy the user account 120 times and you are done.

    B. Create a single user account, assign it to all appropriate groups, and assign the home directory to \\MEGASERVER\USERHOME\%USERID%. Copy the user account 120 times and you are done.

    C. Create a single user account, assign it to all appropriate groups and assign the home directory to \\MEGASERVER\USERHOME\%USERNAME%. Copy the user account 120 times and you are done.

    D. You have to create every single account by assigning groups and home directories yourself.

14. Your network has a PDC and two BDCs. There are also 5 NT Server computers that have no domain role associated with them. You want to assign Becky the task of a backup operator on all these machines. How can you achieve this? Select the best answer:

    A. Add Becky to the Domain Admins group.

    B. Add Becky to the Backup Operators group.

    C. Create a new global group, Domain Backup Operators, and add this group to the local Backup Group on the domain controllers and servers. Add Becky to the Domain Backup Operators group.

    D. Create a new local group, Domain Backup Operators, and add this group to the local Backup Group on the domain controllers and servers. Add Becky to the Domain Backup Operators group.

15. Some users are going to leave for three months for holidays. As you are concerned about security, you want to prevent abuse of these accounts during this time period. How can you achieve this? Select the best answer:

    A. Revoke the right to log on locally for these user accounts.

    B. Select "User may log on to these workstations" in User Manager for these accounts, but don't select any workstations.

    C. Disable the accounts for these users.

    D. Delete the accounts for these users.

16. If you are logged on to a Windows NT computer, of which group do you automatically become a member? Select the best answer:

    A. Power User

    B. Interactive

    C. Everyone

    D. Network

17. Name the four special groups of Windows NT. Select the best answer:

    A. Global, Interactive, Creator Owner, Local

    B. Interactive, Power Users, Global, Local

    C. Network, Creator Owner, Interactive, Everyone

    D. Everyone, Global, Local, Personal

18. Which local user groups are granted the right to shut down a domain controller by default? Select all that apply:

    A. Users

    B. Administrators

    C. Backup Operators

    D. Server Operators

    E. Print Operators

    F. Account Operators

19. Your company has hired a new accountant who is working for a trial period of two months. You need to assure that the account for this new user can be used only two months. How can you achieve this? Select the best answer:

    A. Set the password expiration to two months.

    B. Set the Account Expires option for this user account to a date that is two months away.

    C. Create a logon script that checks the date and automatically logs off the user when the end of the trial period is reached.

    D. You cannot set an account to expire.

20. You have established account lockout after 5 unsuccessful logins with duration Forever selected. On Monday mornings you often get calls from users saying they cannot logon to the computer at the first attempt and the system tells them that the account is locked. They also tell you that they could logon successfully on Friday. What is the most likely cause for this happening? Select the best answer:

    A. They have accumulated five unsuccessful logon attempts in the last few days and now the system locks them out.

    B. One of the users is fooling you: He simply enters five password guesses for a user account he knows in order to stop others from getting to work on Monday morning.

    C. The users have changed their password on Friday, because you have set the password expiration period to seven days and they no longer remember the passwords they have chosen.

    D. A Backup Operator has made a restore on the weekend, including the registry of the PDC.

21. Please refer to question 3.1.20—how could you detect from where these unsuccessful logon attempts were made? Select the best answer:

    A. Audit successful logon attempts.

    B. Audit Use of user Rights.

    C. Audit successful and failed logon attempts.

    D. Audit failed logon attempts.

22. Who has the right to backup and restore files? Select the best answer:

    A. Server Operators, Account Operators, Backup Operators

    B. Administrators, Server Operators, Replicator

    C. Backup Operators, Server Operators, Administrators

    D. Replicator, Backup Operators, Administrators

23. Built-in local groups can be (select all that apply):

    A. Renamed

    B. Deleted

    C. Disabled

    D. Copied

24. Which of the following statements is true?

    A. Local groups and user accounts can be contained in a global group.

    B. Global groups and user accounts can be contained in a local group.

    C. Only user accounts can be contained local groups.

    D. Only local groups can be contained in global groups.

25. Which kinds of groups are known to Windows NT? Select all that apply:

    A. Global

    B. Personal

    C. Local

    D. Special

26. A user is complaining that the time displayed on his computer is incorrect, and that the system keeps telling him that he hasn't got sufficient rights to change it. What action can you take as an administrator to allow the user to change the system time himself? Select the best answer:

    A. Temporarily add the user to the Server Operators group.

    B. Tell him the Administrator password so he can logon as Administrator and change the time.

    C. Add the user the "Change the system time" right.

    D. You have to change the time yourself.

27. When you are connecting to a shared directory on a NT Server, of which group do you automatically become a member? Select the best answer:

    A. Interactive

    B. Local

    C. Network

    D. Creator Owner

28. You are creating a new user account in the domain MEGACORP. By default, of which group is this new user a member? Select the best answer:

    A. Local

    B. Everyone

    C. Domain Users

    D. Domain Guests

29. What is the difference between a locked out user account and a disabled user account? Select the best answer:

    A. A locked out user account does not retain its SID, whereas a disabled user account does.

    B. A system administrator can lock out a user account, but he cannot disable a user account.

    C. A system administrator can disable a user account, but he cannot lock out a user account.

    D. A disabled user account does not retain its SID, whereas a locked out user account does.

3.1 Answers and Explanations: Practice Problems

1. **C** Account Operators are able to manage user accounts without the additional power that is inherent to the Domain Admins group.
2. **C** NT tracks only the SID for resource permissions, therefore, when the account is deleted and with it the SID, simply recreating the username isn't sufficient as the SID isn't reused.
3. **C** Managing permissions with groups is easier than assigning each account the desired permission.
4. **D** You can't restrict users from using their usernames as passwords unless you install specific software to prevent this.
5. **D** Renaming is your only option.
6. **C** You can restrict logon only to eight workstations.
7. **A** Logon hours are used to specify a time period when a specific user is allowed to log on.
8. **B** Auditing allows you to track security and object usage.
9. **C** SIDs are unique in NT and represent a user account.
10. **A, B, C, D** All answers are correct because of the task of backing up and restoring a local computer.
11. **A, C** Only Domain Admins and Server Operators are available for administration on domain controllers.
12. **C** The Administrator has to set a new password.
13. **C** Use templates for creating identical user accounts.
14. **C** You need to create a new global group and add it to local Backup Operators.
15. **C** Disabling prevents anyone from using the account, however, any permissions are retained.
16. **B** You automatically become a member of the Interactive group.
17. **C** Network, Creator Owner, Interactive, and Everyone are the four special groups of Windows NT.
18. **B, C, D, F** Users and Print Operators must not log on to a domain controller.
19. **B** Account expiration is the way to assure that the account for this new user can be used for only two months.
20. **B** When a username is known, everyone can try to figure the password for this account.
21. **D** Auditing can track user logons.
22. **C** The Backup Operators, Server Operators, and Administrators have the rights to backup and restore files.
23. **D** Only copying is allowed for local built-in groups.
24. **B** Only global groups and user accounts can be members of a local group.
25. **A, C, D** Personal is not a group known to NT.

26. **C** Users and groups can be assigned rights.

27. **C** Everyone connecting to a share automatically becomes member of the special Network group.

28. **C** Domain Users is the default group, however, you can remove the user from this one.

29. **C** Lockouts occur when you specified security policy to lock out an account after specified number of retries.

3.1 Key Words

User Group
Local groups Global groups
Creating users Deleting users
Disabling users Creating groups
Renaming users Deleting groups
User rights Auditing
Account policy Account lockout
Built-in groups Special groups
Backup Operators
Server Operators
Print Operators
Administrators Guests
Account Operators
Power Users
Replicator Interactive
Network Everyone
Creator Owner Domain Guests
Domain Admins Domain Users
User Manager Event
ViewerMember Server
Logon scripts

3.2 Managing Policies and Profiles

Policies and profiles are two powerful methods for defining the user environment. Microsoft lists the following objective for the Windows NT Server exam: Create and manage policies and profiles for various situations. Policies and profiles include local user profiles, roaming user profiles, and system policies.

A. User Profiles

A user profile is the entire collection of configuration data that applies to a specific user and only to that user. Because profiles are maintained for each individual user, users can change their own environment without affecting the environment of other users. Profiles contain quite a number of items, including the following:

- Settings for the user-specific Control Panel entries
- Persistent network drive connections
- Remote printer connections
- Personal program groups
- User environment variables
- Bookmarks in Help
- Preferences for Win32 applications
- Most recently accessed documents in Win32 applications

The user's profile subdirectory generally consists of

- an ntuser.dat file (containing Registry information)
- a transaction log file called ntuser.dat.log (which provides fault tolerance for ntuser.dat)
- and a series of folders containing other items such as shortcuts and application-specific profile data

Windows NT provides two types of user profiles:

- **Local Profiles:** Because a local profile resides on the local machine, it does not follow the user if the user logs on to the network from a different machine.
- **Roaming Profiles:** A profile that can follow the user to other computers on the network because it is stored at a central location.

1. Local Profiles

Unless you specify a roaming profile (see the following section), Windows NT obtains user-specific settings from a local user profile on the workstation the user is currently using. You can find a local user profile subdirectory for each workstation user in the <winnt_root>\profiles directory.

When a user logs on for the first time, the Windows NT logon process checks the user account database to see whether a roaming profile path has been specified for the account (see the following section). If the accounts database doesn't contain a profile path for the user, Windows NT creates a local user profile subdirectory for the user in the <winnt_root>\profiles directory and obtains initial user profile information from the local default user profile, which is stored in the subdirectory:

```
<winnt_root>\profiles\Default User
```

Windows NT saves all changes to the user profile in the new local user profile. The next time a user logs on at the workstation, Windows NT accesses the local user profile and configures all user-specific settings to match the information in the profile.

2. Roaming Profiles

A *roaming profile* is a centrally located user profile that other workstations on the network can access at logon. You specify a path to a roaming profile subdirectory in User Manager.

When a user logs on to the domain, the Windows NT logon process checks to see whether the account database contains a roaming profile path for the account.

If the account database contains a path to a roaming profile, Windows NT compares the local version of the profile with the roaming profile specified in the account database. If the local version is more recent, Windows NT asks whether you would like to use the local version rather than the roaming version. Otherwise, Windows NT downloads the roaming version.

At logoff, if the user is a guest or if the profile is a mandatory profile (see next section), Windows NT doesn't save the current user profile to the user profile subdirectory. If the user is not a guest, and if the profile isn't mandatory, Windows NT saves the current profile information. If the profile type is set to Roaming, Windows NT saves the current profile information to both the local copy and the version specified in the account database.

3. Mandatory Profiles

A mandatory profile is a preconfigured roaming profile that the user cannot change. To create a mandatory profile, create a roaming profile subdirectory and specify the path to that directory in User Manager for Domains. Then, copy a user profile to the roaming profile subdirectory (using the Copy To command in the User profile tab of the Control Panel System application) and rename the ntuser.dat file to ntuser.man. The MAN extension makes the profile read-only.

4. Switching Local and Global Profiles

The User Profiles tab of the Control Panel System application will use a locally stored version of the profile, or whether the computer should download a roaming profile at logon. If you are logged on as an administrator, the user profile list in figure 3.2.1 displays all user profiles currently stored on the computer. If you are logged on as a user, the list displays only the profile you are currently using. The Change Type button enables you to specify whether to use the local version of the profile, or whether to download a roaming profile at logon. If you choose the roaming profile option, click on the box labeled `Use cached profile on slow connections` if you want Windows NT to use the local profile when the network is running slowly.

Click on the Copy To button box in the User Profiles tab to open the Copy To dialog box, which enables you to copy the user profile to another directory or to another computer on the network. If a different user will use the profile at its new location, you must give that user permission to use the profile. To add a user to the permissions list for the profile, click on the Change button in the Copy To dialog box.

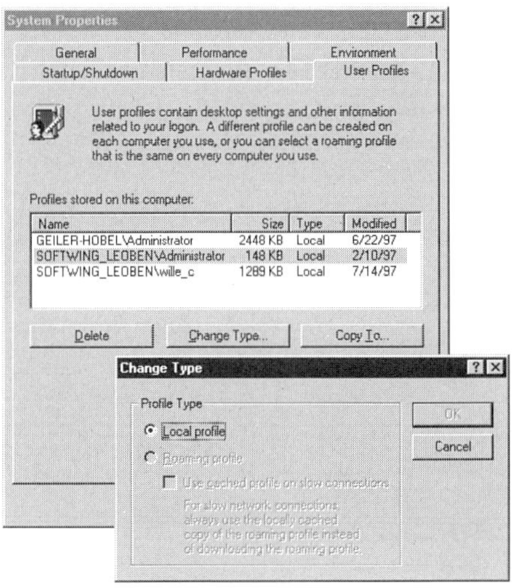

Figure 3.2.1 The System Properties User Profiles tab with the Change Type dialog box opened.

B. Hardware Profiles

Hardware profiles, a new addition to NT, refers to a collection of information about devices, services, and other hardware-related settings. Hardware profiles were designed for portable computers. The hardware configuration of a portable computer might change each time the portable is attached or removed from a docking station. A hardware profile enables the user to define a set of hardware conditions under which the computer will operate at a given time.

If you have defined more than one hardware profile, Windows NT displays a menu of hardware profiles at startup and asks which profile you want to use. The profile you specify becomes the active hardware profile. Any changes to your hardware configuration affect the active hardware profile. You can enable or disable a device for a given hardware profile using the Control Panel Devices application. You can enable or disable a service using the Control Panel Services Application.

C. Managing System Policy with System Policy Editor

System Policy Editor, a powerful configuration tool included with Windows NT Server, enables a network administrator to maintain these options for the entire network from a single location:

- Machine Configurations
- User Policies

System Policy Editor can operate in the following modes:

- Registry mode
- Policy File mode

The exam objectives for the "Managing Resources" section of the NT Server exam specifically mention *system policies*. This implies that, at least for the purposes of the "Managing Resources" section, the Policy File mode functions of System Policy Editor are the more significant. The Windows NT Registry, however, is an extremely important part of Windows NT, and System Policy Editor Registry mode is an able and important interface to the registry.

1. Registry Mode

In Registry mode, System Policy Editor enables whoever is using it to display and change Registry settings of either the local computer or another computer on the network. System Policy Editor does not provide the complete Registry access provided that Registry Editor affords, but it is much easier to use, and it provides powerful access to settings you cannot access via Control Panel. System Policy Editor has a hierarchical structure similar to the Registry and is remarkably simple and convenient when you consider its power. You can use System Policy Editor for the following tasks:

- Set the maximum number of authentication retries
- Prohibit NT from creating 8.3 aliases for long file names
- Define a logon banner to appear prior to logon
- Enable or disable a computer's capability to create hidden drive shares
- Hide the Network Neighborhood icon
- Remove the Run command from the Start menu
- Require a specific desktop wallpaper
- Disable Registry editing tools

The best way to get a feel for the kinds of things you set using System Policy Editor is to browse through the Properties dialog boxes yourself. As you study for the MCSE exam, spend some time familiarizing yourself with System Policy Editor settings.

You can find System Policy Editor in the Administrative Tools program group. Choose Programs in the Start menu, select Administrative Tools, and click on the System Policy Editor icon. Figure 3.2.2 shows System Policy in Registry Mode with the settings for the local computer displayed.

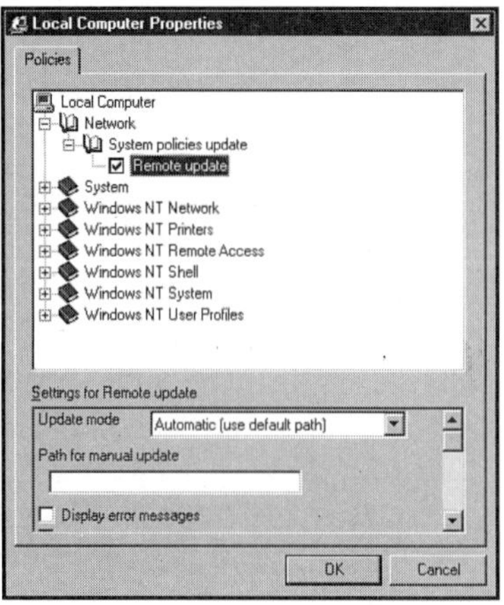

Figure 3.2.2 System Policy Editor Registry mode with the Local Computer Properties dialog box opened.

You are not limited to configuring the local computer's registry settings. You can use System Policy Editor to configure another computer on the network as well.

2. Policy File Mode

System Policy Editor's Policy File mode looks similar to Registry mode, but it is significantly different; System Policy is a kind of meta-Registry. The System Policy file can contain settings that override local Registry settings, you can therefore use System Policy Editor to impose a configuration on a user or machine that the user cannot change.

For Windows NT machines, the System Policy file is called NTConfig.pol. To enable system policy, create the NTConfig.pol file (using System Policy Editor) and place it in the \<winnt_root>\System32\Repl\Import\Scripts folder of the Domain controller's boot partition. This directory is shared as \\PDC_servername\Netlogon$. (Store system policy information for Windows 95 machines in the file Config.pol rather than NTConfig.pol.)

When a Windows NT computer attempts to log on, Windows NT looks for the NTConfig.pol file and checks NTConfig.pol for system policy information that affects the user or computer. Windows NT merges the system policy information with local Registry settings, overwriting the Registry information if necessary.

The types of settings you can define through System Policy Editor's Policy File mode are similar to the settings you can define through Registry mode, but system policy settings override Registry settings. Also, because you can apply system policy settings to groups, you can simultaneously set policies for several users, or even for an entire domain.

A complete set of all system policy information for a given configuration is stored in one big system policy file. You can create different system policy files to test different system policy configurations. The active file (for NT machines), however, must be saved as NTConfig.pol.

Windows NT Server includes some System Policy templates, which contain system policy settings and categories. The template files present on Windows NT are as follows:

- c:\<winnt_root>\inf\common.adm Settings common to both Windows NT and Windows 95 (and not present on the following two files)
- c:\<winnt_root>\inf\winnt.adm Windows NT settings
- c:\<winnt_root>\inf\windows Windows 95 settings

To add a System Policy template, choose Options, Policy Template from the System Policy Editor and choose a template from the list.

The System Policy templates are written in a proprietary scripting language. (See the Windows NT Resource kit for more information on the policy template scripting language.)

3.2.1 Exercise: Creating a New Hardware Profile

The purpose of this exercise is to create a new Hardware Profile.

1. Open Control Panel and double-click on the System application.
2. Click on the Hardware Profiles tab, which enables you to create new hardware profiles and change the order of precedence among hardware profiles. You can also specify whether Windows NT waits indefinitely for you to choose a hardware profile on startup, or whether the choice defaults to the highest-preference profile after a specific time interval.
3. To create the new hardware profile, select an existing profile and click on the Copy button. The new hardware profile will appear in the Available Hardware Profiles list in the Hardware Profiles tab.
4. Close the System application and reboot the computer; select the new profile when prompted by Windows NT during startup.
5. Back in Windows NT, you now you can start to configure this new hardware profile by enabling/disabling services and devices.

3.2.2 Exercise: Applying System Policies

The purpose of this exercise is to show you how to work with System Policy Editor to configure interesting settings of the local computer.

1. Open System Policy Editor in the Administrative Tools menu. Select Open Registry from the File menu.
2. The local registry is being opened. Double-click on Local Computer to start configuring the local machine.
3. Open Network, System Policies Update and enable the Remote Update check box. This entry is used for system policies stored on servers (ntconfig.pol) and their automatic updating on the local computer.
4. Go to Windows NT Network, Sharing and enable (depending on whether the computer is running NT Server or Workstation) the appropriate check box to create hidden administrative shares for the computer.
5. Go to Windows NT System, Logon and enable "Do not display last logged on user name" check box to automatically clear the username in the logon dialog box.
6. Go to Windows NT User Profiles and enable the deletion of cached copies of roaming profiles.
7. Click OK and select Save from the File menu to make your changes persistent.

3.2 Practice Problems

1. You are creating a policy file that is to be used by all computers and users throughout your domain. Where do you have to put this file and which name must it have? Select the best answer:

   A. Put it in <winnt_root>\System32\Repl\Import\Scripts, and name the file config.pol.

   B. Put it in <winnt_root>\System32\Repl\Import\Scripts, and name the file ntconfig.pol.

   C. Put it in <winnt_root>\System32\Repl\Export\Scripts, and name the file config.pol.

   D. Put it in <winnt_root>\System32\Repl\Export\Scripts, and name the file ntconfig.pol.

2. A user logs on to many different workstations and complains that every time he logs on that the changes he made previously to the desktop on another workstation are not available on this workstation. What is the problem? Select the best answer:

   A. The user has a mandatory profile.

   B. The user has a roaming profile.

   C. The user has a local profile.

   D. The user has a per-workstation profile.

3. How can you ensure that a user always gets his current profile independent of the workstation on which he logs on? Select the best answer:

   A. Create a mandatory profile for the user.

   B. Create a roaming profile for the user.

   C. Create a local profile for the user.

   D. Create a per-workstation profile for the user.

4. New summer interns are hired and only a single user account is created for all interns, even though they will be working on different computers. You want to ensure that no single summer intern can mess up the user profile, which means that all changes made to the profile should be ignored. What can you do to achieve this? Select the best answer:

   A. Create a mandatory profile for the interns user account.

   B. Create a mandatory roaming profile for the interns user account.

   C. Create a mandatory local profile for the interns user account.

   D. Create a mandatory per-workstation profile for the interns user account.

5. How do you create mandatory profiles? Select the best answer:

   A. Rename profile.dat to profile.man.

   B. Apply read-only permissions for the interns user account to profile.dat.

   C. Rename ntuser.dat to ntuser.man.

   D. Apply read-only permissions for the interns user account to ntuser.dat.

6. Where do you have to specify the path for roaming profiles? Select the best answer:

   A. In Control Panel, System application, tab User Profiles enter the path to the roaming profile.

   B. In User manager, User Environment Profile, enter the path to the roaming profile.

   C. Enter the information in the Registry under the key HKEY_CURRENT_USER.

   D. Using System Policy Editor, set the path to the roaming profile for a user or an entire group.

7. Which statement best describes Windows 95 and Windows NT policies?

   A. Windows 95 policies can be stored only locally; Windows NT policies can reside on a server share.

   B. Windows 95 doesn't have system policies.

   C. Windows 95 and Windows NT are enforcing the same policies, and therefore they can be interchanged.

   D. The policies are not the same and cannot be interchanged.

8. The finance department was added to the domain yesterday; today all users from this department are complaining that the desktop settings they made are no longer available. What has happened? Select the best answer:

   A. The users didn't save their desktop settings before shutting down their workstations.

   B. The users are not allowed to save changes because their profiles are mandatory.

   C. You have run of licenses for desktop customization on your server.

   D. The group the users belong to doesn't have the right to save desktop settings.

9. Which of the following statements about roaming profiles is *not* true?

   A. Roaming profiles are located on a server share.

   B. Roaming profiles can be stored locally.

   C. You can switch between using roaming and local profiles.

   D. Roaming profiles can't be mandatory.

10. System policies are used to (select all that apply):

    A. Distribute mandatory user profiles.

    B. Restrict access to parts of NT.

    C. Enable administrative shares.

    D. Customize logon.

11. Your boss has bought a new laptop. At his office, he is using a docking station to connect to the LAN; at home he uses a PCMCIA card to dial the office. How can you manage the different hardware setups in NT? Select the best answer:

    A. Install a second copy of NT on the hard disk, one configured for the docking station, the other for use with the modem.

    B. Create a hardware profile for both situations, and activate the devices accordingly.

    C. You don't have to do anything—NT automatically detects docking stations and PCMCIA cards.

    D. You cannot, because NT doesn't support Plug and Play.

12. In System Policy Editor, for which objects can you set a policy? Select all that apply:

    A. Groups

    B. Users

    C. Servers

    D. Computers

3.2 Answers and Explanations: Practice Problems

1. **B** This is the location where NT computers look for policy files.
2. **C** Local profiles are created on every NT computer when a user logs on for the first time.
3. **B** Roaming profiles are stored on a server and retrieved every time a user logs on to a NT computer.
4. **B** Mandatory profiles prevent users from changing any settings.
5. **C** Renaming ntuser.dat must be done in order to make a profile mandatory.
6. **B** You have to specify roaming profiles in User manager, User Environment Profile.
7. **D** Windows 95 and NT use different policy files.
8. **B** Mandatory profiles prevent users from changing any desktop settings.
9. **D** Roaming profiles can be mandatory.
10. **B, C, D** Roaming profiles are not distributed using system policies.
11. **B** Hardware profiles are used for managing different hardware configurations.
12. **A, B, D** There is no specific notion of Servers in system policies.

3.2 Key Words

Profiles

Roaming profiles

System policy editor

Registry mode

Policy templates

Mandatory profiles

Local profiles

Policy file mode

3.3 Managing Windows NT Server from Client Machines

The Network Client Administrator tool, located in the Administrative Tools program group, makes a set of Windows NT administration tools available to Windows NT clients. The Administration tools enable you to perform network administration functions from a client machine. Microsoft lists the following objective for the Windows NT Server exam: Administer remote servers from various types of client computers. Client computer types include Windows 95 and Windows NT Workstation.

There are two packages of client-based network administration tools: one for Windows 95 clients and one for Windows NT Workstation clients. The Windows 95 client-based network administration tools are as follows:

- Event Viewer
- File Security tab
- Print Security tab
- Server Manager
- User Manager for Domains
- User Manager Extensions for Services for NetWare
- File and Print Services for NetWare

Before you can use the Windows 95 client-based network administration package, you must have a 486DX/33 or better Windows 95 computer with 8 MB of RAM (highly recommended) and a minimum of 3 MB of free disk space in the system partition. Client for Microsoft Networks must be installed on the Windows 95 computer.

The Windows NT Workstation client-based network administration tools are as follows:

- DHCP Manager
- Remote Access Administrator
- Remoteboot Manager
- Services for Macintosh
- Server Manager
- System Policy Editor
- User Manager for Domains
- WINS Manager

Before you can use the client-based network administration package, the Windows NT Workstation must be a 486DX/33 or better with 12 MB of RAM and a minimum of 2.5 MB of free disk space in the system partition. The Workstation and Server services must be installed on the Windows NT Workstation.

3.3.1 Exercise: Creating a Server Share for the Client-Based Network Administration Tools

The purpose of this exercise is to copy the client-based network administration tools to a server's hard disk and create a share for these.

1. Open Network Client Administrator from the Administrative Tools menu. Select "Copy client-based network administration tools" and click Continue.
2. In the Share Client-based Administration Tools dialog box you are presented three options: Share Files, Copy Files to a new directory and then share, as well as use existing shared directory. Select the second option and enter the path where to store the files. Leave the share name as proposed. In the path field enter the path to the source location of the tools (the NT Server CD-ROM).
3. The files are copied and the share is created automatically. You are finished with your task.

3.3.2 Exercise: Installing the Client-Based Network Administration Tools on a Windows NT Computer

The purpose of this exercise is to install the NT version of the client-based network administration tools from the server share created in Exercise 3.3.1 to a local NT workstation or server.

1. Open Windows NT Explorer or File Manager to navigate to the servershare you have previously installed the administration tools.
2. Once on the share, go to the Winnt folder and double-click on setup.bat.
3. Let the installation proceed.
4. When the installation is finished, create icons for the tools and start using them as if you were working on the remote machine.

3.3 Practice Problems

1. Which of the following are client-based administration tools for Windows 95? Select all that apply:

    A. Event Viewer

    B. Remoteboot Manager

    C. File and Print Services for NetWare

    D. User Manager for Domains

2. Which of the following are client-based administration tools for Windows NT? Select all that apply:

    A. Event Viewer

    B. Remoteboot Manager

    C. File and Print Services for NetWare

    D. User Manager for Domains

3. For which operating systems are client-based administration tools available? Select all that apply:

    A. Windows 3.x

    B. Windows 95

    C. Windows NT

    D. Apple Macintosh System 7

4. Which of the following are *not* client-based administration tools for Windows 95? Select all that apply:

    A. Server Manager

    B. Remoteboot Manager

    C. File and Print Services for NetWare

    D. System Policy Editor

5. Which of the following are *not* client-based administration tools for Windows NT? Select all that apply:

    A. Services for Macintosh

    B. Remoteboot Manager

    C. File and Print Services for NetWare

    D. System Policy Editor

3.3 Answers and Explanations: Practice Problems

1. **A, C, D** Remoteboot Manager is not available on Windows 95.

2. **A, B, D** File and Print Services for NetWare are not client-based administration tools for Windows NT.

3. **B, C** There are only client-based administration tools for NT and Windows 95.

4. **B, D** Remoteboot Manager and System Policy Editor are not part of the client-based administration tools for Windows 95.

5. **C** File and Print Services for NetWare are not part of the client-based administration tools for NT.

3.3 Key Words

Windows 95 clients

Windows NT clients

Network Client Administrator

3.4 Managing Disk Resources

A big part of an NT administrator's job is managing file resources for the network. Microsoft lists the following objective for the Windows NT Server exam: Manage disk resources. Tasks include copying and moving files between file systems, creating and sharing resources, implementing permissions and security, and establishing file auditing.

A. Copying and Moving Files

When you copy a file within or between partitions with the Copy command, a new instance of that file is created, and the new file inherits the compression and security attributes of the new parent directory.

The same effect results if a file is moved between partitions by using the Move command. (Remember that a move between partitions is really a copy followed by a delete.) When a file is moved within a partition, the file retains its original attributes. The attributes do not change, because the file itself is never altered. Only the source and target directories change.

1. Long File Names

Although all the Windows NT-supported file systems support long file names, you should be aware of certain issues.

a. FAT Long File Names

Only 512 directory entries are permitted in the root directory of any partition. Because each long file name requires a directory entry for every thirteen characters (or portion thereof) in its name and an additional entry for its 8.3 alias, you are in danger of quickly reaching the entry limit if you use excessively long file names in a root directory.

Also, if you are dual-booting between Windows NT and Windows 95, you should be aware that although the long file names are compatible with both operating systems, Windows 95 has a path limitation of 260 characters, including the drive letter. If you use a deep hierarchy of subdirectories with long file names, therefore, you may find that Windows 95 cannot access a file buried deep within that directory tree.

The two operating systems also differ in the way they create the 8.3 alias. Both Windows NT and Windows 95 begin by taking the first six legal characters in the LFN (in other words, stripping spaces and punctuation and converting to uppercase) and following them by a tilde (~) and a number. If the first six legal characters result in a unique identifier for that file, the number following the tilde is 1. If a file in that directory already has the same first six legal characters, the numeric suffix will be 2. For an extension, Windows NT uses the first three legal characters following the last period in the LFN. To give you an idea of what this looks like, here is a sample directory listing:

```
Team Meeting Report #3.Doc        TEAMME~1.DOC
Team Meeting Report #4.Doc        TEAMME~2.DOC
Team Meeting Report #5.Doc        TEAMME~3.DOC
Team Meeting Report #6.Doc        TEAMME~4.DOC
Nov. 1995 Status Report.Doc         NOV199~1.DOC
```

Both Windows 95 and Windows NT generate aliases in this fashion until the fifth iteration of the same first six legal characters. At this point, Windows 95 continues to do so, but Windows NT does something altogether different; it takes only the first two legal characters, performs a hash on the file name to produce four hexadecimal characters, and then appends a ~5. The ~5 remains for all subsequent aliases of those same initial six characters. If additional reports were saved in the directory used in the preceding example, for example, here is how Windows 95 would and Windows NT might generate the aliases:

	Windows 95	Windows NT
Team Meeting	TEAMME~5.DOC	TEA4F2~5.DOC Report #7.Doc
Team Meeting	TEAMME~6.DOC	TE12B4~5.DOC Report #8.Doc
Team Meeting	TEAMME~7.DOC	TE833E~5.DOC Report #9.Doc

If you choose to disable long file name support altogether on a FAT partition, be careful when copying files from a partition that does support LFNs because both the COPY and XCOPY commands always default to using the LFN for their operations.

If you are copying from an LFN-enabled FAT partition or from an NTFS partition, you can use the /n switch with both COPY and XCOPY. The /n switch directs the command to use the alias rather than the LFN.

b. NTFS Long File Names

NTFS generates an alias for each LFN the same way that FAT does. This auto-generation takes time, however. If you won't be using 16-bit MS-DOS or Windows 3.x-based applications, you might consider disabling the automatic alias generation by adding a value called NtfsDisable8dot3NameCreation with a type of REG_DWORD and a value of 1 to HKEY_LOCAL_MACHINE\System\CurrentControlSet\Control\FileSystem. To re-enable alias generation, set the value to 0, or delete the value.

B. Converting a FAT Partition to NTFS

You can convert a FAT partition to NTFS at any time. You cannot, however, convert an NTFS partition to a FAT partition. Therefore, if you aren't certain about what type of file system to use for a partition, you might want to start with FAT and convert after you are sure there will be no ill effects.

To convert from FAT to NTFS, issue this command from the command prompt (there is no GUI utility for this):

```
CONVERT <drive_letter>: /FS:NTFS
```

C. NTFS Compression

Individual files and directories can be marked for compression on NTFS partitions only. (An entire drive can be compressed, too, but all you are really doing is compressing the root directory and the files within it; everything is handled at the file level.)

Compression occurs on the fly. All this is transparent to applications and the rest of the operating system. NTFS compresses each file individually, so you always know the exact amount of disk space you have. You can also choose which files to compress, so you don't have to waste time compressing the entire drive.

NTFS compression does not free up as much disk space as most MS-DOS–compatible compression products. The reason for the loose compression in Windows NT is actually to ensure that performance is not affected adversely.

Typically, disk compression products sacrifice performance for extra compression. In Windows NT, you can get a compression ratio almost as good as the MS-DOS 6.22 DriveSpace compression engine, without sacrificing any noticeable performance. When a user marks files to compress, NTFS analyzes the files to see how much disk space will be saved and the amount of time it will take to compress and decompress the file. If NTFS determines that it is not a fair trade, it does not compress the file, no matter how many times the user issues the compress command.

You can compress any file or directory on an NTFS partition, even if it is the system or boot partition. NTLDR, a hidden, system, read-only file in the root of your system partition, is the only file that you cannot compress.

1. Compressing and Uncompressing Files, Directories, and Drives

One of a few ways to compress a file or directory on an NTFS partition is to select the directories and files in File Manager, and choose File, Compress. To compress NTFS files using Explorer, follow these steps:

1. Select the files you want to compress. Use the Ctrl key to select multiple files.
2. Choose File, Properties. The Properties dialog box appears.
3. In the Attributes frame, select the Compressed check box (see fig. 3.4.1).

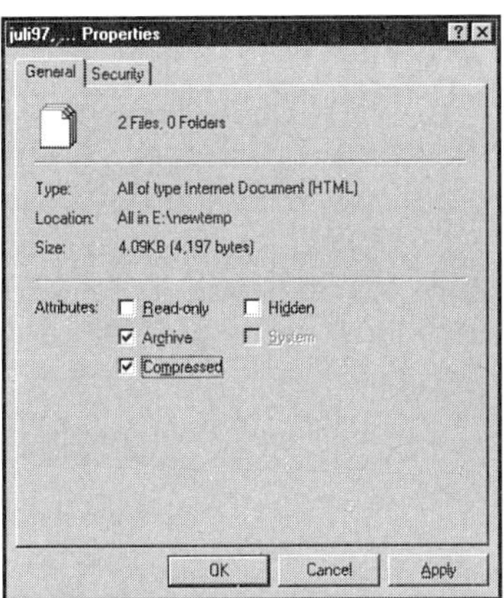

Figure 3.4.1 File Properties dialog box for a file on an NTFS partition.

If you select a directory rather than or along with a file, you are asked whether you want to compress all the files and subdirectories within that directory.

To uncompress files or directories, select them and disable the Compressed check box in the Properties dialog box.

When files and directories are compressed, a new Compression attribute is set for those objects. Note that the Compression attribute does not display for non-NTFS partitions.

The procedure for compressing a drive is similar to the procedure for compressing a file or directory. Select the drive in My Computer or Explorer, and then choose File, Properties. Select the Compress check box at the bottom of the General tab of the Properties dialog box.

2. COMPACT.EXE

You also can use a command-line utility to compress files. The COMPACT.EXE command enables a user to compress files and directories from the command prompt. The following table lists switches you can use with the COMPACT command.

Use	To
COMPACT <filelist> /C	Compress
COMPACT <filelist> /U	Uncompress
COMPACT <filelist> /S	Compress an entire directory tree
COMPACT <filelist> /A	Compress hidden and system files
COMPACT <filelist> /I	Ignore errors and continue compressing
COMPACT <filelist> /F	Force compression even if the objects are already compressed
COMPACT <filelist> /Q	Turn on quiet mode; that is, display only summary information

You also can use the COMPACT command without any switches, in which case it just reports on the compression status, size, and ratio for each file in the file list.

3. Special Notes About Compressed Directories

Directories do not truly get compressed; the Compressed attribute for a directory just sets a flag to tell Windows NT to compress all current files and all future files created in this directory.

With that in mind, it may be easier to understand that when you copy or move compressed files, the files do not always stay compressed.

When a new file is created in an NTFS directory, it inherits the attributes set for that directory. When a file is created in a "compressed" directory, for example, that file will be compressed. When a file is created in an uncompressed directory, the file will not be compressed. So when a compressed file is copied to an uncompressed directory, the new copy of the file will not be compressed. Likewise, if an uncompressed file is copied to a "compressed" directory, the copy of the file will be compressed even though the original is not.

This much probably makes sense. Windows NT includes a MOVE command, however, that, when used within a single partition, swaps directory pointers so that a single file appears to move from one directory to another. Note the word "appears." The file does not actually go anywhere;

it is the source and target directories that actually record a change. When files are moved, attributes do not change. In other words, a compressed file moved into an uncompressed directory stays compressed, and an uncompressed file moved into a compressed directory stays uncompressed.

If you don't think that is complicated enough, Windows NT enables you to use the MOVE command even when the source and target directories are on two different partitions. In this scenario, it is not possible for a directory on one partition to point to a file on another partition. Instead, Windows NT copies the file to the target partition and deletes the original file. Because the target partition now contains a brand-new file, that file inherits the attributes of its new parent directory.

When you copy a file within or between partitions, or move a file between partitions, therefore, the compression attribute of the new copy is inherited from its new parent directory. When you move a file within a single partition, the attributes on the file remain unchanged.

D. Sharing Directories

Sharing refers to publishing resources on a network for public access. When you share a resource, you make it available to users on other network machines. The Windows NT objects most commonly shared are directories and printers. This section (and the following subsections) look at how to share directories.

If you are familiar with NetWare but not with Windows NT, you need to understand the concept that, by default, absolutely no Windows NT resources are available to remote users; resources must be explicitly published (shared) on the network to host network users.

If you are familiar with Windows for Workgroups or Windows 95 but not with Windows NT, you also should understand that Windows NT users cannot share directories on their computers; only administrators and power users have this privilege. Because shares are computer-specific, and because users cannot modify anything that affects the entire computer, shares are off-limits. This restriction is not a default; granting this capability to users is impossible, as is revoking this capability from administrators and power users.

Even if you are an administrator, you must have at least List permissions to the directory before you can share a directory. Any user who has locked you out of a share probably does not want you to publish it on the network.

Three ways to create shared directories are as follows:

- Using Explorer or My Computer (or you can still use File Manager)
- Using the command prompt
- Using Server Manager

1. Sharing with Explorer and My Computer

You can share directories in Windows NT in a number of ways. The easiest, and usually the most efficient, uses Explorer or My Computer.

Right-click on the directory you want to share and choose Sharing from the shortcut menu to open the Sharing tab of the Properties dialog box. You also can reach the Sharing tab by choosing File, Properties. Or, My Computer enables you to choose Sharing directly from the File menu after you select a directory.

The Share Name defaults to the name of the directory. You can change it; it does not affect the actual directory name at all, it just defines the way the directory appears to network users.

You should never have to change the path. As long as you select the appropriate directory before you choose the Sharing command, the Path box should be set correctly.

The comment is optional. It is nothing more than a free-text tag line that appears next to the share name when browsing in Explorer or Network Neighborhood. (Choose View, Details if you want to see the comments.)

Click on the Permissions button to open the Access Through Share Permissions dialog box, from which you can build an Access Control List for the share to prevent unauthorized network access.

The ATS permissions are completely independent from the local NTFS permissions. In fact, ATS permissions can even be applied to FAT partitions. Because they apply to the entire share, however, you cannot assign granular file-level permissions unless the partition on which the share resides is NTFS.

The ATS permissions themselves are not that granular. Here are your choices:

No Access	Users with No Access to a share can still connect to the share, but nothing appears in File Manager except the message `You do not have permission to access this directory.`
Read	Assigns R and X permissions to the share and its contents.
Change	Assigns R, X, W, and D permissions to the share and its contents.
Full Control	Assigns R, X, W, and D permissions to the share and its contents. In addition, for NTFS shares, P and O permissions are added.

Just as with local NTFS permissions, user and group permissions accumulate, with the exception of No Access, which instantly overrides all other permissions.

Remember, however, that ATS permissions are completely independent of local NTFS permissions. If both sets of permissions are assigned, only the most restrictive permissions are retained.

If you don't require security, you don't have to touch the ATS permissions. The default permissions grant the Everyone group Full Control (just as the default NTFS permissions do).

Choose the OK button to enact sharing of the directory. To modify the share configuration, right-click on the directory again and choose Sharing from the shortcut menu.

The Sharing tab looks identical to the New Share dialog box, with the addition of the New Share button. Click on the New Share button to share the directory again, with a different name and ACL. It does not remove the original share, it just shares the directory again. You can share a single directory an unlimited number of times.

2. Sharing from the Command Prompt

To share from the Windows NT command prompt, use the NET SHARE command, using this syntax:

```
NET SHARE <share_name>=<drive_letter>:<path>
```


To share the C:\PUBLIC directory as Documents, use the following command:

```
NET SHARE Documents=C:\PUBLIC
```

To add a comment for browsers, use the /REMARK switch:

```
NET SHARE Documents:=C:\PUBLIC /REMARK:"Public Documents"
```

To set the user limit to Maximum allowed, use the /UNLIMITED switch (although this is the default):

```
NET SHARE Documents:=C:\PUBLIC /REMARK:"Public Documents" /UNLIMITED
```

To set a specific user limit, use the /USERS switch:

```
NET SHARE Documents:=C:\PUBLIC /REMARK:"Public Documents" /USERS:5
```

To stop a share using the NET SHARE command, use the /DELETE switch:

```
NET SHARE Documents /DELETE
```

a. Hidden Shares

Regardless of how you created it, you can hide a share by ending the share name with a dollar sign ($):

```
NET SHARE Documents$=C:\Public
```

Users can still connect to these shares, but they must explicitly supply the entire path to do so. And of course, the shares can still be protected using Access Through Share Permissions.

b. Administrative Shares

Any Windows NT-based computer that has hard-coded ACLs that grant Full Control to Administrators and No Access to everyone else has at least the following two hidden shares:

C$	Shares the root of the computer's drive C—If other partitions exist on the drive, those partitions also will have similar shares (but not for CD-ROM or disk drives). Consequently, administrators can easily connect to other computers on the network.
ADMIN$	Shares the root of the Windows NT installation, regardless of where it may have been installed—it gives administrators easy access to the operating system directory on any Windows NT-based computer.

To permanently disable these shares, open System Policy editor in Registry mode and go to Windows NT Network, Sharing and disable the Create hidden drive shares check box.

3. Monitoring and Managing Shares

To see a list of all the shares on the system, open the Server application in the Control Panel. Although you cannot stop sharing a resource from the Server application, you can see a complete list of shared resources as well as a list of connected users and other server-related items.

The Server application is a subset of Windows NT Server's Server Manager application. It is a front end for administering connections to your computer. In the Server dialog box, you can view the Usage Summary for your server.

The Usage Summary tracks the following statistics:

Sessions	The number of computers connected to this server.
Open Files	The total number of files currently open for access by remote users.
File Locks	The total number of file locks placed against this computer by remote users.
Open Named Pipes	The total number of named pipes between this computer and connected workstations. (Named pipes are an interprocess communication (IPC) mechanism.)

The Server dialog box also acts as the launch pad for five other server-configuration dialog boxes, as follows:

Users Sessions	Shows detailed information about current user sessions on your Windows NT-based server. (Click on the Users button.)
Shared Resources	Displays detailed information about current shares on your server. (Click on the Shares button.)
Open Resources	Displays the resources of your computer currently being used by remote users. (Click on the In Use button.)
Directory Replication	You can configure the Directory Replicator service in this window. (Click on the Replication button.)
Alerts	Enables an administrator to enter a list of users or workstations to whom messages will be sent in the event of a significant server event. (Click on the Alerts button.)

To view the shared resources on your system, click on the Shares button in the Server application's Server dialog box. The Shared Resources dialog box that appears shows a list of all shares presently configured for your system and the path to each share (see fig. 3.4.2).

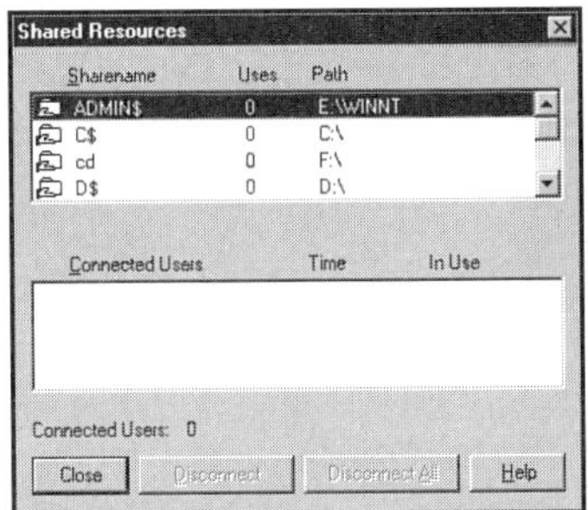

Figure 3.4.2 The Shared Resources dialog box.

Server Manager, in the Administrative Tools group, offers a similar view of shared resources on the local system and on other network computers as well. Click on a computer icon in the Server Manager main screen to open the dialog box.

In the Server Manager, not only can you view the share information for a remote PC, you can actually create a new shared directory. Select a computer in the Server Manager and choose Computer, Shared Directories. The Shared Directories dialog box then shows the shared directories for the computer you selected. Click on the New Share button to add a new share. The New Share dialog box (see fig. 3.4.3) that appears asks you to specify a share name, a path, and an optional comment that will appear in descriptions on the share. You also can limit the number of simultaneous users who can access the share. The Permissions button enables you to specify Access Through Share (ATS) permissions.

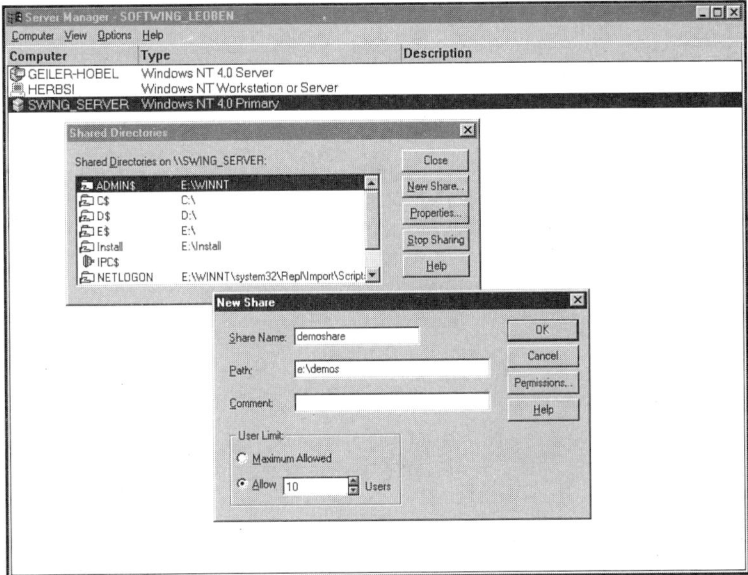

Figure 3.4.3 Server Manager with dialog boxes Shared Directories and New Share opened.

The Stop Sharing button in the Shared Directories dialog box enables you to terminate a share. The Properties button opens the Shared Properties dialog box, which is similar to the New Share dialog box.

E. Working with NTFS File Permissions and Security

The NTFS file system supports a complex arrangement of directory and file security for which there is no equivalent in the FAT file system. The following sections examine important aspects of NTFS security:

- Ownership of NTFS Resources
- Auditing NTFS Resources
- Securing NTFS Resources

1. Ownership of NTFS Resources

Every NTFS file and directory has one account designated as its owner. The owner of a resource is the only account that has the right to access a resource, modify its properties, and secure it from outside access.

By default, the owner of a resource is the user who created the resource. Only one user can own a resource at any given time, except that a user who is a member of the Administrators group cannot be the sole owner of any resource. Any resource created by an administrator, for example, is co-owned by the entire Administrators group.

To identify the owner of any file or directory, follow these steps:

1. Select the file or directory in My Computer or Windows NT Explorer.
2. Choose File, Properties. The Properties dialog box appears.
3. Click on the Security tab.
4. Click on the Ownership button. The Owner dialog box appears.

Remember that only NTFS resources have owners. You also can take ownership away from the current owner by choosing the Take Ownership button in the Owner dialog box. Normally, only administrators can do this—they can take ownership of any resource because they have been granted the Take Ownership of File and Directories user right.

If you are not an administrator, you may still be able to take ownership if the current owner has granted you permission to take ownership. The important concept to grasp for now, however, is that ownership is taken, never given. Ownership involves responsibility, and that responsibility can never be forced on anyone, even by an administrator. Implications to this rule will surface shortly.

2. Auditing NTFS Resources

One of the most important aspects of Windows NT security is that system administrators can *audit* access to objects such as directories files. In other words, you can configure NT to track all attempts (successful or not) to access NTFS resources for various purposes. The record of all access attempts then appear in the Security log of the Event Viewer.

If you copy a file to a directory configured for auditing, the file inherits the directory's auditing configuration. If you move a file (dragging a file in Explorer to another directory in the same partition is a move), the file retains its original auditing configuration.

You can audit the following six access events for success and/or failure:

- Read
- Write
- Execute
- Delete
- Change Permissions
- Take Ownership

3. Securing NTFS Resources

The set of permissions on a file or directory is just another attribute (or stream) attached to the file, called an Access Control List (ACL). Each ACL contains a series of Access Control Entries (ACEs), and each Access Control Entry references a specific user or group SID and a type of access to grant or deny that SID.

a. Discretionary Access

Who gets to assign permissions to a resource? The owner of the resource. Who is the owner of the resource? The user who created it. In other words, unlike other operating systems, security is not the sole domain of the administrator. If you create a file, you, not the administrator, get to secure it. You can, in fact, easily lock administrators out of their resources. And that makes sense in many environments.

Because locking administrators out of files and directories is dangerous, there is a spare key. An administrator cannot be blocked from taking ownership of a resource, and after the administrator owns the resource, he or she can modify the permissions on the resource so that he or she can access it. Remember, though, that ownership can be taken but never given, and that goes for giving back too.

When the administrator owns the resource, he/she can never return ownership to the original user without that user explicitly taking ownership. And that is how it should be for legitimate situations in which a user might be absent from work when a critical file needs to be accessed. The administrator could get into a sticky situation by accessing files without a legitimate reason.

b. Permissions Versus User Rights

You may remember that resource permissions are not the same thing as user rights. User rights are tasks stored with your account information in the Registry, which you can perform on the system as a whole. NTFS permissions are stored with the resource itself, in the ACL property discussed earlier.

It is important to understand the difference between rights and permissions, because that understanding brings light to why the resource permissions assigned to a user cannot be viewed the way trustee assignments in other operating systems such as Novell NetWare are viewed. Displaying all the permissions assigned to a user requires searching all the NTFS files and directories on all the NTFS partitions on the workstation and on shared directories of any other workstation or server on the network. It also requires searching for incidence of the user's SID or group SIDs on the ACL of each of those files.

c. Directory-Level Permissions

Permissions can be placed on both directories and files. When they are, you need to resolve the permissions to figure out the effective permissions for a user.

The owner of a directory may grant a user the following permissions:

No Access	Restricts users from accessing the directory by any means. The directory appears in the directory tree, but instead of a file list, users see the message "`You do not have permissions to access this directory.`"
List	Restricts users from accessing the directory, although they may view the contents list for the directory.
Read	Users can read data files and execute program files from the directory, but cannot make changes.
Add	Users cannot read or even view the contents of the directory, but may write files to the directory. If you write a file to the directory, you receive the message "`You do not have permissions to access this directory, but you still may save or copy files to it.`"
Add & Read	Users may view and read from the directory and save new files into the directory, but cannot modify existing files.
Change	Users may view and read from the directory and save new files into the directory, may modify and even delete existing files, and may change attributes on the directory and even delete the entire directory
Full Control	Users may view, read, save, modify, or delete the directory and its contents. In addition, users may change permissions on the directory and its contents, even if they do not own the resource. Users can also take ownership at any time.

What actually happens with all these levels of permissions is a combination of six basic actions that can be performed against a resource:

- Read (R)
- Write (W)
- Execute (X)
- Delete (D)
- Change Permissions (P)
- Take Ownership (O)

The following table breaks down these permissions by permissions level:

Level	Directory Permissions	File Permissions
No Access	None	None
List	RX	Unspecified
Read	RX	RX
Add	WX	Unspecified
Add & Read	RXWD	RX
Change	RXWD	RXWD
Full Control	RXWDPO	RXWDPO

The two custom levels of permissions are Special Directory Access and Special File Access, both of which enable the owner (or any user granted the "P" permission) to custom build an access control entry by using any combination of the six basic actions mentioned here.

When a new directory or file is created on an NTFS partition, the resource inherits the permissions on its parent directory, the same way it inherits the compression attribute. (See the section, "NTFS File Compression," earlier in this chapter.)

d. File-Level Permissions

Although permissions for files are not as varied as they are for directories, NTFS can store permissions for files also. The owner of a file may grant users the following permissions:

No Access	Cannot access this file at all, although the file name and basic attributes still appear in File Manager.
Read	Can read this file if it is a data file, or execute it if it is a program file, but can not modify it.
Change	Can read, execute, modify, or delete this file.
Full Control	Can read or execute, write to, or delete this file, may change permissions on it, as well as take ownership away from the current owner.

The following table breaks down these file permissions:

Level	Permissions
No Access	None
Read	RX
Change	RXWD
Full Control	RXWDPO

As with Directory permissions, a Special Access level allows anyone who has the capability to change permissions to custom build an access control entry for a user or group.

e. Setting Permissions

To set permissions on a file or directory, first select the resource in Explorer or My Computer, and then choose File, Properties. Click on the Permissions button on the Security tab of the File Properties dialog box to open the File Permissions dialog box.

To remove a user or group from the ACL, select the user and click on the Remove button. To add a user or group to the ACL, click on the Add button. Clicking on the Add button opens the Add Users and Groups dialog box, which includes a list of all the groups in your account database (see fig. 3.4.4).

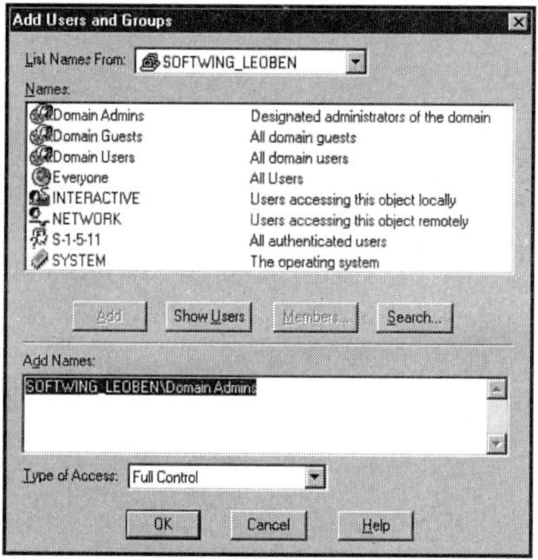

Figure 3.4.4 The Add Users and Groups dialog box.

If you want to grant access to a specific user, click on the Show Users button. Otherwise, only the group names are displayed. Choose the users and groups you want to add to the ACL individually or collectively and click on the Add button to enter their names in the Add Names list box at the bottom of the dialog box. Don't try to set their access level here, unless all of these accounts are going to be granted the same access level. When you click on the OK button, you get another chance to modify the permission level for each individual account on the ACL.

Setting permissions for a directory brings up a slightly different dialog box—you can set the following additional options before the new permissions are applied to the directory:

- **Replace Permissions on Subdirectories:** Modifies the permissions on all directories in the directory tree, but not on any files within those directories, even in the top-level directory.
- **Replace Permissions on Existing Files:** The permissions that apply to the directory also apply to the files within the directory, but not to subdirectories or files within subdirectories.

Selecting both check boxes applies these permissions to the entire directory tree and its contents. Enabling neither check box changes the permissions on the top-level directory only.

f. Local Groups

When working with user rights, assigning rights to user and built-in groups usually suffices. When assigning resource permissions, however, adding individual users may be too time-consuming, and adding built-in groups may be too inclusive. Imagine having a directory that contains meeting minutes for a project on which you are working. You would like to grant permissions to the people on the project team, but the team contains more than 30 people.

Assigning permissions to everybody would take a long time, and assigning permissions to the Users group would give access to too many people.

It is time to introduce local groups, a separate level of user management in Windows NT. Local groups can be created by any user for any purpose (Headquarters, Marketing, Vice Presidents, Portland, Engineering), and once created, can be reused repeatedly. By creating a local group called MyProject and including all the project team members, you need to grant only a single set of permissions for each meeting report.

g. Local Groups versus Built-In Groups

A *local group* is a group used to assign rights and/or permissions to a local system and local resources. Local groups are similar to built-in groups in that both can contain many users to address a single purpose. In fact, technically, the built-in groups in Windows NT Workstation are local groups.

Local and built-in groups also have similar structures. Both can contain local users, domain users, and global groups, and users and global groups from trusted domains. The only type of account that cannot be placed inside a local group is another local group.

The difference between local and built-in groups lies in their intended purposes. The built-in groups are predefined and preassigned to specific rights and capabilities for system management. They are not intended for use in managing access to resources. Local groups are impractical for managing the system, but are ideal for assigning permissions to files and directories.

The only other difference between the two types of groups is that built-in groups are permanent members of a computer's account database, whereas local groups can be created and deleted at will.

h. How User and Group Permissions Interact

At this point, you have probably realized that users are likely to be in many different groups. Abigail's user account, for example, may be a member of the Users group, but also the Marketing group, the Department Managers group, the Philadelphia group, and the Project X group. Each of these user and group accounts is likely to be granted permissions to resources at one time or another, and it is quite likely that some of the accounts might occasionally appear on the same Access Control List. In such scenarios, how should the permissions granted to both a user's user account and group accounts be resolved?

Quite simply, user and group permissions are cumulative; neither takes precedence over the other. If the Marketing group has Read access to a file and the Department Managers group has Change access to the same file, Abigail (a member of both groups) has both—or in other words, Change access, because Change already includes the R and X permissions that Read incorporates.

The one exception to this rule is the No Access permission. No Access overrides all other permissions granted to a user or the user's groups, regardless of where the No Access was assigned. If Abigail were granted Read access to a file but Marketing was granted No Access, for example, Abigail would not be able to access the file. You cannot—and this cannot be emphasized enough—override a No Access permission.

No Access is intended as a "negator" to remove permissions from a user or group that may already have been implicitly added to the ACL through membership in another group.

i. How Directory and File Permissions Interact

When you have permissions on both directories and files—such is the case on an NTFS partition—things get just a bit more complicated. Fortunately, you can resolve this situation pretty easily, although a few odd circumstances might surround the situation.

Simply put, file permissions override directory permissions. Likewise, it is possible to grant a user Read access to a directory and yet still grant Full Control over a single file within that directory.

This can lead to some odd scenarios. Sam may not want anyone to view the contents of his private directory, for example, so he assigns the directory this ACL:

Sam: Full Control

If Beth tries to view this directory, she gets the `You do not have permission to access this directory` message. Yet Sam may still want to occasionally grant Beth access to one or two of his files. One day, he grants Beth Read access to a document in his private directory. Beth can read that file, but how can she access it? She can't view the directory contents in Explorer, and when she does a File/Open in an application, she cannot view the directory contents there either. Before she can access the file, Beth must type the full path to the file, from the application in which she wants to view it.

j. File Delete Child

Consider another odd scenario. Sam decides to grant Everyone Full Control to his private directory, and just apply Read permissions to Everyone for the individual files within the directory. Sam knows that although users might be able to copy and save files in his directory, they can't change the ones already present, because those files have only Read permissions. Sam also knows that no one else can change permissions on the existing files, because those files have only Read permissions. Sam, however, thinks that no one can delete his existing files because they only have Read permissions. On this last count, he is wrong.

In addition to the six basic permissions (RXWDPO) granted with Full Control, there is a seventh, implicit permission, called File Delete Child (FDC). FDC is included for POSIX compatibility, and it grants a user who has Full Control over a directory the capability to delete a top-level file within that directory, even if that user does not have delete permissions to the file itself! Only top-level files can be deleted, not subdirectories or files within subdirectories.

There is a workaround, but you must grant Special Directory Access before you can use it. If you grant Special Directory Access and choose all six permissions rather than grant Full Control to a directory, the user granted this level of access won't have the FDC permission. It looks like you are really just assigning the equivalent of Full Control, but you are doing so minus File Delete Child. By the way, don't waste time searching for File Delete Child in the Explorer interface—it is not there. It's an implicit permission granted only when Full Control is granted over a directory.

An even better workaround is to never grant anyone Full Control over anything, unless you grant it to yourself as the owner. After all, you probably don't want anyone else to have the power to change permissions on the file and lock you out. And you certainly don't want someone to have the capability to take ownership of the file at the same time so that you can't even change permissions back to what they were. A good rule of thumb is never to grant anyone any permissions higher than Change. That is high enough, because a user with Change access can delete the resource itself.

k. Special Considerations for the Boot and System Partitions

When you install Windows NT on an NTFS partition, it is tempting to prevent necessary files from being deleted or overwritten, to try to exclude users from accessing the Windows NT installation directory tree. If you examine the Access Control List for that directory, however, you won't see the customary Everyone/Full Control that you normally find on NTFS resources.

The critical entry on the ACL is the SYSTEM/Full Control ACE. Do not, under any circumstances, remove this ACL from the list, or modify it. Otherwise, Windows NT crashes and you cannot restart the operating system.

If this does happen, don't panic. You can use the Emergency Repair Disk to strip the permissions from the Windows NT installation directory tree.

3.4.1 Exercise: Taking Ownership

The purpose of this exercise is to show how user A, who owns a file or directory, can initiate ownership transfer to user B, who then finishes the ownership transfer by taking it.

1. User A selects the file or directory he wants to transfer ownership to user B. He opens the security tab and clicks on Permissions.
2. Once on there, he selects user B from the user list and assigns Read access. Back in the Permissions dialog box, he selects Special Access and enables Take Ownership. User A's part is finished.
3. Now user B can go to the Security tab, select Ownership and then click Take Ownership to be the new owner of the file.

3.4.2 Exercise: Configuring Auditing

The purpose of this example is to show how to configure auditing for a file using NT Explorer. Follow these steps:

1. Right-click on an NTFS file in Explorer of My Computer and choose Properties.
2. Click on the Security tab of the File Properties dialog box.
3. Click on the Auditing button. The File Auditing dialog box appears (see fig. 3.4.5). You can audit either successful or failed attempts at any of the actions listed, and you can specify which specific groups or users you want to audit.
4. Click on the Add button to add a group or user to the audit list. Click on the Remove button to delete a group or user from the audit list.

The Directory Auditing dialog box is similar. The procedure for reaching the Directory Auditing dialog box is similar to the procedure for reaching the file Auditing dialog box. Right click on a directory, choose Properties, choose the Directory Properties Security tab, then click on the Auditing button. The Directory Auditing dialog box enables you to choose whether the new auditing arrangement you are configuring will replace the auditing on subdirectories or existing files.

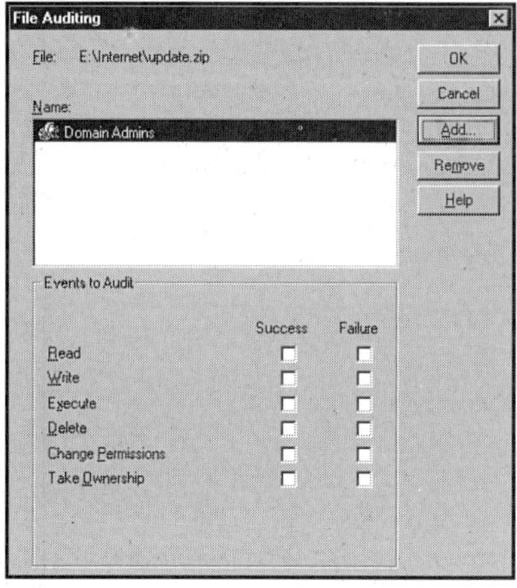

Figure 3.4.5 The File Auditing dialog box.

3.4 Practice Problems

1. You are copying a file that is compressed with permissions set to Read for Everyone to an uncompressed directory in which Everyone has Change permissions. Which of the following statements is true?

    A. The file will be compressed and Change permissions enforced for Everyone.

    B. The file will be compressed and Read permissions enforced for Everyone.

    C. The file will be uncompressed and Read permissions enforced for Everyone.

    D. The file will be uncompressed and Change permissions enforced for Everyone.

2. You are moving a file that is compressed and has permissions set to Read for Everyone to an uncompressed directory in which Everyone has Change permissions. Which of the following statements is true?

    A. The file will be compressed and Change permissions enforced for Everyone.

    B. The file will be compressed and Read permissions enforced for Everyone.

    C. The file will be uncompressed and Read permissions enforced for Everyone.

    D. The file will be uncompressed and Change permissions enforced for Everyone.

3. You are moving a file that is compressed and has permissions set to Read for Everyone to a different disk on an uncompressed directory in which Everyone has Change permissions. Which of the following statements is true?

    A. The file will be compressed and Change permissions enforced for Everyone.

    B. The file will be compressed and Read permissions enforced for Everyone.

    C. The file will be uncompressed and Read permissions enforced for Everyone.

    D. The file will be uncompressed and Change permissions enforced for Everyone.

4. Which of the following statements is true?

    A. You can convert FAT partitions to NTFS at any time using Disk Administrator.

    B. You can convert FAT partitions to NTFS at any time using the command line utility convert.exe.

    C. You can convert NTFS partitions to FAT at any time using Disk Administrator.

    D. You can convert NTFS partitions to FAT at any time using the command line utility convert.exe.

5. Which of the following statements about NTFS compression is true?

    A. Compression is only available for entire drives.

    B. Both FAT and NTFS file systems support compression.

    C. You can tune NTFS compression with Registry editor going to the HKEY_LOCAL_MACHINE\CurrentControlSet\Services\Ntfs and setting the NtfsCompression Factor to a higher number.

    D. NTFS compression is transparent to all applications and can be used only on NTFS formatted volumes.

6. Which of the following command lines forces all files in the directory to be recompressed? Select the best answer:

   A. COMPACT *.* /C

   B. COMPACT *.* /F

   C. COMPACT *.* /R

   D. COMPACT *.* /S

7. You want to format a floppy disk using the NTFS file system. Select the best method of doing this:

   A. Go to Disk Administrator, select the floppy disk drive and run the Format command from the Tools menu. Specify NTFS as file system.

   B. Open File Manager and select Disk, Format NTFS. You are prompted to insert a disk.

   C. You cannot format floppy disks using NTFS.

   D. You have to use the RDISK utility to format removable disks with NTFS.

8. You have set up the computer of your boss as a Windows NT computer with drive C: formatted with NTFS. Now, he wants to test-drive Windows 95b on this computer. What would you need to do to install Windows 95b? Select the best answer:

   A. Nothing. Simply start the installation program of Windows 95b.

   B. Add an MS-DOS entry to the boot.ini file, and restart the computer. Now you can install Windows 95b.

   C. You have to backup the files, format the drive with FAT, install Windows 95b, and then install Windows NT again. Don't forget to restore the files.

   D. You cannot go with solution C because NT can't read the FAT32 entries of Windows 95b.

9. Which file systems are supported by Windows NT? Select all that apply:

   A. CDFS

   B. HPFS

   C. NTFS

   D. FAT

10. Which file systems allow to secure files with ACLs? Select all that apply:

    A. CDFS

    B. HPFS

    C. NTFS

    D. FAT

11. You have set the following permissions on a directory: Change for the Sales group, Read for the SalesManagers group, and No Access for Everyone. Ronnie is member of the SalesManagers group. What kind of access is he granted? Select the best answer:

    A. Change

    B. Read

    C. Take Ownership

    D. No Access

12. You have set the following permissions on a directory: Change for the Sales group, and Read for Ann (who is member of the SalesManagers and the Sales group). What kind of access is she granted? Select the best answer:

    A. Change

    B. Read

    C. Take Ownership

    D. No Access

13. You have created a share on a directory. The directory permissions are as follows: Change for the Sales group, and Read for Ann (who is member of the SalesManagers and the Sales group). The share has Read permission for the Sales group. What kind of access is she granted? Select the best answer:

    A. Change

    B. Read

    C. Take Ownership

    D. No Access

14. You have created a share on a directory. The directory permissions are as follows: Change for the Sales group, and Read for Ann (who is member of the SalesManagers and the Sales group). The share has Read permission for the Sales group. What kind of access has Ronnie, who is member of the SalesManager group? Select the best answer:

    A. Change

    B. Read

    C. Take Ownership

    D. No Access

15. Which of the following statements is true about the following share on the MEGAMACH server: \\MEGAMACH\machine$

    Select the best answer:

    A. It is an administrative share.

    B. It is a hidden share.

    C. The share can be accessed only from Windows NT computers.

    D. The dollar sign ($) is invalid for share names. This share cannot exist.

16. Which of the following statements is true about administrative shares?

    A. Administrative shares cannot be disabled.

    B. Administrative shares are available to Administrators, Server Operators, and Account Operators.

    C. Administrative shares can be turned off.

    D. Administrative shares are available on Windows NT Server only.

17. What are the default file and directory permissions on an NTFS partition? Select the best answer:

    A. Everyone Full Control

    B. Administrators Full Control, Everyone Read

    C. Everyone Change

    D. Everyone No Access

18. Ben has been offered a management position in another company and is about to leave the company. His replacement, Joey, asks him to turn over his project files. Which of the following is best way to achieve this?

    A. Ask the administrator to assign permissions on Ben's files to the Joey.

    B. Ben must grant Take Ownership permission to Joey on his files and then Joey must take ownership on these.

    C. Joey must execute Take Ownership from the Security tab on Ben's files and directories.

    D. None of this works. Ben has to e-mail the files to Joey.

3

3.4 Answers and Explanations: Practice Problems

1. **D** When copying, the file inherits compression and permissions from the destination folder.
2. **B** Moving on the same disk retains compression and permissions.
3. **D** Moving to a different disk is a copy operation followed by a delete operation.
4. **B** You can convert FAT partitions to NTFS at any time using the command line utility convert.exe.
5. **D** NTFS compression is performed on the fly and does not warrant special attention by applications accessing the compressed files.
6. **B** COMPACT *.* /F forces all files in the directory to be recompressed.
7. **C** You can't format a floppy disk with NTFS because of its overhead.
8. **D** NT currently does not support FAT32.
9. **A, C, D** HPFS is no longer supported with NT 4.
10. **C** Only NTFS allows you to set permissions.
11. **D** No Access overrides all other permissions.
12. **A** Permissions are cumulative.
13. **B** Permissions are cumulative.
14. **D** No Access overrides all others.
15. **B** Trailing "$" denotes hidden shares.
16. **C** You can only turn off administrative shares.
17. **A** Standard installation sets permission to Everyone Full Control.
18. **B** Take Ownership enables others to gain control over files owned by a user granting Take Ownership.

3.4 Key Words

Copying
Moving
NTFS compression
Compact.exe
Sharing
Server managers
Share permissions
Net share
Monitoring shares
Managing shares
NTFS permissions
Take Ownership
Auditing
File Delete Child

Practice Exam: Managing Resources

Use this practice exam to test your mastery of Planning. This practice exam is 9 questions long, so you should try to finish the test within 15 minutes or so. Keep in mind that the passing Microsoft score is 76.4 percent. There will be two types of questions:

- Multiple Choice—Select the correct answer.
- Multiple Multiple Choice—Select all answers that are correct.

Begin as soon as you are ready. Answers follow the test.

1. Which of the following groups are built-in global groups on Windows NT domain controllers? Select all that apply:

   A. Domain Users

   B. Domain Operators

   C. Domain Guests

   D. None of the above

2. You want to prevent users on your system from changing back to their original passwords right after they have been forced to change it by your account policy (password expiration set to 25 days). How can you circumvent this problem? Select the best answer:

   A. Enable Password never expires for all users.

   B. Set the maximum password age to 2.

   C. Set the minimum password age to 24.

   D. Keep a password history.

3. You are creating a single account for your summer interns. How can you prevent a single intern from changing the password for the user account? Select the best answer:

   A. Set Password Expires for this account to the amount of time this account is intended to be used.

   B. Use a blank password.

   C. Enable "User cannot change password."

   D. Revoke the right "Change password" from the account the summer interns will be using.

4. System Policy Editor comes with the following policy templates (select all that apply):

   A. common.adm

   B. winnt.adm

   C. windows.adm

   D. user.adm

5. Where are the policy template files stored by default? Select the best answer:

   A. <winnt_root>\inf

   B. <winnt_root>\profiles

   C. <winnt_root>\system32\config

   D. <winnt_root>\System32\Repl\Import\Scripts

6. Which of the following are client-based administration tools for Windows NT? Select all that apply:

   A. Services for Macintosh

   B. Remoteboot Manager

   C. File and Print Services for NetWare

   D. System Policy Editor

3

7. You have created an application pool share named POOL. You want to audit who executes a specific setup program. How can you achieve this? Select the best answer:

   A. Enable auditing on the share for Execute events.

   B. Enable auditing for the specific Setup program for Execute events only.

   C. You cannot do this.

   D. Enable auditing for the specific Setup program for Execute and Read events.

8. Which of the following statements isn't true about account types? Choose all the apply:

   A. Windows NT administrators can create two types of accounts: user accounts and group accounts.

   B. A user account can belong to one person only.

   C. A group account is limited to 256 users.

   D. A group account is a collection of users that holds common rights and permissions by way of its association with the group.

   E. All of the above are true.

9. Windows NT users get their rights and permissions in which of the following ways? Choose all that apply:

   A. They are explicitly assigned a right or permission through user accounts.

   B. They acquire rights after the administrator manually enables such rights.

   C. They are members of a group that has a right or permission.

   D. They acquire rights from another user.

Answers and Explanations: Practice Exam

1. **A, C** Domain Users and Domain Guests are built-in global groups on Windows NT domain controllers.

2. **D** Password history prevents users from using old passwords.

3. **C** You can prevent a single intern from changing the password for the user account by enabling "User cannot change password."

4. **A, B, C** The user.adm file doesn't come with System Policy Editor.

5. **A** <winnt_root>\inf is the default location for system policy templates.

6. **A, B, D** File and Print Services for NetWare are not part of the client-based administration tools for NT.

7. **B** Auditing enables you to monitor which files are accessed.

8. **C** A group account can hold an unlimited amount of users.

9. **A, C** Users get rights when they are explicitly assigned a right or permission through their accounts, or when they are members of a group that has a right or permission.

Chapter 4

Connectivity

The "Connectivity" section of the Microsoft Exam (70-67) includes the following objectives:

- Configure Windows NT Server for interoperability with NetWare servers using various tools. Tools include Gateway Services for NetWare and Migration Tool for NetWare.
- Install and configure Remote Access Service (RAS). Configuration options include configuring RAS communications, configuring RAS protocols, configuring RAS security, and configuring dial-up networking clients.

4.1 NetWare Connectivity

Microsoft Windows NT Server provides features that permit connectivity to NetWare-based systems. The following sections outline these features, which include: NetWare Gateway Service (GSNW), Client Services for NetWare (CSNW), and the Migration Tool for NetWare.

A. Gateway Services for NetWare (GSNW)

Gateway Services for NetWare (GSNW) is available only with Windows NT Server. GSNW performs the following functions:

- Enables Windows NT Server systems to access NetWare file and print resources directly.
- Enables a Windows NT Server to act as a gateway to NetWare resources. Non-NetWare clients on a Windows NT network then can access NetWare resources through the gateway as if they were accessing Windows NT resources without any need for NetWare client licensing (see fig. 4.1.1).

GSNW is a practical solution for occasional NetWare access, but is not designed to serve as a high-volume solution for a busy network. Because all Windows NT clients must reach the NetWare server through a single connection, there is potential for a bottleneck and performance diminishes considerably with increased traffic.

Network clients with operating systems that use Server Message Block (SMB)—Windows NT, Windows 95, and Windows for Workgroups—can access a share through a GSNW gateway. GSNW supports both NDS-based and bindery-based NetWare systems.

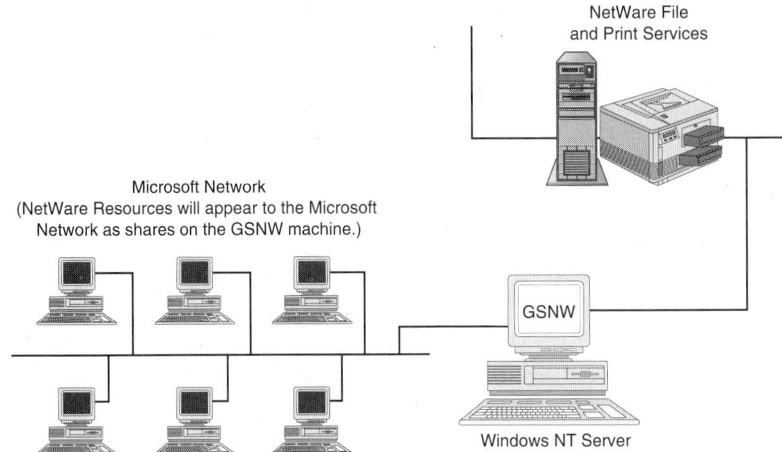

Figure 4.1.1 GSNW enables a Windows NT Server to act as a gateway to NetWare resources.

NetWare Directory Service (NDS) is a distributed database of network resources primarily associated with NetWare 4.x systems. Bindery-based NetWare networks are primarily associated with NetWare 3.x.

1. GSNW Installation and Configuration

In order to install GSNW, you must be logged on the NT Server as an Administrator. Before installing GSNW, you must remove any NetWare redirectors presently on your system (such as Novell NetWare services for Windows NT) and reboot the Server. GSNW is a network service; it is installed using the Services tab of the Control Panel Network application. To install GSNW, follow these steps:

1. Choose Start, Settings/Control Panel. Double-click on the Control Panel Network application icon.
2. In the Network application's Network dialog box, select the Services tab. Click on the Add button to open the Select Network Services dialog box.
3. Select Gateway (and Client) Services for NetWare in the Network Service list; then click on OK.
4. Windows NT prompts you for the location of the files (typically, the installation CD-ROM).
5. Windows NT asks if you want to restart your system. You must restart the system to enable the new service.

2. GSNW as a Gateway

To configure GSNW to act as a gateway to NetWare resources, you must have supervisor equivalence on the NetWare server, and perform the following steps:

1. Using NetWare's Syscon utility, create a group called NTGATEWAY on the NetWare server.
2. Using NetWare's Syscon utility, create a user account on the NetWare server for the gateway and add the gateway user account to the NTGATEWAY group.
3. Double-click on the GSNW icon in the Control Panel. The Gateway Service for NetWare dialog box appears. The Preferred Server, Default Tree and Context, Print Options, and Login Script Options frames are discussed in the following section.

4. To configure Windows NT to act as a gateway, click on the Gateway button. The Configure Gateway dialog box appears.
5. Select the Enable Gateway check box. In the Gateway Account text box, enter the name of the account you created on the NetWare server. Below the account name, enter the password for the account and retype the password in the Confirm Password text box.

GSNW essentially enables you to create a Windows NT share for a resource on a NetWare server. Microsoft network machines that use Server Message Block (SMB), such as Windows NT, Windows 95, and Windows for Workgroups, can then access the share even if they don't have NetWare client software. NetWare directories and volumes presently shared through a gateway appear in the Share name list at the bottom of the Configure Gateway dialog box.

To create a new share for a NetWare directory or volume, click on the Add button in the Configure Gateway dialog box. You are asked to enter a share name and a network path to the NetWare resource. You then can enter a drive letter for the share. The share appears to Windows NT, Windows 95, and Windows for Workgroups machines as a network drive on the gateway machine.

The Remove button in the Configure Gateway dialog box removes a gateway share. The Permissions button lets you set permissions for the share.

B. Client Services for NetWare (CSNW)

Client Services for NetWare (CSNW) enables a Windows NT Workstation to access file and print services on a NetWare server (see fig. 4.1.2). CSNW is incorporated into Windows NT Server's GSNW. GSNW and CSNW both support NDS-based and bindery-based NetWare servers. GSNW and CSNW also support Novell's NetWare Core Protocol (NCP) and Large Internet Protocol (LIP).

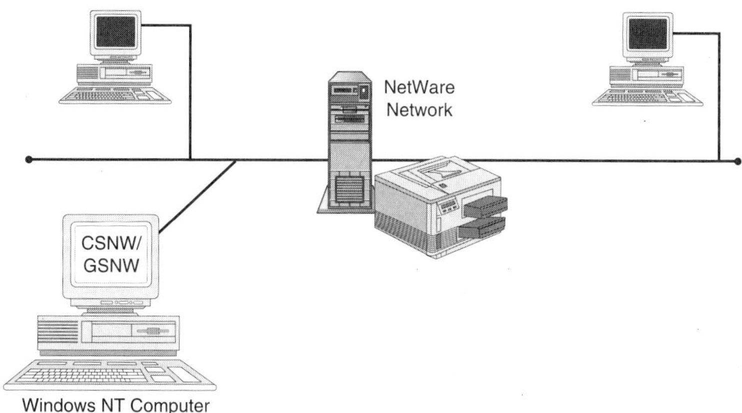

Figure 4.1.2 CSNW enables a Windows NT computer to access file and print services as a client on a NetWare network.

CSNW, like GSNW, is a network service; you install it using the Services tab of the Control Panel Network application. If you're running Windows NT Server, CSNW functions are installed automatically when you install GSNW.

The first time you log on after you install CSNW or GSNW, Windows NT prompts you to enter a preferred server and attempts to validate your credentials for the NetWare network.

The Select Preferred Server for NetWare dialog box shows the name of the user attempting to log on and a drop-down list of available NetWare servers. As implied by the username parameter, this is a per-user configuration parameter. The selected server is stored in HKEY_CURRENT_USER, not HKEY_LOCAL_MACHINE.

Choose <None> in the Select Preferred Server for NetWare dialog box if you don't want to have a preferred server authenticate your logon request. Choosing the Cancel button just defers the decision until the next time you log on.

After you select a preferred server, Windows NT always tries to have that server authenticate the user. If the server is unavailable, the user is prompted for a new preferred server. A user can change his or her preferred server at any time via the new CSNW icon in Control Panel (which was added during installation of CSNW).

Double-clicking on the GSNW icon in Control Panel opens the Gateway Service for NetWare dialog box, which lets you select a preferred server and a default tree and context for the NetWare network.

You also can choose to run a NetWare logon script. To connect to a client to a NetWare server's printer, use the Add Printer Wizard in the Printers folder as you would for any Network attached printer device.

C. Migration Tool for NetWare

To ease the transition process from NetWare to NT Server, Microsoft provides a tool to automate the migration process. The Migration Tool for NetWare transfers file and directory information along with user and group account information from a NetWare server to a Windows NT domain controller. The Migration Tool for NetWare also preserves logon scripts and directory and file effective rights. You can optionally indicate which accounts, files, or directories you want migrated. For obvious security reasons, the Migration Tool for NetWare cannot preserve the original NetWare passwords, but it does provide the capability of setting up new passwords.

The Migration Tool for NetWare can migrate NetWare resources to the domain controller on which it is running, or it can execute from a separate NT Server or Workstation and migrate the NetWare resources to a domain controller somewhere else on the network. NWLink and Gateway Services for NetWare must be running on both the computer running Migration Tool for NetWare and on the domain controller receiving the migration.

To run the Migration Tool for NetWare, choose Start, Run, and type **nwconv** in the Run dialog box.

The Migration Tool for NetWare provides a number of options for transferring file and account information. Always migrate files and directories to an NTFS partition if possible, because NTFS file and directory permissions provide an equivalent to the trustee rights specified for these resources in the NetWare environment.

4.1.1 Exercise: Creating a Gateway to a NetWare Directory Using GSNW

Note: This exercise requires both an NT Server and a NetWare Server.

Exercise 4.1.1 examines the process of establishing a gateway to a NetWare directory using Gateway Services for NetWare.

1. Log on to the NT Server as an Administrator if you have not done so already.
2. From the Control Panel, double-click on the Network icon.
3. Choose the Services tab and click on the Add button.
4. Select Gateway (and Client) Services for NetWare in the Network Service list; then click on OK.
5. After all the required files are copied, click on Yes to restart your system.

   What new icon has been added to the NT Server's Control Panel?
6. From the NetWare server, open the Syscon utility.
7. Create a group called NTGATEWAY.
8. Create a user account for the gateway and add the gateway user account to the NTGATEWAY group.
9. Back at the NT Server, double-click on the GSNW icon in Control Panel. The Gateway Service for NetWare dialog box appears. To configure Windows NT to act as a gateway, click on the Gateway button.

   Under what circumstances would you want to utilize the Gateway Service for NetWare?
10. The Configure Gateway dialog box appears. Click on the Enable Gateway check box. In the Gateway Account text box, enter the name of the account you created on the NetWare server. Below the account name, enter the password for the account and retype the password in the Confirm Password text box.
11. To create a new share for the NetWare directory or volume, click on the Add button. You are asked to enter a share name and a network path to the NetWare resource. You then can enter a drive letter for the share.
12. From another SMB-compatible computer on the Microsoft network (Windows NT, Windows 95, or Windows for Workgroups), access the gateway computer through Network Neighborhood. Look for the drive letter you entered in step 5 for the NetWare directory. Double-click on the drive letter and browse the NetWare files.

4.1 Practice Problems

1. When using GSNW to provide access to NetWare resources for Microsoft clients, what are the NetWare licensing requirements for the clients?

   A. Each of the clients must obtain individual NetWare licensing.

   B. No additional NetWare licensing is required.

   C. You need to obtain NetWare licensing only for the maximum number of clients that will connect at any given time.

   D. None of the above.

2. After installing a NetWare gateway using GSNW, you can then create a share on the gateway machine for NetWare files using what?

   A. GSNW

   B. Control Panel

   C. Explorer or My Computer

   D. Any of the above

3. The Migration Tool for NetWare is not capable of preserving which of the following?

   A. Accounts

   B. Files

   C. Rights

   D. Directories

   E. Passwords

4. Your company currently has several thousand NT clients and several hundred NetWare clients running on separate networks. The NetWare server contains vital information that needs to be accessed continuously by everyone. The managers have requested that you provide a plan for providing equal access between these networks. What course of action would be the best solution?

   A. Install the GSNW service.

   B. Report that a solution is not possible.

   C. Purchase NetWare client licenses for all the NT side clients in order to allow them direct access to the server.

   D. Use the Migration Tool for NetWare, and convert the NetWare clients to NT.

5. How do you attach to a NetWare server's printer?

   A. Use File and Print Services for NetWare (FPNW).

   B. Use the Add Printer Wizard in the Printers folder.

   C. You cannot connect to a NetWare Server printer.

   D. Use the DLC protocol.

6. Installing what service will enable your Windows NT Server machine to access file and print resources on a NetWare server?

   A. File and Print Services for NetWare (FPNW)

   B. Client Services for NetWare (CSNW)

   C. Gateway Services for NetWare (GSNW)

   D. Directory Service Manager for NetWare (DSMN)

7. Which service must be established on an NT Server before you can share NetWare print queues?

   A. FPNW

   B. GSNW

   C. NetWare Migration Tool

   D. DLC

8. Which two statements regarding GSNW are accurate:

   A. GSNW attaches the NT Server to the NetWare server as a client.

   B. GSNW shares user account information between NetWare servers and NT Server.

   C. GSNW emulates a NetWare Server to clients using the NetWare Requester.

   D. GSNW permits NT Server to request resources from the NetWare server, and to share them with clients on the Microsoft network.

9. Some of your Microsoft network clients use an old application that does not send a proper end-of-file message to the printer on the attached NetWare server utilizing GSNW on an NT Server. What simple step could you perform to overcome this situation?

   A. Move the printer to the NT side of the network.

   B. Upgrade the application to a NetWare-aware version.

   C. Open the GSNW tool in the Control Panel and select the Add Form Feed option.

   D. Open the Printer device properties, choose the Device settings tab, and select the Add Dorm Feed option.

10. The Migration Tool for NetWare can migrate NetWare resources to which type of domain controller?

   A. Only to the domain controller on which the Migration Tool for NetWare is currently running.

   B. Besides the domain controller that is running the migration process, it can migrate NetWare resources to any available domain controller running NWLink and GSNW.

   C. Besides the domain controller that is running the migration process, it can migrate NetWare resources to any available domain controller that has an available NTFS partition.

   D. The migration process must transfer resources only to a separate domain controller running NWLink, GSNW, and has an available NTFS partition.

11. What must be running on the NT Server that is going to be receiving the migration, before using the Migration Tool for NetWare?

   A. GSNW

   B. NWLink

   C. NTFS

   D. IP

12. If your Microsoft network has a relatively small number of clients who want to be able to access resources on a NetWare server, what would be the best solution?

   A. Use floppy disks to transfer any needed files.

   B. Purchase additional NetWare client licenses as needed, and attach them to the NetWare server.

   C. Use the NWCONV tool to migrate the NetWare server resources to an NT Server.

   D. Install and configure GSNW.

13. When using the Migration Tool for NetWare, why is it preferable to migrate the NetWare resources to an NT Server utilizing NTFS?

   A. Using a non-NTFS partition will cause significant performance problems.

   B. There is no choice; you must use an NTFS partition during the migration process.

C. NTFS file and directory permissions provide an equivalent to the trustee rights specified in the NetWare environment.

D. NTFS is the only way to properly transfer account password information to the NT Server.

14. Which Microsoft network clients can access NetWare resources through a NetWare gateway on a Windows NT Server?

A. Currently, Windows 95 and Windows NT are supported.

B. Any Microsoft client that uses Server Message Blocks: WFWG, Windows 95, and Windows NT.

C. Any client using Microsoft's NWLink IPX/SPX protocol stack.

D. MS-DOS, Windows 3.x, LAN Manager, WFWG, Windows 95, NT Workstation, and Macintosh.

15. What command is used in the Run box to start the Migration Tool for NetWare?

A. CONVNW.EXE

B. MTNW.EXE

C. CONVNW.COM

D. NWCONV.EXE

16. What tool must be used on the NetWare server to create the necessary group and account on the NetWare server to facilitate the installation of GSNW on a NT Server?

A. SYSCON

B. PCON

C. User Manager

D. DSMN

17. After installing GSNW and rebooting the NT Server, you are prompted to choose a preferred server. Which server option should you choose in the Select Preferred Server for NetWare dialog box if you don't want to have a preferred server authenticate your logon request?

A. <None>

B. The NetWare server with the least amount of activity

C. The name of the NetWare server that was initially established during the installation of GSNW

D. <All>

18. What is the primary purpose of GSNW?

A. GSNW essentially enables you to create a Windows NT share for a resource on a NetWare server.

B. GSNW provides an essential component utilized by the Migration Tool for NetWare.

C. GSNW provides an economical alternative to purchasing NetWare client licensing.

D. A and C.

19. During the installation of GSNW, which tab of the Network application's dialog box is utilized?

A. Identification

B. Services

C. Protocols

D. Adapters

E. Bindings

20. A GSNW gateway can provide Windows NT networks with convenient access to NetWare resources, but isn't an appropriate solution under which of the following circumstances?

A. Serving as a high-volume Microsoft client to NetWare resource solution for a busy network.

B. Sharing multiple NetWare resources with Microsoft clients.

C. Providing an economical solution when only a nominal number of Microsoft clients will be accessing NetWare resources.

D. When reducing administrative overhead is desirable.

4.1 Answers and Explanations: Exercises

The Gateway Services for NetWare icon is the new icon added to the NT Servers Control Panel in step 5.

In step 9, you would want to utilize the Gateway Service for NetWare to permit SMB-compatible computers on the NT network (Windows NT, Windows 95, or Windows for Workgroups) access to resources on the NetWare server.

4.1 Answers and Explanations: Practice Problems

1. **B** It is not necessary for clients accessing the NetWare server through the NT GSNW service to have NetWare client licensing (just the NT Server itself).
2. **A** To create a new share for a NetWare directory or volume, click on the Add button in the Configure Gateway dialog box within the GSNW application.
3. **E** For security reasons, the Migration Tool for NetWare cannot preserve the original NetWare password, but it provides you with the capability of setting a new password from within the tool.
4. **D** Under this scenario, the best option is to use the Migration Tool for NetWare and convert all users to an NT environment. Otherwise, there is tremendous potential for a bottleneck at the GSNW NT server.
5. **B** The connection to a NetWare server's printer is relatively transparent. Simply use the same basic procedures you use to connect to any network attached printer device.
6. **C** GSNW provides access to file and printer resources on a NetWare server.
7. **B** GSNW provides accessibility to NetWare printer queues in addition to file resources.
8. **A** As far as the NetWare server is concerned, the NT Server running GSNW is just another client. The NT Server can then share the NetWare resources among the Microsoft network.
9. **C** By using the Form Feed option, you can often overcome such printing issues.
10. **B** The Migration Tool for NetWare can migrate NetWare resources to the domain controller on which it is running, or it can execute from a separate NT Server or Workstation and migrate the NetWare resources to a domain controller somewhere else on the network. Both the domain controller running the migration process and the domain controller receiving the migration process resources must be running NWLink and GSNW.
11. **A, B** GSNW and the NWLink protocol stack must be running before the Migration Tool for NetWare will function properly.
12. **D** GSNW is a practical solution unless you have a busy, high-volume network with a substantial number of clients who want to utilize the GSNW.
13. **C** Although it is not necessary to migrate NetWare resources to an NTFS partition, it is always the preferred method in order to preserve equivalent rights.
14. **B** Clients must support Server Message Blocks (SMB) in order to access a share through a GSNW gateway.
15. **D** The executable filename is NWCONV.EXE, and is located in the %SYSTEMROOT%\SYSTEM32 directory.
16. **A** NetWare's SYSCON is utilized to create and manage groups and accounts on a NetWare server.
17. **A** If you do not want to have a specific NetWare server assigned as a preferred server, choose the <none> option. This permits any available NetWare server to authenticate your logon request.

18. **A** GSNW essentially enables you to create a Windows NT share for a resource on a NetWare server. By attaching an NT Server to NetWare resources utilizing GSNW, the NT Server can then share the attached resources as needed.

19. **B** The GSNW service, as well as all other network services, is installed under the Services tab within the Network application in the Control Panel.

20. **A** Should the situation indicate that a high volume of traffic is orchestrated through the GSNW, it is advisable to seek an alternative solution, such as migrating the NetWare server resources to NT using the Migration Tool for NetWare.

4.1 Key Words

Gateway Services for NetWare

Client Services for NetWare

Server Message Block

Preferred Server

Migration Tool for NetWare

NetWare Directory Service (NDS)

4.2 Remote Access Service (RAS)

Windows NT *Remote Access Service* (RAS) provides the technology to permit an NT-based computer to connect to a remote network via a dial-up connection and fully participate in the network as a network client. RAS also enables your Windows NT computer to receive dial-up connections from remote computers.

RAS supports SLIP and PPP line protocols, and NetBEUI, TCP/IP, and IPX network protocols. Because so many Internet users access their service providers using a phone line, RAS often serves as an Internet interface.

The dial-up networking application (in the Accessories program group) lets you create phonebook entries, which are preconfigured dial-up connections to specific sites. The Telephony application in the Control Panel enables the remote user to preconfigure dialing properties for different dialing locations.

RAS can connect to a remote computer using any of the following media:

- **Public Switched Telephone Network (PSTN).** (Also known as the phone company.) RAS can connect using a modem through an ordinary phone line.
- **X.25. A packet-switched network.** Computers access the network via a Packet Assembler Disassembler device (PAD). X.25 supports dial-up or direct connections.
- **Null modem cable.** A cable that connects two computers directly. The computers then communicate using their modems (rather than network adapter cards).
- **ISDN.** A digital line that provides faster communication and more bandwidth than a normal phone line. (It also costs more—that's why not everybody has it.) A computer must have a special ISDN card to access an ISDN line.

Windows NT 4 also includes a new feature called Multilink. Using Multilink, a Windows NT computer can form a RAS connection using more than one physical pathway. One Multilink connection, for example, can use two modems at once (or one modem line and one ISDN line) to form a single logical link. By using multiple pathways for one connection, Multilink can greatly increase bandwidth. Of course, the computer has to have access to more than one pathway (that is, it must have two modems installed) or you can't use it.

A. RAS Security

Like everything else in Windows NT, RAS is designed for security. Here are some of RAS' security features:

- **Auditing.** RAS can leave an audit trail, enabling you to see who logged on when and what authentication they provided.
- **Callback security.** You can enable RAS server to use callback (hang up all incoming calls and call the caller back), and you can limit callback numbers to prearranged sites that you know are safe.
- **Encryption.** RAS can encrypt logon information, or it can encrypt all data crossing the connection.

- **Security hosts.** In case Windows NT isn't safe enough, you can add an extra dose of security by using a third-party intermediary security host—a computer that stands between the RAS client and the RAS server and requires an extra round of authentication.
- **PPTP filtering.** You can tell Windows NT to filter out all packets except ultra-safe PPTP packets (described in the section "PPTP").

B. RAS Line Protocols

RAS supports the following line protocols:

- SLIP
- PPP
- PPTP

1. SLIP

Serial Line Internet Protocol (SLIP) is a standard protocol for serial line connections over TCP/IP networks. SLIP is relatively old for the computer age—it was developed in 1984—and lacks some of the features that are available in PPP. SLIP operates only with older modems and will not operate at speeds greater than 19.2 baud. Each node in a SLIP connection must have a static IP address; that is, you can't use Windows NT features such as DHCP and WINS. Unlike PPP, SLIP does not support NetBEUI or IPX; you must use TCP/IP with SLIP. Also, SLIP cannot encrypt logon information.

2. PPP

Point-to-Point Protocol (PPP) was originally conceived as a deluxe version of SLIP. Like SLIP, PPP is an industry standard for point-to-point communications, but PPP offers several advantages over SLIP. Most notably, PPP isn't limited to TCP/IP. PPP also supports IPX, NetBEUI, and several other network protocols, such as AppleTalk and DECnet.

Because PPP supports so many protocols, it allows much more flexibility in configuring network communications. Windows NT automatically binds RAS to TCP/IP, NetBEUI, and IPX if those protocols are installed at the same time as RAS.

Another advantage of RAS is that it supports encrypted passwords.

3. PPTP

Point-to-Point Tunneling Protocol (PPTP) is related to PPP, but is different enough, and important enough, to deserve its own section. PPTP is a protocol that lets you transmit PPP packets over a TCP/IP network securely. Because the Internet is a TCP/IP network, PPTP enables highly private network links over the otherwise highly public Internet. PPTP connections are encrypted, making them a nearly impenetrable to virtual voyeurs.

In fact, PPTP is part of an emerging technology called Virtual Private Networks (VPNs). The point of VPN is to provide corporate networks with the same (or close to the same) security over the Internet that they would have over a direct connection.

Another exciting advantage of PPTP (and another reason that it fits nicely into the scheme of the virtual private network) is that PPTP doesn't discriminate among protocols. Because PPP supports NetBEUI, IPX, and other network protocols, and because a PPTP operates on PPP packets, PPTP actually lets you transmit non-TCP/IP protocols over the Internet.

Because PPTP provides intranet privacy over the open Internet, it can significantly reduce costs in some situations. Networks that once would have depended on extravagant direct connections now can hook up via a local Internet service provider.

C. Routing with RAS

RAS comes with a NetBIOS gateway. A RAS client using the NetBEUI protocol can connect to a RAS server and, using the NetBIOS gateway on the RAS server, can gain access to the remote LAN beyond the gateway regardless of what protocol the LAN is using (see fig. 4.2.1).

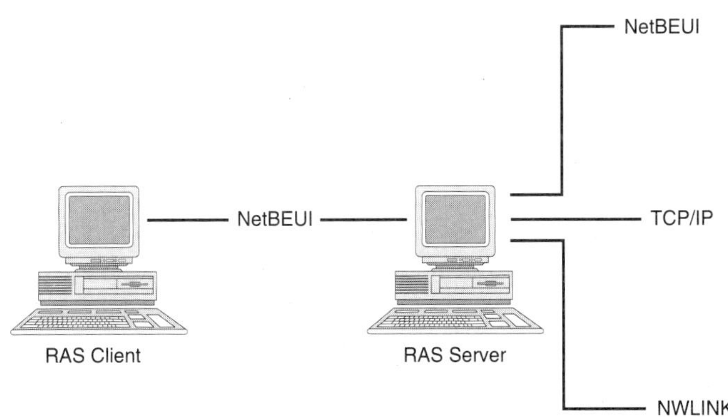

Figure 4.2.1 RAS can act as a NetBIOS gateway, connecting NetBEUI clients with networks using other protocols.

RAS can act as a TCP/IP or IPX router. RAS also is capable of serving as a Service Advertising Protocol (SAP) agent. (*SAP* is a NetWare protocol that lets servers advertise their services to the network.)

D. The Telephony API

The *Telephony Application Program Interface* (TAPI) provides a standard interface with telephony applications. (Telephony applications are applications that enable a computer to interact with telephone services, such as a network fax service or an online answering machine). TAPI oversees communication between the computer and the phone system, including initiating, answering, and ending calls. In effect, TAPI is a device driver for the phone system.

Windows NT's basic TAPI settings are set up in the Dialing Properties dialog box. The Dialing Properties dialog box maintains location and area code settings, as well as calling card settings and a setting for the dialing type (tone or pulse). The first time you run a TAPI-aware application, you have a chance to set dialing properties. Or, you can reach the Dialing Properties dialog box directly in several ways, including through the Control Panel Telephony and Modems applications.

E. Installing and Configuring RAS

RAS is a network service, and, like other network services, is installed and removed using the Services tab of the Control Panel Network application. Install RAS as follows:

1. In the Control Panel, double-click on the Network application icon.
2. In the Network dialog box that appears, click on the Services tab and then click on the Add button. The Select Network Service dialog box appears.
3. In the Select Network Service dialog box, choose Remote Access Service from the Network Service list and click on OK. Windows NT prompts you for the path to the Windows NT Installation CD-ROM.
4. Windows NT prompts you for name of an RAS-capable device and an associated communications port. A modem installed on your system typically appears as a default value. Click on OK to accept the modem, or click on the down arrow to choose another RAS-capable device on your system. You also can install a new modem or an X.25 Pad using the Install Modem and Install X25 Pad buttons.
5. The Remote Access Setup dialog box appears. Click on the Configure button to specify whether to use the port for dial-out connections, dial-in connections, or both. The Port Usage options apply only to the port. In other words, you could configure COM1 for Dial out only and COM2 for Receive only. In the Remote Access Setup dialog box, you also can add or remove a port entry from the list. The Clone button lets you copy a port configuration.
6. Click on the Network button in the Remote Access Setup dialog box to specify the network protocols for your Remote Access Service to support. The Server Settings options in the lower portion of the Network Configuration dialog box appear only if you configure the port to receive calls. Select one or more dial-out protocols. If you want RAS take care of receiving calls, select one or more server protocols, and choose an encryption setting for incoming connections. You also can enable Multilink. Multilink allows one logical connection to use several physical pathways.

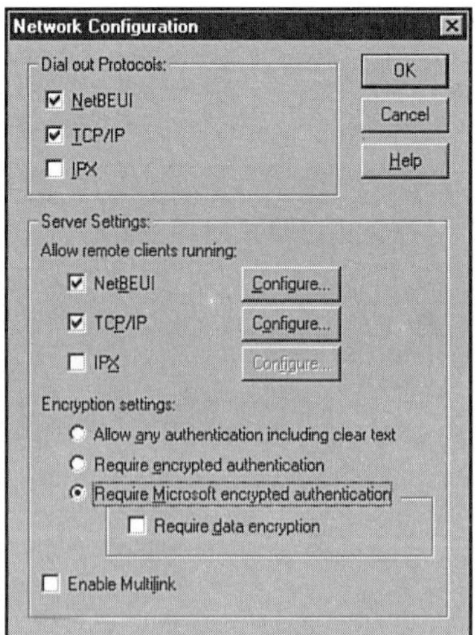

Figure 4.2.2 The Network Configuration dialog box.

Note in figure 4.2.2 that a Configure button follows each of the Server Settings protocol options. Each Configure button opens a dialog box that enables you to specify configuration options for the protocol, as follows:

- The RAS Server NetBEUI Configuration dialog box lets you specify whether the incoming caller will have access to the entire network or to only the RAS server.

  By confining a caller's access to the RAS server, you improve security (because the caller can access only one computer), but you reduce functionality because the caller can't access information on other machines.

- The RAS Server TCP/IP Configuration dialog box lets you define how the RAS server assigns IP addresses to dial-up clients (see fig. 4.2.3). You can use DHCP to assign client addresses, or you can configure RAS to assign IP addresses from a static address pool. If you choose to use a static address pool, input the beginning and ending addresses in the range. To exclude a range of addresses within the address pool, enter the beginning and ending addresses in the range you're excluding in the From and To boxes, then click on the Add button. The excluded range appears in the Excluded ranges box.

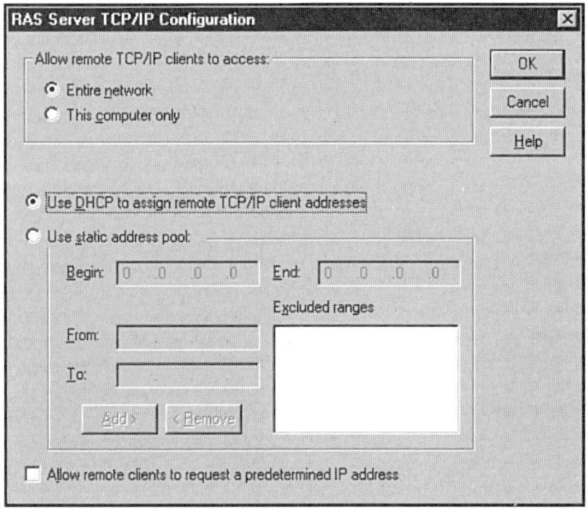

Figure 4.2.3 The RAS Server TCP/IP Configuration dialog box.

  The RAS Server TCP/IP Configuration dialog box lets you specify whether a client can access the entire network or only the RAS server. By confining a caller's access to the RAS server, you improve security (because the caller can access only one computer), but you reduce functionality because the caller can't access information on other machines.

- The RAS Server IPX Configuration dialog box lets you specify how the RAS server assigns IPX network numbers.

  You also can specify whether a client can access the entire network or only the RAS server. By confining a caller's access to the RAS server, you improve security (because the caller can access only one computer), but you reduce functionality because the caller can't access information on other machines.

7. After you define the RAS settings to your satisfaction, click on OK.
8. The Network application's Services tab appears in the foreground. You should see Remote Access Service in the list of services. Click on the Close button.
9. Windows NT asks whether you want to Restart your computer. Choose Yes.

F. Changing the RAS Configuration

To view or change your RAS configuration, follow these steps:

1. Double-click on the Network icon in the Control Panel and select the Network application's Services tab.
2. Select Remote Access Service from the services list and click on the Properties button.
3. The Remote Access Setup dialog box appears. Specify your new RAS configuration as described in steps 5 to 7 in the preceding section.

G. Dial-Up Networking

The Dial-Up Networking application lets you establish remote connections with other computers. The most common uses for Dial-Up Networking are as follows:

- Accessing an Internet service provider
- Accessing a remote Windows NT computer or domain

You can open the Dial-Up Networking application as follows:

1. Choose Start, Programs, Accessories.
2. Click on the Dial-Up Networking icon.

Dial-Up Networking maintains a list of phonebook entries. A *phonebook entry* is a bundle of information that Windows NT needs to establish a specific connection. You can use the Dial-Up Networking application to create a phonebook entry for your access provider, your Windows NT domain, or any other dial-up connection. When it's time to connect, select a phonebook entry from the drop-down menu at the top of the screen and click on the Dial button. If you access the phonebook entry often, you can create a Desktop shortcut that lets you access the phonebook entry directly.

You can create a new phonebook entry as follows:

1. Click on the New button in the Dial-Up Networking dialog box to open the New Phonebook Entry dialog box.
2. In the New Phonebook Entry Basic tab, specify a name for the entry, an optional comment, and the phone number you want Windows NT to dial to make the connection. The Alternates button beside the phone number box lets you specify a prioritized list of alternative phone numbers. You also can specify a different modem or configure a modem from the Basic tab.
3. In the New Phonebook Entry Server tab, specify the communications protocol for the dial-up server (in the Dial-up server type combo box) and the network protocol. If you select the TCP/IP network protocol, click on the TCP/IP Settings button to configure TCP/IP settings.
4. The New Phonebook Entry Script tab defines some of the connection's logon properties. You can tell Windows NT to pop up a terminal window after dialing or to run a logon script after dialing. A terminal window enables you to interactively log on to the remote server in terminal mode. The Run this script radio button option automates the logon process. For more information on dial-up logon scripts, click on the Edit script button, which places you in a file that provides instructions and sample logon scripts, called SWITCH.INF. The Before dialing button lets you specify a terminal window or a logon script to execute before you dial.

5. In the New Phonebook Entry Security tab, you can require encrypted authentication, or you can elect to accept any authentication including clear text. You also can specify data encryption.
6. The New Phonebook Entry X.25 tab serves only for X.25 service. Select an X.25 access provider from the Network combo box and enter the requested information.
7. After you make changes to the New Phonebook Entry tab, click on OK. The new phonebook entry appears in the Dial-Up Networking dialog box.

1. Editing a Phonebook Entry and Other Options

The More button in the Dial-Up Networking dialog box offers several options. Figure 4.2.4 shows the More menu.

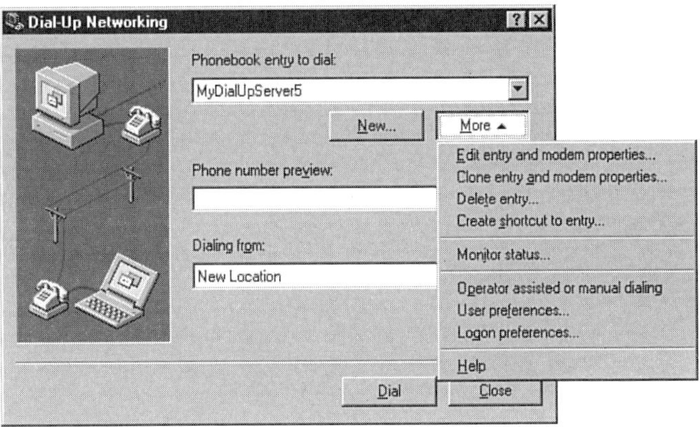

Figure 4.2.4 The Dial-up Networking More menu.

The following list describes the More menu options.

- **Edit entry and modem properties.** Returns you to the setup tabs you configured in the preceding section.
- **Create shortcut to entry.** Creates a shortcut to the active phonebook entry.
- **Monitor status.** Opens the Control Panel Dial-Up Networking Monitor.
- **User preferences.** Opens a User Preferences dialog box that presents the following four tabs:
  - **Dialing.** Lets you specify dialing options, such as the number of redial attempts and the time between redial attempts. You also can use the Dialing tab to enable or disable Autodial (see the following section).
  - **Callback.** Tells Windows NT what to do if the server you connect to offers callback. You can specify a number, you can elect to skip callback, or you can tell NT to prompt at the time callback is offered.
  - **Appearance.** Offers some dial-time interface options.
  - **Phonebook.** Lets you specify a Dial-Up Networking phonebook. Phonebook entries are stored in a file with the .pbk extension. The default phonebook is the system phonebook. Using the Phonebook tab, you can place an entry in your personal phonebook (a user-specific phonebook), or you can choose a different phonebook.

- Logon preferences. Configures Dialing, Callback, Appearance, and Phonebook settings for a remote Windows NT logon. The Logon preferences options are very similar to the User preferences options in the previous discussion. The difference is that the User preferences options apply to a user who is already logged on to Windows NT and is trying to connect to a remote machine. The Logon preferences apply to a user who isn't yet logged on to Windows NT and wants to log on directly to a Windows NT domain via a remote connection. The Windows NT Ctrl+Alt+Del logon dialog box includes the Logon using dial-up networking check box. If you enable this check box and log on using Dial-Up Networking, the preferences you set in the Logon preferences dialog box apply.

The Logon preferences dialog box doesn't appear unless you log on as an Administrator.

The Location button in the Dial-Up Networking dialog box lets you set a dialing prefix or suffix or specify a Telephony dialing location.

2. AutoDial

Windows NT includes a feature called AutoDial. AutoDial automatically associates network connections with Phonebook entries. This means that if you attempt to access a file or directory that can be accessed only via a dial-up connection, Windows NT attempts to make the dial-up connection automatically.

AutoDial supports IP addresses, Internet host names, and NetBIOS names. By default, AutoDial is enabled. You can enable/disable AutoDial for specific calling locations using the Dialing tab of the User Preferences dialog box.

4.2.1 Exercise: Using Windows NT RAS and the AutoDial Feature

Exercise 4.2.1 outlines the process of establishing a RAS connection from a remote client to an NT domain and demonstrates the use of the AutoDial feature.

1. Log on to a Windows NT domain using dial-up networking. (Check the Logon using Dial-up Networking check box below the domain name in the Windows NT Logon dialog box.) Make sure that you are not connecting to the network locally.

   What step should you take to ensure that your network connection is truly remote?

2. Locate a text file or a word processing document on a shared directory somewhere on the domain using Network Neighborhood icon in Explorer. (Use a file type that your computer is configured to recognize automatically—click on Options in the Explorer View menu and choose the File Types tab for a list or registered file types. A .txt file or a Write file should work.) If Explorer can't find the other computers in the domain, pull down the Explorer menu and click on Find with the Computer option. Enter the name of the computer with the shared directory you want to access in the Find: Computer dialog and click on the Find Now button. The computer will appear as an icon in the Find:Computer dialog box. Double-click on the icon for a list of shared resources.

3. When you've located a file on the remote share, right-click on the file and choose Create Shortcut from the shortcut menu that appears. Create a shortcut to the file and drag the shortcut to the Desktop on your own computer.

4. Double-click on the shortcut to make sure it opens the file.
5. Shut down your system.
6. Log on again; this time, don't use dial-up networking. (Deselect the Logon Using Dial-up Networking check box.) You might get a message that says Windows NT could find the domain controller and logged you on using cached account information. Click on OK.
7. Wait until the logon process is finished. Double-click on the shortcut to the file on the remote domain.
8. If you selected the Always prompt before auto-dialing check box in the Appearances tab of the Dial-up Networking User Preferences dialog box, Windows NT will ask if you want to initiate a connection with the remote file. Click on Yes. AutoDial will automatically dial the remote network and attempt to initiate a connection to the file referenced in the shortcut.

4.2 Practice Problems

1. You want remote TCP/IP RAS clients to have access to the entire TCP/IP network, but right now they can only connect to the RAS server machine. What will enable the client to reach the network?

    A. The Entire Network check box in the Server tab of the Dial-up Networking Edit Phonebook Entry dialog box.

    B. The Entire Network radio button in the Remote Access Permissions dialog box of the Remote Access Admin application.

    C. The Entire Network radio button in the TCP/IP Configuration dialog box accessible via the Network button in the Remote Access Setup dialog box.

    D. A, B, and C are all necessary.

2. You have several salespeople who dial in to your network via RAS. How can you configure the security options in RAS so the users can minimize long-distance phone charges?

    A. Configure the user's Dial-Up Networking software to use PPTP, which bypasses the PSTN billing computers, thus giving the users free long-distance service.

    B. Configure the RAS service to perform a callback based on the number specified by the user dialing in to the RAS server. The server authenticates the logon and then disconnects and calls the user back at the specified number.

    C. Issue the users long-distance calling cards and have their RAS calls billed directly to the company.

    D. Make sure the users are calling only from public telephones and are making collect calls to the RAS server. Then configure the RAS server to accept collect calls.

3. Which types of communication-interface hardware can be utilized with RAS?

    A. Modem

    B. Network Interface Card (NIC)

    C. Null modem cable via serial ports

    D. ISDN card

4. A user is trying to dial in to the NT Server-based RAS server. The user is connecting, but is disconnected immediately and receives a message that says he or she isn't an authorized dial-in user. What is the first thing you should do?

    A. Restart the NT Server, because one of the modems must be disabled.

    B. Change the security configuration options on the RAS server to enable any authentication method including clear text.

    C. Check to make sure the user has dial-in permissions in User Manager for Domains.

    D. Tell the user to restart his/her remote system and try again.

5. What's the name of the feature that lets RAS use more than one communication channel at a time for the same connection?

    A. Multinet

    B. Multilink

    C. ISDN

    D. Multichannel

6. What is the primary use of RAS?

    A. To provide a method for connecting a remote client to the network via a dial-up connection and fully participate on the network.

    B. To provide permanent leased line links between LANs.

    C. For Network administrators to establish remote network management capability.

    D. To provide essential prerequisites for DSU/CSU connections.

7. If you're having problems with the RAS server, what can you do to have NT create a log?

   A. Under Remote Access Administrator, configure the logging option.

   B. Under Control Panel, Network, Services, configure RAS to write all connection information to the System log.

   C. In the Registry, set the parameter Logging under the following key to 1 to create a PPP.LOG file in the <winnt root>\system32\Ras directory: `HKEY_LOCAL_MACHINE\System\CurrentControlSet\Services\Rasman\ PPP\`.

   D. Run the program Raslog.exe to create a RAS log in the <winnt root>\system32\Ras directory.

8. You want to let users connect to your local area network using the Internet; however, you're concerned that security might be a problem. Which protocol should you use to ensure a reliable connection and a secure transmission of information?

   A. PPP

   B. SLIP

   C. IEEE 802.2

   D. PPTP

9. What is the name of the utility that enables remote users to access the network through an NT Workstation or Server?

   A. Remote Control

   B. Remote Access Service

   C. Remote Network Service

   D. The Internet

10. Which of the following serial protocols supports the NetBEUI, IPX/SPX, and TCP/IP transport protocols over RAS?

    A. PPP

    B. SLIP

    C. PPTPS

    D. IEEE 802.2

11. The type of connections that RAS supports is/are (select all that apply):

    A. PSTN (Public Switched Telephone Network)

    B. X.25

    C. IEEE X.400

    D. Null Modem Cable

    E. ISDN

    F. RadioLan

12. Identify the two serial protocols that RAS supports.

    A. IEEE 802.2 and X.25

    B. Ethernet and Token Ring

    C. SLIP and PPP

    D. ESLIP and PPTP

13. Your management is concerned that accessing the network via RAS might open up security problems. What features does RAS support that help alleviate some of these concerns?

    A. RAS supports the U.S. Government DES (Data Encryption Standard) and encrypts all data going across the communication channel.

    B. RAS, in fact, can be more secure than a LAN connection because of the Callback security, Encryption of userid and password information, and PPTP features.

    C. RAS is not secure over standard PSTN connections unless data scrambling equipment is used on both ends of the connection.

    D. You can obtain a C2 level version the RAS product that meets U.S. Government standards for security.

14. A user calls you and states that she's getting connected to the NT Workstation via RAS, but cannot see any resources on the network. What could be causing the problem?

    A. The user is using a userid that isn't configured to have network access via RAS.

    B. She's dialing in with a protocol configured for "This computer only" when it needs to configured for "Entire network."

    C. She needs to use a different protocol. NetBEUI isn't routable, so she can't see any other devices on the network if she's using it as the dial-in protocol.

    D. She needs to configure her RAS server to use ISDN because the PSTN can support only a limited amount of bandwidth.

15. You're trying to run a program from a NetWare server over your RAS connection. You have installed the NWLink-compatible transport protocol at your remote computer, but you still cannot connect to the NetWare server. What did you forget to do?

    A. You need to install the Client Service for NetWare (CSNW) so you can access a NetWare server using file and print services.

    B. You need to install the FPNW (File and Print Services for NetWare) on the RAS Server to gain access to the NetWare servers.

    C. You must dial in to the NetWare server directly.

    D. You have to change your protocol to TCP/IP and install TCP/IP on the NetWare server.

16. Users would like to be able to connect to the Internet using the company's T1 connection from home. You configure RAS to allow your users to dial in. What protocol must they use to dial in to the RAS server?

    A. IEEE 802.2

    B. Ethernet

    C. NetBEUI

    D. TCP/IP

17. Which statement below correctly identifies the differences between the RAS software running on Windows NT Workstation and RAS software running on Windows NT Server?

    A. When RAS is running on NT Workstation, you can access only the shared resources on that machine. When it is running on NT Server, you can access resources on the entire network.

    B. When RAS is running on NT Workstation, you can access shared resources on the entire network, except for resources on NetWare Servers. Before you can do so, you must be running RAS on Windows NT Server.

    C. RAS running on Windows NT Workstation supports only one simultaneous connection whereas, if it is running on NT Server, it can support up to 256 connections.

    D. RAS running on Windows NT Workstation supports up to 256 simultaneous connections, whereas if it is running on NT Server, it can support only one simultaneous connection, because the server is running other services that tie up the CPU.

18. Which feature of RAS enhances security and billing situations by calling back the client computer after the client computer initiates a call to the RAS server to request a network connection?

    A. CHAP

    B. Leased links

    C. autodial

    D. callback

19. Which of the following security features are incorporated into RAS?

    A. RAS can leave an audit trail, enabling you to see who logged on when and what authentication they provided.

    B. There is a multilink requirement, forcing the remote user to utilize more than one link.

    C. The callback feature that hangs up the incoming caller and calls back at a predetermined number.

    D. Encryption of the logon process and or all data transferring over the RAS connection.

20. With which protocol can RAS perform routing capabilities?

    A. TCP/IP

    B. NetBEUI

    C. IPX

    D. DLC

4.2 Answers and Explanations: Exercises

In order to ensure that your network connection is truly remote, you must disconnect the cable from the network card. This ensures that you are not connecting to the network locally.

4.2 Answers and Explanations: Practice Problems

1. **C** By default, only the local server can be accessed from RAS clients. You must select the Entire Network option in order to allow RAS clients to browse all of the available network resources.

2. **B** The callback option provides not only the capability to reduce phone use charges, but also increases security by ensuring that the RAS client is legitimate.

3. **A, C, D** A NIC is not supported or utilized by RAS.

4. **C** It is vital to ensure that all RAS clients have the dial-in permissions option selected within the User Manager for Domains.

5. **B** Multilink enables a single logical connection to use several physical pathways, such as two modems.

6. **A** The primary use of RAS is to provide a means for remote, or traveling clients, to connect to the NT Server on an occasional basis. It is not intended for heavy traffic or permanent connections.

7. **C** By changing the registry entry value to True (1), you can create and update the PPP.LOG file for both troubleshooting and additional security auditing purposes.

8. **D** PPTP is a protocol that transmits PPP packets over a TCP/IP network securely.

9. **B** Remote Access Service provides remote connectivity.

10. **A** PPP is not restricted to TCP/IP; it also supports IPX, NetBEUI, and other network protocols.

11. **A, B, D, E** PSTN, X.25, Null Modem Cable, and ISDN are media types that RAS can utilize.

12. **C** SLIP and PPP are the two types of serial protocols that RAS supports.

13. **B** Callback, encryption, and PPTP features ensure a secure connection to the NT Server under RAS.

14. **B** By default, only the local server can be accessed from RAS clients. If no resources are on the local server, you must select the Entire Network option in order to permit RAS clients access to network resources.

15. **A** Client Service for NetWare has to be installed in order to access the NetWare resources.

16. **D** TCP/IP is utilized in conjunction with the T1 link.

17. **C** Whereas NT Workstation supports only a single RAS connection, Windows NT Server supports up to 256 simultaneous RAS connections with the appropriate hardware and licensing.

18. **D** The callback option provides a means of controlling phone bills by calling back the clients at an assigned number. This can be especially economical if your company has a decent long-distance phone rate. The callback option also provides great security from hackers. If hackers obtain a username and password, they are still prevented access to the network because the NT server will disconnect them and try to call them back at a predetermined number.

19. **A, C, D** Multilink option enables one logical connection to use several pathways if they are available.

20. **A, C** RAS can act as a TCP/IP or IPX router. However, the NT Server running RAS comes with a NetBIOS gateway. A RAS client using the NetBEUI protocol can connect to a RAS server and, using the NetBIOS gateway on the RAS server, can gain access to the remote LAN beyond the gateway, regardless of what protocol the LAN is using.

4.2 Key Words

Remote Access Service (RAS)

Integrated Services Digital Network (ISDN)

Serial Line Internet Protocol (SLIP)

Point-to-Point Protocol (PPP)

Point-to-Point Tunneling Protocol (PPTP)

Telephony Application Program Interface (TAPI)

Callback

Phonebook entries

AutoDial

Multilink

Service Advertising Protocol (SAP)

Practice Exam: Connectivity

Use this practice exam to test your mastery of Connectivity. This practice exam is made up of 10 questions. Keep in mind that the passing Microsoft score is 76.4 percent. There will be two types of questions:

- Multiple Choice—Select the correct answer.
- Multiple Multiple Choice—Select all answers that are correct.

Begin as soon as you are ready. Answers follow the test.

1. Your manager has requested that you provide existing NetWare server resource accessibility to a small team of engineers that are Windows 95 clients currently attached to an NT Server. Choose the best course of action:

   A. Install a new NetWare server exclusively for the engineering team.

   B. Install GSNW on the NT Server.

   C. Purchase the necessary NetWare licensing for the team of engineers.

   D. Migrate the NetWare server over to an NT domain server.

2. What two components that must be running on an NT domain server in order to execute the Migration Tool for NetWare?

   A. NWLink

   B. NTFS

   C. RAS

   D. GSNW

3. For what purpose is NetWare's Syscon utility utilized during the installation of GSNW?

   A. To establish the proper rights and permissions for the NT Server to properly use GSNW.

   B. NetWare Syscon tool is not used during the setup and configuration of GSNW.

   C. To establish a user account on the NetWare server to enable GSNW to act as a gateway to NetWare resources.

   D. To establish a group and user account on the NetWare server to enable GSNW to act as a gateway to NetWare resources.

4. How do you create a new share for a NetWare directory or volume on the NT Server running GSNW?

   A. By using the Explorer tool on the NT Server.

   B. With the GSNW tool initial dialog box, which provides the buttons to add, remove, and set Permissions for NetWare directories and volumes.

   C. The shares are determined by the NetWare server.

   D. With the GSNW tool's Gateway button that launches the Configure Gateway dialog box, which in turn provides the buttons to add, remove, and set Permissions for NetWare directories and volumes.

5. Which two of the following must both the local NT Server and remote NT Server using RAS have in order to take advantage of the Multilink option?

   A. Both must have access to more than one physical pathway, such as two modems.

   B. Both must have the Multilink option selected.

   C. Both must be running ISDN compatible hardware.

   D. One of the two must have the Multilink option selected.

6. Which of the following network protocols are supported by RAS?

   A. TCP/IP

   B. NetBEUI

   C. DLC

   D. IPX

7. When is encryption used with a RAS connection (choose three)?

   A. When used with the SLIP protocol.

   B. During the logon process.

   C. Optionally, all data can be set to be encrypted.

   D. In conjunction with the PPTP protocol, which encrypts PPP packets.

8. Which of the following does the AutoDial feature *not* support?

   A. IP addresses

   B. NetBIOS names

   C. MAC addresses

   D. Internet host names

9. Which of the following statements about Server Message Block (SMB) is *not* true?

   A. It is jointly developed by Microsoft, Intel, and IBM.

   B. It is a file-sharing protocol.

   C. It specifies a series of commands utilized to pass information between computers using four message types.

   D. All of the above are true.

10. RAS can connect to a remote computer using which of the following media?

    A. Public Switched Telephone Network (PSTN)

    B. X.25

    C. Null modem cable

    D. ISDN

Answers and Explanations: Practice Exam

1. **B** GSNW is an ideal solution in circumstances where network traffic is minimal through the gateway.

2. **A, D** NWLink and GSNW must be installed and running for the NetWare Migration tool to run.

3. **D** NetWare's Syscon utility is used to establish user groups and accounts on the NetWare server, both of which are required to set up the GSNW gateway.

4. **D** You must use the GSNW tool to establish shares for the gateway connected NetWare resources. This is done with the GSNW tool's Gateway button, which launches the Configure Gateway dialog box (which in turn provides the buttons to add, remove, and set Permissions for NetWare directories and volumes).

5. **A, B** In order to establish a Multilink between two NT Servers, they must both have access to two or more modems or ISDN channels, and both must have the Multilink option selected.

6. **A, B, D** TCP/IP, IPX, and NetBEUI are all network protocols supported with RAS.

7. **B, C, D** Encryption is always used during the logon process, and RAS can optionally be set to use data encryption at all times. If PPTP is used, it encrypts PPP packets. The outdated SLIP protocol does not support encryption.

8. **C** IP addresses, NetBIOS names, and Internet host names can all be used by the AutoDial feature of RAS.

9. **D** All the statements about Server Message Block (SMB) are true.

10. **A, B, C, D** RAS can connect to a remote computer using all of the aforementioned media.

CHAPTER 5

Monitoring and Optimization

The performance of your applications on Windows NT depends on the combination of hardware and software on your system. Microsoft provides the following objectives for the "Monitoring and Optimization" section of the exam, as follows:

- Monitor performance of various functions by using Performance Monitor. Functions include processor, memory, disk, and network.
- Identify performance bottlenecks.

5.1 Performance Optimization

Optimal performance means getting the best results with the hardware and software you have. Optimization of a task consists of measuring and analyzing the resource demands of the task to determine what can be done to make it finish in a shorter period of time.

A. Performance Objectives

Performance objectives vary depending on the role of the computer in the network.

After you optimize performance of your application the next question is whether that level of performance meets your business goals. You may have the best performance possible with your existing system, but to get adequate performance you may need to upgrade one or more components, such as memory, disk, network card, or processor.

The best way to know what you can do to improve performance is to measure it. Gathering data on how your system performs under various circumstances gives you the information you need to make appropriate changes to your system.

B. Windows NT Tunes Itself

One of Microsoft's design goals for Windows NT was that it should not require a user to make changes to Registry settings to get good performance.

Microsoft decided to let the operating system itself handle evaluating settings, such as the size of the disk cache and paging file, and adjust them dynamically as resource demands change.

Windows NT does most of the task of optimizing overall performance of the system without requiring manual changes to Registry parameters.

C. Reasons to Monitor Performance

Although there is little to tune in NT itself, you still have several reasons to monitor system performance, as follows:

- *To optimize specific tasks.*

  If you have a particular application on your server that you want to optimize, monitoring system performance can tell you whether changing your hardware will help your application run faster.

- *To troubleshoot performance problems.*

  One of the most difficult kinds of performance problems to troubleshoot is diagnosing transient network problems.

- *To plan for future needs.*

  Another reason to monitor performance is that it enables you to detect changes in the way that the server is being used by users.

D. Configuration Changes that Affect Performance

You can, however, change many things that affect overall system performance, including adding or upgrading hardware components, removing software components, changing Windows NT performance parameters, and moving or rescheduling time-intensive tasks.

1. Adding or Upgrading Hardware Components

Hardware optimization may be necessary to truly upgrade your server's performance. You may consider upgrading the following components: processor capability, memory capacity, disks, network capabilities, and fault-tolerance issues.

a. Processor

Optimization considerations include:

- Upgrade the speed of the processor.
- Add another processor (for example, two Pentium processors on an SMP system).
- Upgrade the secondary cache.

b. Memory

Optimization considerations include:

- You can never have too much RAM. Having adequate RAM reduces the need for paging memory to and from the hard disk.
- Shadowing of the ROM BIOS in RAM does not improve performance under Windows NT. Disabling this feature can, therefore, make more memory available to the system.

c. Disks

Optimization considerations include:

- Replace slow disks with faster ones.
- Use NTFS for partitions larger than 400 MB.
- Use a defragmentation tool if disks become fragmented.
- Upgrade from IDE to SCSI.
- Use a controller with the highest possible transfer rate and best multitasking functionality.
- Isolate disk I/O-intensive tasks on separate physical disks and/or disk controllers.
- Create a stripe set to gain the advantage of simultaneous writes to multiple disks if your hardware supports it. Stripe sets write data to the drives in 64K segments. Stripe sets without parity offer no fault-tolerance. Should a drive fail, all data on the stripe set will be lost. You should use stripe sets with parity when it is available.

d. Network

Optimization considerations include:

- Get a network card with the widest data bus available on your system.
- Divide your network into multiple networks, attaching the server to each network with a different adapter.

e. Fault Tolerance

Optimization considerations include:

- If using software-based fault tolerance such as mirroring (RAID 1) or striping with parity (RAID-5), use a hardware-based solution instead.
- If the goal is the greatest availability of data, you could consider mirroring (via Windows NT fault-tolerant drivers) two hardware-based RAID-5 arrays.

2. Removing Unnecessary Software Components

You can remove any software components that are using precious processor and memory resources. These software components fall into three categories: device drivers, network protocols, and services.

1. *Device drivers.* Any drivers that are loaded into memory but not used should be removed.
2. *Network protocols.* Remove any unnecessary network protocols. You can remove the bindings for a protocol selectively.

3. *Services.* Any services that this server does not need to provide should be disabled, or configured to start manually.

3. Replacing Inefficient Software

If your system has applications or drivers that use system resources inefficiently, you may not be able to make a particular application run faster.

4. Changing Windows NT Performance Parameters

Several relatively easy-to-change settings can make a substantial difference in performance, as discussed in the following sections.

a. Optimizing the Paging File

You configure the size of the paging file in the Virtual Memory dialog box. To open the Virtual Memory dialog box, click on the Change button in the Performance tab of the Control Panel System application.

The following are general recommendations regarding the virtual memory settings:

- Consider spreading the paging file across multiple physical disks if your hardware supports writing to those disks at the same time.
- Move the paging file to the disk with the lowest amount of total disk activity.
- If you plan to use Windows NT's Recovery feature, which writes out debugging information if a stop error occurs to disk, the swap file located on your system partition must be larger than the amount of physical RAM present on the system.
- Monitor the size of the paging file under peak usage and then set the minimum size to that value.
- To determine the amount of RAM to add to reduce paging activity, use a tool, such as Performance Monitor, to determine the amount of memory each application needs. Then remove applications (noting their working set sizes) until paging activity falls within acceptable limits.

b. Optimizing the Server Service

Another setting that can affect performance is the configuration of the Server service. To access the Server dialog box, choose the Services tab in the Control Panel Network application, select the Server service, and click on the Properties button.

By default, Windows NT Server is configured to work best as a file server for 64 or more users. Table 5.1.1 shows the optimal Server service settings.

Table 5.1.1 Server Service Optimization

Setting	Description
Minimize Memory Used	Up to 10 connections
Balance	Up to 64 connections
Maximize Throughput for File Sharing	64 or more connections, large file cache (best suited for file and print servers)
Maximize Throughput for Network Applications	64 or more connections, small file cache (best suited for PDCs, BDCs and for application servers)

c. Optimizing Other Services

Other services on your system may have Registry settings that you need to adjust for optimal performance. Table 5.1.2 lists some common values for standard Windows NT services that would be a good starting point for evaluation.

Table 5.1.2 Some Common Registry Values for Standard Windows NT Services

Service	Value
Net Logon	Pulse, Pulse Concurrency, Pulse Maximum
Directory Replication	Interval, Guard Time
Computer Browser	Hidden, IsDomainMaster, MaintainServerList
Spooler	DefaultSpoolDirectory, PriorityClass

5. Rescheduling Resource-Intensive Tasks

Demands for resources on a server often fluctuate widely at different times of day. It makes sense, then, that you should shift demands for resources to times when you have a surplus of the resource available.

6. Moving Tasks to Another System

You may be able to move the demand to another machine that has idle resources. If you have two I/O-intensive applications running on a server, consider moving one application to a different server to even out the workload.

E. Before Making Changes

You have to be able to isolate which resource on the system has become the bottleneck; then you have to discover the source of the demand for that resource. You can use Performance Monitor, discussed in the next section after the exercises, to do this kind of investigative work.

5.1.1 Exercise: Practicing Performance Optimization

This exercise is a paper-based exercise. You are presented with a scenario and need to perform the following tasks:

- Determine the goals of the server.
- Identify the problems currently in place.
- Determine the best solutions to resolve these problems.

Scenario: You are a network administrator of a LAN environment. You have one NT Server acting as a PDC and 50 clients on NT Workstation in your domain. In addition to serving as a PDC, your server also acts as a file, print, and application server.

The primary protocol you want to use is TCP/IP, but when installing NT, you choose to install TCP/IP, NetBEUI, and IP/SPX. Currently, you have four SCSI drives in the server, but you are not using any stripe sets with parity or disk mirroring.

From the information presented, complete the following:

1. What should the primary goal(s) of the PDC be?
2. What problems (list at least three based on the information presented) might present themselves in this environment?
3. What is an immediate solution you could make to impact network performance on the PDC?
4. What are some potential changes you might make to enhance this environment?

5.1 Practice Problems

In the following multiple choice questions, more than one answer can be correct; pick all answers that apply.

1. For the most part, how much time should you spend tuning and optimizing Windows NT?
   A. At least an hour a day.
   B. After the initial installation, you should plan on spending most of the first week tuning and optimizing Windows NT.
   C. You should never have to.
   D. NT, for the most part, is self-tuning and requires very little user intervention. On occasion, you should monitor portions of the OS.

2. Name the major tool for gathering information and identifying bottlenecks.
   A. Tune-T.
   B. NT Monitor.
   C. Performance Monitor.
   D. Server Manager.
   E. NT doesn't provide any tools for tuning and performance monitoring.

3. Before you can tune a file server for optimum performance, which one of the following questions must you answer?
   A. How much money do you have available to spend on new hardware?
   B. What types of tasks is the file server expected to perform?
   C. This question has no answer; simply put, tuning is the process of installing the fastest hardware in your computer.
   D. In what type of business is the company using file server? For certain companies, you cannot tune NT because of U.S. government restrictions.

4. A curious user tells you that while reading a major computer periodical, she came across this statement: "All computer systems have a bottleneck of some type." Why is this so?
   A. All computer systems are only as fast as their slowest component. You might remove one bottleneck, but you will always expose another.
   B. The article was incorrect. For example, your file server has absolutely no bottlenecks.
   C. The article was referring to non-Windows NT systems. Microsoft has designed the system to continually self-adjust, thus eliminating bottlenecks.
   D. Because you always upgrade components as soon as new ones are available, you eliminate any potential bottlenecks before they become apparent.

5. Which statement is true regarding the type of hardware you should place in a heavily used file server?
   A. The equipment in the server is not important because nobody actually uses the server to run applications.
   B. You should always spend the most money on the server hardware.
   C. When designing a file server, always pick the hardware that exploits the full bus speed if possible (for example, SCSI hard drives, PCI bus network cards, and so on).
   D. You should use the same type of computer hardware as the workstations so that users get good response time, because hardware from the same vendor works better together.

6. To optimize the network components in an NT Workstation or Server, which *one* of the following should you do?

   A. You do not need to do anything. NT automatically optimizes the network components.

   B. You should remove unused adapter cards and protocols.

   C. You should always have TCP/IP, NetBEUI, and NWLink installed, even if your computers are using only one protocol. This leaves more paths open in case one protocol becomes unusable.

   D. You should disable the server service for a workstation, and disable the workstation service for a server.

7. Select the name of the piece of software that automatically swaps data in physical RAM out to disk and back.

   A. The Virtual Memory Manager

   B. The Virtual Device Driver

   C. Himem.exe

   D. Emm386.exe

8. Choose the paging file that Windows NT creates.

   A. RAMPAGE.SYS

   B. SYS$RAM.SYS

   C. PAGEFILE.SYS

   D. VIRAM.SYS

9. What are some of the things you can do to make the system use virtual memory more efficiently? (Choose all that apply.)

   A. Spread the paging file across multiple hard drives.

   B. Move the paging file to the drive where the Windows NT System files are located.

   C. Move the paging file from the drive where the Windows NT System files are located.

   D. Monitor the size of the paging file under peak usage and then set the minimum size of the paging file to that value, thereby saving time when the system has to expand the paging file.

10. Performance on NT depends on what two variables?

    A. Hardware

    B. Pagefile.sys location(s)

    C. Software

    D. RISC or Intel processor

11. What is optimal performance?

    A. Making NT work faster by editing the registry.

    B. Getting the best result with the hardware and software available.

    C. Making threads process at a higher priority.

    D. Making processors work at their maximum.

12. In addition to servicing LOGON validations from users, what additional tasks are performed at a BDC acting as a File and Print Server? (Choose all that apply.)

    A. Acting as Master Browsers in the domain

    B. Directory replication updates

    C. Servicing resource requests from users

    D. Account database updates from the PDC

13. Windows NT optimizes what components automatically? (Choose all that apply.)

    A. Disk cache

    B. Paging file

    C. Monitor settings

    D. Bindings

14. What hardware changes have an effect on system performance? (Choose all that apply.)

    A. Mouse

    B. Monitor

    C. Processor

    D. Memory

15. What are considerations for hard disks in regard to optimization of a file server? (Choose all that apply.)

    A. Use faster disks.

    B. Combine multiple hard disks into a stripe set with parity.

    C. Use the FAT file system.

    D. Use SCSI over IDE.

16. Why should you use stripe sets?

    A. They require less overhead.

    B. They are easier on system for I/O management.

    C. They enable NT to do simultaneous writes (if supported by hardware).

    D. You should not use stripe sets.

17. Which are considerations with regard to optimizing NT with network cards? (Choose all that apply.)

    A. Get a network card with the widest data bus available.

    B. Always use NetBEUI when available.

    C. Never use NetBEUI.

    D. Divide your network into multiple networks, attaching the server to each network with a different adapter.

18. How many drives do you need to implement fault tolerance under NT Server?

    A. 1

    B. 2

    C. 3

    D. 4

19. You are deciding how to implement fault tolerance on your NT Server. You've heard that using hardware fault tolerance is better than using NT's software fault tolerance. Why is one better than the other?

    A. NT's built-in fault tolerance works only with NTFS.

    B. Software fault tolerance is more reliable than hardware.

    C. Hardware fault tolerance takes the load of parity calculation off the processor.

    D. Hardware fault tolerance does not work with NT because of the HAL.

20. What can you do with device drivers to optimize NT?

    A. Remove unneeded drivers.

    B. Pause any unnecessary drivers through the devices applet in the Control Panel.

    C. Create hardware profiles that use only the drivers needed during that boot-up phase.

    D. There is no need to do anything. NT automatically purges unneeded drivers.

5.1 Answers and Explanations: Exercise

1. In this environment, the primary goals of the PDC are to validate users from the LAN, and serve as the file, print, and application server—all in the most efficient way possible.
2. Possible problems, from the information presented, include:
   - The PDC becomes a bottleneck in the network if it becomes too busy serving client requests.
   - The extra protocols can have detrimental effects on network performance.
   - In a single server environment, fault tolerance is crucial. If a drive in the server were to go bad, the data on that drive would be lost.
   - If the PDC were to be taken off-line, access to network resources on the server, including domain validation, would be denied.
3. To make an immediate impact on the network performance of the PDC, you should remove all unnecessary network protocols. If TCP/IP is the desired protocol, it must be configured as such on the server and on the workstations.
4. Potential changes include:
   - Adding a BDC to the domain to act as a file, print, and application server
   - Evaluating the hardware to see whether hardware upgrades are appropriate
   - Implementing fault-tolerance support—either disk mirroring or stripe sets with parity
   - Removing unnecessary protocols and evaluating bindings of the remaining protocols to see whether they are effective in their current state

5.1 Answers and Explanations: Practice Problems

1. **D** Windows NT, for the most part, is self-tuning. There are portions of the OS, such as memory and network usage, that should be monitored to optimize performance.
2. **C** Performance Monitor is the major tool for gathering information and identifying bottlenecks.
3. **B** The question to ask is, "What types of tasks is the file server expected to perform?" Based on the answer to that question, one can determine what the primary goals of that server should be and optimize accordingly.
4. **A** All computer systems are only as fast as their slowest component.
5. **C** When designing a file server, always pick the hardware that exploits the full bus speed if possible (for example, SCSI hard drives, PCI bus network cards, and so on).
6. **B** You should remove unused adapter cards and protocols in order to optimize the network components in an NT Workstation or Server.
7. **A** Virtual Memory Manager automatically swaps data in physical RAM out to disk and back.
8. **C** PAGEFILE.SYS is the name of the paging file that Windows NT creates.
9. **A, C, D** Spread the paging file across multiple hard drives. Move the paging file to the drive where the Windows NT System files are located. Move the paging file from the drive where the Windows NT System files are located. Monitor the size of the paging file under peak usage and then set the minimum size of the paging file to that value, thereby saving time when the system has to expand the paging file.

10. **A, C** Performance on NT depends on hardware and software.
11. **B** Optimal performance is getting the best result with the hardware and software available.
12. **B, C, D** BDCs can also act as file, print, and application servers. Most BDCs will also participate in Directory Replication.
13. **A, B** Windows NT optimizes the disk cache and the paging file automatically.
14. **C, D** Processor and memory changes have an effect on system performance.
15. **A, B, D** You always want the faster hard drives available; stripe sets can improve performance; and SCSI drives are preferred over IDE.
16. **C** Stripe sets enable NT to do simultaneous writes if it is supported by the hardware.
17. **A, D** Considerations with regard to optimizing NT with network cards include getting a network card with the widest data bus available and dividing your network into multiple networks by attaching the server to each network with a different adapter.
18. **B** Two drives are needed to implement fault tolerance on NT Server.
19. **C** Hardware fault tolerance takes the load of parity calculation off the processor.
20. **A** You can remove unneeded drivers to optimize NT.

5.1 Key Words

Boot partition

Mirrored set fault-tolerance RAID Level 1

Optimal performance

Paging file

Secondary cache

Stripe set

Stripe set with parity

System partition

5.2 Using Performance Monitor

The most useful tool for measuring performance on NT systems is Performance Monitor.

You can use Performance Monitor for the following tasks:

- Measuring the demand for resources on your system
- Identifying bottlenecks in your system performance
- Monitoring the behavior of individual processes
- Monitoring the performance of remote systems
- Generating alerts to inform you that an exception condition has occurred
- Exporting performance data for analysis using other tools
- Collecting data to determine a baseline for the computer system.

You can configure Performance Monitor to record a variety of statistical measurements (called *counters*) for a variety of system hardware and software components (called *objects*). Each object has its own collection of counters.

Windows NT Server exam objectives specify that you should be familiar with how to use Performance Monitor to measure processor, memory, disk, and network functions.

A. Bottleneck—The Limiting Resource

When you understand the tools you need for measuring your system's performance, you are ready to dig into the data to determine how to improve it.

The simplest way to detect the bottleneck on your system is to examine the amount of time that the four major bottleneck areas: memory, disk, processor, and network. Typically, the component that uses the most time to complete its portion of the task is the bottleneck.

B. Overall Performance Indicators

A reasonable place to start in monitoring performance for a server in Windows NT is to watch a number of general counters in Performance Monitor.

1. The Processor Object

The following are useful counters for the processor object. In looking at the processor, be certain to remember that high levels of processor activity can result from two situations other than handling a processor-intensive task:

- A severe memory shortage with the processor busy managing virtual memory (swapping pages of memory to and from the disk).
- The system is busy handling a large number of interrupts.

The following are useful counters for the processor object:

- **% Processor Time.** This counter measures the amount of time the processor spent executing a non-idle thread.
- **Interrupts/sec.** This counter measures the number of interrupts the processor handles per second.
- **System:** Processor Queue Length. This counter measures the number of threads waiting in the queue for an available processor. Generally, if the number of threads in the queue exceeds two, you have a problem with processor performance.

2. The Memory Object

In general, the symptoms of a memory shortage on the system are a busy processor and a high level of disk activity on the disk that contains the page file.

a. Pages/sec

This counter measures the number of times that a memory page had to be paged in to memory or out to the disk.

5

b. Available Bytes

This counter measures the amount of physical memory available. When this value falls below 4 MB, you are getting excessive paging.

c. Committed Bytes

This counter measures the amount of virtual memory that has been committed to physical RAM or to pagefile space. If the amount of committed bytes exceeds the physical memory of a system, more RAM is required on the system.

d. The PhysicalDisk and LogicalDisk Objects

Before you can use Performance Monitor to monitor disk activity, you must enable the disk performance counters. Otherwise, all values for the disk counters report zeroes in Performance Monitor.

To turn on the disk performance counters, log on as a user with administrative privileges and type the following:

```
diskperf -y
```

To start the disk counters on a remote computer, add the computer name to the `diskperf` command.

To complete performance analysis on an NT Server with RAID 5 you must execute diskperf -ye to enable the disk counters.

e. PhysicalDisk: % Disk Time

This counter reports the percentage of time that the physical disk was busy reading or writing.

f. PhysicalDisk: Avg. Disk Queue Length

The average disk queue length is the average number of requests for a physical disk (both read and write requests).

g. LogicalDisk: % Disk Time

This counter reports the percentage of time that the logical disk (for example, C) was busy.

h. LogicalDisk: Avg Disk Queue Length

This counter measures the number of read and write requests waiting for the logical disk to become available.

3. The Server Object

The Server component is responsible for handling all SMB-based requests for sessions and file and print services. If the Server service becomes the bottleneck, requests from clients are denied, forcing retries and creating slower response times and increased traffic. Here are the counters:

- **Bytes Total/sec.** This counter measures the number of bytes sent to and received from the network.
- **Logon/sec.** This counter measures the logon activity to predict if you need to add a BDC on the segment.
- **Pool Nonpaged Failures.** This counter measures the number of times that a request from the server to allocate memory from the nonpaged pool failed. It is generally an indication that the computer's physical memory is not sufficient.
- **Pool Paged Failures.** This counter measures the number of times that a request from the server to allocate memory from the paged pool failed. It is generally an indication that the computer's physical memory or its pagefile size is not sufficient.

C. Establishing Baseline Performance Data

Many of the counters that Performance Monitor provides cannot be interpreted without some baseline data to which to compare it.

It is a good idea to log performance from your servers at various times of the day, regularly, so that you have appropriate baselines with which to compare.

5.2.1 Exercise: Creating a Chart in Performance Monitor

This exercise helps you do the following: become familiar with the process of creating and reading a Performance Monitor chart; understand the basic components of the Performance Monitor main window and the Add to Chart dialog box; and learn how to turn on disk performance counters by using the `diskperf` command.

Estimated Time: 25 minutes

1. Choose Start, Programs, Administrative Tools, and click on Performance Monitor. The Performance Monitor window appears.

2. Choose Edit, Add to Chart. The Add to Chart dialog box appears. You also can open the Add to Chart dialog box by clicking on the plus sign in the toolbar of the Performance Monitor window.

3a. The Computer text box at the top of the Add to Chart dialog box tells Performance Monitor which computer you want to monitor. The default is the local system. Click on the ellipses button to the right of the Computer text box for a browse list of computers on the network.

3b. The Object combo box tells Performance Monitor which object you want to monitor. As you learned earlier in this chapter, an object is a hardware or software component of your system. You can think of an object as a *category* of system statistics. Click on the down arrow to the right of the Object combo box to see a list of object options. Scroll through the list of objects. Look for the Processor, Memory, PhysicalDisk, LogicalDisk, Server, and Network Segment objects described earlier in this chapter. Choose the PhysicalDisk object. If you have more than one physical disk on your system, a list of your physical disks appears in the Instances box to the right of the Object box. The Instances box lists all instances of the object selected in the Object box. If necessary, choose a physical disk instance.

3c. The Counter list box displays the counters (the statistical measurements) available for the object in the Object box. Scroll through the list of counters for the PhysicalDisk object. If you feel like experimenting, select a different object in the Object box. Notice that the different object is accompanied by a different set of counters. Switch back to the PhysicalDisk object and choose the % Disk Time counter. Click on the Explain button. Notice that a description of the % Disk Time counter appears at the bottom of the dialog box.

3d. Click on the Done button in the Add to Chart dialog box. The dialog box closes and you see the Performance main window.

4. In the Performance Monitor main window, you'll see a vertical line sweeping across the chart from left to right. You also might also see a faint colored line at the bottom of the chart recording a % Disk Time value of 0. If so, this is because you have not enabled the disk performance counters for your system. (If the disk performance counters are enabled on your system, you should see a spikey line that looks like the readout from an electrocardiogram. Go to step 5.)

   If you need to enable the disk performance counters, choose click on the Start button go to the command prompt. Enter the command: diskperf -y. Reboot your system and repeat steps 1–4. (You do not have to browse through the Object and Counter lists this time.)

5. You should now see a spikey line representing the percent of time that the physical disk is busy reading or writing. Choose Edit, Add to Chart. Select the PhysicalDisk object and choose the counter Avg. Disk Queue Length. Click on the Add button; then choose the counter Avg. Disk Bytes/Read. Click on the Add button. Click on the Done button.

6. Examine the Performance Monitor main window. All three of the counters you selected should be tracing out spikey lines on the chart. Each line is a different color. A table at the bottom of the window shows which counter goes with which color. The table also gives the scale of the output, the instance, the object, and the computer.

7. Below the chart (but above the table of counters) you find a row of statistical parameters labeled Last, Average, Min, Max, and Graph Time. These parameters pertain to the counter selected in the table at the bottom of the window. Select a different counter and some of these values change. The Last value is the counter value over the last second. Graph Time is the time it takes (in seconds) for the vertical line that draws the chart to sweep across the window.

8. Start Windows NT Explorer. Select a file (a graphics file or a word processing document) and choose Edit, Copy. (This will copy the file you selected to the Clipboard.) Go to another directory and choose Edit, Paste. (This will create a copy of the file in the second directory.) Minimize Explorer and return to the Performance Monitor main window. The disk activity caused by your Explorer session will be reflected in the spikes of the counter lines.

9. Choose Options, Chart. The Chart Options dialog box appears, providing a number of options governing the chart display. The Update Time frame enables you to choose an update interval. The update interval tells Performance Monitor how frequently it should update the chart with new values. (If you choose the Manual Update option, the chart updates only when you press Ctrl+U or choose Options, Update Now.) Experiment with the Chart Options dialog box, or click on the Cancel button.

10. Choose File, Exit to exit Performance Monitor. The Save Chart Settings and Save Chart Settings As options in the File menu enable you to save the collection of objects and counters you are using now so you can monitor the same counters later without having to set them up again. The Export Chart option enables you to export the data to a file that you can open with a spreadsheet or database application. The Save Workspace option saves the settings for your chart as well as any settings for alerts, logs, or reports specified in this session. You will learn more about alerts, logs, and reports in Exercise 5.2.2.

5.2.2 Exercise: Performance Monitor Alerts, Logs, and Reports

In this exercise, you learn about the alternative views (Alert view, Log view, and Report view) available through the View menu of Performance Monitor, and you learn how to log performance data to a log file.

Estimated time: 25 minutes

1. Choose Start, Programs, Administrative Tools, and Performance Monitor. The Performance Monitor main window appears.

2. Open the View menu. You see the following four options:

   - The Chart option plots the counters you select in a continuous chart (refer to Exercise 5.2.1).
   - The Alert option automatically alert a network official if a predetermined counter threshold is surpassed.
   - The Log option saves your system performance data to a log file.
   - The Report option displays system performance data in a report format.

   The setup is similar for each of these view formats. All use some form of the Add to Chart dialog box. All have options configured through the first command at the top of the Options menu. (The name of the first command at the top of the Options menu changes depending on the active view.) It was the Chart command in Exercise 5.2.1.

3a. Choose View, Alert.

3b. Click on the plus sign in the toolbar or choose Edit, Add to Alert. The Add to Alert dialog box appears; it is similar to the Add to Chart dialog box, except you will notice two additional items at the bottom.

The options in the Alert If frame enable you to enter a threshold for the counter. The Over and Under radio buttons specify whether you should receive an alert if the counter value is over or under the threshold value. The Run Program on Alert text box enables you to specify a command line that will execute if the counter value reaches the threshold you specify in the Alert If box. Use the Run Program on Alert text box to execute a command or script that will send a message to your beeper, send you an e-mail message, or notify your paging service.

Do not specify a batch file in the Run Program on Alert text box. Performance Monitor uses Unicode format, which can confuse the command-prompt interpreter. (The < and > symbols, which are used in Unicode format, are interpreted as a redirection of input or output.)

5

3c. The default object in the Object combo box should be the Processor object. The default counter in the Counter list box should be % Processor Time. Enter the value **5%** in the Alert If box and select the Over radio button.

In the Run Program on Alert text box, type **SOL** and select the First Time radio button. This configuration tells Performance Monitor to execute Windows NT's Solitaire program when the % Processor Time exceeds five percent.

It is important to select the First Time radio button; otherwise, Performance Monitor will execute a new instance of Solitaire every time the % Processor Time exceeds five percent, which happens every time Performance Monitor executes a new instance of Solitaire. In other words, if you try this experiment without selecting the First Time radio button, you'll probably have to close Performance Monitor using the X button or reboot your system to stop the incessant shuffling and dealing.

3d. Click on the Add button, and then click on the Done button. The Alert Legend at the bottom of the Performance Monitor window describes the active alert parameters. The Alert Log shows every instance of an alert.

3e. Make some change to your Desktop. (Hide or reveal the taskbar, change the size of the Performance Monitor window—anything that will cause a five percent utilization of the processor.) The Solitaire program should miraculously appear on your screen. In a real alert situation, Performance Monitor would execute an alert application instead of starting a card game.

3f. Choose Edit, Delete Alert.

4a. Choose View, Log. The Log view saves performance data to a log file instead of displaying it on-screen.

4b. Choose Edit, Add to Log. Notice that only the objects appear in the Add to Log dialog box. The counters and instances boxes do not appear because Performance Monitor automatically logs all counters and all instances of the object to the log file.

Select the Memory Object and click on Add. If you want, you can select another object, such as the Paging File object, and then click on Add again. When you are finished adding objects, click on Done.

4c. Choose, Options Log. The Log Options dialog box appears, enabling you to designate a log file that Performance Monitor will use to log the data.

In the File Name text box, enter the name **exer2.log**.

You also can specify an update interval. The update interval is the interval at which Performance Monitor records performance data to the log. The Manual Update radio button specifies that the file won't be undated unless you press Ctrl+U or choose Options, Update Now.

Click on the Start Log button to start saving data to the log. Wait a few minutes, and then return to the Log Options dialog box and click on the Stop Log button.

4d. Choose View, Chart.

4e. Choose Options, Data From. The Data From dialog box enables you to specify a source for the performance data that will appear in the chart. Note that the default source is Current Activity. (That is why the chart you created in Exercise 5.2.1 took its data from current system activity.)

The alternative to the Current Activity option is to use data from a log file. Click on the Log File radio button; click on the ellipses button to the right of Log File; and select the exer2.log file you created in step 4c. Click on OK.

4f. Choose Edit, Add to Chart.

Click on the down arrow of the Object combo box. Notice that your only object choices are the Memory object and any other objects you selected in step 4b. Select the Memory object. Browse through the counter list and select Pages/sec. Click on the Add button. Select any other memory counters you want to display and click on the Add button. Click on Done.

4g. The log file's record of the counters you selected in 4f appear in the chart in the Performance main window. Notice that, unlike the chart you created in Exercise 5.2.1, this chart does not continuously sweep out new data. That is because this chart represents static data from a previous, finite monitoring session.

4h. Choose Edit, Time Window. A time window enables you to focus on a particular time interval within the log file.

In this example (because you only collected data for a few minutes), the Time Window option might seem unnecessary. If you collected data for a longer period, however, and you want to zero in on a particular event, a time window can be very useful.

Set the beginning and end points of your Time window by adjusting the gray start and stop sliders on the Time Window slide bar. The Bookmarks frame enables you to specify a log file bookmark as a start or stop point. (You can create a bookmark by choosing Options, Bookmark while collecting data to the log file or by clicking on the book in the Performance Monitor toolbar.)

Click on OK to view the data for the time interval.

5a. Choose View, Report.

Choose Options, Data From.

In the Data From... dialog box, select the radio button labeled Current Activity. Report view displays the performance data in a report rather than in a graphics format.

9. **C** Three startup disks are made at the time of install. If you lose these disks, you can recreate them by running WINNT /OX.

10. **C** Three startup disks are made at the time of install. If you lose these disks, you can recreate them by running WINNT / OX.

11. **B** CONVERT.EXE is used to convert FAT partitions to NTFS.

6.1 Key Words

Domain name

NTFS partitions

FAT

Startup disks

6.2 Troubleshooting Boot Failures

The boot process is one of the most common sources of problems in Windows NT. The cause may be a lost or corrupt boot file. Try booting from the Windows NT boot disk and perform an emergency repair (a process described later in this chapter) if necessary.

Microsoft lists the following objective for the Windows NT Server exam: Choose the appropriate course of action to take to resolve boot failures.

A. Booting Up

The boot process begins when your computer accesses the hard drive's Master Boot Record (MBR) to load Windows NT. If your system fails during the Power On Self Test (POST), the problem isn't NT-related; instead, it is a hardware issue. What happens after the MBR's program loads depends on the type of computer you are using.

1. The Intel Boot Sequence

On Intel x86-based computers, the boot sector of the active partition loads a file called NTLDR. Similar to IO.SYS for MS-DOS or Windows 95, NTLDR is a hidden, system, read-only file in the root of your system partition, responsible for loading the rest of the operating system. NTLDR carries out the following steps:

1. Switches the processor to the 32-bit flat memory model necessary to address 4 GB of RAM.
2. Starts the minifile system driver necessary for accessing the system and boot partitions. This minifile system driver contains just enough code to read files at boot time. The full file systems are loaded later.
3. Displays a Boot Loader menu that gives the user a choice of operating system to load, and waits for a response. The options for the Boot Loader menu are stored in a hidden, read-only file in the root of your system partition named BOOT.INI.
4. Invokes, if Windows NT is the selected system, the hardware detection routine to determine the hardware required. NTDETECT.COM (the same program that detects the hardware during NTSETUP) performs the hardware detection. NTDETECT.COM builds the hardware list and returns it to NTLDR. NTDETECT.COM is hidden, system, and read-only in the root of the system partition.
5. Loads the kernel of the operating system. The kernel is called NTOSKRNL.EXE, and you can find it in the <winnt_root>\SYSTEM32 directory. At this point, the screen clears and displays OS Loader V4.xx.
6. Loads the Hardware Abstraction Layer (HAL). The HAL is a single file (HAL.DLL) that contains the code necessary to mask interrupts and exceptions from the kernel.
7. Loads SYSTEM, the HKEY_LOCAL_MACHINE\SYSTEM hive in the Registry. You can find the corresponding file in the <winnt_root>\SYSTEM32\CONFIG directory.
8. Loads the boot-time drivers. Boot-time drivers have a start value of 0. These values are loaded in the order in which they are listed in HKEY_LOCAL_MACHINE\SYSTEM\CurrentControlSet\Control\ServiceGroupOrder. Each time a driver loads, a dot is added to the series following the OS Loader V4.00 at the top of the screen. If the /sos switch is used in BOOT.INI, the name of each driver appears on a separate line as each is loaded. The drivers are not initialized yet.
9. Passes control, along with the hardware list collected by NTDETECT.COM, to NTOSKRNL.EXE.

After NTOSKRNL.EXE takes control, the boot phase ends and the load phases begin.

2. The RISC Boot Sequence

On a RISC-based computer, the boot process is much simpler because the firmware does much of the work that NTLDR does on the Intel platform. RISC-based computers maintain hardware configuration in their firmware (also called non-volatile RAM), so they don't need NTDETECT.COM. Their firmware also contains a list of valid operating systems and their locations, so they don't need BOOT.INI either.

RISC-based machines don't look for the Intel-specific NTLDR to boot the operating system; instead, they always look for a file called OSLOADER.EXE. This file is handed the hardware configuration data from the firmware. It then loads NTOSKRNL.EXE, HAL.DLL, and SYSTEM, and the boot process concludes.

3. Booting to Windows 95, MS-DOS, or OS/2

On Intel-based computers, you can install Windows NT with Windows 95 or MS-DOS. The boot loader screen offers the user a choice of Windows NT Workstation 4, Microsoft Windows, and MS-DOS. If the user chooses a non-Windows NT operating system, a file called BOOTSECT.DOS is loaded and executed. BOOTSECT.DOS is a hidden, system, read-only file in the root of the system partition. It contains the information that was present in the boot sector before Windows NT was installed. If a user chooses Windows 95 from the boot menu, for example, BOOTSECT.DOS loads IO.SYS and passes control to it.

6

4. BOOT.INI

To understand the BOOT.INI file, you must understand two things—the ARC syntax and the actual use of the file. Both topics are discussed in the sections that follow.

a. ARC

Because not all machines use MS-DOS–style paths (for example, c:\winnt) for referring to locations on a hard drive, Windows NT uses a cross-platform standard format called Advanced RISC Computer (ARC), within BOOT.INI. An ARC-compliant path consists of four parameters:

Parameter	Description
scsi(x) or multi(x)	identifies the hardware adapter
disk(y)	SCSI bus number: always 0 if multi
rdisk(z)	Physical drive number for multi; ignored for SCSI
partition(a)	Logical partition number

The first three parameters are zero-based; that is, the first physical IDE drive is rdisk(0) and the second is rdisk(1). The partition parameter, however, is one-based, so the first partition on the drive is rdisk(0)partition(1).

All of the parameters—even the ones that are ignored—must be present in the path. For instance, multi(0)disk(0)rdisk(0)partition(1) is a valid path even though disk(0) is essentially unnecessary. multi(0)rdisk(0)partition(1) is not valid.

The first parameter almost always is multi, even for a SCSI controller. The only time you even see SCSI in a BOOT.INI file is if the BIOS on the disk controller is turned off. If this is the case, don't worry; an additional hidden, system, read-only file, NTBOOTDD.SYS, is present in the root of the system partition. NTBOOTDD.SYS is a device driver necessary for accessing a SCSI controller that doesn't have an on-board BIOS or doesn't use INT 13 to identify hard disks. If you have this file present, you probably see a scsi(x) entry in BOOT.INI. If you don't, you probably have upgraded from Windows NT 3.1 (where this setting was more common) without ever deleting the file.

The same holds true for a RISC-based computer; look at the firmware entries for the operating system paths and you should see the same kind of ARC-compliant paths.

b. The BOOT.INI in Use

NTLDR may invoke the Boot Loader menu, but BOOT.INI, an editable text file, controls it. (It is read-only, so you must remove that attribute before editing it.) BOOT.INI is the only INI file that Windows NT uses—if, indeed you can actually say that NT uses it. After all, Windows NT is not loaded when this file is called on.

BOOT.INI has only two sections: [boot loader] and [operating systems], covered next.

[boot loader]—The [boot loader] section of BOOT.INI defines the operating system loaded if the user doesn't make a selection within a defined period of time. By default, you see something like this:

```
[boot loader]
timeout=30
default=multi(0)disk(0)rdisk(0)partition(1)\WINNT
```

The timeout parameter is the length of time (in seconds) that NTLDR has to wait for the user to make a decision. If timeout is set to 0, the default operating system loads immediately. If it is set to -1, the menu displays until the user makes a decision.

The default parameter defines the actual path to the directory that contains the files for the default operating system.

You can edit BOOT.INI directly, but remember that a mistyped character in NOTEPAD.EXE or EDIT.COM could result in your system not booting properly.

[operating systems]—The [operating systems] section contains a reference for every operating system available to the user from the Boot Loader menu, as well as any special switches necessary to customize the Windows NT environment. One of these entries must match the default= entry in the [boot loader] section. Otherwise, you end up with two entries for the same OS on-screen, one of which has (default) following it.

Note that the paths are in ARC format with a label in quotation marks, which display as an on-screen selection. Here's an example of an [operating systems] section:

```
multi(0)disk(0)rdisk(0)partition(1)\WINNT=Windows NT Workstation "Version
4.00"
```

c. BOOT.INI Switches

The following table delineates several useful switches that you can include in the [operating systems] section of BOOT.INI. The only way to include them is to manually edit the BOOT.INI file (take the read-only attribute off first and save the file as a text file).

Switch	Description
/basevideo	Tells Windows NT to load the standard VGA driver rather than the optimized driver written for your video card. Selecting the VGA mode entry uses the standard VGA 640×480, 16-color driver that works with almost every video card.
/sos	Enumerates to the screen each driver as it loads during the kernel load phase. If Windows NT hangs during this phase, you can use the /sos switch to determine which driver caused the problem.
/noserialmice=[COMx|COMx,y,z_]	When Windows NT boots, NTDETECT.COM looks for, among other things, the presence of serial mice. Sometimes this detection routine misfires and identifies modems or other devices as serial mice. Then, when Windows NT loads and initializes, the serial port is unavailable and the device is unusable because Windows NT is expecting a serial mouse. This switch tells NTDETECT.COM not to bother looking for serial mice. Used with a specific COM port(s), NTDETECT.COM still looks for serial mice, but not on the port(s) specified.
/crashdebug	Turns on the Automatic Recovery and Restart capability, which you can also configure using the Control Panel System application. In fact, when you configure this capability through Control Panel, you are adding this switch to the OS path in BOOT.INI.

continues

Switch	Description
/nodebug	Programmers often use a special version of Windows NT that includes debugging symbols useful for tracking down problems with code. This version of Windows NT runs slowly compared to the retail version, owing to the extra overhead in tracking every piece of executing code. To turn off the monitoring in this version of NT, add the /nodebug switch to the OS path in BOOT.INI.
/maxmem:n	Memory parity errors can be notoriously difficult to isolate. The /maxmem switch helps. When followed with a numeric value, this switch limits Windows NT's usable memory to the amount specified in the switch. This switch also is useful for developers using high-level workstations, who want to simulate performance on a lower-level machine.
/scsiordinal:n	If your system has two identical SCSI controllers, you need a way to distinguish one from the other. The /scsiordinal switch is used to assign a value of 0 to the first controller and 1 to the second.

5. Kernel Initialization Phase

After all the initial drivers have loaded, the screen turns blue and the text height shrinks; the kernel initialization phase has begun. Now the kernel and all the drivers loaded in the previous phase are initialized. The Registry begins to flesh out. The CurrentControlSet is copied to the Clone Set, and the volatile HARDWARE key is created. The system Registry hive then is scanned once more for higher-level drivers configured to start during system initialization.

6. Services Load Phase

Here the session manager scans the system hive for a list of programs that must run before Windows NT fully initializes. These programs may include AUTOCHK.EXE, the boot-time version of CHKDSK.EXE that examines and repairs any problems within a file system, or AUTOCONV.EXE, which converts a partition from FAT to NTFS. These boot-time programs are stored in the following:

```
HKEY_LOCAL_MACHINE\SYSTEM\CurrentControlSet\Control\Session
Manager\BootExecute
```

Following these programs, the page file(s) are created based on the locations specified in:

```
HKEY_LOCAL_MACHINE\SYSTEM\CurrentControlSet\Control\Session Manager\Memory
Management
```

Next, the SOFTWARE hive loads from <winnt_root>\SYSTEM32\CONFIG. Session Manager then loads the CSR subsystem and any other required subsystems from:

```
HKEY_LOCAL_MACHINE\System\CurrentControlSet\Control\Session
Manager\SubSystems\Required
```

Finally, drivers that have a start value of 2 (Automatic) load.

7. Windows Start Phase

After the Win32 subsystem starts, the screen then switches into GUI mode. The Winlogon process is invoked, and the Welcome dialog box appears. Although users can go ahead and log on at this point, the system might not respond for a few more moments while the Service Controller initializes automatic services.

The critical file at this point is SERVICES.EXE, which actually starts Alerter, Computer Browser, EventLog, Messenger, NetLogon, NT LM Security Support Provider, Server, TCP/IP NetBIOS Helper, and Workstation. A missing or corrupt SERVICES.EXE cripples your Windows NT-based computer.

After a user successfully logs on to the system, the LastKnownGood control set is updated and the boot is considered good. Until a user logs on for the first time, though, the boot/load process technically remains unfinished, so a problem that Windows NT cannot detect but that a user can see (such as a video problem) can be resolved by falling back on the LastKnownGood configuration.

6

8. Control Sets and LastKnownGood

A *control set* is a collection of configuration information used during boot by Windows NT. A special control set, called LastKnownGood, plays a special role in troubleshooting the boot process.

After the system boots and a user logs on successfully, the current configuration settings are copied to the LastKnownGood control set in the Registry. These settings are preserved so that if the system cannot boot successfully the next time a user attempts to log on, the system can fall back on LastKnownGood, which, as the name implies, is the last configuration known to facilitate a "good" boot. LastKnownGood is stored in the Registry under

```
HKEY_LOCAL_MACHINE\SYSTEM\CurrentControlSet
```

The key to understanding LastKnownGood lies in recognizing that it updates the first time a user logs on to Windows NT after a reboot.

To boot with the LastKnownGood configuration, press the spacebar when prompted during the boot process. You are presented with the Hardware Profile/Configuration Recovery menu. Select a hardware profile and enter L for the LastKnownGood configuration.

Windows NT occasionally will boot using LastKnownGood automatically, but only if the normal boot process produces severe or critical errors in loading device drivers.

LastKnownGood does not do you any good if files are corrupt or missing. You must use the Emergency Repair Process for aid with that.

B. Troubleshooting the Boot Process

If one of the important boot files is missing or corrupt, Windows NT can't boot correctly. If NTLDR, NTDTECT.COM, BOOTSECT.DOS, or NTOSKRNL.EXE fail, NT displays a message that tells you the name of the missing file. Use the Emergency Repair Process to restore the system.

If BOOT.INI is missing, NTLDR tries to start Windows NT without consulting BOOT.INI or the boot menu. This works as long as Windows NT is installed in the default \Winnt directory on the first partition of the first disk. If Windows NT is installed in a different directory, however, NTLDR cannot find it and issues an error message stating that the file, \winnt root\system32\ntoskrnl.exe, is missing or corrupt.

If BOOT.INI contains an invalid path name, or if a BOOT.INI path includes an invalid device, the boot fails. Verify all BOOT.INI paths. If possible, boot from a floppy and edit BOOT.INI to fix the problem. The Emergency Repair Process described later in this chapter can restore BOOT.INI if the error stems from a recent change.

If you need to boot Windows NT from the floppy drive, you can use Setup Boot disks created using the Winnt.exe or Winnt32.exe utilities with the /ox switch.

C. The Emergency Repair Process

As discussed in Chapter 2, the installation process enables you to create an emergency repair directory and emergency repair disk, both of which are backup copies of Registry information (which come in handy if you can't boot Windows NT owing to missing or corrupt files). The following sections examine ways in which the Emergency Repair Process can aid a troubled Windows NT installation.

1. Emergency Repair Directory Versus Emergency Repair Disk

Installation always creates the emergency repair directory. You can find it in <winnt_root>\REPAIR. You can create an emergency repair disk as well.

Both the directory and disk are computer-specific. Keep a separate emergency repair disk for each computer and tag it with the serial number of the computer.

Table 6.2.1 lists and describes the files on the emergency repair disk.

Table 6.2.1 Files on the Emergency Repair Disk

Files	Description
SETUP.LOG	A text file that contains the names of all the Windows NT installation files, along with checksum values for each. If any of the files on your hard drive are missing or corrupt, the Emergency Repair Process should detect them with the aid of this hidden, system, and read-only file.
SYSTEM._	A compressed copy of the Registry's SYSTEM hive. This is the Windows NT control set collection.

Files	Description
SAM._	A compressed copy of the Registry's SAM hive. This is the Windows NT user accounts database.
SECURITY.__	A compressed copy of the Registry's SECURITY hive. This is the Windows NT security information, which includes SAM and the security policies.
SOFTWARE._	A compressed copy of the Registry's SOFTWARE hive. This hive contains all Win32 software configuration information.
DEFAULT._	A compressed copy of the system default profile.
CONFIG.NT	The VDM version of the MS-DOS CONFIG.SYS file.
AUTOEXEC.NT	The VDM version of the MS-DOS AUTOEXEC.BAT file.
NTUSER.DA_	A copy of the file NTUSER.DAT (which contains user profile information) from the directory winnt_root\profiles\Defaultuser.

2. RDISK.EXE

Both the emergency repair disk and directory are created during installation, but neither are updated automatically at anytime thereafter. To update the emergency repair information, use the hidden utility RDISK.EXE (located in \<winnt_root>\SYSTEM32).

RDISK offers two options for administrators: Update Repair Info and Create Repair Disk.

a. Update Repair Info

The Update Repair Info button updates only the emergency repair directory, although it does prompt for the creation/update of an emergency repair disk immediately following successful completion of the directory update. Always update the directory before creating the disk, because the disk will be created using the information in the directory.

b. Create Repair Disk

If the information in the repair directory is up-to-date, you may choose to create or update an emergency repair disk. You don't have to use a pre-formatted disk for the repair disk. RDISK formats the disk regardless.

A significant limitation of RDISK is that it will not update DEFAULT._, SECURITY, or SAM, in the repair directory (or disk). In other words, you may update your repair disk week-to-week, but none of your account changes are being backed up. To do a complete emergency repair update, you must run RDISK.EXE using the /S switch.

3. Starting the Emergency Repair Process

Whether you use the emergency repair directory or the emergency repair disk, you need to recognize that you can't boot from either or use either from within Windows NT. To actually invoke the Emergency Repair Process, you must access the original three Windows NT Setup disks. If you don't have the original disks handy, you generate them from the CD by using the WINNT /OX command on a DOS-based machine.

The Setup process offers the choices either to install Windows NT or repair an existing installation. Pressing R on this screen invokes the Emergency Repair Process.

After you select your repair options, Setup attempts to locate your hard drive. After Setup locates your hard drive, it asks you whether you want to use an emergency repair disk or you want Setup to search for your repair directory. You then encounter a series of restoration choices based on the repair options you selected and the problems Setup uncovers as it analyzes your system. The next few sections discuss the emergency repair options.

a. Inspect Registry Files

At this point, the process gets computer-specific. If your registry becomes corrupt, only your own emergency repair disk can save you—no one else's can. You granularly select to repair any combination of the SYSTEM, SOFTWARE, DEFAULT, and SECURITY/SAM hives, which are copied from the repair directory/disk.

b. Inspect Startup Environment

The files required to boot Windows NT are discussed earlier in this chapter. If any of these files become corrupted, choose Inspect Startup Environment to repair them. You can use anyone's emergency repair disk for this option because these files are generic across all Windows NT installations.

c. Verify Windows NT System Files

This option systematically inspects every file in the Windows NT directory tree and compares them with the checksum values in SETUP.LOG. If it determines that any files are missing or corrupt, the repair process attempts to replace them. Again, you need the original disks or CD before you can do so.

d. Inspect Boot Sector

If you upgrade to a new version of DOS and suddenly find that you cannot boot to Windows NT anymore, your boot sector probably has been replaced. The MS-DOS or Windows 95 SYS command is notorious for trashing the Windows NT boot sector. The emergency repair disk solves this problem, and you don't even need a computer-specific ERD—you can borrow anybody's.

6.2.1 Exercise: Booting with SOS

In Exercise 6.2.1, you learn how to initiate a Windows NT boot by using the /sos switch, which enumerates each driver as the drivers load during the kernel load phase.

Estimated time: 20 minutes

1. Remove the Read-only flag on the BOOT.INI file. Start the Notepad accessory application and open the boot.ini file in the root directory of the system partition. In the Notepad Open dialog box, don't forget to select All Files in the box labeled Files of type. The extension may not appear in the browse list. (The filename may appear as *boot*, without the extension. If you aren't sure you have the right file, right-click on the file and select Properties.) Examine the MS-DOS name setting in the File Properties dialog box.

2. Figure 6.2.1 shows the boot.ini file in Notepad. Find the line with the text string "Windows NT Server Version 4.00 [VGA]." Make sure the string is followed by the switches /basevideo and/sos. If you're confident your system uses a VGA video driver, skip to step 6; otherwise, continue with step 3.

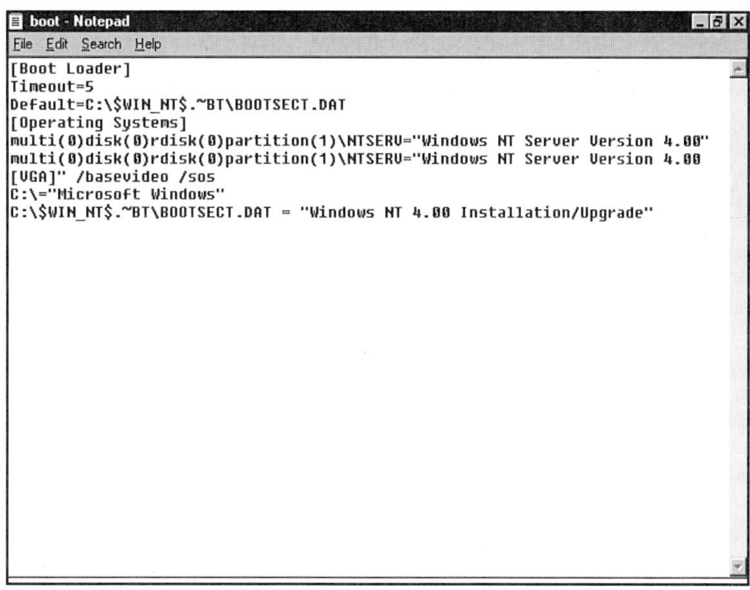

Figure 6.2.1 A boot.ini file.

3. Save the boot.ini file to a different filename (such as boot.tmp) by using the File, Save As command.
4. Delete the /basevideo switch in the line with the text string "Windows NT Server Version 4.00 [VGA]." The /sos switch should remain. Change the text in the square brackets from "VGA" to "sos."
5. Save the file as boot.ini.

   You may have to use the Save As command to save boot.ini. Verify the filename in the File name box. Step 3 may have changed the default filename.
6. Close Notepad and shut down your system.
7. Reboot Windows NT. When the boot menu appears, choose the "sos" option (or the VGA option if you skipped steps 3–5).
8. Watch the drivers display on-screen as they load. (Watch carefully, they will disappear quickly from the screen.) The drivers, like the boot.ini entries, will appear in ARC format. If you experience a boot failure, you can use this technique to determine which driver crashed or hung the system.
9. Log on to Windows NT. Restore the boot.ini file to its original state, either by inserting "VGA" and "/basevideo" using Notepad or by copying the boot.tmp file back to boot.ini. When you're finished, open boot.ini and make sure it is back to normal.

   Note that Step 9 is very important. You may not use the VGA boot option for months or even years, and when you do, you may not remember that you tried this exercise.

6.2 Practice Problems

1. Which of the following files are not on the Emergency Repair Disk?

   A. SETUP.LOG

   B. NTUSER.DA_

   C. CONFIG.NT

   D. NTSYSTEM.DA_

2. Which is a collection of configuration information used during boot by Windows NT?

   A. LastKnownGood

   B. Control set

   C. BOOT.INI

   D. NTLDR

3. Which is a collection of configuration information used in troubleshooting Windows NT boot problems?

   A. LastKnownGood

   B. Control set

   C. BOOT.INI

   D. NTLDR

4. The user screen switches into GUI mode after which phase of startup?

   A. Kernel Initialization

   B. Services Load

   C. Windows Start

   D. Win32 subsystem

5. Before editing the BOOT.INI file, you should (choose two):

   A. Backup the existing file.

   B. Turn off the system attribute.

   C. Turn off the read-only attribute.

   D. Rename the file with a TXT extension.

6. The BOOT.INI file can be changed with which of the following? (Choose all that apply.)

   A. EDIT.COM

   B. NOTEPAD.EXE

   C. The Environment tab of the Control Panel System application

   D. The Startup/Shutdown tab of the Control Panel System application

7. The preferred method of changing the BOOT.INI file is via:

   A. EDIT.COM

   B. NOTEPAD.EXE

   C. The Environment tab of the Control Panel System application

   D. The Startup/Shutdown tab of the Control Panel System application

8. Choices available from the Emergency Repair Process menu do *not* include:

   A. Inspect Registry Files

   B. Event Viewer

   C. Inspect Startup Environment

   D. Verify Windows NT System Files

9. LastKnownGood boot information is stored in the Registry under:

   A. HKEY_LOCAL_MACHINE

   B. HKEY_LOCAL_MACHINE\SYSTEM

   C. HKEY_LOCAL_MACHINE\SYSTEM\CurrentControlSet

   D. HKEY_LOCAL_MACHINE\SYSTEM\CurrentControlSet\LastKnownGood

10. Two of the files needed during an Intel-based boot that are *not* needed for a RISC boot operation are:

    A. NTDETECT.COM

    B. NTLDR

    C. OSLOADER.EXE

    D. NTOSKRNL.EXE

11. To update the SAM information on the Emergency Repair Disk, which switch must you use with RDISK?

    A. /SAM

    B. /S

    C. /OX

    D. SYSTEM

    E. None of the above

12. Which of the following items will RDISK *not* update, by default, in the Emergency Repair Directory?

    A. SAM

    B. SETUP.LOG

    C. DEFAULT._

    D. SYSTEM._

13. Which of the following items will RDISK update, by default, in the Emergency Repair Directory?

    A. SAM

    B. SETUP.LOG

    C. DEFAULT._

    D. SYSTEM._

14. Which is responsible for building the hardware list during boot operations?

    A. HAL.DLL

    B. NTLDR

    C. NTOSKRNL.EXE

    D. NTDETECT.COM

15. Two files that are common to RISC-based boots as well as Intel-based boots:

    A. OSLOADER.EXE

    B. HAL.DLL

    C. NTDETECT.COM

    D. NTOSKRNL.EXE

16. Which is a system file that is read-only, and hidden in the root of your system partition?

    A. HAL.DLL

    B. NTLDR

    C. NTOSKRNL.EXE

    D. NTDETECT.EXE

17. Which is a system file that is in the <winnt_root>\SYSTEM32 directory of your system?

    A. HAL.DLL

    B. NTLDR

    C. NTOSKRNL.EXE

    D. NTDETECT.COM

18. To boot with the LastKnownGood configuration:

    A. Start WINNT with the /L switch.

    B. Select the option from the Boot Loader menu.

    C. Use the /lastknowngood switch in the BOOT.INI file.

    D. Press the spacebar, when prompted, during the boot process.

19. The utility used to update the emergency repair information is:

    A. RDISK.EXE

    B. REPAIR.EXE

    C. DISKPERF

    D. Server Manager

20. Which two items are updated by running the RDISK utility?

    A. The Emergency Repair Directory

    B. The Emergency Repair Disk

    C. The LastKnownGood control set

    D. HKEY_LOCAL_USER

6

21. On Intel x86-based computers, the boot sector of the active partition loads a file called:

    A. NTLDR

    B. IO.SYS

    C. BOOT.INI

    D. MSDOS.SYS

22. Selecting VGA mode during boot uses which settings? (Select all that apply.)

    A. 16 color

    B. 256 color

    C. 640×480

    D. 800×600

23. This BOOT.INI file switch tells Windows NT to load the standard VGA driver rather than the optimized driver written for you video card:

    A. /basevideo

    B. /sos

    C. /crashdebug

    D. /nodebug

24. What are two ways to turn on the Automatic Recovery and Restart capability?

    A. Use the /crashdebug switch in the BOOT.INI file.

    B. Use the /recovery switch in the BOOT.INI file.

    C. From the System application in the Control Panel.

    D. From Server Manager.

25. This BOOT.INI file switch turns on the Automatic Recovery and Restart capability:

    A. /basevideo

    B. /sos

    C. /crashdebug

    D. /nodebug

26. This BOOT.INI file switch limits the amount of usable memory to a specified amount:

    A. /basevideo

    B. /maxmem

    C. /noserialmice

    D. /nodebug

27. This BOOT.INI file switch turns off the tracking of each piece of executing code during the loading of Windows NT:

    A. /basevideo

    B. /sos

    C. /crashdebug

    D. /nodebug

28. This BOOT.INI file switch tells NTDETECT.COM to not look for the presence of serial mice:

    A. /basevideo

    B. /sos

    C. /noserialmice

    D. /nodebug

29. If you need to recreate the Setup Boot disks, which command should be used?

    A. WINNT32

    B. WINNT

    C. WINNT /OX

    D. REPAIR

30. This BOOT.INI file switch is useful in differentiating between multiple SCSI controllers in a system:

    A. /scsiordinal

    B. /scsi

    C. /nononscsi

    D. /nodebug

31. If NT hangs during the loading of system drivers, which switch should be added to the BOOT.INI file to assist with troubleshooting?

    A. /nodebug

    B. /crashdebug

    C. /sos

    D. /drivers

32. This BOOT.INI file switch lists every driver to the screen as it loads during the kernel load phase:

    A. /basevideo

    B. /sos

    C. /crashdebug

    D. /nodebug

33. The NTOSKRNL.EXE file is found, by default, on an x86-based NT Server in:

    A. <winnt_root>

    B. <winnt_root>\SYSTEM32

    C. <winnt_root>\SYSTEM32\CONFIG

    D. <winn_root>\SYSTEM

34. Choices available from the Emergency Repair Process menu do *not* include:

    A. Inspect Security Environment

    B. Inspect Boot Sector

    C. Inspect Startup Environment

    D. Verify Windows NT System Files

35. If Windows NT is installed in a location other than the default directory and an error message indicating that NTOSKRNL.EXE is missing or corrupt occurs, what is the most likely cause of the error?

    A. The BOOT.INI file is missing or corrupt.

    B. The Registry has not saved the new location.

    C. The NTOSKRNL.EXE has been moved.

    D. The LastKnownGood was automatically invoked.

36. The section of the BOOT.INI file that contains a reference for every OS on the Boot Loader menu is:

    A. [initialize]

    B. [common]

    C. [boot loader]

    D. [operating systems]

37. The section of the BOOT.INI file that defines the default operating system that will be loaded if a choice is not made on the Boot Loader menu is:

    A. [initialize]

    B. [common]

    C. [boot loader]

    D. [operating systems]

38. The sections of the BOOT.INI file include (choose all correct answers):

    A. [initialize]

    B. [common]

    C. [boot loader]

    D. [operating systems]

39. Which of the following files are *not* on the Emergency Repair Disk?

    A. DEFAULT._

    B. NTUSER.DA_

    C. BOOT.INI

    D. SYSTEM._

40. A hidden, read-only, system file in the root of the system partition, it contains information that was present in the boot sector prior to the install of Windows NT:

    A. NTBOOT.INI

    B. NTLDR

    C. BOOT.INI

    D. BOOTSECT.DOS

41. Windows NT installation always creates an emergency repair directory. This is located in:

    A. <winnt_root>

    B. <winnt_root>\SYSTEM

    C. <winnt_root>\REPAIR

    D. <winnt_root>\SYSTEM\REPAIR

42. If you upgrade to a new version of DOS and find that you suddenly cannot boot to NT anymore, a possible cause is:

    A. Your boot sector has been replaced.

    B. The BOOT.INI file has been deleted.

    C. NTOSKRNL.EXE has been moved.

    D. The two operating systems are not compatible.

43. It is a single file that contains the code necessary to mask interrupts and exceptions from the kernel:

    A. HAL.DLL

    B. NTLDR

    C. NTOSKRNL.EXE

    D. NTDETECT.COM

44. It is an editable text file that controls the Boot Loader menu:

    A. NTBOOT.INI

    B. NTLDR

    C. BOOT.INI

    D. BOOTSECT.DOS

45. It is the file responsible for starting the minifile system driver necessary for accessing the system and boot partitions on an NT system:

    A. NTLDR

    B. IO.SYS

    C. BOOT.INI

    D. MSDOS.SYS

46. Which of the following files are not the Emergency Repair Disk?

    A. NTLDR

    B. NTUSER.DA_

    C. CONFIG.NT

    D. SYSTEM._

47. The option to Verify Windows NT System Files during the Emergency Repair Process relies upon information contained in what file?

    A. SOFTWARE._

    B. CONFIG.NT

    C. SAM

    D. SETUP.LOG

48. Which file of those on the Emergency Repair Disk contains the names of all Windows NT installation files?

    A. AUTOEXEC.NT

    B. SETUP.LOG

    C. NTLDR

    D. WINNT.LOG

49. The HKEY_LOCAL_MACHINE\SYSTEM file is found, by default, on an x86-based NT Server in:

    A. <winnt_root>

    B. <winnt_root>\SYSTEM32

    C. <winnt_root>\SYSTEM32\CONFIG

    D. <winn_root>\SYSTEM

50. The BOOT.INI file allows for the use of several troubleshooting switches. Those switches are added to which section of the file?

    A. [initialize]

    B. [common]

    C. [boot loader]

    D. [operating systems]

51. Which is *not* a valid BOOT.INI switch?

    A. /maxmem

    B. /msgsvc

    C. /noserialmice

    D. /nodebug

52. Which is *not* a valid BOOT.INI switch?

    A. /maxmem

    B. /readonly

    C. /noserialmice

    D. /nodebug

53. Boot-time drivers are stored in the Registry under:

    A. HKEY_LOCAL_MACHINE

    B. HKEY_LOCAL_MACHINE\SYSTEM

    C. HKEY_LOCAL_MACHINE\SYSTEM32

    D. HKEY_LOCAL_MACHINE\SYSTEM\CurrentControlSet\Control\ServiceGroupOrder

54. The LastKnownGood control set is updated:

    A. After a user successfully logs on to a system

    B. After the Win32 subsystem starts

    C. During Shutdown

    D. During the Kernel Initialization phase

55. To recreate the Setup Boot disks with the WINNT command, the system of choice would be:

    A. A DOS machine with a CD-ROM drive and floppy drive

    B. A Windows NT Workstation machine with a CD-ROM drive and floppy drive

    C. A Windows NT Server machine with a CD-ROM drive and floppy drive

    D. Any RISC-based machine with a CD-ROM drive and floppy drive

56. On an Intel-x86 computer, which set of files is required to boot Windows NT?

    A. NTLDR; BOOT.INI; NTDETECT.COM; NTOSKRNL.EXE; NTBOOTDD.SYS

    B. NTLDR; BOOT.MNU; NTDETECT.EXE; OSLOADER; NTBOOTDD.SYS

    C. OSLOADER; NTOSKRNL.EXE; NTDETECT.COM; NTBOOTDD.SYS

    D. NTLDR; HAL.DLL; BOOT.INI; NTDETECT.COM; NTOSKRNL.EXE

57. Evan calls on Friday, right before it is time to go home. He wants to know if you can reduce the amount of time his computer takes to boot. He also wants to change the default operating system from MS-DOS to NT Workstation. Which utility should be used?

    A. Control Panel, Boot.

    B. Control Panel, System.

    C. Server Manager.

    D. Configure on a user-by-user basis in the users' profiles.

6.2 Answers and Explanations: Exercise

In the preceding exercise, you learned how to initiate a Windows NT boot using the /sos switch. Through careful observation, you saw how it enumerates each driver as the driver is loaded during the kernel load phase.

6.2 Answers and Explanations: Practice Problems

1. **D** A compressed copy of the Registry's SYSTEM hive is stored as SYSTEM._ instead of NTSYSTEM.DA.

2. **B** A control set is a collection of configuration information used during boot, whereas LastKnownGood is a special single control set used for troubleshooting.

3. **A** A control set is a collection of configuration information used during boot, whereas LastKnownGood is a special single control set used for troubleshooting.

4. **D** After the Win32 subsystem starts, the screen switches into GUI mode.

5. **A, C** Always back up the file because an error can cause serious harm; take off the default read-only attribute to save your changes.

6. **A, B, D** An editable text file, BOOT.INI, can be changed with any text editor, but doing so from the Startup/Shutdown tab is preferred because one typographical error in the file can cause serious boot problems.

7. **D** An editable text file, BOOT.INI, can be changed with any text editor, but doing so from the Startup/Shutdown tab is preferred because one typographical error in the file can cause serious boot problems.

8. **B** Event Viewer is a stand-alone utility and not a part of the Emergency Repair Process.

9. **C** HKEY_LOCAL_MACHINE\SYSTEM\CurrentControlSet houses the LastKnownGood information.

10. **A, B** Much of the work of NTDETECT.COM and NTLDR are performed by the firmware on the RISC platform.

11. **B** Neither the DEFAULT._, SAM, or SECURITY._ items are updated with RDISK unless the /S option is used.

12. **A, C** Neither the DEFAULT._, SAM, or SECURITY._ items are updated with RDISK unless the /S option is used.

13. **B, D** Neither the DEFAULT._, SAM, or SECURITY._ items are updated with RDISK unless the /S option is used.

14. **D** NTDETECT.COM builds the hardware list and returns the information to NTLDR.

15. **B, D** NTDETECT.COM is used only on Intel boots, whereas OSLOADER.EXE is used only on RISC boots. HAL.DLL and NTOSKRNL.EXE are common to both boot operations.

16. **B** NTDLR is the system file responsible for the majority of the early boot operations.

17. **C** NTOSKRNL.EXE is the kernel file and it is loaded during boot by the NTLDR.

18. **D** Pressing the spacebar during the boot process presents you with the Hardware Profile/Configuration Recovery menu. Select a hardware profile and enter **L** for LastKnownGood configuration.

19. **A** RDISK will update Emergency Repair Directory and Emergency Repair Directory.

20. **A, B** RDISK will update Emergency Repair Directory and Emergency Repair Directory.

21. **A** Similar to the IO.SYS file in MS-DOS environments, the NTLDR file is a hidden, read-only, system file in the root of the system partition.

22. **A, C** Standard VGA consists of 16 colors displayed at 640×480.

23. **A** The /basevideo switch performs this operation.

24. **A, C** The /crashdebug switch enables this, as does the System application in the Control Panel.

25. **C** The /crashdebug switch performs this operation.

26. **B** The /maxmem switch performs this operation.

27. **D** The /nodebug switch performs this operation.

28. **C** The /noserialmice switch performs this operation. At times, other devices connected to the serial port can be falsely identified as mice. After boot, the serial port is unavailable because the system expects a mouse to be there.

29. **C** The /OX switch, used with WINNT, will recreate the Setup Boot disks.

30. **A** The /scsiordinal switch performs this operation.

31. **C** The /sos switch causes all drivers to be displayed on the screen as they are loaded.

32. **B** The /sos switch performs this operation.

33. **B** The <winnt_root>\SYSTEM32 directory holds the NTOSKRNL.EXE file.

34. **A** The Boot Sector, Startup Environment, and NT System files can all be inspected and verified during the Emergency Repair Process.

35. **A** The BOOT.INI file contains a pointer to the NTOSKRNL.EXE location.

36. **D** The BOOT.INI file contains only two sections, [boot loader] and [operating systems]. The first defines the default operating system, whereas the second contains a reference for each OS on the menu.

37. **C** The BOOT.INI file contains only two sections, [boot loader] and [operating systems]. The first defines the default operating system, whereas the second contains a reference for each OS on the menu.

38. **C, D** The BOOT.INI file contains only two sections, [boot loader] and [operating systems]. The first defines the default operating system, whereas the second contains a reference for each OS on the menu.

39. **C** The BOOT.INI file is not on the Emergency Repair Disk.

40. **D** The BOOTSECT.DOS file contains information about previous operating systems and calls the correct files if a choice other than NT is made from the Boot Loader menu.

41. **C** The directory where the emergency repair directory resides is <winnt_root>\REPAIR.

42. **A** The DOS and Windows 95 SYS command will often overwrite the boot sector—which can be restored from the Emergency Repair Disk.

43. **A** The HAL.DLL file contains the code necessary to mask interrupts and exceptions from the kernel.

44. **C** The NTLDR calls the Boot Loader menu, but it is the BOOT.INI file that controls it and its choices.

45. **A** The NTLDR file is responsible for carrying out the vast majority of the early initialization operations, including starting the minifile system driver.

46. **A** The NTLDR is not on the Emergency Repair Disk.

47. **D** The SETUP.LOG file contains names and checksum values of files used during NT installation.

48. **B** The SETUP.LOG file has the name and checksums of all Windows NT installation files. It can find corrupted files and report which ones need to be fixed.

49. **C** The SYSTEM component of the Registry is stored in <winnt_root>\SYSTEM32\CONFIG.

50. **D** The [operating systems] section contains information about each operating system offered on the menu, whereas the [boot loader] lists only the default operating system if one is not chosen from the Boot Loader menu.

51. **B** There is not a /msgsvc switch for the BOOT.INI file.

52. **B** There is not a /readonly switch for the BOOT.INI file.

53. **D** This is the hive of the Registry responsible for boot-time driver information.

54. **A** When a user successfully logs into a system, the LastKnownGood control set is updated.

55. **A** WINNT works on DOS machines, whereas WINNT32 is used on all other choices.

56. **A** The files needed to load NT on an Intel-x86 platform are NTLDR; BOOT.INI; NTDETECT.COM; NTOSKRNL.EXE; and NTBOOTDD.SYS

57. **B** The System utility will enable you to choose a default operating system and reduce boot time.

6.2 Key Words

Boot

Master Boot Record (MBR)

NTLDR

Control set

Advanced RISC Computer (ARC)

6.3 Troubleshooting Configuration Errors

Microsoft lists the following objective for the Windows NT Server exam: Choose the appropriate course of action to take to resolve configuration errors.

Some common device problems are resource conflicts (such as interrupt conflicts) and SCSI problems. Use Windows NT diagnostics to check resource settings. If the error is the result of a recent configuration change, you can reboot the system and boot to the LastKnownGood configuration.

If a Windows NT service doesn't start, check Event Viewer; or, check the Control Panel Services application to make sure the service is installed and configured to start. Windows NT includes some important tools, as follows:

- Event Viewer
- Windows NT Diagnostics
- System Recovery

A. Event Viewer

If your Windows NT-based computer manages to boot successfully, yet still isn't performing correctly, the first thing to check is the system event log, where all critical system messages are stored.

Windows NT includes the Event Viewer application in the Administrative Tool program group for viewing the messages stored in the system, security, and application log files (see fig. 6.3.1).

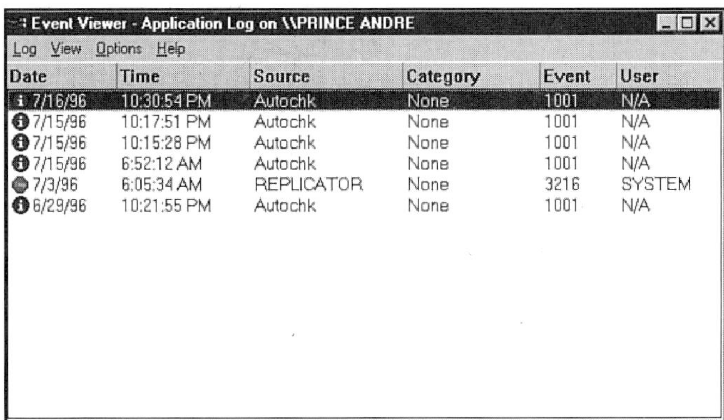

Figure 6.3.1 Event Viewer.

1. System Log

The system log, the default view in Event Viewer, is maintained by the operating system. It tracks three kinds of events:

- **Errors.** Symbolized by Stop signs, and indicative of the failure of a Windows NT component or device, or perhaps an inability to start. These errors are common on notebook computers when Windows NT fails to start the network components because PCMCIA network cards are not present.

- **Warnings.** Symbolized by exclamation points, and indicative of an impending problem. Low disk space on a partition triggers a warning, for example.
- **Information Events.** Symbolized by the traditional "I" in a blue circle, and indicative of an event that isn't at all bad but is still somehow significant. Browser elections often cause information events.

2. Security Log

The security log remains empty until you enable auditing through User Manager. After enabling auditing, the audited events reside here. The security log tracks two types of events:

- **Success Audits.** Symbolized by a key, and indicative of successful security access.
- **Failure Audits.** Symbolized by a padlock, and indicative of unsuccessful security access.

3. Application Log

The application log collects messages from native Windows NT applications. If you aren't using any Win32 applications, this log remains empty.

4. Securing Event Logs

Ordinarily, anyone can view the event log information. Some administrators, however, might not want guests to have this sort of access. There is one restriction, enabled through the Registry, that you can place on Event Viewer—you can prohibit guests from accessing the system or application logs from the following Registry location, in which <log_name> is either System or Application:

```
HKEY_LOCAL_MACHINE\System\CurrentControlSet\Services\EventLog\å<log_name>
```

You need to add a value called RestrictGuestAccess of type REG_DWORD and set it equal to 1. To re-enable guest access to either log, set the appropriate RestrictGuestAccess value to 0 or just delete the value altogether.

5. Configuring Event Viewer

By default, log files can reach 512 KB, and events are overwritten after seven days. You can change these settings in the Event Log Settings dialog box, which you open by choosing Log Settings in the Event Viewer Log menu.

The Save As option in the Log menu enables you to save the log as an event log file (with an EVT extension), making it available for examination on another computer at a future time, or as a comma-separated value text file (also with a TXT extension) for importing into a spreadsheet or database.

6. Using Event Viewer

At some point, every Windows NT user receives this infamous message:

```
One or more services failed to start. Please see the Event Viewer for
details.
```

This message appears when the first user logs on to the system after at least one Windows NT component fails to load successfully. As directed, you should immediately proceed to Event Viewer.

To find the source of the problem, look at the system log, under the Event heading. Somewhere toward the top of the column, you should find an Event code of 6005. By default, the logs list the most recent events at the top of the list, so start scanning at the top of the list or you may not find the most recent 6005 event. Event 6005 means that the EventLog service was successfully started.

To examine an event message, double-click on an event to open the Event Detail dialog box.

Note the identifying information for the event:

- Date of the event
- Time of the event
- User account that generated the event, if applicable (usually found in the security log)
- Computer on which the event occurred
- Event ID (the Windows NT Event code)
- Source Windows NT component that generated the event
- Type of event (Error, Warning, and so on)
- Category of event (Logon/Logoff audit, for example)
- Description of the event
- Data in hexadecimal format, useful to a developer or debugger

B. Windows NT Diagnostics

Windows NT Diagnostics provides a tidy front-end to much of the information in the HKEY_LOCAL_MACHINE Registry subtree. Like its ancestor, MSD from Windows 3.1, Windows NT Diagnostics can create incredibly detailed and valuable system configuration reports. One thing you cannot do with Windows NT Diagnostics is edit the system configuration. Figure 6.3.2 shows the Windows NT Diagnostics dialog box.

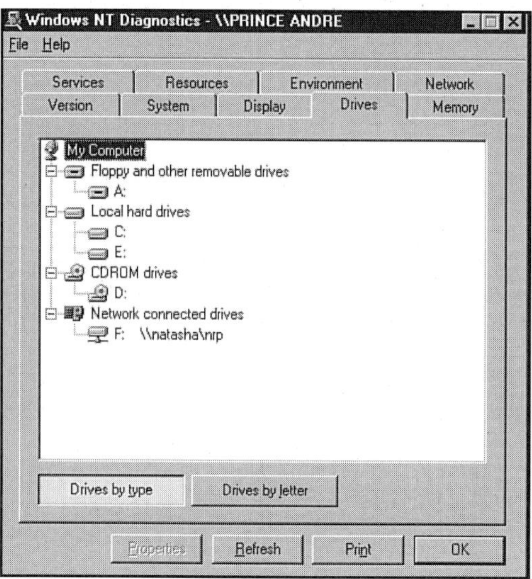

Figure 6.3.2 The Windows NT Diagnostics dialog box.

The Windows NT Diagnostics dialog box includes the following nine tabs:

- **Version.** Displays information stored under HKEY_LOCAL_MACHINE\Software\Microsoft\Windows NT\CurrentVersion, including the build number, registered owner, and Service Pack update information.
- **System.** Displays information stored under HKEY_LOCAL_MACHINE\Hardware, including CPU and other device identification information.
- **Display.** Displays information on the video adapter and adapter settings.
- **Drives.** Lists all drive letters in use and their types, including drive letters for floppy drives, hard disks, CD-ROM and optical drives, and network connections. Double-click on a drive letter to display a drive Properties dialog box. The General tab of the drive Properties dialog box shows byte and cluster information for the drive, while the File System tab shows file system information.
- **Memory.** Displays current memory load, as well as physical and virtual memory statistics.
- **Services.** Displays service information stored under HKEY_LOCAL_MACHINE\System\CurrentControlSet\Services, including status. Click on the Devices button to display driver information stored under HKEY_LOCAL_MACHINE\System\CurrentControlSet\Control, including status.
- **Resources.** Displays device information listed by interrupt and by port, and also by DMA channels and UMB locations in use.
- **Environment.** Displays environment variables for command prompt sessions (set under Control Panel System).
- **Network.** Displays network component configuration and status.

C. System Recovery

The Recovery utility is a tool you can use to record debugging information, alert an administrator, or reboot the system in the event of a Stop error. (A *Stop error* causes Windows NT to stop all processes.) To configure the Recovery utility, start the Control Panel System application and click on the Startup/Shutdown tab.

The bottom frame of the Startup/Shutdown tab is devoted to Recovery options. The options are as follows:

- Write an event to the system log.
- Send an administrative alert.
- Write debugging information to (specify a filename). In the event of a Stop error, the Savedump.exe program dumps everything in memory to the pagefile and marks the location of the dump. When you restart your system, Windows NT copies the memory dump from the pagefile to the file specified in the Startup/Shutdown tab. You can then use a program called Dumpexam.exe in the \Support directory of the Windows NT CD-ROM to study the contents of the memory dump and determine the cause of the Stop error.
- Automatically reboot. You might not want to have your server sit idle after a Stop error. This option instructs Windows NT to automatically reboot after a Stop error.

D. Backing Up the Registry

Before discussing Registry files, you should be familiar with the term hive. A *hive* is a binary file that contains all the keys and values within a branch of the Registry.

Two files are associated with each hive: one file is named after the hive and has no extension, and the other is identically named with a LOG extension (with the exception of SYSTEM, which has a SYSTEM.ALT counterpart for reasons to be explained shortly). Both files reside in the \<winnt_root>\SYSTEM32\CONFIG directory. Most of the hives loaded at any given time are residents of HKEY_LOCAL_MACHINE, and the others belong to HKEY_USERS. Here is a list of the Registry hives:

HKEY_LOCAL_MACHINE\SAM (SAM, SAM.LOG)

HKEY_LOCAL_MACHINE\SECURITY (SECURITY, SECURITY.LOG)

HKEY_LOCAL_MACHINE\SOFTWARE (SOFTWARE, SOFTWARE.LOG)

HKEY_LOCAL_MACHINE\SYSTEM (SYSTEM, SYSTEM.ALT)

HKEY_USERS\.DEFAULT (DEFAULT, DEFAULT.LOG)

HKEY_USERS\<user_sid> (<user_profile>, <user_profile>.LOG)

The LOG files provide fault tolerance for the Registry. Whenever configuration data is changed, the changes are written to the LOG file first. Then the first sector of the actual hive is flagged to indicate that an update is taking place. The data is transferred from the log to the hive, and the update flag on the hive is then lowered. If the computer were to crash after the flag had been raised but before it had been lowered, some, if not all the data, would quite possibly be corrupt. If that happened, when Windows NT restarted it would detect the flag still raised on the hive, and it would use the log to redo the update.

The only exception to this rule is the SYSTEM file. Because the SYSTEM hive contains critical information that must be loaded intact to load enough of the operating system to process the log files, a duplicate of SYSTEM is maintained as SYSTEM.ALT. This file functions identically to a log file, except that the entire file (rather than just the changes) is mirrored. If the computer were to crash during an update to the SYSTEM branch of the Registry, the integrity of the SYSTEM hive is still preserved. If the data had not yet been fully committed to SYSTEM.ALT, the SYSTEM hive is still preserved in its original configuration. If the data had not yet been fully committed to SYSTEM, SYSTEM.ALT would be used to redo the update.

LOG files are so transitory that they would be useless by the time the backup completes, and should not be included in the backup. The files of greatest import are SYSTEM and SOFTWARE.

Registry files almost always are in a state of flux and are constantly open for read/write access. The Windows NT Backup program usually skips over these files for that reason. Probably the best way to back up the SYSTEM and SOFTWARE files is to use the Repair Disk application, another hidden application in the \<winnt_root>\SYSTEM32 directory. The section "RDISK.EXE," earlier in this chapter, discussed the Repair Disk utility, otherwise known as RDISK.EXE.

E. Backing Up Individual Keys

You can create your own hive files by saving an entire branch of the Registry starting from any key you choose. You do so by choosing Registry, Save Key in Registry Editor. To load the hive into the Registry of another Windows NT computer, choose Registry, Restore Key.

If you want to work with the key only temporarily, you can use the Restore Volatile command rather than the Restore Key command. The key still loads into the Registry at the selected location, but it doesn't reload the next time the system restarts.

6.3.1 Exercise: Back up an Individual File

In Exercise 6.3.1, you learn how to start the NTBACKUP utility and back up an individual file.

Estimated time: 10 minutes

1. Start the Backup program by choosing Administrative Tools from the Programs section of the Start Menu. Next, select Backup.
2. Double-click on the root drive, and then Windows, followed by system and viewers.

3. Select the QUIKVIEW.EXE program. Notice what happens to the tree—not only is the file selected, but all the directories above it in the path now have a gray box showing that a portion of their contents has been chosen.
4. Choose Backup and observe as this file is backed up to your tape drive.

6.3.2 Exercise: Restore an Individual File

In Exercise 6.3.2, you learn how to start the NTBACKUP utility and restore the file backed up in Exercise 6.3.1.

Estimated time: 10 minutes

1. Start the Backup program by choosing Administrative Tools from the Programs section of the Start Menu. Next, select Backup.
2. Double-click on the tape drive, and find the file you backed up in the early exercise.
3. Reverse the steps in Exercise 6.3.1 and restore QUIKVIEW.EXE from the tape to your system.

6.3.3 Exercise: Utilize Event Viewer

In Exercise 6.3.3, you learn how to start the Event Viewer utility and examine the System log file.

Estimated time: 15 minutes

1. Start the Event Viewer program by choosing Administrative Tools from the Programs section of the Start Menu.
2. Next, select Event Viewer. Notice that the System log comes up by default.
3. Select the Log option and change to Security, then Application, and back to System.
4. From View, choose Filter Events, then select only for the information entries to display.
5. Select View, All Events to remove the filter.
6. Exit Event Viewer.

6.3.4 Exercise: Examine Windows NT Diagnostics

In Exercise 6.3.4, you learn how to start the Windows NT Diagnostics utility and look at your system.

Estimated time: 10 minutes

1. Start the Diagnostics program by choosing Administrative Tools from the Programs section of the Start Menu.
2. Next, select Windows NT Diagnostics. Notice the tabs which appear.
3. Click through each of the tabs and observe the information each presents.
4. Exit Windows NT Diagnostics.

6.3 Practice Problems

1. The Recovery tool can do which three of the following:

   A. Record debugging information.

   B. Alert an administrator of a stop event.

   C. Alert two administrators on different domains of a stop event.

   D. Reboot the system in response to a stop event.

2. A common cause of information events in the System log would be:

   A. Browser elections

   B. Failure of a service to start

   C. Hard drive errors

   D. Configuration errors

3. By default, who can view Event Log information:

   A. Administrators

   B. Members of Domain Users

   C. Guests

   D. Anyone

4. There is only one restriction you can place on who can see Event Log information. That restriction applies to whom?

   A. Administrators

   B. Members of Domain Users

   C. Guests

   D. Anyone

5. The default directory that system dumps are written to is:

   A. C:\

   B. %SystemRoot%

   C. SYSTEM

   D. DUMP

6. The default filename that system dumps are written to is:

   A. Dump.hex

   B. Dump.txt

   C. Memory.dmp

   D. Memory.txt

7. The Save As option in the Event Viewer log menu will let you save the files as comma-delimited fields. When you choose to do so, what extension is used on the files?

   A. TXT

   B. EVT

   C. DAT

   D. CHK

8. The Save As option in the Event Viewer log menu, by default, saves the event log file with what extension?

   A. TXT

   B. EVT

   C. DAT

   D. CHK

9. What program creates EVT extension hex files?

   A. Event Viewer

   B. Performance Monitor

   C. DiskPerf

   D. System

10. Which extension indicates hex files that were saved from the Event Viewer?

    A. TXT

    B. EVT

    C. DAT

    D. CHK

11. To see information about DMA channels and VMB locations in the Windows NT Diagnostics tool, select which tab?

    A. Services

    B. Memory

    C. Resources

    D. Network

12. Event Viewer can view which three log files?

    A. System

    B. Application

    C. Security

    D. Netlogon

13. If a Windows NT service fails to start, what tool should you use?

    A. Performance Monitor

    B. Event Viewer

    C. Tracert

    D. System Recovery

14. The Windows NT Diagnostics dialog box includes all of the following tabs *except*:

    A. Memory

    B. Network

    C. Global

    D. Resources

15. The System Tab in the Windows NT Diagnostics box displays information stored in the Registry under which hive:

    A. HKEY_LOCAL_MACHINE\SOFTWARE

    B. HKEY_LOCAL_MACHINE\HARDWARE

    C. HKEY_LOCAL_MACHINE\SOFTWARE\MICROSOFT\WINDOWS NT\CurrentVersion

    D. HKEY_LOCAL_MACHINE\SYSTEM

16. Version information is stored in the Windows NT Registry under which hive:

    A. HKEY_LOCAL_MACHINE\SOFTWARE

    B. HKEY_LOCAL_MACHINE\SOFTWARE\MICROSOFT\WINDOWS NT

    C. HKEY_LOCAL_MACHINE\SOFTWARE\MICROSOFT\WINDOWS NT\CurrentVersion

    D. HKEY_LOCAL_MACHINE\SYSTEM

17. Service information is stored in the Windows NT Registry under which hive:

    A. HKEY_LOCAL_MACHINE\SOFTWARE

    B. HKEY_LOCAL_MACHINE\SOFTWARE\MICROSOFT\WINDOWS NT

    C. HKEY_LOCAL_MACHINE\SOFTWARE\MICROSOFT\WINDOWS NT\CurrentVersion

    D. HKEY_LOCAL_MACHINE\SYSTEM

18. A common cause of warning events in the System log would be:

    A. Browser elections

    B. Failure of a service to start

    C. Low disk space on a hard drive partition

    D. Configuration errors

19. To see information about network component configuration in the Windows NT Diagnostics tool, select which tab:

    A. Services

    B. Memory

    C. Resources

    D. Network

20. A common cause of error events in the System log would be:
    A. Browser elections
    B. PCMCIA cards not present on a notebook computer
    C. Low disk space on a hard drive partition
    D. Configuration errors
21. Tools for looking at configuration errors include all of the following *except*:
    A. Event Viewer
    B. Performance Monitor
    C. Windows NT Diagnostics
    D. System Recovery
22. The Windows NT Diagnostics dialog box includes all of the following tabs *except*:
    A. Services
    B. Resources
    C. Environment
    D. Profiles
23. Two common causes of device problems are:
    A. Interrupt conflicts
    B. Installation of graphic-intensive game packages
    C. Installation of new software
    D. SCSI problems
24. To see information stored in HKEY_LOCAL_MACHINE\SYSTEM\CurrentControlSet\Services in the Windows NT Diagnostics tool, select which tab?
    A. Services
    B. Memory
    C. Resources
    D. Network
25. Failure Audits are displayed in the Security log—when viewed with Event Viewer—as:
    A. A stop sign
    B. A key
    C. An exclamation mark
    D. A padlock
26. Success Audits are displayed in the Security log—when viewed with Event Viewer—as:
    A. A stop sign
    B. A key
    C. An exclamation mark
    D. A padlock
27. Which two symbols are displayed in the Security log—when viewed with Event Viewer:
    A. A stop sign
    B. A key
    C. An exclamation mark
    D. A padlock
28. By default, on a busy system with large event log files that reach their maximum default size, you can choose how much information should be maintained in terms of:
    A. hours
    B. days
    C. weeks
    D. months
29. If you are not using any Win32 applications on a system, what are the contents of the Application log:
    A. It is empty.
    B. Only the Win16 application information.
    C. It mirrors the System log.
    D. Only events for those applications manually selected.

30. The backup Registry file for SAM is:
    A. SAM.BACKUP
    B. SAM.BAK
    C. SAM.ALT
    D. SAM.LOG
31. Recovery options are configured by:
    A. Using Regedit to change parameters.
    B. Running the SYSTEM command-line utility.
    C. Changing values in the bottom frame of the Startup/Shutdown tab.
    D. Running Server Manager.
32. By default, on a busy system with large event log files that reach their maximum default size, how many days of information are kept before the information is overwritten?
    A. 1
    B. 7
    C. 14
    D. 21
33. Debugging information from a Stop error can be verified in a dump file using:
    A. Savedump.exe
    B. Dump.exe
    C. Dumpchk.exe
    D. Dumpexam.exe
34. The backup Registry file for System is:
    A. SYSTEM.BACKUP
    B. SYSTEM.BAK
    C. SYSTEM.ALT
    D. SYSTEM.LOG
35. Debugging information from a Stop error can be made viewable in a dump file using:
    A. Savedump.exe
    B. Dump.exe
    C. Dumpchk.exe
    D. Dumpexam.exe
36. The Event Viewer is found on a Windows NT Server in which program group:
    A. User Manager
    B. System
    C. Administrative Tool
    D. Diagnostics
37. Two common reasons for configuration errors are:
    A. Installation of a new device
    B. Failing hard drives
    C. Installation of new software
    D. Incorrect SCSI settings
38. Debugging information from a Stop error is written to a dump file using:
    A. Savedump.exe
    B. Dump.exe
    C. Dumpchk.exe
    D. Dumpexam.exe
39. Until an administrator enables auditing, what are the contents of the Security log?
    A. Only configuration errors.
    B. It is empty.
    C. It mirrors the System log.
    D. Only share permission errors.
40. The Security log tracks which two types of events?
    A. Success Audits
    B. Failure Audits
    C. Permission Audits
    D. Registry Audits

41. If your Windows NT-based computer manages to boot successfully, yet still is not performing correctly, the first thing to check is:

    A. The system event log

    B. The Performance Monitor

    C. Server Manager

    D. BOOT.INI

42. Which of the following logs is the default log displayed in Event Viewer?

    A. System

    B. Application

    C. Security

    D. Netlogon

43. When looking at a series of stop errors in a System log, the most likely source of all the errors is:

    A. The stop error at the top of the list

    B. The stop error at the bottom of the list

    C. Each error stands alone

    D. The error most replicated

44. The System log, which can be viewed with Event Viewer, tracks which three kinds of events?

    A. Warnings

    B. Information

    C. Configuration

    D. Errors

45. Which of the following events is *not* tracked in the System log?

    A. Warnings

    B. Information

    C. Configuration

    D. Errors

46. Windows Diagnostics is a front-end to information contained where?

    A. HKEY_LOCAL_MACHINE

    B. HKEY_LOCAL_USER

    C. USER

    D. SYSTEM

47. To see information about virtual memory statistics in the Windows NT Diagnostics tool, select which tab?

    A. Services

    B. Memory

    C. Resources

    D. Network

48. Error events are symbolized in the System log—as displayed in Event Viewer—by which of the following symbols?

    A. Stop sign

    B. Exclamation mark

    C. Question mark

    D. An "I" in a blue circle

49. Information events are symbolized in the System log—as displayed in Event Viewer—by which of the following symbols?

    A. Stop sign

    B. Exclamation mark

    C. Question mark

    D. An "I" in a blue circle

50. Warning events are symbolized in the System log—as displayed in Event Viewer—by which of the following symbols?

    A. Stop sign

    B. Exclamation mark

    C. Question mark

    D. An "I" in a blue circle

51. Which of the following would not be a symbol found in the System log—as displayed by Event Viewer?

    A. Stop sign

    B. Exclamation mark

    C. Question mark

    D. An "I" in a blue circle

52. The Windows NT Diagnostics dialog box includes all of the following tabs except:

    A. Version

    B. Connections

    C. System

    D. Display

53. The backup Registry file for Security is:

    A. SECURITY.BACKUP

    B. SECURITY.BAK

    C. SECURITY.ALT

    D. SECURITY.LOG

54. Marco, a remote administrator, claims to have received a message during the boot process reading that a dependency service failed to start. Where should you inform him to look for more information?

    A. The file server error log

    B. In Event Viewer, under the security log

    C. In Event Viewer, under the system log

    D. In Server Manager, under the system log

6.3 Answers and Explanations: Exercises

In Exercise 6.3.1, you learned how to start the NTBACKUP utility. An important correlation to make is that NTBACKUP works only with tape devices. Without a tape device, you cannot do the exercise, or utilize any function of NTBACKUP. Additionally, you learned how to back up an individual file.

In Exercise 6.3.2, you started the NTBACKUP utility once more and saw how to restore the file backed up in Exercise 6.3.1.

In Exercise 6.3.3, you learned how to start the Event Viewer utility. You also saw that the default file to examine is the System log file, and you looked at it.

In Exercise 6.3.4, you learned how to start the Windows NT Diagnostics utility and look at your system.

6

6.3 Answers and Explanations: Practice Problems

1. **A, B, D** An individual user or group can be notified of a stop event, but not two administrators on different domains.

2. **A** Browser elections are a common cause of information events in the System log.

3. **D** By default, anyone can view Event Log information. Editing the Registry, you can prevent Guests from seeing the log information, but that is the only restriction available.

4. **D** By default, anyone can view Event Log information. Editing the Registry, you can prevent Guests from seeing the log information, but that is the only restriction available.

5. **B** By default, memory dumps are written to Memory.dmp—a non-viewable hex file in the %SystemRoot% directory.
6. **C** By default, memory dumps are written to Memory.dmp—a non-viewable hex file.
7. **A** By default, the files are saved as EVT hex files, but can also be saved as comma-delimited TXT files for importing into spreadsheets or databases.
8. **B** By default, the files are saved as EVT hex files, but can also be saved as comma-delimited TXT files for importing into spreadsheets or databases.
9. **A** By default, the files are saved as EVT hex files, but can also be saved as comma-delimited TXT files for importing into spreadsheets or databases.
10. **B** By default, the files are saved as EVT hex files, but can also be saved as comma-delimited TXT files for importing into spreadsheets or databases.
11. **C** DMA channel and VMB location information is displayed under the Resources tab.
12. **A, B, C** Event Viewer will show the contents of the System, Application, and Security log files.
13. **B** Event Viewer will show the System log, which indicates what services have started and which ones have failed.
14. **C** Global is a type of group, a function of the user and User Manager for Domains rather than Windows NT Diagnostics.
15. **B** HKEY_LOCAL_MACHINE\HARDWARE stores information about what is available on the machine.
16. **C** HKEY_LOCAL_MACHINE\SOFTWARE\MICROSOFT\WINDOWS NT\CurrentVersion stores information about the current version of NT on the machine.
17. **D** HKEY_LOCAL_MACHINE\SYSTEM\CurrentControlSet\Services stores information about the current services available to NT on the machine.
18. **C** Low disk space in a partition is a common cause of warning events in the System log.
19. **D** Network component configuration information is displayed under the Network tab of the Windows NT Diagnostics tool.
20. **B** On notebook computers, the absence of a PCMCIA card is a common cause of an error event in the System log.
21. **B** Performance Monitor is used to gather statistics on running services and processes, and not to diagnose configuration errors.
22. **D** Profiles are a function of the user and User Manager for Domains rather than Windows NT Diagnostics.
23. **A, D** SCSI problems and interrupt conflicts are common causes of device problems.
24. **A** Services information in the Registry is displayed under the Services tab of the Windows NT Diagnostics tool.
25. **D** Success Audits are displayed as a key and Failure Audits are displayed as a padlock.
26. **B** Success Audits are displayed as a key and Failure Audits are displayed as a padlock.
27. **B, D** Success Audits are displayed as a key and Failure Audits are displayed as a padlock.
28. **B** The default on a busy system is for the event log files to be overwritten every 7 days. This can be changed to any other day value.
29. **A** The Application log only stores information on Win32 applications.

30. **D** The backup files all have the LOG extension except for System, which is ALT.

31. **C** The bottom frame of the Startup/Shutdown tab contains configuration information for the Recovery options.

32. **B** The default on a busy system is for the event log files to be overwritten every 7 days. This can be changed to any other day value.

33. **C** The Dumpchk utility is used to verify the contents of a debugging file.

34. **C** The backup files all have the LOG extension except for System, which is ALT.

35. **D** The Dumpexam utility is used to make the contents of a debugging file viewable.

36. **C** The Event Viewer is located in the Administrative Tool program group.

37. **A, C** The most common causes of configuration errors are the installation of new software or devices.

38. **A** The Savedump utility is used to write out debugging information.

39. **B** The Security log remains empty until auditing is enabled.

40. **A, B** The Security log tracks only success and failure audits.

41. **A** The system event log will show all services that have started, or attempted to start, and results of that operation.

42. **A** The System log is the default log displayed when Event Viewer is started.

43. **B** The System log is written to in sequential order, with new entries at the top. The error most likely to be causing others is the first one written to the file and at the bottom of the list.

44. **A, B, D** The System log tracks warnings, errors, and information events.

45. **C** The System log tracks warnings, errors, and information events.

46. **A** The Windows Diagnostic tool is a front end to the Registry information stored in HKEY_LOCAL_MACHINE.

47. **B** Virtual memory statistics are displayed under the Memory tab of the Windows NT Diagnostics tool.

48. **A** Warning events are shown with an exclamation mark, errors by a stop sign, and information by an "I" in a blue circle.

49. **D** Warning events are shown with an exclamation mark, errors by a stop sign, and information by an "I" in a blue circle.

50 **B** Warning events are shown with an exclamation mark, errors by a stop sign, and information by an "I" in a blue circle.

51. **C** Warning events are shown with an exclamation mark, errors by a stop sign, and information by an "I" in a blue circle.

52. **B** Windows NT Diagnostics contains information about NT, which would not include current connections.

53. **D** The backup files all have the LOG extension except for System, which is ALT.

54. **C** The system log contains information about services

6.3 Key Words

Errors

Information events

Hive

Warnings

Stop error

6.4 Troubleshooting Printer Problems

Microsoft lists the following objective for the Windows NT Server exam: Choose the appropriate course of action to take to resolve printer problems. When you try to isolate printing problems, the following guidelines can be helpful:

- Check the cable connections and the printer port to verify that the printing device is on and the cables are all securely fitted. This precaution may seem rather obvious, but the simplest of things cause some of the most perplexing problems.
- To verify that the correct printer driver is installed and configured properly, establish the type of printing device (such as PCL, PostScript, and so on) and verify that the correct driver type has been installed. If necessary, reinstall the printer driver. If a printer driver needs updating, use the Printers folder to install and configure the new printer driver.
- Verify that the printer is selected, either explicitly in the application or as the default printer. Most Windows NT applications have a Printer Setup menu or toolbar button. When printing by means of OLE or some other indirect means, you need to specify a default printer.
- Verify that enough hard disk space is available to generate the print job, especially on the partition that has the spooler directory specified, which, by default, is the boot partition (that is, the winnt_root partition).
- Run the simplest application possible (for example, Notepad) to verify that printing can occur from other applications within Windows NT. If problems are encountered printing from the application (other than a Win32-based application), check the appropriate application subsystem (for example, DOS, Win16, POSIX, and OS/2).
- Print to a file (FILE:) and then copy the output file to a printer port. If this works, the problem is the spooler, or is data-transmission related. If this doesn't work, the problem is application- or driver-related.

A. Spooling Problems

By default, spooled print jobs reside in the \<winnt_root>\SYSTEM32\SPOOL\PRINTERS directory until completely printed. If a Windows NT-based computer is acting as a print server for the network, make sure plenty of free disk space is available on the partition that contains the default spool directory. Also, keeping this partition defragmented improves printing performance. Because Windows NT doesn't include a defrag utility, you need to use a third-party utility (or boot to MS-DOS if you are using the FAT file system).

If you have more room on another partition, you may change the default spool directory in the Advanced tab of the Server Properties dialog box. You can also change the spool directory in the Registry by adding a value called DefaultSpoolDirectory of type REG_SZ to the following and entering the path to the new spool directory:

```
HKEY_LOCAL_MACHINE\System\CurrentControlSet\Control\Print\Printers
```

You need to restart the spooler service (or the computer itself) for the change to take effect.

You can also assign a separate spool directory for each individual printer. Enter the path to the new spool directory as the data for the value SpoolDirectory in the following, where <Printer> is the name of the printer you want to redirect:

```
HKEY_LOCAL_MACHINE\System\CurrentControlSet\Control\Print\åPrinters\<Printer>
```

Again, you need to restart the spooler service for this change to take effect.

B. Printing from Non-Windows–Based Applications

Non-Windows–based applications—for example, MS-DOS–based applications—require their own printer drivers if the application requires any kind of formatted output other than plain ASCII text. WordPerfect for MS-DOS, for example, does not even allow the user to print a document unless there is a WordPerfect-specific and printer-specific driver installed, for example, because non-Windows-based applications are not written to conform to or take advantage of the Windows APIs. Also, remember that you may need to use the NET USE LPT1: \\servername\printername command to enable the DOS-based application to print.

C. Handling the Computer Crashing

When a document prints, two files are created for the print job in the spool directory (by default, <winnt_root>\SYSTEM32\SPOOL\PRINTERS). One of the files, which has an .SPL extension, is the actual print job spool file. The other file, which has an .SHD extension, is a shadow file that contains information about the job, including its owner and priority. These files remain in the spool directory until the jobs finish printing, at which point they are deleted.

In the event of a system crash, some spool and shadow files may be left over from jobs that were waiting to be printed. When the spooler service restarts (along with the rest of the system), the printer should process these files immediately. They are, however, sometimes corrupted during the crash and get stuck. Be certain, therefore, to check the spool directory every so often, and delete any spool and shadow files with old date/time stamps. How old is old depends on how long it takes to print a job on your printer. Certainly anything from days, weeks, or months ago should be deleted.

If a print job appears stuck in the printer and you cannot delete it, stop the spooler service in Control Panel Services and delete the SPL and/or SHD file for that job from the spool directory (match the date/time stamp on the files and in Print Manager to determine which files are causing the problem).

D. Printing Too Slow or Workstation Too Sluggish

Windows NT Workstation assigns priority 7 to the spooler service, which puts printing on an equal footing with other background applications. Windows NT Server, which favors printing over background applications, assigns priority 9 to the spooler, which puts it neck-and-neck with the foreground applications.

If a Windows NT-based workstation moonlighting as a print server appears to print too slowly, consider raising the priority by one or two classes. If the workstation is responding sluggishly to the user while printing, consider lowering the priority by a class or two. Don't alter the priority by more than two levels under any circumstances without a full understanding of the performance consequences involved.

To change the priority class for the Spooler service, add a value called PriorityClass of type REG_DWORD to HKEY_LOCAL_MACHINE\System\CurrentControlSet\Control\Print and set it equal to the priority class desired. If this value is set to 0 or isn't present, the default is used (7 for Windows NT Workstation, or 9 for Windows NT Server).

6.4 Practice Problems

1. If you cannot print to a printer, one of the first things tried should be:
   A. Change print drivers.
   B. Reconfigure the print spool.
   C. Try a different printer to see if the problem appears there.
   D. Stop and restart the printing services.

2. By default, spooled print jobs reside where?
   A. \<winnt_root>
   B. \<winnt_root>\SYSTEM32
   C. \<winnt_root>\SYSTEM32\SPOOL
   D. \<winnt_root>\SYSTEM32\SPOOL\PRINTERS

3. If an NT-based computer will function as a print server for the network, what is one of the most critical components?
   A. Free disk space
   B. Frequent backups
   C. A fast processor
   D. Accelerated PCI local bus video

4. What priority level is assigned to the print spooler service by Windows NT Server?
   A. 1
   B. 3
   C. 9
   D. 15

5. You can change the location of the spool directory by:
   A. Changing the entry is the Spool tab of the Control Panel\Printers option
   B. In the Registry, adding a value called DefaultSpoolDirectory to HKEY_LOCAL_MACHINE\System\CurrentControlSet\Control\Print\Printers
   C. Mapping a drive to the new location
   D. Changing port settings at the printer

6. A potential solution to problems with printing from non-Window–based applications to a printer that works fine in Windows is:
   A. Install additional printer drivers.
   B. Elect to use RAW data instead of EMF.
   C. Stop spooling services, and send data directly to the printer.
   D. Configure the printer on a different port.

7. If DOS-based applications will not print, what command should you first try?
   A. PRINT
   B. NET PRINT
   C. NET PRINT LPT1: _ HYPERLINK \\\\servername\\printername __\\servername\printername_
   D. NET USE LPT1: \\servername\printername

8. Files in the printer spool should have which two of the following extensions?
   A. TXT
   B. SHD
   C. SHT
   D. SPL

9. Files in the printer spool remain there for what duration?
   A. Until there is a clean boot of the system
   B. Until the system is shut down
   C. Until the job finishes printing
   D. Until the administrator empties the spool

10. What becomes of spooled print jobs in the event of a computer crash?

    A. When the system restarts, the printer should process these files immediately.

    B. They wait until the administrator restarts them before continuing.

    C. They do not restart.

    D. They perform a checksum operation to identify corruption that may have occurred.

11. If a print job appears stuck in the printer after recovering from a system crash, and you cannot delete it, you should:

    A. Continue rebooting the computer until the problem goes away.

    B. Stop the spooler service in Control Panel Services and delete the files for that job in the spool directory.

    C. Invest in a more industrial printer.

    D. Use Regedit to change stuck job parameters.

12. What priority level is assigned to the print spooler service by Windows NT Workstation?

    A. 15

    B. 10

    C. 7

    D. 1

13. If a Windows NT-based workstation moonlighting as a print server appears to print too slowly, what action should be be taken on the priority level of the print service?

    A. Raise the priority by one or two classes.

    B. Raise the priority by three to four classes.

    C. Lower the priority by one or two classes.

    D. Make no change—the priority level does not affect this service.

6.4 Answers and Explanations: Practice Problems

1. **C** Always try to isolate the problem as much as possible before taking other actions.

2. **D** By default, print jobs are in \<winnt_root>\SYSTEM32\SPOOL until they are completely printed.

3. **A** If a Windows NT-based computer is acting as a print server for the network, make sure plenty of free disk space is available on the partition that contains the default spool directory. Spooled print jobs can be quite large and can eat up disk space more quickly than you might think, especially during peak printing periods.

4. **C** Windows NT Server assigns a default priority level of 9 to the print spooler service.

5. **B** You can change the spool directory in the Registry by adding a value called DefaultSpoolDirectory of type REG_SZ to HKEY_LOCAL_MACHINE\System\CurrentControlSet\Control\Print\Printers and entering the path to the new spool directory.

6. **A** Non-Windows-based applications—for example, MS-DOS–based applications—require their own printer drivers if the application requires any kind of formatted output other than plain ASCII text.

7. **D** You might need to use the NET USE LPT1: \\servername\printername command to enable the DOS-based application to print.

8. **B, D** When a document prints, two files are created for the print job in the spool directory (by default, <winnt_root>\SYSTEM32\SPOOL\PRINTERS). One of the files, which has an .SPL extension, is the actual print job spool file. The other file, which has an .SHD extension, is a shadow file that contains information about the job, including its owner and priority.

9. **C** When a document prints, two files are created for the print job in the spool directory (by default, <winnt_root>\SYSTEM32\SPOOL\PRINTERS). One of the files, which has an .SPL extension, is the actual print job spool file. The other file, which has an .SHD extension, is a shadow file that contains information about the job, including its owner and priority. These files remain in the spool directory until the jobs finish printing, at which point they are deleted.
10. **A** In the event of a system crash, some spool and shadow files might be left over from jobs that were waiting to be printed. When the spooler service restarts (along with the rest of the system), the printer should process these files immediately.
11. **B** If a print job appears stuck in the printer and you cannot delete it, stop the spooler service in Control Panel Services and delete the SPL and/or SHD file for that job from the spool directory (match the date/time stamp on the files and in Print Manager to determine which files are causing the problem).
12. **C** Windows NT Workstation assigns a default priority level of 7 to the print spooler service.
13. **A** If a Windows NT-based workstation moonlighting as a print server appears to print too slowly, consider raising the priority by one or two classes. If the workstation is responding sluggishly to the user while printing, consider lowering the priority by a class or two.

6.4 Key Words

Printer

Spool

Priority

6.5 Troubleshooting RAS

Microsoft lists the following objective for the Windows NT Server exam: Choose the appropriate course of action to take to resolve RAS problems.

If RAS isn't working, check the Event Viewer. Several RAS events appear in the system log. You might also check the Control Panel Dial-Up Networking Monitor application. The Status tab of Dial-Up Networking Monitor displays statistics on current conditions, including connection statistics and device errors.

RAS supports TCP/IP, NWLink, and NetBEUI protocols for both dial-in and dial-out connections. TCP/IP benefits from being available on a number of different platforms, easily routable, and the compatibility choice of the Internet.

If you are having problems with PPP, you can log PPP debugging information to a file called PPP.Log in the \<winnt_root>\System32\Ras directory. To log PPP debugging information to PPP.Log, change the Registry value for the following subkey to 1:

```
\HKEY_LOCAL_MACHINE\System\CurrentControlSet\Services\Rasman\PPP\Logging
```

Microsoft has identified the following common RAS problems and some possible solutions:

- **Authentication.** RAS authentication problems often stem from incompatible encryption methods. Try to connect using the `Allow any authentication including clear text` option. If you can connect using clear text and you can't connect using encryption, you know the client and server encryption methods are incompatible.
- **Callback with Multilink.** If a client makes a connection using Multilink over multiple phone lines, with Callback enabled, the server will call back using only a single phone line (in other words, Multilink functionality is lost). RAS can use only one phone number for callback. If the Multilink connection uses two channels over an ISDN line, the server can still use Multilink on the callback.
- **AutoDial at Logon.** At logon, when Explorer is initializing, it might reference a shortcut or some other target that requires an AutoDial connection, causing AutoDial to spontaneously dial a remote connection during logon. The only way to prevent this is to disable AutoDial, or to eliminate the shortcut or other target causing the AutoDial to occur.

6.5 Practice Problems

1. If RAS is suspected of failing, what should be one of the first tools used to look for problems?

   A. Performance Monitor

   B. Event Viewer

   C. Server Manager

   D. User Manager for Domains

2. What tool displays statistics on current conditions of RAS?

   A. Performance Monitor

   B. In Control Panel, the Status tab of Dial-Up Networking Monitor

   C. Event Viewer

   D. User Manager for Domains

3. Which of the following statements are true of PPP logging (choose two):

   A. It is enabled by default.

   B. Information is written to the PPP.Log.

   C. You must edit the Registry to turn it on.

   D. It also contains logging information on modems.

4. The PPP.Log is stored, by default, where:

   A. \<winnt_root>\System32\Ras

   B. \<winnt_root>\System32

   C. \<winnt_root>

   D. C:\

5. If you can connect using clear text, and you can't connect using encryption, what is the most likely problem?

   A. Connection speeds are too low to support verification.

   B. Encryption is not enabled at both client and server.

   C. The client and server encryption methods are incompatible.

   D. The server requires additional resources.

6. If you suspect the client and server encryption methods of being incompatible, what should you try?

   A. Try to connect using the Allow any authentication including clear text option.

   B. Try to avoid using any form of encryption.

   C. Try to discourage users from seeking dial-in functionality.

   D. Try to connect using the Incompatible encryption methods option.

7. Which of the following statements is true in regards to Callback with MultiLink:

   A. RAS can use multiple phone numbers for callback.

   B. RAS can use only one phone number for callback by default, but can use multiple phone numbers after this function is enabled.

   C. RAS can utilize callback only over ISDN lines.

   D. RAS can use only one phone number for callback.

8. If a non-ISDN client makes a connection using Multilink over multiple phone lines, with Callback enabled, the server will call back using:

   A. Only a single phone line

   B. Multiple phone lines

   C. An ISDN line

   D. One phone line unless, the default has been changed to `Utilize Multiple`

9. Which three of the following are RAS problem areas, as identified by Microsoft:

   A. Autodial at Logon

   B. Authentication

   C. Heterogeneous connectivity

   D. Callback with MultiLink

10. Juan complains that AutoDial spontaneously attempts to dial a remote connection during his logon. How should an administrator address this problem?

    A. Move Juan to another machine.

    B. Disable AutoDial.

    C. Restrict Juan's profiles and groups.

    D. Reinstall Windows NT.

11. RAS can use which protocols for dial-in connections (choose all correct answers):

    A. TCP/IP

    B. NWLink

    C. NetBEUI

    D. SMTP

6.5 Answers and Explanations: Practice Problems

1. **B** If RAS isn't working, check the Event Viewer. Several RAS events appear in the system log.

2. **B** In Control Panel, the Status tab of Dial-Up Networking Monitor displays statistics on current conditions, including connection statistics and device errors.

3. **B, C** If you are having problems with PPP, you can log PPP debugging information to a file called PPP.Log in the \<winnt_root>\System32\Ras directory. To log PPP debugging information to PPP.Log, change the Registry value for \HKEY_LOCAL_MACHINE\System\CurrentControlSet\Services\Rasman\PPP\Logging to 1.

4. **A** PPP.Log in the \<winnt_root>\System32\Ras directory.

5. **C** RAS authentication problems often stem from incompatible encryption methods.

6. **A** If you can connect using clear text, and you can't connect using encryption, you know the client and server encryption methods are incompatible. You should try to connect using the Allow any authentication including clear text option.

7. **D** RAS can use only one phone number for callback.

8. **A** If a client makes a connection using Multilink over multiple phone lines, with Callback enabled, the server will call back using only a single phone line—in other words, Multilink functionality is lost.

9. **A, B, D** Autodial at Logon, Authentication, and Callback with MultiLink have all been identified as potential RAS problem areas by Microsoft.

10. **B** At logon, when Explorer is initializing, it might reference a shortcut or some other target that requires an AutoDial connection, causing AutoDial to spontaneously dial a remote connection during logon. The only way to prevent this is to disable AutoDial, or to eliminate the shortcut or other target causing the AutoDial to occur.

11. **A, B, C** RAS supports TCP/IP, NWLink, and NetBEUI protocols for both dial-in and dial-out connections.

6.5 Key Words

RAS

TCP/IP

6.6 Troubleshooting Connectivity Problems

Network problems often are caused by cables, adapters, or IRQ conflicts, or problems with transmission media. Protocol problems also can disrupt the network. Use a diagnostics program to check the network adapter card. Use a cable analyzer to check the cabling. Use Network Monitor to check network traffic, or use a network protocol analyzer.

Microsoft lists the following objective for the Windows NT Server exam: Choose the appropriate course of action to take to resolve connectivity problems.

A. Pinging Other Computers

If you are using TCP/IP, the IP address and the subnet mask must be given when installed in a non-routed environment. You often can isolate problems by *pinging* the other computers on your network. Pinging is a common diagnostic procedure:

1. Ping the 127.0.0.1 (the loopback address).
2. Ping your own IP address.
3. Ping the address of another computer on your subnet.
4. Ping the default gateway.
5. Ping a computer beyond the default gateway.

Check the Control Panel Services application to ensure that the Server service and the Workstation service (and any other vital services that might affect connectivity) are running properly. Check the Bindings tab in the Control Panel Network application to ensure that the services are bound to applications and adapters.

B. Network Monitor

Windows NT Server 4 includes a tool called Network Monitor. Network Monitor captures and filters packets and analyzes network activity. The Network Monitor included with Windows NT Server can monitor only the specific system on which it is installed.

To install Windows NT Server's Network Monitor, start the Network application in Control Panel and click on the Services tab. Click on the Add button and select Network Monitor and Tools from the network services list. After Network Monitor is installed, it appears in the Administrative Tools program group. Figure 6.6.1 shows the Network Monitor main screen.

The Network Monitor window is divided into four sections, or *panes*. The Graph pane (in the upper-left corner) shows the current network activity in a series of five bar charts. Note the scroll bar to the right of the Graph section. To view the bar charts (not shown in fig. 6.6.1), scroll down or drag the lower border down, exposing the hidden charts. The five bar graphs are as follows:

- % Network Utilization
- Frames Per Second
- Bytes Per Second
- Broadcasts Per Second
- Multicasts Per Second

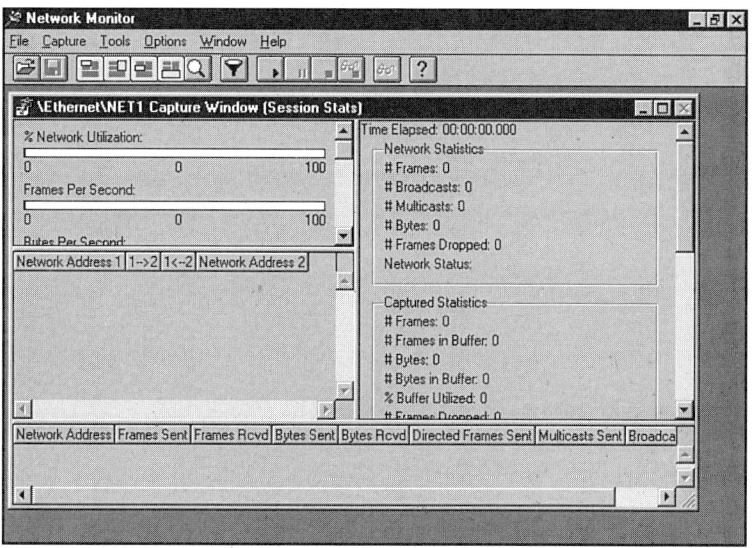

Figure 6.6.1 The Network Monitor main screen.

Below the Graphs pane you see the Session Stats pane. The Session Stats pane indicates the exchange of information from two nodes on the network, the amount of data, and the direction of travel. This data is limited to a per-session basis.

All the Stats panes report only on the first 128 sessions it finds. You can specify a particular session creating a capture filter. The Session Stats pane collects information on the following four areas:

- Network Address 1. The first node included in a network session.
- 1→2. The number of packets sent from the first address to the second.
- 1←2. The number of packets sent from the second address to the first.
- Network Address 2. The second node included in the network session.

On the right side of the display windows is the Total Stats pane, which reveals information relevant to the entire activity on the network. Whether statistics are supported depends on the network adapter. If a given network adapter isn't supported, Unsupported replaces the label.

The Total Stats information is divided into the following five categories:

- *Network Statistics*

  Total Frames
  Total Broadcasts
  Total Multicasts
  Total Bytes
  Total Frames Dropped
  Network Status

- *Captured Statistics*

  Captured Frames
  Captured Frames in Buffer
  Captured Bytes
  Capture Bytes in Buffer
  Percentage of Allotted Buffer Space in Use
  Captured Packets Dropped

- *Per Second Statistics*

  Frames
  Bytes/second
  Broadcasts/second
  Multicasts/second
  % Network Utilization

- *Network Card (MAC) Statistics*

  Total Frames
  Total Broadcasts
  Total Multicasts
  Total Bytes

- *Network Card (MAC) Error Statistics*

  Total Cyclical Redundancy Check (CRC) Errors
  Total Dropped Frames Due to Inadequate Buffer Space
  Total Dropped Packets Due to Hardware Failure(s)

At the bottom of the display window, you see the Station Stats pane. The Station Stats pane displays information specific to a workstation's activity on the network. You can sort on any category by right-clicking on the column label.

The following eight categories constitute the Station Stats pane:

- Network Address
- Frames Sent
- Frames Rcvd
- Bytes Sent
- Bytes Rcvd
- Directed Frames Sent
- Multicasts Sent
- Broadcasts Sent

6.6 Practice Problems

1. Which of the following are common causes of network problems? (Select all correct answers.)

    A. IRQ conflicts

    B. Workstation RAM

    C. Cables and adapters

    D. Transmission media

2. Which of the following tools should be used to check the network adapter card:

    A. Cable analyzer

    B. Diagnostics program

    C. Network Monitor

    D. Performance Monitor

3. Which of the following tools should be used to check the network cabling:

    A. Cable analyzer

    B. Diagnostics program

    C. Network Monitor

    D. Performance Monitor

4. Which of the following tools should be used to check the network traffic:

    A. Cable analyzer

    B. Diagnostics program

    C. Network Monitor

    D. Performance Monitor

5. The Ping utility can be useful in diagnosing network problems. Which address is the "loopback" address?

    A. 0.0.0.0

    B. 0.0.0.1

    C. 127.0.0.1

    D. 255.255.255.255

6. You have used Ping to troubleshoot your problems. After having used the loopback address and having received successful results, what should you try?

    A. Ping the default gateway.

    B. Ping your own IP address.

    C. Ping a computer on your subnet.

    D. Ping a computer beyond the default gateway.

7. When troubleshooting network problems, what information can be gleaned from the Services application in the Control Panel?

    A. Ensure that the Server service is running properly.

    B. Verify that a remote host is up and running.

    C. Verify that the default gateway is operable.

    D. Identify bottlenecks on the system.

8. To verify that services are bound to applications and adapters, which tab should you check in the Control Panel Network application?

    A. Services

    B. Bindings

    C. Protocols

    D. System

9. You have used Ping to troubleshoot your problems. After having pinged your own IP address and having received successful results, what should you try?

    A. Ping the default gateway.

    B. Ping the loopback address.

    C. Ping a computer on your subnet.

    D. Ping a computer beyond the default gateway.

10. Which troubleshooting tool included with NT captures and filters packets and analyzes network activity?

    A. Event Viewer

    B. Performance Monitor

    C. SMTP

    D. Network Monitor

11. Which statement regarding the version of Network Monitor included with Windows NT is true?

    A. It can monitor only the system upon which it was installed.

    B. It can monitor any system on the network.

    C. It is not included with NT, but rather a component of the resource kit.

    D. It will not collect TCP/IP information until SMTP is installed.

12. You have used Ping to troubleshoot your problems. After having pinged a computer on your subnet and having received successful results, what should you try?

    A. Ping the default gateway.

    B. Ping your own IP address.

    C. Ping the loopback address.

    D. Ping a computer beyond the default gateway.

13. Network Monitor appears on which program group tab:

    A. System

    B. Server Manager

    C. Resource Kit

    D. Administrative Tools

14. To install Windows NT Server's Network Monitor, start the Network application in Control Panel and click on which tab:

    A. Install

    B. Services

    C. System

    D. Network

15. You have used Ping to troubleshoot your problems. After having pinged the default gateway and having received successful results, what should you try?

    A. Ping the loopback address.

    B. Ping your own IP address.

    C. Ping a computer on your subnet.

    D. Ping a computer beyond the default gateway.

16. Network Monitor's display is broken into a number of sections called:

    A. Views

    B. Windows

    C. Panes

    D. Corners

17. The Graph pane in Network Monitor shows:

    A. The exchange of information from two nodes on the network

    B. Activity on the entire network

    C. Current network activity, as a series of bar charts

    D. Information specific to a workstation's activity on the network

18. The Station Stats pane in Network Monitor shows:

    A. The exchange of information from two nodes on the network

    B. Activity on the entire network

    C. Current network activity, as a series of bar charts

    D. Information specific to a workstation's activity on the network

19. The Session Stats pane in Network Monitor shows:

    A. The exchange of information from two nodes on the network

    B. Activity on the entire network

    C. Current network activity, as a series of bar charts

    D. Information specific to a workstation's activity on the network

20. The Total Stats pane in Network Monitor shows:

    A. The exchange of information between two nodes on the network

    B. Activity on the entire network

    C. Current network activity as a series of bar charts

    D. Information specific to a workstation's activity on the network

21. Within the Graph Pane of Network Monitor, which of the following is *not* displayed as a bar graph:

    A. % Network Utilization

    B. Total Frames Dropped

    C. Frames Per Second

    D. Bytes Per Second

22. The Session Stats pane of Network Monitor can report on how many sessions at a time:

    A. 1

    B. 32

    C. 64

    D. 128

23. The Session Stats pane collects all of the following information *except*:

    A. The network address of the first node included in a session

    B. The network address of the second node included in a session

    C. The total number of frames dropped from each address

    D. The number of packets sent from each address

24. Within the Graph Pane of Network Monitor, which of the following is not displayed as a bar graph:

    A. % Network Utilization

    B. Multicasts Per Second

    C. Network Status

    D. Bytes Per Second

25. Total Stats information in Network Monitor is divided into which of the following categories? (Choose three.)

    A. Network Statistics

    B. Dropped Frame Statistics

    C. Captured Statistics

    D. Per Second Statistics

26. The Station Stats portion of Network Monitor keeps track of all of the following *except*:

    A. Bytes/second

    B. Bytes Sent

    C. Bytes Recd

    D. Frames Sent

27. Within the Graph Pane of Network Monitor, which of the following is not displayed as a bar graph:

    A. Captured Frames

    B. Multicasts Per Second

    C. Broadcasts Per Second

    D. Frames Per Second

28. The Station Stats portion of Network Monitor keeps track of all of the following *except*:

    A. Broadcasts Sent

    B. Bytes Sent

    C. %Network Utilization

    D. Frames Sent

29. Network Card (MAC) Error Statistics would contain which of the following statistical categories? (Choose all correct answers.)

    A. Total Cyclical Redundancy Check (CRC) Errors

    B. Total Dropped Frames Due to Inadequate Buffer Space

    C. Total Dropped Packets Due to Hardware Failure(s)

    D. Total Dropped Bytes Due to Failure(s)

30. The Station Stats portion of Network Monitor keeps track of all of the following *except*:

    A. Directed Frames Sent

    B. Frames Sent

    C. Bytes Resent

    D. Frames sent

31. Network Card (MAC) Statistics would consist of which of the following (select all correct answers):

    A. Total Dropped Frames Due to Inadequate Buffer Space

    B. Total Broadcasts

    C. Total Multicasts

    D. Total Dropped Bytes Due to Failure(s)

32. The Station Stats portion of Network Monitor keeps track of all of the following *except*:

    A. Network Address

    B. Bytes Sent

    C. Bytes Recd

    D. Frames Resent

33. The minimum number of nodes needed to constitute a session for Session Stats in Network Monitor is:

    A. 0

    B. 1

    C. 2

    D. 3

6.6 Answers and Explanations: Practice Problems

1. **A, C, D** Network problems often are caused by cables, adapters, IRQ conflicts, or problems with transmission media.

2. **B** Use a diagnostics program to check the network adapter card. Use a cable analyzer to check the cabling. Use Network Monitor or a network protocol analyzer to check network traffic.

3. **A** Use a diagnostics program to check the network adapter card. Use a cable analyzer to check the cabling. Use Network Monitor or a network protocol analyzer to check network traffic.

4. **C** Use a diagnostics program to check the network adapter card. Use a cable analyzer to check the cabling. Use Network Monitor or a network protocol analyzer to check network traffic.

5. **C** 127.0.0.1 is the loopback address that Ping can use to verify the status of the internal\local operation.

6. **B** The sequence is: Ping the loopback address, your own IP address, then the address of another computer on your subnet. Following that, Ping the default gateway, and finally a computer beyond the default gateway.

7. **A** Checking the Control Panel Services application can ensure that the Server service and the Workstation service (and any other vital services that might affect connectivity) are running properly.

8. **B** Check the Bindings tab in the Control Panel Network application to ensure that the services are bound to applications and adapters.

9. **C** The sequence is: Ping the loopback address, your own IP address, the default gateway, and finally a computer beyond the default gateway.

10. **D** Network Monitor captures and filters packets and analyzes network activity.

11. **A** The Network Monitor included with Windows NT Server can monitor only the specific system on which it is installed, unlike the Network Monitor in Microsoft's Systems Management Server package, which can monitor other systems on the network.

12. **A** The sequence is: Ping the loopback address, your own IP address, then the address of another computer on your subnet. Following that, Ping the default gateway, and finally a computer beyond the default gateway.

13. **D** After Network Monitor is installed, it appears in the Administrative Tools program group.

14. **B** To install Windows NT Server's Network Monitor, start the Network application in Control Panel and click on the Services tab. Click on the Add button and select Network Monitor from the network services list. After Network Monitor is installed, it appears in the Administrative Tools program group.

15. **D** The sequence is: Ping the loopback address, your own IP address, then the address of another computer on your subnet. Following that, Ping the default gateway, and finally a computer beyond the default gateway.

16. **C** The Network Monitor window is divided into four sections, or *panes*.

17. **C** The Graph pane (in the upper-left corner) shows the current network activity in a series of five bar charts.

18. **D** The Station Stats pane displays information specific to a workstation's activity on the network.

19. **A** The Session Stats pane indicates the exchange of information from two nodes on the network, the amount of data, and the direction of travel. This data is limited to a per-session basis.

20. **B** The Total Stats pane reveals information relevant to the entire activity on the network. Whether statistics are supported depends on the network adapter.

21. **B** The five graphs shown are:

    % Network Utilization

    Frames Per Second

    Bytes Per Second

    Broadcasts Per Second

    Multicasts Per Second

22. **D** The Session Stats pane of Network Monitor can report on only the first 128 sessions that it finds.

23. **C** The total number of frames dropped is displayed in Total Stats, and not Session Stats.

24. **C** The five graphs shown are:

    % Network Utilization

    Frames Per Second

    Bytes Per Second

    Broadcasts Per Second

    Multicasts Per Second

25. **A, C, D** The five categories of Total Stats are:

    Network Statistics

    Captured Statistics

    Per Second Statistics

    Network Card (MAC) Statistics

    Network Card (MAC) Error Statistics

26. **A** The following eight categories constitute the Station pane:

    1. Network Address
    2. Frames Sent
    3. Frames Rcvd
    4. Bytes Sent
    5. Bytes Rcvd
    6. Directed Frames Sent
    7. Multicasts Sent
    8. Broadcasts Sent

27. **A** The five graphs shown are:

    % Network Utilization

    Frames Per Second

    Bytes Per Second

    Broadcasts Per Second

    Multicasts Per Second

28. **C** The following eight categories constitute the Station pane:

    1. Network Address
    2. Frames Sent
    3. Frames Rcvd
    4. Bytes Sent
    5. Bytes Rcvd
    6. Directed Frames Sent
    7. Multicasts Sent
    8. Broadcasts Sent

29. **A, B, C** Network Card (MAC) Error Statistics consist of: Total Cyclical Redundancy Check (CRC) Errors, Total Dropped Frames Due to Inadequate Buffer Space, and Total Dropped Packets Due to Hardware Failure(s).

30. **C** The following eight categories constitute the Station pane:

    1. Network Address
    2. Frames Sent
    3. Frames Rcvd
    4. Bytes Sent
    5. Bytes Rcvd
    6. Directed Frames Sent
    7. Multicasts Sent
    8. Broadcasts Sent

31. **B, C** Network Card (MAC) Statistics consist of: Total Frames, Total Broadcasts, Total Multicasts, and Total Bytes

32. **D** The following eight categories constitute the Station pane:

    1. Network Address
    2. Frames Sent
    3. Frames Rcvd
    4. Bytes Sent
    5. Bytes Rcvd
    6. Directed Frames Sent
    7. Multicasts Sent
    8. Broadcasts Sent

33. **C** The Session Stats pane indicates the exchange of information between two nodes on the network, the amount and data, and direction of travel.

6.6 Key Words

IP address

Subnet mask

Subnet

6.7 Troubleshooting Access and Permission Problems

If you can't log on, you may be using an incorrect username or password. Also, ensure the correct account database is selected in the drop list at the bottom of the dialog box. You can logon to the domain or to the local workstation account database. If you still can't log on, try logging on using another account. If other accounts are working normally, check the settings for your account in User Manager for Domains. If you can't log on from any account, repair the accounts database by using the emergency repair process. One of the worst culprits for logon problems is the Caps Lock key. Make certain that the user isn't typing the password in all caps.

Microsoft lists the following objective for the Windows NT Server exam: Choose the appropriate course of action to take to resolve resource access problems and permission problems.

If a user can't access a file, a share, a printer, or some other resource, check the resource permissions. Try connecting using a different account. Try accessing a similar resource to see whether the problem also appears there. Make certain that the user has spelled the name of the resource correctly.

Check the Control Panel Services application to ensure that the NetLogon service, the Server service, and the Workstation service are running properly, and check the Bindings tab in the Control Panel Network application to ensure that the services are bound to applications and adapters.

You can also check User Manager for Domains to ensure that the user's group memberships haven't changed or that a change to a group rights setting hasn't inadvertently denied the user access to the resource. Finally, check System Policy Editor for restrictions on the user's access to computers or other resources.

6.7 Practice Problems

1. What are two likely reasons for failure to log on to a network from a workstation you have used in the past?

   A. Incorrect password

   B. Incorrect username

   C. Incorrect media

   D. Incorrect frame type

2. If you cannot log on from a workstation you were using earlier, and are certain username and password are correct, what should be checked next?

   A. Verify you are logging on to the correct domain or workgroup.

   B. Check the media.

   C. Verify frame types.

   D. Look for CRC errors.

3. You cannot log on to the network from a workstation you have used earlier, and are certain that username, password, and domain name are correct. What is the next logical step to try?

   A. Down the network and begin an Emergency Repair procedure.

   B. Verify the proper permissions are on the SAM database.

   C. Attempt to log on using another account.

   D. Look for CRC errors.

4. If you cannot log on to a workstation using any account, what is the next logical step in solving the problem?

   A. Repair the accounts database by using the emergency repair process.

   B. Verify the proper permissions are on the SAM database.

   C. Look for CRC errors.

   D. Verify frame types.

5. One of the most common logon problems is:

   A. Programmable keyboards

   B. Hashing table errors

   C. Duplicate SIDs

   D. The Caps Lock key

6. If a user can't access a file, a share, a printer, or some other resource, start by checking:

   A. The resource permissions

   B. The Global groups

   C. The Local groups

   D. TechNet

7. To ensure that a user's group memberships have not changed, thus denying them permissions to a resource, use:

   A. Network Monitor

   B. User Manager for Domains

   C. Server Manager

   D. Performance Monitor

8. If there is a suspected logon problem from a workstation, you should check the Control Panel Services application to ensure that which of the following services are running properly:

   A. The NetLogon service

   B. The Server service

   C. The Workstation service

   D. The Bindings service

9. Checking the Bindings tab in the Control Panel Network application verifies which of the following? (Choose two.)

   A. Services are bound to applications.

   B. Correct frame types have been selected.

   C. Dirty RAM is not causing a failure to update SAM.

   D. Services are bound to adapters.

10. You use which tool to find restrictions on the user's access to computers?

    A. Network Monitor

    B. User Manager

    C. User Manager for Domains

    D. System Policy Editor

6.7 Answers and Explanations: Practice Problems

1. **A, B** If you can't log on, you might be using an incorrect username or password.

2. **A** Enable the check box beneath the password to make certain that you are logging on to the correct domain or workgroup (or the local machine).

3. **C** Try logging on using another account. If other accounts are working normally, check the settings for your account in User Manager for Domains.

4. **A** If you can't log on from any account, repair the accounts database by using the emergency repair process.

5. **D** One of the worst culprits for logon problems is the Caps Lock key. Make certain that the user isn't typing the password in all caps.

6. **A** If a user can't access a file, a share, a printer, or some other resource, check the resource permissions.

7. **B** You can use User Manager for Domains to ensure that the user's group memberships haven't changed or that a change to a group rights setting hasn't inadvertently denied the user access to the resource.

8. **A, B, C** Check the Control Panel Services application to ensure that the NetLogon service, the Server service, and the Workstation service are running properly.

9. **A, D** Checking the Bindings tab in the Control Panel Network application will verify that the services are bound to applications and adapters.

10. **D** Check System Policy Editor for restrictions on the user's access to computers or other resources.

6.8 Recovering from Fault-Tolerance Failures

Even if you are employing a high-tech RAID fault-tolerance system, a well planned backup routine is still your best defense against lost data. Windows NT includes a backup utility (NTBACKUP.EXE). Backup is part of the Administrative Tools group.

Microsoft lists the following objective for the Windows NT Server exam: Choose the appropriate course of action to take to resolve fault-tolerance failures. Fault-tolerance methods include: tape backup, mirroring, stripe set with parity, disk duplexing.

A. Backing Up Files and Directories

The Backup main window shows the disk drives presently accessible to the Backup utility. Double-click on a drive and to see an Explorer-type directory tree. Note that every directory or file has a small box beside it. Click on the box to back up the file or directory and all child files/directories beneath it.

To start a backup, click on the Backup button in the toolbar or choose Operations, Backup. The Backup Information dialog box appears, offering a number of backup options (see fig. 6.8.1). Note the Log Information frame at the bottom of the Backup Information dialog box. You can write a summary or a detailed description of the backup operation to a log file.

6

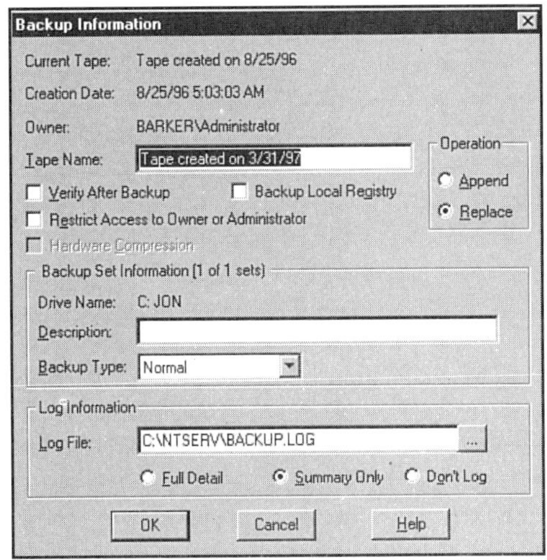

Figure 6.8.1 The Backup Information dialog box.

B. Restoring Files and Directories

To restore a file or directory using the Backup utility, open the Tapes window (if you don't see the Tapes window on your screen, pull down the Window menu and choose Tapes) and select the backup set you want to restore. Like the Drives window, the Tapes window enables you to expand directories and select individual files for restoration.

Select the files/directories you want to restore and click on the Restore button in the toolbar (or choose Operations, Restore). The Restore Information dialog box appears. Select the desired restore options and click on OK to restore the files/directories.

You also can run the NTBACKUP utility from the command prompt. This enables you to automate the backup process through batch files, so you can perform backups at regular intervals. You can only back up directories with the ntbackup command (not individual files). The syntax is as follows:

```
ntbackup operation  path
```

where *operation* is the name of the operation (backup, restore, and so on), and *path* is the path to the directory you're backing up. The NTBACKUP command includes a number of switches, including the following:

> */a* cause the backup set to be appended after the last backup set. (If you don't specify /a will overwrite existing backup sets on the tape.)
>
> */v* verifies the backup operation.
>
> */d* "text" enables you to add a description of the data in the backup set.
>
> */t* {option} enables you to specify the backup type (normal, incremental, daily, differential, copy).

C. Breaking a Mirror Set

A mirror set is the only fault-tolerant option capable of holding the system and boot partitions. When a partition in a mirror set fails, it becomes an orphan. To maintain service until the mirror is repaired, the fault-tolerant device directs all I/0 requests to the healthy partition. If the boot and/or system partitions are involved, a fault-tolerant boot disk is required to restart the system. To create a fault-tolerant boot disk, follow these steps:

1. Format a floppy disk using Windows NT.
2. If you are using an I386 system, copy NTLDR, NTDETECT.COM, NTBOOTDD.SYS (for SCSI disks not using SCSI BIOS), and BOOT.INI to the disk.

   If you're using a RISC-based computer, copy OSLOADER.EXE and HAL.DLL.
3. Modify the BOOT.INI file so that it points to the mirrored copy of the boot partition.

To fix a mirror set, you must first break it by choosing Fault Tolerance, Break Mirror. This action exposes the remaining partition as a separate volume. The healthy partition is given the drive letter that was previously assigned to it in the set, and the orphaned partition is given the next logical drive letter, or one that you manually selected for it.

After the mirror (RAID level 1) has been re-established as a primary partition, selecting additional free space and restarting the process of creating a mirror set can form a new relationship.

D. Regenerating a Stripe Set with Parity

Like a mirror set, the partition that fails in a stripe set with parity (RAID level 5) becomes an orphan. Also, the fault-tolerant device redirects I/O requests to the remaining partitions in the set to enable reconstruction. So that this can be done, the data is stored in RAM by using the parity bits (which may affect the system's performance).

To regenerate a stripe set with parity, follow these steps:

1. Select the stripe set with parity by clicking on it.
2. Select an area of free space as large or larger than the stripe set. The size of the stripe set becomes the size of the smallest amount of free space on any drive multiplied by the number of drives.
3. Choose Fault Tolerance, Regenerate.

You must close the Disk Administrator and restart the system before the process can begin. After the system restarts, the information from the existing partitions in the stripe set are read into memory and re-created on the new member. This process completes in the background, so the stripe set with parity isn't active in the Disk Administrator until it finishes.

E. Troubleshooting Partitions and Disks

When you install Windows NT, your initial disk configuration is saved on the emergency repair disk and in the directory \<winnt_root>\Repair. The RDISK utility does update the disk configuration information stored on the repair disk and in the Repair directory. You can also save or restore the disk configuration by using Disk Administrator.

You should periodically update emergency configuration information in case you ever need to use the Emergency Repair Process or you ever want to you upgrade to a newer version of Windows NT. Otherwise, NT restores the original configuration that was saved when you first installed Windows NT.

6.8.1 Exercise: Familiarize Yourself with Disk Administrator

In Exercise 6.8.1, you learn how to use Disk Administrator to perform some routine tasks.

Estimated time: 20 minutes

1. Start the Disk Administrator program by choosing Administrative Tools from the Programs section of the Start Menu. Next, select Disk Administrator.
2. Select Tools, and then Assign Drive Letter. Change the C: drive to J: and notice how simple the operation is. The mappings are all internal.
3. Change the J: drive back to C:
4. Make note of the size of each partition and the amount of free space.
5. If Fault Tolerance is in use, note the information pertinent to it from the Fault Tolerance menu of Disk Administrator.
6. Exit Disk Administrator.

6.8 Practice Problems

1. What is the best defense against lost data?

   A. RAID hardware implementation

   B. RAID software implementation

   C. Backups

   D. Volume sets

2. The Windows NT backup utility is called:

   A. NTBACK.EXE

   B. NTBACKUP.EXE

   C. BACKUP.EXE

   D. BACKUP.COM

3. When installed, the Backup utility is a part of what program group?

   A. Server Manager

   B. User Domain for Workgroups

   C. Administrative Tools

   D. Backup

4. To start a Backup process in the Windows NT Backup Utility, you could do either of which two options:

   A. Click on the Backup button in the toolbar.

   B. Choose Operations, Backup.

   C. Type BACKUP at a command-line prompt.

   D. Type BACKUP at the RUN line.

5. The Backup operation can be detailed in a log file by making the appropriate radio box selection on the Backup Information screen in what three ways?

   A. Full Detail

   B. Limited Detail

   C. Summary Only

   D. Don't Log

6. To restore a file or directory using the Backup utility, what must be done first?

   A. You must reboot the system.

   B. You must disable logging.

   C. You must select the backup set you want to restore.

   D. You must load the Restore utility from the Resource kit.

7. The Backup utility can be run in which three ways:

   A. Click on the Backup button in the toolbar.

   B. Choose Operations, Backup.

   C. Type NTBACKUP at a command-line prompt.

   D. Type BACKUP at the RUN line.

8. What is an advantage of running NTBACKUP from the command line?

   A. There is none.

   B. It takes up less RAM.

   C. It enables you to automate the backup process.

   D. It enables you to choose files as well as directories.

9. What is a disadvantage of running NTBACKUP from the command line?

   A. There is none.

   B. It takes up more RAM.

   C. It does not allow you to automate the backup process.

   D. It does not allow you to choose files; only directories.

10. Which NTBACKUP command-line switch will cause the backup set to be appended after the last backup set?

    A. /a

    B. /v

    C. /d

    D. /t

11. Which NTBACKUP command-line switch will verify the backup operation?

    A. /a

    B. /v

    C. /d

    D. /t

12. Which NTBACKUP command line-switch enables you to set the backup type to incremental?

    A. /a

    B. /v

    C. /d

    D. /t

13. Which NTBACKUP command-line switch enables you to add a description of the data in the backup set?

    A. /a

    B. /v

    C. /d

    D. /t

14. When a partition in a mirror set fails, it becomes known as:

    A. An orphan

    B. A discard

    C. A non-member

    D. A Lansing-75

15. After a drive in a mirror set fails, all I/O requests are:

    A. Spooled

    B. Directed to the other partition

    C. Ignored

    D. Withdrawn

16. If a mirrored drive fails on a system partition:

    A. The system continues to act normally until the failed drive can be replaced.

    B. The system shuts down automatically and NT must be reinstalled.

    C. A fault-tolerant boot disk might be required to restart the system.

    D. Only a Lansing-75 (or higher) will continue to process requests.

17. Which files are necessary on a fault-tolerant boot disk for an I386 system (choose all that apply):

    A. OSLOADER.EXE

    B. NTDETECT.COM

    C. HAL.DLL

    D. BOOT.INI

18. Which files are necessary on a fault-tolerant boot disk for a RISC-based system? (Choose all that apply.)

    A. OSLOADER.EXE

    B. NTDETECT.COM

    C. HAL.DLL

    D. BOOT.INI

19. In the event of a mirror failure, which file must be modified to point to the mirrored copy of the boot partition?

    A. NTBOOTDD.SYS

    B. BOOT.INI

    C. NTBOOT.INI

    D. NTLDR

20. Which file is needed on a fault-tolerant boot disk for systems with SCSI controllers that are non-BIOS enabled:

    A. NTBOOTDD.SYS

    B. BOOT.INI

    C. NTBOOT.INI

    D. NTLDR

21. To fix a mirror set, you must first:
    A. Break it by choosing Fault Tolerance, Break Mirror.
    B. Replace the bad drive with a new one.
    C. Stop transaction logging.
    D. Expose the bad partition as a separate volume.
22. When you break a mirror set due to a fault, what drive letter is given to the faulty drive, by default?
    A. The one it originally had.
    B. The next logical letter.
    C. It does not need one.
    D. The last free letter of the alphabet.
23. After a broken mirror has been re-established as a primary partition, selecting additional free space and restarting the process of creating a mirror set will do what?
    A. Remove all old references.
    B. Re-enable transaction logging.
    C. Form a new relationship.
    D. Start parity checking again.
24. When a partition in a stripe set with parity fails, it becomes known as:
    A. An orphan
    B. A discard
    C. A non-member
    D. A Lansing-75
25. To recreate a stripe set with parity after replacing a failed drive:
    A. First break the set it by choosing Fault Tolerance, Break Mirror.
    B. Choose Fault Tolerance, Regenerate.
    C. Do nothing, the stripe set will recreate itself.
    D. Enable Pulse via the Regedit utility.
26. If you employ fault-tolerance via a stripe set with parity over six drives, what must you do if two drives fail (and are replaced) after a lightning strike?
    A. Choose Fault Tolerance, Regenerate.
    B. Restore the lost data from tape backup.
    C. Do nothing; the stripe set will recreate itself.
    D. Enable Pulse via the Regedit utility.
27. The Regenerate command is located beneath Fault Tolerance in what utility?
    A. Network Monitor
    B. Disk Administrator
    C. Emergency Repair
    D. Server Manager
28. What utility updates the disk configuration information stored on the repair disk and in the Repair directory?
    A. Server Manager
    B. Network Monitor
    C. RDISK
    D. Regenerate
29. In addition to RDISK, you can also save or restore the disk configuration information by using:
    A. Disk Administrator
    B. Server Manager
    C. Network Monitor
    D. Regenerate
30. Volume information can be viewed on the NT Server by using which utility?
    A. Disk Administrator
    B. Server Manager
    C. Network Monitor
    D. Regenerate

31. When first using NTBACKUP, the default is that all files and directories are:

    A. Checked for inclusion in the backup.

    B. There is no default setting.

    C. Not checked to be included in the backup.

    D. Marked to archive, but not backup.

32. Which utility is used to create an emergency repair disk?

    A. Disk Administrator

    B. ERD.EXE

    C. BOOTNT.COM

    D. RDISK.EXE

33. Fault-Tolerance can be provided at which two RAID levels in Windows NT?

    A. 1

    B. 2

    C. 3

    D. 5

34. What is the minimum number of physical disks needed to implement mirroring?

    A. 1

    B. 2

    C. 3

    D. 4

35. What is the minimum number of physical disks needed to implement disk striping with parity?

    A. 1

    B. 2

    C. 3

    D. 4

36. What is the minimum number of physical disks needed to implement disk striping without parity?

    A. 1

    B. 2

    C. 3

    D. 4

37. Data can be recovered in the event of *either* a hardware *or* software failure using which redundancy techniques? (Choose all correct answers.)

    A. Disk mirroring

    B. Disk duplexing

    C. Disk striping

    D. Disk striping with parity

38. If disk striping with parity is implemented on three drives with free space of 250 MB, 400 MB, and 900 MB, respectively, what is the size of the stripe set?

    A. 250 MB

    B. 750 MB

    C. 1550 MB

    D. 2700 MB

39. What is the maximum number of drives RAID level 1 will support?

    A. 1

    B. 2

    C. 4

    D. unlimited

40. The System and boot partitions can be included in which fault-tolerance strategies? (Choose all correct answers.)

    A. Mirror

    B. Stripe set with parity

    C. Stripe set

    D. Volume set

41. Which can be thought of as the graphical equivalent of FDISK.EXE?

    A. Disk Administrator

    B. ERD.EXE

    C. BOOTNT.COM

    D. RDISK.EXE

42. If disk striping with parity is implemented on five drives with free space of 100 MB, 200 MB, 300 MB, 400 MB and 500 MB, respectively, what is the size of the stripe set?

    A. 100 MB

    B. 500 MB

    C. 1000 MB

    D. 1500 MB

6.8 Answers and Explanations: Exercise

In Exercise 6.8.1, you learned how to use Disk Administrator to perform some routine tasks. This is a tool you should become very familiar with and consider indispensable.

6.8 Answers and Explanations: Practice Problems

1. **C** Even if you are employing a high-tech RAID fault-tolerance system, a good backup routine is still your best defense against lost data.

2. **B** Windows NT includes a backup utility called NTBACKUP.EXE.

3. **C** Backup is part of the Administrative Tools group.

4. **A, B** To start a backup, click on the Backup button in the toolbar or choose Operations, Backup.

5. **A, C, D** You can write a summary or a detailed description of the backup operation to a log file as Full Detail or Summary Only. You can also choose to not create a log file.

6. **C** To restore a file or directory using the Backup utility, open the Tapes window and select the backup set you want to restore.

7. **A, B, C** You also can run the NTBACKUP utility from the command prompt.

8. **C** This enables you to automate the backup process through batch files, so you can perform backups at regular intervals.

9. **A** The command line utility is less intuitive in nature than the graphical version.

10. **A** Ntbackup /a cause the backup set to be appended after the last backup set. (If you don't specify /a will overwrite existing backup sets on the tape.)

11. **B** Ntbackup /v verifies the backup operation.

12. **D** Ntbackup /t {option} enables you to specify the backup type (normal, incremental, daily, differential, copy).

13. **C** Ntbackup /d "text" enables you to add a description of the data in the backup set.

14. **A** When a partition in a mirror set fails, it becomes an orphan.

15. **B** To maintain service until the mirror is repaired, the fault-tolerant device directs all I/0 requests to the healthy partition.

16. **C** If the boot and/or system partitions are involved, a fault tolerant boot disk is required to restart the system.

17. **B, D** If you are using an I386 system, NTLDR, NTDETECT.COM, NTBOOTDD.SYS (for SCSI disks not using SCSI BIOS), and BOOT.INI are needed on the disk.

18. **A, C, D** OSLOADER.EXE and BOOT.INI are needed on a RISC-based fault tolerant boot disk.

19. **B** BOOT.INI must be modified to point to the mirrored copy of the boot partition.

20. **A** NTBOOTDD.SYS must be included on a fault tolerant disk if SCSI drives are used without SCSI BIOS.

21. **A** To fix a mirror set, you must first break it by choosing Fault Tolerance, Break Mirror. This action exposes the remaining partition as a separate volume.

22. **B** The healthy partition is given the drive letter that was previously assigned to it in the set, and the orphaned partition is given the next logical drive letter or one that you manually selected for it.

23. **C** After the mirror has been re-established as a primary partition, selecting additional free space and restarting the process of creating a mirror set can form a new relationship.

24. **A** When a partition in a mirror set or a stripe set with parity fails, it becomes an orphan.

25. **C** The Regenerate command is used to reestablish a stripe set with parity after replacing the fault disk.

26. **B** A stripe set with parity keeps a system running during the failure of one drive but cannot handle more than that.

27. **B** Disk Administrator is the utility for all disk-related operations.

28. **C** The RDISK utility does update the disk configuration information stored on the repair disk and in the Repair directory.

29. **A** You can also save or restore the disk configuration by using Disk Administrator.

30. **A** The Disk Administrator is used to view all information relevant to the drives, partitions, and volumes.

31. **C** By default, files are not marked for backup, and you must select which ones you want to include in the set.

32. **D** RDISK is used to create an emergency repair disk.

33. **A, D** RAID level 1 (mirroring) and RAID level 5 (disk striping with parity) are both supported by Windows NT.

34. **B** Two physical disks are needed to implement disk mirroring.

35. **C** Three physical disks are needed to implement disk striping with parity.

36. **B** Two physical disks are needed to implement disk striping without parity. It is not considered a fault-tolerant solution because it does not support data redundancy.

37. **A, B, D** Disk Striping does not offer fault tolerance or data redundancy whereas mirroring, duplexing, and striping with parity do.

38. **B** The size of the stripe set becomes the size of the smallest amount of free space on any drive multiplied by the number of drives.

39. **B** Disk mirroring (RAID level 1) supports only two drives.

40. **A** A mirror is the only fault tolerant strategy capable of containing the system and boot partitions.

41. **A** Disk Administrator is the graphical equivalent of FDISK.EXE. It enables you to partition drives, create stripe sets, etc.

42. **B** The size of the stripe set becomes the size of the smallest amount of free space on any drive multiplied by the number of drives.

6.8 Key Words

Mirror set

Disk Administrator

Fault-tolerance

Orphan

Practice Exam: Troubleshooting

Use this practice exam to test your mastery of Connectivity. This practice exam is made up of 20 questions. Keep in mind that the passing Microsoft score is 76.4 percent. There will be two types of questions:

- Multiple Choice—Select the correct answer.
- Multiple Multiple Choice—Select all answers that are correct.

Begin as soon as you are ready. Answers follow the test.

1. The utility used to convert NTFS partitions to FAT is:

   A. NTFS.EXE

   B. CONVERT.EXE

   C. MIGRATE.EXE

   D. There is no utility to perform this operation.

2. Spencer calls to say that he was playing around and accidentally changed the SCSI controller card driver, and now the computer won't boot NT. It stops at the blue screen and gives him a system error. What should Spencer do?

   A. Boot into DOS and rerun the Windows NT Setup program.

   B. Purchase and install the SCSI device that he selected.

   C. Reinstall NT.

   D. Select the LastKnownGood configuration during NT booting, then remove the incorrect driver.

3. Annie works in the South Building. She calls to say that the message "`I/O Error accessing boot sector file multi(0)disk(0)rdisk(0)partition(1):\bootsect.dos`," is showing up on her screen. Which one of the critical boot files is *really* missing?

   A. NTLDR

   B. NTDETECT.COM

   C. BOOTSECT.DOS

   D. MSDOS.SYS

4. What information does the BOOTSECT.DOS file contain?

   A. A copy of the information that was originally on the boot sector of the drive before NT was installed. You use it to boot an operating system other than NT.

   B. A copy of the information needed to boot a RISC-based computer.

   C. The file that detects the hardware installed on a PC with a Plug-and-Play BIOS.

   D. The file that contains the boot menu selections.

5. If BOOTSECT.DOS becomes corrupted on one machine, can you copy it from another machine?

   A. Yes, the file is standard on every machine.

   B. Only if the other machine is identical to the corrupted one in every way.

   C. Only with the RDISK utility.

   D. No, the file is machine specific.

6. Marco calls back to say that he is looking for a particular message in the system log under Event Viewer, but there are so many messages that he can't find the one you told him to look for. Can he display messages of a certain type?

   A. He cannot. Event Viewer shows all the messages in the system log.

   B. He must set up Event Viewer to store only messages of the type he is looking for and then restart the system.

   C. He can filter the log by choosing View, Filter Events.

   D. He must first export the data to an ASCII file and then use the Edit program to find the specific data sought.

7. The pointy-headed manager informs you that an inventory of all company PCs running NT Workstation and NT Server needs to be done. Which NT utility can you use to find the amount of RAM, type of CPU, and other information about the computers in question?

   A. You must purchase the 32-bit version of PC Tools. This program gives you the required information.

   B. No tools will run under NT because they would have to access the hardware directly, which isn't allowed under NT.

   C. You must manually edit the Registry and search for the information you need.

   D. Use the Windows NT Diagnostics utility.

8. Kristin knows just enough to be dangerous. She calls and says that while running Windows NT Diagnostics, she attempted to change the type of CPU that was reported but could not. Why?

   A. NT Diagnostics only shows information. You cannot make any modifications using this tool.

   B. The type of CPU cannot be changed with NT Diagnostics. The user must use Registry Editor to make the change manually.

   C. The user must make the CPU change in CMOS setup, not in NT Diagnostics.

   D. Kristin does not have sufficient permissions to make the change.

9. If a Windows NT-based workstation moonlighting as a print server appears too sluggish to the user while printing is taking place, what action should be done on the priority level of the print service?

   A. Raise the priority by one or two classes.

   B. Raise the priority by three to four classes.

   C. Lower the priority by one or two classes.

   D. Make no change—the priority level does not affect this service.

10. To change the priority class of a print service, edit which component of the Registry?

    A. HKEY_LOCAL_MACHINE\System\CurrentControlSet

    B. HKEY_LOCAL_MACHINE\System\CurrentControlSet\Control

    C. HKEY_LOCAL_MACHINE\System\CurrentControlSet\Control\Print

    D. HKEY_LOCAL_MACHINE\System\CurrentControlSet\Control\Printers

11. RAS can use which protocols for dial-out connections? (Choose all correct answers.)

    A. TCP/IP

    B. NWLink

    C. NetBEUI

    D. SMTP

12. Of the protocols RAS supports for dial-in and dial-out, which benefits from being available on a number of different platforms and is easily routable?

    A. TCP/IP

    B. NWLink

    C. NetBEUI

    D. SMTP

13. Which statement regarding the version of Network Monitor included with Windows NT Resource Kit is true?

    A. It can monitor only the system upon which it was installed.

    B. It can monitor any system on the network.

    C. It is not included with the Resource Kit, but rather a component of the NT distribution disks.

    D. It will not collect TCP/IP information until SMTP is installed.

14. Common causes of physical network problems include which two of the following:

    A. Transmission media

    B. NIC cards

    C. Fax/Data modems in Workstations

    D. Insufficient video RAM

15. Which of the following tools should be used to check network traffic:

    A. Cable analyzer

    B. Diagnostics program

    C. A network protocol analyzer

    D. Performance Monitor

16. Mary calls to say that she is having trouble with networking in a non-routed TCP/IP environment. What two pieces of information had to be given to enable networking in this environment:

    A. Number of servers

    B. IP address

    C. Subnet mask

    D. Host name

17. Karen calls to report that she cannot log on to the system. She is getting a message that says "`NT cannot log you on. Check your userid and password information and try again`" As an administrator, what should you check first?

    A. Make sure that she types in the correct password and userid combination. Also check that she has entered the password in the correct case and is specifying the correct domain name.

    B. Nothing. It's a normal message that a user would get when the server is down for maintenance.

    C. Log on as administrator and restart the domain controller to clear out any unused connections. When the server comes back up, Karen should be able to log on.

    D. Check the System log in Event Viewer.

18. If disk striping with parity is implemented of three drives with free space of 250 MB, 400 MB, and 900 MB, respectively, what is the size of the data that can be stored on the stripe set?

    A. 250 MB

    B. 500 MB

    C. 750 MB

    D. 2700 MB

19. When do changes take place in Disk Administrator?

    A. When they are implemented.

    B. When they are committed.

    C. When you exit the program.

    D. When you reboot the server.

20. What is stored in the BOOT.INI file?

    A. Information about the previous operating system.

    B. Properties associated with the video card.

    C. Information on services and drivers that fail to start.

    D. The ARC path of partitions.

Answers and Explanations: Practice Exam

1. **D** There is no such utility for converting NTFS back to FAT.

2. **D** Booting with LastKnownGood boot gets around recent driver change problems.

3. **C** Never try to make a problem harder than it is. If the error message says BOOTSECT.DOS is missing, it is probably BOOTSECT.DOS that is missing.

4. **A** BOOTSECT.DOS is a copy of the information that was originally on the boot sector of the drive before NT was installed. You use it to boot an operating system other than NT.

5. **B** BOOTSECT.DOS can be borrowed from another machine if the two machines are identical in every way.

6. **C** You can filter the log by choosing View, Filter Events.

7. **D** The Windows NT Diagnostics utility is perfect for this task.

8. **A** NT Diagnostics only shows information. You cannot make any modifications using this tool.

9. **C** If a Windows NT-based workstation moonlighting as a print server appears to print too slowly, consider raising the priority by one or two classes. If the workstation is responding sluggishly to the user while printing, consider lowering the priority by a class or two.

10. **C** To change the priority class for the Spooler service, add a value called PriorityClass of type REG_DWORD to HKEY_LOCAL_MACHINE\System\CurrentControlSet\Control\Print and set it so that it is equal to the priority class desired.

11. **A, B, C** RAS supports TCP/IP, NWLink, and NetBEUI protocols for both dial-in and dial-out connections.

12. **A** TCP/IP benefits from being available on a number of different platforms, being easily routable, and having the compatibility choice of the Internet.

13. **B** The Network Monitor included with Windows NT Server can monitor only the specific system on which it is installed, unlike the Network Monitor in Microsoft's Systems Management Server package, which can monitor other systems on the network.

14. **A, B** Network problems often are caused by cables, adapters, IRQ conflicts, or problems with transmission media.

15. **C** Use a diagnostics program to check the network adapter card. Use a cable analyzer to check the cabling. Use Network Monitor to check network traffic, or use a network protocol analyzer.

16. **B, C** The IP address and the subnet mask must be given when TCP/IP is installed in a non-routed environment.
17. **A** If users can't log on, they might be using an incorrect username or password.
18. **B** The size of the stripe set becomes the size of the smallest amount of free space on any drive multiplied by the number of drives. The stripe set is then divided by the number of drives to come up with the parity information, and what remains is used for data storage.
19. **B** Disk Administrator changes are not made until you commit the changes.
20. **D** BOOT.INI stores the ARC path to partitions. It must be edited to reflect changes in the event of a mirrored drive failure.

Part II

MCSE TestPrep

Windows NT Server 4 Enterprise

CHAPTER 7

Planning

This chapter helps you prepare for the exam by covering the following Planning objectives:

- Select the appropriate directory services architecture for given scenarios (considerations include selecting the appropriate domain model, supporting a single logon account, and allowing users to access different resources in different domains).
- Plan the disk drive configurations for various requirements. Requirements include fault tolerance, stripe sets, and volume sets.
- Select the proper protocol for various situations. Protocols include:
    - TCP/IP
    - TCP/IP with WINS and DHCP
    - NWLink IPX/SPX Compatible Transport Protocol
    - Data Link Control (DLC)
    - AppleTalk

7.1 Selecting the Appropriate Directory Services Architecture

To prepare for this part of the exam, you need to recognize which domain model is appropriate for a given network environment. You need to know how to set up the trusts for each of these models and how to assign groups to give permissions across the trust relationship.

A. Goals of Windows NT 4 Directory Services

A logical grouping of servers and clients in Windows NT is called a *domain*. Domains can be linked together to enable users from one logical group to access servers in another logical group. Administering the accounts in domains and providing links between domains are the main tasks of directory services.

A single domain maintains all the directory database information in the Security Account Manager (SAM). The *SAM* contains all user accounts, Windows NT computer accounts, group accounts, and any account settings assigned in the domain, all of which contribute to the SAM's size. Microsoft recommends that SAM not exceed 40 MB. Table 7.1.1 shows the size of each account or group included in the SAM database.

Table 7.1.1 SAM Database Limitations

SAM Database Item	Size Per Item
User accounts	1.0 KB
Local groups	512 bytes per group plus 36 bytes per user
Global groups	512 bytes per group plus 12 bytes per user
Computer accounts	0.5 KB

The maximum size of the SAM is a physical limitation of the domain. Domains are also often broken into logical units, such as departments within a company. The organizational chart and political influences usually need to be addressed in the design. Individual departments may require control of their own resources.

Directory services are implemented to help you administer and maintain a consistent network environment throughout a WAN or LAN. The main goals of directory services are:

- One user, one account
- Universal resource access
- Centralized administration
- Directory synchronization

1. One User, One Account

Each user in your network should not have more than one account name or password. Administration is simplified with only one account per user. With one account per user, you can easily assign permission to a single user for resources located anywhere on the network, you can audit your system for any type of access by this user, and it is easier to modify the permissions of a user because the account is located in one place. Having one account is also easier for users because they have to remember only one username and one password.

> **BackOffice applications also can use Windows NT usernames and passwords so that you maintain the goal of one user, one account.**

2. Universal Resource Access

With this single account, users should be able to access all resources, regardless of physical location. This is known as *universal resource access.*

By having universal resource access, a user from one domain can access resources in other domains without having a separate account in these resource domains. However, users may not even be aware that they are accessing resources outside of their own domain. When the administrator configures permissions correctly, universal resource access should be transparent to the user.

3. Centralized Administration

The goal of centralized administration is to consolidate the administration of user accounts and resource access to one central location. It's easier to manage user accounts when they are in one central place than when they are scattered on different servers throughout the enterprise.

4. Directory Synchronization

All directory services information must be available to all the computers in the network so that users can access resources whenever they need. This information is copied to all domain controllers through *directory synchronization*. Directory synchronization is automatic within domains in Windows NT Server 4. By using trust relationships (discussed in the next section), domains communicate with each other to share the database information.

Setting up a trust relationship does not synchronize one domain's accounts with another. Rather, a trust allows one domain's directory services database to be accessed from another domain. Accounts are not copied from one domain to another; the domains cross-reference the other domain's databases through the trust.

B. Trust Relationships

A *trust relationship* is a secured communication link between two domains implemented as a Remote Procedure Call, or RPC. One of the domains acts as the trusted domain, and the other is the trusting domain. The trusting domain permits users from the trusted domain to access its resources. 7

Because a user can access resources in another domain through the trust, the user doesn't need a new account in the resource domain. This one account can access resources throughout the network on different domains as long as trust relationships are properly configured. Accounts can be administered in one central place while still allowing access to remote resources. With more than one domain in the network, using trust relationships is critical to meeting the goals of directory services.

1. Trusted Versus Trusting

Every trust relationship has a trusted and a trusting domain. The trusted domain is the domain that contains the user accounts. The trusted domain is also referred to as the *account domain*.

The trusting domain uses the accounts from the trusted domain. Located in the trusting domain are the resources that you need to share. The trusting domain assigns security permissions to any user in its SAM and any user in a trusted domain's SAM. By creating a trusting domain, departments can maintain control of their resources while still allowing the users to be administered centrally. A trusting domain is also referred to as a *resource domain*.

2. Graphically Representing a Trust Relationship

When drawing trust relationships, domains are represented as circles and the direction of the trust relationship is depicted by an arrow. The direction of the arrow always points to the trusted domain. One way to remember the direction of the arrow is to always point to whom you can trust. The arrow head in a trust diagram points to the trusted (account) domain.

A trust relationship always involves two domains. One domain contains user accounts. The other domain has resources, such as files, printers, or applications, that users in the account domain need to access. The account domain is known as the trusted domain. The resource domain is known as the trusting domain, so in a trust diagram the trust arrow points from the resource domain to the account domain. If you become unsure during the test, try drawing the trust relationship on paper.

3. Planning Trust Relationships

Administrators from both domains in a trust relationship must configure their domains to participate in the trust. A trust relationship cannot be established from one domain. The requirements for setting up a trust are the following:

- The trust relationship can only be established between Windows NT Server domains.
- The domains must be able to make an RPC connection. Basically, the PDC from each domain should be able to make a network connection. However, the PDCs cannot have an existing network connection when you try to establish the trust.

You can use the following command to terminate all sessions with any other computers:

```
net use * /d
```

- The trust relationship must be set up by a user with administrator access.
- The number of trusts and type of trusts should be determined prior to the implementation.
- Determine where the user accounts reside; this is the trusted domain.
- Determine where the resources reside; this is the trusting domain.

Always define the role of your domain before configuring the trust. When implementing a trust, you must specify in the interface which domain is trusted and which domain is trusting.

4. Establishing Trust Relationships

Establishing a trust relationship must be completed by an administrator from each domain in the trust relationship by using the Trust Relationships dialog box. This dialog box is accessed from User Manager for Domains by selecting Trust Relationships from the Policies menu.

This dialog box has two different sections. The administrator specifies in the dialog box the relationship of the other domain in the trust relationship. The name of the administrator's own domain never appears in the Trust Relationships dialog box; only the name of the trust partner appears:

- The trusted domains section is filled in by the trusting domain.
- The trusting domains section is filled in by the trusted domain.

You can configure the trust in either order; however, Microsoft recommends the trusted domain initiate the trust by entering the name of the trusting domain. When the trusting domain completes the trust by entering the name of the trusted domain, a message "Trust Successfully Established" is displayed.

If the trust relationship was established in the opposite order (trusting domain initiates the trust), it can still be completed; however, you receive a dialog box warning that the trust could not be verified. In this case, the trust is not immediately established (it can take up to 15 minutes), and you need to manually verify the trust later.

The steps needed to establish a trust relationship are as follows:

1. From a command prompt, type **net use** to see if you have any connections with the PDC in the other domain. If you have connections, type the following in the command prompt to end these connections:

   ```
   net use * /d
   ```

2. From the trusted domain, start User Manager for Domains, and then select the Trust Relationship command from the Policies menu.
3. From the trusted domain, add the name of the trusting domain. A password for the trust can be entered, but is optional.
4. When the trusting domain has been added into the Trust Relationships dialog box, the trusted domain can then close the screen.
5. From the trusting domain, open the Trust Relationships dialog box and add the name of the trusted domain. Type the password specified by the administrator in the trusted domain.
6. After the trusted domain is added, you should see the "Trust Successfully Established" message.

When a trust is established, Windows NT changes the password that was used to establish the trust. The domain controllers in both domains know the new password, however it is not visible to the users. Frequently, this password is changed by Windows NT for added security. If one of the domains in the trust relationship was to break the trust, the trust could not be reestablished without breaking both sides and starting the trust relationship from the beginning. This is because the administrators do not know the current correct password.

a. One-Way Trusts

A *one-way trust* is a trust relationship with a single trusted domain and a single trusting domain.

The accounts exist in the trusted domain, and the trusting domain has resources that are assigned permissions to users in the trusted domain.

b. Two-Way Trusts

A *two-way trust* is nothing more than two one-way trusts. In a two-way trust, both domains are trusted domains and trusting domains. This type of trust is necessary because each domain has user accounts and also has resources that users in the other domain need to access.

c. *Non-Transitive Trusts*

Trust relationships are non-transitive, in other words you cannot pass through one trust into another. A trust relationship involves only two domains. The domain with user accounts must be explicitly trusted by the domain with the resources the users need to access.

Assume an environment in which DomainA trusts DomainB and DomainB trusts DomainC. Because trusts are not transitive, a user from DomainC can access resources in DomainB, but cannot access any resources in DomainA, even though DomainB and DomainA also have a trust relationship. There isn't a trust relationship between DomainA and DomainC, which are the two domains in question. DomainA must trust DomainC if a user in DomainC wants to access resources in DomainA.

5. Removing Trusts

You remove a trust relationship by removing the name of the other domain from the Trust Relationships dialog box. If either domain, trusted or trusting, removes the opposite domain, the trust is broken. If the broken half of the trust tries to reestablish the trust, the trust fails because the password assigned to the trust relationship has been changed by Windows NT.

A trust also can be broken if the domain name of one of the members of the trust relationship is changed. The trust relationship will not be reestablished even if the name of the domain is changed back.

> **When the domain controllers in a domain are stopped, the trust is temporarily broken. If any domain controller for the domain comes back up, the trust is reestablished.**

6. Accounts in Trust Relationships

When a trust relationship is established, you have access to accounts in trusted domains as well as your own domain accounts.

You can create two types of user accounts, but only one of them can be used across a trust—global accounts.

a. *Global Accounts*

A *global account* is the default user account type. Every user account is a global account unless you specify the type of account as local. Global accounts are designed to be used across trusts and can be assigned access in the local domain and all the trusting domains.

b. *Local Accounts*

A local account is a special account type with some limitations:

- Cannot be given permissions across trusts, thus they are only used for accounts in non-trusted domains.
- Do not support interactive logon processes.
- Require their own passwords. Users will not be able to automatically synchronize passwords from one local account to another.

The local account cannot be used across trusts and is used only locally in your own domain. This type of account can be used to assign permissions to a user who only needs access to one domain in your enterprise. You, for example, can use local accounts for temporary employees who only need to access specific applications or resources. Because the temporary employees are set up as local accounts, they can never access resources outside the domain the account is created in, which provides additional security. Users from another domain can use a local account if they connect to a share by specifying the local account's username and password.

To specify a local account, select the account options in the User Properties dialog box, and select the Local Account option.

c. Global Groups and Local Groups

Microsoft recommends using groups for assigning all permissions. Users then inherit permissions from the groups to which they belong. Assigning permissions through groups is preferred to assigning permissions directly to individual users.

In Windows NT Server, the two types of groups are local and global. Local groups are restricted to being used where they are created, such as within a domain for local groups created on a domain controller. On the other hand, global groups are designed to contain users used across trusts.

The recommended strategy is to collect users together in global groups and to assign permission to local groups. Users get permission to use resources when global groups they belong to are added to local groups for resources they want to access. Users could be placed in global groups based on job function, department membership, or a common need to access certain resources on the network. Local groups are created where the resource is located. Resources could be file shares, printers, or applications. Permissions to use the resource are assigned to the local group. Then, the global groups with the users are added to the local groups with the permissions.

If you need to have different levels of access for one resource, you need to create more than one local group. If, for example, you wanted users of an application to have read rights while allowing administrators full control rights, you would create one local group with read permission. The global group with the application users would be assigned to this local group. You would also create another local group with full control permission. The global group with the application administrators would be assigned to this local group.

This method of granting permissions enables resource administrators to control access to their resources without having to control which groups users belong to. Assigning users to groups is typically done by account administrators. The resource administrator just controls which rights are given to a local group and which global group is added to the local group.

However, the resource administrator does not control who belongs to this global group. The membership of global groups is controlled by the administrator in the accounts domain. The resource administrator must "trust" the account administrator to assign the appropriate users to the global group. Because the resource administrator is controlling permissions, all the accounts administrator needs to do to give a user rights is to add that user to the appropriate global group. To take rights away from a user, the administrator removes the user from a global group.

Built-in groups are automatically created in a Windows NT domain. Table 7.1.2 shows the built-in local groups and Table 7.1.3 shows the built-in global groups.

Table 7.1.2 Built-In Local Groups

Local Group	Initially Contains	Rights
Administrators	Domain Admins, Administrator	Administrator account, to manage and maintain the entire system.
Users	Domain Users	Access resources, day-to-day operation of computer system.
Guests	Domain Guests	Guest account disabled by default.
Server Operators	None	Share and Stop sharing resources. Shut down/Lock servers. Stop and Start services. Server Maintenance. Backup and restore server.
Print Operators	None	Share and Stop sharing printers. Manage printers.
Backup Operators	None	Backup and restore server.
Account Operators	None	Create and manage user and group accounts.
Replicators	None	Used for the Directory Replicator service.

Table 7.1.3 Built-In Global Groups

Global Group	Initial Accounts	Member of...
Domain Admins	Administrator	Administrators
Domain Users	Administrator	Users
	All accounts created in domain.	
Domain Guests	Guests	Guests

Remember that only global groups and global user accounts can be used across trust relationships.

d. Assigning Permissions Across a Trust

Assigning permissions across a trust uses Microsoft's strategy to give users rights—global groups with users are added to local groups with permissions. When trusts are involved, a global group from a trusted domain is added to a local group in a trusting domain. Adding global groups from another domain to a local group is done in much the same way as adding global groups from the same domain. Create or edit the local group in User Manager, and then choose the Add button to add members to the group. Then, select the trusted domain from the List Names pull-down menu. The global groups and users from the trusted domain are listed and can be added to the local group.

Local groups and local accounts cannot be seen from this view because local accounts and local groups cannot be used across trusts.

7. The NetLogon Service in a Trust

After trust relationships are set up and permissions assigned, users from trusted domains must be authenticated to get access to the resources in a trusting domain. Similar to logging on to a domain, the user account must be verified and the security permissions must be assigned to the user account. The NetLogon service is responsible for handling logon requests and authentication. When requests are made across a trust, the action is called *pass-through authentication.*

a. *Pass-Through Authentication*

Pass-through authentication enables the trusting domain to handle the logon request, but it looks into the SAM of the trusted domain to verify that the account is valid.

If a user is using a computer in DomainB to log on to DomainA, the request to validate the logon must be passed on to DomainA from DomainB because DomainB does not have any record in its SAM for this user account. The communication between the two domains to validate the user is called pass-through authentication.

C. Windows NT Server 4 Domain Models

Windows NT domains can be organized into one of four different domain models. Each of these models supports the goal of directory services. Although there are other ways to combine domains, these four domain models (single domain, single master, multiple master, and complete trust) are the ones Microsoft expects you to know for the exam.

1. Selecting your Domain Model

When you are selecting a domain model, you should consider a number of points:

- Number of user accounts
- Number of organizational, or departmental, domains required
- Whether centralized account administration is required
- Whether centralized or distributed resource administration is required

Responses to these questions help you select the correct domain model.

2. Single Domain Model

The single domain model is the easiest to implement. It places all users, groups, and resources into a single domain. The single domain is the starting point of all the domain models; in any implementation you must ensure that each domain can function as a single domain before you should consider any of the other models.

The single domain model is ideal for smaller organizations. The benefits in a single domain model are as follows:

- Simple installation; just install the first server as a Primary Domain Controller and you have a single domain model.
- Centralized administration of accounts because there is only one domain database.

- Centralized administration of resources because all the resources are in one domain.
- No trust relationships to establish.

The limitations of the single domain model affect larger organizations that have a distributed WAN environment. The limitations of the single domain model are as follows:

- Can only support a SAM database of 40 MB, which is the maximum size Microsoft recommends for a single domain.
- No departmental administrative controls (decentralized administration) can be assigned because there is only one domain database for assigning security permissions.
- Browsing is slow if the domain contains a large number of servers and resources.

The total size of a domain is determined by the number of user, computer, and group accounts. The size of each of these accounts is discussed earlier in the section "Goals of Windows NT 4 Directory Services."

3. Single Master Domain Model

The single master domain model has one domain with user accounts and other domains to control access to resources. This model maintains the centralized administration of user accounts while allowing decentralized management of resources.

These resource domains can maintain their own resources and permissions, with all user accounts residing in the master domain. From a user's perspective, the domain appears to be one large system, every user logs on to the master. The users can connect to other domains in the environment without requiring additional user accounts or passwords.

The benefits of a single master domain model are

- Centralized administration of user accounts.
- Resources can be distributed and administered throughout resource domains.
- Each resource domain can have a domain administrator to maintain its resources, without giving access to the master domain.
- The trust relationships are fairly easy to implement.
- Maintains one user, one account goal of directory services.
- Global groups can be maintained from the master domain.

The limitations of a single master domain model are similar to those of the single domain model. The single master domain model still uses one domain database for all the users, so the number of user accounts this model supports is limited. The limitations of the single master domain model are

- Local groups must be defined in each domain, both master and resource domains.
- Maximum number of users is limited by the 40 MB maximum size of the SAM database.

- Resource domains have no control over group memberships of global groups from the master domain.
- Trust relationships have to be established in the proper direction to maintain the directory services structure.

The single master domain model is best suited for organizations with less than 20,000 users that require some departmental resource administration. This model is excellent for companies with locations spread across a WAN, because the trust relationships allow for the centralized administration of user accounts.

a. Trusts in a Single Master Domain Model

The trust relationships in a single master domain model are relatively easy to implement. In this model, the master domain holds all the user accounts and global groups, and may also have resources. The other domains in the organization become resource domains. The master domain is the trusted domain, whereas the resource domains are the trusting domains. All resource domains trust the master domain.

b. Accounts in a Single Master Domain Model

All user accounts in this model reside in the master domain, so all the global groups for the organization must also be defined in the master domain. Users or global groups from the master domain can then be accessed by any of the resource domains.

At the resource domains, local groups must be created with permissions for resources. Global groups and users from the master domain are then added to these local groups to give users access to the local resources. Remember that Microsoft stresses adding global groups rather than individual user accounts to local groups.

To assign administrator rights for the resource domains, administrators from the master domain are added to the resource domain's local administrators group. The simplest way to do this is to add the Domain Admins global group from the master domain to the local administrators group in each of the resource domains.

4. Multiple Master Domain Model

The multiple master domain model is designed for very large organizations that have users distributed across multiple domains. In this model, there is more than one master domain. Each master domain contains user and global group accounts to be used by all other domains in the environment. In this model, account administration can still be centralized. For all administrators to manage accounts, the Domain Admins global group from each master domain must be added to the local administrators group in each master domain.

The multiple master domain model is the most scaleable of the domain models. Each master domain can be the maximum recommended size of 40 MB. Additional master domains can be added to this model to enable the network to expand to include an unlimited number of users. The number of master domains available in this model is not limited.

The advantages of the multiple master domain model are the following:

- Scaleable to networks with a large number of users.
- Resources are grouped into resource domains to enable distributed resource management.
- Each master domain can have a domain administrator, or can be grouped to achieve centralized administration.
- User accounts and global groups are maintained in the master domains.

The limitations of the multiple master domain model are the following:

- Complex trust relationships have to be configured to maintain this domain model.
- User accounts are distributed across multiple master domains.
- Global groups may have to be defined multiple times, one in each master domain.

The multiple master domain model requires more planning than the single domain or the single master domain models. Domain planners must decide how the master domains are divided. Master domains can be based on geographical areas or different parts of an organization, such as unique business units. Centralized account administration can still be achieved in this model by adding the global Domain Admins group from each master domain into the local administrators group in all the other master domains. The trust relationships are more complex in this model.

a. Trusts in a Multiple Master Domain Model

The trust relationships in a multiple master domain model are configured similar to the single master domain. All resource domains trust the master domain. However, the multiple master domain model has more than one master domain so each resource domain must trust *all* master domains. Each master domain must have a two-way trust with all other master domains. There are no trusts between the resource domains.

You can determine the number of trusts required for a multiple master domain model by using the following formula:

```
M*(M-1)+(R*M)
```

M is the number of master domains, and *R* is the number of resource domains. The formula indicates that every master domain must trust every other master domain (M*M–1) and every resource domain must trust each master domain (R*M).

> **Remember that two-way trusts are actually two one-way trusts.**

b. Accounts in a Multiple Master Domain Model

The accounts in the multiple master are distributed across multiple master domains. Each user still has only one account; however, global groups may have to be duplicated in all the master domains. If, for example, an organization has members of the marketing department spread across both master domains, a marketing global group must be created in each master domain because users can only be assigned to global groups in their own domains. To give these marketing users access to a resource, the marketing global group from each master domain must be added to the local group for that resource.

The key points to remember regarding accounts in a multiple master domain are the following:

- User accounts are located in one of the master domains.
- Global groups are defined in all the master domains.
- Local groups are defined in resource domains, and contain global groups from all the master domains.

The multiple master domain model is best suited for large organizations that have more than 20,000 users and want to maintain centralized control of user accounts, while allowing resources to be administered departmentally.

5. Complete Trust Model

The complete trust model enables each domain to maintain their own control of users and resources with the opportunity to assign permissions to users of any other domain in the model. The complete trust model implements two-way trust relationships between every domain in the environment. Each domain is both an account domain and a resource domain.

This model is scaleable and flexible because domains can easily be added and removed from the model. However, the model does not allow for centralized administration of user accounts or resources.

7

a. Trusts in a Complete Trust Model

The complete trust model requires more trust relationships than any other domain model. Every domain has a two-way trust with every other domain.

You can use the following formula to determine the number of trusts required in a complete trust model:

```
N*(N-1)
```

N is the total number of domains in the model.

b. Accounts in a Complete Trust Model

Every domain is responsible for administering the user accounts and global groups in their own domains. The local administrators are also responsible for creating local groups and assigning members to them. This domain model makes it difficult to centrally manage the user accounts, and is designed for environments that do not require centralized administration.

7.1.1 Exercise: Selecting the Appropriate Directory Services Architecture

The type of questions you will see on the enterprise exam will be scenario-based questions. The questions will supply you with some basic information and you will have to select the appropriate domain model for a given situation. Try out a few questions to determine whether you understand the directory services architecture:

1. ABC Corporation has locations in Toronto, New York, and San Francisco. They want to install Windows NT Server 4.0 to encompass all its locations in a single WAN environment. The head office is located in New York, and all user accounts will be created at that location. In Toronto and San Francisco, ABC has numerous applications and resources that users from all three locations may need to access. What is the best domain model for ABC's directory services implementation? Pick only one answer.

   A. Single domain model

   B. Single master domain model

   C. Multiple master domain model

   D. Complete trust domain model

2. JPS Printing has a single location with 1,000 users spread across the LAN. They have special printers and applications installed on the servers in their environment and need to be able to centrally manage the user accounts and the resources. Which domain model would best fit their needs? Choose one.

   A. Single domain model

   B. Single master domain model

   C. Multiple master domain model

   D. Complete trust model

3. Worldwide Training has locations spread across the world. The North American headquarters are located in Seattle, the European headquarters in London, England. Smaller locations are distributed throughout the world. All the user accounts would be maintained from the two corporate headquarters, but each location needs to manage their own resources. Which domain model would best fit their scenario?

   A. Single domain model

   B. Single master domain model

   C. Multiple master domain model

   D. Complete trust model

4. ABC Corporation has a single domain model to maintain the directory services in its Toronto location. They manage all users and resources for their current network. ABC Corporation is merging with DEF Corporation. The two companies will still run as separate companies, but want to share network resources. Each domain would be completely responsible for user accounts and resources in their separate domains. Which domain model would allow the two domains to maintain account and resource control, but still allow access between the two domains?

   A. Single domain model

   B. Single master domain model

   C. Multiple master domain model

   D. Complete trust model

7.1.2 Exercise: Synchronizing the Domain Controllers

Exercise 7.1.2 shows how to manually synchronize a Backup Domain Controller within your domain.

1. Click Start, Programs, Administrative Tools, and select the Server Manager.
2. Highlight the BDC (Backup Domain Controller) in your computer list.
3. Select the Computer menu, then select Synchronize with Primary Domain Controller.

7.1.3 Exercise: Establishing a Trust Relationship Between Domains

Exercise 7.1.3 shows how to establish a trust relationship between multiple domains. To complete this exercise, you must have two Windows NT Server computers, each installed as Primary Domain Controllers in unique domains.

1. From the trusted domain select Start, Programs, Administrative Tools, and click User Manager for Domains. The User Manager for Domains application starts.
2. Select the Policies menu and select Trust Relationships. The Trust Relationships dialog box appears.
3. In the trusting domain section, click Add and enter the name of your trusting domain. You can leave the password blank.
4. When the trusting domain information has been entered, click OK and close the Trust Relationships dialog box.
5. From the trusting domain, start the User Manager for Domains.
6. Select the Policies menu and select Trust Relationships.
7. In the trusted domain box, click Add and press Enter. Type in the same password that you entered in step 3, and then click OK. If you left the password blank, do not enter a password here.
8. A message should appear stating that the trust relationship was successfully established.
9. To test the trust relationship, log off from the trusting domain. When logging back on, select the drop-down list from the Domain section of the logon screen. You should see the name of the trusted domain and your current domain.

7.1.4 Exercise: Designing a Network Domain Model

Exercise 7.1.4 steps you through the planning phases of your Windows NT domain model. Look at the situation below, then work through the planning of a domain model.

Situation: The ABC Corporation has a building in Los Angeles, a production department in San Francisco, and a satellite location in San Diego. The Los Angeles location has 1,500 users and holds the central IT department that is responsible for all network administration. The other two locations, San Francisco and San Diego, each have a local administrator who is responsible for network servers and resources but does not need administrator access in Los Angeles.

Answer the following questions to help step you through the planning phases of your network.

1. How many domains would you require for this situation?
2. Which domain would hold all the user accounts?
3. Sketch the domain diagram for the scenario; make sure you include all trust relationships in the diagram.
4. What groups would the local administrator for the resource domains need to be placed in?

7.1 Practice Problems

1. ABC Company has 500 users located in a single location. The MIS Director wants to administer the accounts and resources for the network in one central place. Which domain model is best for this situation?

    A. Single domain model

    B. Single master domain model

    C. Multiple master domain model

    D. Complete trust model

2. The Acme Corporation has 20 locations. Administrators at each location want to manage the user accounts for their location. Resource access will be controlled by departments at each location. Which domain model is best for this situation?

    A. Single domain model

    B. Single master domain model

    C. Multiple master domain model

    D. Complete trust model

3. Riverton City wants to install an NT network. They have 600 employees located in five divisions. The network administrator wants to manage all the user accounts, but will allow administrators in each division to control access to their resources. Which domain model is best for this situation?

    A. Single domain model

    B. Single master domain model

    C. Multiple master domain model

    D. Complete trust model

4. Mid-Size Inc. has 30,000 users who each have an NT Workstation for their desktop computers. The network needs to have centralized control of user accounts while allowing branch offices to control their resources. Which domain model is best for this situation?

    A. Single domain model

    B. Single master domain model

    C. Multiple master domain model

    D. Complete trust model

5. Big Company has 20,000 users who each have a Windows NT workstation. For their domain, the MIS Director wants the MIS department to maintain user accounts and to manage the resources on the network. Which domain model is best for this situation?

    A. Single domain model

    B. Single master domain model

    C. Multiple master domain model

    D. Complete trust model

6. XYZ, Inc. has 100 users scattered in three locations. The administrators at each location want to control their own resources. However, the administrators at headquarters insist on creating all the user accounts. Which domain model is best for this situation?

    A. Single domain model

    B. Single master domain model

    C. Multiple master domain model

    D. Complete trust model

7. Disagree Corp. has seven locations. Administrators at each location refuse to allow others to manage their users or control access to their resources. The administrators will, however, allow other users to access their resources if the local administrators allow it. Which domain model is best for this situation?

    A. Single domain model

    B. Single master domain model

C. Multiple master domain model

D. Complete trust model

8. The Getting Bigger By The Minute Company has 50,000 users. Each user has a Windows 95 workstation. Company management wants the corporate network administrators to administer all user accounts. Management also wants resources to be controlled by local administrators who understand who needs access to each resource. Which domain model is best for this situation?

   A. Single domain model

   B. Single master domain model

   C. Multiple master domain model

   D. Complete trust model

The following scenario applies to questions 9–12. A different solution to the scenario is proposed for each question.

Scenario: MCSEs-R-Us has three locations—Headquarters, R&D, and Manufacturing. Users in Manufacturing use files at Headquarters and R&D in addition to files on their own servers. Users at the other locations access files only on local servers.

9. *Required results*: Centrally manage all user accounts; centrally manage access to all resources; users at Manufacturing must access resources at Headquarters and R&D. *Optional results*: Users at Headquarters can access resources at Manufacturing; users at R&D can access resources at Manufacturing.

   Solution: Implement a single master domain model with the master domain at Headquarters. Add the Domain Users group from Headquarters to the local Users group on each server to which users need access.

   A. The proposed solution produces the required results and produces both optional results.

   B. The proposed solution produces the required results and produces only one optional result.

   C. The proposed solution produces the required results but does not produce any optional results.

   D. The proposed solution does not produce the required results.

10. *Required Results:* Headquarters manages all user accounts; manufacturing must access resources at Headquarters and R&D. *Optional Results*: R&D can access resources at Manufacturing; headquarters can access resources at R&D.

   Solution: Implement a single domain model. Add the Domain Users group to the local Users group on any server that needs to be accessed by users.

   A. The proposed solution produces the required results and produces both optional results.

   B. The proposed solution produces the required results and produces only one optional result.

   C. The proposed solution produces the required results but does not produce any optional results.

   D. The proposed solution does not produce the required results.

11. The question is based on the scenario presented for question 9. *Required Result*: Users at Manufacturing need to access resources at Headquarters and R&D. *Optional Results*: Administrators at each location manage their own accounts; access to resources is managed from a central location.

Solution: Implement a complete trust domain model. Create accounts for each user in the domain for their location. Add the Domain Users groups from each domain to the local Users group on each server to which users need access.

A. The proposed solution produces the required result and produces both optional results.

B. The proposed solution produces the required result and produces only one optional result.

C. The proposed solution produces the required result but does not produce any optional results.

D. The proposed solution does not produce the required result.

12. *Required Result*: Users at Manufacturing must access resources at Headquarters and R&D. *Optional Results*: Users at Headquarters can access resources at Manufacturing; users at R&D can access resources at Manufacturing.

Solution: Create a domain for each location. Create trust relationships in which Manufacturing trusts R&D, and Manufacturing and Headquarters trust each other with a two-way trust. Assign domain users from each domain to the local Users group where users need to access resources.

A. The proposed solution produces the required result and produces both optional results.

B. The proposed solution produces the required result and produces only one optional result.

C. The proposed solution produces the required result but does not produce any optional results.

D. The proposed solution does not produce the required result.

13. How are the trusts configured in a single master domain model?

A. The master domain trusts all the resource domains in a one-way trust.

B. The resource domains trust the master domain with a one-way trust and trusts the other resource domains with two-way trusts.

C. The master domain is trusted by all the resource domains.

D. All the domains trust each other with two-way trusts.

14. What can be added to a local group in a resource domain in a multiple master domain model?

A. Members of the resource domain

B. Members of the resource domain and any master domain

C. Members of resource domain and global groups from the resource domain

D. Members of the resource domain and any master domain and global groups from any of these domains

15. An administrator in a resource domain is administering a local group on a server in his domain. The administrator adds members to the group by selecting a trusted domain. What can the administrator add to the local group from the trusted domain?

A. Local groups from the trusted domain

B. Global groups from the trusted domain

C. Global and local groups from the trusted domain

D. Users and global groups from the trusted domain

16. Which utility is used to create trust relationships?

    A. Server Manager

    B. User Manager for Domains

    C. Trust Manager

    D. DNS Manager

17. The Sales domain trusts the HR domain. The HR domain trusts the Accounting domain. How can users in the Accounting domain access resources in the Sales domain?

    A. Add a global group from the Accounting domain to a local group in the Sales domain.

    B. Add a global group from the Accounting domain to a global group in the HR domain, and then add the global group from the HR domain to a local group in the Sales domain.

    C. Add a global group from the Sales domain to a local group in the Accounting domain.

    D. Users in the Accounting domain cannot access resources in the Sales domain.

18. What best describes the trust relationships in a complete trust domain model?

    A. Each domain trusts every other domain.

    B. Each domain trusts the complete domain.

    C. All the resource domains and the master domain share a one-way trust.

    D. All the resource domains and the master domain share a two-way trust.

19. How should trust relationships be established?

    A. The trusting domain should specify the name of the trusted domain, and then the trusted domain should specify the name of the trusting domain.

    B. The trusting domain should specify the name of the trusted domain and the trusting domain along with a password; the trusted domain then enters the password.

    C. The trusted domain should specify the name of the trusting domain and the trusted domain along with a password; the trusting domain then enters the password.

    D. The trusted domain should specify the name of the trusting domain, and then the trusting domain should specify the name of the trusted domain.

20. What happens if the trust relationship is initiated by the trusting domain?

    A. A dialog box appears indicating that the trust relationship is established.

    B. The trust relationship is established without a dialog box confirming the trust.

    C. The trust relationship cannot be established.

    D. A two-way trust is established.

The following scenario applies to questions 21–24. A different solution to the scenario is proposed for each question.

Scenario: Contra Costa County has domains at each of their county offices in Concord, Martinez, and Richmond. The domains have member servers in addition to domain controllers. Each of the users has a Windows NT workstation.

21. *Required Result*: Server administrators in Concord need to configure domain controllers in all three domains. *Optional Results*: Server administrators in Concord need to configure member servers in all three domains; server administrators in Concord need to configure Windows NT workstations in all three domains.

    Solution: The Martinez and Richmond domains are configured to trust the Concord domain. The Server Operators group from the Concord domain is added to the Server Operators group in the Martinez and Richmond domains.

    A. The proposed solution produces the required result and produces both optional results.

    B. The proposed solution produces the required result and produces only one optional result.

    C. The proposed solution produces the required result but does not produce any optional results.

    D. The proposed solution does not produce the required result.

22. *Required Result*: Administrators for the Concord domain need to administer the Richmond and Martinez domains. *Optional Results*: Administrators for the Concord domain need to administer the member servers of the Richmond and Martinez domains; administrators for the Concord domain need to administer the Windows NT workstations of the Richmond and Martinez domains.

    Solution: The three domains are configured in a single master domain model with the Concord domain as the master domain. The Domain Admins group from the Concord domain is added to the Administrators group of the Martinez and Richmond domains.

    A. The proposed solution produces the required result and produces both optional results.

    B. The proposed solution produces the required result and produces only one optional result.

    C. The proposed solution produces the required result but does not produce any optional results.

    D. The proposed solution does not produce the required result.

23. *Required Result*: Administrators need to configure user accounts in any domain. *Optional Results*: Administrators need to back up any Windows NT machine in any domain; Administrators need to modify network settings on the member servers in any domain.

    Solution: The three domains are configured in a complete trust model. The Domain Admins group from each domain is added to the administrators group in the other domains and the administrators group on each Windows NT member server in each domain.

    A. The proposed solution produces the required results and produces both optional results.

    B. The proposed solution produces the required results and produces only one optional result.

    C. The proposed solution produces the required results but does not produce any optional results.

    D. The proposed solution does not produce the required results.

7

24. *Required Result*: Administrators from the Concord domain need to administer member servers in the Richmond and Martinez domains. *Optional Results*: Administrators from the Concord domain need to manage domain accounts in the Richmond domain; administrators from the Concord domain need to back up domain controllers in the Martinez domain.

    Solution: The three domains are configured in a complete trust domain model. Domain Admins from the Concord domain is added to the Account Operators group in the Richmond domain. The default group assignments are used for the Concord to Martinez domain.

    A. The proposed solution produces the required result and produces both optional results.

    B. The proposed solution produces the required result and produces only one optional result.

    C. The proposed solution produces the required result but does not produce any optional results.

    D. The proposed solution does not produce the required result.

25. You are planning a complete trust domain model with four domains. How many trust relationships are required for this model?

    A. 4

    B. 6

    C. 10

    D. 12

7.1.1 Answers and Explanations: Exercise

For more information regarding directory services, see the section in this chapter titled "Selecting the Appropriate Directory Services Architecture." The following are the solutions to the exercise questions.

1. **B** Single master domain model; the key phrase that led to the answer was the centralized account administration, with distributed resource management.
2. **A** Single domain model; small network environment requiring centralized user and resource administration.
3. **C** Multiple master domain model; large organizations that require multiple account or master domains for user administration with distributed resource management.
4. **D** Complete trust domain model; each domain is completely independent of the other, allowing access into resources across the domains.

If you get into the habit of drawing out the domain models, or more importantly, the trust relationships in the scenario-based questions, you will find them easier to understand. Watch for key phrases in the questions; they generally lead you to the selection of the appropriate domain model. Some key phrases to watch for are the following:

- **Centralized user accounts:** When centralized user accounts are required, it narrows your selection to single domain, single master, or multiple master.
- **Distributed resource management:** This distribution of resources is available in single master domain model, multiple master domain model, and complete trust domain model.

- **Distributed users and resources:** The only model that offers both of these is the complete trust model.
- **Select domains to maintain user accounts with distributed resources:** The multiple master allows for numerous account (master) domains and distributed resource domains.
- **Large organization with 20,000 or more users:** This is restricted to multiple master or complete trust domain models.
- **Small organizations with less than 20,000 users:** Best models are single domain or single master domain.

By combining all these items, you should be able to select the appropriate domain model in any situation with which you are presented on the Enterprise exam.

7.1.2 Answers and Explanations: Exercise

This exercise taught you how to manually synchronize a Backup Domain Controller within your domain.

7.1.3 Answers and Explanations: Exercise

This exercise taught you how to establish a trust relationship between multiple domains.

7.1.4 Answers and Explanations: Exercise

1. Three domains would be required for this situation. One domain is needed for all user accounts in Los Angeles. Another domain is needed for the resource admin in San Franscisco. A third domain is necessary for the resource admin in San Diego. Only one account domain is needed to hold all the user accounts because the 1,500 accounts will easily fit in the 40 MB limit for the SAM database.
2. The Los Angeles domain would contain all the user accounts because the department is centrally located there.
3. See the following figure.

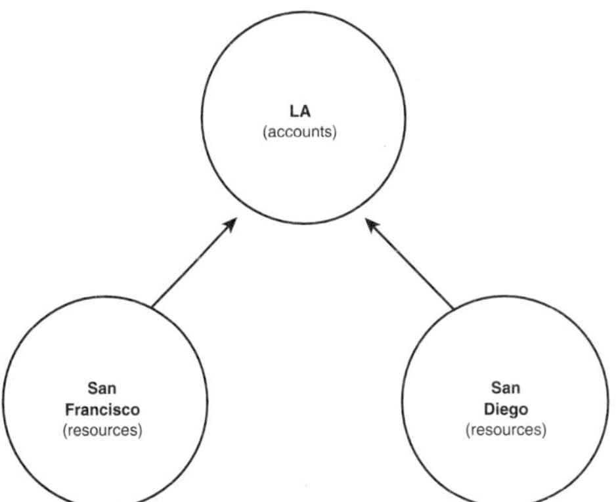

4. The resource administrator would be placed into a global group on the Los Angeles domain. That global group would then be placed into the Administrators group on each of the resource domains.

7.1 Answers and Explanations: Practice Problems

1. **A** With a small number of users in one location and centralized administration of both accounts and resources, the single domain is the only possible answer.
2. **D** Each domain controls both accounts and resource administration. The only way to give all these users access to resources in all the other domains is by using the complete trust model.
3. **B** A small number of users with centralized account administration means a single accounts domain. With the demand for decentralized resource administration, separate resource domains must be created, thus necessitating the single master domain model.
4. **C** Centralized control of users with decentralized administration suggests the single master domain model. However, with 30,000 users and 30,000 computer accounts, the SAM database would be 45 MB (30 MB for users and 15 MB for

7

computer accounts), which exceeds the recommended size for a single master. Therefore, multiple master is needed.

5. **B** Centralized administration of accounts and decentralized control of resources implies the single master model. Checking the size of the SAM for 20,000 users and computers yields a total SAM of 30 MB (20 MB for users and 10 MB for computers). This is small enough for a single master.

6. **B** Although the number of users is small, with the requirement for decentralized resource administration, the single master is the best choice.

7. **D** Each site wants to maintain control of both users and resources. The only way to enable all users to access all resources in all domains is to implement the complete trust model.

8. **C** Centralized account administration with distributed resource administration suggests the single master model. However, the size of the SAM is 50 MB with 50,000 users and no computer accounts, so the multiple master model must be used.

9. **D** Although the single master model enables centralized administration of accounts, it does not enable centralized administration of resources, which was one of the required results.

10. **A** With the single domain model, administration is centralized. In a single domain, the location of users is not important, so if the Domain Users group is added to all the servers where access is needed, all users can access all required resources regardless of location.

11. **B** The complete trust model lets all users access everything. It also allows decentralized account administration, but does not allow centralized resource administration.

12. **D** The trust between R&D and Manufacturing is in the wrong direction for the required result to be met.

13. **C** All the domains with resources trust the single domain with user accounts.

14. **D** Individual users and global groups from the local domain as well as any trusted domain can be added to local groups.

15. **D** Both users and global groups can be added.

16. **B** The Policies menu within User Manager for Domains is used to create trusts.

17. **D** No trust relationship exists between the Sales and Accounting domains. Users from one domain cannot access resources in another domain unless a trust relationship is explicitly created between them.

18. **A** Each domain has accounts and resources; therefore, every domain must trust every other domain.

19. **D** The trusted domain starts the process by naming its partner. The trusting domain then finishes the process by naming its partner.

20. **B** Although this is not the preferred method for creating a trust, the trust is still established. However, the user will not receive a dialog box with a positive confirmation that the trust has been created.

21. **D** The trust is correct, but Server Operators is the local group that cannot be copied across a trust and also cannot be assigned to another local group.

22. **C** The trust is correct, but Domain Admins is added only to the administrators group in the domain, which allows domain administration but not administration of member servers or Windows NT workstations.

23. **B** The complete trust model creates the proper trust relationships. Adding Domain Admins to the domain administrators group allows account administration. Adding Domain Admins to the member server administrators groups

allows server configuration. However, nothing is added to groups on the Windows NT workstations.

24. **D** The trusts will work but no group assignments are automatically made across a trust, so the required result is not produced.

25. **D** All four domains must trust the other three domains, 4×3=12.

7.1 Key Words

Complete trust domain model

Directory services

Directory synchronization

Domain

Multiple master domain model

Non-transitive trusts

One-way trust

Security Account Manager (SAM)

Single domain model

Single master domain model

Trust relationships

Two-way trust

Universal resource access

7.2 Planning the Fault-Tolerance Configurations for Windows NT Server 4.0

To prepare for this section of the exam, you must understand each of the fault-tolerant disk arrays supported by Windows NT Server and know which method should be used for a given scenario.

A. RAID Systems in Windows NT Server 4.0

Windows NT Server supports fault-tolerant disk arrays that provide data recovery if a single physical disk fails. These fault-tolerant arrays are not supported on Windows NT Workstation. However, the disk arrays supported by Windows NT Workstation (striping and volume sets) are also supported by Windows NT Server.

Windows NT Server 4.0 supports RAID (Redundant Array of Inexpensive Disks)—Level 0 (Disk Striping), Level 1 (Disk Mirroring), and Level 5 (Disk Striping with parity). Disk duplexing is also supported, which is an extension to disk mirroring. RAID 0 is not a fault-tolerant disk array, but RAID 1 and RAID 5 are fault tolerant (the data is protected from the failure of a single disk).

1. RAID Level 0: Stripe Sets

Stripe sets are not a fault-tolerant disk array. You can combine several disks into a single partition with a stripe set. The stripe set is similar to a RAID 5 array (striping with parity). RAID 0 is supported on both Windows NT Workstation and Server.

Disk striping divides the data into 64 KB blocks and writes the data across multiple physical disk drives. This process writes data to all the disks in the array at the same time, increasing write performance. Read performance is also improved because data can be read simultaneously from several disks at once. If one disk in the array fails, all the data on the stripe set is lost because the disks work together as a unit. A disk stripe set consists of multiple physical disks. A minimum of two disks is required to create a stripe set; a stripe set can include as many as 32 disks.

After a stripe set is created, no disks can be added to or removed from the array. When a stripe set is created, equal portions of disk space from each physical drive are used. The benefits of a disk stripe set are the following:

- Increased disk read performance
- Increased disk write performance

The limitations of a disk stripe set are the following:

- No data redundancy, or fault tolerance
- Cannot contain the system or boot partition in a stripe set

2. RAID Level 1: Disk Mirroring

Disk mirroring duplicates writes to the hard drive onto two physical disks. If each disk has a separate hard drive controller, a mirror is called disk duplexing, which provides redundancy for both hard drive failure and controller failure.

This method of fault tolerance is considered to be more expensive per megabyte of data due to the complete duplication of data. Every disk mirror requires two physical disks. Disk mirroring (and disk duplexing) are supported only on Windows NT Server. The benefits of disk mirroring are the following:

- All drives and partitions can be mirrored, including boot and system partitions.
- Complete data duplication is done, allowing a complete recovery of data.

The drawbacks to using disk mirroring are the following:

- Per megabyte cost is higher; 50 percent of total available disk space is utilized.
- Read and write performance is moderate.

3. RAID Level 5: Stripe Sets with Parity

Disk striping with parity is the more common of the fault-tolerant methods available through Windows NT Server 4.0. Disk striping with parity uses the same basic process of disk striping; it writes the data in 64 KB blocks across multiple physical disks.

A stripe set uses the stripes on disk to store redundant information, known as *parity*. The parity is basically a checksum that can be used to restore the rest of the data if a disk is lost. For example, consider a stripe set with parity with three disks. 7

If the data values 1 and 2 were written to the stripe set, the parity 3 (which is the sum of 1 and 2) would be written to the third disk. If one of the disks were lost, the data could still be recovered because an algebraic statement would exist. If disk 2 were lost, the equation 1+?=3 would exist. The value 2 could be computed as the missing data and Windows NT could recover from the missing drive.

To implement the disk striping with parity, a minimum of three physical disks is required and a maximum of 32 disks can be used. Note that an extra disk is required over striping without parity. This extra disk is devoted to parity information. If any one of the disks in the stripe set with parity fail, the data can be regenerated from the remaining disks. Striping with parity is supported only on Windows NT Server.

The cost for the fault tolerance is one disk in the array. For the smallest array (3 disks), the cost is the largest (1/3 or one disk of the three). For the largest array (32 disks), the cost is relatively small (1/32 or one disk of the 32). The benefits of a stripe set with parity include the following:

- Data can be regenerated from parity information.
- Read performance from stripe sets with parity is excellent.
- Cost per megabyte is lower with stripe sets than with disk mirroring.

The limitations and drawbacks of the stripe set with parity include the following:

- A minimum of three disks and a maximum of 32 disks is required.
- Write performance is moderate.
- More system memory is required to implement stripe set due to calculation of parity.
- System or boot partition cannot be included.

4. Hardware RAID

Hardware solutions for fault tolerance are by far the best solutions available. RAID 5 is commonly implemented in a hardware array of disks. For a hardware implementation, the disk controllers calculate the parity and control the striping of information on the disks. The operating system sees a hardware RAID 5 array as a single disk. Windows NT uses software emulation for its RAID 5 implementation. This is slower than the hardware method, but it allows you to use disks of different sizes and types. Hardware RAID is typically more expensive than buying individual drives and implementing software RAID.

Hardware RAID 5 does offer several advantages over the software implementation. First, you can install a system or boot partition on a hardware array. In fact, Windows NT recognizes an entire hardware array as a single disk; the operating system doesn't see the multiple drives because the disk controllers control the management of these drives as one physical unit. Also, many hardware arrays support *hot swapping*, which allows you to replace a bad drive while the computer is still running. When the new drive is added to the array, the information on the new disk is automatically written there.

B. Summary of Supported RAID Levels

Table 7.2.1 includes a summary of the RAID levels supported by Windows NT.

Table 7.2.1 Summary of Fault-Tolerance Options in Windows NT Server 4.0

Disk Striping	Disk Mirroring/ Disk Duplexing	Disk Striping w/Parity
No fault-tolerance	Complete disk duplication	Data regeneration from stored parity information
Minimum of two physical disks; maximum of 32 disks	Two physical disks	Minimum of three physical disks; maximum of 32 disks
100 percent available disk utilization	50 percent available disk utilization	Dedicates the equivalent of one disk's space in the set for parity information; the more disks, the higher the utilization
Cannot include system/boot partition	Includes all partition types	Cannot include system/boot partition
Excellent read/write performance	Moderate read/write performance	Excellent read; moderate write performance

C. Implementing RAID in Windows NT Server 4.0

The steps required to implement fault tolerance in Windows NT Server 4.0 are covered in detail in Chapter 8, "Installation and Configuration."

D. Sector Sparing

Sector sparing automatically fixes data on bad sectors of a hard drive. This is also known as *hot fixing*. Sector sparing is supported only on SCSI drives in RAID 1 or RAID 5 arrays that are formatted as NTFS partitions. Sector sparing is supported only on Windows NT Server. Sector sparing verifies each write of data onto the disk and, if it does not reread the data successfully, it will move the data to another sector of the drive. The operating system never receives a message about the bad write because the sector sparing automatically corrects the error. After a sector of the disk has been marked bad, the system will not use the bad sector until a disk defragmentation utility, or a disk tool utility, has been executed.

7.2.1 Exercise: Selecting the Proper Fault-Tolerance Method for Given Scenarios

1. Select all the disk fault-tolerance functions that are supported by Windows NT Server 4.0. Select all that apply.

   A. Disk mirroring

   B. Disk striping

   C. Disk striping with parity

   D. Sector sparing

2. List two differences between disk striping with parity and disk mirroring.
3. Your company wants to implement a fault-tolerance scheme. You have a Windows NT Server system with two hard disks. Which disk fault-tolerance method can be used?
4. Your organization has implemented a stripe set with parity; you have four physical disks: Disk 1 is a 1 GB disk that contains the system files and all Windows NT files. Disk 2 is a 2 GB disk to be used for data. Disk 3 is a 1.5 GB disk to be used for data. Disk 4 is a 2 GB drive also for data. What is the largest working disk space that can be used in a disk stripe set with parity?

7.2 Practice Problems

1. On which disk partitioning scheme can you place a system partition?

    A. Volume set

    B. Stripe set without parity

    C. Stripe set with parity

    D. Disk mirror

2. Which fault-tolerant disk scheme requires the least overhead in disk storage?

    A. Striping with parity

    B. Disk mirroring

    C. Disk duplexing

    D. Striping without parity

3. How many physical disks are required for a RAID 5 array?

    A. 2

    B. 3

    C. 4

    D. 32

4. How many physical disks can be included in a RAID 5 array?

    A. 2

    B. 3

    C. 4

    D. 32

5. Which file system can be used for a stripe set with parity? Select all that apply.

    A. HPFS

    B. FAT

    C. CDFS

    D. NTFS

6. Which file system supports sector sparing?

    A. HPFS

    B. FAT

    C. CDFS

    D. NTFS

7. What happens to data on a bad sector when sector sparing occurs?

    A. The data is copied to a good sector.

    B. The data is copied to a file called FILExxxx.chk.

    C. The data is copied to the sparing partition.

    D. The data can be recovered with the **SECTCHK** command.

The following scenario applies to questions 8–11. A different solution to the scenario is proposed for each question.

Scenario: Your SQL Server has four physical disks. The first disk is where the Windows NT files are located. SQL data is stored on the other three disks. You are asked to implement a fault-tolerant disk scheme for this SQL server.

8. *Required Result*: The boot partition must be protected from a single disk failure. *Optional Results*: The SQL data must have the fastest read and write access possible; the SQL data must be protected from a single disk failure.

    Solution: Mirror the first physical drive to the second physical drive. Make a stripe set without parity with the remaining two disks. Store the SQL data on the stripe set without parity.

    A. The proposed solution produces the required results and produces both optional results.

    B. The proposed solution produces the required results and produces only one optional result.

C. The proposed solution produces the required results but does not produce any optional results.

D. The proposed solution does not produce the required results.

9. *Required Result*: The SQL data is protected from a single disk failure. *Optional Results*: The system partition is protected from a disk crash; the disk space overhead used for fault tolerance is the least amount possible.

   Solution: Mirror the first physical disk to the second physical disk. Mirror the third physical disk to the fourth physical disk. Place the SQL data on the third physical disk.

   A. The proposed solution produces the required results and produces both optional results.

   B. The proposed solution produces the required results and produces only one optional result.

   C. The proposed solution produces the required results but does not produce any optional results.

   D. The proposed solution does not produce the required results.

10. *Required Result*: Access to the SQL data is maximized for read and write performance. *Optional Results*: Extra space from the first physical disk is used for SQL data; the SQL data can be accessed with one drive letter.

    Solution: Create a volume set with the second, third, and fourth physical disks. Add extra space from the first physical disk to the volume set. Place the SQL data on the volume set.

    A. The proposed solution produces the required results and produces both optional results.

    B. The proposed solution produces the required results and produces only one optional result.

    C. The proposed solution produces the required results but does not produce any optional results.

    D. The proposed solution does not produce the required results.

11. *Required Result*: Provide the system partition with the maximum amount of failure for a hardware failure. *Optional Results*: Improve the read access for the SQL data; protect the SQL data from a single disk failure.

    Solution: Install an additional physical disk with a separate controller. Mirror the system partition to the new disk. Create a RAID 5 array with disks 2–4 and place the SQL data on this array.

    A. The proposed solution produces the required results and produces both optional results.

    B. The proposed solution produces the required results and produces only one optional result.

    C. The proposed solution produces the required results but does not produce any optional results.

    D. The proposed solution does not produce the required results.

12. What best describes a volume set?

    A. It allows a system partition to be duplicated.

    B. It combines disk space from several disks into one logical drive.

    C. It requires equal disk space from each drive included in the volume set.

    D. It provides faster read access to data.

13. What type of information can be put on a stripe set? Select all that apply.

    A. The boot sector

    B. Spool directory

    C. Data files

    D. Registry hives

14. What type of drives can be used to create a RAID 5 array? Select all that apply.

    A. Removable drives

    B. SCSI drives

    C. IDE drives

    D. EIDE drives

15. A server is currently used to store data on its single disk drive. How many disks must be added to protect the operating system from disk failure and also to protect the data?

    A. 0

    B. 1

    C. 2

    D. 3

16. A server currently has two EIDE controllers with a physical drive attached to each controller. What must be added to the server to enable sector sparing?

    A. Two SCSI hard drives with controller

    B. A tape device

    C. A PCI controller for the EIDE drives

    D. A Y-cable connecting the two EIDE drives

17. Which of the following best describes striping with parity?

    A. Provides fastest write access to the disk for any disk array

    B. Enables addition of new disks to an existing partition

    C. Can be used only with NTFS

    D. Requires at least three disks to implement

18. A Windows NT Server has four physical disks. The first disk, which contains the WINNT directory on a 400 MB FAT partition, has 200 MB of free space. The second disk has a 400 MB NTFS partition and 100 MB of free space. The third and fourth disks are unformatted with 500 MB of free space on each disk. Which fault-tolerant scheme would allow a 300 MB application to be installed on the disks? Select all that apply.

    A. Make a stripe set with parity using all the free space on disks 1, 3, and 4.

    B. Make a volume set using the remaining disk space on disk 2.

    C. Make a mirror using all the free space on disks 3 and 4.

    D. Make a mirror with the boot partition using free space on disk 4. Make a stripe set with parity using the remaining disk space on all four disks.

19. Which tool is used to create a RAID 5 array in Windows NT?

    A. RAID Configuration Wizard

    B. DNS Manager

    C. Disk Administrator

    D. Server Manager

20. Which platforms support disk mirroring? Select all that apply.

    A. Windows NT Workstation

    B. Windows NT Server

    C. Windows 95

    D. Windows for Workgroups

The following scenario applies to questions 21–24. A different solution to the scenario is proposed for each question.

Scenario: Your department manager wants you to create a web site to publish data to other departments within the company. Your manager wants to protect data, but also wants to do it at the lowest possible cost.

21. *Required Result*: Protect web server data from disk failure using the cheapest fault-tolerant disk scheme. *Optional Results*: Provide faster read access to web data; provide capability to expand storage for web data without moving existing data.

    Solution: Install Peer Web Services on a Windows NT machine. Create a stripe set with parity. Put the web data on this stripe set.

    A. The proposed solution produces the required results and produces both optional results.

    B. The proposed solution produces the required results and produces only one optional result.

    C. The proposed solution produces the required results but does not produce any optional results.

    D. The proposed solution does not produce the required results.

22. *Required Result*: Protect web server data from disk failure using the cheapest fault-tolerant disk scheme. *Optional Results*: Provide faster read access to the Web data; provide capability to expand storage for web data without moving existing data.

    Solution: Install IIS on a Windows NT machine. Create a volume set and place the web data on the volume set.

    A. The proposed solution produces the required results and produces both optional results.

    B. The proposed solution produces the required results and produces only one optional result.

    C. The proposed solution produces the required results but does not produce any optional results.

    D. The proposed solution does not produce the required results.

23. *Required Result*: Protect the operating system and web data from a single disk failure. *Optional Result*: Provide faster read access for web data; enable file level permissions for the web data.

    Solution: Install Windows NT Server on a machine with three physical disks. Mirror the boot partition to another disk. Use the remaining disk space on the system disk and the other disks to create a stripe set with parity. Format the partition as NTFS. Place the web data on the stripe set.

    A. The proposed solution produces the required results and produces both optional results.

    B. The proposed solution produces the required results and produces only one optional result.

    C. The proposed solution produces the required results but does not produce any optional results.

    D. The proposed solution does not produce the required results.

24. *Required Result*: Protect the operating system and web data from a single disk failure. *Optional Results*: Provide faster read access for web data; enable file-level permissions for the web data.

    Solution: Install Windows NT Server on a machine with three physical disks. Create a stripe set with parity on the three

7

physical disks. Format the stripe set with parity as NTFS. Install Windows NT and the web data on the stripe set with parity.

A. The proposed solution produces the required results and produces both optional results.

B. The proposed solution produces the required results and produces only one optional result.

C. The proposed solution produces the required results but does not produce any optional results.

D. The proposed solution does not produce the required results.

25. Which of the following is required for sector sparing?

A. A disk controller for each disk

B. An NTFS partition

C. A PCI disk controller

D. BIOS that supports hot swapping

7.2.1 Answers and Explanations: Exercise

1. The correct answer for this question is A and C. Disk mirroring and disk striping with parity are the supported disk fault-tolerance methods.

2. The differences between disk striping with parity and disk mirroring are the following:

   - System and Boot Partitions can be mirrored.
   - Mirroring uses two disks and striping with parity requires a minimum of three and a maximum of 32 disks.

3. The only fault-tolerance method that can be used is disk mirroring due to the two-disk limit.

4. Disk 1 cannot be used for the stripe set because it contains the boot and system partition. Disks 2, 3, and 4 can be used to create the stripe set with parity. The stripe set would use equal amounts of disk space on each disk. With this restriction, the largest available disk space that could be used for the stripe set with parity is 4.5 GB with 3 GB of working disk space. To obtain this disk space, the system would use 1.5 GB from each of the three disks.

7.2 Answers and Explanations: Practice Problems

1. **D** Only a disk mirror allows a system partition.

2. **A** Although striping without parity requires no overhead, it's not a fault-tolerant scheme.

3. **B** At least three disks are required for a RAID 5 array; two disks are for data and one disk is for parity.

4. **D** Up to 32 disks can be part of a RAID 5 array.

5. **B, D** Any supported file system can be used for any of the disk arrays. HPFS is not supported for Windows NT 4.0. CDFS is the file system used to read data from CD-ROMs.

6. **D** Only NTFS supports sector sparing.

7. **A** The data is automatically copied to a new sector and the process is transparent to the user.

8. **B** Mirroring the first disk protects the boot partition. The stripe set without parity provides the fastest read and write access, but it isn't a fault-tolerant disk array.

9. **B** This method protects both the system partition and the SQL data. However, mirroring uses more disk overhead than striping with parity.

10. **D** A volume set can use all available space on different drives, but does not improve read or write performance.

11. **A** Disk duplexing was used for the system partition and RAID 5 for SQL, which gives SQL faster read access and fault tolerance.

12. **B** A volume set joins dissimilar disk space together in a single drive letter, but it does not improve access times, nor is it fault tolerant.

13. **B, C** Data can be placed on any partition. Although the spool directory is part of the boot partition by default, it can be moved to any partition.

14. **B, C, D** Any fixed type of hard drive can be used in a RAID 5 array.

15. **B** An additional drive would allow mirroring of both the operating system and data.

16. **A** Sector sparing is supported only on SCSI drives.

17. **D** Striping without parity is faster, and a stripe set cannot be modified after it's created. A stripe set can be formatted as FAT or NTFS.

18. **A, C, D** The mirror would be 1 GB, with 500 MB of usable space. A stripe set on three disks would yield 600 MB total, with 400 MB of usable space. A stripe set on four disks would yield 400 MB total, with 300 MB of usable space.

19. **C** Disk Administrator is the tool used to create any disk scheme.

20. **B** Only Windows NT Server supports fault-tolerant disk arrays.

21. **D** Peer Web Services is installed on a Windows NT Workstation. Windows NT Workstations do not support fault-tolerant disk arrays.

22. **D** IIS indicates this is a Windows NT Server, but a volume set is not a fault-tolerant disk array.

23. **A** Mirroring the boot partition protects the operating system. The stripe set with parity protects the web data and provides faster read access. The NTFS file system allows file-level permissions.

24. **D** Windows NT cannot be installed on a stripe set.

25. **B** NTFS on SCSI drives in a fault-tolerant array is required for sector sparing.

7.2 Key Words

Disk duplexing

Disk mirroring

Disk striping

Disk striping with parity

Fault tolerance

Parity

RAID (Redundant Array of Inexpensive Disks)

Sector sparing

Striping

Volume sets

7.3 Selecting the Proper Protocol

The interconnectivity of Windows NT with other operating systems and other Windows NT systems is critical to the proper functioning of your enterprise system. The protocols installed on a server determine the type of systems with which Windows NT can communicate. They include:

- NetBEUI
- TCP/IP
- NWLINK IPX/SPX Compatible
- DataLink Control (DLC)
- AppleTalk Protocol

A. NetBEUI

The NetBEUI protocol is the easiest to implement. The *NetBEUI* protocol uses NetBIOS broadcasts to locate other computers on the network. This broadcasting generates extra traffic on the network, which increases to excessive amounts on larger networks. Also, the broadcasts that NetBEUI uses are not routable; in other words, you cannot access computers that are not on your physical network segment. For these reasons, NetBEUI is recommended only for small- to medium-sized networks that are on a single segment. NetBEUI does not provide connectivity to many other network types. This protocol is supported by most Microsoft clients as well as IBM OS/2 clients.

B. TCP/IP

Transmission Control Protocol/Internet Protocol, or TCP/IP, is the most common protocol. *TCP/IP* is an industry standard protocol that is supported under most network operating systems. Because of this acceptance throughout the industry, TCP/IP allows a Windows NT system to connect to other systems running TCP/IP.

TCP/IP is a routable protocol that lends itself directly to enterprise or WAN communication. You can communicate with any number of physical network segments with TCP/IP. The advantages of using TCP/IP in a Windows NT environment include the following:

- Capability to connect dissimilar systems using numerous standard connectivity utilities; utilities include File Transfer Protocol, Telnet, and Ping.
- Internet access

Configuring TCP/IP is more difficult than configuring the other supported protocols.

1. Heterogeneous Connectivity with TCP/IP

TCP/IP allows Windows NT to connect with many non-Microsoft systems. Some of the systems with which it can communicate include the following:

- Any Internet-connected system
- UNIX systems
- IBM Mainframe systems

- DEC Pathworks
- TCP/IP printers directly connected to the network

TCP/IP has increased in popularity and is now supported by virtually all the new operating systems being released today. Using TCP/IP gives you the widest possible choice of connectivity options.

2. WINS, DHCP, DNS, and IIS

TCP/IP is required for several Windows NT services. Because these services depend on TCP/IP, they cannot be installed if TCP/IP is not installed on the server. WINS, DHCP, DNS, and IIS all require TCP/IP.

DHCP (Dynamic Host Configuration Protocol) is a service that allocates TCP/IP addresses automatically to all the clients configured for DHCP. When clients use DHCP to obtain IP addresses and configuration information, the administrator does not have to manually configure these clients.

WINS (Windows Internet Name Service) Server is a dynamic database to resolve NetBIOS names to IP addresses. It is often used in conjunction with WINS because an administrator does not know which client will receive a particular IP address. WINS automatically registers a client's current IP address in the WINS database. In addition to the computer name, any networking services a computer provides are also registered with WINS.

DNS (Domain Name System) is used to resolve domain names, such as `www.microsoft.com`, to IP addresses. DNS is often used to resolve Internet names or to resolve names on a local intranet. *IIS* (Internet Information Server) provides World Wide Web publishing, FTP publishing, and Gopher server capabilities. You can use IIS to provide Web pages for Internet access or for local intranet use.

7

C. NWLink IPX/SPX Compatible Protocol

NWLink is Microsoft's version of IPX/SPX, the protocol suite that has been used within the NetWare environment for years. NWLINK is best suited for networks requiring communication with existing NetWare servers, and for existing NetWare clients.

1. NetWare Connectivity

A Windows NT Server running NWLink can serve as an application server for NetWare clients. However, the NetWare clients also need client software to communicate with the application; NWLink provides the common protocol. Other services can be installed on a Windows NT Server to enable additional NetWare connectivity. All these services depend on NWLink.

The NetWare clients also can use the Windows NT Server for file and print access if an additional service is installed (File and Print Services for NetWare [FPNW]). If the Gateway Service for NetWare (GSNW) is installed on the Windows NT Server, clients on the Windows NT network can communicate with NetWare servers without having NetWare client software installed.

If GSNW and NWLink are installed on a Windows NT Server, the Migration Tool for NetWare can be used to migrate NetWare users and files to the Windows NT Server. Microsoft also provides Client Services for NetWare (CSNW) to allow Windows NT Workstation computers to connect to NetWare servers.

Windows NT also can communicate with NetWare using TCP/IP if the NetWare servers have TCP/IP installed. However, NWLink (IPX/SPX) is usually thought of as the protocol used to connect to NetWare.

D. DLC (Data Link Control)

DLC is used to provide connectivity to IBM mainframes and AS400 servers. The BackOffice product SNA is used to connect to these IBM servers and requires DLC as its underlying protocol. DLC also can be used for HP network printers. However, if an HP printer has a JetDirect card installed, it can be assigned a TCP/IP address and thus use TCP/IP rather than DLC for its printing protocol. DLC is not used by any Microsoft clients—it is only used on a Windows NT Server to support IBM and HP connections.

E. AppleTalk Protocol

Apple Macintosh clients can connect to Windows NT servers running the AppleTalk protocol. This protocol is installed when Services for Macintosh is installed. This service (and the underlying AppleTalk protocol) allows Macintosh computers on your network to be able to access files and printers on the Windows NT Server. It also enables Windows NT clients to print to AppleTalk printers.

7.3.1 Exercise: Selecting the Proper Protocol for a Given Scenario

1. The production department needs to access a software product that can be installed only on a NetWare Server. They currently connect to the Windows NT system and would like be able to connect to both systems with one common protocol. Which of the following protocols can access both a NetWare system and a Windows NT system?

   A. NetWare Connect Protocol

   B. NetBEUI

   C. NWLink IPX/SPX Compatible

   D. GSNW

2. Users from your Windows NT system want to access your NetWare server, but you do not want to set up each one with the NetWare client. Which of the following is required to enable your Windows NT system to share a NetWare connection for the Windows NT users? Select all that apply.

   A. NWLink IPX/SPX Compatible

   B. NetBEUI

   C. GSNW

   D. Services for the Macintosh

7.3.2 Exercise: Selecting the Appropriate Protocol for Connectivity

Exercise 7.3.2 has you select the appropriate protocols to use for a specific scenario. Select the best protocols for each scenario.

1. Users need to access the Internet and to communicate with each other locally.
2. Users need to access a Novell server both running IPX and communicating with the Windows NT Server.
3. Users need to access resources on Novell servers, Windows NT systems, and UNIX systems.
4. A small number of users want to be able to share resources with no network configuration requirements. They do not need to access any computers outside their local network.

7.3 Practice Problems

1. You are installing Windows NT on a departmental LAN that will support 20 users. The network is wired on a single segment. Which of the following is the most efficient networking protocol you can use for this LAN configuration?

   A. NetBEUI

   B. NWLink

   C. TCP/IP

   D. AppleTalk

2. You are installing a Windows NT Server to support connections for Macintosh clients. This server will also have IIS installed to publish the company employee handbook. Which of the following protocols need to be installed on this server to support these functions? Select all that apply.

   A. NetBEUI

   B. NWLink

   C. TCP/IP

   D. AppleTalk

3. Your network includes Windows NT Servers and NetWare Servers running the IPX/SPX protocol. Which of the following protocols must be installed on the Windows NT Servers so that NetWare clients can connect to these servers?

   A. NetBEUI

   B. NWLink

   C. TCP/IP

   D. AppleTalk

4. You have several IBM AS400 servers in your environment that will communicate with a Windows NT server using SNA. You also have several HP network printers that will be managed by a Windows NT print server. Which of the following protocols must be installed on the Windows NT Server to support connections to peripherals? Select all that apply.

   A. NWLink

   B. NetBEUI

   C. PrintTalk

   D. DLC

5. A Windows NT Server will be a RAS Server for incoming client calls. This server will provide file access to a NetWare Server and print support for a TCP/IP printer. Which of the following protocols must be installed on the RAS Server to provide client access to these resources and to enable the clients to connect over RAS using the most efficient protocol? Select all that apply.

   A. NetBEUI

   B. NWLink

   C. TCP/IP

   D. DLC

6. Which protocol uses broadcasts in attempts to communicate with other computers on the network?

   A. NetBEUI

   B. NWLink

   C. TCP/IP

   D. DLC

7. You want to configure a Windows NT Server to provide DHCP and WINS services. Which of the following protocols needs to be installed on the server to support these services?

   A. NetBEUI

   B. NWLink

   C. TCP/IP

   D. DLC

8. A Windows NT Primary Domain controller will be used to migrate accounts from several NetWare servers. This PDC will also provide domain-name resolution for web servers to the rest of the domain. Which of the following protocols need to be installed on this server? Select all that apply.

   A. NetBEUI

   B. NWLink

   C. TCP/IP

   D. DLC

9. Which of the following protocols can be used to support network printers? Select all that apply.

   A. NetBEUI

   B. NWLink

   C. TCP/IP

   D. DLC

The following scenario applies to questions 10–13. A different solution to the scenario is proposed for each question.

Scenario: Your company is adding two new servers to its network for applications, file serving, and print serving. The applications will be used by clients in the domain and also by NetWare clients.

10. *Required Result*: Allow both NetWare and Microsoft clients access to the file and print services. *Optional Results*: Minimize the number of protocols used on the network; allow UNIX hosts to access printers on the Windows NT network.

    Solution: Install File and Print Services for NetWare on the Windows NT servers. Install JetDirect cards into the network printers. Install the NetBEUI protocol on the servers.

    A. The proposed solution produces the required results and produces both optional results.

    B. The proposed solution produces the required results and produces only one optional result.

    C. The proposed solution produces the required results but does not produce any optional results.

    D. The proposed solution does not produce the required results.

11. *Required Result*: Allow Microsoft clients to access all the services on the new servers. *Optional Results*: Allow the NetWare clients to access file and print services on the new servers; allow Macintosh clients to access files on the new servers.

    Solution: Install NWLink on the servers.

    A. The proposed solution produces the required results and produces both optional results.

    B. The proposed solution produces the required results and produces only one optional result.

    C. The proposed solution produces the required results but does not produce any optional results.

    D. The proposed solution does not produce the required results.

12. *Required Result*: Allow both NetWare and Microsoft clients to access the client/server application on the new servers. *Optional Results*: Minimize the protocols used on the network; allow NetWare clients to access the file and print services of the new servers.

    Solution: Install the client software needed for the application on the Microsoft and NetWare clients. Install NWLink on the servers.

    A. The proposed solution produces the required results and produces both optional results.

    B. The proposed solution produces the required results and produces only one optional result.

7

C. The proposed solution produces the required results but does not produce any optional results.

D. The proposed solution does not produce the required results.

13. *Required Result*: Allow access to the application for both Microsoft and NetWare clients. *Optional Results*: Minimize broadcast traffic on the network; minimize the number of protocols used on the network.

Solution: Install TCP/IP and the client software on the NetWare and Microsoft clients. Install TCP/IP on the new servers. Install a WINS Server and configure the Microsoft clients as WINS clients. Install WINS proxy agents on the network segments where the NetWare clients reside.

A. The proposed solution produces the required results and produces both optional results.

B. The proposed solution produces the required results and produces only one optional result.

C. The proposed solution produces the required results but does not produce any optional results.

D. The proposed solution does not produce the required results.

14. Which protocols can be used in a segmented network with routers separating the segments? Select all that apply.

A. NetBEUI

B. NWLink

C. NDIS

D. TCP/IP

15. Which of the following protocols must be installed before File and Print Services for NetWare can be installed?

A. NetBEUI

B. NWLink

C. DLC

D. TCP/IP

16. Which of the following protocols must be installed so that a server can be used as a DNS server?

A. NetBEUI

B. NWLink

C. DLC

D. TCP/IP

17. Windows NT supports printing to network printers that have a specific address assigned to the printer. Which of the following protocols supports this type of printing?

A. NetBEUI

B. NWLink

C. NDIS

D. TCP/IP

18. A RAS Server will allow a RAS client to connect by using only one protocol while routing information to other servers using several protocols. Which protocol is most efficient for the RAS client/server connection?

A. NetBEUI

B. NWLink

C. DLC

D. TCP/IP

19. Which protocol allows the greatest variety of non-Microsoft clients to connect to a Windows NT Server?

A. NetBEUI

B. NWLink

C. DLC

D. TCP/IP

20. Which protocols allow connections to both servers and network printers? Select all that apply.

    A. NetBEUI

    B. NWLink

    C. DLC

    D. TCP/IP

21. A friend runs a small warehouse. She wants to install a network to connect the warehouse parts workstations with the office server and the office workstations. The network will be used internally without outside access. Which of the following protocols would be the most efficient and easiest to configure for this environment?

    A. NetBEUI

    B. NWLink

    C. DLC

    D. TCP/IP

22. A friend runs a small warehouse. She wants to install a network to connect the warehouse parts workstations with the office server and the office workstations. She also wants to connect to parts suppliers through the Internet. Which of the following protocols is best for this environment?

    A. NetBEUI

    B. NWLink

    C. DLC

    D. TCP/IP

23. You want a server to provide WINS and DHCP services on the network. You also want this server to be a Gopher Server. How many protocols must be installed to support these services?

    A. 1

    B. 2

    C. 3

    D. 4

24. You want Macintosh clients to save data on a Windows NT Server. You also want Microsoft clients to have access to this data. How many protocols must be installed on the server to provide this access?

    A. 1

    B. 2

    C. 3

    D. 4

25. Which of the following protocols can be used by Microsoft clients to access file and print services on a Windows NT server? Select all that apply.

    A. NetBEUI

    B. NWLink

    C. DLC

    D. TCP/IP

    E. AppleTalk

7.3.1 Answers and Explanations: Exercise

1. **C** NWLink is the protocol that Microsoft provides to work with NetWare. NetBEUI is not supported on NetWare. GSNW is a service that allows Microsoft clients to access NetWare servers through a Windows NT Server without having NetWare client software installed.

2. **A, C** You need the protocol to let the Windows NT Server talk to NetWare (NWLink) and the service to let the Windows NT Server function as a gateway for Microsoft clients (Gateway Service for NetWare or GSNW).

7.3.2 Answers and Explanations: Exercise

1. TCP/IP. TCP/IP is the protocol required for Internet connections, but it also can be used for local network connections.
2. NWLink IPX/SPX Compatible. NWLink is the protocol used to connect with NetWare, but it also can be used by Microsoft clients.
3. TCP/IP, NWLink IPX/SPX Compatible. NWLink is required for NetWare connectivity. TCP/IP is required for UNIX connectivity. The Microsoft clients can use either of these protocols.
4. NetBEUI. All protocols would work; NetBEUI, however, is the easiest to configure and set up. It would also provide complete connectivity on the local network because no routers would be used in this environment.

7.3 Answers and Explanations: Practice Problems

1. **A** NetBEUI is the most efficient protocol for this small, single segment LAN.
2. **C, D** AppleTalk is needed for the Mac clients and IIS requires TCP/IP.
3. **B** NWLink is Microsoft's implementation of IPX/SPX.
4. **D** DLC provides support for IBM mainframes and AS400s in addition to HP network printer support.
5. **A, B, C** NWLink and TCP/IP must be installed so that the server can connect to these resources. NetBEUI is the most efficient protocol to use over a RAS link. The RAS Server functions as a NetBIOS gateway, converting the NetBEUI protocol to the protocols used by the servers with which the RAS client is trying to communicate.
6. **A** NetBEUI is broadcast-based.
7. **C** TCP/IP is needed for DHCP and WINS.
8. **B, C** NWLink supports the NetWare migration and TCP/IP supports DNS for domain-name resolution.
9. **C, D** DLC supports HP network printers and TCP/IP supports network printers, including HP network printers with JetDirect cards that can be assigned an IP address.
10. **C** Installing File and Print Services for NetWare forces the installation of NWLink. This allows both Microsoft and NetWare clients file and print access. Adding NetBEUI is not necessary. TCP/IP was not installed to allow UNIX printing support.
11. **C** NWLink allows Microsoft clients to connect to the server, but without additional services (FPNW). NetWare clients cannot access the file and print server. The Macintosh clients require the AppleTalk protocol on the server.
12. **B** The client software combined with the NWLink protocol allows both Microsoft and NetWare clients to access the application. However, the NetWare clients require FPNW on the server before they can connect for file and print access.
13. **A** NetWare clients can connect by using TCP/IP if they have the protocol installed. TCP/IP uses few broadcasts, and a single protocol can be used for these requirements.
14. **B, D** Both NWLink and TCP/IP can be used in this environment. NetBEUI is the only protocol limited to a single segment.
15. **B** FPNW depends on NWLink.
16. **D** DNS depends on TCP/IP.
17. **D** TCP/IP fits this description.

18. **A** NetBEUI is the most efficient protocol for a RAS connection.
19. **D** TCP/IP is the most common protocol.
20. **C, D** DLC allows connections to IBM servers (AS400s) and HP network printers, whereas TCP/IP connects to a variety of servers and printers.
21. **A** NetBEUI is most efficient for a small, single segment LAN.
22. **D** With Internet connectivity as a requirement, TCP/IP is the only possible choice.
23. **A** TCP/IP is the only protocol needed to support these services. A Gopher Server is part of IIS.
24. **B** The Macintosh clients require the AppleTalk protocol. Because Microsoft clients cannot use this protocol, you must install one additional protocol to support these clients.
25. **A, B, D** DLC is intended for specialized use, whereas AppleTalk is only for Mac clients.

7.3 Key Words

DHCP (Dynamic Host Configuration Protocol)

DLC (Data Link Control)

DNS (Domain Name System)

IIS (Internet Information Server)

TCP/IP

WINS (Windows Internet Name Service)

Practice Exam: Planning

Use this practice exam to test your mastery of the Planning objective. This practice exam is 15 questions long. The passing Microsoft score is 78.4 percent.

1. Where can computer accounts for a domain be created?

    A. Computer Manager for Domains

    B. User Manager for Domains

    C. Account Administrator

    D. Server Manager

2. How can you reestablish a broken trust?

    A. Enter the password used for the original trust.

    B. Remove the domains from the Trust Relationships dialog box and set up the trust again.

    C. Synchronize domain controllers in each domain in the trust.

    D. Choose the Reestablish Trust option in Trust Administrator.

3. You have created a stripe set with parity that uses five physical disks with 200 MB used on each disk. How much storage is available for data?

    A. 500 MB

    B. 600 MB

    C. 800 MB

    D. 1 GB

4. You have created a stripe set with parity that uses three physical disks. The stripe set is now filled and you want to expand it. How can you do this?

    A. Add a new volume to the stripe set.

    B. Regenerate the stripe set.

    C. Back up the data, create a new stripe set, and restore the data.

    D. Install the new drive and configure the stripe set to recognize the new drive.

5. Which disk arrays are supported by Windows NT Workstation?

    A. Striping

    B. Striping with parity

    C. Disk mirroring

    D. Volume sets

6. You are creating a stripe set with parity from five physical drives. One drive has 300 MB of free space left, another drive has 500 MB left, and the other three drives have 700 MB left. What is the maximum size of a stripe set with parity that can be created by using a combination of these disks, including both usable space and parity space?

    A. 1.5 GB

    B. 2.0 GB

    C. 2.1 GB

    D. 2.9 GB

7. What is the best way to protect the partition where the Windows NT files are stored from disk failure?

    A. Install the operating system on a stripe set with parity.

    B. Automate a backup of the Windows NT drive by using the interface in the Windows NT Backup utility.

    C. Use disk duplexing.

    D. Configure directory replication to copy the Windows NT directory to another server.

8. SNA is a BackOffice product that provides a connection from a Windows NT server to AS400s. Which of the

following protocols must be installed to support SNA?

A. NetBEUI

B. NWLink

C. DLC

D. TCP/IP

9. You want to install Gateway Services for NetWare to allow clients on your domain to access files on NetWare servers. You also want to provide file and print services to Microsoft clients on this server. How many protocols need to be installed on this server?

A. 1

B. 2

C. 3

D. 4

10. You want to provide Web services on a Windows NT Server. This server must also have NetBIOS support for a network application. How many protocols need to be installed on the server?

A. 1

B. 2

C. 3

D. 4

11. You want to have a single protocol on your network that can be routed and provides connectivity for the greatest variety of clients. Which protocol should you use?

A. NetBEUI

B. NWLink

C. DLC

D. TCP/IP

12. You want to use the Migration Tool for NetWare to copy files from a NetWare Server to a new Windows NT Server. Which of the following protocols must be installed on the Windows NT Server so that the Migration Tool can be used?

A. NetBEUI

B. NWLink

C. DLC

D. TCP/IP

13. You have established a trust relationship between two domains. Users in the trusted domain cannot log in to the trusting domain. What is the problem?

A. Users in the trusted domain do not have access to accounts in the trusting domain.

B. The trust is broken.

C. The Domain Users group from the trusting domain has not been assigned to the Users group of the trusted domain.

D. The pass-through authentication service must be started.

14. A trust is established between a master domain and two resource domains. Which of the following can be added to local groups in each of the resource domains? Select all that apply.

A. Global groups from the other resource domain

B. Global groups from the master domain

C. Users from the master domain

D. Global groups from the same resource domain

15. Your domain has 5,000 Windows 95 clients and 1,000 Windows NT Workstation clients. How much space in the SAM database is required for these clients?

A. 500 KB

B. 1 MB

C. 3 MB

D. 6 MB

Answers and Explanations: Practice Exam

1. **D** Server Manager is the tool used to create computer accounts.
2. **B** A trust must be manually broken and then reestablished.
3. **C** One disk is used for overhead; only 800 MB of the stripe set is usable space.
4. **C** You cannot expand a stripe set. You must remove it and create a larger one. To protect data, you should back it up first and then restore it to the larger stripe set.
5. **A, D** Fault-tolerant arrays are supported only on Windows NT Server.
6. **C** Stripe sets must use an equal amount of space from each disk. The largest possible combination is to use the three 700 MB disks, for a stripe set of 2.1 GB. Using four disks with 500 MB yields 2.0 GB while using all five disks with 300 MB results in a 1.5 GB stripe set.
7. **C** Disk mirroring or disk duplexing is the only way to provide instant backup of a system disk. By the way, Windows NT Backup does not have an automated backup utility. Disk replication wouldn't copy open files.
8. **C** DLC is required for this connection.
9. **A** NWLink can be used to provide access to NetWare and as the protocol for Microsoft clients.
10. **A** TCP/IP provides the Web support. TCP/IP (or any protocol on a Windows NT Server) also provides NetBIOS connectivity.
11. **D** TCP/IP is routable and provides the greatest connectivity options.
12. **B** NWLink is required for the Migration Tool.
13. **A** A trust allows accounts in the trusted domain to be visible to the trusting domain. Users in the trusted domain don't see anything from the trusting domain.
14. **B, C, D** You can always add users and global groups from the local domain. You also can add users and global groups from any trusted domain.
15. **A** Windows 95 computers do not require computer accounts. Each Windows NT computer account uses .5 KB of space; therefore, 1,000 computers would require 500 KB of disk space.

Chapter 8

Installation and Configuration

This chapter prepares you for the exam by covering the following objectives:

- Installing Windows NT Server in the various server roles of Primary Domain Controller, Backup Domain Controller, and member server.
- Configuring network protocols and protocol bindings (including TCP/IP with DHCP and WINS, NWLink IPX/SPX Compatible Transport Protocol, DLC, and AppleTalk).
- Configuring Windows NT Server core services, including Directory Replication and Computer Browser.
- Configuring hard disks to provide redundancy and to improve performance.
- Configuring printers, such as adding and configuring a printer, implementing a printer pool, and setting print priorities.
- Configuring NT Server for various types of clients, including Windows NT Workstation, Windows 95, and Macintosh.

This chapter focuses on the installation and configuration of your Windows NT Server computer in an enterprise environment. It also covers the additional components and services that can be used in an enterprise environment.

The Enterprise exam does not place a great deal of emphasis on the installation process. You need to have a strong knowledge of the configuration options, however, and an understanding of the reasons for selecting a specific configuration. As you go through the sections of this chapter, you will be introduced to the configuration options and the steps required to install and to configure each component.

8.1 Installing Windows NT Server 4 in Various Server Roles

This chapter begins with a quick overview of the entire installation process to provide you with a solid understanding of the steps involved in installing a Windows NT Server system.

A. An Overview of the Installation Process

To install Windows NT Server, run the appropriate WINNT.EXE setup program. If you are installing from a 16-bit operating system, such as MS-DOS, Windows 3.*x*, or Windows 95, run WINNT.EXE. To install from a 32-bit operating system, use WINNT32.EXE.

1. The first phase of Windows NT copies the source files into temporary directories held locally on your computer, and then restarts the system.
2. After the setup program has copied all the files to your system and the computer has been restarted, you are presented with a screen welcoming you to the installation of Windows NT Server.
3. If you are installing Windows NT, press Enter to continue with a new install, or select to repair a damaged NT installation or to upgrade your Windows NT system. You also can access help screens that give you additional information about the Windows NT Server installation process.
4. The setup program then attempts to detect any mass storage devices in your system. To continue with this detection, press Enter.
5. The detected mass storage devices are displayed. If you have any SCSI devices that are not recognized automatically by the setup program, you can press S to specify additional mass storage devices. When all mass storage devices have been recognized, press Enter to continue with the setup. Microsoft's End-User Licensing Agreement (EULA) is presented to you; read the agreement and continue with the installation.
6. Next, system settings that the setup program has detected for your installation are displayed. Review the settings to ensure they are correct and continue with the installation. If any of the settings are incorrect, select the item to change and press Enter to view the options available.
7. Next, select the disk partition in which to install Windows NT Server or to create a new partition by selecting the free space on your drive and pressing C. Partitions can be removed by selecting the partition and pressing D. The partition that holds the temporary files used by your NT installation cannot be removed by this method.
8. After disk partition, you are prompted to select the file system for your installation partition. The default is to use the current file system; alternately, you can select to convert the partition to NTFS or to format the partition using FAT or NTFS.
9. You then are prompted to enter the directory for Windows NT Server. The default directory is \WINNT. After you have entered the installation directory, press Enter to continue.
10. In the next screen, you are prompted to do an exhaustive check of the hard disk. Press Enter to do the search; press Esc to skip the search.
11. Press Enter to restart your system. When it restarts, you will be running the GUI portion of the installation.
12. The graphical portion of the Windows NT Server setup has been broken into three sections. Complete each section to properly configure your new Windows NT Server system.

13. Enter the registration information for your software and press Enter or click Next to continue.
14. Next, select the client licensing mode based on your licensing agreement with Microsoft. The two options available are Per Server and Per Seat.
15. Each computer in a Windows NT environment must have a unique NetBIOS computer name with a maximum length of 15 characters. Enter your computer name and press Enter or click Next to continue.
16. Next, select your server role. For more information about server roles, see the next section, "Defining Server Roles in Windows NT Server."
17. The first account created in Windows NT Server is Administrator. This account cannot be deleted, so assign a password that is secure. You can assign a password to this account during the installation.
18. The next option enables you to create an Emergency Repair Disk. It is recommended that you always have an up-to-date Emergency Repair Disk to help you recover from unforeseen accidents.
19. You now see the list of components available when installing your Windows NT Server system. Select any desired components, then press Enter or click Next to continue.
20. You are ready to install Windows NT Networking. Press Enter or click Next to continue.
21. The first option in this section is connectivity. You must clarify whether you are wired directly to the network or using a dial-up adapter for remote access, or using both for connectivity.
22. Internet Information Server (IIS) can be installed automatically at this point or installed later. You will learn more about installing IIS in a later section.
23. Next, the Windows NT Server 4 installation program attempts to automatically detect a network adapter on your computer. If you have multiple adapters, click Find Next to search for any additional adapters. If your adapter is not detected, you can click the Select from list button and manually select your network adapter. After all adapters have been selected, press Enter or click Next to continue.
24. Select the protocols you want to install. Three basic protocols are already listed. Select all required protocols and continue.
25. The default or core networking services are listed on the next screen. Additional network services can be added by clicking Select from the list. Add the additional networking services you want and continue the installation.
26. Each service, protocol, and adapter is then added to the binding list. You can configure the binding list for your networking needs.
27. If you previously elected to install a Primary Domain Controller from the Server Type screen, you are prompted to define the name of your domain. If you are installing a Backup Domain Controller or a Member Server, you have the option to join an existing domain.
28. Now you can add the final touches to your Windows NT Server installation. Press Enter or click Next to continue with the installation.
29. You can select the correct time zone and set the date and time. Enter the appropriate information and click Next.
30. Next, you select the proper video card driver and video settings.

Make sure you test all the video settings by clicking Test. This ensures that your selection works with Windows NT Server.

31. Setup then saves your configuration and displays a message informing you that the installation was completed successfully.
32. After the installation has been successfully completed, you can restart your system to verify the Windows NT Server setup.

B. Defining Server Roles in Windows NT Server

The different server roles in which Windows NT Server can be installed are as follows:

- Primary Domain Controller
- Backup Domain Controller
- Member Servers

Each server role provides a specific function in your Windows NT system. The next three sections address each of the roles. You gain an understanding of both the function each role performs and the reasons for selecting a particular server role for your Windows NT Server system.

1. Primary Domain Controllers

The Primary Domain Controller (PDC) is the first domain controller installed into a domain. As the first computer in the domain, the PDC creates the domain. Each domain can contain only one PDC. All other domain controllers in the domain are installed as Backup Domain Controllers (BDCs). In addition to standard Windows NT Server functionality, the PDC contains the original copy of the Security Accounts Manager (SAM) database, which contains all user accounts and security permissions for your domain and handles user requests and logon validation. The PDC runs the Netlogon service.

The three main functions of the Netlogon service are covered in different sections of this chapter. The three main functions are as follows:

- **To handle logon requests from users**
- **To control database synchronization between PDCs and all BDCs**
- **To enable pass-through authentication of users across trust relationships**

2. Backup Domain Controllers

The Backup Domain Controller (BDC) is an additional domain controller used to handle logon requests by users in the network. To handle the logon requests, the BDC must have a complete copy of the domain database, or SAM. The BDC also runs the Netlogon service.

A PDC will announce that there have been changes to one of the three SAM databases. The BDCs then will connect to the PDC and will request the changes that they do not have in their copy of the database. The entire database is not present, only the changes to the database are. The BDC helps the PDC handle user requests and logon validation. It also acts as a Windows NT Server, offering all the available options and functionality.

3. Member Servers

A computer that handles the server functionality you require without the overhead of handling logon validation is called a *Member Server*. A Member Server either is a part of the domain or is simply a participant in the Workgroup environment, but it does not need a copy of the SAM database nor does it handle logon requests. The main function of a Member Server is to share resources.

C. Changing Server Roles

After you install your computer in a specific server role, you might decide to change the role of the server. This can be a relatively easy task if you are changing a PDC to a BDC, or vice versa. If you want to change a domain controller to a Member Server or Member Server to a domain controller, however, you must reinstall into the required server role.

1. BDC to PDC

To change the server role of a domain controller, use the Promote to Primary Domain Controller option in the Computer menu of the Server Manager. You can only access this option by highlighting the appropriate BDC from the Server Manager list.

Selecting this option stops the Netlogon service of both the existing PDC and the BDC to be promoted. The Netlogon is then restarted with the role change in effect. The BDC starts as the PDC, and the old PDC restarts as a BDC. This is a relatively easy change and does not affect any of the other BDCs in the enterprise.

2. Member Server to Domain Controller

The only way to change the server role from a Member Server to a domain controller (or vice versa) is to do a reinstall, not an upgrade.

8

8.1.1 Exercise: Installing Windows NT Server 4 as a Primary Domain Controller

In this exercise, you step through the process of installing Windows NT Server 4 as a PDC. The setup also includes some additional services and protocols. This exercise should take approximately 45 minutes to complete. Your system should have at least 150 MB of free disk space to complete this exercise.

1. Access the Windows NT Server 4 source directory from a CD-ROM, or copy all of the source files for Windows NT Server onto the local hard drive. The I386 directory contains the files you use to install the Intel-based software.

Make sure SMARTDRV.EXE is loaded prior to starting the installation of Windows NT because it dramatically reduces the time required to complete the first stage of the setup.

2. From the Windows NT Server directory, enter the command line **WINNT /B**. This starts Windows NT Setup and enables you to complete the setup without creating the three boot disks.
3. The setup program copies the Windows NT Server 4 software into temporary directories on your computer. When finished copying the files, it prompts you to restart the system.
4. After the system has been restarted, you should notice that the Windows NT boot menu is now configured to autostart Windows NT. At this time, you should prepare to start the DOS-based portion of the Windows NT setup. Read the Welcome to Windows NT Setup screen and press Enter to start the setup of Windows NT.
5. The program then attempts to detect all mass-storage devices in your system. Review the selection and, if correct, press Enter to continue.
6. The End User Licensing Agreement screen is displayed for you to review. Read the screen, pressing Page Down to view the entire document. When you reach the bottom, press F8 to accept the terms of the agreement.
7. You then are prompted for the type of installation to complete. If this is the first occurrence of Windows NT on this system, press Enter to install Windows NT. If an existing installation of Windows NT is still on this system, pressing Enter upgrades the installation. If you want a new installation of Windows NT, press N to cancel the upgrade.
8. The hardware and software found on your computer is displayed. Press Enter to continue with the installation.
9. Select the drive on which you want to install Windows NT Server. Make sure it has at least 120 MB of free disk space to complete the installation. You also want to make sure the current file system is left intact, so FAT is the file system for your Windows NT system.

If you want to use NTFS as the file system, this screen enables you to convert your file system to NTFS.

10. Press Enter to use the default directory, \WINNT.
11. Press Enter to have the setup program examine your hard disks.
12. The system then prompts you to restart. When the system is restarted, it is in the graphical portion of the setup.
13. When the Windows NT Server Setup Wizard appears, click Next to start using the Setup Wizard.
14. Enter your name and organization information; click Next.
15. Type your CD Key, located on the Windows NT Server CD-ROM, and click Next.
16. Select the licensing mode you want to use. For this exercise, select Per Server with 10 concurrent connections; click Next.
17. Enter the computer name for your Windows NT Server computer. For this exercise, enter **Comp1** as the computer name; click Next.

The computer name can be a maximum of 15 characters and must be unique on the network to which it is attached.

18. Select the Primary Domain Controller option and click Next.
19. Enter a password for the Administrator account. For this exercise, use **password** as the password. Make sure you confirm the password and then click Next.
20. You might get a prompt regarding a floating point workaround. Select Do Not Enable the Floating Point Workaround and click Next to continue.
21. Click Yes, create an Emergency Repair Disk, and then click Next.
22. Click Next to select the default components. You are then presented with Phase 2 of the setup, "Installing Windows NT Networking."
23. Click Next to begin Phase 2.
24. Make sure Wired to the network is selected and click Next.
25. Clear the Install Microsoft Internet Information Server check box and click Next.
26. Click Start Search to have the setup program automatically detect your network cards. If you have multiple cards, click Find Next until all have been located. If your card is not located automatically, click Select from list and choose your network card manually. When the proper network adapters have been selected, click Next to continue.
27. Select TCP/IP and NetBEUI as your protocols and click Next.
28. All of the default network services should be used, so click Next to continue.
29. Click Next to install the network components.
30. If you are prompted to confirm the settings for your network adapter, make sure they are displayed correctly and click Next to continue.
31. You are prompted to use DHCP. If you have a DHCP server, click Yes. If you do not have a DHCP server, click No.
32. Click Next to accept the default bindings for your system.
33. Click Next to start the network.
34. If you did not use DHCP, when you are prompted for your TCP/IP settings, use 131.107.2.100 for your IP Address and 255.255.255.0 for a subnet mask. No default gateway is required for this exercise.
35. When prompted for your domain name, enter **DomainA** and click Next.
36. Phase 3 of the setup starts. Click Finish to start the last phase of the setup.
37. When prompted, enter the date, time, and time zone information for your location; click Next.
38. You must then configure your video adapter. Click OK to confirm the detected video adapter.
39. Click Test to verify the settings for your video adapter.
40. If the settings appear correctly, click Yes. Click OK to continue the installation.
41. The system then prepares to create the Emergency Repair Disk. Get a blank high-density floppy disk and, when prompted, insert it into drive A: and click OK.
42. When the emergency repair information has been written to disk, the system removes the temporary files and prompts you to restart.
43. When the system restarts, Windows NT Server has been installed successfully.

8.1 Practice Problems

1. You need to install a new Member Server in the Pittsburgh Domain, but you are in St. Louis. What is the best method to install and configure a Member Server when it is not physically attached to the Domain?

    A. Install the new server as a PDC; then, convert it to a Member Server when it can be attached physically.

    B. Install it as a BDC of the St. Louis domain and change its domain when in the correct location.

    C. Install the machine as a computer in the workgroup. When it is in the correct location, add the computer to the Pittsburgh domain.

    D. None of the above.

2. You have correctly installed your NT server, but it has developed a problem that requires the Emergency Repair Disks. You do not have the three disks created during the original installation. How can you create them?

    A. SETUP32.EXE /B

    B. WINNT /OX

    C. WINNT /B

    D. WINNT32 /UDF

3. Your company has one server running Windows NT and has no plans to add additional servers. With 40 employees and 30 workstations, what kind of licensing do you choose?

    A. Purchase 30 CALs and configure them as Per Seat.

    B. Purchase 40 CALs and configure them as Per Seat.

    C. Purchase 30 CALs and configure them as Per Server.

    D. Purchase 40 CALs and configure them as Per Server.

4. You have installed four NT server machines in one domain (one PDC and three BDCs). Your company has grown and the following objectives have been set for the changing company network.

    Primary Objective: You want to add another domain to the network, but must use only the existing domain controllers.

    Secondary Objective: When the new domain has been created, you want to move several users and their machines to the new domain.

    Proposed Solution: To accomplish this, you want to promote one BDC to a PDC and rename it. You then plan to change another BDC to belong to the new domain by changing the domain name from the Network option in Control Panel.

    In addition, you want to migrate several NT Workstation computers by changing the domain name and by creating the computer account from the system option in the Control Panel.

    How well does this solution work?

    A. This solution fills the primary and the secondary objectives.

    B. This solution fills the primary but not the secondary objective.

    C. This solution does not fill the primary objective but does fill the secondary objective.

    D. This solution does not fill the primary or the secondary objectives.

5. What installation options are available when installing NT Server?

    A. Custom, Typical, Portable

    B. Typical, Custom

    C. Custom

    D. Typical

6. If an NT Workstation machine needs to migrate to another domain, what needs to happen? Select all that apply.

   A. From the Server Manager, use Add to Domain; then, from the workstation machine, change the workstation name from My Computer properties.

   B. From the Server Manager, use Add to Domain; then, from the workstation machine, change the workstation name from Network Neighborhood properties.

   C. Reinstall and create the computer account during the installation.

   D. On the local computer, add the computer account from the network applet in Control Panel.

7. Which of the following will create a server-based installation? Select all that apply.

   A. Copy the platform-specific folder to the server and share the folder.

   B. Share the platform-specific folder on the Windows NT Server compact disk.

   C. Copy the platform-specific files to the workstation.

   D. Connect the workstation to the shared files on the distribution server.

8. You already have created NT setup boot disks and do not want to create them again. How can you avoid creating the disks and use your original set?

   A. Start the installation with WINNT /X.

   B. Start the installation with WINNT /OX.

   C. Start the installation with WINNT /B.

   D. Start the installation with WINNT /disks:0.

9. You want to upgrade a Windows NT Workstation 3.51 to a Windows NT Server 4 domain controller. How do you do so?

   A. Run WINNT and choose yes to the upgrade question.

   B. Run WINNT32 and choose yes to the upgrade question.

   C. There is no direct upgrade path from NT Workstation 3.51 to an NT Server 4 domain controller.

   D. Run UPGRADE.EXE.

10. You want to upgrade a Windows NT Server 3.51 Member Server to a Windows NT Server 4 domain controller. How do you do this?

   A. Run WINNT and choose yes to the upgrade question.

   B. Run WINNT32 and choose yes to the upgrade question.

   C. There is no direct upgrade path from an NT Server 3.51 Member Server to an NT Server 4 domain controller.

   D. Run UPGRADE.EXE.

11. You want to upgrade a Windows NT Server 3.51 Member Server to a Windows NT Server 4 Member Server. How do you do this?

   A. Run WINNT and choose yes to the upgrade question.

   B. Run WINNT32 and choose yes to the upgrade question.

   C. There is no direct upgrade path from NT Workstation 3.51 to an NT Server 4 domain controller.

   D. Run UPGRADE.EXE.

12. You want to upgrade a Windows NT Server 3.51 domain controller to a Windows NT Server 4 domain controller. How do you do this?

    A. Run WINNT and choose yes to the upgrade question.

    B. Run WINNT32 and choose yes to the upgrade question.

    C. There is no direct upgrade path from an NT Workstation 3.51 to an NT Server 4 domain controller.

    D. Run UPGRADE.EXE.

13. You want multiple servers to contain the source files to increase the performance for installation of NT machines. How do you do this?

    A. Run WINNT /s

    B. Run WINNT32 /d

    C. Run WINNT32 /m

    D. Run WINNT /m

14. You have to remove NT from a logical partition formatted with NTFS and want to remove just the partition. How can you do this? Select all that apply.

    A. Use the NT Disk Administrator. Choose to remove the partition and it will do so the next time NT starts.

    B. Use the NT setup program and, when choosing a partition, highlight the NT partition and press D to delete.

    C. Use the OS/2 1.*x* installation disks.

    D. Use MS-DOS FDISK from versions 5.0 or earlier.

15. You want to automate the installation of 50 NT Workstations. You have created UNATTEND.TXT. How do you start your installations?

    A. WINNT /U:UNATTEND.TXT

    B. WINNT /A:UNATTEND.TXT

    C. WINNT /UDF:UNATTEND.TXT

    D. WINNT /I:UNATTEND.TXT

16. What is the name of the setup program for an upgrade installation of Windows NT Server 3.51 to 4?

    A. SETUP.EXE

    B. SETUP32.EXE

    C. WINNT.EXE

    D. WINNT32.EXE

17. What is the name of the setup program if you are not installing from a 32-bit operating system?

    A. SETUP.EXE

    B. SETUP32.EXE

    C. WINNT.EXE

    D. WINNT32.EXE

8.1.1 Answers and Explanations: Exercise

In this exercise, you reviewed the process of installing Windows NT Server 4 as a PDC. This setup also included some additional services and protocols. To perform this setup, you need 150 MB of free space, and SMARTDRV.EXE needs to be loaded prior to starting the installation of Windows NT. You can update your file system to NTFS at the time of installation as well.

8.1 Answers and Explanations: Practice Problems

1. **C** It is not possible to change a domain controller to a Member Server without reinstalling.

2. **B** Use WINNT /OX to create the three disks without performing a complete.

3. **C** Because there are only 30 workstations, only 30 connections would be used.

4. **D** It is not possible to migrate domain controllers, and although computer accounts can be made from an NT Workstation, they are created through the Network icon in the Control Panel.

5. **C** Custom is the only option under NT Server.

6. **B, D** Reinstalling is not necessary.

7. **A, B, D** Although it is possible to copy the files to the workstation and then install them, it isn't a server-based installation.

8. **B** /OX will create the startup disks. /X will start an installation and use previously created disks.

9. **B** When upgrading NT use WINN32.

10. **C** Although 3.51 Member Servers are upgradable, they can be upgraded only to Member Servers.

11. **B** Version 3.51 Member Servers are upgradable to 4 Member Servers.

12. **B** Run Winnt32 to perform the upgrade from the Run line and keep your domain controller down time to a minimum.

13. **A** WINNT /s and the source code paths.

14. **A, B, C** FDISK will work if it is MS-DOS 6.0 or later and if the NTFS partition is a primary partition.

15. **A** /UDF often accompanies an unattended installation, but it will provide information specific to each workstation.

16. **D** WINNT32.EXE is used to upgrade 32-bit environments like NT 3.51.

17. **C** WINNT.EXE is used for installing from DOS, Windows 3.1, or Windows 95.

8.1 Key Words

Primary Domain Controller

Backup Domain Controller

Member Server

WINNT

WINNT32

8.2 Configuring Networking Protocols and Protocol Bindings

In this section, you examine the configuration process for each protocol. You also learn the installation steps required to add any protocols.

Installing and configuring network protocols is controlled in the network properties of your Windows NT system. The installation of all the protocols is identical. The configuration of each protocol is different, however, so you must understand the process required for configuring each of the supported protocols.

A. Installing Protocols

The installation of a new protocol in Windows NT Server is done through the Network dialog box. To open the Network dialog box, double-click the Network icon in the Control Panel.

To install a new protocol using the Network dialog box, select the Protocols tab. To see a list of the protocols available for you to install, click Add. Highlight the protocol you are installing; then click OK.

The system tries to locate the Windows NT installation files. If it cannot locate them, you are prompted to enter the directory path of the Windows NT Server 4 source files.

After the protocol has been installed, you cannot configure it until it has been bound to your network adapter. After the binding process is completed, you can configure the protocol. Click OK at the bottom of the Network dialog box when finished. When the binding process is completed, you will then be prompted to configure the protocol.

B. Configuring Protocols

Each protocol is configured by changing its properties. The properties of each protocol can be accessed in the Protocols tab of the Network dialog box. On the Protocols tab, highlight the protocol you want to configure and then select the Properties button.

1. TCP/IP

TCP/IP is the most common protocol because it is accepted across most platforms. It is the protocol that allows access to the Internet. The TCP/IP protocol also enables communication between various platforms, including UNIX systems.

Many of the questions on the Enterprise exam relate to the use of the TCP/IP protocol. Be sure you understand all the options available with the TCP/IP protocol.

To access the properties of the TCP/IP protocol, highlight TCP/IP Protocol in the Network dialog box and click Properties. The tabs available for configuration in the Microsoft TCP/IP Properties dialog box are as follows:

- IP Address
- DNS

- WINS Address
- DHCP Relay
- Routing

You must configure each tab in the Microsoft TCP/IP Properties dialog box to complete the configuration of your TCP/IP settings. Note that on the IP Address tab, you have the option to select the network adapter you want to configure. Each network adapter card in your system can and should have different TCP/IP settings.

a. Configuring the IP Address

The IP Address tab allows configuring of the IP address, the subnet mask, and the default gateway. You also can enable the system to automatically obtain an IP address through the use of the DHCP server.

An IP address is a 32-bit address that is broken into four octets and is used to identify your network adapter card as a TCP/IP host. Each IP address must be unique. If users have IP address conflicts on the network, they cannot use the TCP/IP protocol until the conflict is resolved.

Your IP addresses then are grouped into a subnet. To subnet your network, assign a subnet mask. A *subnet mask* is used to identify the computers local to your network. Any address outside your subnet is accessed through the default gateway. The *default gateway* is the address of the router that passes your TCP/IP information to computers, or hosts, outside your subnet.

If your IP address was 131.107.2.100 and your subnet mask was 255.255.0.0, the first two octets would represent the network (131.107) and the last two octets would represent the unique host on the subnet (2.100).

b. Configuring DNS for TCP/IP

8

The *Domain Name System* (DNS) server translates TCP/IP host names of remote computers into IP addresses. The DNS server contains a database of all the computers you can access by hostname. This database is used when you access a web page on the Internet.

The DNS tab shows you the options available for configuring your TCP/IP protocol to use a DNS server. In configuring your DNS settings for the TCP/IP protocol, you must start by assigning a hostname to your computer. This *hostname* is part of the name other computers use to make TCP/IP connections to your computer system. The hostname is then combined with the TCP/IP domain name.

After your computer hostnames have been entered, enter the IP address of the DNS server containing your name database. Multiple DNS servers can be entered. The top DNS server is the first DNS searched by your system; other configured DNS servers will be used if the first server is unavailable. The Up and Down buttons directly beside your DNS servers can be used to modify your search order.

c. Assigning a WINS Address for TCP/IP

The WINS Address tab enables you to configure your primary and secondary *Windows Internet Names Services* (WINS) server addresses. WINS is used to reduce the number of NetBIOS broadcast messages sent across the network to locate a computer. By using a WINS server, the names of computers on your network are kept in a WINS database. Each computer or NetBIOS service registers its name into the database, enabling immediate lookup of computer names.

In configuring your WINS servers, you can enter a secondary WINS server. Your system first searches the primary WINS server database; your system searches the secondary database if the first server is unavailable.

Two other options are available on this tab. The first enables your system to search the DNS database if a computer name cannot be resolved to an IP address. The second option enables a local file, LMHOSTS, to be used as a local database of computer names. You then can configure the LMHOSTS file to enable named connections to your most common systems without using a DNS or WINS lookup.

d. Using a DHCP Relay Agent with TCP/IP

The DHCP relay agent is used to find your DHCP servers across routers. IP addresses are handed out by the DHCP servers. The client request, however, is made with local subnet broadcast messages. Broadcast messages do not normally cross routers. The solution is to use a DHCP relay agent to assist the clients in finding the DHCP server across a router.

After the DHCP Relay Agent Service is installed, you can configure your DHCP relay agent. Settings include the seconds threshold, the maximum number of hops to use in searching for the DHCP servers, and the IP addresses of the DHCP servers you want to use.

e. Routing

In an environment in which multiple subnets are used, you can configure your Windows NT Server as a multihomed system. By installing multiple network adapters, each connecting to a different subnet, you can enable the Enable IP Forwarding option: your computer acts as a router, forwarding the packets through the network cards in the multihomed system to the other subnet.

2. NWLink IPX/SPX Compatible

The NWLink IPX/SPX-compatible protocol was designed for NetWare connectivity, but it can be used for network connectivity between any systems running IPX-compatible protocols. The configuration of the NWLink protocol is simple in comparison to the TCP/IP protocol. To configure your NWLink protocol, highlight NWLink IPX/SPX Compatible Transport in the Network dialog box; then click Properties. The NWLink IPX/SPX Properties dialog box appears. The NWLink IPX/SPX Properties dialog box has two tabs: General and Routing.

On the General tab, you have the option to assign an internal network number. This eight-digit, hexadecimal number format is used by some programs with services that can be accessed by NetWare clients.

You also have the option to select a frame type for your NWLink protocol. The frame type you select must match the frame type of the remote computer with which you need to communicate. By default, Windows NT Server uses the Auto Frame Type Detection setting, which scans the network and loads the first frame type it encounters. If multiple frame types are detected, NT will default to using the 802.2 frame type. The topologies and frame types are listed in Table 8.2.1.

Table 8.2.1 Supported Frame Types

Topology	Supported Frame Types
Ethernet	802.2, 802.3, Ethernet II, SNAP
Token ring	802.5, SNAP
FDDI	802.2, SNAP

The default frame type is 802.2 in NetWare 3.12 and later. Earlier versions of NetWare used 802.3 as a default frame type.

The Routing tab of the NWLink IPX/SPX Properties dialog box is used to enable or disable the Routing Information Protocol (RIP). If you enable RIP routing over IPX, your Windows NT Server can act as an IPX router. This also requires the installation of the RIP for NWLink IPX/SPX Compatible Transport Service to be installed.

3. AppleTalk

To install the AppleTalk protocol, you must install Services for Macintosh. You will examine the requirements for that later in this chapter. Select the AppleTalk protocol; then, click Properties. The Microsoft AppleTalk Protocol Properties dialog box appears.

C. Configuring the Binding Order

The *binding order* is the sequence your computer uses to select which protocol to use for network communication. Each protocol is listed for each network-based service, protocol, and adapter available. Setting the binding order of your network services and protocols can optimize your network configuration. To modify the binding order, go to the Bindings tab in the Network dialog box.

The Bindings tab contains an option, Show bindings for, that can be used to select the service, adapter, or protocol that you want to modify in the binding order. By clicking the appropriate option, each binding can be enabled or disabled, or it can be moved up or down in the binding order.

8.2.1 Exercise: Configuring TCP/IP Protocol

In this exercise, you modify the TCP/IP protocol to use a DHCP server and to manually input an IP Address. This exercise should take about 15 minutes to complete.

1. Select Start, Settings, Control Panel, and double-click the Network icon.
2. Select the Protocols tab.
3. Highlight TCP/IP Protocol, then click Properties.
4. On the IP Address tab of the Microsoft TCP/IP Properties dialog box, enable Obtain an IP address from a DHCP server.
5. Click OK to close the Microsoft TCP/IP Properties dialog box; then click OK to close the Network dialog box.
6. The system prompts you to restart the system for the new settings to take effect. Restart the system.
7. When the system restarts, open a command prompt and enter **IPCONFIG /ALL** to view your current TCP/IP settings.

If a DHCP server is not available when you run the IPCONFIG command, all of the addresses should be set to 0.0.0.0. If these are already the current settings, it is configured properly and you are only missing the DHCP server.

8. Next, you will reset the IP address back to a manual IP address. Right-click the Network Neighborhood icon and select Properties. The Network dialog box appears.
9. Select the Protocols tab.
10. Highlight TCP/IP Protocol and click Properties.
11. In the Specify an IP address section, enter **131.107.2.100** as the IP Address.
12. For the Subnet Mask, enter **255.255.255.0**.
13. For the Default Gateway, enter **131.107.2.1**.
14. Next, select the WINS Address tab.
15. Enter **131.107.2.2** for the Primary WINS Server.
16. Select the DNS tab.
17. Enter **131.107.2.2** in the list of DNS servers.
18. Click OK to save all settings.
19. Click OK in the Network properties dialog box. You are now using your new settings.
20. Start a command prompt and enter **IPCONFIG /ALL**.
21. Note that your current IP information has been changed to the settings you just entered.

8.2 Practice Problems

1. What is a subnet mask used for?

   A. It is the address of the router.

   B. It is used to determine whether a target host is on the same subnet or on a remote subnet.

   C. It is a unique 32-bit address that identifies your machine across a TCP/IP network.

   D. It passes addressing information to the Internet.

2. Your company is using TCP/IP as the primary network protocol. Users on the network randomly complain that they get messages about IP address conflicts. What could be a potential solution to this?

   A. Implement IIS

   B. Implement DNS

   C. Implement WINS

   D. Implement DHCP

3. Which service can be used to reduce the number of NetBIOS broadcast messages sent across the network to locate a computer?

   A. TCP/IP

   B. HOST files

   C. WINS

   D. DNS

4. By default, how are DHCP servers used to allocate an IP address to a client?

   A. Each client is configured to request an IP address from a specific DHCP server.

   B. Each client sends out a broadcast requesting a number from any DHCP server that can respond.

   C. Each client is configured to look for an LMHOSTS file with the IP address of the DHCP server.

   D. A DHCP server sends out broadcasts announcing itself across the network. Any client needing an address will respond to the broadcast.

5. Your multihomed system is connected to multiple TCP/IP subnets. What must be enabled to transfer packets between subnets?

   A. IP repeating

   B. IP forwarding

   C. Default Gateway

   D. DNS

6. What is the default frame type setting for Windows NT?

   A. 802.2

   B. 802.3

   C. Auto Frame

   D. SNAP

7. What needs to be installed to configure AppleTalk?

   A. Gateway Services for Macintosh

   B. NWLINK

   C. Services for Macintosh

   D. LocalTalk

8. To optimize your binding order, the protocols should be placed in what order?

   A. The protocols used most often should be at the top of the binding order.

   B. The least used protocols should be at the top of the binding order.

   C. Binding order will not affect speed.

   D. Stagger the protocols to keep a balanced load.

8.2.1 Answers and Explanations: Exercise

In this exercise, you modified the TCP/IP protocol to use a DHCP server and then manually inserted an IP address. You did this from the Settings, Control Panel, Network icon area. For more information on the TCP/IP protocol, review the section titled "Configuring Protocols."

8.2 Answers and Explanations: Practice Problems

1. **B** A subnet mask number will identify whether an address is local or needs to be passed on the default gateway.
2. **D** DHCP will assign IP addresses as needed. This will provide users with a unique address and will minimize the possibility of conflicts.
3. **C** WINS will keep a list of all NetBIOS names for machines.
4. **B** Machines broadcast a request for an address and will accept an address from any server that responds unless configured otherwise.
5. **B** A router works at the network layer of the OSI model and can filter protocol information.
6. **A** 802.2 is used in Windows NT as the preferred frame type.
7. **C** Services for Macintosh must be installed from the Service tab of the Network icon.
8. **A** To optimize the protocols, place the most used at the top of the list.

8.2 Key Words

Subnet mask

IP address

DNS

WINS

DHCP relay

Default gateway

8.3 Configuring Windows NT Server Core Services

Windows NT takes full advantage of its multithreaded, multitasking capabilities by running services in the background. In this section, you look at configuring some of the core services in Windows NT Server. These services are the following:

- Server service
- Workstation service
- Computer Browser service
- Directory Replication service

A. Server Service

The Server service answers network requests. By configuring Server service, you can change the way your server responds and, in a sense, the role it plays in your network environment. Servers in a network environment can be grouped into three different classes or roles:

- Logon server (domain controller)
- Application server
- File/print server

When configuring the Server service, the first step is to select the role your computer will play in your network environment. To configure Server service, you must open the Network dialog box. To do this, double-click the Network icon in Control Panel and select the Services tab.

To configure Server service, highlight Server and click Properties. You are then able to view the properties of your Server service. In the Server dialog box, you have four optimization settings. Each of these settings modifies memory management based on the role the server plays. These options are described in the following sections.

For the enterprise exam, you need to know when each optimization setting should be used and the differences between the four settings.

1. Minimize Memory Used

The Minimize Memory Used setting is used when your Windows NT Server system is accessed by a small number of users (less than 10). This setting is used when the Windows NT Server computer is used as a user's desktop computer, not in a true server role. This setting allocates memory so a maximum of 10 network connections can be properly maintained. By restricting the memory for network connections, more memory is available at the local or desktop level.

2. Balance

The Balance setting can be used for a maximum of 64 network connections. This setting is the default when using NetBEUI software. Like the Minimize setting, Balance is best used for a relatively low number of users connecting to a server that also can be used as a desktop computer.

3. Maximize Throughput for File Sharing

The Maximize Throughput for File Sharing setting allocates the maximum amount of memory available for network connections. It is the default on any Windows NT Member Server computer. This setting is excellent for large networks in which the server is accessed for file and print sharing.

4. Maximize Throughput for Network Applications

If you are running distributed applications, such as SQL Server or Exchange Server, the network applications do their own memory caching. Therefore, you want your system to enable the applications to manage the memory. This is accomplished using the Maximize Throughput for Network Applications setting. This setting also is used for very large networks and is suggested for domain controllers.

B. Workstation Service

The Workstation service is your redirector in Windows NT Server. The Workstation service handles all outgoing network communication. The Workstation service has no configuration options through the Control Panel, unlike the other services discussed. You can make some Registry changes. Registry modification is not recommended unless you have a strong understanding of the Registry and its entries.

To make Registry changes, run the REGEDT32.EXE program. The Registry in Windows NT is a complex database of configuration settings for your computer. If you want to configure the Workstation service, open the HKEY_LOCAL_MACHINE hive. The exact location to configure your Workstation service is:

```
HKEY_Local_Machine\System\CurrentControlSet\Services\LanmanWorkstation\Parameters
```

C. Computer Browser Service

The Computer Browser service is responsible for maintaining the list of computers on the network that are running the Server service or that have file and print sharing enabled. The browse list contains all the computers located on the physical network. As a Windows NT Server, your system plays a big role in the browsing of a network. The Windows NT Server acts as a master browser or backup browser.

The functions of a master or backup browser are to hold the list of computers in the domain and to share that list with other computers. In the Microsoft networking environment, all computers send broadcast messages across the network containing the domain/workgroup to which they belong as well as their computer names.

A master browser will gather all of these broadcasts for their subnets. The domain master browser will collect the lists from all master browsers to build a total domain browse list. Periodically, the master browsers will copy the browse list to backup browsers. When clients request a browse list, they receive it from a backup browser on their subnet.

Browsing happens automatically, so no configuration is required. You can, however, configure whether you want your server to be a master or backup browser. The configuration is done in the Registry. The settings are found in

```
HKEY_Local_Machine\System\CurrentControlSet\Services\Browser\Parameters
```

Two entries can be modified to select whether your server is a preferred master. The first entry is `IsDomainMaster=True/False`. You select `True` if you want your computer to be the master browser; select `False` if you do not want it to be the master browser.

The other entry is `MaintainServerList=Auto`. If this entry is set to `Auto`, your server is able to act in a browser role on the network.

The selection of browsers is through an election. The election is called by any client computer when it cannot connect to a master browser or when a preferred master browser computer starts up. The election is based on broadcast messages. Every computer has the opportunity to nominate itself, and the computer with the highest settings wins the election. The election criteria are based on three things:

- The operating system (Windows NT Server, Windows NT Workstation, Windows 95, Windows for Workgroups)
- The version of the operating system (NT 4, NT 3.51, NT 3.5)
- The current role of the computer (master browser, backup browser, potential browser)

This is a simplified breakdown of the election criteria. Look in the Windows NT Resource Kit for detailed information about the election criteria.

D. Directory Replication Service

In any network environment, it is a challenge to maintain consistent logon scripts and system policies across multiple servers. In Windows NT Server, this is handled through the use of the Directory Replication service. The Directory Replication service can be configured to synchronize an entire directory structure across multiple servers.

In configuring the directory replication service, you must select the export server and all the import servers. The export server is the computer with the original copy of the directory structure and files. Each import server receives a complete copy of the export server's directory structure, which is monitored by the Directory Replication service. If the contents of the directory change, the changes are copied to all the import servers. A special service account you create is needed by the service. You configure the Directory Replication service to use this service account.

8

The Directory Replication service can be used to maintain consistent logon scripts, system policies, or data files across the distributed network environment.

1. Directory Replication Service Account

The Directory Replication service account must have proper access on all the servers participating in the directory replication process. The following access is required for your Directory Replication service account:

- The account should be a member of the Backup Operators and Replicator groups.
- There should be no time or logon restrictions for the account.
- The Password Never Expires option should be selected.
- The User Must Change Password At Next Logon option should be turned off.
- This account also must be assigned the user right to log on as a service. This happens when replication is configured through the Services icon in Control Panel.

If you are not running the service packs for Windows NT Server, this replication account does not work properly. To fix this problem, apply the Windows NT service packs or assign the Administrators group membership to the service account. Another solution is to edit the Registry in the following area:

```
HKEY_LOCAL_MACHINE\System\CurrentControlSet\Control\SecurePipeServers\WinReg\AllowedPaths
```

You can modify the `Machine` **value to include the entry System\CurrentControlSet\Services\Replicator.**

2. Installing Directory Replication Service

The Directory Replication service is installed during the installation of Windows NT Server. To get the Directory Replication service to work, you need to configure the service. Prior to configuring the service, be sure your Directory Replication service account has been created and assigned the appropriate permissions. Open the Control Panel and double-click the Services icon. You then are presented with a list of all the services installed on your Windows NT Server. Locate the Directory Replication service.

The Directory Replication service's start up option is set to manual. The service is not started at this time, and you should not start the system until all configuration has been completed. To change the properties for the Directory Replication service, make sure it is selected in the Service list and then click Startup.

To configure the service to work with the Directory Replication service account, you must change the Startup Type to Automatic. Fill in the Log On As This Account option with the name and password of your service account.

You have now configured the Directory Replication service, but you still need to configure replication. The export and import servers must be selected and prepared before starting the Directory Replication service.

a. Export Server

To configure the export server, start Server Manager and double-click the export server. Click Replication in the Server Properties dialog box. When configuring the export server, you have the option to specify the export directory. The default export directory is as follows:

```
%SystemRoot%\system32\repl\export\
```

All subdirectories and corresponding files are sent to all the computers listed as import computers in the Export Directories section of the Directory Replication dialog box. It is critical that you include all systems requiring the files. It is possible for your own computer to act as both an export and import computer.

b. Import Server

The import computer also is configured in the Server Manager, Properties dialog box. To configure the import computer, click Replication to open the Directory Replication dialog box. The import computer can be the same computer as the export server.

In the Import Directories section of the Directory Replication dialog box, you can select the import directory. The default import directory is as follows:

```
%SystemRoot%\system32\repl\import.
```

Remember that the default directory for executing logon scripts in a Windows NT system is as follows:

```
%SystemRoot%\system32\repl\import\scripts
```

The netlogon share points to the same directory. You must also select the export server from which the import computer should receive the information. Make sure your import computer does not receive updates from multiple export servers, or you might have difficulty maintaining consistency across your servers.

3. Managing Directory Replication

You can control directory replication from both the export and import servers. You can place locks on certain directories to exclude them from the replication process. You also can designate a stabilization time to ensure that the files in your directories are not modified during a replication.

The import server has similar options. Directory locking can be managed from either the export server or the import server.

8.3.1 Exercise: Configuring Directory Replication on a Windows NT Server

In this exercise, you configure the Directory Replication service to automatically replicate logon scripts.

1. Before you can configure directory replication, you must create a Directory Replication service account. Start User Manager for Domains and create a new user named **replacct**. This account should be a member of the Replicator and Backup Operators groups. Make sure there are no password or time restrictions on this account. When the user has been created, click Add and close the User Manager.
2. Select Start, Settings, Control Panel, and double-click the Services icon.
3. Highlight Directory Replicator in the Services dialog box and click Startup.
4. In the Service dialog box, select Automatic in the Startup Type section.
5. In the Log on As section, click This Account and select **replacct**. Click Add to add the account. If you created a password for this account, make sure you enter it in the password fields. Click OK and the Services dialog box is displayed again.
6. Click Close to exit the Services dialog box.
7. Select Start, Programs, Administrative tools, Server Manager.
8. Locate your computer in the list and double-click to view the properties of your computer.
9. Click Replication.
10. The Directory Replication dialog box appears.
11. Enable the Export Directories radio button.

12. Click Add to add a new computer for exporting. Select your computer name in the list; then, click OK to add it to the list.
13. Enable the Import Directories radio button.
14. Click the Add button in this section and select your computer name; then, click OK.
15. Click OK to close the Directory Replication dialog box. The Directory Replication Service should start when you click OK to close the dialog box.
16. Start the Windows NT Explorer and locate the \WINNT\System32\Repl\Export\scripts directory.
17. Create a text file called LOGIN.TXT in this directory.
18. Open the \WINNT\System32\Repl\Import\Scripts directory. Watch this directory until the LOGIN.TXT file appears. This might take a few minutes, so be patient.
19. When you see the file in the directory, close Explorer.
20. Select Start, Programs, Administrative Tools, Server Manager.
21. Locate your computer and double-click to view its properties.
22. Click Replication.
23. In the Export Directories section of the Directory Replication dialog box, click Manage. You should see status information about your directory replication.
24. Click Manage in the Import Directories section to view the status from the import computer.

At the completion of this exercise, you might want to set the Directory Replication service back to a manual start.

8.3 Practice Problems

1. Where do you go to configure your server service?
   A. Double-click the System icon in Control Panel and select the Services tab.
   B. Double-click the Network icon in Control Panel and select the Services tab.
   C. Double-click the Services icon in Control Panel and select the Services tab.
   D. From the Run line, type **Net Start server /config**.

2. When an NT server is utilized as a desktop machine, which server configuration is appropriate?
   A. Minimize Memory Used
   B. Balance
   C. Maximize Throughput for File Sharing
   D. Maximize Throughput for Network Applications

3. If a server needs to run distributed applications, which server configuration is appropriate?
   A. Minimize Memory Used
   B. Balance
   C. Maximize Throughput for File Sharing
   D. Maximize Throughput for Network Applications

4. Which server configuration is appropriate if a server needs the most amount of memory available for network connections?
   A. Minimize Memory Used
   B. Balance
   C. Maximize Throughput for File Sharing
   D. Maximize Throughput for Network Applications

5. Which server configuration is appropriate when a machine will never have more than 64 network connections?
   A. Minimize Memory Used
   B. Balance
   C. Maximize Throughput for File Sharing
   D. Maximize Throughput for Network Applications

6. Where do you go to use a graphical interface to configure your workstation service?
   A. Double-click the System icon in Control Panel and select the Services tab.
   B. Double-click the Network icon in Control Panel and select the Services tab.
   C. There are no GUI interface configuration options for the Workstation service.
   D. From Run, type **Net service / workstation**.

7. What does the Workstation service provide?
   A. It maintains a list of computer resources available to the current user.
   B. When requests are made that are not local, the Workstation service forwards the request to the network.
   C. When requests are made to a computer, the Workstation service provides the information to the requesting client.
   D. It enables replication information broadcasts to be made.

8. Which service will initiate synchronizing the domain controllers?
   A. Server
   B. Replication
   C. Network DDE
   D. Netlogon

9. Which service maintains the dynamic list of computers on the network?
   A. DHCP
   B. Computer Browser service
   C. DNS
   D. Messenger service

10. How is a computer registered with the browser?
    A. Every computer with file and print sharing enabled sends a broadcast across the network with domain and computer name information that is picked up by the browser.
    B. Browsers send out broadcast requests across the network asking for domain and computer names.
    C. A machine is configured during installation to be the browser. All machines automatically send an identity packet to this machine on startup.
    D. The network administrator manually logs NetBIOS names into a file on the browser computer.

11. Where can you configure the role an NT Server plays in Browsing?
    A. Right-click Network Neighborhood and choose Properties.
    B. Run the Registry Editor and open the HKEY_Local_Machine hive.
    C. Browsing roles are automatic. Configuration is not possible.
    D. Open Control Panel Services and edit the Computer Browser Startup tab.

12. Which operating system is going to take precedence in a browser election?
    A. NT Server 3.51
    B. NT Server 4
    C. NT Workstation 4
    D. Either of the Server versions have equal criteria

13. When directory replication occurs, how much information is copied over to import servers?
    A. Initially, the whole directory structure is copied—subsequent imports copy only changes.
    B. The whole directory structure is copied each time.
    C. The directory structure is copied in stages. This prevents excessive traffic on the network.
    D. The entire directory structure is copied once a week. In between, full transfers of changed information are replicated.

14. Where must information be placed for replication to occur?
    A. Folders are placed in *Systemroot*\system32\repl\import.
    B. Folders are placed in *Systemroot*\system32\repl\import\scripts.
    C. Folders are placed in *Systemroot*\system32\repl\export\scripts.
    D. Folders are placed in *Systemroot*\system32\repl\export.

15. What can you use Directory Replication to maintain? Select all that apply.
    A. Directory database information
    B. System Policies
    C. Logon scripts
    D. User profiles

16. What groups should the Directory Replication service account be a member of? Select all that apply.
    A. Administrators
    B. Backup Operators
    C. Power Users
    D. Replicators

17. How do you change the properties of the Directory Replication service?

    A. Make sure it is selected in the Service list; then click Startup.

    B. From the Policy menu in User Manager for Domains.

    C. Run **replication /configure**.

    D. Replication is automatically configured when NT is first installed.

8.3.1 Answers and Explanations: Exercise

In this exercise, you configured the Directory Replication service to automatically replicate logon scripts. You did this from the Services icon in the Control Panel. Before you can configure directory replication, you must create a Directory Replication service account.

Consider setting the Directory Replication service back to a manual start after finishing this exercise. For more information on Directory Replication, review the section titled "Installing Directory Replication Service."

8.3 Answers and Explanations: Practice Problems

1. **B** Services are configured through the Network icon in Control Panel, or by right-clicking Network Neighborhood.
2. **A** Minimize Memory Used if no more than 10 users are going to connect to the machine.
3. **D** Applications running across the network are going to benefit from this if they do not perform memory management themselves.
4. **C** Maximize Throughput for File Sharing is the default selection.
5. **B** Balance is not recommended for more than 64 connections.
6. **C** Workstation is a service not generally configured. If needed, there are some settings in the Registry that can be modified.
7. **B** This service enables a client to request information from a server.
8. **D** The PDC announces changes and the BDCs will request them using the Netlogon service.
9. **B** Browse lists contain machines on the network. DNS servers do have computer names but are resolved to IP addresses and are static.
10. **A** Browse lists are gathered through broadcasts.
11. **B** Browse roles are configured in the Registry.
12. **B** Election criteria includes OS versions, time available, and others.
13. **A** When replication first occurs, the entire structure is copied only after the changed files are replicated out.
14. **D** Files must be placed in Folders under the export folder to replicate.
15. **B, D** Only information that will be applied to a number of users is practical to replicate. Policies and profiles will typically apply to many users on a network.
16. **B, D** The account must be a member of both.
17. **A** Replication is also configured in Server Manager.

8.3 Key Words

Browser election

Directory Replication service

Export server

Import server

Server service

8.4 Configuring Hard Disks to Improve Performance

In Windows NT Server, various hard disk options and fault tolerance options are available to help you improve disk performance. In this section, you look at configuring your system to use the disk options available in Windows NT Server. All hard disk configuring can be done using the Disk Administrator tool. The different disk configurations you need to understand for the enterprise exam are as follows:

- Stripe set
- Volume set
- Disk mirroring
- Stripe set with parity

To start the Disk Administrator, select Start, Programs, Administrative Tools (common), Disk Administrator. When the program is first started, you see a progress bar initializing your hard disk configuration.

A. Configuring a Stripe Set

Implementing a stripe set improves disk performance. Information is written across multiple physical disks and can increase the speed of disk reads and writes.

A stripe set is created from free space on a non-boot or system partition of your hard disks. A stripe set is created using free disk space across multiple physical disks. A stripe set must use equal amounts of disk space on each physical disk. A stripe set requires a minimum of 2 disks and is limited to a maximum of 32 disks.

To create a stripe set, start the Disk Administrator and select the free space from each of the disks to be used in the stripe set. To select multiple disks, hold down Ctrl and click with the mouse on each section. When all the sections have been selected, select Partition, Create Stripe Set. The stripe set is created, and the space is treated as one drive letter.

B. Configuring a Volume Set

A volume set enables you to extend a drive. The partitions can be on multiple physical disks or on the same physical disk. When setting up a volume set, select the free space from all the drives you want to include and then select Partition, Create Volume Set.

After the volume set has been created, you then must format the volume set. To format the drive, select Tools, Format in the Disk Administrator. If formatted with NTFS, you can extend the volume set if more space is required.

To extend a volume set, select the volume set and the free space to be added to it. Then select Partition, Extend Volume Set. The volume set can be extended across the entire disk space, or it can be spread across multiple physical disks and treated as one partition.

Volume sets are discussed on the Windows NT Server exam. They also might be mentioned on the enterprise exam, especially as a question involving extending a volume set. Only an NTFS partition can be extended in a volume set. If the file system is FAT, it cannot be extended.

C. Configuring Disk Mirroring

To establish a disk mirror, you are required to have two physical disks in your NT system. With disk mirroring, you are able to use an existing disk partition—including the system and boot partitions. Disk mirroring provides a duplicate set of your data on a spare disk. To establish a disk mirror, select the drive to mirror, and then select the free space to use on a second physical disk. Select Establish Mirror from the Fault Tolerance menu. The mirror set begins to duplicate all existing information from the first drive onto the mirror copy. Any new data is written to both drives by FTDISK.SYS.

After the disk mirror has been created, you might need to break the mirror. As part of configuration, however, you should know how to break a mirror set. The mirror set is split across two physical disks. Both partitions, however, are labeled E:. To remove or break a mirror set, select the mirror set and then select Break Mirror from the Fault Tolerance menu.

Adding a second controller to the machine will provide extra redundancy. By placing each disk in a mirror set on a separate controller, there is a lesser chance of both disks being made unavailable. This is commonly referred to as *disk duplexing*.

D. Configuring a Stripe Set with Parity

A stripe set with parity writes data and parity information across a minimum of 3 and a maximum of 32 physical disks. If any one of the disks fails, the data can be regenerated from the remaining data and the parity. As with a stripe set, you cannot create a stripe set with parity from an existing partition. By holding down the Ctrl key, you can select multiple sections of free space. Only after the three sections have been selected can you select Create Stripe Set with Parity in the Fault Tolerance menu.

After you select Create Stripe Set with Parity, you are prompted to enter the size of the stripe set with parity. By default, the value shown is the maximum size available. The minimum size also is listed for your information. The stripe set is then configured. In the Disk Administrator, you can see the stripe set is written across multiple physical disks. The legend across the bottom of the Disk Administrator shows which partitions belong to the stripe set with parity.

After the creation of any new partition, you also must format your drive. To format, select the stripe set with parity and then select Format from the Tools menu.

8.4.1 Exercise: Planning for Fault Tolerance Scenarios

This exercise tests your knowledge of recovering from a disk failure with different fault-tolerant partitioning schemes.

The Scenario: The ABC Company wants to install a Windows NT Server that will have the following disks installed:

DISK 0: IDE 2 GB

DISK 1: IDE 2 GB

DISK 2: SCSI 8 GB

DISK 3: SCSI 8 GB

DISK 4: SCSI 8 GB

The following disk partitions are created on the computer:

DISK 0 and DISK 1 are mirrored and Windows NT is installed to the mirrored partitions.

DISK 2, DISK 3, and DISK 4 are members of a stripe set with parity.

Answer the following questions based on disk failure:

1. How would you recover if DISK 1 were to crash?
2. How would you recover if DISK 0 were to crash?
3. How would you recover if DISK 3 were to crash?
4. Can you recover if both DISK 3 and DISK 4 were to crash?
5. How much disk space will be available on the mirror set for storage?
6. How much disk space will be available on the stripe set with parity for storage?

8.4 Practice Problems

1. You have several areas of free space on a hard disk. What is the best way to collect this area for use?

   A. Create a stripe set.

   B. Create a volume set.

   C. Create a new logical drive.

   D. Create a new primary partition.

2. You are running out of space on your NT boot partition and want to make it bigger. How do you do so?

   A. Select an empty section of the disk and extend the NT partition as a volume set.

   B. Select an empty section on another disk and create a stripe set.

   C. Choose a separate disk and mirror the NT partition.

   D. Back up the NT partition, create a larger partition, and restore the data.

3. You want to create a volume set. What is the minimum number of disks required to do so?

   A. 1

   B. 2

   C. 3

   D. 4

4. You want to create a stripe set. What is the minimum number of disks required?

   A. 1

   B. 2

   C. 3

   D. 4

5. You want to create a stripe set with parity. What is the minimum number of disks required?

   A. 1

   B. 2

   C. 3

   D. 4

6. You created a volume set and now need to reclaim part of the space for another drive. What is the best way to do this?

   A. In the Disk Administrator, select the volume set. From the Partition menu, choose to break the volume.

   B. In the Disk Administrator, select the volume set. Right-click the area to be reclaimed and choose to remove it.

   C. Back up the data and delete the volume set; then, re-create the volume and restore the data.

   D. Run FDISK and delete the volume set.

7. How is data written to a volume set?

   A. Each new file is written to a different section.

   B. One volume is filled before the next one is used.

   C. Data is broken up into 64 KB chunks and is evenly spread across the volume.

   D. Data is broken up into 32 KB chunks and is evenly spread across the volume.

8. Disk striping is considered to be which RAID level?

   A. 0

   B. 1

   C. 2

   D. 5

9. Volume sets are which RAID level?

   A. 1

   B. 5

C. 0

D. Volume sets are not any RAID level

10. How many areas of unformatted free space can be combined into one volume set?

 A. 6

 B. 12

 C. 24

 D. 32

11. How many disks can be combined into one stripe set?

 A. 12

 B. 22

 C. 32

 D. 42

12. With what file systems can a volume set be formatted?

 A. FAT, HPFS, NTFS

 B. HPFS, NTFS

 C. FAT, NTFS

 D. FAT, HPFS

13. How many types of hard disks can be used in a stripe set?

 A. SCSI only

 B. IDE only

 C. ESDI or SCSI or IDE

 D. A combination of disk types can be used

14. What type of fault tolerance can contain a system or boot partition?

 A. RAID 0

 B. RAID 1

 C. RAID 5

 D. RAID cannot be used on a system or boot partition

15. With what file systems can a stripe set be formatted?

 A. FAT, HPFS, NTFS

 B. HPFS, NTFS

 C. FAT, NTFS

 D. FAT, HPFS

16. With what file system can a volume set be formatted to extend it?

 A. FAT

 B. NTFS

 C. FAT or NTFS

 D. HPFS

17. How many partitions can removable media contain?

 A. 2

 B. 3

 C. 4

 D. 1

18. What does an administrator need to do to add another hard disk to the system?

 A. Run WINNT and choose to update.

 B. Nothing; NT will automatically detect the new disk.

 C. Run the Disk Administrator and choose Update from the Disk menu.

 D. In the Control Panel, go to the System icon and then to the Hardware Profiles tab.

19. You have formatted your D: drive with NTFS and need it to be FAT without losing data. What is the best method to do this?

 A. From a command prompt, type **Convert d: /fs:NTFS**.

 B. From a command prompt, type **Format d: /fs:NTFS"**.

C. Back up the D: drive to tape. Format the drive with FAT and restore the data.

D. You cannot restore a drive to FAT after it is NTFS.

20. Your computer has two hard disks installed in a master/slave combination. On the first disk you have two primary partitions and one extended partition with three logical drives. On the second disk you have one primary partition and one extended partition with two logical drives. What arc name would appear in the BOOT.INI file if Windows NT were installed in the default directory on the second logical drive of the first disk?

A. multi(0)disk(0)rdisk(0)partition(4)\WINNT

B. multi(1)disk(0)rdisk(0)partition(4)\WINNT

C. multi(0)disk(0)rdisk(0)partition(3)\WINNT

D. multi(1)disk(0)rdisk(0)partition(3)\WINNT

21. Your computer has two hard disks installed in a master/slave combination. On the first disk you have two primary partitions and one extended partition with three logical drives. On the second disk you have one primary partition and one extended partition with two logical drives. What arc name would appear in the BOOT.INI file if Windows NT were installed in the default directory on the primary partition of the second disk?

A. multi(0)disk(0)rdisk(0)partition(0)\WINNT

B. multi(1)disk(0)rdisk(0)partition(0)\WINNT

C. multi(0)disk(0)rdisk(1)partition(1)\WINNT

D. multi(1)disk(0)rdisk(1)partition(1)\WINNT

22. Your computer has two hard disks installed in a master/slave combination. On the first disk you have two primary partitions and one extended partition with three logical drives. On the second disk you have one primary partition and one extended partition with two logical drives. What arc name would appear in the BOOT.INI file if Windows NT were installed in the default directory on the second logical drive on the second disk?

A. multi(0)disk(0)rdisk(1)partition(3)\WINNT

B. multi(1)disk(0)rdisk(0)partition(2)\WINNT

C. multi(1)disk(0)rdisk(0)partition(3)\WINNT

D. multi(1)disk(0)rdisk(1)partition(7)\WINNT

23. After adding a new partition, NT will no longer boot. What needs to be done to correct the problem?

A. Edit the BOOT.INI file to reflect the new partition numbering.

B. Run WINNT and change the partition information.

C. Select MS-DOS from the Boot menu. At the C:\ prompt, copy the NTOSKRNL file to the boot partition.

D. You must reinstall NT.

24. You have installed NT on a FAT partition (D:) and want the partition to be NTFS. How do you change it?

A. From the command prompt, type **Convert D: /FS:ntfs**. This will immediately start the conversion.

B. From the command prompt, type **Convert D: /FS:ntfs**. This will start the conversion the next time NT is started.

8

C. From the command prompt, type **Format D: /FS:ntfs**. This will immediately start the conversion.

D. Back up the data, and then reformat the drive to NTFS and restore the data.

25. You have three drives with extra space on them. One has 400 MB, another has 500 MB, and a third has 300 MB. What is the largest stripe set that can be created?

    A. 1,200 MB

    B. 1,500 MB

    C. 900 MB

    D. 500 MB

26. You have three drives with extra space on them. One has 400 MB, another has 500 MB, and a third has 300 MB. What is the largest volume set that can be created?

    A. 1,200 MB

    B. 1,500 MB

    C. 900 MB

    D. 600 MB

27. A user is complaining that he has lost all of his long filenames. He is currently running Office 97 and using Norton Utilities 5.0. What might have caused the problem?

    A. The user converted from FAT to NTFS and all LFNs are lost during a conversion.

    B. The use of the third-party disk utilities included with Norton Utilities 5.0 has destroyed the LFN entries.

    C. The user has been moving files from an NTFS to a FAT partition.

    D. Long filenames were supported only under Windows 3.1

28. Which RAID level provides the better I/O performance?

    A. Mirror sets.

    B. Stripe sets with parity.

    C. Mirror and stripe sets with parity offer equal I/O performance benefits.

    D. Mirror and stripe sets with parity offer no I/O performance increase.

29. Which RAID level provides the better read performance?

    A. Mirror sets.

    B. Stripe sets with parity.

    C. Mirror and stripe sets with parity offer equal read performance benefits.

    D. Mirror and stripe sets with parity offer no read performance increase.

30. Your computer has four hard disks with the following amounts of free disk space: 250 MB, 400 MB, 450 MB, and 500 MB. What is the largest usable space that can be created with a stripe set with parity using any combination of the four hard disks?

    A. 1,000 MB

    B. 750 MB

    C. 1,200 MB

    D. 800 MB

8.4.1 Answers and Explanations: Exercise

1. How would you recover if DISK 1 were to crash? If DISK 1 were to crash, you would probably still be able to boot the system as the primary hard disk will still be functioning. You would have to break the mirror set using the Disk Administrator program. After the mirror is broken, you could replace the defective drive and re-establish the mirror set.

2. How would you recover if DISK 0 were to crash? If DISK 0 were to crash, you would not be able to boot the computer as the primary boot disk has failed. You would need to create a fault-tolerant boot disk and have the BOOT.INI file on this disk point to the Windows NT installation on DISK 1. After you have booted the computer, you could use the Disk Administrator program to break the mirror partition, re-assign Disk 1 the original drive letter that the mirror set used, replace the defective drive, and re-establish the mirror.

3. How would you recover if DISK 3 were to crash? If DISK 3 were to crash, you would still be able to work with the data. A stripe set with parity will make use of its parity information to rebuild the data stored on the failed drive. After DISK 3 is diagnosed as being the failed drive, a new SCSI 8 GB disk will need to be installed. Using the Disk Administrator program, you can then regenerate the stripe set with parity using the Disk Administrator program

4. Could you recover if both DISK 3 and DISK 4 were to crash? If both DISK 3 and DISK 4 were to crash, you could only resort to restoring the data from a recent tape backup. Stripe sets with parity only protect against a single-disk failure.

5. How much disk space will be available on the mirror set for storage? The mirror set will have 2 GB of available disk space.

6. How much disk space will be available on the stripe set with parity for storage? The stripe set with parity will have 16 GB of usable disk space. 8 GB will be used to maintain parity information.

8.4 Answers and Explanations: Practice Problems

1. **B** Volume sets can take areas on the same disk and collect them into a larger drive.

2. **D** Volume sets and stripe sets are not supported on system or boot partitions.

3. **A** Because areas on the same disk can be used in a volume, only one disk is required.

4. **B** A striped set requires a minimum of two disks.

5. **C** Because parity information is written across all disks, a minimum of three disks is needed.

6. **C** The only way to retrieve space from a volume set is to delete and recreate the volume. Make sure to back up any needed data before reformatting.

7. **B** One area on the volume is filled before another one is used.

8. **A** Disk striping will not provide any fault tolerance and is considered to be RAID 0.

9. **D** Volumes are not part of RAID.

10. **D** Up to 32 areas can be used in one volume set.

11. **C** Up to 32 disks can be combined.

12. **C** A volume can be created and formatted with FAT or NTFS.

13. **D** A combination of disk types may be used.

14. **B** Only Disk Mirroring can be used on a system or boot partition.

15. **C** A stripe set can be created and formatted with FAT or NTFS.

16. **B** Only NTFS can be used on an extended volume.

17. **D** Only one partition on removable media is supported.

18. **B** NT will recognize the new drive when the computer is back on line.

19. **C** FAT can be converted to NTFS but not the other way around.

20. **A** The Arc Name that would appear in the BOOT.INI that would represent the second logical drive on the first disk would be multi(0)disk(0)rdisk(0)partition(4)\WINNT. Remember that all primary partitions are first assigned numbers and then the logical drives are assigned numbers. Partitions start numbering at 1.

21. **C** Remember that the second disk is a slave disk on the first controller. The Arc Name would be multi(0)disk(0)rdisk(1)partition(1)\WINNT.

22. **A** The slave disk would be represented as RDISK(1), and the second logical drive on this disk would be represented as partition(3) on the second disk.

23. **A** The BOOT.INI file uses ARC paths to locate NT.

24. **B** Because the Boot partition is in use, it can't be converted until the machine is restarted.

25. **C** Stripe sets require that each area is of similar size.

26. **A** A volume set can use various sized areas to create a new drive.

27. **B** Third-party disk programs will not recognize the secondary directory entries that store the LFNs and will attempt to "fix" them. This results in the loss of long filenames.

28. **B** Stripe sets with parity result in better I/O performance due to the use of additional disk controllers.

29. **B** With multiple disks read operations will be faster.

30. **D** The largest usable disk space that can be created is 800 MB. This is created by using 400 MB from the three disks with free space greater than 400 MB. Remember that 400 MB of the total 1,200 MB is used to store parity information in case of data loss.

8.4 Key Words

Stripe set

Volume set

Disk mirroring RAID level 1

Stripe set with parity RAID level 5

Disk Administrator

8.5 Configuring Printers

In this section, you examine the options available for configuring a printer. You also go through the installation steps required to configure a network printer.

All the settings for installing and configuring printers are found by clicking the Printer icon in My Computer or by selecting Start, Settings, Printers. The Printers dialog box contains all of your installed printers as well as an icon used for installing new printers. To configure an existing printer, right-click the printer and select Properties from the shortcut menu.

A. Adding a Printer

Add printers in Windows NT by accessing the Add Printer Wizard. When adding a printer, you must follow these steps:

1. Make sure the print device is on the Hardware Compatibility List (HCL) or have the driver for your printer available.
2. Log on to the system as a user with Print Operator, Administrator, or Server Operator access privileges.
3. Run the Add Printer Wizard and follow all prompts.

When installing a printer in a Windows NT system, you can connect to an existing network printer, or install your own printer and share it with other computers. To add a new printer to your computer, follow these steps:

1. Double-click the Add Printer icon to start the Add Printer Wizard.
2. Select whether you are installing a printer on your computer or connecting to a network printer server. For example, select the My Computer option and click Next.
3. Select the port on which you're installing your printer and click Next.
4. You are then prompted to select the manufacturer and model of your print device from the list boxes. You can click Have Disk if your print device is not listed and you have the printer driver for the computer. After your printer has been selected, click Next to continue.
5. Assign a name for your printer. The default is the printer model name, but you can assign any name to the actual printer. Then specify whether you want your Windows programs to use this printer as the default printer.
6. If you want to share your printer with other users on the network, assign a share name and select which client operating systems can access your shared printer. If you are not sharing the printer, select Not shared. After the screen has been completed, click Next to continue.
7. Finally, you get the option to print a test page to verify that your printer is communicating properly. Select the appropriate test option and click Finish.

The printer driver is now installed. If you are prompted for the location of the NT source files, enter the directory that contains the printer driver.

B. Connecting to an Existing Network Printer

If you are adding an existing network printer to your system, you can use the Add Printer Wizard to configure the printer with the following steps:

1. Start the Add Printer Wizard by double-clicking the Add Printer icon.
2. Select the Network printer server option and click Next.
3. Enter the network path to the network printer or select it from the Shared Printers list. When you have located the network printer, click OK to continue.
4. Select whether to use this printer as your default Windows printer, then click Next.
5. Click Finish and the printer driver is installed. You also can assign a name to this printer.

C. Implementing a Printer Pool

A printer pool enables one print driver to send documents to multiple print devices. Up to eight print devices can be combined to use the same printer driver and print spooler. This method can help to meet your organization's printing needs and to speed up the printing process. To implement a printer pool, follow these steps:

1. Double-click the Add Printer icon.
2. Select My Computer for the location or management of the printer pool and click Next.
3. When selecting the port for your printer pool, you must select all ports to be managed by this printer. The order the printer will use to send documents to the print device depends on which ports are selected first. Make sure you enable the printer pooling option in the lower-left corner of the dialog box first.

If you need to configure a jet-direct printer or other network-based printers not connected to your physical computer, click the Add Port option. Select the appropriate printer port to establish your connection. After all the ports have been configured and selected, click Next to continue with the installation. Continue by following these steps:

1. Select the printer driver to be used by all the printers in your printer pool and click Next.
2. Assign a printer name to the printer pool. Specify whether this printer pool should be your default Windows printer and click Next.
3. Share the printer with clients. Make sure all operating systems that can connect are selected. By selecting all the operating systems, your clients do not need to load the driver locally. When they first make a connection to the network printer, the printer driver is copied locally to their computer system.
4. After all the Wizard dialog boxes have been completed, click Finish. The printer driver is now loaded, and your printer is ready for use.

All of the printers in a printer pool must be able to use the same printer driver.

8.5.1 Exercise: Adding a Printer in a Windows NT Server 4 Environment

In this exercise, you add a printer and share it so others in your domain can access it as a network printer.

1. Select Start, Settings, Printers.
2. Double-click the Add Printers icon.
3. Enable the My Computer radio button and click Next.
4. Under Available ports, select the LPT1 check box. Click Next to continue.
5. Under Manufacturers, select HP (Hewlett Packard).
6. Under Printers, select the HP LaserJet 4. Click Next to continue.
7. In the Printer name box, enter **HP LaserJet 4** and click Next.
8. Enable the Shared radio button.
9. In the Share Name box, enter **Laser** and click Next.
10. When asked if you want to print a test page, select No and click Finish.
11. You should now see the HP LaserJet 4 icon in the Printers dialog box.
12. To view the print queue for the HP LaserJet 4 printer, double-click the printer's icon.
13. This dialog box is where all print jobs are transferred. The printer also can be paused from this screen.
14. Close the Printers dialog box.

8.5.2 Exercise: Creating a Printer Pool in Windows NT Server 4

8

In this exercise, you install and configure a printer pool on your Windows NT Server.

1. Select Start, Settings, Printers.
2. Double-click the HP LaserJet 4 printer icon.
3. Select Printer, Pause Printing.
4. Close the HP LaserJet 4 dialog box.
5. Right-click the HP LaserJet 4 printer icon and select Properties.
6. Select the Ports tab.
7. Turn on the Enable Printer Pooling option.
8. Click LPT2, but make sure LPT1 is still selected.
9. Click OK.

With printer pooling enabled, the print jobs can be redirected to any of the ports configured in the printer pool.

8.5 Practice Problems

1. What is the default permission granted to the Everyone group with Printer Permissions?

   A. Manage documents

   B. Print

   C. Full Control

   D. Creator Owner

2. Who can install a printer on a Domain Controller?

   A. Administrators, Power Users, and Print Operators

   B. Administrators, Power Users, and Server Operators

   C. Administrators, Server Operators, and Print Operators

   D. Administrators

3. After sharing a network printer for Windows NT and 95 clients, what else needs to be done to allow NT Workstation clients to use the printer?

   A. Users just connect to the printer.

   B. Users must right-click the printer under network neighborhood and choose to configure it to the appropriate port.

   C. Users must install a printer driver locally.

   D. Nothing else needs to be done. The printer will automatically be available for use.

4. For DOS-based clients using LAN Manager, what is the syntax to point LPT1 to the correct network location?

   A. `Capture quename`

   B. `lpr -Sserver_name -Pshare_name`

   C. `net use LPT1 = \\server_name\share_name`

   D. `net use LPT \\server_name\share_name`

5. When Joe prints, he needs his documents to be processed as soon as possible. Where should you set a printer priority and what should it be?

   A. In User Manager for Domains, edit Joe's account and set the priority to 99.

   B. In User Manager for Domains, edit Joe's account and set the priority to 1.

   C. Go to the Printer properties for each of the printers using the Print device and, on the Security tab, set Joe's account to use priority 99.

   D. Go to the Scheduling tab on the properties of the printer that Joe is using and set the priority to 99.

6. By default, who can take ownership of a printer?

   A. Only the Administrator

   B. Everyone

   C. Administrators, Print Operators, and Server Operators

   D. Creator Owner

7. What clients can access an NT printer? Select all that apply.

   A. Macintosh

   B. NetWare

   C. OS/2 (with LAN Manager 2.2C)

   D. Windows 3.1

8. When do you want to create a printer pool?

   A. When all of your print devices are identical and are located in the same general area. Some printers are used more heavily and you want to balance the load.

   B. When print devices are dissimilar and need to be grouped together.

   C. When employees are in different buildings, but all use the same kind of print devices.

D. When identical print devices are located in each wing of a building.

E. When some printers are used more heavily and you want to balance the load.

9. What permission is necessary for users to delete their own documents?

A. Assign each user the Print permission, and then they can delete their own documents.

B. Only Administrators with Full Control can delete a document.

C. Creator Owner with the Manage Document permission.

D. Creator Owner with Print permission.

10. To connect to a shared network printer, a user can do which of the following? Select all that apply.

A. Browse Network Neighborhood and right-click a printer to install it.

B. Use the Add Printer Wizard and choose Local Printer and install the printer.

C. Use the Add Printer Wizard and choose Network Printer and install the printer.

D. The administrator will need to install printers on workstations.

8.5.1 Answers and Explanations: Exercise

In this exercise, you added a printer and shared it so others in your domain could access it as a network printer. To do this, you chose Settings, Printers, and then selected the Add Printers icon. For more information on adding printers, review the section titled "Adding a Printer."

8.5.2 Answers and Explanations: Exercise

In this exercise, you installed and configured a printer pool on your Windows NT Server. The printer pool enables you to redirect the print jobs to any of the ports configured in the printer pool. For more information on adding printer pools, review the section titled "Implementing a Printer Pool."

8.5 Answers and Explanations: Practice Problems

1. **B** Unlike shared folder permissions, which give everyone Full Control, printer permissions allow Print.

2. **C** Administrators, Server Operators, and Print Operators may install printers.

3. **A** A user may connect to a printer to install the driver.

4. **D** `net use LPT \\server_name\share_name`.

5. **D** Priorities are set on the Print Properties.

6. **C** Anyone with Full Control can take ownership.

7. **A, B, C, D** NT will allow a variety of clients to connect.

8. **A** Printer pools are most effective with similar printers in close proximity.

9. **C** By default, the Creator Owners can delete their own documents.

10. **A, C** If users have permissions to use a printer, they just need to browse to it to gain access.

8.5 Key Words

Printer

Print device

Printer pool

Network printer

Local printer

8.6 Configuring Windows NT Server for Various Types of Clients

Your Windows NT Server is the selected server for various client operating systems. In this section, you look at the configuration requirements for the following:

- Windows NT Workstation clients
- Windows 95 clients
- Macintosh clients

Windows NT Server handles all the requests from each of these clients automatically. The Windows NT Workstation and Windows 95 clients use Windows NT logon security and provide complete functionality as a Windows NT client right out of the box. To enable connectivity with Apple Macintosh computers, the services for the Macintosh must be installed. The Network Client Administrator can be used to simplify the installation of your client computers.

The Network Client Administrator is found in the Administrative Tools group. You can use the Network Client Administrator program to do the following:

- **Make a network installation startup disk.** This option requires an MS-DOS boot disk. It will install the necessary files to connect to the network and start an installation of your client software.
- **Make an installation disk set.** This option enables the creation of installation disks for the DOS network client, LAN Manager 2.2c for DOS, or LAN Manager 2.2c for OS/2.
- **Copy client-based Network Administration Tools.** This option enables you to share the network administration tools with client computers. The client computers that can use the network administration tools are Windows NT Workstation and Windows 95 computers.
- **View remoteboot client information.** This option enables you to view the remoteboot client information. To install remoteboot, go to the Services tab of the Network dialog box.

A. Windows NT Workstation Clients

Windows NT Workstation computers require a computer account to be created in order to join a domain. The computer account is then used by the Remote Procedure Call (RPC) service to make a secured communication. This verifies when the computer is started and can be used for monitoring services on your NT Workstation computer. Windows NT Workstation can be installed as a standalone system and then, in the Network dialog box, joined to the domain. You must, however, have Account Operator or Administrator access, or be assigned the User Right "Add Workstations to the Domain" to create this computer account. If you want to create the computer account in the Windows NT Server computer, you can use Server Manager.

After you have a Windows NT Workstation client configured, the users and the client computer can use the Windows NT security. You also can install the client-based Network Administration Tools. These tools enable you to manage your Windows NT Server from your Windows NT Workstation client computer.

The system requirements for installing the Windows NT Workstation server tools are as follows:

- Windows NT Workstation must be installed.
- It must have a 486DX/33 or higher processor.
- A minimum of 12 MB RAM is needed.
- There must be 2.5 MB of free disk space in the system partition.
- The Workstation and Server service must be installed on the NT Workstation computer.

The tools found in the Windows NT Workstation Server are listed in Table 8.6.1.

Table 8.6.1 Windows NT Workstation Server Tools

Tools	Use this Tool To...
Server Manager	Manage Windows NT-based computers and domain controllers.
User Manager	Manage users, groups, and user rights for Windows for Domains NT domains.
WINS Manager	Administer the WINS servers.
DHCP Manager	Administer the DHCP servers.
Remote Access Admin	Administer the remote access service on a computer running Windows NT.
Service for Macintosh	Share Windows NT resources with Macintosh clients.
System Policy Editor	Modify and maintain user and system policies.

B. Windows 95 Clients

Using the Network Client Administrator program, you can create an automated installation from a floppy disk. Any installation of Windows 95 with a Microsoft Network client loaded, however, can be configured to log on to a Windows NT domain. This can be configured in the Network properties of a Windows 95 computer.

8

Windows 95 also has server tools available to enable Windows 95 computers to administer a Windows NT system. The system requirements for the Windows 95 computer to use the server tools are as follows:

- Windows 95 must be installed.
- A 486DX/33 or higher processor is required.
- A minimum of 8 MB of RAM is required.
- There must be 3 MB of free disk space available at the system partition.
- The client for Microsoft networks must be installed.

C. Macintosh Clients

For Windows NT to integrate with Apple Macintosh clients, you must first install Services for Macintosh on your Windows NT Server. Services for Macintosh enable file and print sharing between the Macintosh clients and the Windows NT Server. The Windows NT Server also is able to share Macintosh printers with the other clients of Windows NT Server. When Services for Macintosh is installed, the AppleTalk protocol is installed as well.

1. Server and Client Requirements

A few requirements must be met prior to installing Services for Macintosh onto your network. The requirements for the Windows NT Server computer are as follows:

- 2 MB of free disk space
- An NTFS partition to be used as the Macintosh volume

Requirements for the Macintosh computer are as follows:

- Version 6.0.8 or later of the Macintosh operating system
- Version 2.0 of the AppleTalk Filing Protocol
- Network cards that enable connectivity into the same network as the Windows NT Server system

2. Installing Services for Macintosh

To install Services for Macintosh, open the Network dialog box of your Windows NT system. Change to the Services tab and click Add to add a new service. Services for Macintosh should be found in the list of available services. Select Services for Macintosh and click OK. Services for Macintosh is installed automatically, and you are prompted to restart your system.

8.6.1 Exercise: Setting Up a Central Network Share

This exercise reviews the steps necessary to set up a central network share for the installation of client software. This exercise will create the installation disks for the MS-DOS client.

1. Log in as the Administrator of your Windows NT Server.
2. Install the Windows NT Server CD-ROM.
2. Select Start, Programs, Administrative Tools, Network Client Administrator.
3. From the Network Client Administrator dialog box, select the option to Make Installation Disk Set. Click the Continue button.
4. In the Share Network Client Installation Files dialog box, you must configure where the Client directory is located. If your CD-ROM is drive letter Z:, this would be Z:\Clients. Click the Use Existing Path option and click OK to continue.

You also can use this dialog box to create a network share for the client installation files. This process will copy the clients directory from the CD-ROM to a network share location. This directory will need about 64 MB of disk space.

5. From the Make Installation Disk Set dialog box, select the Network Client v3.0 for MS-DOS and Windows option. Select the format disks check box and click OK.
6. When prompted, insert each of the required disks. These can now be used to install the DOS client software on a system.

8.6 Practice Problems

1. The client Network Administration Tools are available for which operating systems on the Windows NT 4 Server CD-ROM? Select all that apply.
   - A. Windows for Workgroups
   - B. Windows 95
   - C. Windows NT Workstation
   - D. DOS

2. Which tools are available for network administration when the Network Administration Tools are installed on a Windows 95 client system? Select all that apply.
   - A. Event Viewer
   - B. DHCP Manager
   - C. User Manager for Domains
   - D. Server Manager

3. Which tools are installed when the Network Administration Tools are added to a Windows NT Workstation computer? Select all that apply.
   - A. Event Viewer
   - B. DHCP Manager
   - C. User Manager for Domains
   - D. Server Manager

4. How do you install the Windows 95 Network Administration Tools?
   - A. Run SETUP.EXE from the CD:\Clients\srvtools\win95 directory.
   - B. Right-click the SRVTOOLS.INF file in the CD:\clients\srvtools\win95 directory and choose install.
   - C. Use the Add/Remove programs applet in Control Panel and run SETUP.EXE from there.
   - D. Use the Add/Remove programs applet in Control Panel and use the Have Disk option to point to the CD:\clients\srvtools\win95 directory.

5. How do you install the Windows NT Workstation Network Administration Tools?
   - A. Run SETUP.BAT from the CD:\Clients\srvtools\winnt directory.
   - B. Right-click the SRVTOOLS.INF file in the CD:\clients\srvtools\winnt directory and choose install.
   - C. Use the Add/Remove programs applet in Control Panel and run SETUP.BAT from there.
   - D. Use the Add/Remove programs applet in Control Panel and use the Have Disk option to point to the CD:\clients\srvtools\winnt directory.

6. What manual configuration step must be performed on a Windows 95 client when the Network Administration Tools are installed?
   - A. All icons must be created for the Network Administration Tools.
   - B. Security must be set to use User level security on the Windows 95 system.
   - C. C:\srvtools must be added to the path.
   - D. No manual configuration must be performed.

7. What print data type is used when a Macintosh client sends a print job to a network-shared HP LaserJet II non-postscript printer?
   - A. RAW
   - B. EMF
   - C. PSCRIPT1
   - D. You cannot print to a PCL printer with a Macintosh client. Macintosh clients can print only to PostScript printers.

8. Which Network Client Administrator program option is used to install TCP/IP support for a Windows for Workgroups client?

   A. Make a network installation startup disk

   B. Make an installation disk set

   C. Copy client-based network administration tools

   D. View remoteboot client information

9 Which protocols can be used by an MS-DOS v3.0 network client? Select all that apply.

   A. NetBEUI

   B. IPX/SPX

   C. TCP/IP

   D. DLC

10. What file formats are supported for Macintosh Accessible Volumes?

   A. FAT

   B. NTFS

   C. HPFS

   D. FAT and NTFS

8.6.1 Answers and Explanations: Exercise

This exercise reviewed the steps necessary to set up a central network share for the installation of client software and created the installation disks for the MS-DOS client. For more information about setting up central network shares, review the section titled "Windows NT Workstation Clients."

8.6 Answers and Explanations: Practice Problems

1. **B, C** The Windows NT Server 4 CD-ROM ships with Network Administration Tools for Windows 95 and Windows NT Workstation. You also can administer Windows NT using Windows for Workgroups. The client software is available on the Windows NT Server 3.51 CD-ROM.

2. **A, C, D** You cannot perform DHCP administration from a Windows 95 system running the Network Administration Tools.

3. **B, C, D** The Event Viewer is already included with Windows NT Workstation administrative tools.

4. **D** The Network Administration Tools are added using the Add/Remove Programs applet in Windows 95.

5. **A** The Network Administration Tools are installed using SETUP.BAT on Windows NT Workstation. The batch file determines the platform that Windows NT Workstation is running on and then installs the correct version of the files.

6. **C** The directory where the Network Administration Tools are installed (C:\srvtools) must be added to the path to use the Explorer extensions.

7. **C** The job data type would be PSCRIPT1. The PostScript information is translated into bitmaps that are downloaded to the PCL printer.

8. **B** Using the Make an installation disk set option, you can create the TCP/IP 32B for Windows for Workgroups installation disks.

9. **A, B, C** All of the standard protocols can be used with the MS-DOS client software.

10. **B** MAC-accessible volumes must be formatted using NTFS.

8.6 Key Words

Network Client Administrator

Services for Macintosh

Network Administration Tools

Practice Exam: Installation and Configuration

Use this practice exam to test your mastery of Chapter 8, "Installation and Configuration." This practice exam is 37 questions long. The passing Microsoft score is 76.4 percent. Questions are in multiple-choice format.

1. Your company currently is running Windows NT Server in a single-domain model. You are finding that logon requests are very slow, and you want to install a new server into your network to help handle logon requests. What type of server should you install into your environment?
   A. File and Print server
   B. Primary Domain Controller
   C. Backup Domain Controller
   D. Member Server

2. What is the name of the setup program used for an upgrade installation of Windows NT Server 3.51 to 4?
   A. SETUP.EXE
   B. SETUP32.EXE
   C. WINNT.EXE
   D. WINNT32.EXE

3. What is the name of the setup program if you are not installing from a 32-bit operating system?
   A. SETUP.EXE
   B. SETUP32.EXE
   C. WINNT.EXE
   D. WINNT32.EXE

4. You can upgrade Windows NT Server when installed as a Member Server to a domain controller under what circumstances?
   A. The Member Server was installed with NT 3.51.
   B. The Member Server was installed with NT.
   C. It is not possible to upgrade NT servers from one server type to another.
   D. Reinstalling is the only way to upgrade Member Servers to domain controllers.

5. What action would you take if you needed to take your Primary Domain Controller down for repairs, and you wanted to set up one of your Backup Domain Controllers to act as the PDC?
   A. Demote the PDC, and then promote the BDC to take its place.
   B. Just turn off the PDC. The first BDC to detect the absence of a PDC will automatically be promoted to a PDC.
   C. Demote the PDC. This will automatically promote the BDC.
   D. Promote a BDC. This will automatically demote the PDC.

8

6. What service is used to send a copy of the SAM database from the PDC to the BDCs?
   A. Netlogon
   B. Redirector
   C. Replication
   D. Alert service

7. Which of the following network protocols are supported by Windows NT Server? Select all that apply.
   A. TCP/IP
   B. XNS
   C. AppleTalk
   D. DLC

8. What network protocol can be used to connect to the Internet?

   A. NWLink IPX/SPX

   B. AppleTalk

   C. DLC

   D. TCP/IP

9. What configuration options are mandatory when installing TCP/IP?

   A. DNS and IP address

   B. Default gateway and subnet mask

   C. IP address and subnet mask

   D. IP address and default gateway

10. What is the function of the default gateway?

    A. To translate IPX packets to TCP/IP.

    B. To route TCP/IP packets outside of your physical network to TCP/IP hosts on remote subnets.

    C. To allow for automatic assignment of TCP/IP addresses to clients.

    D. To identify the Host and Network portions of the IP address.

11. What service enables automatic configuration of IP addresses for client computers?

    A. DHCP

    B. WINS

    C. DNS

    D. Internet Explorer

12. What service must be installed to configure the AppleTalk protocol?

    A. Macintosh Gateway service

    B. LocalTalk

    C. Services for Apple

    D. Services for Macintosh

13. What is the function of the Server service?

    A. To route requests for information to local or network locations

    B. To handle incoming network communication

    C. To ensure information from the Security accounts database will be copied from the PDC to the BDC

    D. To register computer names

14. What is the default import directory for the Directory Replication Service?

    A. *%systemroot%*\system32\repl\export

    B. *%systemroot%*\system32\repl\import\scripts

    C. *%systemroot%*\repl\import

    D. *%systemroot%*\repl\import\scripts

15. You have three computers that you want to put into a printer pool. The printers are an HP LaserJet 4, an IBM Lexmark, and a Panasonic dot matrix. What will be the best way to do this?

    A. Install the dot matrix printer driver and configure the pool.

    B. Install an HP Series II printer driver and configure the pool.

    C. Install each printer driver appropriately and make all of them printer pools.

    D. You cannot configure these three printers to participate in a printer pool.

16. Mary is trying to add a new NT Workstation to her NT Domain. What is the maximum number of characters allowed?

    A. 14

    B. 20

    C. 15

    D. 10

17. Harry has installed a new NT Workstation computer. The next morning the machine starts up with the error "One or more services failed to start." Where should Harry go to try and troubleshoot the problem?

    A. Server Manager

    B. Event viewer

    C. NT diagnostics

    D. Disk Administrator

18. In the Directory Replication service, which types of computers can act as export computers? Select all that apply.

    A. Windows NT Server computers (domain controllers only)

    B. Windows NT Workstation computers

    C. Windows NT Server computers

    D. Windows 95 computers

19. To enable Macintosh users to store files on a Windows NT Server computer, what must be installed?

    A. GSNW

    B. Services for Macintosh

    C. WINS

    D. DNS

20. What is the disk-partitioning scheme that enables equal areas of disk space from 2 to 32 physical drives to be combined into one logical drive?

    A. Volume set

    B. Stripe set with parity

    C. Stripe set

    D. Mirror set

21. What type of disk system makes an exact copy of all data from one disk to another disk?

    A. Stripe set with parity

    B. Stripe set

    C. Volume set

    D. Mirror set

22. Select the types of disk systems that are fault tolerant.

    A. Volume sets

    B. Disk striping

    C. Disk striping with parity

    D. Disk mirroring

23. What is the name of the utility used to implement fault tolerance in Windows NT Server?

    A. User Manager for Domains

    B. Server Manager

    C. Disk Administrator

    D. Control Panel

24. You installed Windows NT Server 4, but during the installation process, you selected Server as the type of installation. You now want to make the server a Backup Domain Controller. What must you do to convert the server?

    A. Run the Convert command.

    B. Do nothing. The Member Server can act as a domain controller.

    C. Reinstall Windows NT Server as a domain controller.

    D. Under Control Panel, Network, change the server type to Backup Domain Controller.

25. What is the main difference between an NT Server installed as a domain controller and an NT Server not installed as a domain controller?

    A. A domain controller maintains a copy of the domain directory database; a non-domain controller does not.

    B. A non-domain controller validates user logons; a domain controller does not.

C. A domain controller is best suited to an application server role in the network.

D. There is no difference in the domain controller and the non-domain controller.

26. To set up a printer pool, which of the following criteria must be met? Select all that apply.

A. All printers should be in the same general area.

B. The printers should be able to use the same printer driver.

C. The printers must be managed by the same print server.

D. The printer must be connected to the same type of port.

27. How do you install a new printer? Select all that apply.

A. Select Start, Settings, Printers. Click the Add Printers icon.

B. Start Print Manager and add the printer from the Printer menu.

C. Open Control Panel and click the Printer icon; then double-click the Add Printer icon.

D. Run the Windows NT Setup program and install the printer under the Configuration menu.

28. How do you configure a network protocol in Windows NT Server? Select all that apply.

A. Select Start, Settings, Control Panel. Double-click the Network icon.

B. Right-click the Network Neighborhood icon and select the Properties.

C. From Server Manager.

D. From the Network Client Administrator.

29. If you want to convert your C: drive from FAT to NTFS as the file system, what is the correct syntax?

A. Format C: /FS:NTFS

B. Convert /FAT:NTFS

C. Convert C: /FS:NTFSD.

D. You cannot convert FAT to NTFS

30. What is the amount of usable space provided by a stripe set with parity consisting of four disks and the smallest open space being 300 MB?

A. 600 MB

B. 1,200 MB

C. 900 MB

D. 1,500 MB

31. When a drive that is part of a mirror fails, how can you make the system available again?

A. Open the computer case and physically swap out the drives, and then from the Fault Tolerance menu of the Disk Administrator, break the mirror.

B. Use a Fault Tolerance boot disk to start the mirrored drive, and then from the Fault Tolerance menu of the Disk Administrator, break the mirror.

C. Use a Fault Tolerance boot disk to start the mirrored driver, and then from the Partition menu of the Disk Administrator, break the mirror.

D. Boot to DOS and edit the BOOT.INI.

32. What files are required on a Fault Tolerance boot disk?

A. COMMAND.COM, IO.SYS, MSDOS.SYS

B. Ntldr, Ntoskrnl, BOOT.INI

C. Ntldr, NTDETECT.COM, BOOT.INI

D. COMMAND.COM, BOOTSECT.DOS

33. What file is required on a Fault Tolerance boot disk using a SCSI controller with the BIOS disabled?

A. OSLOADER.EXE

B. NTBOOTDD.SYS

C. Ntoskrnl

D. HAL.DLL

34. What happens if a stripe set with parity has a failed member?

A. Nothing; performance will continue unchanged.

B. The drive will continue to work; however, the system performance will slow.

C. The drive will not work until replaced.

D. An NT dialog box will let the administrator know of the problem.

35. If an ARC path reads `Multi(0)disk(0)rdisk(1)partition(3)`, it means which of the following?

A. NT is on the 1st controller, 1st disk, 4th partition.

B. NT is on the 1st controller, 1st disk, 3rd partition.

C. Would not be a possible ARC path.

D. NT is on the 1st controller, 2nd disk, 3rd partition.

36. If an ARC path reads `scsi(0)disk(0)rdisk(0)partition(3)`, it means which of the following?

A. NT is on the 1st controller, 1st disk, 4th partition.

B. NT is on the 1st controller, 1st disk, 3rd partition.

C. Would not be a possible ARC path.

D. NT is on the 1st controller, 2nd disk, 3rd partition.

37. What level of fault tolerance is available on NT Workstation?

A. 1

B. 5

C. 3

D. NT Workstation does not provide disk fault tolerance

Answers and Explanations: Practice Exam

1. **C** Because a domain is already in use, only a BDC would be able to assist.
2. **D** WINNT32 is designed to allow for the system to remain up for as long as possible.
3. **C** WINNT is for installing from DOS, Windows, or Windows 95.
4. **D** Reinstalling is the only way to upgrade Member Servers to domain controllers.
5. **D** By promoting a BDC, the PDC is automatically demoted to a BDC.
6. **A** Netlogon provides that service.
7. **A, C, D** These are all supported transport protocols.
8. **D** TCP/IP is the standard for the Internet.
9. **C** Every network device on a TCP/IP network must include IP address and subnet mask.
10. **B** If an address is not part of the local subnet, it is passed on to the gateway.
11. **A** DHCP uses a pool of addresses and assigns them to clients.
12. **D** Services for Macintosh must be installed.

13. **B** The Server service enables remote computers to connect to resources on the local computer.

14. **B** The default directory replication import directory is *%systemroot%*\system32\repl\import\scripts.

15. **D** It is not possible to create a printer pool with printers that cannot use a single print driver between them.

16. **C** Computer names must be 15 characters or less.

17. **B** Event viewer will give information, errors, and warnings regarding services in the system log.

18. **A, C** Any NT server machine may be a replication server.

19. **B** Services for Macintosh enables Macintosh clients to access Windows NT network resources.

20. **C** Stripe sets require a minimum of 2 and a maximum of 32 spaces to be combined.

21. **D** Mirroring gives two identical drives.

22. **C, D** These are fault tolerant.

23. **C** The Disk Administrator is used for disk management.

24. **C** NT cannot change a Member Server to a domain controller without reinstalling.

25. **A** Domain controllers will validate users and maintain directory database information.

26. **A, B, C** Printers in printing pools should be close together, part of the same print server, and able to use the same printer driver.

27. **A, C** The printer folder is in several locations.

28. **A, B** Network properties can be found in several locations.

29. **B** From the command prompt, type the command to convert.

30. **C** 900 MB is correct because one fourth of the disk space will be used for parity if four disks are used.

31. **B** With the Fault Tolerance disk, the system will start, and then use Disk Administrator to break the mirror.

32. **C** You will require NTLDR, NTDETECT.COM, and the BOOT.INI file for your Fault Tolerant boot disk.

33. **B** Also the ARC path on the BOOT.INI will read SCSI instead of Multi.

34. **B** Because parity information is being generated, performance will slow.

35. **D** NT is on the 1st controller, 2nd disk, 3rd partition.

36. **B** NT is on the 1st controller, 1st disk, 3rd partition.

37. **D** Disk fault tolerance is only provided in the Windows NT Server Disk Administrator program.

CHAPTER 9

Managing Resources

This chapter helps you prepare for the exam by covering the following objectives:

- Managing user accounts and rights
- Managing group accounts and rights
- Creating and managing policies and profiles for various situations
- Administering remote servers from various types of client computers
- Managing disk resources

9.1 Managing User and Group Accounts

Managing user and group accounts is best understood when divided into the following topics:

- Managing Windows NT user accounts
- Managing Windows NT user rights
- Managing Windows NT groups
- Administering account policies
- Auditing changes to the user account database

A. Managing Windows NT User Accounts

Windows NT user accounts, with their unique identifiers, enable users to log on to the Windows NT network. Their user account/password combinations are their tickets to all the resources on the NT network.

Create Windows NT user accounts in User Manager for Domains. To create a new account, the user running User Manager for Domains must be a member of either the Administrators local group or the Account Operators local group.

1. User Properties

Each user has several property pages. When creating a new user, the first screen contains individual settings. Each setting in the User Properties dialog box is described as follows:

- **Username:** The name that each user uses to log in to the network. The name must be unique, no longer than 20 characters, and cannot contain "/\[]:;|=,+*?<> as characters. The goal of enterprise networking is for each user in the enterprise to have only *one* user account.
- **Full Name:** Enables the display of the user's full name. This can be used as a sort setting by choosing Sort by Full Name from the View menu.
- **Description:** Used to further describe a user, and if you use description as a template, you can copy the description from account to account.
- **Password/Confirm Password:** The password can be up to 14 characters. If the user is working at an NT class system, the password is also case-sensitive. If the user is at a Windows 95 or lower system, the password is case-insensitive.

Of the four properties at the top of the dialog box, only the description will be copied from account to account. All other settings must be re-entered for a copied user.

The lower settings in the User Properties dialog box relate to how passwords are handled. The settings are as follows:

- **User Must Change Password at Next Logon:** Forces users to change their password when they next log on to the network. This option should not be selected if the account policy Users Must Log On in Order to Change Password has been set.
- **User Cannot Change Password:** Used in higher security networks in which the users are assigned passwords for their accounts.
- **Password Never Expires:** Overrides the account policy of password expiration and should only be used for service accounts in Windows NT.
- **Account Disabled:** The Account Disabled setting prevents users from using the disabled account.
- **Account Locked Out:** Active only if a user's account has been locked out by the operating system by failing the Account Lockout settings. To reactivate an account, simply clear the check box for this setting.

2. Group Properties Tab

Use the Group Properties tab to assign the user whose account you are modifying to various groups. This dialog box enables you to assign users to global and local groups in only the same domain as the user (generally, you assign users to global groups). To assign a user to a group in a different domain, you must use that domain's local group properties.

The Primary Group option at the bottom of the dialog box is used by Services for Macintosh when it assigns permissions to Mac Shares. You can designate a primary Global Group for the account.

3. User Environment Profiles Page

The User Environment Profiles page is one of the main configuration pages used in an Enterprise Network. It enables the administrator to configure the following as centrally located:

- User Profile Path
- Login Script
- Home Directory

The main purpose in centrally locating these options is that you can have all these items stored on a central server. By having the users store their profiles and home directories in a central location, you make the process of backing up their data more manageable.

a. User Profile Path

The User Profile Path designates a specific location on a specified server where the user's profile is stored. As the directory structure reveals, the profile path contains the user portion of the Registry in the file NTUSER.DAT. The directory structure itself also contains a user's Start menu, desktop layout, and a recently used file listing. By using the profile path, the users can have their desktops and personal configuration settings follow them to each NT computer they use.

The most common path entered for the user profile path is \\SERVER\PROFILESHARE\%USERNAME%. You should note that this location is server-specific. To limit WAN traffic, consider locating the user's profile on a server in the same subnet as the client.

b. Login Script

The login script enables an administrator to configure common drive mappings, run central batch files, and configure the system. When configuring a login script, put the name of the *.bat or *.cmd file that you want to execute. The logon scripts are stored by default in the following directory:

```
\%systemroot%\system32\repl\import\scripts
```

This directory is shared as the netlogon share, and the logon script presents a common network layout to all clients on the network.

9

c. Home Directory

The home directory setting for the user's profile creates a personal directory where users can store their data on a network server. To create home directories, the most common entry is a common share called USERS. Assuming this share has been created, you enter that path for each home directory as `\\COMPUTER\USERS\%USERNAME%`.

4. Logon Hours Properties

The Logon Hours Properties tab enables the administrator to set the hours the user account is able to access to the network. If the user attempts to log on to the network during restricted hours, a dialog box appears that states that the user is not permitted to log on during the hours.

If users are currently logged on when their allotted logon hours end, they cannot connect to any more net shares. Likewise, they cannot use any of their current shares. If the users actually log out, they will not be able to log back on until the unrestricted hours begin.

5. Logon to Properties

The Logon to Properties page restricts users to working at specific workstations. You can specify up to eight computer names. They are entered as the computer name, not UNC format. For example, you would type **INSTRUCTOR**, not **\\INSTRUCTOR**.

6. Account Properties

An administrator uses the account properties page to define one of two options:

- **Setting an account expiration date:** Used for any short-term employees. The administrator sets when the account expires.
- **Setting whether the account is a global or local account:** Global is the default, as local accounts cannot cross trusts.

7. Dial-In Properties

The Dial-In Properties page enables administrators to determine which users are granted dial-in access to the network and whether the administrators should implement call-back security.

If you choose No Call Back, the users will immediately be able to use network resources. No Call Back is commonly used in low-security networks and for users working out of hotel rooms.

If you choose Set by User, the users are prompted to enter their phone number, and the Remote Access Server calls them back at that number. If you choose Preset To, the users dial in to the office network. After connecting, the line is dropped, and the user will be called back at a predefined phone number.

B. Managing Windows NT User Rights

User rights define security rights when the user's activity cannot be associated with one particular object. Several predefined user rights can grant these nondiscretionary levels of access to the system. The User Rights policy is implemented via the User Manager for Domain's User Rights option from the Policy menu.

1. The Default User Rights

User rights are automatically implemented in Windows NT 4. The user rights are stored in the SAM Account Database. This is in the Security hive of the HKEY_LOCAL_MACHINE subtree in the Registry. Table 9.1.1 describes each of the basic and advanced user rights as defined in Windows NT Workstation and Windows NT Server.

Table 9.1.1 User Rights Assignments in Windows NT 4

User Right	This Right Enables:	Initially Assigned to:
Access This Computer from the Network	Enables users to connect to the computer via the network.	Administrators, Everyone, Power Users
Act as Part of the Operating System	Enables a process to perform as a secure, trusted part of the operating system. For example, the Microsoft Exchange 5.0 Server Service account requires this right to handle POP3 mail requests from clients.	None
Add Workstations to the Domain	Enables users to add workstations to the domain so that workstation can recognize the domain's user and global accounts.	None, but this is a predefined right for all members of the Administrators and Server Operators local groups, and the right cannot be revoked.
Backup Files and Directories	Enables users to back up files and directories on the computer, no matter what file and directory permissions they have.	Administrators, Backup Operators, and Server Operators
Bypass Traverse Checking	Enables users to change directories and traverse the directory structure, even if the user has no permissions for the traversed directory structures.	Everyone
Change System Time	Enables a user to set the time of the computer's internal clock.	Administrators, Server Operators, Power Users
Create a Pagefile	Determines which users can create a pagefile for the Virtual Memory Manager to use.	Administrators

9

continues

Table 9.1.1 Continued

User Right	This Right Enables:	Initially Assigned to:
Create a Token Object	Gives the right to create access tokens.	None; this is a predefined right of the Local Security Authority.
Create Permanent Shared Objects	Enables a user to create shared objects, such as \\Device, used within Windows NT. The right has nothing to do with creating file or printer shares.	None
Debug Programs	Enables a user to debug various low-level objects such as threads.	Administrators
Force Shutdown from a Remote System	This right is not currently implemented in Windows NT 4, but it has been reserved for future use.	Administrators, Server Operators, Power Users
Generate Security Audits	Enables a process to generate security audit logs.	None
Increase Quotas	This right is not currently implemented in Windows NT 4, but it has been reserved for future use. Products such as Disk Quota Manager might use this right.	Administrators
Increase Scheduling Priority	Enables a user to boost the execution priority of a process by using the Task Manager.	Administrators, Power Users
Load and Unload Device Drivers	Enables a user to install and remove device drivers.	Administrators
Lock Pages in Memory	Enables a user to lock pages into memory so that the pages cannot be paged out to the paging file.	None

User Right	This Right Enables:	Initially Assigned to:
Log On as a Batch Job	This right is not currently implemented in Windows NT 4, but it has been reserved for future use.	None
Log On as a Service	Enables users to register with the systems as a Service. This right is automatically granted to any account set up as a service account.	None
Log On Locally	Enables users to log on to the system by typing their usernames and passwords into the User Authentication dialog box.	Account Operators, Administrators, Backup Operators, Everyone, Print Operators, Server Operators, Power Users, Guests, Users
Manage Auditing and Security Log	Enables users to specify which files to audit, which groups to audit, and which printers to audit. The right does not enable the user to change the audit policy, but to work only within the framework defined by a member of the Administrators group. This right also enables the user to view and clear the security log in the event viewer.	Administrators
Modify Firmware Environment Variables	Enables a user to modify system environment variables stored in non-volatile RAM on RISC-based systems.	Administrators
Profile Single Process	Enables a user to perform performance sampling on a process.	Administrators, Power Users

continues

9

Table 9.1.1 Continued

User Right	This Right Enables:	Initially Assigned to:
Profile System Performance	Enables a user to perform performance sampling on a computer.	Administrators
Replace a Process Level Token	The system uses this right to modify a process's security access token. The right is used by the process of impersonation.	None
Restore Files and Directories	Enables users to restore backed-up files and directories regardless of their personal permissions on these files and directories.	Administrators, Backup Operators, Server Operators
Shut Down the System	Enables a user to shut down the Windows NT computer system.	Account Operators, Administrators, Backup Operators, Print Operators, Server Operators, Everyone Users, Power Users
Take Ownership of Files or Other Objects	Enables users to take ownership of any object on the computer, even if they do not have sufficient permissions to access the object.	Administrators

2. Modifying User Rights

Generally, you do not want to adjust the default user rights. If you do change the user rights, a possibility exists that the server might be rendered unusable. The following are some suggested guidelines to further secure your system's user rights. Two of the rights that have been granted default *excess* rights are as follows:

- **Log on Locally:** The default membership includes the Everyone and Guest groups on Windows NT Workstation. Remove these two groups and replace them with the Users local group from the local account database. Be sure that the Domain's Domain Users global group is a member of the Users local group.
- **Shut Down the System:** The default membership in Windows NT Workstation includes the Everyone group. This group should not be assigned the shut-down privilege. You may also want to consider revoking this right from the Everyone group if you want all systems to run during the night.

C. Managing Windows NT Groups

Using the global and local groups in an enterprise Windows NT environment is one of the key concepts tested in the exam. This section looks into the following areas:

- Differences between global and local groups
- Creation of global groups
- Built-In global groups
- Creation of local groups
- Built-In local groups
- Special groups
- Management of global and local groups in a multidomain environment

1. Differences Between Global and Local Groups

One of the most difficult enterprise concepts to get a handle on is the difference between global and local groups. In an Enterprise network, the acronym AGLP helps to define the use of global and local groups.

AGLP stands for Accounts/Global Groups/Local Groups/Permissions. This means that when you want to assign permissions to any resource, the following steps must be performed.

1. Make sure that user accounts exist for each user that needs access to the resource.
2. Assign all user accounts to a common global group. If the users are spread across multiple domains, you have to create a global group in each domain because global groups can contain only users from the domain in which they are located.
3. Assign the global groups from each domain to a local group in the domain where the resource exists. If the resource is on a Windows NT domain controller, create the local group on a domain controller. If the resource is on a Windows NT Workstation or Windows NT Member Server, create the local group on that system's local account database.
4. Assign necessary permissions to the local group.

Local groups are the only groups that you should assign permissions. When assigning local group permissions, the administrator should always determine whether there is an existing local group with the appropriate permissions. For example, if you want to grant a user the capability to create new users or change group memberships, the Account Operators local group already has these permissions. You have no reason to create a new local group to perform this task. Instead, make the user a member of the Account Operators local group.

Think of it this way: Global groups exist across the domain, whereas local groups are local to the machine in question.

9

2. Creation of Global Groups

You create global groups by using the User Manager for Domains utility. When you create a global group, it is initially written to the SAM database on the Primary Domain Controller. Then the global group is synchronized with the Backup Domain Controllers during the synchronization process. The global groups are accessible from any domain controller.

To create a new global group, choose User, New Global Group from the menus of User Manager for Domains.

The New Global Group dialog box enables you to add and remove users as members of the global group in the current domain. After you have added all users, click the OK button to complete the creation of the global group.

3. Built-in Global Groups

When you first install an NT domain, three global groups are predefined. They are described in Table 9.1.2.

Table 9.1.2 Initial Global Group Memberships

Global Group	Initial Membership
Domain Admins	Administrator
Domain Guests	Guest
Domain Users	All user accounts except for Guest

4. Creation of Local Groups

To create a new local group, choose User, New Local Group from the menus of User Manager for Domains.

To add a global group to the local group, click the Add button in the New Local Group dialog box. A list of global groups and global accounts appears that you can make members of the local group. Note that the drop list at the top enables you to add global accounts and global groups from trusted domains to the local group.

5. Built-In Local Groups

The built-in groups that you have depends on the version of Windows NT you are running. They vary depending on whether you are on Windows NT Workstation, Windows NT Member Servers, or Windows NT domain controllers. The local groups found only on domain controllers include:

- Account Operators
- Print Operators
- Server Operators

The local group found only on Windows NT Workstations or member servers is Power Users. The local groups found on all Windows NT systems include:

- Administrators
- Backup Operators
- Guests
- Replicator
- Users

a. Account Operators Local Group

Members of the Account Operators local group have the capability to create and manage users and groups within the domain. They cannot modify membership in the following groups:

- Administrators
- Account Operators
- Backup Operators
- Print Operators
- Server Operators
- Domain Admins

If they were able to modify the membership of these groups, they ultimately could increase their own rights. Only administrators can change the membership of these groups. Account operators cannot modify users who are members of the operator groups, either.

b. Print Operators Local Group

The Print Operators local group can create new printers and maintain existing printers in the domain. The maintenance activities include sharing printers and managing all jobs in a printer queue.

c. Server Operators Local Group

Members of the Server Operators local group can create shared directories on a domain controller. Other capabilities include:

- Locking or unlocking the server console
- Formatting disks on a server
- Backing up and restoring files to a server
- Managing all facets of printing
- Shutting down servers

d. *Administrators Local Group*

The Administrators local group is found on all Windows NT class computers. This group can manage any and all aspects of the Windows NT domain. The initial membership in the Administrators group is the pre-created Administrator account and the Domain Admins global group.

e. *Backup Operators Local Group*

The members of the Backup Operators local group can back up and restore any files on the system. This right supersedes any permissions assigned to these files and directories. Backup Operators can also shut down a server.

f. *Guests Local Group*

The Guests local group can grant access to specific resources to guests of the domain. The initial membership in the Guests local group is the Domain Guests global group from the domain.

g. *Replicator Local Group*

The Replicator local group is used by the Directory Replicator service. Membership in this group enables a member to be involved in the process of maintaining a directory structure and its contents on multiple domain controllers.

h. *Users Local Group*

The Users Local group contains the global group Domain Users. This group is most often used when increasing the security on a Windows NT domain. Rather than keeping the default share and NTFS permissions, use the local group users instead of everyone.

6. Special Groups

In addition to the predefined local and global groups in Windows NT 4, there are special groups. The membership in these groups is not based as much on usernames as on how the user is functioning on the network. The special groups implemented in Windows NT 4 are as follows:

- **Everyone:** The Everyone group membership includes absolutely everyone that can connect to your network. The everyone group includes users that are not defined in the Account database.
- **Creator/Owner:** The Creator/Owner group membership is applied to every object created in Windows NT. If you take ownership of a file or directory, you automatically become a member of the Creator/Owner group.
- **Network:** The Network group membership is based on whether the user is connecting remotely to a resource.
- **Interactive:** The Interactive group membership is based on whether the user is sitting locally at the server where the data is stored. If the data is stored on a local drive, assigned permissions to the Interactive group affect any users working with that data.
- **System:** This special group never includes users. The System group refers to the Windows NT operating system itself when it must access resources on the network.

7. Management of Global and Local Groups in a Multidomain Environment

The real art of using global and local groups emerges in a multidomain environment. When working with groups across trust relationships, the following guidelines are useful:

- Always gather users into global groups. Remember that global groups can contain user accounts only from the same domain. You may have to create global groups with the same name in multiple domains.
- If you have multiple account domains, use the same name for a global group that has the same types of members as another global group in a separate domain. Remember that when multiple domains are involved, the group name is referred to as DOMAIN\GROUP.
- Before you create the global groups, determine whether an existing local group meets your needs. There is no sense in creating duplicate local groups.
- Remember that you must create the local group where the resource is located. If the resource is on a domain controller, create the local group in the Domain Account database. If the resource is on a Windows NT Workstation or Member Server, create the group in that system's local account database.
- Be sure to set the permissions for a resource before you make the global groups members of the local group assigned to the resource so that security has been set for the resource.

D. Administering Account Policies

Before you start implementing user accounts, one of the most important policies to set is your account policy. These policies affect every account in the domain—you cannot pick and choose which ones are affected. The account policies define how password changes and improper passwords are handled.

The password portion of account policy determines your rules for password security. Options within the account policy include:

- Maximum password age
- Minimum password age
- Minimum password length
- Password uniqueness
- Account lockout
- Account lockout duration
- Handling remote users whose logon hours have expired
- Changing passwords

Template Accounts

As an administrator, consider creating template user accounts for the various types of users that you plan to create. The template enables you to quickly create new user accounts when required. You should disable these template accounts to prevent their use for network access.

To use the template account to your advantage, just choose the template account in User Manager for Domains and create a copy of the account by choosing Copy from the User menu (or press F8). Doing so copies all properties of the template account except:

- **Username**
- **Full Name**
- **Password**
- **Confirm Password**

Template accounts also work best when you make use of the %USERNAME% environment variable for both the User Profile Path and the Home Directory. The environment enables the option User Must Change Password at Next Logon while it disables the Account Disabled box.

E. Auditing Changes to the User Account Database

When an organization implements decentralized administration of the Windows NT Account database, you may want to audit all changes to the Accounts database. Remember, only members of the local groups Administrators and Account Operators can add, modify, and delete users in User Manager for Domains.

To enable auditing of changes to the Account database, a member of the Administrators group must enable Auditing User and Group Management. If you want to know exactly what files are being updated, enable File and Object Access.

The addition of File and Object Access helps you determine when Account Operators attempt to add a member to the Operators or Administrators local groups. When this attempt is made, they see a dialog box that states that their attempt was unsuccessful. Auditing User and Group Management will not catch this error. You must enable File and Object access so that you see the unsuccessful attempt to write to the SAM database.

9.1.1 Exercise: Viewing the SAM and SECURITY Hives

The following steps enable you to view the SAM and SECURITY hives of the HKEY_LOCAL_MACHINE subtree:

1. Start a Command prompt.
2. Start the schedule service by typing **NET START SCHEDULE** at the command prompt. This also can be done from the Services applet of the Control Panel.

3. Type the following AT command. The time portion should be set to a minute or two later than the current time. Remember that you must be logged on as a member of the Administrators group to do this.

   AT [time] /interactive "regedt32.exe"

4. When [time] arrives, the Registry Editor will launch and then give you access to the SAM and SECURITY hives.

9.1.2 Exercise: Application of User Rights When Implementing the Directory Replication Service

The Directory Replication service requires a service account that it uses to perform its tasks of maintaining a consistent NETLOGON share on all domain controllers. You must complete the following steps to set up the service:

1. Create an account in the User Manager for Domains that will be used as the service account.
2. Set the account properties as shown in Figure 9.1.1. Be sure to deselect User Must Change Password at Next Logon and to select Password Never Expires. All service accounts should be set this way so that the accounts will never be prompted to change their passwords.

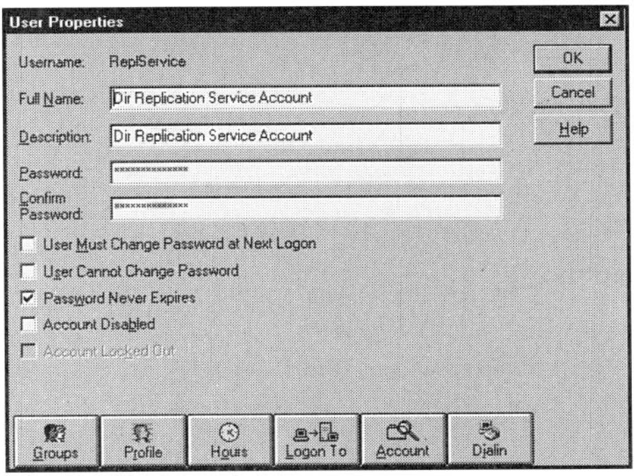

Figure 9.1.1 Setting up the Directory Replication Service Account in User Manager for Domains.

3. Make the user a member of the Replicator local group and the Backup Operators group. These groups grant the service account the necessary rights to perform its predetermined tasks. The Replicator local group enables the account to perform the directory replication task. The Backup Operators group enables the account to read all files in the `REPL$\scripts` directory of the export server regardless of the permissions on the share. The Backup Operators group also enables the account to write these files to the NETLOGON share of all import servers no matter what permissions exist on these directories.
4. From the Policies menu, choose User Rights. Grant the newly created account to the user right Log On as a Service. This right displays only when you select the advanced check box.
5. Open the Control Panel.
6. Open the Service applet.
7. From the list of services, choose the Directory Replicator Service and click the Startup Button.
8. Fill in the dialog box as shown in Figure 9.1.2. Change the startup type to Automatic. Also be sure to change Log On As option to Use the Account that You Have Set Up. Use the ... button to select the account name from the list as it must be the full domain\username. Finally, enter the password you set for the account.

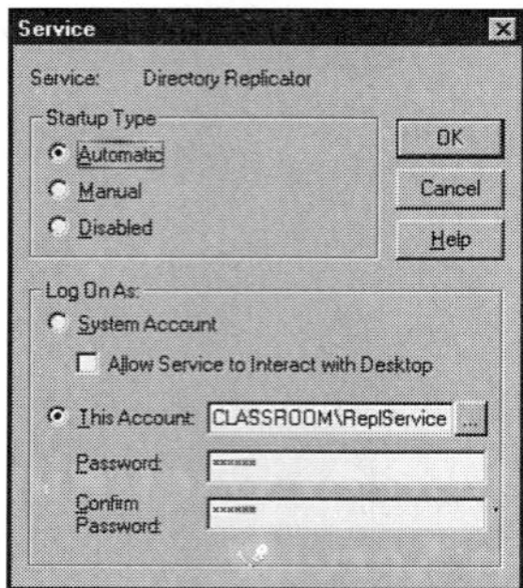

Figure 9.1.2 Configuring the Directory Replicator Service to use your pre-created service account.

9. Click the Start button to start the service. The next time you restart the system, the service will start automatically because of your Automatic Start setting.

9.1 Practice Problems

1. Which option enables Windows NT users to access accounts and log on to a network?
   A. Unique identifiers
   B. Bindery entries
   C. NDS entries
   D. Policies

2. Accessing resources and identifying yourself to a network requires which two items?
   A. Policies
   B. User ID
   C. Password
   D. Group accounts

3. Windows NT user accounts are created in:
   A. User Manager
   B. Server Manager
   C. Network Administrator
   D. User Manager for Domains

4. To create a new account, the user running the utility must be a member of either of which two groups?
   A. Administrators
   B. Account Operators
   C. Domain Users
   D. Guest

5. Which portion of account policy determines your rules for password security?
   A. User
   B. Group
   C. Logon
   D. Password

6. Options within the account policy include all the following except?
   A. Maximum Password Age
   B. Minimum Password Age
   C. Maximum Password Length
   D. Minimum Password Length

7. Template accounts work best when you make use of which environment variable for both the User Profile Path and the Home Directory?
   A. %root%
   B. %Winnt%
   C. %username%
   D. %path%

8. Which setting does not normally appear in the User Properties dialog box unless there is a problem?
   A. User Must Change Password at Next Logon
   B. User Cannot Change Password
   C. Password Never Expires
   D. Account Locked Out

9. Which two statements are true of the Password Never Expires setting in the User Properties dialog box?
   A. This setting overrides the account policy of password expiration.
   B. This setting forces users to change their password when they next log on to the network.
   C. This setting is used in higher security networks in which the users are assigned passwords for their accounts.
   D. This setting should be used only for service accounts in Windows NT.

10. The %username% variable must be unique in the domain, and no longer than how many characters?

    A. 14

    B. 20

    C. 26

    D. 256

11. The password for each username must be no longer than how many characters?

    A. 14

    B. 20

    C. 26

    D. 256

12. The goal of enterprise networking is for each user in the enterprise to have how many user accounts?

    A. 1

    B. 2

    C. 14

    D. 256

13. If the user is working at an NT class system, the password is:

    A. Lowercase

    B. Uppercase

    C. Case-sensitive

    D. Case-insensitive

14. Which feature enables an administrator to configure common drive mappings, run central batch files, and configure the system?

    A. User Manager for Domains

    B. Server Manager

    C. Login scripts

    D. User Manager

15. When configuring a login script, the recommended extensions are? Select two.

    A. *.bat

    B. *.cmd

    C. file

    D. *.txt

16. The logon scripts are stored by default in which directory?

    A. \%systemroot%

    B. \%systemroot%\system32

    C. \%systemroot%\system32\scripts

    D. \%systemroot%\system32\repl\import\scripts

17. The netlogon directory is which directory?

    A. \%systemroot%

    B. \%systemroot%\system32

    C. \%systemroot%\system32\scripts

    D. \%systemroot%\system32\repl\import\scripts

18. Which properties page enables the administrator to determine whether call-back security is to be implemented?

    A. RAS

    B. Dial-in properties

    C. System

    D. Modem

19. This call-back option is commonly used in low-security networks and for users working out of hotel rooms.

    A. No Call Back

    B. Set by User

    C. Preset to

    D. Permanent Connection

20. Which key should you press in User Manager for Domains to create a copy of the template account?

    A. F3

    B. F5

    C. F8

    D. F10

21. A security risk—the user right to shut down the system in Windows NT Workstation—is granted by default to whom?

    A. Everyone group

    B. Backup group

    C. NT Users group

    D. PPP group

22. Global groups, as a general rule, contain:

    A. Resources

    B. Users

    C. Domains

    D. Text files

23. Local groups, as a general rule, are related to:

    A. Resources

    B. Users

    C. Domains

    D. Text files

24. Global groups can contain what? Select all correct answers.

    A. Local groups

    B. Global groups from the same domain

    C. Users from the same domain

    D. Users from a trusted domain

25. Local groups can contain what? Select all correct answers.

    A. Local groups

    B. Global groups from the same domain

    C. Global groups from a trusted domain

    D. Users from the same domain

    E. Users from a trusted domain

9.1.1 Answers and Explanations: Exercise

In Exercise 9.1.1 you learned that when viewing the hives, you must start the Registry Editor in system mode. You viewed the values of the SAM and SECURITY hives of the HKEY_LOCAL_MACHINE subtree.

9.1.2 Answers and Explanations: Exercise

In Exercise 9.1.2, you saw the interaction between user rights and the directory replication service. It is important to note that after established, the service will automatically start for all future sessions.

9.1 Answers and Explanations: Practice Problems

1. **A** Unique identifiers enable a user to log on to the Windows NT network.

2. **B, C** User ID and password combinations are the access tickets to all resources on the NT network.

3. **D** You create Windows NT user accounts in User Manager for Domains.

4. **A, B** To create a new account, the user running User Manager for Domains must be a member of either the Administrators local group or the Account Operators local group.

5. **D** The password portion of account policy determines your rules for password security.

6. **C** Options within the account policy include Maximum Password Age, Minimum Password Age, and Minimum Password Length.

7. **C** Template accounts work best when you make use of the %username% environment variable for both the User Profile Path and the Home Directory.

8. **D** The Account Locked Out setting is only active if a user's account has been locked out by the operating system for failing the Account Lockout settings.

9. **A, D** The Password Never Expires setting will override the account policy of password expiration and should be used for service accounts in Windows NT.

10. **B** The %username% variable must be no longer than 20 characters.

11. **A** The password for the user can be up to 14 characters long.

12. **A** The goal of enterprise networking is for each user in the enterprise to have only *one* user account.

13. **C** When the user is working at an NT class system, the password is case-sensitive.

14. **C** The login scripts enable an administrator to configure common drive mappings, run central batch files, and configure the system.

15. **A, B** When configuring a login script, recommended extensions are *.bat or *.cmd.

16. **D** The logon scripts are stored by default in the directory:

```
\%systemroot%\system32\repl\
import\scripts
```

17. **D** The \%systemroot%\system32 \repl\import\scripts directory is shared as the netlogon share.

18. **B** The dial-in properties page enables the administrator to determine which users are granted dial-in access to the network and whether call-back security should be implemented.

19. **A** If No Call Back is selected, the user immediately is able to use network resources.

20. **C** F8 in User Manager for Domains will create a copy of the template account.

21. **A** The default membership in Windows NT Workstation includes the Everyone group.

22. **B** As a general rule, global groups contain users and local groups contain resources. The local groups are then related to resources and assigned the appropriate permissions.

23. **A** Local groups contain resources and global groups contain users. The local groups are then related to resources and assigned the appropriate permissions.

24. **A, B** Global groups can contain local groups and other global groups.

25. **A** Local groups cannot contain global groups, but can contain other local groups.

9.1 Key Words

Global group

Local group

Replication

Replication service

User Manager

User Manager for Domains

9.2 Creating and Managing System Policies and User Profiles

System policies and user profiles assist in the centralization of management in a Windows NT Enterprise network. System policies help an administrator implement common Registry settings across the enterprise. User Profiles store the user portion of the Registry, and you can implement the user profiles as either local profiles or roaming profiles. A roaming profile enables users to have the user portion of their configuration follow them wherever they log in on the Windows NT network.

A. Local Profiles Versus Roaming Profiles

When users log in at a system, they create a local profile on that system. The local profile is implemented as a set of directory structures. This directory structure includes the desktop folder and the Start menu folder. The user portion of the Registry is stored in the file NTUSER.DAT.

When a user logs in to the network, their desktop and Start menu are also based on the local system that they are logging in to. The desktop is based on the user's profile directory and the ALL USERS directory. The same is true for the Start menu directory.

The problem with local profiles is that every workstation that you log in to will have its own version of the local profile. User configuration settings will have to be set at each workstation that they log in to.

To overcome this problem, you must implement Roaming profiles. Roaming profiles include the user portion of the Registry, which is downloaded from a designated system to the system that the users are currently logged on to. Any changes to their settings will be stored in the central location so that the next workstation can retrieve the settings.

1. Configuring Roaming Profiles in Windows NT

To configure a roaming profile for a user account, first set the profile path in the User Manager for Domains for that account. If you are configuring a block of users, the best method is to do a group property change by choosing all users you want to have roaming profiles, and then choosing Properties from the User menu.

9

The most common setting is to have a directory shared with a share name such as profiles. It should enable the local group USERS the permission FULL CONTROL. With this share, you can now set the user's profile path to \\server\share\%username%. The next time the users log on, their profile information is saved to this central profile directory.

2. Tuning Roaming Profiles

An administrator can determine whether the User Profiles stored on the local system are roaming or local profiles by viewing the User Profiles tab in the System applet in Control Panel.

The dialog box shows all the profiles currently stored on the system and whether they are roaming or local profiles. You can change the profile between a roaming and local profile by clicking the Change To button. A dialog box appears.

You also use this dialog box to configure how to handle roaming profiles when the user logs in to the network over a slow WAN link. This is an extremely useful setting for laptop users that may log in to the enterprise network from various locations. Remember that the roaming profile is stored on a specific server even though the user can be authenticated on any domain controller within the domain.

3. Implementing Roaming Profiles in Windows 95

Windows 95 users can also have roaming profiles configured so that their user-based configurations can follow them from workstation to workstation. Implementing roaming profiles in Windows 95 differs from Windows NT in the following ways:

- Separate user profiles are not implemented automatically in Windows 95 as they are in Windows NT.
- The user portion of the Registry is saved in the file USER.DAT in Windows 95, whereas it is stored in NTUSER.DAT in Windows NT.
- The user profile path setting in the user's properties has no effect on Windows 95 clients. The roaming profile information is stored in their Windows NT Home Directory.

B. Understanding System Policies

System policies help the network administrator restrict the configuration changes users can perform to their profiles. By combining roaming profiles and system policies, the administrators cannot provide the users a consistent desktop, but they can control what the users can do to that desktop. Likewise, the administrator can ensure that the users cannot modify certain settings.

System policies work like a merge operation. Think of system policies as a copy of your Registry. When you log in to the network and the NTCONFIG.POL file exists on the domain controller, it merges its settings into your Registry, changing your Registry settings as indicated in the system policy.

You implement system policies by using the System Policy Editor. The System Policy Editor is automatically installed with any Windows NT domain controller.

You can configure system policies to do the following:

- Implement defaults for hardware configuration for all computers or for a specific machine using the profile.
- Restrict the capability to change specific parameters that affect the hardware configuration of the participating system.
- Set defaults for all users on the areas of their personal settings that they can configure.
- Restrict the users from changing specific areas of their configurations to prevent them from tampering with the system. An example is disabling all Registry editing tools for a specific user.
- Apply all defaults and restrictions on a group level rather than just a user level.

You can also use the System Policy Editor to change settings in the Registry of the system on which the System Policy Editor is executed. Many times it is easier to use the System Policy Editor because it has a better interface for finding common restrictions.

1. Implementing System Policies

To create Computer, User, and Group policies, you must use the System Policy Editor. The System Policy Editor is automatically installed on all domain controllers, and you can find the editor in the Administrative Tools Group of the Start menu.

When you create a new policy file, you see two default icons within the policy:

- **Default Computer:** Used to configure all machine-specific settings. All property changes within this section affect the HKEY_LOCAL_MACHINE subtree of the Registry.
- **Default User:** Used for any client that uses the policy and does not have a specific machine entry created for itself in the policy file. Used to specify default policy settings for all users that use the policy. It affects the HKEY_CURRENT_USER subtree of the Registry. If the users are configured to use a roaming profile, this information is stored in their centralized version of NTUSER.DAT in their profile directories.

2. Configuring Computer Policies

You can configure computer policies to lock down common machine settings that affect all users of a Windows NT system. Common settings that are configured include:

- Programs to automatically run at startup of the computer system. These can include virus scans. Opening the System/Run option in the Default Computer Properties sets this.
- Ensuring that all Windows NT clients will have the administrative shares automatically created on startup of these systems. This enhances the capability of the administrator to centrally manage the network. Opening the Windows NT Network/Sharing option in the Default Computer Properties sets this option.
- Implementing customized shared folders. These include the Desktop folder, Start menu folder, Startup folder, and Programs folder. These can be set to point to an actual network share location so that multiple machines have common desktops or Start menus. Opening the Windows NT Shell/Custom Shared Folders option in the Default Computer Properties sets this.
- Presenting a customized dialog box called the Logon Banner that you can use to inform users of upcoming maintenance to the network or for other network information. Opening the Windows NT System/Logon option in the Default Computer Properties sets this option.
- Removing the last logged on user from the Authentication dialog box. Many users have predictable passwords, and knowing the user's login name can help lead to guessing their passwords. This is also set in the Windows NT System/Logon option in the Default Computer Properties.

You also can implement computer policies on a computer-by-computer basis by choosing Add Computer from the Edit Menu. This adds a new icon to the policy with that computer's name.

3. Configuring User Policies

Implement user policies through the System Policy Editor. These policies affect the HKEY_CURRENT_USER Registry subtree. Each user is affected individually by these settings.

You can also implement user policies on a user-by-user basis. To create an individual user policy, choose Add User from the Edit menu. When a user logs in, NTCONFIG.POL will be checked to see whether there is a policy for the specific user. If there is not, the default user policy is used for the login process.

Some of the common implementations of user profiles are the following:

- Locking down display properties to prevent users from changing the resolution of their monitors. You can lock down display properties as a whole or on each individual property page of display properties. Adjust this setting in the Control Panel/Display/Restrict Display option of the Default User Properties sheet.
- Setting a default color scheme or wallpaper. You can set the default in the Desktop option of the Default User Properties sheet.
- If you want to restrict access to portions of the Start menu or Desktop, you can do this via the Shell/Restrictions option of the Default User Properties sheet.
- If you need to limit the applications run at a workstation, set this in the System/Restrictions option of the Default User Properties sheet. You can use the System/Restrictions option to prevent the users from modifying the Registry.
- You can prevent users from mapping or disconnecting network drives by setting the options in the Windows NT Shell/Restrictions option of the Default User Properties sheet.

4. Implementing Group Policies

If you need to have user settings affect multiple users, you can implement group policies. Group policies add another level of complexity to the processing of the policies. Some of the additional considerations include:

- The System Policy Editor uses global groups for group membership. Appropriate trust relationships must be implemented to see the necessary global groups.
- Because a user can belong to multiple global groups, the order in which the groups are processed is very important. One group's settings could be the opposite of another group's. Set group order in the Group Priority option of the Options menu.

5. Processing Order for System Policies

When a user logs on to a network in which system policies have been implemented, the following steps occur:

1. The user successfully logs in to the network.
2. The user profile is read from the NETLOGON share of the authenticating domain controller.
3. If a predefined policy exists for a user, that policy is merged into the HKEY_CURRENT_USER Registry subtree. Then the processing moves to step 6.
4. If no predefined user policy exists, the default user policy is processed.
5. The group priority list is examined. If the user is a member of any of the global groups for which policy exists, the account is processed according to the group priority order. The priority is ordered from bottom to top of the group priority list. Each of the group policies is applied to the HKEY_CURRENT_USER Registry subtree.
6. After the user and group policies have been processed, the machine policies are determined. If there is a predefined machine policy, that policy is merged with the HKEY_LOCAL_MACHINE Registry subtree. If there is no predefined machine policy for the system from which the user is logging in, the default machine policy is merged with the HKEY_LOCAL_MACHINE subtree.

6. Differences Between Windows NT and Windows 95 Profiles

Although Windows NT automatically implements system policies in its clients, there is more configuration required for Windows 95 if you want Windows 95 to recognize group policies. First, you must individually configure the Windows 95 clients to recognize group policies, as follows:

1. Open the Windows 95 Control Panel.
2. In the Control Panel, open the Add/Remove Programs applet.
3. Change to the Windows Setup tab and click the Have Disk button.
4. The System Policy installation files are located on the Windows 95 CD in the directory \ADMIN\APPTOOLS\POLEDIT. Choose this directory by using the Browse button.
5. When the options to install appear, choose Group Policies.

Following these steps installs the necessary files. After you configure the client to use system policies, one more change is recommended in a Windows NT network environment. By default, the Windows 95 client only looks for the file CONFIG.POL on the Primary Domain Controller's NETLOGON share. If you want the Windows 95 client to be able to process the system policy from any domain controller as in Windows NT, you must enable the Load Balancing option under the Network/System Policies Update/Remote Update option.

9.2.1 Exercise: Changing Windows 95 from Shared to Separate Profiles

To change Windows 95 from using shared user profiles to separate profiles, perform the following steps:

1. Open the Control Panel.
2. Open the Password applet in the Control Panel.
3. Choose the User Profile Tab. You must change the setting to Users Can Customize Their Preferences and Desktop Settings. Be sure to also enable the options to Include Desktop Icons and Network Neighborhood Contents in User Settings and Include Start Menu and Program Groups in User Settings.
4. Then you must restart the computer for the change to take effect.

9.2.2 Exercise: Creating a New System Policy

Creating a system policy is outlined in the following steps:

1. From the Start menu, choose Programs, Administrative Tools (Common), System Policy Editor.
2. Verify that the proper template files are loaded by choosing Policy Template from the Options menu. The default templates that should be loaded are:
    - `c:\%winntroot%\INF\COMMON.ADM`
    - `c:\%winntroot%\INF\WINNT.ADM`

3. From the File menu, choose New Policy.
4. To adjust settings affecting the HKEY_LOCAL_MACHINE subtree, double-click the Default Computer icon. To adjust settings affecting each user's HKEY_CURRENT_USER subtree in the Registry, double-click the Default User icon. The following settings are available:
   - **Clear:** Changes the client's Registry to not implement the Registry setting. If it has been previously enabled in the client's Registry, it will be disabled after the policy is implemented.
   - **Shaded:** Leaves the client's Registry exactly as it is before the policy is implemented. If the option was enabled in the client's Registry, it remains enabled. If the option was disabled, it remains disabled.
   - **Checked:** Changes the client's registry to match exactly what the system policy has configured. There is no choice on the part of the client.
5. After you make all your desired setting changes, you must save the file. The location that all Windows NT clients will look for the file is in the NETLOGON share of the domain controller that authenticates the user. The best place to save this file is in the following location:

   ```
   \\CENTRAL SERVER\REPL$\SCRIPTS\NTCONFIG.POL
   ```

   where *NTCONFIG.POL* is the name of your policy. This file is available only if you set up directory replication among your domain controllers.

9.2 Practice Problems

1. What two items are used to assist in the centralization of management in a Windows NT Enterprise network?
   A. System policies
   B. Local groups
   C. User profiles
   D. Global groups

2. Which of the following help an administrator implement common Registry settings across the enterprise?
   A. System policies
   B. User profiles
   C. Regedt32
   D. Login scripts

3. Which of the following store the user portion of the Registry?
   A. System policies
   B. User profiles
   C. Regedt32
   D. Login scripts

4. User profiles can be implemented in which two ways?
   A. Local
   B. Global
   C. Roaming
   D. Group

5. Which user profile type enables users to have the user portion of their configurations follow them wherever they log on to the Windows NT network?
   A. Local
   B. Global
   C. Roaming
   D. Group

6. The user portion of the Windows NT Registry is stored in which file?
   A. USER.DAT
   B. USER.MAN
   C. NTUSER.DAT
   D. NTUSER.MAN

7. If you want to configure a user account to use a roaming profile, the first thing to do is:
   A. Set the profile path in the User Manager for Domains for that account.
   B. Rename USER.DAT to USER.MAN.
   C. Move USER.DAT to the NETLOGON directory.
   D. Enable TTS.

8. An administrator can determine whether the User Profiles stored on the local system are roaming or local profiles by viewing the User Profiles tab in which Control Panel applet?
   A. Network Neighborhood
   B. Passwords
   C. System
   D. Users

9. If a roaming profile is only stored on one specific server, the user can be authenticated:
   A. Only on that server
   B. On any domain controller within the domain
   C. Only on the local workstation
   D. At any workstation within the domain

10. Implementing roaming profiles in Windows 95 differs from Windows NT in which of the following ways? Select all correct answers.

    A. Separate user profiles are not implemented automatically in Windows 95 as they are in Windows NT.

    B. The user portion of the Registry is saved in the file USER.DAT in Windows 95, whereas it is stored in NTUSER.DAT in Windows NT.

    C. The user profile path setting in the user's properties has no effect on Windows 95 clients.

    D. Windows NT roaming profile information is stored in the Windows NT Home Directory.

11. Which of the following help the network administrator restrict what configuration changes users can perform to their profiles:

    A. Roaming profiles

    B. System policies

    C. Group assignments

    D. Login scripts

12. The System Policy file on NT is, by default, named:

    A. CONFIG.POL

    B. NTCONFIG.POL

    C. SYSTEM.DAT

    D. SYSTEM.POL

13. Implement system policies by using:

    A. System Policy Editor

    B. User Manager for Domains

    C. Server Manager

    D. Regedit

14. The System Policy Editor is installed by default:

    A. From the Resource Kit

    B. On any Windows 95 workstation

    C. On any NT Workstation

    D. On any Windows NT domain controller

15. You can configure system policies to do all the following except:

    A. Implement defaults for hardware configuration for all computers.

    B. Restrict the capability to change specific parameters that affect the hardware configuration of the participating system.

    C. Eliminate the need for backups of user-specific information.

    D. Set defaults for all users on the areas of their personal settings that they can configure.

16. Using the System Policy Editor, you can create policies for which of the following? Select all correct answers.

    A. Domain

    B. Computer

    C. User

    D. Group

17. The System Policy Editor can be found in what group of the Start menu?

    A. System

    B. User Manager

    C. Administrative Tools

    D. Programs

18. When you create a new policy file, what two default icons appear within the policy?

    A. Default Computer

    B. Default User

C. Default Domain

D. Default Group

19. Which item is used to configure all machine-specific settings?

A. Default Computer

B. Default User

C. Default Domain

D. Default Group

20. All property changes within the Default Computer section affect which subtree of the Registry:

A. HKEY_USER

B. HKEY_SYSTEM

C. HKEY_CURRENT_USER

D. HKEY_LOCAL_MACHINE

21. Which item is used to specify default policy settings for all users that use the policy:

A. Default Computer

B. Default User

C. Default Domain

D. Default Group

22. The default user settings affect which subtree of the Registry:

A. HKEY_USER

B. HKEY_SYSTEM

C. HKEY_CURRENT_USER

D. HKEY_LOCAL_MACHINE

23. Which of the following do you use to lock down common machine settings that affect all users of a Windows NT system:

A. System policies

B. User policies

C. Computer policies

D. Domain policies

24. Which type of policies should you use to prevent users from changing the resolution of their individual monitors:

A. System policies

B. User policies

C. Computer policies

D. Domain policies

25. Which type of policies should you use to set a default color scheme or wallpaper for individual users:

A. System policies

B. User policies

C. Computer policies

D. Domain policies

9.2.1 Answers and Explanations: Exercise

Any user that logs on for the first time is informed that they have not logged on to this network. Then they are asked if they want to have this user's settings maintained in their own personal profile.

9.2.2 Answers and Explanations: Exercise

A new system policy is created by systematically following the steps outlined earlier in the chapter. It is important to load the template files first, and enable the directory replication service at the conclusion—to ensure that an up-to-date version of the policy is stored in each domain controller to which the export server has been configured to replicate.

9.2 Answers and Explanations: Practice Problems

1. **A, C** The use of system policies and user profiles assists in the centralization of management in a Windows NT Enterprise network.

2. **A** System policies help an administrator implement common Registry settings across the enterprise.
3. **B** User Profiles store the user portion of the Registry.
4. **A, C** You can implement user profiles as either local profiles or roaming profiles.
5. **C** A roaming profile enables users to have the user portion of their configurations follow them wherever they log on to the Windows NT network.
6. **C** The user portion of the Registry is stored in the file NTUSER.DAT.
7. **A** If you want to configure a user account to use a roaming profile, the first thing to do is set the profile path in the User Manager for Domains for that account.
8. **C** An administrator can determine whether the user profiles stored on the local system are roaming or local profiles by viewing the User Profiles tab in the System applet in Control Panel.
9. **B** Although the roaming profile is stored on a specific server, the user can be authenticated on any domain controller within the domain.
10. **A, B, C** Implementing roaming profiles in Windows 95 differs from Windows NT in the following ways: Separate User profiles are not implemented automatically in Windows 95 as they are in Windows NT; the user portion of the Registry is saved in the file USER.DAT in Windows 95, whereas it is stored in NTUSER.DAT in Windows NT; and the user profile path setting in the user's properties has no effect on Windows 95 clients.
11. **B** System policies help the network administrator restrict the configuration changes the users can perform to their profiles.
12. **B** NTCONFIG.POL is the default system policy filename on NT networks.
13. **A** System policies are implemented by using the System Policy Editor.
14. **D** The System Policy Editor is automatically installed with any Windows NT domain controller.
15. **C** System policies do not eliminate the need for backups of user-specific information.
16. **B, C, D** To create Computer, User, and Group policies, you must use the System Policy Editor.
17. **C** The System Policy Editor is automatically installed on all Domain Controllers, and you can find the editor in the Administrative Tools Group of the Start menu.
18. **A, B** When you create a new policy file, it presents you with two default icons within the policy: Default Computer and Default User.
19. **A** Use the Default Computer item to configure all machine-specific settings.
20. **D** All property changes within this section affects the HKEY_LOCAL_MACHINE subtree of the Registry.
21. **B** Use the Default User item to specify default policy settings for all users that use the policy.
22. **A, C** The default user setting affects the HKEY_CURRENT_USER subtree of the Registry and the HKEY_USER subtree.
23. **C** You can configure computer policies to lock down common machine settings that affect all users of a Windows NT system.
24. **B** User policies can be used to prevent users from changing the resolution of their monitors.
25. **B** User policies can be used to set a default color scheme or wallpaper.

9.2 Key Words

Domain controller
Primary Domain Controller
Backup Domain Controller
System Policy Editor
System policies
User policies
User profiles
Local profiles
Roaming profiles

9.3 Administering Remote Servers from Various Client Computers

A common initial misconception is that you must be located at a Windows NT domain controller to manage a Windows NT Domain. On the contrary, you can choose from several versions of the Remote Administration Tools for Windows NT that enable you to administer Windows NT Domains from Windows 95 and from Windows NT Workstation.

A. Remote Administration Tools for Windows 95

The Windows 95 Remote Administration Tools allow a client running Windows 95 to manage the following aspects of a Windows NT Server domain:

- You can manage users in a domain with User Manager for Domains.
- Manage servers in the domain using Server Manager.
- Troubleshoot servers using the Event Viewer to view System, Application, and Audit Logs.
- Extensions to the Windows 95 Explorer enable you to manage NTFS permissions, auditing, and print permissions through the Network Neighborhood.
- Manage servers running File and Print Services for NetWare from the Windows 95 system through the FPNW tab of any drive on that server.

B. Remote Administration Tools for Windows NT

The Windows NT Server Tools for Windows NT Workstation enable you to manage a Windows NT domain from either a Windows NT Workstation or a Windows NT Member Server. The Windows NT Server Tools for Windows NT Workstation include the following utilities:

- **DHCP Manager:** Covered in Chapter 10, "Connectivity."
- **System Policy Editor:** As discussed in the previous section, you implement system policies by using the System Policy Editor.
- **Remote Access Admin:** Covered in Chapter 10.
- **Remote Boot Manager:** Covered in Chapter 8, "Installation and Configuration."
- **Server Manager:** Covered in Chapter 8.
- **User Manager for Domains:** As discussed in Section 9.1, you create Windows NT user accounts in the User Manager for Domains.
- **WINS Manager:** Covered in Chapter 10.
- **Extensions for Managing Services for Macintosh:** Covered in Chapter 8.

C. Web-Based Administration Tools

The Windows NT Server Resource Kit includes a new utility that enables you to remotely administer Windows NT Servers from Windows, Macintosh, and UNIX hosts running web browser software. This utility is also available for download from the Microsoft web site. Implement Web Administration tools as an Internet Information Server extension. The only caveat is that the person connecting to the NT Administration page must be a member of the Domain's Administrators local group.

To install the Web Administration tools on a Domain Controller, use the following steps:

1. Insert the Windows NT Server Resource Kit CD into the CD Drive of the domain controller to be managed.
2. From the autorun screen presented, choose the Web Administration link.
3. On the next screen, choose the Install Now link.
4. To continue the installation, you must agree to the End User License Agreement by clicking the Yes button.
5. To start the installation, click the Continue button.
6. To complete the installation, click the Exit to Windows button. The Readme file for the Web Administration tools is displayed to finalize the installation.
7. To access the web-based administration tools, start your web browser and go to the address `http://<your_server_name>/ntadmin/ntadmin.htm`.

The Web Administration tools are intended for an experienced NT administrator. These tools allow limited administration of a Windows NT domain controller using HTML forms. Management tasks that can be performed from Web Administration tools include:

- Managing user accounts.
- Managing global and local accounts.
- Adding and removing Windows NT computer accounts to/from a domain.
- Stopping and starting devices on the system.
- Viewing the System, Audit, and Application.
- Managing shared directories and their permissions.
- Managing NTFS file and directory permissions.
- Sending a broadcast message to all users with open sessions to the server.
- Setting up the server to run the Windows NT Resource Kit Remote Console Utility.
- Rebooting the server using the web page.
- Setting the preferences for the Web Administration Tools.
- Managing printers hosted by the server.
- Stopping, starting, and configuring services running on the server.
- Managing all active sessions. This includes disconnecting all or specific sessions.
- Viewing the server configuration. This makes use of the WINMSDP utility from the resource kit. This utility provides the same information as the graphical WINMSD utility, but in text-only format.
- Viewing a report format on selected performance counters.
- Viewing server statistics.

9.3.1 Exercise: Installing Remote Administration for Windows NT Server on Windows 95

To install the Remote Administration for Windows NT Server, perform the following steps:

1. Open the Windows 95 Control Panel.
2. Open the Add/Remove Programs applet in Control Panel.
3. On the Windows Setup tab, click the Have Disk button.
4. Insert the Windows NT Server CD and on the CD select the `\CLIENTS\SRVTOOLS\WIN95` directory where the SRVTOOLS.INF file is located using the Browse button.
5. In the dialog box that appears after clicking the OK button, select the Windows NT Server Tools option and click the Install button. This installs the Server Tools into the c:\srvtools directory by default using about 3 MB of disk space.
6. You must manually adjust the path statement in AUTOEXEC.BAT to include the directory `c:\srvtools`.
7. After the path has been adjusted in AUTOEXEC.BAT, you must reboot the system for all changes to take place.

9.3.2 Exercise: Installing Server Tools for Windows NT Workstation

To install the Server Tools for Windows NT Workstation, perform the following steps:

1. Insert the Windows NT 4 Server CD.
2. Run SETUP.BAT from the `\clients\srvtools\winnt` folder. This copies all the necessary files to the NT Workstation and makes the necessary Registry setting changes to enable you to manage Windows NT domains.
3. The installation program does not automatically create the Windows NT Server Tools icons in the Start menu. You must create the server tool icons manually in the Start menu.

9.3 Practice Problems

1. Versions of the Remote Administration Tools for Windows NT that shipped on the Windows NT 4.0 Server CD enable you to administer Windows NT domains from which two of the following operating systems?

   A. Windows 95

   B. Windows for Workgroups

   C. Windows NT Workstation

   D. LAN Manager

2. The Windows 95 Remote Administration Tools enable a client running Windows 95 to manage all but which of the following aspects of a Windows NT Server domain?

   A. You can manage users in a domain with User Manager.

   B. Servers in the domain.

   C. Troubleshooting of servers.

   D. Extensions to the Windows 95 Explorer enable you to manage NTFS permissions.

3. When using the Windows 95 Remote Administration Tools, which of the following can you manage on a Windows NT Server Domain? Select all correct answers.

   A. Auditing

   B. Print permission management

   C. NTFS permissions

   D. Dial-up connections

4. Which tool do you use from Windows 95 Remote Administration to manage servers in a domain?

   A. Event Viewer

   B. User Manager

   C. Server Manager

   D. Network Neighborhood

5. Which tool do you use from Windows 95 Remote Administration to manage users in a domain?

   A. Event Viewer

   B. User Manager

   C. Server Manager

   D. Network Neighborhood

6. Which tool do you use from Windows 95 Remote Administration to troubleshoot servers in a domain?

   A. Event Viewer

   B. User Manager

   C. Server Manager

   D. Network Neighborhood

7. You can manage servers running File and Print Services for NetWare from the Windows 95 system through:

   A. Network Neighborhood

   B. User Manager

   C. Event Viewer

   D. The FPNW tab of any drive on that server

8. The Windows NT Server Tools for Windows NT Workstation include which of the following utilities? Select all correct answers.

   A. DHCP Manager

   B. System Policy Editor

   C. Remote Access Admin

   D. User Manager

9. The Windows NT Server Tools for Windows NT Workstation include which of the following utilities? Select all correct answers.

   A. Remote Boot Manager

   B. Server Manager

C. WINS Manager

D. Extensions for Managing Services for Macintosh

10. The Web Administration tools are available from what two sources:

A. The Microsoft web site.

B. The NT Server Resource Kit.

C. Through mail-order houses.

D. A subdirectory on the original distribution CDs.

11. The Web Administration tools enable you to remotely administer Windows NT Servers from what platforms? Select all correct answers.

A. OS/2 Workstations

B. Macintosh

C. UNIX hosts

D. CP/M

12. The Web Administration tools are implemented as:

A. A CMD script

B. An ActiveX plug-in

C. A DirectX extension

D. An Internet Information Server extension

13. When using the Web Administration tools, the person connecting to the NT Administration page must be a member of:

A. The domain's Administrators local group

B. Any domain's Administrators local group

C. The domain's Administrators global group

D. Any domain's Administrators global group

9.3.1 Answers and Explanations: Exercise

In this exercise, you installed Remote Administration for Windows NT Server on a Windows 95 client. Whenever a user tries to administer an NT domain using the Windows NT Remote Administration tools, users are asked to enter their passwords before running the utility. This ensures that the users have sufficient privileges to run the Administration Tools.

9.3.2 Answers and Explanations: Exercise

In this exercise, you installed the Server Tools for Windows NT Workstation. The Windows NT Server Tools for Windows NT Workstation enable you to manage a Windows NT domain from either a Windows NT Workstation or a Windows NT Member Server.

9.3 Answers and Explanations: Practice Problems

1. **A, C** You can choose among several versions of the Remote Administration Tools for Windows NT that enable you to administer Windows NT domains from Windows 95 and from Windows NT Workstation.

2. **A** You can use User Manager for domains, but not User Manager.

3. **A, B, C** The Windows 95 Remote Administration Tools enable a client running Windows 95 to manage NTFS permissions, auditing, and print permissions through the Network Neighborhood.

4. **C** Manage servers in the domain by using Server Manager.

5. **B** You can manage users in the domain by using User Manager.

6. **A** You can troubleshoot servers by using the Event Viewer to view System, Application, and Audit Logs.

7. **D** You can manage servers running File and Print Services for NetWare from the Windows 95 system through the FPNW tab of any drive on that server.
8. **D** The Windows NT Server Tools for Windows NT Workstation include User Manager for Domains and not User Manager (a Workstation utility).
9. **A, B, C, D** The Windows NT Server Tools for Windows NT Workstation include all four utilities listed.
10. **A, B** The Web Administration tools are available from the Microsoft web site or on the Server Resource Kit.
11. **B, C** The Web Administration tools enable you to remotely administer Windows NT from Windows, Macintosh, and UNIX hosts running web browser software.
12. **D** The Web Administration tools are implemented as an Internet Information Server extension.
13. **A** The person connecting to the NT Administration page must be a member of the domain's Administrators local group.

9.3 Key Words

Remote server

Web Administration tools

9.4 Managing Disk Resources

After you create your groups in Windows NT, the next step in securing your system is to protect your disk resources. Windows NT has two levels of security for protecting disk resources:

- Share permissions
- NTFS permissions

The management of both sets of permissions protects your Windows NT system from inappropriate access.

A. Creating and Sharing Resources

Share-level security enables a Windows NT administrator to protect resources from Network users. Shares have a level of security, and they are also used as the entry point into the system for Windows NT users.

There are four explicit share permissions that you can implement, as follows:

- **Read:** Enables users to connect to the resource and run programs. They also can view any documents that are stored in the share, but they cannot make any changes to the documents.
- **Change:** Enables users to connect to a resource and run programs. It also enables them to create new documents and subfolders, to modify existing documents, and to delete documents.
- **Full Control:** Enables users to do anything they want in the share. It also enables them to change the share permissions to affect all users. The full control permission generally is not required for most users. Change is sufficient for most day-to-day business needs.
- **No Access:** The most powerful permission. When it is implemented, the user assigned this permission has no access to the specified resource. It does not matter what other permissions are assigned. The No Access permission overrides any other assigned permissions.

1. Determining Effective Share Permissions

When users, through group membership, have been assigned varying levels of share permissions, the users' effective shared permissions are the accumulation of their individual shared permissions.

The only time that this is not the case is when you assign the user or a group to which the user belongs the explicit permission of No Access. The No Access permission always takes precedence over any other permissions you assign.

Remember you must create the local groups in the accounts database where the resource is located. If the resource is located on a domain controller, you can create the local group in the domain's accounts database. If the resource is located on a Windows NT Workstation or a Windows NT Member Server, you must create the local group in that system's accounts database.

B. Implementing Permissions and Security

NTFS permissions enable you to assign more comprehensive security to your computer system. NTFS permissions can protect you at the file level. Share permissions, on the other hand, can apply only to the directory level. NTFS permissions can affect users logged on locally or across the network to the system where you apply the NTFS permissions. Share permissions are in effect only when the user connects to the resource via the network.

You can apply NTFS permissions, when applied at the directory level, as one of the following default assignments shown in Table 9.4.1.

Table 9.4.1 NTFS Directory Permissions

NTFS Permission	Meaning
No Access (none)(none)	The No Access NTFS permission means that the user will have absolutely No Access to the directory or its files. This will override any other NTFS permissions they may have been assigned to them through other group memberships.
List (RX) (Not Specified)	The List NTFS permission enables the user to view the contents of a directory and to navigate to its subdirectories. It does not grant them access to the files in these directories unless specified in file permissions.
Read (RX) (RX)	The Read NTFS permission enables the user to navigate the entire directory structure, view the contents of the directory, view the contents of any files in the directory, and to execute programs.
Add (WX) (Not Specified)	The Add NTFS permission enables the user to add new subdirectories and files to the directory. It does not give the user access to the files within the directory unless specified in other NTFS permissions.
Add & Read (RWX) (RX)	The Add & Read NTFS permission enables a user to add new files to the directory structure. After the file has been added, the user has read only access to the files. This permission also enables the user to run programs.
Change (RWXD) (RWXD)	The Change NTFS permission enables the user to do the most data manipulation. They can view the contents of directories and files, run programs, modify the contents of data files, and delete files.
Full Control (All) (All)	The Full Control permission gives the user all the capabilities of the Change Permission. In addition, the user can change the permissions on that directory or any of its contents. They also can take ownership of the directory or any of its contents.
Special Directory	You can set the NTFS permissions as desired to any combination of (R)ead, (W)rite, E(X)ecute, (D)elete, Change (P)ermissions, and Take (O)wnership.

You can apply NTFS permissions to individual files in directories. The NTFS file permissions are shown in Table 9.4.2.

Table 9.4.2 NTFS File Permissions

NTFS Permission	Meaning
No Access (none)	The No Access NTFS file permission means that the users have absolutely No Access to that file. This overrides any other NTFS directory and file permissions they may have assigned to the users through other group memberships.
Read (RX)	The Read NTFS file permission enables the users to view the contents of files but make no changes to the contents. The users can also execute the file if it is a program.
Change (RWXD)	The Change NTFS file permission enables the users to make any editing changes they want to a data file, including deleting the file.
Full Control (All)	The Full Control file permission gives the users all the capabilities of the Change permission. The users can also change the permissions on that file and take ownership of that file, if they are not the present owner.
Special File	You can set the NTFS file permissions as desired to any combination of (R)ead, (W)rite, E(X)ecute, (D)elete, Change (P)ermissions, and Take (O)wnership.

1. Determining Effective NTFS Permissions

The determination of NTFS permissions is based on the cumulative NTFS permissions based on group membership. As with share permissions, the only wildcard is the No Access permission. If you assign users or a local group to which users belong the No Access permission, the other assigned permissions do not matter. Users have no access.

2. The Effects of Moving and Copying on NTFS Permissions

If a file is moved or copied to a new directory, this could change the permissions on an NTFS file. The permissions depend on whether the target directory is on the same NTFS volume as the current directory.

If a file is copied from one directory to another on a single NTFS volume, the file inherits the directory permissions for new files of the target directory. If a file is moved from one directory to another directory on the same NTFS volume, it retains the same NTFS permissions it had from the original directory.

The permissions get confusing when files are moved or copied from one NTFS volume to another NTFS volume. When you copy a file from an NTFS volume to another NTFS volume, the file always inherits the permissions of the target directory. This is also the case when you move a file between NTFS volumes because the file is not actually moved between NTFS volumes. The process is as follows:

- The file is copied to the target directory. This causes the file to inherit the permissions of the target directory.
- The file in the target directory is compared to the original file to verify that it is identical.
- The original file is deleted from the original directory.

3. Setting NTFS Permissions

You set NTFS permissions from the Security page of an NTFS file or directory object. To set NTFS permissions, users must meet one of the following criteria:

- Be a member of the Administrators local group.
- Be a member of the Server Operators local group.
- Be a member of the Power Users local group in a Windows NT Workstation or Windows NT Member Server environment.
- Be assigned the NTFS Permission of Change Permission (P) for a directory or file resource.
- Be the owner of a file or directory object. The owner of any object can change the permissions of that object at any time.
- Have the permission to Take Ownership so that they can become the owner of the file or directory object and change the permissions of that object.

When combining NTFS and share permissions, remember the following tips:

- You can assign users only to global groups in the same domain.
- Only global groups from trusted domains can become members of local groups in trusting domains.
- You assign NTFS permissions only to local groups in all correct test answers.
- Only NTFS permissions give you file-level security.

C. The Windows NT Security Model

In the Windows NT security model, users are associated with resources. Each resource has an Access Control List (ACL) that contains Access Control Entries (ACEs). When you determine whether you should grant users access to resources, the users' access tokens are compared to the ACL for the resources they are trying to access.

When users log in to the system, they receive access tokens that are attached to any processes that they run during the logon session. The access tokens contain their security IDs (SID) and all their group memberships. The access tokens serve as the credentials for the logon session. Whenever users try to access an object, they present the access tokens as their credentials. Because the access token is built during the logon process, group membership is not modified until the next user logon.

When the user attempts to open a resource, the user's access token is compared to the Access Control List for the resource. The Access Control Entries within the Access Control List are, by default, sorted with all No Access permissions at the top of the list. The evaluation of whether the user should be granted access to the resource is as follows:

1. If the users or any group that they belong to is explicitly denied access (assigned the No Access permission), the access to the resource is denied.
2. The ACEs are next checked to see whether any of the entries explicitly assigns the users or a group to which the users belong the type of access that they are attempting. If there is such an entry, access is granted to the resource.

3. Each entry in the ACL is investigated to determine whether the accumulated permissions enable the users to have the access that they attempt.
4. If the necessary rights cannot be accumulated from the ACL, the users are denied the access that they have attempted.

When a user opens the object successfully, the user's process is given a handle to the object. The handle is used to identify the user accessing the object. The system also creates a list of granted access rights to the object. This way, if the user attempts different transactions with the object, only the list of granted rights needs to be evaluated. The entire process of checking the object's ACL does not have to be performed on every transaction attempt.

Not checking the object's ACL is both good and bad. It is good because subsequent actions on a resource do not require a check against the ACL every time that the user attempts to manipulate the data. This reduces network traffic, because the Windows NT Challenge/Response transaction does not have to perform over and over again. It is bad because the users have the same access to the object as they did when they opened the object, even if the ACL is modified for the object after access occurs. The list of granted rights to the object stored in the users' process tables for that handle is not modified. They have the same level of access until they close the object and ultimately close the handle to the object.

D. Implementing File-Level Auditing

File-level auditing enables an administrator to review the security log to determine who may have created, deleted, or modified a specified file or directory. This can help identify problems in the security model implemented in a domain. To set up file-level auditing, two separate steps are required:

- Enable File and Object Access Auditing in the domain's Audit policy.
- Enable the detail of file level auditing you want to employ on specific file and directory objects on an NTFS volume.

A member of the Administrators local group must enable the File and Object Access auditing. After this has been enabled, administrators and any users or groups that you assign the User Right Manage Auditing and Security Log can set auditing on specific directories and review the security log for audit successes and failures.

To set up auditing on a specific directory or file on an NTFS volume, the person you assign the task of setting up auditing must bring up the properties for that directory or file object. By choosing the Security tab of the object, they can click the Auditing button to set the auditing levels for that object.

1. Setting the Permissions to Audit

Figure 9.4.1 provides an example of the Auditing property sheet of an object's Security properties.

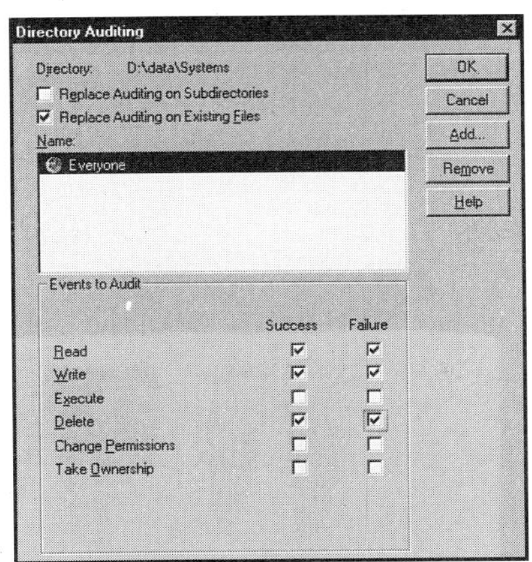

Figure 9.4.1 Setting auditing on a folder.

The administrator has to answer the following questions:

- Who are you going to audit?
- What actions are you going to audit?
- Do you want to apply this auditing to files and subfolders?

When determining the users to audit, remember that you are more likely to determine who performed a task by auditing the Everyone group rather than a smaller local group. The Everyone group is preferred when auditing because it includes all users that connect to the network (whether they are a known user is not important). If you know that only members of the local group Accounting_Users have access to a folder and its subfolders, it is fine to audit just this group.

After you select the users to audit, you now must select the actions to audit. Auditing is always based on either successes or failures. Be careful what you choose here. The actions that you can audit for a file or folder directly match the six different NTFS permissions. You must choose the correct combination of permissions that are being used to determine who is performing the task that causes the need for an audit. For example, if you are trying to determine who has been deleting the General Ledger, you must audit delete successes (as they have been very successful in deleting the file). The actions that you can audit include

- By enabling the Read event, you can determine whether an attempt was made to open a file.
- By enabling the Write event, you can determine when a user attempted to modify the contents of a file.
- By enabling the Execute event, you can determine when a user attempted to run a program.
- By enabling the Delete event, you can determine when a user attempted to delete a file object.
- By enabling the Change Permissions event, you can determine when a user tried to change the permissions on a file or directory.
- By enabling the Take Ownership event, you can determine when a user attempted to take ownership of a file or directory object.

After you set the auditing, you can check the Event Viewer's Security Log to determine the access done to the file or directory on which auditing was enabled. Figure 9.4.2 shows an event where bkomar attempted to delete the file named SECRET.DOC. It records as a failure event in the event viewer. The event shows that bkomar from the classroom domain was denied when attempting to delete the file `d:\data\systems\secret.doc`. If you scrolled down in the dialog box, it reveals that the access tried was DELETE.

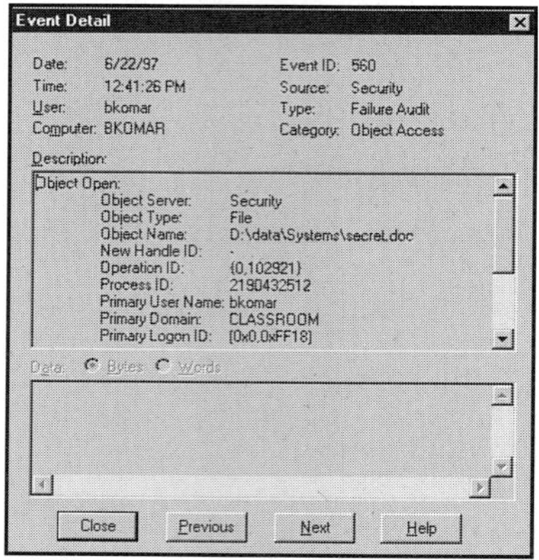

Figure 9.4.2 Security Failure Event for an attempt to delete a file.

2. The Effects of Moving and Copying Files on Auditing

As with NTFS permissions, the task of copying and moving files directly affects the auditing on files. If you copy a file from one NTFS directory to another NTFS directory, the new copy of the file inherits the auditing set on the target directory.

If you move a file from one NTFS directory to another NTFS directory on the same logical volume, the file maintains the same auditing settings that it had in the first directory.

If you move a file from one NTFS directory to another NTFS directory but they reside on different NTFS logical volumes, the file inherits the audit settings of the new folder. Anytime a file is moved between volumes on Windows NT, the actual chain of events is a copy, verify, and delete. That is, a copy of the original file is placed in the new directory. This copy is verified against the original copy of the file. Finally, if they match, the original file is deleted.

E. Auditing Logons and Logoffs

If you feel that your network has been compromised and unwanted users are accessing the network, the auditing of logons and logoffs can help determine what account they are using to access the network and what computer they are accessing the network from.

By auditing the successes and failures of the Logon and Logoff audit category, you can determine the location of the access point to your network. It is recommended that you monitor both successes and failures, because you want to know where the attempts to access the network are taking place and whether the attempts are successful.

9.4.1 Exercise: Creating a Shared Folder

To create a shared folder, complete the following:

1. Right-click the folder that you want to share in either My Computer or the Windows NT Explorer. Remember that this folder is an artificial root directory for all users who access the share.
2. From the pop-up menu, choose the Sharing option.
3. The Sharing property sheet enables you to give a name to the share and set limits to the number of users who can access the share simultaneously.
4. Click the Permissions button.
5. You should first determine whether you can use an existing local group to grant access to the resource. If you can, grant access to the share by clicking the Add button and choosing the local group from the list of groups. If no local group exists, you may need to switch briefly into User Manager for Domains and add the local group to the appropriate accounts database. To remove a group from the list, choose the group you want to remove and click the Remove button.
6. Click the OK button to finalize the permissions for the share.
7. Click the OK button to close the Sharing Properties page.

9.4.2 Exercise: Setting NTFS Permissions

To set the NTFS permissions on a directory or file object, complete the following steps:

1. Right-click the NTFS Resource.
2. Choose Properties from the pop-up menu for the object.
3. Switch to the Security Page of the object. This appears only if the resource is on an NTFS volume.
4. Click the Permissions button.
5. Click the Add button to add new groups and users to assign NTFS permissions to the resource.
6. Click the local group or user to which you want to assign permissions and choose the NTFS permission you want to assign from the bottom drop list.
7. Click the OK button to return to the Directory Permissions dialog box. From the top of the dialog box, choose whether you want to replace the permissions on all existing files in the directory and whether you want the changes to propagate to all subdirectories.
8. Click OK to make effective your changes to NTFS permissions.
9. Answer Yes to the dialog box that asks whether you want the change in security information to replace the existing security information on all files in all subdirectories.
10. Click OK to exit the Directory's Properties dialog box.

9.4 Practice Problems

1. Which two of the following are the two levels of security for protecting your disk resources in Windows NT?

   A. Share permissions

   B. NTFS permissions

   C. User permissions

   D. Attributes

2. Which of the following enables Windows NT administrators to protect their resources from Network users?

   A. Share-level security

   B. User-level security

   C. Resource security

   D. Attributes

3. Which of the following is used as the entry point into the system for Windows NT users?

   A. Share-level security

   B. User-level security

   C. Resource security

   D. Attributes

4. Which of the following explicit share permissions can you implement? Select all correct answers.

   A. Modify

   B. Read

   C. Full Control

   D. No Access

5. Which is the minimum permission that enables users to connect to a resource and run programs?

   A. Full Control

   B. Read

   C. No Access

   D. Change

6. Which permission enables users to view documents that are stored in the share, but does not enable them to make changes to the documents?

   A. Full Control

   B. Read

   C. No Access

   D. Change

7. Which minimum share permission enables users to connect and to create new documents and subfolders?

   A. Full Control

   B. Read

   C. No Access

   D. Change

8. Which minimum permission enables users to modify existing documents and delete documents?

   A. Full Control

   B. Read

   C. No Access

   D. Change

9. Which permission enables users to do anything they want in the share?

   A. Full Control

   B. Read

   C. No Access

   D. Change

10. Which permission is sufficient for most day-to-day business needs?

    A. Full Control

    B. Read

    C. No Access

    D. Change

11. As a general rule, which permission is considered the most powerful?

    A. Full Control

    B. Read

    C. No Access

    D. Change

12. Users whom you assign varying levels of permissions through group memberships have effective shared permissions of:

    A. The accumulation of their individual shared permissions.

    B. The lowest possible permissions.

    C. Those permissions assigned the highest priority.

    D. The permissions assigned to the highest priority group of which they belong.

13. The only time the situation in question 12 differs is when the user or a group to which the user belongs has been assigned the explicit permission of:

    A. Full Control

    B. No Access

    C. Change

    D. Read

14. To what level of depth can share permissions go?

    A. Root level

    B. Directory level

    C. Subdirectory level

    D. File level

15. To what level of depth can NTFS permissions go?

    A. Root level

    B. Directory level

    C. Subdirectory level

    D. File level

16. At what levels do share permissions affect users? Select all correct answers.

    A. Locally.

    B. When logged across the network.

    C. When running other operating systems locally.

    D. They do not affect them.

17. At what levels do NTFS permissions affect users? Select all correct answers.

    A. Locally.

    B. When logged across the network.

    C. When running other operating systems locally.

    D. They do not affect them.

18. Which of the following NTFS directory permissions enables users to view the contents of a directory and to navigate to its subdirectories?

    A. No Access

    B. List

    C. Read

    D. Add

19. Which of the following NTFS directory permissions overrides all other permissions?

    A. No Access

    B. List

    C. Read

    D. Add

20. Which of the following NTFS directory permissions enables users to do the most data manipulation?

    A. No Access

    B. List

    C. Read

    D. Change

21. Which of the following NTFS directory permissions enables users to navigate the entire directory structure, view the contents of the directory, view the contents of any files in the directory, and execute programs?

    A. No Access

    B. List

    C. Read

    D. Add

22. Which of the following NTFS directory permissions enables users to add new subdirectories and files to the directory, but does not enable them to access files within the directory?

    A. No Access

    B. List

    C. Read

    D. Add

23. Which set of NTFS directory permissions enables users to add new files to the directory structure, and after the files have been added, users have read-only access to the files?

    A. No Access

    B. List

    C. Read

    D. Add

24. If an NTFS file is moved to a new directory on the same volume, what will become of the permissions?

    A. The file will maintain its existing permissions.

    B. The file will assume permissions from the source.

    C. The file will assume permissions from the target.

    D. The file will abandon permissions.

25. If an NTFS file is copied to a new directory on the same volume, what will become of the permissions?

    A. The file will maintain its existing permissions.

    B. The file will assume permissions from the source.

    C. The file will assume permissions from the target.

    D. The file will abandon permissions.

9.4.1 Answers and Explanations: Exercise

The exercise illustrated how to create a shared folder and share it in Windows NT. You should be very familiar with this operation.

9.4.2 Answers and Explanations: Exercise

In this exercise, you created and changed NTFS permissions and saw the effects it created through the Directory's Properties dialog box.

9.4 Answers and Explanations: Practice Problems

1. **A, B** Windows NT has two levels of security for protecting disk resources: Share permissions and NTFS permissions.

2. **A** Share-level security enables Windows NT administrators to protect their resources from Network users.

3. **A** Shares have a level of security, and they are also used as the entry point into the system for Windows NT users.

4. **B, C, D** There are four explicit share permissions that can be implemented. They are: Read, Change, Full Control, and No Access.

5. **B** The Read permission enables a user to connect to the resource and run programs.

6. **B** With the Read permission, users can view any documents that are stored in the share, but they cannot make any changes to the documents.
7. **D** The Change permissions setting enables users to connect to a resource and run programs. It also enables them to create new documents and subfolders, modify existing documents, and delete documents.
8. **D** See answer to 7.
9. **A** The Full Control permission enables users to do anything they want in the share.
10. **D** Change permission is sufficient for most day-to-day business needs.
11. **C** The No Access permission is the most powerful permission. When it is implemented, the user that you assign this permission has no access to that resource.
12. **A** When users, through group membership, have been assigned varying levels of share permissions, their effective shared permissions are the accumulation of their individual shared permissions.
13. **B** The No Access permission always takes precedence over any other assigned permissions.
14. **C** Share permissions can be applied only to the subdirectory level.
15. **D** NTFS permissions protect you at the file level.
16. **B** Share permissions are in effect only when the user connects to the resource via the network.
17. **A, B** NTFS permissions can affect users logged on locally or across the network to the system where the NTFS permissions apply.
18. **B** List enables the user to view the contents of a directory and to navigate to its subdirectories.
19. **A** No Access overrides all other permissions.
20. **D** Change enables the user to do the most data manipulation.
21. **C** Read enables the user to navigate the entire directory structure, view the contents of the directory, view the contents of any files in the directory, and execute programs.
22. **D** Add enables the user to add new subdirectories and files to the directory, but Add does not enable the user to access files within the directory.
23. **C, D** Add enables a user to add new files to the directory structure, and after the files have been added, the users have read-only access to the files.
24. **A** If a file is moved from one directory to another directory on the same NTFS volume, it retains the same NTFS permissions it had.
25. **C** If a file is copied from one directory to another on a single NTFS volume, the file inherits the directory permissions for new files of the target directory.

9.4 Key Words

Access Control List

Access Control Entries

Security log

Practice Exam: Managing Resources

Use this practice exam to test your mastery of "Managing Resources." This practice exam is 17 questions long. The passing Microsoft score is 78.4 percent (13 right on this practice test). Questions are in multiple-choice format.

1. If you take ownership of a file or directory, you are automatically a member of which group?
    A. Domain Local
    B. Domain User
    C. Creator/Owner
    D. Admin

2. To enable auditing of changes to the account database, a member of which group must enable auditing User and Group Management?
    A. Creator/Owner
    B. Administrators
    C. Local
    D. Global

3. To know exactly what files are being updated, what component of auditing must you enable?
    A. File and Object Access
    B. Account Operator
    C. TTS
    D. SAM

4. This is the Security hive of the HKEY_LOCAL_MACHINE subtree in the Registry:
    A. File and Object Access
    B. The SAM Account Database
    C. Audit records
    D. TTS

5. Built-in global groups include all the following except:
    A. Everyone
    B. Domain Admins
    C. Domain Guests
    D. Domain Users

6. The System Policy Editor uses which types of groups for group membership?
    A. Local
    B. Global
    C. Domain
    D. Admin

7. If you use group policies, and a user belongs to more than one group, the order in which the group settings are processed becomes critical. What setting can you use to change the processing order?
    A. Group Priority
    B. Group Process
    C. Group Order
    D. Group Rank

8. When Kristin logs in to the network, her login script executes only some of the time. What would be a likely reason for this?
    A. She is not using the correct password.
    B. She is not logging out of one session before beginning the next.
    C. Group policies are overriding user policies.
    D. Directory Replication is not functioning properly.

9. System policy files are stored where on a NetWare 4.x network?
   A. SYS:PUBLIC
   B. In individual users' mail directories
   C. NETLOGON share
   D. Locally

10. System policy files are stored where on a NetWare 3.x network?
    A. SYS:PUBLIC
    B. In individual users' mail directories
    C. NETLOGON share
    D. Locally

11. The Web Administration tools enable limited administration of a Windows NT domain controller using:
    A. HTTP protocols
    B. HTML forms
    C. RPC calls
    D. UDP sessions

12. Management tasks that you can perform from the Web Administration tools include which of the following?
    A. Manage user accounts
    B. Manage global and local groups
    C. Reboot connected workstations
    D. Add and remove Windows NT computer accounts to/from domains

13. If an NTFS file is moved to a new directory on a different NTFS volume, what will become of the permissions?
    A. The file will maintain its existing permissions.
    B. The file will assume permissions from the source.
    C. The file will assume permissions from the target.
    D. The file will abandon permissions.

14. Where are NTFS permissions set?
    A. From the Security page of an NTFS object
    B. From the NET USE command line
    C. From User Manager
    D. From DiskPerf

15. To set NTFS permissions, a user must meet one of which two of the following criteria?
    A. Be a member of the Administrators local group
    B. Be a member of the Administrators global group
    C. Be a member of the Server Operators local group
    D. Be a member of the Server Operators global group

16. To enable the File and Object Access auditing, a member of which group must enable this auditing feature:
    A. Administrators global
    B. Administrators local
    C. Domain Users global
    D. Domain Users local

17. Susan has been told to enable auditing for a specific NTFS file. What must she do, assuming that auditing is already turned on?
    A. Select the Security tab of the object from Properties and click the Auditing button.
    B. Issue the appropriate NET USE command.
    C. Place the Audit attribute on the file.
    D. Turn Auditing on from User Manager.

9

Answers and Explanations: Practice Exam

1. **C** If you take ownership of a file or directory, you are automatically a member of the Creator/Owner group.
2. **B** To enable auditing of changes to the account database, a member of the Administrators group must enable auditing User and Group Management.
3. **A** To know exactly what files are being updated, you should enable File and Object Access.
4. **B** The SAM Account Database is the Security hive of the HKEY_LOCAL_MACHINE subtree in the Registry.
5. **A** Built-in global groups are: Domain Admins, Domain Guests, and Domain Users.
6. **B** The System Policy Editor uses global groups for group membership.
7. **A** Group order is set in the Group Priority option of the Options menu.
8. **D** Directory Replication ensures that each domain controller in the domain contains the same files and versions of the files in their NETLOGON share. If there is a problem with replication, login scripts can execute only some of the time when a user accesses the network.
9. **A** System policy files are stored in the SYS:PUBLIC directory in Novell NetWare 4.x networks.
10. **B** System policy files are stored in individual users' mail directories in Novell NetWare 3.x networks.
11. **B** The Web Administration tools enable limited administration of a Windows NT domain controller using HTML forms.
12. **A, B, D** With Web Administration tools, you have the capability to Manage User Accounts, Manage Global and Local Accounts, and Add and Remove Windows NT Computer accounts to a domain, among others.
13. **C** When you move a file from an NTFS volume to another NTFS volume, the file always inherits the permissions of the target directory.
14. **A** NTFS permissions are set from the Security page of an NTFS file or directory object.
15. **A, C** To set NTFS Permissions, a user must meet be a member of one of the two local groups.
16. **B** To enable the File and Object Access auditing, a member of the Administrators local group must enable this auditing feature.
17. **A** To set up auditing on a specific directory or file on an NTFS volume, the person assigned the task of setting up auditing must bring up the properties for that directory or file object. By choosing the Security tab of the object, they can click the Auditing button to set the auditing levels for that object.

CHAPTER 10

Connectivity

This chapter helps you prepare for the exam by covering the following objectives:

- Configure Windows NT Server for interoperability with NetWare servers using Gateway Services for NetWare and Migration Tool for NetWare.
- Install and configure multiprotocol routing to serve various functions including Internet Router, BOOTP/DHCP Relay Agent, and IPX Router.
- Install and configure Internet Information Server (IIS).
- Install and configure Internet services including World Wide Web and DNS.
- Install and Configure Remote Access Service (RAS) including communications, protocols, and security.

10.1 Interoperability with NetWare

Although organizations continue to rapidly deploy Windows NT in the enterprise, many organizations still have legacy NetWare systems that must be able to interoperate with Windows NT. Microsoft ensured compatibility with NetWare servers by including the NWLINK IPX/SPX compatible protocol, but they did not end there. Microsoft bundles in the Gateway Services for NetWare (GSNW) and also includes a utility to help smooth the conversion from NetWare into Windows NT Server. In the following sections you learn about:

- Gateway Services for NetWare (GSNW)
- Installing and configuring GSNW
- NWCONV: Migration Tool for NetWare

A. Gateway Services for NetWare

Gateway Services for NetWare performs the following functions:

- Enables Windows NT Servers to access NetWare file and print resources.
- Enables the Windows NT Servers to act as a gateway to the NetWare file and print resources. The Windows NT Server can share off the connection to the NetWare server.

GSNW can provide Windows NT networks with convenient access to NetWare resources. GSNW enables one single connection to be shared by multiple Windows NT clients. This sharing of a connection is very convenient. However, it also causes a significant performance loss for the NetWare resource. GSNW is ideal for occasional NetWare resource access, but it is not recommended for large-scale routing.

1. Installing GSNW

GSNW is a network service, and you install it using the Services tab of the Control Panel Network icon. Click the Add button to view a list of available services, and in the list, find the Gateway Services for NetWare option, and then click OK. You may be prompted for the location of your Windows NT source files—give the location, and then you will be prompted to restart your system.

2. Configuring GSNW

After the system restarts, you can configure GSNW to act as a gateway to the NetWare resources. To enable GSNW to act as a gateway for your Windows NT clients, you must perform the following steps:

1. On the NetWare server, create a group called NTGATEWAY.
2. Create a user account on the NetWare server for the gateway to use and add the account to the NTGATEWAY group.
3. From the Control Panel, double-click the GSNW icon to start the Gateway Services for NetWare dialog box.
4. To configure the gateway options, click the Gateway button located on the right corner of the dialog box.
5. The Configure Gateway dialog box appears.
6. Click the Enable Gateway check box. In the account box, enter the name of the gateway account and password matching the account you created on the NetWare server.
7. You can then create shares to the NetWare resources in the bottom section of the Configure Gateway dialog box. Click the Add button to create a share to the NetWare resources.
8. After you create the share, you can apply the standard Windows NT share permissions to the NetWare share. Click the Permissions button to assign specific permissions to your Windows NT users.
9. After you complete the Configure Gateway screen, click OK to close the dialog box. You can then select your preferred NetWare server, default tree and context, and print options for your Windows NT Server to connect to the NetWare server.
10. After you establish all configuration settings, click OK to close the Gateway Services for NetWare dialog box.

Gateway Services for NetWare is now available to the users of the Windows NT Server. A user can use GSNW by making a network connection to the NetWare share created on the Windows NT Server computer.

B. NWCONV: Migration Tool for NetWare

The Migration Tool for NetWare transfers file and directory information and user and group account information from a NetWare server to a Windows NT domain controller. The Migration Tool can preserve the directory and file permissions if it is being transferred to an NTFS partition. Table 10.1.1 displays the corresponding NetWare and Windows NT NTFS rights that are being converted.

Table 10.1.1 Conversion of Rights

Novell NetWare Permission	Windows NT Permission
Supervisor (S)	Full Control (All)
Read (R)	Read (RX)
Write (W)	Change (RWXD)
Erase (E)	Change (RWXD)
Modify (M)	Change (RWXD)
Create (C)	Add (WX) Custom right
File Scan (F)	List (RX) Custom right
Access Control (A)	Change Permission (P)

If the partition to which you are migrating is a FAT partition, no rights or permissions are maintained.

To start the Migration Tool for NetWare, run the NWCONV.EXE file. For test purposes, it must be executed from a command prompt or from the Start, Run command.

1. Steps for Migrating from NetWare

When the Migration Tool for NetWare is first started, a dialog box displays that enables you to select the NetWare and Windows NT Server domain controller with which you will be working.

To be able to accomplish the migration from the NetWare server onto your Windows NT Server computer, you must have supervisor access to the NetWare system, and you must be an administrator in the Windows NT domain to which you will be migrating.

To complete the migration from a NetWare server to a Windows NT Server, follow these steps:

1. From the Start menu choose the Run command, type **NWCONV**, and press Enter.
2. Click the Add button and select your NetWare server and Windows NT domain controller, and then click OK.
3. You then have the option to configure the User Options or the File Options. After you configure each of these sections, you can either click the Start Migration button, or you can do a trial migration first to verify your settings (which is highly recommended).

2. User and Group Options

All the user accounts from your NetWare server are migrated by default to the Windows NT domain controller. To disable the transfer of users and groups, click the Transfer Users and Groups check box located at the top of the User and Group Options dialog box.

The User and Group Options dialog box holds all the options available on four pages: Passwords, User Names, Group Names, and Defaults.

3. Passwords

The passwords from the NetWare server cannot be migrated across for security reasons; however, the Migration Tool can be used to specify how the passwords for the migrated users should be handled:

- **No Password:** The migrated users have no passwords assigned to them.
- **Password is Username:** The migrated users have passwords the same as their usernames.
- **Password is:** Assigns a single password to all migrated users.
- **User must Change Password:** Forces the migrated users to change their passwords the first time they log on to the Windows NT Server.

4. User Names and Group Names

You need to configure the Migration Tool in case it runs into a duplicate username or group name during the migration. The User Names page enables you to select how the Migration Tool should react to the duplicates.

- **Log Error:** Adds an error to the ERROR.LOG file.
- **Ignore:** Causes the account to be skipped with no error messages or warnings. This is the default option.
- **Overwrite with New Information:** The existing account would be overwritten with the new NetWare user information.
- **Add Prefix:** Includes a prefix with the user account to enable you to distinguish between the existing account and the migrated account.

5. Defaults Page Tab

The Defaults page tab contains two options:

- **Use Supervisor Defaults:** You can use the supervisor account restrictions for the migrated users instead of using the account policies in the Windows NT Server.
- **Add Supervisors to the Administrators Group:** The migrated users that have supervisor equivalent access are added into the Windows NT domains Administrators group. By default, the supervisors from the NetWare system are not added into this group.

10.1.1 Exercise: Installing Gateway Services for NetWare

This exercise assumes several things:

- The NetWare server is version 3.x.
- The NTGATEWAY groups has been created on the NetWare server.
- The gateway account has been created on the NetWare server and is a member of the NTGATEWAY group.

This exercise steps you through the process of installing Gateway Services for NetWare, and setting up a gateway from the Windows NT Server into the NetWare Server.

1. Click the right mouse button on the Network Neighborhood, and choose the Properties option.
2. Click the Services page tab.
3. Click the Add button, and then select the Gateway (and Client) Services for NetWare.
4. Click OK.
5. Windows NT prompts you for the location of your Windows NT Server source directory. Enter the location of the source files, and then click Continue.
6. Click Close to close the Network Properties dialog box. The network is reconfigured.
7. The system prompts you to restart your computer. Click OK to enable the restart.
8. When the system restarts, log on to the Windows NT domain, and the system prompts you for the NetWare server to which you want to log on. Select the NetWare server available, and then click OK to log on to the NetWare server.
9. After the system completes the logons, click the Start menu, Settings, Control Panel option.
10. After the Control Panel opens, locate the GSNW icon and double-click it to launch the GSNW dialog box.
11. In the Select Preferred Server dialog box, choose your NetWare server.
12. Click the Gateway button. The Configure Gateway dialog box opens.
13. Click Enable Gateway.
14. Enter the Gateway account name and password information. Remember that the Gateway account must be a valid account on the NetWare server, and it must be a member of the NetWare NTGATEWAY group.
15. Click the Add button to create a NetWare share to the NetWare server.
16. Enter the share name. For this example, enter NetWare as the share name.
17. In the network path, enter the UNC path to the NetWare server SYS volume. Type **\\NWSERVER\SYS**.
18. In the Use Drive box, click Z:, and then click OK.
19. Click OK to close the Configure Gateway dialog box.
20. Click OK to close the Gateway Services for NetWare dialog box.

10.1.2 Exercise: Running a Trial Migration from a NetWare Server to a Windows NT Domain Controller

This exercise steps you through the configuration settings for the migration process, and then through a trial migration.

1. To start a NetWare migration, click the Start menu and choose the Run command.
2. In the Run command box, type **NWCONV.EXE** and press Enter.
3. When the NWCONV utility starts, the system prompts you to select the NetWare and Windows NT servers to use for the migration. After you select the servers, click OK.
4. Click the User Options button.
5. Select the Transfer Users and Groups check box.
6. In the Passwords page tab, select the No Password option.
7. Click on the User Names page tab, and select the Add Prefix command and enter **NW** for the prefix.
8. Click on the Group Names page tab, and select the Add Prefix command and enter **NW** for the prefix.
9. Click OK on the User and Group Options dialog box.
10. Click the File Options Button, and select the files and directories to transfer.
11. After you select the files and directories, click OK to close the File Options dialog box.
12. After you configure the User and File Options, click the Trial Migration button.
13. After the Trial Migration completes, view the log files to see whether there are any potential problems in your migration, which are signified by error messages.
14. After the Trial Migration completes and you have reviewed the log files, click Exit to close the Migration Tool for NetWare.

10.1 Practice Problems

1. Microsoft ensured compatibility with NetWare servers by including what protocol with NT Server?

   A. NWLINK

   B. IPX/SPX

   C. TCP/IP

   D. NetBEUI

2. What utility has Microsoft bundled with NT to help smooth the conversion from NetWare into Windows NT Server?

   A. Migration Tool for NetWare

   B. NetBEUI

   C. Gateway Services for NetWare

   D. IIS

3. Which of the following two functions does Gateway Services for NetWare perform? Choose all that apply.

   A. Enables Windows NT Servers to access NetWare file and print resources.

   B. Provides additional security for NetWare servers.

   C. Enables login scripts to be processed.

   D. Enables the Windows NT Servers to act as a gateway to the NetWare file and print resources.

4. How many connections to the NetWare server does GSNW require?

   A. 1

   B. 2

   C. 4

   D. 8

5. What utility transfers file and directory information and user and group account information from a NetWare server to a Windows NT domain controller?

   A. Gateway Services for NetWare

   B. Migration Tool for NetWare

   C. NTFS

   D. NetBEUI

6. For the Migration Tool for NetWare to maintain directory and file permissions, what type of partition must the target be?

   A. FAT

   B. VFAT

   C. NTFS

   D. CDFS

7. For the Migration Tool for NetWare to maintain directory and file permissions, what type of partition must the source be?

   A. FAT

   B. VFAT

   C. NTFS

   D. CDFS

8. To what NetWare permission does the NT Full Control permission map?

   A. Read

   B. Write

   C. Modify

   D. Supervisor

9. To what NetWare permission does the NT Read permission map?

   A. Read

   B. Write

   C. Modify

   D. Supervisor

10. To what NetWare permission does the NT Change permission map? Choose all that apply.

    A. Read

    B. Write

    C. Modify

    D. Supervisor

11. To what NT permission does NetWare's Create permission map?

    A. Change Permission

    B. List

    C. Add

    D. Change

12. To what NT permission does NetWare's File Scan permission map?

    A. Change Permission

    B. List

    C. Add

    D. Change

13. To what NT permission does NetWare's Access Control permission map?

    A. Change Permission

    B. List

    C. Add

    D. Change

14. What rights and permissions are maintained when migrating from NetWare to an NT FAT partition?

    A. All rights and permissions.

    B. All rights but no permissions.

    C. No rights but all permissions.

    D. No rights and no permissions.

15. What utility is used to start the Migration Tool for NetWare?

    A. NWCONV.EXE

    B. MIGRATE.COM

    C. MIGRATE.EXE

    D. MGTOOL.EXE

16. What becomes of passwords from the NetWare server during migration?

    A. Duplicate ones are discarded.

    B. Duplicate ones are written to an error file.

    C. All passwords are maintained.

    D. All passwords are discarded.

17. What is the result of selecting "Password Is:" in the Migration Tool?

    A. Migrated users have no passwords assigned to them.

    B. Migrated users' passwords are the same as their usernames.

    C. A single password is assigned to all migrated users.

    D. Migrated users are forced to change their passwords the first time they log on to the Windows NT Server.

18. What is the result of selecting "User Must Change Password:" in the Migration Tool?

    A. Migrated users have no passwords assigned to them.

    B. Migrated users' passwords are the same as their usernames.

    C. A single password is assigned to all migrated users.

    D. Migrated users are forced to change their passwords the first time they log on to the Windows NT Server.

19. What is the result of selecting "Password is Username:" in the Migration Tool?

    A. Migrated users have no passwords assigned to them.

    B. Migrated users' passwords are the same as their usernames.

    C. A single password is assigned to all migrated users.

    D. Migrated users are forced to change their passwords the first time they log on to the Windows NT Server.

10.1.1 Answers and Explanations: Exercise

In this exercise, you walked through the process of installing Gateway Services for NetWare. After the installation, you set up a gateway from the Windows NT Server into the NetWare server.

10.1.2 Answers and Explanations: Exercise

In this exercise, you walked through the configuration settings for the migration process, and then attempted a trial migration. You should also examine the log files for errors that occurred.

10.1 Answers and Explanations: Practice Problems

1. **A** Microsoft ensures compatibility with NetWare servers by including the NWLINK IPX/SPX-compatible protocol.

2. **C** Microsoft also bundles Gateway Services for NetWare (GSNW) to help smooth the conversion from NetWare to Windows NT Server.

3. **A, D** Gateway Services for NetWare performs the following functions: enables Windows NT Servers to access NetWare file and print resources, and enables the Windows NT Servers to act as a gateway to the NetWare file and print resources.

4. **A** GSNW enables multiple Windows NT clients to share a single connection.

5. **B** The Migration Tool for NetWare transfers file and directory information and user and group account information from a NetWare server to a Windows NT domain controller.

6. **C** The Migration Tool for NetWare can preserve the directory and file permissions if it is being transferred to an NTFS partition.

7. **A** NetWare partitions are always FAT.

8. **D** Full Control equates to NetWare's Supervisor permission.

9. **A** The Read permission is identical on both NetWare and NT.

10. **B, C** Change equates to NetWare's Write, Erase, and Modify permissions.

11. **C** NetWare's Create permission equates to NT's Add permission.

12. **B** NetWare's File Scan permission equates to NT's List permission.

13. **A** NetWare's Access Control permission equates to NT's Change Permission (P) permission.

14. **D** If the partition to which you are migrating is a FAT partition, no rights and permissions are maintained.

15. **A** To start the Migration Tool for NetWare, you must run the NWCONV.EXE file from the command prompt.

16. **D** For security reasons you cannot migrate across the passwords from the NetWare server.
17. **C** "Password Is:" assigns a single password to all migrated users.
18. **D** "User Must Change Password:" forces the migrated users to change their passwords the first time they log on to the Windows NT Server.
19. **B** "Password is Username:" means that the migrated users' passwords are the same as their usernames.

10.1 Key Words

File and Print Sharing

IPX/SPX

NetWare

NWLink

10.2 Installing and Configuring Multiprotocol Routing

This section discusses installing and configuring multiprotocol routing, including Internet router and IPX router. Multiprotocol routing enables you to send more than one protocol across the router.

A. Internet Router

Windows NT can act as a router between the Internet and the internal network. With a router, all incoming packets from the Internet are forwarded into the network.

Setting Windows NT up as an Internet router is as simple as installing two network adapters in the system, and then enabling IP routing via Control Panel, Networks, the TCP/IP protocol configuration. This option enables Windows NT to act as a static router. Take note that Windows NT cannot exchange Routing Information Protocol (RIP) routing packets with other IP RIP routers unless the RIP routing software is installed.

To enable IP RIP routing, you must install the RIP routing software from Control Panel, Networks. This enables Windows NT to send out RIP packets once every 60 seconds, to exchange routing information with other dynamic RIP routing routers.

NT supports RIP I routing. Steelhead (RRAS) supports RIP II routing.

Without the RIP protocol, you must manually set up router tables using the ROUTE ADD command.

B. DHCP Server Service

DHCP is a service available on NT that dynamically assigns IP addresses to clients. Instead of manually assigning an IP address to each new computer you purchase, DHCP can assign an IP address to the computer each time it boots. This simplifies administration tremendously.

Setting up the DHCP Server Service requires Windows NT Server, with DHCP installed as a service. To install the DHCP Server Service, add the service under Control Panel, Networks.

After you install the DHCP Server Service, you can configure the service using the Administrative Tools, DHCP Manager option.

The local machine always appears on the list, but you can remotely administrate other servers by adding a server using the Servers menu option. After clicking on the local machine (or any other server that might appear in the list), you set up the DHCP scope—the range of available IP addresses.

The DHCP database is created in JET format and stored in the `\%systemroot%\system32\dhcp` subdirectory. You should back up the database occasionally using the JETPACK command, which also clears out deleted records.

10

1. DHCP Relay

The DHCP Relay tab enables a Windows NT system to relay DHCP messages for clients across an IP router. Normally, you configure IP routers not to forward broadcasts, so a client asking (broadcasting) for an IP address on a local segment when the DHCP server is located on a remote segment does not receive an answer. You also can specify optional timeout parameters in the DHCP Relay tab.

Add the addresses of any DHCP servers on the DHCP Relay tab so that DHCP requests (IP packets) can be directed appropriately.

The DHCP protocol originated as an expansion of the BOOTP protocol that enables diskless workstations to get their boot information from a server.

C. IPX Router

IPX is another protocol common to networks interacting with NetWare's IPX/SPX protocol. You enable the IPX router by installing the IPX RIP router software via Control Panel, Networks, Services.

After installing the IPX RIP router, Windows NT can route IPX packets over the installed network adapters. It uses the RIP to exchange its routing table information with other RIP routers. The default sending interval is once every 60 seconds, so you must be careful in deploying hundreds of RIP routers in an enterprise environment; these packets can consume a big chunk of network bandwidth (especially on WANs, where the bandwidth commonly is limited to 64 Kbps).

The configuration screen for the IPX Rip router is straightforward, and only prompts for whether the administrator wants to propagate NetBIOS broadcasts (type 20) packets over the router.

You have to propagate NetBIOS broadcasts over the router only if both sides of the Windows NT router contain Microsoft Clients (such as Windows 95 or Windows for Workgroups) that need to communicate browsing information over the router.

Although RIP does offer a number of benefits—including a reduction in administrative overhead associated with updating router tables—it does have a drawback in that RIP can increase network traffic in large networks as it routes table updates.

10.2.1 Exercise: Setting Up a DHCP Scope

In this exercise, you are working in the DHCP Manager to set up the DHCP scope. To do so, use the following steps:

1. Click on the Scope option and select Create Scope. The Create Scope dialog box appears.
2. Fill in the start and end address of the pool of addresses that will be distributed. For example, you might enter 177.22.34.100 for the Start Address field and 177.22.34.200 in the End Address field.
3. You also can exclude a set of addresses. You normally do this when the network consists of machines that aren't DHCP-aware, such as printers or legacy operating systems.
4. You should give the scope a name to identify the batch of systems to which this pool of addresses will be distributed.
5. Specifying the lease duration, which indicates how long a client machine may keep an address before it must reapply, is an important step. Keep the lease period short (a few days) when users are highly mobile. Lengthen the lease period to several months or years if you want the workstation to keep the IP addresses for a long time. You also can set the period to unlimited, in which case the workstations keep their assigned addresses forever.

10.2.2 Exercise: Backing Up the DHCP Database

In this exercise, you learn to back up the DHCP database and compress it with two simple steps:

1. Stop the DHCP Server Service via Control Panel, Services, because this service holds the files open, preventing the files to close for backup.
2. To check database consistency and back up the database in the `C:\backup.dir` directory, execute the following command from the DHCP subdirectory:

```
JETPACK DHCP.mdb C:\backup.dir\dhcp.mdb
```

10.2 Practice Problems

1. To set up Windows NT as an Internet router, what two steps should you follow?
   A. Install two network adapters in the system.
   B. Enable IP routing.
   C. Start GSNW.
   D. Enable the NetBEUI protocol.

2. An NT router cannot exchange Routing Information Protocol (RIP) routing packets with other IP RIP routers unless
   A. GSNW is running.
   B. The RIP routing software is installed.
   C. NetBEUI is enabled.
   D. The Default Gateway has been defined.

3. After you enable RIP, how often are RIP packets sent?
   A. Every 5 seconds
   B. Every 30 seconds
   C. Every minute
   D. Every 5 minutes

4. What is the purpose of the RIP packets?
   A. To exchange queued messages
   B. To exchange e-mail
   C. To exchange routing information
   D. To verify host existence

5. To whom are the RIP packets sent?
   A. Hosts
   B. Clients
   C. Other routers
   D. Domain controllers

6. Without the RIP protocol, router tables are maintained ______________.
   A. By OSPF
   B. Manually
   C. Automatically
   D. At startup

7. If administrators decide to manually add an entry to the routing table, what command must they use?
   A. ROUTE ADD
   B. TRACERT
   C. NBSTAT
   D. NETSTAT

8. After the DHCP Server Service has been installed, you can configure the service using which tool?
   A. Server Manager
   B. DHCP Manager
   C. DHCP Administrator
   D. DHCP Client Configuration

9. The DHCP database is created in which format?
   A. Access
   B. JET
   C. DNS
   D. IP

10. Where is the DHCP database stored?
    A. `\%systemroot%\system32\dhcp`
    B. `\%systemroot%\system32\jet`
    C. `\%systemroot%\dhcp`
    D. `\%systemroot%\jet`

11. Spencer, the new administrator, is complaining about the size of the DHCP database. Which command should Spencer use to clear deleted records from the DHCP database?

    A. COMPRESS

    B. DELETE

    C. JETPACK

    D. CLEAR

12. What is the primary purpose for the DHCP Relay tab?

    A. To allow an NT system to relay DHCP broadcasts for clients across an IP router.

    B. To block broadcast messages from foreign networks.

    C. To relay alerts regarding the DHCP database to the administrator.

    D. To relay inventory messages to a central JET database.

13. Under normal conditions, IP routers are configured to do what with broadcasts?

    A. Forward them

    B. Ignore them

    C. Answer them

    D. Send them continuously

14. Given the situation in question 13, if a client asks for an IP address on a local segment when the DHCP server is located on another network segment, what becomes of the request?

    A. It goes unanswered.

    B. It is answered immediately.

    C. It is routed for answer.

    D. It is continuously sent until an answer is received.

15. When the IPX RIP router is installed, Windows NT can route IPX packets over the installed network adapters, and it uses what to exchange routing table information?

    A. IP

    B. RIP

    C. TCP/IP

    D. UDP

10.2.1 Answers and Explanations: Exercise

In this exercise, you learned to establish a scope for a DHCP server, and looked at the values used to do so.

10.2.2 Answers and Explanations: Exercise

In this short exercise, you learned to back up and pack the DHCP database.

10.2 Answers and Explanations: Practice Problems

1. **A, B** To set up Windows NT as an Internet router, install two network adapters in the system, and then enable IP routing.
2. **B** An NT router cannot exchange Routing Information Protocol (RIP) routing packets with other IP RIP routers unless the RIP routing software is installed.
3. **C** RIP packets are sent out once every 60 seconds.
4. **C** RIP packets are used to exchange routing information.
5. **C** RIP packets are sent to other dynamic RIP routing routers.

6. **B** Without the RIP protocol, router tables must be set up manually when using Windows NT to route information.
7. **A** Without the RIP protocol, router tables must be set up manually using the ROUTE ADD command.
8. **B** After you install the DHCP Server Service, you can configure the service using the DHCP Manager option.
9. **B** The DHCP database is created in JET format.
10. **A** The DHCP database is stored in the `\%systemroot%\system32\dhcp` subdirectory.
11. **C** You should back up the database occasionally using the JETPACK command, which also clears out deleted records.
12. **A** The DHCP Relay tab enables a Windows NT system to relay DHCP broadcasts for clients across an IP router.
13. **B** Normally, you configure IP routers not to forward broadcasts.
14. **A** A client asking (broadcasting) for an IP address on a local segment when the DHCP server is located on a different network segment does not receive an answer.
15. **B** It uses the RIP to exchange its routing table information with other RIP routers.

10.2 Key Words

Gateway Services for NetWare

Migration Tool for NetWare

DHCP Scope

RIP for IP

RIP Packets

Multiprotocol Routing

DHCP Server Service

10.3 Installing and Configuring Internet Information Server

Internet Information Server is bundled into Windows NT 4, and you can automatically install it during the initial installation of your Windows NT Server system.

Internet Information Server, or IIS, serves primarily as a World Wide Web (WWW), server, but it also offers FTP and Gopher support. Because this software is included with the Windows NT Server software, it makes perfect sense to learn about what IIS can do for you. The enterprise exam has a few questions relating to installation and configuration of IIS. Before you can look into the installation and configuration of IIS, though, you must understand the different components and functions of IIS.

A. Overview of IIS

Internet Information Server uses Hypertext Transfer Protocol (HTTP), File Transfer Protocol (FTP), and the Gopher services to provide Internet publishing services to your Windows NT Server computer.

1. HTTP: Hypertext Transfer Protocol

HTTP is a client/server protocol used on the World Wide Web. HTTP web pages allow the client and server machines to interact and be updated very quickly using Windows Sockets. HTTP is, of course, pervasive on the Internet and more information on this standard can be found at `http://www.ics.uci.edu/pub/ietf/http/`.

2. FTP: File Transfer Protocol

FTP is the protocol used to transfer files from one computer to another using the TCP/IP protocol. In any FTP file transfer, the two computers must each play a role in the connection. One system must be designated the FTP server and the other the FTP client. The FTP client does all the work in the transfer; the FTP server is a depository only. This protocol is very handy for quick transfer of files across the Internet.

3. Gopher Service

The Gopher service provides a means to create a set of hierarchical links to other computers or to annotate files or directories. This service is not as common as FTP or HTTP, but is included with IIS for backward compatibility with the older Gopher Internet technology.

B. Installation Steps for IIS

Installing IIS is very simple. During the initial install of your Windows NT Server software, you were prompted about whether you wanted to install IIS at that time. However, if you said no, you still have the opportunity to install it at anytime from a working installation of Windows NT Server.

Exercise 10.3.1, "Installing Internet Information Server," walks you through the steps to installing IIS.

When the installation steps are complete, your Windows NT Server is ready to host your Internet publications. If you want to test your IIS installation, from a Web browser enter `http://your_computername` and verify that you can see the default web page installed with IIS. If you can see this web page, your installation and all the Internet services are functional. If you do not see the default web page, begin the process anew and look for errors along the way.

Getting the Internet Information Service installed is the easy part. You may need to configure the system based on your specific needs. Each of the services can be configured, and in the following sections you learn about the configuration options for each of the IIS services.

C. Overview of Internet Service Manager

Internet Information Server provides a graphical administration tool called the *Internet Service Manager*. With this tool, you can centrally manage, control, and monitor the Internet services in your Windows NT network. The Internet Service Manager uses the built-in Windows NT security model so it offers a secure method of remotely administering your web sites and other Internet services. To start the Internet Service Manager from the Start Menu, click Programs, Microsoft Internet Information Server, and then select the Internet Service Manager icon. When the Internet Service Manager has started, you can view the status of your Internet services.

The Internet Service Manager has three views that you can select to more easily monitor the information that you need. The three main views are as follows:

- **Report view:** This is the default view. The report view lists each computer alphabetically with each Internet service shown on a separate line in the screen.
- **Servers view:** This view groups all the services on each server and lists only computers with an Internet service loaded on them. The servers can then be expanded to display the loaded services.
- **Services view:** Each Internet service is listed with the corresponding servers grouped by service.

In each of the views, you can double-click on an entry to view the Properties dialog box for the selected item. You can make the configuration of the servers and services in these dialog boxes.

10.3.1 Exercise: Installing Internet Information Server

This exercise steps you through the installation of IIS, with the services for WWW, FTP, and Gopher enabled.

1. Click the right mouse button on the Network Neighborhood, and choose the Properties command.
2. Click the Services page tab.
3. Click the Add button, and then click the Microsoft Internet Information Server 2.0 option. Click OK.
4. The Internet Information Server Welcome dialog box displays. Click OK to continue.
5. Review the installation options to ensure that all are selected, and then click OK .
6. You may be prompted to create the installation directory for IIS; click Yes to create the directory.

7. The Publishing Directories dialog box appears. Click OK to select the default publishing directories.
8. Again, you may be prompted to create the directories. Click Yes to create them.
9. When the Internet Domain Name Warning dialog box appears, click OK.
10. Select the SQL Server entry on the ODBC Drivers dialog box, and click OK.
11. When the setup is complete, click OK.

10.3 Practice Problems

1. Internet Information Server, or IIS, serves primarily as a server of what?
   A. World Wide Web (WWW)
   B. FTP
   C. Gopher
   D. Archie

2. What three servers is Internet Information Server capable of being or supporting?
   A. World Wide Web (WWW)
   B. FTP
   C. Gopher
   D. Archie

3. What version of IIS ships with NT Server 4?
   A. 2.0
   B. 3.0
   C. 4.0
   D. 5.0

4. What three publishing services does Internet Information Server use?
   A. WWW
   B. HTTP
   C. HTML
   D. FTP
   E. Gopher

5. Which of the following is a client/server protocol used on the World Wide Web?
   A. WWW
   B. HTTP
   C. HTML
   D. FTP
   E. Gopher

6. Which of the following is a protocol used to transfer files from one computer to another over TCP/IP?
   A. WWW
   B. HTTP
   C. HTML
   D. FTP
   E. Gopher

7. Which of the following is a means to create a set of hierarchical links to other computers?
   A. WWW
   B. HTTP
   C. HTML
   D. FTP
   E. Gopher

8. In any FTP file transfer, what two roles must the computers play?
   A. Client
   B. Server
   C. Router
   D. Bridge

9. Internet Information Server provides a graphical administration tool called:
   A. Internet Tool
   B. Server Manager
   C. User Manager
   D. Internet Service Manager

10. Using the tool mentioned in question 9, you can centrally perform what three functions?
    A. Manage
    B. Add and Delete
    C. Control
    D. Monitor

11. The Internet Service Manager has three views that you can select to enable you easily to monitor the information that you need. What are the three main views?
    A. Report view
    B. Log view
    C. Servers view
    D. Services view

12. In reference to question 11, which is the default view?
    A. Report view
    B. Log view
    C. Servers view
    D. Services view

13. What does the Report view do?
    A. Groups all the services on each server and only lists each computer with an Internet service loaded on it.
    B. Reports each computer's load and capacity.
    C. Lists each Internet service, with the corresponding servers grouped by service.
    D. Lists each computer alphabetically with each Internet service shown on a separate line on the screen.

10.3.1 Answers and Explanations: Exercise

In this exercise, you installed Internet Information Server (IIS) on your Windows NT machine. Version 2.0 is the IIS version shipping with all current versions of Windows NT.

10.3 Answers and Explanations: Practice Problems

1. **A** Internet Information Server, or IIS, serves primarily as a World Wide Web (WWW) server.
2. **A, B, C** Internet Information Server serves primarily as a World Wide Web (WWW) server, but it also offers FTP and Gopher support.
3. **A** IIS 2.0 ships with NT Server 4.
4. **B, D, E** Internet Information Server uses Hypertext Transfer Protocol (HTTP), File Transfer Protocol (FTP), and the Gopher services to provide Internet publishing services to your Windows NT Server computer.
5. **B** HTTP is a client/server protocol used on the World Wide Web.
6. **D** FTP is the protocol used to transfer files from one computer to another using the TCP/IP protocol.
7. **E** The Gopher service provides a means to create a set of hierarchical links to other computers or to annotate files or directories.
8. **A, B** One system must be designated the FTP server and the other the FTP client.
9. **D** Internet Information Server provides a graphical administration tool called the Internet Service Manager.
10. **A, C, D** Using Internet Service Manager, you can centrally manage, control, and monitor the Internet services in your Windows NT network.
11. **A, C, D** The three main views are Report view, Servers view, and Services view.
12. **A** Report view is the default view.
13. **D** The Report view lists each computer alphabetically with each Internet service shown on a separate line on the screen.

10.3 Key Words

FTP

Gopher

HTML

HTTP

Internet Information Server (IIS)

Internet Service Manager

10.4 Installing and Configuring Internet Services

Installing and configuring Internet services can be broken into a number of components: installing the service World Wide Web, FTP, or Gopher (WWW is used for all the examples here, as it is the most popular) and configuring DNS services. Intranet services are identical to Internet with the exception of the clients accessing them, and thus only Internet is examined.

A. Configuring WWW Services

To view the configuration for your WWW service, double-click on the WWW service in the Internet Service Manager application.

After you are in the properties dialog box for the WWW service, you notice the page tabs across the top of the dialog box. Each of these pages contains the configuration options available, as described in the following sections.

1. The Services Property Page

The Services Property page tab enables you to set user logon and authentication requirements, as well as port and connection information for the service.

2. The Directories Property Page

The Directories Property page shows you the location of your home directories and the location in which to place all your Internet publications. This page also sets the name of the default document to be used and whether or not directory browsing is enabled.

3. The Logging Property Page

The Logging Property page enables you to select logging of the activity of the services. You can select a log filename and the log format, and you can also specify how often you should start a new log file. A nice feature of this page is the option to log to a SQL/ODBC database. This option is available only if the ODBC drivers are installed on your system.

4. The Advanced Property Page

The Advanced Property page enables you to prevent access to the service based on IP addresses. This enables you to secure an intranet very easily by selecting an IP address range and then limiting the access allowed to the site. You can also use this page to limit the network bandwidth available for outbound traffic from the server.

B. The DNS Service

You use the Domain Name Server Service on the Internet and UNIX-based systems primarily to resolve Fully Qualified Domain Names (FQDN) to IP addresses. You install the service via Control Panel, Networks. This installs the service into the service database, and after rebooting, starts the service automatically. The service is configured using the DNS Manager application in the Administrative Tools menu. After you install it, you must set up the records in the DNS database.

You set up information concerning DNS (Domain Name System) servers on the DNS tab. The first two optional entries are the Host Name and Domain fields. You can use the Domain field to identify your computer on a smaller, local network, such as the one in your company. By default, this is your Windows NT computer name, but the network administrator can assign a different name. The host name is combined with a domain name or suffix to create your Internet address.

Take note that a DHCP server can supply the DNS Service information as well. If a DHCP server supplies the DNS server information, you can leave these fields empty.

The next entries are more important, especially if your machine is connected to the Internet. The DNS Service Search Order section lists the Domain Name System (DNS) servers. These servers contain a database that Windows NT searches to find the name assigned to your computer or other hosts on the internetwork. Servers are searched in the order listed.

The servers are searched in the order listed until the first server is contacted. If you always contact the first DNS server in the list, the second server will never be used for Internet name resolution. It only checks the second DNS server listed when a connection cannot be made to the first server in the list.

10.4.1 Exercise: Installing and Configuring the DNS Service in Windows NT Server 4

This exercise steps you through the installation and configuration of the DNS service under Windows NT Server 4.

1. Get the IP address of your computer by typing **IPCONFIG** at the command line. You need the IP address for the upcoming steps.
2. Right-click the Network Neighborhood, and choose the Properties option.
3. Click the Services page tab.
4. Click Add.
5. In the Network Service list, select Microsoft DNS Server and click OK.
6. Enter the path to the Windows NT Server source directory and click Continue.
7. Click Close in the Network Properties dialog box.
8. Click Yes to restart the computer.
9. After the system restarts, log on.
10. Click the Start menu, Programs, Administrative Tools, and then click the DNS Manager.
11. Click the DNS menu, and then click the New Server option.

12. In the DNS Server box, type your computer name and click OK.
13. Highlight your computer name in the DNS Manager window.
14. Click the DNS menu, and click the New Zone command.
15. Click the Primary check box, and then click Next.
16. In the Zone Name type **xyz.com**, and then press the tab key to move to the Zone file box. The Zone file is automatically filled in as **xyz.com.dns**.
17. Click Next to finish.
18. To add a computer into your DNS Server, right click the Zone name, and then click the New Host option.
19. In the Host name, enter the computer name.
20. In the Host IP address, enter the IP address for the new computer.
21. Click the Add Host button.
22. Click Done.

10.4.2 Exercise: Configuring the DNS Manager

After you install DNS, you must configure the DNS Manager. This exercise walks you through the configuration process using two imaginary systems.

In this example, the two systems are located in the `imaginary.com` domain. The two hostnames are referred to as `www.imaginary.com` and `ftp.imaginary.com`, and the relevant IP addresses are provided. To set up the example in the DNS Manager, follow these steps:

1. Create the top domain structure first. In this case, it is COM. Choose the DNS menu and add the server. Enter the IP address of the DNS Server. You can use the loopback address of 127.0.0.1 for the current system.
2. Select the server, and then from the DNS menu, choose New Zone. Select Primary, and type **com** for the zone name. A tab automatically fills in the zone filename. Then click Finish.
3. Create the subdomain, imaginary, using the same approach as you used for the previous domain; that is, choose New Zone from the DNS menu and step through the wizard.
4. Create the two hosts, ftp and www, in the domain by selecting New Host and entering the hostname (for example, ftp or www) and the IP address for the host. Be sure to enable the Create PTR Record option to ensure that reverse lookups can also work.
5. Enable the Update Server Data Files option to refresh the server records and you're finished. To test the DNS setup, open a command prompt and try the following command:

```
ping ftp.imaginary.com
```

The command should return the proper IP address for the server if the DNS entries are complete.

10.4 Practice Problems

1. Internet services can be broken into what three components?

   A. Reverse lookup

   B. WWW

   C. Gopher

   D. FTP

2. In the Internet Service Manager application, which page enables you to set user logon and authentication requirements?

   A. The Services Property page

   B. The Directories Property page

   C. The Logging Property page

   D. The Advanced Property page

3. In the Internet Service Manager application, which page enables you to select logging of the activity of the services?

   A. The Services Property page

   B. The Directories Property page

   C. The Logging Property page

   D. The Advanced Property page

4. In the Internet Service Manager application, which page shows you the location of your home directories and the location in which to place all your Internet publications?

   A. The Services Property page

   B. The Directories Property page

   C. The Logging Property page

   D. The Advanced Property page

5. In the Internet Service Manager application, on which page do you set the name of the default document to be used and whether to enable directory browsing?

   A. The Services Property page

   B. The Directories Property page

   C. The Logging Property page

   D. The Advanced Property page

6. In the Internet Service Manager application, which page enables you to prevent access to the service based on IP addresses?

   A. The Services Property page

   B. The Directories Property page

   C. The Logging Property page

   D. The Advanced Property page

7. In the Internet Service Manager application, which page can you use to limit the network bandwidth available for outbound traffic from the server?

   A. The Services Property page

   B. The Directories Property page

   C. The Logging Property page

   D. The Advanced Property page

8. What is the primary use of the DNS Service on the Internet and UNIX-based systems?

   A. Page delivery

   B. FQDN Name resolution to IP addresses

   C. Management statistics

   D. Monitoring and optimization of existing resources

9. DNS is the abbreviation for:

   A. Domain Name System

   B. Domain Name Service

   C. Dynamic Name System

   D. Dynamic Name Service

10. The DNS Service Search Order section lists the DNS servers. These servers contain a database that Windows NT searches to find the name assigned to

your computer or other hosts on the internetwork. Servers are searched in what order?

A. Alphabetically

B. By region

C. Order listed

D. Frequency

10.4.1 Answers and Explanations: Exercise

In this exercise, you walked through the installation and configuration of the DNS service under Windows NT Server 4.

10.4.2 Answers and Explanations: Exercise

This exercise stepped you through the process of configuring DNS to provide Internet name resolution for two imaginary hosts in an Internet domain.

10.4 Answers and Explanations: Practice Problems

1. **B, C, D** Internet services can be broken into three components: World Wide Web services, FTP services, and Gopher services.
2. **A** The Services Property page enables you to set user logon and authentication requirements.
3. **C** The Logging Property page enables you to enable logging of the activity of the services.
4. **B** The Directories Property page shows you the location of your home directories and the location in which to place all your Internet publications.
5. **B** The Directories Property page enables you to set the name of the default document to use and whether to enable directory browsing.
6. **D** The Advanced Property page enables you to prevent access to the service based on IP addresses.
7. **D** You can use the Advanced Property page to limit the network bandwidth available for outbound traffic from the server.
8. **B** You use the Domain Name Server Service on the Internet and UNIX-based systems primarily to resolve Fully Qualified Domain Names (FQDN) to IP addresses.
9. **A** DNS is the abbreviation for Domain Name System.
10. **C** Servers are searched in the order listed in the file.

10.4 Key Words

DNS

FQDN

10.5 Installing and Configuring Remote Access Service (RAS)

The enterprise exam contains a few questions on the use of RAS. To be successful with these questions, you must have a solid understanding of RAS, including the installation and configuration of RAS.

Windows NT Remote Access Service extends the power of Windows NT networking to anywhere you can find a phone line. Using RAS, a Windows NT computer can connect to a remote network via a dial-up connection and fully participate in the network as a network client. RAS also enables your Windows NT computer to receive dial-up connections from remote computers.

RAS supports SLIP and PPP line protocols, and NetBEUI, TCP/IP, and IPX network protocols. NT supports SLIP only as a client. PPP, on the other hand, is supported as both a server and client protocol. Because so many Internet users access their service providers using a phone line, RAS often serves as an Internet interface.

The Dial-Up Networking application (in the Accessories program group) enables you to create phonebook entries. A phonebook entry is a pre-configured dial-up connection to a specific site. The Control Panel Telephony application enables the remote user to preconfigure dialing properties for different dialing locations.

RAS can connect to a remote computer using any of the following media:

- **Public Switched Telephone Network (PSTN):** (Also known as the phone company.) RAS can connect using a modem through an ordinary phone line.
- **X.25:** A packet-switched network. Computers access the network via a Packet Assembler Disassembler device (PAD). X.25 supports dial-up or direct connections.
- **Null modem cable:** A cable that connects two computers directly. The computers then communicate using their modems (rather than network adapter cards).
- **ISDN:** A digital line that provides faster communication and more bandwidth than a normal phone line. (It also costs more, which is why not everybody has it.) A computer must have a special ISDN card to access an ISDN line.

Windows NT also includes a new feature called Multilink. Using Multilink, a Windows NT computer can form a RAS connection using more than one physical pathway. One Multilink connection, for example, can use two modems at once (or one modem line and one ISDN line) to form a single logical link. By using multiple pathways for one connection, Multilink can greatly increase bandwidth. Of course, the computer has to have access to more than one pathway (that is, it must have two modems installed). Multilink, however, is not supported for callback features; you can configure only one number for callback.

A. RAS Security

Like everything else in Windows NT, RAS is designed for security. As standard practice, all events are written to the system log, and you can view them with Event Viewer (which is used to view event logs). The following are some of RAS's other security features:

- **Auditing:** RAS can leave an audit trail, enabling you to see when users logged in and what authentication they provided.

- **Callback security:** You can enable RAS server to use callback (hang up all incoming calls and call the caller back), and you can limit callback numbers to prearranged sites that you know are safe.
- **Encryption:** RAS can encrypt logon information, or it can encrypt all data crossing the connection.
- **Security hosts:** In case Windows NT isn't safe enough, you can add an extra dose of security by using a third-party intermediary security host—a computer that stands between the RAS client and the RAS server and requires an extra round of authentication.
- **PPTP filtering:** You can tell Windows NT to filter out all packets except ultra-safe PPTP packets (described later in this chapter).

B. RAS Line Protocols

RAS (Remote Access Service) supports the SLIP, PPP, and PPTP line protocols. The following sections define these protocols in more detail.

1. SLIP

Serial Line Interface Protocol (SLIP) is a standard protocol for serial line connections over TCP/IP networks. SLIP is relatively old for the computer age—it was developed in 1984—and, although it is not yet completely obsolete, it does lack some of the features that are available in PPP. Each node in a SLIP connection must have a static IP address; that is, you can't use Windows NT features such as DHCP and WINS. Unlike PPP, SLIP does not support NetBEUI or IPX. You must use TCP/IP with SLIP. Also, SLIP cannot encrypt logon information.

2. PPP

Point-to-Point Protocol (PPP) was originally conceived as a deluxe version of SLIP. Like SLIP, PPP is an industry standard for point-to-point communications, but PPP offers several advantages over SLIP. Most notably, PPP isn't limited to TCP/IP. PPP also supports IPX, NetBEUI, and several other network protocols, such as AppleTalk and DECnet. Because PPP supports so many protocols, it enables you to have much more flexibility in configuring network communications, and also provides secure authentication.

3. PPTP

PPTP is a protocol that enables you to securely transmit PPP packets over a TCP/IP network. Because the Internet is a TCP/IP network, PPTP enables highly private network links over the otherwise highly public Internet. PPTP connections are encrypted, making them nearly impenetrable to virtual voyeurs.

In fact, PPTP is part of an emerging technology called Virtual Private Networks (VPNs). The point of VPN is to provide corporate networks with the same (or close to the same) security over the Internet that they would have over a direct connection.

Another exciting advantage of PPTP (and another reason that it fits nicely into the scheme of the VPN) is that PPTP doesn't discriminate among protocols. Because PPP supports NetBEUI, IPX, and other network protocols, and because PPTP operates on PPP packets, PPTP actually lets you transmit non-TCP/IP protocols over the Internet.

Because PPTP provides intranet privacy over the open Internet, it can significantly reduce costs in some situations. Networks that once would have depended on extravagant direct connections now can hook up via a local Internet service provider.

C. Installing a RAS Server

Remote Access Service is installed using the Services tab of the Network Properties dialog box. Prior to the installation, you should gather some basic information that you use during the installation of RAS:

- The type of modem to be used by RAS.
- Whether the device will be used for outgoing RAS communication, incoming RAS communication, or both.
- The protocols to be used by RAS.
- Whether the callback security feature needs to be configured.

After you have all the required information, you are ready to begin the installation of RAS. To complete the RAS installation, follow these steps:

1. In Control Panel, double-click on the Network Application icon.
2. In the Network dialog box, choose the Services tab. Click on the Add button, invoking the Select Network Service dialog box.
3. In the Select Network Service dialog box, choose Remote Access Service from the service list and click OK. Windows NT prompts you for the path to the Windows NT Installation CD-ROM.
4. Windows NT prompts you for name of a RAS-capable device and an associated communications port. A modem installed on your system typically appears as a default value. Click OK to accept the modem, or click on the down arrow to choose another RAS-capable device on your system. You also can install a new modem or an X.25 Pad using the Install Modem and Install X25 Pad buttons.
5. The Remote Access Setup dialog box appears. Click on the Configure button to specify whether to use the port for dial-out connections, dial-in connections, or both. The Port Usage options apply only to the port. In other words, you could configure COM1 for dial out only and COM2 for receive only. In the Remote Access Setup dialog box, you also can add or remove a port entry from the list. The Clone button enables you to copy a port configuration.
6. Click on the Network button to specify the network protocols for your Remote Access Service to support. The Server Settings options in the lower portion of the Network Configuration dialog box only appear if you configure the port to receive calls. Select one or more dial-out protocols. If you want RAS to take care of receiving calls, select one or more server protocols, and choose an encryption setting for incoming connections. You also can select Multilink, which enables one logical connection to use several physical pathways.

   A Configure button follows each of the Server Settings protocol options. Each Configure button opens a dialog box that enables you to specify configuration options for the protocol, as follows:

   - The RAS Server NetBEUI dialog box enables you to specify whether the incoming caller will have access to the entire network or to only the RAS server.

By confining a caller's access to the RAS server, you improve security (because the caller can access only one PC), but you reduce functionality because the caller can't access information on other machines.

- The RAS Server TCP/IP Configuration dialog box enables you to define how the RAS server assigns IP addresses to dial-up clients. You can use DHCP to assign client addresses, or you can configure RAS to assign IP addresses from a static address pool. If you choose to use a static address pool, input the beginning and ending addresses in the range. To exclude a range of addresses within the address pool, enter the beginning and ending addresses in the range you're excluding in the From and To boxes. Then click on the Add button. The excluded range appears in the Excluded Ranges list box.

  The RAS Server TCP/IP Configuration dialog box enables you to specify whether a client can access the entire network or only the RAS server. By confining a caller's access to the RAS server, you improve security (because the caller can only access one PC), but you reduce functionality because the caller cannot access information on other machines.

- The RAS Server IPX Configuration dialog box enables you to specify how the RAS server assigns IPX network numbers.

  You also can specify whether a client can access the entire network or only the RAS server. By confining a caller's access to the RAS server, you improve security (because the caller can only access one PC), but you reduce functionality because the caller can't access information on other machines.

7. After you define the RAS settings to your satisfaction, click OK.
8. The Network Services tab appears in the foreground. You should see Remote Access Service in the list of services. Click the Close button.
9. Windows NT asks whether you want to restart your computer. Choose Yes.

D. Configuring RAS

When configuring Remote Access Service, you need to configure the communication ports, network protocols, and encryption settings required for remote users when they dial into your Windows NT Server using the RAS as a server.

1. The Remote Access Setup Dialog Box

The RAS server is configured using the Control Panel Network icon located on the Services page tab. Locate the Remote Access Service and click the Properties button. The Remote Access Setup dialog box opens. A number of configuration options are available from this dialog box:

- **Add:** Add a port to be used by RAS. May be accessed by a modem or X.25 pad.
- **Remove:** Remove a port being used by RAS.
- **Configure:** Change the settings for a port being used by RAS.
- **Clone:** Copy the settings being used from one port to another.
- **Network:** Configure the network protocols and encryption to be used by RAS.

To make configuration changes to an existing port being used by RAS, click the Configure button. The following list describes each of the options:

- **Dial Out Only:** Port only used for outgoing RAS connections.
- **Receive Calls Only**: Port only used for receiving calls from RAS clients.
- **Dial Out and Receive:** Port used for both outgoing and incoming RAS connections.

You can configure each port that is listed in the RAS Setup dialog box for different roles. Com1 can be configured for dial-out only, whereas Com2 is used for Receive Calls Only. By allowing each port to be configured separately, you have a great deal of flexibility in the Remote Access Service.

2. The Network Configuration Dialog Box

After you configure the ports, you must configure the network settings. Start from the Remote Access Setup dialog box. Click the Network Button to view the Network Configuration dialog box.

The Network Configuration settings apply to all the ports that are enabled in RAS. Notice in the top section of the screen that you can select which protocols to use for dial-out calls. By clicking the check box next to the required protocols, you can enable or disable each of the protocols.

For the RAS server settings, you must configure the middle section of the screen. As a RAS server, you can control how far each of the selected protocols can go, or whether RAS clients accept the protocols at all. Again the check box directly next to each of the protocols enables or disables the protocols.

Clicking the Configure button located to the right of the listed protocols can also restrict each of the protocols. You can configure each protocol slightly differently.

E. Dial-Up Networking

The Dial-Up Networking application lets you establish remote connections with other computers. The most common uses for Dial-Up Networking are as follows:

- Accessing an Internet service provider
- Accessing a remote Windows NT computer or domain

You can reach the Dial-Up Networking application as follows:

1. Choose Programs from the Start menu.
2. Choose Accessories from the Programs list.
3. Click the Dial-Up Networking icon.

Dial-Up Networking maintains a list of phonebook entries. A phonebook entry is a bundle of information that Windows NT needs to establish a specific connection. You can use the Dial-Up Networking application to create a phonebook entry for your access provider, your Windows NT domain, or any other dial-up connection. When it's time to connect, select a phonebook entry from the drop-down menu at the top of the screen and click the Dial button. If you access the phonebook entry often, you can create a desktop shortcut that enables you to access the phonebook entry directly by following these steps:

1. Click on the New button in the Dial-Up Networking main screen to open the New Phonebook Entry dialog box.
2. In the New Phonebook Entry Basic tab, specify a name for the entry, an optional comment, and the phone number you want Windows NT to dial to make the connection. The Alternates button beside the phone number box enables you to specify a prioritized list of alternative phone numbers. You also can specify a different modem or configure a modem from the Basic tab.
3. In the New Phonebook Entry Server tab, specify the communications protocol for the dial-up server (in the drop-down menu at the top of the screen) and the network protocol.

   If you select the TCP/IP network protocol, click the TCP/IP button to configure TCP/IP settings.
4. The New Phonebook Entry Script dialog box defines some of the connection's logon properties. You can tell Windows NT to pop up a terminal window before or after dialing or to run a logon script after dialing. A terminal window enables you to interactively log on to the remote server in terminal mode. The Run This Script option option automates the logon process. For more information on dial-up logon scripts, click the Edit Script button. The Edit Script button places you in a file called SWITCH.INF that provides instructions and sample logon scripts. The Before Dialing button enables you to specify a terminal window or a logon script to execute before you dial.
5. The New Phonebook Entry Security tab offers some encryption options. You can require encrypted authentication, or you can accept any authentication including clear text. You also can specify data encryption.
6. The New Phonebook Entry X.25 tab serves only for X.25 service (described earlier in this chapter). Select an X.25 access provider from the drop-down menu and enter the requested information.
7. After you make changes to the New Phonebook Entry tab, click OK. The new phonebook entry appears in the drop-down menu at the top of the Dial-Up Networking screen.

F. Troubleshooting RAS

If you have problems with PPP, you can log PPP debugging information to a file called PPP.LOG in the `\<winnt_root>\System32\Ras` directory. To log PPP debugging information to PPP.LOG, change the Registry value for `\HKEY_LOCAL_MACHINE\System\CurrentControlSet\Services\Rasman\PPP\Logging` to 1. 10

RAS authentication problems often stem from incompatible encryption methods. If you can connect using clear text and you can't connect using encryption, you know the client and server encryption methods are incompatible. You should try to connect using the Allow any Authentication Including Clear Text option.

10.5.1 Exercise: Installation of Remote Access Service on a Windows NT Server

This exercise helps you install the RAS service and configure it only to receive calls.

1. Right-click the Network Neighborhood Icon, and click the Services page tab.
2. Click the Add Button.
3. Select the Remote Access Service, and then click OK.
4. Enter the location of the source files for your Windows NT Server software.
5. The Remote Access Setup dialog box opens, prompting you to allow the Setup Wizard to detect your modem. Click Yes. If your modem is not found, start the wizard again and click the Don't Detect my Modem, I Will Select it from the List option, and then click Next.
6. Select the Dial-Up Networking Serial Cable Between Two PCs, and then click next.
7. Select COM1 as the selected port and click Next.
8. In the Location Information dialog box, enter the appropriate country.
9. Enter your area code in the What Area (or City) Code Are You in Now box.
10. Click Next.
11. Click Finish.
12. Click OK to add the Modem into your Remote Access Setup dialog box.
13. Click the Configure button.
14. Click to select the Receive Calls Only option.
15. Click OK to close the Port Configuration dialog box.
16. Click OK to close the Remote Access Setup dialog box.

10.5.2 Exercise: Configuring RAS for Dial Out and Receiving Communication

This exercise enables you to configure your RAS settings to allow your RAS server to dial out and receive RAS calls.

1. In the Control Panel, double-click the Network icon.
2. Click the Services page tab.
3. Locate the Remote Access Service, and then click the Properties button.
4. In the Remote Access Setup dialog box, click the Configure button.
5. Click the Dial Out and Receive Calls option, and then click OK.
6. Click the Network button.

7. In the dial out protocols, disable all protocols except for TCP/IP.
8. In the Server Settings, go to the Allow Remote Clients section and disable all protocols except TCP/IP.
9. Click the TCP/IP configure button.
10. Ensure that the remote clients can access the entire network through TCP/IP.
11. Click to enable the Remote clients to use the DHCP server.
12. Click OK to close the TCP/IP settings.
13. Click OK to close the Network Configuration dialog box.
14. Click OK to close the Remote Access Server Setup dialog box.

10.5 Practice Problems

1. Karen, a remote administrator, complains that RAS is not working properly, and that it keeps failing. What should be one of the first tools used to look for problems?

   A. Performance Monitor

   B. Event Viewer

   C. Server Manager

   D. User Manager for Domains

2. To justify additional expenses, you need to gather statistics on RAS. Which of the following tools displays statistics on current conditions of RAS?

   A. Performance Monitor

   B. The Status tab of the Dial-Up Networking Monitor in Control Panel

   C. Event Viewer

   D. User Manager for Domains

3. A sure way to find problems with RAS is to check the PPP.LOG. Which of the following statements are true of PPP logging? Choose two.

   A. It is enabled by default.

   B. Information is written to the PPP.LOG.

   C. You must edit the Registry to turn it on.

   D. It also contains logging information on modems.

4. Madonna, in customer service, must gather statistics about RAS. She needs to view the PPP.LOG, but she cannot find it. The PPP.LOG is stored, by default, where?

   A. `\<winnt_root>\System32\Ras`

   B. `\<winnt_root>\System32`

   C. `\<winnt_root>`

   D. `C:\`

5. Susan, a remote user, can connect using clear text, but cannot connect using encryption. What is the most likely problem?

   A. Connection speeds are too low to support verification.

   B. Encryption is not enabled at both client and server.

   C. The client and server encryption methods are incompatible.

   D. The server requires additional resources.

6. If you, as the RAS administrator, suspect that the client and server encryption methods are incompatible and cause problems, what should you do?

   A. Try to connect using the Allow Any Authentication Including Clear Text option.

   B. Try to avoid using any form of encryption.

   C. Try to discourage users from seeking dial-in functionality.

   D. Try to connect using the Incompatible Encryption Methods option.

7. Which of the following statements is true in regards to Callback with MultiLink?

   A. RAS can use multiple phone numbers for callback.

   B. RAS can use only one phone number for callback by default, but can use multiple phone numbers with the MultiLink function enabled.

   C. RAS can utilize callback only over ISDN lines.

   D. RAS can use only one phone number for callback.

8. If a non-ISDN client makes a connection using Multilink over multiple phone lines with Callback enabled, the server will call back using:

   A. Only a single phone line.

   B. Multiple phone lines.

   C. An ISDN line.

   D. One phone line unless, the default has been changed to Utilize Multiple.

9. Which three of the following are RAS problem areas, as identified by Microsoft?

   A. AutoDial at logon

   B. Authentication

   C. Heterogeneous connectivity

   D. Callback with MultiLink

10. Jerry complains that AutoDial spontaneously attempts to dial a remote connection during his logon. How should an administrator address this problem?

    A. Move Jerry to another machine.

    B. Disable AutoDial.

    C. Restrict Jerry's profiles and groups.

    D. Reinstall Windows NT.

11. RAS can use which protocols for dial-in connections? Choose all correct answers.

    A. TCP/IP

    B. NWLink

    C. NetBEUI

    D. SMTP

12. RAS can use which protocols for dial-out connections? Choose all correct answers.

    A. TCP/IP

    B. NWLink

    C. NetBEUI

    D. SMTP

13. Of the protocols RAS supports for dial-in and dial-out, which one benefits from being available on a number of different platforms and being easily routable?

    A. TCP/IP

    B. NWLink

    C. NetBEUI

    D. SMTP

14. Each node in a SLIP connection must:

    A. Have its own phone number

    B. Have a static IP address

    C. Be PPP enabled

    D. Be DHCP configured

15. Which of the following protocols cannot be used on DHCP and WINS?

    A. PPP

    B. TCP/IP

    C. SLIP

    D. PPTP

16. Which of the following protocols does PPP support?

    A. TCP/IP

    B. NetBEUI

    C. IPX

    D. Appleshare

17. Which of the following protocols does SLIP support?

    A. TCP/IP

    B. NetBEUI

    C. IPX

    D. Appleshare

18. Which protocol enables you to securely transmit PPP packets over a TCP/IP network?
    A. SLIP
    B. PPP
    C. PPTP
    D. UDP

19. Which protocol is part of an emerging technology called Virtual Private Networks?
    A. SLIP
    B. PPP
    C. PPTP
    D. UDP

20. What is the purpose of Virtual Private Networks (VPNs)?
    A. To provide corporate networks with the same security over the Internet that they would have over a direct connection.
    B. To provide corporate networks with the same support over the Internet that they would have over a direct connection.
    C. To provide corporate networks with the same speed over the Internet that they would have over a direct connection.
    D. To provide corporate networks with the same access over the Internet that they would have over a direct connection.

21. Which configuration option is used to copy the settings being used from one RAS port to another?
    A. Copy
    B. Clone
    C. Add
    D. Duplicate

10.5.1 Answers and Explanations: Exercise

In this exercise, you installed the RAS service and configured it to only receive calls.

10.5.2 Answers and Explanations: Exercise

In this exercise, you configured your RAS settings to enable your RAS server to dial out and receive RAS calls.

10.5 Answers and Explanations: Practice Problems

1. **B** If RAS isn't working, check the Event Viewer. Several RAS events appear in the system log.
2. **B** In Control Panel, the Status tab of Dial-Up Networking Monitor displays statistics on current conditions, including connection statistics and device errors.
3. **B, C** If you have problems with PPP, you can log PPP debugging information to a file called PPP.LOG in the `\<winnt_root>\System32\Ras` directory. To log PPP debugging information to PPP.LOG, change the Registry value for `\HKEY_LOCAL_MACHINE\System\CurrentControlSet\Services\Rasman\PPP\Logging` to 1.
4. **A** The PPP.LOG is stored, by default, in the `\<winnt_root>\System32\Ras` directory.
5. **C** RAS authentication problems often stem from incompatible encryption methods.
6. **A** If you can connect using clear text, and you can't connect using encryption, you know the client and server encryption methods are incompatible. You should try to connect using the Allow Any Authentication Including Clear Text option.
7. **D** RAS can use only one phone number for callback.

8. **A** If a client makes a connection using MultiLink over multiple phone lines with Callback enabled, the server calls back using only a single phone line—in other words, MultiLink functionality is lost.
9. **A, B, D** AutoDial at logon, authentication, and callback with MultiLink have all been identified as potential RAS problem areas by Microsoft.
10. **B** At logon, when Explorer initializes, it might reference a shortcut or some other target that requires an AutoDial connection, causing AutoDial to spontaneously dial a remote connection during logon. The only way to prevent the AutoDial is to disable AutoDial, or to eliminate the shortcut or other targets causing the AutoDial to occur.
11. **A, B, C** RAS supports TCP/IP, NWLink, and NetBEUI protocols for both dial-in and dial-out connections.
12. **A, B, C** RAS supports TCP/IP, NWLink, and NetBEUI protocols for both dial-in and dial-out connections.
13. **A** TCP/IP benefits from being available on a number of different platforms and being easily routable (as well as having the compatibility choice of the Internet).
14. **B** Each node in a SLIP connection must have a static IP address.
15. **C** SLIP cannot be used with DHCP and WINS.
16. **A, B, C** PPP supports TCP/IP, NetBEUI, and IPX.
17. **A** Unlike PPP, SLIP does not support NetBEUI or IPX. You must use TCP/IP with SLIP.
18. **C** PPTP is a protocol that enables you to securely transmit PPP packets over a TCP/IP network.
19. **C** PPTP is part of an emerging technology called Virtual Private Networks (VPNs).
20. **A** The point of VPNs is to provide corporate networks with the same (or close to the same) security over the Internet that they would have over a direct connection.
21. **B** The Clone option copies the settings being used from one port to another.

10.5 Key Words

Dial-Up Networking

Event Viewer

ISDN

Phonebook Entry

RAS

Virtual Private Networks

Practice Exam: Connectivity

Use this practice exam to test your mastery of "Connectivity." This practice exam is 17 questions long. The passing Microsoft score is 78.4 percent (13 right on this practice test). Questions are in multiple-choice format.

1. Which of the four configuration options is the default for how the Migration Tool is to react in the event that duplicate usernames are found on the NetWare server and the NT server?

   A. Add an error to the ERROR.LOG file.

   B. Skip the account with no error messages or warnings.

   C. Overwrite the existing account with new information.

   D. Include a prefix with the user account to distinguish between the existing account and the migrated account.

2. To migrate files from NetWare to NT using the Migration Tool for NetWare, what must be running on the NT Server?

   A. TCP/IP

   B. Client Services for NetWare

   C. File and Print Sharing

   D. NWLink

3. What would be a reason for NetBIOS broadcasts to be propagated over RIP routers?

   A. Routing tables need to be automatically updated.

   B. NetBIOS is the default protocol of the network.

   C. Windows 95 clients on both sides of the router need to communicate browsing information over the router.

   D. The Default Gateway is not configured.

4. The Migration Tool for NetWare can specify which of the following options for migrated passwords?

   A. No Password: The migrated users have no passwords assigned to them.

   B. Exact Password: The migrated users will have the same passwords as before.

   C. Password is: Assigns a single password to all migrated users.

   D. User must change password: Forces the migrated users to change their passwords the first time they log on to the Windows NT Server.

5. Kristin is trying to convince management that RIP for IP should be installed on every router. One justification she can use is that it reduces?

   A. Administrative overhead

   B. DNS usage

   C. Dependence on automatic router updates

   D. Network traffic

6. Evan works for the same company as Kristin, and is trying to convince management that RIP for IP should not be installed on every router. One justification he has is that it increases:

   A. Administrative overhead

   B. DNS usage

   C. Dependence on automatic router updates

   D. Network traffic

7. What does the Server view do?

   A. Groups all the services on each server and only lists each computer with an Internet service loaded on it.

   B. Reports each computers load and capacity.

C. Lists each Internet service, with the corresponding servers grouped by service.

D. Lists each computer alphabetically with each Internet service shown on a separate line in the screen.

8. What does the Services view do?

A. Groups all the services on each server and only lists each computer with an Internet service loaded on it.

B. Reports each computers load and capacity.

C. Lists each Internet service, with the corresponding servers grouped by service.

D. Lists each computer alphabetically with each Internet service shown on a separate line in the screen.

9. DNS is the abbreviation for:

A. Domain Name System

B. Domain Name Service

C. Dynamic Name System

D. Dynamic Name Service

10. Which configuration option do you use to configure the protocols and encryption used by RAS?

A. Add

B. Configure

C. Clone

D. Network

11. The Network Configuration settings apply to?

A. Individual ports

B. All the ports that are enabled in RAS

C. Dial-in ports only

D. Dial-out ports only

12. What is a collection of information that Windows NT needs to establish a specific connection?

A. A phonebook entry

B. A property

C. A configuration

D. A setting

13. To what NetWare permission does the NT Full Control permission map?

A. Read

B. Write

C. Modify

D. Supervisor

14. Which of the following statements is false about the Domain Name Server Service?

A. You can use it on the Internet and UNIX-based systems primarily to resolve Fully Qualified Domain Names (FQDN) to IP addresses.

B. You install the service via Control Panel, Networks.

C. DNS Service information can be supplied via a DHCP server as well.

D. You set up information concerning DNS (Domain Name System) servers on the Networks tab.

15. Which of the following statements is false?

A. Gateway Services for NetWare transfers file and directory information and user and group account information from a NetWare server to a Windows NT domain controller.

B. Gateway Services for NetWare enables Windows NT Servers to access NetWare file and print resources.

C. The passwords from the NetWare server can be migrated across to NT by setting the right option.

D. RIP packets are sent out once every 60 seconds.

16. Which of the following statements is not true about Gateway Services for NetWare?

A. GSNW enables Windows NT Servers to access NetWare file and print resources.

B. GSNW is ideal for large-scale routing.

C. GSNW enables the Windows NT Servers to act as a gateway to the NetWare file and print resources.

D. GSNW enables multiple Windows NT clients to share a single connection.

17. RAS can connect to a remote computer using which of the following media?

A. The phone company

B. X.25

C. Null modem cable

D. ISDN

Answers and Explanations: Practice Exam

1. **B** The Migration Tool for NetWare default is Ignore, which causes the account to be skipped with no error messages or warnings.
2. **D** NWLink must be running on the NT Server to use the Migration Tool.
3. **C** You only propagate NetBIOS broadcasts over RIP routers if both sides of the Windows NT router contain Microsoft clients that need to communicate browsing information over the router.
4. **A, C, D** The passwords from the NetWare server cannot be migrated to NT for security reasons, but other options are available.
5. **A** RIP for IP reduces administrative overhead.
6. **D** RIP for IP can increase network traffic.
7. **A** Server view groups all the services on each server and only lists computers with an Internet service loaded on them.
8. **C** With Services view, each Internet service is listed with the corresponding servers grouped by service.
9. **A** DNS is the abbreviation for Domain Name System.
10. **B** You use the Network configuration option to configure the network protocols, and encryption to be used by RAS.
11. **B** The Network Configuration settings apply to all the ports that are enabled in RAS.
12. **A** A phonebook entry is a bundle of information that Windows NT needs to establish a specific connection.
13. **D** Full Control equates to NetWare's Supervisor permission.
14. **D** You set up information concerning DNS (Domain Name System) servers on the DNS tab, not the Networks tab.
15. **C** For security reasons, the passwords from the NetWare server cannot be migrated to NT.
16. **B** GSNW enables multiple Windows NT clients to share a single connection. This sharing causes a significant performance loss for the NetWare resource. For this reason, it is not recommended for large-scale routing.
17. **A, B, C, D** RAS can connect to a remote computer using all mentioned methods.

CHAPTER 11

Monitoring and Optimization

This chapter covers the following Microsoft exam objectives:

- Establishing a baseline for measuring system performance. Tasks include creating a database of measurement data.
- Monitoring performance of various functions by using Performance Monitor. Functions include Processor, Memory, Disk, and Network.
- Monitoring network traffic by using Network Monitor. Tasks include collecting, presenting, and filtering data.
- Identifying performance bottlenecks.
- Optimizing performance for various results. Results include controlling network traffic and controlling server load.

Some of the tools that Microsoft provides for monitoring system performance are as follows:

- **Server Manager:** Monitors the number of users connected, open files, idle time, shared resources, and so on.
- **Windows NT Diagnostics:** Displays the current configuration for the processor, memory, disk, and network.
- **Response Probe:** A utility used to apply a controlled stress on a system and monitor the response.
- **Performance Monitor:** An administrative tool for monitoring NT workstations and servers. Performance Monitor helps you to better plan for future use and, at the same time, to optimize its current performance.
- **Task Manager:** Enables the viewing, stopping, and starting of applications and processes. It also contains the Performance Monitor capabilities that enable the viewing of memory and CPU utilization.
- **Network Monitor:** Captures and views the network traffic going in and out of the system on which Network Monitor is running.

All these tools come with Windows NT 4 (Network Monitor must be installed) except Response Probe, which comes with the Resource Kit.

11.1 Analysis Using Performance Monitor

To conduct analysis and optimization, do the following:

- Create a baseline of current use.
- Monitor the use over a period of time.
- Analyze data to determine non-optimum system use.
- Determine how the system should be used.
- Determine whether additional resources should be added to the system or whether the system needs to be upgraded.

Performance Monitor helps you to better plan for future use and, at the same time, to optimize its current performance.

A. An Overview of Performance Monitor

This section identifies some of the options available in Performance Monitor for monitoring, analyzing server performance, and gathering specific data. Some of the options include:

- Viewing data from multiple computers simultaneously
- Seeing how changes affect the computer
- Changing charts of current activity while viewing them
- Starting a program or procedure automatically, or sending a notice when a threshold is exceeded
- Exporting Performance Monitor data to spreadsheets or database programs, or using it as raw input for programs
- Saving different combinations of counter and option settings for quick starts and changes
- Logging data about various objects from multiple computers over time
- Creating reports about current activity or trends over time

A number of other factors can adversely affect the data gathered by using Performance Monitor:

- If the sample interval is too short, the log file becomes very large.
- If sampled too often, the processor has additional burden.
- If the interval is too long, significant changes in data may be missed.
- Monitoring too soon after startup records all the processes and services being initiated.
- Take the computer off the network to stop the burden of network resources skewing the performance of other resources.

B. What Resources Should You Monitor?

The throughput of each resource should be monitored both individually during installation and after installation is complete with all resources in use. The following four resources have the greatest impact on the performance of the server:

- Memory
- Processor
- Disk
- Network

Monitoring the four resources—memory, processor, disk, and network—simultaneously shows the effects the resource combinations have on each other and the server system.

1. Memory

Two main types of memory need to be considered when analyzing server performance:

- Physical random access memory (RAM)
- Virtual memory (pagefile)

The more physical memory the better because the disk drive does not have to be accessed as often for the pagefile. The pagefile can be moved to another partition to reduce access to the boot partition, but it prevents debugging system problems if the system tends to crash often. The best option is to leave the pagefile in its default location with its size set to be the same as physical memory and to create a large secondary pagefile on another physical drive.

2. Processor

The type and number of processors greatly affects the performance of the system. Windows NT Server 4 can scale up to 32 processors.

3. Disk

A number of factors affect disk performance, and all of them should be taken into account when analyzing and optimizing the system. The factors include:

- **Type and number of controllers:** Whether they are IDE, EIDE, SCSI, fast SCSI, and so on, can make a big difference.
- **Types of drives implemented:** Disk drives come with varying specs as far as access speed and rotation speed.
- **Controllers that support RAID:** RAID can provide fault tolerance.
- **Disk striping with parity:** If you are using Microsoft's disk striping with parity, write performance can improve greatly.
- **Busmaster controllers:** Have a processor on board to handle requests and reduce the load on the system processor.
- **Caching:** Read and write performance can improve due to requests being held in onboard memory until free time is available.

- **Type of work being performed:** Application server, file and print server, network protocol(s) being used, number of users, type of network adapter(s), services being run (DHCP, WINS, IIS, and so on).
- **Matching disk controllers to disk types:** Ensure that disk controllers are matched to the disk types. A fast-wide SCSI disk should be used with a fast-wide SCSI controller.

4. Network

A number of different topologies as well as network architecture standards are available. The two main architectures in use today are Ethernet and Token Ring:

- Ethernet is the most commonly implemented type of network that operates anywhere from 10 MHz to 100 MHz and more.
- Token Ring is a standard that was developed by IBM and operates anywhere from 4 MHz to 16 MHz and more.

In each case, whether Ethernet or Token Ring is used, it is always advisable to use the fastest network card with the largest bus. Both Ethernet and Token Ring are available in 32-bit formats, and 64-bit cards should be available soon if they are not already.

C. Objects in Performance Monitor

When monitoring a computer system, what is really being monitored is the behavior of its objects. An *object* is a standard mechanism for identifying and using a system resource. Objects are created to represent individual threads, processes, physical devices, and sections of shared memory. Performance Monitor groups counters by their object type. Each object has a unique set of counters assigned to it. Certain objects and their respective counters are available on all systems; others are available only when the computer is running the associated software or service.

Each object type can have more than one component installed in the computer. These components are referred to as *instances* and are displayed in the Instance box of any Add to dialog box. The Instance box also can contain the Total instance. This instance represents the total of all instances. Some objects are dependent on or a part of another object. This type of object also can be referred to as a *child object*. An object that has one or more dependent objects can be referred to as a *parent object*.

A *thread* is an object with a process that executes program instructions. By having multiple threads, a process can carry out different parts of its program on different processes concurrently. Threads dependent on a process or parent object are indicated by an arrow from parent object to child object.

Microsoft designed Performance Monitor to cause as little impact on Windows NT as possible. It still, however, has an effect on the system. Therefore, when monitoring anything other than network performance, it is recommended that you monitor the server system from a different computer. When monitoring for network performance, it is best to do so in Log mode.

The core objects that can be monitored on any Windows NT 4 system are described in Table 11.1.1.

Table 11.1.1 Core Objects Capable of Being Monitored

Core Object Name	Description of Object
Cache	An area of physical memory that holds recently used data
LogicalDisk	Partitions and other logical views of disk space
Memory	Physical random access memory used to store code and data
Objects	Certain system software objects
Paging File	File used to back up virtual memory locations to increase memory
PhysicalDisk	A single spindle-disk unit or RAID device
Process	Software object that represents a running program
Processor	Hardware unit (CPU) that executes program instructions
Redirector	File system that diverts file requests to the network servers; also referred to as the Workstation service
System	Contains counters that apply to all system hardware and software
Thread	The part of a process that uses the processor

D. Counters in Performance Monitor

A *counter* defines the type of data available from a type of object. Performance Monitor can display, collect, and average data from counters by using the Windows NT Registry and the Performance Library DLLs. Counters can be divided into three types:

- **Instantaneous:** Instantaneous counters always display the most recent measurement. In the case of the Process:Thread Count, the number of threads found in the last measurement is displayed.
- **Averaging:** Averaging counters measure a value over a period of time and display the average of the last two measurements.
- **Difference:** Difference counters subtract the last measurement from the preceding measurement and display the difference if it is a positive value. A negative value is shown as zero.

Other performance monitoring applications can read the data gathered from Performance Monitor and can display and use the negative values.

Data is broken down into either absolute or relative information, with the difference being that an *absolute* value is exactly the duration taken or the amount reached, whereas a *relative* value is one measurement compared to another. (See Table 11.1.2 for an example of absolute values.)

Table 11.1.2 Absolute Transfer Rates

Counter	5-Second Interval	5-Minute Interval
Disk time	4.652 seconds	263.89 seconds
Bytes transferred	82,524 bytes	4,978,335 bytes

11

It is difficult to tell which measurement is showing a faster rate of transfer. If you look at the same information in Table 11.1.3 that uses relative counters, however, it is easier to compare the results.

Table 11.1.3 Relative Transfer Rates

Counter	5-Second Interval	5-Minute Interval
Disk time	93.04%	87.96%
Bytes transferred	16504.8 bytes/sec	16594.45 bytes/sec

A brief description displays at the bottom of the dialog box if the Explain button is selected. This is useful if you are unsure to what a counter refers.

E. Views in Performance Monitor

You can view data in Performance Monitor in various ways. The Chart, Report, Log, and Alert views are described in Table 11.1.4.

Table 11.1.4 Various Ways to View Data in Performance Monitor

View	Description
Chart	A chart is a graphical display of the value of a counter over a period of time.
Report	A report shows the value of the counter. A report of all the counters can be created.
Log	The selected data is stored in a file on a disk for future analysis.
Alert	An alert can be set on an individual counter. This causes an event to display if the counter attains the specified value.

The four views are always available, but only one can be viewed at a time. The default view is the Chart view. To highlight an individual chart line, select the desired line in the legend and press Ctrl+H. This turns the corresponding line white and makes it much wider than the other lines. After the highlight is enabled, it can be moved from one chart line to another by using either the up/down arrow keys or the mouse. To disable the highlight, press Ctrl+H again.

If you want to view the contents of the log while it is still collecting data, open a second instance of Performance Monitor. Switch to the desired view (Chart or Report) and set the Data values displayed from option to the name of the running log file.

F. Performance Analysis

Now that the process for creating a baseline has been established, analysis of the system and resource requirement forecasting can start. Analysis on a system takes four steps:

- Determine what is normal for the system and how to deal with the abnormal.
- Set expectations of how the system or resource should respond under specific conditions.

- Help plan for upgrades and additions.
- Provide better input into system budgeting requirements.

When a system is to be analyzed, you should first determine what functions the server performs. Three types of Windows NT Servers exist, as described in Table 11.1.5.

Table 11.1.5 Windows NT Servers

Server Type	Description
File and print server	Used for data storage and retrieval. It also can be used for loading application software over the network.
Application server	The server runs the application engine that users access by using a local version of the application front end.
Domain server	A domain server validates user account logons. Domain controllers synchronize the account database among themselves.

To set expectations, you must know what is to be expected of a system. This is referred to as *workload characterization*. A *workload unit* is a list of requests made on the system or a resource. An example of a workload unit might be the number of bytes transferred per second.

To determine workload characterization, you must understand what is taking place in each environment.

Many Windows NT installations have the servers acting in one, two, or all three server roles. In these situations, the administrator might have to sacrifice or reduce the performance of one server role to bring the performance of another role up to a satisfactory level to get the best overall performance.

A resource that restricts the workflow is referred to as a *bottleneck*. Sometimes the performance of one resource makes another resource appear to be the bottleneck.

Because Windows NT is self-tuning to a certain degree, a good percentage of optimization involves upgrading hardware, not changing Registry settings. It is important, however, to know what needs to be upgraded and what doesn't.

1. Analysis of a File and Print Server

File and print servers generally are accessed for data storage and retrieval and sometimes for loading applications across the network. Therefore, the largest load applied is from users who access the server at the same time and demand resource requirements. Events that need to be monitored for this type of server are listed in Table 11.1.6.

Table 11.1.6 File and Print Server Monitoring

Workload Unit	Performance Monitor Counter
Concurrent user sessions	Server: Server Sessions
The number of open files	Server: Files Open
Average transaction size	PhysicalDisk: Avg. Disk Bytes/Transfer
Amount of disk activity	PhysicalDisk: %Disk Time
Type of disk activity	PhysicalDisk: %Disk Read Time PhysicalDisk: %Write Time
Network use	Network Segment: %Network Utilization

In addition to the preceding, you might find that additional resources (such as memory) are being consumed and should also be monitored. All four of the main system components are important in any server; however, some resources are more important than others, depending on the type of server being analyzed. For a file and print server, the order of importance is explained in Table 11.1.7.

Table 11.1.7 Order of Importance in a File and Print Server

Priority	Resource	Implications
1	Memory	Memory is used for caching opened files; if RAM is insufficient for caching, performance takes a big hit.
2	Processor	The processor is used for each network connection. This means all network traffic must pass through the processor.
3	Disk	The disk drive is the primary resource that users are going to access. The speed of the disk drives affects the general perception of how the server operates.
4	Network	A number of factors affect the network system (adapter type, number of adapters, protocols used, and so on). It does not matter, however, how fast the disk drive is, how much RAM exists, or how many processors exist if the network adapter is slow.

When forecasting resource requirements, keep the following in mind:

- Monitor the number of user sessions and the effect each session has on the four main system resources.
- If the server is used to retrieve and update data files, monitor the disk and network resources.
- If the server is used for data files and to load applications, monitor memory, disk, and network resources.
- Make sure Maximize Throughput for File Sharing is selected in the Server dialog box. This is found in the Network Applet of the Control Panel on the Services tab.

2. Analysis of an Application Server

Workload units are key when analyzing an application server. (Workload units that need to be monitored are shown in Table 11.1.8.)

Table 11.1.8 Monitoring Workload

Workload Unit	Performance Monitor Counter
Concurrent user sessions	Server: Server Sessions
Processor usage	Processor: %Processor Time
Average disk transaction size	PhysicalDisk: Avg. Disk Bytes/Transfer
Amount of disk activity	PhysicalDisk: %Disk Time
Network use	Network Segment: %Network Utilization
Average network transaction	NetBEUI: Frame Bytes/sec (similar size counter for each protocol)
Available memory	Memory: Available Bytes
Amount of paging	Memory: Pages/sec
Usage of cache	Cache: Copy Read Hits %

In addition to the counters that Performance Monitor provides, certain applications (such as Microsoft Exchange Server) provide additional counters and predefined charts. If application-specific counters are available, be sure to utilize them when analyzing the server.

Table 11.1.9 lists the four main resources in order of importance and briefly describes their role in an application server.

Table 11.1.9 Resources and Their Roles in an Application Server

Priority	Resource	Roles
1	Processor	Applications run on the server instead of the client side of the network.
2	Memory	Memory is needed at the server to support both the server needs and the application needs.
3	Disk	Client/server applications typically access large amounts of data; therefore, they demand more of the disk drives.
4	Network	Client/server applications transfer many requests across the network. These requests often are queries or commands that are small in size.

11.1.1 Exercise: Monitoring Memory Performance

The purpose of this exercise is to illustrate the monitoring of the memory resource in a server. To this exercise, edit the BOOT.INI file and add the switch /MAXMEM:16 so that the available memory is limited to 16 MB. Then follow these steps and note the Average, Minimum, and Maximum measurements.

1. Start Performance Monitor.
2. Click Add to Chart to open the dialog box.
3. Add the counters of Pages/sec and Page Faults/sec for the Memory object.
4. Open the Chart Options dialog box and change the time interval to one second.
5. Open Disk Administrator, and then open Server Manager.
6. Return to Performance Monitor and view the results.

11.1.2 Exercise: Monitoring the Network Performance

The purpose of this exercise is to illustrate the monitoring of the network services using one or multiple protocols.

1. Ensure that all three protocols are installed (TCP/IP, NetBEUI, IPX/SPX) on your server.
2. Ensure that SNMP Service is installed to activate the TCP/IP network counters.
3. Ensure that Network Monitor Agent Service is installed to activate the network segment object.
4. Open Performance Monitor if it is not already open and ensure that no counters have been added.
5. Add all the counters for the Workstation object.
6. Open Server Manager.
7. Open Explorer to the *WindowsNtroot*\System32 directory.
8. Map a drive to a computer share on the network.
9. Copy the files from the current directory on your computer to the mapped drive.
10. Although the files are being copied, switch to Server Manager and open the properties of a computer on the network.
11. Return to Performance Monitor to view the results and make note of the Average, Minimum, and Maximum values during file transfer.

11.1 Practice Problems

1. How is Performance Monitor installed on a Primary Domain Controller?

   A. It is installed from the Windows NT 4.0 Resource Kit.

   B. Performance Monitor is automatically installed as part of Windows NT 4.

   C. Performance Monitor is purchased as an add-on package.

   D. Performance Monitor is a separate service that must be installed after Windows NT has been installed.

2. Performance Monitor can be used to monitor the activity of the disk. To activate the disk counters, diskperf -y must first be run. What must be run if you want to monitor a disk system that is a RAID?

   A. diskperf -yr

   B. diskperf -y stripe

   C. diskperf -ye

   D. diskperf -raid

3. Which is the default window in Performance Monitor?

   A. Report

   B. Chart

   C. Objects, Counters, Instances

   D. Sessions, Real Time, Transfer Statistics

4. What does a Counter represent in Performance Monitor?

   A. A process that executes a set of program instructions

   B. A mechanism for identifying system resources

   C. The type of data available from an object

   D. The type of data available from a thread

5. What does an Object represent in Performance Monitor?

   A. A process that executes a set of program instructions

   B. A mechanism for identifying system resources

   C. The type of data available from a type of object

   D. The type of data available from a thread

6. What does an Instance represent in Performance Monitor?

   A. The type of data available from a thread

   B. The type of data available from an object

   C. One of multiple installed objects

   D. One of multiple installed counters

7. What command is used to enable the disk monitoring counters in Performance Monitor?

   A. perfdisk -y

   B. perfdisk /y

   C. diskperf /yes

   D. diskperf -y

8. What is used to enable the TCP/IP network counters in Performance Monitor?

   A. perfnet -y

   B. perfnet /yes

   C. netperf -y

   D. SNMP service

9. How often do you have to enable the disk counters for Performance Monitor?

   A. Each time Performance Monitor is restarted.

   B. Each time the computer is restarted.

   C. It never has to be re-enabled.

   D. Each time an administrator logs onto the server.

10. Jack has added the 15 counters that his supervisor recommended to monitor for his file and print server. Now when he views the chart he has a hard time distinguishing which line corresponds with which counter. How can Jack make it simpler to distinguish one line from the other? Choose the best answer.

    A. Start three separate Performance Monitor sessions and add just five of the counters to each of the sessions.

    B. Press Ctrl+C to highlight the selected counter.

    C. Press Ctrl+H to highlight the selected counter.

    D. Modify the color selections to make each line more obvious.

11. Susan wants to get the most accurate reading on the network counters on her file and print server. What should she do? Choose the best answer.

    A. Run Performance Monitor on the file and print server while running multiple applications on the server.

    B. Run Performance Monitor on a different server while running multiple applications on the server.

    C. Run Performance Monitor on the file and print server while transferring files to another computer.

    D. Run Performance Monitor on a different server while transferring files to another computer.

12. What is Response Probe used for, and how is it enabled?

    A. Like Performance Monitor, it is automatically installed as part of Microsoft Windows NT 4.

    B. Like Performance Monitor, it is a service that can be installed from the Microsoft Windows NT 4 CD.

    C. Response Probe doesn't exists.

    D. Response Probe is an application for creating a workload that is available on the Resource Kit.

13. Select the three types of counters available in Performance Monitor.

    A. Averaging

    B. Maximum

    C. Difference

    D. Instantaneous

14. What are the two types of data that are gained from Performance Monitor?

    A. Average and Maximum

    B. Absolute and Refined

    C. Relative and Accrued

    D. Relative and Absolute

15. Mike needs to compare disk transfer rates between two computers. What counter should he select in Performance Monitor? Choose the best answer.

    A. Bytes Transferred

    B. %Disk Time

    C. Bytes Transferred/sec

    D. Disk Time

11.1.1 Answers and Explanations: Exercise

The purpose of this exercise was to illustrate the monitoring of the memory resource in a server. You edited the BOOT.INI file and added the switch /MAXMEM:16 so that the available memory was limited to 16 MB. Be sure to note the Average, Minimum, and Maximum measurements.

11.1.2 Answers and Explanations: Exercise

The purpose of this exercise was to illustrate the monitoring of the network services using one or multiple protocols. (For more information, see the section "Performance Analysis.")

11.1 Answers and Explanations: Practice Problems

1. **B** Performance Monitor is a built-in utility of Windows NT 4.
2. **C** The *-y* enables the disk counters and the *e* indicates that every drive should be monitored.
3. **B** The chart is the default view in Performance Monitor.
4. **C** A counter represents the type of data that is available from an object.
5. **B** An object represents a mechanism for identifying system resources.
6. **C** An instance represents one of multiple installed objects. For example, if two disk drives exist, two instances for the object Physical Disk exist.
7. **D** diskperf -y enables the disk counters the next time the system is restarted.
8. **D** The SNMP service enables the TCP/IP network counters in Performance Monitor.
9. **C** The disk counters remain enabled until an administrator disables them by running diskperf -n.
10. **C** The best answer is to press Ctrl+H while viewing Performance Monitor to highlight the selected counter.
11. **C** Run Performance Monitor on the file and print server while transferring files so that additional network traffic is not generated by monitoring.
12. **D** Response Probe is an application that is available on the Resource Kit that is used to create a workload on the server.
13. **A, C, D** Maximum is not one of the types of counters that are available in Performance Monitor.
14. **D** Relative and Absolute are the two types of data that is generated in Performance Monitor.
15. **C** Bytes Transferred/sec is the best selection because it gives relative information. Mike can see how many bytes are transferred in one second. Bytes Transferred provides the number of bytes transferred but no indication of how long it took.

11.1 Key Words

Pagefile
Object
Counter
Thread
RAID
Striping
Cache
Logical disk

11.2 Establishing a Baseline

Whenever you analyze a system's performance, you must first create a baseline from which to measure. After you have an established baseline, you can always compare system performance to that baseline whenever changes are made to the system, whether they are good or bad.

The method in which data is collected can provide a wide variety of information. Taking a measurement, for example, adding all the components, and then measuring again displays the effect of having all the components working together. Another way of measuring is to take a separate measure as each component is added. This provides data about how each individual component affects the performance of the system. Yet another way is to add components one at a time, but in different combinations. This provides a better understanding of how each component affects the performance of the others.

A. Creating a Baseline Using Performance Monitor

You should always include memory, processor, disk, and network objects in the baseline. After the initial set of data is captured, use the same settings and capture data on a regular basis. Place this information in a database and analyze the performance of the system.

You must use the Log view to create a baseline measurement; this is the only way to create a log of activity. While measuring, you log, relog, and append logs to get a complete set of information. Objects that should be included are as follows:

- Cache
- Logical disk
- Memory
- Network adapter
- Network segment activity on at least one server in the subnet
- Physical disk (if using a RAID system)
- Processor
- Server
- System

Measurements should be taken for a full week at different times of the day so that information can be recorded at both peak and slack times. Ideally, you should have enough data to know whether the different counters experience significant change during different times of the day.

To automate the collection of data, a utility is available on the Resource Kit that enables Performance Monitor to be started as a service.

> **Performance Monitor log files can grow to be quite large. Set up monitoring to be done on a system that is not being monitored and that has a large amount of free disk space. Practice taking logs that use different time intervals to get a feel for the size of the created file.**

B. Establishing a Database

The second step in preparing for analysis is to take the collected data and put it into a database so that it can be analyzed. This involves collecting the information over a period of time and adding it to a database. After it's in a database, the information can be used to identify bottlenecks and trends.

11.2.1 Exercise: Establishing a Baseline

This exercise reinforces the concept of establishing a baseline regardless of the tool(s) used. Scenario: You are assigned the task of being the network administrator for the new office that your company is opening. Two logon servers exist, as well as a file and print server controlling four printers.

The network protocol is TCP/IP, with 150 users. Because the office is smaller, they only work one shift—8:00 a.m. to 4:30 p.m. weekdays. From the information you have, what kind of schedule would you set up for creating the baseline?

11.2.2 Exercise: Using a Baseline

This exercise reinforces the use of a baseline to qualify assumptions. Scenario: You have inherited the role of administering a network. When the network was first set up, a baseline was created. Now that six months have passed and a few new users have been added, you want to see whether performance has improved, deteriorated, or stayed the same.

Explain what steps should be taken to judge how performance has faired over the last six months.

11.2 Practice Problems

1. Which is the primary tool used for creating a baseline in Windows NT Server? Choose the best answer.
   - A. Server Manager
   - B. User Manager
   - C. Network Monitor
   - D. Performance Monitor
2. Which monitoring tool that Microsoft provides does not come on the Microsoft Windows NT Server CD?
   - A. Task Manager
   - B. Response Probe
   - C. Network Monitor
   - D. Performance Monitor
3. What is a baseline?
   - A. The performance specifications for all hardware components.
   - B. The performance specifications for all software components.
   - C. A collection of performance information to which all future measurements can be compared.
   - D. A baseline in Microsoft Windows NT is like "Safe Mode" in Windows 95. It is the minimum standard configuration for the system.
4. How many baselines should be created? Choose the best answer.
   - A. One for each server, even if they have "identical" configurations
   - B. One for each Primary Domain Controller
   - C. One for each domain controller (Primary and Backup)
   - D. One for each computer on the network
5. Which components should be included in the creation of the baseline? Choose all that apply.
   - A. Memory
   - B. Processor
   - C. Disk
   - D. Network
6. Which component is the most important when creating a baseline? Choose all that apply.
   - A. Memory
   - B. Processor
   - C. Disk
   - D. Network
7. When should a baseline be created?
   - A. When the server is first configured.
   - B. After two months, so that the system has stabilized.
   - C. At the first sign of problems on the network.
   - D. At the first sign of problems on the server.
8. What time of day should data for the baseline be recorded? Choose the best answer.
   - A. 7:00 a.m. to 10:00 a.m.
   - B. 2:30 p.m. to 6:30 p.m.
   - C. All day
   - D. 10:00 a.m. to 2:00 p.m.
9. How often should the baseline be upgraded? Choose the best answer.
   - A. Every two weeks.
   - B. Whenever changes have been made to the server or the network.
   - C. Once a year.
   - D. The baseline does not need to be upgraded.
10. Your server has to be shut down during business hours. What is the first thing that should be done? Choose the best answer.
    - A. Notify the users that the server will be shut down so that they can close any files that may be open on the server.

B. Go to the server that is to be shut down and stop the Server Service.

C. Disconnect the network cable from the server so that it cannot be accessed.

D. Just turn off the server. Windows NT automatically saves and closes files before it shuts down.

11. Bill is planning to shut down his file and print server but wants to make sure that no one has files open. How can Bill check for open files?

A. Open User Manager for Domains to see who is logged onto the network.

B. Start Windows NT Diagnostics to see which resources are being used.

C. Open the Services dialog box to see who is using the Server Service.

D. Open Server Manager to see which files are open and who has them open.

12. Jane has inherited the role of network administrator and finds that a baseline has never been created on any of the five servers. Two of the servers are logon servers and the other three are file and print servers. What should she do?

A. Create a baseline for each of the five servers.

B. Because the hardware is the same on all servers, create a baseline on one of the logon servers and one of the file and print servers.

C. Because the hardware is the same on all servers, create a baseline on only one of the servers.

D. Because the network has been up and running for eight months, it is too late to create a baseline.

13. When Sean creates a baseline for his application server by using Performance Monitor, which view should he use?

A. Chart

B. Report

C. Log

D. Alert

The following scenario applies to questions 14 and 15.

Scenario: Alice has taken over as administrator of a small network. The network consists of 150 users with two domains that fully trust each other. Three file servers are in DomainA of which the Primary Domain Controller is one. In DomainB, the Primary Domain Controller is a print server, and an application server also exists. No baseline has been created for the domain controllers of either domain also exists.

Required Result: A baseline must be created for each of the domain controllers. *Optional Result 1:* A baseline must be created for the application server. *Optional Result 2:* A baseline must be created for the print server.

14. *Proposed Solution*: Alice uses Performance Monitor on each domain controller and file server each day, throughout the day, for two weeks. She uses the Log view so that a log file can be created and referenced at a later date. Ratings:

A. The required result is met, and both optional results are also met.

B. The required result and one optional result is met.

C. The required result is met, and neither optional result is met.

D. The required result is not met, and one optional result is met.

E. None of the results is met.

15. *Proposed Solution*: Alice uses Performance Monitor on each file server, print server, and application server each day, throughout the day, for two weeks. She uses the Log view so that a log file can be created and referenced at a later date. Ratings:

A. The required result is met, and both optional result are also met.

B. The required result and one optional result is met.

C. The required result is met, and neither optional result is met.

D. The required result is not met, and one optional result is met.

E. None of the results is met.

11.2.1 Answers and Explanations: Exercise

To establish a baseline for any network, it is important to take a sampling of data for all parts of the day. The peak periods for the logon servers will be shortly after the working day starts, lunch time, and again at the end of the day. For the file and print server, peak times could be spread throughout the day depending on a number of factors. Because the office is only operational during the day, sample data for evening or night is not necessary, except maybe to compare with a non-loaded network.

11.2.2 Answers and Explanations: Exercise

First review the baseline to see which objects were selected when it was created. Collect data into a log file with the same objects selected, being sure to run the log at the same times of day with the same polling interval. Take the log files and compare them with the baseline and use whatever application you want to draw your conclusions.

11.2 Answers and Explanations: Practice Problems

1. **D** Performance Monitor can capture data for all aspects of the computer performance.
2. **B** Response Probe is available on the Resource Kit for Windows NT 4.
3. **C** A baseline is a collection of performance information to which all future measurements can be compared.
4. **A** One baseline should be created for each server, even if hardware and software seems to be "identical," because nothing is ever really "identical."
5. **A, B, C, D** Memory, Processor, Disk, and Network should all be included when creating a baseline.
6. **A, B, C, D** All components are important because any one of them could cause a computer to perform poorly.
7. **A** A baseline should be created when a server is first configured so that configuration changes can be evaluated for performance.
8. **C** The performance should be monitored at all times during the day to compare "load" to "no load" times.
9. **B** The baseline should be upgraded each time the configuration has been changed.
10. **A** Notify the users so that any files that are open can be saved and closed.
11. **D** Open Server Manager to view the users who have files open.
12. **A** Create a baseline for each of the servers.
13. **C** The Log view creates a file that can be referenced at a later date.
14. **B** Both domain controllers and the print server had a baseline created. The application server did not get a baseline created.
15. **A** Both domain controllers as well as both the print server and the application server had a baseline created.

11.2 Key Words

Baseline

Log

Subnet

11.3 Identifying and Resolving Performance Bottlenecks

Bottlenecks are the problem areas that need to be addressed to improve the performance of the system. Trends are useful for capacity planning and preparing for future needs.

Any spreadsheet or database application can be used to analyze the data collected.

A. Finding Memory Bottlenecks

The reason memory has the greatest impact on the system is that a shortage of memory causes the system to read and write from the disk more often. The RAM in Windows NT is broken down into two categories:

- **Nonpaged:** Data placed directly into a specific memory location that cannot be written to or retrieved from disk.
- **Paged:** Virtual memory, in which all applications believe they have a full range of memory addresses available.

The best indicator that memory is the bottleneck is when a sustained, high rate of hard page faults is present. Table 11.3.1 shows some of the memory counters to watch and the range that is acceptable.

Table 11.3.1 Page Fault Counters

Counter	Description
Pages/sec	This is the number of requests that had to access the disk because the requested pages were not available in RAM.
Available Bytes	This is the amount of available physical memory.
Committed Bytes	This is the amount of virtual memory allocated either to physical RAM for storage or to the pagefile.
Pool Nonpaged Bytes	This is the amount of RAM in the pool nonpaged memory area, where space is used by operating system components as they carry out their tasks.

B. Finding Processor Bottlenecks

The two most common problems when the processor is a bottleneck are CPU-bound applications and drivers and excessive interrupts generated by inadequate disk or network components. Table 11.3.2 shows the counters to watch and the type of values for which to look.

Table 11.3.2 Bottleneck Indicators

Counter	Description
Processor: %Processor Time	This is the amount of time the processor is busy. It is the %Privileged Time plus the %User Time. When the processor is consistently above 75%–80%, it has become a bottleneck.
Processor:% Privileged Time	This is the amount of time the processor spends performing operating system services. Like %Processor Time, this value should average below 75%.
Processor: %User Time	This is the amount of time the processor spends running user services such as desktop applications. Again, this value should average below 75%.
Processor: Interrupts/sec	This is the number of interrupts the processor is handling from applications and hardware devices.
System: Processor Queue Length	This is the number of requests the processor has in its queue. Each of these requests is a thread waiting to be processed. Normally, this value is at zero, but if the queue length is consistently two or greater, the queue has a problem.
Server Work Queues: Queue Length	This is the number of requests in the queue for a particular processor. Again, if the queue length is two or greater, the queue has a problem.

C. Finding Disk Bottlenecks

Performance Monitor has counters for both the PhysicalDisk and LogicalDisk objects. The LogicalDisk monitors the logical partitions of physical drives that indicate when a service or application is making excessive requests. The PhysicalDisk is used to monitor the physical disk drive as a whole.

> Remember to activate Performance Monitor disk counters before trying to monitor the disk drives. By default, the counters are not enabled and do not show activity when added in Performance Monitor.
>
> Type **diskperf -y** at a command prompt to enable the counters on the local computer.
>
> Type **diskperf -y \\servername** at a command prompt to enable the counters on a remote computer.
>
> Type **diskperf -ye** at a command prompt to enable the counters on the local computer with a RAID implementation.
>
> Type **diskperf -n** at a command prompt to disable the counters on the local computer.

Table 11.3.3 shows some of the counters to use and the values to watch for when monitoring the physical disk—logical disks also have similar counters.

Table 11.3.3 Disk Monitoring

Counter	Description
%Disk Time	This is the amount of time the disk is busy with reads and writes. An acceptable value is around 50%.
Disk Queue Length	This is the number of waiting disk I/O requests. If this value is consistently two or higher, upgrade the disk.
Avg. Disk Bytes/ Transfer	This is the average number of bytes transferred to or from the system during read and write operations.
Disk Bytes/ sec	This is the rate at which bytes are transferred to or from the disk during read and write operations.

D. Finding Network Bottlenecks

Table 11.3.4 shows some counters to monitor and some values to watch for when a lot of activity from the network is at the server.

Table 11.3.4 Finding Bottlenecks

Counter	Description
Server: Bytes Total/sec	This is the number of bytes the server has sent and received over the network. If this value is low, try adding an adapter.
Server: Logon /sec	This is the number of logon attempts for local, across-the-network, and service-account authentication in the last second. Add domain controllers if the value is low.
Server: Logon Total	This is the number of logon attempts for local, across-the-network, and service-account authentication since the server was started.
Network Segment: % Network utilization	This is the percentage of bandwidth in use for the local network segment. This is used to monitor the effects of different network operations, such as account synchronization and logon validation. Limit the number of protocols used if this number is high.
Network Interface: Bytes Sent/sec	This is the number of bytes sent by using the selected adapter. Upgrade the network adapter if a problem exists.
Network Interface: Bytes Total/sec	This is the number of bytes sent and received by using the selected adapter. Upgrade the network adapter if a problem exists.

To have the network segment available in Performance Monitor, the Network Monitor Agent service must first be installed.

11.3.1 Exercise: False Bottlenecks

This exercise illustrates how the poor performance of one resource can make another resource appear to be a bottleneck.

1. From a Command prompt enter **diskperf -y** on the server and reboot the system.
2. Open Performance Monitor on the server and select Physical Disk: Bytes Read/sec and Bytes Written/sec.
3. Go to a client system and try copying about 20 MB of data to the server and then about 20 MB from the server. Take note of the results in Performance Monitor.
4. Restore the memory in your server to its original amount prior to the Performance Monitor exercise by removing the /MAXMEM switch that was added in the previous exercise.
5. Carry out the procedure in step 3 again and compare the transfer rates. The rate should have improved.

11.3.2 Exercise: Memory as a Bottleneck

This exercise illustrates how memory can be a bottleneck for running applications and transferring files by comparing results with the Pages/sec and Page Faults/sec results from Exercise 11.1.1.

1. Recall the notes you made during the Performance Monitor exercise. In that exercise you reduced the amount of memory that was available to your server and started some applications.
2. Start Performance Monitor.
3. Click Add to Chart to open the dialog box.
4. Add the counters of Pages/sec and Page Faults/sec for the Memory object.
5. Open the Chart Options dialog box and change the time interval to one second.
6. Open Disk Administrator, and then open Server Manager.
7. Return to Performance Monitor and view the results.

11.3 Practice Problems

1. What is a bottleneck? Choose the best answer.

    A. A slow network card

    B. A faulty memory simm

    C. A crashed disk drive

    D. A resource that restricts workflow

2. Jackie wants to check to see whether the disk drive in the server is a bottleneck. What should she do?

    A. Use Performance Monitor to compare byte transfer rates to the baseline.

    B. Use Task Manager to view the amount of memory that is being used.

    C. Use Windows NT Diagnostics to verify the size, speed, and type of disk drive that is installed.

    D. Open Disk Administrator to adjust the cluster size being used on the disk drive.

3. What is the meaning of Nonpaged RAM?

    A. Data that is placed on disk before it gets moved into physical memory.

    B. Data that is placed directly physical memory.

    C. Data that is stored to a text file prior to being moved into memory.

    D. Windows NT has no such thing as Nonpaged RAM.

4. What is the meaning of Paged RAM?

    A. Data that is placed on disk before it gets moved into physical memory.

    B. Data that is placed directly into physical memory.

    C. Data that is stored to a text file prior to being moved into memory.

    D. Windows NT has no such thing as Nonpaged RAM.

5. Chuck has been running some tests on one of his file and print servers and has come to the conclusion that the disk drives are the bottleneck. What is the best solution for Chuck's network?

    A. Add another disk to his server.

    B. Add a faster disk to his server.

    C. Redistribute the load across all the file and print servers.

    D. Reinstall Windows NT Server 4, making sure to choose the disk optimization option during installation.

6. John discovered that the processor was the bottleneck on his application server but found that when he added another processor to the system, the server's performance did not improve. What could be the problem?

    A. John forgot to activate the new processor in the System dialog box.

    B. The application is not written to be multithreaded.

    C. More memory has to be added to enable the new processor.

    D. Windows NT cannot work with multiple processors unless it is an OEM version.

7. Sharon found that the processor in her server was a bottleneck and upgraded to a faster one. Although the processor was rated much faster, the performance did not improve as expected. What other option did Sharon have?

    A. Install the latest Service Pack.

    B. Upgrade to Windows NT 4 b-release.

    C. Add a second processor instead of upgrading the existing processor.

    D. The application needs to be rewritten.

8. What two counters make up the %Processor Time?
   A. %Privileged Time
   B. Bytes Processed/sec
   C. %Free Time
   D. %User Time
9. When monitoring memory, to what does Available Bytes refer?
   A. The amount of space available in the pagefile that has not been committed to an application
   B. The amount of space available on the disk drive that has not been committed to the pagefile
   C. The amount of cache that has not been written back to the disk
   D. The amount of physical memory that has not been used
10. When monitoring memory, to what does Committed Bytes refer?
   A. The amount of physical memory being used
   B. The difference between the amount of physical memory and virtual memory
   C. The amount of virtual memory that has been allocated to either physical RAM for storage or to the pagefile
   D. The total amount of both physical and virtual memory that is being used
11. Silvia has been monitoring her application server for a few days and has found that the processor has exceeded 95% for %Processor Time quite frequently. What should she do to rectify the situation?
   A. Nothing.
   B. Stop the Server service to see if the %Processor Time is reduced.
   C. Have the application rewritten to make better use of the resources.
   D. Upgrade the processor.
12. To ensure that no one can see what applications are being run on the server, Sam has set up a screen saver. Whenever the screen saver comes on, however, people complain about poor server performance. What should Sam do?
   A. Change the screen resolution.
   B. Disable the screen saver.
   C. Turn the monitor off when not sitting at the server.
   D. Upgrade the processor.
13. What other counter, besides %Processor Time, indicates that the processor is not fast enough?
   A. %Free Time.
   B. System: Processor Queue Length.
   C. Processor: Bytes/sec.
   D. No other counters exist.
14. Which bottleneck makes the access time to a disk seem slow to a locally logged on user? Choose all that apply.
   A. Memory
   B. Processor
   C. Disk
   D. Network
15. You suspect your processor to be the bottleneck of your system. What two counters should you check?
   A. %DPC Time, %User Time
   B. %Processor Time, Avg. Disk Queue Length
   C. Interrupts/sec, Processor Queue Length
   D. Processor Queue Length, %Processor Time

16. A file server is being used by 65 users for storing files, as well as for installation source files. The server has 64 MB of RAM, a 9.2 GB fast SCSI drive, a 16-bit network card, and enabled shadow RAM. The users complain that access to the server is slow at different times of the day.

    Required Result: Determine whether memory is the bottleneck. *Optional Result 1:* Determine whether the disk is the bottleneck. *Optional Result 2:* Improve the performance of the server.

    Proposed Solution: Run Performance Monitor at different times throughout the day for a number of days, watching the counters of %Processor Time, Page Faults/sec, and Processor Queue Length. Ratings:

    A. The required result is met, and both optional results are also met.

    B. The required result and one optional result is met.

    C. The required result is met, and neither optional result is met.

    D. The required result is not met, and one optional result is met.

    E. None of the results is met.

17. A file server is being used by 65 users for storing files, as well as for installation source files. The server has 64 MB of RAM, a 9.2 GB fast SCSI drive, a 16-bit network card, and enabled shadow RAM. The users complain that access to the server is slow at different times of the day.

    Required Result: Determine whether memory is the bottleneck. *Optional Result 1*: Determine whether the processor is the bottleneck. *Optional Result 2*: Improve the performance of the server.

    Proposed Solution: Run Performance Monitor at different times throughout the day for a number of days watching the counters of %Processor Time, Page Faults/sec, and Processor Queue Length. Ratings:

    A. The required result is met, and both optional result are also met.

    B. The required result and one optional result is met.

    C. The required result is met, and neither optional result is met.

    D. The required result is not met, and one optional result is met.

    E. None of the results is met.

11.3.1 Answers and Explanations: Exercise

By looking only at the transfer rates, it appeared as though the disk drives were the bottleneck. When the memory was increased, however, the performance improved, indicating that memory was the bottleneck. For this reason, it is important to look at counters for all objects when analyzing a server.

11.3.2 Answers and Explanations: Exercise

By increasing the amount of memory, the number of page faults was reduced. As indicated, memory was the bottleneck; without ample memory, the virtual memory manager performs excessive page swapping.

11.3 Answers and Explanations: Practice Problems

1. **D** A bottleneck is a resource that restricts workflow.

2. **A** Use Performance Monitor to compare byte transfer rates to the baseline.

3. **B** Nonpaged RAM is data that is placed directly into physical memory without being written to or retrieved from disk.

4. **A** Paged Ram is data that has been written to or read from disk prior to being moved to physical memory.

5. **C** Redistribute the load across multiple file and print servers so that they have more equal usage.

6. **B** If the application is not written to be multithreaded, all requests must go through the one processor.

7. **C** If the application is written to be multithreaded, it is more beneficial to have multiple processors than to have one processor that is fast.

8. **A, D** %Privileged Time and %User Time together make up %Processor Time.

9. **D** Available Bytes refers to the amount of physical memory that is not being used.

10. **C** The amount of virtual memory that has been allocated to either physical RAM for storage or to the pagefile.

11. **A** It is normal for the %Processor Time to go over 95% on numerous occasions.

12. **B** Disable the screen saver. No one should be logged onto the server except for administrative tasks.

13. **B** System: Processor Queue Length indicates how many requests are waiting to be processed.

14. **A, B, C, D** All resources could have an affect on a locally logged on user.

15. **D** Processor Queue Length and %Processor Time should be checked.

16. **C** Monitoring Page Faults/sec can help determine whether memory is a bottleneck.

17. **B** Monitoring Page Faults/sec can help determine whether memory is a bottleneck and monitoring %Processor Time and Processor Queue Length can help determine whether the processor is a bottleneck.

11.3 Key Words

Bottleneck
Nonpaged Memory
Paged Memory

11.4 Analysis Using Network Monitor

Network Monitor is a tool that enables monitoring of the network traffic going in and out of the system running the monitor. A second format that comes with Systems Management Server permits traffic to be monitored anywhere on the network.

Windows NT 4 provides a number of network services that enable users to carry out specific requirements on their network. Table 11.4.1 lists some of the more commonly installed network components. Some are installed by default; others are not.

Table 11.4.1 Network Components

Component	Description
Computer Browser	Enables users to find or browse resources on the network without having to remember specific paths or the correct syntax
DHCP	The automatic distribution and administration of TCP/IP addresses and related parameters to DHCP clients
Directory Replicator	The automatic duplication of directories among Windows NT computers
Domain Name System (DNS)	The resolution of TCP/IP host names to IP addresses
Internet Explorer	An Internet browser that provides access to the World Wide Web (WWW) to view and download files
Netlogon	Service that performs user account logon validation and synchronization of user accounts in a domain
Server	Enables network clients to access shared resources
WINS	A centralized database that resolves NetBIOS names to TCP/IP addresses
Workstation	Provides network access to shared resources

A. Traffic Analysis

To optimize or capacity plan your network, as with the optimization of a server, the administrator must know what traffic is currently being generated. Analysis involves determining what effect each Windows NT Server service has on the network. This is done with a network analyzer. You can optimize network traffic in two ways:

- Provide users with better response time by implementing network services that can increase network traffic.
- Provide users with more bandwidth on the network by reducing network traffic generated by services.

11

Each method is valid and deserves consideration, but a properly optimized network is going to strike a compromise between the two. *Capacity planning* is the method of analyzing the network as one or more factors are increased. As the network grows, different services are added.

1. Classifying Services

Classifying services enables an administrator to better predict the effects on a network as changes are made. Each of the Windows NT Server services can be classified with three simple questions:

- What kind of traffic does this service generate?
- How often is this traffic generated?
- What impact does this traffic have on the network?

Following are some basic guidelines for classifying services on the server:

1. Isolate a network segment. This helps to prevent other network traffic from skewing the results of monitoring.
2. Use Network Monitor or some third-party program to monitor the network traffic.
3. Capture the appropriate traffic by initiating the service to be classified.
4. Identify each captured frame to ensure that all the traffic is generated by the service and not by some other function.

2. Frame Types

Frames are divided into three types: broadcast, multicast, and directed. Table 11.4.2 provides a description of each frame type.

Table 11.4.2 Frame Types

Frame Type	Description
Broadcast	Broadcasts are sent with the destination of FFFFFFFFFFFF. No host can be configured with this address, but all hosts on the network (subnet) accept this frame and process it. The frame is passed up the stack until it is determined whether the frame is meant for that computer or not.
Multicast	Multicasts are sent to a portion of the computers on the network. Like broadcast frames, multicast frames are not sent to a specific Media Access Control (MAC) address, but to a select few addresses on the network. Each host on the network must register its multicast address to become a member of a multicast set. NetBEUI and some TCP/IP applications utilize multicasting.
Directed	Directed frames are the most common type of frame. Each of these frames has a specific address for a host on the network. All other hosts disregard this frame because it does not contain the host's MAC address.

3. Contents of a Frame

All frames are broken down into different pieces, or fields, that can be analyzed. Some contain addressing information, others contain data, and so on. By analyzing the addressing portion of the frame, you can determine whether the frame was a broadcast type. This helps administrators determine which service created the frame and whether it can be optimized.

4. Network Protocols and Frames

The type of network traffic generated often depends on the protocol used to send the frames. As more companies want connectivity over WANs and more people want access to the Internet, TCP/IP has become the protocol of choice.

B. Installing Network Monitor

Network Monitor is a network packet analyzer that comes with Windows NT Server 4. The advantage of the version that comes with Systems Management Server is that any system can be monitored on the network.

1. Hardware

Network Monitor does not require special hardware other than a network adapter supported by the system on which it is installed; Windows NT 4 supports NDIS 4 and allows the viewing of local traffic only or full network traffic. In Windows NT 3.51, a special adapter (which is available with Microsoft Systems Management Server) was needed to support the promiscuous mode of Network Monitor.

2. Software

Network Monitor is made up of two components:

- **Network Monitor application:** Enables a system to capture and display network data, to display network statistics, and to save the captured data for future analysis
- **Network Monitor Agent:** Enables a computer to capture all network traffic and to send it over the network to the computer running the Network Monitor application

3. Network Monitor Window

The Capture Window is the default view of Network Monitor. (Table 11.4.3 describes each area of the Network Monitor window.)

Table 11.4.3 Network Monitor Window Areas

Window Area	Description
Graph	A horizontal bar chart that displays the current activity as a percentage of network utilization
Session Statistics	A summary of the transactions between two hosts and a display of which host initiated the broadcasts or multicasts
Total Statistics	Statistics for the traffic on the network as a whole, the frames captured, the per second statistics, and the network adapter statistics
Station Statistics	A summary of the number of frames and bytes sent and received, the number of frames initiated by a host, and the number of broadcasts and multicasts

C. Capturing and Displaying Data

Capturing data by using Network Monitor is quite simple and can be initiated in one of three ways:

- Select Capture, Start from the menu bar.
- Click the Start Capture button in the toolbar.
- Press F10, the function key.

Stopping the capture of data is just as simple as starting it. It can been done in one of four ways:

- Select Capture, Stop from the menu bar.
- Click the Stop Capture button in the toolbar.
- Press F11, the function key.
- Click the Stop and View button in the toolbar.

To control the amount of data captured, the user can set a capture filter. A *filter* describes what type of data should be captured and displayed. The most common items to filter are either the protocol (NetBEUI, IPX, TCP/IP, and so on) or the destination or source address (MAC address, IP address, and so on).

Captured data can be displayed for analysis, or it can be saved to a capture file (*.CAP) for analysis later. After the data is captured, it needs to be analyzed. To analyze the data, it must be displayed. Displaying the data can be done in one of three ways:

- Select Capture, Display Captured Data from the menu bar.
- Click the Display Captured Data button in the toolbar.
- Press F12, the function key.

As with capturing data, filters can be applied while viewing the data. This enables the capture of numerous types of information, but it also permits the user to filter for frames of particular interest during analysis. The following three areas make up the display window for Network Monitor:

- **The Summary pane:** Shows a list of all the frames that were captured and information about each of them.
- **The Detail pane:** Shows protocol information for the frame selected in the Summary pane.
- **The Hexadecimal pane:** Displays the contents of the frame in hexadecimal format. The actual contents of data sent can be viewed in this area.

D. Analyzing Data

As with any kind of monitoring and analysis, the analysis is the difficult part.

1. Client Traffic

One of the first provisions to a user is the capability to log on to the network and to be validated by a server. Other considerations for the network administrator follow:

- When do people log on? Are they all logging on at 8 a.m. or randomly over an hour during the morning from 7:30 a.m. to 8:30 a.m.?
- Are all the users logging on from a local network computer, or are some users logging on from remote sites?

a. Locate a Logon Server

The first action that must take place is finding the logon server. In a Windows NT network, that can be done in two ways, depending on what has been implemented:

- Send a broadcast message across the network to the NETLOGON mail slot (only located on domain controllers).
- Send a query to the WINS server for all registered domain controllers in the selected domain (appears as a domain [1C] entry in WINS). If found, send a request through directed frames.

b. Logon Validation

After the requests have all been sent out, the client computer then accepts the first server response to that request. It does not matter whether the request was generated from a broadcast or from a directed message. Four factors are involved in validating the logon:

- The amount of traffic generated by establishing the session
- The amount of traffic generated if the client is at a Windows 95 computer
- The amount of traffic generated if the client is at a Windows NT computer
- The termination of the session

c. File Session Traffic

Almost all communication between computers requires the establishment of a session before the communication actually takes place. DHCP, WINS, and DNS are a few of the communications in a Windows NT network that do not require an established session before communication starts. Establishing a session occurs in five steps:

1. Resolve the NetBIOS name (computer name) to an IP address.
2. Resolve the IP address to the MAC address (hardware address) of the computer.
3. Establish a TCP session.
4. Establish a NetBIOS session.
5. Negotiate the computer's SMB protocols.

2. Client-to-Server Browser Traffic

Client-to-server traffic is the communication a client has with a server. Browser traffic is all the traffic generated during the browser process, both in announcing available resources and in retrieving lists of available resources. The entire process is as follows:

1. Servers (any computer with sharing enabled) are added to the browse list by announcing themselves to the master browser.
2. The master browser shares the list of servers with the backup browsers and the master browsers of other domains.

3. The client computer retrieves a list of backup browsers from the master browser.
4. The client retrieves a list of servers from a backup browser.
5. The client retrieves a list of shared resources from the server.

3. Server to Server Traffic

A large amount of traffic is generated between servers. The basics of server browsing are as follows:

1. At startup, the PDC assumes the role of domain master browser for its domain.
2. At startup, each BDC becomes either a backup browser or the master browser of its subnet, if no PDC is on the subnet.
3. Each master browser announces itself every 12 minutes to the master browsers of other domains on the local subnet.
4. Every 12 minutes, each domain master browser contacts the WINS server for a listing of all domains.
5. Every 12 minutes, each master browser contacts the domain master browser for an update of the browse list.
6. Each backup browser contacts its local master browser to retrieve an updated list every 15 minutes.

Along with the announcement traffic a server generates, it also can create additional traffic by taking part in other browser traffic.

- Browser elections take place if a client cannot find a master browser, if the master browser announces it is being shut down, or if a domain controller is being initialized.
- Master browsers in different domains share their browse lists to permit servers and resources to be accessed throughout the network.
- Backup browsers retrieve updated browse lists from their local master browser.

The three areas that Trust Relationships generate traffic are as follows:

- Creating the trust creates a lot of traffic (about 16,000 bytes), but it only takes place at the time the trust is created.
- Using trusted accounts creates traffic. When the administrator of the trusting domain assigns permissions to an account from the trusted domain, much traffic is generated.
- Pass-through authentication creates additional traffic.

11.4.1 Exercise: Browser Traffic

This exercise illustrates the amount of traffic that can be generated by browsing the network to find a resource.

1. Open the Network dialog box from the Control Panel and ensure that NetBEUI, IPX/SPX, and TCP/IP are all installed.
2. Open Explorer.

3. Open Network Monitor and start capturing traffic data.
4. Return to Explorer and click Network Neighborhood.
5. Double-click a domain or workgroup name.
6. Select one of the computers within the selection.
7. Return to Network Monitor and stop capturing.
8. Open the Details window in Network Monitor to see how much traffic was generated by browsing the network.

11.4.2 Exercise: Client to Server Traffic

This exercise illustrates the amount of network traffic generated by a client logging onto a domain.

1. Open Network Monitor on your Primary Domain Controller.
2. Start capturing data.
3. Log on to the domain from another computer (any computer that is a part of the domain).
4. After you are logged onto the network, log off again.
5. Switch to Network Monitor and stop capturing data.
6. Open the Details window to view the traffic generated by a user logging on and off of the network.
7. Close Network Monitor.

11.4 Practice Problems

1. Nancy is trying to verify that logon requests are reaching the server with the correct user name because a number of users are not getting validated. How can she verify that particular user names are being forwarded to the logon server?

   A. Have each user go to the server and logon locally.

   B. Have Nancy watch them enter their name and password to ensure that they are not making typos.

   C. Run Network Monitor on the logon server and check the Hexadecimal pane to see whether the names are getting to the server.

   D. It's not possible to verify that the information is reaching the server.

2. What are the areas of the Network Monitor window when it is capturing data?

   A. Network Statistics, Session Statistics, Counters

   B. Graph, Session Statistics, Total Statistics, Station Statistics

   C. Objects, Counters, Instances

   D. Sessions, Real Time, Transfer Statistics

3. What areas can be displayed while viewing the captured data in Network Monitor?

   A. Resource pane, Data pane

   B. Summary pane, Detail pane, Hexadecimal pane

   C. Report pane, Alert pane, Detail pane

   D. None of the above

4. What are the two versions of the Network Monitor?

   A. Real mode and Protected mode

   B. Local traffic only and full network traffic

   C. Promiscuous mode and Server mode

   D. LAN mode and WAN mode

5. A network has a large number of Windows 95 and Windows NT Workstation 4 systems. Select all that could help reduce network traffic.

   A. Reduce the number of protocols being used at the workstations and servers.

   B. Increase the number of network cards in the servers.

   C. Turn off file and print sharing on the desktop systems.

   D. Install SNMP.

6. Which of the following services helps to reduce network traffic?

   A. WINS

   B. DHCP

   C. Remote Access Service

   D. SNMP

7. A user says that he cannot connect to a resource displayed for a remote system in Explorer. Why would a resource be displayed if it is not available?

   A. The Browser service has been disabled.

   B. The WINS server is providing an old list of resources.

   C. The system is down or has removed the share, but the browse list has not been updated.

   D. Browsing was enabled before the browse list was updated.

8. Jack is administering a network that has three distinct groups. Approximately 200 users share the network, and most of them complain that network response time is slow. What can be done to increase performance?

   A. Subnet the network and put each of the groups onto its own subnet.

B. Move the pagefile to a different directory.

C. Remove file and print sharing from the workstations and have all access go through a server.

D. Add another network card to the server.

9. How can logon validation be speeded up over a slow link?

A. Add another WINS server.

B. Install a Proxy server.

C. Add more resource domains.

D. Put a Backup Domain Controller at each of the remote sites.

10. Why is TCP/IP the default protocol for Windows NT?

A. TCP/IP was designed for use on LANs and WANs.

B. It reduces the number of bytes sent across the network.

C. TCP/IP is the fastest protocol.

D. It is the simplest to set up.

11.4.1 Answers and Explanations: Exercise

You can see that a great deal of traffic is generated just to find out what resources are available on the network. First, broadcasts are sent to discover which computer is the master browser. From the master browser, the client receives a list of backup browsers. The client must then find the addresses of the servers on the network so that it can "talk" to them. Finally, the selected server must provide the client with a list of the available resources.

11.4.2 Answers and Explanations: Exercise

You can see the traffic generated by a client logging onto the domain. First, the client computer broadcasts to find an available domain controller. Then it sends the logon request to the server for validation. At this time, it checks the username and password in the SAM to determine whether it is a valid name and then to see what group memberships exist. After all this information is gathered, a token is generated and passed back to the client. When the client logs back off again, similar traffic is generated to inform the domain controller that the user is no longer active on the network.

11.4 Answers and Explanations: Practice Problems

1. **C** Run Network Monitor at the logon server and view the Hexadecimal pane to see whether the names are getting to the server correctly.

2. **B** Graph, Session Statistics, Total Statistics, Station Statistics.

3. **B** Summary pane, Detail pane, Hexadecimal pane.

4. **B** Local traffic only and full network traffic.

5. **A, C** Reduce the protocols being used and disable file and print sharing from the workstations.

6. **A** WINS helps to reduce network traffic.

7. **C** The browse list has not been updated as of yet.

8. **A, C, D** Subnet the network, remove all sharing and have all access go through the server, and add an additional network card(s) to the server.

9. **D** Put a Backup Domain Controller at each remote location.

10. **A** TCP/IP was designed for use on LANs and WANs.

11.4 Key Words

Promiscuous

Global group

Local group

11.5 Performance Optimization

The most common and now the least expensive method of optimizing memory is to add more physical memory (RAM). Adding more memory to a server, whatever function that server serves, helps performance.

A. Processor Optimization

When the processor becomes a bottleneck, you have two options depending on the situation:

- Upgrade the processor.
- Add a processor(s).

If the server hardware is not capable of handling additional processors, then the processor can be upgraded to a faster, more robust one.

If the server is capable of handling multiple processors, then the decision has to be made depending on what type of server it is and what kind of requests it is handling. In the case of an application server where the application is written to be multithreaded, multiple processors may be the best choice. In the case of a server that is controlling a single printer and files, for example, it might be more realistic to just upgrade the processor.

B. Disk Optimization

If the disk is the bottleneck, you have a number of possible solutions:

- Offload some of the processes to another system.
- Add a faster controller or an on-board caching controller.
- Add more memory to permit more caching by Windows NT.
- Add more disk drives in a RAID environment. This spreads the data across multiple physical disks and improves performance.

C. Network Optimization

If the network is found to be the bottleneck, a number of things can be done:

- On the server, add an adapter, upgrade to a better adapter, or upgrade to better routers/bridges.
- Add more servers to the network to distribute the load.
- Segment the network to isolate traffic to appropriate segments.

1. Optimizing Logon Traffic

To have the optimum response time for logon validation, the proper number and configuration of domain controllers must be set up. This creates four things to consider when optimizing the logon validation:

- Determine the hardware required for better performance.
- Configure the domain controllers to increase the number of logon validations.
- Determine the number of domain controllers needed.
- Determine the best location for each of the domain controllers.

2. Optimizing File Session Traffic

Although file session traffic is minimal when compared to the amount of traffic generated during the transfer of a file, a few things can still be done to reduce traffic.

- Remove excess protocols, or at least disable them for functions or services where they are not needed. To change the binding configurations, open the Network applet in Control Panel and select the Bindings tab.
- Try to make sure the servers are in a location close to the people that use them most, especially if they can be kept on the same subnet.

3. Optimizing Browser Traffic

Browsing is provided to enable efficient use of network resources by a typical end user. By making it easy for users to access resources on the network, the efficiency of the network has been sacrificed due to the increase in network traffic.

A few things can be done to help reduce the network traffic generated by browsing:

- Disable the Server component on all computers that do not need to share resources.
- Configure which systems can be browsers.
- Reduce the number of protocols used.
- Create internal web sites.
- Limit the size of the intranet web pages.
- Increase the cache at the client computers.

4. Optimize Server Browser

Most of the traffic generated by browsing takes place automatically and at intervals that cannot be configured. However, server browser traffic can be reduced in three ways:

- Reduce the number of protocols.
- Reduce the number of entries in the list.
- Increase the amount of time between browser updates.

5. Optimize Trust Relationship Traffic

Normally, trust relationships do not create a lot of network traffic. However, traffic from a trust relationship can be reduced in two ways:

- Create fewer trust relationships.
- Assign global groups from the trusted domain to local groups and then assign permissions to the local group.

11.5.1 Exercise: Virtual Memory Optimization

This exercise illustrates the performance degradation when virtual memory is minimal.

1. Right-click My Computer on the Desktop and select Properties.
2. Select the Performance tab and then select Virtual Memory.
3. Change the pagefile size to be the minimum size of 2 MB and select Set.
4. Close the dialog boxes and select Yes to restart the system.
5. Open Explorer, Disk Manager, Performance Monitor, and Network Monitor.
6. Return to Explorer and copy 20 MB of data to another computer.
7. Take note of how long it takes to copy the data.
8. Change the pagefile size to what it was originally.
9. Delete the files that were copied to the other computer.
10. Ensure that Explorer, Disk Manager, Performance Monitor, and Network Monitor are all open.
11. Transfer the same files to the other computer again and take note of how long it takes.

11.5.2 Exercise: Broadcast Traffic

This exercise illustrates the amount of traffic generated by broadcasts with multiple protocols installed.

1. Ensure that NetBEUI, IPX/SPX, and TCP/IP protocols are installed.
2. Open Network Monitor and start capturing data.
3. Select Start, Run.
4. Enter **net view** and select OK. Net view may be run from a command prompt if you want to see the results of the command.

5. Return to Network Monitor after you have received the results of the `net view` command.
6. Stop capturing data and open the Details window.
7. Notice the number of broadcasts that were generated by all three protocols.
8. Open the Network dialog box and remove the NetBEUI and IPX/SPX protocols.
9. Repeat steps 2 through 7.
10. Close Network Monitor.

11.5 Practice Problems

1. Jane wants to optimize the network components on her server. What should she do?

   A. Remove unused adapter cards and protocols.

   B. Disable the Server service.

   C. Make sure that TCP/IP, IPX/SPX, and NetBEUI are all installed to create the maximum number of network paths possible.

   D. Nothing needs to be done because Windows NT is self-optimizing.

2. Which of the following items can make the system use virtual memory more efficiently? Choose all that apply.

   A. Move the pagefile to the partition where the Windows NT system files are located.

   B. Move the pagefile from the partition where the Windows NT system files are located.

   C. Spread the pagefile over multiple drives.

   D. Set the minimum pagefile size to that which it reaches during peak system load.

3. Optimum performance in Windows NT 4 depends on which two components?

   A. Pagefile location

   B. Software

   C. Hardware

   D. Processor type (RISC, Intel, MIPS, and so on)

4. What is the definition of optimal performance?

   A. To make threads process at a greater speed

   B. To make processors work at a higher percentage capacity

   C. To have the maximum number of services running possible

   D. To get the best performance result with the available hardware and software

5. Although the Backup Domain Controller is used to validate logons, what other functions does it perform if it is also a file and print server?

   A. Account database updates from the Primary Domain Controller

   B. Service resource requests from users

   C. Act as Master Browser in the domain

   D. Directory replication updates

6. What are the advantages of using a stripe set? Select all that apply.

   A. They are more efficient for I/O management.

   B. Stripe sets are not advantageous.

   C. Less overhead is required.

   D. Simultaneous writes may be accomplished if multiple controllers exist.

7. How many disk drives are needed to implement a stripe set with parity?

   A. 2

   B. 3

   C. 8

   D. 32

8. What can be done with device drivers to optimize Windows NT?

   A. You don't need to do anything because Windows NT is self-tuning.

   B. Remove unneeded drivers.

   C. Create separate hardware drivers that use only specific drivers.

   D. Pause all unnecessary devices in the Network dialog box from the Control Panel.

9. Which of the following components are automatically optimized by Windows NT?

    A. Pagefile

    B. Mouse

    C. Disk cache

    D. Bindings

10. To optimize your network cards, what should you consider? Choose all that apply.

    A. Never use NetBEUI.

    B. Always use NetBEUI.

    C. Use a card with the widest available bus.

    D. Split your network into multiple subnets, with each subnet attaching to a separate network card in the server.

11. Why is hardware fault tolerance considered to be better than software fault tolerance?

    A. Hardware fault tolerance does not work with the HAL of Windows NT.

    B. Windows NT's version of fault tolerance only works with NTFS.

    C. Software fault tolerance works only with FAT.

    D. Hardware fault tolerance removes the parity calculation from the processor.

12. When tuning a file server for optimum performance, what question must you first ask?

    A. For what type of tasks is the file server going to be used?

    B. How large is the budget for upgrading hardware?

    C. For what type of business is this unit being used? Companies that do business for the government or military, have a restriction on tuning.

    D. Is the fastest hardware installed?

13. When choosing disk drives for a server, what should be considered? Choose all that apply.

    A. Use the FAT file system.

    B. Use the fastest drives.

    C. Use stripe sets with parity when possible.

    D. Use SCSI over IDE.

14. A user tells you that his Windows NT 4 Workstation system is running slowly. Which is the best way you can monitor the performance of the system?

    A. Connect to the administrative share C$, and then run Performance Monitor.

    B. Go to the workstation and run Performance Monitor.

    C. You cannot monitor a Windows NT 4 Workstation system.

    D. Use Performance Monitor to connect to the workstation and monitor it across the network.

15. Where is the best place to modify the virtual memory settings in Windows NT 4?

    A. Through the Registry

    B. Through Control Panel, Services, Virtual Memory

    C. Through Control Panel, System, Virtual Memory

    D. Through WinMSD

16. The Server Service Properties dialog box has a number of options, of which

Balance is one. When would the Balance option be selected?

A. When the number of users is between 10 and 64

B. When the number of users is 10 or less

C. When the number of users is greater than 64

D. When setting up an application server or when a domain has only the Primary Domain Controller

17. The Server Service Properties dialog box offers a number of options, of which Minimize is one. When would the Minimize option be selected?

A. When the number of users is between 10 and 64

B. When the number of users is 10 or less

C. When the number of users is greater than 64

D. When setting up an application server or when a domain has only the Primary Domain Controller

18. Jane has been monitoring the Total Bytes/sec on each of the servers on her network. When she adds up the total, she finds that it is nearly as much as the maximum capacity for her network. What should she do to improve general network performance?

A. Upgrade her NIC drivers.

B. Subnet her network.

C. Upgrade the network cards.

D. Increase the amount of memory on each server.

19. The Server Service Properties dialog box offers a number of options, of which Maximize Throughput for Network Applications is one. When would the Maximize Throughput for Network Applications option be selected?

A. When the number of users is between 10 and 64.

B. When the number of users is 10 or less.

C. When the number of users is greater than 64.

D. When setting up an application server or when a domain has only the domain controller.

20. What may occur on the network if the Server service becomes a bottleneck on a server? Choose all that apply.

A. Response times become longer.

B. Client requests are denied.

C. Logon requests may be denied.

D. Database synchronization may not occur between domain controllers.

21. What is the most common hardware upgrade that generally provides the greatest performance increase?

A. Install a faster processor.

B. Install a faster disk controller.

C. Install more memory.

D. Install a faster network card.

22. Fred's network has a number of machines that are using different protocols (NetBEUI and IPX/SPX) because of specific needs. The server is also used to access different web sites to download the drivers. What can Fred do to improve performance?

A. Remove all except one protocol from all systems.

B. Unbind TCP/IP from the Workstation service and unbind NetBEUI and IPX/SPX from the Server service.

C. Unbind NetBEUI and IPX/SPX from the Workstation service and unbind TCP/IP from the Server service.

D. Bindings can be rearranged, but they cannot be disabled.

23. The Server Service Properties dialog box offers a number of options, of which Maximize Throughput for File Sharing is one. When would the Maximize Throughput for File Sharing option be selected?

A. When the number of users is between 10 and 64

B. When the number of users is 10 or less

C. When the number of users is greater than 64

D. When setting up an application server or when a domain has only the domain controller

24. What is one reason why the NetBEUI protocol causes the most broadcast messages on a network?

A. NetBEUI does not cache broadcast results.

B. NetBEUI cannot perform directed messaging.

C. NetBEUI cannot use multicasts.

D. NetBEUI does not use broadcasts.

25. Joe has decided that the amount of traffic on his network has become too great, so he is going to split it into three subnets with his NT Server as the router. This enables each user to have the server available on his subnet. Since this implementation, the network performance has not changed or has become worse. What could be the problem?

A. Windows NT Server cannot act as router.

B. Because of the subnetting, additional cable had to be added, which caused resistance problems.

C. The system that is acting as a router doesn't have enough memory.

D. The server was configured to forward broadcast messages, so traffic was not reduced.

26. Albert has organized his subnets so that the people who need access to certain servers are on the same subnet, but network traffic is still bad. What could be the problem with Albert's network?

A. The network cards must have specific IP addresses for optimum performance.

B. The disk controllers on the servers all need to be synchronized.

C. The server that is acting as the router is configured to forward broadcast packages.

D. WINS is only enabled on one subnet.

27. While monitoring the Disk Queue length, it is determined that the disk is the bottleneck. What could be done to improve this? Choose all that apply.

A. Implement RAID.

B. Use asynchronous disk drives.

C. Add more memory.

D. Use a faster disk interface.

28. While monitoring the Disk Queue Length, John was trying to remember which value indicated that the disk was a bottleneck. Which number indicates that the disk is a bottleneck?

A. A value of less than 2

B. A value of greater than 2

C. A value of less than 4

D. A value of greater than 4

11

11.5.1 Answers and Explanations: Exercise

This exercise illustrates that not only physical memory but also virtual memory is important to the operation of Windows NT 4. The operation of Windows NT 4 was definitely hampered by the lack of ample virtual memory.

11.5.2 Answers and Explanations: Exercise

This exercise illustrates that having more protocols can cause unnecessary traffic on the network. By removing protocols or stripping unnecessary bindings, network traffic can be reduced.

11.5 Answers and Explanations: Practice Problems

1. **A** Always remove unused hardware and software when trying to optimize a server.
2. **B, C, D** Spread the pagefile across multiple drives. Move the pagefile from the boot partition. Set the minimum pagefile size to the size it needs to be during peak load.
3. **B, C** Performance depends on both hardware and software because the hardware can restrict performance, and if the software is written to use the full potential of the hardware, it becomes a bottleneck (16-bit as opposed to 32-bit applications).
4. **D** To get the best performance possible by using the available hardware and software.
5. **A, B, D** Backup Domain Controllers receive database updates from the Primary Domain Controller. A file and print server responds to requests for access to files. Most Backup Domain Controllers participate in Directory Replication.
6. **D** If more than one controller is installed, disks may be written to simultaneously.
7. **B** Three drives are needed to implement a fault-tolerant stripe set.
8. **B** Remove unneeded drivers.
9. **A, C** The pagefile and Disk cache are automatically optimized by Windows NT.
10. **C, D** Use a card with the largest possible bus. Subnet the network to reduce the amount of traffic on each subnet.
11. **D** Hardware fault tolerance removes the parity calculation from the processor.
12. **A** You must ask what type of tasks the server is expected to perform.
13. **B, C, D** Use the fastest drives. Use stripe sets with parity. Use SCSI instead of IDE. The use of faster drives and SCSI improves disk access time and the use of stripe sets with parity adds fault tolerance.
14. **D** Systems may be monitored from across the network.
15. **C** The settings are in Control Panel, System, Performance tab.
16. **A** Balance is chosen when the number of users is between 10 and 64.
17. **B** Minimize is selected when the number of users is 10 or less.
18. **B** Subnet the network to decrease the amount of traffic on each segment.
19. **D** Maximize Throughput for Network Applications is chosen when setting up an application server or when a domain has only one domain controller.
20. **A, B, C** The Server service is set to start automatically on all servers to share resources.
21. **C** Install more memory.
22. **C** The Server must act as a Workstation on the Internet and act as a Server to the local network.
23. **C** Maximize Throughput for File Sharing is chosen when the number of users is greater than 64.

24. **A** NetBEUI does not cache the results of broadcast messages.

25. **D** If the client computers are all creating their own shares and they are accessing each other's resources across the three, traffic is slowed by having to go through the router.

26. **C** If broadcast packages are being forwarded across the router, then the purpose of subnetting has been defeated.

27. **A, B, D** RAID helps reduce degradation; asynchronous drives boost performance; and faster controllers reduce disk access time.

28. **B** If the Disk Queue Length becomes greater than 2, the disk is a bottleneck.

11.5 Key Words

Trust

Optimize

Practice Exam: Monitoring and Optimization

Use this practice exam to test your mastery of "Monitoring and Optimization." The passing Microsoft score is 76.4 percent.

1. Which of the following protocols utilize broadcast messages? Choose all that apply.
   A. NetBEUI
   B. IPX/SPX
   C. TCP/IP
   D. None of the above

2. What type of counter should an Alert be assigned to? Choose all that apply.
   A. Low disk space
   B. Byte transfer rate over 80%
   C. %Processor time over 80%
   D. High number of page faults

3. What Registry settings should be monitored and modified on a regular basis to optimize the server?
   A. Nothing. Windows NT Server 4 is self-tuning.
   B. DiskRotationSpeed
   C. FileTransferRate
   D. NetworkBindings

4. What is a workload unit when referring to Performance Monitor?
   A. Workload units are the counters that are added in Performance Monitor to monitor the server.
   B. A workload unit is any service that is installed and running on the server.
   C. A workload unit is a list of requests made on a server.
   D. No such thing as a workload unit exists when referring to Performance Monitor.

5. Which resource seems to have the greatest impact on a file and print server? Choose the best answer.
   A. Processor
   B. Disk
   C. Network
   D. Memory

6. Which resource seems to have the greatest impact on an application server? Choose the best answer.
   A. Processor
   B. Disk
   C. Network
   D. Memory

7. Which resource seems to have the greatest impact on a domain controller (logon server)? Choose the best answer.
   A. Processor
   B. Disk
   C. Network
   D. Memory

8. Sara has a server that is both a file and print server and a domain controller. The server doesn't seem to be performing as well as it should. What is the best way to monitor the system to get the most accurate results? Choose all that apply.

   A. Use Performance Monitor on another system to gather data from the server.

   B. Monitor all possible counters from the server at the same time.

   C. Stop certain services to isolate the resource usage by the different server roles.

   D. Monitor the power supply to ensure that it is supplying the proper voltage.

9. Performance Monitor has a counter named Memory: Pages/sec. What does this counter indicate?

   A. The number of pages that can be swapped in one second from RAM to pagefile.sys by the Virtual Memory Manager

   B. The general activity of the pages being swapped

   C. The number of pages that can be swapped in one nanosecond from RAM to PAGEFILE.SYS by the virtual memory manager

   D. The number of RAM pages that can be read in one second

10. Which Performance Monitor object and counter measures the amount of time that the CPU is busy?

   A. System: TotalProcessorUsage

   B. System: % Total Processor Time

   C. Processor: % Processor Time

   D. Processor: % Busy Time

11. What answer best explains what the System:Processor Queue Length counter's purpose in Performance Monitor?

   A. A measure of the amount of activity at the CPU

   B. The total CPU usage across the entire network for all CPUs

   C. The number of threads waiting for a response to their request for CPU time

   D. The number of users waiting for a response to their request for CPU time

12. Cathy is just learning how to use Performance Monitor and wants to know whether and how she can be notified when the server is becoming low on disk space. Can it be done, and if so, how would she set it up?

   A. It cannot be done with Performance Monitor.

   B. When a counter is added while in the Alert view, threshold values can be set and computer or user names may be specified to receive the alert.

   C. When a counter is added while in the Report view, threshold values can be set, and computer or user names may be specified to receive the report.

   D. The Chart view automatically notifies all Administrators on the network.

13. Janice wants to analyze the data generated from Performance Monitor with a database program. What view does she have to use to generate the proper information?

   A. Chart

   B. Report

   C. Log

   D. Alert

14. Alice is creating a baseline for network traffic on her logon server using the Log view in Performance Monitor. What must she do to view the data as it is being recorded?

   A. Open a second instance of Performance Monitor and select the Chart view.

B. Start Performance Monitor on another server on the network to monitor the logon server.

C. Nothing has to be done because the Log view enables you to view the data as it is being recorded.

D. The Log view is not the correct view for creating a baseline.

15. To which hardware items do changes make a difference to performance? Choose all that apply.

A. Memory

B. Keyboard

C. Disk Controller

D. Video Resolution

16. What is the name of the virtual memory file that is used in Windows NT 4?

A. SWAPFILE.386

B. PAGEFILE.386

C. SWAPFILE.SYS

D. PAGEFILE.SYS

17. Alice has taken over as administrator of a small network. It consists of 150 users with two domains that fully trust each other. There are three file servers in DomainA of which the Primary Domain Controller is one. In DomainB, the Primary Domain Controller is a print server and there is also an application server. No baseline has been created for the domain controllers of either domain.

Required Result: A baseline must be created for each of the domain controllers. *Optional Result 1*: A baseline must be created for the application server. *Optional Result 2:* A baseline must be created for the print server.

Proposed Solution: Alice uses Performance Monitor on each of the file servers and the application server each day, throughout the day, for two weeks. She uses the Log view so that a log file can be created and referenced at a later date. Ratings:

A. The required result is met, and both optional results are also met.

B. The required result and one optional result is met.

C. The required result is met, and neither optional result is met.

D. The required result is not met, and one optional result is met.

E. No result is met.

18. A file server is being used by 65 users for storing files, as well as for installation source files. The server has 64 MB of RAM, a 9.2 GB fast SCSI drive, a 16-bit network card, and shadow RAM is enabled. The users complain that access to the server is slow at different times of the day.

Required Result: Determine whether memory is the bottleneck. *Optional Result 1:* Determine if the disk is the bottleneck. *Optional Result 2:* Improve the performance of the server.

Proposed Solution: Run Performance Monitor at different times throughout the day for a number of days, watching the counters of %Processor Time, and Processor Queue Length. Off-load the application source files onto a different server. Ratings:

A. The required result is met, and both optional results are also met.

B. The required result and one optional result is met.

C. The required result is met, and neither optional result is met.

D. The required result is not met, and one optional result is met.

E. No result is met.

19. How should users and groups be arranged when assigning permissions across domain trusts?

A. Assign the users to local groups, and then assign the local groups to global groups in the appropriate domain.

B. Create a global group in the resource domain and add the users from the account domain to the global group. Assign the global group to the local group and then assign the permissions to the local group.

C. Users from an account domain do not have access to resources in a resource domain.

D. Assign users to a global group in their domain and add that global group to a local group in the resource domain. Assign permissions to the local group.

20. A server has two hard drives and one partition for each drive. What can be done to make the pagefile more efficient?

A. Keep a pagefile in the default location that is a little more than the size of the physical memory, and place a large pagefile on the other partition.

B. Remove the pagefile from the default location and place the pagefile on the other partition.

C. Move the pagefile to a different directory on the same partition.

D. Remove the pagefile because it is not needed as long as there is 32 MB or more of RAM.

Answers and Explanations: Practice Exam

1. **A, B, C** All three protocols utilize broadcast messages. The difference is how they implement broadcasts.
2. **A, C, D** These three items are something with which any network administrator would be concerned.
3. **A** For the most part, Windows NT 4 is self-tuning; therefore, the administrator should not have to make many changes to the Registry.
4. **B** A workload unit is any service that is installed and running on the server.
5. **D** Memory seems to have the greatest impact on a file and print server because of the amount of caching used while files are being written and read from the disk.
6. **A** Because the application is being run on the server for multiple users, the processor plays a large role in an application server.
7. **C** During logon, very little processor time or memory is needed; therefore, the speed at which the requests are transferred has the greatest impact.
8. **A, C** Monitoring from a different system does not skew readings on the server, except for the network counters. By stopping different services, the resource usage can be isolated.
9. **B** The Memory: Pages/sec indicates the general activity of the pages being swapped.
10. **B, C** Both System: % Total Processor Time and Processor : % Processor Time are valid answers. If only one processor exists, these readings are the same. If multiple processors exist, then the System counter provides an average of all the processors.
11. **C** The number of threads waiting for CPU time.
12. **B** When a counter is added in the Alert view, a threshold value may be entered and a computer or user name may be entered that receives the alert.
13. **C** The log view creates a file that may be used in other applications.
14. **A** Open a second instance on the server that is to be monitored. If you monitored the server from another machine, additional network traffic would be generated.
15. **A, C** Changes to memory and the disk controller can alter the performance of a server.
16. **D** PAGEFILE.SYS is the name of the virtual memory file in Windows NT 4.
17. **D** The application server had a baseline created. Neither of the other results was achieved.
18. **D** The processor is the only resource being monitored and by off-loading the application source files, more resources should be available for performing as a file server.
19. **D** Assign users to a global group in their domain and add that global group to a local group in the resource domain. Assign permissions to the local group.
20. **A** Leave a pagefile in its original location (boot partition) that is the same as the physical memory and place a larger pagefile on another physical disk.

Chapter 12

Troubleshooting

This chapter covers the following Microsoft exam objectives:

- Installation failures
- Boot failures
- Configuration failures (including backing up and editing the Registry)
- Printer problems
- RAS problems
- Connectivity problems
- Resource access and permission problems
- Fault-tolerance failures: mirroring, striping with parity, and tape backup
- Advanced problem resolution, including diagnosing and interpreting a blue screen, configuring a memory dump, and using the event log service

12.1 Solving Installation Failures

This section discusses choosing the appropriate course of action to solve installation failures. These failures occur for two basic reasons: hardware-related problems and configuration-related problems. This section also discusses some of the methods available for automating the installation process.

A. Hardware-Related Problems

Windows NT supports a wide variety of hardware. As such, a variety of problems can occur with these hardware devices. Windows NT has very specific minimum hardware requirements, as you can see in the following list:

- **CPU:** For Intel-based systems, any 486 or higher processor is sufficient. For RISC-based systems, any supported RISC processor (MIPS 4×00, Alpha, PreP-compliant PPC) is sufficient.
- **Video adapter:** A VGA or better is required.
- **Hard disk drive:** A minimum of 110 MB of free space is required.

- **Floppy disk drive:** A 3.5 or 5.25 floppy drive for Intel systems (used for setup boot disks) is required.
- **CD-ROM drive:** A supported CD-ROM drive is necessary. It can be located on the system on which NT Server is being installed or on another computer connected by a network.
- **Memory:** At least 16 MB is recommended for Intel- or RISC-based systems (although 12 MB is sufficient for installation of NT Workstation on an Intel platform). The price of memory has decreased dramatically and it significantly improves system performance. Therefore, a larger quantity is advisable (32 MB being a reasonable minimum).
- **Network adapter:** Although a network adapter is not absolutely necessary, networking is not available unless a network adapter is installed.
- **Pointing device:** A mouse or other pointing device is not absolutely necessary, but it is highly recommended.

In addition to the minimum hardware requirements, it is essential to consider the Windows NT Hardware Compatibility List (HCL). If your system and all its installed components are on the HCL, many potential difficulties can be avoided. Before installing Windows NT, make a list of all the components on your system and the resources they use. Having this information available can greatly simplify the installation process.

> **If you are unsure whether your computer's hardware is on the Windows NT HCL, you can use the Hardware Quantifier tool. This tool itemizes and identifies all hardware on your system necessary for Windows NT. The program runs from a floppy disk created by running the MAKEDISK.BAT batch file in the `\SUPPORT\HQTOOL` directory on the Windows NT Server CD-ROM.**

1. Hard Disk Errors and Unsupported Hardware Errors

Installation failure most commonly occurs due to media errors or hardware problems, including hard disk errors. Problems also can arise from unsupported CD-ROMs and network adapters. Boot sector viruses affect the master boot record and can cause problems with Windows NT. Therefore, you might want to scan each of your hard drives for viruses.

The actual boot error you receive when a boot sector virus is encountered during installation is reported as `0X4,0,0,0`. This error message occurs after the first reboot during an installation. To fix this error, you can boot with a write-protected disk with anti-virus software loaded. Another method is to run the command `fdisk /mbr` after booting into DOS. This command rewrites the master boot record for the hard disk.

If you are using small computer system interface (SCSI) drives, make sure your SCSI chain is properly terminated. The BIOS on the boot SCSI adapter should be enabled, and the BIOS on all other SCSI adapters should be disabled. All SCSI devices should have unique SCSI IDs.

For enhanced integrated drive electronics (EIDE) drives, make sure the system drive is on the first controller on the motherboard. In addition, the file I/O and disk access should be set to standard.

For IDE/EIDE or EDSI drives, the controller should be functional before installing Windows NT. If the disk lights come on briefly upon starting the computer, you know the controller is working. You also will hear the disk start up. If drives are larger than 1024 cylinders, make sure Windows NT supports the disk configuration utility you are using. Finally, the jumpers should be set correctly for master or slave drives.

Even if Windows NT does not support your CD-ROM drive, it still is possible to perform the installation. Assuming you have DOS or Windows 95 drivers for your CD-ROM, you can copy the \i386 directory from the CD-ROM to the local hard disk. You then can run the command `winnt_ /b` from the newly created directory. The `/b` parameter installs the Windows NT boot files to the local hard disk in the directory `c:\$WIN_NT$.~bt` instead of generating the three boot disks. Windows NT also can be installed from a network share of the target computer that is participating in a network.

> **The three startup disks are still necessary to perform an Emergency Repair Process. To create the three startup disks for Windows NT, run the command WINNT /OX from DOS or Windows 95 and the command WINNT32 /OX from Windows NT.**

2. Adapter Card Problems

Network adapters and their associated hardware also can cause problems during installation. Prior to starting Windows NT installation, you should obtain a list of which resources are used by your network adapter cards and make sure there are no conflicts within your system. Typically, a network adapter requires an interrupt (IRQ) and an I/O port, and might require other resources such as a DMA channel. These resources should not be in use by other components of your system before starting the Windows NT installation. Cabling, adapter settings, and terminators are the most likely problem areas.

Other adapter cards in the machine also can create problems. This generally is observed in the area of conflicting settings for IRQ and I/O ports:

- **Sound adapters:** Make sure you have the correct values for interrupts, I/O ports, and DMA channels prior to installing Windows NT. The default installation process does not install sound adapter cards. Sound cards are installed using the Multimedia applet in the Control Panel.

> **Windows NT provides minimal support for Plug and Play ISA drivers by installing the PNPISA drivers, located in the `\Drvlib\PNPISA\%platform%` directory on the Windows NT CD-ROM. They are installed by right-clicking the INF file in this directory and choosing INSTALL. When the system is restarted, all Plug and Play ISA cards are detected and installation routines run automatically.**

- **SCSI devices:** Each device on your SCSI chain should have a unique SCSI ID, and your host adapter should be configured to operate with each device. Also make sure your SCSI bus is terminated correctly.
- **PCMCIA cards:** If your system supports PCMCIA cards and you want to use them with Windows NT, make sure they are present in your system during installation.

You should check the following networking connections:

- **10Base2 (or thinwire) Ethernet networks:** Make sure both ends of the segment are terminated properly. Also make sure your cabling does not run next to (or over) electrical conduits.
- **10Base-T (twisted pair) Ethernet networks:** Make sure the connectors are properly crimped. (The RJ-45 connectors should make solid contact with the wires in the unshielded twisted-pair cable.) A concentrator or hub is required as the connection backbone for the network. Note that 10Base-T equipment has a *link light*, which indicates whether you have a connection to your concentrator. Finally, make sure you have not exceeded the recommended cable length (usually 100 meters from the repeater to your computer, including all path cables and cross-connects).
- **10Base-F networks (or FDDI or any other fiber-optic networks):** You must pay special attention to the cabling. Fiber-optic cable is extremely fragile and can easily be broken. Make sure the cable has not been bent or broken.

  When diagnosing faults in fiber-optic cables, never look directly into the end of a live cable. Retinas can be damaged easily, even by low-level emissions.
- **Asynchronous Transfer Mode (ATM) networks:** ATM networks have very strict requirements for cabling. Be sure to follow all the manufacturer's recommendations for your cabling plant.
- **Token-ring networks:** Make sure your cabling connections are reliable. As with 10Base-T, a centralized network connection point known as a Media Access Unit (MAU) is required. Diagnostic tools can diagnose and resolve problems with the token-ring environment.

B. Configuration-Related Problems

During Windows NT installation, you are asked several questions that can lead to problems if not answered correctly. Common mistakes made during installation include the following:

- Computer name
- Role of server
- Inability to communicate with the Primary Domain Controller (PDC)

1. Computer Name Issues

The computer name for each participating computer must be unique within the network. The NetBIOS name is limited to 15 characters, none of which can be the following:

```
/ \ []":;¦<>+=,?*
```

If a duplicate name is detected, the computer's network services will not start.

2. Computer Role Issues

During Windows NT Server installation, the installer is asked what role the computer will play in the network. The choices are Primary Domain Controller, Backup Domain Controller, and Member Server. This selection is critical because an incorrect selection generally requires reinstallation of the NT Server product into a new directory. Installing a Primary Domain Controller requires that a unique domain name be entered. This name must be a unique NetBIOS name on the network (including computer names and other domain names). When installing a Backup Domain Controller, make sure the domain name is entered correctly.

3. Communication with the Primary Domain Controller

If you install a Backup Domain Controller (BDC) or a member server that participates in the domain, the Windows NT Server computer requires communication with the Primary Domain Controller (PDC). The BDC needs to communicate with the PDC at two stages of the installation:

- During the creation of the computer account for the BDC
- During the initial synchronization of the Accounts database

A member server that participates in the domain requires communication with the PDC during the creation of the computer account in the PDC's Accounts database. If the PDC is not available during installation, a member server can be initially installed as a member of a workgroup. The member server then can join a domain when the PDC is available on the network.

C. Automating the Installation Process

When performing large numbers of Windows NT installations, the main areas of concern are speed and consistency. Windows NT enables you to script, or automate, installation. This provides a consistent method of performing the installations and reduces the amount of user interaction required during the installation process. Automated installation makes use of two files: an unattended script and a uniqueness database file.

The *unattended script* can be configured using the SETUPMGR.EXE utility. This application is located on the Windows NT Server CD in the `\support\deptools\%platform%` directory. SETUPMGR.EXE generates a text file containing all the basic information required for installation of Windows NT. The script can be configured for either Windows NT Workstation or Windows NT Server.

The *uniqueness database file* defines unique parameter settings for individual computers when multiple installations are performed using the same unattended script. The uniqueness database file defines what definitions are included in the file and what included sections are referenced by the definitions.

1. Performing an Unattended Installation

To perform an automated installation, run the WINNT program with the following parameters:

```
WINNT /t:<drive letter> /s:<source directory> /u:<unattended file> /udf:<id,udf file>
```

The `/t` parameter defines to which drive letter Windows NT will be installed. The rule is: Where the temp files go, so goes the Windows NT installation. The `/s` option enables you to select the source file directory. This is especially useful when installing from a local or network directory location. The `/u` option enables the installation to make use of a preconfigured unattended-installation script file. Use the full path when defining the filename. The `/udf` option enables the installation to use unique entries for each machine. The ID is used to identify which computer is being installed with the script. The ID also identifies the sections of the UDF file that will be used for the installation process.

2. Including Applications in the Unattended Installation

The Windows NT Server CD includes another deployment application that assists with the installation of application software during unattended installations. The application is called SYSDIFF.EXE and is located in the `\support\deptools\%platform%` directory of the Windows NT Server CD-ROM.

The SYSDIFF utility is run in three phases. The first phase takes a snapshot of a computer before any applications are installed. The second phase takes a snapshot of all changed files, *.ini configuration files, and Registry entries after the applications have been installed. The final phase applies these changes to other systems that do not yet have the applications installed. The parameters of the SYSDIFF utility are as follows:

- **SYSDIFF /SNAP *snapfile*:** Creates the original snapfile that contains the current files, the *.ini configuration files, and the Registry settings before applications are installed.
- **SYSDIFF /DIFF *snapfile diff-file*:** After all applications are installed, this command creates the difference file based on the original snapfile. The file outlines what files, *.ini settings, and Registry entries have been added during the installation of the application software.
- **SYSDIFF /APPLY *diff-file*:** This command is used to apply the difference file to a workstation on which applications have not yet been installed.
- **SYSDIFF /INF *diff-file oemroot*:** This command applies the contents of a difference file to an installation directory. It generates an .inf file to perform .ini file and Registry changes contained in a Sysdiff package. It also generates an `$OEM$\` directory tree for file changes contained in a SYSDIFF package. This information can be incorporated into an automated installation.

12.1.1 Exercise: Creating Windows NT Startup Disks

This exercise shows you how to create the three Windows NT startup disks.

1. Format three 1.44 MB floppy disks by right-clicking the A drive icon in My Computer. Repeat for each disk.
2. Insert the Windows NT CD into your CD-ROM drive.
3. From the Start menu, select Run and type the following command:

   ```
   WINNT32 /ox
   ```

4. When prompted, insert Windows NT disk #3 into your floppy drive.
5. When prompted, insert Windows NT disk #2 into your floppy drive.
6. When prompted, insert the Windows NT Startup disk into your floppy drive.

12.1.2 Exercise: Viewing Your Current Hardware Resource Allocations

This exercise shows how the Windows NT diagnostics program can be used to determine what resources your computer system has.

1. From the Start menu, select Programs, Administrative Tools, Windows NT Diagnostics.
2. Select the Resources tab.
3. The Resources tab shows the currently allocated hardware interrupts (IRQs). You should note common interrupt assignments, such as the floppy drive being assigned IRQ 6. If you were to install a new network adapter, you could scrutinize the IRQ listing to determine which IRQs are free, and therefore, where to install the network adapter.
4. By clicking the I/O Port button near the bottom of the dialog box, you likewise can determine which I/O ports are in use on your system.
5. The DMA button enables you to determine which DMA channels are in use.

12.1 Practice Problems

1. The most likely cause of a dependency service failure during Windows NT installation is which of the following?

   A. Improper configuration of the Service applet.

   B. Incorrect service account information.

   C. The network adapter is improperly configured.

   D. You must be a member of the Administrators group to install Windows NT.

2. What must be configured correctly for a newly created BDC to communicate with a PDC on a remote TCP/IP subnetwork? Select all that apply.

   A. WINS server IP address

   B. DNS server IP address

   C. LMHOSTS file

   D. HOSTS file

3. In a Master Domain Model, where are Windows NT computer accounts most commonly created? Select all that apply.

   A. Master domain

   B. Resource domain

   C. Trusted domain

   D. Trusting domain

4. You are upgrading a Windows 95 system to Windows NT Workstation. You notice that none of your applications are running now. This is due to which of the following?

   A. You must run SETUP.EXE and select the Search for All Applications option.

   B. They are now located under Programs in the Start Menu.

   C. Only 32-bit applications are migrated to Windows NT Workstation.

   D. You cannot upgrade Windows 95 to Windows NT Workstation.

5. You are upgrading a Windows NT 3.51 Workstation to Windows NT Server. Which role can the newly created NT Server take on during the upgrade?

   A. Primary Domain Controller

   B. Backup Domain Controller

   C. Windows NT Member Server

   D. All the above

6. You are upgrading a Windows NT 3.51 Member Server to Windows NT Server. Which role can the newly created NT Server take on during the upgrade?

   A. Primary Domain Controller

   B. Backup Domain Controller

   C. Windows NT Member Server

   D. All the above

7. You are installing Windows NT Server on a RISC-based system. The system partition can be formatted as which file system?

   A. FAT

   B. NTFS

   C. CDFS

   D. HPFS

8. During Windows NT Server installation, you accidentally chose to install the computer as a Member Server. How do you change the role of the computer to a Backup Domain Controller?

   A. Reinstall Windows NT Server.

   B. In Server Manager, promote the Member Server to a Backup Domain Controller.

C. Edit the Registry.

D. In the Networks applet, change the role of the computer on the Identification tab.

9. Which situation causes the installation of a Backup Domain Controller named MARKETING in the HEAD_OFFICE domain to fail? Select all that apply.

   A. The PDC for the HEAD_OFFICE domain is not available.

   B. The MARKETING BDC does not share a common protocol with the PDC.

   C. There are no other BDCs in the domain.

   D. Another computer named MARKETING already exists on the network.

   E. All the above.

10. If the incorrect video driver is selected during Windows NT Workstation installation, what should be the next course of action?

   A. Reinstall Windows NT Server.

   B. Select the LastKnownGood boot option.

   C. Select the [VGA Mode] option from the Boot menu.

   D. Hold Shift during the boot process to enable the VGA driver.

11. Which Windows NT utility do you use to troubleshoot the failure of a dependency service to start?

   A. Server Manager

   B. Windows NT Event Viewer

   C. Windows NT Diagnostics

   D. The Services applet in the Control Panel

12. If your CD-ROM drive is not on the Windows NT Hardware Compatibility List, what alternative method can be used to install Windows NT? Select all that apply.

   A. Run the installation over the network using WINNT /B.

   B. Generate the three startup disks using WINNT32 /ox.

   C. Copy the installation files to a local directory and run WINNT /B from the directory.

   D. Order the 3.5-inch floppy installation disk set from Microsoft.

13. How many PDCs can be installed in a single domain?

   A. 4

   B. Any number

   C. 1

   D. 100

14. Which of the following systems meet the minimum hardware specifications to run Windows NT Server? Select all that apply.

   A. Pentium 100 MHz, 16 MB RAM, 100 MB free disk space

   B. 486 33 MHz, 16 MB RAM, 200 MB free disk space

   C. Dec Alpha, 12 MB RAM, 300 MB free disk space

   D. Pentium II 233 MHz, 32 MB RAM, 500 MB free disk space

15. Which of the following computers can be upgraded to a Windows NT 4.0 Primary Domain Controller? Select all that apply.

   A. Windows NT 3.51 PDC

   B. Windows NT 3.51 BDC

   C. Windows NT 3.51 Member Server

   D. Windows NT 3.51 Workstation

16. Which computer types require computer accounts when participating in a domain environment? Select all that apply.

    A. Backup Domain Controllers

    B. Windows NT Workstations

    C. Windows 95 Computers

    D. Windows for Workgroups Computers

17. Which methods can be used to add a computer account during the installation process? Select all that apply.

    A. Have an administrator precreate a computer account using User Manager.

    B. Have an administrator precreate a computer account using Server Manager.

    C. Indicate the domain that the computer will be a member of.

    D. Indicate the domain that the computer will be a member of and provide an account/password combination that is a member of the domain's Administrators local group.

18. Which program is used to speed up the installation of client software during the deployment of computers?

    A. APPDIFF.EXE

    B. USERDIFF.EXE

    C. SYSDIFF.EXE

    D. SOFTDIFF.EXE

The following scenario applies to questions 19 and 20. A different solution to the scenario is proposed for each question.

Scenario: The Orion Organization has hired a consultant to assist with the deployment of 1,000 new computer systems, all of which will all be running Windows NT 4 Workstation.

Required Result: The IS Manager wants the installations to be completely automated and be consistent between computers. *Optional Result 1:* The workstations should be installed to different resource domains based on their geographic locations and should have the correct time zone settings. *Optional Result 2:* All applications used in the Orion Organization should be included in the deployment process.

19. *Proposed Solution*: Create an unattended script file for the installation process. Install all necessary software onto the first system using the unattended script file. Run the SYSDIFF utility to take a snapshot of all the software installed. Perform all remaining installations using the unattended script file and the SYSDIFF snapshot.

    This solution:

    A. Meets the required result and both optional results

    B. Meets the required result and only one optional result

    C. Meets only the required result

    D. Does not satisfy any required or optional results

20. *Proposed Solution*: Create an unattended script file for the installation process. Create a uniqueness database file to contain the computer names, domains, and time zone settings for each computer. Install the first system using the unattended script file. Run the SYSDIFF utility using the /SNAP option to capture the current configuration of the system. Install all necessary software onto the system. Run the SYSDIFF utility using the /DIFF option to take a snapshot of all the software installed. Run the SYSDIFF utility a third time using the /INF option to create a OEM directory structure. Modify the unattended script file to include this software in the installation. Perform all remaining installations using the unattended script file and the uniqueness database file.

This solution:

A. Meets the required result and both optional results

B. Meets the required results and only one optional result

C. Meets only the required results

D. Does not satisfy any required or optional results

21. Which of the following is not required for using Windows NT Workstation?

A. Hard disk

B. Mouse

C. 12 MB memory

D. VGA monitor

22. During the installation of Windows NT Workstation, the installation program does not recognize a SCSI adapter. How can the third-party driver be installed?

A. Install with the default SCSI driver and apply the third-party driver after the installation is complete.

B. Press **S** to specify the third-party driver when the SCSI device-selection screen is presented.

C. If the SCSI adapter cannot be selected, it is not on the NT Hardware Compatibility List and cannot be used.

D. Replace the SCSI adapter with an adapter on the HCL list.

23. When installing Windows NT onto a SCSI drive, what issue can arise that does not come into play when installing to EIDE drives?

A. Unique SCSI IDs.

B. Master/Slave settings.

C. Whether the SCSI controller is BIOS-enabled.

D. There are no issues when using SCSI drives.

24. If you want to install the TCP/IP protocol to test Internet Information Server, but you do not have a physical network card, what can you install that will provide an adapter for TCP/IP to bind to?

A. Any supported Network Adapter Driver.

B. Microsoft Loopback Adapter.

C. Virtual Network Adapter.

D. This cannot be done.

25. Windows NT Workstation can be dual-booted with which of the following? Select all that apply.

A. Windows NT Server

B. Windows 95 (upgrade version)

C. Windows 95 (OSR2) using FAT

D. Windows for Workgroups

E. Windows 95 (OSR2) using FAT32

12.1.1 Answers and Explanations: Exercise

Exercise 12.1.1 reviewed how to create the three startup disks for Windows NT. These disks can be used for either of the following:

- Performing an installation of Windows NT
- Performing an emergency repair process on a Windows NT system

You should be aware that the startup disks are operating system dependent. If you have both a Windows NT Workstation and Windows NT Server, you need a separate set of boot disks for each operating system.

12.1.2 Answers and Explanations: Exercise

Exercise 12.1.2 reviewed how to determine your existing hardware configuration. The process described in this exercise often is used when installing a new adapter on a system. Inspecting the current resources in use can greatly reduce installation time because open resources are already known.

This process also should be used to document what resource allocations have been performed on a computer. This can greatly reduce reinstallation scenarios if the actual resource allocations are known before the installation occurs.

12.1 Answers and Explanations: Practice Problems

1. **C** All Windows NT networking services depend on the initialization of the network adapter drivers to start.
2. **A, C** Both WINS and LMHOSTS provide NetBIOS name resolution. For a BDC to be installed successfully, it must be able to communicate with the PDC, even if it is on a remote subnet. The NetBIOS name of the PDC must be resolved to an IP address for this to occur.
3. **B, D** Computer accounts generally reside in the Resource (or trusting) domain. This reduces the size of the SAM database in the Master (or account) domain.
4. **C** You cannot upgrade Windows 95 to Windows NT Workstation. Upgrades are supported only for Windows 3.x and Windows NT 3.x.
5. **C** A Windows NT Workstation can only be upgraded to a Windows NT Member Server. Its Registry does not contain the necessary entries to become a Primary or Backup Domain Controller.
6. **C** A Windows NT Member Server can only remain a Windows NT Member Server. Its Registry does not contain the necessary entries to become a Primary or Backup Domain Controller.
7. **A** A RISC-based system requires that the SYSTEM partition be formatted using the FAT file system.
8. **A** To change the role of an NT Server computer from Member Server to Backup Domain Controller, you must reinstall the software.
9. **A, B, D** The installation of a BDC will fail if the BDC cannot communicate with the PDC. Lack of a common protocol or the unavailability of the PDC can cause this. Likewise, if another computer named MARKETING exists on the network, the networking services on the BDC will fail. This also prevents communication with the PDC.
10. **C** You can choose to boot Windows NT using the /BASEVIDEO option, which loads Windows NT using a VGA 16-color, 600×480 display driver.
11. **B** The Windows NT Event Viewer's system log reports the cause of a dependency service failure.
12. **A, C** Without the generation of boot disks, the installation of Windows NT can be performed from a local folder or from a network share if the CD-ROM is not on the HCL.
13. **C** There can be only a single PDC in a domain.
14. **B, D** The only systems that meet the minimum requirements for installing Windows NT Server are the 486-33 and Pentium II systems. The Pentium 100 does not meet the minimum disk space requirement, and all RISC-based installations require 16 MB of RAM.
15. **A, B** Only domain controllers can be upgraded to domain controllers. The Backup Domain Controller would technically be upgraded to a Backup Domain Controller. It then can be promoted to a Primary Domain Controller.
16. **A, B** Only Windows NT–class computers require computer accounts when participating in a domain environment.

17. **B, D** Either an Administrator can create the account before the installation is performed, or the installer can create the account by providing the logon credentials of a member of the Administrators local group.

18. **C** The SYSDIFF utility captures the files, *.ini settings, and Registry entries associated with a software installation.

19. **D** Although this solution appears to answer the required result, a uniqueness database file is required to do 1,000 installs. The UDF provides the unique settings required by each computer. Without the UDF, the computers would have to be renamed manually after the install is completed. In addition, the SYSDIFF procedure is performed incorrectly. The initial snapshot must be performed before the software is installed to the master template system.

20. **A** This solution meets all the business requirements. The unattended script and the UDF file methodology meet the required results. The first optional result also is met with the UDF file. The second optional result is met with the proper use of the SYSDIFF utility.

21. **B** A mouse is not required to use Windows NT (although it is desired).

22. **B** You can specify third-party SCSI drivers during the SCSI-detection routine of the Windows NT installation.

23. **A** When installing SCSI drives, each SCSI drive must have a unique SCSI ID to be accessible. EIDE drives are configured using a master/slave relationship.

24. **B** The MS Loopback Adapter can be used to assign an IP configuration if no network card is present in the local system.

25. **A, B, C, D** Windows NT Workstation can be dual-booted with all the operating systems listed. Windows 95 OSR2 cannot be dual-booted with Windows NT when the FAT32 file system is used, however, because Windows NT does not recognize this file system.

12.1 Key Words

10Base2

10Base-T

Concentrator

Enhanced integrated drive electronics (EIDE)

Hardware Compatibility List (HCL)

Hardware Quantifier Tool

Media Access Unit (MAU)

NetBIOS name

Small computer system interface (SCSI)

SYSDIFF

12

12.2 Solving Boot Failures

When configuration changes take place on a Windows NT system, they sometimes result in the inability to restart Windows NT. This section reviews common problems that occur during the boot process and their resolutions. This section discusses the boot process, the emergency repair process, and using the Last Known Good (LKG) configuration.

A. The Boot Process

The boot process is a series of operations that load, initialize, and start the various subsystems, services, and device drivers required to operate Windows NT. Knowing the sequence of the boot process and the files involved can help troubleshoot Windows NT boot failures. The process differs slightly on Intel- and RISC-based platforms.

1. Files Involved in Booting

The Windows NT boot process involves several files working together to start the Windows NT operating system. On the Intel and RISC platforms, the initialization files initially are platform specific, then are common during the later stages of the boot process. The platform-specific files required for the startup of an Intel-platform Windows NT system are as follows:

- **NTLDR:** The NTLDR file loads the Windows NT operating system. It is located in the root directory of the C: drive.
- **BOOT.INI:** This text file contains the entries for the Operating System Selection menu that appears during the startup of the computer. It is located in the root directory of the C: drive.
- **BOOTSECT.DOS:** This file contains the boot sector of the hard disk that existed before Windows NT was installed. It is machine specific and should not be copied between systems. It is loaded by NTLDR if an operating system other than Windows NT is selected during the boot process. It is located in the root directory of the C: drive.
- **NTDETECT.COM:** This file examines the available hardware on the system and builds the hardware list that will be contained in the HKEY_LOCAL_MACHINE\Hardware key of the Registry. It is located in the root directory of the C: drive.
- **NTBOOTDD.SYS:** This driver is used by Windows NT systems that have a non-BIOS–enabled SCSI adapter. This driver is used to access devices attached to the adapter. It is located in the root directory of the C: drive. It is not required for BIOS-enabled SCSI adapters.

The platform-specific files required for the startup of an RISC-platform Windows NT system are as follows:

- **OSLOADER.EXE:** This is the operating system loader file (similar in function to NTLDR on Intel systems).
- ***.pal:** On Alpha systems, these files contain software subroutines that enable the Windows NT operating system to directly control the microprocessor.

The common files involved in the boot sequence include the following:

- **NTOSKRNL.EXE:** The Windows NT kernel file. It is located in the `%SystemRoot%\System32` directory.
- **SYSTEM hive:** This file contains the SYSTEM hive of the Registry. It contains the configuration settings for the device drivers and servers loaded during the initialization process of the operating system. The SYSTEM hive is stored in the `%SystemRoot%\System32\Config` directory.
- **Device drivers:** All hardware on the computer requires device drivers that can interface with Windows NT. They are commonly stored in the `%SystemRoot%\System32\drivers` directory.
- **HAL.DLL:** The hardware abstraction layer (HAL) protects the NT Kernel and the Windows NT Executive from recognizing platform-specific hardware differences. All procedures make their calls to the HAL layer, and the HAL controls the underlying hardware.

2. The Boot Sequence

The boot sequence in Windows NT is composed of five distinct phases:

- Boot-up
- Kernel load
- Kernel initialization
- Services load
- Win32 Subsystem start

These phases are the same for both Intel- and RISC-based computers; however, there are some differences in implementation.

a. The Boot-Up Phase

On an Intel system, the boot-up phase proceeds as follows:

1. The power on self-test (POST) determines what hardware components are present on the system, including memory and disks.
2. The master boot record (MBR) is loaded into memory from the system's boot device. The program stored in the MBR is executed.
3. The MBR program locates the active partition for the system by scanning the partition boot record. The boot sector on the active partition is loaded into memory.
4. NTLDR is loaded and initialized on a Windows NT system.
5. NTLDR switches the CPU to a 32-bit flat memory model.
6. The minifile system drivers are started by NTLDR to enable NT to read the hard disk. There are minifile system drivers for FAT and NTFS.
7. The BOOT.INI file is read, and the Boot Loader Operating System Selection menu is presented to the user.
8. If an operating system other than Windows NT is selected, NTLDR runs BOOTSECT.DOS. NTLDR then passes control to the selected operating system, and the NT boot process is completed. If Windows NT is selected, the boot process continues.

9. NTDETECT runs and detects installed hardware components. The list of detected hardware is passed back to NTLDR for inclusion in the HKEY_LOCAL_MACHINE\Hardware key of the Registry.
10. NTLDR loads NTOSKRNL.EXE, HAL.DLL, and the SYSTEM hive.
11. NTLDR scans the SYSTEM hive and loads the device drivers that are configured to start at boot time.
12. NTLDR starts NTOSKRNL.EXE and the boot-up phase is complete.

The RISC boot-up phase is more streamlined than the Intel boot-up phase. This is a result of the RISC architecture. The RISC boot-up phase process is as follows:

1. The ROM firmware—system software—selects a boot device by reading the boot precedence table in non-volatile RAM(NVRAM).
2. The firmware reads the Master Boot Record (MBR) and determines whether the Windows NT system partition is present.
3. The firmware reads the first sector of the system partition into memory. It examines the BIOS parameter block to make sure the volume's file system is supported by the firmware.
4. The firmware loads OSLOADER.EXE from the root directory of the system partition. It then passes control to the OSLOADER.EXE, along with the list of available hardware on the system (from the RISC POST routines).
5. OSLOADER.EXE loads NTOSKRNL.EXE, HAL.DLL, the *.pal files, and the SYSTEM hive.
6. OSLOADER.EXE scans the SYSTEM hive and loads any device drivers that are configured to start at boot time.
7. OSLOADER.EXE passes control to NTOSKRNL.EXE, and the boot-up phase is complete.

b. The Kernel Load Phase

From this phase forward, the boot process is identical on the Intel and RISC platforms. The kernel load phase is the actual loading of NTOSKRNL.EXE. The HAL is loaded after the kernel to mask differences in the underlying hardware. Finally, the SYSTEM hive is loaded and scanned again. This time, it is scanned for device drivers and services that are configured to a System Startup type. The drivers and services are loaded into memory but are not initialized. They are loaded in the order set by the ServiceGroupOrder subkey found in the Registry under:

```
HKEY_LOCAL_MACHINE\System\CurrentControlSet\Contrl\ServicesGroupOrder
```

c. The Kernel Initialization Phase

The screen is now blue. The drivers and services loaded during the kernel load phase are now started. The SYSTEM hive again is scanned. This time any drivers configured to start automatically are loaded. They are initialized after the kernel is fully initialized. The CurrentControlSet is saved, and the Clone set is created and initialized for the creation of the Last Known Good configuration.

Finally, the Hardware key of the Registry is created based on information passed from NTDETECT.COM (for Intel systems) or OSLOADER.EXE (for RISC systems).

d. The Service Load Phase

This phase starts the Session Manager, which then starts the higher-order subsystems for Windows NT. These include the following:

- The BootExecute item runs programs (such as the NT version of Checkdisk) and performs conversions of FAT volumes to NTFS.
- The Memory Management key sets up the defined Paging files.
- The DOS Devices key is used by the Session Manager to create symbolic links. These links direct certain classes of commands to the correct components in the file system.
- The Subsystems key loads the required subsystems on the computer. By default, this only includes the Win32 subsystem.

e. Win32 Subsystem Start Phase

When the Win32 subsystem starts, the WINLOGON.EXE process is started. The WINLOGON.EXE process calls the local security authority that displays the Press Control+Alt+Delete logon dialog box.

The service controller makes a final pass through the SYSTEM hive, looking for services that are configured to start automatically. They are loaded based on their configured dependencies. The Last Known Good configuration is not saved until the user successfully logs on to the system.

B. Troubleshooting the BOOT.INI File

The BOOT.INI file presents a menu of selectable operating systems during the boot-up phase on an Intel system. An error in BOOT.INI can lead to a boot failure of Windows NT. BOOT.INI also can contain additional parameters to help troubleshoot a system failing to start or suffering from Blue Screen STOP errors.

1. Use of ARC Names in the BOOT.INI File

The BOOT.INI file makes use of Advanced RISC Computing (ARC) names to represent the locations of installed operating systems on a computer. A typical ARC name is as follows:

```
multi(0)disk(0)rdisk(1)partition(1)
```

The ARC name components can be described as:

- **MULTI/SCSI:** This component identifies the hardware adapter/disk controller that is controlling the disk on which the operating system is installed. SCSI is used as the first parameter only if the adapter is a SCSI adapter with BIOS disabled. All other controllers (including SCSI controllers with BIOS enabled) use the designation MULTI.

The multi() syntax indicates to Windows NT that it should rely on the system BIOS to load system files. This means that NTLDR, the boot loader for x86-based computers, will be using interrupt (INT) 13 BIOS calls to find and load NTOSKRNL.EXE and any other files it needs to get the system running. The scsi() syntax indicates that Windows NT needs to load a SCSI device driver and use that driver to access the boot partition.

12

- **DISK:** The SCSI bus number (or ID) of the disk. If the first parameter is MULTI, the value is set to 0.
- **RDISK:** The ordinal number of the disk. If the disk is a SCSI disk (controlled by a BIOS-enabled SCSI controller), it is the SCSI ID of the disk.
- **PARTITION:** The ordinal number of the partition on which the operating system is installed.

Errors that can occur due to a misconfigured BOOT.INI file include the following:

- **The BOOT.INI file is missing:** If the BOOT.INI file is missing, the Windows NT operating system will not start unless it is located on the first partition of the first disk of the first controller in a directory named WINNT. All other locations will fail because the NTLDR file only looks in the default installation directory.
- **An entry for NT (default) appears in the Boot menu:** This entry appears only if the ARC name for the default entry does not match the ARC name for an entry on the [operating system] section of BOOT.INI.
- **An invalid path name exists in BOOT.INI:** If BOOT.INI points to the incorrect partition or path for the Windows NT installation, the following error appears:

```
Windows NT could not start because the following file was missing or corrupt:
<winnt root>\system32\ntoskrnl.exe

Please reinstall a copy of the above file.
```

- **An invalid device is referenced by BOOT.INI:** If the BOOT.INI file points to a nonexistent disk or partition, the following error message displays:

```
OS Loader v4.0

Windows NT could not start because of a computer disk hardware configuration
problem.
Could not read from the selected boot disk. Check boot path and disk hardware.

Please check the Windows NT (TM) documentation about hardware disk
configuration and your hardware reference manuals for additional
information.
```

2. Additional Parameters Within BOOT.INI

Within BOOT.INI, a series of options can be added to entries for troubleshooting and debugging purposes. The following switch options can be appended to the multiline in the BOOT.INI file:

- **`/SOS`:** Displays kernel and driver names during system startup. If you suspect a driver is missing or corrupted, append the `/SOS` switch to the BOOT.INI line that loads Windows NT.
- **`/MAXMEM:##`:** Enables you to specify the quantity of memory Windows NT will use. If you suspect a problem with a faulty memory chip, for example, this option enables you to boot your system using less than the total quantity of available RAM. A value of less than 12 MB should never be specified because Windows NT Workstation requires at lest 12 MB for normal operation (NT Server requires 16 MB). If you want to limit the amount of memory to 16 MB, enter the parameter as **/MAXMEM:16**.

- **/BASEVIDEO:** Forces Windows NT to use the standard VGA display driver. If your display no longer appears correctly, or if a driver upgrade has made your display unreadable, this option can be added to BOOT.INI.
- **/DEBUG:** Tells NT to load the kernel debugger during boot and to keep it in memory.
- **/CRASHDEBUG:** Similar to the /DEBUG option, except the debugging code is available only if the system crashes. In most cases, this is a better option because the debugger code will not be in memory and, therefore, won't interfere with the problem.
- **/DEBUGPORT:** Indicates the communications port you use.
- **/BAUDRATE:** Selects the baud rate for the connection you use for debugging.
- **/NOSERIALMICE:** This parameter disables NTDETECT from looking for serial mice on the designated serial port. This often is used when a UPS is connected to a COM port. The technique that NTDETECT.COM uses can cause many UPSs to think a power failure has occurred. The setting /NOSERIALMICE:COM1 indicates not to detect serial mice on COM1. If no COM port is indicated, no COM ports are searched for serial mice.

C. Creating a Windows NT Boot Disk

A boot disk can be created for a Windows NT system. This disk enables you to reboot your system if the startup files located in the system partition are damaged or missing. The procedure to create a boot disk is quite straightforward, as follows:

- Format the disk from within Windows NT. This is required because the boot sector must look for the NTLDR file, not the IO.SYS file as under DOS or Windows 95.
- For Intel systems: Using My Computer, Windows NT Explorer, or a command prompt, copy the following files to the disk: NTLDR, BOOT.INI, NTDETECT.COM, and possibly NTBOOTDD.SYS (if using a non-BIOS–enabled SCSI controller).
- For RISC systems: Copy the following files to the newly formatted disk: OSLOADER.EXE, HAL.DLL, and *.pal (for Alpha systems only). Note that for RISC systems, a few more steps are required. In order to boot from a disk, you have to add an alternate boot selection in your system firmware. Refer to your system's documentation for information about how to add a boot selection.

D. Using the Last Known Good Configuration

The Last Known Good option can be selected during the boot process to select the prior successful boot configuration. Basically, the Last Known Good option enables you to boot your system using the Registry settings in effect the last time you successfully booted your system and logged on. If your system configuration has changed, and you are no longer able to boot your computer, this option reverts your configuration to the settings in effect the last time you successfully booted your computer.

It should be noted that the Last Known Good configuration is available to the users only when they have successfully logged on to the system. To use the Last Known Good option, press the space bar when prompted during the Windows NT boot sequence. You will be presented with a screen informing you that the Last Known Good option can be used. Press the L key to use the Last Known Good configuration.

E. The Emergency Repair Process

An emergency repair disk can be used to rebuild corrupted Registry files. The repair process requires an emergency repair disk and the three Windows NT startup disks.

1. Creating the Three Windows NT Startup Disks

For Intel-based systems, place the Windows NT CD-ROM into a system running Windows NT or any other operating system, and then locate either WINNT.EXE or WINNT32.EXE. (WINNT is for 16-bit operating systems and Windows 95; WINNT32 is for 32-bit operating systems.) Execute the appropriate file using the /OX command-line parameter. You are prompted to insert startup disks 3, 2, then 1. These disks can be used to install the operating system or to perform an emergency repair process. RISC-based systems, unlike Intel systems, do not require startup disks. Instead, the firmware is used to provide a series of boot options.

2. Creating an Emergency Repair Disk

The emergency repair disk is created during the actual installation of the Windows NT operating system. It should be updated whenever changes are made to the computer. The application file for creating and updating the emergency repair disk is RDISK.EXE. This executable file starts the repair disk utility.

Update Repair Info updates the data files stored in `the %SystemRoot%\System32\Config` directory. If no emergency repair disk is provided during an emergency repair process, the information in this directory is used.

By default, the Security and SAM hives are not updated when updating the repair information. If you want this information to be updated, you must run RDISK /S.

The Create Repair Disk is used for the initial creation of a recovery disk, and it requires a blank floppy disk. Note that the disk need not be formatted (or even blank) because RDISK formats the disk.

A recovery disk has copies of a Windows NT system's configuration files. Thus, a recovery disk created for one specific computer cannot be used on a different computer. In addition, recovery disks should be updated whenever your system configuration changes. The recovery disk contains the following files:

- **SETUP.LOG:** A log of files installed and the cyclic redundancy check (CRC) checksums for each file. This file is Read Only, Hidden, and System.
- **SYSTEM._:** The contents of the HKEY_LOCAL_MACHINE\SYSTEM Registry key in compressed format.
- **SOFTWARE._:** The contents of the HKEY_LOCAL_MACHINE\SOFTWARE Registry key in compressed format.
- **SECURITY._:** The contents of the HKEY_LOCAL_MACHINE\SECURITY Registry key in compressed format.
- **SAM._:** The contents of the HKEY_LOCAL_MACHINE\SAM Registry key in compressed format.

- **DEFAULT._:** The contents of the HKEY_LOCAL_MACHINE\DEFAULT Registry key in compressed format.
- **NTUSER.DA_:** The contents of `%systemroot%\Profiles\Default User\Ntuser.day` in compressed format.
- **AUTOEXEC.NT:** A copy of `%systemroot%\System32\Autoexec.nt` (a configuration file for the MS-DOS environment under Windows NT).
- **CONFIG.NT:** A copy of `%systemroot%\System32\Config.nt` (a configuration file for the MS-DOS environment under Windows NT).

3. Performing the Emergency Repair Process

The following options apply to the standard emergency repair on an Intel-based machine. These options, however, are similar for other systems. Insert the Windows NT Server Disk 1 and boot the computer. When prompted, insert Disk 2 and proceed. At the next prompt, select R in order to begin the recovery process. The following four options are presented:

- Inspect Registry files
- Inspect startup environment
- Verify Windows NT system files
- Inspect boot sector

All four tasks are selected by default, but tasks can be deselected as required. Note that to select or deselect items, you must use the cursor keys because no mouse driver is loaded at this point. These four tasks perform the following operations:

- **Inspect Registry files:** This option can be used to repair Registry keys. When this option is selected, you are provided with a list of Registry files it can restore. A warning also is shown, indicating that information can be lost. Proceed until you are prompted with a list of information that can be restored. Select the Registry keys you want to restore, and then select Continue.
- **Inspect startup environment:** This option verifies that the Windows NT files in the system partition are not missing or corrupted. If required, Repair will replace these with files from the Windows NT Server CD. On Intel-based systems, Repair ensures that Windows NT is listed in BOOT.INI. If this is not the case (or if BOOT.INI is missing), Repair changes or creates it as required. On RISC-based systems, startup information in NVRAM is inspected and repaired if required.
- **Verify Windows NT system files:** This option verifies that the Windows NT system files are not corrupt or missing. The file SETUP.LOG on the recovery disk contains a list of every file installed. It also has a cyclic redundancy check (CRC) checksum for every file. The checksums are computed for each file present on the system and are compared with SETUP.LOG. If the checksums do not match, the repair process asks whether it should replace the files from the Windows NT Server CD. If you have applied service packs to your system, these might need to be reinstalled after the repair process is completed.
- **Inspect boot sector:** On Intel systems, this option verifies that the boot sector on the system partition is configured to load NTLDR on startup. If this is not the case, the boot sector will be repaired. This part of the recovery process is not required for RISC systems. After the entire process has been completed, your system is configured as a bootable system, and all errors encountered are repaired.

12.2.1 Exercise: Creating a Windows NT Boot Disk

This exercise reviews the steps necessary to create a Windows NT boot disk. This disk can be used if any files are damaged in the system partition of a Windows NT computer.

1. Insert a new 1.44 MB disk into your floppy drive.
2. Open the My Computer icon on the desktop.
3. Right-click the A: drive icon and choose Format.
4. Ensure that the format is set to 1.44 MB and the FAT file system, and then select OK. (You can perform a quick format if you want.)
5. From the Start menu, select Programs, and then select Windows NT Explorer.
6. From the View menu, select Options.
7. Make sure the Show all Files option is selected, and then click OK.
8. Copy the following files to the A: drive:
    - NTLDR
    - BOOT.INI
    - NTDETECT.COM
    - NTBOOTDD.SYS (if it exists)
9. Shut down Windows NT.
10. Leaving the newly created boot disk in the A: drive, restart the system. If created correctly, the computer should boot as normal.

12.2.2 Exercise: Updating the Emergency Repair Disk

This exercise reviews how to update the emergency repair information for a system.

1. From the Start menu, select Run.
2. Type **RDISK** and click OK.
3. In the Repair Disk Utility dialog box, click the Update Repair Info button. This updates the information stored in the `%SystemRoot%\System32\Config` directory.
4. Place a 1.44 MB floppy disk into the A: drive.
5. Click the Create Repair Disk button. This copies the files in the `%SystemRoot%\System32\Config` directory to the floppy disk.
6. Label the disk as the emergency repair disk for the system and store it in a secure location.

12.2 Practice Problems

1. Which files are located in the Windows NT boot partition on an Intel system? Select all that apply.

   A. HAL.DLL

   B. NTLDR

   C. BOOT.INI

   D. NTOSKRNL.EXE

2. The file NTBOOTDD.SYS is used to what end?

   A. To identify whether Windows NT is installed on a system

   B. To activate a BIOS-enabled SCSI adapter

   C. To activate a non-BIOS–enabled SCSI adapter

   D. By Windows 95

3. Which NT startup files are common to both the Intel and RISC platforms? Select all that apply.

   A. OSLOADER.EXE

   B. BOOT.INI

   C. NTOSKRNL.EXE

   D. HAL.DLL

4. Which files are located in the Windows NT system partition on an Intel system?

   A. HAL.DLL

   B. NTLDR

   C. BOOT.INI

   D. NTOSKRNL.EXE

5. What information is included in the SYSTEM hive of the Registry?

   A. The operating system version

   B. The name of the file system in use

   C. The configuration settings for the device drivers and services

   D. A listing of all installed operating systems on the computer

6. What is contained in the boot partition?

   A. The files necessary to start Windows NT

   B. The previous operating system before Windows NT was installed

   C. The BOOT.INI file

   D. The \WINNT directory structure

7. What is used to collect a list of all the hardware present on an Intel computer system?

   A. NTDETECT.COM

   B. NTLDR

   C. OSLOADER.EXE

   D. CMOS information

8. How can you force a user to select an operating system from the Boot menu when starting Windows NT?

   A. Do not enable a default choice.

   B. Set the timeout value to 0 in BOOT.INI.

   C. Set the timeout value to –1 in BOOT.INI.

   D. In the System applet of the Control Panel, set the Show List option on the Startup/Shutdown tab to 999 seconds.

9. Which Registry subkey is used to determine the order in which device drivers and services are started?

   A. HKEY_CURRENT_USER\ So ftware\Microsoft\Windows NT

   B. HKEY_LOCAL_MACHINE\ Software \Microsoft\ Windows NT

C. HKEY_LOCAL_MACHINE\System\CurrentControlSet\Control\ServiceGroupOrder

D. HKEY_LOCAL_MACHINE\System\CurrentControlSet\Services\ServiceGroupOrder

10. When is the Last Known Good Configuration saved?

    A. When control is passed to the NTOSKRNL

    B. When the kernel has completed initialization

    C. When the user successfully logs on to the computer

    D. When the Control+Alt+Delete to Logon dialog box appears

11. Where is the Last Known Good configuration stored in the Registry?

    A. HKEY_LOCAL_MACHINE\System\ControlSet001

    B. HKEY_LOCAL_MACHINE\System\Select

    C. HKEY_LOCAL_MACHINE\Software\Select

    D. HKEY_LOCAL_MACHINE\System\Startup

12. If Windows NT was installed on the second partition of the slave disk in a directory named WINNT4, the ARC name in the BOOT.INI for this installation would be which of the following?

    A. SCSI(0)disk(1)rdisk(0)partition(1)\WINNT4

    B. MULTI(0)disk(1)rdisk(0)partition(1)\WINNT4

    C. SCSI(0)disk(0)rdisk(2)partition(2)\WINNT4

    D. MULTI(0)disk(0)rdisk(1)partition(2)\WINNT4

13. Your system has been encountering frequent STOP errors resulting in a blue screen on the computer. What settings can be added to BOOT.INI to assist in debugging the problem? Select all that apply.

    A. /SOS

    B. /DEBUG

    C. /ENABLEDEBUG

    D. /BAUDRATE

14. Under what circumstances might Windows NT boot when the BOOT.INI file has been deleted?

    A. When Windows NT is the only operating system on the computer.

    B. When Windows NT is installed in the directory C:\WINNT.

    C. When the boot sequence in the BIOS has been set to C: then A:.

    D. It is not possible to boot Windows NT without a BOOT.INI file.

15. You have received an error message stating `<WINNT ROOT>\SYSTEM32\NTOSKRNL.EXE IS MISSING OR CORRUPT` during the startup of Windows NT. The cause of the problem could be which of the following? Select all that apply.

    A. The file NTOSKRNL.EXE is missing or corrupt.

    B. The file NTLDR is corrupt and cannot find NTOSKRNL.EXE.

    C. The Registry contains the incorrect location for NTOSKRNL.EXE.

    D. The BOOT.INI file has an incorrect ARC name path for the Windows NT installation.

16. You want to test a software package on your computer. The actual computer that will run the software has only 32 MB of RAM while your computer has 128 MB

of RAM. What setting do you add to BOOT.INI to restrict memory usage to 32 MB of RAM?

A. /RESTRICTMEM:32000

B. /RESTRICTMEM:32

C. /MAXMEM:32000

D. /MAXMEM:32

17. What settings are added to the ARC name path for the [VGA mode] entry in the BOOT.INI? Select all that apply.

A. /DEBUG

B. /VGA

C. /SOS

D. /BASEVIDEO

18. When creating a boot disk for a RISC-based system, what files must be included on the boot disk? Select all that apply.

A. NTLDR

B. OSLOADER.EXE

C. HAL.DLL

D. BOOT.INI

19. Which file is not located on the emergency repair disk?

A. SETUP.DAT

B. SETUP.LOG

C. SAM._

D. AUTOEXEC.NT

20. After adding a new network adapter to your Windows NT Workstation computer, the computer suffers a blue screen STOP error when restarting. To repair this problem, you have to do which of the following?

A. Use a Windows NT boot disk and remove the adapter using the Network applet in the Control Panel.

B. Perform an emergency repair process.

C. Use the Last Known Good configuration.

D. Reinstall Windows NT Workstation.

21. To create the three startup disks for Windows NT, which command do you use?

A. WINNT /B

B. WINNT /O

C. WINNT /OX

D. RDISK /S

22. To back up the entire Registry to the emergency repair disk, which command do you use?

A. REGBACK.EXE

B. RDISK

C. RDISK /E

D. RDISK /S

23. Which files are normally not adjusted when the repair disk utility is run to update configuration info? Select all that apply.

A. SAM._

B. SOFTWARE._

C. SYSTEM._

D. SECURITY._

24. After performing an emergency repair process, all the user accounts in the domain have been lost. This is most likely due to which of the following?

A. Somebody has deleted all the accounts.

B. The SAM database was restored.

C. The Registry is still corrupt.

D. The emergency repair process always removes all user accounts from the domain.

12.2.1 Answers and Explanations: Exercise

In Exercise 12.2.1, a Windows NT boot disk was created. This is useful for troubleshooting corrupt files in the Windows NT system partition. It can be used in the following circumstances:

- When NTLDR, NTDETECT.COM, or BOOT.INI has been deleted or corrupted.
- When somebody has run the DOS SYS command and changed the boot sector of the computer to look for IO.SYS instead of NTLDR.
- If the system partition has been mirrored and a disk failure has occurred, the BOOT.INI file on the boot disk can be modified to boot to the other disk of the mirror set.

The only issue that might arise is when the computer CMOS settings have been adjusted to use the boot sequence C,A rather than A,C. This must be set to A,C for the Windows NT boot disk to work.

12.2.2 Answers and Explanations: Exercise

In Exercise 12.2.2, an emergency repair disk was created. This process should be repeated whenever a configuration change is made to the Windows NT system. This includes:

- The addition of a new hard disk
- The changing of a partition's file format from FAT to NTFS
- New software installed to the computer

It should be noted that repair information can only be updated by members of the Administrators or Power Users local groups.

12.2 Answers and Explanations: Practice Problems

1. **A, D** Remember that the Windows NT boot partition is where the operating system is located.
2. **C** If you do not have a non-BIOS–enabled SCSI adapter, the file NTBOOTDD.SYS will not be installed.
3. **C, D** Both the Intel and RISC versions of Windows NT use the NTOSKRNL.EXE and HAL.DLL files during the boot sequence.
4. **B, C** Remember that the system partition is where platform-specific startup files are located in Windows NT.
5. **C** The System hive contains configuration information for all device drivers and services. This includes parameter settings, dependency services, and how to handle errors during startup.
6. **D** The operating system itself is stored in the boot partition for Windows NT.
7. **A** NTDETECT.COM collects a list of all detected hardware on an Intel-based Windows NT computer.
8. **C** Setting the timeout value to –1 eliminates the countdown timer for selecting the default operating system.
9. **C** The List value is found in HKEY_LOCAL_MACHINE\System\CurrentControlSet\Control\ServiceGroupOrder. It sets the order for starting services.
10. **C** The Last Known Good configuration is saved after a user successfully logs on to the system.
11. **B** The Last Known Good configuration's location in the Registry is stored in the value LASTKNOWNGOOD in the HKEY_LOCAL_MACHINE\System\Select key.

12. **D** Because Windows NT was installed to a slave disk, the disk is not a SCSI disk. Therefore, the first parameter in the ARC name must be MULTI. Remember that partitions start numbering at 2; therefore, answer D is correct in referring to the second partition as partition(2).

13. **B, D** To enable debugging on a Windows NT system, you need to add /DEBUG, /BAUDRATE, and /DEBUGPORT to an ARC name in the BOOT.INI.

14. **B** When the BOOT.INI file is missing, Windows NT boots only if it is installed to the first partition of the first disk in the directory \WINNT.

15. **A, D** This error appears when NTOSKRNL.EXE is missing or corrupt and when an ARC name in the BOOT.INI points to the wrong partition.

16. **D** The correct setting to restrict memory usage on a Windows NT system to 32 MB is /MAXMEM:32. This also is useful if you suspect you have a defective memory SIMM module.

17. **C, D** The [VGA Mode] entry in the BOOT.INI file has both the /SOS and /BASEVIDEO parameters. You only need /BASEVIDEO to start up in VGA 16-color mode.

18. **B, C** The boot disk for a RISC system requires the OSLOADER.EXE, HAL.DLL, and *.pal files. The *.pal files are required only on an Alpha system.

19. **A** The file SETUP.DAT is not located on an emergency repair disk.

20. **C** When the computer prompts you to press the spacebar for the Last Known Good configuration, do so. Also remember to press L to select the Last Known Good configuration.

21. **C** The command WINNT /OX generates the three startup disks for Windows NT. They are used to install Windows NT and to perform emergency repairs.

22. **D** The parameter /S, when included with the RDISK command, also backs up the SECURITY and SAM hives that are not normally backed up.

23. **A, D** The SAM and SECURITY hives normally are backed up only during the initial installation of the Windows NT system into the directory `%SystemRoot%\System32\Config`. Running RDISK /S updates these two files along with the rest of the recovery files.

24. **B** If all Registry files are recovered, the SAM will be restored to its initial state from installation. The SAM now must either be re-created or restored from backup. If RDISK /S has been run, the accounts created up until that point of time are restored.

12.2 Key Words

BOOT.INI

Cyclic redundancy check (CRC)

Last Known Good option

SETUP.LOG

RDISK

12.3 Solving Configuration and Registry Failures

The Registry is used to store most of the configuration information for Windows NT. It is organized as a series of keys, subkeys, and values. A file system is similar in organization: a file is stored with a filename consisting of a drive letter, a directory, and a filename (C:\USERS\MYFILE.TXT), and the file can contain data. In much the same way, the Registry stores information as a key, subkey, and value (HKEY_LOCAL_MACHINE\MySubkey\MyValue).

A. NT Registry Subtrees

The primary keys located in the Registry (known as the subtrees of the Registry) are:

- **HKEY_LOCAL_MACHINE:** Contains information about the hardware installed on the computer as well as operating system data, device drivers configuration, service configuration information, and startup control data.
- **HKEY_USERS:** Contains all actively loaded user profiles (including HKEY_CURRENT_USER) and the default profile. The currently active user profile is listed as a subkey under the user Security ID.
- **HKEY_CURRENT_USER:** Contains the user profile for the currently logged on user. The profile includes desktop settings, network connections, the installed printer, and user-based configuration information.
- **HKEY_CURRENT_CONFIG:** Contains configuration data for the current hardware profile.
- **HKEY_CLASSES_ROOT:** Contains information about how all installed applications open and print their data files. Application extensions are associated to the applications. This key also contains information about object linking and embedding for the applications.

> **You might also see the term *hive* when reading about the Registry. A hive is a section of the Registry that is backed up to a combination of a data file and a .log file. Hives are located either in the `%SystemRoot%\System32\Config` or the `%SystemRoot%\Profiles\%Username%` directories.**

The Registry can be viewed using REGEDT32, a tool provided with Windows NT. This tool provides a graphical interface to examine and modify Registry information on either local or remote computers. All information in the Registry can be edited using this tool. Much of the key information, however, also can be changed using standard administrative tools such as the Control Panel. It is preferable to use standard tools to modify the Registry; this reduces the likelihood of accidental changes or deletions. The most common standard tools used are the applets in the Control Panel.

Wherever possible, use administrative tools such as the Control Panel and System Policy Editor to make configuration changes, rather than editing the Registry. It is safer to use administrative tools because they are designed to store values properly in the Registry. If you make errors while changing values with a Registry editor, you are not warned. Registry-editing applications do not recognize and cannot correct errors in syntax or other semantics.

> **Note that REGEDIT also can be used to edit the Registry files. REGEDIT has better search capabilities but cannot edit all value types. Also, you cannot set security permissions on the Registry using the REGEDIT command.**

B. Datatypes in the Registry

Each value in the Registry stores data as a specific value type. Some value types, however, can be used only for certain types of data. The value types used in Windows NT are as follows:

- **REG_BINARY:** Binary information, entered either as a sequence of binary digits or as hexadecimal digits.
- **REG_SZ:** A string value (human-readable text).
- **REG_EXPAND_SZ:** A string value that also contains a variable, such as %SystemRoot%.
- **REG_DWORD:** A four-byte hexadecimal value.
- **REG_MULTI_SZ:** A large string value (multiple lines of text, such as a list of configured IP addresses).

Values can be added anywhere in the Registry by selecting the desired key, and then selecting Edit, Add Value from the REGEDT32 menu. You then are asked for the name of the new value, its data type, and the data itself.

Existing Registry values can be modified by double-clicking the desired value in its Registry key. Depending on the value type of the selected value, you are presented with an appropriate editor. After the desired modifications have been completed, click OK to save the new value.

C. Setting Permissions in the Registry

Windows NT defines a series of Registry permissions that can be set for users and groups. The following list describes the permissions:

- **Read:** Users or groups are allowed to read the Registry key, but they cannot change its information.
- **Full control:** Users or groups have permission to read, modify, delete, or take ownership of a key.
- **Special access:** Allows fine-tuning of access permissions and is broken down as follows:
  - **Query value:** Permission to read a value.
  - **Set value:** Permission to modify a value.
  - **Create subkey:** Permission to create a subkey under an existing key.
  - **Enumerate subkey:** Permission to list the subkeys of a Registry key.
  - **Notify:** Permission to open a key with notify access.
  - **Create link:** Permission to create a symbolic link (a "shortcut") for a Registry key.
  - **Delete:** Permission to delete a Registry key.
  - **Write DAC:** Permission to modify permissions (discretionary access control) for a key.
  - **Write owner:** Permission to take ownership of a Registry key.
  - **Read control:** Permission to read the security information for a key.

These permissions can be changed by selecting Security, Permissions from the REGEDT32 menu.

D. Backing up the Registry

The REGEDT32 tool can be used to back up the Registry of other computers in the domain as well. In REGEDT32, select Save from the Registry menu. You are prompted to enter a filename. This procedure creates a binary file containing the selected Registry information.

Select Restore from the Registry menu to restore this information at a later time. You are prompted to select a file to be restored. Note that because the Registry is open when Windows NT is running, you cannot restore the entire Registry from within REGEDT32. This is because some of the keys currently are opened by the operating system. After a file has been selected, a warning message displays before the Registry values are restored.

Another way to back up the Registry is to use the RDISK utility. The RDISK utility saves the current configuration to the `%SystemRoot\Repair` directory and can be used by the emergency repair process. The RDISK utility saves all information except the SAM and SECURITY hives. If you want to save the complete Registry using RDISK, you must run RDISK /S. This also creates a backup, compressed version of the Registry that includes updated versions of the SAM and SECURITY hives.

The Windows NT Resource Kit includes the REGBACK and REGREST utilities, which also can be used to back up the Registry. These utilities enable you to back up the entire Registry to a specified directory. A separate file is created for each hive of the Registry.

A final method to back up the Registry is to use the Windows NT Backup program. If you select the Backup Local Registry option and at least one file on the Windows NT boot partition, Windows NT Backup also can back up the local Registry. If you are running NTBACKUP from a batch file, you must include the /b option to back up the local Registry. Remember, you must include at least a single file from the boot partition of Windows NT to back up the Registry.

> **The Backup Local Registry option cannot be used to back up remote Registries. NT Backup only supports backing up the local Registry.**

12.3.1 Exercise: Using the Policy Editor to Modify the Registry

The System Policy Editor can be used to edit the local Registry. It provides an easy-to-use interface that prevents syntax errors when modifying values in the Registry. The System Policy Editor is installed on any domain controller in the environment. It also can be installed on a Windows NT Workstation or a Windows NT Member Server. This is accomplished by installing Server Tools for Windows NT from the Windows NT Server CD-ROM.

1. From the Start menu, select Programs, Administrative Tools, System Policy Editor.
2. In the System Policy Editor, select Open Registry from the File menu. A window appears containing two icons. The Local Computer icon affects settings in the HKEY_LOCAL_MACHINE subtree of the Registry. The Local User icon affects the HKEY_CURRENT_USER subtree.

3. Double-click the Local User icon.
4. In the Local User Properties window, select the '+' next to the Shell option in the list of items.
5. Beneath the Shell option, open the Restrictions option.
6. Enable the Hide Network Neighborhood option.
7. Click OK to finish the settings.
8. From the File menu, select Save.
9. Close the System Policy Editor. Note that the Network Neighborhood icon still exists on the desktop.
10. Log off, and then log on to the system again. Note that the Network Neighborhood icon now has disappeared.

12.3.2 Exercise: Comparing the Search Utilities of REGEDT32 and REGEDIT

This exercise compares the search capabilities of the REGEDT32 and REGEDIT utilities. Although both utilities can be used to view the Windows NT Registry, each has its own strengths. Knowing these strengths can help you decide which editor to use under specific circumstances.

1. From the Start menu, select Run and type **REGEDT32.EXE** to start the native format of the Registry Editor.
2. From the Start menu, select Run and type **REGEDIT.EXE** to start the Windows 95 version of the Registry Editor.
3. Right-click an open space on the Taskbar and select Tile Windows Horizontally from the pop-up menu. This arranges both versions of the Registry Editor on your screen.
4. Note that the Windows 95 Registry Editor uses a single window, whereas the Windows NT version uses a separate window for each subtree of the Registry.
5. In each window, select the HKEY_LOCAL_MACHINE subtree.
6. In the Windows NT Registry Editor, select Find Key from the View menu. Note that you only can search for keys in this version of the Registry Editor. Search for the string ServiceGroupOrder. Note that the value in the right window is named LIST and is a REG_MULTI_SZ data type.
7. In the Windows 95 Registry Editor, select Find from the Edit menu. Note that you can search for Keys, Values, or Data in this version. Enter the string ServiceGroupOrder in the Find dialog box and click OK. The LIST value also appears in this version of the Registry Editor.
8. Double-click the List value. Note that this version of the Registry Editor determines List is a binary value. The Windows 95 editor does not recognize the REG_MULTI_SZ data type.
9. Close both Registry Editors.

12.3 Practice Problems

1. What information is stored in the Registry? Select all that apply.
   A. Programs
   B. Configuration information
   C. Hardware detected during the startup process
   D. Only application information

2. Which utilities can be used to view portions of the HKEY_LOCAL_MACHINE subtree of the Registry? Select all that apply.
   A. Windows NT Diagnostics
   B. The System applet of the Control Panel
   C. The SCSI applet of the Control Panel
   D. Solitaire

3. You have updated your video drive, and when you reboot, Windows NT fails to start. What can you do to fix this problem? Select the best answer.
   A. Boot using the [VGA Mode] setting.
   B. Use the Last Known Good configuration.
   C. Perform an emergency repair procedure.
   D. Boot into DOS and rename the REG.BAK file REG.DAT.

4. You have updated your tape backup device's driver, and when you reboot, Windows NT fails to start. What can you do to fix this problem? Select the best answer.
   A. Boot using the [VGA Mode] setting.
   B. Use the Last Known Good configuration.
   C. Perform an emergency repair procedure.
   D. Boot into DOS and rename the REG.BAK file REG.DAT.

5. What is the organization of the Registry?
   A. Keys, values
   B. Keys, text, values
   C. Values
   D. Keys, subkeys, values

6. How do you create a mandatory user profile?
   A. In the System applet of the Control Panel, change the user's profile type to Mandatory on the User Profile tab.
   B. Rename the NTUSER.DAT file to NTUSER.MAN in the `%Systemroot%\profiles\%username%` directory.
   C. In the System Policy Editor, configure the user profile to be Mandatory.
   D. In User Manager, configure the Profile path to a central network location.

7. Which Windows NT Resource Kit file can be used to research an unknown Registry entry?
   A. Windows NT Server Resource Guide
   B. Windows NT Workstation Resource Guide
   C. RESGUIDE.HLP
   D. REGENTRY.HLP

8. What is a hive?
   A. The file that contains the entire Registry
   B. Another name for the HKEY_LOCAL_MACHINE subtree

C. A portion of the Registry contained in a single file/.log file combination

D. A multiple-value data type in the Registry

The following scenario applies to questions 9 and 10. A different solution to the scenario is proposed for each question.

Scenario: The Grabling Group has installed two Windows NT Server computers in its Vancouver office. It has set up the RESOURCE server as the primary file location. It also is functioning as the print server for the office.

The BACKEND server is running Microsoft Exchange and SQL Server. It also is functioning as the PDC for the GRABLING domain. A consultant has been hired to configure these computers to optimize network performance.

Required Result: The Grabling group wants to make sure its PDC is running efficiently, so the 100 users do not suffer any delays when authenticating with the network. *Optional Result 1*: The users need fast access to their data stores. *Optional Result 2:* The Grabling group is planning to install a BDC next year and wants to make sure its user account database is protected.

9. *Proposed Solution*: Configure the Server service of the BACKEND server to Maximize Throughput for Network Applications. Configure the RESOURCE server's Server service to be Balanced. Install a tape backup unit on the RESOURCE server. Configure NT Backup to back up the Registries of both the BACKEND and RESOURCE servers as well as all the data files on the BACKEND and RESOURCE servers.

   This solution:

   A. Meets the required result and both optional results

   B. Meets the required result and only one optional result

   C. Meets only the required results

   D. Does not satisfy any required or optional results

10. *Proposed Solution*: Configure the Server service of the RESOURCE server to Maximize Throughput for File Sharing. Configure the BACKEND server's Server service to Maximize Throughput for Network Applications. Install a tape backup unit on the BACKEND server. Configure NT Backup to back up the local Registry as well as all the data files on the BACKEND and RESOURCE servers.

    This solution:

    A. Meets the required result and both optional results

    B. Meets the required result and only one optional result

    C. Meets only the required result

    D. Does not satisfy any required or optional results

11. Using REGEDT32.EXE, where do you look to determine which subkey contains the Last Known Good configuration?

    A. The LastKnownGood subkey in the HKEY_LOCAL_MACHINE subtree.

    B. The LastKnownGood value located in HKEY_LOCAL_MACHINE\Select.

    C. The LastKnownGood value located in HKEY_LOCAL_MACHINE\System\CurrentControlSet.

    D. The LastKnownGood value located in HKEY_LOCAL_MACHINE\System\Select.

12. Which editing tools can be used to edit the Registry? Select all that apply.

    A. Notepad

    B. REGEDIT

C. REGEDT32

D. SysEdit

13. How can you optimize the pagefile to provide better virtual memory performance? Select all that apply.

 A. Spread the paging file across multiple logical disks.

 B. Spread the paging file across multiple physical disks.

 C. Include the paging file on the volume that contains the Windows NT boot partition.

 D. Exclude the paging file from the volume that contains the Windows NT boot partition.

14. Which of the following is the text version of the Windows NT Diagnostics program that can be used to read Registry information from a command prompt?

 A. WINMSDT.EXE

 B. WINMSD.EXE

 C. WINMSDP.EXE

 D. WINDIAG.EXE

15. Which of the following data types can be used in the Registry? Select all that apply.

 A. REG_HEX

 B. REG_BYTE

 C. REG_BINARY

 D. REG_SZ

16. The text string values in the Registry are stored as which type?

 A. REG_SZ

 B. REG_TEXT

 C. REG_WORD

 D. REG_EXPAND

17. What is the purpose of the ServiceGroupOrder subkey?

 A. It contains the order in which services were installed on a system.

 B. It organizes the services into logical groups.

 C. It determines the order in which device drivers and services are loaded.

 D. It determines where memory services and device drivers are loaded.

18. Where would you find the TCP/IP settings for a DHCP client in the Registry of a computer that had an IEEPRO network card?

 A. HKEY_LOCAL_MACHINE\System\CurrentControlSet\Services\TCPIP\Parameters

 B. HKEY_LOCAL_MACHINE\System\CurrentControlSet\Services\IEEPRO\Parameters\TCPIP

 C. HKEY_LOCAL_MACHINE\System\CurrentControlSet\Control\TCPIP\Parameters

 D. HKEY_LOCAL_MACHINE\System\CurrentControlSet\Services\IEEPRO1\Parameters\TCPIP

19. Where are the physical data files that store the Registry on the computer? Select all that apply.

 A. %SystemRoot%\Repair

 B. %SystemRoot%\System32\Config

 C. %SystemRoot%\Profiles\%Username%

 D. %SystemRoot%\Config

20. When editing the Registry file, what is true of each data type?

 A. Only the text data can be edited.

 B. Each has its own editor.

C. All are edited with the same editor.

D. All are edited in hex.

21. On the Intel platform, the information collected by NTDETECT.COM during the startup process is stored in which key of the HKEY_LOCAL_MACHINE subtree?

A. SAM

B. SOFTWARE

C. HARDWARE

D. SECURITY

22. What does RDISK /S do?

A. Copies only selected Registry keys.

B. Copies boot files, not Registry files.

C. It is not a valid program.

D. Makes a complete copy of the Registry, including the SAM and SECURITY.

23. If the start value for a driver is set to Automatic, when is the driver loaded during the Windows NT startup process?

A. By NTLDR

B. During the NTOSKRNL.EXE initialization

C. During the system startup phase

D. By a dependency service

24. From within REGEDT32, which of the following is true?

A. You cannot save the resource profiles.

B. You cannot save or restore the entire Registry.

C. You can save only selected keys.

D. You cannot save the information.

25. What is the difference between REGEDITand REGEDT32?

A. They are the same program.

B. REGEDIT allows saving the Registry, REGEDT32 doesn't.

C. REGEDT32 allows restoring the Registry, REGEDIT doesn't.

D. REGEDIT provides better search options.

12.3.1 Answers and Explanations: Exercise

Exercise 12.3.1 reviewed using the System Policy Editor to edit the Registry. Another use of the System Policy Editor is to create system policies that can be merged with the Registry.

When using the System Policy Editor to work with policy files, the information is stored in a separate file named NTCONFIG.POL for Windows NT systems. The contents of NTCONFIG.POL merge with the user's and the computer's Registry settings when they authenticate with their domain. NTCONFIG.POL is read from the NETLOGON share of the authenticating domain controller.

You also can connect to a remote Registry using File, Connect and can edit the Registry using the System Policy Editor. It is common practice to create your own system policy templates to modify the Registry more safely.

12.3.2 Answers and Explanations: Exercise

Exercise 12.3.2 outlined the differences between REGEDT32.EXE and REGEDIT.EXE. REGEDT32.EXE is best used for editing information under Windows NT because it has native data editors for all data types stored in the Windows NT Registry. REGEDIT.EXE is best used for finding information in the Registry because it allows searches to be performed on keys, values, and data. REGEDT32.EXE can search only for keys.

12

12.3 Answers and Explanations: Practice Problems

1. **B, C** The Registry contains information about hardware detected during startup and configuration information for installed devices, services, and applications.

2. **A, B, C** Windows NT Diagnostics, the System applet, and the SCSI applet all can be used to view configuration information stored in the Windows NT Registry.

3. **A** Windows NT has BOOT.INI settings that enable Windows NT to boot in a VGA 16-color mode. The setting that performs this is /BASEVIDEO. It is listed as [VGA Mode] in the Windows NT boot menu.

4. **B** If your computer fails to start due to a newly installed driver, you can use the Last Known Good configuration to revert to the previous setup. Remember, you must not log on to Windows NT if you plan to use the Last Known Good configuration.

5. **D** The Registry is organized into keys, subkeys, and values contained in the subkeys.

6. **B** You create a mandatory profile by renaming the user's NTUSER.DAT file as NTUSER.MAN. NTUSER.DAT is stored in the `%SystemRoot%\Profiles\%Username%` directory. Remember that if the user has been configured with a roaming profile, you must rename the NTUSER.DAT file in the configured roaming profile directory.

7. **D** The Windows NT Resource Kit contains a help file named REGENTRY.HLP that holds all Registry entries, data types, and default values.

8. **C** A hive is a portion of the Registry that is stored in a single distinct file/.log file combination. The combination is stored in the `%SystemRoot%\System32\Config` directory.

9. **C** The RESOURCE server should have been set to Maximize Throughput for File and Print Sharing. In addition, Windows NT Backup can perform only a local Registry backup. Because the tape backup unit is located on the resource server, the NT account database will not be backed up in this scenario.

10. **A** This solution meets all the requirements. The BACKEND server is configured to Maximize Throughput for Network Applications, which increases login response for authentication. The RESOURCE server is optimized for file and print sharing. By locating the tape backup unit on the RESOURCE server, the NT account database will be backed up.

11. **D** The LastKnownGood value stored in the HKEY_LOCAL_MACHINE\System\Select subkey contains a REG_DWORD data type that contains a number. If the number is 2, it means that HKEY_LOCAL_MACHINE\System\CurrentControlSet002 contains the Last Known Good configuration information.

12. **B, C** You can use the REGEDT32 and REGEDIT programs to edit the Registry.

13. **B, D** To obtain the best virtual memory performance, spread the paging file across multiple physical drives to increase system performance. Excluding it from the boot partition drive also increases performance because this drive is frequently accessed by the operating system, which can cause delays in access for virtual memory. Remember that if you do not include the page file on the boot partition, Windows NT cannot store crashdump information because it requires a paging file the size of physical RAM on the boot partition.

14. **C** The WINMSDP.EXE utility can access the same information from the Registry as Windows NT Diagnostics. It can be run through a remote command session on a remote computer.

15. **C, D** REG_BINARY and REG_SZ are recognized data types in the Windows NT Registry.

16. **A** String values in the Registry are stored in the REG_SZ data type.

17. **C** The ServiceGroupOrder subkey contains a list of service groups. It determines the order in which these groups are loaded during the Windows startup process.

18. **D** DHCP configuration information is stored under the HKEY_LOCAL_MACHINE\System\CurrentControlSet\Services\ Netcard1\Parameters\TCPIP subkey. A common mistake is to look only in the NETCARD subkey. The configuration is in the specific instance of the network card.

19. **B, C** The hives located in HKEY_LOCAL_MACHINE are stored in `%SystemRoot%\System32\Config`. The current user information is stored in the `%SystemRoot%\Profiles\ %UserName%\NTUSER.DAT` file.

20. **B** Each data type has its own editor in the Windows NT Registry Editor.

21. **C** The information collected by NTDETECT is stored in the Hardware subkey. This information is volatile and is rebuilt every time Windows NT is restarted.

22. **D** Running RDISK with the /s parameter backs up the entire Registry to the `%SystemRoot%\Repair` directory. It also includes updated copies of the SAM and SECURITY hives.

23. **C** A driver configured to start automatically starts during the system startup phase.

24. **B** You cannot restore or save the entire Registry using the REGEDT32 utility because a portion of the Registry is always open when operating Windows NT.

25. **D** The REGEDIT utility allows searches for keys, values, and data; REGEDT32 only allows searches for keys.

12.3 Key Words

Hive

NT Backup

RDISK

REGEDIT

REGEDT32

System Policy Editor

12.4 Solving Printer Problems

Before examining the print model, it is necessary to discuss the vocabulary used by Microsoft to explain the model. Microsoft does not use the same terminology as other network operating systems, and this can lead to some confusion when first working with the Windows NT print model.

Print devices are the actual hardware devices that produce hard copy output. *Printers* are the software interfaces between the operating system and the print device. A printer can be configured to send output to multiple physical printer devices. Multiple printers also can be configured to send output to the same printing device at different priority levels or at different hours of the day. A *print spooler* is the software responsible for receiving, distributing, and processing print jobs. A spooler consists of many components that perform the functions.

A *print job* is data destined for a print device. It can be sent in various formats in the Windows NT print model. A *queue* is a series of print jobs waiting to be printed. *Print processors* work with the print drivers to de-spool the spooled print jobs during print spool file playback. The print processor makes the final alterations to print jobs, based on the data type of the print job. Data types include Text, Enhanced Metafile (EMF), RAW FF(Appended), and RAW FF(Auto).

A. Files Involved in the Windows NT Print Process

Most files involved in printing are in the %systemroot%\SYSTEM32 directory. One notable exception is the spooler's workspace, which can be placed on any given drive or directory. By default, it is located in %systemroot%\SYSTEM32\SPOOL\Printers. You can change this location in the Advanced Property page of the Server Properties dialog box. You can access this dialog box from the Printers applet by selecting Server Properties from the File menu. The following list shows the major print-related files used under Windows NT:

- The print spooler uses WINSPOOL.DRV, SPOOLSS.EXE, and SPOOLSS.DLL.
- Local print providers (used for printers connected to a local port, such as LPT1 or COM1) use LOCALSPL.DLL.
- Remote print providers (used for printers not connected to a local port, such as a printer equipped with a network interface card) use WIN32SP.DLL for NT print servers. For NetWare print servers, NWPROVAU.DLL is used instead. For AppleTalk print servers, SFMPSPRT.DLL is used.
- Print monitors (used to send jobs from the spooler to the print device) can use one of a series of files, depending on how the printer is connected. For local printers, LOCALMON.DLL is used. For network-connected printers, a DLL specific to the network connection is used (HPMON.DLL or LPRMON.DLL).

B. The Printing Process

When a job is printed from a remote client to a printer located on a Windows NT printer server, the following process occurs:

1. The application (such as MS Word) makes a series of GDI calls. The GDI uses the printer driver to perform a partial rendering of the print job.

> **Windows 16-bit programs and DOS applications perform full rendering of the print job.**

2. The print job is sent to the print spooler on the workstation that generated the print job.
3. The print job is sent using a remote print provider, which connects the workstation to the remote print spooler.
4. The print spooler on the NT system receives the print job and performs whatever final processing is required (if any).
5. Finally, the print job is sent to the actual print device. If all is OK, a paper copy is generated.

C. Support for Other Operating Systems

Windows NT supports printing from other operating systems. Special services are required to provide support for UNIX, NetWare, and Macintosh clients.

1. Print Support for UNIX Hosts

Windows NT includes an LPD service (the Microsoft TCP/IP Print Server service), which can accept print jobs from UNIX clients using Line Printer Remote (LPR) clients. Windows NT clients also can use the LPR command when they have installed the TCP/IP Print Server service. The syntax of the LPR command is as follows:

```
lpr -S{server} - P{printer} -J{job} -C{class} -o {option} -x -d {filename}
```

> **The options `-S` and `-P` are case sensitive. They must be uppercase.**

Another command included with the TCP/IP Print Server service is the LPQ command, which can display the queue information for an LPD Print Server. The syntax of the LPQ command is:

```
lpq -S{server} - P{printer}
```

2. Print Support for NetWare Clients

Two services provide print support when the NetWare operating system is involved. Gateway services for NetWare enables Windows NT clients to print to NetWare print servers. File and print services for NetWare enables Windows NT Server printers to receive print jobs from NetWare clients.

3. Print Support for Macintosh Clients

The Services for Macintosh print processor (SFMPSPRT.DLL) enables Macintosh clients to send print jobs to Windows NT printers. This print processor has a specific data type named PSCRIPT1. This data type enables Macintosh clients to send Level 1 PostScript jobs to non-PostScript printers. The spooler sends the PostScript code through a Microsoft TrueImage raster image processor (RIP), supplied with Services for Macintosh. The raster image processor creates a series of one-page, monochrome bitmaps at a maximum of 300 DPI. The Windows NT print spooler sends the rasterized images, or bitmaps, to the print driver for the target printer. The print driver returns a job that prints the bitmaps on the page. If the printer is a PostScript printer, the Services for Macintosh print processor sends the job using the RAW data type.

D. Typical Print Problems

Typical problems encountered during the printing process include:

- The print device is turned off.
- The print device is offline.
- The print device is out of paper.
- The print permissions do not allow a user access to the printer.
- The print driver on the client is corrupt.
- The print spooler on either the client or the print server is corrupt.
- The print spool directory is out of disk space.

The following basic troubleshooting steps can be used to diagnose a printing problem:

1. Make sure the print device is properly connected, is online, and has paper.
2. On the print server, click the Print Test Page button. This determines whether the print driver on the print server is corrupt. If the test page does not print correctly, make sure all required files are present on the print server. This can be done by reloading the print driver.
3. On the printer's Sharing property page, make sure all necessary operating systems' print drivers are loaded for the printer. This enables the auto-downloading of drivers for each installed operating system's print drivers.
4. If the test print works correctly, try printing using a basic application such as Notepad or WordPad. If printing works for these applications, you might need to reinstall the application that does not print correctly.
5. If only specific users cannot print, verify that the permissions for the printer have been set correctly by inspecting the Permissions option on the Security page of the Printer dialog box. The permissions that can be set include:

    - **Full Control:** Allows the configured groups or users to change printer settings. This is assigned by default to members of the Administrators, Server Operators, Print Operators, and Power Users groups.
    - **Manage Documents:** Allows the configured groups or users to pause documents in the queue, to delete jobs, and to reorder jobs. The Creator/Owner special group has this permission assignment by default.
    - **Print:** Allows the configured groups or users to print a job. This permission is assigned to the Everyone special group by default.
    - **No Access:** Prevents the configured users and groups from printing. This is not assigned to any groups or users by default.

E. Downloading Print Drivers

Automatic downloading of print drivers can be configured for the following platforms:

- Windows NT Alpha platforms (Windows NT versions 3.1, 3.5x, and 4.0)
- Windows NT MIPS platforms (Windows NT versions 3.1, 3.5x, and 4.0)
- Windows NT PPC platforms (Windows NT 3.51 and 4.0)
- Windows NT Intel platforms (Windows NT versions 3.1, 3.5x, and 4.0)
- Windows 95 (true 32-bit print drivers only)

When a Windows NT client connects to a printer on a remote print server, its version of the print driver is compared to the version on the print server. If the version on the print server is newer, the newer version is downloaded and then used on the client. If the driver does not exist on the client, it also is downloaded and then used on the client.

On Windows 95 clients, the driver is downloaded only during the initial installation of the printer. If the Windows 95 print driver on the print server has been updated at all, the printer should be deleted from all Windows 95 clients and then reloaded.

12.4.1 Exercise: Installing Multiple Print Drivers for a Printer

This exercise reviews the steps necessary to install multiple print drivers for a Windows NT printer. Installing all necessary platforms' drivers to a print server assists in the distribution of updated print drivers on the network.

1. From the Start menu, select Settings and then select Printers.
2. Double-click the Add Printers icon to start the Add Printer Wizard.
3. Select My Computer and click the Next button.
4. Select the Enable Printer Pooling option to enable the creation of a printing pool. Select LPT1:, LPT2:, COM1:, and COM2: from the list of ports.

   The order in which you select the ports is extremely important because it is the order in which the ports are accessed when sending a print job to the pool.
5. From the Manufacturer listing, select LexMark. From the Printers listing, select the LexMark 4039 Plus PS printer. Click the Next button to continue.

   When configuring a printer pool, all component printing devices must be able to use the same print driver.
6. Accept the default for printer name. Do not set this printer to be your default printer. Click the Next button to continue.
7. Share the printer with the name LEXMARK. The share name can be up to 256 characters in length. Click the Next button to continue.

> **Although print shares can be up to 256 characters in length, this is not supported by all operating systems. Windows NT 4 clients can connect to printer shares up to 256 characters in length. Windows 95 and Windows NT 3.x clients can connect to printer shares up to 12 characters in length. Win16 and DOS clients can only connect to print shares up to 8.3 characters in length.**

8. Answer No when asked whether you want to print a test page. Click the Finish button to complete the printer installation.
9. When prompted, insert the Windows NT Server CD-ROM and indicate the <Drive Letter>:\i386 directory to install the necessary support files.

12.4.2 Exercise: Installing the TCP/IP Print Server Service

This exercise reviews the steps to install the TCP/IP Print Server service. It then reviews usage of the LPR and LPQ commands. This exercise assumes that the printer created in Exercise 12.4.1 exists and that the current user is a member of the Administrators local group.

1. From the Start menu, select Settings and then select Control Panel.
2. Double-click the Printers applet.
3. Right-click the LexMark 4039 Plus PS printer and select the Pause Printing option.
4. Switch back to the Control Panel and double-click the Network applet.
5. Select the Services tab of the Network Properties dialog box.
6. Click the Add button, and then select the Microsoft TCP/IP Printing option to install the TCP/IP Print Server service.
7. When prompted, indicate the path for the Windows NT Server CD-ROM and the %platform% directory (such as d:\i386).
8. When prompted to restart the computer, select Yes.

> **If you have installed any service packs on your Windows NT Server computer, you should always select No when asked any question about restarting the computer until you have reinstalled the service pack. If you do not reapply the service pack at this point, you could end up with a STOP error that will not allow Windows NT to start.**

9. When the computer restarts, log on as Administrator.
10. Start the Control Panel again.
11. In the Control Panel, double-click the Service applet.
12. Change the Startup setting for the TCP/IP Print Server service to Automatic, and then start this service.
13. Start a command prompt.

14. Make C:\ the current directory.

15. Type the following command to print the BOOT.INIfile to your LEXMARK print share:

    ```
    LPR -S<Your Computer Name> -PLEXMARK c:\boot.ini
    ```

    You should replace <Your Computer Name> with the NetBIOS name of your computer.

16. To view the queue of the paused printer, type the following command:

    ```
    LPQ -S<Your Computer Name> -PLEXMARK
    ```

17. Switch back to the Printers Window. Double-click the LexMark 4039 Plus PS printer to view the contents of the queue. The contents should be the same as you saw in step 16.

12.4 Practice Problems

1. When a new printer is installed on a print server, which of the following statements is true about the default permissions assigned to the printer? Select all that apply.

   A. Everyone can delete any job in the printer.

   B. Only Administrators can change the properties of the printer.

   C. Administrators, Server Operators, and Printer Operators can change the properties of the printer.

   D. The owner of a job can delete the job.

2. What does the print spooler do?

   A. Receives, processes, and prints jobs

   B. Receives jobs and reroutes to remote printers

   C. Reprints jobs

   D. Translates hex to ASCII

3. Which operating systems support the automatic downloading of printer drivers by Windows NT? Select all that apply.

   A. Windows NT Server

   B. Windows NT Workstation

   C. Windows 95

   D. Windows for Workgroups

4. Which service must be installed to enable a UNIX system to print to a Windows NT printer?

   A. TCP/IP

   B. Simple TCP/IP services

   C. SNMP Service

   D. TCP/IP Printing service

5. Where are permissions for a print share set?

   A. Windows NT Explorer

   B. Property pages of a printer

   C. Print Manager

   D. Server Manager

6. Your department is using an HP LaserJet 3 SI printer that is unable to switch dynamically between PCL and PostScript modes. Which separator page do you use before all PostScript jobs to make sure the printer is in PostScript mode?

   A. PCL.SEP

   B. PSCRIPT.SEP

   C. SYSPRINT.SEP

   D. SWITCH.SEP

7. You are supporting a mainframe emulation program that requires form feeds appended to each job. You want to change the default data type for the WINPRINT print processor to which of the following?

   A. RAW

   B. RAW (FF After)

   C. FF After

   D. Text (FF After)

8. Users in your office are unable to print large documents. You suspect that the drive where your spool files are stored has run out of disk space. How do you change the default location for the spool directory?

   A. Change the location on the Spool tab of the Printer's Properties dialog box.

   B. Change the Spool Settings in the System Applet of the Control Panel.

   C. On the Advanced tab of the Server Properties dialog box, which can be reached from the Server Properties option in the File menu of the Printer dialog box.

D. This setting cannot be changed. You must delete files to free up disk space.

9. If you find there is a job in the printer that will not print and cannot be deleted, how can you remove this job from the printer?

   A. Delete all files in the %System Root%\System32\spool\PRINTERS directory.

   B. Log on as Administrator and delete the job. The Administrator account has the right to delete stuck jobs.

   C. Ignore the job. After the configured time-out period has passed, the job removes itself from the queue.

   D. Stop and start the Spooler Service.

10. What factors must be considered when creating a printer pool? Select all that apply.

   A. All printers should be in the same area of the office.

   B. The print server must have a digiboard installed.

   C. The HP JetAdmin utility must be installed on the print server.

   D. The printers that make up the printer pool must be able to use the same print driver.

   E. The order in which the ports are selected determines the order in which the printing devices are accessed.

11. What is the name of the administrative share that is set up to download print drivers?

   A. PRINTER$

   B. SPOOL$

   C. PRINT$

   D. SPOOLER$

12. What is the syntax of the command a UNIX client would use to print the file OUTPUT.DOC to a share named HPLJ on the server SPARKY?

   A. `lpd -SSPARKY -PHPLJ output.doc`

   B. `lpr -SSPARKY -PHPLJ output.doc`

   C. `lpd -SHPLJ -PSPARKY output.doc`

   D. `lpq -SHPLJ -PSPARKY output.doc`

13. You have installed all your HP Laserjet printers with HP Jet Direct cards, yet you cannot manage any of them with Windows NT. What is the missing component that enables Windows NT to manage these printers?

   A. HP Jet Direct Service

   B. HP Print Service

   C. DLC Protocol

   D. Need to install the NT Patch to the HP Laserjet firmware on each printer

14. Can a Windows NT Server support the automatic downloading of print drivers for Intel, PPC, Alpha, and MIPS clients on the same print server?

   A. Yes

   B. No

15. What permissions are required to pause, delete, and reorder jobs in the print queue?

   A. No Access

   B. Print

   C. Manage Documents

   D. Full Control

16. What is the main difference in the printing process when a Windows 3.x client prints to a Windows NT print share compared to when a Windows NT client prints to a Windows NT print share?

A. There is no difference.

B. Windows 3.x clients cannot print to a Windows NT print share.

C. Windows 3.x clients can only submit text jobs.

D. Windows 3.x clients fully process their jobs before submitting them to a Windows NT print share.

17. You have installed the TCP/IP Print Server service on your print server and have restarted the print server, yet UNIX clients cannot print to any of the print shares. Which of the following could be the reason for this?

    A. Windows NT does not support printing for UNIX clients.

    B. The SNMP Service also must be installed.

    C. The TCP/IP Print Server service is set to be manually started. It should be switched to start automatically.

    D. The UNIX clients must first capture the print port.

18. What must be installed to enable Macintosh clients to print to a Windows NT printer?

    A. TCP/IP Print Server service

    B. Services for Macintosh

    C. Mac Print Services

    D. AppleTalk Protocol

The following scenario applies to questions 19–22. A different solution to the scenario is proposed for each question.

Scenario: The Xavier group has offices in Boston, Montreal, and Seattle. Each office has its own domain, with the Boston domain functioning as the master domain in a Master Domain Model. Global groups have been created to represent the Boston users, the Montreal users, and the Seattle users. The resource domains each have their own printer resources that are shared throughout the entire enterprise.

Required Result: The Systems group comprised of Bob, Mary, and Jane should be the only users with Full Control on all printers in the ènterprise. *Optional Result 1:* The Xavier group wants all print servers to be capable of hosting jobs sent by UNIX computers. *Optional Result 2:* The Xavier group wants to provide printing support to all Macintosh clients in the enterprise.

19. *Proposed Solution*: When a printer is installed, change the permissions on each print share to assign Bob, Mary, and Jane to manage all documents for the printer. Be sure to install the TCP/IP and AppleTalk Protocols on each print server. This enables print support for UNIX and Macintosh clients.

    This solution:

    A. Meets the required result and both optional results

    B. Meets the required result and only one optional result

    C. Meets only the required result

    D. Does not satisfy any required or optional results

20. *Proposed Solution:* In each domain, add the user accounts for Bob, Mary, and Jane to the Print Operators local group. At each print server, install the TCP/IP protocol and the SNMP Service. Also add the Services for Macintosh service.

    This solution:

    A. Meets the required result and both optional result

    B. Meets the required result and only one optional result

    C. Meets only the required result

    D. Does not satisfy any required or optional results

21. *Proposed Solution*: In the Boston domain, add the user accounts for Bob, Mary, and Jane to the Print Operators local group. At each print server, install the TCP/IP protocol and the Microsoft TCP/IP Print Server service. Also add the Services for Macintosh service.

    This solution:

    A. Meets the required result and both optional results

    B. Meets the required result and only one optional result

    C. Meets only the required result

    D. Does not satisfy any required or optional results

22. *Proposed Solution*: In each domain, add the user accounts for Bob, Mary, and Jane to the Print Operators local group. At each print server, install the TCP/IP protocol and the Microsoft TCP/IP Printing service. Also add the Services for Macintosh service.

    This solution:

    A. Meets the required result and both optional results

    B. Meets the required result and only one optional result

    C. Meets only the required result

    D. Does not satisfy any required or optional results

23. You have updated the HP LaserJet 4 print driver on your print server for Windows 95 to enable duplex printing. Your Windows 95 clients are not able to take advantage of this new option. What is the problem?

    A. Windows 95 clients do not support duplex printing.

    B. You must load Windows 95 print drivers at the client systems.

    C. You must restart the Windows 95 system for the changes to take effect.

    D. You have to delete the existing printer and reconnect to the printer to download the newer version of the driver.

24. How can you prevent print job information events from being written to the System Log of the Event Viewer?

    A. In the Registry, configure which events are logged to the Event Viewer for the Spooler service.

    B. In the Printers dialog box, select Server Properties from the File menu. On the Advanced tab, deselect the Log Spooler Information Events option.

    C. On a printer's Advanced Property page, configure the printer so it does not record information events to the Event Viewer.

    D. This cannot be done.

25. What is the syntax a login script uses to connect the printer shared as SHOPPRINT that is located on the print server named SHOP_FLOOR to LPT2:?

    A. `Capture l=2 s=SHOP_FLOOR q=SHOPPRINT`

    B. `NET PRINT LPT2: Error! Reference source not found. \SHOPPRINT`

    C. `CAPTURE LPT2:=\\SHOP_FLOOR\SHOPPRINT`

    D. `NET USE LPT2: \\SHOP_FLOOR\SHOPPRINT`

26. If a physical printing device has broken down, and the printer that was sending jobs to the printing device still has jobs in its queue, how do you redirect the jobs to a similar printing device?

    A. You cannot redirect jobs.

    B. Have the users recall their jobs and readdress them to a different printer.

    C. Add a new local port to the printer using the UNC name of a printer that prints to a similar printing device.

    D. Use the Redirect option in the printer's property pages.

27. What data type is used when a Macintosh client sends a print job to a LaserJet III printer that does not have PostScript support?

    A. RAW

    B. PSCRIPT1

    C. EMF

    D. You cannot print PostScript to a PCL printer.

28. What data type is used when a Macintosh client sends a print job to a PostScript Laser printer?

    A. RAW

    B. PSCRIPT1

    C. EMF

    D. TEXT

12.4.1 Answers and Explanations: Exercise

Exercise 12.4.1 reviewed the steps necessary to create a printer pool. The following are the key concerns when creating a printer pool:

- Make sure the print devices are near each other in the office because it is not known which print device is used to output a job.
- All printers must be able to use the same print driver.
- When selecting the ports for a printing pool, be sure to select the fastest ports first.
- If the print devices are different models, select the faster print devices before the slower print devices.

12.4.2 Answers and Explanations: Exercise

Exercise 12.4.2 reviewed the steps to install the TCP/IP Print Server service. This service also added a new print monitor, known as the LPR Print Monitor (LPRMON.DLL). This print monitor can be used to redirect print jobs to an LPD print server.

When configuring an LPR print port, you must configure the network address of the LPD print server and the name that the LPD service associates with its print device.

12.4 Answers and Explanations: Practice Problems

1. **C, D** The default permissions grant Administrators, Print Operators, and Server Operators the Full Control permissions. The special group Creator Owner is granted the Manage Documents permissions, which enable users to delete their own print jobs.
2. **A** The spooler receives jobs from clients, performs further processing on jobs received from 32-bit clients, and prints the jobs.
3. **A, B, C** Windows NT Server, Windows NT Workstation, and Windows 95 all support the automatic downloading of print drivers. Windows 95 has this support only when working with true 32-bit drivers.
4. **D** The TCP/IP Printing service enables a UNIX system to print to a Windows NT printer. After installation, it is referred to in the list of installed services as the TCP/IP Print Server service.
5. **B** Print permissions are set from the Security tab of a printer's properties. The Print Manager application was used in Windows NT 3.x.

6. **B** The PSCRIPT.SEP separator page switches the printer into PostScript mode before a job is printed.
7. **B** The data type RAW (FF After) is used to automatically eject the page after printing has been completed.
8. **C** On the Server Properties pages, you can set the default spool directory when configuring the advanced properties.
9. **D** Stopping and starting the Spooler service flushes all jobs from the printer.
10. **A, D, E** When setting up a printer pool, the printers should be in the same general location and must use the same print driver. When selecting the ports used for the printer pool, be sure to select faster ports before slower ports.
11. **C** The print drivers are downloaded from the administrative share named PRINT$ on the print server.
12. **B** The syntax of the LPR command is LPR -S<Server name or IP address> -P<printer or share name>. Remember, the –S and –P are case sensitive and must be uppercase.
13. **C** The HP print monitor is loaded when the DLC protocol is added to a Windows NT computer.
14. **A** Yes. You must install print drivers for each platform that will connect to the print server for printing.
15. **C** The Manage Documents permission allows a user to pause, delete, and reorder print jobs.
16. **D** Windows for Workgroups uses its own 16-bit drivers to fully process a job before sending the job to a Windows NT print share. Windows NT clients partially process their print jobs, and then send them to the print share. The print share's spooler completes the processing of the job.
17. **C** The TCP/IP Print Server service is not configured to automatically start after installation. You must change its startup setting to automatically start the service.
18. **B** Services for Macintosh installs the Services for Macintosh print processor (SFMPSPRT), which enables Macintosh clients to print to Windows NT print shares.
19. **D** According to the requirements, Bob, Mary, and Jane require Full Control permissions, not Manage Documents permissions. This could have been achieved without granting excess permissions by making them members of the Print Operators local group in each of the three domains.
20. **B** This solution grants the three users sufficient permissions to meet the primary requirement. Only Macintosh clients, however, can access the print shares. You need the TCP/IP Print Server service to grant print access to UNIX hosts.
21. **D** This does not meet the primary requirement. Bob, Mary, and Jane are only able to fully manage the printers in the Boston domain. They must be added to the Print Operators local group in each of the three domains.
22. **A** This solution fully meets all requirements. Remember that if any member servers or Windows NT workstation computers are functioning as print servers, the three users must be added to the Print Operators local group in the account database on each of the member servers or NT Workstation computers.
23. **D** Windows 95 clients only download the server's version of the print driver when they initially connect to the printer. You must delete the printer and then reinstall it to download the new version of the driver. Windows NT clients *do* check the version of their driver and the version stored on the print server. If the version on the print server is newer, they download the newer version.
24. **B** You can choose whether to log information, warnings, and STOP errors

for the print spooler in the Advanced properties page of the Server Properties dialog box.

25. **D** The syntax for connecting a print share to a DOS print port is `NET USE <PORT>Error! Reference source not found.`**`Error! Reference source not found.`** `SHARE>`.

26. **C** A local port can be added that points to the UNC name of a printer. The printer must use the same print driver as the original printer because the job will be fully processed when downloaded to the new printer.

27. **B** The Services for Macintosh print processor (SFMPSPRT) downloads the job using the PSCRIPT1 data type. This data type indicates that the job is Level 1 PostScript code from a Macintosh client, but the target printer is not a PostScript printer.

28. **A** When a Macintosh client prints to a PostScript printer, the data is downloaded in its native RAW format.

12.4 Key Words

LPD Service

LPQ

LPR

Print device

Print drivers

Print job

Print spooler

Printer

Queue

12.5 Troubleshooting Remote Access Service

One of the many challenges faced by network administrators today is the user's need to dial in to the network. The popularity and convenience of laptops and telecommuting makes this process necessary. Windows NT comes with a dial-in service known as Remote Access Service (RAS). This section presents an overview of RAS and investigates troubleshooting the RAS client and server.

A. An Overview of RAS

Essentially, RAS enables users to function as if they are physically connected to a remote network. RAS has two main components—the server (Remote Access Service) and the client (Dial-Up Networking). The RAS server can be Windows NT Server, Windows NT Workstation, or Windows 95 (either through Service Pack 1 or OEM Service Release 2). The RAS server enables users to connect to the network from a remote location. The Microsoft RAS server always uses the Point-to-Point Protocol (PPP) when users are dialing in to the network.

When clients connect to a server using a modem, there are two popular line protocols. *Serial Line Internet Protocol* (SLIP) frequently is used in UNIX implementations. SLIP is the older of the two line protocols and is geared directly for TCP/IP communications. Windows NT can dial in as a client to a SLIP server. However, it does not provide a SLIP server. Because SLIP requires a static IP address and does not provide secured logon (passwords are sent as clear text), Microsoft's RAS server uses Point-to-Point Protocol (PPP).

PPP, developed as a replacement for SLIP, provides several advantages over the earlier protocol. PPP can automatically provide the client computer with an IP address and other configuration. It provides a secure logon and has the capability to transport protocols other than TCP/IP (such as AppleTalk, IPX, and NetBEUI).

Two important extensions to PPP are implemented in Windows NT RAS Server. These extensions are the Multilink Protocol (MP) and the Point-to-Point Tunneling Protocol (PPTP). Windows NT supports both of these protocols.

Multilink Protocol enables a client station to connect to a remote server using more than one physical connection. This capability provides better throughput over standard modems. You will, however, need multiple phone lines and modems to enable this protocol. This can be an easy interim solution if you need to temporarily connect to offices, but do not have the time or budget to set up a leased line or other similar connection.

Point-to-Point Tunneling Protocol facilitates secure connections across the Internet. Using PPTP, users can connect to any Internet Service Provider (ISP) as well as the office network. During the session initialization, the client and server negotiate a 40-bit session key. This key then is used to encrypt all packets to be sent back and forth over the Internet. The packets are encapsulated into PPP packets as data. The PPTP-encapsulated protocol can be NetBEUI, NWLink IPX/SPX, or TCP/IP.

You can connect to the Windows NT server in other ways. In addition to connections over Public Switched Telephone Networks (PSTN), RAS can connect networks in two other ways—using Integrated Services Digital Networks (ISDN) and using X.25 (a wide area networking standard).

1. ISDN

ISDN is becoming a common method of communicating. It is a good choice for connecting to remote sites or for individuals and small organizations connecting to the Internet. Whereas today's standard phone lines can handle transmission speeds of up to 56 Kbps, ISDN transmits at 64 or 128 Kbps—depending on whether it is one or two channels.

ISDN is a point-to-point communications technology, and special equipment must be installed at both the server and the remote site. You need to install an ISDN card (which acts as a network card) in place of a modem in both computers. As you probably have guessed by now, ISDN connections are more expensive than modems. If you truly require the higher speed, however, the cost most likely is justified. Be aware that in some parts of the world, this is a metered service; the more you use, the more you pay.

2. X.25

The X.25 protocol is not a communication device; rather, it is a standard protocol for connections. It is a packet-switching communication protocol designed for WAN connectivity.

RAS supports X.25 connections using Packet Assemblers/Disassemblers (PADs) and X.25 smart cards. These are installed as a network card, just like ISDN.

B. Client Issues When Using RAS

Several issues must be investigated when configuring and troubleshooting the Dial-Up Networking client. These issues include installing and configuring the modem, configuring dialing locations, creating phonebook entries, setting dial-in permissions, and setting callback security levels on a user-by-user basis.

1. Installing and Configuring Modems

Installing a modem is simple in Windows NT. After the hardware is connected, go to the Control Panel and double-click the Modems icon. If no modem is installed, the modem installer starts automatically. This wizard steps you through the installation of the modem.

If you have already used the installer once and it was unable to detect the modem, you probably have one of two problems. Either the modem cannot be detected and you will have to install it manually, or the system can't see the modem, in which case you should check the port. If you need to install the modem manually, check the option Don't detect my modem, I will select it from a list. This selection brings up a screen that enables you to select the modem.

Windows NT can use Windows 95 configuration files to install a modem. If you are unable to find a Windows NT 4.0 driver, you can use a Windows 95 driver in its place.

When you have installed the modem, you can check modem properties using the Modems icon in the Control Panel. After you have selected the modem to configure, you can change the configuration of the modem using its property pages. On the General tab of the modem's properties, you can set the following items:

- **Port:** Displays the port that the modem was installed on. You should check this if the hardware has been changed. Also check the port settings if the modem is not working.
- **Speaker Volume:** Determines the volume of the speaker during the connection phase. This should be turned up so you can verify the dial tone and that the other end is, in fact, a modem.
- **Maximum Speed:** Sets the fastest rate attempted by the system when communicating with the modem. If this is set too high, some modems are not able to respond to the system. In this case, try lowering the rate.
- **Only connect at this speed:** Instructs the modem to connect to the remote site at the same speed you set for communications with the modem. If the other site is unable to support this speed, you are not able to communicate.

In the Connection tab of the modem's properties dialog box, you also can set the manner in which the modem connects. Settings that might need to be adjusted include

- **Call Preferences:** Configures how the modem reacts to events that occur during a dial-up session. Options include:
    - Wait for Tone Before Dialing
    - Cancel the Call if Not Connected Within...
    - Disconnect a Call if Idle for More Than...
- **Advanced Modem Settings:** The advanced modem settings are configured by clicking the Advanced button on the Connection page. This enables the configuration of the following properties of a modem:
    - **Use Error control:** Turns on or off some common settings that affect the way the system deals with the modem.
    - **User flow control:** Overrides the flow control setting for the port. Both types of flow control (Xon/Xoff and hardware) are available. In most cases, you should choose to use hardware flow control. Using flow control enables you to set the speed of the transmission between the computer and the modem.
    - **Modulation Type:** Enables users to set the modem's frequency modulation to match that of the phone system being used. The modulation is either standard or Bell, and deals with the sound frequency that is used for the send and receive channels of the communicating hosts.
    - **Extra settings:** Enables you to enter extra modem initialization strings to be sent to the modem whenever a call is placed.
    - **Record a log file:** Enables you to record a file that permits you to see the communications that take place between the modem and the computer during the connection phase of the communications. This is probably the most important setting from the troubleshooting perspective.

2. Configuring Dialing Locations

Some dial-in users call from varying locations. Depending on their location, they might need to dial long distance to reach the office network or use different prefixes to access an outside line. You can create various Dialing Locations from the Telephony applet in the Control Panel. This information is used with a phonebook setting to determine how to dial an access number to dial-in to the office network. If a user cannot reach the point in which the two modems are attempting to connect, dialing location is generally one of the first areas to check. The settings that can be configured for a dialing location include:

- **I am dialing from:** This is the configured name of the location. To create a new entry, click the New button and enter a name in the box. The user needs to know which entry to use when dialing. Be sure to use a descriptive name that has meaning for the user.
- **The area code is:** The computer uses this information to determine whether it needs to dial the number as a long distance number or as a local number.
- **I am in:** Sets the country code for dialing purposes, so the system is able to connect to international numbers.
- **To access an outside line, first dial:** Sets the prefix to be used to access an outside line. This setting enables configuration of separate prefixes for local and long distance calls.
- **Dial using Calling Card:** Enables you to have the computer enter calling card information to make the connection with the remote host. Click the Change button to review or change the calling card information. You can select from common calling cards available or create your own template for your calling card.
- **This location has call waiting:** The call waiting tone often causes a connection to be dropped. You can enter information here to temporarily disable call waiting for the location you are dialing from.
- **The phone system at this location uses:** Enables you to select whether the system you are calling from uses tone or pulse dialing.

3. Configuring the Phonebook Entry

After your modem has been configured and dialing locations have been created, you need to configure a phonebook entry for the network you want to dial-in to. Dial-Up Networking is the component used to connect to the RAS server. In Dial-Up Networking, you create a phonebook entry for each remote network you call. The steps required to create an entry are as follows:

1. Double-click the My Computer icon, and then double-click the Dial-Up Networking folder.
2. Click the New button to create an entry. You also can select an existing entry from the list, click More, and choose Edit the Entry.

   If you choose New, the New Entry Wizard appears. You have the option to enter information manually. Because this chapter discusses troubleshooting, this section covers manual entries (they provide more options).
3. The New (or Edit) Phonebook Entry dialog box appears. Enter or verify the information. The options are as follows:
   - **Entry Name:** The name of the entry.
   - **Comment:** Any comment you want to make about the entry.

- **Phone Number:** This is the phone number for the entry; you should verify this. You can enter multiple numbers by clicking the Alternates button. These numbers are tried in the sequence entered. You also have the option to move a successful number to the top of the list.
- **Use Telephony-Dialing Properties:** This tells the system to use the properties set for your location when dialing the number.
- **Dial Using:** Informs the system which modem you want to use when dialing. Verify that the modem exists. If Multilink is selected, choose Configure and verify the phone numbers entered for each modem listed.
- **Use Another Port if Busy:** This tells the system to use another modem if the modem specified is busy.

4. Select the Server tab, and enter or verify the information. The options are as follows:
   - **Dial-up server type:** Tells the system what type of server you are trying to connect to. You can use three different types of servers—PPP (such as Windows NT), SLIP, and Windows NT 3.1 RAS.
   - **Network protocols:** Select the protocols you want to be able to use. If the client computer uses the Internet, TCP/IP needs to be selected. If the client uses the services of a remote NetWare server, IPX/SPX must be selected.
   - **Enable software compression:** If you are working with a Windows NT server, you can select this to turn on software compression. For troubleshooting purposes, you should turn this off.
   - **Enable PPP LCP extensions:** Tells the system that the PPP server can set up the client station and can verify the user name and password. This also should be turned off when you are troubleshooting.
5. If you are using TCP/IP for this connection, you also should set or verify the TCP/IP settings. The TCP/IP setting screen appears; the screen is different depending on the type of server you selected. The options are as follows:
   - **Server Assigned IP Address:** Tells the computer that the server will assign the IP address for this station. The server must have some means of assigning IP address to use this option.
   - **Specify an IP Address:** Enables you to give the station an IP address. The address needs to be unique and must be correct for the server's network. The server also must enable the client to request an IP address.
   - **Server Assigned Name Server Addresses:** Tells the system that the server will assign IP addresses for DNS and WINS servers.
   - **Specify Name Server Addresses:** Enables you to set the addresses for DNS and WINS servers. This enables you to see if the server is giving you correct addresses.
   - **Use IP Header Compression:** Using IP header compression reduces the overhead transmitted over the modem. For troubleshooting, you should disable this.
   - **Use Default Gateway on the Remote Network:** If you are connected to a network and dialed-in to a service provider, this tells Windows NT to send information bound for a remote network to the gateway on the dial-in server.

6. Set the script options on the Script tab, as follows:
    - **After dialing (logon):** You can choose three different settings here; make sure the correct one is used. For NT-to-NT communications, you can select None. For other connections, you might have to enter information. For troubleshooting, you should try the terminal window. This enables you to enter the information manually rather than using the script. If this works, you should verify the script.
    - **Before dialing:** If you click this button, you are presented with basically the same options. This can be used to bring up a window or to run a script before you dial the remote host.
7. Enter or check the security information on the Security tab. This security should be set to the same level as the security on the server or the connection will probably fail. The options are as follows:
    - **Authentication and encryption policy:** Set the level of security you want to use. For troubleshooting, you can try Accept any authentication including clear text. This setting should be set to match the setting on the server.
    - **Require data encryption:** If you are using Microsoft-encrypted authentication, you have the option to encrypt all data being sent over the connection. This option should be set the same as the server.
    - **Use current name and password:** Enables Windows to use the current username and password as your logon information. If you are not using the same name and password on the client as you do on the network, do not check this box. You will be prompted for the username and password to log on, just as when you attempted to connect.
    - **Unsave password:** If you told the system to save the logon password for a connection, you can clear it by clicking this button. You should do this in the case of a logon problem.
8. Finally, you can check or enter the information for X.25 connections.

You can configure many different options; therefore, a great potential exists for errors. Client errors tend to be either validation problems or errors in the network protocols. Remember that you also might need to check the configuration of the server to verify that the client configuration is correct.

4. Dial-In Permissions

Remote Access Server uses integrated Windows NT security. To access the network using Dial-Up Networking, a client has to provide the same account/password combination that is used when connecting directly to the network. In addition, the account needs to have dial-in permissions set.

You can grant users dial-in permissions through the User Manager (or User Manager for Domains) or through the Remote Access Admin program. If you receive an error message that you do not have permission to dial in to the network, this is one of the first things you should check. In User Manager for Domains, the dial-in permissions are set in the property pages for an individual user. Each user has a Dial-in button. From the Dial in property page, the user can be configured as a dial-in user.

You also can set dial-in permissions from the Remote Access Admin utility. In the Remote Access Admin program, select Permissions from the Users menu. You can select each user and set whether the user has dial-in permissions or not. You also can use the Grant All button to grant dial-in permissions to all accounts in the domain.

You can only grant dial-in permissions on a user-by-user basis. You cannot grant dial-in permissions to a global group or a local group.

5. Configuring Call-Back Security

You also can set call-back options in the Dial-in property pages of User Manager for Domains or Remote Access Admin. Call-back adds another level of security to your network. It also is used to assign long distance charges primarily to the RAS server rather than to the dial-in clients. The call-back levels that can be set include the following:

- **No Call Back:** This is the default; it means the call-back feature is disabled.
- **Set By Caller:** With this option, the user is able to specify the number to be be used when the server calls back. This is useful if you have a large number of users that travel and you want to centralize long distance.
- **Preset To:** This enhances the security of the network by forcing the user to be at a predetermined phone number. If this option is set, the user only can call from that one location.

In some cases, call-back security cannot be implemented. If the user dials in from a hotel and does not have a direct line to the room, call-back security cannot be implemented.

6. Troubleshooting Other Issues with the Client

As mentioned earlier, Windows NT acts as a PPP server. This means the client station and the server undergo a negotiation during the initial phase of the call.

During the negotiation, the client and the server decide on the protocol to be used and the parameters for the protocol. If there are problems when attempting to connect, you might want to set up PPP logging to actually watch the negotiation between the server and the client. This is set up on the server by changing the Logging option, as follows:

```
HKEY_LOCAL_MACHINE\SYSTEM\CurrentControlSet\Services\RASMAN\PPP\Parameters
```

The log file is in the system32\RAS directory and, like the modem log, can be viewed using any text editor. Some other problems you might encounter when dialing in to the network include:

- You must make sure the protocol you are requesting is available on the RAS server. There must be at least one common protocol or the connection fails.
- If you are using NetBEUI, make sure the name used on the RAS client is not in use on the network you are attempting to connect to.
- If you are attempting to connect using TCP/IP, the RAS server must be configured to provide you with an address.

C. Server Issues When Using Remote Access Server

The server side of the dial-in process also can have some configuration and installation issues that affect whether a successful dial-in session is established.

After Remote Access Server is installed, several configuration issues can affect the dial-in clients. You can configure Remote Access Service by opening the Network applet in the Control Panel. On the Services tab, select the Remote Access Service and click the Properties button. The Remote Access Setup dialog box contains the following configuration options:

- **Add:** Enables you to add another port to the RAS server. This could be a modem, an X.25 PAD, or a PPTP Virtual Private Network. Note that to add a Virtual Private Network port, you also must have installed the PPTP Protocol.
- **Remove:** Removes the port from RAS.
- **Configure:** Brings up a dialog box that enables you to configure how this port is used. You can configure the port to be used only for dialing out, only for receiving calls, or it can support both. Check this option if users are not able to dial in.
- **Clone:** This setting enables you to copy a port. Windows NT Server has been tested with up to 256 ports.

Due to product restrictions, Windows NT Workstation and Windows 95 (with service pack 1 or the OSR2 release) can only enable one client to dial in.

After the ports are configured, you need to configure the network settings. These affect what users are able to see, how they are authenticated, and what protocols they are able to use when they dial in to the network. The network settings include:

- **Configuring Dial Out Protocols:** Sets which protocols you can use to dial in to another server.
- **Configuring Dial in Protocols:** Sets the protocols used to connect to you. The following sections detail protocol-specific configuration options.
- **Configuring Server-Side Encryption Settings:** As with the client side of Remote Access Service, encryption levels can be set. The level of security you choose also must be set on the client computer. If the client cannot use at least the same level of security, it cannot be validated by the server.
- **Enabling Multilink Connections:** By enabling the multilink option, the RAS server can accept multilink connections from clients.

a. Configuring NetBEUI on the RAS Server

Very little configuration is required for the NetBEUI protocol. Only one option can be configured—whether to give dial-in users access to the entire network or just to the RAS server.

Built within the NetBEUI protocol is a NetBIOS gateway. The NetBIOS gateway can take requests bound for a server that does not speak NetBEUI and forward them on your behalf. In other words, you can dial in to a server using NetBEUI and connect to file shares on a remote server that only runs NWLink or TCP/IP.

b. Configuring IPX on the RAS Server

If your environment is a mix of both Windows NT and NetWare, you probably want to enable the IPX protocol on the RAS server. This enables clients to communicate with the NetWare servers over the RAS connection (if they also are using a NetWare client).

Again, you have the option to let clients see either the entire network or only this computer. The other options deal with the IPX node numbers that identify a station using IPX. Normally, you do not need to change the defaults; if you are having problems, however, try resetting the dialog box to the default.

The only case in which you might have a problem is when a secure package reads the node number. In this case, do not assign the same node number to all clients. If the numbers need to be entered in the software, either assign a group of node numbers you are able to enter or enable the client to request a specific number.

c. Configuring TCP/IP on the RAS Server

If you run a mixed network that could include UNIX hosts, you should enable the TCP/IP protocol on the RAS server. This also enables your clients to use an Internet connection on your network.

The TCP/IP configuration dialog box enables the administrator to restrict network access to the RAS server or to allow access to the entire network. The other options all deal with assigning TCP/IP addresses to clients dialing in. By default, the RAS server uses a Dynamic Host Configuration Protocol (DHCP) server to assign the addresses. If your DHCP server has a long lease period, you might want to assign the numbers from a pool of addresses given on the server. If you enable the client to request an address, you need to configure the client stations for all the other parameters.

If your clients are having problems connecting, assign a range of addresses to the RAS server. This eliminates any problems related to the DHCP server and still enables you to prevent clients from requesting specific IP addresses.

D. Monitoring the Dial-In Connections

When you are unable to determine whether the client or server portion is causing the problem in a failed dial-up session, you might need to monitor the actual connection. Tools that can be used include the Remote Access Admin monitoring option and the Dial-Up Network Monitor.

1. Monitoring from the RAS Server

From the server, you can use the Remote Access Admin tool to monitor the ports. Select the server you want to look at and double-click it. A list of communication ports appears. For each port available on the server, you will see the user currently connected and the time connected.

From this dialog box, you can disconnect users or you can send a message to all users (or a single user) connected to the server. You also can check the port status, which shows you all the connection statistics for the selected port.

2. Dial-Up Networking Monitor

On the client side, the Dial-Up Networking Monitor is an application you can use to check the status of communications. There are three tabs in the monitor:

- **The Status tab:** Provides the dial-in user with basic information about the connection. From here, you have the option to hang up the connection or to view details about the connection. The details include names the client has registered on the network and the IP address assigned to the client (if using TCP/IP).
- **The Summary tab:** Summarizes all the connections the client currently has open.
- **The Preferences tab:** Enables the dial-in user to control the settings for Dial-Up Networking. Options that can be set include controlling when a sound is played and how the Dial-Up Networking monitor is presented to the user.

D. Other Issues that Affect RAS Connections

Other issues can affect a RAS connection, including authentication problems and the use of multilink when call-back security is enabled. Authentication can be a problem in two areas. First, a client might attempt to connect using the incorrect username and password. This easily can happen if the user is dialing from a home system. The RAS client can be set to attempt the connection using the current username and password, or it might have to unsave the previous password if it has changed on the network.

The other authentication problem occurs if the security settings on the server and the client do not match. You can get around this using the Allow Any Authentication setting or possibly by using the After Dial terminal window. If connection can be achieved using clear text, you must increase the encryption level on both the client and the server to use the highest level of encryption shared by both.

In the case of using call-back security with the multilink protocol, it is not supported over a Public Switched Telephone Network. The initial connection to the server uses multilink. When the server hangs up, however, it only has one number configured for the call-back configuration. The client only uses one line from this point on.

> **The only case in which call-back can be enabled for a multilink session is over an ISDN connection using two channels. The two channels must share the same phone number for this to work.**

12.5.1 Exercise: Creating a New Dialing Location

This exercise reviews the steps to create a new dialing location. The scenario is this—you are on the road and need to create a new dialing location to access an outside line from your hotel room to access your office network.

1. Open the Windows NT Control Panel by selecting Settings, Control Panel from the Start menu.
2. Open the Telephony applet to create a new dialing location.

3. Click the New button and name the new location Hotel.
4. Set the Area Code to 604 and the country to Canada.
5. Configure the options so you dial 8 to access an outside line for a local call and dial 9 to access an outside line for a long distance call.
6. Enable the checkbox to use a calling card and click the Change button to select the calling card type.
7. Select the Calling Card via 0 option. Enter the card number 80755512121234.
8. Click OK to save the new dialing location.

12.5.2 Exercise: Configuring a Phonebook Entry

This exercise creates a new phonebook entry and uses the dialing location setup in Exercise 12.5.1.

1. Double-click the My Computer icon on the desktop.
2. Double-click the Dial-Up Networking folder in the My Computer window.
3. Click the New button to create a new phonebook entry.
4. Name the new entry New Riders.
5. Set the phonebook entry to use Telephony properties.
6. Set the Area Code to 317.
7. Set the phone number to 555-1234.
8. Click the Alternates button to enter alternative phone numbers.
9. Add the phone number 555-2345. Try reordering the phone numbers. You also can select the option to move successful numbers to the top of the list.
10. Select the modem you want to use for the dial-up entry.
11. On the Server tab, select the NetBEUI protocol.
12. On the Security tab, select to use Microsoft Encrypted Authentication with data encryption. Note that on this tab, you can configure to use the current user and password combination. You also can erase a saved password.
13. Click OK to save the configuration.
14. In the Dial-Up Networking dialog box, set Hotel as the location. Note that the phone number appears as `9 0 317 555-1234 [Calling Card via 0]`.
15. Click the Location button.
16. Change the area code for the Hotel to 317 and click OK.
17. Note that the phone number now has changed to `8 555-1234`.

12.5 Practice Problems

1. Windows NT RAS Server can accept connections using which line protocols? Select all that apply.

    A. SLIP

    B. PPTP

    C. PPP

    D. TCP/IP

2. What does the Multilink Protocol provide?

    A. The capability to connect to a RAS server with multiple protocols.

    B. The capability to dial in to a RAS server from two or more clients at the same time.

    C. The capability to connect to a RAS server using multiple phone lines from the same client.

    D. The capability to connect with ADSL.

3. You have purchased a new modem for use with Dial-Up Networking in Windows NT Workstation., There is only a Windows 95 driver on the modem driver disk, and the Windows NT Workstation CD-ROM does not contain a driver for your new modem. How do you configure your modem for use?

    A. Edit the SWITCH.INFfile.

    B. Edit the MODEM.INFfile.

    C. Use a driver for an older version of the modem.

    D. Use the Windows 95 driver.

4. What advantages does PPP offer over SLIP when connecting to the Internet? Select all that apply.

    A. Auto configuration of TCP/IP

    B. Advanced scripting options for PPP versus SLIP

    C. Support for dial-in protocols other than TCP/IP

    D. Encrypted user authentication

5. How can RAS Server be configured to auto assign IP addresses to dial-in clients? Select all that apply.

    A. Use a DHCP server.

    B. Use the current IP address of the client.

    C. Have its own pool of IP addresses to assign to clients.

    D. This cannot be done. Clients must request their own IP addresses.

6. You want to install Internet tunnels to allow access to the corporate network over the Internet. What must be installed before you configure RAS to provide this capability?

    A. VPN Service

    B. PPTP protocol

    C. L2TP protocol

    D. This functionality is built into RAS and just needs to be configured.

7. You want to install an ISDN adapter on your Windows NT Server. Where do you add the adapter?

    A. On the Adapters page of the Net-works applet in the Control Panel.

    B. In the Modems applet of the Control Panel.

    C. In the SCSI Adapter applet of the Control Panel.

    D. In the WAN Adapter applet of the Control Panel.

8. What is the maximum number of inbound connections supported by Windows NT Server?

    A. 1

    B. 64

C. 256

D. Unlimited

9. What network protocols can be used over a PPP connection? Select all that apply.

A. NetBEUI

B. NWLink

C. TCP/IP

D. AppleTalk

10. Under what conditions can a dial-in Windows NT Workstation client access NetWare resources by dialing into a Windows NT Server? Select all that apply.

A. The client dials in via a SLIP connection to a RAS Server running Gateway Services for NetWare.

B. The client dials in via a PPP connection to a RAS Server running Gateway Services for NetWare.

C. The client dials in via a NWLink PPP connection and has Client Services for NetWare installed.

D. The client dials in via a NetBEUI PPP connection and has Client Services for NetWare installed.

11. What security features are included with RAS Server? Select all that apply.

A. Call-back Security

B. Integrated Domain Security

C. Kerberos Server Certificates

D. Support for Intermediary Security Hosts

12. Ruby is dialing in to the RAS server on your network. She complains that the line disconnects right after her user name has been authenticated. This happens every time she attempts to connect to the network, and no further communication exists. This is most likely due to which of the following?

A. The client is using the wrong network protocol.

B. Ruby has entered the wrong password for her account.

C. Ruby does not have dial-in permissions.

D. Call-back security has been set to a specific phone number for the client and is configured incorrectly.

13. What utilities can be used to assign dial-in permissions to user accounts? Select all that apply.

A. Remote Access Admin

B. Server Manager

C. User Manager for Domains

D. Registry Editor

14. What operating systems can be used to connect to a RAS Server over a PPTP tunnel? Select all that apply.

A. Windows for Workgroups 3.11

B. Windows 95

C. Windows NT Workstation 3.51

D. Windows NT Workstation 4.0

The following scenario applies to questions 15-17. A different solution to the scenario is proposed for each question.

Scenario: Your office wants to enable users to access the office network from home. The office is connected to the Internet through a fractional T1 line.

Required Result: The office has decided to provide only managers with dial-in access to the network. *Optional Result 1:* Because the network is being accessed from the homes of personnel, the office wants to encrypt all information transferred to and from the network. *Optional Result 2:* Due to the nature of the files the managers have access to on the network, it has been determined that call-back security will be implemented. The managers will be called back at a predetermined phone number.

15. *Proposed Solution*: Install a RAS Server that contains a digiboard on the local network. Set up four modems to enable the users to access the network. In User Manager for Domains, create a global group containing all the managers' accounts. In Remote Access Admin, assign the newly created global group the Dial-In permission. Set call-back security on the global group so the users can set the number to be called back at.

    This solution:

    A. Meets the required result and both optional results.

    B. Meets the required result and only one optional result.

    C. Meets only the required result.

    D. Does not meet the required result.

16. *Proposed Solution*: Install a RAS Server that contains a digiboard on the local network. Set up four modems to enable the users to access the network. Configure so that all clients require Microsoft Encrypted Authentication using data encryption. In User Manager for Domains, select each of the managers' user accounts and grant them Dial-In permissions. Set call-back security on each user account so the users can set the number at which to be called back.

    This solution:

    A. Meets the required result and both optional results.

    B. Meets the required result and only one optional result.

    C. Meets only the required result.

    D. Does not meet the required result.

17. *Proposed Solution*: Install a RAS Server that contains a digiboard on the local network. Set up four modems to enable the users to access the network. Configure so that all clients require Microsoft Encrypted Authentication using data encryption. In Remote Access Admin, select each of the managers' user accounts and grant them dial-in permissions. Set call-back security on each user account so each user is called back at a preconfigured phone number.

    A. Meets the required result and both optional results.

    B. Meets the required result and only one optional result.

    C. Meets only the required result.

    D. Does not meet the required result.

18. What methods can clients use to connect to RAS servers? Select all that apply.

    A. ISDN

    B. X.25

    C. RadioLan

    D. PSTN

19. What methods can be used to reduce dial-in phone charges? Select all that apply.

    A. Have all users use the same Internet account.

    B. Set call-back security by user.

    C. Establish a modem on an 800 line for remote users.

    D. Set logon preferences so each dial-in client disconnects if idle for at least 120 seconds.

20. A user notes that when logging on to the network using Dial-Up Networking, it seems to take an exceptionally long time for the logon process to complete. This is most likely due to which of the following?

    A. A roaming profile is being downloaded.

    B. A login script is being executed.

C. A virus scan is being run.

D. Authentication is always slow over a dial-in connection.

21. A user dials in to your RAS Server using multilink. The server uses call-back security to a user-specified number. The server successfully calls the user back, but the connection is not using multilink anymore. This is due to which of the following?

   A. The user must provide both phone numbers for multilink to work.

   B. The call-back security feature only works with multilink if it is configured to call back a preconfigured phone number.

   C. The user's modems are not on the multilink HCL.

   D. Multilink is not supported for call-back security.

22. Autodial can be enabled by which of the following?

   A. NetBIOS name

   B. Location

   C. IP address

   D. Time of day

23. Which service needs to be running to enable Autodial functionality?

   A. Server Service

   B. Remote Access Service

   C. Remote Access Autodial Manager

   D. Dial-Up Networking Service

24. Where is the file PPP.LOG stored on a NT Server?

   A. %SystemRoot%

   B. %SystemRoot%\System32

   C. %SystemRoot%\System32\PPP

   D. %SystemRoot%\System32\RasMan

25. Where can a network administrator view which users have connected to the network using the RAS service, how much data they transferred to and from the network, and how long the users were connected to the RAS server?

   A. PPP.LOG

   B. Remote Access Admin

   C. Event Viewer's System Log

   D. Dial-Up Network Monitor

26. Where can a network administrator view actual compression ratios as the user is connected to a Remote Access Server?

   A. PPP.LOG

   B. Network Monitor

   C. Event Viewer

   D. Dial-Up Network Monitor

27. What is the one case in which callback security over a multilink connection works?

   A. All modems on the server and the client are the same brand and model.

   B. The client is using Windows NT Server as the operating system.

   C. The connection is established using PPTP.

   D. The link between the server and the client uses ISDN with two channels that have the same phone number as the client.

28. A remote client has connected to the office's RAS Server using a NetBEUI PPP connection. The RAS Server is running the NWLink, TCP/IP, and NetBEUI protocols. The DATA server is only running the TCP/IP protocol, and the OFFICE server is only running the NWLink protocol. The MAIL server is only running the NetBEUI protocol. Which servers can the remote client connect to (and use file shares) if the

12

NetBEUI protocol has been configured to allow access to the entire network? Select all that apply.

A. The RAS server

B. The DATA server

C. The OFFICE server

D. The MAIL server

12.5.1 Answers and Explanations: Exercise

This exercise configured a new dialing location for use with Dial-Up Networking. By configuring a dialing location, you can automate how a phonebook entry is dialed. Dialing locations enable you to configure information such as the area code you are in, prefixes for accessing outside lines, whether the phone line is tone or pulse, and whether you want to use a calling card.

12.5.2 Answers and Explanations: Exercise

This exercise guided you through creating a new phonebook entry. It then investigated how the phone number changes as the location is modified.

You also could investigate changing your location rather than editing the existing location. This indicates how Dial-Up Networking can be configured to change the phone number dialed simply by changing the dialing location.

12.5 Answers and Explanations: Practice Problems

1. **B, C** PPP and PPTP are the only line protocols that a Windows NT RAS Server can accept connections over. SLIP is supported as a client protocol only in Windows NT RAS.
2. **C** Multilink enables multiple phone lines to be used to provide more bandwidth to the client.
3. **D** Windows 95 and Windows NT Workstation can use the same modem configuration files.
4. **A, C, D** PPP provides for auto-configuration, dial-in support for NetBEUI and NWLink, and the encryption of a user's name and password when authenticating.
5. **A, C** When using TCP/IP as a dial-in protocol, a RAS server can assign IP addresses using the network's DHCP server or from its own private pool.
6. **B** By installing the PPTP protocol, you can add Virtual Private Networks (VPNs) to RAS Server.
7. **A** Wide Area Network (WAN) adapters are added in the Adapters property page of the Network applet in the Control Panel.
8. **C** Windows NT has been tested to support 256 inbound RAS connections.
9. **A, B, C** NetBEUI, NWLink, and TCP/IP are all supported network protocols for a PPP session.
10. **B, C** A dial-in client can access a NetWare server if the dial-in server is running Gateway Services for NetWare or if the client is running Client Services for NetWare and using the NWLink protocol when dialing in to the network.
11. **A, B, D** Windows NT RAS Server includes support for call-back security, fully integrated domain authentication, and third-party security hosts such as radius servers.
12. **D** This situation can occur if call-back security has been implemented for a specific user and is set to call the user back at a predetermined number. In this case, the predetermined number is either incorrect or entered incorrectly.
13. **A, C** Dial-in permissions can be set in Remote Access Admin and User Manager for Domains.

14. **B, D** The PPTP protocol can be used in Windows 95 (using Dial-Up Networking version 1.2) and Windows NT Workstation 4.0.

15. **D** Dial-in permissions are granted to individual users, not groups.

16. **B** This solution fulfills the required result of granting secure access to the network. It also assigns the managers access using the User Manager for Domains. It does not meet the second optional result because if a user breaks into the network with a manager's account, he can configure the network to call him back at his own phone number.

17. **A** This solution fulfills all requirements. Remember that dial-in permissions also can be granted in Remote Access Admin. Implementing predetermined phone numbers ensures that the managers are calling in from an approved phone number.

18. **A, B, D** Remote Access Server supports connections via Public Switched Telephone Networks, ISDN, and X.25 networks.

19. **B, C, D** Setting call-back security can reduce costs if the office network is able to take advantage of reduced long distance charges. Likewise, use of an 800 number reduces long distance charges. Setting auto-disconnect times prevents charges from accumulating if the line is not active.

20. **A** If a roaming profile has been configured for a user, configure the client to use a locally cached version of the profile if a slow connection is detected. This is set in the User Profiles tab of the System applet in the Control Panel.

21. **D** Multilink is not supported for call-back security when using modems over Public Switched Telephone Networks.

22. **B** You configure auto-dial functionality by dialing location. This is enabled on a location-by-location basis by viewing the User Preferences in the Dial-Up Network Phonebook.

23. **C** The Remote Access Autodial Manager must be running for Autodial to be available.

24. **D** The PPP.LOG file is stored in the %Systemroot%\System32\RasMan directory.

25. **C** The Windows NT Event Viewer shows an information event after a RAS session has ended. The event contains information about who was connected, how long they were connected, and how much data was transferred over the connection.

26. **D** The Dial-Up Network Monitor shows actual compression information for incoming and outgoing data during a dial-up session.

27. **D** Multilink functionality is available only if the link between the client and the server is an ISDN line using two channels configured to use the same phone number. This is because call-back accepts only a single phone number as a parameter.

28. **A, B, C, D** All servers can be accessed because NetBEUI functions as a NetBIOS gateway, enabling access to servers not running the NetBEUI protocol

12.5 Key Words

Call-back Security

Multilink Protocol (MP)

PPP

PPTP

RAS

SLIP

12

12.6 Solving Connectivity Problems

Network connectivity problems center around the inability of a client to find the destination server on the network. This can be due to:

- Protocol issues
  - The protocol does not allow routing in a Wide Area Network.
  - The client and the server do not share a common protocol.
  - The protocol is configured improperly.
- Name resolution not being performed correctly
- A physical problem with the network

A. Protocol Issues that Affect Connectivity

Each protocol has issues that can affect network connectivity. Common to all protocols is the use of NetBIOS computer names in the Windows NT Networking model. When a client connects to a server, the client uses the Computer Name in the Universal Naming Convention (UNC) address. A UNC name is represented in the format *\\SERVER\SHARE.*

If a Microsoft networking-participant computer starts and finds that another computer has already registered its NetBIOS name, the networking services will not start. The remedy is to give the computer a unique name on the network. This problem can be diagnosed in the Windows NT Event Viewer in the System Log.

Each protocol has specific issues that can affect connectivity. The following sections detail potential problems with the NetBEUI, NWLink, and TCP/IP protocols.

1. NetBEUI Configuration Issues

NetBEUI is the simplest protocol to use on the network because it automatically configures itself to perform at its best possible level. The major issue with NetBEUI is that it is non-routable. If your network is broken into separate segments, clients using NetBEUI cannot communicate with servers on remote segments of the network. The only physical device that enables this connectivity is a bridge. A bridge logically connects two physical network segments into one large segment.

2. NWLink Configuration Issues

NWLink is Microsoft's 32-bit implementation of the IPX/SPX protocol standard. NWLink is a routable network commonly associated with Novell NetWare networks.

By default, NWLink alone enables you to interact with client/server class applications running on NetWare servers. It also enables a NetWare client to connect to a SQL server running on a Windows NT box. (The client must be running NetBIOS, which is optional in NetWare.)

If you want to be able to work with the file and print services of a Novell NetWare system, you need to add either Client Services for NetWare (on Windows NT Workstation) or Gateway (and Client) Services for NetWare (on Windows NT Server). These services enable your Windows NT system to become a Novell client.

If you want NetWare clients to use file and print resources on a Windows NT Server, you must load File and Print Services for NetWare. This enables a Windows NT server to emulate a NetWare 3.12 server, which a NetWare client can connect to using its native protocols.

> **Client Services for NetWare enables a user to authenticate to a Novell NetWare 4.x server by indicating the Preferred Tree and the default context. Unfortunately, you cannot manage the Directory Services using NetAdmin or NWAdmin because you have not fully authenticated into the Directory Services. You can do this only if you use NetWare's Windows NT client.**

The only configuration that needs to be checked when NWLink is installed is the frame type. NetWare servers use different frame types depending on the network topology and the version of NetWare in use. If you are having problems communicating with a Novell server, make sure the frame types are the same.

When the frame type is set to Automatic, only a single frame type is loaded. If both Ethernet 802.2 (the default for NetWare 3.12 and later versions) and Ethernet 802.3 (the default for NetWare 3.11 and later versions) are loaded, Windows NT defaults to the Ethernet 802.2 frame type. This prevents communication with any NetWare servers using only the 802.3 frame type.

3. TCP/IP Configuration Issues

The TCP/IP protocol is designed to enable wide area networking and is a routable protocol.

Most problems you encounter using the TCP/IP protocol deal with the actual configuration of the protocol. TCP/IP uses a 32-bit binary address to uniquely identify each host connected to a network. These 32 bits are separated into a network component and a host component.

The number of bits used to identify the network and host components is determined by the subnet mask configuration setting. The network portion is set to all 1s, and the host portion is set to all 0s. This is used to extract the network ID from the IP address, so the computer is able to determine whether a given address is local or remote. (If the network IDs match, it is local; otherwise, it is remote.)

Normally, the IP address is not viewed as a string of 32 1s and 0s; rather, look at it as four decimal numbers between 0 and 255, separated by dots (hence the name *dotted decimal notation*).

You can configure TCP/IP in two ways. You can enter all the information manually, or you can use a DHCP server that provides all the configuration information automatically for the participating hosts.

a. Manual IP Configuration

Be sure you enter each and every IP address used in communication correctly. A common problem with assigning IP addresses manually is that duplicate addresses can be assigned. It is imperative to use an organized method to distribute IP addresses when working with manual IP addresses.

After you have manually configured TCP/IP, you can use the Packet Internet Groper (ping) utility to verify your connectivity to the network.

After you have verified that you are able to communicate using these steps, you should attempt to ping other computers using their Fully Qualified Domain Names (FQDNs).

b. *Automatic TCP/IP Configuration*

For dynamically allocating IP address, the DHCP Server service is used to create a pool of IP addresses to be assigned to DHCP clients.

When a DHCP server is installed, the first configuration issue is setting up a pool of IP addresses to assign to DHCP clients. Another common issue is that the pool should not contain any IP addresses that have already been assigned on the network. In addition, if there are multiple DHCP servers on the network, the pool of addresses on each DHCP server should not overlap.

The DHCP server also must be assigned a lease duration. When setting the lease duration, keep these factors in mind:

- If the number of clients is very close to the number of IP addresses available to lease, the lease duration should be kept short.
- If the number of clients is low compared to the number of IP addresses available, longer lease durations can be set.
- Lease duration is applied on a scope-by-scope basis.
- DHCP clients renew their DHCP lease every time the computer is restarted, at 50 percent of the lease duration and at 87.5 percent of the lease duration.

In order to verify the IP configuration that a DHCP server has assigned to a DHCP client, you can use the IPCONFIG command. The IPCONFIG command—when entered without parameters—returns your IP address, your subnet mask, and your default gateway settings.

Microsoft DHCP clients not only can get their IP addresses and subnet mask settings from the DHCP server, several other options can be assigned as well, including:

- **[003] Router:** The Router setting contains the IP address for the default gateway for the subnet the DHCP client is on.
- **[006] DNS Server:** The DNS Server setting contains the IP addresses of the DNS server that the DHCP client can query when it needs to resolve a hostname or Fully Qualified Domain Name to an IP address.
- **[015] Domain Name:** The Domain Name setting contains the domain name the host is using in an intranet. The host www.company.com, for example, has its domain name set to company.com and its hostname to www.
- **[044] WINS/NBNS Servers:** The WINS/NBNS (NetBIOS Name Server) setting contains the IP addresses of servers that will provide a NetBIOS name to IP address-resolution services.
- **[046] WINS/NBT Node Type:** The WINS/NBT (NetBIOS over TCP/IP) Node Type determines what methods will be implemented (and in what order) to resolve a NetBIOS name to an IP address.

- **[047] NetBIOS Scope ID:** The NetBIOS Scope ID setting can segment NetBIOS clients into working groups that cannot communicate with each other (even if they are on the same network segment).

B. Name Resolution Issues

Microsoft networking clients use two methods of name resolution in their day-to-day transactions. When performing native Windows NT networking, they commonly use *NetBIOS name resolution*. When using intranet or Internet technologies, they use *hostname resolution*.

All protocols included with Windows NT support NetBIOS name resolution methods. The TCP/IP protocol requires that an additional service be installed for efficient resolution of NetBIOS names to IP addresses. This service is known as the WINS Server service.

Only the TCP/IP protocol provides the capability to resolve hostnames or Fully Qualified Domain Names to IP addresses. The TCP/IP protocol requires that a Domain Name Service (DNS) server assist in the resolution of hostnames to IP addresses.

1. The WINS Server Service

The WINS Server service provides a centralized database of NetBIOS names to IP address mappings. WINS clients automatically register their NetBIOS names and IP address to the WINS server every time they start.

WINS clients can be configured to use the WINS server as their primary method of NetBIOS name resolution. There are four methods of NetBIOS name resolution that the WINS clients can use: B-node, P-Node, M-Node, or H-Node.

2. The DNS Server Service

The DNS Server service provides hostname-to-IP address resolution. Hostnames are used for most common Internet applications, such as FTP, Web browsing, Telnet, and IRC. The resolution of hostnames to IP addresses is performed by three components:

- **Domain Name Space:** Every host on the Internet requires a unique Fully Qualified Domain Name. The registration of each unique name is managed by Internic to ensure that duplication does not occur.
- **Name Resolver:** Any client that needs to resolve a hostname to an IP address is functioning as a name resolver.
- **Name Server:** The name server contains lists of hostnames and their IP addresses. The name server can contain records that represent services (for example, a Mail Exchanger record to represent that a host is the mail server for a domain) or aliases for hosts.

If you are unable to resolve hostnames on the Internet using a Web browser or FTP client, you must check whether you have configured the correct IP address for your DNS server. The NSLOOKUP command can be used to determine whether the hostname is being resolved correctly on your DNS Server. The NSLOOKUP commands syntax is as follows:

```
NSLOOKUP <hostname>
```

This returns the resolved IP address for the entered hostname. It also can be run in a batch mode by simply typing **NSLOOKUP**.

C. Physical Network Problems

If the network has suffered breakdowns in its physical components, this also can lead to the inability of clients to connect to servers. If information cannot flow between two sites due to a downed router, connectivity cannot take place. A Simple Network Management Protocol (SNMP) management utility can assist in diagnosing a breakdown in the physical network in a timely fashion. Windows NT includes SNMP services that enable an NT client to be managed by an SNMP manager. It does not provide any management software itself. These are generally third-party products such as HP OpenView.

D. Tools for Troubleshooting Connectivity Problems

Windows NT contains several tools that can be used to troubleshoot connectivity problems. These include

- The Network Monitor
- The Server Manager
- The TRACERT command
- The NETSTAT command

The Network Monitor application can be used to examine network traffic and to monitor network performance. The Network Monitor is a network sniffer and can be used to check for the following:

- **Bad packet cyclic redundancy checks (CRCs):** A packet with a bad CRC value indicates that the packet is corrupted.
- **Network saturation:** This is caused by a network card constantly sending broadcast packets.
- **Packet Recognition:** Understanding what common traffic flows should look like can help in diagnosing a communication error. Detecting where communication is breaking down can assist in determining where the problem lies and can lead to a quicker resolution. You might notice, for example, that the DHCP client is placing Discover packets onto the network, but the DHCP server is not sending offers. You can rule out that the problem is on the client.

The Server Manager program can be used to manage services running on a Windows NT computer. If the workstation or server service is not functioning on a Windows NT computer, this can lead to connectivity failure if the computer is part of an equation.

The TRACERT command can be used to determine what route is taken when a computer attempts to communicate with a host on a remote network. It also reports how many routers have been crossed when the remote host is communicated with.

The NETSTAT command can be used to determine what ports are in use when a communication session is taking place. TCP/IP Winsock applications use preconfigured ports to connect. Many networks now have firewalls in place that prevent certain ports from being used. The NETSTAT command can be used to determine which ports might need to be opened on a firewall.

12.6.1 Exercise: Investigating NetBIOS Names

This exercise guides you through using the NBTSTAT command to investigate what NetBIOS names your computer has registered on the network. This exercise assumes that the TCP/IP protocol is installed on your system.

1. Start a command prompt.
2. At the command prompt, type the following command:

   ```
   C:\>nbtstat -n
   ```

   You will see output similar to the following:

   ```
   Node IpAddress: [131.107.2.200] Scope Id: []

         NetBIOS Local Name Table

     Name         Type     Status
   ---------------------------------------------
   SIDESHOWBRI  <00> UNIQUE   Registered
   CLASSROOMB   <00> GROUP    Registered
   CLASSROOMB   <1C> GROUP    Registered
   SIDESHOWBRI  <20> UNIQUE   Registered
   CLASSROOMB   <1B> UNIQUE   Registered
   SIDESHOWBRI  <03> UNIQUE   Registered
   CLASSROOMB   <1E> GROUP    Registered
   INet~Services <1C> GROUP    Registered
   IS~SIDESHOWBRI.<00> UNIQUE   Registered
   CLASSROOMB   <1D> UNIQUE   Registered
   ..__MSBROWSE__.<01> GROUP    Registered
   ADMINISTRATOR <03> UNIQUE   Registered
   ```

3. Based on the information you see, is this computer a Primary Domain Controller? If so, what entry tells you this? What is the name of the domain?
4. What is the name of the user logged in to this system? Which entry tells you this?
5. Is the computer a master browser on the subnet where it is located? Which entry tells you this?

12.6.2 Exercise: Troubleshooting NWLink Configuration Errors

This exercise shows you how to troubleshoot if a client is unable to connect to any resources when using the NWLink protocol. This exercise assumes the NWLink protocol is installed on your computer.

1. Start a command prompt.
2. Type the following command:

   ```
   C:\>ipxroute config
   ```

You should see output similar to the following:

```
NWLink IPX Routing and Source Routing Control Program v2.00
net 1: network number 00000000, frame type 802.2, device CE31
(0080c72254bf)
```

3. What is the network number assigned to your network card?
4. When would you see multiple network numbers?
5. What is the MAC address of your network adapter?
6. What issues are involved with the frame type configuration?

12.6 Practice Problems

1. What connectivity feature of Windows NT enables secure access to a Windows NT network over public networks?

   A. PPP

   B. SLIP

   C. PPTP

   D. NetBIOS Scope ID

2. The two offices of MNO Office Supplies are linked by a dedicated T1 line. The network is configured to use NetBEUI as its network protocol. Users can connect to any servers on their network segment, but cannot view resources on the remote network segment. This is due to which of the following?

   A. They require a WINS server.

   B. They need to configure LMHOSTS files at each computer.

   C. A static route needs to be added on the router to direct traffic between the two segments.

   D. NetBEUI does not support routing.

3. You want to connect to a client/server application located on a NetWare server. What must be configured on your Windows NT Workstation to enable connectivity?

   A. NWLink protocol

   B. RIP for IPX

   C. Client Services for NetWare

   D. SAP Agent

4. You want to connect to a printer hosted by a NetWare server. What must be configured on your Windows NT Workstation to enable connectivity? Select all that apply.

   A. NWLink protocol

   B. RIP for IPX

   C. Client Services for NetWare

   D. SAP Agent

The following scenario applies to questions 5–7. A different solution to the scenario is proposed for each question.

Scenario: Your network is running a mix of NetWare and Windows NT servers. All your client systems are using the Windows NT Workstation operating system.

5. *Required Result:* Connectivity must be established to file and print services in both the NetWare and Windows NT environments. *Optional Result 1:* You want to be able to manage the users in the Windows NT domain from your own Windows NT Workstation computer. *Optional Result 2:* You want to be able to manage the users on the NetWare 4.x servers in your environment.

   Proposed Solution: Add Client Services for NetWare and the NWLink protocol to all your Windows NT client systems. Configure Client Services for NetWare to authenticate to the correct Directory Tree and to set the correct default context. Perform user management on the Windows NT domain with the User Manager utility, and use the NWADMIN.EXE utility to manage the NetWare servers.

   This solution:

   A. Meets the required result and both of the optional results.

   B. Meets the required result and only one of the optional results.

   C. Meets only the required result.

   D. Does not meet the required result.

6. *Required Result:* Connectivity must be established to file and print services in both the NetWare and Windows NT environments. *Optional Result 1:* You want to be able to manage the users in the Windows NT domain from your own Windows NT Workstation computer. *Optional Result 2:* You want to be able to manage the users on the NetWare 3.x servers in your environment.

Proposed Solution: Add Client Services for NetWare and the NWLink protocol to all your Windows NT client systems. Configure Client Services for NetWare with the correct Preferred Server setting. Perform user management on the Windows NT domain with the User Manager utility, and use the SYSCON.EXE utility to manage the NetWare servers.

This solution:

A. Meets the required result and both optional results.

B. Meets the required result and only one optional result.

C. Meets only the required result.

D. Does not meet the required result.

7. *Required Result:* Connectivity must be established to file and print services in both the NetWare and Windows NT environments. *Optional Result 1:* You want to be able to manage the users in the Windows NT domain from your own Windows NT Workstation computer. *Optional Result 2:* You want to be able to manage the users on the NetWare 3.x servers in your environment.

   Proposed Solution: Add Client Services for NetWare and the NWLink protocol to all your Windows NT client systems. Configure Client Services for NetWare with the correct Preferred Server setting, and install Server Tools for Windows NT. Perform user management on the Windows NT domain using the User Manager for Domains utility, use the SYSCON.EXE utility to manage the NetWare servers.

   This solution:

   A. Meets the required result and both optional results.

   B. Meets the required result and only one optional result.

   C. Meets only the required result.

   D. Does not meet the required result.

8. Your network has a mix of NetWare 3.x and NetWare 4.x servers. A Windows NT workstation cannot connect to all the NetWare servers even though Client Services for NetWare and NWLink appear to be properly configured. What potentially is the problem?

   A. There are frame type issues.

   B. Preferred Server is configured incorrectly.

   C. The default context is set incorrectly.

   D. You need to switch the default network provider to NetWare from Microsoft.

9. What service is used in TCP/IP networks to resolve NetBIOS names to IP addresses?

   A. DNS

   B. WINS

   C. DHCP

   D. SNMP

10. What service is used in TCP/IP networks to resolve Fully Qualified Domain Names to IP addresses?

    A. DNS

    B. WINS

    C. DHCP

    D. SNMP

11. Which protocol in the TCP/IP protocol suite is used to resolve an IP address to a physical MAC address?

    A. WINS

    B. Services for Macintosh

    C. SNMP

    D. ARP

The following scenario applies to questions 12–14. A different solution to the scenario is proposed for each question.

Scenario: The Cosmos Corporation wants to use TCP/IP as the primary protocol on the wide area network between two sites. The corporation has had issues assigning IP addresses to all the hosts on its network and has brought in your consulting firm to assist with the IP address rollout.

Required Result: The Cosmos Corporation wants to reduce the number of hosts that require manual IP address configuration. *Optional Result 1:* The Cosmos Corporation wants to provide fault tolerance in case the primary IP address-assignment server fails. *Optional Result 2*: The Cosmos Corporation wants to reduce the broadcast traffic on the network.

12. *Proposed Solution:* Set up two DHCP servers on separate segments with the Scope of IP addresses set as shown in Table 12.6.1:

    Also configure a DHCP relay agent on each network segment to forward any DHCP packets to the DHCP server on the remote segment.

    This solution:

    A. Meets the required result and both optional results.

    B. Meets the required result and only one optional result.

    C. Meets only the required result.

    D. Does not meet the required result.

13. *Proposed Solution*: Set up two DHCP servers on separate segments with the Scope of IP addresses set as shown in Table 12.6.2:

    Also configure a DHCP relay agent on each network segment to forward any DHCP packets to the DHCP server on the remote segment.

    This solution:

    A. Meets the required result and both optional results.

    B. Meets the required result and only one optional result.

    C. Meets only the required result.

    D. Does not meet the required result.

14. *Proposed Solution*: Set up two DHCP servers on separate segments with the Scope of IP addresses set as shown in Table 12.6.3:

    Also configure a DHCP relay agent on each network segment to forward any DHCP packets to the DHCP server on the remote segment.

    This solution:

    A. Meets the required result and both optional results.

    B. Meets the required result and only one optional result.

    C. Meets only the required result.

    D. Does not meet the required result.

Table 12.6.1

	Server1	Server2
Scope	192.168.2.10–192.168.3.254 with subnet mask 255.255.0.0	192.168.2.10–192.168.3.254 with subnet mask 255.255.0.0
Scope Options	Def Gateway—192.168.2.1 DNS Server—192.168.3.9	Def Gateway—192.168.3.1 DNS Server—192.168.3.9

Table 12.6.2

	Server1	Server2
Scope1	192.168.2.10–192.168.2.200 with subnet mask 255.255.255.0	192.168.3.10–192.168.3.200 with subnet mask 255.255.255.0
Scope2	192.168.3.201–192.168.3.254 with subnet mask 255.255.255.0	192.168.2.201–192.168.2.254 with subnet mask 255.255.255.0
Scope1 Options	Def Gateway—192.168.2.1 WINS Server—192.168.2.8 WINS Node Type—Mixed	Def Gateway—192.168.3.1 WINS Server—192.168.2.8 WINS Node Type—Mixed
Scope 2 Options	Def Gateway—192.168.3.1 WINS Server—192.168.2.8 WINS Node Type—Mixed	Def Gateway—192.168.2.1 WINS Server—192.168.2.8 WINS Node Type—Mixed

Table 12.6.3

	Server1	Server2
Scope1	192.168.2.10–192.168.2.200 with subnet mask 255.255.255.0	192.168.3.10–192.168.3.200 with subnet mask 255.255.255.0
Scope2	192.168.3.201–192.168.3.254 with subnet mask 255.255.255.0	192.168.2.201–192.168.2.254 with subnet mask 255.255.255.0
Scope1 Options	Def Gateway—192.168.2.1 WINS Server—192.168.2.8 WINS Node Type—Hybrid	Def Gateway—192.168.3.1 WINS Server—192.168.2.8 WINS Node Type—Hybrid
Scope 2 Options	Def Gateway—192.168. 3.1 WINS Server—192.168.2.8 WINS Node Type—Hybrid	Def Gateway—192.168.2.1 WINS Server—192.168.2.8 WINS Node Type—Hybrid

15. What file can be used instead of WINS to provide NetBIOS name resolution?

    A. HOSTS

    B. LMHOSTS

    C. LMHOSTS.SAM

    D. HOSTS.SAM

16. How do you optimize network protocol usage when multiple protocols are installed on a system?

    A. Adjust the network bindings.

    B. Set a default protocol.

    C. Install the protocols in the order you prefer to use them.

    D. This cannot be done.

17. Which methods are used to reduce browser traffic on a network? Select all that apply.

    A. Disable file and print sharing on any clients that do not require these services.

    B. Disable the Browser service on all clients.

    C. Adjust the binding order on all clients.

    D. Reduce the number of protocols on the network.

The following scenario applies to questions 18–20. A different solution to the scenario is proposed for each question.

Scenario: The Pelican Insurance Company wants to enable file and print connectivity to its Windows NT server for its NetWare clients. Pelican created the following requirements for this system.

Required Result: Pelican wants to create common file-storage locations for both the NetWare and Windows NT clients. *Optional Result 1*: Pelican wants to establish common drive-letter mappings for both NetWare and Windows NT users. *Optional Result 2*: Pelican wants to limit the number of protocols in use on the network.

18. *Proposed Solution*: Install Gateway Services for NetWare on the Windows NT server to enable connectivity to Windows NT resources. Set a login script in the %systemroot%\System32\repl\import\scripts directory that establishes common drive letters for NetWare and Windows NT clients. Install the TCP/IP protocol on all servers and clients.

    This solution:

    A. Meets the required result and both optional results.

    B. Meets the required result and only one optional result.

    C. Meets only the required result.

    D. Does not meet the required result.

19. *Proposed Solution*: Install File and Print Services for NetWare on the Windows NT server to enable connectivity to Windows NT resources by NetWare clients. Set a login script in the %systemroot%\System32\repl\import\scripts directory that establishes common drive letters for Windows NT clients. Install the NWLink protocol on all servers and clients.

    This solution:

    A. Meets the required result and both optional results.

    B. Meets the required result and only one optional result.

    C. Meets only the required result.

    D. Does not meet the required result.

20. *Proposed Solution*: Install File and Print Services for NetWare on the Windows NT server to enable connectivity to Windows NT resources by NetWare clients. Set a login script in the %systemroot%\System32\repl\import\scripts directory that establishes common drive letters for Windows NT clients. Configure a login script in the NetWare compatibility settings so that each NetWare client uses the same drive mappings. Install the NWLink protocol on all servers and clients.

    This solution:

    A. Meets the required result and both optional results.

    B. Meets the required result and only one optional result.

    C. Meets only the required result.

    D. Does not meet the required result.

21. Which protocol offers routing capabilities with the least amount of configuration?

    A. NetBEUI

    B. NWLink

    C. TCP/IP

    D. DLC

22. Your Windows NT server is configured with both the TCP/IP and NWLink protocols. The TCP/IP protocol is used only for enabling connections from Microsoft clients; the NWLink protocol is used to connect to a client/server application hosted on a NetWare server. What binding adjustments can be performed to optimize the network protocols? Select all that apply.

    A. Disable the TCP/IP protocol for the Workstation Service.

    B. Disable the NWLink protocol for the Workstation Service.

    C. Disable the TCP/IP protocol for the Server Service.

    D. Disable the NWLink protocol for the Server Service.

23. Which protocols can be used to connect to IBM mainframes? Select all that apply.

 A. NetBEUI

 B. NWLink

 C. TCP/IP

 D. DLC

24. You use the network monitor to diagnose why clients on a remote subnet are taking a long time to authenticate on the network. It is discovered that the clients are all authenticating with a BDC on a remote subnet rather than the local BDC. What setting should you use to configure the NetBIOS node type on this subnet to speed up authentication, yet enable authentication from remote BDCs if the local BDC is down?

 A. Pointed

 B. Broadcast

 C. Mixed

 D. Hybrid

25. Which command can be used to determine how many routers are crossed when communicating with a remote TCP/IP network?

 A. ROUTE.EXE

 B. TRACERT.EXE

 C. NETSTAT.EXE

 D. NET CONFIG

26. What command can be used to determine which ports are in use during a network session?

 A. ROUTE.EXE

 B. NBTSTAT.EXE

 C. NETSTAT.EXE

 D. NET CONFIG

27. Which commands can be used to view your network adapter's MAC address? Select all that apply.

 A. IPCONFIG /ALL

 B. ARP -A

 C. NBTSTAT -n

 D. NET CONFIG WORKSTATION

28. You can connect to any computers on your local network segment using TCP/IP, but not to any computers on remote network segments. Which of the following is a likely cause of the problem?

 A. Incorrect subnet mask

 B. Incorrect default gateway

 C. Incorrect DNS setting

 D. Incorrect WINS setting

29. What line can be entered in the LMHOSTS file to preload the address 172.16.3.16 for the Primary Domain Controller XERXES in the XANADU domain?

 A. `172.16.3.16 XERXES #CACHE #DOM:XANADU`

 B. `XERXES 172.16.3.16 #CACHE #DOM:XANADU`

 C. `172.16.3.16 XERXES #PRE #DOM:XANADU`

 D. `XERXES 172.16.3.16 #PRE #DOM:XANADU`

12.6.1 Answers and Explanations: Exercise

This exercise helped you recognize the NetBIOS names a computer registers on the network. Knowing the NetBIOS name registrations can help you recognize when a service has failed. You also can use the NBTSTAT command to view your NetBIOS name cache. The NetBIOS name cache contains the NetBIOS names that have been resolved by your computer. The answers to the specific questions posed in the exercise are:

3. This computer is a Primary Domain Controller. The entry `CLASSROOMB <1B>` is registered only by the PDC for a domain. This computer is a PDC for the CLASSROOMB domain.

4. The Administrator is currently logged on to the system. This is based on the `Administrator <03>` entry. The <03> entry is registered by the messenger service.

5. Yes. This computer is a master browser on the subnet. This is based on the `..__MSBROWSE__.<01>` entry. The master browser for a workgroup or domain on a subnet registers this NetBIOS name.

12.6.2 Answers and Explanations: Exercise

This exercise investigated the use of the IPXROUTE command. The IPXROUTE command also can be used to determine which servers are using the Server Advertising Protocol (SAP) and to display routing statistics if RIP for IPX/SPX is installed. The answers to the specific questions asked in this exercise are:

```
NWLink IPX Routing and
Source Routing Control
Program v2.00

net 1: network number
00000000, frame type
802.2, device CE31
(0080c72254bf)
```

3. The network number assigned to this network card is 00000000. This is the default value used when automatic frame configuration is chosen.

4. You would see multiple network numbers in one of two cases. First, if the network card has been configured to use multiple frame types, each frame type would be assigned a unique network number. The other case is when multiple network cards are installed on the system. Each card would have a unique network number.

5. The MAC address of the network card in question is 0080C72254BF.

6. If the Windows NT computer is using a different frame type than the rest of the computers on the network, then communication will not take place on the network segment using NWLink.

12.6 Answers and Explanations: Practice Problems

1. **C** PPTP enables secure tunnels to be established over public networks such as the Internet.

2. **D** NetBEUI is fast performing and requires no configuration, but it does not support routing. This protocol cannot be used to link two remote offices.

3. **A** Connecting to a client/server application on a NetWare server only requires the NWLink protocol.

4. **A, C** To use file and print services on a NetWare server, a Windows NT Workstation computer requires both the NWLink protocol and Client Services for NetWare.

5. **A** This solution meets only the required result. You must use User Manager for Domains (not User Manager) to manage users in a Windows NT domain. The NWAdmin utility cannot be used with Client Services for NetWare because the user has not logged in to the directory services of NetWare. To run NWAdmin, you must load the NetWare client for Windows NT.

6. **B** You can manage a NetWare 3.x server running both Client Services for NetWare and SYSCON.EXE, but you must run User Manager for Domains to manage users in a Windows NT domain.

7. **A** If you install the Server Tools for Windows NT Workstation, you can manage the Windows NT domain with User Manager for Domains.

8. **A** If Windows NT is set to auto-detect frame types, it defaults to an Ethernet 802.2 frame if it detects both Ethernet 802.2 and Ethernet 802.3 frame types on the network. NetWare 3.11 (and earlier versions) used 802.3 as the default frame type. NetWare 3.12 and 4.x use Ethernet 802.2 as the default frame type.
9. **B** WINS provides NetBIOS-to-IP address resolution in a Windows NT network.
10. **A** DNS provides FQDN-to-IP address resolution in a Windows NT network.
11. **D** The Address Resolution Protocol (ARP) is used to resolve an IP address to a MAC address.
12. **A** This solution does not work. You do not want to create overlapping scopes on the two servers. Even though the DHCP relay agent would pass requests to the other server, the clients would receive incorrect default gateway information if they received an IP address from the other subnet's server.
13. **B** The first two requirements are met. Using DHCP assists in reducing manual configuration by properly configuring the scopes on each server to not overlap. By using a mixed node type, however, NetBIOS name resolution is performed first using a broadcast and then a WINS lookup.
14. **A** This solution meets all the requirements.
15. **B** The LMHOSTS file can be used to provide NetBIOS name resolution in Microsoft networking. It must be located in the %Systemroot%\System32\Drivers\Etc directory.
16. **A** To optimize network protocols, you should order the bindings for each network service to use the desired protocols first.
17. **A, D** By disabling file and print sharing on unnecessary clients, you reduce the number of computers making browser announcements on the network. By reducing the number of protocols on the network, you reduce the total number of browser election packets as a separate election for browse masters that occur for each protocol.
18. **D** Gateway Services for NetWare enable Microsoft clients to intermittently use file and print services on a NetWare server. This scenario requires NetWare clients to connect to resources on a Windows NT server.
19. **B** Only Windows NT clients can process login batch files in the NETLOGON share. This does not meet the first optional result.
20. **A** This solution meets all requirements.
21. **B** NWLink requires the least configuration for a routable protocol.
22. **A, D** The TCP/IP protocol is not used when acting as a client, and the NWLink protocol is not used to enable other systems to connect to file shares. You can disable these bindings to optimize the network bindings on the system.
23. **C, D** TCP/IP and DLC can be used to connect to IBM mainframes.
24. **C** By using Mixed for the NetBIOS node type, the client first broadcasts and then uses a WINS lookup.
25. **B** The TRACERT command indicates how many routers are crossed when communicating with a remote host.
26. **C** The NETSTAT command shows which ports are in use during a network session.
27. **A, D** The IPCONFIG /ALL and NET CONFIG WORKSTATION commands can be used to view your network adapter's MAC address.

28. **B** If the default gateway is configured incorrectly, you can connect only to local hosts.

29. **C** The correct syntax for an LMHOSTS entry is `<IP Address> <NetBIOS Name> #PRE #DOM:<Domain name>`.

12.6 Key Words

Client Services for NetWare (CSNW)

File and Print Services for NetWare

Frame types

Gateway Services for NetWare

IPCONFIG

NBTSTAT

NetBEUI

NetBIOS

NETSTAT

NWLink

Ping

TCP/IP

TRACERT

12.7 Solving Resource Access and Permissions Problems

When resources cannot be accessed, and there is not a network connectivity problem, it generally can be attributed to incorrect share or NTFS permissions. This section discusses how to troubleshoot resource access problems that result from incorrect permissions, and how share and NTFS permissions interact with each other.

Another issue is group usage in a multidomain environment. Planning your domain environment for growth and using groups in your security assignments can assist you in creating a security environment that will expand into a multidomain environment.

A. Share Permissions

In Windows NT networking, shares provide an access point into a server's file stores. Setting share permissions determines which users have access to a file share and what level of access they have.

Share permissions do not change from the entry-point directory. In other words, if a user only has Read access to a shared directory, that user also only has Read access to all subdirectories. The shared permissions that can be assigned to a directory include:

- **No Access:** No Access permissions override all other permissions assigned to a shared directory. If a user (or a group the user is a member of) is assigned No Access permissions, he cannot gain access to the file share.
- **Read:** Read permissions enable the assigned user to view documents, to copy information from the shared directory, and to run programs.
- **Change:** Change permissions include all the privileges of the Read permission, plus the capability to modify and to delete any files contained in the shared directory.
- **Full Control:** Full Control permissions include all the privileges of the Change permission, plus the capability to change the share permissions on the shared directory.

By default, a newly created file share is assigned to the EVERYONE special group with Full Control permissions. This default generally should be changed because it grants access rights to the file share.

It is recommended that you never use the EVERYONE special group when assigning permissions. The EVERYONE special group includes all users that connect to the file share, including users you do not know about. It is better to use the local group USERS.

Some final issues that must be considered when you use share permissions are:

- Share permissions can be applied only to directory objects. You cannot apply share permissions to the file's level of access.
- On FAT volumes, share permissions are the only level of security that can be applied.
- Share permissions can be applied only to users connecting through the network. Share permissions do not apply to local security.

B. NTFS Permissions

When you use NTFS volumes, you can apply NTFS permissions. NTFS permissions can be applied to both directories and files. This enables the administrator to assign varying levels of access to files within the same directory structure. It is therefore possible to have many different files in a directory that have their own individual permissions. There are six specific NTFS permissions that can be assigned to directories and files. They are:

- **Read (R):** Allows viewing the names of files and subdirectories.
- **Write (W):** Allows adding files and subdirectories.
- **Execute (X):** Allows changing to subdirectories in the directory.
- **Delete (D):** Allows deleting the directory.
- **Change Permissions (P):** Allows changing the directory's permissions.
- **Take Ownership (O):** Allows taking ownership of the directory.

Due to POSIX compliance, Windows NT has an exception rule that appears to break the NTFS permissions. If an NTFS folder is assigned the NTFS Full Control permissions, users can delete a file even if they have been assigned No Access permissions on the file. This is because, under POSIX, if users have full control of a directory, they can perform any task to the underlying files.

If you do not want this to be the case, assign the special permissions Read, Write, Execute, Delete, Permissions, and Ownership. Even though this is equivalent to Full Control permissions, the Windows NT operating system recognizes that they have been assigned separately. The Windows NT operating system then does not allow the deletion of a file if file-level permissions prevent it.

C. Combining Permissions

One thing that complicates matters is that you can assign both NTFS permissions and share permissions to a folder. In addition, the files in a share also can have NTFS file permissions. The effective permissions will be the most restrictive of the share and NTFS permissions. Evaluate each set of permissions separately, then compare them to determine which is most restrictive.

A good rule of thumb is to set the share permissions to the maximum level of NTFS permissions required within the directory structure. If you use this rule, you only have to troubleshoot the NTFS permissions. This is because the NTFS permissions are always the most restrictive.

D. Implementing Permissions in a Multidomain Environment

When assigning permissions, make sure you use the Account-Global Groups-Local Groups-Permissions (AGLP) methodology, as follows:

- An account is created for each user.
- The accounts are grouped together into global groups. Global groups can only contain accounts from the same domain. If multiple domains exist, you need to create a global group in each of the domains.

- The global groups are made members of local groups in the domain in which the resource exists. If the resource exists on a domain controller, the local group is created in the domain account database. If the resource exists on a Windows NT Member Server or NT Workstation, you create the local group in the account database of that system.

> **You do not have to go to the specific system to add a local group to a Member Server or NT Workstation account database. In User Manager for Domains, you can modify a computer's account database by typing \\\\computername in the dialog box presented when you choose Select Domain from the User menu.**

- The local group(s) are assigned the appropriate permissions.

This methodology should be applied to both NTFS and share permissions. If you use this methodology, it expands well into a multidomain environment.

Remember that in a multidomain environment, appropriate trust relationships must be established. A trust relationship should be established so the Resource domains trust the Account domains. In this case, local groups in the Resource domains can have global groups from the Account domains assigned as members.

E. Other Issues with NTFS Permissions

When a file is copied or moved on an NTFS partition, the permissions might change. This can lead to unexpected resource access problems when the NTFS permissions are not what was expected. Remember the following rules for moving and copying files:

- When a file is copied into an NTFS directory, the file assumes the NTFS permissions of the target directory.
- If a file is moved to an NTFS directory on the same NTFS partition, the file retains its original NTFS permissions.
- If a file is moved to an NTFS directory on a different NTFS partition, the file assumes the NTFS permissions of the target directory.
- If a file is moved or copied to a non-NTFS partition, all NTFS permissions are lost.

12.7.1 Exercise: Testing NTFS Permissions

This exercise requires a single NTFS partition to test NTFS permission assignments.

1. Open the Windows NT Explorer.
2. Select the NTFS drive in the left pane and select File, New, Folder from the menus. Name the folder NTFSTEST.
3. Right-click the NTFSTEST folder and select Properties from the pop-up menu.
4. Select the Security tab and click the Permissions button.
5. Note that security is set to EVERYONE with Full Control permissions by default. Click the Remove button to remove the EVERYONE permission assignment.

6. Click the Add button and select the Users local group. Set the type of access to Change.
7. Click the OK button to set the new permissions and click the following OK button to close the properties of the folder.
8. Select the NTFSTEST folder in the left pane.
9. Select File, New, Text File from the menu to create a new document in the folder. Name it RIGHTS.
10. Right-click the RIGHTS file in the right pane and select Properties.
11. From the menu, select the Security tab and select Permissions.
12. Note that the permissions for the newly created file also are Change permissions. This is because new files inherit the permissions of the parent directory.
13. Change the type of access to No Access. You are warned that No Access permissions prevent any users from accessing the object after you click the OK button to change the permissions. Click the Yes button to acknowledge the warning.
14. Attempt to open the file. What is the error message you receive?
15. Start a command prompt and change the current directory to NTFSTEST.
16. Attempt to delete the file. Can you delete the file? Why or why not?
17. Change the permissions on the directory to Full Control for the Users group. Be sure not to apply the changes to the files in the directory.
18. Attempt to delete the file again. Can you delete the file? Why or why not?

12.7.2 Exercise: Testing the Effects of Copying and Moving

This exercise tests how copying and moving affects NTFS permissions. This exercise assumes the NTFSTEST directory still exists and the USERS group has Full Control permissions.

1. Start the Windows NT Explorer.
2. In the root directory of your NTFS partition, create a new text file. Name it Change.
3. Assign the new text file Administrators permissions and Change permissions.
4. Create another text file in the root directory. Name it READ.
5. Assign this file Administrators permissions and Read permissions.
6. Copy the Change file to the NTFSTEST directory.
7. Move the Read file to the NTFSTEST directory.
8. What are the permissions on each file?

12.7 Practice Problems

1. What are the default permissions assigned to a new file share?

   A. Users, Change permissions

   B. Everyone, Change permissions

   C. Users, Full Control

   D. Everyone, Full Control

2. The ACME Corporation has offices in St. Louis, Vancouver, and New Orleans. Each office has been installed with its own Windows NT domain. The ACME Corporation wants all user accounts in the domain to be managed at the head office in St. Louis. Select the trust relationships that must be established. Select all that apply.

   A. St. Louis must trust Vancouver.

   B. Vancouver must trust St. Louis.

   C. New Orleans must trust St. Louis.

   D. St. Louis must trust New Orleans.

3. The ACME Corporation wants all administrators in the St. Louis domain to be able to manage the two remote domains. What group memberships must be implemented to accomplish this?

   A. Assign the Administrators group from the St. Louis domain to be a member of the Domain Admins group in the New Orleans and Vancouver domains.

   B. Assign the Administrators group from the St. Louis domain to be a member of the Administrators group in both the New Orleans and Vancouver domains.

   C. Assign the Domain Admins group from the St. Louis domain to be a member of the Administrators group in the New Orleans and Vancouver domains.

   D. Assign the Domain Admins group from the Vancouver and New Orleans domains to be members of the Administrators group in the St. Louis domain.

4. Which Windows NT utilities can be used to set share permissions on the local computer? Select all that apply.

   A. User Manager for Domains

   B. Server Manager

   C. Windows NT Explorer

   D. File Manager

5. When Jim attempts to log on to a Windows NT workstation, he receives the message that he cannot log on locally. What configuration change must be made to grant Jim permission to log on locally?

   A. Make Jim a member of the Administrators local group.

   B. Configure Jim's account so he only can log on to the workstation that he has problems logging on to.

   C. Configure Jim's account to ignore warnings.

   D. Grant Jim's account the user right Log on Locally.

6. The Red domain trusts the Blue domain. The Blue domain trusts the White domain. If you are attempting to log on to the network at a Windows NT workstation that is a member of the Red domain, what account databases can you authenticate with? Select all that apply.

    A. The Red domain

    B. The White domain

    C. The Blue domain

    D. The Windows NT Workstation account database

7. Which Windows NT utilities can be used to set NTFS permissions on the local computer? Select all that apply.

    A. User Manager for Domains

    B. Server Manager

    C. Windows NT Explorer

    D. File Manager

Questions 8–10 are based on a two-domain network in which DOMAIN1 trusts DOMAIN2. The computers involved in each question are located in the domains as shown in Figure 12.7.1

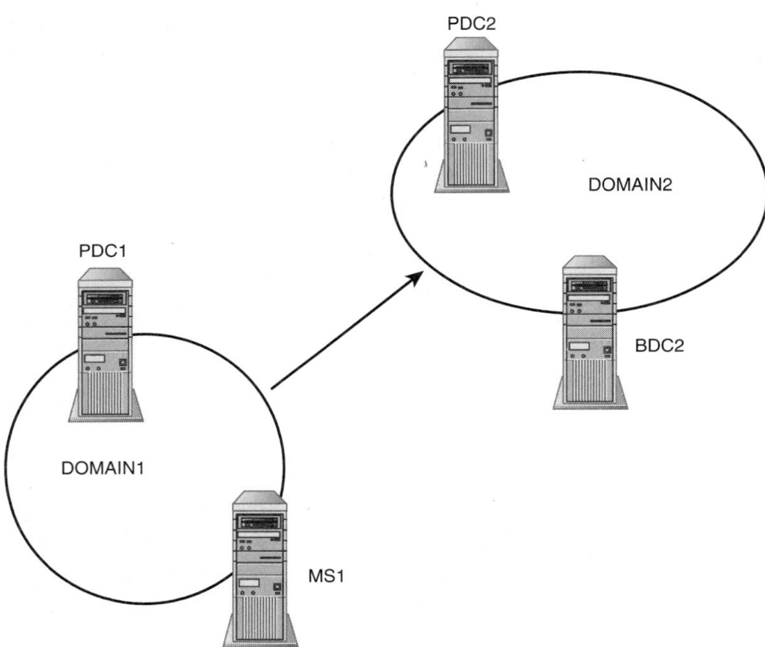

Figure 12.7.1 The Omaha National Network.

8. Greg's account on the Omaha National Network is located in DOMAIN1. If you were to grant Greg access to a printer located on BDC2, what permission assignments need to be performed?

   A. Create a new global group in DOMAIN1 and make Greg's account a member of the group. Create a local group in DOMAIN2 and assign it Print permissions. Remove the Everyone group from the permissions for the printer. Finally, assign the global group from DOMAIN1 to the local group in DOMAIN2.

   B. Create a new local group in DOMAIN1 and make Greg's account a member of the group. Create a local group in DOMAIN2 and assign it Print permissions. Remove the Everyone group from the permissions for the printer. Finally, assign the local group from DOMAIN1 to the local group in DOMAIN2.

   C. Create a new local group in DOMAIN1 and make Greg's account a member of the group. Create a global group in DOMAIN2 and assign it Print permissions. Remove the Everyone group from the permissions for the printer. Finally, assign the local group from DOMAIN1 to the global group in DOMAIN2.

   D. This cannot be done because the trust relationship has been established in the wrong direction.

9. Charlene and Ron have user accounts in DOMAIN2. Anthony and Bernice have accounts in DOMAIN1. You need to grant all these users access to the accounting system on the member server MS1 in DOMAIN1. What group assignments must be performed?

   A. Create a global group in DOMAIN1 and make all four users members of the group. Create a local group on PDC1 and assign permissions to it on the MS1 computer. Make the global group a member of the local group.

   B. Create a global group in DOMAIN1 and make all four users members of the group. Create a local group on MS1 and assign permissions to it on the MS1 computer. Make the global group a member of the local group.

   C. Create a global group in DOMAIN1 and make Anthony and Bernice members. Create another global group in DOMAIN2 and make Charlene and Ron members. Create a local group on PDC1 and assign permissions to it on the MS1 computer. Make the two global groups members of the local group.

   D. Create a global group in DOMAIN1 and make Anthony and Bernice members. Create another global group in DOMAIN2 and make Charlene and Ron members. Create a local group on MS1 and assign permissions to it on the MS1 computer. Make the two global groups members of the local group.

10. Adam has an account in DOMAIN2 and needs to manage file and print shares on the PDC1 computer in DOMAIN1. What group assignments enable Adam to perform this task without assigning excess rights?

    A. Assign Adam to the Server Operators group in DOMAIN2 and make the group a member of the Server Operators group in DOMAIN1.

B. Assign Adam to the Domain Admins group in DOMAIN2 and make the group a member of the Administrators group in DOMAIN1.

C. Assign Adam to a newly created global group in DOMAIN2 called FILENPRINT. Make the FILENPRINT global group a member of the Server Operators group in DOMAIN1.

D. Assign Adam to a newly created global group in DOMAIN2 called FILENPRINT. Make the FILENPRINT global group a member of the Account Operators group in DOMAIN1.

11. Which of the following groups are not found in Windows NT Workstation?

  A. Backup Operators

  B. Server Operators

  C. Power Users

  D. Administrators

12. Which of the following are the default groups for new users?

  A. Administrators, users

  B. Users, domain users

  C. Domain users

  D. Logon users

13. When you log on to Windows NT Workstation as an Administrator, you notice that the sharing symbol no longer appears below any of your shared folders. Which of the following is the probable cause of this?

  A. The View options in Windows NT Explorer have been configured to not show the shared folder symbol.

  B. The Server service has stopped.

  C. The Workstation service has stopped.

  D. On Windows NT Workstation, shares are only viewed in the Server Manager.

14. A file within Users local group that is assigned NTFS Change permissions is located in the c:\USERS directory. The directory d:\DATA has been assigned the NTFS Administrators permissions with Full Control permissions. If the file is moved to the d:\DATA directory, what are the permissions after the file is moved?

  A. Everyone, Full Control

  B. Users, Change

  C. Administrators, Full Control

  D. Users, Change
  Administrators, Full Control

15. A file in the Users local group that is assigned NTFS Change permissions is located in the c:\USERS directory. The directory C:\DATA has been assigned the NTFS Administrators permissions with Full Control permissions. If the file is moved to the C:\DATA directory, what are the permissions after the file is moved?

  A. Everyone, Full Control

  B. Users, Change

  C. Administrators, Full Control

  D. Users, Change
  Administrators, Full Control

16. All users' home directories have been generated using the setting \\SERVER\USERS\%USERNAME% in the home directory field of each user's properties. What permissions are assigned to the home directories by default?

    A. Users, Full Control

    B. Everyone, Full Control

    C. %USERNAME%, Change

    D. %USERNAME%, Full Control

17. The file DATA.TXT has been assigned the NTFS permissions Users, Read. The directory the file is in has the NTFS permissions Users, Change. The share permissions for the folder are set to Administrators, Full Control and Users, Full Control. What are the effective permissions on the file DATA.TXT?

    A. Users, Read

    B. Users, Change

    C. Users, Full Control

    D. Users, Full Control
Administrators, Full Control

Questions 18 and 19 are based on the directory structure shown in Figure 12.7.2. The SALARIES.XLS file is located in the Payroll folder, which is located in the Accounting folder, which is located in the Data folder. Varying share and NTFS permissions are set on these directories and files in each question.

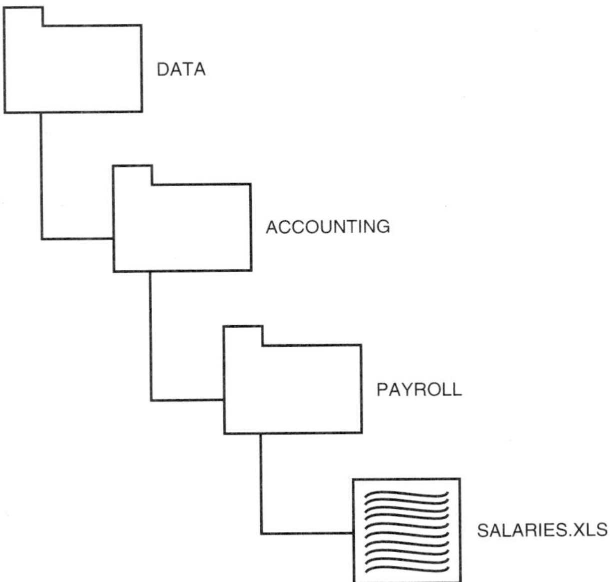

Figure 12.7.2 A sample directory structure.

12

18. Using the directory structure in Figure 12.7.2, the following security has been set. The Data directory has been shared with the Administrators group, which is assigned Full Control permissions. The Accounting folder has been shared with the Accountants local group, which is assigned Full Control permissions. The Payroll folder has NTFS Read permissions assigned to the Accounting group, and the SALARIES.XLS file has been assigned NTFS Change permissions. Dale, an accountant, has been assigned NTFS Read permissions. What are Dale's effective permissions on the file SALARIES.XLS if he connects using the Accounting share? Choose the best answer.

    A. Full Control permissions, based on the shared permission for the Accounting folder.

    B. Read permissions, based on the NTFS permissions for the Payroll folder.

    C. Read permissions, because Read is the more restrictive of the NTFS permissions assigned to the SALARIES.XLS file.

    D. Change permissions, because Dale is a member of the Accounting group and, when you combine the NTFS permissions on the file SALARIES.XLS, his effective permissions are Change.

19. The Data folder is shared with Full Control permissions for the Users group. The Accounting folder has been shared with the Change permission assigned to the Users group. Finally, the Payroll folder has been assigned the Read share permission to the Users group. What are the effective permissions on the SALARIES.XLS file if Anna connects using the Data share and the default NTFS permissions are in effect?

    A. Full Control

    B. Change

    C. Read

    D. No Access

The following scenario applies to questions 20–22. A different solution to the scenario is proposed for each question.

Scenario: The Really Big Corp. has three domains in its organization: Canada, USA, and Mexico. It wants to set up a Windows NT domain structure that meets the following requirements.

Required Result: Administrators in the Canada domain must be able to administer all three domains. *Optional Result 1*: Backup Operators in the Mexico domain must be able to perform backups in all three domains. *Optional Result 2:* Users in the Canada domain must be able to connect to a shared program located on a BDC in the Mexico domain.

20. *Proposed Solution*: Set up the following trust relationships:

    USA trusts Canada
    Mexico trusts Canada
    Mexico trusts USA

    Perform the following group assignments:

    - Make the Domain Admins group in Canada a member of the Administrators groups in USA and Mexico.
    - Make the Backup Operators group in Mexico a member of the Backup Operators groups in USA and Canada.
    - Make the Users group in Canada a member of a newly created local group in Mexico that has been assigned appropriate permissions for the shared program.

This solution:

A. Meets the required result and both optional results.

B. Meets the required result and only one optional result.

C. Meets only the required result.

D. Does not meet the required result.

21. *Proposed Solution*: Set up the following trust relationships:

USA trusts Canada
Mexico trusts Canada
USA trusts Mexico
Canada trusts Mexico

Perform the following group assignments:

- Make the Domain Admins group in Canada a member of the Administrators groups in USA and Mexico.
- Make the Backup Operators group in Mexico a member of the Backup Operators groups in USA and Canada.
- Make the Domain Users group in Canada a member of a newly created local group in Mexico that has been assigned appropriate permissions for the shared program.

This solution:

A. Meets the required result and both optional results.

B. Meets the required result and only one optional result.

C. Meets only the required result.

D. Does not meet the required result.

22. *Proposed Solution*: Set up a complete trust model between the three domains.

Perform the following group assignments:

- Make the Domain Admins group in Canada a member of the Administrators groups in USA and Mexico.
- Create a new global group in Mexico that includes all members of Mexico that perform backups. Make this new global group a member of the Backup Operators groups in Mexico, USA, and Canada.
- Make the Domain Users group in Canada a member of a newly created local group in Mexico that has been assigned appropriate permissions for the shared program.

This solution:

A. Meets the required result and both optional results.

B. Meets the required result and only one optional result.

C. Meets only the required result.

D. Does not meet the required result.

Questions 23, 24, and 25 are based on the permissions outlined in Table 12.7.1, which are assigned to the DATASTORE folder on the RESOURCES server.

Table 12.7.1

Share Permissions	NTFS Permissions
Users, Change	Users, Read
Accountants, Full Control	Accountants, Change
Actuaries, Read	Actuaries, Full Control
Irwin, No Access	Irwin, Read

23. If Alexander, a member of the Accountants group, attempted to access the \\RESOURCES\DATASTORE share, what would his effective permissions be?

    A. Full Control

    B. Change

    C. Read

    D. No Access

24. If Amy, a member of the Accountants and Actuaries groups, attempted to access the \\RESOURCES\DATASTORE share, what would her effective permissions be?

    A. Full Control

    B. Change

    C. Read

    D. No Access

25. If Amy were to walk over to the actual RESOURCES server and use Windows NT Explorer to view the DATASTORE folder, what would her effective permissions be?

    A. Full Control

    B. Change

    C. Read

    D. No Access

26. An organization has three domains named Alberta, Saskatchewan, and Manitoba. The trust relationships have been established so that Alberta trusts Saskatchewan and Saskatchewan trusts Manitoba. Andrea's account is in the Alberta domain, Sandy's account is in the Saskatchewan domain, and Max's account is in the Manitoba domain. Select all statements that are correct.

    A. Max can use resources in the Saskatchewan domain.

    B. Max can use resources in the Alberta domain.

    C. Sandy can use resources in the Alberta domain.

    D. Sandy can use resources in the Manitoba domain.

    E. Andrea can use resources in the Saskatchewan domain.

27. In a multimaster domain mode, how many trust relationships must be implemented if there are three master domains and four resource domains?

    A. 7

    B. 10

    C. 14

    D. 18

28. Which of the following groups can Account Operators modify the membership of?

    A. Replicators

    B. Backup Operators

    C. Domain Users

    D. Administrators

29. Harry, a user who handed in his resignation three weeks ago, had his account deleted. He now has returned to his former job. When you re-create his account, he can no longer access the files that he accessed before his resignation. Why is this?

    A. The account should have been undeleted in the User Manager for Domains.

    B. The account now has a new SID.

    C. The password has changed.

    D. The account must be regenerated.

12.7.1 Answers and Explanations: Exercise

This exercise tested the POSIX-compliant feature of Windows NT. This feature enables users with NTFS Full Control permissions to delete a file to which they have been assigned No Access permissions.

It should be noted that if you are working in the Graphical environment of Windows NT Explorer, you are prevented from actually deleting the file when the permissions are set to No Access. This is because you are working entirely in the Windows NT environment. For a command prompt, you could be working in a POSIX environment, so the POSIX rules are enforced.

12.7.2 Answers and Explanations: Exercise

This exercise investigated the effects of moving and copying a file in an NTFS environment. When you copied the Change file from the root directory to the NTFSTEST directory, the permissions changed to Users, Full Control from the original settings of Administrators, Full Control.

This exercise helps you recognize that permissions can be affected when files are moved or copied between directories. This realization can help you troubleshoot permission problems.

12.7 Answers and Explanations: Practice Problems

1. **D** The default permissions assigned to a shared directory are Everyone, Full Control.

2. **B, C** If St. Louis is going to act as the Master Domain, both Vancouver and New Orleans must trust St. Louis.

3. **C** If you assign the Domain Admins group from the St. Louis domain to the Administrators group in the Vancouver and New Orleans domains, administrators in the St. Louis domain are able to manage the remote domains.

4. **B, C, D** Server Manager, Windows NT Explorer, and File Manager all can be used to set share permissions on the local computer.

5. **D** If you grant the users' accounts (or groups that they have membership in) the user right Log on Locally, users can log on to the NT Workstation computer.

6. **A, C, D** You are able to authenticate with all account databases except the White domain. This is because trust relationships are non-transitive. Even though the Blue domain trusts the White domain, there is not an explicit trust relationship between the Red and White domains.

7. **C, D** Only Windows NT Explorer and File Manager can be used to set NTFS permissions on the local computer.

8. **D** The trust relationship is pointing in the wrong direction. If you want Greg to access any resources in DOMAIN2, DOMAIN2 must trust DOMAIN1.

9. **D** Because the resource is located on a Member Server in DOMAIN2, the local group must be created in the account database of the Member Server.

10. **C** The Server Operators group in DOMAIN1 grants Adam sufficient rights to manage file and print shares. He also could do this with the answer in B, but this grants excess rights.

11. **B** The Server Operators group is only found on a Windows NT domain controller.

12. **C** Users are members of the Domain Users global group by default. They have membership in the Users local group only because the global group Domain Users is a member of the Users local group.

13. **B** If the Server service stops operating, share symbols do not appear below shares because they are not being shared at that time. When you restart the Server service, the share symbols reappear.

14. **C** Because the file is moved between NTFS partitions, the file assumes the NTFS permissions of the target directory.

15. **B** Because the file is moved to a directory on the same NTFS partition, it retains its original permissions.

16. **D** When a home directory is generated on an NTFS partition, only the user's account is granted the Full Control permission.

17. **A** File permissions always take precedence over directory permissions in NTFS permissions assignments. Because the share permissions will effectively be Full Control, the Read permissions on the file DATA.TXT are the most restrictive and are the effective permissions.

18. **D** Dale's effective rights would be Change. Even though he has been assigned NTFS Read permissions, he also is a member of the Accounting group, which has Change permissions. When you combine Read and Change permissions, they are effectively Change permissions.

19. **A** The default NTFS permissions are Everyone with Full Control permissions. This means they are definitely not the most restrictive. The user is entering the directory structure at the Data directory, which has shared permissions of Full Control. This is the permission for the entire directory structure. Only Windows 95 looks at the share permissions assigned to subdirectories.

20. **C** This solution only meets the required result. You cannot assign local groups to other local groups. The Users group and the Backup Operators group are both local groups. Also, the trust relationships do not allow the optional requirements to work.

21. **B** This answer does not meet the requirement to have Backup Operators in the Mexico domain perform backups in all three domains. You cannot make a local group a member of another local group.

22. **A** This solution meets all objectives, but it uses excess trust relationships. There is no need for Canada to trust USA. There also is no need for Mexico to trust USA. Because there was no objective to minimize trust relationships, however, this meets all the objectives.

23. **B** Alexander would have share permissions of Full Control and NTFS permissions of Change. The most restrictive permissions are the NTFS permissions. This gives him effective permissions of Change.

24. **D** Amy has been assigned the explicit No Access permission on the share. This always overrides any other permission assignments.

25. **A** Because Amy is not connecting to the DATASTORE folder over the network, share permissions are not in effect. Her

effective NTFS permissions on the folder would be Full Control, due to her membership in the Actuaries local group.

26. **A, C** An account can only use resources in its own domain or in a domain that explicitly trusts its domain. Trust relationships are not transitive.

27. **D** The formula for calculating the number of trust relationships in a multimaster domain model is

    M*(M-1) + M*R

    where M is the number of Master domains, and R is the number of Resource domains.

28. **A, C** Account Operators are not allowed to affect the membership of the Administrators group, the Domain Admins group, or any of the Operators groups.

29. **B** When you delete an account and re-create it with the same User ID, the account has a different SID and does not retain any of its previous group memberships.

12.7 Key Words

Accounts-Global Groups-Local Groups-Permissions (AGLP) global group

Local group

NTFS permissions

Share permissions

SID

12.8 Solving Fault-Tolerance Failures

There are two levels of fault tolerance that are built into Windows NT Server: disk mirroring/duplexing (RAID 1) and disk striping with parity (RAID 5). Each fault-tolerant method has advantages and issues when being implemented. No matter which fault-tolerant method you implement, a good backup strategy is essential to prevent data loss in an organization. This section details issues with disk mirroring, stripe sets with parity, and backup strategies.

A. RAID 1: Disk Mirroring

Disk mirroring writes the contents of a single disk on two physical disks. Mirroring duplicates each write action to both disks in the mirror set. This protects against a disk failure because the system can continue to function using the other disk in the mirror set. If the disks are on separate controllers, this also protects against a controller failure. If they are on separate controllers, this is commonly known as disk duplexing. The cost associated with disk mirroring is 50%, which means that 50% of the total disk space in the mirror set is used to maintain fault-tolerant information.

Disk mirroring is the only fault-tolerant partitioning scheme provided with Windows NT that can contain the System and boot partitions. There are some issues to consider when you do mirror the System or boot partitions. It is possible that the disk that the computer uses to start the system may not be functioning at that time. For that, you need a fault-tolerant boot disk.

Remember that any time you update the disk configuration, you must update the Emergency Repair Disk. Doing so copies the disk configuration changes so that you can recover the fault-tolerant set in case of Registry problems.

1. Recovering from a Mirror Set Failure

If a mirror set fails, you may need to use a fault-tolerant boot disk. You only need to do use this if the Boot or system partitions of Windows NT are located on the failed drive in the mirror set. If the Boot or system partitions were located on the failed disk, the following steps must be followed:

1. Diagnose which disk is the failed hard disk in the mirror set. This disk probably needs to be replaced.
2. Start the system using the fault-tolerant boot disk. Select the startup entry for the functioning disk in the system.
3. Start the Disk Administrator program.
4. Select the mirror set. (You may not be able to determine which disk has failed until you have started the Disk Administrator program.)
5. From the Fault Tolerant menu, select Break Mirror.
6. Assign to the remaining member of the mirror set the original drive letter assigned to the mirror set.

7. After the defective drive has been replaced, you should reestablish the mirror. This is done by selecting the remaining member of the mirror set, and then Ctrl-clicking an area of free disk space on the newly installed disk that is the same size or larger than the original member of the mirror set.

8. When prompted, restart the computer.

B. RAID 5: Stripe Sets with Parity

Disk striping with parity also protects against the failure of a single disk on a Windows NT system. A stripe set with parity writes data across all the disks in a 64 KB stripe. On a different disk in each stripe, parity information is written that assists in recovering from a disk failure. The movement of the parity information between the drives in the stripe set with parity helps to improve performance when a disk fails. If a disk fails, the information that was on the missing disk can be rebuilt using the information on the remaining disk and the information stored in the parity information for that stripe. For some of the stripes, the parity information will have been stored on the disk that failed. No calculations are required to read information for stripes where this scenario occurs.

Windows NT–created stripe sets with parity cannot be used to store the Windows NT System and boot partitions. For data partitions, they offer better write and read performance due to the additional disk controllers involved in a stripe set with parity. A stripe set with parity requires a minimum of three disks and can be created using up to 32 disks. These disks can be any mix of disk formats, including SCSI, IDE, EIDE, and ESDI.

Windows NT can store its System and boot partitions on hardware RAID 5 stripe sets with parity because Windows NT sees the stripe set with parity as a single physical disk.

The cost of utilizing a stripe set with parity is 1/n, where n is the number of disks involved in a stripe set with parity. If you have six disks making up your stripe set with parity, 1/6th of the total disk space is used to store parity information.

If you are asked a question about fault-tolerant disk schemes, remember that although stripe sets and volume sets are supported under Windows NT, they provide absolutely NO fault tolerance.

1. Recovering from a Disk Failure with RAID 5

When a disk fails in a stripe set with parity, the Windows NT system can continue to use the disk array. When reading information from a stripe, the computer rebuilds any of the missing information from the failed disk using the parity information and the remaining disks for that stripe.

An example might be the best way to explain how parity information is calculated and used when a single disk fails in a stripe set with parity. Stripe sets with parity use the Exclusive OR function

12

to create the parity information for each stripe. The Exclusive OR function is based on the following series of calculations:

- 0 Exclusive OR 0 = 0
- 0 Exclusive OR 1 = 1
- 1 Exclusive OR 0 = 1
- 1 Exclusive OR 1 = 0

Table 12.8.1 shows how the parity information would have been calculated for a single stripe as the data was written to the stripe.

Table 12.8.1

Calculating the Parity Information for a Stripe Set with Parity

Drive	Drive Status	Bit Pattern
Data drive 1	Running	11100011
Data drive 2	Running	11101101 XOR
Check Byte drive	Running	00001110

If Data drive 1 were to fail, the calculation shown in Table 12.8.2 would be used to re-create the data missing from Data drive 1.

Table 12.8.2

Calculating the Parity Information for a Stripe Set with Parity

Drive	Drive Status	Bit Pattern
Data drive 1	Running	11100011
Check Byte drive	Running	00001110 XOR
Data drive 2	Failed	11101101

The system regenerates the information from Data drive 2 in memory on-the-fly. Due to the amount of calculations that are required, system performance suffers. Therefore, you need to quickly replace the failed disk and regenerate the stripe set with parity.

If two or more disks fail in a stripe set with parity, the only way to recover is to restore from a backup tape.

2. Recovering from a Failed Stripe Set with Parity

If a stripe set with parity fails, you should replace the defective disk as quickly as possible. The following process is used:

1. Start the Disk Administrator program to determine which disk has failed.
2. Replace the failed disk. Windows NT does not support hot swapping functionality, so the system must be shut down to replace the drive with a new drive that is at least the same size as the original drive.

3. Start the Disk Administrator again.
4. Click the stripe set with parity that you need to repair, and then Ctrl+click the free space of the drive you want to add to the stripe set with parity.
5. From the Fault Tolerant menu, select Regenerate. Note that this process can take some time, although it takes less time than restoring from tape.
6. If there were any other partitions on the failed drive, they may need to be restored from a tape backup.

You cannot increase the size of a stripe set with parity unless you back up its information. To back up a stripe set with parity, delete the previous stripe set with parity and create a new one made up of additional disks. After the new stripe set with parity is running, you have to restore the original data from the backup.

C. Backup Strategies for Disaster Recovery

Windows NT comes with its own proprietary backup software named NT Backup. Windows NT Backup can be run in either a graphical mode or a command-line mode. Both modes require a Windows NT HCL-compliant tape backup unit. Windows NT supports five different backup types, as follows:

- **Normal:** Backs up all selected files during the backup process and resets the archive bit to an off position on each file to indicate that the file has been backed up.
- **Differential:** Backs up only the files that have the archive bit set on from the selected files. A differential backup does not reset the archive bit.
- **Incremental:** Backs up the files that have the archive bit set to an on position from the selected files. After the files have been backed up, the archive bit for the backed up files is reset to an off position.
- **Copy:** Backs up all files that are selected for backup, but does not change the status of the archive bit.
- **Daily Copy:** Backs up only the files that have their archive bits set to an on position and were modified on that day. This backup type does not reset the archive bit for the files it backs up.

Other options that can be set during a backup include the following:

- Verify After Backup
- Backup Local Registry

Selecting the Backup Local Registry option works only if at least one file located on the Windows NT boot partition is selected.

- Restrict Access to Owner or Administrator
- Hardware Compression
- Log Options

1. Scheduling Backups

The Windows NT Backup program does not support the scheduling of backups. If you want to schedule backups, you must use the text version of the NTBACKUP command and the Automatic Transaction (AT.EXE) command that comes with Windows NT. The NTBACKUP command uses the following syntax:

```
NTBACKUP BACKUP paths [/A] [/V] [/R] [/D "TEXT"] [/B] [/HC:ON¦OFF] [/T type]
[/L "LOGFILE"]
```

Where:

- /A indicates that the new backup operation should be appended to the tape.
- /V indicates that the backup set should be verified after the backup process is completed.
- /R indicates that restoration should be restricted to Administrators or Owners of the file.
- /D "Text" enables an electronic description to be associated with the backup.
- /B indicates that the local Registry should be included in the backup operation.
- /HC:ON|OFF turns the hardware compression feature on or off.
- /T sets the backup type. Options include Normal, Incremental, Differential, Copy, or Daily.
- /l "logfile" indicates that logging should occur and should be written to the indicated log file.

A batch file can be written that can be called by the Windows NT AT.EXE command. The AT command enables you to schedule a batch file to be run at regular intervals.

```
AT time [ /EVERY:date[,...] ¦ /NEXT:date[,...]] "command"
```

For example, if you created a batch file named fullback.bat that you want to run every Friday at 11:30 p.m., you use the command.

```
AT 23:30 /EVERY:Friday "FULLBACK.BAT"
```

The AT command requires that the Schedule service be running on the computer on which you want to run the scheduled backup.

2. Backup Strategies

There are some very common backup strategies that are implemented to ensure that data is not lost on a system. These include the following:

- Daily full backups
- Weekly full backups with differentials
- Weekly full backups with incrementals

A backup methodology of full backups can be implemented when the total amount of data that needs to be backed up can be handled by your tape backup device and can be performed in a timely fashion. As the size of your backup set increases, this backup methodology generally evolves into a weekly full backup set with differentials or incremental occurring on the other days of the week. With the increase in data storage over the last few years, this often requires that a tape changer be in place to enable the automatic changing of tapes. If data is lost and needs to be restored from tape, it takes a single restore function to restore the entire system to the state it was in after the last completed backup.

When using a backup with differential method, full backups are usually run once a week. During the other days of the week, a differential backup is run. The differential backs up all the files that have changed since the previous week's full backup. If the system needs to be restored fully from backup, it requires two restore operations—one from the previous week's full backup and one from the previous day's differential backup. A common practice is to store the full backups off-site to prevent a loss of data from a natural disaster or fire.

When using a backup with incremental method, full backups are usually run once a week. During the other days of the week, an incremental backup is run. The incremental backups save all the files that have changed since the last backup. It does not matter whether it was a full or incremental backup the day before. If the system needs to be restored fully from backup, it requires many restore operations. You first restore the previous week's full backup. You then restore, in order, the incremental backups. A common practice is to store the full backups off-site to prevent a loss of data from a natural disaster or fire.

12.8.1 Exercise: Choosing a Disk Partitioning Scheme

Your computer has Windows NT Server installed. Your computer currently contains a single 2 GB drive. You want to install another 4 GB disk and two 2 GB disks to your computer. Based on this scenario, answer the following questions:

1. What fault-tolerant disk-partitioning schemes would you use to protect your Windows NT Server System and boot partitions and to provide the best access speeds for data stores?
2. What disks would you use to create these fault-tolerant disk-partitioning schemes?
3. If the 4 GB disk were to fail, could you still access all data on the computer?
4. If the 4 GB disk were to fail, what steps would you have to perform to restore the computer back to its fault-tolerant status?

12.8.2 Exercise: Creating a Batch File for Backup

In this exercise, you write a batch file that meets the following backup scenario. The computer that you are backing up is named MARKETING and has Windows NT Server installed into the default directory location.

- You need to back up all the data files in the \\CORPORATE\DATA network share.
- You need to back up all data on the local D: drive.
- You want to verify that the backup proceeded correctly.
- You want to create a logfile named BIGBACK.LOG and store it in the d:\LOGS directory.
- You want to back up the local Registry.
- You want to take advantage of the hardware compressions of your tape backup unit.

12.8 Practice Problems

1. How many total disks can be combined into a stripe set with parity?

   A. 3

   B. 10

   C. 32

   D. As many as can be installed in the system

2. What is required to boot a system that has a mirrored system partition and a default startup disk that is not operating?

   A. Emergency Repair Disk

   B. Fault-tolerant boot disk

   C. DOS boot disk

   D. Windows NT startup disks

   The following scenario applies to questions 2–5. A different solution to the scenario is proposed for each question.

   Scenario: Your computer system has four 8 GB hard disks. You want to configure the system to be fault tolerant based on the following specifications:

   Required Result: Protect the operating system from a boot failure. *Optional result 1:* The user data must be available at all times. *Optional result 2:* You want to get the best performance with the lowest cost for the user data.

3. *Proposed Solution:* Create a mirror set between the first two disks and install the Windows NT boot and System partitions to the mirrored disks. Create a second mirror between the remaining two disks and install the user data to the remaining disk in the system.

   This solution:

   A. Meets the required solution and both optional solutions.

   B. Meets the required solution and only one optional solution.

   C. Meets only the required solution.

   D. Does not meet the required solution.

4. *Proposed Solution:* Create a software-based stripe set with parity using all four disks and install the Windows NT boot partition, Windows NT System partition, and the user data to the newly created stripe set with parity. This solution:

   A. Meets the required solution and both optional solutions.

   B. Meets the required solution and only one optional solution.

   C. Meets only the required solution.

   D. Does not meet the required solution.

5. *Proposed Solution:* Create a hardware-based stripe set with parity using all four disks and install the Windows NT boot partition, Windows NT System partition, and the user data to the newly created stripe set with parity.

   This solution:

   A. Meets the required solution and both optional solutions.

   B. Meets the required solution and only one optional solution.

   C. Meets only the required solution.

   D. Does not meet the required solution.

6. Which option in backup can prevent unauthorized users from restoring the data on the backup tapes? Select all that apply.

   A. Select the Only Approved Users check box.

   B. Select the Restrict Access to Owner or Administrator check box.

   C. Run the backup command from a command prompt using the /r parameter.

   D. Run the ntbackup command from a command prompt using the /r parameter.

7. What software-fault-tolerant solutions can be used to protect the System and boot partitions of Windows NT? Select all that apply.

   A. Disk mirroring

   B. Stripe set

   C. Disk duplexing

   D. Stripe set with parity

8. How do you recover from a MIRROR failure?

   A. Use the Disk Regenerate command in Disk Administrator.

   B. Use the Rebuild Mirror command in Disk Administrator.

   C. Break the mirror, replace the defective disk, and re-establish the mirror.

   D. Replace the defective disk. The Disk Administrator automatically re-creates the mirror set.

9. Does a Windows NT system keep running if a single disk fails in a mirrored solution?

   A. Yes

   B. No

10. Is data still accessible if two disks fail in a stripe set with parity solution?

    A. Yes

    B. No

11. What disk driver does Windows NT use when implementing a mirror set?

    A. NTFS.SYS

    B. FTDISK.SYS

    C. MIRROR.SYS

    D. DISK.SYS

12. In your computer, you have four disks with free disk space. Disk 0 has 300 MB of free disk space. Disks 1, 2, and 3 have 500 MB of free disk space each. What is the largest usable disk space that can be provided using a stripe set with parity made up of any combination of disks in the computer?

    A. 900 MB

    B. 1500 MB

    C. 1200 MB

    D. 1000 MB

13. What types of disks can be combined to form a stripe set with parity in Windows NT 4.0 Server?

    A. SCSI

    B. EIDE

    C. JAZZ

    D. ESDI

14. Under what conditions can the Windows NT boot partition be installed to a RAID 5 stripe set with parity?

    A. It cannot be done.

    B. The RAID 5 stripe set with parity is formatted using NTFS.

    C. If the system partition is installed to the same partition.

    D. If the RAID 5 stripe set with parity is implemented as a hardware RAID solution.

15. What program is used to create a stripe set with parity?

    A. FTDISK

    B. Disk Administrator

    C. FDISK

    D. RAIDUTIL

16. Your stripe set with parity is running out of disk space. You add a new 4 GB drive to your system and want to expand the stripe set with parity to include the new disk. What must be done?

    A. In Disk Administrator, select the previous stripe set with parity, Ctrl-click the free space in the new disk, and select Disk Regenerate from the Fault Tolerant menu.

B. In Disk Administrator, select previous stripe set with parity, Ctrl-click the free space in the new disk, and select Disk Expand in the Fault Tolerant menu.

C. Back up all the data on the existing stripe set with parity, delete the partition, and create a new stripe set with parity using all the disks of the previous stripe set with parity, including the new disk. After the system has been restarted, restore all data and re-create any shares that were on the partition.

D. In Disk Administrator, select previous stripe set with parity, Ctrl-click the free space in the new disk, and select Expand Stripe Set with Parity from the Disk Menu.

17. What can be done to protect against both a disk and a disk controller failure?

    A. Stripe set

    B. Stripe set with parity

    C. Disk mirroring

    D. Disk duplexing

18. If Windows NT is installed to a Windows NT RAID 5 disk set, what would the ARCNAME appear as?

    A. SCSI(0)DISK(0)RDISK(3) PARTITION(0)\WINNT

    B. MULTI(0)DISK(0)RDISK(3) PARTITION(0)\WINNT

    C. SCSI(0)DISK(0)RDISK(3) PARTITION(1)\WINNT

    D. Windows NT cannot be installed to a software RAID 5 disk set.

19. Which disk-partitioning scheme provides the best disk access performance?

    A. Striping

    B. Mirror set

    C. Striping with parity

    D. Volume set

20. Two disks have failed in a stripe set with parity. How do you recover?

    A. Replace the two disks, restart the system, and allow the automatic recovery to take place.

    B. Replace the two disks, re-create the stripe set with parity, and restore from a tape backup.

    C. Replace the two disks and select the Disk Regenerate command from the Fault Tolerant menu in Disk Administrator.

    D. Replace the two disks. Start the Disk Administrator, right-click the remaining disks in the stripe set with parity, and select Rebuild.

21. Which fault-tolerant methodology is the most efficient in its usage of disk space?

    A. Disk duplexing

    B. Disk mirroring

    C. Disk striping

    D. Disk striping with parity

22. Which fault-tolerant disk strategy results in only 50% disk utilization?

    A. Disk duplexing

    B. Disk mirroring

    C. Disk striping

    D. Disk striping with parity

23. What steps are required to recover from a failed disk in a mirror set? Select all that apply.

    A. Boot with a fault-tolerant boot disk.

    B. Replace the defective disk.

    C. Select Regenerate from the Fault Tolerant menu.

    D. Re-create the mirror.

    E. Assign the desired drive letter to the remaining member of the mirror set.

24. What RAID levels are supported in Windows NT Server?

    A. 0

    B. 1

    C. 3

    D. 5

25. What RAID levels are supported in Windows NT Workstation?

    A. 0

    B. 1

    C. 3

    D. 5

The following disk space scenario applies to questions 26 and 27.

Scenario: Disk 0 has 1000 MB of free disk space, Disk 1 has 1200 MB of free disk space, Disk 2 has 200 MB of free disk space, Disk 3 has 400 MB of free disk space, and Disk 4 has 500 MB of free disk space.

26. What is the largest usable disk space RAID 5 stripe set with parity that can be created using any available disks?

    A. 1500 MB

    B. 1600 MB

    C. 1200 MB

    D. 1000 MB

27. What is the largest stripe set that can be created using any of the available disks?

    A. 2200 MB

    B. 2000 MB

    C. 1600 MB

    D. 1500 MB

The following scenario applies to questions 28–30. A different solution to the scenario is proposed for each question.

Scenario: The Omega Organization needs to establish a backup strategy. It has two Windows NT Server computers named PDC and BDC that require backups to be performed. Both computers have the System and boot partitions on the C drive, and all organizational data is stored to the D drive. The tape backup device is on the Windows NT HCL and is located on the PDC. The following requirements have been defined:

Required functionality: The backup of the PDC must include the Registry.

Optional result 1: The backup process should be automated.

Optional result 2: The backup process should restrict access to the data files to the owner or to an administrator.

28. *Proposed solution:* Map a network drive on the PDC connecting to the D$ share on the BDC computer. Run the Windows NT Backup program, and then select to back up all files on the local D: drive and the drive letter mapped to the \\BDC\D$ share. Select the options to restrict access to the owner or administrator, backup the Registry, and run the backup process each night at midnight.

    This solution:

    A. Meets the required solution and both optional solutions.

    B. Meets the required solution and only one optional solution.

    C. Meets only the required solution.

    D. Does not meet the required solution.

29. *Proposed solution:* Create the following batch file to perform the backup:

```
        Ntbackup backup
c:\boot.ini d:\*.*
\\BDC\D$\*.* /t:normal
/r /b /23:00
```

    This solution:

    A. Meets the required solution and both optional solutions.

    B. Meets the required solution and only one optional solution.

12

C. Meets only the required solution.

D. Does not meet the required solution.

30. Proposed solution: Create the following batch file to perform the backup:

```
Ntbackup backup
c:\boot.ini d:\*.*
\\BDC\D$\*.* /t:normal
/r /b
```

Run the following command to automate the backup procedure:

```
AT 23:00 /
EVERY:MONDAY,TUESDAY,WEDNESDAY,
THURSDAY,FRIDAY
"batchfile.bat"
```

This solution:

A. Meets the required solution and both optional solutions.

B. Meets the required solution and only one optional solution.

C. Meets only the required solution.

D. Does not meet the required solution.

12.8.1 Answers and Explanations: Exercise

Your computer has Windows NT Server installed. Your computer currently contains a single 2 GB drive. You want to install another 4 GB disk and two 2 GB disks to your computer.

1. A mirror set would provide fault tolerance for the boot and System partitions on the original 2 GB disk. You could then create a stripe set with parity to provide the best disk access times for data.
2. You would probably choose to create a mirror set between the original disk in the computer using 2 GB of the 4 GB disk. You could then create a stripe set with parity using the 2 GB of disk space from the 4 GB drive and the two 2 GB drives.
3. Yes. Because the 4 GB disk has failed, you would still be able to boot into Windows NT using the original boot disk without requiring a fault-tolerant boot disk. If the original 2 GB disk had failed, you would require a fault-tolerant boot disk with the BOOT.INI configured to point to the 4 GB disk's first partition instead. You would also be able to access data on the stripe set with parity, as it can rebuild the missing information from the 4 GB disk using the parity information that it has stored.
4. You would have to turn off the computer and replace the 4 GB drive with another 4 GB or larger disk drive. When the system restarted, you would need to start the Disk Administrator program. You would re-create the mirror set to provide fault tolerance to the boot and System partitions. You would then select the stripe set with parity and the remaining 2 GB of disk space on the newly added disk. You would restore the stripe set with parity using the Disk Regenerate command on the Fault Tolerance menu.

12.8.2 Answers and Explanations: Exercise

The following batch file would meet the backup scenario in this question:

```
Net use X:
\\Corporate\DATA
NTBACKUP BACKUP
C:\boot.ini d:\*.* x:\*.*
/V /l
"D:\LOGS\BIGBACK.LOG" /B
/HC:ON
NET USE X: /D
```

Another correct answer is:

```
NTBACKUP BACKUP
C:\boot.ini d:\*.*
\\corpoarte\data\*.* /V /
l "D:\LOGS\BIGBACK.LOG" /
B /HC:ON
```

You need to back up the file BOOT.INI because the /b option to back up the local Registry only works if you back up a file on the partition where the Windows NT Registry is stored. Because Windows NT was installed to the default location, you must assume that this is c:\WINNT.

12.8 Answers and Explanations: Practice Problems

1. **C** A stripe set with parity requires a minimum of three disks and can use up to 32 disks.
2. **B** A fault-tolerant boot disk contains the necessary files for the operating system to start. On an Intel system, these include NTLDR, BOOT.INI, NTDETECT.COM, and possibly NTBOOTDD.SYS. You edit the BOOT.INI to use the other component disk of the mirrored set.
3. **B** This solution does protect all user data and protects the operating system from boot failure. A mirrored partition does not give a performance boost for disk access for the user data volume.
4. **D** This solution does not meet the required solution because Windows NT cannot have its System or boot partition located on a software-created stripe set with parity.
5. **A** Windows NT can have its System and boot partitions installed on a hardware-created stripe set with parity. This protects the operating system and user data from a single disk failure. It also gives the best performance. The cost of this setup is 1/4 of the disk space; 8 GB will be used to store parity information.
6. **B, D** By selecting the Restrict Access to Owner or Administrator option in the GUI version of Windows NT Backup or by using the /r parameter in the NTBACKUP command-line version of the backup, you can restrict who can restore from the backup.
7. **A, C** Windows NT can only protect the System and boot partitions using disk mirroring or disk duplexing when using a software raid solution.
8. **C** You must replace the defective disk and then re-establish the mirror using the remaining disk of the mirror set and the free space of the new disk.
9. **A** Yes, the computer continues to operate; however, if the system is rebooted, it may not restart. It depends on whether the failed disk is the disk referenced in the BOOT.INI file.
10. **B** Stripe sets with parity only protect against a single disk failure. You can only be protected from two disks failing if you are using a hardware RAID 10 solution in which two disk stripes with parity are mirrored.
11. **B** Windows NT uses the fault-tolerant disk driver (FTDISK.SYS) when implementing a mirrored set.
12. **D** The largest usable disk space that you can create from this set of disks is 1000 MB. This is done by creating a stripe set with parity using the three 500 MB disks. 500 MB is allocated to parity information.
13. **A, B, D** Jazz drives cannot be component drives in a stripe set with parity.
14. **D** Windows NT can only have its boot partition installed on a stripe set with parity if the stripe set with parity is hardware-based. Windows NT recognizes only the disk array as a single disk.
15. **B** The Disk Administrator program is used to create all disk partitioning schemes in Windows NT.
16. **C** Windows NT does not support increasing the number of disks in the stripe set with parity without re-creating the stripe set with parity and reloading the contents from a tape backup.

17. **D** A disk duplexing scheme protects against both disk and controller failure as each disk in the mirror set is controlled by an independent disk controller.

18. **D** Windows NT cannot be installed to a software RAID 5 disk array.

19. **A** Disk striping offers the fastest disk access performance, but offers no fault tolerance.

20. **B** Disk striping with parity only protects against a single disk failure. You must re-create the stripe set with parity with new disks and restore the data from backup.

21. **D** Disk striping with parity only uses 1/n of the total disk space for parity information (where n is the total number of disks in the array).

22. **A, B** Both disk mirroring and disk duplexing use 50% of their total disk space to maintain a fault-tolerant copy of the data.

23. **A, B, D** To recover from a failed mirror set, you may have to boot with a fault-tolerant disk if the failed disk is the disk and partition referenced in the BOOT.INI. You must also replace the defective disk and re-create the mirror set in Disk Administrator.

24. **A, B, D** Windows NT supports RAID 0 (stripe sets), RAID 1 (mirror sets), and RAID 5 (stripe sets with parity).

25. **A** Windows NT does not provide any fault-tolerant disk schemes.

26. **C** The largest stripe set with parity that can be created using any of these five disks is 1200 MB. It would be created using 400 MB from disks 0, 1, 3, and 4.

27. **C** The largest stripe set that can be created using any of the available disks is 1600 MB, using 400 MB from disks 0, 1, 3, and 4.

28. **D** To back up the Registry using Windows NT Backup, you must include at least a single file from the partition where the Registry is stored.

29. **B** The required objective is met because /b for backing up the Registry is included in the NTBACKUP statement and a file is being backed up from the C drive of the PDC. The /r parameter does restrict access to the data to owners or administrator. There is no such parameter as /time.

30. **A** This solution meets all the requirements. The use of the AT command enables the backup to be scheduled for 11:00 p.m. Monday through Friday.

12.8 Key Words

Disk duplexing

Disk mirroring

Disk striping

Disk striping with parity

Exclusive OR function

NTBackup

12.9 Advanced Problem Resolution

Advanced problem resolution requires the use of the Event Log, the System Log, and the Application Log to determine what is causing the problem. Often, what the user sees is the result of a more significant failure. The three event logs that are maintained by Windows NT are as follows:

- **The system event log:** Used to record events generated by Windows NT system components, such as drivers and services.
- **The security event log:** Records events related to system security. In the case of the security log, the system audit policy determines which events are logged. System audit policies are created and maintained with User Manager for Domains.
- **The application event log:** Used to record messages generated by applications.

The first place you should look for information is the Event Viewer. There are five basic events that you see in the logs. The first is informational items that are letting you know when things are happening on the system. These are represented by blue circles with the letter "i" in them. Warning messages indicate there are more severe problems, but do not stop the system. These are yellow circles with an exclamation point (!) in them. Warnings often lead to a STOP error. Most STOP errors indicate that some part of Windows NT is not functioning and are shown as red stop signs. Event fields are described in the following list:

- **Date:** The date the event message was logged.
- **Time:** The time the event message was logged.
- **User:** The user who caused the event.
- **Computer:** The name of the computer where the event occurred.
- **Event ID:** A numeric value for a specific message as defined by the source of the message.
- **Source:** The application or system component that logged the event.
- **Type:** A Windows NT classification of the event, such as an Error, Warning, or Information message.
- **Category:** A classification of the event, as defined by the source of the message.
- **Description:** A textual explanation of the event.
- **Data:** Binary data specific to an event, shown either as a series of Byte or Word values.

A. Filtering

Thousands of events that can be listed in the event logs. To make the job of finding the problem easier, you can filter the log. Filters can be set on any of the event fields in the preceding list. To filter the log, choose View, Filter from the menu.

B. Searching for Events

Searching for an Event is similar to Filtering, but in many cases it is more useful for troubleshooting, because it enables you to see the events around the one for which you are looking. You can find an event by going to View, Find.

The Find dialog box appears, which enables you to enter the search criteria. The options are almost the same as the Filter Events dialog box; however, you will notice that dates are missing. You can now look for any piece of text in the details of the event and choose to search up or down.

C. Other Errors

There are two other errors that are normally found in the security log. Violations of security are shown as locks, and access events are shown as keys. Blue screen errors are cases in which the operating system fails to start or abruptly stops working.

There are two ways to deal with a blue screen. You may reboot the system, and if the problem continues, you may have to diagnose which driver or component of Windows NT is causing the STOP error. Interpreting the information reported when a STOP error has occurred can help in diagnosing which driver may be at fault. You can also use some of the tools that are provided by Windows NT to diagnose the problem and fix it.

Debug port status indicators, bugcheck information, driver information, kernel build number and stack dump, and debug port information are the informational items used to determine the root of a system crash.

You can also configure the computer to create a dump file and debug it, or use a kernel debugger to isolate the problem. Boot options associated with a debug are /DEBUG, /CRASHDEBUG, /DEBUGPORT, and /BAUDRATE. You can keep the system debug-ready by setting the /DEBUG switch in the BOOT.INI. This enables the host computer running a kernel debugger to interrupt processing on the target computer whenever it is desired. If you use the /CRASHDEBUG switch, kernel debugging is enabled only after a STOP error has occurred.

D. Information on the Blue Screen

When a STOP error occurs and the system gives the character mode stop screen, there are five main sections on the screen. The five are listed here:

- **Debug Port Status Indicators:** Describes the status of the serial port. If it is in use, that information is used for debugging.
- **BugCheck Information:** Displays the actual error code and any parameters that the developer included in the error trapping routines. If only the top line is displayed, the error has also affected the areas that are used to display such information. This is the most useful portion of information for diagnosing the cause of the STOP screen.
- **Driver Information:** In this area, the drivers that were loaded when the STOP error occurred are listed. There are three items of information given for each driver:
    1. The memory location into which the driver was loaded.
    2. The time the driver was created (this is the offset in seconds from Jan 1, 1970; use CVTIME.EXE to convert these to readable dates).
    3. The name of the driver is listed. The BugCheck Information sometimes includes a pointer to the instruction that caused the ABEND (abnormal end), and you can use this information to discover which driver was involved.

- **Kernel Build Number and Stack Dump:** Provides the information on the current build number and a dump of the last instructions that were executed.
- **Debug Port Information:** Indicates the baud rate and other COM settings for the debug port in use.

E. Interactive Debugging

In some cases you need to go further than just looking at the screen. You can do this in two ways. You can set up the problematic computer to create a dump file and use utilities to verify it, or you can interactively debug the problematic computer using another computer, either with a RAS null modem cable or remotely using a modem.

In the \support\debug directory on the distribution CD, there is a kernel debugger for each platform that can be used for installation. The kernel debuggers use basic serial communications and each needs some configuration. The steps involved in preparing for a debugging session are listed here:

1. Set up the serial connection.
2. Configure the problematic computer (target).
3. Place the symbol tree on the diagnostic computer (host).
4. Start the computer in debugging mode.
5. Start the debugger on the diagnostic computer.

1. Setting up the Serial Connection

You may not be able to use an off-the-rack null modem cable to perform kernel debugging. Table 12.9.1 shows the cabling requirements for a 9-pin cable. Table 12.9.2 shows the cabling specifications for a 25-pin cable. Kernel debugging does not function correctly if the null modem cable you used does not meet these specifications.

Table 12.9.1

9-Pin Null Modem Cabling

Remote host	Calling system	Signal
3	2	Transmit Data
2	3	Receive Data
7	8	Request to Send
8	7	Clear to Send
6,1	4	Data Set Ready and Carrier Detect
5	5	Signal Ground
4	6,1	Data Terminal Ready

Table 12.9.2

25-Pin Null Modem Cabling

Remote host	Calling system	Signal
3	2	Transmit Data
2	3	Receive Data
4	5	Request to Send
4	4	Clear to Send
6,8	20	Data Set Ready and Carrier Detect
7	7	Signal Ground
20	6,8	Data Terminal Ready

After you have created the null modem cable, connect the host and target computers. Be sure to plug the Remote Host end of the null modem cable into the target computer and the Calling System end of the cable into the host computer.

2. Configuring the Target Computer

For the system that you debug to properly route the information (to the serial port rather than the screen), you need to modify the BOOT.INI file. The following list provides the switches that you should add to the version of Windows NT you will boot:

- **`/Debug:`** Tells NT to load the kernel debugger during boot and kept it in memory.
- **`/Crashdebug:`** Similar to the `/Debug` option; however, the debugging code is available only if the system crashes. In most cases, this is a better option because the debugger code is not in memory and therefore doesn't interfere with the problem.
- **`/Debugport:`** Indicates the communications port that you use.
- **`/Baudrate:`** Selects the baud rate for the connection that you use for debugging.

You must also configure the target computer to not reboot in the case of a STOP error so that kernel debugging can be performed at that time. This is done by deselecting the Automatically Reboot option on the Startup/Shutdown tab of the System applet in Control Panel.

3. Configuring the Host Computer

The host computer requires that the necessary tools for debugging are located on a local disk drive. The symbol tree is used in debugging to provide the information about what the code does at various locations. This information is different for every version of Windows NT. The symbol library for a standard single processor version of Windows NT is in the `\support\debug\%platform%\symbols` directory on the CD-ROM.

If you have installed a service pack or you are working with a HAL other than the basic single processor HAL, you need to create a symbol set for the system. The following list outlines how to do this:

1. Copy the correct directory structure from the Support directory on the CD to your hard drive.
2. For the updates you have applied, copy the symbols from the distribution media for them in the same order that you applied them. Depending on your service pack version, these may need to be expanded first.
3. For multiprocessor systems, you have to rename some of the symbol files. The standard kernel debugger files are named NTOSKRNL.DBG for kernel and HAL.DBG for the HAL. On a multiprocessor computer, you need to rename NTKRNLMP.DBG to NTOSKRNL.DBG. These files are in the \Exe subdirectory.

Next, you need to set up the host with a series of environment variables so that the debugger has the basic information that it needs. You can do this using the SET command (for help on this, type **SET /?** at a prompt).

- **_NT_DEBUG_PORT:** COM port being used.
- **_NT_DEBUG_BAUD_RATE:** Baud rate for port.
- **_NT_SYMBOL_PATH:** Directory in which the symbols directory is located.
- **_NT_LOG_FILE_OPEN:** The name of a log file; this is optional.

> **To automate the process of performing kernel debugging, you may want to create a batch file that sets the previous environment variables and starts the kernel debugger.**

4. Starting the Target Computer in Debugging Mode

After the necessary parameters have been added to the BOOT.INI file and the computer has been configured so as not to automatically reboot in the case of a STOP error, you must restart the target computer so that the debug parameters are enabled.

5. Starting the Debugger on the Host Computer

After you have restarted the host system, you can perform kernel debugging on the remote system. To do this, you run the kernel debugger for the platform of the target machine. You need to be aware of some command-line switches, as follows:

- **-b:** Sends a debug breakpoint to the remote system, which causes execution on the target computer to stop as soon as possible.
- **-c:** Requests a communications resync when the systems connect.
- **-m:** Watches the modem control lines. This places the debugger in terminal mode if there is no CD (carrier detect).
- **-n:** Loads the symbols immediately. They usually are loaded in a deferred mode.
- **-v:** Activates verbose mode.
- **-x:** Forces the debugger to immediately break in when an exception occurs. The application is usually left to deal with it.

If you want to invoke the debugger, you must use the Ctrl+C combination. After you have started the debugger, you need to use some of the commands in Table 12.9.3 to diagnose the problems.

Table 12.9.3

Kernel Debugging Commands

Command	Usage
!reload	Reloads the symbol files if an updated symbol file has been copied to the host system.
!trap	Dumps the computer state when the trap frame occurs. It shows the state of the computer when an access fault has occurred.
!errlog	Displays the contents of an error log that the system builds as kernel errors occur. If there are contents in the log, this can assist in determining which component or process has caused the STOP error.
!process	Lists information about the current process running on the active processor.
!process 0 0	Lists all running processes and their headers.
!thread	Lists all the currently running threads.
!drivers	Displays a list of all drivers currently loaded. The most useful information can be the link date, which can be used to determine whether non-service pack versions of drivers are used correctly.
!vm	Lists the system's virtual memory usage.
g	Releases the target computer if kernel debugging was invoked by the person performing kernel debugging.
.reboot	Restarts the target computer.

F. Analyzing Memory Dump Files

Sometimes you are unable to resolve the problem using the kernel debugger. When this happens, you might want to have Windows NT create a dump file and either try to analyze it yourself or send it to Microsoft for analysis.

To create a dump file, you must have the page file existing on the boot partition of Windows NT. The page file on this partition must be larger in size than the total memory installed on the computer because the contents of memory are copied into the page file when a STOP error occurs.

After the system is restarted, the contents of the page file are copied to the configured memory dump file. The default is %SystemRoot%\memory.dmp. This can be configured in the System applet of Control Panel on the Startup/Shutdown tab. You must ensure that there is enough free disk space on the partition where the MEMORY.DMP file is to be created. It will be the size of the installed RAM on the system.

1. Configuring NT to Create a Dump File

Configuring Windows NT to create a dump file is very easy. You must configure the DumpCrash settings. The steps for setting this up are as follows:

1. Right-click the My Computer Icon.
2. Choose the Startup/Shutdown tab.
3. Under Recovery, click the "Write debugging information to" check box.

   You can select to overwrite an existing dump file by checking "Overwrite any existing file."

   You can enter another location for the dump file by entering the location (and name) into the text box.
4. Click OK.

2. Dump File Utilities

Three utilities come with Windows NT that enable you to work with the memory dump files. These utilities are listed here with a brief description:

- **DUMPCHK:** Checks that the dump file is in order by verifying all the addresses and listing the errors and system information.
- **DUMPEXAM:** Creates a text file that can provide the same information that was on the blue screen at the time the STOP error occurred. You need the symbol files and the kernel debugger extensions, as well as IMAGEHLP.DLL to run dump exam. The DUMPEXAM utility can only be used for STOP 0×0000000A and 0×0000001E errors.
- **DUMPFLOP:** Backs up and compresses the dump file to a series of floppies so that they can be sent to Microsoft.

G. Finding More Information

If you have worked with the event logs in Windows NT, you know that the information displayed in the event details can sometimes be cryptic. This means that you need to be able to find more information using the event ID or other clues that are in the information. There are three very good sources for information about Windows NT errors:

- Microsoft TechNet is a solid and very current source of information that is available as a monthly subscription. TechNet is probably the best source for troubleshooting information for Windows NT and all the Microsoft products. Shipped to subscribers on a monthly basis, it comes on at least two CDs.
- The Microsoft Support site, at `http://www.microsoft.com/support`, has a full suite of information about problems that other users have already experienced. One of the more helpful items on the support site is a group of the troubleshooting wizards. These wizards step you through the process of troubleshooting and provide you with solutions that come from the Microsoft technical staff.
- The Microsoft Knowledge Base contains articles on errors with the Windows NT operating system and their solutions. The Knowledge Base is accessible on the Internet at `http://www.microsoft.com/kb`.

12.9.1 Exercise: Configuring the Target Server for Kernel Debugging

This exercise guides you through the necessary steps to enable kernel debugging on a Windows NT computer that will be functioning as the target computer.

1. Start the Windows NT Explorer.
2. From the View menu, select Options. Ensure that the option to Show all files is enabled and the Hide file extensions for known file types is deselected. Click the OK button to confirm your changes.
3. In the c:\ directory, right-click the BOOT.INI file and select properties.
4. Clear the Read-only attribute and click the OK button.
5. Double-click the BOOT.INI file to edit the file.
6. In the section titled [Operating Systems], add the following parameters to the end of the line:

   ```
   /debug /debugport=com1 /baudrate=9600
   ```

7. Save and close the file.
8. Restart Windows NT. Note that the Boot menu now displays the words [Debugger Enabled] for the selection to which you have added the parameters.

12.9.2 Exercise: Configuring the Host Server for Kernel Debugging

This exercise guides you through the necessary steps to enable kernel debugging on a Windows NT computer that will be functioning as the host computer. This exercise assumes that your CD-ROM is assigned the drive letter Z.

1. Insert the Windows NT Server CD in the CD-ROM drive.
2. Start a command prompt.
3. On the C drive, create a new directory named \debug.
4. On the Z drive (the CD-ROM), make the current directory \support\debug.
5. Run the following command to install the symbol files on the host computer:

   ```
   expandsym z: c:\debug
   ```

   where z: is the drive letter of your CD-ROM and the c:\debug directory is the target directory where you want to install the symbol files.
6. Now copy the contents of the directory z:\support\debug\i386 to the c:\debug folder.
7. Close the command prompt.
8. In the c:\debug folder, create a DBG.BAT file. It should contain the following information:

   ```
   REM loca debug batch file
   Set _NT_DEBUG_PORT=com2
   Set _NT_DEBUG_BAUD_RATE=9600
   Set _NT_SYMBOL_PATH=c:\debug\symbols
   Set _NT_LOG_FILE_OPEN=c:\debug\debug.log
   -i386kd -M -v
   ```

9. Close the DBG.BAT file and save changes.

12.9 Practice Problems

1. When running a kernel debugger, what key combination interrupts processing on the target computer and enables the technician to perform kernel debugging?

   A. Ctrl+D

   B. Ctrl+C

   C. End

   D. Ctrl+Break

2. How does Windows NT provide the capability to perform kernel debugging?

   A. By providing checked versions of all programs.

   B. By providing debug files of all programs.

   C. By providing symbol files for all programs.

   D. By providing kernel files for all programs.

3. Although checked versions of files provide the capability to perform kernel debugging, which of the following is a performance issue?

   A. They cannot be run in a production environment.

   B. They cannot be run in debug mode.

   C. They result in larger, possibly slower executables.

   D. They can only be used on the Intel platform.

4. In Windows NT debugging, the host computer is which of the following?

   A. The computer that is suffering the STOP errors.

   B. The computer running the kernel debugger.

   C. The computer running the Remote Access Service.

   D. The file where the Windows NT Symbol files are stored on the network.

5. In Windows NT debugging, the target computer is which of the following?

   A. The computer that is suffering the STOP errors.

   B. The computer running the kernel debugger.

   C. The computer running the Remote Access Service.

   D. The file where the Windows NT Symbol files are stored on the network.

6. What program writes the contents of memory to a disk file when a STOP error occurs?

   A. CRASHDUMP

   B. DUMPCHK.EXE

   C. DUMPFLOP.EXE

   D. DUMPEXAM.EXE

7. What settings must be set in the BOOT.INI of the system that is encountering STOP errors? Choose all that apply.

   A. /DEBUG

   B. /CRASH

   C. /BAUDRATE

   D. /DEBUGPORT

8. Which setting in the BOOT.INI file enables debugging ionlyn the event of a STOP error?

   A. /DEBUG

   B. /CRASH

   C. /CRASHDEBUG

   D. /WAIT

9. Where are CRASHDUMP parameters set?

   A. Registry

   B. Server Manager

   C. RDISK

   D. Startup/Shutdown tab of the System Applet in Control Panel

10. In which file are the contents of a CRASHDUMP stored by default?

    A. Paging file

    B. %SystemRoot%\crashdmp.log

    C. %SystemRoot%\memdump.log

    D. %SystemRoot%\memory.dmp

11. Which Windows NT dump analysis tool validates the contents of a dump file after a STOP error has occurred?

    A. CRASHDUMP

    B. DUMPCHK.EXE

    C. DUMPFLOP.EXE

    D. DUMPEXAM.EXE

12. What size will the crash dump file be when it is created?

    A. 16 MB

    B. 32 MB

    C. 64 MB

    D. Size of physical RAM on computer

13. For a memory dump to be successful, what conditions must be met? Choose all that apply.

    A. The paging file must be at least 64 MB.

    B. The paging file must be at least as large as physical RAM.

    C. The paging file must be located on the Windows NT boot partition.

    D. The paging file must be located on the Windows NT system partition.

14. What utility can be used to reduce the size of a memory dump file by extracting the crucial information that Microsoft Technical services requires to diagnose a problem?

    A. CRASHDUMP

    B. DUMPCHK.EXE

    C. DUMPFLOP.EXE

    D. DUMPEXAM.EXE

15. What utility can be used to copy the contents of a memory dump to floppy disks to be sent to Microsoft technical support?

    A. DUMPDISK.EXE

    B. DUMPCHK.EXE

    C. DUMPFLOP.EXE

    D. DUMPEXAM.EXE

16. When troubleshooting errors occur during the startup of Windows NT, which event log should be viewed in the Windows NT event viewer?

    A. Startup

    B. System

    C. Application

    D. Security

17. How can you narrow down the number of items being viewed in the Windows NT Event Viewer?

    A. Use the Extract command in the NT Event Viewer.

    B. Export the contents of the Windows NT Event Viewer to a comma-separated value file and import into a database product.

    C. Use Crystal Reports.

    D. Apply a filter.

18. What is the default behavior for the Windows NT Event viewer when an Event log becomes full?

    A. Overwrite Events as Needed.

    B. Overwrite Events older than seven days.

    C. Do not overwrite events (Clear log Manually).

    D. Shut down the Windows NT Server.

19. When running a kernel debugger, what command is entered to display all device drivers in use and their link dates?

    A. devices

    B. !devices

C. drivers

D. !drivers

20. When performing kernel debugging on a multiprocessor computer, what additional steps must be performed before starting the debugging process?

    A. Add the /MULTI parameter to the BOOT.INI file of the target computer.

    B. Set the environment variable _DEBUG_PROCESSOR to MULTI on the host computer.

    C. Rename the file NTKRNLMP.DBG to NTOSKRNL.EXE on the host computer.

    D. Rename the file NTKRNLMP.DBG to NTOSKRNL.EXE on the target computer.

21. What must be configured on both the host and target computers for successful kernel debugging to take place?

    A. Debug ports

    B. Identical version of the kernel debugger

    C. Port speed settings

    D. The NT Symbol path

22. If you encounter a STOP error that you do not recognize, where can you research information that may help troubleshoot the problem?

    A. The knowledge base on the Microsoft web site

    B. TechNet Compact Disks

    C. The Windows NT README.DOC file

    D. The Windows NT Help files

23. Which STOP errors are supported by the DUMPEXAM utility? Select all that apply.

    A. STOP: 0x0000007F UNEXPECTED_KERNEL_MODE_TRAP

    B. STOP: 0x0000000A IRQL_NOT_LESS_OR_EQUAL

    C. STOP: 0x0000001E KMODE_EXCEPTION_NOT_HANDLED

    D. STOP: 0x0000007B INACCESSIBLE_BOOT_DEVICE

24. What utility on the Windows NT Server CD-ROM enables a dial-in client to perform kernel debugging on a computer?

    A. REMOTE.EXE

    B. REMDEBUG.EXE

    C. KRNDEBUG.EXE

    D. RCMD.EXE

25. If you have installed a Windows NT Service Pack, what additional steps must be completed to perform kernel debugging?

    A. No additional steps are required.

    B. Ensure that the same level of service packs is applied to the computer performing the kernel debugging.

    C. Delete the previous symbol files and install the new symbol files for the service pack.

    D. Download the symbol files for the service pack and replace all updated symbol files.

The following scenario applies to questions 26–29. A different solution to the scenario is proposed for each question.

Scenario: You have a computer that is crashing several times a day. You want to have Microsoft Technical Support assist you with diagnosing the cause of the problem.

Required Result: You want to be able to perform kernel debugging at any time, even when a STOP error has not

12

occurred. *Optional Result 1:* You want to have the Administrator of the network notified when a STOP error has occurred. *Optional Result 2:* When a STOP error occurs, you want to have the system restart automatically, because the computer is housing crucial information that must be available at all times.

26. *Proposed Solution:* On the computer that is crashing, add the parameter /CRASHDEBUG to the BOOT.INI file. Also configure the messenger service to forward all alerts to the Administrator's computer. Finally, set the computer to reboot in the event of a STOP error.

    This solution:

    A. Meets the required solution and both optional solutions.

    B. Meets the required solution and only one optional solution.

    C. Meets only the required solution.

    D. Does not meet the required solution.

27. *Proposed Solution:* On the computer that is crashing, add the parameters /DEBUG and /REBOOT to the BOOT.INI file. Configure the computer to send an administrative alert to the Administrator of the network.

    This solution:

    A. Meets the required solution and both optional solutions.

    B. Meets the required solution and only one optional solution.

    C. Meets only the required solution.

    D. Does not meet the required solution.

28. *Proposed Solution:* On the computer that is crashing, add the parameter /DEBUG to the BOOT.INI file. Configure a computer that will be connected directly to the machine that is suffering the STOP errors. Run the following command on the host computer:

```
        remote /s "i386kd
-v" debug
```

    Configure a separate RAS server to allow Microsoft Technical support to dial in to the network. Configure the RAS server to allow access only to that computer. Provide Microsoft with an account to access the network, grant that account the dial-in permission, and tell them to run the command:

```
        Remote /c
\\hostcomputername debug
```

    Whenever a crash occurs, run the DUMPFLOP utility to transfer the dump the memory dump file to floppy disks.

    This solution:

    A. Meets the required solution and both optional solutions.

    B. Meets the required solution and only one optional solution.

    C. Meets only the required solution.

    D. Does not meet the required solution.

29. *Proposed Solution:* On the computer that is crashing, add the parameter /DEBUG to the BOOT.INI file. Configure a computer that will be connected directly to the machine that is suffering the STOP errors. Run the following command on the host computer:

```
        remote /s "i386kd
-v" debug
```

    Configure the RAS service on the host computer to enable Microsoft Technical support to dial in to the network. Configure the RAS server to allow access only to that computer. Provide Microsoft with an account to access the network, grant that account the dial-in permission, and tell them to run the command:

```
        Remote /c
\\hostcomputername debug
```

    Any time that a crash occurs, run the DUMPFLOP utility to transfer the dump the memory dump file to floppy disks.

This solution:

A. Meets the required solution and both optional solutions.

B. Meets the required solution and only one optional solution.

C. Meets only the required solution.

D. Does not meet the required solution.

30. If you have not configured your computer to store the results of a STOP error into a memory dump file, where might you look to see what the actual STOP error was?

A. Server Manager

B. DRWATSON.LOG

C. MEMORY.DMP

D. Windows NT Event Viewer

12.9.1 and 12.9.2 Answers and Explanations: Exercises

These two exercises investigated how to configure the host and target computers to perform kernel debugging.

Additional steps must be included to complete the debugging process. The target computer could have been configured with the /crashdebug switch instead of the /debug switch. This would have only enabled kernel debugging when a STOP error occurred. The /debug switch enables the kernel debugger to STOP processing at any time and investigate the target system.

12.9 Answers and Explanations: Practice Problems

1. **B** Ctrl+C interrupts processing on the target computer and enables a technician to perform kernel debugging without a crash taking place.

2. **C** Windows NT provides symbol files for all Windows NT operating system files. These symbol files are used with the actual executable files when kernel debugging is performed.

3. **C** Checked versions of files do provide debugging capabilities, but are larger in size and can result in slower execution.

4. **C** The host computer is the computer running the kernel debugging software.

5. **A** The target computer is the computer in which the STOP errors are occurring. This computer is the target of the kernel debugging.

6. **A** Although not a true executable, the CRASHDUMP routine writes the contents of memory to the page file with an indicator that a memory dump has been written to the page file. When the system is restarted, the contents of the page file are written to the file `%SystemRoot%\Memory.dmp` by default.

7. **A, C, D** The parameters /DEBUG, /BAUDRATE, and /DEBUGPORT must be included in the BOOT.INI of the target computer in kernel debugging.

8. **C** The /CRASHDEBUG parameter in the BOOT.INI of the target computer enables kernel debugging only in the event of a STOP error. It does not enable kernel debugging when the host computer presses Ctrl+C to interrupt processing.

9. **D** The CRASHDUMP parameters are set on the Startup/Shutdown tab of the System applet in Control Panel.

10. **D** The contents of a memory dump are stored in the file `%SystemRoot%\memory.dmp` by default. The actual memory dump is originally written to the page file on the boot partition in Windows NT with an indicator that a memory dump has taken place. When the

system is restarted, the page file contents are then copied to the MEMORY.DMP file. You might receive a warning that you are running out of virtual memory space when the system initially restarts.

11. **B** The DUMPCHK utility verifies that the contents of a MEMORY.DMP file are not corrupt.

12. **D** The MEMORY.DMP file will be the size of physical RAM on the computer. If the computer has 512 MB of RAM, the MEMORY.DMP file will be 512 MB in size. Be sure to have enough available disk space for the file.

13. **B, C** The Paging file must be located on the Windows NT boot partition and be at least as big as the physical RAM pool for a memory dump to occur successfully.

14. **D** The DUMPEXAM utility reduces the size of a memory dump file for transport to Microsoft Technical support. It includes only the relevant information and, by default, stores the information in a file named MEMORY.TXT.

15. **C** Not only does the DUMPFLOP copy the entire MEMORY.DMP file to floppy disk, it also compresses the information.

16. **B** The System log in Windows NT Event Viewer will contain errors related to the Windows NT startup process.

17. **D** You can apply a filter to reduce the displayed events in the Windows NT Event Viewer. Filters can include error codes, reporting services, and event types.

18. **B** The default Event Log behavior is to overwrite events that are older than seven days.

19. **D** The command !drivers is executed within the kernel debugger. The command drivers is a Windows NT resource kit tool that displays the same results for the computer on which the program is run.

20. **C** You must rename the NTKNRLMP.DBG file on the host com-puter to NTOSKRNL.EXE. A multiprocessor computer will be using the multiprocessor and the symbol file must match the executable.

21. **A, C** Both the target and host computer must configure which port and what speed will be used for the debugging to take place.

22. **A, B** You can research STOP error messages by searching the knowledge base at `www.microsoft.com/support/` or searching the TechNet CD with the actual STOP message error.

23. **B, C** The DUMPEXAM utility only works with 0x0000000A or 0x0000001E errors.

24. **A** The REMOTE.EXE command enables a dial-in client to take over a remote session on the host computer that is connected by a direct cable to the target computer.

25. **D** You must update each symbol file to match the current version of the Windows NT system file. Some of the files may not have been updated in the service pack, so replacing all symbol files with the new symbol files for the service pack may omit some necessary files.

26. **D** The /CRASHDEBUG setting in the BOOT.INI only enables kernel debugging when a STOP error occurs. This does not meet the required result.

27. **B** There is no such setting as /REBOOT in the BOOT.INI. To set the reboot parameters, you edit the Start/Shutdown tab of the System applet in Control Panel.

28. **B** With the RAS Server only enabling a connection to resources on the local computer, Microsoft Technical Support will not be able to connect to the host computer to perform the kernel debugging.

29. **A** When the RAS Server is running on the host computer, the remote user can connect to the host computer using the REMOTE.EXE program. It does not matter that the target computer is running on a separate computer.

30. **D** The Windows NT Event Viewer's System log can contain an entry with the actual STOP error message if the Startup/ Shutdown tab in the System applet has been configured to write an event to the system log.

12.9 Key Words

Application event log

DUMPCHK

DUMPEXAM

DUMPFLOP

Host computer

Kernel debugger

Memory dump file

Security event log

Stop event

System event log

Target computer

Practice Exam: Troubleshooting

Use this practice exam to test your mastery of "Troubleshooting." The passing Microsoft score is 76.4 percent.

1. What is the syntax of the SYSDIFF command that applies the changes created by a new application to another system?
   A. SYSDIFF /APPLY SNAPFILE
   B. SYSDIFF /DIFF SNAPFILE
   C. SYSDIFF /APPLY DIFFFILE
   D. SYSDIFF /DIFF DIFFFILE
2. Why must a Backup Domain Controller communicate with a Primary Domain Controller during the installation process? Choose all that apply.
   A. To verify that the account being used to install the BDC has sufficient permissions.
   B. To synchronize the BDC's copy of the accounts database.
   C. To create the computer account for the BDC in the accounts database.
   D. To verify the network protocols that must be installed on the BDC.
3. During the installation of an NT Workstation, you encounter an error message that states the hard disk cannot be accessed. The error message is 0x4,0,0,0. The cause of this error is which of the following?
   A. Another installation of NT Workstation using the same serial number has been found on the network.
   B. There is insufficient disk space on the NT Workstation.
   C. The CD-ROM is damaged.
   D. A boot sector virus is on the computer.
4. Which program is used to add a Tape Backup Device to an existing installation of Windows NT Server?
   A. The Add/Remove Hardware applet in the Control Panel.
   B. The Tape Devices applet in the Control Panel.
   C. The Windows NT Setup program.
   D. The SCSI Devices applet in the Control Panel.
5. What partitions can Windows NT Server be installed to? Select all that apply.
   A. Mirrored sets
   B. Volume sets
   C. Stripe sets
   D. Stripe sets with parity
6. When starting your computer, Windows NT's boot menu is not presented and the computer starts Windows 95 immediately. Some of the likely causes of this are which of the following?
   A. Windows NT has been removed from the computer.
   B. Windows 95 has been set as the default operating system.
   C. Somebody has run the SYS command on drive C.
   D. The timeout setting in BOOT.INI has been set to 0.
7. You have been asked to update the Emergency Repair Disk, but it appears to be failing. What is the probable cause?
   A. The Emergency Repair Disk that you have tried to update is corrupt.
   B. The Emergency Repair Disk must be blank and formatted under Windows NT.
   C. You must be a member of the local group Administrators or Power Users to run RDISK.

D. The Registry must have been in use when you tried to update the Emergency Repair Disk.

8. During the start of Windows NT, you encounter an error message that states that the file NTFS.SYS is corrupt. You decide to perform an emergency repair on the system. Which option do you select to fix this problem?

   A. Inspect Registry Files

   B. Inspect Startup Environment

   C. Verify Windows NT System Files

   D. Inspect Boot Sector

9. After creating a stripe set with parity on your computer, Windows NT refuses to restart. You receive an error message that states <WINNT ROOT>\SYSTEM32\NTOSKRNL.EXE IS MISSING OR CORRUPT. You decide to perform an emergency repair on the computer. Which option do you select?

   A. Inspect Registry Files

   B. Inspect Startup Environment

   C. Verify Windows NT System Files

   D. Inspect Boot Sector

10. If the Windows NT boot sector has been replaced with the Windows 95 Boot sector, how do you reinstall the Windows NT boot sector?

    A. Reinstall Windows NT.

    B. Run an Emergency Repair Process and select the Inspect Startup Environment option.

    C. Run an Emergency Repair Process and select the Inspect Boot Sector option.

    D. Boot with a Windows NT Boot disk and select the SYS option in Disk Administrator.

11. If you wanted to determine the name of each file installed by Windows NT, what file could be viewed on the Emergency Repair Disk that contains this information?

    A. LOADED.LOG

    B. SETUP.LOG

    C. FILES.LOG

    D. EVENTS.LOG

12. NTBackup enables what options on Registry files?

    A. All Registry files on the network can be backed up and restored.

    B. Backup on the Registry file is not enabled.

    C. Only the local Registry file can be backed up and restored.

    D. Only the changes from the prior Registry file can be saved.

13. If the Registry becomes corrupted, how can the entire Registry be restored?

    A. It can't be; you must reinstall it.

    B. By using the Emergency Repair Disk.

    C. By copying an older version to registry.sys.

    D. By renaming the backup Registry to registry.nt.

14. Which of the following is the name of the registry file?

    A. REG.DAT

    B. It has multiple names.

    C. SYSTEM.INI

    D. SYSTEM.REG

15. If the start value is set to System for a driver, when is the driver loaded during the Windows NT startup process?

    A. By NTLDR

    B. During the NTOSKRNL.EXE initialization

C. During the system startup phase

D. By a dependency service

16. When are changes to the Registry file implemented? Choose all that apply.

    A. At boot up for the local machine

    B. When changed

    C. When acknowledged by the administrator

    D. When the user logs in again

17. Your printer is unable to send any jobs to the physical print devices and you have verified that the correct port has been selected. What other configuration property can you change?

    A. Start printing after last page is spooled

    B. Start printing immediately

    C. Stop the Spooler Service

    D. Print directly to printer

18. Which option can be set for a Printer to prevent PostScript jobs from being printed to a connected PCL Print Device?

    A. Print directly to printer

    B. Hold mismatched jobs

    C. Print spooled documents first

    D. Check print format

19. What can be configured in the Telephony applet of Control Panel? Choose all that apply.

    A. Modem configuration

    B. Dialing locations

    C. Calling card information

    D. Whether the phone line uses pulse or tone

20. Mary, a user, receives a message that her user account could not be authenticated. Which debugging feature can be used to troubleshoot this problem?

    A. Use the Event Viewer

    B. Enable the logging option in Remote Access Admin

    C. Enable PPP logging in the Registry

    D. Server Manager

21. You want to use a centralized LMHOSTS file for all your servers and want to reference this LMHOSTS file located in the PUBLIC share of the computer name LOCALSRV. What entries are required in the LMHOSTS file if the LOCALSRV computer is located on a remote subnet?

    A. #BEGIN_ALTERNATE

       #INCLUDE \\localsrv\public\lmhosts

       #END_ALTERNATE

       172.16.2.1 LOCALSRV

    B. 172.16.2.1 LOCALSRV

       #BEGIN_ALTERNATE

       #INCLUDE \\localsrv\public\lmhosts

       #END_ALTERNATE

    C. #INCLUDE \\localsrv\public\lmhosts

    D. 172.16.2.1 LOCALSRV

       #INCLUDE \\localsrv\public\lmhosts

22. You want to have Jody use her account and password to make Windows NT computers members of the SCHOOL-HOUSE domain. What methods can be used to enable Jody to add computers to the domain?

    A. Make Jody a member of the Administrators group in the SCHOOLHOUSE domain.

    B. Make Jody a member of the Account Operators group in the SCHOOLHOUSE domain.

C. Make Jody a member of the Server Operators group in the SCHOOLHOUSE domain.

D. Grant Jody the User Right to "Add Workstations to Domain."

Answers and Explanations: Practice Exam

1. **C** The syntax for applying a difference file is SYSDIFF /APPLY DIFFFILE.

2. **B, C** During the installation of a BDC, the SAM database is synchronized to the BDC, and a computer account is created in the SAM database for the BDC.

3. **D** This message occurs when a boot sector virus is found during the installation of Windows NT.

4. **B** Tape Devices are added via the Tape Device applet in Control Panel.

5. **A** Windows NT can be installed only to mirror sets in the list of options. Volume sets and stripe sets have no fault tolerance and cannot house the Boot or system partitions. The Boot and system partitions also cannot be stored on a Windows NT created RAID 5 partition. This is supported only under hardware RAID 5.

6. **B, C, D** If Windows 95 is set to be the default operating system and the timeout value in the BOOT.INI is set to 0, the computer will automatically start Windows 95 without presenting a boot menu. Likewise, if the SYS command was run in Windows 95 on the C drive, this would replace the boot sector and now look for IO.SYS instead of NTLDR.

7. **C** To update the Emergency Repair Disk, you must be a member of either the Administrators or Power Users local group and using the computer on which you are running RDISK.

8. **C** To replace a corrupted driver file, you select the Verify Windows NT System Files option. If you had applied any service packs, they must be re-applied after this, because the file is restored to the pre-service-pack version.

9. **B** The Inspect Startup Environment option searches for the partition and disk on which Windows NT is installed and rebuilds the BOOT.INI. If the SYSTEM partition was installed on a FAT partition, editing the BOOT.INI also could have been performed to fix this problem (as long as you knew the new partition number for the installation).

10. **C** By inspecting the boot sector, the Emergency Repair Process resets the boot sector to load the file NTLDR.

11. **B** The file SETUP.LOG contains the name of every file installed under Windows NT. It also contains a CRC value to determine whether a file has been corrupted.

12. **C** The NTBackup utility only enables the local Registry to be backed up to tape.

13. **B** By performing an Emergency Repair process, you can read in a previously saved version of the Registry, assuming that you have updated the repair information using RDISK.

14. **B** The Windows NT 4 Registry is made up of several hives that are stored in the %SystemRoot%\System32\Config directory.

15. **B** System drivers are started at the same time that the Windows NT kernel is initialized.

16. **A, B, D** It depends on what you have adjusted. Some of the changes are immediate, some require the system to be restarted, and some take effect the next time the user logs in to the network.

17. **D** When you print directly to the printer, you bypass the Print Spooler entirely. You can do this to test for a corrupt print spooler.

18. **B** When you choose the option to Hold mismatched jobs, the print spooler detects that the job was intended for a PostScript printer when the printer only supports PCL jobs. It prevents the job from printing, but enables other jobs to continue printing.

19. **B, C, D** The Telephony applet enables dialing locations to be configured. The dialing location information includes calling card information and indicates whether the phone line used pulses or tones.

20. **C** By enabling PPP logging in the Registry, authentication problems can be determined using the PPP.LOG file.

21. **B, D** When you reference a centrally stored LMHOSTS file, you must first have an entry for the SERVER where the LMHOSTS file is located. If the entry does not exist, there is no way for the client to resolve the NetBIOS name to an IP address when the LMHOSTS file resides on a remote subnet. The LMHOSTS file is parsed sequentially line by line.

22. **A, B, D** The Administrators and Account Operators groups can add Workstations to the domain by default. You can also grant users this right by granting them the user right Add Workstations to Domain.

Part III

MCSE TestPrep

Windows NT Workstation 4

Chapter 13

Planning

This chapter helps you prepare for the exam by covering the following objectives:

- Creating unattended installation files
- Choosing the appropriate file system to use in a given situation, including NTFS, FAT, HPFS, security, and dual boot scenarios
- Planning strategies for sharing and securing resources

This chapter focuses on planning the unattended installation of Windows NT Workstation 4.0, planning how to most effectively share and secure resources, and planning the appropriate file system to use on your Windows NT Workstation. Planning is a key element in the implementation of any new operating system. Microsoft emphasizes this fact by devoting an entire section of the exam to test your knowledge on planning for a Windows NT Workstation 4.0 implementation. A planning session answers questions such as what file system to use, how to set up security for users and applications, and whether or not Windows NT Workstation is the best operating system, given your requirements and objectives.

13.1 Creating Unattended Installation Files

The Windows NT Workstation setup application normally prompts the user for information about the current installation. Some parameters the user must supply are as follows:

- File system type (NTFS or FAT)
- Computer Name
- Network Options, such as protocols to install or domain membership
- Video hardware and resolution
- Time Zone information

Windows NT setup can retrieve the information for these parameters through various text files that are created prior to beginning the setup. When setup is launched, command-line switches specify the locations of these files. These files can automate portions of or the entire setup process, eliminating the need for a user to be present at each machine during setup.

A. Files Used for Unattended Installation

In a relatively small environment, one with less than 10 machines, manually installing Windows NT Workstation might be an option. In larger environments, however, time is better spent developing and implementing an unattended installation plan for rolling out Windows NT across the enterprise. Some of the files and tools related to this unattended installation process are as follows:

- Unattended answer file (unattend.txt)
- Uniqueness database file (UDF)
- Sysdiff

Windows NT 4.0 uses a combination of an unattended answer file with unique database files to do both the customization and automation of the installation of Windows NT Workstation. A third utility used in the installation process, sysdiff, enables the administrator to automate the installation of other applications in addition to the operating system itself. By using these three tools, an administrator can perform an entire installation of the operating system and all needed applications.

1. Understanding Answer Files

Answer files eliminate the need for an administrator to sit at a particular computer and manually reply to the prompts of the setup program. Windows NT setup uses an unattended answer file to provide specific information about setup options. The path to the text file is specified with the /u switch when starting Windows NT setup. You can use the same unattended answer file across a number of installations. If you use an unattended answer file only, however, it is difficult to completely automate the setup process because of the unique information required to install Windows NT Workstation—for example, machine name, domain memberships, and applicable network information such as IP address or DNS hostname.

To circumvent this problem, one option is to create an unattend.txt file for each computer and specify the unique name and path when starting setup on each machine. This drastically increases the management effort required during the installation and can lead to errors during the installation.

Another option is to selectively automate portions of the setup. For those parameters that require unique responses, you can force the installation program to pause for user input. However, this approach reduces much of the benefit of automating the setup process.

2. Using Uniqueness Database Files (UDF)

The best solution to the problem of providing unique information in the unattended answer file during the installation process is to create what is called a uniqueness database file or UDF. A UDF is a text file that enables you to supply the information that must be unique to each computer or each user. Uniqueness database files are used with an unattended answer file to provide a complete installation of Windows NT Workstation without any user intervention during the setup process. The uniqueness database file provides the capability to specify per-computer parameters for a truly unique installation.

The UDF is used to merge or replace sections of the unattended answer file during the GUI portion of the Windows NT setup process. For the installation of Windows NT Workstation 4.0, you can use one unattended answer file for the information that applies to all installations, and one or more UDF files to specify the settings intended for a single computer or for a group of computers. It is possible to have one UDF that contains settings for multiple computers or users within it. As with the unattended answer file, the name and path to the UDF file is specified with the /UDF switch when starting Windows NT setup.

3. Using the Sysdiff Utility

In addition to installing Windows NT Workstation, you might need to install other applications. If those applications do not support a scripted installation, you can use the sysdiff utility to install the additional applications on the destination computers. Sysdiff requires three steps:

- Create a snapshot file
- Create a difference file
- Apply the difference file

Sysdiff is also alternatively used to:

- Create an INF file
- Dump the contents of a difference file

B. Creating an Unattended Answer File

The unattended answer file is a simple text file that provides responses to the Windows NT Setup application prompts. A sample unattended answer file, called unattend.txt, is included with the Windows NT Workstation CD. You can use it as a template for creating or customizing your specific unattended installation file. You can also use the Windows NT Setup Manager, a graphical application included with the Windows NT Workstation Resource Kit CD, to create an unattended answer file.

1. Modifying the Unattend.txt Sample File

On the Windows NT Workstation 4.0 CD, open the unattend.txt file with a text editor such as Notepad. The information found in the unattend.txt file is categorized as section headings, parameters, and values associated with those parameters. Most of the section headings are predefined and do not require changes. An example of the format used follows:

```
[section]
;comments
;comments
parameter=value
```

Information in the unattend.txt file is divided into main sections. You might or might not choose to modify these sections, depending on your particular environment. Those sections are as follows:

- [Unattended]. This section is used during text mode setup and can be modified only in the answer file; there is no valid entry in the UDF. This section tells the setup that this is an unattended setup.

This section specifies settings such as installation type (upgrade/new), installation path, and file system type (NTFS/FAT).

- [OEMBootFiles]. This section is used to specify OEM boot files and can be specified only in the answer file, not in the UDF.
- [MassStorageDrivers]. This section is used to specify SCSI drivers to install and is used during the text mode portion of setup. If this section is missing, setup tries to detect SCSI devices on the computer. This section can be specified only in the answer file, not in the UDF.
- [DisplayDrivers]. This section contains a list of display drivers to be loaded by the text mode setup process. If this section is missing, setup tries to detect the display devices on the computer.
- [KeyboardDrivers]. This section includes a list of keyboard drivers to be loaded by setup. This setting can be specified only in the answer file, not in the UDF.
- [PointingDeviceDrivers]. This section contains a list of pointing device drivers to be used during setup and is run during the text mode portion of setup. This section must be specified in the answer file, not in the UDF.
- [OEM_Ads]. This section can be used to modify the default user interface of the setup program. It is used to modify the banner, background bitmap, and logo used during the GUI portion of setup.
- [GuiUnattended]. This section is used to specify settings for the GUI portion of setup. It can be used to indicate the time zone and to hide the administrator password page.
- [UserData]. This section is used to provide user-specific data such as username, organization name, computer name, and product ID.
- [LicenseFilePrintData]. This section is only valid when installing Windows NT Server. It enables you to specify the licensing option you want to use for your Windows NT server.
- [Network]. This section is used to specify network settings such as network adapters, services, and protocols. If this section is missing, networking won't be installed. This is the section used to specify the domain or workgroup to join, as well as to create a computer account in the domain.

If a [Network] section is not specified in your unattended answer file, no networking for Windows NT Workstation is installed. If the computer you are installing does not have a CD-ROM and you are installing across the network, you have a Windows NT system that has no way to connect to the installation files to add the networking components.

If the [Network] section is specified but is empty, the user is presented with a number of different error messages during the installation.

- [Modem]. This section is used to identify whether or not a modem should be installed. This section must be specified if you want to install RAS in unattended mode.
- [Display]. This section is used to indicate specific display settings for the display adapter being installed. These settings must be correct and supported by the adapter.
- [DetectedMassStorage]. This section is used to specify which mass storage devices setup should recognize, even if they are not currently connected to the system during installation. This setting must be specified in the answer file, not in the UDF.

> **The sections of the unattended answer file that pertain to individual user settings are the most likely candidates for inclusion in a UDF. Those are: [GuiUnattended], [UserData], and [Network].**

Those items that can be specified only in the answer file and not the UDF must be the same for all installations from that answer file. If, for example, you need to install different keyboard drivers or SCSI drivers on various machines, you must create a different answer file for each instance.

2. Using Setup Manager to Create an Unattended Answer File

Setup Manager is a graphical application that comes with the Windows NT Workstation Resource Kit CD. You can use it to graphically create an unattended answer file instead of directly editing the template file on the Resource Kit CD. You can specify the following three areas in the Setup Manager:

- General Setup
- Network Setup
- Advanced Setup

a. General Setup

The *General Setup* button is used to specify the installation type and directory, display settings, time zone, license mode, user information, computer role, and general information for hardware detection and upgrade information.

b. Network Options

The *Network Options* button is used to specify the network adapters, protocols, and services, as well as modem settings, and whether this portion of the GUI setup should be manual or automatic.

c. Advanced Options

The *Advanced Options* button is used to specify device drivers to install, the file system to use, and the banner and background information to use during the GUI portion of setup. This section also is used to control the reboots during the setup process, as well as to skip the display of the administrator password page.

You can use a combination of Setup Manager to configure most of the settings for the unattended answer file and then use a text editor to make changes to that file directly.

C. Creating Uniqueness Database Files

The uniqueness database file extends the functionality of the unattended answer file, enabling the specification of per-computer settings. Its function is to merge with sections of the answer file to provide these computer-specific settings. The UDF is a text file that should be located with the other Windows NT installation files on the distribution server.

The UDF contains two sections—one for Unique IDs and one for the Unique ID parameters. The first section identifies which areas of the answer file will be replaced or modified. It is used to specify the particular users or computers that will have unique information specified. The Unique ID parameters section contains the actual data that will be merged into the answer file, such as the computer name or time zone information. As with the Unattned.txt file, the path and name of the uniqueness database file is specified through the /UDF switch when launching the setup application from the command line.

The first section of the UDF lists the Uniqueness IDs. Following the Uniqueness IDs are the sections to which they refer. For example:

```
[UniqueIDs]
User1 = UserData, GuiUnattended, Network
User2 = UserData, GuiUnattended, Network
[User1:UserData]
FullName = "User 1"
OrgName = "MyCompany"
ComputerName = "Computer1"
[User1:GuiUnattended]
TimeZone = "(GMT-08:00) Pacific Time (US & Canada); Tijuana"
[User1:Network]
JoinDomain = "DomainName"
[User2:UserData]
FullName = "User 2"
OrgName = "MyCompany"
ComputerName = "Computer2"
[User2:GuiUnattended]
TimeZone = "(GMT-08:00) Pacific Time (US & Canada); Tijuana"
[User2:Network]
JoinDomain = "OtherDomain"
```

So, how do you combine the use of the unattended answer file and the UDF? For each environment (similar hardware, certain department, certain geography), create a single unattended answer file. Additionally, create at least one UDF file that specifies the unique IDs of all machines that will be installed. For each Unique ID, indicate those parameters that should be defined on a per-computer basis or per-user basis.

Understanding how the unattended answer file and UDFs function is important for the exam. Not only is it one of the exam objectives, but there tend to be quite a few questions about this area on the exam.

D. Using Sysdiff

Sysdiff, unlike the unattended answer file and the uniqueness database file, is not used to actually install the Windows NT operating system itself. Instead, it is used to install applications after the operating system is in place. You can use it with an unattended installation to create a fully automated install of both the operating system and your applications.

Sysdiff gives you the ability to track the changes between a standard installation of Windows NT Workstation and an installation that has been modified to your particular environment. It does this by creating a *snapshot* of your system before the changes. The snapshot is of a freshly installed Windows NT Workstation, configured from the automated installation. After you have made the desired changes to your system (adding applications), sysdiff records a *difference file*, which tracks the changes that were made.

1. Creating a Snapshot File

The first step to use sysdiff is to complete an installation of Windows NT Workstation on a sample system. This computer's hardware configuration should be identical to the systems on which you intend to install Windows NT Workstation. Also, the installation method on this machine should be identical to the method you will use during the roll out. After the operating system is installed, use sysdiff to take a snapshot of that reference machine by using this command:

```
Sysdiff /snap [/log:log file] snapshot file
```

where the following is true:

log file is the name of an optional log file that can be created by sysdiff.

snapshot file is the name of the file that will contain the snapshot of the system.

This process creates the snapshot file, which is referred to as the original configuration. The original configuration is the baseline system for comparing with the changed system. In addition to being an identical hardware platform, the Windows NT root directory (d:\winnt, for example) must be the same on the reference machine and the target machines that will have the difference file applied.

2. Creating a Difference File

After the snapshot has been taken, install all desired applications on the baseline machine. After the applications have been installed, apply the second step of sysdiff, which is to create the difference file. The difference file is created by using this command:

```
Sysdiff /diff [/c:title] [/log:log file] snapshot file difference file
```

where the following is true:

/c:title is the title for the difference file.

log file is the name of an optional log file that can be created by sysdiff.

snapshot file is the name of the file that contains the snapshot of the system. This file must be created from the same snapshot file created with the /snap command. If you use a file created on another system, sysdiff will not run.

difference file is the name of the file that contains the changes from when the snapshot was created to the current configuration of the system.

This mode uses the snapshot file (the original configuration) created in the first step to determine the changes in the directory structure and the Registry entries created by the application installations.

3. Applying the Difference File

The final step in the sysdiff process is to apply the difference file to a new installation as part of the unattended setup. This is done with the following command:

```
Sysdiff /apply /m [/log:log file] difference file
```

where the following is true:

/m makes the changes made to the menu structure map to the Default User profile structure, rather than to the currently logged on user. Otherwise, these menu changes would be made only to one user account, not globally to the system, and that one user account might not even exist on the destination workstation.

log file is the name of an optional log file sysdiff uses to write information regarding the process. This is good to use for troubleshooting if sysdiff fails during the apply process.

difference file is the file created by the /diff command. The Windows NT root must be the same (d:\winnt, for example) as the system that created the difference file. This means that all the unattended installs that you will perform using this difference file must be identical in the location of this system root.

You do not have to run this command as part of the unattended installation. You can run it at any time after Windows NT Workstation is installed. To make the installation of Windows NT and your applications fully automated, you might want to have it run as part of the install.

Because this difference file contains all the files and Registry settings for the applications you installed, it can be quite large (depending on how many applications you install). Applying such a potentially large package as part of the installation can add a significant amount of time to your setup process. One way to alleviate this problem is to create an INF file from this difference file.

4. Creating an INF File

An INF file created from the difference file contains only the Registry and the initialization file directives. It is, therefore, significantly smaller than the difference file itself. The command to initiate the INF portion of the installation is as follows:

```
Sysdiff /inf /m [/u] sysdiff_file oem_root
```

where the following is true:

/m makes the changes made to the menu structure map to the Default User profile structure rather than to the currently logged on user. Otherwise, these menu changes would be made only to one user account, not globally to the system, and that one user account might not even exist on the destination workstation.

/u indicates that the INF be generated as a Unicode text file. The default is to generate the file by using the system ANSI codepage.

Sysdiff_file is the path to the file created by the /diff process.

Oem_root is the path of a directory. This is where the OEM structure required for the INF is created and where the INF is placed.

This command creates the INF file, as well as a OEM directory structure, which contains all the files from the difference file package. You should create this directory under the I386 directory (if installing x86 machines) on the distribution server. If the directory is not under the I386 directory, you can move it.

The initial phase of Windows NT installation is DOS-based and cannot copy directories with path names longer than 64 characters. Make certain that the directory length under the OEM directory does not exceed 64 characters.

5. Using the INF File

To use this INF file after it has been created, you must add a line to the file Cmdlines.txt under the OEM directory. This line is used to invoke the INF that you created. The format of the command is as follows:

```
"RUNDLL32 syssetup,SetupInfObjectInstallAction section 128 inf"
```

where the following is true:

section specifies the name of the section in the INF file.

inf specifies the name of the INF file. This needs to be specified as a relative path.

Using an INF file rather than the entire difference file package can save you time in your unattended installation.

6. Dumping the Difference File

You can use the /dump option to dump the difference file into a file that you can review. This command enables you to read the contents of the difference file. The syntax of this command is as follows:

```
Sysdiff /dump difference file dump file
```

where the following is true:

difference file specifies the name of the difference file that you want to review.

dump file specifies the name you want to give to the dump file.

After creating the dump file, you can view it with a text editor such as Notepad.

E. Activating an Automated Install

After creating the unattend.txt, the uniqueness database, and the sysdiff file, you can launch Windows NT setup from the command line in one of two ways:

- From an existing Windows NT installation:

```
X:\i386\winnt32.exe /s:<source_path> /u:v:\unattend.txt /UDF:user1;v:\udf.txt
```

- From an existing Windows 95, Windows 3.1, or DOS installation:

```
X:\i386\winnt.exe /s:<source_path> /u:v:\unattend.txt /UDF:user1;v:\udf.txt
```

Where *X:* is the drive mapped to your installation CD-ROM or network share point, *<source_path>* is the path pointing to the /i386 directory of the distribution files, and *v:* is the drive mapped to the directory containing your unattend.txt and uniqueness database files.

13.1.1 Exercise: Using the Setup Manager to Create an Unattended Answer File

Objective: Create an unattended answer file by using the Setup Manager utility included with the Windows NT Resource Kit.

The following exercise helps you work with the Setup Manager to create an unattended answer file, which can then be used to automate an installation of Windows NT Workstation.

1. Log on to Windows NT Workstation as an administrator.
2. Install the Setup Manager from the Windows NT Resource Kit CD-ROM. Follow the instructions provided with the Resource Kit for installing the utilities included on the CD-ROM.
3. Launch the application from the Setup Program Group in the Windows NT Resource Kit 4 Program Group.
4. Click the General button. Fill in the following fields on the User Information tab:

User Name	**Your name**
Organization Name	Acme
Computername	ACME1
Product ID	Leave blank

Fill in the following information on the Computer Role tab:

Role	**Workstation in Workgroup**
Workgroup Name	WebWorks

On the Time Zone tab, select your time zone from the list. Click the OK button.

5. Click the Networking Setup button. On the General tab, select Automatically detect and install first adapter. Click the OK button.

6. Click the Advanced Setup button. On the Advertisement tab, Banner text, type **Acme Setup for Windows NT Workstation**. On the General tab, put a check mark in the following check boxes:
   - Reboot After Text Mode
   - Reboot After GUI Mode
   - Skip Welcome Wizard Page
   - Skip Administrator Password Page

   Click OK.
7. Click the Save button and save this file as c:\unattend.txt. Exit Setup Manager.
8. Launch Notepad from the Start button, Programs, Accessories menu. From the File menu, choose Open. In the File Name field, type **c:\unattend.txt**. Review the contents of the file.
9. Exit Notepad and log off Windows NT Workstation.

Answers and Explanations: Exercise

This exercise showed you how to use the Setup Manager to create an unattended answer file. For more information about the concepts raised by the exercise, refer to the section entitled “Using Setup Manager to Create an Unattended Answer File.”

13.1 Practice Problems

1. You have to roll out 200 copies of Windows NT Workstation with Office 97 installed. What tools can you use to assist you in this task?

   A. Sysdiff

   B. Windiff

   C. UNATTEND.TXT

   D. Uniqueness database file

2. How can you create an unattend.txt file? Select all options that apply.

   A. Use a text editor such as Windows Notepad.

   B. Use Setup Manager, included with the Windows NT Resource Kit.

   C. Use the Windows NT system editor in the Control Panel.

   D. Modify the unattend.txt file, included with the Windows NT Resource Kit, to fit your environment.

3. *Situation:* You need to roll out 300 copies of Windows NT Workstation. All have identical hardware configurations. All will use the NWLink network protocol to communicate with the corporate Novell 3.*x* servers. Each Windows NT Workstation installation will be identical.

   Desired Result: Install and configure Windows NT Workstation 4.0 on all workstations so that when they are booted for the first time after installation they will operate in the corporate environment without modification.

   Optional Result #1: Minimize the installation time.

   Optional Result #2: Minimize user intervention.

   Proposed Solution: Create a single unattended installation file. There will be a single UDF created to specify unique machine names.

   A. The proposed solution meets the desired result and all optional results.

   B. The proposed solution meets only the desired result.

   C. The proposed solution meets the desired result and one optional result.

   D. The proposed solution does not meet the desired result or either of the optional results.

4. How can you create a uniqueness database file? Select all that apply.

   A. Use Setup Manager, included with the Windows NT Resource Kit.

   B. Use the Windows NT Workstation Policy Editor.

   C. Use a text editor such as Notepad.

   D. Use a commercial desktop database such as Microsoft Access.

5. Select all the tools you can use to automate the installation of Windows NT Workstation 4.0.

   A. SYSDIFF.EXE

   B. WINDIFF.EXE

   C. UNATTEND.TXT

   D. Uniqueness data list

6. What switch enables you to instruct Windows NT Workstation 4.0 setup to run by using an unattended text file during the installation?

   A. /u

   B. /b

   C. /c

   D. /UDF

7. What switch enables you to instruct Windows NT Workstation 4.0 setup to run by using a uniqueness database file during setup?

   A. /U

   B. /UDF

   C. /x

   D. /OC

8. What are the three steps required to use sysdiff to install additional applications after installing the base operating system?

   A. Create a snapshot file, create a difference file, and apply the difference File.

   B. Create a baseline file, create a modification file, and apply the modification file.

   C. Create a snapshot file, create an installable file, and apply the installable file.

   D. Create a baseline file, create a difference file, and apply the difference file.

9. What switch forces sysdiff to create a snapshot file?

   A. /start

   B. /baseline

   C. /bl

   D. /snap

10. Which of the following commands forces sysdiff to create a difference file named diff1wks with the sysdiff application if your snapshot file is name snap1wks?

    A. sysdiff - diff - snap1wks - diff1wks

    B. sysdiff /diff /snap1wks / diff1wks

    C. sysdiff /diff snap1wks diff1wks

    D. sysdiff - diff snap1wks diff1wks

Answers and Explanations: Practice Problems

1. **A, C, D** Sysdiff enables you to automate the installation of the Office 97 suite. Unattend.txt enables you to automate the majority of the Windows NT Setup process. The uniqueness database file enables you to provide machine-specific information to the installation routine, such as the NetBIOS machine name.

2. **A, B, D** Because unattend.txt is a plain text file, you can start from scratch or edit the sample unattend.txt with any text editor. Additionally, you can use the Setup Manager included with the Windows NT Resource Kit.

3. **A** The only parameter that needs to change between machines is the NetBIOS machine name. Using a uniqueness database file enables the administrator to specify a unique name for each machine.

4. **C** The uniqueness database is a simple text file.

5. **A, C** Sysdiff.exe and unattend.txt are two of the tools supplied by Microsoft that you can use to automate the installation of Windows NT Workstation 4.0.

6. **A** The /u switch enables you to specify the use and location of the unattended text file when running Windows NT setup.

7. **B** The /UDF switch enables you to specify the use, name, and location of a uniqueness database file when running Windows NT setup.

8. **A** You must create a snapshot file on the baseline system, add the desired application and create a difference file, and finally apply the difference file.

9. **D** The /snap switch instructs sysdiff to create a snapshot file.

10. **C** The /diff switch followed by the snapshot filename and the difference filename instructs sysdiff to create a difference file.

13.1 Key Words

UDF

Sysdiff

difference file

Setup Manager

unattended answer files (unattend.txt)

13.2 Choosing the Appropriate File System

Windows NT Workstation 4.0 supports two file systems: FAT and NTFS. Earlier versions of Windows NT also supported HPFS (High Performance File System supported by OS/2); Windows NT 4.0, however, has eliminated HPFS support.

Windows NT 4.0 supports the use of either or both the NTFS and FAT file systems. An important decision in planning your Windows NT Workstation environment is which file system to use. Which file system you use depends on the needs of your particular environment. Some of the issues to consider when choosing a file system are the following:

- Performance
- Partition size
- Recoverability
- Dual-boot capabilities
- Security
- File compression

A. The High Performance File System (HPFS)

High Performance File System (HPFS) is the file system used with OS/2. Windows NT 3.51 supported partitions formatted with the HPFS file system, although it did not support formatting new drives as HPFS. In Windows NT 4.0, the support for HPFS has been eliminated entirely. Thus, if you have a system that currently has an HPFS partition, you need to change the file system on the partition prior to installing or upgrading Windows NT Workstation 4.0. You must remove the HPFS partition before setting up Windows NT 4.0 or else you cannot proceed with the installation. You can do this in one of two ways:

- Format the HPFS partition to either FAT or NTFS.
- Convert the HPFS partition to NTFS prior to the installation.

The option you choose depends on what is stored on the existing HPFS drive. If you do not want to lose the data on your HPFS or FAT partition, you can use the Convert command (from within Windows NT 3.51) to convert the HPFS or FAT partition to NTFS before you upgrade to Windows NT 4.0. Run the Convert command from the command line with the following syntax:

```
Convert drive: /FS:NTFS /v
```

where the following is true:

drive is the drive letter of the HPFS partition you want to convert.

/FS:NTFS specifies the file system to which you want to convert (NTFS is the only option).

/v runs in verbose mode.

You cannot convert the Windows NT boot partition while you are running Windows NT. If the boot partition is the partition you are attempting to convert, you receive a prompt to convert it the next time the machine is rebooted. Additionally, the convert utility can be used with Windows NT 3.51 and 4.0 at any time to convert FAT partitions to NTFS without data loss.

B. Using the FAT File System

Windows NT Workstation 4.0 supports the FAT file system, which is named after its method of organization—the File Allocation Table. The File Allocation Table resides at the top, or beginning, of the volume. Two copies of the FAT are kept in case one is damaged. FAT supports the following four file attributes:

- Read only
- Archive
- System
- Hidden

1. Benefits of FAT

The FAT file system is typically a good option for a small-sized partition. Because FAT is required for DOS, it is also a good option for a dual-boot system with Windows 95 or Windows 3.*x*. The FAT file system on Windows NT has a number of advantages over using FAT on a DOS-based system. Used under Windows NT, the FAT file system supports the following:

- Long filenames up to 255 characters
- Multiple spaces
- Multiple periods
- Filenames that are not case-sensitive but that do preserve case

The FAT file system has a fairly low file-system overhead, which makes it good for smaller partitions.

2. Limitations of FAT

Although the FAT file system is necessary for dual-boot configurations, there are some significant limitations to using it with Windows NT, including the following:

- *Inefficient for larger partitions.* There are two reasons that FAT is inefficient on larger partitions (over about 400MB). One reason is that FAT uses a linked list for its directory structure. If a file grows in size, the file can become fragmented on the disk and will have slower access time for retrieving the file because of fragmentation. The other reason is the default cluster size used on a FAT partition. For partitions up to 255MB, FAT uses a 4KB cluster size. For partitions greater than 512MB, however, FAT uses 16KB cluster sizes and up to 256KB cluster sizes for drives above 8192MB on Windows NT 4. Thus, if you use FAT under Windows NT and have a partition that is 800MB and you have many smaller (under 32KB) files on the drive, you waste a lot of space on the drive due to the cluster size.
- *Has no local security.* The FAT file system does not support local security, so there is no way to prevent a user from accessing a file if that user can log on locally to the workstation.

- *Does not support compression under Windows NT.* Although the FAT file system supports compression by using DriveSpace or DoubleSpace, neither of those are supported under Windows NT. For this reason, there is no way to use compression on FAT under Windows NT.

Whether or not you choose to use the FAT file system depends on what needs you have on your particular workstation.

C. Using the NTFS File System

NTFS tends to be the preferred file system for use under Windows NT if your environment can support it (you don't need to dual boot, for instance). Only Windows NT supports NTFS.

1. Benefits of NTFS

Using NTFS has many benefits, including the following:

- *Support for long filenames.* NTFS supports filenames up to 255 characters long.
- *Preservation of case.* NTFS is not case-sensitive, but it does have the capability to preserve case for POSIX compliance.
- *Recoverability.* NTFS is a recoverable file system. It uses transaction logging to automatically log all file and directory updates so that, in the case of a power outage or system failure, this information can be used to redo failed operations.
- *Security.* NTFS provides the user with local security for protecting files and directories.
- *Compression.* NTFS supports compression of files and directories to optimize storage space on your hard disk.
- *Size.* NTFS partitions can support much larger partition sizes than FAT. Theoretically, NTFS can support partitions up to 16 exabytes in size. (An exabyte is one billion gigabytes.)

Using NTFS gives you security and enhanced functionality compared with the FAT file system.

2. Limitations of NTFS

The main limitations of NTFS are compatibility with other operating systems and overhead. If you need to dual boot or if you have a partition size smaller than 400MB, use FAT rather than NTFS.

D. Comparison of FAT and NTFS

There are benefits to using both FAT and NTFS partitions on Windows NT Workstation. Many of these are dependent on your particular configuration and what you need to support. Table 13.2.1 provides a comparison of the two file systems.

Table 13.2.1 Comparison of NTFS and FAT File Systems

Feature	FAT	NTFS
Filename length	255	255
Compression	No	Yes
Security	No	Yes

continues

Table 13.2.1 Continued

Dual-boot capabilities with non-Windows NT systems	Yes	No
File/partition size	4GB	16EB
Recommended partition size	0–200 MB	100MB–16EB
Can use it to format a floppy	Yes	No
Recoverability (transaction logging)	No	Yes

E. Implementing Security

When talking about security as it relates to file systems, it is necessary to define what is meant by security. The NTFS file system gives you the ability to implement "local security," which is defined as being able to restrict access to a file or directory to someone who is sitting at the keyboard of that particular machine. Even if users can log on to your Windows NT workstation locally or interactively, for example, you can still prevent them from accessing your files and directories if you use NTFS security.

NTFS is the only file system used with Windows NT 4.0 that has the capability to provide local security. The FAT file system can secure a directory with only share-level permissions, not local permissions. Share-level permissions apply only to users accessing the directory across the network. Because of this, share-level permissions cannot prevent said user, logged on locally, from accessing your files or directories.

F. Choosing Dual-Boot Scenarios

If you want to dual boot between Windows NT 4.0 and any other non-Windows NT operating system, you must use the FAT file system for universal access across operating systems. The NTFS file system is accessible only by Windows NT. Thus, if you are dual booting with Windows 95, the NTFS partition will not be visible under Windows 95.

If you have a machine that you dual boot between Windows NT Workstation 4.0 and Windows 95, you can use an NTFS partition if you choose to, even though it is inaccessible from within Windows 95. You must make sure in doing this, however, that you do not format your active partition (your C: drive) or the partition that has the windows directory on it. Otherwise, you can't boot into Windows 95.

If you are using the FAT32 file system with Windows 95, you must remove it before installing Windows NT for dual boot. The FAT32 file system for Windows 95 is inaccessible from within Windows NT.

If you choose to dual boot between Windows 95 and Windows NT Workstation 4.0, any applications that you have installed under one operating system must be reinstalled under the other operating system, as well. For further comparison between Windows NT Workstation 4.0

and other Microsoft Operating Systems, see the sidebar "Comparison of Windows NT Workstation 4.0 with Other Microsoft Operating Systems."

Comparison of Windows NT Workstation 4.0 with Other Microsoft Operating Systems

An important element of the exam is your ability to determine the proper operating system for a given situation. You must be able to decide when it is advantageous for you to select Windows 3.1, Windows 95, or Windows NT Server instead of Windows NT Workstation.

Windows 3.11 (Windows for Workgroups). Windows 3.11 is a much simpler operating system than Windows NT. Therefore, it is much more limited in the services it can provide; as a result, however, it is much simpler to install and maintain.

Windows NT has many advantages over Windows 3.11. Windows NT is built on a 32-bit architecture, whereas Windows 3.11 has minimal 32-bit support for applications. Windows NT has achieved a C2-level security rating whereas security is very limited in Windows 3.11. Lastly, Windows NT provides a much more stable environment with preemptive multitasking. Windows 3.11 is a cooperative multitasking environment. Because of the cooperative multitasking, a single application failure on a Windows 3.*x* system has a good chance of crashing the entire operating system.

Windows 3.11 does have less stringent hardware requirements, but the most likely feature to steer your decision away from Windows NT is DOS support. Windows NT has a good DOS emulator, but certain applications require the native DOS support afforded by Windows 3.11. If you have one or more corporate applications that require DOS, you might have to look at Windows 3.11 as your operating system.

Windows 95. There are strong, valid reasons to select either Windows 95 or Windows NT. On most single-processor machines, with less than 24 megabytes of RAM, Windows 95 demonstrates better application performance. Although Windows 95 does operate as a 32-bit operating system with native 32-bit applications, it is still tied to a cooperative multitasking model. Also, Windows 95 has less stringent system requirements.

Windows NT still offers better security and true 32-bit performance for all applications in a preemptive multitasking environment. Also, if you are looking at multiprocessor machines or alternative platforms such as RISC-based machines, Windows NT is your only choice because Windows 95 is written specifically to the Intel architecture and does not offer the portability of Windows NT. Lastly, as available memory increases, Windows NT delivers better application performance than an equivalent Windows 95 machine.

Windows NT Server. The choice of Windows NT Server will largely be based on capacity. Windows NT Server does not impose the limits inherent in Workstation for the number of processors supported, the number of inbound network connections

continues

continued

serviced, and the number of inbound remote access sessions than can be concurrently sustained.

There are also performance issues associated with each operating system. Windows NT Server is optimized to handle network requests such as file and print services at a higher priority than applications. The opposite is true with Windows NT Workstation.

Windows NT Server includes additional tools for creating and managing domains and integrating with other network operating systems such as Novell NetWare. Lastly, Windows NT Server includes additional applications for establishing an Internet presence with Internet Information Server.

Upgrading Existing Operating Systems. **To make the best decision on which operating system to select, you also need to understand the various upgrade paths to Windows NT Workstation.**

When upgrading from Windows 3.11, user settings and applications are migrated during the upgrade. Additionally, program groups are maintained. The same is true with an upgrade from Windows NT Workstation 3.5 or 3.51.

The upgrade path from Windows 95 is not as simple. Windows 95 configuration is Registry-based, as in Windows NT Workstation 4.0. However, the Registries are not compatible. Therefore, when installing Windows NT over Windows 95, all user settings and applications are lost. You must reinstall all user applications after installing Windows NT.

13.2.1 Exercise: Creating a Partition with Disk Administrator and Converting an Existing FAT Partition to NTFS

This exercise teaches you how to convert a FAT partition to NTFS:

1. Log on to Windows NT Workstation as an administrator.
2. Go to a command prompt, type **convert *drive letter:* /fs:ntfs**, and then press Enter. Windows NT begins the conversion process. If files are in use on this partition, you receive a message that `Convert cannot gain exclusive access to your drive, would you like to schedule it to be converted the next time the system restarts`. Type **Y** to answer Yes and press Enter.
3. Exit the command prompt by typing **Exit**. Restart Windows NT Workstation by clicking the Start button, Restart the Computer.

When the computer reboots, it converts the drive to NTFS. After the conversion has happened, the system restarts again and boots into Windows NT Workstation.

Answers and Explanations: Exercise

This showed you how to convert an existing FAT partition to NTFS. For more information about the concepts raised by the exercise, refer to the section entitled “Converting HPFS and FAT Partitions.”

13.2 Practice Problems

1. John needs to dual boot his machine with Windows 95 and Windows NT Workstation. He has three partitions of 200 megabytes, 400 megabytes, and 800 megabytes on his machine. He wants to have 100 megabytes available for certain files that he will use only with Windows NT Workstation that must be secure. He also has some data and applications that Windows 95 and Windows NT will use. How should he format his partitions?

    A. All partitions should be formatted with FAT.

    B. All partitions should be formatted with NTFS.

    C. Format the 400- and 800-megabyte partitions with the FAT file system and the 200-megabyte partition with NTFS.

    D. Format the 200- and 800-megabyte partitions with the FAT file system and the 400-megabyte partition with NTFS.

2. Mary wants to upgrade her OS/2 machine to Windows NT Workstation 4.0. It is a 486 system with a 1.2 gigabyte hard disk (formatted with HPFS), 32 megabytes of RAM, and a 6x CD-ROM. What steps should she complete to upgrade her system?

    A. Format the partition with FAT prior to starting the Windows NT Workstation installation.

    B. You cannot upgrade to Windows NT Workstation from OS/2.

    C. Install Windows NT as an upgrade that automatically converts the partition to NTFS.

    D. Do nothing; Windows NT 4.0 Workstation can read and write to HPFS partitions.

3. Jamie is running a dual-boot system with Windows NT Workstation 4.0 and Windows 3.11. The system has a single hard disk with one 800-megabyte partition. She is running out of disk space and wants to use Windows NT compression. How should she proceed?

    A. Use the Windows 3.11 shrink.exe utility.

    B. Use the MS-DOS DoubleSpace utility.

    C. She cannot use compression.

    D. Enable compression on the selected files when she is running Windows NT Workstation to compress the files.

4. Select all benefits of using FAT over NTFS:

    A. FAT requires less file system overhead on the partition.

    B. FAT is more efficient for partitions less than 800 megabytes.

    C. FAT is supported by more operating systems.

    D. FAT is fault tolerant.

5. Windows NT FAT formatted partitions support filename lengths up to:

    A. 120 characters

    B. 255 characters

    C. 256 characters

    D. 512 characters

6. Windows NT NTFS formatted partitions support filenames up to which size?

    A. 128 characters

    B. 255 characters

    C. 256 characters

    D. 512 characters

7. You currently have 23 Windows 95 machines. You want to upgrade the systems to Windows NT Workstation while maintaining the same set of applications on the machines for users. Select all the steps you need to complete to perform this upgrade.

   A. Start Windows NT Setup.

   B. Reinstall all user applications.

   C. Run upgrade.exe after the installation to migrate all user and application settings.

   D. Ensure that Windows NT Setup does not reformat the partition with NTFS.

8. You currently have 50 Windows 3.11 machines that need to be upgraded to Windows NT Workstation 4.0 while maintaining the same set of applications and users on the original machines. Select all the steps you need to perform to accomplish the upgrade.

   A. Create an unattended installation of Windows NT Workstation to facilitate the upgrade and complete the installation.

   B. Run upgrade.exe from the Windows NT Resource KIT to ensure users are upgraded appropriately.

   C. Reinstall all applications to ensure the users have the same work environment as they did before the installation.

   D. Use sysdiff to take a snapshot of the Windows 3.11 installation and apply the changes after the upgrade to Windows NT Workstation 4.0.

9. James has a Windows NT 3.51 workstation with a single HPFS partition. He wants to upgrade to Windows NT Workstation 4.0. What steps should he perform? Select all that apply.

   A. Start the upgrade to Windows NT Workstation 4.0. Setup automatically converts the partition to NTFS.

   B. Run setup; Windows NT Workstation runs on this system without modification.

   C. Run convert.exe from the console prompt to convert the current HPFS partition to NTFS.

   D. Reformat the existing partition during setup with either FAT or NTFS.

10. What are the benefits of using NTFS over FAT? Select all that apply.

    A. NTFS is fault tolerant.

    B. NTFS requires less file-system overhead on the partition.

    C. NTFS supports file- and folder-level permissions.

    D. NTFS supports share-level permissions.

11. How can you upgrade user and application settings from Windows 3.11 to Windows NT Workstation 4.0?

    A. You cannot do so.

    B. This is done automatically during setup.

    C. You must do it manually by running upgrade.exe from the command line after the installation is complete.

    D. You must back up the data prior to completing the upgrade and restore the data after the upgrade.

12. Select all the advantages of using Windows NT Workstation over Windows 3.11.

    A. Windows NT is more secure than Windows 3.11.

    B. Windows NT is a 32-bit operating system.

C. Windows NT requires less memory and disk space.

D. Windows NT has improved DOS support.

13. Select all the advantages of using Windows NT Workstation over Windows 95.

A. Windows NT Workstation requires less memory.

B. Windows NT supports file- and folder-level security.

C. Windows NT offers better performance on an equivalent system with less than 24 megabytes of memory.

D. Windows NT runs on multiple platforms such as MIPS and RISC architecture machines.

14. How can you upgrade user and application settings in Windows 95 to Windows NT Workstation?

A. You cannot do so.

B. This is done automatically during setup.

C. You must do it manually by running upgrade.exe from the command line after the installation is complete.

D. You must back up the data prior to completing the upgrade and restore the data after the upgrade.

15. NTFS is most efficient for partitions that are greater than how many megabytes?

A. 200MB

B. 400MB

C. 600MB

D. 800MB

Answers and Explanations: Practice Problems

1. **D** The 400-megabyte partition should be formatted with NTFS. Because he wants file level security, he must format that partition with NTFS. Windows NT Workstation requires approximately 120 megabytes for an installation, he cannot use the 200-megabyte partition for Windows NT and 100 megabytes of files. Because only Windows NT can access NTFS partitions, it is only logical to format the largest partition with FAT so that Windows 95 and Windows NT can both access the applications on that partition. Lastly, the Windows 95 system files easily fit on a 200 megabyte partition, which must be formatted with FAT.

2. **B** Windows NT Workstation 4.0 cannot be installed as an upgrade on OS/2 systems.

3. **C** Because this is a dual-boot system with a single partition, it must be formatted with FAT. Windows NT Workstation supports compression on Windows NT formatted with only NTFS. DOS-based compression utilities are not compatible with Windows NT.

4. **A, C** FAT typically requires 1 to 2 megabytes of file system overhead and supports the DOS, Windows 3.*x*, Windows 95, and Windows NT operating systems.

5. **B** FAT supports long filenames up to 255 characters under Windows NT.

6. **B** NTFS supports long filenames up to 255 characters.

7. **A, B** There is no upgrade path from Windows 95 to Windows NT. Therefore, you must install Windows NT with Windows NT Setup and reinstall all user applications.

8. **A** The simplest way to complete this number of upgrades is to use an unattended installation. Windows NT Workstation automatically upgrades your user and application settings from Windows 3.*x*.
9. **C** Windows NT Workstation 4.0 no longer supports HPFS. The conversion must be completed prior to completing the upgrade.
10. **A, C** NTFS supports Transaction Logging for fault tolerance and file/folder permissions for security.
11. **B** User and application settings in Windows 3.11 are automatically upgraded during the installation of Windows NT Workstation 4.0.
12. **A, B** Windows NT offers a better security model and is a true 32-bit operating system.
13. **B, D** Windows NT Workstation can offer file- and folder-level support, as well as support for multiple hardware platforms.
14. **A** There is no upgrade from Windows 95 to Windows NT Workstation 4.0. You must re-create all users and reinstall all applications after installing Windows NT Workstation 4.0.
15. **B** NTFS is most efficient for partitions greater than 400 megabytes.

13.2 Key Words

FAT

NTFS

HPFS

local security

dual boot

13.3 Planning Strategies for Sharing and Securing Resources

When planning a Windows NT Workstation installation, you must consider how resources will be made available to users while remaining secure. To effectively share and secure resources for Windows NT Workstation, you must understand the built-in groups and what rights those give the users within them, as well as how sharing one folder affects the other folders in the hierarchy below it.

Before sharing any resources, you must determine the networking model your Windows NT Workstation installation will participate in. Networking model selection can directly impact your strategy of sharing and securing resources.

A. Windows NT Network Support

Windows NT Workstation supports two network models in a homogeneous Microsoft networking environment—the Domain Model and the Workgroup Model. In a heterogeneous networking model, in which the enterprise network does not exist or uses another network operating system such as Novell NetWare, Windows NT Workstation will more than likely be installed as a standalone member of a Workgroup.

Regardless of the networking model, you must select a protocol that the workstations will use to communicate with other workstations, servers, and legacy systems. Microsoft provides support for TCP/IP, NetBEUI, and NWLink protocols.

1. Microsoft Domain Model

To implement a Microsoft domain model, you also must have a base of Windows NT Servers installed to manage the domain and authenticate logons. In the Domain (or Enterprise) Model, user and group accounts are centrally maintained in a domain account database, known as the Domain Security Account Manager (SAM) database. In this model, users should be able to log on to the domain from any workstation and receive the same rights and privileges.

Resources also are maintained centrally. Therefore, the Access Control Lists, or ACLs (see Chapter 15, "Managing Resources," for more information on ACLs) are centrally maintained. This enables users to access domain resources by authenticating only to the domain, not the individual SAM databases residing on the machines where the resources are located.

There are various derivatives of the Domain Model, such as Single Domain Model, Master Domain Model, and Multiple Master Domain Model. An in-depth description of these models is beyond the scope of the Workstation exam and this text, but you should be familiar with the terminology for the exam.

2. Workgroup Model

The Workgroup Networking Model, also known as the Peer-to-Peer model, is much easier to implement than the Domain Model. It does, however, lack the scalability and centralized management of the Domain Model, and management can become unwieldy with more than a few machines. In this model, each workstation acts as a server and a workstation. Access to resources on the workstation is determined by the ACL residing on the machine on which the resource is located. Therefore, users must authenticate to each workstation containing resources they want to utilize. Frequently, this means that each machine must have as many user accounts as there are members in the workgroup. Because these accounts are not synchronized, even trivial tasks such as changing a password become major efforts for administrators. Each workstation is responsible for managing the accounts and resources for that machine.

Additionally, in the Workgroup model, each Windows NT Workstation can only support 10 inbound connections to resources. Because of this limitation, the Workgroup Model is best utilized in small networks that have a limited number of users requiring resources on other workstations.

3. Microsoft Network Protocols

Windows NT Workstation provides support for various network protocols, including TCP/IP, NetBEUI, AppleTalk, DLC, and NWLink. Additionally, various third-party manufactures can provide support for their proprietary protocols. For more information on all the network protocols supported by Windows NT Workstation 4.0, see Chapter 16, “Connectivity.”

B. Using Built-In NTW Groups

Windows NT Workstation has six built-in groups created during the installation process. Each of these groups has certain associated rights by default. You can utilize these built-in groups to give users certain rights and permissions on the Windows NT system. These groups are as follows:

- Users
- Power Users
- Administrators
- Guests
- Backup Operators
- Replicators

When administering user accounts and assigning user rights and permissions, it typically is easier to assign rights and permissions to a group rather than to an individual. When rights and permissions are given to a group, all members of that group automatically inherit those rights and permissions. Before progressing any further in the discussion of user rights and permissions, there is an important distinction that must be made: *Rights* define what a user can do. *Permissions* define where a user can exercise those rights.

When trying to determine whether to add a particular user account to the list of default user rights or to simply add the user to an existing Windows NT Workstation group that has the desired right, you should consider that, in addition to default user rights, Windows NT also has built-in user capabilities associated with each of the default groups. You cannot modify these built-in capabilities or add them to user-defined groups. The only way to give a user one of these abilities is to put that user in a group that has the capability. If you want to give a user the right to create and manage user accounts on a Windows NT workstation, for example, you must put that user into either the Power Users or the Administrators group. Table 13.3.1 lists the built-in capabilities on Windows NT Workstation.

Table 13.3.1 Built-In User Capabilities

Built-In Capabilities	Admin	Power Users	Users	Guests	Everyone	Backup Operators
Create and manage user accounts	X	X				
Create and manage local groups	X	X				
Lock the workstation	X	X	X	X	X	X
Override the lock of the workstation	X					
Format the hard disk	X					
Create common groups	X	X				
Share and stop sharing directories	X	X				
Share and stop sharing printers	X	X				

These built-in user rights on Windows NT Workstation are important in understanding how to give users access to perform certain tasks on the system. The groups are defined as follows:

- *Users.* The Users group provides the user with the necessary rights to use the computer as an end user. By default, all user-created accounts on Windows NT Workstation are members of the Users group.
- *Power Users.* The Power Users group gives members the ability to perform certain system tasks without giving the user complete administrative control over the machine. One of the tasks a Power User can perform is the sharing of directories.
- *Administrators.* The Administrators group has full control over the Windows NT Workstation. As a member of the Administrators group, however, the user does not automatically have control over all files on the system. If using an NTFS partition, a file's permissions could be to restrict access from the Administrator. If the Administrator needs to access the file, she or he can take ownership of the file to gain access.
- *Guests.* The Guests group is used to give someone limited access to the resources on the Windows NT Workstation. The Guest account is automatically added to this group. By default, the Guest account is disabled.
- *Backup Operators.* The Backup Operators group gives a user the ability to back up and restore files on the Windows NT system. Users have the right to back up any files or directories to which they have access without being part of this group. By being a part of the Backup Operators group, users have the ability to back up and restore files to which they normally would not have access.

- *Replicators.* The Replicators group is used to identify the service account when Directory Replication is configured with a Windows NT Server.

C. Sharing Home Directories for User's Private Use

One of the issues that you have to decide in the planning process is whether to give your users their own home on the server or on their local workstation. A home directory is used as a location for users to be able to store their own data or files. Typically, the user is the only account that has access to the user's home directory. Table 13.3.2 outlines the benefits of storing a user's home directory on the server versus his local workstation.

Table 13.3.2 Benefits of Storing Users' Home Directories on the Server versus the Local Computer

Server-Based Home Directories	Local Home Directories
Are centrally located so that users can access them from any location on the network.	Available only on the local machine. If user is a *roaming user*, information is not accessible from other systems.
If a regular backup of the server is being done, information in users' home directories is also backed up.	Often users' local workstations are not backed up regularly as part of a scheduled backup process. If the user's machine fails, the user cannot recover the lost data.
Windows NT does not provide a way to limit the size of a user's directory. Thus, if a lot of information is being stored in home directories, it uses up server disk space.	If a user stores a lot of information in his home directory, the space is taken up on his local hard drive rather than the server.
If the server is down, the user won't have access to her files.	The user has access to his files regardless of whether the server is up, because the files are stored locally.
Some network bandwidth is consumed due to the over-the-network access of data or files.	No network traffic is generated by a user accessing his or her files.

1. Setting the Directory Structure

Typically when you are creating home directories on the server for users, it is best to centralize those directories under one directory (for example, "UserData") If you have two accounts—named LStanton and HStanton—your directory structure would look like that shown in Figure 13.3.1.

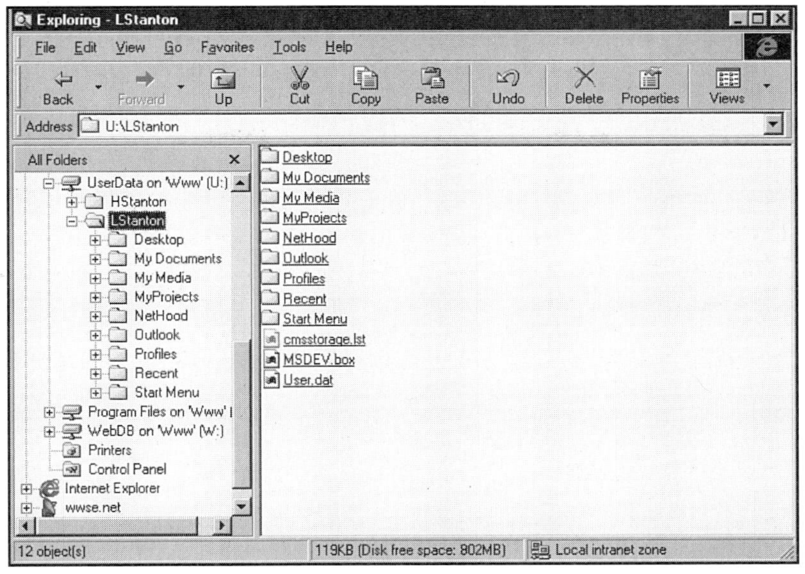

Figure 13.3.1 The directory structure of the two users' directories.

By establishing a share at the UserName level, all users are allowed access to all directories on a FAT partition. Recall that FAT partitions do not enable you to establish file and folder permissions. Thus, if Tina wants to access Mark's directory, using this setup, you cannot prevent her from doing so. If you use share permissions only, you must share each user's directory individually at the folder level. In this case, therefore, you would share Tina's directory to just Tina, Mark's to just Mark, and so on. (For a more thorough discussion of NTFS, FAT, and Share permissions, see Chapter 15.)

2. Setting Permissions

Sharing each individual user's home directory separately at the folder level is probably tedious, especially if you have a large environment with many users. One way around this problem is to create the "Users" directory on an NTFS partition rather than a FAT partition. By doing that, you can use NTFS permissions for each specific directory (for example, the directory called "Tina"), and then share with share permissions the top level "Users" directory to the Users group. By combining NTFS and share permissions in this manner, you solve the problem of giving individual access, without a lot of extra work on the part of the administrator. Table 13.3.3 lists the directory permissions.

Table 13.3.3 Directory Structure Permissions for Users' Home Directories Using NTFS and Share Permissions

Directory	User/Group	Permission
\UserData	Users	Full Control
\LStanton	LStanton	Full Control
\HStanton	HStanton	Full Control

This example provides a situation in which all users can access the top level Users folder, but only a particular user can access his or her own home directory. Only Fritz has Full Control of his own home directory, for example. Because Fritz is not listed in the directory permissions for Carla's home directory, he does not have access to it or anything inside of it.

D. Sharing Application Folders

Another resource you might have to plan for is giving your users access to shared network applications. Shared application folders are typically used to give users access to applications that they run from a network share point. Another option is to have users run applications locally from their own computers. Table 13.3.4 shows a comparison.

Table 13.3.4 Shared Network Applications versus Locally Installed Applications

Shared Network Applications	Locally Installed Applications
Take up less disk space on the local workstation.	Use more local disk space.
Easier to upgrade/control.	Upgrades must "touch" every machine locally.
Use network bandwidth.	Use no network bandwidth for running applications.
Slower response time because applications are accessed from the server.	Faster, more responsive.
If the server is down, users can't run applications.	Users can run applications regardless of server status.

Table 13.3.4 points out advantages and disadvantages to both shared network and locally installed implementations.

1. Planning the Directory Structure

If you choose to use shared network applications, you must plan your server directory structure so that these folders can be shared in the most efficient and secure method. If, for example, you use a shared copy of Word, Excel, and PowerPoint, your directory structure might look something like that shown in Figure 13.3.2.

In this example, you want all your users to be able to access these folders for running applications, but you do not want them to be able to change the permissions or delete any files from within these directories. A group (the "Applications group") is in charge of updates to these applications. That group, therefore, needs the ability to modify the application directories but not to modify the permissions on the directory structure.

2. Setting Share Permissions

The permissions on this shared network applications directory structure must enable the Applications group update files within any of the three directories as needed, and enable the users to access the directories to execute the applications. To do this, set up the directory structure, as shown in Table 13.3.5.

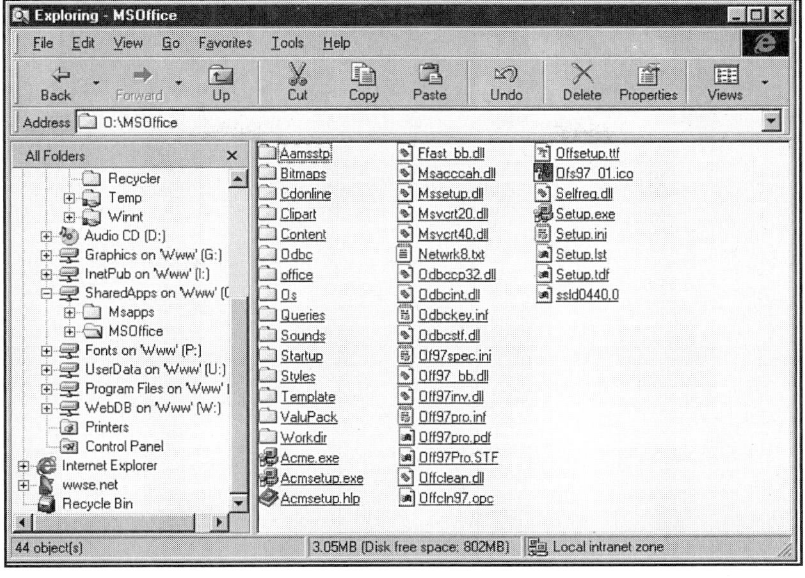

Figure 13.3.2 The directory structure of shared applications folders.

Table 13.3.5 Directory Structure Permissions for Shared Network Applications

Directory	Group	Permission
\SharedApps	Administrators Applications group Users	Full Control Change Read
\Word	Inherited from SharedApps	Inherited from SharedApps
\Excel	Inherited from SharedApps	Inherited from SharedApps
\PowerPoint	Inherited from SharedApps	Inherited from SharedApps

Because you are sharing the top-level folder *SharedApps*, you do not need to share the lower-level folders *Word*, *Excel*, and *PowerPoint* unless you want them to be individually available to users. By giving administrators full control, you give them the ability not only to add files but also to change the permissions on the directory structure. By giving the Applications group the change permission, you are allowing them to upgrade the applications in these directories, as needed.

E. Sharing Common Access Folders

Another situation that you might face when planning how to appropriately share and secure resources is the need to have a directory structure, which enables certain groups to work together on files and have access to directories based on this group membership. You might have a top-level directory called *Departments*, for example, with subdirectories of Sales, Accounting, HumanResources, and Finance.

1. Planning the Directory Structure

To create a directory structure to support the need for certain groups to share access over certain directories, you might want to create your directory structure like that shown in Figure 13.3.3.

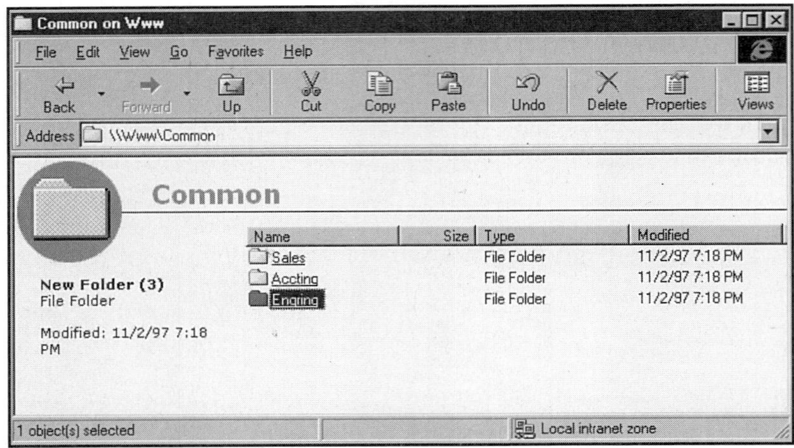

Figure 13.3.3 The directory structure of company departments' common access folders.

By creating the departmental folders under one main folder, you centralize the administration of the folder hierarchy. This structure enables you to have a common location for the accounting personnel to store their files and access information. Because you might not want the engineering personnel to access the accounting data, however, you need to plan your shared directories accordingly.

2. Setting Share Permissions

To set share permissions on this folder hierarchy, you need to assign permissions separately to each directory, as shown in Table 13.3.6.

Table 13.3.6 Directory Structure Permissions for Common Access Folders

Directory	Group	Permission
\Common	Administrators	Full Control
\Sales	Sales	Change
\Accting	Accountants	Change
\Engring	Eningeering	Change

Giving the Administrators group Full Control over the Common share makes the administration of the shared hierarchy possible and enables the administrators to have access to all the shared folders below the top-level folder Common. No specific department can be given access at the Common level, because you do not want any department having access to any other department's data. Because this is the case, you need to share each departmental folder at the folder level and only to that particular department.

The Sales folder, for example, is shared to the Sales group with Change permission. The Sales group will probably need to add or modify data in this directory but not modify the directory itself or the directory's permissions. Because of this, the Sales group is given the Change permission rather than Full Control. (For a more thorough definition of share permissions, see Chapter 15.)

13.3.1 Exercise: Creating a Shared User Home Directory Structure

This exercise shows you how to create a shared user home directory structure that is easy to maintain, yet secure. This exercise assumes you have an NTFS partition available.

Although the users' home directories should be created on a server, this exercise creates them on a local workstation partition for simplicity. The steps and structure are identical on a server.

This exercise demonstrates the structure required to create a flexible, secure, and easy to maintain user home directory structure on an NTFS partition.

1. Log on to Windows NT Workstation as the Administrator.
2. From the root of any drive on an NTFS partition, create a folder called users.
3. From the context menu, select sharing. Create a share named users and set the permissions to Everyone Full Control.
4. Right-click the User folder and select Properties.
5. Click the Security tab and then the Permissions button. Are the permissions set to Everyone Full Control? This is the default permission assigned by Windows NT when a new folder is created.
6. Now create a subfolder within the users folder. Name this subfolder Administrator. This is the home directory for the Administrator.
7. From the context menu, select properties and click the security tab. Click permissions and add the Administrator account with Full Control. Remove the Everyone group and click OK.
8. Create another subfolder within the users folder named BobQ. Follow the same steps for setting permissions, except add BobQ with Full Control instead of the Administrator. This is BobQ's home directory.
9. Now try to view the contents of the BobQ folder. Were you successful?

Answers and Explanations: Exercise

This exercise showed you how to create and share a directory structure to provide users with secure, easily accessible home directories. In Chapter 15, you will see how you can skip the step of creating a folder for each user. Instead, you can utilize User Manager to automatically create a folder for each user within the users folder and assign the appropriate permissions.

For more information about the concepts raised by this exercise, refer to the section entitled "Sharing Home Directories for User's Private Use."

13.3 Practice Problems

1. Patrick needs to secure files on his workstation, which is shared with another user. What are his options with a workstation that is running Windows 95?

   A. Enable the hidden FAT property.

   B. Convert the partition to NTFS by using the convert utility available from Microsoft's web site.

   C. Windows 95 does not support file level security on the local machine.

   D. Set the Access option from the Network Neighborhood properties sheet to NT Style Access.

2. Cindy needs to share files on her hard disk for people to access through a network share. What built-in group must Cindy belong to to create network shares on her machine?

   A. Administrator

   B. User

   C. Replicator

   D. Backup Operators

3. Bob is an administrator of a 200-person network. He needs to set up home directories for all the users on the network. The data that users will store in their home directories is sensitive and should not be viewed by other users. This data is vital to the company's business. Users need to access this data from anywhere on the network. How should Bob set up the home directories?

   A. Create a home directory for each user on his or her primary workstation.

   B. Create a common directory on a server and share the folder so that everyone has access.

   C. Create a shared folder on an NTFS partition and grant everyone access. Create subfolders for each user and set the permissions so that each user has access to only his or her home directory.

   D. Create a folder on an NTFS partition on one user's workstation and give everyone full access.

4. Patrick needs to secure files on his workstation, which is shared with another user. What are his options with a workstation that is running Windows NT Workstation with a FAT-formatted partition?

   A. He must reinstall the operating system and format the partition with NTFS to secure the files.

   B. He should use share-level permissions.

   C. He should convert the partition to NTFS.

   D. He should place the files in My Briefcase and enable the password protection option.

5. What are the two Microsoft networking models in which Windows NT Workstation can participate?

   A. Shared and Standalone

   B. Domain and Workgroup

   C. Domain and Bindery

   D. Master and Workgroup

6. Select all the advantages of the Domain networking model over the Workgroup networking model.

   A. The domain model offers centralized account and resource management.

   B. The domain model does not require Windows NT Server.

   C. The domain model is simpler to implement.

   D. The Domain Model does not limit the number of inbound connections of any network resource to 10 simultaneous connections.

7. Select all the derivatives of the Microsoft Domain networking model.
   A. Master Domain model
   B. Multiple Domain model
   C. Segregated Domain model
   D. Integrated Trust

8. What Windows NT Workstation built-in groups have the built-in capability to Share and Stop Sharing Printers?
   A. Administrators
   B. Server Operators
   C. Print Operators
   D. Power Users

9. Select all advantages of using the Workgroup network model over the Domain network model.
   A. It is easier to set up.
   B. It is scaleable.
   C. Users have to authenticate only once to gain access to all workgroup resources.
   D. Management tasks, such as changing a user password, are much easier.

10. You are creating a five-user network for a small law firm. What networking model should you use?
    A. Workgroup
    B. Master Domain
    C. Multiple Master Domain
    D. Complete Trust Domain model

11. Select all the file systems supported by Windows NT that also support share-level permissions.
    A. NTFS
    B. FAT
    C. FAT32
    D. HPFS

12. How many built-in groups does Windows NT Workstation 4.0 install?
    A. 4 groups
    B. 6 groups
    C. 8 groups
    D. 10 groups

13. Select all the advantages of using Locally Installed Applications over Shared Network Applications.
    A. Less network traffic
    B. Less space is required on the system hard disk
    C. Better performance
    D. Centralized control

14. From the following list of groups, select all that are built-in to Windows NT.
    A. Power Users
    B. Domain Users
    C. Server Operators
    D. Guests

15. Which Windows NT Workstation 4.0 built-in groups have permission to Share and Stop Sharing Directories?
    A. Users
    B. Guests
    C. Administrators
    D. Power Users

Answers and Explanations: Practice Problems

1. **C** Windows 95 supports FAT and FAT32. Only NTFS enables file- and folder-level permissions.

2. **A** Of the built-in groups listed, only the Administrator account can create network shares. Additionally, the Power User group also has the built-in capability to create network shares.

3. **C** Because subfolders inherit the share permissions of their parent directories, you must utilize an NTFS partition to set the folder permissions for individual users. You must place the directory on a server because Windows NT Workstation 4.0 supports only 10 concurrent inbound connections.

4. **C** Because Windows NT only supports file- and folder-level security on NTFS formatted partitions, he must utilize the convert utility to change the partition file system to NTFS.

5. **B** Microsoft supports the Domain and Workgroup network models.

6. **A, D** The Domain model enables centralized administration of accounts and resources. Additionally, the number of licenses purchased only limits the number of inbound connections to any network resource.

7. **A, D** The three Microsoft Domain models are the Single Domain model, the Master Domain model, and the Multiple Master Domain model.

8. **A, D** Only the Administrator and Power Users Windows NT Workstation built-in groups have the capability to share and stop sharing printers. Server Operators and Print Operators are Windows NT global groups available only on Windows NT Servers installed as Primary Domain Controllers.

9. **A** Peer-to-Peer, or workgroups, are easier to set up than domains.

10. **A** In this situation, a workgroup is the most cost effective and the easiest network model to set up and maintain.

11. **A, B** Both NTFS and FAT support share-level permissions.

12. **B** Windows NT Workstation creates the Users, Backup Operators, Power Users, Administrators, Guest, and Replicators built-in groups.

13. **A, C** By running applications from the local workstation, you can reduce the amount of network traffic and increase performance. You lose centralized control, however, and must have larger hard disks in the workstations.

14. **A, D** Windows NT Workstation creates the Users, Backup Operators, Power Users, Administrators, Guest, and Replicators built-in groups.

15. **C, D** The only two built-in groups that have the right to Share and Stop Sharing Directories are the Power Users and Administrators groups.

13.3 Key Words

Users group

Power Users group

Administrators group

Guests group

Backup Operators group

Replicators group

Workgroup network model

Domain network model

Practice Exam: Planning

Use this practice exam to test your mastery of Planning. This practice exam is 17 questions long. The passing Microsoft score is 70.4 percent. Questions are in multiple-choice format.

1. *Situation*: You need to roll out 300 copies of Windows NT Workstation. All have identical hardware configurations. All will use the TCP/IP network protocol and will join the same domain. Each Windows NT Workstation installation is identical.

   Desired Result: Install and configure Windows NT Workstation 4.0 on all workstations so that when booted for the first time after installation they operate in the domain environment without modification.

   Optional Result #1: Minimize the installation time.

   Optional Result #2: Minimize user intervention.

   Proposed Solution: Create a single unattended installation file. Additionally, create a single UDF to specify unique computer names and IP addresses.

   A. The proposed solution meets the desired result and all optional results.

   B. The proposed solution meets only the desired result.

   C. The proposed solution meets the desired result and one optional result.

   D. The proposed solution does not meet the desired result or any of the optional results.

2. *Situation*: You need to roll out 300 copies of Windows NT Workstation. All have identical hardware configurations. All will utilize the TCP/IP network protocol and join the same domain. Each Windows NT Workstation installation will be identical.

   Desired Result: Install and configure Windows NT Workstation 4.0 on all workstations so that when booted for the first time after installation, the workstations operate in the domain environment without modification.

   Optional Result #1: Minimize the installation time.

   Optional Result #2: Minimize user intervention.

   Proposed Solution: Create a single unattended installation file. There will be no UDFs utilized. IP addressing will be completed with DHCP.

   A. The proposed solution meets the desired result and all optional results.

   B. The proposed solution meets only the desired result.

   C. The proposed solution meets the desired result and one optional result.

   D. The proposed solution does not meet the desired result or any of the optional results.

3. Select all the operating systems that currently support NTFS.

   A. MS-DOS

   B. Windows NT

   C. Windows 95

   D. OS/2

4. What is the correct command to initiate a conversion from HPFS to NTFS? The HPFS drive is assigned the drive letter C.

   A. convert c:

   B. convert c: /FS:HPFS

   C. convert c:\ /FS:HPFS

   D. convert c: /FS:NTFS

5. Select all the operating systems that currently support HPFS.

   A. OS/2

   B. Windows 95

   C. Windows NT 4.0

   D. Windows NT 3.51

6. Select all the file systems supported by Windows NT Workstation 4.0.

   A. FAT

   B. NFS

   C. NTFS

   D. FAT32

7. Select all files systems supported by Windows 95.

   A. HPFS

   B. NTFS

   C. FAT

   D. FAT32

8. What is the maximum file size supported by FAT?

   A. 2 gigabytes

   B. 4 gigabytes

   C. 6 gigabytes

   D. 8 gigabytes

9. FAT is most efficient for partitions that are less than how many megabytes in size?

   A. 200MB

   B. 400MB

   C. 600MB

   D. 800MB

10. Select all the file systems supported by Windows NT Workstation that also support recoverability in the event that data was not completely written to the disk.

    A. HPFS

    B. NTFS

    C. FAT

    D. FAT32

11. Select all the operating systems that can be dual-booted with Windows NT Workstation.

    A. Windows NT Server

    B. DOS

    C. Windows 95

    D. Windows NT Workstation 3.51

12. Which Windows NT Workstation 4.0 built-in groups have permission to create common groups?

    A. Power Users

    B. Users

    C. Administrators

    D. Replicators

13. Select all the advantages of using Server-based home directories over Local-based user home directories.

    A. Centralized location for backup.

    B. Home directories are available from any workstation.

    C. Less network traffic.

    D. Better availability of data for users.

14. Select two advantages of using Shared Network Applications over Locally Installed Applications.

    A. Centralized control enables easier upgrades.

    B. Less hard disk space is required on the workstation.

C. Reduces the amount of network traffic.

D. Controls application access.

15. Select all the file systems supported by Windows NT Workstation 4.0 that also support file- and folder-level permissions.

A. NTFS

B. FAT

C. FAT32

D. HPFS

16. Users'_______ define where users can exercise their _______? (Fill in the blanks.)

A. rights, permissions

B. permissions, rights

C. authority, rights

D. permissions, privileges

17. You are creating a 500-user corporate network. What network model should you use?

A. Large

B. Corporate

C. Domain

D. Workgroup

Answers and Explanations: Practice Exam

1. **A** The uniqueness database file can supply the unique machine names, and IP addresses for each machine completely identify a unique machine on the network without user intervention.

2. **C** Without the use of a UDF, when the machine is booted for the first time, the user must change the machine name. If a uniqueness database file is used, a unique machine name can be specified during the installation. Also, to change the machine name, the user that logs on needs to be a member of the Administrators group.

3. **B** Only Windows NT Workstation and Server support NTFS.

4. **D** You must specify the drive and the new file system of the target drive.

5. **A, D** OS/2 and Windows NT 3.51 currently support HPFS. Windows NT 4.0 no longer supports HPFS.

6. **A, C** NFS is not natively supported by Windows NT, and FAT32 is only supported by Windows 95.

7. **C, D** Windows 95 supports the FAT and FAT32 file systems.

8. **B** The FAT file system can support file sizes up to 4 gigabytes.

9. **B** FAT is considered more efficient for partitions less than 400 megabytes.

10. **B** Of all the file systems supported by Windows NT 4.0, only NTFS is fault tolerant by supporting Transaction Logging.

11. **A, B, C, D** Windows NT can be dual-booted with DOS, Windows 95, Windows NT Server, and previous versions of Windows NT Workstation.

12. **A, C** The only two built-in groups that have the right to create common groups are the Power Users and Administrators groups.

13. **A, B** Centralized home directory locations enable the user's data to be included with the server backup. Also, the directories will be available from any workstation on the network. Storing data on the server creates some additional network traffic as the users access files, and the server must be up and available for the users to access their data.

14. **A, B, D** Using shared applications enables the administrator to more easily control upgrades and access, and requires less hard disk space on the workstations.

15. **A** Windows NT Workstation 4.0 only supports FAT and NTFS. Of those, only NTFS supports file- and folder-level permissions. However, both FAT and NTFS support share-level permissions.

16. **B** User permissions define where users can exercise their rights.

17. **C** With a network of this size, creation and management of a Workgroup model would be an impossible task. A workgroup would also be ineffective due to the 10-inbound-network-connection limit imposed by Windows NT Workstation 4.0.

Chapter 14

Installation and Configuration

This chapter prepares you for the exam by covering the following objectives:

- Installing Microsoft Windows NT Workstation 4.0 on an Intel platform in a given situation.
- Setting up a dual-boot system in a given situation.
- Removing Microsoft Windows NT Workstation 4.0 in a given situation.
- Upgrading to Windows NT Workstation 4.0 in a given situation.
- Configuring server-based installation for wide-scale deployment in a given situation.
- Installing, configuring, and removing hardware components for a given situation. Hardware components include the following:

    Network adapter drivers

    SCSI device drivers

    Tape device drivers

    UPSs

    Multimedia devices

    Display drivers

    Keyboard drivers

    Mouse drivers

- Using Control Panel applications to configure a Microsoft Windows NT Workstation 4.0 computer in a given situation.

14.1 Installing Windows NT Workstation 4.0 on an Intel Platform

Before you try to install Microsoft Windows NT Workstation 4.0, you must be able to answer the following questions:

- Is your hardware on the Microsoft Windows NT 4.0 Hardware Compatibility List (HCL)?
- Does your hardware meet the minimum requirements for processor, RAM, and hard disk space?
- Are you attempting to install Microsoft Windows NT Workstation 4.0 on a "clean" system? Or are you planning to upgrade a computer with an existing operating system?
- If you are upgrading a computer with an existing operating system, will the Microsoft Windows NT 4.0 operating system replace the other operating system? Or do you want to be able to use both operating systems and be able to switch between them by "dual booting?"
- Do you want to use the FAT or NTFS file system?
- Will your Windows NT Workstation 4.0 computer be a member of a workgroup or a member of a domain?
- Which type of installation do you want to perform: typical, portable, compact, or custom?
- Where are the installation files that you will use to install Microsoft Windows NT Workstation 4.0 located: on a local floppy disk or CD-ROM, or on a network-distribution server?

When you know the answers to the preceding questions, write them down. Those answers help you choose the proper options during the setup process. The Hardware Compatibility List (HCL) specifies all the computer systems and peripheral devices that have been tested for operation with Microsoft Windows NT 4.0. Devices not listed on the HCL can cause intermittent failures or, in extreme cases, system crashes.

A. Using the Windows NT Hardware Qualifier Tool (NTHQ.EXE)

One way to make sure that all your hardware is on the official Hardware Compatibility List (HCL) is to execute the Windows NT Hardware Qualifier Tool (NTHQ.EXE), which is only available for Intel x86-based computers or compatibles. Microsoft provides a batch file (Makedisk.bat) that actually creates a special MS-DOS bootable disk that contains NTHQ.EXE. Makedisk.bat is located in the \Support\HQTool folder on the Windows NT Workstation 4.0 installation CD. You will find full instructions on how to create the special bootable disk and then use NTHQ in Exercise 14.1.1, which appears at the end of this section.

NTHQ lists detected hardware devices in four categories: System, Motherboard, Video, and Others. The Others category is used for device types that the tool cannot positively identify. For example, if the system has an old PCI adapter that does not support PCI version 2.0 or later, the tool might not be able to identify its device type.

Click the appropriate tabs to view detection results for each category. Alternatively, you can save the results to a text file named NTHQ.TXT. You should then check the list of detected devices with the Windows NT 4.0 HCL to avoid unpleasant surprises during installation. The information in NTHQ.TXT is also very useful for avoiding IRQ conflicts when adding new hardware because, unlike Windows 95, Windows NT does not support Plug and Play. Note that IRQ, DMA, and I/O addresses for detected devices are included in the NTHQ.TXT file.

Plug and Play (PnP) devices can be automatically configured (with the proper operating system) to work with any combination of other peripheral devices. Windows NT 4.0 does not support PnP automatic configuration of devices; Windows 95 does.

If you have several different computers that you want to examine with the NTHQ utility, follow these steps:

1. Boot the first computer with the NTHQ floppy disk.
2. Execute the NTHQ program, as described in Exercise 14.1.1.
3. Rename the Nthq.txt file to *computername*.TXT.
4. Use the same NTHQ floppy disk on the next computer.
5. Repeat, as necessary, on all your computers.

B. Minimum Requirements for Installation

You also have to make sure that your computer hardware meets the minimum requirements for installing Windows NT Workstation 4.0 (see Table 14.1.1). If your hardware does not meet the minimum requirements, you need to make the necessary upgrades before you attempt to install Windows NT Workstation 4.0. If your computer has devices not listed in the HCL, you should check with the devices' manufacturers to see if device drivers that support Windows NT 4.0 are available. Unlike with Windows 95, you cannot use older 16-bit device drivers with Windows NT. If you cannot obtain the proper device drivers, you cannot use unsupported devices after you install Windows NT.

If you have unsupported devices, see if they emulate another device that has drivers for Windows NT 4.0. Then try to use the drivers for the emulated device (for example, standard VGA for video, Sound Blaster for audio, Novell NE2000-compatible for generic network adapter cards).

Table 14.1.1 Windows NT Workstation 4.0 Minimum Installation Requirements

Component	Minimum Requirement
CPU	32-bit Intel x86-based (80486/33 or higher) microprocessor or compatible (the 80386 microprocessor is no longer supported) Intel Pentium, Pentium Pro, or Pentium II microprocessor Digital Alpha AXP-based microprocessor
Memory	Intel x86-based computers: 12MB RAM RISC-based computers: 16MB RAM
Hard disk	Intel x86-based computers: 110MB RISC-based computers: 148MB
Display	VGA or better resolution

continues

Table 14.1.1 Continued

Component	Minimum Requirement
Other drives	Intel x86-based computers: high-density 3.5-inch floppy disk and a CD-ROM drive (unless you are planning to install Windows NT over a network)
Optional	Network adapter card Mouse or other pointing device (such as a trackball)

Microsoft Windows NT 4.0 actually requires slightly more hard disk space during the installation process to hold some temporary files than it requires after installation. If you don't have at least 119MB of free space in your partition, the Setup routine displays an error message and halts. The Setup routine also displays an error message and halts if you attempt to install Windows NT Workstation 4.0 to a Windows NT software-based volume set or stripe set (RAID 0). If you have a hardware-based volume set or stripe set, you might be able to install Windows NT Workstation 4.0 on it; ask your manufacturer.

Keep in mind that Table 14.1.1 lists the *minimum* requirements for installing Windows NT Workstation 4.0. After you install your actual application software and data, you will probably find out that your hardware requirements are higher than these minimum values.

If you are upgrading a Windows 95-based computer to Windows NT Workstation 4.0, make sure that you do not have any compressed drives and that you are not using FAT32. FAT32 is the new optional partitioning format that is supported only by Windows 95 OEM Service Release 2 (which is also called Windows 95b). Windows NT cannot access Windows 95 compressed drives and FAT32 partitions.

C. Installation Options

During installation, you can make use of your knowledge from Chapter 13, "Planning," to decide whether you want to change the partitioning of your hard disk and/or convert hard disk partitions from FAT to NTFS.

Regardless of whether you install Microsoft Windows NT Workstation 4.0 locally via the three floppy disks and the CD or by means of a network connection to a network distribution server, you have four setup options: typical, portable, compact, and custom. The four setup options install varying components from several categories (see Table 14.1.2).

Table 14.1.2 Varying Components in Four Setup Options

	Typical	Portable	Compact	Custom
Accessibility options	X	X	None	All options
Accessories	X	X	None	All options
Communications programs	X	X	None	All options

	Typical	Portable	Compact	Custom
Games			None	All options
Windows Messaging			None	All options
Multimedia	X	X	None	All options

Note that the compact setup option is designed to conserve hard disk space and installs no optional components. The Portable setting should be used for installing Windows NT Workstation on laptop computers; it installs only the necessary components and leaves the others as optional to make the best use of limited disk space. The only way to install Windows Messaging or games during installation is to choose Custom setup. You can change installation options after installation via the Add/Remove Programs application in Control Panel.

D. Beginning the Installation

You actually have several choices on how to install Microsoft Windows NT Workstation 4.0. These are the ways:

- Locally, via three Setup floppy disks and a CD.
- Locally, using the CD and creating and using the three Setup floppy disks.
- Over the network, creating and using the three Setup floppy disks.
- Over the network, not requiring any Setup floppy disks.

Step-by-step instructions on the actual installation procedures are detailed in Exercises 14.1.2, 14.1.3, and 14.1.4. After you install Microsoft Windows NT Workstation 4.0, you need to install all your applications.

E. Installing Windows NT Workstation 4.0 on an Intel Computer with an Existing Operating System

If your computer already has an existing operating system with support for CD-ROM, you can install Windows NT Workstation 4.0 directly from the installation CD. All you have to do is execute WINNT.EXE, which is a 16-bit program compatible with MS-DOS, Windows 3.x, and Windows 95. WINNT.EXE is located in the \I386 folder on the Microsoft Windows NT 4.0 CD. It performs the following steps:

- Creates the three Setup boot disks (requires three blank high-density formatted disks).
- Creates the WIN_NT.~LS temporary folder and copies the contents of the \I386 folder to it.
- Prompts the user to restart the computer from the first Setup boot disk.

You can also modify the installation process (see Table 14.1.3).

Table 14.1.3 Modifying the WINNT.EXE Installation Process

Switch	Effect
/b	The system does not make the three Setup boot disks. Create a temporary folder named WIN_NT.~BT and copy to it the boot files that would normally be copied to the three floppy disks. Then when the user is prompted to restart the computer, the files in the temporary folder are used to boot the machine instead of the Setup boot disks.
/c	The system skips the check for available free space.
/I:*inf_file*	This enables you to specify the name of the Setup information file. (The default file name is Dosnet.inf.)
/f	The system does not verify files as they are copied.
/l	The system creates a log file called $WINNT.LOG that lists all errors that occur as files are being copied to the temporary directory.
/ox	The system creates the three Setup boot disks and then stops.
/s:*server_path*	Enables you to specify the location of the installation source files.
/u	All or part of an installation proceeds unattended as explained in Chapter 13. When you use the */u* switch, the */b* option for floppyless installation is automatically invoked, too, and the */s* option for location of the source files must be used. The */u* option can be followed with the name of an answer file to fully automate installation.
/udf	During an unattended installation, this enables you to specify settings unique to a specific computer by creating a uniqueness data file, as explained in Chapter 13.
/w	This *undocumented* flag enables the WINNT.EXE program to execute in Windows instead of requiring execution from a MS-DOS command prompt.
/x	The system does not create the three Setup boot disks. You must already have the three boot disks.

There is also a 32-bit version of the installation program called WINNT32.EXE that is used to upgrade earlier versions of Windows NT; it cannot be used to upgrade Windows 95. WINNT32.EXE does not support the */f, /c*, or */l* options. See the section titled "Upgrading to Windows NT Workstation 4.0" for more information. Remember that WINNT.EXE and WINNT32.EXE are the installation programs for Windows NT.

14.1.1 Exercise: Creating and Using an NTHQ Boot Floppy

Objective: Determine whether the hardware in your computer is supported by Windows NT.

Time Estimate: 20 minutes

This exercise shows you how to create a Windows NT Hardware Qualifier (NTHQ) boot floppy. You then use the NTHQ boot floppy disk to examine the hardware configuration of your computer. Follow these steps:

1. Insert the Windows NT Workstation 4.0 CD into your CD-ROM drive.
2. At the command prompt, type **D:** (or whatever the correct drive letter is for your computer) to switch the default drive to the CD-ROM drive.
3. Type **CD \Support\HQTool** to switch to the HQTool directory.
4. Insert a formatted 3.5-inch floppy disk into drive A.
5. Type **Makedisk** at the command prompt.
6. When the Makedisk utility finishes transferring all the necessary files to the floppy disk, reboot your computer, leaving the disk that you just made in drive A.
7. When the NTHQ dialog box appears, click Yes to approve device detection.
8. Click Yes to approve comprehensive detection.
9. Wait for the system detection process to end. Then click the various buttons at the bottom of the screen and observe the details that were detected for the various devices in your computer.
10. Click the Save button at the bottom of the screen.
11. Click OK to save the detection results to A:\NTHQ.TXT.
12. Click the Exit button at the bottom of the screen.
13. Remove the disk from drive A.
14. Reboot your computer.
15. Reinsert the NTHQ floppy disk into drive A.
16. View the contents of A:\NTHQ.TXT.

Answers and Explanations: Exercise

In this section, you created a Windows NT Hardware Qualifier (NTHQ) boot floppy disk. After the NTHQ disk analyzed your hardware, you were presented with details about the various hardware on your system. To save the information, you can create a text file (NTHQ.TXT, for example), which you can later view and analyze to determine which hardware devices are compatible with Windows NT.

For more information, refer to the section titled "Using the Windows NT Hardware Qualifier Tool (NTHQ.EXE)."

14.1.2 Exercise: Installing Windows NT Workstation 4.0 from CD on a Computer That Doesn't Have an Existing Operating System

Objective: Install Windows NT Workstation on an Intel platform.

Time Estimate: 70 minutes

This exercise shows you how to perform a CD-based installation of Windows NT on a computer that doesn't have an existing operating system.

1. Before starting the installation, make sure that your hardware (especially your CD-ROM drive) is listed on the Windows NT HCL.
2. Locate your Windows NT Workstation 4.0 CD and the three floppy disks that came with it.
3. Insert the Windows NT Workstation CD into the CD-ROM drive.
4. Insert the Windows NT Workstation Setup Boot Disk into your floppy disk drive and restart your computer.
5. When prompted, insert Windows NT Workstation Setup Disk #2.
6. At the Windows NT Workstation Setup—Welcome to Setup screen, press Enter to start the installation process.
7. Press Enter to detect mass storage devices.
8. When prompted, insert Windows NT Workstation Setup Disk #3.
9. Press Enter to approve the list of detected mass storage devices. (Don't worry if your IDE hard disk controller isn't detected; the installation process should proceed just fine anyway.)
10. Press Page Down repeatedly, until you reach the last page of the Windows NT Licensing Agreement.
11. Press F8 to approve the Windows NT Licensing Agreement.
12. Press Enter to approve the list of detected hardware components.
13. Select the desired installation partition, and then press Enter.
14. Press Enter to *not* convert the installation partition to NTFS.
15. Press Enter to install to the default directory named \WINNT.
16. Press Enter to examine the hard disk for errors.
17. Wait for the hard disk to be examined.
18. Wait while files are copied.
19. When prompted, remove the floppy disk from the drive. Then press Enter to restart the computer and begin the graphical portion of the setup process.
20. When the computer restarts, click Next.
21. Select the Typical installation option, and then click Next.

22. Enter your Name and Organization, and then click Next.
23. Enter your CD-ROM key, and then click Next.
24. Enter your Computer Name (in this case, specify a computer named **Test**), and then click Next. The maximum length for a computer name is 15 characters.
25. Enter and confirm the password for the administrator account, and then click Next. Make sure that you write down your password and keep it in a secure location. If you forget your administrator password, you will be locked out of your own system, and you will have to reinstall Windows NT to restore access.
26. Click Yes to create an emergency repair disk (ERD).
27. Click Next to install the most common components.
28. Click Next to install Windows NT Networking.
29. Specify whether your computer will be part of a network, and then click Next. If your computer will not be part of a network, skip ahead to step 36.
30. Click Start Search for Your Adapter, or click Select from List.
31. Select your adapter from the list, and then click Next.
32. Make sure that NetBEUI is the only specified protocol, and then click Next.
33. Click Continue to approve the network card settings. (Remember that Windows NT 4.0 doesn't support Plug and Play, and your network card settings *must* be correct.)
34. Click Next to start the network.
35. Click Next to install the computer named Test into a workgroup named Workgroup.
36. Click Next to finish setup.
37. Select the proper time zone, and then click Close.
38. Click OK to approve the detected video adapter.
39. Click Test to test the video adapter.
40. Click OK to start the video test and wait 5 seconds.
41. Click Yes if you saw the bitmap properly.
42. Click OK to save the video settings.
43. Click OK in the Display Properties dialog box.
44. Wait while files are copied.
45. Wait while the configuration is saved.
46. Insert a floppy disk that will become your ERD, and then click OK.
47. Wait while the ERD is formatted and files are copied.
48. Wait while the temporary configuration files are removed.
49. Restart your computer. The installation process is now complete.

Answers and Explanations: Exercise

For more information, refer to the section titled "Installing and Configuring Windows NT 4.0."

14.1.3 Exercise: Upgrading an Existing System to Windows NT Workstation 4.0 from CD-ROM Without the Setup Disks

Objective: Install Windows NT Workstation on an Intel platform.

Time Estimate: 80 minutes

This exercise shows you how to re-create the Setup disks and then upgrade an existing system to Windows NT Workstation 4.0 from CD-ROM.

1. Format three high-density floppy disks and label them like this:

   Windows NT Workstation Setup Boot Disk

   Windows NT Workstation Setup Disk #2

   Windows NT Workstation Setup Disk #3

2. Place the Windows NT Workstation 4.0 CD in the CD-ROM drive. (This exercise assumes that your CD-ROM drive is drive D.)
3. From a command prompt, type **D:\I386\WINNT** to upgrade a 16-bit system, or type **D:\I386\WINNT32** to upgrade a previous version of Windows NT.
4. Insert Windows NT Workstation Setup Disk #3, into the floppy disk drive.
5. When prompted by the Windows NT 4.0 Upgrade/Installation screen, click Continue.
6. Wait while files are copied.
7. When prompted, insert Windows NT Workstation Setup Disk #2.
8. When prompted, insert Windows NT Workstation Setup Boot Disk.
9. When prompted, restart your computer, leaving the Windows NT Workstation Setup Boot Disk in the drive.
10. Wait while the computer restarts and files are copied.
11. When prompted, insert Windows NT Workstation Setup Disk #2.
12. At the Windows NT Workstation Setup—Welcome to Setup screen, press Enter to start the installation process.
13. Press Enter to detect mass storage devices.
14. When prompted, insert Windows NT Workstation Setup Disk #3.
15. Press Enter to approve the list of detected mass storage devices. (Don't worry if your IDE hard disk controller isn't detected. The installation process should proceed just fine anyway.)
16. Press Page Down repeatedly, until you reach the last page of the Windows NT Licensing Agreement.

17. Press F8 to approve the Windows NT Licensing Agreement.
18. Press Enter to approve the list of detected hardware components.
19. Select the desired installation partition, and then press Enter.
20. Press Enter to *not* convert the installation partition to NTFS.
21. Press Enter to install to the default directory named \WINNT.
22. Press Enter to examine the hard disk for errors.
23. Wait for the hard disk to be examined.
24. Wait while files are copied.
25. When prompted, remove the floppy disk from the drive. Then press Enter to restart the computer and begin the graphical portion of the setup process.
26. When the computer restarts, click Next.
27. Select the Typical installation option, and then click Next.
28. Enter your Name and Organization, and then click Next.
29. Enter your CD-ROM key and click Next.
30. Enter your Computer Name (in this case, specify a computer named **Test**), and then click Next.
31. Enter and confirm the password for the administrator account, and then click Next.
32. Click Yes to create an emergency repair disk (ERD).
33. Click Next to install the most common components.
34. Click Next to install Windows NT Networking.
35. Specify whether your computer will be part of a network, and then click Next. If your computer will not be part of a network, skip ahead to step 42.
36. Click Start Search for Your Adapter, or click Select from List.
37. Select your adapter from the list, and then click Next.
38. Make sure that NetBEUI is the only specified protocol, and then click Next.
39. Click Continue to approve the network card settings. (Remember that Windows NT 4.0 doesn't support Plug and Play, and your network card settings *must* be correct.)
40. Click Next to start the network.
41. Click Next to install the computer named Test into a workgroup named Workgroup.
42. Click Next to finish setup.
43. Select the proper time zone, and then click Close.
44. Click OK to approve the detected video adapter.
45. Click Test to test the video adapter.
46. Click OK to start the video test, and then wait 5 seconds.
47. Click Yes if you saw the bitmap properly.

48. Click OK to save the video settings.
49. Click OK in the Display Properties dialog box.
50. Wait while files are copied.
51. Wait while the configuration is saved.
52. Insert a floppy disk that will become your ERD, and then click OK.
53. Wait while the ERD is formatted and files are copied.
54. Wait while the temporary configuration files are removed.
55. Restart your computer. The installation process is now complete.

Answers and Explanations: Exercise

If you want to speed up the process, you can use the */b* option, which doesn't require the three floppy disks because it copies the temporary files to your hard disk.

For more information, refer to the section titled "Installing and Configuring Windows NT 4.0" and Table 14.1.3, "Modifying the WINNT.EXE Installation Process."

14.1.4 Exercise: Installing Windows NT Workstation 4.0 from a Network Server

Objective: Install Windows NT Workstation on an Intel platform.

Time Estimate: 60 minutes

This exercise details how to upgrade an existing MS-DOS system to Microsoft Windows NT Workstation 4.0 when the installation files are located on a network server.

1. Format three high-density floppy disks and label them like this:

   Windows NT Workstation Setup Boot Disk

   Windows NT Workstation Setup Disk #2

   Windows NT Workstation Setup Disk #3

2. From a command prompt, enter the appropriate command to connect a network drive to drive letter X. For example, the appropriate command for a Microsoft-based network would be:

   NET USE X: *server**sharename*

3. Change to drive X.
4. Start the Windows NT installation process by typing **WINNT** and pressing Enter.
5. Insert Windows NT Workstation Setup Disk #3 into the floppy disk drive.
6. When prompted by the Windows NT 4.0 Upgrade/Installation screen, click Continue.
7. Wait while files are copied.
8. When prompted, insert Windows NT Workstation Setup Disk #2.

9. When prompted, insert Windows NT Workstation Setup Boot Disk.
10. When prompted, restart your computer, leaving the Windows NT Workstation Setup Boot Disk in the drive.
11. Wait while the computer restarts and files are copied.
12. When prompted, insert Windows NT Workstation Setup Disk #2.
13. At the Windows NT Workstation Setup—Welcome to Setup screen, press Enter to start the installation process.
14. Press Enter to detect mass storage devices.
15. When prompted, insert Windows NT Workstation Setup Disk #3.
16. Press Enter to approve the list of detected mass storage devices. (Don't worry if your IDE hard disk controller isn't detected. The installation process should proceed just fine anyway.)
17. Press Page Down repeatedly, until you reach the last page of the Windows NT Licensing Agreement.
18. Press F8 to approve the Windows NT Licensing Agreement.
19. Press Enter to approve the list of detected hardware components.
20. Select the desired installation partition, and then press Enter.
21. Press Enter to *not* convert the installation partition to NTFS.
22. Press Enter to install to the default directory named \WINNT.
23. Press Enter to examine the hard disk for errors.
24. Wait for the hard disk to be examined.
25. Wait while files are copied.
26. When prompted, remove the floppy disk from the drive. Then press Enter to restart the computer and begin the graphical portion of the setup process.
27. When the computer restarts, click Next.
28. Select the Typical installation option, and then click Next.
29. Enter your Name and Organization, and click Next.
30. Enter your CD-ROM key, and then click Next.
31. Enter your Computer Name (in this case, specify a computer named **Test**), and then click Next.
32. Enter and confirm the password for the administrator account, and then click Next.
33. Click Yes to create an emergency repair disk (ERD).
34. Click Next to install the most common components.
35. Click Next to install Windows NT Networking.
36. Specify whether your computer will be part of a network, and then click Next. If your computer will not be part of a network, skip ahead to step 43.
37. Click Start Search for Your Adapter, or click Select from List.

38. Select your adapter from the list, and then click Next.
39. Make sure that NetBEUI is the only specified protocol, and then click Next.
40. Click Continue to approve the network card settings. (Remember that Windows NT 4.0 doesn't support Plug and Play, and your network card settings *must* be correct.)
41. Click Next to start the network.
42. Click Next to install the computer named Test into a workgroup named Workgroup.
43. Click Next to finish setup.
44. Select the proper time zone, and then click Close.
45. Click OK to approve the detected video adapter.
46. Click Test to test the video adapter.
47. Click OK to start the video test, and then wait 5 seconds.
48. Click Yes if you saw the bitmap properly.
49. Click OK to save the video settings.
50. Click OK in the Display Properties dialog box.
51. Wait while files are copied.
52. Wait while the configuration is saved.
53. Insert a floppy disk that will become your ERD, and then click OK.
54. Wait while the ERD is formatted and files are copied.
55. Wait while the temporary configuration files are removed.
56. Restart your computer. The installation process is now complete.

Answers and Explanations: Exercise

If you want to speed up the process, you can use the */b* option, which doesn't require the three floppy disks because it copies the temporary files to your hard disk.

For more information, refer to the section titled "Installing and Configuring Windows NT 4.0" and Table 14.1.3, "Modifying the WINNT.EXE Installation Process."

14.1 Practice Problems

1. Before installing Windows NT Workstation 4.0, you want to make certain your system's hardware will be compatible. What can you do? (Choose two.)

   A. You cannot know if your hardware is compatible until after Windows NT is installed.

   B. Use the NTHQ tool included on the Windows NT Workstation 4.0 CD.

   C. You must contact the hardware manufacturer first and ask about your specific hardware.

   D. Consult the Windows NT 4.0 Hardware Compatibility List.

2. Using the tools found in the \Support\HQTool directory on the Windows NT Workstation 4.0 CD, you can do which of the following?

   A. Create a bootable floppy disk with the NTHQ.EXE program to help determine your hardware's compatibility with NT 4.0.

   B. Query the hardware after installation to determine whether IRQ settings are conflicting.

   C. Query the hardware before installation to determine whether IRQ settings are conflicting.

   D. Install the latest drivers for outdated hardware.

3. If your hardware is not listed in the Windows NT 4.0 Hardware Compatibility List, which of the following is true?

   A. The hardware will not operate properly with Windows NT 4.0.

   B. The hardware will not be detected by Windows NT 4.0.

   C. The hardware might work with Windows NT 4.0 anyway, or it might require a third-party driver.

   D. The item should be replaced with a comparable piece of hardware that is on the Hardware Compatibility List.

4. You have a video card that is not recognized by Windows NT 4.0. What can you do to attempt to get your card working with Windows NT? (Choose two.)

   A. Contact the manufacturer of the card to find out if any Windows NT 4.0 drivers are available for the card.

   B. Nothing. If Windows NT cannot recognize the card as a listed piece of hardware, the card cannot be made to work.

   C. Try to install the card as a generic video card with similar settings.

   D. Run the NTHQ.EXE utility.

5. Which processor type is not supported by Windows NT 4.0?

   A. Intel 80386

   B. Intel 80486/33

   C. Intel Pentium 75

   D. Alpha AXP

6. What is the minimum memory requirement for Windows NT Workstation 4.0 running on an Intel processor?

   A. 8MB RAM

   B. 12MB RAM

   C. 16MB RAM

   D. 24MB RAM

7. What is the minimum memory requirement for Windows NT Workstation 4.0 running on a RISC processor?

   A. 8MB RAM

   B. 12MB RAM

   C. 16MB RAM

   D. 24MB RAM

8. What is the minimum hard disk requirement for running Windows NT Workstation 4.0 on an Intel processor computer?

   A. 80MB

   B. 100MB

   C. 110MB

   D. 512MB

9. What is the minimum hard disk requirement for running Windows NT Workstation 4.0 on a RISC processor computer?

   A. 100MB

   B. 110MB

   C. 120MB

   D. 148MB

10. Which of the following are valid setup options that you can choose when installing Windows NT Workstation 4.0? (Choose all that apply.)

    A. Typical

    B. Compact

    C. Laptop

    D. Multimedia

11. When installing Windows NT Workstation 4.0 on the same hard disk with Windows 95 OSR2, what happens if the hard disk is formatted with the FAT32 file system?

    A. Windows NT recognizes it and carries on normally with the installation.

    B. The FAT32 partition is automatically converted to NTFS.

    C. Windows NT does not recognize the FAT32 file system.

    D. The FAT32 partition is automatically converted to FAT.

12. When you're using the winnt32.exe installation program, which switch do you use for an unattended installation?

    A. /ox

    B. /e: *command*

    C. /u

    D. /b

13. When you're using the winnt32.exe installation program, which switch do you use to create the three Windows NT 4.0 setup disks?

    A. /x

    B. /ox

    C. /u

    D. /b

14. When you're using the winnt32.exe installation program, which switch do you use to copy all necessary files to the hard disk so you can install Windows NT 4.0 without boot floppy disks?

    A. /o

    B. /u: *script*

    C. /u

    D. /b

15. When you're using the winnt32.exe installation program, how do you perform an unattended installation using a prewritten script file?

    A. Use the /ox switch.

    B. Use the /u switch, which tells the system to prompt you for the name of the script file.

    C. Use the /u: *script* switch, where *script* is the name of the prewritten script file.

    D. Use the /u switch with the /ox switch to create a script file on the setup boot disk.

16. When you're using the winnt.exe installation program in DOS, which switch do you use to prevent file verification as the files are being copied?

    A. /ox

    B. /e

    C. /u

    D. /f

17. You are installing Windows NT Workstation 4.0 over a previous installation of Windows 3.1. Assuming you will use the FAT file system, what can you do to ensure that you can perform a multiple boot into either operating system? (Choose only one.)

    A. Install Windows NT 4.0 into a separate directory.

    B. Install Windows NT 4.0 into the existing Windows 3.1 directory.

    C. Windows NT 4.0 will allow a multiboot with Windows 3.1 regardless of whether Windows NT is in a new directory or the existing Windows 3.1 directory.

    D. Windows NT 4.0 will not allow a multiboot with Windows 3.1.

18. You are installing Windows NT 4.0 and want to be able to connect to the Internet and UNIX servers. Which network protocol must be installed?

    A. NetBEUI

    B. TCP/IP

    C. NWLink IPX/SPX

    D. DLC

19. You are installing Windows NT 4.0 and need to connect to a Windows 3.1 workgroup. Which network protocol must be installed?

    A. NetBEUI

    B. TCP/IP

    C. NWLink IPX/SPX

    D. DLC

20. You are installing Windows NT 4.0 and will need to connect to a Novell NetWare network. Which network protocol must be installed?

    A. NetBEUI

    B. TCP/IP

    C. NWLink IPX/SPX

    D. DLC

21. Which of the following are not valid names for a Windows NT account? (Choose all that apply.)

    A. T_Arrington

    B. E*McElroy

    C. User1891

    D. Admin/SU

22. Which of the following options are not automatically installed when you choose the Typical installation option during Windows NT 4.0 setup? (Choose all that apply.)

    A. Accessibility options

    B. Windows Messaging

    C. Games

    D. Accessories

23. Which of the following options are not automatically installed when you choose the Compact installation option during Windows NT 4.0 setup? (Choose all that apply.)

    A. Accessibility options

    B. Windows Messaging

    C. Games

    D. Accessories

24. To install components such as Microsoft Mail or Solitaire during the initial installation, which installation option must you use?

    A. Typical

    B. Compact

    C. Custom

    D. Portable

25. A FAT partition is only necessary: (Choose two.)

    A. When you choose the Compact installation option.

    B. On the bootable partition of a RISC system.

    C. To preserve existing DOS, Windows 3.x, or Windows 95 installations that use FAT.

    D. On the system partition.

26. You want to install Windows NT Workstation 4.0 from MS-DOS. Assuming you have an installed CD-ROM drive (that's recognized by DOS), which methods can you use? (Choose all that apply.)

    A. Use the winnt32.exe setup program on the Windows NT 4.0 CD-ROM.

    B. Use the setup.exe program on the Windows NT 4.0 CD-ROM.

    C. Use the winnt.exe setup program on the Windows NT 4.0 CD-ROM.

    D. Use the three setup disks along with the Windows NT 4.0 CD-ROM.

27. You just FDISKed your hard disk and installed MS-DOS. Now you find that you do not have the appropriate CD-ROM drivers and thus cannot access your CD-ROM under DOS. What is the best course of action for installing Windows NT Workstation 4.0 on this computer? (Choose one.)

    A. Install Windows NT 4.0 over the network using a network share point for the \I386 directory on the CD-ROM.

    B. Install a bootable CD-ROM drive.

    C. Use the Windows NT Workstation 4.0 setup disks to begin the installation.

    D. Windows NT Workstation 4.0 cannot be installed on this system until the MS-DOS CD-ROM drivers are installed.

28. What three things do the winnt.exe and winnt32.exe do (without switches) during Windows NT installation?

    A. Create three setup disks for installation.

    B. Create the WIN_NT.~LS temporary folder and copy the contents of the \I386 folder to it.

    C. Configure limited network transport for remote installations.

    D. Prompt the user to reboot.

Answers and Explanations: Practice Problems

1. **B, D** The NTHQ.EXE tool can be used to create a special boot disk that checks your hardware configuration for compatibility with Windows NT 4.0. The Hardware Compatibility List (HCL) is included with Windows NT 4.0 and can be found on Microsoft's Web site as well.

2. **A** The MAKEDISK.BAT file in this directory can be used to create the bootable disk that contains NTHQ.EXE, which determines hardware compatibility.

3. **C** Although hardware that's not listed may not work properly with Windows NT 4.0, the HCL may not contain the latest information for your piece of hardware and/or the manufacturer may have a Windows NT 4.0 driver for the hardware.

4. **A, C** Often, manufacturers write Windows NT drivers for their hardware list and then post them on their Web sites or bulletin board services.
5. **A** The 80386 processor is no longer supported in Windows NT.
6. **B** 12MB RAM is the minimum for Windows NT running on an Intel processor.
7. **C** 16MB RAM is the minimum for Windows NT running on a RISC processor.
8. **C** The Intel version of Windows NT requires 110MB of hard drive space to install and run.
9. **D** The RISC version of Windows NT requires 148MB of hard drive space to install and run.
10. **A, B** Typical and Compact are valid installation options.
11. **C** Windows NT does not recognize FAT32. You have to reformat the drive.
12. **C** The */u* switch is used for unattended installation.
13. **B** The */ox* switch is used to create the three setup boot disks.
14. **D** The */b* switch is used for a diskless installation from the hard drive.
15. **C** You must use the */u: filename* switch when you want to use a prewritten installation script file for an unattended installation.
16. **D** The */f* switch is used in the DOS version (winnt.exe) of Windows NT installation to forego file verification.
17. **C** Windows NT can multiboot with Windows 3.x even if you installed Windows NT as an upgrade to 3.x.
18. **B** TCP/IP is necessary for Internet and UNIX connectivity.
19. **A** Windows 3.x workgroups standardize on the NetBEUI network protocol for small networks.
20. **C** Novell NetWare networks use the NWLink IPX/SPX network protocol.
21. **B, D** The characters * and / are not allowed in Windows NT user names.
22. **B, C** Games and Windows Messaging are not installed automatically during a Typical Windows NT installation.
23. **A, B, C, D** No optional components are installed during Compact installation.
24. **C** Custom installation allows you to install any component.
25. **B, C** RISC systems require at least a small FAT partition for their boot partition, and Windows 3.x or Windows 95 installations using the FAT file system are not accessible if the disk is converted to NTFS.
26. **C, D** Only the winnt.exe program will run under MS-DOS. Using the setup boot disks always works.
27. **C** The setup disks will likely recognize your CD-ROM drive during installation.
28. **A, B, D** The setup programs create the setup boot disks, copy the installation files to a temporary directory on the hard drive, and then ask the user to reboot. No networking transport protocols are installed at this time.

14.1 Key Words

Hardware Compatibility List (HCL)

Windows NT Hardware Qualifier Tool (NTHQ.EXE)

batch file

IRQ conflicts

FAT32

14.2 Setting Up a Dual-Boot System

Dual-boot systems are computers that have more than one operating system installed. When a dual-boot system is restarted, the user can choose which system he or she wants to start.

If you are in the process of transitioning your users to Windows NT Workstation, they might feel better if they could continue to use their previous operating system for a limited period of time. Additionally, they might need to be able to execute applications that are not compatible with Windows NT. Another possibility is that you might need to support users running different operating systems, and you need to be able to use only one computer. If you need to solve any of these problems, you might want to set up a dual-boot system.

Dual booting is a term for having more than one operating system on a single computer. A dual-boot system also has, typically, a boot menu that appears whenever the computer is restarted. The boot menu then enables users to choose which of the available operating systems they would like to start. It is possible to install Windows NT Workstation 4.0 to operate as a dual-boot system. The other operating system can be any version of MS-DOS, Microsoft Windows, or even OS/2. Some operating systems, such as some versions of UNIX, can dual boot with Windows NT but may need to use their own boot loader. Also remember that other operating systems may use different file systems for their partitions.

Installing Windows NT as a second operating system is similar to installing it as the sole operating system. During installation, you choose a separate system directory from the existing operating system's directory, and Windows NT automatically configures the boot loader to display selections for Windows NT and the other operating system.

To change the default boot menu options, either edit the boot.ini file or change the default operating system selection on the Startup/Shutdown tab of the System applet in Control Panel.

Although it is possible to set up a dual-boot system with Windows 95 and Windows NT, this configuration is not recommended. In this configuration, you must install all of your Windows applications twice—once for each operating system. No system or application settings are migrated or shared between the two operating systems. You should also install Windows 95 first because it installs its own boot track and can effectively disable a Windows NT boot loader.

14.2 Practice Problems

1. Dual booting means:

   A. Choosing between Windows NT in normal video mode and Windows NT in VGA mode.

   B. Using Windows NT's capability to run on different types of computers (that is, Intel, Alpha, and so on).

   C. Choosing between booting two separate operating systems on one computer.

   D. Two operating systems share the same system directory, such as Windows NT 4.0 and Windows 3.1 sharing the C:\Windows directory.

2. Windows NT Workstation 4.0 can be installed to dual boot with which of the following operating systems? (Choose all that apply.)

   A. Windows 3.1

   B. Windows 95

   C. Another installation of Windows NT

   D. OS/2

3. What advantages are there to installing Windows NT Workstation 4.0 in the same directory with a Windows 3.x installation? (Choose all that apply.)

   A. 16-bit applications will run as 32-bit apps under Windows NT.

   B. Windows NT will be able to dual boot with Windows NT 3.x.

   C. Windows 3.x applications and settings will migrate to the Windows NT installation.

   D. Applications from each operating system will work on the other operating system.

4. Which of the following are true about installing Windows NT 4.0 on the same system with Windows 95? (Choose all that apply.)

   A. Windows 95 uses the FAT32 file system and cannot be dual booted on the same partition as Windows NT.

   B. Windows 95 applications and file settings cannot be migrated to Windows NT.

   C. Windows NT cannot install over Windows 95 and, therefore, must be configured as a dual boot.

   D. Applications needed under both operating systems must be installed twice—once for each operating system.

5. Which Windows NT file determines the options presented on the boot menu when your Windows NT system first boots up?

   A. BOOTSECT.DOS

   B. AUTOEXEC.BAT

   C. CONFIG.SYS

   D. BOOT.INI

6. Which of the following are valid reasons for setting up a dual-boot system between Windows NT Workstation 4.0 and Windows 3.x?

   A. You want your users to make a gradual transition from their old operating system to Windows NT.

   B. You need to support multiple operating systems per user need, but you have only one computer available.

   C. You want to run 16-bit and 32-bit Windows applications.

   D. Your development team needs to compile and test software under two different Windows operating systems.

7. You want to change your default operating system selection on the boot menu to Windows 95. How do you go about doing this?

   A. Use the Registry Editor.

   B. Use the Network applet in Control Panel.

   C. Use the System applet in Control Panel.

   D. Edit the BOOTSECT.DOS file.

8. You have a system running MS-DOS, and you want to be able to dual boot between Windows NT Workstation 4.0 and Windows 95. Which step must you take? (Choose only one.)

   A. Install Windows NT Workstation before Windows 95.

   B. Install Windows 95 before Windows NT Workstation.

   C. Create two partitions for each operating system.

   D. Create two partitions for each file system, FAT and NTFS.

Answers and Explanations: Practice Problems

1. **C** Dual booting refers to having two separate operating systems on one computer.

2. **A, B, C, D** Windows NT 4.0 can dual boot with all of these operating systems, even though dual booting with Windows 95 is not generally advised because Windows 95 cannot be upgraded or converted to Windows NT 4.0.

3. **B, C** Dual booting and migration will both be possible. Answer A is incorrect because 16-bit applications are not converted to 32-bit simply by switching to a 32-bit operating system. Answer D is incorrect because, although 16-bit applications will more than likely run on Windows NT, 32-bit apps will not run on Windows 3.x.

4. **B, C, D** Applications and settings cannot be migrated, and they must be installed for both operating systems.

5. **D** BOOT.INI, which can be edited, determines the order of the operating systems and the choices given upon bootup.

6. **A, B, D** Although some 16-bit Windows applications will not run properly with Windows NT, Windows NT is designed to run both 16-bit and 32-bit Windows applications.

7. **C** Use the Startup/Shutdown tab in the System applet of the Control Panel to change the default startup operating system.

8. **B** You should install Windows 95 before installing Windows NT because Windows 95 will overwrite the Windows NT boot loader.

14.2 Key Words

dual booting

14.3 Removing Windows NT Workstation

To remove Windows NT Workstation from a computer, you must first determine whether there are any NTFS partitions on the computer. If there are NTFS partitions on the computer, you must remove them because Windows 95 or MS-DOS cannot use them. If the NTFS partitions contain only data and no Windows NT system files, you can use the Windows NT Disk Administrator program to remove them. However, if the NTFS partitions contain Windows NT system files or if they are logical drive(s) in an extended partition, the MS-DOS FDISK utility cannot be used to remove them and you should use the procedure detailed in Exercise 14.3.1.

After you have removed all the NTFS partitions, you need to start the computer with a Windows 95 or MS-DOS system disk that contains the sys.com file. Type the command **sys c:** to transfer the Windows 95 or MS-DOS system files to the boot track on drive C. You then need to remove all the remaining Windows NT Workstation files, as outlined here:

- All paging files (C:\Pagefile.sys)
- C:\BOOT.INI, C:\BOOTSECT.DOS, C:\NTDETECT.COM, C:\NTLDR (these are hidden, system, read-only files)
- The *winnt_root* folder
- The c:\Program files\Windows Windows NT folder

If you fail to remove the Windows NT boot track from your computer, the following error message appears when you restart your computer:

```
BOOT: Couldn't find NTLDR.
Please insert another disk.
```

You can now proceed with installing your choice of operating system on your computer.

14.3.1 Exercise: Removing NTFS Partitions

Objective: Remove Windows NT Workstation from a computer.

Time Estimate: 30 minutes

This exercise gives instructions on how to remove Windows NT from a computer in which there are NTFS partitions that are logical drives in extended partitions. Logical NTFS partitions cannot be removed using FDISK.

1. Insert the Windows NT Workstation Setup Boot Disk into your floppy disk drive and restart your computer. (If you don't have the three Setup boot disks, you can create them with the command WINNT /OX.)
2. When prompted, insert Windows NT Workstation Setup Disk #2.
3. At the Windows NT Workstation Setup—Welcome to Setup screen, press Enter to start the installation process.

4. Press Enter to detect mass storage devices.
5. When prompted, insert Windows NT Workstation Setup Disk #3.
6. Press Enter to approve the list of detected mass storage devices. (Don't worry if your IDE hard disk controller isn't detected. The installation process should proceed just fine anyway.)
7. Press Page Down repeatedly, until you reach the last page of the Windows NT Licensing Agreement.
8. Press F8 to approve the Windows NT Licensing Agreement.
9. Press Enter to approve the list of detected hardware components.
10. Select the desired installation partition, and then press Enter.
11. Specify that you want to convert the desired partition from NTFS to FAT.
12. When the conversion to FAT is complete, press F3 to exit from the Setup program.
13. Restart your computer with an MS-DOS system disk that contains the sys.com program.
14. From a command prompt, type **sys c:**, which transfers an MS-DOS boot sector to the hard disk.

Answers and Explanations: Exercise

In this exercise, you used the Windows NT 4.0 Setup disks to delete existing Windows NT partitions on your system, and then you reformatted the partitions as FAT. You used an MS-DOS system disk to transfer the MS-DOS boot sector to the C: drive, thus enabling the system to boot. All Windows NT system files were deleted when the partitions were deleted and reformatted.

Several shareware programs also remove all partitions from a hard disk. Check your favorite shareware collections for details. For more information, refer to the section titled "Removing Windows NT Workstation."

14.3 Practice Problems

1. What should be your first consideration when removing a Windows NT Workstation 4.0 installation completely from a computer?

    A. Removing the system files

    B. Restoring the regular MS-DOS bootup by using sys.com

    C. Removing any NTFS partitions

    D. Removing the pagefile(s)

2. Your Windows NT system's C: drive is formatted with FAT, whereas your D: drive is formatted NTFS. You remove and reformat the D: drive as FAT. What should you do next to uninstall Windows NT?

    A. Remove the pagefile(s).

    B. Reboot with an MS-DOS disk and use the SYS C: command.

    C. Remove the system files.

    D. Reformat drive C:.

3. Which of the following *does not* have to be specifically deleted during a removal of Windows NT 4.0? (Choose one.)

    A. All pagefiles

    B. The Windows NT system root folder (ex: c:\winnt)

    C. The Registry files

    D. The C:\Program Files\Windows NT folder

4. After removing Windows NT Workstation 4.0 from your computer, you reboot and receive the following message: `BOOT: Couldn't find NTLDR. Please insert another disk.` What is wrong with your installation?

    A. The BOOT.INI file has not been deleted.

    B. The Windows NT system files were not deleted.

    C. The Windows NT boot track was not removed from your computer.

    D. You must use the emergency repair disk to finish removing your installation of Windows NT 4.0.

5. Which of the following are Windows NT 4.0 hidden system files that should be deleted during removal of Windows NT 4.0 from your computer? (Choose all that apply.)

    A. BOOT.INI

    B. BOOTSECT.DOS

    C. AUTOEXEC.BAT

    D. NTLDR

6. Your Windows NT system has logical drives in extended partitions, all of which are formatted with NTFS. You want to remove Windows NT 4.0 from your system and install Windows 95, which must access all hard drives. What should you do first?

    A. Use FDISK to wipe the drives.

    B. Use the Windows NT 4.0 Setup boot disks to reformat the drives.

    C. Reboot in MS-DOS and reformat the drives.

    D. Reboot in MS-DOS and use the sys c: command to transfer boot tracks.

7. If you want to completely remove Windows NT from your computer and you are not running any other operating system, you can forego manually deleting system files and other data by doing which of the following?

    A. Booting with an MS-DOS disk and using the FDISK.EXE utility to wipe each drive

    B. Booting with an MS-DOS disk and formatting each drive

14

   C. Booting with the Windows NT Setup disks, deleting each partition, and reformatting the partitions as FAT

   D. Installing Windows 95 or MS-DOS over the current installation

8. You are dual booting between Windows 95 and Windows NT, and you want to remove Windows NT but keep your Windows 95 installation intact. What steps do you take? (Choose all that apply.)

   A. Use the Windows NT Setup boot disks to delete the Windows NT boot and system partition.

   B. Use the Windows NT Setup boot disks to delete all NTFS partitions and reformat them as FAT.

   C. Use a Windows 95 boot disk to copy the Windows 95 boot loader.

   D. Delete the Program Files directory.

Answers and Explanations: Practice Problems

1. **C** NTFS partitions must be removed first because they cannot be accessed by other operating systems.

2. **B** It is best to copy the DOS boot files to the boot track in order to boot up in MS-DOS. Old Windows NT pagefiles and system files can then be deleted easily.

3. **C** The Registry files do not have to be specifically deleted; they are deleted when the system root folder and subdirectories are deleted.

4. **C** Use the sys c: command under DOS to remove the Windows NT boot track and copy the MS-DOS boot files to the boot track.

5. **A, B, D** Autoexec.bat is a DOS or Windows 95 file.

6. **B** DOS's FDISK cannot delete logical drives in extended partitions. Beginning the Windows NT installation and going as far as deleting and reformatting the drives is the preferred way of removing NTFS partitions.

7. **C** You can easily delete all NTFS and FAT partitions by using the setup process with the Windows NT Setup disks.

8. **B, C** You need to delete and reformat all NTFS partitions and then copy the Windows 95 boot record to the boot partition in order to override the Windows NT boot record.

14.3 Key Words

FDISK.EXE

partition

14.4 Upgrading to Windows NT Workstation 4.0

If you are upgrading an earlier version of Microsoft Windows NT Workstation to Microsoft Windows NT Workstation 4.0, you need to use the 32-bit version of the installation program WINNT32.EXE. WINNT32.EXE was explained earlier in this chapter, in the section titled "Installing Windows NT Workstation 4.0 on an Intel Computer." Installations of any version of Windows NT Server cannot be upgraded to Windows NT Workstation 4.0, and you must install into a new folder and reinstall all of your Windows applications.

If Windows NT Workstation 3.x is upgraded to Windows NT Workstation 4.0, all the existing Registry entries are preserved, including the following:

- User and Group settings
- Preferences for applications
- Network settings
- Desktop environment

To upgrade Windows NT Workstation 3.x to Windows NT Workstation 4.0, install to the same folder as the existing installation and answer Yes to the upgrade question that you are asked during the installation process. Then follow the instructions.

Because of differences in hardware device support and differences in the internal structure of the Registry, there is no upgrade path from Microsoft Windows 95 to Microsoft Windows NT 4.0. You need to perform a new installation of Windows NT to a new folder and then reinstall all your Windows applications. No system or application settings are shared or migrated. After you install Microsoft Windows NT Workstation 4.0 and your applications, you should delete the Windows 95 directory.

To attain a significant performance increase in the file transfer portion of a network-based upgrade from a previous version of Windows NT Workstation to Windows NT Workstation 4.0, use multiple */s* switches with WINNT32.EXE to specify multiple servers that contain the source files (see section 14.5).

14.4 Practice Problems

1. If you are upgrading from a previous installation of Windows NT, which program do you use to begin the upgrade?

   A. WINNT.EXE

   B. WINNT32.EXE

   C. UPGRADE.EXE

   D. SETUP.EXE

2. If you are upgrading Windows 3.x to Windows NT 4.0, which program do you use to begin the upgrade?

   A. WINNT.EXE

   B. WINNT32.EXE

   C. UPGRADE.EXE

   D. SETUP.EXE

3. Which of the following are preserved in an upgrade from Windows NT 3.x to Windows NT Workstation 4.0? (Choose all that apply.)

   A. User and group settings

   B. Application preferences

   C. Windows NT 3.x interface

   D. Desktop environment

4. You want to upgrade an existing installation of Windows NT 3.x to Windows NT 4.0, yet still maintain all of your Windows NT 3.x application settings and configuration. What must you do?

   A. Install Windows NT 4.0 in a separate directory and manually migrate applications and settings.

   B. Install Windows NT 4.0 in a separate directory and choose the Upgrade option.

   C. Nothing. Windows NT will automatically detect and update a Windows NT 3.x installation without prompting you for any other information.

   D. Install Windows NT 4.0 in the same directory as Windows NT 3.x and choose the Upgrade option.

5. Which operating systems cannot be directly upgraded to Windows NT Workstation 4.0? (Choose all that apply.)

   A. Windows NT 3.51 Workstation

   B. Windows 95

   C. Windows NT 3.51 Server

   D. Windows NT 4.0 Server

6. You want to begin installing Windows NT Workstation 4.0 while in Windows 95. Which setup program do you use?

   A. WINNT.EXE

   B. WINNT32.EXE

   C. UPGRADE.EXE

   D. SETUP.EXE

7. You want to upgrade from Windows 95 to Windows NT Workstation 4.0. Considering that Windows 95 cannot be directly upgraded to Windows NT, what must you do to make this transition? (Choose two.)

   A. You must install Windows NT Workstation 4.0 in a separate directory.

   B. You must convert the file system to NTFS.

   C. You must migrate user profiles to Windows NT.

   D. You must reinstall all 32-bit applications under Windows NT.

8. Why can't you directly upgrade a system from Windows 95 to Windows NT Workstation 4.0? (Choose two.)

   A. Windows NT requires the NTFS file system and cannot be upgraded over Windows 95's FAT file system.

   B. There are differences in Registry structure.

   C. Windows 95 supports FAT32, and Windows NT cannot access FAT32 volumes.

   D. There are differences in hardware device support.

Answers and Explanations: Practice Problems

1. **B** WINNT32.EXE is the 32-bit installation program used within Windows NT to begin an upgrade or a reinstallation.

2. **A** WINNT.EXE is the 16-bit program used to install Windows NT from a Windows 3.x installation.

3. **A, B, D** Application settings, user and group settings, and desktop environment are preserved, but the new Windows NT 4.0 interface will replace the Windows 3.x interface.

4. **D** Windows NT will upgrade Windows 3.x and migrate all necessary information and settings.

5. **B, C, D** Neither Windows 95 nor any version of Windows NT Server can be upgraded to Windows NT Workstation 4.0.

6. **A** You should use the 16-bit WINNT.EXE program to begin installing Windows NT 4.0 under Windows 95.

7. **A, D** Install Windows NT in a separate directory, and then reinstall all 32-bit apps under Windows NT. You can then delete the Windows 95 system files.

8. **B, D** Differences in hardware device support and Registry structure prohibit Windows 95 from being upgraded to Windows NT.

14.4 Key Words

WINNT.EXE

WINNT32.EXE

14.5 Configuring Server-Based Installation for Wide-Scale Deployment

The quickest way to install Windows NT Workstation 4.0 on a large number of computers is to use a network distribution server as the source of the installation files (especially when you need to install Windows NT Workstation 4.0 on computers that have network connectivity but don't have CD-ROM drives).

This is the basic procedure for setting up a network distribution server:

1. Use the Windows NT Explorer, the Windows 95 Explorer, or the MS-DOS XCOPY command to copy the I386 folder from the Windows NT Workstation 4.0 CD to a folder on the network server. Make sure that you copy all the subfolders, too.
2. Share the folder on the network server with the appropriate permissions so that authorized users can access the files. (Alternatively, you could share the I386 folder on the Windows NT Workstation 4.0 CD, but your installations will be performed significantly more slowly. Therefore, that method should be used only if you must conserve hard disk space on your network server.)

Keep in mind that if you use Windows NT Explorer or Windows 95 Explorer to copy the files, the default options must be changed to allow for hidden files and system files with extensions such as .dll, .sys, and .vxd to be displayed and copied. Choose the View, Options command. Then, in the dialog box that appears, select Show All Files from the Hidden Files list.

If you are using WINNT32.EXE to upgrade an existing copy of Windows NT, you can use more than one network server to significantly speed up the rate at which the installation files are downloaded to your client computers. If you set up two network servers called SERVER1 and SERVER2 with installation shares called NTW, for example, the proper command line option to use both servers during the installation process is:

```
WINNT32 /B /S:\\SERVER1\NTW /S:\\SERVER2\NTW
```

14.5 Practice Problems

1. Which of the following describes the best method for installing Windows NT Workstation 4.0 on a large number of computers in a network?

   A. Install from the CD-ROM and Setup boot disks.

   B. Install from the CD-ROM using the */b* switch to avoid using Setup boot disks.

   C. Install from a network distribution server that contains a share point to the installation files.

   D. Install from a workstation with a share point to the appropriate directory (such as \i386, \ppc) on the CD-ROM.

2. Which of the following enables you to greatly increase the speed of the file transfer portion of your network Windows NT installations?

   A. Choosing the */b* switch for installation without Setup disks.

   B. Choosing the */f* switch for installation without file verification.

   C. Using the fastest server on your network for the share point of the Windows NT installation files.

   D. Using multiple */s* switches and multiple servers containing the Windows NT installation files.

3. In order to copy the Windows NT installation files necessary for creating a network share for remote installation, what option must be set in the Windows NT or Windows 95 Explorer?

   A. Hide Files of Specified Types

   B. Show All Files

   C. The Shared-As radio button must be selected and a share name specified for the CD-ROM installation directory

   D. None

4. You're installing Windows NT 4.0 on your 100-workstation network, and your primary goal is to remotely upgrade all workstations. Your secondary goal is to copy files as quickly and efficiently as possible. You make a share on the Windows NT 4.0 CD-ROM's \i386 directory and use this for network installation. How well does this accomplish your goals?

   A. It does not accomplish the primary goal or the secondary goal.

   B. It accomplishes both the primary goal and the secondary goal.

   C. It does not accomplish the primary goal, but it does accomplish the secondary goal.

   D. It accomplishes the primary goal but not the secondary goal.

5. Which steps must you take to create a network share point for installation files taken from the Windows NT 4.0 CD-ROM? (Choose all that apply.)

   A. Use the winnt32.exe /s command and switch to copy files into directories on multiple servers.

   B. Copy all installation files to a directory on one or more servers, making sure all hidden files are copied.

   C. Create a share on the directory or directories used for installation.

   D. Set the appropriate file permissions on any installation directories.

6. The command winnt32 /b /s:\\SVR1\NTWS /s:\\SVR2\NTWS accomplishes what?

    A. It installs Windows NT on the computers SVR1 and SVR2 in each computer's specified NTWS directory.

    B. It performs a diskless installation, creating the setup information on SVR1 and SVR2.

    C. It installs Windows NT without setup boot disks, copying installation files from both SVR1 and SVR2.

    D. It copies setup files from the local computer to \\SVR1\NTWS and \\SVR2\NTWS.

7. A network distribution server for Windows NT can be described as which of the following?

    A. A server with a shared CD-ROM drive in which the Windows NT Workstation CD-ROM is inserted

    B. A server with a shared directory for installing Windows NT 4.0 drivers

    C. A server with a shared directory that includes all of the files from the required Windows NT Workstation 4.0 installation directory

    D. A Windows NT server capable of remote booting other Windows NT Workstations

Answers and Explanations: Practice Problems

1. **C** A server (or multiple servers) with a share to a copy of the installation files on the server's hard disk offers the fastest and easiest way to install Windows NT over the network.

2. **D** The */s* switch with multiple servers enables the installation to simultaneously copy files from all multiple servers specified.

3. **B** Show All Files must be selected because several hidden system files need to be copied over to the hard disk before creating the share on the directory.

4. **D** Although the solution allows you to install over the network, creating the share on one server and on the CD-ROM (slower than a hard disk) does not adequately provide speed and efficiency.

5. **B, C, D** All of these files should be copied first, then a share should be created on the installation directory or directories, and finally the share access permissions should be configured as desired.

6. **C** Using the */s* switch, this installation copies files from both servers, which speeds up the file copying process considerably.

7. **C** Network distribution servers are used to install software across the network. The easiest and fastest way to do this is to copy installation files from the CD-ROM to a hard disk and then create a share to the directory.

14.5 Key Words

network distribution server

14.6 Installing, Configuring, and Removing Hardware Components

Configurable hardware components in Windows NT Workstation include the following:

- Network adapter drivers
- SCSI device drivers
- Tape device drivers
- UPSs
- Multimedia devices
- Display drivers
- Keyboard drivers
- Mouse drivers

This section covers each of the preceding items, which are accessible via programs in Control Panel. The discussion looks at how you can configure these types of devices in Windows NT.

A. Working with Network Adapter Drivers

You can configure network adapters by double-clicking the Network icon in the Control Panel and then selecting the Adapters tab.

Windows NT 4.0 allows for an unlimited number of network adapters, as discussed in Chapter 16, "Connectivity." You can also configure each network adapter separately. To configure a specific network adapter, select the Adapters tab of the dialog box, and then click the Properties button.

You also need to make sure that you have the proper device drivers for your network adapter. Windows NT 4.0 is compatible with any device drivers compliant with Network Driver Interface Specification (NDIS) version 4.0 or version 3.0. However, Windows NT cannot use any 16-bit legacy device drivers or device drivers from Windows 95, which uses NDIS 3.1 drivers.

When you modify the settings in the Network Adapter Properties dialog box, be careful to select the proper settings. Microsoft Windows NT does not support Plug and Play and has no way to determine whether the values that you select are correct. Choosing incorrect values in this dialog box can lead to loss of network connectivity and, in extreme cases, system crashes.

B. Working with SCSI Device Drivers

The user interface for viewing configuration information on SCSI host adapters in Windows NT 4.0 has now been moved to the Control Panel.

To view device properties, open the SCSI Adapter dialog box. Select the Devices tab, select the device, and then click the Properties button. You can then view information on the device properties, as well as the revision data on its device drivers.

Although the dialog box is titled SCSI Adapters, this is also where you can view and modify information on your IDE adapters and devices. You must restart Windows NT 4.0 if you add or delete any SCSI or IDE adapters.

C. Working with Tape Device Drivers

The user interface for viewing configuration information on tape devices in Windows NT 4.0 has also been moved to the Control Panel.

If you want to have Windows NT 4.0 automatically detect tape devices, click the Devices tab, and then click Detect. If you would rather view device properties, click Properties. You can also add and remove device drivers by using the Add and Remove buttons located on the Drivers tab. You do not have to restart Windows NT if you add or delete tape devices.

D. Working with UPSs

An Uninterruptible Power Supply (UPS) provides backup power in case your local power source fails. Power for UPS units is typically provided by batteries that are continuously recharged and are rated to provide power for a specific (usually highly limited) period of time.

During a power failure, the UPS service of Windows NT communicates with the UPS unit until one of the following events occur:

- Local power is restored.
- The system is shut down by the UPS service or by an administrator.
- The UPS signals to Windows NT that its batteries are low.

During a power failure, the Windows NT Server service is paused (which prevents any new users from establishing sessions with the server). Any current users are warned to save their data and to close their open sessions. All users are notified when normal power is restored.

Communications between the UPS and the Windows NT system is via a standard RS-232 port. The cable is not, however, a standard cable. A special UPS cable *must* be used to ensure proper communications between the UPS system and your computer.

You must also be sure to test the UPS unit after it has been configured. On startup of Intel-based computers, ntdetect.com sends test messages to all serial ports to determine whether a serial mouse is attached. Some UPS units misinterpret these test messages and shut down. To prevent your UPS unit from doing so, add the /NoSerialMice switch to the boot.ini file.

E. Working with Multimedia Devices

Use the Multimedia icon in Control Panel to install, configure, and remove multimedia devices. Categories of multimedia devices that can be modified include audio, video, MIDI, and CD music. There is also a Devices tab, with which you can view information on all the multimedia devices and drivers installed on your system.

You must install drivers for sound cards after you have successfully installed Windows NT. You cannot configure them during an unattended install. For step-by-step instructions on how to install a sound driver, see Exercise 14.6.4.

F. Working with Display Drivers

Use the Settings tab of the Display program in Control Panel to choose display options, including refresh frequency, font sizes, video resolution, and the number of colors.

The Settings tab also enables you to choose options for your display (see Table 14.6.1).

Table 14.6.1 Options for Configuring Display Settings

Option	Description
Color Palette	Lists color options for the display adapter.
Desktop Area	Configures screen area used by the display.
Display Type	Displays options about the display device driver and allows installation of new drivers.
Font Size	Allows selection of large or small display font sizes.
List All Modes	Gives the option to configure color and desktop area, and to refresh frequency simultaneously.
Refresh Frequency	Configures the frequency of the screen refresh rate for high-resolution drivers only.
Test	Tests screen choices. (If you make changes and do not test them, you are prompted to test your choices when you try to apply them.)

Whenever you make changes to your display driver settings, you are prompted to test them before saving them. If you ignore the test option and save incompatible values, your screen may become unreadable. You can restore normal operations by restarting your computer and selecting the VGA option from the Boot menu. The VGA option forces your video card into 16-color standard VGA. You can then try different values in the Display Properties dialog box.

Be careful when changing settings for your display driver. In extreme cases, it is possible to damage your display card or monitor by choosing incorrect settings.

G. Working with Keyboard Drivers

The three tabs of the Keyboard program on the Control Panel enable you to configure the following options:

- *Speed.* Enables you to control repeat character delay, character repeat rate, and cursor blink speed.
- *Input Locales.* Enables you to specify the proper international keyboard layout.
- *General.* Enables you to view or change the keyboard driver. You might want to change your keyboard driver if you need to support an international keyboard, or if your prefer a Dvorak-style keyboard to the standard QWERTY keyboard.

To configure a system to match the capabilities of a physically impaired user, you can specify keyboard options in the Accessibility Options program in Control Panel.

H. Working with Mouse Drivers

Use the Mouse program in Control Panel to change mouse options, including Buttons, Pointers, Motion, and General. Table 14.6.2 details the various options that you can configure with the Mouse program.

Table 14.6.2 Configuring Mouse Options

Tab	Available Options
Buttons	Configure mouse for right-handed or left-handed operation and for double-click speed.
Pointers	Choose the pointer shapes to associate with various system events.
Motion	Control pointer speed and specify if you want the mouse pointer to snap to the default button in dialog boxes.
General	View current mouse driver, and change to new mouse driver if desired.

All of the mouse options outlined in Table 14.6.2, with the exception of the mouse driver, can be configured individually for each user account and are saved in the user's profile.

14.6.1 Exercise: Changing Hardware Settings for a Network Adapter

Objective: Install, configure, and remove network adapter drivers.

Time Estimate: 10 minutes

This exercise shows the necessary steps to change the hardware settings for a network adapter.

1. Double-click the Network program in Control Panel.
2. Click the Adapters tab.

3. Select the desired network adapter in the Network Adapters section.
4. Click Properties.
5. Modify the network card properties to the desired settings, and then click OK.
6. Click Close in the Network dialog box.
7. Wait while your bindings are recalculated.
8. Click Yes to restart your computer.

Answers and Explanations: Exercise

In this exercise, you used the Network applet in Control Panel to modify the settings of your network card. Incorrect network adapter settings sometimes have very adverse effects on your Windows NT installation, ranging from inability to access the network to system crashes.

If you enter incorrect information for your hardware settings, your computer might experience problems when you try to restart it. If it does, try selecting Last Known Good Configuration to solve the problem. For more information, refer to the section entitled "Working with Network Adapter Drivers."

14.6.2 Exercise: Adding Additional SCSI Adapters

Objective: Install, configure, and remove SCSI device drivers.

Time Estimate: 10 minutes

This exercise shows how to add additional SCSI adapters to a computer already running Windows NT 4.0.

1. Double-click the SCSI Adapters program in Control Panel.
2. Click the Drivers tab.
3. Click Add.
4. Wait while the driver list is being created.
5. Select the appropriate SCSI adapter from the list, or click Have Disk.
6. Insert the installation CD or the device manufacturer's installation disk when prompted, and then click OK.
7. Click Close to close the SCSI Adapters box.

Answers and Explanations: Exercise

In this exercise, you used the SCSI Adapters applet in Control Panel to install a new SCSI driver for your SCSI device. You can also use the SCSI Adapters applet to configure and remove SCSI device drivers. The new SCSI host adapter driver becomes active the next time you restart your system. For more information, refer to the section titled "Working with SCSI Device Drivers."

14.6.3 Exercise: Adding Tape Devices

Objective: Install, configure, and remove tape device drivers.

Time Estimate: 10 minutes

This exercise shows how to add tape devices to a computer already running Windows NT Workstation 4.0.

1. Double-click the Tape Devices program in Control Panel.
2. Click Detect to see whether your tape drive can be automatically detected.
3. If your tape drive is not automatically detected, click the Drivers tab.
4. Click Add.
5. Select the appropriate SCSI adapter from the list, or click Have Disk.
6. Click OK.
7. Insert the installation CD or the device manufacturer's installation disk when prompted, and then click OK.
8. Click Close to close the Tape Devices dialog box.

Answers and Explanations: Exercise

In this exercise, you used the Tape Devices applet in Control Panel to install a new driver for your tape device. You can also use the Tape Devices applet to configure and remove SCSI device drivers. In many cases, you can have the tape devices detected automatically by clicking the Detect button; however, if that doesn't work, they can still easily be installed using a drivers disk. New tape drives are activated immediately; you do not have to restart your computer.

For more information, refer to the section titled "Working with Tape Device Drivers."

14.6.4 Exercise: Installing a Sound Card

Objective: Install, configure, and remove multimedia devices.

Time Estimate: 10 minutes

This exercise leads you through the steps to install a driver for a sound card.

1. Double-click the Multimedia program in Control Panel.
2. Click the Devices Tab.
3. Click Add.
4. Select the appropriate device from the list (or select Unlisted or Updated Driver if you have a manufacturer's installation disk).
5. Click OK.
6. Place the installation CD (or manufacturer's installation disk) in your drive and click OK.

7. Configure the appropriate hardware settings for your sound card in all the dialog boxes that appear.
8. Restart your computer when prompted.

Answers and Explanations: Exercise

You can use the Multimedia applet in Control Panel to configure or remove a sound card, along with many other multimedia devices. If your particular sound card isn't listed, try selecting Sound Blaster Compatible.

For more information, refer to the section titled "Working with Multimedia Devices."

14.6.5 Exercise: Configuring Display Settings

Objective: Install, configure, and remove display devices.

Time Estimate: 10 minutes

This exercise leads you through the steps to change your display settings.

1. Double-click the Display program in Control Panel.
2. Click the Settings tab in the Display Properties dialog box.
3. Click Display Type.
4. In the Display Type dialog box, click Change.
5. Select the appropriate device from the list (or select Have Disk if you have a manufacturer's installation disk).
6. Click OK.
7. Place the installation CD (or manufacturer's installation disk) in your drive and click OK.
8. In the Display Type dialog box, click Close.
9. Click Test to test the new video settings.
10. Click OK and wait 5 seconds for the video test to be performed.
11. Click Yes if you saw the test bitmap correctly.
12. In the Display Properties dialog box, click OK.
13. If prompted, restart the computer.

Answers and Explanations: Exercise

Setting display properties is an important step and should be approached with some caution. Incorrect drivers or unsupported refresh frequencies can damage your monitor. Always make sure your settings comply with the capabilities of both your video card and your monitor.

Another way to bring up the Display Properties dialog box is to right-click on any vacant area of the desktop and choose Properties from the menu.

For more information, refer to the section titled "Working with Display Drivers."

14.6.6 Exercise: Adjusting Keyboard Drivers

Objective: Install, configure, and remove keyboard drivers.

Time Estimate: 5 minutes

This exercise shows you how to adjust the repeat delay and the repeat speed for your keyboard.

1. Double-click the Keyboard program in Control Panel.
2. Adjust the Repeat delay to the desired setting.
3. Adjust the Repeat rate to the desired setting.
4. Click OK to save your settings.

You can use the test box near the middle of the Keyboard Properties dialog box to test your settings for repeat delay and repeat rate.

Answers and Explanations: Exercise

In this exercise, you used the Keyboard applet in Control Panel to adjust the repeat delay and the repeat speed of your keyboard. Using this applet, you can also install, configure, and remove keyboard drivers, as well as change and switch to different keyboard locales. For more information, refer to the section titled "Working with Keyboard Drivers."

14.6.7 Exercise: Configuring Your Mouse

Objective: Install, configure, and remove mouse drivers.

Time Estimate: 5 minutes

This exercise leads you though the steps of configuring your mouse.

1. Double-click the Mouse program in Control Panel.
2. Click the Buttons tab to specify right-handed or left-handed operation, and then double-click Speed.
3. Click the Pointers tab to specify the desired style for the mouse pointer.
4. Click the Motion tab to specify the pointer speed and the snap-to default.
5. Click the General tab to view the current mouse driver.
6. Click OK to save your mouse settings.

Answers and Explanations: Exercise

When you change the double-click settings in the Buttons tab, make sure that you test them in the test area. If you are trying to configure a system for a user with a physical disability, look at the settings in the Accessibility Options program in Control Panel. For more information, refer to the section titled "Working with Mouse Drivers."

14.6 Practice Problems

1. You have just installed a new network card in your computer, and you now need to install the new network adapter in Windows NT. Where do you do this?

   A. The Network applet in Control Panel.

   B. The Windows NT Setup tab on the Add/Remove Programs applet in Control Panel.

   C. The Devices applet in Control Panel.

   D. The Server applet in Control Panel.

2. The Network Adapter dialog box used to configure network adapters lets you configure which of the following information?

   A. IRQ settings

   B. IP address-specific information

   C. I/O port

   D. This is dependent on your network adapter card

3. From the Adapters tab in the Network applet in Control Panel, what actions can you perform? (Choose all that apply.)

   A. Add a new network adapter.

   B. Remove an existing network adapter.

   C. Change the IP address for an adapter card.

   D. Configure routing for the adapter card.

4. Which of the following actions can you *not* do from the Adapters tab in the Network applet? (Choose all that apply.)

   A. View properties for the adapter card.

   B. Configure network bindings for the adapter card.

   C. Enable IP forwarding.

   D. Update the adapter card driver.

5. To view device properties for SCSI adapters, which of the following do you use?

   A. The Devices applet in Control Panel

   B. The System applet in Control Panel

   C. The Tape Devices applet in Control Panel

   D. The SCSI Adapters applet in Control Panel

6. In the SCSI Adapters applet in Control Panel, you can perform which of the following actions? (Choose all that apply.)

   A. View SCSI device information.

   B. View IDE device information.

   C. Add or remove SCSI drivers.

   D. Format SCSI hard disks.

7. You can make Windows NT Workstation 4.0 automatically detect Tape Backup Devices using what tool?

   A. The Registry Editor

   B. The Tape Devices applet in Control Panel

   C. The System applet in Control Panel

   D. Windows NT cannot be configured to detect tape devices.

8. Which of the following actions *can* be performed with the Tape Devices applet in Control Panel? (Choose all that apply.)

   A. Back up selected files onto the tape drive

   B. Automatically detect installed tape devices

   C. Add/remove device drivers for tape devices

   D. View properties of each installed tape device

9. Your Windows NT Workstation 4.0 computer is equipped with a UPS. During a power outage, the computer stills runs, but it will not accept remote logons. Why is this so?

   A. You have not configured Windows NT to accept remote resource access during power failures.

   B. Networking services on Windows NT Workstation are stopped when the UPS signals Windows NT that it is providing power.

   C. The Server Service has been stopped.

   D. The Workstation Service is stopped when the UPS signals Windows NT that it is providing power.

10. You have a UPS installed on your computer, but when you boot up in Windows NT, the UPS automatically shuts down. You suspect that the UPS may be interpreting Windows NT's serial port test messages. How can you determine whether this is the problem?

    A. Disconnect your serial mouse or install a PS2 mouse.

    B. Use the UPS applet in Control Panel to alter the configuration settings until the UPS is recognized.

    C. Install the UPS on a different COM port.

    D. Edit the BOOT.INI file and add the /NoSerialMice switch to the end of the boot entry you want to use.

11. From within the UPS applet in Control Panel, you can configure the way Windows NT 4.0 works with your UPS in which of the following ways? (Choose all that apply.)

    A. Specify a program to run upon shutdown.

    B. Specify the time to wait between a power failure and the initial warning message.

    C. Specify a user or computer to warn upon signaling the UPS.

    D. Specify whether the UPS Interface Voltages are positive or negative for the power failure signal.

12. You want to run a program automatically before the UPS shuts down the system. What is the estimated time constraint for executing a command file before shutdown?

    A. 30 seconds

    B. 60 seconds

    C. Two minutes

    D. Half of the expected battery life of the UPS

13. You want to install a new sound card on your Windows NT Workstation 4.0 computer. Which applet in Control Panel would you use to install the drivers?

    A. Devices

    B. Add/Remove Programs

    C. Multimedia

    D. Sounds

14. The Multimedia applet in Control Panel enables you to set and view configurations on which of the following? (Choose all that apply.)

    A. Audio

    B. Video

    C. MIDI

    D. CD music

15. You need to install a new MIDI device on your system. Which is a step you would take to install this device under Windows NT 4.0? (Choose one.)

    A. Select the MIDI tab on the Multimedia applet in Control Panel.

    B. Select the Devices tab on the Multimedia applet in Control Panel.

C. Select the Audio tab on the Multimedia applet in Control Panel.

D. Select the Devices applet in Control Panel.

16. You have removed the sound card from your computer and want to remove the drivers under Windows NT 4.0. How would you go about doing this?

A. Use the Devices tab in Control Panel to remove the device driver.

B. Use the Multimedia applet to determine the names of the drivers, and then delete them from your hard disk.

C. Use the Devices tab in Control Panel to disable the device associated with your sound card.

D. Select the sound card on the Devices tab in the Multimedia applet, and then click the Remove button.

17. Which of the following can be configured using the Settings tab in the Display applet found in Control Panel? (Choose all that apply.)

A. Color Palette

B. Desktop Area

C. Show Icons Using All Possible Colors

D. Windows Wallpaper settings

18. Which of the following *cannot* be configured using the Settings tab in the Display applet? (Choose all that apply.)

A. Refresh Frequency

B. Screen Saver

C. Display Type

D. Show Window Contents While Dragging

19. The Test button on the Settings tab in the Display applet should be used for which of the following? (Choose only one.)

A. Testing screen colors

B. Previewing the screen saver

C. Testing screen resolution and refresh frequency

D. Testing display adapter drivers

20. You have changed the display adapter settings on your Windows NT Workstation 4.0 computer. Upon rebooting, your monitor does not work properly with Windows NT 4.0, and you cannot view the screen. What should be your first step toward fixing the problem?

A. Reinstall Windows NT as an upgrade and use the default display adapter settings.

B. Use the emergency repair disk.

C. Reboot Windows NT and select the [VGA] version.

D. Try using another monitor temporarily.

21. Of the following, which are tabs for configuration in the Keyboard applet in Control Panel? (Choose three.)

A. Speed

B. Keyboard Map

C. Input Locales

D. General

22. You need to configure the keyboard to match the capabilities of a physically impaired user. What do you do?

A. Use the Keyboard Locale tab in the Keyboard applet to select a scheme appropriate for the user.

B. Use the General tab in the Keyboard applet.

C. Use the Speed tab in the Keyboard applet to change the response speed of the keyboard to suit the user.

D. Use the Accessibility Options applet in Control Panel to configure this.

23. Which of these options are configurable from the Mouse applet in Control Panel? (Choose all that apply.)

A. Buttons

B. Pointers

C. Dragging

D. General

24. Which of the following options are configurable for individual users and stay unique to each user? (Choose all that apply.)

A. Mouse drivers

B. Double-click speed

C. Mouse pointers

D. Mouse pointer speed

25. You need to change the international keyboard layout for your Windows NT 4.0 computer. Where do you do this?

A. The System applet in Control Panel.

B. You must reinstall or upgrade Windows NT to make this change.

C. The General tab in the Keyboard applet.

D. The Input Locale tab in the Keyboard applet.

Answers and Explanations: Practice Problems

1. **A** The Network applet is where you add, remove, and configure network adapters.

2. **D** Different network adapter drivers will allow you to configure different settings, or often none at all.

3. **A, B** Adding and removing adapters is done in the Adapters tab. IP configuration is handled in the Protocols tab.

4. **B, C** Network bindings are configured in the Bindings tab, while IP configuration is configured in the Protocols tab.

5. **D** The SCSI Adapters applet shows information on both SCSI and IDE devices and drivers.

6. **A, B, C** You can view both SCSI and IDE devices with the SCSI Adapter applet. You can also add and remove device drivers for both SCSI and IDE devices.

7. **B** You can select the Detect button on the Devices tab in the Tape Devices applet, and Windows NT will begin detecting any tape devices installed on your computer. This is done manually.

8. **B, C, D** The Tape Devices applet is used only for installing and removing tape devices and drivers, not for backing up data on the tape devices.

9. **C** The Server Service is automatically stopped when the UPS is signaled to run. This ensures that no other connections can be made to the Windows NT Workstation 4.0 during power failures.

10. **D** Some UPS devices misinterpret the serial mouse test signals that Windows NT sends to serial ports during bootup. The /NoSerialMice switch disables these test signals.

11. **A, B, D** A command file can be run about 30 seconds before initial shutdown; the time between Windows NT's warning of power failure and the actual shutdown by the UPS can be configured; and the positive or negative voltage setting can be set. You cannot specify a specific user or computer that's to be warned, but all connected users will receive a warning message.

12. **A** A command file needs to run in under 30 seconds, or it may interfere with proper Windows NT shutdown.

13. **C** The Multimedia applet's Devices tab can be used to add new multimedia hardware.

14. **A, B, C, D** The Multimedia applet lets you configure audio, video, MIDI, and CD Audio properties for your multimedia devices.

15. **D** Click the Add button on the Devices tab. You then use the MIDI tab to configure your MIDI settings, not install your hardware.

16. **D** To remove a multimedia device driver, simply go to the Devices tab in the Multimedia applet, select the device, and click Remove.

17. **A, B** The color palette and desktop area can be configured with the Settings tab. This tab basically offers configuration options for your monitor and viewing area.

18. **B, D** Windows color schemes, wallpaper, screen savers, and desktop options are not configured with the Settings tab. They are all covered in the other tabs of the Display applet.

19. **C** You should use the Test button before committing to a resolution and frequency scheme.

20. **C** If your display settings have rendered your display unworkable, you can boot Windows NT with the [VGA] option, which uses a standard 16-color VGA display setting.

21. **A, C, D** Keyboard mapping is not done with the Keyboard applet. The Keyboard applet is used for configuring the repeat rates, the international keyboard settings, and the keyboard device.

22. **D** You need to use the Accessibility Options to configure a keyboard layout for physically impaired users. If the Accessibility Options icon is not present, install the options by choosing them in the Add/Remove Programs applet under the Windows NT Setup tab.

23. **A, B, D** Buttons, pointers, and general setup are configured through the Mouse applet.

24. **B, C, D** The device drivers stay the same for all users. Other mouse configurations such as buttons, speed, and so on are saved to each user profile.

25. **D** The Input Locale tab lets you change the international settings for your keyboard.

14.6 Key Words

network adapter

UPS (Uninterruptible Power Supply)

Keyboard Input Locale

14.7 Using Control Panel Applications to Configure Windows NT Workstation

In addition to the Control Panel applications used to configure hardware that were described in the section titled "Installing, Configuring, and Removing Hardware Components," you can use several other options to configure Windows NT Workstation.

A. Adding and Removing Programs

You can modify the installation option (typical, portable, compact, and custom) that you chose when you originally installed Windows NT Workstation 4.0 by choosing the Add/Remove Programs program in Control Panel and then selecting the Windows NT Setup tab.

The Windows NT Setup tab enables you to add and delete optional components and applications in the following categories:

- Accessibility options
- Accessories
- Communications
- Games
- Multimedia
- Windows messaging

Note that the appearance of the check boxes actually indicates one of the following three states:

- *Clear boxes.* Indicate that *none* of the selected components or applications in that category is installed.
- *Clear and checked boxes.* Indicate that *all* of the selected components or applications in that category are installed.
- *Gray and checked boxes.* Indicate that *some* of the selected components or applications in that category are installed. For details on which of the components or applications are actually installed, click the Details button.

You can also add and remove applications from your system by choosing the Add/Remove Programs program in Control Panel and then selecting the Install/Uninstall tab. You could attempt to delete a program by deleting the appropriate program folder, but you will fail to remove any files that program needs that are in different folders, as well as any Registry entries that have been made by that program.

B. Modifying Date/Time or Time Zone

You can also use the Control Panel to modify your computer's date and time or to change which time zone it is located in. You must be an administrator or power user or have been granted the "Change the System Time" user right to be able to access this dialog box.

14.7.1 Exercise: Adding Additional Optional Components

Objective: Use Control Panel applications to configure a Windows NT Workstation computer.

Time Estimate: 10 minutes

This exercise shows you how to add any additional optional components that you didn't select when you installed Windows NT Workstation 4.0.

1. Double-click the Add/Remove program in Control Panel.
2. Click the Windows NT Setup tab.
3. Click the appropriate category from the displayed list.
4. Click Details.
5. Click the optional component(s) that you want to add.
6. Click OK.
7. Click OK in the Add/Remove Properties dialog box.
8. If prompted, insert the installation CD in your CD-ROM drive, and then click OK.

Answers and Explanations: Exercise

Depending on which version of setup you chose (Typical, Custom, and so on), you may need to use the Windows NT Setup tab in the Control Panel's Add/Remove Programs applet to install other Windows NT components. You should have your Windows NT CD-ROM available when installing new components.

You can also use the same techniques outlined in this exercise to remove optional components. For more information, refer to the section titled "Adding and Removing Programs."

14.7 Practice Problems

1. You need to add accessibility options to a Windows NT Workstation 4.0 computer to allow a physically disabled user to use the workstation, but the Accessibility Options icon does not appear in the Control Panel. What can you do to use accessibility options?

   A. Reinstall Windows NT.

   B. Use the Keyboard applet to customize the keyboard to the user's needs.

   C. Use the Add/Remove Programs icon to install Accessibility Options.

   D. Configure the User Profile using the System applet in Control Panel.

2. Which of the following are categories of components that can be installed using the Add/Remove Programs icon in the Control Panel? (Choose all that apply.)

   A. Multimedia

   B. Modems

   C. Games

   D. Display

3. Which of the following are *not* categories of components that can be installed using the Add/Remove Programs icon in the Control Panel? (Choose all that apply.)

   A. Audio

   B. Keyboard

   C. Accessibility Options

   D. Windows Messaging

4. You want to uninstall your Internet Explorer installation. Which Windows NT applet can you use to uninstall it?

   A. System

   B. Internet

   C. Add/Remove Programs

   D. Network

5. Who can change the Windows NT system time? (Choose all that apply.)

   A. Administrators

   B. Power Users

   C. Users

   D. Guests

6. You want to install more components from the Accessories options. In the Windows NT Setup tab, the check box next to the Accessories tab is gray. What does this mean?

   A. You cannot install any components from this option.

   B. You have already installed all of these components.

   C. You have installed some, but not all of these components.

   D. None of the components are installed.

7. You use the Windows NT Setup tab in Add/Remove Programs to install which of the following components?

   A. SCSI device drivers

   B. A new network adapter

   C. Windows wallpaper

   D. Display adapters

8. Which of the following components can *not* be installed by using the Windows NT Setup tab in Add/Remove Programs?

   A. HyperTerminal

   B. CD Player

   C. Microsoft Mail

   D. ODBC database components

Answers and Explanations: Practice Problems

1. **C** The Accessibility Options are a component in Windows NT Setup and can be added or removed using the Add/Remove Programs icon in Control Panel.
2. **A, C** Accessibility Options, Accessories, Communications, Games, Multimedia, and Windows Messaging are all component categories in the Windows NT Setup tab.
3. **A, B** Accessibility Options, Accessories, Communications, Games, Multimedia, and Windows Messaging are all component categories in the Windows NT Setup tab.
4. **C** The Install/Uninstall tab of the Add/Remove Programs applet lets you uninstall many types of Windows programs, including Internet Explorer and most web browsers.
5. **A, B** Administrators and Power Users, as well as any user granted the "Change the System Time" user right can change the system time.
6. **C** A gray checked area means some of the components in this category are already installed, but not all of them.
7. **C** Windows desktop wallpaper can be installed under the Accessories category in the Windows NT Setup tab.
8. **D** ODBC database components are not installed using the Windows NT Setup tab. The other answers are all components installable through the Windows NT Setup tab, however.

14.7 Key Words

Accessibility Options

Windows NT Setup

Practice Exam: Installation and Configuration

Use this practice exam to test your mastery of Installation and Configuration. This practice exam is 20 questions long. The passing Microsoft score is 70.4 percent (15 questions correct). Questions are in multiple-choice format.

1. Mitch has a system configured with Windows 95 and Office 97. He wants to dual-boot with Windows NT Workstation 4.0 and still be able to use his Office applications. His machine is a Pentium 100 that has 32MB RAM, 1GB hard disk formatted with FAT32. What should he do to upgrade his machine?

    A. Install Windows NT 4.0 using the winnt32 command, and then reinstall Office 97 under Windows NT.

    B. Upgrade Windows 95 to Windows NT Workstation by deleting his Windows directory after he installs Windows NT Workstation.

    C. Mitch cannot install Windows NT Workstation on this machine in its current configuration.

2. You want to install Microsoft Windows NT Workstation 4.0 on 10 Microsoft Windows for Workgroups computers that are connected to your Microsoft Windows NT Server 4.0. What is the fastest way to perform the installation?

    A. Using floppies

    B. Using the Setup boot floppy disks and CD

    C. Over the network

    D. Over the network specifying the */b* option for WINNT

3. You want to upgrade a Windows 95 computer to Windows NT Workstation 4.0. You have the installation CD and a CD-ROM drive. What program should you use to perform the upgrade?

    A. SETUP

    B. WINNT

    C. WINNT32

    D. UPGRADE

4. You want to upgrade a Windows NT 3.51 Workstation computer to Windows NT Workstation 4.0. You have the installation CD and a CD-ROM drive. What program should you use to perform the upgrade?

    A. SETUP

    B. WINNT

    C. WINNT32

    D. UPGRADE

5. You are setting up a network-based distribution server so that you can perform over-the-network based installations of Microsoft Windows NT Workstation 4.0. What program should you use to place the necessary files on your server? (Choose two.)

    A. SETUP /A

    B. XCOPY

    C. SERVER MANAGER

    D. Explorer

6. What version of network adapter drivers does Microsoft Windows NT Workstation 4.0 support? (Choose two.)

    A. ODI

    B. NDIS 3.0

    C. NDIS 3.1

    D. NDIS 4

7. You need to re-create the three Setup boot disks that originally came with your installation CD. What command enables you to re-create the disks without installing Windows NT Workstation 4.0?
   A. /B
   B. /A
   C. /OX
   D. /X

8. How do you configure network hardware and software?
   A. Use Windows Setup.
   B. In Control Panel, click the Network applet.
   C. In Control Panel, click the Devices applet.
   D. In Control Panel, click the Services applet.

9. What command uses a script file to install Windows NT?
   A. Netsetup
   B. Setup setup.txt
   C. WINNT /U:setup.txt /s:\\server1\ntw
   D. WINNT32 /b

10. You need to upgrade a computer from Windows 95 to Windows NT Workstation 4.0. It is Pentium-based, has 32MB of RAM, and has 750MB of free hard disk. What method should you use?
    A. Run WINNT and install Windows NT Workstation 4.0 in the same directory as Windows 95.
    B. Run WINNT and install Windows NT Workstation 4.0 in a different directory from Windows 95.
    C. Run WINNT32 and install Windows NT Workstation 4.0 in the same directory as Windows 95.
    D. Run WINNT32 and install Windows NT Workstation 4.0 in a different directory from Windows 95.
    E. You cannot perform this upgrade.

14

11. When you upgrade a computer from a previous version of Windows NT Workstation, which Registry settings are preserved? Choose all that apply.
    A. User and group accounts.
    B. All desktop settings.
    C. Network adapter settings and protocols.
    D. You cannot perform this upgrade.

12. You need to upgrade a computer to Windows NT Workstation 4.0. It is Intel 386-based, has 32MB of RAM, and has 750MB of free hard disk. What method should you use?
    A. Run WINNT to install Windows NT Workstation 4.0.
    B. Run SETUP to install Windows NT Workstation 4.0.
    C. You cannot perform this upgrade.

13. What is the maximum length of a computer name?
    A. 15 characters
    B. 12 characters
    C. 32 characters
    D. 256 characters

14. What is the minimum amount of RAM required to install Windows NT Workstation 4.0 on an Intel processor?

    A. 4MB

    B. 12MB

    C. 16MB

    D. 32MB

15. You need to install the Windows Messaging system when you install Windows NT Workstation 4.0. Which Setup option should you choose?

    A. Compact

    B. Portable

    C. Typical

    D. Custom

16. Your computer has Windows 95 installed. You want to install Windows NT Workstation 4.0 and configure it to dual-boot both operating systems. Which of the following statements are true? (Choose two.)

    A. You must reinstall all your 32-bit Windows applications before they will run under Windows NT Workstation 4.0.

    B. Do nothing after you install Windows NT Workstation 4.0. All your 32-bit Windows applications will continue to execute.

    C. All your user profile settings will be migrated from Windows 95 to Windows NT Workstation 4.0.

    D. None of your user profile settings will be migrated from Windows 95 to Windows NT Workstation 4.0.

17. You have 50 Pentium-based computers with network cards that you want to upgrade to Windows NT Workstation 4.0. To prepare for over-the-network installations, which folder on the installation CD needs to be shared?

    A. \I386

    B. \NETSETUP

    C. OEMSETUP

    D. \WINNT

18. You're performing an over-the-network based installation of Windows NT Workstation 4.0. What is the name of the temporary folder that contains the installation files?

    A. WIN_NT.TMP

    B. $WINNT.LS

    C. WIN_NT.~LS

    D. WIN_NT.TMP

19. You need to upgrade a computer from Windows NT 3.51 Workstation to Windows NT Workstation 4.0. It is Pentium-based, has 32MB of RAM, and has 750MB of free hard disk. What method should you use?

    A. Run WINNT and install Windows NT Workstation 4.0 in the same directory as Windows NT 3.51.

    B. Run WINNT and install Windows NT Workstation 4.0 in a different directory from Windows NT 3.51.

    C. Run WINNT32 and install Windows NT Workstation 4.0 in the same directory as Windows NT 3.51.

    D. Run WINNT32 and install Windows NT Workstation 4.0 in a different directory from Windows NT 3.51.

    E. You cannot perform this upgrade.

20. What switch needs to be specified along with the */s* switch to enable an unattended installation of Windows NT Workstation 4.0?

    A. /B

    B. /U

    C. /OEM

    D. /OX

Answers and Explanations: Practice Exam

1. **C** Because Mitch's system is formatted with FAT32, he cannot install Windows NT Workstation on it. For more information, refer to the section titled "Minimum Requirements for Installation."

2. **D** Performing an over-the-network installation with the */b* option does not waste time creating the three Setup boot disks and reading them back. For more information, refer to the section titled "Installing Windows NT Workstation 4.0 on an Intel Computer."

3. **B** You cannot use WINNT32 with Windows 95. For more information, refer to the section titled "Installing Windows NT Workstation 4.0 on an Intel Computer."

4. **C** You cannot use WINNT to upgrade Windows NT. For more information, refer to the section titled "Installing Windows NT Workstation 4.0 on an Intel Computer."

5. **B, D** There is no SETUP /A option for Windows NT, and Server Manager is used for other functions. For more information, refer to the section titled "Installing Windows NT Workstation 4.0 on an Intel Computer."

6. **B, D** ODI and NDIS 3.1 are types of network device drivers that are supported by Windows 95. For more information, refer to the section titled "Working with Network Adapter Drivers."

7. **C** The */ox* switch creates the Setup boot disks without continuing Windows NT installation. For more information, refer to the section titled "Installing Windows NT Workstation 4.0 on an Intel Computer."

8. **B** The Network applet in Control Panel offers network adapter and network protocol setup and configuration. For more information, refer to the section titled "Working with Network Adapter Drivers."

9. **C** The /U:setup.txt switch signifies an unattended installation that uses the setup.txt script file. For more information, refer to the section titled "Installing Windows NT Workstation 4.0 on an Intel Computer."

10. **B** There is no upgrade path from Windows 95, and you can use WINNT32 only when you are upgrading previous versions of Windows NT. For more information, refer to the section titled "Upgrading to Windows NT Workstation 4.0."

11. **A, B, C** When you upgrade a previous version of Windows NT, all Registry settings are preserved. For more information, refer to the section titled "Upgrading to Windows NT Workstation 4.0."

12. **C** Windows NT Workstation 4.0 is not supported on Intel 386 microprocessors. For more information, refer to the section titled "Upgrading to Windows NT Workstation 4.0."

13. **A** Fifteen characters is the maximum length for a Windows NT computer name. For more information, refer to Exercise 2.2.

14. **B** 12MB RAM is the minimum requirement for installing Windows NT on an Intel system. For more information, refer to the section titled "Minimum Requirements for Installation."

15. **D** You can only install the messaging components if you choose a custom installation. For more information, refer to the section titled "Installation Options."

16. **A, D** When you dual boot Windows NT and Windows 95, neither program settings nor user profiles are migrated to Windows NT. Your applications must be reinstalled before they will run under Windows NT. For more information, refer to the section titled "Setting Up a Dual-Boot System."

17. **A** There is no upgrade path from Windows 95 to Windows NT. For more information, refer to the section titled "Configuring Server-Based Installation for

Wide-Scale Deployment."

18. **C** WIN_NT.~LS contains the installation files for an over-the-network installation. For more information, refer to the section titled "Installing Windows NT Workstation 4.0 on an Intel Computer with an Existing Operating System."

19. **C** The 16-bit version of the installation program does not work under Windows NT. For more information, refer to the section titled "Upgrading to Windows NT Workstation 4.0."

20. **B** The */u* switch is used for unattended installations. For more information, refer to the section titled "Installing Windows NT Workstation 4.0 on an Intel Computer."

Chapter 15

Managing Resources

This chapter helps you prepare for the exam by covering the following exam objectives:

- Creating and managing local user accounts and local group accounts to meet given requirements
- Setting up and modifying user profiles
- Setting up shared folders and permissions
- Setting permissions on NTFS partitions, folders, and files
- Installing and configuring printers

Managing resources is an important part of implementing and administering Windows NT Workstation. In a Windows NT environment, *resources* refer to the user and group accounts on the workstation, disks, partitions, Volume Sets and Stripe Sets, local and network shares, local files, and folders and printers.

15.1 Creating and Managing Local User Accounts and Local Group Accounts

Every user who uses Windows NT Workstation must have a username and password in order to gain access to the workstation. Windows NT stores this information in a user account. Other items, such as a description of the user, the user's home directory and profile path, and password options are also stored with the account. User and group accounts are stored on the local machine in the Security Account Manager database, also known as the SAM database.

In addition to user accounts, Windows NT Workstation provides local groups to ease administrative burdens. By placing individual user accounts that require similar access to resources in Local Groups, the administrator can apply the required permissions and rights to the Local Group. All members of that Local Group automatically inherit those rights and privileges.

Accounts and groups are created and managed through the Windows NT Workstation utility called User Manager. You can launch User Manager from the Administrative Tools (Common) program group or by executing the musrmgr.exe from the file Run dialog box.

A. Creating Built-In Accounts and Groups

During Windows NT Workstation installation, two default accounts are created: Administrator and Guest. The Administrator account is assigned as a member of the local Administrator group. The individual performing the installation is prompted for an account password. The guest account is created without a password. This account is automatically disabled for security reasons. Although both accounts can be renamed, neither can be deleted.

Additionally, by default, Windows NT Workstation provides six built-in local groups. Table 15.1.1 outlines these groups and their associated privileges.

Table 15.1.1 Default Rights and Privileges of Built-In Groups

Administrators	This group has complete administrative control over the computer. Can create users and assign them to any group, and can create and manage network shares. Can gain access to any file or resource on the local machine.
Power Users	Similar to Administrators, but they cannot fully administer the computer. Can create accounts in any group but Administrators.
Users	Default group for all new user accounts. This group has enough rights and privileges to productively operate the machine on a daily basis.
Guests	This group has the least access to resources of all groups. The default Guest account is disabled during installation.
Backup Operators	Members of this group have enough access to all files and folders to enable data backups and restoration.
Replicator	When directory replication is configured, this group identifies the Windows NT service account used to perform replication.

In addition to these six default groups, Windows NT Workstation allows administrators to create and define additional Local Groups for managing resources.

B. Creating User Accounts

To create user accounts, you must be logged on with an account that has the appropriate rights to create the account and assign it to the desired local group. The only two built-in Windows NT groups that can create user accounts are the Administrators group and the Power Users group. Only a member of the Administrators group can create and add other accounts to the Administrator group, while members of the Power User group can assign accounts to any group except Administrators. To create a user account, start User Manager, and the main User Manager screen appears.

The top pane of the User Manager window lists existing users, and the bottom pane shows existing Local Groups. To create a new account, select New User from the User menu. The New User window appears (see Figure 15.1.1).

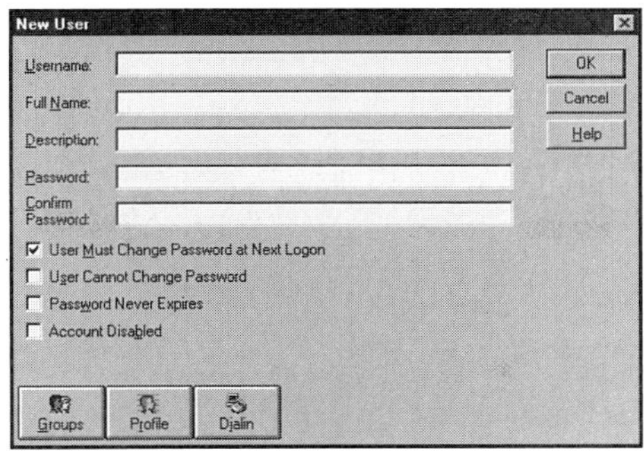

Figure 15.1.1 The New User window allows you to create new users.

When you create a new user, Windows NT requires you to complete only one field, the Username. All other information is optional but recommended. The username can be a maximum of 20 characters and cannot contain special characters. Special characters include the following:

“ / \ [ ] : ; | = , + * ? < >

The Full Name and Description fields are used for informational purposes. If you choose to preassign a password to users when creating their accounts, you specify that password in the Password field as well as the Confirm Password field. The password in Windows NT can be up to 14 characters long. If you have specified an account policy that requires a minimum password length, you must enter a password that is at least that long when creating the user account. (Account policies are covered later in this chapter.)

The password options consist of the four check boxes immediately below the Confirm Password field. These options are:

- *User Must Change Password at Next Logon.* This is the only option enabled by default. When this option is selected, the user is prompted to change the password when logging on to Windows NT. This setting is not compatible with the account policy that forces a user to log on to change the password. If both are selected, the user must contact the administrator to change the password.
- *User Cannot Change Password.* Setting this option prevents a user from changing the password. If this setting is selected along with User Must Change Password, you get an error message when you attempt to add the account stating that you cannot check both options for the same user. This option is not selected by default.
- *Password Never Expires.* This option overrides the setting for password expiration in the Account Policy. If you have this option selected along with User Must Change Password at Next Logon, a warning tells you that the user will not be required to change the password. This option is not selected by default.
- *Account Disabled.* This prevents use of the account until this option is deselected. This option is not selected by default.
- *Account Locked Out.* This option is visible only if you have Account Lockout enabled in the Account Policy. You, as an administrator, can never check this box—it will be grayed out. This box is available only when a user’s account has been locked out because he or she has hit the specified

number of bad logon attempts. If the Lockout Duration is set to Forever, the administrator must go into that user's account and remove the check from the Account Locked Out check box.

1. Assigning Local Group Memberships

You can assign membership in any Local Group by clicking the Groups button from the New User screen. The Group Memberships window appears.

To add a user to a group, select the appropriate group from the Not Member Of box and click the Add button. This user will become a member of that group, automatically inheriting all the rights and permissions assigned to that group. To remove a user from a group, select the group from which you want to remove the user in the Member Of list and click Remove.

It is important to note that group membership changes will not take effect until the user logs out and logs back on to the workstation. As an example, if you add a user to a group to grant access to a file, those permissions will not take effect until the user logs off and logs back on.

2. Configuring a User Environment Profile

You can access the User Environment Profile Settings by clicking the Profile button from the New User window. There are three items you can configure from the User Profile Environment window within User Manager:

- *User Profile Path.* This setting is used to specify a path for a user profile to be available centrally on a server or to assign a mandatory user profile for this user. To use a roaming or mandatory user profile, you must create a share on a server and then specify the path to that share in the user's profile, where the path follows the syntax of the standard Universal Naming Convention, or UNC, which follows:

  *servername**sharename**profilename*

  For more information on mandatory user profiles, see the section titled "Mandatory User Profiles," later in this chapter.

- *Logon Script Name.* This setting is used to specify a logon script to be used (if desired). If a logon script is specified, it will be launched when the user logs on to the Windows NT Workstation. If the logon script is not in a subdirectory of the machine's logon script path (typically c:\winnt\system32\repl\import\scripts), you must specify the subdirectory where it is located in the logon script name (for example, users\LailaL.bat). Logon scripts can have the extension .cmd, .bat, or .exe.

- *Home Directory.* To specify a home directory for a user's personal use, specify it here. You can configure two types of home directories: local or remote. A remote home directory will always be available to the user, regardless of where he or she logs on. If you choose to use a remote home directory, you must select a drive letter and specify the path to that remote share in a UNC format such as this:

  servername\users\JillB

A local home directory will always be local to the machine from which the user logs on. Therefore, if users use multiple machines, they may not always be able to access information stored in their home directories on other machines. If you choose to use local home directories, specify the full path in this setting like this:

C:\users\JillB

3. Granting Dial-In Permission

The final set of parameters you can set for an individual user account is Dial-In Permissions. If you have users who will be working from home or who travel and are on the road and need to access your network remotely, you need to grant those users dial-in access. By default, Windows NT does not grant the right to dial in to the network remotely. These are the call-back options for dial-in access:

- *No Call Back.* This setting disables call back for a particular user account. If this is set, the user initiates the phone call with the RAS server, and the user is responsible for the phone charges.
- *Set by Caller.* This enables the remote user to specify the number where the server can call back the user. This is typically used so that the server is responsible for the phone charges instead of the user.
- *Preset To.* When set, this specifies a number at which the server can call the user back when the user initiates a dial-in session. This tends to be used for security so that a user is called back at a predefined number only.

C. Managing User Accounts

After you create user accounts, you might find it necessary to modify, rename, or delete them. It is important to understand when it is advantageous to rename or disable an account as opposed to deleting the account.

1. Modifying User Accounts

Modifying a user account is very similar to creating a new user. To modify an existing account, select the account from the top pane of the User Manager window and select Properties from the User menu, or simply double-click the user account. This brings up the User Properties window.

The only difference between this window and the similar window you saw when creating a new user is that all user information for this account already appears in the fields. You can set any of the values as you did when creating a new user. In addition, the Groups, Profile and Dial-In buttons perform the same tasks as they do when you're creating a new user.

When a user account is created in Windows NT, it is given a unique identification called a security identifier (SID). This SID is designed to be unique in all of space and time. Because the SID is not related to the account name, renaming the user account does not make a difference to Windows NT. When an account is renamed, all the rights, permissions, and group associations for that account remain and are transferred to the new username.

2. Deleting User Accounts

In Windows NT, it is not usually a good idea to delete a user account. When you delete an account, you delete the SID, and the deleted account can never be retrieved. And after deleting an account, creating a new account with the same name will not restore the rights, privileges, or local group memberships associated with the original account.

Because the SID is eliminated when an account is deleted, it is generally better to disable an account using the User Manager than to delete the account. If you are certain that another user will not require the same permissions, rights, and local group associations of the account, you can delete the account. As an example, if an employee is fired, the account should be disabled and then renamed when a new employee is hired to take his place. However, if a worker was let go because his position was being eliminated (and, therefore, a replacement will not be hired), it is safe to delete the account.

D. Setting Account Policies

In addition to physically creating user accounts, an important part of administering a Windows NT environment is setting account policies. Account policies are global: They affect all accounts equally, regardless of local group membership. Some account policies, such as Maximum Password Age, can be overridden by your selection of password options (such as Password Never Expires, which you learned about earlier). Account policies address such issues as how often do you want users to have to change their passwords? What do you want to happen if a user makes multiple bad logon attempts? How many passwords do you want "remembered?" You configure the Account Policy within User Manager by choosing Account from the Policies menu (see Figure 15.1.2).

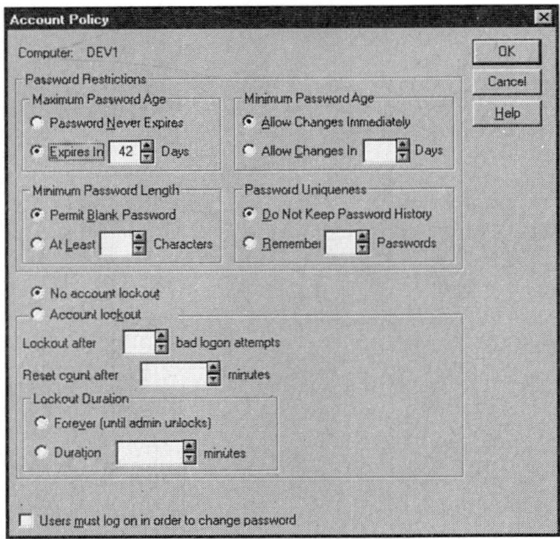

Figure 15.1.2 The Account Policy dialog box.

The following is a list of the password restrictions available:

Maximum Password Age. This option enables you to specify how long a user's password is valid. The default is that passwords expire in 42 days. Note that this policy will be overridden if you select Password Never Expires for a user account.

Minimum Password Age. This specifies how long a user must keep a particular password before the password can be changed. Setting this option to a reasonable amount of time will prevent users from reusing passwords, thereby increasing your security.

Minimum Password Length. By default, Windows NT allows blank passwords. You can set a minimum password length of up to 14 characters, which is the maximum password length allowed under Windows NT.

Password Uniqueness. If you want to force users to use different passwords each time they change their passwords, you can set a value for password uniqueness. If you set the password uniqueness value to remember two passwords, when a user is prompted to change her password, she cannot use the same password again until she changes the password for the third time.

The following is a list of the Account Lockout options:

Lockout After Bad Logon Attempts. Setting a value for this option prevents the account from being used after this number of unsuccessful login attempts. Once an account is locked out, only an administrator can restore the account if there is no lockout duration specified. When this option is enabled, Windows NT sets this option to five by default.

Reset Counter After. This value specifies when to reset the counter for bad logon attempts. The default value is 30 minutes. That means if Account Lockout is set to five and a user tries to log on unsuccessfully four times and then tries again in 45 minutes, the counter will have been reset and the account will not be locked out.

Lockout Duration. This value specifies how long the account should remain locked out if the lockout counter is exceeded. It is generally more secure to set Lockout Duration to Forever so that the administrator must unlock the account. That way the administrator is warned of the activity on that account.

User Must Log On in Order to Change Password. This setting requires a user to log on successfully before changing the password. If a user's password expires, the user cannot log on until the administrator changes the password for the user.

E. Account Rights

Account rights define *what* a user can do. Permissions, discussed later in this chapter, define *where* a user can do things. Account rights define whether the user can do such things as log on locally or set the system time on the workstation. Account rights are set from the User Rights Policy window. You access the User Rights Policy window by selecting User Rights from the Policies menu.

Select the appropriate right from the drop-down list, and then select the individual user account or group to which this right should be applied.

F. Template Accounts

A template account can ease the administrative task of creating multiple similar accounts. For example, suppose you have a group of salespeople for whom you will be creating Windows NT accounts, and the description field should show Sales Reps. Additionally, perhaps you want to assign each account a membership in the user-defined local group called Sales. Instead of entering the description and assigning local group membership to each account, you can create a user account called Template for which the description is complete and the group membership is assigned.

You can create a template account for any other groups of user accounts that require the same description, groups, home directories, logon scripts, user profile paths, or dial-in access.

In addition, you can also assign home and profile directories based on the Username field. In the User Environment Profiles window's fields, you can use the %USERNAME% variable to facilitate the creation of the home and profile directories. When the new account is created from the template, User Manager automatically substitutes the Username you entered for the %USERNAME% variable. After the Template account has been created, you can use that account to create the user accounts for the sales representatives. To create such accounts, complete the following steps:

1. Highlight the Template account in User Manager.
2. Choose Copy from the User menu, or press F8.
3. Enter the Username and Full Name for the new account.

G. Creating Group Accounts

To create a local group account, you must be logged on to Windows NT with an account that has administrative permissions. The tool used to create local group accounts is User Manager.

To create a local group account on Windows NT Workstation, select the New Local Group command from the User menu. Fill in the Group Name text box and the Description text box. Then click the Add button to select local user accounts to populate the group. When all desired members have been added, click the OK button to create the group. The lower pane of the User Manager window will be updated to reflect the change.

If you have one or more user accounts highlighted when you create a new local group, the selected user account(s) will automatically be put in that group.

1. Managing Local Group Accounts

You might have to manage your local group accounts after they have been created. This might consist of adding additional user accounts to the group, renaming the group, or deleting the group. If you need to add additional users to a local group, double-click the local group account within User Manager. To add a user account to the local group, click the Add button and select the desired user account.

2. Renaming Local Group Accounts

You cannot rename a local group account. If you decide that you want to change the name of a group, you must create a new group with the new name. You then give the new group the appropriate rights to resources.

3. Deleting Local Group Accounts

If you choose to delete a group account, that group will be gone forever. In the same way that an individual user account is given a SID when it is created, so is a group account. If you delete the group accidentally, you must re-create the group and reassign all the permissions for the group.

Deleting a group does not delete the individual user accounts within the group, just the group itself. You cannot delete any of the six default Windows NT Workstation local groups.

15.1.1 Exercise: Creating User Accounts and Groups

Objective: Create and manage local users accounts and local groups to meet given requirements.

This exercise demonstrates how to create groups and users and how to add users to groups. During this exercise, you will create a new group called Web Masters, create a new user account for Jack Smith, and add that user to the new group.

To create a local group, follow these steps:

1. Log on to Windows NT with an account that has administrative permissions.
2. Launch User Manager by opening the Start menu and selecting Programs, Administrative Tools, User Manager.
3. Create a new local group by opening the User menu and choosing New Local Group.
4. In the Group Name field, type **Web Masters**.
5. In the Group Description field, type **Local Server Web Masters**.
6. Make sure no user accounts are included in the group. (You will add the user accounts later in the exercise.)
7. Click OK to create the local group.

To create the user account, follow these steps:

1. Log on to Windows NT with an account that has administrative permissions.
2. Launch User Manager opening the Start menu and selecting Programs, Administrative Tools, User Manager.
3. Create a new user account by opening the User menu and choosing New User.
4. In the Username field, type **JackS**.
5. In the Full Name field, type **Jack Smith**.
6. In the Description field, type **Web Master**.
7. In the password field, type **password**.
8. In the Confirm Password field, type **password**.
9. Click the Groups button.
10. In the Not Member Of list, find and click the new Web Masters group.
11. Click the Add button.
12. In the User Properties window, click the OK button.

Answers and Explanations: Exercise

This exercise showed you how to create a new local group, create a new user account, and add new users to existing Local Groups. For more information, see the section titled "Implementing Local User and Group Accounts."

15.1 Practice Problems

1. By default, Windows NT Workstation installs two accounts during setup: the Administrator and Guest accounts. You are concerned about security and would like to minimize the chances that anyone could gain unauthorized access to your network through these accounts. What can you do? (Select all that apply.)

   A. Delete the accounts and create new ones.

   B. Delete the built-in Guest account and change the password for the built-in Administrator account.

   C. Create difficult passwords for both accounts.

   D. Rename both accounts.

2. Bob contacts you and asks why he cannot log on. He is certain he entered the proper password. You check his account with User Manager and find that the Account Locked Out check box is checked. What should you do to help Bob?

   A. Uncheck the Account Locked Out box on Bob's account.

   B. Reset the Accounts Policy so Bob will not be locked out again.

   C. Change Bob's password and have him try to log on again.

   D. Ask Bob to make sure the Caps Lock key is not set.

3. Which of the following are built-in groups on a Windows NT Workstation? (Select all that apply.)

   A. Administrators

   B. Users

   C. Power Users

   D. Account Operators

   E. Replicators

4. Alice is taking a leave of absence for six months. What should you do with her account?

   A. Delete it and then re-create it when she returns.

   B. Rename the account so that no one else can use it.

   C. Disable the account while she is gone.

   D. Leave the account alone.

5. Which of the following groups have the capability by default to create and manage network shares? (Select all that apply.)

   A. Administrators

   B. Power Users

   C. Users

   D. Server Operators

6. When creating a new user account, what information must you supply? (Select all that apply.)

   A. Password

   B. Maximum Password Length

   C. Username

   D. Description

7. Which of the following are functional tasks that by default can be completed by an account with membership in the Administrators group?

   A. Create network shares

   B. Delete default Guest account

   C. Change workstation time

   D. Create users in the Users group

8. Which of the following are functional tasks that by default can be completed by the Power Users group.

A. Create printers shares
B. Delete users accounts in the Administrator group
C. Take ownership of any file
D. Change workstation time

9. Which of the following are functional tasks that by default can be completed by members of the Backup Operators group?
   A. Back up files and directories
   B. Load and unload device drivers
   C. Manage auditing and security log
   D. Lock the workstation

10. Phil, a member of the Users group, complains that he cannot change the time on his Windows NT Workstation. What should you do to solve this problem?
   A. Tell him to reboot his machine. After his machine restarts, it will automatically resynchronize with other members in the workgroup.
   B. Add Phil to the Administrator group of his workstation.
   C. Remotely edit the Registry on his machine and set the time from your workstation.
   D. Use the User Manager program to assign Phil's account the right to change system time.

11. What is the minimum password length imposed with a default installation of Windows NT?
   A. 8 characters
   B. 0 characters
   C. 13 characters
   D. 6 characters

12. How do you set the Minimum Password Age property for user accounts?
   A. In User Manager, select Account from the Policies menu.
   B. In User Manager, select Passwords from the User menu.
   C. In User Manager, select Rights from the Policy menu.
   D. In User Manager, select Permissions from the User menu.

15

13. You want to change the name of the local Administrator group to Admins. How should you proceed?
   A. Delete the Administrator group and create a new group named Admins.
   B. You cannot rename Windows NT's built-in groups.
   C. Double-click the group in User Manager and select New Name.
   D. Select the desired group, and then select Rename from the User menu.

14. You create a local group named Web Managers. A week later, you decide you need to change the name to Web Masters. How should you proceed? (Select all steps that apply.)
   A. Delete the group.
   B. Double-click the group in User Manager and click New Name.
   C. Select the group from User Manager, and then select Rename from the User menu.
   D. Re-create the group with the new name.

15. James needs to access your workstation remotely through a Dial-Up connection. When he connects, he is unable to log on. What is wrong?
   A. He is probably using the wrong networking protocol. Have him change his protocol to TCP/IP and try again.

B. You need to enable dial-in permission through the User Manager.

C. Windows NT Workstation cannot support dial-in clients.

D. You must add his account to the Remote Users group built into Windows NT Workstation 4.0.

16. What application allows you to enable auditing on Windows NT resources?

A. User Manager

B. Disk Manager

C. System Applet (Control Panel)

D. Security Service (Services Manager)

17. What application allows you to assign a user a home directory?

A. Server Manager

B. Account Manager

C. Disk Manager

D. User Manager

18. Which of the following are true statements about accounts installed during a Windows NT Workstation installation? (Select all that apply.)

A. The Administrator account is enabled and can be renamed. The Guest account is enabled and can be renamed.

B. The Administrator account is enabled and can be deleted. The Guest account is disabled and can be renamed.

C. The Administrator account is enabled and can be renamed. The Guest account is disabled and can be renamed.

D. The Guest account is disabled and can be deleted. The Administrator account is enabled and can be deleted.

19. A user needs to be able to create shares on a local workstation, but you do not want to make the user an Administrator. What can you do?

A. By default, users can create and maintain shares on a workstation.

B. Add the user to the Backup Operator group.

C. Add the user to the Power Users group.

D. Assign the permission “Create Local Shares” through the User Manager.

20. Which of the following are true statements about local and global groups? (Select all that apply.)

A. Local groups and global groups can exist on a Windows NT Domain controller.

B. Local and global groups can exist on a Windows NT Workstation.

C. Global groups, but not local groups, can exist on a Windows NT Domain Controller.

D. Global groups, but not local groups, can exist on a Windows NT Workstation.

21. Which of the following are true statements about local groups? (Select all that apply.)

A. Local groups can contain global groups.

B. Local groups can be deleted and renamed.

C. Local groups can contain users and resources.

D. Local group SIDs are maintained in the Workstation SAM.

22. What is the maximum username length on a Windows NT Workstation?

A. 11 characters

B. 20 characters

C. 16 characters

D. 10 characters

23. What is the maximum password length on a Windows NT Workstation?

    A. 10 characters

    B. 12 characters

    C. 14 characters

    D. 16 characters

24. Your boss notifies you that DaveS has been fired and will not be replaced. She wants to ensure that DaveS does not have access to his files. What should you do?

    A. Delete his account immediately.

    B. Disable his account.

    C. Rename his account.

    D. Enable auditing on his account.

25. Derek calls to inform you that he will be on vacation for three weeks. He wants to ensure that no one can access his account while he is gone. What should you do?

    A. Delete his account and re-create it when he returns.

    B. Change his password.

    C. Disable the account.

    D. Lock the account.

26. You have a default installation of Windows NT Workstation. You have not changed any of the audit or account policies. You suspect that someone is trying to hack the administrator's account. What can you do to confirm this suspicion? (Select the best two options.)

    A. Enable auditing on logon attempt failures.

    B. Disable the Administrator account.

    C. Delete the Administrator account.

    D. Implement a Lock Out Policy.

Answers and Explanations: Practice Problems

1. **C, D** The default Administrator and Guest accounts cannot be deleted, so they should be renamed and given difficult passwords to prevent unauthorized access.

2. **A, D** A common cause for login failure is not entering the case-sensitive password correctly. Changing the account lock out policy is not prudent because this will affect all accounts and overall system security.

3. **A, B, C, E** All are built-in groups on a Windows NT Workstation except Account Operators.

4. **C** Because the user will be coming back to the company, you should disable the account so that it will not be used while she is gone. Do not delete the user account because that will delete the SID as well.

5. **A, B** Only Administrators and Power Users can share directories on Windows NT Workstation. The Server Operator group is only found on Windows NT servers.

6. **C** You need to specify only a unique username.

7. **A, C, D** The default Guest account can never be deleted.

8. **A, D** Power Users do not have the right to create or delete users in the administrator group. Only Administrators have the right to take ownership of any file.

9. **A, D** Only Administrators can manage the audit and security logs and load and unload device drivers.

10. **D** You can assign users the right to perform specific functions on a workstation yet still limit their authority in other areas; therefore, answer D is the best answer.

11. **B** By default, the Windows NT Workstation account policy does not require a minimum password length.

12. **A** The minimum password age is set from the Account option on the Policy menu.
13. **B** You can rename a group only by deleting and re-creating the group with a new name. You cannot delete the built-in Windows NT groups.
14. **A, D** You cannot rename local groups. You must delete and re-create them.
15. **B** By default, users are not granted dial-in permission.
16. **A** Auditing must be enabled through User Manager.
17. **D** Home directories are assigned through User Manager.
18. **C** Neither account can be disabled. The Guest account is disabled.
19. **C** Both Administrators and Power Users can create and maintain shares.
20. **A, C** Local groups can exist on Windows NT Workstation and Windows NT Server; however, global groups exist only on Windows NT servers configured as domain controllers.
21. **A, D** Local groups cannot be deleted and cannot contain resources, only users.
22. **B** Usernames must be 20 characters or fewer.
23. **C** Passwords must be 14 characters or fewer.
24. **A** Because the user will not be replaced, it is best to delete the account.
25. **C** When the employee will be absent for a period of time, it is best to disable the account.
26. **A, D** To confirm a suspicion of someone hacking into the system, enable auditing on logon attempt failures and implement a lockout policy.

15.1 Key Words

built-in accounts

built-in groups

local groups

SID

account policies

account rights

Template account

User Manager

15.2 Setting Up and Modifying User Profiles

User profiles are automatically created when a user logs on to a computer running Windows NT. A user profile maintains the settings that contribute to a user's working environment. This includes such things as wallpaper, desktop shortcuts, and network connections. The user's profile contains all user-definable settings for the user's environment.

User profiles in Windows NT are completely different and incompatible with user profiles in Windows 95 or Windows NT 3.51. On Windows NT Workstation, a user profile is automatically created for every user who logs on to the workstation. Windows 95, on the other hand, enables you to select whether to use user profiles. If you have users that will use Windows 95 and Windows NT 4.0, you need to maintain multiple profiles for those users.

User profiles are primarily used for convenience, but they can be used by an administrator to establish control over the user's environment. (For more information, see the section entitled "Mandatory User Profiles.") A user profile can be stored either locally on the user's Windows NT Workstation or centrally on a server so it's accessible from any location in the network. If user profiles are stored on the server and set as roaming user profiles, they can be accessed from any machine on the network running Windows NT 4.0.

A. User Profile Settings

A user profile stores information associated with a user's work environment. Table 15.2.1 identifies these items.

Table 15.2.1 Items Included in a User's Profile

Item	Description
Accessories	Any user-specific settings that affect the user's environment, such as Calculator, Clock, Notepad, and Paint.
Control Panel	Any user-defined settings defined within the Control Panel, such as Mouse Pointers, Modem Dialing properties, and Mail and Fax properties.
Printers	Any printer connections made within Windows NT Workstation to network printers.
Start menu	Any personal program groups and their properties, such as the working directory.
Taskbar	Any taskbar settings, such as Always on Top or Auto Hide.
Windows NT Explorer	Any user-specific settings for Windows NT Explorer, such as whether to view the toolbar, whether to show large icons, and how to arrange icons.

B. User Profile Directory Structure

By default, when a user logs on to a machine running Windows NT Workstation, the user profile is stored locally on that machine for the user. The profile is located in a folder whose name matches the username that is under the Profiles folder in the Windows NT root folder. Windows NT creates the initial profile by copying the information stored in the Default User Profile into the new directory and combining the settings in the All User Folder.

After the user logs off the Windows NT Workstation, any changes that the user made to her environment while logged on, such as rearranging the Start menu items or desktop icons, are saved to the user's profile. Below the user's directory within the Profiles directory is a structure of settings relating to the user's profile. Table 15.2.2 describes that structure.

Table 15.2.2 Folders Within a User's Profile Directory

Folder	Description
Application Data	Application-specific data. The contents of this folder are determined by application vendors.
Desktop	Desktop items, such as shortcuts, folders, documents, or files.
Favorites	A list of favorite locations, such as Internet URLs for different web sites.
NetHood	Shortcuts to Network Neighborhood items.
Personal	Shortcuts to program items.
PrintHood	Shortcuts to printers.
Recent	Shortcuts to recently used items.
SendTo	Shortcuts to items in the SendTo context menu. You can add items to this folder, such as Notepad or a printer.
Start menu	Shortcuts to the program items found in the Start menu.
Templates	Shortcuts to any template items.

The NetHood, PrintHood, Recent, and Templates folders are not visible by default. If you would like to display these folders, you must go into the View menu within Windows NT Explorer and choose Options, the View tab, and then the Show All Files option button.

1. All Users

The All Users public folder is used for Start menu shortcuts that apply to all users of a local workstation. These settings are not added to the user's profile, but they are used along with it to define the user's working environment. The common program groups—common to all users who log on to the Windows NT Workstation—are stored under the All Users directory.

Only members of the Administrators group can add items to the All Users folder for common access.

2. Default User

The Default User folder contains the settings that new users inherit the first time they log on to the workstation. If no preconfigured profile exists for a user when he logs on, he inherits the settings from the Default User folder. Those settings are copied into the user's new profile directory. Any changes that the user makes while logged on are saved into his user profile, which means the Default User folder remains unchanged.

C. User Profiles Types

Setting user profiles can help you to configure a user's environment. User profiles enable you to restrict users and enable users to retain their own settings when they move from one machine to another throughout your network. There are three types of user profiles: mandatory, local, and roaming.

1. Mandatory User Profiles

Use mandatory user profiles when you need a higher level of control than that of the standard user profile environment. Although the user can change items associated with the profile while logged on (such as screen colors or desktop icons), these changes are not saved when the user logs off. Mandatory user profiles are configured through the Control Panel's System icon.

> **In Windows NT 4.0, user profiles are configured through the Control Panel, the System icon, and the User Profiles tab. In Windows NT 3.51, user profiles were manipulated through the Setup Editor.**

2. Local User Profiles

The term *local user profile* refers to a user's profile that is created and stored on the Windows NT Workstation machine that she is logging on to. Local user profiles are the default in Windows NT Workstation, and one is created the first time that a user logs on to a Windows NT Workstation. Local user profiles are stored locally on the Windows NT Workstation. Local profiles are most effective if a user uses only one machine and never needs the settings while sitting at another Windows NT Workstation.

3. Roaming User Profiles

If you have users who will "roam" from one Windows NT Workstation computer to another in your environment, default local user profiles do not enable the users to maintain a consistent work environment on each machine. However, the administrator can configure a roaming user profile to allow the user to retain consistent settings regardless of which machine the user logs on to. Roaming profiles work with Windows NT 4.0 only. When the user makes a change to a roaming personal profile, that change is saved on the server where the profile is stored.

If the user is logged on to two machines simultaneously, the settings that were used in the *last* session from which she logs off will be the settings retained for the user's profile. If the administrator decides to create a roaming mandatory profile, the user cannot change it. A roaming mandatory profile can be used for multiple users. If a change needs to be made to the profile, the administrator has to make the change only once, and it affects all users who have that mandatory profile.

D. Creating a User Profile

To create a user profile, complete the following steps:

1. Log on to Windows NT Workstation with an account that has administrative permissions.
2. Create a test user account.
3. Log off and log on as the test user account. This creates a folder under the Profiles directory for that test user.
4. Configure the desktop environment as you would like it to be for the new mandatory profile.
5. Log off and log back on with the administrative account.
6. Create a centralized location for storing user profiles on a server and share that directory (for example, *servername\Profiles\username*).
7. Open the Control Panel, click the System icon, and select the User Profiles tab.
8. Select the profile for the test user and click Copy To. Under Copy Profile To, enter the path to the shared profile's directory: **\\servername\Profiles\username**.
9. Under Permitted to Use, make sure the correct user name is selected.
10. Within the folder that you created for the test user's roaming profile, find the file Ntuser.dat and rename it **Ntuser.man** to make the profile mandatory.
11. Launch User Manager and double-click the test user's account.
12. Click the Profile button and enter the UNC path to the mandatory profile: **\\servername\Profiles\username**.

Regardless of whether they are used for the convenience of the user or to restrict user actions, user profiles can be helpful in managing the Windows NT Workstation environment.

15.2 Practice Problems

1. When a user first logs on to a Windows NT Workstation, what folders are copied to the user's profile directory?

   A. Default User

   B. All Users

   C. Default Profiles

   D. Common User Profiles

2. Which of the following statements about a mandatory user profile are true? (Select all that apply.)

   A. Users with mandatory profiles can edit their desktops while logged on.

   B. A mandatory profile must be stored on the server.

   C. User changes to a mandatory profile are saved when the user exits.

   D. If a user's mandatory profile is not available at the time of log on, the user cannot log on.

3. Which of the following statements about a roaming profile are true?

   A. Roaming profiles are stored only on the local workstation.

   B. Users cannot change roaming profiles.

   C. Roaming profiles are compared to the locally stored profile for the user when the user logs on. If the locally stored profile is newer, it will be used.

   D. Both the roaming profile and the locally stored profile are updated when a user logs off.

4. What utility should you use to assign a roaming profile for a user? (Select all that apply.)

   A. User Manager

   B. System applet in Control Panel

   C. Account Manager

   D. Server Manager

5. You create a default installation of Windows NT in the C:\WINNT folder. What is the complete path to the Recent folder on the Start menu for a user with the username of RobertP? (RobertP has been assigned a local profile.)

   A. C:\Winnt\System32\Profiles\RobertP\ Desktop\Recent

   B. C:\Winnt\System32\Profiles\RobertP\Recent

   C. C:\Winnt\System\Profiles\RobertP\Recent

   D. C:\Winnt\System32\Profiles\RobertP\Applications\Recent

6. You need to add a shortcut for Microsoft Word to all users' desktops. Which of the following tasks do you need to complete in order to ensure that all users who log on to the workstation can access the shortcut? (Select all that apply.)

   A. Log in with an account in the Administrator group.

   B. Add the shortcut to the Default User folder in the Profiles folder.

   C. Add the shortcut to the All Users folder in the Profiles folder.

   D. Copy the shortcut to the Desktop folder of every user who maintains a local profile on the workstation.

7. As an administrator, you browse into C:\Winnt\system32\profiles\LutherS\ to find the network shortcuts mapped for the user LutherS, but you cannot find the NetHood folder. What is wrong?

   A. By default, the NetHood folder is hidden.

   B. The NetHood folder does not exist if the user does not have any shortcuts mapped.

   C. The NetHood folder is located in the Desktop folder.

   D. The NetHood folder is located in the Personal folder.

8. What is the Default User folder used for?

   A. The contents of this folder are used to build the common options of the Start menu every time the user logs on.

   B. This folder contains the machine's default profile.

   C. This folder is used by the Recycle Bin.

   D. This folder holds the SAM database entries for each user account on the machine.

9. By default, when is a user's profile created?

   A. When the user account is created.

   B. When the user logs on for the first time.

   C. When the user logs off for the first time.

   D. None of the above.

10. By default, where is a user's profile stored?

   A. C:\Winnt\system32\profiles

   B. C:\Winnt\profiles

   C. C:\Winnt\system32\users\profiles

   D. C:\Users\profiles

Answers and Explanations: Practice Problems

1. **A** The only file copied to the new user's profile folder is the Default User folder. The All Users folder is used to create the common section of the Start menu.

2. **A, B, D** Mandatory profiles must be stored on the server. Users can change the components, such as the desktop, of a mandatory profile while logged on; however, changes are never saved. If a mandatory profile is not available at the time of login, the user will be denied access to the workstation.

3. **C, D** Roaming profiles must be server-based. When a user logs on, the newer of the roaming profile or local profile is used. When a user logs out, both the local and roaming profiles are updated.

4. **A, B** User Manager is used to specify the path of the profile, while the Service applet is used to specify the profile as roaming.

5. **B** The complete path to the Recent folder on the Start menu for a user with the username of RobertP is C:\Winnt\System32\Profiles\RobertP\Recent.

6. **A, C** Only administrators can add shortcuts in the All Users folder.

7. **A** You must select View, Options, Show All Files in Windows Explorer in order to see the NetHood folder.

8. **B** The All Users folder builds the common section of the Start menu when a user logs on.

9. **B** The user's local profile folder structure is created when a user first logs on to the workstation.

10. **B** By default, a user's profile is created in C:\Winnt\profiles.

15.2 Key Words

user profiles

All Users folder

Default User folder

mandatory user profile

local user profiles

roaming user profiles

15.3 Setting Up Shared Folders and Permissions

To allow remote access of your resources, you must make them available on the network to users on other computers. Windows NT enables you to selectively choose which folders you want to allow access to, also known as *sharing*, and which you want to keep private to that workstation. Before you delve into folder sharing and permissions, you need to understand how Windows NT Workstation implements security.

A. Understanding Windows NT Security

All security functions provided by Windows NT 4.0 are handled through the Security Reference Monitor. Whenever a user attempts to complete a task, the request is reviewed by the Security Reference Monitor. It is the Security Reference Monitor that determines where and to what extent a given user can exercise his rights. User rights define *what* a user is allowed to do, such as changing the time on the local workstation. User permissions define *where* a user can use his assigned rights.

Windows NT allows administrators to define two types of permissions: share level and resource level. Share-level permissions are exercised through network connections, such as connecting to a shared folder. Resource-level permissions are exercised on the resource itself, such as copying a file from one local folder to another. Permissions are assigned to the resource or share and reside with the resource or share in the resource's Access Control List (ACL).

When a user authenticates to Windows NT, the user is given an access token. This token remains with the user until the user logs off the system. Along with other information, the access token contains the user's SID. When a user logs on to a local workstation that is not participating in a Windows NT domain, that access token contains a SID that is valid only for the local machine.

When a user attempts to access a resource, the Security Reference Monitor compares the information in the access token with the information contained in the ACL for the resource to which the user requested access. This ACL only contains SIDs in the local SAM database. Therefore, to access resources on another workstation that's not participating in a domain, the user must also have a SID in the remote workstation's SAM database.

Windows NT will automatically attempt to log the user on to the remote machine when a user is accessing resources on a remote machine. Instead of sending the user's SID, which would be useless on the remote machine, Windows NT passes the username and password in an attempt to create a new access token on the remote machine.

When the user requests access to a remote resource, the Security Reference Monitor on the remote machine compares the user's SID with the SIDs in the remote resource's ACL to determine the level of access to grant to the user.

It is important to understand that a user's access token is not dynamic. It cannot change during a given session. Even if an administrator adds a user to the ACL during that user's session, the user will not have access to the resource until he gains another access token by logging off and logging back on to the workstation.

B. Creating Shared Folders

Only Administrator and Power Users group members can create network shares.

Sharing can only be done at the folder or directory level; it cannot be done at the individual file level. In addition, it is important to note that all subfolders inherit the share access level of the parent directory. Therefore, you must plan your directory structure to ensure that users and groups do not inadvertently gain access to folders you want to remain local to the workstation. Remember to consider the type of client that will be accessing a share. Windows 3.x and DOS clients can only access shares that conform to the 8.3 naming convention.

1. Establishing Shared Folder Permissions

Windows NT provides four levels of access that you can give to users or groups that will connect to the shared folder. These permissions include:

- *No Access.* If a user or group is given the No Access permission to a shared folder, that user or group cannot even open the shared folder—although users will see the shared folder on the network. The No Access permission overrides all other permissions that a user or group may have to the folder.
- *Read.* Read permission allows the user or group to view files and subfolders within the shared folder. It also allows the user or group to execute programs that might be located within the shared folder.
- *Change.* Change permission allows the user or group to add files or subfolders to the shared folder, as well as to append or delete information from existing files and subfolders. The Change permission also encompasses everything included within the Read permission.
- *Full Control.* If a user or group is given the Full Control permission, that user or group has the ability to change the file permissions, to take ownership of files, and to perform all tasks allowed by the Change permission. This is the default permission applied by Windows NT when the share is created.

2. Sharing a Folder Locally

When you share a folder locally, you are logged on to the workstation that holds the folder you would like to share. To access that folder, right-click the folder and choose the Sharing option. This brings up the properties of the folder, with the focus on the Sharing tab. All tasks associated with sharing this folder are accessible from this tab. Each element of this dialog box is discussed here:

- *Shared.* Click this option button to enable users to share this resource across the network.
- *Not Shared.* Click this option button to stop sharing a resource.
- *Share Name.* Enter a name users will see when browsing the resources on this machine. Note that if you will have DOS or Windows 3.x clients, you must use the 8.3 naming convention.
- *Comment.* This is a text comment that will appear next to the share when users browse available resources on this machine
- *User Limit.* This option allows you to limit the number of inbound connections. It is important to remember that Windows NT Workstation has a built-in limit of 10 inbound networking connections.

- *Permissions.* This button allows you to set individual user and group permissions for access to this share. Remember that all subfolders will inherit this permission. (See the next section for the options available for setting share permissions.)

You'll find detailed instructions for sharing a folder in an exercise at the end of this section.

3. Setting Permissions on a Shared Folder

You set permissions on shares by right-clicking the folder and choosing Sharing from the context menu that appears. Click the Permissions button to activate the dialog box. Note that the default permissions on a shared folder are Everyone: Full Control. These default share permissions should be changed if there is a need for security because the group Everyone includes just that—everyone from your workstation (or your domain if this workstation is part of a Windows NT domain).

To change the default permissions, click the Add button. By default, just groups are shown. To grant access to a specific user account, click the Show Users button and select the appropriate user or group. Then from the Type of Access field, select the access you want to assign to that user or group. After you have granted permissions to the user or group to make the share more secure, you should remove the permission for Everyone: Full Control.

Before you remove the permissions for Everyone: Full Control, make sure that you have added permission for another user or group to have access to the shared directory or you may have a situation in which the directory is shared but no one has been granted access.

C. Managing Shared Folders

After you create your shared folders, you will likely need to manage them at a later point. Managing folders includes creating a new share from an existing share, stopping sharing for a folder, modifying permissions on a shared folder, and modifying the share name after a folder has been shared.

1. Creating a New Share

Many reasons may prompt you to create a new share for an existing shared directory. Perhaps you want to assign the permissions to the two shares differently, or maybe you need to add another reference to the share for additional departments' use.

The steps for creating a new share are slightly different from those for creating the shared directory from the beginning. It's important that you understand the differences because of the real-life need for implementation and for the exam. When you configure a new share for an existing shared directory, a button labeled New Share appears.

To create a new share from an existing shared directory, complete the following steps:

1. Right-click the existing shared folder and choose the Sharing option.
2. Click the New Share button. (Notice that you cannot change the existing share name through this dialog box.)

3. Enter the new share name and any comments, and then set the permissions for this new shared directory.
4. Click OK to close the New Share dialog box. Then click OK to close the folder's Properties dialog box and create the new share.

2. Stopping Sharing

After a directory has been shared, it may be necessary to stop sharing that directory. To stop sharing a directory on Windows NT Workstation, complete the following steps:

1. Right-click the directory that you would like to stop sharing and choose Sharing from the context menu that appears.
2. Click the Not Shared option button.
3. Click OK. This stops sharing the directory.

One way to prevent any access to your Windows NT Workstation is to stop the Server service through Control Panel, Services. Although this also stops the Computer Browser service, it is the most effective way of preventing access to your workstation.

3. Modifying Permissions on a Shared Directory

Having set up your shared directories, you may need to change the directory permissions at a later time. To modify the permissions of a shared directory after it has been shared, complete the following steps:

1. Right-click the shared directory and choose Sharing from the context menu that appears.
2. On the Sharing tab, click the Permissions button.
3. Add or remove groups as needed from the list of users and groups with permissions.

4. Modifying Share Names

Another aspect of managing shared resources is changing the name of a shared resource after it has been shared. To change the name of a share, you must actually get rid of the first share (stop sharing it) and create a new share with the new name. The order in which you do this is not critical: You can create a new share (as described in "Creating a New Share," earlier in this chapter), or you can stop sharing the resource (as described in "Stopping Sharing," earlier in this chapter) and then re-create the share (as described in "Sharing a Folder," earlier in this chapter). You cannot modify a share name without re-creating the share.

D. Implementation of Shared Folder Permissions

When setting up permissions on shared folders, it is important that you understand how those permissions will apply or be implemented in your environment. Before you set up shared folder permissions, you need to know how user and group permissions will interact, as well as how the No Access permission can override any other permission set for that user or group.

You can grant shared folder permissions to both users and groups. Because of this, you might have a situation in which a user is given permission to a shared resource and a group that the user is a member of is given different permissions. Another possible scenario is one in which a user is a member of more than one group that has been given access to the resource. In those cases, you need to understand how user and group permissions interact in shared folder permissions.

When determining the combined permissions of users and groups assigned to a share, Windows NT combines all the associated permissions and applies the least restrictive one. As an example, suppose HeidiS is given Read permission on a network shared folder. HeidiS is also a member of the Web Masters group, which has Change permission on the share. HeidiS's combined access to the share will be Change control because it is the least restrictive of the individual user and group permissions.

If any user or any group that a user belongs to is assigned the No Access permission to the share, that user will not have access to the share, regardless of any other permissions. Continuing our previous example, if HeidiS were given No Access to the share as a user, HeidiS would have no access to the share—no matter what—because No Access overrides all other assigned permissions, whether they are individual user permissions or group permissions.

If access is not specified for a particular group or user, this permission has no effect on determining the net permissions. Again, assume that HeidiS has Change access to a share but the Web Master group, of which HeidiS is a member, is not included in the ACL. In that case, HeidiS's net permission for the share is Change control.

15.3.1 Exercise: Creating and Managing Shared Directories

Objective: Set up shared folders and permissions.

This exercise shows you how to create a shared directory, set the permissions for it, and manage the shared directory after it is created.

1. Log on to Windows NT Workstation using an account with administrative permissions on that workstation.
2. On an NTFS partition (or FAT if you do not have NTFS), create a directory called **Atlanta**.
3. Right-click the directory and choose Sharing from the context menu that appears.
4. Click the Shared As button and leave the share name as Antigua.
5. In the Comment field, type **My Shared Directory**.
6. Click the Permissions button.
7. Remove the group Everyone from the list of shared permissions. Add Administrators with Full Control and add Users with Read access.
8. Click OK to create the shared directory.
9. Double-click the Network Neighborhood icon on your desktop. Double-click your computer, and you should see "Atlanta."
10. Close Network Neighborhood.
11. Launch Windows NT Explorer. Right-click the Antigua directory and choose Sharing from the context menu that appears.
12. Click the New Share button to create a new share.

13. Type **Georgia** for the new share name. For the Comment, type **Another Share**.
14. Click the Permissions button and remove the Everyone: Full Control permission. Do not add any other permissions.
15. Click OK. You receive a prompt with a warning that your shared directory will be inaccessible because you have removed all the permissions. Click the Yes button to continue.
16. Double-click the Network Neighborhood icon on your desktop. Then double-click your computer. Does "Atlanta" appear? Does "Georgia" appear?
17. Double-click Georgia. What happens?
18. Close Network Neighborhood.

Answers and Explanations: Exercise

This exercise showed you how to create shared directories and modify them after they have been created. It also showed you how permissions affect shared directories. For more information, see the section titled "Setting Up Shared Folders and Permissions."

15.3 Practice Problems

1. You need to enable both shared folder permissions and NTFS permissions on your Windows NT Workstation computer. Your workstation has a single partition formatted with FAT. What should you do?

   A. First set the share permissions, and then set the NTFS permissions.

   B. First set the NTFS permissions, and then set the Shared Folder permissions.

   C. You cannot share folders on a FAT partition.

   D. You cannot implement NTFS permissions on a FAT partition.

2. You have a shared folder with the following permissions:

Account	*Permissions*
AimeeL	Full Control
Accountants	Read
Users	(none specified)

   If AimeeL is a member of the Accountants and the Users group, what are AimeeL's effective permissions?

   A. Full Control

   B. Change

   C. Read

   D. This cannot be determined from the given information.

3. You have assigned the following NTFS permissions on a folder:

Account	*Permissions*
KathyS	Full Control
Sales	(none specified)
Users	Read

   If KathyS is a member of the Sales and the Users groups, what are KathyS's effective permissions?

   A. Full Control

   B. Change

   C. Read

   D. This cannot be determined from the given information.

4. You have a shared folder with the following permissions:

Account	Shared Folder Permissions	NTFS Permissions
AlexA	(none specified)	(none specified)
Sales	Read	Change
Users	(none specified)	Read

   If AlexA is a member of the Sales group and the Users group, what are AlexA's effective permissions when accessing this resource from across the network?

   A. No Access

   B. Change

   C. Read

   D. This cannot be determined from the given information.

5. Where does Windows NT maintain the Access Control List defining access to a specified resource?

   A. In the SAM database

   B. With the user's access token

   C. With the resource

   D. In the HKEY_LOCAL_MACHINE/Hardware Registry key

6. All resource access requests must pass through which of the following resources?

   A. Access Control List

   B. Windows NT Security Manager

   C. SAM Data Manager

   D. Security Reference Monitor

7. When does a user receive an access token? (Select all that apply.)
   A. When a user receives permission to access a resource.
   B. When a user successfully logs on.
   C. When a user requests access to a resource.
   D. When a user account is created.

8. What is an Access Control List (ACL)?
   A. A list of users that can log on locally to the workstation.
   B. A list of SIDs currently logged on to the workstation.
   C. A list of SIDs and permissions maintained with every resource.
   D. The list of users in the SAM database.

9. What is the default permission on a shared folder?
   A. Everyone: No Access
   B. Everyone: Full Control
   C. Users: Full Control
   D. Creator/Owner: Full Control

10. To stop sharing a resource, you must do what? (Select all that apply.)
   A. Be logged on with an account in the Administrators group.
   B. Choose Sharing from the resource's context menu.
   C. Delete and re-create the resource.
   D. Click the Stop Sharing command on the Sharing tab of the resource's properties sheet.

Answers and Explanations: Practice Problems

1. **D** You cannot use NTFS permissions on a FAT partition.
2. **A** When combining user and group permissions, the effective permissions are the cumulative permissions.
3. **A** When combining user and group permissions, the effective permissions are the cumulative permissions.
4. **C** When combining user and group permissions, the effective permissions are the cumulative permissions.
5. **C** The ACL resides with the resource.
6. **D** All security access requests must pass through the Security Reference Monitor.
7. **B** A user receives an access token only after successfully logging on.
8. **C** An Access Control List is a list of SIDs and associated permissions that define the access to a resource. The ACL is maintained with the resource.
9. **B** By default, all shares are assigned the permission Everyone: Full Control.
10. **A, B** To stop sharing a resource, you must be logged on with an account in the Administrators group and then choose Sharing from the resource's context menu.

15.3 Key Words

shared folder

Security Reference Monitor

ACL

No Access

Read

Change

Full Control

15.4 Setting NTFS Partitions, Folders, and File Permissions

One of the benefits of using NTFS over FAT as a file system on a Windows NT Workstation is the added security that NTFS enables you to take advantage of under Windows NT. NTFS permissions enable you to get beyond the security limitations of shared folder permissions (they are effective only when accessing the directory from across the network) and implement local security on both the folder and the file level. Shared permissions can be assigned only at the folder level. NTFS permissions can also apply to a user who is accessing a shared network resource or a local resource.

> **FAT formatted partitions do not allow you to set permissions on local files and folders.**

As an administrator, you must be careful and remember that by default, Windows NT allows Full Permission to the Everyone local group. Although it is often a good idea to change this permission to limit access, before you commit your changes, make sure that you have given at least one user or group access. If you don't, you may find everyone—including you, the administrator—locked out.

A. Understanding NTFS Permissions

You can assign NTFS permissions to files or folders. Table 15.4.1 describes each NTFS permission and what it allows a user to do.

Table 15.4.1 Standard NTFS Permissions

Permission	Folder	File
Read (R)	Display the folder and subfolders, attributes, and permissions	Display the file and its attributes and permissions
Write (W)	Add files or folders, change attributes for the folder, and display permissions	Change file attributes and add or append data to the file
Execute (X)	Make changes to subfolders, display permissions, and display attributes	Run a file if it is an executable and display attributes and permissions
Delete (D)	Remove the folder	Remove the file
Change Permission (P)	Modify folder permissions	Modify file permissions
Take Ownership (O)	Take ownership of the folder	Take ownership of a file

These NTFS permissions are combined into standard groupings of NTFS permissions at both the file and the folder level.

1. NTFS File Permissions

NTFS file permissions are a combination of the various NTFS permissions. You can set NTFS file permissions on a per-file basis; they override NTFS folder permissions if there is a conflict. Table 15.4.2 shows the standard NTFS file permissions.

Table 15.4.2 Standard NTFS File Permissions

Standard File Permission	Individual NTFS Permissions
No Access	(None)
Read	(RX)
Change	(RWXD)
Full Control	(All Permissions)

These standard NTFS file permissions are combinations of the individual NTFS permissions.

2. NTFS Folder Permissions

NTFS folder permissions are also combined into a standard set of permissions. Table 15.4.3 shows the NTFS folder permissions. In a list of NTFS folder permissions, each permission is typically followed by two sets of parentheses. The first set represents the standard permissions on the folder itself. The second set represents the permissions inherited by any file created within that folder.

Table 15.4.3 Standard NTFS Folder Permissions

Standard Folder Permission	Individual NTFS Permissions
No Access	(None)(None)
Read	(RX)(RX)
Change	(RWXD)(RWXD)
Add	(WX)(Not Specified)
Add & Read	(RWX)(RX)
List	(RX)(Not Specified)
Full Control	(All)(All)

When a file permission is "Not Specified," it means that the particular permission does not apply at a file level, only at a folder level. The List permission, for example, allows you to display that which is contained within a folder: It allows you to list all the files within the folder. That permission would not make sense at a file level, only at a folder level.

3. Setting NTFS Permissions

When a partition is created, the default NTFS permission is Everyone: Full Control. NTFS permissions can enhance shared folder permissions that you may have already implemented on your Windows NT Workstation. You set NTFS permissions through the properties of a file or folder from the Security tab.

4. Assigning NTFS Permissions

To assign NTFS permissions, you must be a part of a group that has been given that right, or your user account must be given that right. By default, the group Everyone is assigned Full Control when an NTFS partition is created. If that default permission is left, part of the Full Control permission includes the right to Change Permissions (P).

Suppose that the default Everyone: Full Control is changed. To assign NTFS permissions, you must either be:

- The file/folder creator.
- Have full control (ALL) or change permissions (P) for NTFS permission.
- Given special access to Take Ownership (O). With the ability to Take Ownership, a user can give himself the right to Change Permissions (P). (For a description of the Take Ownership permission, see the section entitled "Taking Ownership of Files or Folders," later in this chapter.)

5. NTFS File and Folder Permission Interaction

Because NTFS permissions can be implemented at both a file and a folder level, you must have an understanding of how these two levels interact.

If a file is created within a folder that has NTFS permissions set, the default is for the file to inherit the permissions of the folder in which it is created. It is possible, though, to assign different permissions to a file that contradict the permissions of the folder in which it is created. Suppose, for example, that you create the following environment:

Resource	*User or Group Account*	*Permission*
Folder: Test	Everyone	Full Control
File: Top Secret	MyAccount	Full Control

The permissions for the Test folder are Everyone: Full Control. You create a file called Top Secret with the permissions Full Control for your account only. Because file permissions always override folder permissions, only the account MyAccount has full control over the Top Secret file. All other users are denied access. Even though Everyone has Full Control at the folder level, the fact that there is only one account specified at the file level effectively excludes all other accounts.

6. NTFS User and Group Permission Interaction

With NTFS permissions, as with shared folder permissions, user and group permissions interact so that the cumulative permission is the effective permission. NTFS permissions can be granted to both users and groups. Because of this, you might have a situation in which a user is given access to a resource through NTFS permissions and a group of which the user is a member is also given access through NTFS permissions.

There also might be a scenario with NTFS permissions in which a user is a member of more than one group that has been given different NTFS permissions to the resource. In those cases, you need to understand how user and group permissions interact in NTFS permissions. When user and group NTFS permissions overlap, the effective permission is always the cumulative, or least restrictive, permission except in the case of the No Access permission.

7. Using Special Access Permissions

The Special Access permission is a combination of the individual NTFS permissions that is not one of the standard NTFS permissions. Typically, the standard permissions are what you will assign to files or folders; however, it is possible that you may want to implement a customized version of the individual NTFS permissions. If you need to assign individual permissions, you can assign Special Access permissions. The Special Access permissions are the same for both files and folders—they are just a listing of the individual NTFS permissions.

To assign Special Access permissions to a file or a folder, complete the following steps:

1. Right-click the file or folder and select the properties from the context menu that appears.
2. Click the Security tab, and then click the Permissions button.
3. Under the Type of Access, select Special File or Folder Access.
4. Select the Other option button, and then check each individual NTFS permission that you would like to use.

Special directory access can be used when you have a situation that requires customizing the NTFS permissions assigned to a resource.

8. Taking Ownership of Files or Folders with NTFS

Taking ownership of files or folders is one of the NTFS permissions that can be assigned through special directory or file permissions. The user who creates a file or a folder is the owner of that file or folder. As the owner, that individual has Full Control to that file or folder. To take ownership, you have to have been given that right through the NTFS permissions. If a user removes everyone but himself from the list of permissions on the resource, only an administrator can take ownership of the files. An administrator can always take ownership, even if he has been given No Access permission to the file or folder.

You cannot actually give ownership to another user or group; you can give only the *permission* to take ownership. Because of this, if an administrator takes ownership of a user's files, that administrator remains the owner. This prevents any user or administrator from altering or creating files or folders and then making it look like those files or folders belong to another user.

To give someone the right to take ownership, you must grant that person Full Control, Take Ownership special permission, or Change Permission special permission.

9. Using the No Access Permission for NTFS Permissions

The No Access permission overrides all other permissions. As in shared folder permissions, in NTFS permissions, the No Access permission is unique in that it can override all other permissions granted for a user or group if it exists in the list of permissions for that user or group. For example, consider the permissions outlined in Table 15.4.4.

Table 15.4.4 Using No Access in NTFS Permissions

Account	File Permission
BillC	Full Control
Democrats	Change
Politicians	No Access

In Table 15.4.4, BillC is a member of the Democrats and the Politicians groups. Even though BillC's account has been given Full Control of the file, the Politicians group has been assigned the No Access NTFS permission. Because BillC is a Politician, his effective NTFS permission is No Access. One way to give BillC access yet still restrict access for the Politicians group is to set the NTFS file permissions as shown in Table 15.4.5).

Table 15.4.5 Example of NTFS File Permissions

Account	File Permission
BillC	Full Control
Democrats	Change
Politicians	

In Table 15.4.5, the effective NTFS permissions for BillC are Full Control. Politicians have not been granted the No Access permission, they have just not been specified in the list of NTFS permissions. This means that users who are members of the Politicians group still do not have access to the file, but BillC's effective NTFS permissions are Full Control.

10. File Delete Child with NTFS Permissions

File Delete Child refers to a specific scenario relating to NTFS permissions under Windows NT. If a user has been given the NTFS No Access permission to a particular file but has Full Control of the directory that contains the file, the user can actually delete the file even though he doesn't even have the ability to read it. This is true only if the user actually tries to delete the file, not if he attempts to move it to the Recycle Bin.

This situation is called File Delete Child. It is a part of Windows NT that meets the POSIX-compliance requirements. To get around this problem and prevent users from being able to delete a file that they should not have access to, follow these steps:

1. Get the properties for the directory that contains the file.
2. Instead of selecting Full Control as the directory permission, select Custom.
3. When the list of Custom Options appears, put a check in each check box. This is the same as Full Control, except that it bypasses the File Delete Child problem.
4. Make sure the file permissions are still set to No Access for that user.

B. Combining Shared Folder and NTFS Permissions

When combining shared folder permissions with NTFS permissions, it is important that you understand how NTFS file and folder permissions interact with the applied shared permissions.

When different permissions exist for the file or folder level and the folder share, Windows NT applies the most restrictive permission.

For example, JohnA is a member of the Security group. The Security group is assigned Read permission to the folder share and Change control to the folder. When accessing the folder through the share, JohnA's net permission will be Read. However, if JohnA accesses the folder locally (if he's logged on to the workstation where the folder resides), his permission will be Change.

Understanding the interaction between shared folder permissions and NTFS permissions is critical to understanding how to manage the security of resources in your Windows NT environment and is a critical part of successfully completing the exam. Remember these key points when determining a user's net access permissions to files or folders:

- When combining user and group permissions for shared folders, the effective permission is the cumulative permission.
- When combining user and group permissions for NTFS security, the effective permission is the cumulative permission.
- When combining shared folder permissions and NTFS permissions, the most restrictive permission is always the effective permission.
- With NTFS permissions, file permissions override folder permissions.
- Using NTFS permissions is the only way to provide local security.
- Shared folder permissions present the only way to provide security on a FAT partition and are effective only when the folder is accessed from across the network.

C. Moving and Copying Files

When you *copy* a file from one folder to another, the file assumes the permissions of the new folder. The original file is deleted, and a new file is created in the target folder. When you *move* a file between folders, the file maintains its original permissions. In this case, the file remains in the same physical location on the disk, and a new pointer to the file is stored in the target directory.

However, a move is only a move when it is between folders within the same partition. When you move a file between partitions, the file is first deleted and then re-created in the target folder, so the file assumes the permissions of the target folder. (Note that this also applies to compression attributes discussed earlier in this chapter.)

15.4.1 Exercise: Implementing NTFS Permissions and Using No Access

Objective: Set up permissions on NTFS partitions, folders, and files.

This exercise helps you set up NTFS permissions on folders and files and see how the No Access permission works. (This exercise requires that you have an NTFS partition on your Windows NT Workstation.)

1. Log on to Windows NT Workstation using an account with administrative permissions on that workstation.
2. Launch Windows NT Explorer. Right-click the Atlanta directory you created in Exercise 15.3.1 and choose Properties from the context menu that appears.
3. Click the Security tab.
4. Click the Permissions button to see what the default NTFS permissions are for the Antigua directory.
5. Delete the permission Everyone: Full Control.
6. Click the Add button and add Administrators: Full Control.
7. Click the Add button and add Users: Read access.
8. Log off Windows NT.
9. Log on with an account that has user permissions.
10. Launch Windows NT Explorer. Double-click the Atlanta directory. Can you open it?
11. From the File menu, choose New, and then choose Folder to create a new folder within the Atlanta directory. Were you successful? Why or why not?
12. Log off Windows NT.
13. Log on to Windows NT Workstation using an account with administrative permissions on that workstation.
14. Launch Windows NT Explorer. Right-click the Atlanta directory you created in Exercise 15.3.1 and choose Properties from the context menu that appears.
15. Click the Security tab, and then click the Permissions button.
16. Highlight the Users group and change the permission from Read to No Access.
17. Log off Windows NT.
18. Log on with an account that has user permissions.
19. Launch Windows NT Explorer. Double-click the Atlanta directory. Can you open it? Why or why not?
20. Log off Windows NT.

Answers and Explanations: Exercise

This exercise showed you how to modify NTFS permissions on a directory. For more information, see the section titled "Setting Permissions on NTFS Partitions, Folders, and Files."

15.4 Practice Problems

1. You have a folder on an NTFS partition with the following permissions:

Account	*Shared NTFS Permissions*	*NTFS Permissions Folder*
HeidiS	Full Control	(none specified)
Sales	List	(none specified)

You also have a file in the folder with the following NTFS permissions:

Account	*NTFS Permissions*
HeidiS	Read
Sales	Change

If HeidiS is member of the Sales group, what are HeidiS's effective permissions when accessing the file?

   A. Full Control

   B. Change

   C. List

   D. This cannot be determined from the given information.

2. What are the default permissions that you can apply to files located on an NTFS formatted partition? (Select all that apply.)

   A. Read

   B. Delete

   C. Accept Ownership

   D. No Access

3. What are the default permissions that you can apply to a file located on a FAT formatted partition?

   A. Read

   B. Change

   C. No Access

   D. None of the above

4. By default, which of the following local groups are allowed to take ownership on a share that is created with the default permissions? (Select the best answer.)

   A. Everyone

   B. Administrators

   C. Power Users

   D. Backup Operators

5. Cindy, a member of the Sales group, moves a file with Users: Full Control and Sales: Change NTFS permissions to a folder on the same partition with the permissions Everyone: Full Control. After the move, what permissions will the file have?

   A. Users: Full Control, Everyone: Full Control, Sales: Change

   B. Users: Full Control, Sales: Change

   C. Everyone: Full Control

   D. This cannot be determined from the given information.

6. Cindy, a member of the Sales group, copies a file with Users: Full Control and Sales: Change NTFS permissions to a folder on the same partition with the permissions Everyone: Full Control. After the copy, what permissions will the file have?

   A. Users: Full Control, Everyone: Full Control, Sales: Change

   B. Users: Full Control, Sales: Change

   C. Everyone: Full Control

   D. This cannot be determined from the given information.

7. Matt, a member of the Users group, moves a file from a folder on one NTFS partition to a folder in a different NTFS partition. The original folder had the permissions Everyone: Full Control. The new folder has the permissions Users: Full Control, Power Users: No Access. What are the permissions on the new file after the move?

   A. Everyone: Full Control

   B. Everyone: Full Control, Power Users: No Access, Users: Full Control

C. Everyone: No Access

D. Users: Full Control, Power Users: No Access

8. Matt, a member of the Users group, moves a file between folders on the same partition. The original folder had Administrators: No Access and Users: Change permissions. The target folder has the permission Users: Full Control, Power Users: No Access. What are the new permissions on the file after the move? (Select all that apply.)

   A. Administrators: No Access

   B. Users: Change

   C. Power Users: No Access

   D. Users: Full Control

9. You have a folder on an NTFS partition with the following permissions:

Account	*Shared Folder Permissions*	*NTFS Permissions*
HeidiS	Full Control	(none specified)
Sales	No Access	(none specified)

   You also have a file in the folder with the following NTFS permissions:

Account	*NTFS Permissions*
HeidiS	Read
Sales	Change

   If HeidiS is member of the Sales group, what are HeidiS's effective permissions when accessing the file?

   A. Full Control

   B. Change

   C. List

   D. No Access

10. When viewing the directory permissions for the Docs directory, you see that the Sales group is assigned the permissions: Special Access (RWX). What could members of the Sales group do with files and subfolders contained in the Docs directory? (Select all that apply.)

   A. Read

   B. Execute

   C. Change File Permissions

   D. Take Ownership

Answers and Explanations: Practice Problems

1. **B** When both file and folder permissions are applied, the file permissions always supersede the folder permissions.

2. **A, D** There is no delete permission. Ownership can only be taken, not accepted.

3. **D** File permissions cannot be applied to files in a FAT formatted partition.

4. **A** The default permission is Everyone: Full Control, which includes the (O) permission.

5. **B** When files are moved within the same partition, they retain their original permissions.

6. **C** When files are copied, they assume the permissions of the new directory.

7. **D** When files are moved between partitions, the file is essentially copied. Copied files assume the permissions of the target folder.

8. **A, B** When a file is moved between folders on the same partition, it retains the permissions of the source folder.

9. **D** No Access overrides all other permissions.

10. **A, C** With the RWX permissions, members of the Sales group can Read files and Subfolders (R), Write Files (W), and Execute Files (X) within the Docs folder.

15.4 Key Words

NTFS file permissions

NTFS folder permissions

File Delete Child

file moves

file copies

15.5 Installing and Configuring Printers

One of the key elements of successfully completing the Windows NT Workstation exam is a solid understanding of both local and network printing and printer management in a Windows NT environment.

A. Installing a Printer

As with any hardware device, you must ensure that the device is listed on the most recent version of the Windows NT Hardware Compatibility List (HCL) prior to installing the device. If the print device is not listed on the HCL, consult the manufacturer to ensure that a Windows NT 4.0 driver is available. To install a printer, you must also be logged on with an account that has the right to install or create a printer. The groups in Windows NT Workstation that have that right are:

- Administrators
- Power Users

To install a printer in Windows NT 4.0, use the Add Printer Wizard. Print Manager is no longer used in Windows NT 4.0; the Add Printer Wizard took its place. Be careful of exam questions that refer to configuring or adding printers by using Print Manager.

When you install a printer, you have the option of either installing the printer to My Computer (locally) or installing to a network print server. You see these options when you use the Add Printer Wizard to install a printer.

1. My Computer (Creating a Printer)

When installing a printer that's physically attached to the computer through a parallel or serial port, use the My Computer option. Also, when installing a network printer (one that your computer accesses indirectly across the network) that will be managed by your computer, you select the My Computer option. Using My Computer designates the machine on which the printer is being installed as the print server.

Remember that if you are using Windows NT Workstation as a print server, Windows NT Workstation accepts only 10 inbound network connections simultaneously. If you must support more than that, you might want to consider installing a Windows NT Server to act as the print server.

To begin installing a printer, launch the Add Printer Wizard by double-clicking the Add Printer icon from the Printers folder in the Settings group on the Start menu.

Select the My Computer option button and click the Next button. This brings up the Port Selection window. Select the local port to which the print device will be attached. If this is a network print device, you may need to click the Add Port button to define a different port. When the proper port is selected, click Next.

The next screen enables you to select the appropriate driver for the printer. If the printer is not on the HCL, you must select the Have Disk button to load the proper Windows NT 4.0 drivers for your print device.

The next step in defining a local printer is selecting a name for the printer. You should also indicate whether this should be the default print device. When you finish, click Next.

The next dialog box enables you to set up this printer as a shared network device. If you set the print device as shared, other workstations can connect to the printer through the network. If this print device is to be shared, enter a share name. Additionally, you can indicate the type of clients that will use the print device, and the proper drivers will be loaded. When the proper selections are made, click Next.

The final step is to load the appropriate drivers. You can print a test page to verify the installation of the local printer.

2. Network Print Server (Connecting to a Printer)

If a printer has already been defined and you just need to send a print job to it from your Windows NT Workstation, you can use the Network Print Server option to install that network printer. You use this option when the print device is being managed by another Windows NT 4.0 system.

If the print device is being managed by a non-Windows NT 4.0 computer (server or workstation), you must create the printer on your own system using the My Computer option.

Notice that when you install a printer using the Network Print Server option, you never have to specify the printer driver as you do when you install a printer using the My Computer option. That is because the driver is automatically downloaded to your workstation from the print server when you select the Network Print Server option.

To install a printer that has already been defined and is being managed by another print server, use the Network Print Server in the Add Printer Wizard to have the driver downloaded to your local machine. You are required to supply only the network path of the print server.

B. Managing Printer Properties

Managing printer properties involves the following actions:

- Configuring printer drivers and general properties
- Managing ports
- Scheduling print jobs
- Sharing printers
- Managing printer security
- Managing device options

Understanding the ins and outs of printer management is essential to being able to administer printing effectively and to successfully completing the Microsoft exam.

1. Configuring Printer Drivers and General Properties

The printer drivers and general properties are accessed through the General Tab on the Printer properties sheet. From this tab, you can assign a comment and location to help describe this device and the functionality it provides.

Also from this tab, you can specify a new device driver for this printer. The three command buttons on the bottom of the General tab enable you to specify whether you want a separator page, specify and alternate print processors, and generate a test page.

Separator pages, also known as banner pages, supply information such as the name of the user who sent the print job and the time. Additionally, these separator pages can switch the mode of the printer, such as forcing an HP device to enter PCL mode or switch to PostScript mode. Besides the three default pages, administrators may define additional separator pages for specific functions.

The Print Process command button enables you to specify an alternate print processor for the print device. As an example, WINPRINT offers five default print-job types that specify such parameters as form feed generation after completing the print job.

2. Managing Ports

The Ports tab displays which ports have associated printers and print devices and enables you to change those port associations. For example, if COM1 experiences a hardware failure, you could switch the defined device to COM2 instead of creating a new printer.

Additionally, this tab allows you specify additional ports, configure existing ports, and delete ports. You may need to add additional ports, such as a port for network print devices. In the Configure Ports area, you can change the baud rate of COM ports or the retransmission retry value for LPT ports. Finally, you can use Delete Port to remove any unneeded ports.

Also from this tab, you can enable bidirectional support from printers so that the printer can return a status update, such as a paper jam, to the selected port.

Lastly, you can enable *printer pooling* from this tab. A printer pool is the association of a single printer with multiple print devices. This allows one set of drivers to control more than one print device, which is effective for printers serving a large number of print jobs. As print jobs are received, they are automatically routed to free printers to balance the load amongst the print devices in order to speed print job completion. However, the print devices should be located within close proximity to each other because the user cannot determine which print device will actually service the print job. You must also ensure that all the print devices associated with the pool printer driver are compatible so the users don't get garbled output.

Setting up the printer pool is a simple task. To enable a printer pool, follow these steps:

1. Check the Enable Printer Pooling option on this tab.
2. Select the ports with print devices attached that will participate in the pool.

3. Scheduling Print Jobs

To manage the scheduling of print jobs, select the Scheduling tab from the Printer properties sheet. The first option on this tab enables you to specify the times when this printer will be available to service print jobs. By specifying two printers for one print device and staggering their availability times, you can manage the order in which documents are printed and alleviate congestion. By having users send large, low-priority print jobs to the printer that's available only during non-business hours, you can effectively ensure the print device will be available for smaller, higher-priority jobs during business hours.

In addition, you can define printer priorities. This option is most effective when two or more printers are associated with a single print device (which is the exact inverse of printer pooling). By setting different priorities for each printer, you can manage the priorities of documents sent to the print device through the different printers.

> **Print priorities do not affect documents that have begun printing.**

Lastly, this tab allows you to manage spooler settings on a per printer basis. You can configure spool settings to make the printing process more efficient. The spool settings that can be set include the following:

- *Spool Print Documents So Program Finishes Printing Faster.* If you choose this option, the documents will spool. This option has two choices within it:

  Start Printing After Last Page Is Spooled. Documents will not print until they are completely spooled.

  Start Printing Immediately. Documents will print before they have spooled completely, which speeds up printing.

- *Print Directly to the Printer.* This prevents the document from spooling. Although this option speeds up printing, it is not an option for a shared printer, which has to support multiple incoming documents simultaneously.
- *Hold Mismatched Documents.* This prevents incorrect documents from printing. Incorrect documents are those that do not match the configuration of the printer.
- *Print Spooled Documents Faster.* Spooled documents will print ahead of partially spooled documents, even if they have a lower priority. This speeds up printing.
- *Keep Documents After They Have Been Printed.* Documents remain in the spooler after they have been printed.

Setting the spool settings to fit your environment can greatly increase the efficiency of your printing.

4. Sharing Printers

You can designate a printer as shared when you create it, or you can designate an existing printer as shared by using the options on the Sharing tab of the printer's properties sheet. You can do this only if your account has sufficient rights to share the printer.

The Sharing tab enables you to provide a share name and select all the appropriate operating system drivers that should be loaded. Remember that with any share, long share names are supported only under Windows NT and Windows 95.

After you have selected those alternative operating systems from the list, you receive a prompt for the location of the drivers for each operating system. This is so the drivers for each operating system that you have selected can be downloaded when the client tries to print to your printer.

You can only share a printer that has been defined by your computer. You cannot share a printer that you connect to using the Network Print Server option.

5. Managing Printer Security

The Security tab from the printer's properties sheet enables you to set permissions for the printer. The four types of printer permissions are:

- Full Control
- Manage Documents
- Print
- No Access

By default, all users are given the Print permission; the creator owner is given Manage Documents permission; administrators are given Full Control. As you will see in this chapter, you may want to change these default printer permissions after the printer is installed. Table 15.5.1 shows the capabilities granted with each of the four types of print permission.

Table 15.5.1 Capabilities Granted with Printer Permissions

Capability	Full Control	Manage Documents	Print	No Access
Print documents	X	X	X	
Pause, resume, restart, and cancel the user's own documents	X	X	X	
Connect to a printer	X	X	X	
Control job settings for all documents	X	X		

Capability	Full Control	Manage Documents	Print	No Access
Pause, restart, and delete all documents	X	X		
Share a printer	X			
Change printer properties	X			
Delete printers	X			
Change printer permissions	X			

15

6. Managing Device Options

The final tab of the printer's properties sheet is Device Options. This tab enables you to set specific device options such as color, resolution, and paper tray selection. The options available here will be specific to the print device and should be covered in the particular print device's documentation.

C. Pausing and Resuming a Printer

Pausing and resuming a printer might be necessary for troubleshooting printing problems. To pause a printer, complete the following steps:

1. Open the Printers folder by opening the Start menu, choosing Settings, and choosing Printers.
2. Double-click the printer to open it.
3. From the Printer menu, choose Pause Printing.

After the printer has been paused and the problem has been solved, you must resume printing by completing the following steps:

1. Open the Printers folder by opening the Start menu, choosing Settings, and choosing Printers.
2. Double-click the printer to open it.
3. From the Printer menu, choose Pause Printing. This removes the check mark next to it and resumes printing.

D. Troubleshooting Printing

In addition to the previously covered items of troubleshooting printing, you must understand a few more issues about troubleshooting printing in order to create a support environment and to be successful on the exam.

1. Spooler Service

The Spooler service is what controls the print spooling process under Windows NT. If your users cannot print to a printer, and if there are documents in the print queue that will not print and cannot be deleted (even by the administrator), you may need to stop and restart the Spooler service.

To stop and restart the Spooler service, complete the following steps:

1. Open the Control Panel by opening the Start menu, choosing Settings, and choosing Control Panel.
2. Click the Spooler service in the list of services.
3. Click Stop. When you're prompted to verify that you want to stop the service, click Yes.
4. After the service has been stopped, click the Start button in the Services dialog box to restart the Spooler service.

While the Spooler service is stopped, no one can print to the shared printer.

Stopping and restarting the Spooler service clears only the jammed print job from the queue. Then it allows the other print jobs to continue printing.

2. Spool Directory

In addition to the Spooler service in Windows NT, there is also a *spool directory*, which is the location on the hard disk where print jobs are stored while spooling. By default, this directory is located under the Windows NT Root\system32\spool\printers directory.

This one directory is used for spooling all printers defined on the print server.

If you notice the hard disk thrashing or find that documents are not printing or are not reaching the print server, make sure that available space exists on the partition where the spool directory is located. If sufficient disk space is not available (minimally about 5MB free, more for complex print jobs), you must free up some disk space. If that is not possible, you must move the spool directory to another location. You can do this by going into the Server properties sheet in the Printers folder.

To change the spool directory's location, complete the following steps:

1. Open the Printers folder by opening the Start menu, choosing Settings, and choosing Printers.
2. From the File menu, choose Server Properties.
3. On the Advanced tab, type in the new location for the spool directory.

15.5.1 Exercise: Printer Installation and Configuration

Objective: Install and configure a local printer.

This exercise walks you through installation and configuration of a printer in Windows NT Workstation. Follow these steps:

1. Log on to Windows NT Workstation using an account with administrative permissions on that workstation.

2. Open the Printers folder by opening the Start menu, choosing Settings, and choosing Printers.
3. Double-click the Add Printer Wizard.
4. Leave the default option of My Computer selected, and then click Next.
5. Click Enable Printer Pooling, and then click LPT2 and LPT3.
6. From the list of printers, select HP on the left and select HP LaserJet 4 on the right. Click Next.
7. For the printer name, type **My Printer**.
8. When prompted to share the printer, click the Shared option button. Do not share the printer to other operating systems.
9. When prompted to print a test page, select No.
10. Click Finish. When prompted, enter the path to the Windows NT Workstation installation files.

To set printer permissions, follow these steps:

1. Log on to Windows NT Workstation using an account with administrative permissions on that workstation.
2. Open the Printers folder by opening the Start menu, choosing Settings, and choosing Printers.
3. Right-click My Printer and choose Properties from the context menu that appears.
4. Click the Security tab.
5. Click the Permissions button to see what the default permissions are for your newly created printer.
6. Click the Add button and select an existing Windows NT Workstation group to add to the list of permissions. Under Type of Access, select Manage Documents.
7. Click OK to exit the printer properties sheet for My Printer.

Answers and Explanations: Exercise

This exercise showed you how to create a printer and modify common properties. For more information, see the sections titled "My Computer (Creating a Printer)" and "Managing Printer Properties."

15.5 Practice Problems

1. In Windows NT terminology, what is a print device?
   A. The associated DLL that controls the output to the printer.
   B. The hardware that places information on an output medium.
   C. The hard disk partition where the print job is stored before it is sent to the printer.
   D. None of the above.

2. In Windows NT terminology, what is a printer?
   A. The hardware used to create output.
   B. The software interface between the application and the print device.
   C. A Windows NT Workstation or Server that has a local print driver installed.
   D. A Windows NT Server or Workstation that is sharing a print device.

3. You want to print to a printer managed by a Windows NT Server 4.0. What should you do?
   A. Use Print Manager to connect to the printer.
   B. Use Print Manager to create a printer.
   C. Use the Add Printer Wizard to connect to the printer.
   D. Use the Add Printer Wizard to create a printer.

4. What is the appropriate method for clearing a jammed print job from the queue?
   A. Delete the printer and re-create it.
   B. Stop the Printer service.
   C. Delete the spool directory.
   D. Stop and restart the Spooler service.

5. What network protocol should you load if you want to install an HP network print device?
   A. TCP/IP
   B. DLC
   C. NetBEUI
   D. NetWare Compatible Transport

6. Which of the following are functions of the print processor? (Select all that apply.)
   A. Renders the print job for the specific printer
   B. Transfers the print job to the spooler directory
   C. Monitors the status of the print device
   D. Manages the print job flow and assigns priorities to the incoming print jobs

7. Which of the following are functions of the Print Monitor? (Select all that apply.)
   A. Tracks print job location
   B. Tracks print job status
   C. Monitors print device status (such as paper outages and low toner conditions)
   D. Releases the port when printing is complete

8. Which of the following are functions of the Print Spooler? (Select all that apply.)
   A. Sends print jobs to the appropriate ports
   B. Assigns priorities to print jobs
   C. Assigns print jobs to appropriate ports
   D. Connects to the spooler on remote print servers

9. How do you create a printer in a Windows NT 4.0 environment?
   A. Use the Printer Manager applet in the Control Panel.
   B. Launch the Add New Hardware applet from Control Panel and let Windows NT autodetect the printer.
   C. Double-click the Add Printer icon in the Printers folder.
   D. You can add printers only during Windows NT Workstation 4.0 installation.

10. How can you share a local printer that is already defined on your Windows NT 4.0 Workstation?
    A. You can share printers only when they are defined.
    B. From the printer's context menu, select Sharing.
    C. From the printer's properties sheet, select the General tab.
    D. From the printer's properties sheet, select the Sharing tab.

11. How can you set the priority for a printer?
    A. From the printer's properties sheet, select the Device Settings tab.
    B. From the printer's properties sheet, select the General tab.
    C. From the printer's properties sheet, select the Scheduling tab.
    D. From the printer's properties sheet, select the Ports tab.

12. Which of the following are attributes of a Windows NT 4.0 Workstation printer that you can control from the General tab? (Select all that apply.)
    A. Provide a comment and description for the printer
    B. Enable printer pooling
    C. Specify a separator page
    D. Enable bidirectional support

13. Where can you delete unneeded ports from the printer's properties sheet?
    A. The General tab
    B. The Ports tab
    C. The Device Options tab
    D. The Sharing tab

14. Where can you select an alternative print processor for a printer?
    A. From the General tab of the printer's properties sheet
    B. From the Ports tab of the printer's properties sheet
    C. From the Device Options tab of the printer's properties sheet
    D. From the Sharing tab of the printer's properties sheet

15. Which of the following statements are true regarding when you enable the Start Printing After the Last Page Is Spooled property for a print spooler? (Select all that apply.)
    A. Documents will not start to print until they're completely spooled.
    B. This reduces space requirements for the spool directory.
    C. This allows the application to return control to the user faster.
    D. This results in a slower print time.

16. After a printer has finished spooling a document, how does changing the printer's priority affect current documents?
    A. It will have no effect on spooled documents.
    B. Printing of the current document will be paused if the printer receives a new job with a higher priority.

C. The current print job will be deleted if the printer receives a new job with a higher priority.

D. This cannot be determined from the given information.

17. How can you enable sharing on a printer after it has been created? (Select all that apply.)

    A. You cannot. Printers can be designated as shared only during creation.

    B. Select the Sharing option from the printer's context menu.

    C. Select the Sharing tab from the printer's properties sheet.

    D. Select the Security tab from the printer's Properties tab.

18. How can you enable bidirectional support for a printer port?

    A. Select the Sharing tab from the printer's properties sheet.

    B. Select the Ports tab from the printer's properties sheet.

    C. Select the Device Options tab from the printer's properties sheet.

    D. You cannot. Only Windows NT Server supports bidirectional support.

19. Which of the following statements are true about printer pools? (Select all that apply.)

    A. Printer pools assign one printer for multiple print devices.

    B. Printer pools can contain no more than four devices.

    C. Printer pools allow the user to determine to which print device the job should spool.

    D. Printer pools distribute print jobs across multiple print devices.

20. Which of the following tasks can be completed from the Scheduling tab of a printer's properties sheet? (Select all that apply.)

    A. Set printer availability times

    B. Set spooler options

    C. Define which accounts can access the printer

    D. Change the spooler directory

21. How can you set the availability times for a printer?

    A. Use the Scheduling tab from the printer's properties sheet.

    B. Use the Ports tab from the printer's properties sheet.

    C. Use the Security tab from the printer's properties sheet.

    D. Use the Device Settings tab from the printer's properties sheet.

22. Which application do you use to add a printer?

    A. Add Printer icon

    B. Server Manager

    C. Device Manager

    D. Print Manager

23. Which two types of printers can you install in Windows NT 4.0 workstation?

    A. Default and Optional

    B. My Computer and Network

    C. My Computer and Network Print Server

    D. Local and Remote

24. The My Computer option should be used for which of the following types of printers? (Select all that apply.)

A. Network print devices managed by other Windows NT Workstations

B. Printers connected to COM1

C. Printers connected to LPT1

D. Network print devices managed by the local workstation

25. How many inbound printer connections will Windows NT Workstation support?

A. 10

B. 6

C. 15

D. 20

26. Which of the following functions are available via the Add Port command button when installing a printer?

A. Create a new monitor

B. Add a new local port

C. Configure the baud rate of any serial ports

D. Configure the retransmission retry time for parallel ports

27. Joe sends a print job to the printer, but nothing happens. He notices an excessive amount of hard disk activity, but the job is never printed. What is the most likely cause of the printing failure?

A. He has the incorrect print drivers loaded.

B. His print queue is stalled.

C. There is a problem with the print device.

D. He does not have enough free space in his spooling directory.

28. Jane calls to ask you why she was not prompted to load the Windows 3.1 printer drivers for a new printer she is creating on her Windows NT 4.0 Workstation. What should you tell her?

A. That particular printer probably does not support downloading the files to Windows 3.1 clients.

B. She needs to download a patch from the Microsoft web site.

C. She must install the printer as a network print server in order to specify the drivers.

D. Windows NT 4.0 will not support downloading drivers to Windows 3.1 clients.

29. Bob asks you why he has to load Windows 95 printer drivers when he connected to a print server on a Windows NT Workstation. What should you do?

A. Delete the printer. Then re-create the printer and ensure that you specify the location of the Windows 95 drivers.

B. Tell him he has to load the drivers whenever he connects from Windows 95. Windows NT 4.0 can only download printer drivers for Windows 3.1.

C. Stop sharing the printer. Then re-enable printer sharing and make sure that you check the Auto Driver Download box.

D. From the printer's properties sheet, select the Sharing tab and select the additional drivers that should be loaded for the printer.

30. From the options listed, select all valid permissions you can apply to a printer.

A. Full Control

B. No Access

C. Print

D. Delete Print Jobs

31. Which of the following are valid methods of stopping the Spooler service? (Select all that apply.)
    A. Use Server Manager.
    B. Use Service Manager (Control Panel).
    C. Use Print Manager.
    D. Log off the workstation and log back on.
32. What will happen to a jammed print job when the Spooler service is stopped?
    A. The print job will be restarted when the spooler is restarted.
    B. The print job will be deleted.
    C. The print job will resume.
    D. The print job will be rescheduled.
33. By default, what directory is used by the spooler service to spool print jobs?
    A. C:\Winnt\system\spoolers\printers
    B. C:\Winnt\system32\spool\printers
    C. C:\Winnt\i386\printers\spooler
    D. C:\Winnt\temp
34. How can you modify the spooler directory's location?
    A. You cannot.
    B. Use the Device Properties tab on the printer's properties sheet.
    C. Use the Scheduling tab on the printer's properties sheet.
    D. From the Printers folder, open the File menu, select Server Properties, and use the Advanced tab.
35. How can you start Print Manager in Windows NT 4.0?
    A. From the Control Panel.
    B. From the Printers folder.
    C. From the Administrative Tools (common) program group.
    D. Windows NT 4.0 no longer uses Printer Manager.

Answers and Explanations: Practice Problems

1. **B** A print device is the actual hardware that the paper comes out of.
2. **B** A printer is the software component that interfaces between the application and the print device.
3. **C** Because the printer is already managed by the Windows NT Server, all the user needs to do is use the Add Printer Wizard to connect to the printer.
4. **D** The appropriate course of action when troubleshooting jammed print jobs is to stop and restart the Spooler service.
5. **B** Most HP network printers use the DLC protocol.
6. **A** The print processor is responsible for rendering the print job into a format that the selected printer can use.
7. **B, C, D** The location of the print job is tracked by the print spoolers.
8. **A, B, C, D** They are all functions of the print spooler.
9. **C** The only way to create a printer in Windows NT 4.0 is by using the Add Printer Wizard.
10. **D** The Sharing tab of the printer's properties sheet contains printer sharing properties.
11. **C** Use the Scheduling tab on the printer's properties sheet to manage the printer priority.
12. **A, C** Printer pooling and bidirectional support are located on the Ports tab.

13. **B** Go to the Ports tab of the printer's properties sheet to delete unneeded ports.

14. **A** The General tab enables you to specify the driver, choose whether to use a separator page, print a test page, and select an alternative print processor.

15. **A, D** The application will not be available during spooling, regardless of when the job starts to print. This option actually increases space requirements for the spool directory because the entire job must be saved to disk.

16. **A** Changing print priorities has no effect on spooled documents.

17. **B, C** You can enable sharing on a printer after it has been created by selecting the Sharing option from the Printers context menu and then selecting the Sharing tab from the printer's properties sheet.

18. **B** Use the Ports tab to enable bidirectional support.

19. **A, D** Printer pools can contain more than four devices, and they distribute print jobs across multiple print devices.

20. **A, B** You can set the spooler options and define times when the printer is available.

21. **A** Go to the Scheduling tab of the printer's properties sheet to set printer availability times.

22. **A** The Add Printer icon is the only way to install printers in Windows NT Workstation 4.0.

23. **C** The Add Printer Wizard allows you to select the My Computer and Network Printer Server options when installing a printer.

24. **B, C, D** Use the Network Printer Server option when connecting to network print devices managed by other Windows NT Workstations.

25. **A** Windows NT Workstation can support 10 inbound network connections.

26. **A, B** You can configure ports by clicking the Configure Port button.

27. **D** A significant increase in hard disk activity and lack of output from the print device indicates that the amount of free space on the hard disk should be questioned.

28. **D** Drivers are downloaded only to Windows NT and Windows 95 clients.

29. **D** You can add drivers at any time for a My Computer printer by using the Sharing tab of the printer's properties sheet.

30. **A, C, D** Delete Print Jobs is not a valid printer permission.

31. **B** You stop the spooler service by using the Service Manager applet found in the Control Panel.

32. **B** Any current print jobs that have already been spooled will be deleted when the spooler service is stopped.

33. **B** By default, the C:\Winnt\system32\spool\printers directory is used by the spooler service to spool print jobs.

34. **D** To modify the spooler directory location, open the Printers folder, open the File menu, select Server Properties, and use the Advanced tab.

35. **D** Printers are managed through the Printers folder in Windows NT 4.0.

15.5 Key Words

printer

print device

print spooler

print server

print driver

printer pool

spool directory

15.6 Disk Resources

Disk resource management does not specifically appear as any Microsoft published objective for the Windows NT Workstation 4.0 exam. However, many of the questions you'll encounter in the exam require you to understand basic principles about disk resources such as creating, deleting, converting, and formatting partitions; creating, formatting, and extending volume sets; creating and formatting stripe sets; and managing data backups and restores. This necessary information about managing disk resources is included here to provide you with the level of understanding needed to successfully answer those questions that appear on the exam.

Before any computer can be used effectively, you must install an operating system. Because of the size of today's 32-bit operating systems, such as Windows NT Workstation 4.0, the operating system must be installed on the local hard disk that has been partitioned. Creating and managing disk resources involves the definition, creation, and maintenance of disk partitions.

A. Disk Partitions

Two types of partitions are recognized: primary and extended. Under MS-DOS, a primary partition holds the files needed to start and initialize the system. In order for MS-DOS to boot, this partition must also be marked active. The primary partition cannot be further subdivided, and only one primary partition can be defined for the physical hard disk. With Windows NT, there can be up to four primary partitions. A Windows NT primary partition could contain application or data files in addition to operating system files.

Extended partitions allow you to exceed the primary partition limits of both Windows NT and DOS. Extended partitions can be defined in addition to the primary partition and can be further divided into logical drives. With Windows NT and DOS, a logical drive refers to the same physical drive as the partition, but the logical drive is contained within the extended partition. The operating system sees logical drives as multiple separate drives even though there is only one physical hard disk in the machine. The use of logical drives provides greater control over the storage of applications and data on the hard disk.

When Windows NT is installed, the partition in which the boot files are stored is termed the *system partition*. The partition in which the operating system files are located is called the *boot partition*. These may be in the same physical partition.

B. File System Support

Windows NT provides support for two file systems: File Allocation Table (FAT) and New Technology File System (NTFS). Previous versions of Windows NT also supported the High Performance File System (HPFS). When selecting a file system, you need to consider many factors. HPFS support has been dropped in Windows NT 4.0. If you want to upgrade the operating system on an HPFS partition to Windows NT 4.0, you must convert the partition to NTFS prior to upgrading.

FAT support under Windows NT is somewhat better than it is under DOS. The FAT file system must be selected when more than one operating system will access the partition, such as in a dual-boot environment. You cannot apply permissions to individual files and folders on a FAT partition, and security can be set only through network shares on FAT formatted partitions.

Listed below are some characteristics of Windows NT 4.0 support for the FAT file system:

- FAT is the only file system accessible to Windows NT, Windows 95, and MS-DOS.
- It supports filenames of up to 255 characters.
- It supports network shares.
- It does not support file security.
- It's considered most efficient for partition sizes of 400MB or less.
- The largest supported partition size is 4GB.
- It requires less than 1MB of system overhead.

NTFS provides better file system support than FAT; however, only Windows NT systems can read local NTFS partitions. NTFS allows you to set security on individual files and folders on the partition. NTFS also supports automatic Transaction Tracking that logs all disk activity to provide improved fault tolerance over FAT partitions. NTFS has a higher system overhead: NTFS partitions typically require 4–5MB of storage space dedicated to the file system.

Listed below are some characteristics of Windows NT 4.0 support for the NTFS file system:

- NTFS is only accessible to Windows NT systems.
- It supports filenames of up to 255 characters.
- It supports network shares.
- It supports file and folder security.
- It's considered most efficient for partition sizes of 400MB or greater.
- The largest supported partition size is 16 exabytes (theoretically).
- It requires 4–5MB of system overhead.
- It provides Transaction Tracking for enhanced robustness.

Windows NT provides a mechanism for converting FAT partitions to NTFS without data loss. However, this is a one-way conversion. Once a partition is converted to NTFS, it can be returned to FAT only by reformatting the partition. This utility is named convert.exe and is located in the WINNT\SYSTEM32 directory. The command line for launching CONVERT is

```
CONVERT C: /FS:NTFS
```

where C: is the drive letter you want to convert. If the operating system is currently accessing files on the drive, you will be asked if the conversion should take place during the next boot.

C. Long FileName Support

Windows NT 4.0 provides long filename support under both the FAT and NTFS file systems. Windows NT provides an algorithm to convert long files to the 8.3 naming convention standard to accommodate operating systems that do not provide long filename support. The first six characters of the name, less any spaces, are retained. The seventh character becomes the tilde character (~). The eighth character becomes a numeric increment to accommodate for files that have the same first six characters. Table 15.6.1 illustrates how the algorithm works.

Table 15.6.1 Long Filename Algorithm

Long Filename	8.3 Truncated Name
wwse ytd books 93.xls	wwseyt~1.xls
wwse ytd books 94.xls	wwseyt~2.xls
wwse ytd books 95.xls	wwseyt~3.xls
wwse ytd books 96.xls	wwseyt~4.xls
wwse ytd books 97.xls	ww5ght~1.xls

This works well for the first four iterations. However, after the fourth iteration, Windows NT eliminates the numeric increment. Instead it retains the first two characters and replaces the remaining 5 characters with a random sequence of characters.

D. Compression

Windows NT 4.0 provides file and folder compression on NTFS formatted partitions. Unlike many other utilities, compression is allowed for individual files and folders, not just entire volumes. Any NTFS formatted disk or folder could conceivably contain both compressed and noncompressed files. Windows NT file compression is completely transparent to the user. The compression algorithm can provide up to 2:1 compression; however, the amount of compression achieved is a tradeoff of file type and system performance. If Windows NT determines that maximum compression will cause system performance to suffer, it automatically reduces the file compression ratio.

There are two ways to enable file compression. You can access the properties sheet for the selected file or folder and check the Compression attribute on the General tab. Alternatively, Windows NT provides a command line utility called COMPACT.EXE. This utility is located in the WINNT\SYSTEM32 directory. This is the basic syntax for this command:

```
COMPACT /C <drive>:\<path>
```

The following table enumerates the available switches for the COMPACT utility.

Table 15.6.2 Compress.exe Switches

Switch	Description
/C	Enables compression of selected file/folder
/D	Disables compression of selected file/folder
/S	Applies compression recursively

Switch	Description
/A	Displays hidden and system files
/I	Disregards any errors
/F	Forces compression on all files
/Q	Displays summary information

E. Managing Disk Resources

15

You manage disk resources through Disk Administrator. Disk Administrator can be launched from the Administrative Tools menu or from the Run dialog box with the command windisk.exe. The Disk Administrator utility is a graphical version of the MS-DOS FDISK utility.

The initial display shows all available disks and their current partitions. From Disk Administrator, you can create and manage partitions, volume sets, and stripe sets.

1. Partition Creation

Creating a new partition from free space is a simple task. Click any available free space, open the Partition menu, and select Create. In the resulting dialog box, you can select the partition size and type (Primary or Extended). Then click OK to establish your changes, and the new partition appears as unformatted in the Disk Manager main window.

If you opted to create an extended partition, you must now define the logical drives in the partition. Click an area of free space in the extended partition, open the Partition menu, and select Create. In the resulting Create Logical Drive box, enter the desired size. Then click OK to return to the Disk Manager main window, and the new logical drive appears as unformatted.

2. Partition Formatting

After creating a partition, you must format it before you can use it. But prior to formatting, you must confirm any partition creations or changes by selecting the Commit Changes Now option from the Partition menu.

To begin the format process, click the new partition you want to format in Disk Manager. From the Tools menu, select Format. Then from the Format Drive dialog box, select FAT or NTFS. Leave the Allocation Unit Size set at its default. Optionally, you can enter a volume label.

You can select the Quick Format option if this disk has been previously formatted and there are no known errors. In addition, you can select Enable Compression if this is an NTFS format and you want to enable compression on the entire drive.

3. Deleting Partitions and Drives

Deleting a partition or drive with Disk Manager is a simple process. Click the drive or partition you want to delete and select Delete from the Partition menu.

4. Volume Sets

A volume set allows you to merge areas of free space on any hard disk into a single partition. The initial volume set must contain at least two and no more than 32 areas of free space. These areas of free space do not have to be contiguous or even on the same physical drive. Once a volume set is created, it is treated similar to a partition for formatting. If the volume set is formatted with NTFS, you can add additional areas of free space to extend the volume set. Volume sets are not available to non-Windows NT operating systems. If any disks or areas of free space fail, the entire volume set will fail and become inaccessible.

To create a volume set, select at least two and no more than 32 areas of free space to include in the volume set. Next, select Create Volume Set from the Partition menu. In the Create Volume Set of Total Size dialog box, select the desired size for the new volume set. Click OK, and the new volume set appears in the main Disk Manager window. Format the new volume set as you would a partition.

You can also extend any NTFS formatted partition, logical drive, or volume set into an extended volume set. To create an extended volume set, select the partition, logical drive, or existing volume set, and then click on the area of free space you want to add. From the Partition menu, select Extend Volume Set. In the resulting Extend Volume Set dialog box, select the desired size for the new volume set and click OK. Disk Manager formats the newly added free space with NTFS. The Disk Manager window will be updated to reflect the changes.

5. Stripe Sets

Creation and management of stripe sets is very similar to that of volume sets. With volume sets, you can add 2–32 areas of free space. With stripe sets, the areas you add must be the same size. For example, if you have three areas with 100, 200, and 300 megabytes of free space, the largest stripe set you could create would be 300 megabytes (3 × 100 megabytes). If one member of the stripe set fails, the entire stripe set will become unavailable. Also, as with volume sets, non-Windows NT operating systems will not be able to access the stripe set or any of its members individually. Unlike volume sets, Windows NT boot and system partitions cannot participate in stripe sets.

When data is written to a stripe set, the data is written in 64KB blocks to each member of the stripe set. Because the data can be written concurrently, you may notice an increase in I/O performance if members of the strip set can be written to concurrently, as in the case where disks are on separate controllers.

Creating a stripe set is a simple process. Select the areas of free space from the Disk Manager display, and then select Create Stripe Set from the Tools menu. Select the desired size of the stripe set and click OK. Format the Stripe Set as you would any partition or logical drive. Regardless of the file system used for stripe sets, they cannot be extended once they're created.

F. Creating and Managing Backups

Another important area of Windows NT disk resource management is creating backups of your data. Only certain users and groups have permissions to back up and restore data. These accounts are:

- Administrators
- Backup Operators

- Users who are granted the "Backup (Restore) Files and Directories" right from User Manager
- Users that have Read permissions to the selected files and folders, including the file or folder creator/owner

Backups are created and managed through the Windows NT Backup utility. You can launch this application from the Administrative Tools program group or by executing ntbackup.exe from the Run dialog box.

The Backup utility provides an Explorer-type interface for selecting files and folders for backup. Select the appropriate files and directories for backup from the volume and folders listed in the Backup dialog box. Selection is hierarchical: Selecting a folder selects all files and subfolders within that folder.

To start the backup, click the Backup button, or select Backup from the Operations menu. The Backup Information dialog box appears. In the Tape Name box, enter a name for this tape using up to 32 characters. Also, complete your selections from the Operations options described in Table 15.6.3.

Table 15.6.3 Tape Name Operations Options

Option	Description
Append	Adds this backup set at the end of the tape
Replace	Overwrite this backup set on the existing tape
Verify After Backup	Compares selected files for backup with files on tape for accuracy
Back Up Registry	Backs up the Registry (at least one other file from the partition containing the Registry must have been selected)
Restrict Access	Limits access so that only administrators, backup operators, and the user who completes the backup can restore the data
Hardware Compression	Enables tape drive compression if hardware supports this option

In the Backup Set Information area of the Backup Information dialog box, enter a description for the backup set and the type of backup. Options for the backup type are listed in Table 15.6.4.

Table 15.6.4 Backup Type Options

Option	Description
Normal	Backs up all files/folders and sets archive property
Copy	Backs up all files/folders but does *not* set archive property
Differential	Backs up only those files/folders that have changed since the last backup, but does not set archive property

continues

Table 15.6.4 Continued

Option	Description
Incremental	Backs up only those files/folders that have changed since the last backup and does set archive property
Daily	Backs up only those files/folders that have changed that particular day but does *not* set archive property

The last options you can modify are the logging options and the location of the log file. When all the information is complete, click OK to finish the backup operation.

G. Restoring Data

The restore process is very similar to the backup process—in reverse. First, your account must be assigned to a group that has the right to restore data. To begin the restore process, start the Windows Backup Utility either from the Administrative Tools program group or by launching ntbackup.exe from the Run dialog box.

The tapes window displays the name of the backup set on the currently loaded tape. You can load the tape catalog to view other backup sets by choosing Catalog from the Operation menu. In the Catalog Status dialog box, choose OK. A new window with the tape's name is displayed. From this window, select the appropriate backup set and load its catalog. Then select the drives, folders, and files to restore and click the Restore button to initiate the restore process.

In the Restore Information dialog box, you can change the options for restoring the data from the chosen backup set. The Restore to Drive field enables you to select an alternative path to restore the data. Table 15.6.5 describes the restore options.

Table 15.6.5 Restore Options

Option	Description
Restore Registry	Restores the workstation's Registry.
Restore Permissions	Restores the NTFS permission to each file as the file is restored. If this option is not selected, the file will assume the permissions of the parent folder.
Verify After Restore	Compares restored files with those on tape for accuracy.

As with the backup operation, you can customize the logging options in the Log Information section. After all the options have been set appropriately, click OK to complete the restore process.

15.6.1 Exercise: Creating and Formatting a Partition

Objective: To create and format an area of free space on your Windows NT Workstation hard disk.

This exercise walks you through the task of creating and formatting a partition. This exercise assumes you have an area of free space available on your hard disk.

1. Start Disk Administrator by opening the Start menu and selecting Programs, Administrative Tools (common), Disk Administrator.

2. Click on an area of free space.
3. From the Partition menu, select Create to create a new primary partition.
4. In the Create Primary dialog box, select a partition size that is one half of the maximum size.
5. Click OK.
6. Commit the changes by selecting Commit Changes Now from the Partition menu. Click OK in the Confirm dialog box.
7. Click the new partition.
8. Select Format from the Tools menu.
9. In the File System box, select NTFS.
10. Choose Start.
11. Close Disk Administrator.
12. Double-click My Computer. Does the new partition appear as an additional drive?

Answers and Explanations: Exercise

This exercise showed you how to create and format a new NTFS partition from free space on your hard disk. For more information, see the section entitled "Partition Creation."

15.6.2 Exercise: Creating a Volume Set

Objective: Extend a volume set from a formatted partition and an area of free space.

This exercise walks you through the task of extending a volume set. This exercise assumes you have an area of free space available on your hard disk and an NTFS formatted partition.

1. Start Disk Administrator by opening the Start menu and selecting Programs, Administrative Tools (common), Disk Administrator.
2. Select an available NTFS formatted partition by clicking anywhere in the partition.
3. Press and hold Ctrl and click an area of free space.
4. From the Partition menu, select Extend Volume Set.
5. In the Create Volume Set of Total Size field, enter the total size you want for the volume set.
6. Click OK. Notice that the new volume set is NTFS formatted.
7. Close Disk Administrator.
8. Double-click My Computer. Can you see the drive with the new size?

Answers and Explanations: Exercise

This exercise showed you how to extend a volume set from an existing NTFS partition and an area of free space. For more information, see the section titled "Volume Sets."

15.6 Practice Problems

1. You have three areas of free space on your hard disk with sizes of 200 megabytes, 280 megabytes, and 60 megabytes, respectively. What is the largest stripe set you can create?

   A. 200MB

   B. 280MB

   C. 540MB

   D. 180MB

2. You have three areas of free space on your hard disk with sizes of 200 megabytes, 280 megabytes, and 60 megabytes, respectively. What is the largest volume set you can create?

   A. 200MB

   B. 280MB

   C. 540MB

   D. 180MB

3. You wish to extend a 400 megabyte volume set formatted with FAT with 100 megabytes of free space. What is the largest volume set you can have on this workstation?

   A. 400MB

   B. 500MB

   C. 450MB

   D. 475MB

4. What is the best method for converting an NTFS formatted partition to FAT?

   A. Use CONVERT.EXE.

   B. Reformat the partition.

   C. From the Disk Manager utility, select Convert from the Tools menu.

   D. Use rdisk.exe with the /Restore option.

5. You want to upgrade a Windows NT 3.51 installation on an HPFS partition to Windows NT 4.0 on an NTFS partition. What is the proper sequence for completing the upgrade?

   A. Start the upgrade. You will be given the option to perform the conversion during the upgrade.

   B. Perform the NTFS conversion after the upgrade is complete.

   C. Perform the conversion to NTFS under Windows NT 3.51 before starting the Windows NT 4.0 upgrade.

   D. Start the upgrade. Windows NT automatically converts the partition to NTFS during the first bootup.

6. What is the smallest element supported by Windows NT 4.0 compression?

   A. Folder

   B. File

   C. Volume

   D. Partition

7. What utility is used to manage disk resources in Windows NT 4.0?

   A. Server Manager

   B. Disk Manager

   C. Windows NT Explorer

   D. Partition Manager

8. A volume set can consist of what ranges of free space?

   A. 2, 20

   B. 4, 30

   C. 2, 32

   D. 6, 64

9. The FAT file system is considered most efficient for partitions less than how many megabytes?

   A. 200

   B. 300

   C. 400

   D. 500

10. What is the maximum number of characters for a filename supported by FAT under Windows NT 4.0?

    A. 64 characters

    B. 256 characters

    C. 255 characters

    D. 1,024 characters

11. What is the best method for changing the file system from FAT to NTFS?

    A. Reformat the partition.

    B. Use the convert utility included with Windows NT.

    C. Use Disk Manager.

    D. Use CHKDSK with the /convert option.

12. What does the Full backup type do?

    A. Backs up all files/folders and sets the archive property.

    B. Backs up all files/folders but does not set the archive property.

    C. Full Backup is not a Windows NT backup option.

    D. Backs up all files/folders that have changed since the previous backup.

13. What does the Incremental backup type do?

    A. Backs up all files/folders that have changed since the last backup and sets the archive bit.

    B. Backs up all files/folders that have changed since the last backup but does not set the archive bit.

    C. Backs up all selected files/folders but does not set the archive property.

    D. Backs up all selected files/folders and sets the archive property.

14. What does the Copy backup type do?

    A. Backs up all files/folders but does not set the archive property.

    B. Backs up all files/folders that have changed since the last Daily backup.

    C. Copies the contents of the currently selected backup set to the local hard disk.

    D. Backs up all files/folders and sets the archive property.

15. What utility is used to create and manage backups?

    A. Server Manager

    B. Backup Manager

    C. Windows NT Backup Utility

    D. Disk Manager

16. What does the Daily backup type do?

    A. Backs up all files/folders that have changed that particular day and sets the archive property.

    B. Backs up all files/folders that have changed that particular day but does not set the archive property.

    C. Backs up all files/folders and sets the archive property.

    D. Backs up all files/folders but does not set the archive property.

17. From the following list of share names, select all that can be accessed by Windows 3.1 clients.

    A. Heidi's Laser Printer

    B. HP5SI-MX

    C. Delta Quadrant Printer

    D. LP34

18. Which of the following file systems can the Windows NT Workstation 4.0 system partition be formatted with? (Select all that apply.)

    A. FAT

    B. FAT32

    C. NTFS

    D. HPFS

19. Your boot partition is an 800 megabyte partition formatted with NTFS. You have 200 megabytes of free space on another hard disk installed in the system. What is the largest volume set you can create?

    A. 800MB

    B. 400MB

    C. 1,000MB

    D. 200MB

20. How can you extend a stripe set?

    A. You cannot.

    B. Select any existing stripe set and at least one area of free space, and then select Extend Stripe Set from the Tools menu of Disk Administrator.

    C. Select any NTFS formatted existing stripe set and at least one area of free space, and then select Extend Stripe Set from the Tools menu of Disk Administrator.

    D. Select any formatted existing stripe set and at least one area of free space that is not in the boot or system partition, and then select Extend Stripe Set from the Tools menu of Disk Administrator.

21. Which of the following file systems are supported by Windows NT 4.0? (Select all that apply.)

    A. NTFS

    B. HPFS

    C. FAT32

    D. FAT

22. Logical drives are created in which type of partitions?

    A. Extended

    B. Primary

    C. Active

    D. System

23. Windows NT installs the boot files in which partition?

    A. System

    B. Boot

    C. Primary

    D. Extended

24. NTFS is considered more efficient than FAT for partition sizes in excess of how many megabytes?

    A. 200MB

    B. 300MB

    C. 400MB

    D. 500MB

25. When comparing FAT and NTFS on the amount of disk space consumed by file system overhead, which of the following are true? (Select all true statements.)

    A. FAT requires more disk space for overhead than NTFS.

    B. NTFS requires more disk space for overhead than FAT.

C. NTFS and FAT require the same amount of disk space for overhead.

D. The amount of overhead is strictly dependent upon partition size.

Answers and Explanations: Practice Problems

1. **D** Stripe sets must be created from areas of free space that are of equal size.
2. **C** Volume sets can be created with unequal sized areas of free space.
3. **A** You cannot extend a FAT formatted volume set. Therefore, the largest possible volume set is the one already in existence.
4. **B** The only way to convert a partition to FAT from NTFS is to reformat the partition.
5. **C** Windows NT 4.0 no longer supports HPFS. You must perform the conversion prior to starting the upgrade.
6. **B** NTFS supports compression down to the file level.
7. **B** Disk Manager is used to manage disk resources.
8. **C** 2, 32.
9. **C** FAT is considered the most efficient file system for partitions of less than 400 megabytes.
10. **C** 255 characters.
11. **B** Although the partition could be reformatted, you would lose all data on that partition.
12. **C** The valid backup options are: Normal, Copy, Differential, Incremental, and Daily.
13. **A** The Incremental backup type does set the archive bit.
14. **B** The Copy backup type creates a tape copy of the files currently selected for backup.
15. **C** The Windows NT Backup Utility enables you to create and manage backups.
16. **B** The Daily option does not set the archive bit.
17. **B, D** "Heidi's Laser Printer" and "Delta Quadrant Printer" do not conform to the 8.3 naming convention.
18. **A, C** FAT and NTFS are the only file systems supported by Windows NT 4.0.
19. **C** Boot and system partitions can participate in a volume set.
20. **A** Stripe sets cannot be extended because the data is written across the stripe set in 64KB data blocks.
21. **A, D** FAT32 is supported by Windows 95 only, and HPFS is not supported in Windows NT 4.0.
22. **A** Logical drives are created in extended partitions.
23. **A** Boot files are located in the system partition; system files are located in the boot partition.
24. **C** NTFS is considered more efficient for partitions larger than 400 megabytes.
25. **B** FAT typically requires less than 1 megabyte of overhead, whereas NTFS typically requires 4–5 megabytes.

15.6 Key Words

primary partition

extended partition

system partition

boot partition

FAT

NTFS

volume sets

stripe sets

Disk Manager

Windows NT Backup Manager

Practice Exam: Managing Resources

Use this practice exam to test your mastery of Managing Resources. This practice exam is 20 questions long. The passing Microsoft score is 70.4 percent. Questions are in multiple-choice format.

1. In order to increase security on your network, you want to ensure that users have a minimum password length of eight characters, that users change their passwords every two months, and that no user can use the same password for half the year. Which of the following account policies will ensure that you meet the goals of your policy?

   A. Minimum Password Length: 8
   Minimum Password Age: 60 days
   Maximum Password Age: 61 days
   Password Uniqueness: 3

   B. Minimum Password Length: 8
   Minimum Password Age: 61 days
   Maximum Password Age: 61 days
   Password Uniqueness: 6

   C. Minimum Password Length: 8
   Minimum Password Age: 30 days
   Maximum Password Age: 61 days
   Password Uniqueness: 3

   D. Minimum Password Length: 8
   Minimum Password Age: 61 days
   Maximum Password Age: 60 days
   Password Uniqueness: 3

2. A user needs Read access to a network share on a FAT partition, but she is currently assigned No Access permission. You change the permissions for the user, but nothing happens. What went wrong?

   A. The user needs to log out and log back on to refresh the access token.

   B. You must also change the file permissions in order for the user to gain access.

   C. You must change the user's password for the share when you change access permissions.

   D. Once a user has been assigned No Access, you cannot reassign a less-restrictive permission.

3. How can you add an existing user to the Backup Operators group? (Select all steps that apply.)

   A. Log on as the administrator.

   B. Start User Manager.

   C. From Account Manager, double-click the username and click the Group button.

   D. In the Group Membership window, click the Backup Operators group and click Add.

4. By default, what groups have permissions to create and manage backups?

   A. Backup Operators

   B. Power Users

   C. Users

   D. Replicators

5. Where is a user's logon script path set?

   A. System applet in Control Panel

   B. Account Manager

   C. User Manager

   D. Logon Manager

6. Select all the groups whose members can create a member in the Administrators group.

   A. Users

   B. Power Users

   C. Account Managers

   D. Administrators

7. When creating a new user, you set the "User Must Change Password at Next Logon" and "Password Never Expires" password properties. What will happen when you attempt to create the user?

   A. You will receive an error because these two properties conflict.

   B. You will receive a warning that this user will not be required to change the password.

   C. This user will have to change the password at logon; however, once it's changed, the password will never expire.

   D. The user will not be able to logon.

8. What application should you use to create a new user account?

   A. User Manager

   B. Server Manager

   C. Account Manager

   D. Logon Manager

9. To change a share name you must do what? (Select all that apply.)

   A. Log on with Power User authority

   B. Delete the folder

   C. Have an NTFS formatted partition

   D. Delete the existing share

10. By default, how many separator pages are installed with a print driver?

    A. 2 pages

    B. 3 pages

    C. 4 pages

    D. 5 pages

11. How can you configure a printer to insert a form feed after completing a print job?

    A. Specify a Separator Page on the General tab of the printer's properties sheet.

    B. Specify an Alternate Print Processor on the General tab of the printer's properties sheet.

    C. Select Insert Form Feed on the Port tab of the printer's properties sheet.

    D. Specify Insert Form Feed on the Device Settings tab of the printer's properties sheet.

12. What is the maximum number of inbound network connections supported by Windows NT 4.0 Workstation?

    A. 10

    B. 15

    C. 20

    D. 25

13. In Windows NT, the active partition is also known as what?

    A. Boot partition

    B. System partition

    C. Primary partition

    D. Extended partition

14. Select two types of partitions that Windows NT 4.0 recognizes.

    A. Extended

    B. Logical

    C. Primary

    D. Secondary

15. Windows NT installs the system files in which partition?

    A. Boot

    B. Extended

    C. System

    D. Primary

16. How many primary partitions can you have on one physical hard disk with Windows NT 4.0?

    A. 1 partition

    B. 4 partitions

    C. 2 partitions

    D. 8 partitions

17. Your boot partition resides in an extended partition. This partition has one logical drive consisting of 800 megabytes formatted with NTFS, as well as 800 megabytes of free space. Additionally, you have two areas of free space on the hard disk. One area is 1.6 gigabytes; the other is 2 gigabytes. What is the largest stripe set you can create?

    A. 1.6 gigabytes

    B. You cannot create a stripe set with these areas of free space.

    C. 2.4 gigabytes

    D. 3.2 gigabytes

18. You create two printers for one print device. The first printer has a priority of 30. The other has a priority of 60. If a print job is sent to the printer with the priority of 30 while the printer with a priority of 60 is printing, what will happen?

    A. The print job with a priority of 30 will cause the print job being printed by the printer with a priority of 60 to be deleted.

    B. Nothing.

    C. The print job with a priority of 30 will cause the print job being printed by the printer with a priority of 60 to pause.

    D. The print queue will be jammed.

19. Where can you specify a separator page for a printer?

    A. On the General tab of the printer's properties sheet.

    B. On the Device Options tab of the printer's properties sheet.

    C. On the Ports tab of the printer's properties sheet.

    D. On the Sharing tab of the printer's properties sheet.

20. John asks you how he can switch his HP print device from PCL to PostScript mode without manually changing the device settings. What should you tell him.

    A. He needs to write a batch file.

    B. He can use a separator page.

    C. He cannot automate the task.

    D. He can use the Device Settings tab of the printer's properties sheet.

Answers and Explanations: Practice Exam

1. **A** You must specify the minimum password age to be two months and the maximum password age to be two months plus one day. Specify the password uniqueness to be three passwords, and set the minimum length at eight characters.

2. **A** Permission changes will not take effect until the user logs out and logs back in.

3. **A, B, D** The Account Manager does not exist in Windows NT workstation.

4. **A, B** Power Users, Backup Operators, and Administrators are the only built-in groups that can create and manage backups by default.

5. **C** User Manager is used to set the user's logon script path.

6. **D** Only members of the Administrators group can add other users to that group.

7. **B** Both properties can be set; however, the user will not be required to change the password.

8. **A** The only application that allows you to create new users is User Manager.

9. **A, D** You do not have to have NTFS permissions for shares, only for file and folder permissions.

10. **B** Three separator pages are installed with Windows NT 4.0.

11. **B** By selecting an alternative print processor, you can specify the insertion of a form feed between print jobs.

12. **A** The maximum number of inbound network connections supported by Windows NT 4.0 Workstation is 10.

13. **B** The boot files must be on the active partition. Windows NT places the boot files in the system partition.

14. **A, C** There are no logical partitions, only logical drives. Secondary partitions do not exist.

15. **A** The system files are placed in the boot partition.

16. **B** Windows NT will support up to four primary partitions on one hard disk.

17. **D** You can combine two 1.6 gigabyte areas of free space.

18. **B** Priority changes do not affect spooled documents.

19. **A** You specify separator pages on the General tab of the printer's properties sheet.

20. **B** Windows NT provides separator pages, available on the General tab of the printer's properties sheet.

CHAPTER 16

Connectivity

This chapter helps you prepare for the exam by covering the following objectives:

- Adding and configuring the network components of Windows NT Workstation
- Using various methods to access network resources
- Implementing Windows NT Workstation as a client in a NetWare environment
- Using various configurations to install Windows NT Workstation as a TCP/IP client
- Configuring and installing Dial-Up Networking in a given situation
- Configuring Peer Web Services in a given situation

16.1 Adding and Configuring the Network Components of Windows NT Workstation

You can configure all of your network components when you first install Windows NT Workstation 4.0. If you want to examine how your network components are configured or make changes to your network configuration, double-click the Network program in Control Panel to view the Network Properties dialog box. You must be an administrator to make changes to the network settings on your computer.

A. Identification Options

Use the Identification tab in the Network properties sheet to view your computer name and your workgroup or domain name. Click the Change button to change your computer name (maximum length for a computer name is 15 characters) or to join a workgroup or domain (maximum length for a workgroup or domain name is 15 characters).

The Windows NT security system requires that all Windows NT computers in a domain have accounts. Only domain administrators and other users that have been granted the user right of "Add Workstations to Domain" by a domain administrator can create computer accounts in a Windows NT domain.

If you are a domain administrator, you can give any user or group the user right of "Add Workstations to Domain." First, open User Manager for Domains. From the Policies menu, choose User Rights. Then make sure that you check the Show Advanced User Rights box.

How you change your domain name on the Identification tab depends on whether or not you already have an account:

- If a domain administrator has already created a computer account for your computer, type the domain name into the Domain box and click OK.
- To create your own computer account in the domain, the user name you specify must be that of a domain administrator or it must have been granted the user right of "Add Workstations to Domain" by a domain administrator. If you use a user name with legitimate rights, you can type the domain name into the Domain box and click OK.

Regardless of which method you use to join a domain, you should see a status message welcoming you to your new domain. You must then restart your computer to complete the process of joining the new domain.

To join a domain, you must have network connectivity to the primary domain controller (PDC) in the domain you want to join. Also, make sure that you do not have a network session open with that PDC. If you must have open network sessions with that PDC, close all open files. Then join that domain, restart your computer, and reopen the files.

B. Services Options

Use the Services tab in the Network properties sheet to view and modify the network services for your computer. You might want to add some of the following network services to a Windows NT workstation:

- *Client Services for NetWare (CSNW).* Enables you to access files or printers on a NetWare server.
- *Microsoft Peer Web Services.* Installs an intranet web server on your computer.
- *Microsoft TCP/IP Printing.* Configures your computer to act as a print server to which TCP/IP-based clients, such as UNIX systems, can submit print jobs.
- *Remote Access Server.* Enables your computer to connect via telephone lines or the Internet to remote networks.
- *SNMP Service.* Enables your computer to transmit status information via TCP/IP to network management stations.

C. Protocols Options

Use the Protocols tab in the Network properties sheet to view and modify the transport protocols for your computer. Windows NT Workstation 4.0 allows an unlimited number of network transport protocols. You might want to add some of the following network transport protocols to a Windows NT workstation:

- *TCP/IP.* The default protocol for Windows NT Workstation 4.0. It is required for Internet connectivity.
- *NWLink IPX/SPX Compatible Transport.* Required for connectivity to NetWare servers.
- *NetBEUI.* Typically allows connectivity only to other Microsoft-based computers and does not support routing.

You can also add third-party transport protocols compatible with TDI and NDIS. (Third-party components are those not developed by Microsoft.)

D. Adapters Options

You can use the Adapters tab in the Network properties sheet to add, remove, view properties of, or update your network adapter drivers. Windows NT Workstation 4.0 allows an unlimited number of network adapters.

Even if you don't have a network adapter, you can practice installing some of the network services that will not function without a network adapter. For example, select the MS Loopback Adapter from the Network Adapter list. (Keep in mind that although the services will be installed, they will not do much without an actual network adapter.)

E. Bindings Options

Network bindings are the connections between network services, transport protocols, and adapter card drivers. You can use the Bindings tab in the Network properties sheet to view, enable, disable, and change the order of the bindings on your computer. The current default protocol for each network service appears at the top of each section in the display. The default protocol for the Server service is TCP/IP.

If the binding from the Server service to the NetBEUI protocol is disabled, client *computers* that are configured with only the NetBEUI protocol cannot establish network sessions with this computer. This computer can still establish network sessions with *servers* configured with the NetBEUI protocol only, however, because the Workstation service is still bound to the NetBEUI protocol. For maximum performance, remove any unnecessary protocols and always make sure that your most frequently used protocol is configured to be your default protocol.

16.1.1 Exercise: Adding a New Network Adapter Driver

Objective: Add a new network adapter driver.

Time Estimate: 10 minutes

To add a new network adapter in Windows NT Workstation, follow these steps:

1. Right-click Network Neighborhood.
2. Choose Properties from the shortcut menu.

3. Click the Adapters tab.
4. Click Add.
5. Select MS Loopback Adapter from the Network Adapter list.
6. Click OK.
7. In the MS Loopback Adapter Card setup box, click OK.
8. Insert your Windows NT Workstation 4.0 installation CD when requested, and then click Continue.
9. Click Close in the Network Properties dialog box.
10. Answer any questions having to do with any protocols that you might have installed.
11. Click Yes to restart your computer.

Answers and Explanations: Exercise

Although the MS Loopback Adapter enables your network services to install without errors, your computer cannot actually communicate with any other computers on your network until you configure it with a real network adapter and the appropriate driver software.

You should use the Loopback Adapter only if you do not have access to a network on which you can experiment.

16.1.2 Exercise: Installing DUN and Configuring a Modem

Objective: Set up your computer to access remote networks via a modem.

Time Estimate: 15 minutes

To install Dial-Up Networking (DUN) and configure your modem, follow these steps:

1. Double-click the Dial-Up Networking program in My Computer.
2. Click the Install button to start the Installation Wizard.
3. Insert your installation CD when prompted.
4. Click Yes to start the Modem installer.
5. Click the Don't Detect My Modem; I Will Select It from a List check box, and then click Next.
6. Select your modem from the list, or click Have Disk.
7. Point the Installation Wizard to your modem's install files.
8. Click Next to install the modem.
9. Select the port to which the modem is connected, and then click Next.
10. Wait while the modem is installed.
11. Click Finish.

12. At the Add RAS Device screen, click OK.
13. In the Remote Access Setup dialog box, click Configure.
14. Notice that the default setting for Microsoft NT Workstation 4.0 is Dial Out Only. Click OK to return to the Remote Access Setup dialog box.
15. Click Network. In the Network Configuration dialog box, notice that you can choose which of the protocols you want to use after you connect to the remote network.
16. Click OK to return to the Remote Access Setup dialog box.
17. Click Continue.
18. Wait while the remainder of the RAS software is installed and the bindings are reset.
19. Press Restart to restart your computer, which finishes the installation of DUN.

Answers and Explanations: Exercise

This exercise illustrated how to set up your computer to access remote networks via a modem. One word of caution, however: When purchasing a modem to be used with DUN, make sure that it has a Windows NT-compliant device driver. If it does not, you will not be able to use this feature.

16.1 Practice Problems

1. Which of the following Control Panel applets enables you to view the Network Properties dialog box?
   A. System
   B. Services
   C. Network
   D. Device Manager
2. To make changes to network settings, what is the minimum security logon required?
   A. User
   B. Administrator
   C. Guest
   D. Domain User
3. What is the maximum length allowed for a computer name?
   A. 8 characters
   B. 8.3 characters
   C. 15 characters
   D. 255 characters
4. Who of the following can create computer accounts in a Windows NT domain?
   A. Domain administrators
   B. Users
   C. Guests
   D. Users that have been granted the user right of "Add Workstations to Domain"
5. What is the maximum length allowed for a domain name?
   A. 8 characters
   B. 8.3 characters
   C. 15 characters
   D. 255 characters
6. Which tab in the Network properties sheet is used to view and modify the network services for your computer?
   A. System
   B. Connectivity
   C. Protocols
   D. Services
7. What is the maximum length allowed for a workgroup name?
   A. 8 characters
   B. 8.3 characters
   C. 15 characters
   D. 255 characters
8. Which tab in the Network Properties sheet is used to view and modify the transport protocols for your computer?
   A. System
   B. Connectivity
   C. Protocols
   D. Services
9. Which of the following protocols are included with Windows NT Workstation?
   A. NetBEUI
   B. TCP/IP
   C. AppleShare
   D. IPX/SPX-compatible
10. Which protocol is installed by default in Windows NT Workstation 4.0?
    A. NetBEUI
    B. TCP/IP
    C. AppleShare
    D. IPX/SPX-compatible
11. To join a domain, you must have network connectivity to which of the following?
    A. A member server
    B. The backup domain controller
    C. The primary domain controller
    D. Another workstation

12. Suppose you have a laptop computer configured with Dial-Up Networking, and you want to configure your system to use a calling card. Which of the following is correct?

    A. You can't program calling card numbers.

    B. Enter the calling card number after the phone number you want to dial.

    C. Edit the Dialing Location, click Dial Using Call Card, click Change, and enter the number.

    D. Go to Control Panel, start the Network program, select the Services tab, and edit the properties for the Remote Access Service.

13. Which three components listed enable a Windows NT Workstation 4.0 computer to access files and printers on a NetWare server?

    A. Client Services for NetWare

    B. Gateway Services for NetWare

    C. NWLink IPX/SPX Compatible Transport

    D. File and Print Services for NetWare

14. What do you need to do before you install Peer Web Services?

    A. Install NetBEUI

    B. Download the files from the Microsoft web site

    C. Remove all other Internet services from the computer

    D. Create a dedicated FAT partition

Answers and Explanations: Practice Problems

1. **C** The Network program in Control Panel is used to view the Network Properties dialog box.
2. **B** You must be an administrator to make changes to the network settings on your computer.
3. **C** Maximum length for a computer name is 15 characters.
4. **A, D** Only domain administrators and other users that have been granted the user right of "Add Workstations to Domain" by a domain administrator can create computer accounts in a Windows NT domain.
5. **C** Maximum length for a domain name is 15 characters.
6. **D** Use the Services tab in the Network properties sheet to view and modify the network services for your computer.
7. **C** Maximum length for a workgroup name is 15 characters.
8. **C** Use the Protocols tab in the Network properties sheet to view and modify the transport protocols for your computer.
9. **A, B, D** NetBEUI, TCP/IP, and the IPX/SPX-compatible protocols ship with Windows NT Workstation.
10. **B** TCP/IP is installed as the default protocol.
11. **C** To join a domain, you must have network connectivity to the primary domain controller (PDC) in the domain that you want to join.
12. **C** You enter your calling card information when you edit your Dialing Location.
13. **A, B, C** FPNW enables NetWare clients to access files and printers on a Windows NT Server.
14. **C** PWS requires TCP/IP.

16.1 Key Words

domain

TCP/IP

NetBEUI

IPX/SPX

16.2 Using Various Methods to Access Network Resources

Windows NT Workstation 4.0 offers several methods of working with network resources, and each of those methods offers different ways of determining what network resources are available to you and the different types of connections you can make to those network resources.

A. Universal Naming Convention

The *Universal Naming Convention* (UNC) is a standardized way of specifying a share name on a specific computer. Share names can refer to folders or to printers. The UNC path takes the form of *computer_name**share_name*. For example, the UNC path to a share called Accounting on a server called ACCTSERVER is \\ACCTSERVER\Accounting.

It is important to note that connections made via UNC paths take place immediately and do not require the use of a drive letter. It is also important to note that if a dollar sign ($) is placed at the end of a share name, the share becomes "hidden" and does not show up in listings, but it can still be accessed by using the UNC name.

You can also use UNC connections to connect to network printers. For example, \\ACCTSERVER\ACCTPRINT is the UNC path to a printer named ACCTPRINT on a server named ACCTSERVER.

Many 16-bit applications do not work with UNC paths. If you need to use a 16-bit application that doesn't work with UNC paths, you must either map a drive letter to the shared folder or connect a port to the network printer.

B. Network Neighborhood

If your Windows NT Workstation 4.0 computer has a network card installed, the Network Neighborhood icon appears on your desktop. When you double-click the Network © Neighborhood icon, a list of all computers in your workgroup or domain appears. By double-clicking the Entire Network icon, you can also view all computers connected to your network that are not members of your workgroup or domain.

When you view lists of computers in Network Neighborhood, you are actually viewing a graphical representation of what is called a *browse list*. The browse list is actually maintained by a computer that has been designated as a *Browse Master*. All computers on the network (that have an active Server service) periodically announce their presence to the Browse Master to keep the browse list current.

Note that Windows 95 computers in a workgroup that have the same name as a Windows NT domain are listed with the Windows NT computers in the browse list.

1. Net View Command

You can access the current browse list from the command prompt by typing **NET VIEW**. The current browse list is displayed on your screen. A sample browse list looks like this:

```
C:\>net view
Server Name            Remark

---------------------------------------------------
\\TEST1
\\TEST2
\\TESTPDC
The command completed successfully.
```

2. Net Use Command

You can assign network resources to drive letters from the command prompt by using the Net Use command and the UNC path of the resource. To connect drive letter X: to a share called GoodStuff on a server named SERVER1, for example, you would type the following command at a command prompt:

```
Net Use X: \\SERVER1\GoodStuff
```

You can also use the Net Use command to connect clients to network printers. For instance, if you wanted to connect port Lpt1: to a network printer named HP5 on a server named SERVER1, you could use the following command:

```
Net Use Lpt1: \\SERVER1\HP5
```

To disconnect the network resources for these two, use the following two commands:

```
Net Use X: /d
Net Use Lpt1: /d
```

16.2.1 Exercise: Using UNC Names

Exercise 16.2.1 illustrates the use of a UNC name. For this exercise, you must be connected to a network and be able to browse file shares on other computers on the network.

1. Open Network Neighborhood from the desktop. The other computers in your workgroup or domain are displayed.
2. Double-click another computer that contains a share to which you have access. The shares on that computer are displayed.
3. Note the computer name and share name that you can access on a piece of paper.
4. From the Start menu, choose Programs, MS-DOS Prompt. A command prompt window opens.

5. Enter **NET USE *computername**sharename***, using the computer name and share name you recorded. If the command succeeds, you receive the message "The command was completed successfully."
6. To remove the connected share, enter **NET USE *computername**sharename* /DELETE** at the prompt.

Answers and Explanations: Exercise

In this exercise, you accessed a shared resource on another computer. You could have mapped a drive letter to the share by using the following command: **NET USE [Drive:] *computername**sharename***. In order to properly complete the mapping procedure, you must be connected to a network and be able to browse file shares on other computers on the network.

16.2 Practice Problems

1. How many characters is the share name traditionally limited to?

   A. 8.3 characters

   B. 10 characters

   C. 15 characters

   D. 255 characters

2. How many characters is the computer name traditionally limited to?

   A. 8.3 characters

   B. 10 characters

   C. 15 characters

   D. 255 characters

3. Which of the following is the correct format for the UNC path?

   A. *computername**sharename* [*optional path*]

   B. *sharename**computername* [*optional path*]

   C. *sharename* [*optional path*]

   D. *computername* [*optional path*]

4. To make a share "invisible," which of the following characters must be added to the name?

   A. #

   B. $

   C. ;

   D. <backspace>

5. The character referenced in question 4 is included where in the name?

   A. At the beginning

   B. Anywhere within the name

   C. At the end of the name

   D. Within quotes anywhere within the name

6. UNC names are supported by what percent of Windows NT Workstation functions?

   A. 50%

   B. 75%

   C. 78%

   D. 100%

7. UNC names can be used to access which two of the following?

   A. Windows NT servers

   B. Routers

   C. Gateways

   D. NetWare servers

8. Which of the following is the UNC path for a file named SPENCER.DAT in a directory named EVAN in a share named KRISTIN on a server named KAREN?

   A. \\KRISTIN\KAREN\EVAN\SPENCER.DAT

   B. \\SPENCER.DAT\EVAN\KRISTIN\KAREN

   C. \\KAREN\KRISTIN\EVAN\SPENCER.DAT

   D. //SPENCER.DAT/EVAN/KRISTIN/KAREN

9. Which of the following is the UNC path for a file named ANN on the server MICHAEL in the share SCOTT?

   A. \\MICHAEL\SCOTT\ANN

   B. \\ANN\SCOTT\MICHAEL

   C. //ANN/SCOTT/MICHAEL

   D. //MICHAEL/SCOTT/ANN

10. Which of the following is the UNC path for a file named SPENCER on the server MICHAEL in the share JOYCE?

    A. \\MICHAEL\JOYCE\SPENCER

    B. \\SPENCER\JOYCE\MICHAEL

    C. //SPENCER/JOYCE/MICHAEL

    D. //MICHAEL/JOYCE/SPENCER

16

Answers and Explanations: Practice Problems

1. **C** The share name is limited to 15 characters.
2. **C** The computer name is limited to 15 characters.
3. **A** The UNC path takes the form of *computername**sharename* [*optional path*].
4. **B** If a dollar sign ($) is added to the end of the share name, it makes the share name invisible to other computers through a browser, such as Network Neighborhood.
5. **C** If a dollar sign ($) is added to the end of the share name it makes the share name invisible to other computers through a browser, such as Network Neighborhood.
6. **D** All Windows NT Workstation functions support the use of UNC names, including the Run option on the Start menu and the command prompt.
7. **A, D** NetWare servers, like Windows NT servers, can be accessed through a UNC name.
8. **C** \\KAREN\KRISTIN\EVAN\SPENCER.DAT is the correct UNC path.
9. **A** \\MICHAEL\SCOTT\ANN is the correct UNC path.
10. **A** \\MICHAEL\JOYCE\SPENCER is the correct UNC path.

16.2 Key Words

Universal Naming Convention

$ character

browse list

Browse Master

16.3 Implementing Windows NT Workstation as a Client in a NetWare Environment

When it comes to non-homogenous networks, Windows NT Workstation cannot run Services for Macintosh—only Windows NT Server can. Workstation, however, can run NetWare connectivity services and access NetWare networks quite easily. To enable a Windows NT Workstation 4.0 computer to access and share resources on a NetWare server, you might have to install additional software besides the NWLink protocol on the Windows NT Workstation 4.0 computers. The type of access you are trying to establish determines whether you need to install the additional software. NWLink can establish client/server connections, but does not provide access to files and printers on NetWare servers.

If you want to be able to access files or printers on a NetWare server, you must install the Microsoft Client Service for NetWare (CSNW), which is included with Windows NT Workstation 4.0. CSNW enables Windows NT Workstation 4.0 to access files and printers at NetWare servers running NetWare 2.15 or later (including NetWare 4.x servers running NDS). CSNW installs an additional network redirector.

Windows NT Workstation 4.0 computers that have NWLink and CSNW installed gain the following benefits:

- A new network redirector compatible with NetWare Core Protocol (NCP). NCP is the standard Novell protocol for file and print sharing.
- Freedom to use long filenames (when the NetWare server is configured to support long filenames).
- Large Internet Protocol (LIP) to automatically negotiate and determine the largest possible frame size to communicate with NetWare servers.

The Microsoft Client Service for NetWare (CSNW) enables Windows NT Workstation 4.0 to access files and printers on NetWare servers. Although NWLink and CSNW enable Windows NT Workstation 4.0 to access files and printers on a NetWare server running NDS, it does not support administration of NDS trees.

Also, although CSNW enables Windows NT Workstation 4.0 to access files and printers on a NetWare server, it doesn't enable NetWare clients to access files and printers on Windows NT Workstation 4.0. If you need NetWare clients to be able to access files and printers on a Windows NT 4.0 computer, you must install Microsoft File and Print Services for NetWare (FPNW) on Windows NT Server 4.0. FPNW is available separately from Microsoft.

A Windows NT Workstation 4.0 computer can access files and printers on a NetWare server without adding CSNW by connecting through a Windows NT Server configured with Gateway Services for NetWare (GSNW). GSNW can be installed only on Windows NT Server.

A. Installing CSNW

CSNW is installed the same way as any other network service, through the Network program in the Control Panel. After you install CSNW, you will notice a new CSNW program listed in the Control Panel.

If, after you install NWLink and CSNW, you cannot establish connectivity to your NetWare servers, you should check to see what IPX frame type they are configured for. There are actually two different, incompatible versions: 802.2 and 802.3. Windows NT Workstation 4.0 attempts to automatically determine the correct frame type, but you might have to manually specify the frame type to make the connection work.

B. Configuring CSNW

After you install CSNW on your computer, users logging on receive a prompt to enter the details of their NetWare accounts. Users can enter a preferred server for NetWare 2.15 or above, or 3.x, or they can enter their default trees and context for NDS (the default in NetWare 4.x), or they can specify <None> if they do not have NetWare accounts. Every time the same user logs on to that computer, that user automatically connects to the specified NetWare account in addition to the Windows NT account.

Each user is requested to enter the NetWare account information only once. The only way to change a user's recorded NetWare account information is to double-click the CSNW program in Control Panel and make the change there. You can also use the CSNW program in Control Panel to modify your print options for NetWare printers—to add form feeds or print banners, for example.

Even though Windows NT Workstation 4.0 attempts to automatically connect you to your NetWare system, there is no direct link between the two account databases. If you change either network password, the other password does not automatically change to match your new network password. If you press Ctrl+Alt+Del and choose Change Password, you have the option of selecting NetWare or Compatible Network in the Domain field. From there you can change the NetWare password. (On NetWare servers running in bindery mode, you can also use the Setpass utility.)

C. Connecting to NetWare Resources

After you install NWLink and CSNW, you access the NetWare servers in your network using the same methods you use to connect to any other Windows NT server. You can connect to files and printers on the NetWare servers without any special procedures:

- **Browsing.** After you install NWLink and CSNW, when you double-click Network Neighborhood and then double-click Entire Network, you can choose to browse either the Microsoft Windows Network or the NetWare or Compatible Network.
- **Map command.** After you install NWLink and CSNW, right-click Network Neighborhood and choose Map Network Drive from the shortcut menu. You can then assign any drive letter to any shared directory on a NetWare server.
- **Other commands.** The Capture, Login, Logout, and Attach commands, all from NetWare, can cause problems if run from Windows NT Workstation. However, their functionality is available from other utilities supplied with Workstation. You should avoid these four utilities to prevent execution failures.

16.3.1 Exercise: Installing Client Service for NetWare (CSNW)

Objective: Enable your computer to access files and printers on a NetWare server.

Time Estimate: 20 minutes

To install the Client Service for NetWare, follow the steps outlined here:

1. Double-click the Network program in Control Panel.
2. Click the Services tab.
3. Click Add.
4. Select Client Service for NetWare in the Network Service list, and then click OK.
5. Insert your Windows NT Workstation 4.0 installation CD when prompted, and then click Continue.
6. Click Close and wait while the bindings are reset.
7. Click Yes to restart your computer.
8. Press Ctrl+Alt+Delete and log on to your computer.
9. When the Select NetWare Logon dialog box appears, select your NetWare 3.x preferred server or your NetWare 4.x default tree and context. Then click OK.
10. When your desktop appears, right-click Network Neighborhood.
11. In the Network Neighborhood menu, choose Who Am I. Your NetWare user information appears.

Answers and Explanations: Exercise

CSNW enables a Windows NT Workstation 4.0 computer to access files and printers located on a NetWare server. However, you must install the Microsoft File and Print for NetWare (FPNW) service in order for NetWare clients to be able to access files and printers located on Windows NT Workstation 4.0.

16.3.2 Exercise: Changing the Frame Type of the NWLink Protocol

Objective: Adjust the properties of the NWLink protocol to change the frame type from auto-detect to 802.2.

Time Estimate: 10 minutes

To change the NWLink's protocol frame type, follow these steps:

1. Double-click the Network program in Control Panel.
2. Click the Protocols tab in the Network Properties dialog box.
3. Select the NWLink IPX/SPX Compatible Transport protocol.
4. Click Properties.
5. In the Frame Type drop-down box, select Ethernet 802.2.

6. Click OK.
7. In the Network Properties dialog box, click Close.
8. Restart your computer when prompted.

Answers and Explanations: Exercise

The default setting for the NWLink frame type in Windows NT Workstation 4.0 is Automatic. You must modify this setting if you are using more than one frame type. The purpose of this exercise was to illustrate how that is done.

16.3.3 Exercise: Connecting to a NetWare Print Server

Objective: Connect your computer to a NetWare print server.

Time Estimate: 10 minutes

To implement Windows NT Workstation as a client in a NetWare environment, follow these steps:

1. Double-click the Printers program in My Computer.
2. Double-click Add Printer.
3. In the Add Printer Wizard, select Network Printer Server, and then click Next.
4. In the Connect to Printer dialog box, select the desired network printer, and then click OK. (Note: You can double-click the desired print server to see a list of the printers available on that print server.)
5. In the Connect to Printer dialog box, click OK.
6. Select the proper printer from the list, and then click OK.
7. Insert your installation CD when prompted, and then click OK.
8. Indicate whether you want this new printer to be your default Windows printer, and then click Next.
9. Click Finish.

Answers and Explanations: Exercise

After you install CSNW, connecting to a printer on a NetWare server is just as easy as connecting to a printer on a Windows NT server. This exercise illustrated that and walked you through the steps required to establish such a connection.

16.3 Practice Problems

1. In order to access files or printers on a NetWare server, which of the following must you install in addition to NWLink?

   A. Gateway Services for NetWare

   B. Microsoft Client Service for NetWare Networks

   C. Microsoft File and Print Services for NetWare

   D. IPX/SPX

2. To enable NetWare clients to access files on a Windows NT 4.0 computer, you must install which of the following (in addition to NWLink) on a Windows NT Server?

   A. Gateway Services for NetWare

   B. Microsoft Client Service for NetWare Networks

   C. Microsoft File and Print Services for NetWare

   D. IPX/SPX

3. Which of the following is the standard Novell protocol for file and print sharing?

   A. IPX

   B. SPX

   C. NCP

   D. LIP

4. Which of the following is the protocol used to negotiate and determine the largest possible frame size that can be used to communicate with NetWare servers?

   A. IPX

   B. SPX

   C. NCP

   D. LIP

5. A Windows NT Workstation computer can access NetWare servers via a Windows NT server as long as the Windows NT server is running which of the following?

   A. Gateway Services for NetWare

   B. Microsoft Client Service for NetWare Networks

   C. Microsoft File and Print Services for NetWare

   D. IPX/SPX

6. CSNW is installed from which Control Panel applet?

   A. Network

   B. System

   C. Services

   D. User Manager for Domains

Answers and Explanations: Practice Problems

1. **B** Microsoft Client Service for NetWare Networks (CSNW) must be installed with Windows NT Workstation in order to access files or printers on a NetWare network.

2. **C** If you need NetWare clients to be able to access files and printers on a Windows NT 4.0 computer, you must install Microsoft File and Print Services for NetWare (FPNW) on Windows NT Server 4.0. FPNW is available separately from Microsoft.

3. **C** NCP is the standard Novell protocol for file and print sharing.

4. **D** The protocol used to determine the largest possible frame size that can be used to communicate with NetWare servers is Large Internet Protocol (LIP).

5. **A** A Windows NT Workstation computer can access NetWare servers via a Windows NT server as long as the server is running Gateway Services for NetWare.
6. **A** CSNW is installed in the same way as any other network service, through the Network program in the Control Panel.

16.3 Key Words

NCP

LIP

CSNW

16.4 Using Various Configurations to Install Windows NT Workstation as a TCP/IP Client

TCP/IP, the default protocol for Windows NT Workstation 4.0, is a suite of protocols originally designed for the Internet and, as such, is ideally suited for WANs. TCP/IP is supported by most common operating systems and is required for connectivity to the Internet.

When you manually configure a computer as a TCP/IP host, you must enter the appropriate settings required for connectivity with your network. The most common network settings include the following:

- *IP Address.* A logical 32-bit address used to identify a TCP/IP host. Each network adapter configured for TCP/IP must have a unique IP address, such as 10.100.5.43. IP address values are 1–223.0–255.0–255.0–255, with the exception of the number 127, which cannot be used in the first octet because it is a reserved address.
- *Subnet Mask.* A subnet is a division of a larger network environment that's typically connected with routers. Whenever a TCP/IP host tries to communicate with another TCP/IP host, the subnet mask is used to determine whether the other TCP/IP host is on the same network or a different network. If the other TCP/IP host is on a different network, the message must be sent via a router that connects to the other network. A typical subnet mask is 255.255.255.0. All computers on a particular subnet must have identical subnet masks.
- *Default Gateway (Router).* This optional setting is the address of the router for the subnet that controls communications with all other subnets. If this address is not specified, this TCP/IP host can communicate only with other TCP/IP hosts on its subnet.
- *Windows Internet Name Service (WINS).* Computers use IP addresses to identify each other, but users generally find it easier to use another means of identification, such as computer names. Therefore, some method must be used to provide *name resolution*, which is the process in which references to computer names are converted into their corresponding IP addresses. WINS provides name resolution for Microsoft networks. If your network uses WINS for name resolution, your computer needs to be configured with the IP address of a WINS server. (The IP address of a secondary WINS server can also be specified.)
- *Domain Name System (DNS) Server Address.* DNS is an industry standard distributed database that provides name resolution and a hierarchical naming system for identifying TCP/IP hosts on the Internet and on private networks. A DNS address is required for connectivity with the Internet or with UNIX TCP/IP hosts. You can specify more than one DNS address and a search order that indicates the order in which they should be used.

Name resolution is the process of translating user-friendly computer names to IP addresses. If the specified settings for the TCP/IP protocol are incorrect, you will experience problems that keep your computer from establishing communications with other TCP/IP hosts in your network. In extreme cases, communications on your entire subnet can be disrupted.

You can specify all the settings for the TCP/IP protocol manually, or you can have them configured automatically through a network service called Dynamic Host Configuration Protocol (DHCP).

A. Understanding DHCP

One way to avoid the possible problems of administrative overhead and incorrect settings for the TCP/IP protocol—which occur during manual configurations—is to set up your network so that all your clients receive their TCP/IP configuration information automatically through DHCP. DHCP automatically centralizes and manages the allocation of the TCP/IP settings required for proper network functionality for computers that have been configured as *DHCP clients*.

One major advantage of using DHCP is that most of your network settings have to be configured only once—at the DHCP server. Also, the TCP/IP settings configured by the DHCP server are only *leased* to the client and must be periodically renewed. This lease and renewal sequence gives a network administrator the opportunity to change client TCP/IP settings if necessary.

1. Using DHCP

To configure a computer as a DHCP client, all you do is select Obtain an IP Address from a DHCP Server in the TCP/IP properties sheet.

2. Testing DHCP

To find out the network settings a DHCP server has leased to your computer, type the following command at a command prompt:

```
IPCONFIG /all
```

The following is sample output that the IPCONFIG program might return in response to the C:\>ipconfig/all command:

```
Windows NT IP Configuration
Host Name . . . . . . . . . : TEST1
DNS Servers . . . . . . . . : 10.1.45.1
Node Type . . . . . . . . . : Hybrid
NetBIOS Scope ID. . . . . . :
IP Routing Enabled. . . . . : No
WINS Proxy Enabled. . . . . : No
NetBIOS Resolution Uses DNS : No
Ethernet adapter CE31:
Description . . . . . . . . : Xircom CE3 10/100 Ethernet Adapter
Physical Address. . . . . . : 00-10-45-81-5A-96
DHCP Enabled. . . . . . . . : Yes
IP Address. . . . . . . . . : 10.100.5.140
Subnet Mask . . . . . . . . : 255.255.255.0
Default Gateway . . . . . . : 10.100.5.1
DHCP Server . . . . . . . . : 10.100.5.16
Primary WINS Server . . . . : 10.100.5.16
Lease Obtained. . . . . . . : Saturday, August 09, 1997 12:31:29 PM
Lease Expires . . . . . . . : Sunday, August 10, 1997 6:31:29 PM
```

Note that IPCONFIG also gives you full details on the duration of your current lease. You can verify whether a DHCP client has connectivity to a DHCP server by releasing the client's IP address and then attempting to lease an IP address. You can conduct this test by typing the following sequence of commands from the DHCP client at a command prompt:

```
IPCONFIG /release
IPCONFIG /renew
```

B. Manually Configuring TCP/IP

To manually configure your TCP/IP settings, you must enter all the required values into the TCP/IP properties sheet. The three required items you must supply are:

- IP address
- Subnet mask
- Default gateway

C. Name Resolution with TCP/IP

DNS and WINS are not the only name resolution methods available for Windows NT Workstation 4.0 TCP/IP hosts. Microsoft also provides for two lookup files: LMHOSTS and HOSTS. You can find both LMHOSTS and HOSTS in the *winnt_root*\SYSTEM32\DRIVERS\ETC folder.

16

16.4.1 Exercise: Adding the TCP/IP Protocol

Objective: Add and configure the TCP/IP protocol.

Time Estimate: 10 minutes

To add and configure the network components of Windows NT Workstation, follow these steps:

1. Double-click the Network program in Control Panel.
2. Click the Protocols tab in the Network Properties dialog box.
3. Click Add.
4. Select the TCP/IP protocol and click OK.
5. In the TCP/IP Setup box, click No to the question about DHCP.
6. When prompted, insert your installation CD and click Continue.
7. When the Network Properties dialog box appears, click Close.
8. In the Microsoft TCP/IP Properties dialog box, specify this IP address: **10.100.5.27**.
9. Specify this subnet mask: **255.255.255.0**. (The default subnet mask for a Class A network (10.x.x.x) is 255.0.0.0.) Then click OK.
10. Restart your computer when prompted.

Answers and Explanations: Exercise

This exercise showed you the steps for adding and configuring the TCP/IP protocol using arbitrary numbers. When you set up a computer on a real network, make sure you enter the exact values specified by your network designer.

16.4.2 Exercise: Changing TCP/IP Properties to Use DHCP

Objective: Change the properties of the TCP/IP protocol from a static IP address to that of a DHCP client. You must have a DHCP server set up in order for this exercise to work.

Time Estimate: 10 minutes

To use various configurations to install Windows NT Workstation as a TCP/IP client, follow these steps:

1. Double-click the Network program in Control Panel.
2. Click the Protocols tab in the Network Properties dialog box.
3. Select the TCP/IP protocol.
4. Click Properties.
5. Select Obtain an IP Address from a DHCP Server.
6. Click Yes to enable DHCP.
7. In the TCP/IP Properties dialog box, click OK.
8. In the Network Properties dialog box, click Close.
9. If prompted, restart your computer.
10. To verify if DHCP is functional, go to a command prompt and type **IPCONFIG /ALL**.
11. If you don't see a valid IP address and lease information and you didn't already restart your computer, restart your computer now.

Answers and Explanations: Exercise

This exercise showed you how to change the properties of the TCP/IP protocol from a static IP address to that of a DHCP client. You must have a DHCP server set up on your network for this exercise to work.

DHCP eliminates virtually all the network problems caused by TCP/IP hosts that have been configured with incorrect TCP/IP address information.

16.4 Practice Problems

1. Which of the following is the default protocol for Windows NT Workstation 4.0?
   A. IPX/SPX
   B. NCP
   C. TCP/IP
   D. NetBEUI

2. Which of the following is defined as a unique, logical 32-bit address used to identify a TCP/IP host?
   A. Default gateway
   B. Subnet mask
   C. IP address
   D. DNS server address

3. Which of the following is defined as a value used to determine whether a host is on the same network or a different network?
   A. Default gateway
   B. Subnet mask
   C. IP address
   D. DNS server address

4. Which of the following is the optional setting that identifies the router?
   A. Default gateway
   B. Subnet mask
   C. IP address
   D. DNS server address

5. Name resolution is commonly performed on which of the following?
   A. Default gateway
   B. Subnet mask
   C. IP address
   D. DNS server

6. Which two of the following are used for name resolution processes?
   A. DHCP
   B. WINS
   C. IPCONFIG
   D. DNS

7. Of the following, which addresses are valid TCP/IP addresses?
   A. 192.200.14.7
   B. 1.1.1.200
   C. 34.56.76.256
   D. 127.120.200.14

8. Which of the following commands displays your computer's IP address?
   A. IPCONFIG
   B. DHCP
   C. IPX
   D. NETCONFIG

9. IP addresses given to clients from a DHCP server are said to be which of the following?
   A. Issued
   B. In use
   C. Leased
   D. Reserved

10. Host name lookup files provided for Windows NT Workstation by Microsoft include which of the following?
    A. Services
    B. Networks
    C. Hosts
    D. LMHOSTS

Answers and Explanations: Practice Problems

1. **C** The default protocol for Windows NT Workstation 4.0 is TCP/IP.
2. **C** The IP address is a unique, logical 32-bit address used to identify a TCP/IP host.
3. **B** A value used to determine whether a host is on the same or a different network is the subnet mask.
4. **A** The optional setting that identifies the router is the default gateway.
5. **D** The DNS server address is used for name resolution, for identifying TCP/IP hosts on the Internet.
6. **B, D** WINS and DNS are used for name resolution.
7. **A, B** IP addresses take the form of 0–223.0–255.0–255.0–255, with the exception of the number 127, which cannot be used as a class address.
8. **A** IPCONFIG /ALL shows the local computer's TCP/IP configuration information.
9. **C** TCP/IP settings issued through DHCP are leased.
10. **C, D** Host name lookup files provided for Windows NT Workstation by Microsoft include HOSTS and LMHOSTS.

16.4 Key Words

DHCP

WINS

DNS

HOSTS

LMHOSTS

16.5 Configuring and Installing Dial-Up Networking

Remote Access Service (RAS) and Dial-Up Networking (DUN) enable you to extend your network to unlimited locations. RAS servers and DUN clients enable remote clients to make connections to your LAN either via ordinary telephone lines or through higher-speed techniques, such as ISDN or X.25. The incoming connections can also be made via industry standard Point-to-Point Protocol (PPP) or the newer Point-to-Point Tunneling Protocol (PPTP) that makes use of the Internet. DUN also supports the use of Serial Line Internet Protocol (SLIP) to initiate dial-up connections with SLIP servers.

The *Point-to-Point Tunneling Protocol* (PPTP) is an extension of PPP that enables clients to connect to remote servers over the Internet. PPTP was designed to provide secure VPN access to networks, especially via the Internet.

Whether using PPP or PPTP, after a client establishes a connection to a RAS server, he is registered into the local network and can take advantage of the same network services and data that he could if he were actually physically connected to the local network. The only difference that a client might notice is that WAN connections are much slower than a direct physical connection to the LAN.

A. Line Protocols

The network transport protocols (NetBEUI, NWLink, and TCP/IP) were designed for the characteristics of LANs and are not suitable for use in phone-based connections. To make the network transport protocols function properly in phone-based connections, they must be encapsulated in a line protocol. Windows NT Workstation 4.0 supports two line protocols: SLIP and PPP.

1. Serial Line Internet Protocol (SLIP)

SLIP is an industry standard that supports TCP/IP connections made over serial lines. Unfortunately, SLIP has several limitations, as outlined here:

- SLIP supports TCP/IP only; it does not support IPX or NetBEUI.
- SLIP requires static IP addresses; it does not support DHCP.
- SLIP transmits authentication passwords as clear text; it does not support encryption.
- SLIP usually requires a scripting system for the logon process.

Windows NT Workstation 4.0 supports SLIP client functionality only; it does not support operation as a SLIP server.

2. Point-to-Point Protocol (PPP)

The limitations of SLIP prompted the development of a newer industry standard protocol: Point-to-Point Protocol (PPP). Some of the advantages of using PPP include the following:

- It supports TCP/IP, IPX, NetBEUI, and others.
- PPP supports DHCP or static addresses.

- PPP supports encryption for authentication.
- It doesn't require a scripting system for the logon process.

New to Windows NT Workstation 4.0 is support for *PPP multilink*, which enables you to combine multiple physical links into one logical connection. A client with two ordinary phone lines and two 28.8KBps modems, for example, could establish a PPP multilink session with a RAS server and maintain an effective throughput of up to 57.6KBps. The two modems do not have to be the same type or speed; however, both the RAS server and the DUN client must have PPP multilink enabled.

B. Point-to-Point Tunneling Protocol

New to Windows NT Workstation 4.0 is an extension to PPP called Point-to-Point Tunneling Protocol (PPTP). PPTP enables a DUN client to establish a communications session with a RAS server over the Internet. PPTP supports multiprotocol virtual private networks (VPNs), so remote users can gain secure encrypted access to their corporate networks over the Internet. Because PPTP encapsulates TCP/IP, NWLink, and NetBEUI, it makes it possible for the Internet to be used as a backbone for NWLink and NetBEUI.

To use PPTP, you first establish a connection from the DUN client to the Internet and then establish a connection to the RAS server over the Internet.

C. Installing the Dial-Up Networking Client

You can install DUN when you install Windows NT Workstation 4.0 or later. If you select Remote Access to the Network during setup, both RAS and DUN are installed. However, either or both services can be installed separately after installation of Windows NT Workstation 4.0.

To install DUN after installation of Windows NT Workstation 4.0, you double-click the Dial-Up Networking icon in My Computer, click Install to start the Installation Wizard, and then follow the wizard's instructions. Windows NT Workstation 4.0 is limited to one RAS session at a time—either dial-out or receive. If you need to support more than one simultaneous RAS session, you should purchase Windows NT Server 4.0.

D. Configuring the Dial-Up Networking (DUN) Client

The first step in configuring the Dial-Up Networking (DUN) client is to install the DUN software and a modem. The entire installation process is automated and is invoked when you double-click the Dial-Up Networking program in My Computer. When you click Yes to start the Modem Installer, the Install New Modem Wizard appears.

The wizard gives you three options: You can allow the Install New Modem Wizard to automatically detect your modem; you can select your modem from a list; or you can supply a manufacturer's installation disk. The next step in the installation process is to add the modem as a RAS device, and after you add the modem, you must configure it.

After you configure your modem, you must specify how RAS should use the phone line. You have the following options:

- Dial Out Only (the default setting for Microsoft Windows NT Workstation 4.0)
- Receive Calls Only
- Dial Out and Receive Calls

You can also select which of the network transport protocols (TCP/IP, IPX, or NetBEUI) you want to use after you have made a connection to the remote network.

Follow these steps to change your RAS configuration after you finish the installation process:

1. Double-click the Network program in Control Panel.
2. Click the Services tab.
3. Double-click the Remote Access Service in the list.
4. In the Remote Access Setup dialog box, make the following selections:

   Click Configure to configure port usage.

   Click Network to select dial-out protocols.

You must restart your computer after you change your RAS configuration.

1. Authentication

Security is a major consideration in the design of DUN. You can choose from several security settings, including the following:

- *Accept any authentication method including clear text.* Use this setting when you don't care about security.
- *Accept only encrypted authentication.* RAS supports several industry standard encrypted authentication procedures (such as RSA, DES, and Shiva) to support connections to non-Microsoft remote networks.
- *Accept only Microsoft encrypted authentication.* If you select this option, you can also choose to have your entire session with the remote network encrypted, not just your logon. This setting is available only if you are connecting to a Windows NT RAS server.

The authentication and encryption settings are set individually for each phonebook entry (see the following section).

2. Creating a Phonebook Entry

Each user on a computer has a unique phonebook stored as part of his or her User Profile. Every user can customize his or her own phonebook by adding entries for numbers he or she might want to call.

You can create new phonebook entries by starting Dial-Up Networking and clicking New. The New Phonebook Entry Wizard appears. Select the I Know All About Phonebook Entries and Would Rather Edit the Properties Directly check box, and the New Phonebook Entry properties sheet appears. If you choose manual phonebook entry and want to be able to use the New Phonebook Entry wizard again, follow these steps:

1. Double-click the Dial-Up Networking icon in My Computer.
2. Click More.
3. Click User Preferences.
4. Click the Appearance tab.
5. Click Use Wizard to Create New Phonebook Entries.

The New Phonebook Entry Wizard automatically starts the next time you run Dial-Up Networking.

3. Configuring a Location

When you double-click the Telephony applet in Control Panel, the Dialing Properties dialog box appears. You can enter Calling Card information by clicking the Dial using Calling Card check box and then clicking Change.

16.5.1 Exercise: Adding a New Dial-Up Networking (DUN) Phonebook Entry

Objective: Add a new DUN phonebook entry.

Time Estimate: 5 minutes

To manually add a phonebook entry, follow these steps:

1. Double-click the Dial-Up Networking program in My Computer.
2. Click New.
3. Enter **New Server** for the name of the new phonebook entry, and then click Next.
4. Click Next for the Server settings.
5. Enter the phone number **555-5555**, and then click Next.
6. Click Finish.
7. Click Close.

To select an existing phonebook entry, you simply click the Phonebook Entry to Dial drop-down list and choose the phone number you want to dial.

Answers and Explanations: Exercise

This exercise lead you though the steps of adding a new DUN phonebook entry. Each user of a Windows NT Workstation 4.0 computer has his or her own phonebook and can personalize it by adding any entries he or she wants.

16.5.2 Exercise: Adding a New Dial-Up Networking (DUN) Dialing Location

Objective: Add a new dialing location so that you can use your DUN client from a new location.

Time Estimate: 5 minutes

To understand the methodology behind configuring and installing Dial-Up Networking, follow these steps:

1. Double-click the Dial-Up Telephony program in My Computer.
2. Click New.
3. Click OK in the dialog box that tells you a new location was created.
4. Change the area code to your new area code.
5. Specify Dial 9 for an Outside Line and Dial 8 for Long Distance, if necessary.
6. Check the Dial Using Calling Card check box, and then click Change.
7. Select your calling card from the list, and then click OK.
8. Click OK to close the Dialing Properties dialog box.

Answers and Explanations: Exercise

This exercise showed you how to add a new dialing location so that you can use your DUN client from a new location. Having multiple dialing locations can greatly benefit mobile users who need to initiate remote network sessions from several locations.

16.5 Practice Problems

1. Which of the following is an extension to PPP that enables clients to connect to remote servers over the Internet?

   A. SLIP

   B. POP

   C. PPTP

   D. PPP+

2. Windows NT Workstation 4.0 supports which two line protocols?

   A. SLIP

   B. PPP

   C. PPTP

   D. TCP/IP

3. Which of the following is an industry standard that supports TCP/IP connections made over serial lines?

   A. SLIP

   B. PPP

   C. PPTP

   D. TCP/IP

4. Which of the following protocols work with SLIP?

   A. TCP/IP

   B. NetBEUI

   C. IPX/SPX

   D. PPTP

5. How does Windows NT Workstation support SLIP functionality?

   A. As a server

   B. As a client

   C. As a client and a server

   D. Windows NT Workstation does not support SLIP

6. Which of the following protocols works with PPP?

   A. TCP/IP

   B. NetBEUI

   C. IPX/SPX

   D. PPTP

7. Which of the following line protocols supports DHCP addresses?

   A. SLIP

   B. PPP

   C. IPX/SPX

   D. TCP/IP

8. Which of the following is the protocol used to create virtual private networks over the Internet?

   A. SLIP

   B. PPP

   C. POP

   D. PPTP

9. How many RAS sessions can Windows NT Workstation serve at one time?

   A. 1

   B. 2

   C. 5

   D. 255

10. RAS can be configured in which three of the following ways?

    A. Dial Out Only

    B. Receive Calls Only

    C. Dial Out and Receive Calls

    D. Manual

Answers and Explanations: Practice Problems

1. **C** Point-to-Point Tunneling Protocol (PPTP) is an extension to PPP that enables clients to connect to remote servers over the Internet.
2. **A, B** Windows NT Workstation 4.0 supports two line protocols: SLIP and PPP.
3. **A** SLIP is an industry standard that supports TCP/IP connections made over serial lines.
4. **A** SLIP supports TCP/IP only.
5. **B** Windows NT Workstation supports SLIP client only in functionality.
6. **A, B, C** PPP supports TCP/IP, NetBEUI, and IPX/SPX among others.
7. **B** TCP/IP and IPX/SPX are not line protocols. SLIP does not support DHCP addressing—only static addressing. PPP supports DHCP addressing.
8. **D** PPTP is used to create virtual private networks over the Internet.
9. **A** Windows NT Workstation is limited to one RAS session at a time.
10. **A, B, C** Dial Out Only, Receive Calls Only, and Dial Out and Receive Calls are the three settings for RAS.

16.5 Key Words

protocol

PPTP

SLIP

PPP

RAS (Remote Access Service)

encryption

Telephony

16.6 Configuring Peer Web Services

Peer Web Services (PWS) gives users the ability to publish information on private intranets. PWS includes capabilities for hypertext documents, interactive web applications, and client/server applications, and it is optimized for use as a small scale web server. PWS supports the following industry standard Internet services:

- *Hypertext TransportProtocol (HTTP).* Used for the creation and navigation of hypertext documents.
- *File Transfer Protocol (FTP).* Used to transfer files between TCP/IP hosts.
- *Gopher.* A hierarchical indexing system that identifies files in directories to make searching for data easier.

PWS also supports Microsoft's Internet Server Application Programming Interface (ISAPI). You can use ISAPI to create interactive web-based applications that enable users to access and enter data into web pages. Internet Information Server (IIS), which is included with Windows NT Server 4.0, should be deployed for larger scale requirements.

A. Installing Peer Web Services

Before you start the installation of Peer Web Services (PWS), make sure you remove all other Internet services (Gopher, FTP, and so on) that are already installed. Also make sure that you have properly configured your computer to function as a TCP/IP host.

Then start the installation process of PWS through the Network program in Control Panel. Select the installation of the Peer Web Services service, which starts the PWS Installation Wizard. The PWS Installation Wizard also asks you to choose which of the PWS services to install.

B. Configuring Peer Web Services

When you install PWS, a new program group containing the PWS utilities is added to your desktop. The Internet Service Manager enables management of multiple web servers from any location on your network. Some of the capabilities of the Internet Service Manager include the following:

- Find and list all PWS and IIS servers on your network
- Connect to servers and view their installed services
- Start, stop, or pause any service
- Configure service properties

You can also choose to install a version of the Internet Service Manager accessible via HTML that enables you to manage your PWS server with any standard web browser. However, it does not include the properties sheet, which means you cannot remotely start, stop, or pause services.

16.6.1 Exercise: Installing Peer Web Services (PWS)

Objective: Install a Peer Web Server on a Windows NT Workstation 4.0.

Time Estimate: 20 minutes

To walk through configuring Microsoft Peer Web Services, follow these steps:

1. Before starting the installation of Peer Web Services, make sure that the TCP/IP protocol is installed and properly configured.
2. Double-click the Network program in Control Panel.
3. Click the Services tab.
4. Click Add.
5. Select Microsoft Peer Web Services from the Network Service list, and then click OK.
6. Insert your Windows NT Workstation 4.0 installation CD when prompted, and then click OK.
7. Click OK to start Peer Web Services Setup.
8. Click OK to select which PWS services to set up.
9. Click Yes to create the Inetsrv directory.
10. Click OK to specify the names for the publishing directories.
11. Click Yes to create the publishing directories.
12. Wait while the PWS files are installed.
13. Click OK in the Install Drivers dialog box.
14. Click OK to end the PWS installation.
15. Click Close in the Network Properties dialog box. You do not have to restart your computer; PWS is now active.

Answers and Explanations: Exercise

This exercise detailed the step-by-step process required to install a Peer Web Server on a Windows NT Workstation 4.0. Note that PWS is designed for smaller performance requirements than is the Internet Information Server (IIS) that's included with Windows NT Server 4.0. If you need a more powerful service, consider using IIS instead of PWS.

16.6 Practice Problems

1. The capability to publish information on private intranets is provided in Windows NT Workstation by which service?

   A. IIS

   B. Peer Web Services

   C. FrontPage

   D. FTP

2. Which Internet services does PWS support?

   A. HTTP

   B. WAIS

   C. Gopher

   D. FTP

3. Which of the following is the service used to transfer files between TCP/IP hosts?

   A. HTTP

   B. ISAPI

   C. Gopher

   D. FTP

4. Which of the following is a hierarchical indexing system that identifies files in directories and is included with PWS?

   A. HTTP

   B. ISAPI

   C. Gopher

   D. FTP

5. Which of the following programs is used to create interactive web-based applications?

   A. HTTP

   B. ISAPI

   C. Gopher

   D. FTP

Answers and Explanations: Practice Problems

1. **B** Peer Web Services gives users the capability to publish information on private intranets.

2. **A, C, D** PWS supports HTTP, FTP, and Gopher.

3. **D** FTP is used to transfer files.

4. **C** Gopher is a hierarchical indexing system that identifies files in directories to make searching for data easier.

5. **B** ISAPI is used to create interactive web-based applications that enable users to access and enter data into web pages.

16.6 Key Words

Peer Web Services

Practice Exam: Connectivity

Use this practice exam to test your mastery of "Connectivity." This practice exam contains 17 questions. The passing Microsoft score is 70.4 percent (12 questions correct). Questions are in multiple-choice format.

1. Which components must be installed on Windows NT Workstation 4.0 to enable it to access a print queue on a NetWare server?
   A. Client Services for NetWare
   B. Gateway Services for NetWare
   C. NWLink IPX/SPX Compatible Transport
   D. File and Print Services for NetWare

2. Which of the following tools should you use to configure Peer Web Services (PWS) after it is installed on your Windows NT Workstation 4.0?
   A. Internet Service Manager
   B. The Network program in Control Panel
   C. Windows Setup
   D. None of the above. You can configure PWS only during installation.

3. Which of the following is the UNC path for a file named ALLAN on the server GOOB in the share HP?
   A. \\ALLAN\HP\GOOB
   B. //ALLAN/HP/GOOB
   C. //GOOB/HP/ALLAN
   D. \\GOOB\HP\ALLAN

4. Which two frame types are used by NetWare and detected by CSNW?
   A. 802.1
   B. 802.2
   C. 802.3
   D. 802.4
   E. 802.5

5. Microsoft provides two lookup files: LMHOSTS and HOSTS. These files are located in which of the following directories?
   A. \winnt_root\SYSTEM32\DRIVERS\ETC
   B. \winnt_root\
   C. \winnt_root\ETC
   D. \winnt_root\SYSTEM32

6. Which of the following is not a valid IPCONFIG command?
   A. IPCONFIG /ALL
   B. IPCONFIG /RENEW
   C. IPCONFIG /RELEASE
   D. IPCONFIG /CACHE

7. Which of the following pieces of information does not show in IPCONFIG information?
   A. NIC card physical address
   B. ARP cache location
   C. Subnet mask
   D. Date of lease expiration

8. Which transport protocol provides connectivity with the Internet?
   A. DLC
   B. NetBEUI
   C. NWLink IPX/SPX Compatible Transport
   D. TCP/IP

9. Which of the following network settings are needed to manually configure a

Windows NT Workstation 4.0 to communicate in a routed WAN configuration? Choose all that apply.

A. IP address

B. Subnet mask

C. DHCP server address

D. Address of the default gateway

10. Which of the following configurations settings is the default for RAS?

A. Dial Out Only

B. Receive Calls Only

C. Dial Out and Receive Calls

D. Manual

11. Authentication and encryption settings are set in what manner?

A. For each workstation

B. For each domain

C. For each phonebook entry

D. For each user

12. From which Control Panel applet can you access the Dialing Properties dialog box?

A. System

B. Services

C. RAS

D. Telephony

13. Which of the following are limitations of SLIP for Dial-Up Networking (DUN) clients?

A. DUN doesn't support use as a SLIP client.

B. SLIP doesn't support NWLink or NetBEUI.

C. SLIP doesn't support DHCP.

D. SLIP doesn't support encrypted authentication.

14. What methods are supported by Dial-Up Networking to establish sessions with remote networks?

A. ISDN

B. X.25

C. Dial-up with modems and ordinary phone lines

D. XNS

15. Which of the following utilities is used to manage multiple web servers from any location in your network?

A. User Manager

B. System Manager

C. Internet Service Manager

D. Web Manager

16. Which of the following functions does the HTML version of the Internet Service Manager *not* let you do?

A. Find and list all PWS and IIS servers on your network

B. Connect to servers and view their installed services

C. Configure service properties

D. Start, stop, or pause any service

17. Suppose you have a TCP/IP network connected to the Internet. What name resolution service enables you to connect to web sites?

A. WINS

B. DHCP

C. DNS

D. Browser service

Answers and Explanations: Practice Exam

1. **A, C** GSNW is supported only for Windows NT Server.
2. **A** The Microsoft Internet Service Manager is used to configure PWS after installation.
3. **D** \\GOOB\HP\ALLAN is the correct UNC path.
4. **B, C** 802.2 and 802.3 are the two NetWare frame types CSNW detects.
5. **B** The files are located in \winnt_root\SYSTEM32\DRIVERS\ETC.
6. **D** IPCONFIG /CACHE is not a valid command.
7. **B** IPCONFIG does not show ARP Cache information.
8. **D** The TCP/IP protocol provides connectivity with the Internet.
9. **A, B, D** You need to configure the default gateway to enable TCP/IP connectivity in a WAN.
10. **A** Dial Out Only is the default RAS setting.
11. **C** Authentication and encryption settings are set individually for each phonebook entry.
12. **D** Telephony is the Control Panel applet that gives access to Dialing Properties.
13. **B, C, D** Windows NT Workstation 4.0 supports use as a SLIP client, but not as a SLIP server.
14. **A, B, C** DUN doesn't support XNS.
15. **C** Internet Service Manager is used to manage multiple web servers from any location on your network.
16. **D** The HTML version does not let you stop, start, or pause services.
17. **C** UNIX TCP/IP hosts do not support WINS.

Chapter 17

Running Applications

This chapter prepares you for the exam by covering the following objectives:

- Starting applications on Intel and RISC platforms in various operating system environments.
- Starting applications at various priorities.

Understanding how the Windows NT architecture handles applications from different operating systems enables an administrator to better work with the Windows NT operating system. Knowing what operating systems' applications are supported and on what platforms of Windows NT is an important aspect of using the Windows NT operating system.

This chapter discusses the following areas of managing applications:

- Windows NT's architectural design, which enables Windows NT to support applications from other operating systems
- Specifics on how Windows NT handles DOS, Win16, Win32, OS/2, and POSIX applications on Intel and RISC platforms
- Starting applications at various priorities and changing the priority of a running application

17.1 Starting Applications on Intel and RISC Platforms in Various Operating System Environments

Windows NT is designed to run applications originally designed to run under other operating systems. Windows NT can support running applications designed for the following operating systems:

- Windows 95 and Windows NT
- MS-DOS
- Windows 3.x
- OS/2
- POSIX

Windows NT accomplishes this by using the subsystems discussed in the following sections.

A. Win32 Subsystem Support

The Win32 subsystem (also known as the Client/Server subsystem) supports all 32-bit Windows applications and the rest of the environment subsystems. Some of the primary features of Win32-bit applications include the following:

- Reliability (due to each application having its own 2GB address space)
- Support of multithreaded applications
- Capability to take advantage of multiprocessor systems
- Capability to take advantage of preemptive multitasking

Each Windows 32-bit application runs in its own 2GB address space. This design prevents one 32-bit application from overwriting the memory space of another 32-bit application. In other words, a failure of one 32-bit application does not affect other running 32-bit applications.

The most common example of a multithreaded application is a 32-bit setup program. A 32-bit setup program generally has the following three threads of execution:

- A decompression thread that decompresses all files from a centralized archive file
- A copying thread that copies the decompressed files to the appropriate installation directory
- A system configuration thread that modifies all necessary configuration files to enable the application to execute correctly

While independent of each other, the threads of execution must be timed correctly by the developer of the application. The copying thread must wait for the decompression thread to finish expanding the necessary file before the copying thread can place it in the proper directory. Likewise, the system configuration thread must ensure that a file has been copied to the proper directory if it needs to execute the program in order for configuration to take place. In a typical setup progress meter for a 32-bit setup program, separate setup bars show the progress of expansion, copying, and configuration.

Multiple threads in a process share the same memory space. It is imperative that one thread does not overwrite another thread's address space.

Having multiple threads also enables 32-bit applications to take full advantage of Windows NT's capability to support Symmetric Multiprocessing (SMP). SMP enables each thread of an application to execute on the first available processor. In Symmetric Multiprocessing, both threads 1 and 2 display an improvement in execution time because less time is spent in wait states while one is waiting for the other to relinquish control of the processor. Windows NT 32-bit multithreaded applications can take full advantage of a multiprocessor system.

B. Supporting MS-DOS Applications

Windows NT supports any MS-DOS applications that do not attempt to directly access hardware. The Windows NT architecture does not allow any User mode processes to directly access the system hardware.

MS-DOS applications run in a special Win32 application known as a Windows NT Virtual DOS Machine (NTVDM). The NTVDM creates a pseudo MS-DOS environment in which the application is capable of running. Each NTVDM has a single thread of execution and its own address space. This enables preemptive multitasking between MS-DOS applications and protection from other MS-DOS application failure. The following components make up the NTVDM:

- **NTVDM.EXE** Provides the MS-DOS emulation and manages the NTVDM.
- **NTIO.SYS** The NTVDM equivalent of IO.SYS in MS-DOS.
- **NTDOS.SYS** The NTVDM equivalent of the MS-DOS kernel.
- **Instruction Execution Unit (IEU)** On RISC systems, this emulates an Intel 80486 microprocessor. On x86 computers, the IEU acts as a trap handler. Any instructions that cause hardware traps have their control transferred to the code in Windows NT that handles them.

Prior to Windows NT 4.0, NTVDMs provided only 80286 emulation. This did not greatly affect MS-DOS applications, but it did affect Win16 applications because they could run only in Standard mode, not 386 Enhanced mode.

Because applications cannot directly access the hardware in the Windows NT architectural model, the NTVDM's virtual device drivers intercept any attempt by an application to access the hardware. The virtual device drivers translate the calls to 32-bit calls and pass them to the Windows NT 32-bit device drivers. This entire process is hidden from the MS-DOS-based applications. The NTVDM provides virtual device drivers for the mouse, keyboard, parallel ports, and COM ports.

If there isn't a virtual device driver for a particular hardware device, any application trying to access that hardware device directly cannot run in an NTVDM. Many MS-DOS applications do not execute in Windows NT for this reason.

You configure a Windows NT Virtual DOS Machine by customizing the application's Program Information File (PIF). (A shortcut to an MS-DOS application is assigned the extension .PIF.) To modify an application's PIF settings, right-click the shortcut to the application and choose Properties from the shortcut menu.

1. Configuring the Program Properties of a PIF

In the Program Properties dialog box for a PIF, you can configure default locations for where the program is located on the hard disk and the directory in which the program will execute. Table 17.1.1 shows the settings you can configure in the Program Properties dialog box.

Table 17.1.1 Program Property Settings

Setting	Description
Cmd Line	The full path to the MS-DOS application's executable file.
Working	Default directory to which you want to save an application's data files.
Batch File	The name of a batch file that runs each time the application is run. (This is functional only in the Windows 95 operating system.)
Shortcut key	Used to set a shortcut key combination for launching the application. To remove a shortcut key combination, use the Backspace key.
Run	Determines which windows state the program starts in. Choices include normal windows, minimized, or maximized.
Close on Exit	When selected, automatically closes the MS-DOS window in which the MS-DOS application runs.
Windows NT	Enables the application to specify tailored Autoexec and Config files that are processed every time the application is run.
Change Icon	Enables the user to change the icon displayed for the shortcut.

Each MS-DOS shortcut can point to a different Autoexec and Config file. By default, these are Autoexec.nt and Config.nt, which are located in the %Systemroot%\System32 directory. These configuration files must follow MS-DOS 5.0 conventions. This does not include multiple configurations.

2. Configuring the Memory Properties of a PIF

Running MS-DOS applications under Windows NT does ease one area of configuration. MS-DOS applications use one of two methods for providing additional memory beyond conventional memory:

- Expanded memory
- Extended memory

To configure these types of additional memory, you make configuration changes to the Config.sys file by modifying the Himem.sys and Emm386.exe drivers. In addition, you have to reboot the system every time that a configuration change is made in order to see the results. In Windows NT, these configuration changes have been moved from the Config.sys file to the Memory property tab of a PIF.

You can use the Memory dialog box of a PIF to allocate the exact amount of expanded memory specification (EMS) or extended memory specification (XMS) to allocate to a program. Instead of rebooting the system, you just restart the application for the new settings to take effect. You can also use the Memory page to set the amount of environment space that will be allocated to the Windows NT Virtual DOS Machine. That environment space is used to store all environment variables declared for the application.

One of the most difficult configurations for a DOS application is the proper memory setting. Most applications support only EMS or XMS memory. Be certain to select the appropriate type of memory you need to provide. If an application states that it is LIM-compatible, you need to provide EMS memory. If the application uses DPMI, you need to provide XMS memory.

C. Supporting Win16 Applications

Windows NT supports Windows 16-bit applications by using Win16 on Win32 (WOW). Note that the WOW environment runs within a Windows NT Virtual DOS Machine. This is just like Windows 3.x, which ran over MS-DOS. Table 17.1.2 describes the WOW components.

Table 17.1.2 WOW Components

Component	Description
Wowexec.exe	The Wowexec provides the Windows 3.1 emulation for the NTVDM.
WOW32.dll	The supporting dynamic link library for the Wowexec.
Win16 application	The Windows 16-bit application that is being executed. This application must not use any Windows 16-bit VxDs. Support may not be provided for them in Windows NT.
Krnl386.exe	This is a modified version of the Windows 3.x kernel. It translates calls meant for the Windows 3.x kernel to Win32 calls. Basic operating system functions are handled by Krnl386.exe.
User.exe	The User.exe is a modified version of the Windows 3.x User.exe. It handles all user interface API calls and translates them to Win32 calls.
Gdi.exe	The Gdi.exe captures API calls related to graphics and printing. These calls are translated to Win32 calls.

1. Running Multiple Win16 Applications

By default, the WOW environment provides non-preemptive multitasking as provided in Windows 3.x. This means that one application voluntarily gives up control of the processor to give another application access to the processor. The implication of this is that one 16-bit application can cause another 16-bit application to fail.

By default, Windows NT starts each 16-bit Windows application in the same Windows NT Virtual DOS Machine, and all Win16 applications share a single thread of execution. Therefore, if one Win16 application were to hang, all other Win16 applications would also hang.

Suppose Win16 App1, Win16 App2, and Win16 App3 are all running within a single NTVDM. Within the NTVDM, the three Win16 applications are non-preemptively multitasked. The NTVDM does have one thread of execution. This thread is preemptively multitasked with the two threads of Win32 App1 and the one thread of Win32 App2. If one of the Win16 applications fails, it affects only the other Win16 applications that share its memory space within the NTVDM. It does not affect the two Win32 applications because each of them is running in its own memory space.

You can determine what Win16 applications are running by viewing the processes in the Task Manager.

2. Running Win16 Applications in Individual NTVDMs

Multiple Win16 applications can be executed within their own individual NTVDMs under Windows NT. To do this, you must configure each Win16 application to run in a separate memory space. This enables Win16 applications to preemptively multitask because each Win16 application's NTVDM has a separate thread of execution.

Advantages to running Win16 applications in their own memory spaces include the following:

- *Preemptive multitasking.* Win16 applications can use preemptive multitasking, which means an ill-behaved Win16 application will not affect other Win16 applications. The other Win16 applications continue to execute normally because each Win16 application has its own memory space and thread of execution.
- *Reliability.* Win16 applications are more reliable because they are affected by the problems of other Win16 applications.
- *Multiprocessing capabilities.* Win16 applications can take advantage of multiprocessor computers. When Win16 applications are run in a common NTVDM, they must share a single thread of execution. When they're run in individual NTVDMs, they have individual threads of execution. Each thread can potentially be executed on a different processor.
- *OLE and DDE capabilities.* Windows NT enables Win16 applications running in separate memory spaces to continue to participate in OLE and dynamic data exchange (DDE).

As with any configuration change, there are some tradeoffs for the advantages gained by running Win16 applications in separate memory spaces. Disadvantages include the following:

- *Overhead.* Additional overhead is involved in running separate NTVDMs. If you do not have enough memory installed on the server, this could result in decreased system performance.
- *OLE and DDE problems.* Some older Win16 applications did not use the standards of OLE and DDE. These applications would not function properly if they were run in separate memory spaces. These applications must be run in a common memory space to function correctly. Lotus for Windows 1.0 is an example of this type of application.

Expect at least one question on running Win16 applications in separate memory spaces. The key concept is that you can load multiple Win16 applications into the same memory space only if it is the only Win16 NTVDM. It is impossible, for example, to run Word for Windows 6.0 and Excel for Windows 5.0 in one shared memory space and PowerPoint 4.0 and Access 2.0 in another shared memory space.

3. Configuring Win16 Applications to Run in Separate Memory Spaces

There are a few ways to run Win16 applications in separate memory spaces. These include the following:

- Anytime you start a Win16 application from the Start menu using the Run option, you can select the Run in Separate Memory Space option.

  The Run in Separate Memory Space option is available only when you type the path to a Win16 application. This is not available for any other type of applications because other types of applications run in their own memory space by default. Only Win16 applications share the same memory space by default.

- At a command prompt, type **start /separate *application*.exe**.
- Configure shortcuts that point to Win16 applications to always run in a separate memory space by using the option on the Shortcut tab of the Spinner Properties dialog box.
- Configure any file with a particular extension to always run in a separate memory space when the data document is double-clicked in the Windows NT Explorer. To configure this type of process, follow these steps:

  1. Start the Windows NT Explorer.
  2. From the View menu, choose Options.
  3. Click the File Types tab.
  4. For example, suppose your default application for displaying bitmap images is a 16-bit Windows application. To change its properties for execution, select Bitmap Image from the Registered File Types list, and then click the Edit button.
  5. From the list of possible actions, select Open, and then click the Edit button to modify the Open action.
  6. Change the Application Used to Perform Action option to make the application always run in a separate memory space. For example, to run the executable Imgmgr.exe in a separate memory space, you would set the executable to be **cmd /c start /separate c:\cw\imgmgr.exe %1** (see Figure 17.1.1).

17

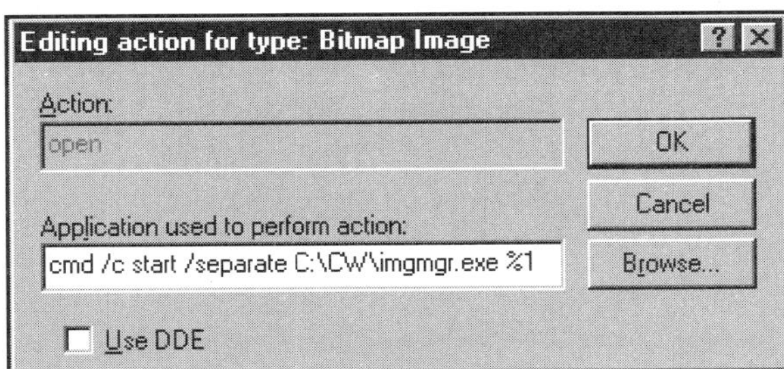

Figure 17.1.1 Configuring the Open action to always run in a separate memory space.

D. Supporting OS/2 Applications Under Windows NT

Windows NT has limited support for OS/2 applications. This list outlines the essentials of the OS/2 support Windows NT provides by default:

- OS/2 1.x-character-based applications are supported only on the Intel platform running the OS/2 subsystem.

- If the OS/2 application makes any calls to the Presentation Manager, by default they are not supported in the OS/2 subsystem.
- OS/2 applications can be executed on RISC-based Windows NT systems if the OS/2 applications are *bound* applications. Bound applications are those that have been written to execute in either OS/2 or MS-DOS. Because there is no OS/2 subsystem for RISC-based systems, these bound applications execute only in an NTVDM.

  You can force a bound application to execute in an NTVDM on an Intel-based Windows NT system by using the Forcedos command. By default though, bound applications always choose to run in the OS/2 subsystem because they execute faster in their native environment.

Expect at least one exam question that deals with the concept of bound applications and the Forcedos command. Remember that the only way to execute OS/2 applications on RISC-based systems is to use the Forcedos command for bound applications.

1. Configuring OS/2 Applications

As with all Windows NT configuration, the OS/2 configuration data is stored in the Windows NT Registry. This configuration data is stored in the following two locations:

- Hkey_Local_Machine\System\CurrentControlSet\Control\Session Manager\Subsystems
- Hkey_local_machine\Software\Microsoft\OS/2 Subsystem for NT

The OS/2 subsystem stores all its configuration information in the files Config.sys and Startup.cmd. When the OS/2 subsystem is started (when an OS/2 application is executed), Windows NT interprets the Config.sys and Startup.cmd files and adds the necessary configuration information to its Registry.

The suggested method for configuring the OS/2 subsystem is to edit the Config.sys file with an OS/2 text editor. You *must* use an OS/2 text editor because it places a header in the file that indicates the file is an OS/2 configuration file.

A common question on the exam tests your knowledge of configuring the OS/2 subsystem. Above all, remember that the Config.sys file must be edited with an OS/2 text editor.

2. Removing Support for the OS/2 Subsystem

The Windows NT Resource Kit includes a utility called the C2 Configuration Tool. The National Computer Security Center has created a set of security standards that are called the Orange Book. Windows NT 3.5x was evaluated as being C2 secure according to the specifications of the Orange Book. The Windows NT operating system supports security that is not part of the C2 security definition.

The OS/2 subsystem is not included in the current C2 security definition. Therefore, in order for Windows NT to meet the C2 security standards, the OS/2 subsystem must be disabled. The C2

Configuration Tool accomplishes this by deleting the OS2.exe and OS2ss.exe files from the %systemroot%\system32 subdirectory.

Another reason you might disable the OS/2 subsystem is that you are not using any OS/2 applications. However, if you need to restore the OS/2 subsystem later, you can do so by restoring the OS2.exe and OS2ss.exe files from the original Windows NT distribution files using the Expand command.

If you have the Windows NT Resource Kit, you can use the following steps to disable the OS/2 subsystem:

1. Start the C2 Configuration Tool (open the Start menu and choose Programs, Resource Kit 4.0, Configuration, C2 Configuration).
2. In the list of Security Features, double-click the OS/2 Subsystem entry. A dialog box appears.
3. Click the OK button to disable the OS/2 subsystem. A confirmation dialog box asks you to verify that you do want to remove the OS/2 subsystem from the computer and tells you that this action is not reversible. If this is acceptable, click the OK button. The icon to the left of the OS/2 subsystem now appears as a red closed lock, indicating full C2 Orange Book compliance.

E. Supporting POSIX Applications

POSIX (Portable Operating System Interfaced based on UNIX) support is provided in Windows NT because of a U.S. government requirement for government computing contracts. Because it includes support for POSIX applications, Windows NT can be considered for government quotes. The implementation of POSIX in Windows NT enables portability of common applications from a UNIX system to Windows NT running the POSIX subsystem.

Windows NT provides POSIX.1 support in its POSIX subsystem. POSIX.1 defines a C language source-code-level application programming interface (API) to an operating system environment. To have full POSIX.1 compliance, the NTFS file system must be implemented on the computer that will be executing POSIX applications. This provides the user with the following POSIX.1 compliance features:

- *Case-sensitive file naming.* NTFS preserves case for both directories and file names.
- *Hard links.* POSIX applications can store the same data in two differently named files.
- *An additional time stamp on files.* This tracks the last time the file was accessed. The default on FAT volumes is to track when the file was last modified.

1. Modifying Support for the POSIX Subsystem

For full POSIX.1 compliance, one of the Windows NT user rights must be modified. By default, the user right Bypass Traverse Checking is granted to the special group Everyone. This right enables a user to change directories through a directory tree even if the user has no permission for those directories. This user right must be disabled for all accounts that will be using POSIX applications.

To disable the Bypass Traverse Checking right, follow these steps:

1. Start the User Manager. To perform this process, you must be logged on as a member of the Administrators local group.
2. Create a Global group that contains all users who will *not* be running POSIX applications. It is imperative that no POSIX users be members of this Global group.
3. From the Policies menu, choose User Rights.
4. Ensure that the Show Advanced User Rights check box is selected.
5. Select the User Right Bypass Traverse Checking.
6. Click Remove to remove the Everyone group.
7. Click the Add button and select the New Global Group of Non-POSIX Users that you created in step 2. Then click the OK button to add this group.
8. Click the OK button to complete this user rights change.

2. Removing Support for the POSIX Subsystem

Like the OS/2 subsystem, the POSIX subsystem is not included in the current C2 security definition. Again, you can disable the POSIX subsystem by using the C2 Configuration Tool in the Windows NT Resource Kit. The C2 Configuration Tool accomplishes this by deleting the Psxss.exe file from the %systemroot%\system32 subdirectory.

To disable the POSIX subsystem, follow these steps:

1. Start the C2 Configuration Tool (open the Start menu and choose Programs, Resource Kit 4.0, Configuration, C2 Configuration).
2. In the list of Security Features, double-click the POSIX Subsystem entry.
3. Click the OK button to disable the POSIX subsystem.
4. Click the OK button to confirm that you do want to permanently remove support for the POSIX subsystem. The icon to the left of the POSIX subsystem now appears as a red closed lock, indicating full C2 Orange Book compliance.

Most exam questions on the POSIX subsystem focus on what features of NTFS provide support for POSIX.1 requirements. These include case-sensitive file naming, hard links, and access date information. Remember that if a POSIX application does not access file system resources, it can run on the FAT file system.

F. Application Support on RISC and Intel Platforms

Although you can run Windows NT on both the Intel and RISC platforms, you face compatibility issues when considering applications to support. Applications are either *source-compatible* or *binary-compatible.* Source-compatible applications must be recompiled for each hardware platform on which they are going to be executed. Binary-compatible applications can be run on any

Windows NT platform without recompiling the application. Table 17.1.3 outlines application compatibility on the Windows NT platforms.

Table 17.1.3 Application Compatibility Across Windows NT Platforms

Platform	MS-DOS	Win16	Win32	OS/2	POSIX
Intel	Binary	Binary	Source	Binary	Source
Alpha	Binary	Binary	Source*	Binary**	Source
Mips	Binary	Binary	Source	Binary**	Source
PowerPC	Binary	Binary	Source	Binary**	Source

* Third-party utilities such as Digital FX!32 enable Win32-based Intel programs to execute on Digital Alpha AXP microprocessors. Although these utilities interpret the code on-the-fly, they end up performing faster on the Alpha due to the increased speed of the processor.

** Only bound applications can be run on the three RISC hardware platforms. They will run in a Windows NTVDM because the OS/2 subsystem is not provided in RISC-based versions of Windows NT.

Typically, the exam tests your knowledge of the terms *source-compatible* and *binary-compatible*. Be sure to know the difference between the two and how each type of application is supported on each platform.

Although products such as Digital's FX!32 exist, the exam still considers Win32-based applications to be source-compatible across platforms, not binary-compatible.

G. Building Distributed Applications Across Platforms with DCOM

Distributed application development is based on creating applications made up of multiple components that can be spread across multiple platforms. The Distributed Component Object Model (DCOM) integrates the following capabilities to make the rapid development of distributed applications possible:

- DCOM supports communications between components over connection and connectionless network transports including TCP/IP, UDP/IP, IPX/SPX, AppleTalk, HTTP, and Remote Procedure Calls (RPCs). These objects can communicate over public networks such as the Internet.
- DCOM is an open technology capable of running on multiple implementations of UNIX-based systems, including Solaris.
- DCOM can lead to lower integration costs because DCOM is based on a common set of interfaces for software programs. This will lead to a lesser requirement for customization when implementing components from outside vendors.
- DCOM supports remote activation. A client can just start an application by calling a component on another computer.
- DCOM is capable of implementing Internet certificate-based security or Windows NT-based Challenge/Response security. This ensures the best of both worlds for security. Security is supported

for the launch of objects, access to objects, and context. Security can also be based on whether the application is launched locally or remotely.

In a pure Windows NT environment, RPCs can be used to allow communication and interoperability between various DCOM objects. RPCs make it possible for an application to execute procedures and call objects on other remote computers.

These steps outline the flow of communication for a DCOM application when a client makes a call to a DCOM object located on another server:

1. A client initiates a Remote Procedure Call.
2. The RPC client stub packages the call for transport across the network. The RPC runtime library on the client transmits the package to the indicated server, which it finds by using a name resolution method (this might include NetBIOS Name Server or Domain Name Server methods).
3. The RPC runtime library on the server receives the package and forwards it to its own RPC stub, which converts the package into the same RPC that was sent from the client.
4. The Remote Procedure Call is carried out at the security level specified in the Server object.
5. The RPC server stub packages the results of the procedure call, and the server's RPC runtime library transmits this package back to the calling client application.
6. The RPC runtime library on the client receives the package and forwards it to the client's RPC stub, which unpacks the data for the client application to use.

You need to know the basic configuration of DCOM objects. This includes where the application resides; who can access, launch, or modify a DCOM object; and whose security context is used to run the DCOM object.

17.1.1 Exercise: Configuring a Windows NT Virtual DOS Machine

Objective: To create a shortcut to an MS-DOS application and to modify a PIF for an MS-DOS application.

Time Estimate: 5 minutes

This exercise investigates some of the configuration that can be done to an NTVDM. Follow these steps:

1. Right-click the desktop and choose New Shortcut from the shortcut menu.
2. Enter **c:\winnt\system32\edit.com** as the command line. (This assumes that Windows NT is installed in the c:\winnt directory; substitute your directory if it differs.)
3. Click the Next button, and the Create Shortcut dialog box should suggest MS-DOS Editor as the shortcut name.
4. Click Finish to complete the creation of the shortcut.
5. Double-click the newly created shortcut to start the MS-DOS Editor.

6. Press the Esc key to bypass the display of the survival guide. The MS-DOS Editor runs in a DOS window and, by default, enables you to use the mouse. By pressing the Alt and Enter keys simultaneously, you can switch to full-screen mode. Note that the mouse pointer switches to a box on-screen.

   You will now modify the NTVDM to automatically run full screen and to disable the capability to switch between Full-Screen and Windowed modes.

7. Exit the MS-DOS Editor by choosing Exit from the File menu.
8. Right-click the shortcut to the MS-DOS Editor and choose Properties from the pop-up menu.
9. On the Program tab, change the command line to read **c:\winnt\system32\edit.com /h** to change the display of the editor to 32 lines.
10. On the Screen tab, set the Usage to Full Screen. Also increase the initial size to 43 lines.
11. On the Misc tab, deselect the check box next to Alt+Enter. This prevents the switching between Full-Screen and Windowed modes.
12. Click the OK button to apply all your changes to the MS-DOS Editor's NTVDM, and then double-click its shortcut to start the MS-DOS Editor.

    Note that the MS-DOS Editor now runs full screen with 43 display lines. Try switching to Windowed mode by using the Alt+Enter key combination. This should not work!

Answers and Explanations: Exercise

This exercise shows how easy it is to create a PIF because Windows NT now recognizes that the application is an MS-DOS-based application and the shortcut's properties sheet now contains PIF settings. Try making additional settings to the configuration of the PIF and test the implications of each change.

For more information about the topics covered in this exercise, refer to the sections titled "Supporting MS-DOS Applications," "Configuring the Program Properties of a PIF," "Configuring the Memory Properties of a PIF," and "Configuring a PIF's Miscellaneous Settings."

17.1.2 Exercise: Running Win16 Applications in Separate Memory Spaces

Objectives: To run Win16 applications in the same memory space, to run Win16 applications in separate memory spaces, and to use Task Manager to view running processes.

Time Estimate: 10 minutes

This exercise makes use of a 16-bit Windows utility to investigate how by default, Windows NT runs Win16 applications in the same memory space. It doesn't matter which 16-bit Windows application is used. Please use one that you download or have installed. This exercise then investigates how Windows NT can run Win16 applications on a separate memory space.

1. Locate a 16-bit Windows program, and then double-click it.
2. Double-click the 16-bit Windows program again to open a second instance of the program.
3. Right-click the taskbar and choose Task Manager from the pop-up menu.

4. On the Process tab, look for the NTVDM.EXE process. Note that both instances of the program are running in the same NTVDM.EXE.
5. Close both instances of the program.
6. From the Start menu, choose Run.
7. Using the Browse button, select the 16-bit Windows program, and then click OK to return to the Run dialog box.
8. Select the Run in Separate Memory Space option and click the OK button to start the program.
9. Repeat steps 6 through 9 to run a second instance of the program in its own separate memory space.
10. Start the Task Manager. Note that each instance of the program is running in its own NTVDM. In fact, you should also see the default NTVDM with only Wowexec.exe running in it.
11. Close all instances of the program and the Task Manager.

Answers and Explanations: Exercise

This exercise shows that by default, Windows NT runs Win16 applications in a shared memory space. To run applications in separate memory spaces requires configuration beyond the defaults. The Task Manager enables the user to view which processes are running and whether Win16 applications are running in separate or shared memory spaces. For further investigation, try creating a shortcut to Spind16.exe on the desktop and configuring the shortcut to run in a separate memory space.

For more information about the topics covered in this exercise, refer to the sections titled “Supporting Win16 Applications,” “Running Multiple Win16 Applications,” “Running Win16 Applications in Individual NTVDMs,” and “Configuring Win16 Applications to Run in Separate Memory Spaces.”

17.1 Practice Problems

1. Which of the following types of multitasking are taking place when a system is running two 16-bit Windows applications (not in separate memory spaces), one DOS session, and two 32-bit Windows applications?

   A. Multithreaded

   B. Multiprocessor

   C. Cooperative

   D. Preemptive

2. Which of the following types of multitasking are taking place when a system is running one 16-bit Windows application (not in a separate memory space), one DOS session, and two 32-bit Windows applications?

   A. Multithreaded

   B. Multiprocessor

   C. Cooperative

   D. Preemptive

3. Which of the following types of multitasking are taking place when a system is running two 16-bit Windows applications in separate memory spaces, one DOS session, and two 32-bit Windows applications?

   A. Multithreaded

   B. Multiprocessor

   C. Cooperative

   D. Preemptive

4. You have a new DEC Alpha system, and you need to run software from the corporate IS department. Which types of applications will you be able to run without recompiling or purchasing additional software?

   A. DOS-based

   B. Windows 3.1-based

   C. OS/2-based, non-bound

   D. POSIX

5. You frequently run multiple Windows 3.1 applications on your machine and want to increase the performance of these applications. You have a Pentium 133 with a dual processor-capable motherboard. What is the *best* way to improve performance?

   A. Add a second processor.

   B. Install a faster processor.

   C. Install a second processor, add memory, and run each application in a separate memory space.

   D. Set up a dual boot with Windows 3.1 and run the Windows 3.1 apps in Windows 3.1.

17

6. If you want to run a DOS program with special settings, which file should you use?

   A. A PIF file

   B. CONFIG.NT

   C. AUTOEXEC.NT

   D. DOSOPT.CFG

7. How much memory can a 32-bit application access?

   A. 16MB

   B. 1GB

   C. 2GB

   D. 4GB

8. You've installed a new 32-bit accounting system to replace the previous 16-bit system. You're concerned about other applications crashing and taking down the new accounting system. What should you do?

   A. Run the accounting application in a separate memory space.

   B. Run all 16-bit Windows applications in separate memory spaces.

C. Run all DOS applications in separate memory spaces.

D. Nothing.

9. Which of the following are advantages of running Win16 applications in their own separate memory spaces?

A. More efficient OLE capabilities

B. Preemptive multitasking

C. Non-preemptive multitasking

D. Greater reliability (one Win16 application that crashes does not affect other Win16 applications)

E. Support for multiple processors

10. An OS/2 application that can also be executed in an NTVDM is known as what type of application?

A. Dynamic

B. 32-bit

C. Flexible

D. Bound

Answers and Explanations: Practice Problems

1. **C, D** Multithreaded and multiprocessor are not types of multitasking. Cooperative multitasking exists whenever two or more 16-bit Windows programs are running in the same memory space, and preemptive is used for any non-16-bit Windows applications.

2. **D** Multithreaded and multiprocessor are not types of multitasking. Cooperative multitasking isn't being used because there is only one 16-bit Windows application. Preemptive multitasking is always used by Windows NT.

3. **D** Multithreaded and multiprocessor are not types of multitasking. Cooperative multitasking isn't being used here because each 16-bit Windows application is in a separate memory space. Preemptive multitasking is always used in Windows NT.

4. **A, B** All versions of Windows NT support 16-bit Intel applications, either via native processor support or via translation. However, RISC-based (read Alpha) systems can't run 32-bit Intel applications without additional software. OS/2 isn't supported unless a DOS version is bound in, and POSIX is a source code standard, not a binary compatibility standard.

5. **C** Adding a second processor as suggested in answer A won't help because the applications are running in the same VDM. Adding a faster processor will improve performance, but only marginally. Adding the processor, adding memory, and changing each app to run in a separate memory space will give the most improvement because the applications will be able to use both processors, effectively doubling performance. The additional memory is to offset the additional memory requirement necessary to run each application in its own memory space. Answer D, using Windows 3.1, will actually decrease performance because the caching function and asynchronous disk I/Os are much better in Windows NT.

6. **A** A PIF, or Program Information File, tells Windows NT how to run a DOS application. Although CONFIG.NT and AUTOEXEC.NT are the default files used by the DOS PIF, they aren't typically modified for a single application. DOSOPT.CFG is a fictional file; it doesn't exist.

7. **C** Each 32-bit application is given 2GB of virtual memory to use. Although Windows NT supports 4GB per application, 2GB of that is reserved for the operating system.

8. **D** 32-bit Windows applications are automatically protected from other applications that crash. No additional configuration is necessary. Option A isn't

valid: Because each 32-bit Windows application already runs in a separate memory space, running in a separate memory space is not an option.

9. **B, D, E** Running Win16 applications in their own separate memory spaces enables them to participate in preemptive multitasking because each Win16 application has a separate thread of execution. Running the applications in separate memory spaces also prevents the crash of one Win16 application from affecting other Win16 applications. Finally, when each Win16 application has a separate thread of execution, they can take advantage of multiple processors in the system because Windows NT can schedule each thread independently. For more information on this issue, refer to the section titled "Running Win16 Applications in Individual NTVDMs."

10. **D** Bound applications run more efficiently under OS/2 environments, but they can also run in MS-DOS environments. This is the only type of OS/2 application that can be run on a RISC-based Windows NT system. For more information, refer to the section titled "Supporting OS/2 Applications Under Windows NT."

17.1 Key Words

bound

NTVDM

process

SMP

thread

17.2 Starting Applications at Different Priorities

Under preemptive multitasking, Windows NT determines which application should get access to the processor for execution by using priority levels. Each application starts at a base priority level of eight. The system dynamically adjusts the priority level to give all applications processor access. The process or thread with the highest priority base at any one time has access to the processor. Some of the factors that cause Windows NT to adjust the priority of a process or thread include the following:

- Windows NT boosts the base priority of whichever process is running in the foreground. This ensures that the response time is maximized for the currently used application.
- Windows NT randomly boosts the priority for lower-priority threads. This has two major benefits. The first benefit is that low-priority threads that would normally not be able to run can do so after their priority base is raised. The second benefit is that if a lower-priority process has access to a resource that is to be shared with a higher-priority process, the higher-priority process could end up monopolizing the resource. The boost in the lower-priority thread's base priority frees up the resource sooner.
- Anytime a thread has been in a voluntary wait state, Windows NT boosts its priority. The size of the boost depends on how long the resource has been in a wait state.

Priority levels 0 through 15 are used by dynamic applications. Anything running at a dynamic level can be written to the Windows NT Pagefile. By default, this includes user applications and operating system functions that are not imperative to the performance of the operating system. Priority levels 16 through 31 are reserved for real-time applications that cannot be written to the Windows NT Pagefile. This includes all Executive Services and the Windows NT Kernel.

A. Starting Applications at Different Levels

The user can change the default priority level from Normal by using the command prompt to start an application, or he can adjust the priority level after the application has started by using the Task Manager. Table 17.2.1 shows the four priority levels the user can set.

Table 17.2.1 Base Priority Levels Under Windows NT

Priority Level	Base Priority	Command Line
Low	4	Start /low executable.exe
Normal	8	Start /normal executable.exe
High	13	Start /high executable.exe
Realtime	24	Start /realtime executable.exe

Be very careful about running any application at the Realtime base priority. This could slow down the performance of your system because no other applications will be able to access the processor for I/O. Windows NT protects against the usage of Realtime base priority by allowing only members of the Administrators group to run applications at this level.

After an application is running, you can use the Task Manager to change the base priority. To change the priority of a running application, follow these steps:

1. Right-click the taskbar and select Properties from the shortcut menu.
2. Click the Task Manager option on the taskbar.
3. Click the Processes tab to view all running processes.
4. If the Base Priority column is not visible, add it to the view by choosing Select Columns from the View menu. In the resulting dialog box, ensure that Base Priority is selected.
5. Right-click the process in the Process list.
6. Click Set Priority, and then click the desired priority at which you want the process to run.

B. Changing the Default Priority Boost for Foreground Applications

On some Windows NT computers, you might want to improve the responsiveness of background applications. By default, the foreground application is given a priority boost of two levels. This changes the base priority for foreground applications to 10 from the default of 8 in the case of Normal priority applications. If you want to change that level, follow these steps:

1. In Control Panel, double-click the System applet.
2. In the System Properties dialog box, click the Performance tab.
3. The Performance tab contains an Application Performance setting that determines whether foreground applications are given a priority boost over background applications. Select from these three settings:
   - If the slider is set to None, no boost is given to foreground applications over background applications. This setting is preferred for file and print servers and application servers so that running a utility on the server will not affect any client connection performance.
   - If the slider is set to the middle setting, the foreground application receives a boost of one level over background applications.
   - The default setting is to have the priority boost set to Maximum. This gives a foreground application a priority increase of two levels over background applications. This is the preferred setting for Windows NT Workstation acting as a client's workstation.

Common questions about base priorities include how to start an application at a different base priority using the start command with the /low, /normal, /high, and /realtime switches.

17.2.1 Exercise: Changing Priorities of Applications

Objective: To start programs at different base priority levels and then change the base priority on-the-fly.

Time Estimate: 5 minutes

Follow these steps:

1. Log on as the administrator of your Windows NT Workstation computer.
2. Start a command prompt by choosing Start, Programs, Command Prompt.
3. Type **start /low sol.exe** to start Solitaire at a low base priority. This sets the base priority to four.
4. Type **start /realtime freecell.exe**.
5. Close the command prompt.
6. Start the Task Manager.
7. Change focus to the Processes tab. If you do not see the Base Priority column, you must add it by choosing Select Columns from the View menu. In the Select Columns dialog box, click the Base Priority check box .
8. Note that the Freecell.exe process is currently running at a base priority of Realtime. Right-click the Freecell.exe process in the Process list to change the base priority. In the pop-up menu that appears, choose Set Priority. Then select Normal to reset the base priority to the default level.
9. Use the same basic procedure to change the base priority for Sol.exe to Normal.

Answers and Explanations: Exercise

This exercise shows that you can start applications at base priorities other than Normal. Remember, however, that you must be an administrator to change the base priority to Realtime.

For more information on the topics covered in this exercise, refer to the sections titled "Starting Applications at Different Priorities," "Starting Applications at Different Levels," and "Changing the Default Priority Boost for Foreground Applications."

17.2 Practice Problems

1. What is the default priority of an application that is run from the Explorer or the Run command?

   A. NORMAL

   B. BASE

   C. STANDARD

   D. INTERACTIVE

2. Without changing the priority of an application, what can you do to make it run more quickly?

   A. Terminate other applications

   B. Bring that application to the foreground

   C. Maximize the application window

   D. Move the mouse in circles

3. How do you start MYAPP.EXE with a low priority?

   A. START /LOW MYAPP.EXE

   B. START MYAPP.EXE /LOW

   C. START /IDLE MYAPP.EXE

   D. START MYAPP.EXE /IDLE

4. Which of the following are valid switches for the Start command?

   A. /base

   B. /separate

   C. /high

   D. /kernel

5. What methods can you use to stop an unresponsive program?

   A. Task Manager

   B. Control Panel's System applet

   C. Kill.exe

   D. Server Manager

6. Which groups have the capability to run applications at the Realtime base priority?

   A. Server operators

   B. Administrators

   C. Account operators

   D. Replicator

7. You have several macros in Excel that you want to run faster in the background when you are working on other applications. How do you accomplish this?

   A. Run the foreground processes using the /separate switch

   B. Run Excel in its own memory space

   C. Increase the base priority for Excel spreadsheets in the Registry

   D. Use the System option in the Control Panel to lower the boost given to foreground applications

8. Which priority should users select if they want an application to run quickly?

   A. LOW

   B. NORMAL

   C. HIGH

   D. REALTIME

9. You want to run a realtime application on your workstation. The application will use 32MB of RAM. How much RAM must you have to run Windows NT?

   A. 12MB

   B. 32MB

   C. 44MB

   D. 64MB

Answers and Explanations: Practice Problems

1. **A** The standard priority for all applications is normal. Other priorities include low, high, and realtime.

17

2. **A, B** Terminating applications obviously removes any contention and makes the application run faster. If you put the application in the foreground, the system will boost its priority automatically. Maximizing the window has no effect on the priority given to the application, and moving the mouse in circles actually increases the run time because redrawing the mouse pointer steals CPU cycles from the application.

3. **A** The correct command line option is /LOW, and it must precede the application name. Any parameters listed after the application are assumed to be the application's parameters, not parameters for start.

4. **B, C** The /separate switch is used to start Win16 applications in their own separate memory spaces, and the /high switch is used to start an application with a base priority of 13 instead of the default of 8. For more information, refer to the sections titled "Configuring Win16 Applications to Run in Separate Memory Spaces" and "Starting Applications at Different Levels."

5. **A, C** You can stop most applications by using the Task Manager. In addition, the Resource Kit's Kill utility enables you to kill any process. For more information, refer to "Running Win16 Applications in Individual NTVDMs."

6. **B** Only administrators can start an application using the /realtime switch. This level is normally reserved for operating system functions. For more information, refer to the section titled "Starting Applications at Different Levels."

7. **D** Even though the Excel application is running in the background, changing the priority boost for foreground applications works in this case because lowering the boost for the application that you are working on enables the macro to execute in the background. For more information, refer to the section titled "Changing the Default Priority Boost for Foreground Applications."

8. **C** Realtime is the highest priority, but is available only to administrators. The highest priority a user can set is HIGH.

9. **C** Windows NT Workstation requires 12MB of RAM to run, and the realtime application requires 32MB. Because realtime applications can't be swapped out, the machine must have 44MB of RAM.

17.2 Key Words

HIGH priority

LOW priority

NORMAL

REALTIME

START

Practice Exam: Running Applications

Use this practice exam to test your mastery of Running Applications. This practice exam contains 21 questions. The passing Microsoft score is 70.4 percent. Questions are in multiple-choice format.

1. What command causes an OS/2 application to execute in an NTVDM?

   A. start /ntvdm os2app.exe

   B. start /separate os2app.exe

   C. Forcedos

   D. Forcecmd

2. POSIX.1 support in Windows NT includes which of the following features?

   A. Additional time stamp

   B. Hard links

   C. Binary compatibility

   D. Case-sensitive naming

3. What utility is used to configure DCOM applications?

   A. DCOMCONF.EXE

   B. SRVMGR.EXE

   C. REGEDT32.exe

   D. Dcomcnfg.exe

4. What files are used to configure an NTVDM by default?

   A. Autoexec.bat

   B. Autoexec.nt

   C. Config.sys

   D. Config.nt

5. You have made changes to the Config.sys file to reflect the configuration changes you want for the OS/2 subsystem, but the changes are ignored. What's the cause of this?

   A. There is a boot-sector virus.

   B. You configure the OS/2 subsystem by modifying the Registry.

   C. You cannot use an OS/2 configuration editor to edit Config.sys

   D. OS/2 configuration is saved to the %systemroot%\system32\config.os2 file.

6. You download a new POSIX utility from the Internet to run on your DEC Alpha AXP system running Windows NT. The application does not run. Why?

   A. POSIX applications are binary-compatible.

   B. The POSIX subsystem must be configured to auto start in the Control Panel in order to run POSIX applications.

   C. POSIX applications are source-compatible.

   D. The POSIX subsystem must be unloaded.

7. MS-DOS applications are compatible across which platforms? (Pick any that apply.)

   A. Source

   B. Processor

   C. Thread

   D. Binary

8. Applications belonging to which of the following operating systems can be run in Windows NT?

   A. Windows 95

   B. VMS

   C. IRIX

   D. Windows 3.1

9. How many POSIX applications can run on Windows NT at one time?

   A. 1

   B. 10

   C. 16

   D. 32

10. Which types of applications have the option of being run in separate memory spaces?

    A. Windows 95

    B. Windows 3.1

    C. OS/2

    D. DOS

11. If you are running one DOS session, one 32-bit Windows application, and one 16-bit Windows application, how many separate tasks is Windows NT managing?

    A. 1

    B. 2

    C. 3

    D. 4

12. If you are running one DOS session and one 32-bit Windows application, how many separate tasks is Windows NT managing?

    A. 1

    B. 2

    C. 3

    D. 4

13. If you are running one DOS session, two 16-bit Windows applications, and one 32-bit Windows application, how many separate tasks is Windows NT managing?

    A. 1

    B. 2

    C. 3

    D. 4

14. Two users want to get 600MHz DEC Alpha computers to replace their 486 computers, but they are concerned about the speed of their 16-bit Windows applications. What do you tell them?

    A. The DEC Alpha won't run their applications.

    B. The DEC Alpha will run their 16-bit applications more slowly.

    C. The DEC Alpha will run their 16-bit applications more quickly.

    D. The DEC Alpha will run their programs at about the same speed.

15. You're standardizing your corporate environment on Windows 95 and Windows NT machines. The engineering department wants to get DEC Alpha-based workstations but you tell them no. Why?

    A. DEC Alpha-based computers' data files are incompatible with Intel based data files.

    B. The network won't support DEC Alpha-based computers.

    C. The building isn't wired for Alpha computers.

    D. Alpha computers cannot run all 32-bit applications.

16. Through which subsystem are all graphics routed?

    A. WOW (Windows on Windows)

    B. Win32

    C. OS/2

    D. POSIX

17. How many processors does Windows NT Workstation support?

    A. 1

    B. 2

    C. 4

    D. 32

18. What does SMP stand for?
    A. Symmetric Multi-Processing
    B. System Multiple Process
    C. Systemic Mutation Processing
    D. Symmetric Media Processing

19. Which programs can take advantage of multiple threads?
    A. DOS
    B. Windows 3.1
    C. OS/2
    D. POSIX

20. Each thread can run on how many processors simultaneously?
    A. 1
    B. 2
    C. 3
    D. As many as the machine has installed

21. Which of the following are requirements of DCOM? Choose all that apply.
    A. The same protocol be running on all systems.
    B. The operating system must support RPC.
    C. The application must be written in C++.
    D. The application must be written in Visual Basic.

Answers and Explanations: Practice Exam

1. **C** The Forcedos command must be used to run bound applications in MS-DOS mode on RISC-based Windows NT systems. For more information, refer to the section titled "Supporting OS/2 Applications Under Windows NT."

2. **A, B, D** With the NTFS file system, Windows NT provides hard links (the capability to store the same data in two files with different names, where changing the data in one also changes the data of the other). Case-sensitive naming is also supported for POSIX applications, which means that Data.txt and DATA.txt are two different files. Finally, POSIX support provides for not only a last-modified time stamp, but also a last-accessed time stamp. For more information, refer to the section titled "Supporting POSIX Applications."

3. **D** The Dcomcnfg.exe utility is used to configure DCOM applications. It must be run on both the client computer that will call the DCOM object and the server computer that will host the DCOM object. For more information, refer to the section titled "Building Distributed Applications Across Platforms with DCOM."

4. **B, D** The Autoexec.nt and Config.nt files are stored in the %systemroot%\System32 subdirectory. Remember that each PIF can have its own Config and Autoexec files. These are set by using the Advanced button on the Program tab of the PIF. For more information, refer to the section titled "Configuring the Program Properties of a PIF."

5. **C** The Config.sys file is not simply a text file as it is under MS-DOS, and it must be saved using an OS/2 configuration editor. For more information, refer to the section titled "Configuring OS/2 Applications."

6. **C** POSIX applications must be compiled for each platform on which they are going to run. Be careful: Most applications that you find by default on the Internet for Windows NT are compiled for the Intel platform. For more information, refer to the section titled "Application Support on RISC and Intel Platforms."

7. **D** MS-DOS applications are binary-compatible across platforms and do not need to be recompiled to run under RISC

systems. The Intel Instruction Unit provides the Intel emulation, and the NTVDM provides an environment for the MS-DOS applications to run under. For more information, refer to the section titled "Application Support on RISC and Intel Platforms."

8. **A, D** Windows NT can run applications that were written for Windows 95, Windows 3.1, OS/2 1.x, Windows NT, and DOS.

9. **D** Windows NT supports 32 simultaneous POSIX applications.

10. **B** Although all of those listed can run in separate memory spaces, Windows 3.1 applications are the only ones for which you have the *option* of running in a separate memory space.

11. **C** Each application is running in a separate memory space. Additional 16-bit applications won't run separately.

12. **C** Even though no 16-bit Windows applications are running, there is still a process running for 16-bit application support.

13. **C** Even though four applications are running, the two 16-bit Windows applications are running in the same virtual machine and are considered one task by the Windows NT scheduler.

14. **C** Even though the DEC Alpha has to translate the instructions, it's much faster and will improve the speed of their applications.

15. **D** Windows NT supports only 16-bit Intel applications on Alpha. Digital's FX!32 doesn't work for all applications.

16. **B** The Win32 subsystem is considered the master subsystem and handles all graphics calls.

17. **D** Windows NT Workstation has been run on OEM HALs with 32 processors.

18. **A** SMP stands for Symmetric Multi-Processing.

19. **C, D** Both OS/2 and POSIX have multithreaded support; 16-bit DOS and Windows applications do not.

20. **A** A thread is limited to running on a single processor at one time.

21. **A, B** DCOM is built upon RPC calls, which may be on different operating systems but must use the same protocol.

Chapter 18

Monitoring and Optimization

Monitoring and optimization of the Windows NT Workstation 4.0 product can be broken into three parts. This chapter prepares you for the exam by covering each of these objectives:

- Monitoring system performance
- Identifying and resolving performance problems
- Optimizing system performance

Based on whether it's running as a standalone system or networked in a Windows NT domain, the Windows NT Workstation 4.0 product will have very different issues to be considered. This chapter focuses on Windows NT Workstation 4.0 in a simple Windows NT domain networked environment. Four tools are used frequently in this chapter:

- Task Manager
- Performance Monitor
- The Server applet in Control Panel
- The WinMSD Utility

To implement changes, you must make use of several Windows NT features. For this reason, a fair understanding of Windows NT is required before you can start to monitor and modify performance.

18.1 Monitoring System Performance

This section takes a close look at the activities going on behind the scenes of Windows NT Workstation 4.0. Unfortunately, no absolute correct answer or value can be given to a specific reading. The goal here is to explain the purpose and use of each tool.

The only method of evaluating a given result is to compare it to a benchmark value. These benchmarks will be gathered over time and should be kept on record. Microsoft and some third-party magazines publish some guideline values that are mentioned in this chapter. However, these guidelines are only examples and suggestions. Remember that each system and situation differs. Thus you may not be able to implement some of the suggestions mentioned in this chapter.

A. Using the Task Manager

The Task Manager tool offers a quick overview of key system resources, such as memory and CPU usage, the status of applications currently running, and processes in use on the system. You can invoke the Task Manager in several ways, including the following:

- Right-click the taskbar and select Task Manager.
- Press Ctrl+Alt+Delete, and then select Task Manager.
- Press Ctrl+Shift+Esc.

There are three tabs in the Task Manager that can be used for monitoring certain system resources and shutting down applications. These tabs are the Applications tab, the Processes tab, and the Performance tab, all described in the next sections.

1. Applications Tab

This tab displays all running applications and allows you to terminate applications. Terminating an application from the Task Manager is useful when a program crashes and cannot be shut down normally. An application may be "frozen" and unable to respond to commands, possibly using valuable system resources.

Remember that DOS and 32-bit applications run in their own memory address spaces with very little sharing of resources between them. On the other hand, 16-bit applications share the same memory address space and message queue with all other running 16-bit applications. When one application fails to respond to the user or the operating system, it blocks all other 16-bit applications from responding.

2. Processes Tab

Each application may run several processes simultaneously. The Windows NT operating system runs several processes at a time. You can consider a process a subset of programming code used to run applications.

Windows NT services are also processes: They use system resources such as memory and CPU time. You can monitor each process in the Processes tab of the Task Manager. To free system resources for other applications and processes, you should end services not being used (see the section titled "Running Windows NT Services").

You can sort the processes in the Task Manager in ascending or descending order based on data in any visible column. You can change columns to reflect different information. Fourteen information columns are available. By changing the sort order and/or the columns listed, you can organize information by importance; thus less time is wasted on idle or low-impact processes.

The Processes tab of the Task Manager has four default-selected columns (see Table 18.1.1). You can choose to add several other columns for more fine-tuned monitoring by selecting the Select Columns choice from the View menu.

Table 18.1.1 Default-Selected Columns in the Processes Tab of Task Manager

Column	Description
Image Name	The process currently running
PID	Process identifier (a unique number)
CPU Usage	Current percentage of CPU's usage allocated to this process
CPU Time	Total time the process has used on the CPU
Memory Usage	The amount of memory allocated to this process

3. Performance Tab

The Performance tab displays a summary of memory, CPU usage, and general indicators. The first part of the Performance tab shows the CPU usage and CPU history. These indicators show the total usage of the CPU by either the operating system or an application. The CPU usage indicates the percentage of the CPU in use at the last update count. The history displays the last few updates. The default update time is approximately one second. You can change this value by using the Update Speed command in the View menu. Selecting a low update count allows for a longer time in the history window. Table 18.1.2 lists the four main categories in the Performance tab.

Table 18.1.2 Main Categories in the Performance Tab

Category	Description
Totals	
Handles	The number of file handles opened on the system.
Threads	The total number of application threads in use by all applications.
Processes	Total number of processes in use by all applications.
Physical Memory	
Total	Actual RAM in the computer.
Available	Physical RAM available that can be allocated to a process.
File Cache	The amount of physical RAM used by the file cache.
Commit Charge	
Total	The total amount of memory allocated. This includes physical and virtual memory.
Limit	Total amount of memory the system can use before the pagefile needs to be increased. This is using the current size of the pagefile, not the maximum or minimum necessarily.
Peak	The largest amount of memory that has been used this session.

continues

Table 18.1.2 Continued

Category	Description
Kernel Memory	
Total	The total amount of memory, both paged and nonpaged, being used by the kernel.
Paged	The amount of memory that the kernel is using and that can be swapped to the pagefile.
Nonpaged	The memory that cannot be paged while in use.

The Performance Monitor tool shows all these counters in much more detail. The Task Manager is used to obtain a quick overview of the system. Information cannot be logged or printed from the Task Manager.

B. Using the Performance Monitor

The Performance Monitor takes the Task Manager to the next level of detail. The entire system's operations as well as the application's performance can be monitored, charted, logged, or displayed in a report. The Performance Monitor enables remote monitoring of other Windows NT 4.0 systems, assuming that administrative rights are available for the remote system.

Information is presented under the following three components:

- Performance monitoring items (such as the Processor, Memory, and so on) are categorized as objects.
- Each object has counters that can be monitored.
- There may be several instances of each counter.

An object is broken down into several counters, and counters are broken down into instances. There are three types of counters: instantaneous, averaging, and difference. Windows NT 4.0 now includes a total instance for most counters, as well as individual instances for more detail. Instances shown may vary depending on the applications or features running. The number of objects available depends on the Windows NT features installed. A special set of TCP/IP counters shows up only if SNMP protocol is loaded along with Service Pack 1 or later. Disk performance counters show up only if DISKPERF -y is run.

Objects found in the Performance Monitor may vary depending on the current configuration of Windows NT. Table 18.1.3 shows common objects that are always available.

Table 18.1.3 Common Objects Always Available in the Performance Monitor

Object	Description
Cache	The file system cache, an area of physical memory that holds recently used data.
Logical Disk	Disk partitions and other logical views of disk space.
Memory	Random access memory used to store code and data.
Objects	Certain system software objects.

Object	Description
Paging File	The file used to support virtual memory allocated by the system.
Physical Disk	Hardware disk unit.
Process	Software object that represents a running program.
Processor	Hardware unit that executes program instructions.
Redirector	File system that diverts file requests to network servers.
System	Counters that apply to all system hardware and software.
Thread	The part of a process that uses the processor.

1. Using Charts

The Performance Monitor can show the system's performance in an easy-to-read chart format. The default view is the Chart view. It is the easiest to use initially. Data can be viewed in a chart format as live data or from a prerecorded log file. Live data must be monitored constantly and evaluated on the spot. A prerecorded log file can gather data for several hours or more and can be monitored at a more convenient time. Current or live data is explained in this section; log files are covered in the next section.

To decide which data is going to be presented on the chart, use the Data From command on the Options menu. Two choices are presented: Current Activity (to view live data) and Log File (to open a previously recorded log file). Using the ellipsis button (...), you can browse the hard drive to find and obtain the log file.

18

Each charted value uses a scale shown at the bottom of the screen just before the counter name. A scale of 1.000 indicates that the counter was not scaled up or down. Imagine a point on the performance chart where the counter value is 50. A scale ratio of 0.100 shows that 50 has been multiplied by 0.1 (divided by 10) for a true value of 5. A ratio of 10 shows that the value was multiplied by 10 for a true value of 50. Multiply the value on the chart by the scale to get a true value.

Another useful option for easier viewing and analysis of performance charts is the grid option. Select Chart from the Options menu (or press Ctrl+O) to display the Chart Options dialog box. Here you can check or uncheck Vertical and Horizontal Grid Lines to control whether gridlines are displayed on your chart. You can also change the chart display from a graph to a histogram, as well as tweak and customize some other viewing preferences.

You can obtain further statistics on any chart line by clicking the counter name at the bottom of the screen. Just above the list of displayed counters are the last, average, minimum, and maximum values of the current item. To highlight a chart item on the screen, click the item name and press Ctrl+H. The emphasized counter is shown in a thick white line.

You cannot print charts from Performance Monitor, but you can export them to a tab separated value (.TSV) file or a comma separated value (.CSV) file. These files contain the data without the chart lines. The Export Chart menu is found under File. You can open these files from a spreadsheet or database for analysis and further charting.

You can gain more information about the role of the performance counters of each object by selecting the object and counter in the Add Counter dialog box and clicking the Explain>> button.

2. Using Logs

In most cases, just watching current data flowing across the screen is not a thorough analysis. Log files are designed to watch the system and record activity in a file that can be reviewed later. You can also use log files to compare the system's performance at different times. All object information that can be monitored live can also be logged to a file.

Creating a log and analyzing data from a log are two distinct processes. Creating a log involves selecting the objects to be monitored, selecting the file in which to store the logged information, and specifying an interval time at which to collect data. Notice that you are not selecting counters or instances for each object; all counters and instances are recorded in the log file. The individual counters and instances are selected when the log file is analyzed. When you create a log file, you specify only the performance objects you want to log. Once the log file has run for the necessary amount of time, you can open it with the other Performance Monitor tools and choose specific counters for all of the specified objects.

The smaller the update time interval, the larger the file will be. Such a file will, however, offer a lot of detail. On the other hand, a larger interval will show a trend, but it may not reflect a specific problem. If a log is to run overnight, do not use a 15-second interval. Try 15-minute (900 second) or 30-minute (1800 second) intervals instead.

If you create a new log file using the same name, it overwrites the old one. To stop a log file, use the same Log command in the Options menu. Stop the log only when all data has been collected. After a log file has been stopped, it cannot be restarted. You can view the log file after a log has been stopped or while the log file is still running.

Performance Monitor also enables you to view or analyze the data captured in a log file. You can display the logged file through the Chart or Report views. The following steps show you how to view a log file (after it has been stopped) in a Chart view and how to change the data source:

1. In the Options menu, choose Data From.
2. Change from Current Activity to Log File and specify the name of the log file to be viewed. If you don't know the name of the file, you can use the ellipsis button (...) to browse the hard drive and find the log file.
3. Add the counters by using the Add Counter button or by choosing the Add to Chart item in the Edit menu.

To remove items from the chart, select a counter and press the Delete key. The process of viewing data is similar to using the Chart view in Current Data mode. Notice that only objects selected to be logged appear in the list. All counters and instances of those objects, however, are available.

The Time Window is a graphical tool that you can drag to indicate the start and end of a section within the log file to be viewed. You can use a Time Window to view the data one hour at a time by continuously moving the Time Window graph. If bookmarks were recorded during the logging process, you can use them to mark the start or end of the Time Window. All other chart options, such as scales and gridlines (mentioned earlier in this chapter), apply to viewing logged data in the Chart view.

3. Using Reports

The Report view displays data in a numeric format. With current data, it shows an average of the last three updates. When you're viewing data from a log file, it shows the average value for the Time Windows selected.

To view reports, choose the Reports command from the View menu or press Ctrl+R. To see the source of the data, select the Data From command in the Options menu. You must add each counter or instance to the report by using the Add Counter button or the Add to Report command on the Edit menu. To remove items from the report, select a value and press the Delete key.

The Report view cannot show trends or large fluctuations. You cannot print a report from Performance Monitor, but you can export it as a .CSV (comma separated value) file or a .TSV (tab delimited) file and open it in a spreadsheet or word processor.

In Report view, you have only one option: the update interval. The interval determines how often the report is updated with new information. This update interval can be set on a report displaying current data only, not logged data.

4. Using Alerts

The Alert view (which can be easily accessed anywhere in Performance Monitor with the Ctrl+A hot key) is very different from the Chart, Log, and Report views. No data is reported or displayed until a system passes a threshold set by the administrator. The administrator can set up to 1,000 alerts on a given system. The same objects, counters, and instances are used, and one other item is added as a condition. When an alert is generated, the system sends an administrative alert message or runs a program. You can set the alerts to react only the first time the threshold is attained or on each and every time.

You might, for example, set the following condition:

> Only alert the administrators if the computer's hard drive space falls below 10 percent free.
>
> or
>
> Alert the administrators when the server's total logons are above 150.

In both of these cases, you can set up the system to inform the administrator of the situation via a message. The alert's destination must be set separately using the Alert command in the Options menu. All alerts are sent to the same destination. You can enter the destination as either a user name or a computer name, and you can specify a program to run the first time or each time the condition occurs.

The following steps describe how to set up the alert's destination:

1. Change to the Alert view by choosing the Alerts command in the View menu.
2. Select the Options menu and choose Alerts.
3. Enter the user or computer name you want Performance Monitor to notify in case of an alert.
4. Select Log Event in Application Log to enable this log feature for all alerts. Note that for the alerts to be generated from a computer, both the Alerter and Messenger service must be started.

For alerts to function, the Performance Monitor must be running at all times. However, because this may slow down a workstation, it should be used for short-term monitoring and troubleshooting only.

5. Using Remote Monitoring

You can use the Performance Monitor to monitor other computers on the network. Each time a counter is added to a chart, log, report, or alert, the current computer is used. Any computer that can be remotely administered can be remotely monitored as well.

To select a remote computer to monitor, type the computer name in the Add Counter dialog box, or click the ellipsis (...) button next to the Computer name field and select the specific computer on the network.. The full computer name is usually preceded by two backslashes (\\). To add a counter for a computer named salesvr1, for example, you would type \\salesvr1. The person doing the remote monitoring must be a member of the Administrators group of the target computer. In a Windows NT domain environment, the group Domain-Admins is always a member of each workstation's local Administrators group and thus can remotely administer or monitor the system.

6. Saving Settings

Charts, reports, logs, and alerts are modified each time a counter is added or removed and each time options are set. You can save all these settings in a separate Settings file. This means that charts, reports, logs, or alerts will be generated one time. They can, however, be used several times on current data or several log files, which provides consistency for comparing systems or situations. To save the settings for the current view, choose the Save Settings command in the File menu or press Shift+F12. For example, to save the current Alert settings, you select Save Alert Settings from the File menu.

The Performance Monitor can be shut down and restarted quickly when a Settings file is opened. You can even move the Settings file from one computer to another. The Settings page stores the objects, counters, and instances for the computer on which they were set up. Just copying the file to another computer does not monitor the new computer; it just makes remote monitoring a little easier to set up.

C. Using the Server Tool

The Server tool can be found in the Control Panel. This tool is used to monitor network activity related to sharing folders or printers, to set up the Replication utility, and to set up alert destinations for Windows NT Workstation 4.0. The component of interest here is the capability to monitor the number of remote users and the types of access they are getting on the system.

The Server tool provides three methods of viewing remote users and their activity on the system. Those three methods offer pretty much the same information, but each has a slightly different focus. These methods are listed and described in Table 18.1.4.

Table 18.1.4 Remote User Monitoring Tools in the Server Tool

Button	Description
Users	Lists all users remotely connected to the system. You can select a specific user to see a list of all the shares to which the user is connected. Additionally, information such as how long the users have been connected and whether they are using the Guest account is available. From here, you can also disconnect any user from a share.
Shares	The Shares button shows the same information as the Users button, except the shares are listed first. You can select a specific share to see a list of all the users connected to it. You can also disconnect someone from a given share.
In Use	The In Use button goes one step further than the two previous items: It lists the resource to which a user is connected and the type of access. A list of files that may be opened with read-only permission is listed as such. You can also close off resources, which disconnects the current users.

The Server icon exists on all Windows NT Workstations and Servers alike. A Windows NT domain controller also includes a Server Manager icon that gives you access to the same tasks as the Server icon on all Windows NT systems in the domain.

Disconnecting a user or a share has little effect initially on remote users because Windows NT and Windows 95 use a persistent connection technique to reconnect lost connections as soon as the resource is needed. The feature for disconnecting a user is primarily used to close connections from systems after hours or to prepare for a backup in which all files must be closed. To completely remove someone permanently from a share, you must change the share permissions and then disconnect the user. When the persistent connection is attempted, the permissions are re-evaluated, and access is denied.

D. Using the WinMSD Utility

The WinMSD (Windows Microsoft Diagnostic) utility is part of Windows NT Workstation 4.0 and can be run from the Start, Run menu. This utility is not used to make changes to a system. Its primary function is to provide a summary report on the current status of the system. This utility displays nine categories of information, ranging from the services' status to the size of the current pagefile and the device drivers used on the system.

You can have WinMSD produce a printed report with all details from all the tabs. This information is accurate only at the time WinMSD is started; it does not monitor or update information automatically while it's running. There is, however, a Refresh button at the bottom of the dialog box that you can use to update information.

WinMSD proves very useful when comparing two systems. Network administrators can use WinMSD to view the following information about remote systems. (Slightly less information is available with remote viewing of WinMSD.)

- *Version.* Shows the Licensing screen, which displays the registered owner and the CD key.
- *System.* Shows the type of computer and CPU chip used. The system BIOS date and version can also be found here.
- *Display.* Shows the display adapter BIOS information and the current adapter settings, including memory on the card and display drivers being used.
- *Drive.* Shows all local drives on the system. The properties of each drive reveal the usage in bytes and clusters.
- *Memory.* Shows the pagefile size and usage, displayed in kilobytes.
- *Services.* Shows all Windows NT services, along with their current status.
- *Resources.* Lists the four critical resources for each device: IRQ, I/O port, DMA, and memory. Information can also be listed per device.
- *Environment.* Shows the environment variables for the system as well as the local user.
- *Network.* Shows general information about the logon status, transport protocols, device settings of the network card, and overall statistics of network use.

Most of the information available in WinMSD can be configured through the Control Panel and the Registry Editor.

18.1.1 Exercise: Reducing Available Memory

Objective: Modify the Boot.ini file to enable Windows NT to access a restricted amount of memory.

Time Estimate: 5–10 minutes

In order to create a situation that results in a memory bottleneck, you may need to reduce the amount of RAM a computer has. On an Intel-based computer, there is a startup switch called MAXMEM that is added to the Boot.ini and is used to limit the amount of memory the system can use. You might be able to create the same bottleneck without having to use the /maxmem switch, but on computers with 16MB of RAM or more, it may take more time to manifest itself.

To reduce the amount of physical RAM that Windows NT uses, change the startup command in the Boot.ini file by adding the /maxmem switch. The minimum amount of RAM that Windows NT Workstation will run on is 12MB. Reduce the amount of RAM to 12, and the system will show a memory bottleneck almost immediately. Use this /maxmem switch only to test or simulate a shortage of memory; it should not be left on the system after the test. Note that the /maxmem switch can be used only on an Intel-based computer.

To reduce the system's memory to 12MB, follow these steps:

1. Open the Start menu, choose Programs, and select the Windows NT Explorer.
2. Open the C: drive and locate the Boot.ini file in the right pane of the Explorer window.

3. You should always make a copy of files that you intend to modify in case you need to restore the file later. To do so, right-click the file and select Copy. Then right-click anywhere on the C: drive and select Paste. The copy of the file is now called "copy of BOOT."
4. Right-click the original Boot.ini file and select Properties. Remember that if the extensions are hidden you will not see "Boot.ini" only "Boot."
5. Click once to clear the Read-Only check box so that the file can be modified. Then close the Properties dialog box.
6. Double-click the Boot file to open and edit it. (If the file is not associated with any program, you can select Notepad from the dialog box that appears.)
7. At the end of the first line in the [operating system] section, add the following entry: **/maxmem:12**.
8. Exit and save the file with the new entry. The Boot file is now ready to start Windows NT with only 12MB of RAM available.
9. Restart the computer.

Answers and Explanations: Exercise

In this exercise, you added the /maxmem switch to the Boot.ini file to limit the maximum memory used by Windows NT in order to simulate a memory bottleneck. Remember to remove the /maxmem switch when you are finished. At the end of this exercise, you can return the Boot file to its original state, or you can keep it this way until the end of Exercise 18.2.1 and then reverse the settings.

18.1 Practice Problems

1. Which tool can provide information about CPU utilization? (Choose all that apply.)
   - A. Performance Monitor
   - B. WinMSD
   - C. Task Manager
   - D. CPU Manager
2. Where or how can someone find a list of all applications currently running on the system?
   - A. From the Start menu
   - B. Using the Task Manager
   - C. Using the Control Panel's Application icon
   - D. Looking at the taskbar
3. You are thinking of stopping an unused service. Before doing so you want to check on service dependencies. Which Windows NT tool can you use to do so?
   - A. The Services icon in the Control Panel
   - B. The Task Manager's Services tab
   - C. WinMSD and the properties of a service
   - D. The System icon
4. You want to print out a detailed summary of the current state of your system, including drivers, system services, and IRQ settings. Which tool do you use?
   - A. Task Manager
   - B. WinMSD
   - C. Performance Monitor
   - D. The System applet in Control Panel
5. You are looking at the Processes tab of Task Manager, but certain information regarding memory usage is not listed. How can you have more information displayed in this same window? (Choose all that apply.)
   - A. Use the Performance Monitor's memory counters.
   - B. Open two Task Managers.
   - C. Use the View menu's Select Columns command.
   - D. Change the size of the window using the mouse.
6. Which is not an available view in the WinMSD tool?
   - A. Network
   - B. Environment
   - C. Version
   - D. Alerts
7. What is the relationship between counters, instances, and objects in Performance Monitor?
   - A. Objects are categories that contain specific counters for all instances.
   - B. An object is a unit of each instance. A counter is used only to determine the number of events occurring on a system.
   - C. Performance Monitor uses counters only.
   - D. All objects are divided into counters. Each counter can be monitored for a given instance or a total instance.
8. A baseline log created a few weeks ago is stored on the local hard drive in a logs folder. How can you view this log? (Choose all that apply.)
   - A. Click the System icon, choose Log view, and select the log file.
   - B. Use the Performance Monitor.
   - C. A log file can be viewed only by Microsoft.
   - D. Use the Event Viewer.

9. You want to know the BIOS version and date for your computer. Which tool can you use to find out this information?

   A. The System applet in Control Panel

   B. The System tab in WinMSD

   C. The NET COMPUTER command at the command prompt

   D. Performance Monitor

10. The Performance Monitor graph window displays five separate parameters for the statistics of each running counter. Which of the following is not one of these counters?

    A. Last

    B. Maximum

    C. Current

    D. Average

11. Which of the following is not a standard view in the Performance Monitor?

    A. Log View

    B. Chart View

    C. Statistics View

    D. Reports View

12. When you're using Performance Monitor to set alerts on specific counter values, with what frequency can alerts be reported? (Choose all that apply.)

    A. The first time the counter exceeds the set value.

    B. At specified intervals, such as every time a counter exceeds the set value.

    C. Each time the counter exceeds the set value.

    D. Only every 15 minutes.

13. Which tool can you use to monitor the remote users connected to your Windows NT Workstation?

    A. User Manager

    B. Event Viewer

    C. Server applet in Control Panel

    D. Performance Monitor, using the Server object

14. Which is not a tab selection in the Task Manager?

    A. Processes

    B. Memory

    C. Applications

    D. Performance

15. You are using the Task Manager to monitor your CPU usage, but you want the chart to be updated more frequently. What can you do?

    A. You must use the Performance Monitor's Processor object to tailor CPU monitoring in this way.

    B. Close all other applications while the Task Manager is running.

    C. Change the Update Speed parameter in Task Manager.

    D. Run Task Manager using the /high or /realtime switch.

16. You want to configure Performance Monitor alerts on your hard disk capacity. What can you configure Performance Monitor to do when alerts occur? (Choose all that apply.)

    A. Send a message to the Administrator.

    B. Start a program the first time the alert is triggered.

    C. Start a program every time the alert is triggered.

    D. Email or page an administrator or technician.

17. Which two services must be running on your Windows NT 4.0 machine in order for Performance Monitor alerts to work properly?

    A. SNMP Service

    B. Server Service

    C. Messenger Service

    D. Alerter Service

18. You want to monitor the resources being used by remote users on your Windows NT 4.0 Workstation, and you want the option of disconnecting them from a resource. Which tool do you use?

    A. User Manager

    B. Server Manager

    C. Task Manager

    D. The My Computer icon

19. In order to understand and effectively use the results of Performance Monitor charts, you must first have:

    A. An established baseline of each monitored counter's average or optimal running efficiency.

    B. Published benchmarks for your computer and hardware running Windows NT 4.0 Workstation.

    C. The Alerter Service running.

    D. Microsoft's published guidelines for system optimization, which are included in the online help.

20. The Performance Monitor can chart system performance on other Windows NT computers on the network by:

    A. Viewing charts created previously on the other Windows NT computers.

    B. Using the Saved Settings file generated on the other Windows NT computers.

    C. Connecting to the remote computer when adding a new counter.

    D. Doing nothing; Performance Monitor can only monitor the local system.

21. You want to be able to easily start Performance Monitor and begin monitoring a pre-established group of objects and their counters. Which is the best method of doing this? (Choose one.)

    A. Leave Performance Monitor running in the background at all times.

    B. Create a Settings file with all the settings, counters, and information you need to begin monitoring.

    C. You must reconfigure Performance Monitor with each use.

    D. Decide on the configuration you want, and then stick with it. Performance Monitor automatically restores the last settings used.

22. What tool do you use to view all the shares on your Windows NT 4.0 Workstation computer, as well as the users currently connected to each share?

    A. File Explorer

    B. Performance Monitor

    C. Disk Administrator

    D. Server Manager

23. Which of the following functions can you accomplish from the Applications tab in the Task Manager? (Choose all that apply.)

    A. End tasks

    B. Monitor memory usage

    C. Boost application thread priority

    D. Start new tasks

24. To view Performance Monitor data, you select the Data From menu choice. Then you have which two of the following options?

    A. Remote Data

    B. Current Activity

    C. Saved Settings

    D. Log File

Answers and Explanations: Practice Problems

1. **A, C** Performance Monitor gives detailed CPU utilization information while Task Manager gives at-a-glance information. WinMSD (Answer B) does not offer CPU utilization information, and the CPU Manager (Answer D) is not a Windows NT tool.
2. **B** Task Manager's Application tab shows running applications.
3. **C** The WinMSD offers a list of all services, and their properties show the dependencies.
4. **B** WinMSD displays nine different categories of information on the current state of the system; all of the categories can be printed together using the Print command in the File menu.
5. **C** The View menu offers a Select Column item that offers up to 14 columns of information. If all columns are selected, a scrollbar is available. The size of the window cannot be changed.
6. **D** Alerts are configured and viewed with Performance Monitor.
7. **B** For more information, see the section entitled "Using the Performance Monitor."
8. **B** Performance Monitor logs can be viewed only by using the Performance Monitor.
9. **B** WinMSD displays BIOS and processor information on the System tab.
10. **C** There is no Current parameter.
11. **C** There is no Statistics view. Statistics on Performance Monitor counter instances are determined with the other views.
12. **A, C** Alerts can be handled the first time or every time they are triggered.
13. **C** The Server applet can be used to view remote users' connection to shares and other resources, and it can be used to disconnect them.
14. **B** Memory information is found on the Performance tab.
15. **C** The Update Speed parameters in the View menu enable you to change the update frequency to Low, Normal, or High.
16. **A, B, C** Performance Monitor can send an alert message to specified users if the Messenger service is running. Programs can be set to run the first time or every time an alert occurs. You could configure a custom program to email or page someone, but this is not supported directly.
17. **C, D** The Messenger and Alerter services must be running for Performance Monitor to properly use alerts.
18. **B** Server Manager can be used to monitor connected users and to disconnect them from resources such as shares.
19. **A** You should have a baseline figure of the average or optimal figure for each counter in order to compare it to the current number given.
20. **C** Performance Monitor can connect to a remote Windows NT computer (if the user has appropriate permissions) and can remotely monitor it.
21. **B** The Settings file saves the object, counter, and instance information of the current configuration. This can be used to quickly begin monitoring several counters on a regular basis.

22. **D** Server Manager displays all shares on the computer (even the administrative share), as well as all users connected to each share.

23. **A, D** You can end and start tasks. You monitor memory usage with the Processes tab, and you boost application thread priority by right-clicking processes in the Processes tab.

24. **B, D** Current Activity enables real-time monitoring, whereas Log File provides a means of analyzing saved data.

18.1 Key Words

Performance Monitor

Task Manager

alert

Server tool

WinMSD utility

remote monitoring

18.2 Identifying and Resolving Performance Problems

The Task Manager and Performance Monitor are used to determine whether performance is suffering in any way. A major cause of performance degradation is the bottleneck—that is, one or more resources operating at or near 100 percent of capacity.

The major components that can be monitored and enhanced fall under the following four groupings:

- Memory
- Processor
- Disks
- Network

These items are discussed in the following sections.

A. Identifying Bottlenecks

By properly identifying one or more bottlenecks, you can help focus the attention on the appropriate resources and determine a course of action. The tricky part is that a particular resource may seem to be the culprit causing the bottleneck when, in fact, another resource is really at fault.

Consider, for example, a CPU running at or near 100 percent consistently. At first it may seem that a new and faster CPU is in order. When you look deeper, however, you may find that the CPU is so busy swapping memory pages from RAM to the pagefile and back that it has no time for anything else. Adding more RAM reduces page swapping would be a satisfactory solution in this scenario—not a faster CPU.

Note that one single reading of CPU usage may lead you to believe the CPU is inadequate when, in fact, the CPU is very busy each time an application was started due to lack of memory. Memory bottlenecks are described in full detail later in this chapter.

You should always look at all bottlenecked resources, not just the first one you find, because resources are often dependent on each other.

To determine what constitutes a bottleneck, you must understand each resource and know its baseline or optimum-operating level. Is it a bottleneck if the hard drive is reading 150 bytes per second, or if the CPU is functioning at 75 percent? No exact figure can be given for each resource, but Microsoft has a few guidelines you can follow. The best way for an individual to analyze a given situation is to maintain a baseline log of appropriate resource counters under normal or basic operation and use of the system. You can then compare that baseline log to situations of extreme stress or to determine whether a change to the system has any impact on performance.

1. Creating a Baseline Log

You can create a baseline log by using the Log feature from Performance Monitor (as explained in the section titled "Using Logs," earlier in this chapter). A log file does not have to be very large to show pertinent information, so long as the log was created while the system was being used in its normal or basic state. You can create a baseline log for each object individually or for a complete set. Creating a complete set gives you more flexibility, but the file will be larger. The following sections show which counter to follow and log to pinpoint possible bottlenecks and system deficiencies.

2. Pinpointing Memory Bottlenecks

The amount of physical memory (RAM) in a computer is probably the most significant factor when it comes to system performance. More is definitely better in respect to memory. The amount of RAM depends on the typical use of the workstation (running applications or sharing folders) and the expectations of the user.

Windows NT Workstation 4.0 uses a virtual memory mechanism to store and retrieve information for the processor. Along with real memory capacity that is the amount of physical RAM, Windows NT also makes use of a pagefile system. As soon as Windows NT Workstation runs out of RAM to store information, it makes up virtual memory by using space on the hard drive. The action of moving information between the pagefile and physical memory is called *paging*.

If information cannot be retrieved from physical memory, the system returns a *page fault*. Two kinds of page faults can occur:

- *Soft page fault.* The information is found in physical RAM, but it is in a different location.
- *Hard page fault.* The information must be retrieved from the pagefile on the hard disk, which takes more time and resources.

The Virtual Memory Manager is responsible for keeping track of each application's address space, the real list of physical memory, and the pagefile memory used to store the information. When physical memory reaches its limit, Windows NT moves some information from the physical space that it occupies to the pagefile. When the system needs the information again, it is paged back into physical space.

You should monitor the size of the pagefile to see if it is always increasing. Excessive paging may just be a short-term phenomenon and could be due to a one-time increase in demand. However, if the pagefile is constantly pushing the upper limits, there may be cause for concern. The pagefile can grow to its maximum size as more space is needed. The default size of the pagefile is based on the amount of physical RAM that was present when Windows NT Workstation was installed. The installation procedure creates a pagefile with a minimum size of RAM plus 11MB, and a maximum of RAM plus 11MB plus 50MB.

All Microsoft documentation shows the pagefile calculation to be RAM plus 12MB for the minimum and RAM plus 12MB plus 50MB for the maximum on Windows NT Workstation. On the exam, always quote Microsoft's numbers. There is never a choice of answers showing 11 and 12; only 12 is listed.

The memory object is definitely of interest, but you cannot forget that Windows NT Workstation uses logical disks to create a pagefile (used as virtual memory) as well as processor time to perform the paging. The Performance Monitor objects of interest in monitoring and pinpointing memory bottlenecks are:

- Memory
- Paging File
- Process
- Logical Disk
- Processor

These items are listed in order of importance and, if monitored as a group, will indicate whether a bottleneck has occurred due to lack of physical memory. As you should remember, when you select an object for a log, all the counters and instances are included as well.

a. The Memory Object

From the Memory object, three specific counters should be monitored:

- *Page Faults.* Includes soft and hard page faults. Microsoft suggests that a count of more than five page faults per second on an ongoing basis is problematic.
- *Pages Input/Sec.* Represents the number of pages the system had to retrieve from the hard drive to satisfy page faults.
- *Page Reads/Sec.* Shows the number of times per second that pages are transferred into memory from the pagefile. This indicator can also be used to show a disk bottleneck that might be created by a memory shortage.

b. The Paging File Object

You should monitor the size of the pagefile to see whether it is always increasing. Excessive paging may just be a short-term phenomenon and could be due to a one-time increase in demand. The following two counters are used by the Paging File object to monitor pagefile activity:

- *% Usage.* The percentage of the paging file in use.
- *% Usage Peak.* The peak usage of the page file, measured as a percentage.

c. The Process Object

The Process object offers two useful counters for monitoring pagefile performance:

- *Page File Bytes.* Shows the current amount of the pagefile being used in bytes.
- *Pool Nonpaged Bytes.* Represents the amount of physical memory an application is using that cannot be moved to the pagefile. If this number keeps increasing while an application runs, it can indicate that an application is using up physical memory.

d. The Logical Disk Object

The Logical Disk object does not have the same significance that the previous objects do, but it might help point out inefficiencies with the disks instead of memory. The pagefile is stored on one or more physical disks. The Logical Disk object provides one important counter that may be of use:

- *Average Disk Queue Length.* Shows the number of entries waiting to be read or written to the disk. Pagefile items fall into the queue like any other requests. If the queue is too slow and cannot process paging requests fast enough, the system appears to be slow due to paging when, in fact, it is the disk that cannot handle the request. This number should be less than two in an optimum scenario.

e. The Processor Object

The counters to follow for the processor are:

- *% Processor Time.* Shows just how busy the processor is performing all tasks.
- *% Privilege Time.* Excludes all tasks being performed for applications.
- *DPC Rate.* The DPC stands for Deferred Procedure Call. These are tasks that are placed in a queue and are waiting to be processed.

3. Pinpointing Processor Bottlenecks

The processor (CPU) of any computer is always busy processing information. Even when no real process is running, Windows NT runs an idle process. Most counters take this idle process into account and display information on all processes except the idle process. A bottleneck may occur if too many items are waiting in a queue to get processed at one time or if an item takes a long time to make it through the queue.

Microsoft's recommendation is that a single processor system should not be above 90 percent usage for any significant length of time. A multiple processor system should not exceed 50 percent usage for any significant length of time.

Another main component of CPU usage is the queue of items waiting to be processed. Microsoft's guideline on the queue is that it should contain no more than two entries most of the time. In a multiprocessor system, there can be two types of processing: synchronous and asynchronous. Windows NT Workstation uses a synchronous environment in which all processors can be used simultaneously. Several single-threaded applications can share a processor, and multithreaded applications can run several threads on one processor or can spread the threads across processors.

The objects and counters listed in Table 18.2.1 can be monitored to determine a possible processor bottleneck.

Table 18.2.1 Objects and Counters Used to Monitor Processor Bottlenecks

Object	Counter	Description
Processor	% Processor Time	The total amount of time the processor is busy, excluding the idle process. This includes user-processing and privilege-processing time. This counter should be below 90 percent over time.
System	Processor Queue Length	The number of threads waiting to be processed by all processors on the system. This does not include threads being processed.

The solution to resolving CPU bottlenecks depends on the number of processors, as well as their speed and the type of applications (single-threaded or multithreaded) being run on the system.

Multithreaded applications can take advantage of multiple processors by distributing threads among processors. Single-threaded applications, on the other hand, benefit more from faster processors.

When you find a bottleneck caused by the processor, you need to complete a further investigation on processes, threads, and priorities. This additional investigation will help clarify whether a single application or thread is generating the bottleneck. If you know that a specific application is causing the problem, you might have the alternative of upgrading the application instead of the CPU. Some 16-bit applications monopolize the CPU, whereas the 32-bit counterpart works quite well. Note that 16-bit applications will not generally benefit from multiple processors, and in extreme cases, may monopolize one CPU while the other is idle.

4. Pinpointing Disk Bottlenecks

Disk performance affects many components of Windows NT Workstation 4.0. The pagefile system runs off a disk, the processor is busy searching or seeking for information on a disk, and file sharing uses the disk along with disk caching to provide information to clients.

These same components can create disk bottlenecks due to their limitations. When at all possible, eliminate memory or CPU bottlenecks before trying to monitor disk performance. All components such as memory, CPU, caches, and disk must work together to accomplish proper overall system throughput. Calculating the speed of a disk might not be very relevant because a faster disk might not enable the overall system to perform faster if other bottlenecks are present.

A log of disk activity can aid you in comparing results from several disks under similar circumstances. You should use the Save Settings feature to start tests on different machines or several hard drives. You can find more information on how to use the Save Settings feature in the section titled "Saving Settings," earlier in this chapter.

The most important objects and counters are not available by default in Windows NT Workstation 4.0. They must be activated with the Diskperf utility. The only reason these objects and counters are not active is that they use system resources and slow down most systems. If they are needed, you can activate them and then deactivate them after completing the analysis. Table 18.2.2 shows the DiskPerf utility and its switches.

Table 18.2.2 Disperf.exe and Its Switches

Command	Description
diskperf	Shows whether the diskperf objects are active.
diskperf -y	Activates the disk counters.
diskperf -ye	Activates the disk counters on mirror, stripe sets, and other noncontiguous partition sets.
diskperf -n	Deactivates disk counters.

Only a member of the Administrators groups can run the diskperf utility on a standalone Windows NT Workstation 4.0. If you are activating or deactivating counters with the Diskperf utility, you must restart the computer for the change to take effect. Do not forget to deactivate the Diskperf objects by using diskperf -n.

Another method of activating the DiskPerf utility is to start it using the Device Manager in the Control Panel. After the appropriate objects and counters have been activated, two objects are available:

- *Physical Disk* refers to the actual hard drive placed in the system.
- *Logical Disk* refers to subsets of the physical disks.

Two types of possible bottlenecks exist when it comes to disks: the amount of disk space available and the access time of the disk. The counters used and the necessary solutions differ greatly.

The second area of concern is the efficiency at which requests are being handled by the hard drive and the overall use of the hard drive. Microsoft makes the following three recommendations regarding use of a typical hard drive:

- Disk activity should not be above 85 percent usage as shown by the % Disk Time counter in the Physical Disk or Logical Disk object.
- The number of requests waiting in the queue should not exceed two, as shown in the Current Disk Queue Length counter of the Physical Disk or Logical Disk object.
- Paging should not exceed five page faults per second as shown in Page Reads/Sec, Page Writes/Sec, and Page Faults counters of the Memory object. (Refer to the section "Identifying Bottlenecks" for a more thorough discussion.)

Monitoring drives for a comparison is fairly simple as long as the same conditions apply to both disks. Certain factors might affect how one disk performs compared to another. Examples of those factors include the file system (FAT versus NTFS), the type of disk (IDE versus SCSI), and the type of controller card. Table 18.2.3 shows a list of common counters used to determine the cause of a bottleneck.

Table 18.2.3 Disk Bottleneck Counters

Object	Counter
Logical Disk/Physical Disk	% Disk Time
Logical Disk/Physical Disk	Avg. Disk Queue Length
Logical Disk/Physical Disk	Current Disk Queue Length (known in previous versions as Disk Queue Length)
Logical Disk/Physical Disk	Avg. Disk sec / Transfer
Logical Disk/Physical Disk	Disk Bytes / Sec
Logical Disk/Physical Disk	Avg. Disk Bytes / Transfer
Logical Disk/Physical Disk	Disk Transfers / Sec
Logical Disk/Physical Disk	% Free Space
Logical Disk/Physical Disk	Free Megabytes

You can use several other counters to interpret disk activity. This may not necessarily show a bottleneck, but it can help you understand how the system resources are being used by certain applications.

5. Pinpointing Network Bottlenecks

You can monitor network activity only on a system connected to the network. Network terminology is used throughout this chapter, and there is an expectation of networking basics on the part of the reader. Non-networked systems do not require monitoring of network activities; therefore, some readers can skip this section. Typically a Windows NT Workstation's primary function is not that of a file or print server, and the number of requests made of the system does not have any negative effects.

You have two main tools to monitor network activity on the system:

- The Performance Monitor offers counters that can monitor the number of bytes transmitted, as well as errors encountered over several protocols, the Server service, and the Redirector service (client).
- The Server tool in the Control Panel can display all the shares on a system, as well as which user at which computer is connected to that share.

The Performance Monitor counters are not all initially present for network monitoring. Some counters that deal specifically with TCP/IP network traffic are not installed and must be added separately. Installing the SNMP (Simple Network Management Protocol) service adds the TCP/IP counters. The network or system administrators are the only users who can add network services. To add SNMP services, follow these steps:

1. From the Control Panel open the Network icon.
2. Select the Services tab.
3. Select the Add button and select SNMP services.

4. Accept all dialog boxes and identify the Windows NT Workstation 4.0 source files if needed.
5. Restart the computer.

After the SNMP service is loaded, a TCP/IP system has five additional counters available: TCP, UDP, IP, ARP, and ICMP. The full detail of these counters is beyond the scope of this book. The focus here is on counters that show information about data transmission.

Regardless of the network protocol being used, there are counters to monitor simple read or write requests from the network card. These counters are always available under the Redirector and Server objects. Individual protocol counters are under the protocol name itself. Table 18.2.4 displays a list of relevant counters from various objects used to monitor network activity on the system.

Table 18.2.4 Network Counters

Object	Counter	Description
Server	Bytes Total/Sec	The total activity of the system as a peer server on the network.
Server	Files Opened Total	The total number of files opened by remote systems. This calculates the amount of I/O requests.
Server	Errors Access Permission	The number of client requests that have failed. A remote user may be attempting to access resources that have been restricted. The system must process these requests, using system resources for nothing. It may also identify possible hackers trying to gain access to the system.
Redirector	Bytes Total/Sec	The client portion of the network initiated by the local system.
NetBEUI	Bytes Total/Sec	The NetBEUI protocol only. This can be useful in determining which protocols are not used much and can be removed.
TCP	Segments/Sec	The amount of information being handled by the TCP/IP protocol.
NWLink	Bytes Total/Sec	There are three objects for NWLink: IPX, SPX, and NetBIOS. All three have the same counter of bytes transferred per second using the NWLink protocol.

B. Monitoring with the Event Viewer

A part of the operating system is constantly monitoring for possible errors committed by either applications or other parts of the operating system. Event monitors are always active and keep track of these errors in the following three separate logs, which you can view with the Event Viewer. It should be noted that only 32-bit applications can log errors in the Application log.

- **System log.** Reports errors originating from the operating system, including services and devices.
- **Security log.** Tracks errors during security auditing. Not relevant in performance monitoring, but when security auditing is active, writing events to the Security log does take up resources.
- **Application log.** Keeps track of 32-bit application errors.

1. Reading Event Viewer Logs

In both the System and Application logs, Windows NT categorizes the entries as Information, Warning, or Error. In the Security log, it records Success or Failure to perform the activity sections. The Event Viewer records three general types of events:

- **Information.** Mostly information about successful activities.
- **Warnings.** The results of critical errors. (However, the system can still function properly.)
- **Errors.** Error message indicating that a service or device failed to start properly. The system may still function, but none of the dependent features are available. You should address these errors quickly.

18

Understanding the error codes and types can make it easier to solve the problem. You can expand any log entry by double-clicking anywhere on the line.

The Event Viewer logs provide extended information on each event, including the date and time of the event, the computer originating the event, the source of the event, and its type and category.

2. Filtering for Events

The size of a current log or an archive file can make it very difficult to find a specific problem. Using a filter can remove from the view all events that do not match a criteria. You can set criteria based on time, type of event, source of event, category, and event ID.

Windows NT performs the filter only on the currently displayed information. The log may need to be refiltered if new information is added during the analysis. The full list of events does not have to be displayed between filtered views; the system always bases the filter criteria on all events currently in the log.

3. Managing Log Settings

All three logs have settings that you can manage separately. Using the Log Settings command on the Log menu, you can set the size of each log as well as the actions to be taken when a log is full. The default values for a log are that it can use up to 512KB of memory to store events and that entries are removed when they have been in the log for seven days. Three options can be set to clear out logs: Overwrite Events as Needed, Overwrite Events Older Than X Days, and Do Not Overwrite Events (Clear Log Manually). The system warns with a message box that the log is full—except when the option Overwrite Events as Needed is used. If the log is full and is not cleared manually, new events cannot be logged.

A larger log keeps track of more information, but it also uses more system resources. Clearing and saving logs is a more efficient method of tracking events and possible trends.

4. Archiving and Retrieving a Log

The file format used is an .EVT file format and can be viewed only from the Event Viewer. *Archiving a log* refers to saving the event log in a separate file. You can do this while clearing the log or by using the Save As command in the Log menu. The Event Viewer is a 32-bit utility. Its Save As routine uses all the standard 32-bit saving features, such as long file names and Create New Folder. All three logs must be saved separately.

To open an archived log file, choose Open from the Log menu and select the appropriate .EVT file. An archive file contains only one of the three types of logs. When you open an archive file, the system prompts for the type of log you want to open.

18.2.1 Exercise: Creating a Memory Log

Objective: To create a log to monitor memory usage and determine whether a bottleneck is being created by lack of memory on the system.

Time Estimate: 20–30 minutes

Exercise 18.2.1 is guaranteed to show a bottleneck if Exercise 18.1.1 has been completed already. For a true test of the system, either do not complete Exercise 18.1.1, or reverse the effects of that exercise before proceeding with this one.

To create a memory bottleneck log, complete the following steps:

1. Start Windows NT under basic conditions. No additional software or hardware conflicts are occurring. This may not always be possible, but you should try to reduce as many factors as possible to focus the analysis on the memory component.
2. Open the Start menu, and choose Programs, Performance Monitor, Administrative Tools (Common).
3. To change to the Log view, choose Log from the View menu.
4. Select the Add Counter icon, or select Add from the Edit menu.
5. From the list of objects, select the following items and add them to the log.

    Memory

    Process

    Page File

    Logical disk

6. Choose the Log command from the Options menu.
7. Give the log file a name, such as **Memtest.log**, and then select a folder for storage. The size of this log should not be considerable. (Always make sure the hard drive used to store the log file has sufficient space if the log is going to run overnight.)
8. Change the interval to 30 seconds and click the Start Log button.
9. Let the log record for at least 20 to 30 minutes while the system is performing normal tasks. (A longer logging period offers more accurate averages and trends.)
10. Minimize the Performance Monitor and startup programs that are used frequently on the system.
11. After 20 or 30 minutes, return to Performance Monitor and stop the log.

Answers and Explanations: Exercise

The objects logged in this exercise may be more than is strictly required to identify a memory bottleneck. The log file will not be significantly larger, and this data may provide insight into other areas of concern that are masquerading as memory bottlenecks.

Do not overdo this test; a memory bottleneck always occurs if enough applications are started simultaneously. You do not want to show a bottleneck if none really exists. Run the system under normal circumstances.

18

For more information on the topics covered in this exercise, refer to the sections titled "Creating a Baseline Log" and "Pinpointing Memory Bottlenecks."

18.2.2 Exercise: Evaluating the Log File

Objective: To understand and interpret the results found in the log that was recorded in Exercise 18.2.1.

Time Estimate: 10–15 minutes

1. In the Performance Monitor, choose the Data From command from the Options menu.
2. Select to view data from a log, and then type or browse for the log file **Memtest.log**.
3. Choose Chart from the View menu.
4. Add the following counters to the chart:

   Memory: Page Faults/sec

   Memory: Page Inputs/Sec

   Paging File: % Use

Answers and Explanations: Exercise

This exercise should have helped you understand and interpret the results of the log file recorded in Exercise 18.2.1. Using Performance Monitor to analyze log files is an effective way of keeping detailed historical information about your computer, as opposed to immediate real-time logging, which may not always be practical.

If the Page Faults/Sec are consistently above 10, and the Page Inputs/Sec are also spiking, the system is low on RAM. Verify the % Use of the pagefile to see whether it is increasing over time. This indicates whether the pagefile demands are becoming more extensive as new applications are loaded, or whether it is only used when the application starts up. Additional paging that occurs when an application starts up may not be much of a concern as long as paging demands return to lower or normal levels after the application is running.

Many other counters mentioned in this chapter can be used in this analysis. You can use them to further investigate a situation. Other sources of information can be used to arrive at the same conclusions. The Task Manager offers memory counters for a simple look in addition to the CPU and Logical Disk objects in the Performance Monitor.

For more information on the topics covered in this exercise, refer to the section titled "Pinpointing Memory Bottlenecks."

18.2.3 Exercise: Creating a Hardware Profile

Objective: To create a hardware profile that will be used to make and test hardware and software changes without the risk of permanently damaging the Windows NT Workstation 4.0 operating system. (You must complete this hardware profile before you can start Exercise 18.3.1.)

Time Estimate: 5–10 minutes

1. Right-click the My Computer icon and select Properties. (This is the same as opening the System icon in the Control Panel.)
2. Select the Hardware Profiles tab.
3. Click the Copy button.
4. Type **Test Configuration** as the new name for the test profile.
5. Select Wait Indefinitely so you will have the time to make a choice and Windows NT will not load any default configuration. The default hardware profile is always the first listed.
6. Restart the system and choose the Windows NT Workstation 4.0 command from the Boot menu. Two new hardware configurations are listed: the Original Configuration and your Test Configuration. At this first logon, the Test Configuration is identical to the Original Configuration because no changes have been made.

Answers and Explanations: Exercise

Using hardware profiles is the safest and fastest way of testing new hardware-specific configurations without posing a threat to your original Windows NT installation. You create new hardware profiles by copying the original hardware profile and then making necessary changes to the copy. When multiple hardware profiles exist, Windows NT allows you to choose at boot time which profile you will use.

This exercise prepares the system to enable you to test various scenarios with less risk of causing damage. For more information on the topics covered in this exercise, see the section titled "Creating Hardware Profiles."

18.2 Practice Problems

1. Which two objects are used to monitor disk activity?

   A. DiskPerf

   B. Physical disk

   C. Hard disk

   D. Logical disk

2. You have decided to stop unused service using hardware profiles. Which services can be stopped without preventing the user from connecting with other computers? (Choose all that apply.)

   A. Browser

   B. Redirector

   C. Spooler

   D. Server

3. You have been monitoring disk activity in a log for the last eight hours. Yet when you display the counters, they all read 0. What is the meaning of these readings?

   A. The disk has been still for the entire logging period.

   B. The Performance Monitor is not functioning correctly and needs to be reinstalled.

   C. The Diskperf utility was not enabled.

   D. The PhysicalDisk counter was not enabled.

4. After making several configuration changes to the system, you reboot and log on. Several seconds after you log on, the system presents an error dialog box. You reboot again and use the Last Known Good Configuration command. The same error appears. What could be the problem?

   A. The Last Known Good Configuration works only with hardware profiles.

   B. The Last Known Good Configuration was updated after you logged on, which replaced the good configuration with the current one.

   C. The Last Known Good Configuration was not told to update on exit. You must boot up using the letter L and tell the system to update the Last Known Good Configuration.

   D. None of the above.

5. What are some of the factors that affect disk performance? (Choose all that apply.)

   A. The partition size

   B. The amount of information on the disk

   C. The name of the files

   D. The Diskperf utility

6. You need to monitor activity on your system. You suspect a lot of network activity. How can you substantiate your suspicions? (Choose all that apply.)

   A. Use the Performance Monitor and make sure DiskPerf is enabled.

   B. Use the Server Service icon in the Control Panel.

   C. Use the Task Manager's Network tab.

   D. Use the Server icon in the Control Panel.

7. How does upgrading to 32-bit applications make a difference on the system? (Pick all that apply.)

   A. 32-bit applications run faster because they are only written by Microsoft.

   B. 32-bit applications run directly in the system's win32 module, and no emulation is required.

C. 32-bit applications cannot run under Windows NT.

D. 32-bit applications run faster because they can be multithreaded, they are designed to make better use of the processor, and they run at a higher priority.

8. The hard drive on your Windows NT 4.0 computer seems to be full. You investigate the C: drive using Explorer and find very little software loaded. What could be using up so much hard drive space? (Choose all that apply.)

   A. The disk is fragmented.

   B. There are several Recycle Bins at full capacity.

   C. The Diskperf utility is active.

   D. The size of a FAT partition is very large, using large clusters.

9. You have lost your emergency repair disk. You can create a new one from which of the following?

   A. Any Windows NT 4.0 Workstation computer

   B. Any Windows NT 4.0 Workstation or 4.0 Workstation computer

   C. Only the Windows NT 4.0 computer for which you need the disk

   D. Any computer as long as you use the Windows NT 4.0 Workstation CD-ROM

10. The system has generated an error code. What tool can you use to review the error code? (Choose all that apply.)

    A. The Performance Monitor

    B. The System icon in the Control Panel

    C. The Event Viewer

    D. The Task Manager

11. You need to quickly free up system memory without restarting the system. What can you do? (Choose all that apply.)

    A. Close any applications or files that are not required.

    B. Minimize all background applications.

    C. Run a 16-bit application in its own memory address space.

    D. Increase the size of the pagefile.

12. You have been logging disk objects for the last few days. What are you looking for in the log to indicate whether a disk bottleneck is occurring?

    A. CPU activity consistently above 85 percent

    B. PageFaults/Sec counter above 2

    C. Consistent increase in the size of the pagefile

    D. Disk usage above 85 percent

13. From the following list of performance counters, which can be used to determine excessive processor time spent in Privileged Processor Mode? (Choose all that apply.)

    A. % DPC Time

    B. % User Time

    C. % Processor Time

    D. % Privileged Time

14. Hardware-related tasks such as disk access consume processor time by doing what?

    A. Causing the processor to handle I/O interrupts.

    B. Causing the processor to handle page faults.

    C. Causing the processor to spend more time in user mode.

    D. Hardware-related tasks do not consume processor time; only software and operating system tasks consume processor time.

15. Devices often use valuable CPU time while the processor is executing other tasks. When device interruption is suspected of being too much of a burden on the processor, which Performance Monitor counter can best be used to monitor frequency?

    A. DPC Rate

    B. % Privileged Time

    C. Interrupts/Sec

    D. APC Bypasses/Sec

16. Deferred Procedure Calls (DPCs) are placed in a queue and given lower priority than hardware interrupts. This can potentially do what to processor efficiency?

    A. Increase it

    B. Decrease it

    C. Have no effect on it

    D. All of the above

17. While running several applications at once, Windows NT displays a dialog box stating that the system is low on virtual memory. What can you do to increase virtual memory?

    A. Buy more RAM.

    B. Buy a faster hard drive.

    C. Buy a bigger hard drive.

    D. Expand the pagefile.

18. Your hard drive regularly churns during application usage, even when files are not being accessed. Assuming nothing is wrong with your hardware, this could be an indication of what?

    A. The need for more RAM

    B. Excessive page files

    C. Low virtual memory

    D. The wrong ODBC drivers

19. Which of the following is *not* a feature of Windows NT 4.0 automatic optimization?

    A. Avoiding physical memory fragmentation

    B. Disk space quota management

    C. Symmetric multiprocessing

    D. Process and thread prioritizing.

20. Windows NT 4.0 uses multiple processors by distributing both kernel and application processes evenly across all processors. This method of multiprocessor use is known as:

    A. Demand paging

    B. Asymmetric multiprocessing

    C. Priority Level Processing

    D. Symmetric multiprocessing

21. The following Performance Monitor performance counters can be used to monitor the use and efficiency of Windows NT pagefiles. (Choose two.)

    A. % Page File Use

    B. % Usage

    C. % Usage Peak

    D. % Virtual Memory Usage

22. If you are concerned that running a certain application is taking up too much physical memory, leaving other processes and applications to depend more upon virtual memory, what performance counter can you run to test this?

    A. Pages/Sec

    B. System Cache Resident Bytes

    C. Pool Paged Bytes

    D. Pool Nonpaged Bytes

23. You are using the Performance Monitor % Processor Time counter to monitor your CPU usage. Normally this counter averages at around 40%, but when you first load an application, the % Processor Time spikes to 100%. What can you determine from this?

    A. Your processor is unable to properly handle your processing needs.

    B. You should add more RAM for less processor-intensive load time.

    C. Your processor is probably not causing a bottleneck.

    D. You may need to consider a dual-processor computer.

24. For the past several weeks, you have been frequently monitoring your processor performance with the Performance Monitor using % Processor Time. The graph shows that most processor spikes are above 80%. What does this indicate? (Choose the best answer.)

    A. Your processor may be causing a major bottleneck for your system, and you should consider upgrading to a faster one after more performance testing.

    B. You need more physical memory (RAM) to offset your processor load.

    C. There is little need to worry about upgrading the processor; spikes over 80% are the norm.

    D. The pagefile should be increased.

25. You are using Performance Monitor to analyze your system processor. Based on the System object's System Processor Queue counter, which of the following indicates your processor is too slow?

    A. The Processor Queue length drops below 2.

    B. The Processor Queue length is always greater than 2.

    C. The Processor Queue length never drops below 8.

    D. The Processor Queue Length does not fluctuate.

Answers and Explanations: Practice Problems

1. **B, D** Physical disks and Logical disks can be monitored using the Performance Monitor.

2. **A, C, and D** The Redirector is the client software that connects the workstation to a Server service on another system.

3. **C** The DiskPerf utility enables disk counters.

4. **B** Last Known Good Configuration updates when the user logs on.

5. **A, B, D** Large FAT partitions may waste disk space. A full disk tends to be fragmented because there is less room to store data continuously, and running the DiskPerf utility slows down the disk.

6. **A, D** The DiskPerf can show file and print sharing accessing the drives. The Server icon can show users who are connected and resources that are being used.

7. **B, D** 32-bit applications run directly in the system's win32 module, so no emulation is required. They also run faster because they can be multithreaded, they are designed to make better use of the processor, and they run at a higher priority.

8. **A, B, D** Large FAT partitions may waste disk space. A full disk tends to be fragmented because there is less room to store data continuously, and running the DiskPerf utility slows down the disk.

9. **C** Parts of Registry are stored on the ERD and are unique to each system.

10. **C** The Event Viewer stores errors generated by applications and the operating system.

11. **A, B** Applications that are open will be stored in memory, and full-screen applications take up more memory than minimized applications do.
12. **D** The Disk Usage counter may spike above 85 percent, but it should not remain that high. Page faults and the pagefile have to do with memory bottlenecks. CPU usage reflects CPU or memory bottlenecks.
13. **A, D** % DPC Time is the time spent servicing deferred procedure calls, which are interrupts with lower priority; it is a component of % Privileged Time.
14. **A** Disk access and other hardware-related tasks cause the processor to handle I/O interrupts.
15. **C** Interrupts/Sec monitors the number of hardware interrupts the processor receives each second.
16. **B** Longer queues can decrease processor efficiency.
17. **D** Expand or create another pagefile using the System applet in Control Panel.
18. **A** Your system may be paging virtual memory too often because it needs more physical memory (RAM).
19. **B** Windows NT 4.0 does not feature disk quota management.
20. **D** Symmetric Multi Processing (SMP) distributes the OS and application load evenly across multiple processors.
21. **B, C** % Usage is the amount of pagefile usage that occurs in one second, whereas % Usage Peak is the peak usage of the pagefile. The counters mentioned in A and D do not exist.
22. **D** Pool Nonpaged Bytes shows memory that cannot be paged to a pagefile and takes up physical memory.
23. **C** Sudden 100% spikes frequently occur when an application is being loaded.
24. **A** Spikes over 80% indicate that the processor is beginning to cause a bottleneck.
25. **B** If the processor queue length is always over two, your processor is too slow to efficiently handle its queue.

18.2 Key Words

bottleneck

Virtual Memory Manager

pagefile

paging

page fault

Event Viewer

filter

18.3 Optimizing System Performance

Microsoft has shipped Windows NT Workstation 4.0 optimized for the majority of users working in a typical environment. The improvement in performance might only be a slim one or two percent, but it could require a lot of work and money to make it happen.

Messing around with system configuration can be hazardous. In all cases, you should perform a backup of critical system files and settings before making any changes. The effect of the changes should also be monitored and compared with a baseline log that you created before the changes were implemented. (See the section entitled "Creating a Baseline Log," earlier in this chapter.)

A. Making a Safe Recovery

You can make a safe recovery if you took the proper steps before making any major changes to the system. Several methods enable users to recover from system configuration changes:

- Creating an emergency repair disk
- Using Windows NT's Backup to store the Registry
- Using Last Known Good Configuration
- Creating hardware profiles

1. Creating and Maintaining an Emergency Repair Disk

The best way to make a copy of all necessary Registry files is to create and maintain an *emergency repair disk* (ERD). The disk includes all hardware and software configuration items as well as security account database information. You can use this disk to restore a corrupted Registry. The backup copy of these files can be stored in two locations when an ERD is created. The disk has a copy, and the %winroot%\repair folder has a second identical copy. However, the copy on the hard drive is not very useful if the system has crashed.

There is no menu or icon to create the emergency repair disk. Instead, you run the RDISK utility from a command prompt or from the Run dialog box (which you access by choosing Start, Run). This brings up a graphical tool used to create the disk or just update the repair folder.

The RDISK utility presents two options: Update Repair Info and Create Repair Disk. Update Repair Info updates the repair folder and then prompts you to create a disk. Create Repair Disk creates a disk without updating the repair folder. You should create and maintain an emergency repair disk. You should also have a backup copy of the disk on a system dealing with critical information.

2. Creating Hardware Profiles

Creating a hardware profile is one of the safest and fastest methods for making and testing changes to a system without running the risk of losing system integrity. Hardware profiles are also used to control when the network settings are loaded on laptops that may be connected to the network or when they are set up to run as a standalone. You can quickly change this setting by using the Properties button of the profile.

A hardware profile starts off as an identical copy of the current system's configuration. Part of the Registry is duplicated, and all device and device-related configuration changes are made to the copy profile and are tested. If a particular configuration fails, the system can just be rebooted into the original configuration without any ill effects. Only device and device-related items are stored in a profile. Most Registry settings are always available to all profiles. The Registry Editor should not be used to modify profiles, however; using the devices or services icon is a safer method for changing a profile.

Once a copy exists, Windows NT displays a prompt prior to logon (but after the Boot.ini displays the list of operating systems), asking which hardware profile is to be used for this session. If no choice is made, the system has a timeout of 30 seconds and then loads the default profile. Note that you can modify the timeout period as well as the default choice in the system's Properties dialog box.

The hardware profiles are easier to use than the ERD. However, the ERD might still be needed if any changes made to the system corrupt the Registry. The hardware profiles are stored in the Registry.

3. Using the Last Known Good Configuration

A temporary copy of the hardware's Original Profile is made after a successful logon. This temporary copy is called the Last Known Good Configuration. It is replaced each time the user logs on.

Configuration changes are written to the Registry in the Current Control Set. Upon successful logon, a copy of this Control Set is copied to the LastKnownGood set. This set can be retrieved when a system is restarted after failed configuration changes. During the startup procedure, Windows NT display's the message `Press the space bar now to load Last Known Good Configuration`. This message appears for a short time only. If you choose to load the Last Known Good Configuration, it replaces the last set that failed. All the changes to the system made during the last session are lost.

The Last Known Good Configuration is updated after the user logs on using the Ctrl+Alt+Del logon sequence. Always wait for the system to load all devices and services before you log on. If a device or service fails, Windows NT displays an error message. Then you can turn off the system's power and restart with the Last Known Good Configuration still intact. Because the Last Known Good Configuration is not always reliable, hardware profiles and emergency repair disks are recommended as well.

B. Configuring the Operating System

You can tune several aspects of Windows NT. Having faster hardware is always an asset, but is not always realistic in the short term. From the operating system's perspective, Windows NT is a set of services that run devices to provide resources to the user. You can tune these items quickly, without having to upgrade or invest a large amount of money. The following sections cover these components:

- Windows NT services
- Windows NT device drivers
- Registry components

1. Running Windows NT Services

Windows NT Workstation 4.0 is made up of a series of services that run with each other to provide the operating system. A default set of services is loaded with a typical installation, and the user or applications can install additional services. Not all services are necessary in order to run Windows NT Workstation 4.0. The default set of services is chosen to satisfy the needs of most common users and systems. Disabling unused services frees up system resources, such as memory and the CPU. You cannot disable all services through hardware profiles, but you can stop them manually.

2. Disabling Devices

Devices, like services, can be disabled on a per hardware profile basis. Most devices that are set up initially are required to run the hardware attached or included in the system. During normal operation of the system, some devices may not be used. They are using system resources for nothing. To disable a device, always use the hardware profiles first to test their impact on the system. The following steps show how to disable a device safely:

1. Open the Devices icon in the Control Panel.
2. Select the device from the list.
3. Click the HW/Profiles button.
4. Select a test profile if one exists.
5. Click the Disable button.

The Original Configuration should be left intact. You can use this profile to return the system to a proper working order at any time.

3. Running Tasks and Applications

Each application runs one or more tasks in the Task Manager. There are several tricks and tips to reducing the demand on memory and processor resources by effectively handling tasks and applications:

- Close unused tasks to free up system resources.
- If an application is needed but is not currently in use, minimize it. Surprisingly, an application running in a window takes up significantly more memory than the same application that is minimized.

Threads in Windows NT are assigned priorities by the operating system, and the threads determine the frequency of processor time each is assigned with relation to all other threads. These priorities, from 1 (the lowest) to 31 (the highest) are typically set by the application programmer. The normal thread level for applications is 8, while most system services run above level 15.

A simple method to change the overall responsiveness of foreground versus background tasks is to set the Application Performance Boost found in the System icon's Performance tab. A Maximum boost increases the thread's priority by two levels when running in the foreground. The Minimum boost increases the priority by one, and the None boost does not increase the thread priority at all.

You can boost individual applications at the command line using the "start" command. Four start command switches can be used to change the priority of a given application. They all use the Start command and are listed in Table 18.3.1.

Table 18.3.1 Start Command Switches to Change Priority

Start Switch	Effects on Priority
Start /low	This actually lowers the base priority of the application to 4. The effect is to increase the overall performance of other applications. Running an application with a priority of 4 as a background application takes longer to complete any task.
Start /Normal	This switch runs the application using the normal priority of 8. It can be used for applications that normally run at a value lower than 8.
Start /High	The High switch sets application priority to a value of 13. Most applications run much faster if they require a lot of CPU time. This improves the performance of an application that reads and writes to the hard disk.
Start /Realtime	This switch increases the base priority to 24. Realtime is not recommended for applications that use the CPU extensively because you may not be able to interact with the system. The mouse or keyboard commands may not be able to interrupt the CPU. Only users with Administrator privileges can use the /Realtime switch.

To start the Notepad application with a priority of 13, follow these steps:

1. From the Start menu, choose Programs, Command Prompt.
2. Type **Start/High Notepad.exe**.

4. Virtual versus Physical Memory

You can almost always add physical memory to a computer with positive results. *Memory is the single most significant factor in overall system performance.* Adding more memory may not be possible in the short term for several reasons. For instance, the cost of upgrading can be a barrier, or the system may not have any space to quickly add additional RAM.

There are alternatives to purchasing more memory. After Windows NT has been tuned to make the best use of its current memory levels, you can do several things to increase the efficiency of the pagefile:

- On a system with several hard drives, move the pagefile to a drive that is faster or is not used as much in order to improve read and write requests.
- Create additional pagefiles stored on different drives, and the read/write operations may be handled faster depending on the hardware.

You can make all changes to the pagefile from the Performance tab of the System Properties dialog box. Select the Change button in the Virtual Memory section. The maximum size of the pagefile could be left intact. The recommendation is to always keep a 50MB buffer between the minimum and maximum sizes. This buffer ensures that the pagefile can grow to accommodate short-term demands.

C. Reviewing Disk Usage

In addition to pagefile activity, the disks are used constantly by the operating system to read information and write data. The speed and efficiency of the drive is important, and hardware issues are very important when selecting a type and speed of hard drive.

1. Making Hardware Choices

Hard drive and controller types can make a big difference on performance. SCSI hard disks, for instance, are much faster than IDE hard disks. Using a 32-bit controller card instead of a 16- or 8-bit controller will have significant impact on the system, too. Although these options improve performance, they may not be realistic in the short term. The cost of these new controller cards may prevent an upgrade.

2. Choosing Partition Size and Disk Format

You can partition each hard drive into different sizes and format them using FAT or NTFS. Large partitions may be easier to use because a single drive letter references them. It is not always better to use one logical disk per physical disk. The size and format of the partition determines the size of the cluster that's used for storage. A *cluster* is the smallest storage unit on a hard drive.

There are several points to consider when choosing partition and disk format options:

- FAT partitions typically have larger cluster sizes, which means that smaller amounts of data can inefficiently take up more space than they actually require.
- NTFS partitions are not bound by the same cluster size limitation that FAT partitions are.
- Partitions larger than 512MB should be converted to NTFS to reduce the size of the cluster that's used.
- Partitions smaller than 512MB can be converted to NTFS, but because NTFS requires additional space to operate, it may in fact offer less disk space.

3. Disk Access Issues

You should be aware of several disk access issues when optimizing your Windows NT Workstation 4.0 system:

- Use the diskperf -n command and reboot the system to disable any disk performance counters after you finishing monitoring performance.
- It is often inefficient to store the operating system, pagefile, programs, and data on a single hard drive.
- Placing the operating system on a separate partition improves the I/O request.

- When a pagefile is used constantly, it should be placed on a different partition than the operating system is on.
- Applications and data files should share the same physical disk so the hard disk does not have to search multiple locations.
- You should never compress heavily used files and programs that access the hard disk frequently. Compression under NTFS was designed for the Windows NT Workstation and does not have a major impact, but it can be noticeable is some cases.

4. Cleaning Up Disk Space

Fragmentation occurs in all cases when the operating system saves, deletes, and moves information on a hard drive. A file is fragmented if it is stored in several nonconsecutive clusters on the hard drive. Windows NT attempts to store information in the first continuous block of clusters. When a continuous block is not available, the file is stored in several nonconsecutive blocks. A disk can be fragmented even if files are not fragmented. There may be unused clusters in areas that are not large enough to store any one complete file. Fragmentation slows down disk access time because the read heads must move to several locations on the disk to read one file.

Currently, Windows NT Workstation 4.0 does not offer a defragmentation tool. There are third-party disk utilities that can do the job. There are also several methods you can use to help reduce fragmentation, especially on multiuser workstations:

- Move information between drives. From within Windows NT, just moving large amounts of information from one drive to another and back again re-creates a larger continuous block of clusters that will store data more efficiently.
- Reduce the size of the Recycle Bin; the deleted files it stores can take up a large percentage of your hard disk.
- Use only one hard drive for the Recycle Bin.
- Delete unused user profiles.

All improvements in performance come at a price. As you learned earlier, there will always be faster and newer hardware available. Changing Windows NT's internal configuration might improve performance slightly, but in some cases, it will do so at the expense of losing a service or resource. Always consider the repercussions of a change before implementation, and be prepared to reverse the change if problems occur. The basic configuration generated with a standard installation may be more than adequate for most systems.

18.3.1 Exercise: Improving Memory Performance

Objective: To see the impact on memory usage that occurs when certain services are stopped.

You must complete Exercise 18.2.3 before attempting this exercise. The changes you make can be quickly reversed if the desired results are not achieved.

Time Estimate: 10–15 minutes

Follow these steps to stop certain services and see the impact of that action on memory usage:

1. Use the Memtest.log file you created in Exercise 18.2.1 as a baseline log to represent the system before changes were made. If the Memtest.log file is not available, create one.
2. Boot the computer in the Test Configuration. No changes have been made yet to this profile.
3. From the Control Panel, select the Services icon.
4. Click the Spooler service.
5. Click the HW Profile button and disable only the Test Configuration. Disabling the Spooler removes printing capabilities.
6. Click the Server service and disable it for the Test Configuration. Administrators cannot remotely administer your system, and you will not be able to share folders.
7. Click any other service you think is not required and disable it as well for the Test Configuration.
8. Restart the computer using the same Test Configuration.
9. Create a new memory log called **MemTestAfter.log** and perform the same operations you did for Memtest.log for about the same amount of time.
10. Compare the values in the Memtest.log (no system improvements) with the values in MemTestAfter.log (with the system improvements). If the values are not significantly better in the latter, it may not have been worth making the improvements.
11. Reboot the computer using the Original Configuration. If the changes did not improve the system, delete the Test Configuration from the System icon in the Control Panel.

Answers and Explanations: Exercise

This exercise showed the impact stopping services has on memory usage. You disabled the print Spooler service, the Server service, and any others you decided by using a test hardware profile. After rebooting into your Test Configuration hardware profile and monitoring memory just as you did in Exercise 18.2.1, you probably saw improvements in memory usage because fewer services were running and using resources. By using hardware profiles to test your system, you can safely determine whether disabling various unneeded services creates a significant performance and optimization benefit. For more information on topics covered in this exercise, see the section titled "Running Windows NT Services."

18.3 Practice Problems

1. Your Windows NT 4.0 Workstation alerts you that virtual memory is too low. Where can you increase virtual memory?
   A. Disk Administrator
   B. System applet in Control Panel
   C. Device Manager
   D. File Explorer

2. How many pagefiles can be created per physical disk?
   A. 1
   B. 2
   C. 4
   D. 32

3. Windows NT 4.0 automatically assigns a priority level to each thread and process, depending on each one's importance. Can these priorities be changed by the user, or are they solely controlled by the operating system?
   A. Thread priorities can be changed by a user with the necessary privileges.
   B. Only the operating system can change thread priorities.
   C. Some thread priorities can be changed only by the operating system, whereas some can be changed by a user with the necessary privileges.
   D. Thread priorities are set by the operating system once and do not change.

4. In terms of performance and efficiency of disk space, what is the recommended file system for volumes over 512MB?
   A. FAT
   B. NTFS
   C. HPFS
   D. There are no performance or disk space issues.

5. You are running a mission-critical application on your Windows NT Workstation 4.0 system, and you want it to receive as much processor time as possible. How do you change the performance boost for the foreground application?
   A. Use the Performance tab in the System applet in Control Panel.
   B. Use Performance Monitor.
   C. Restart the application using the /realtime switch.
   D. Reduce the pagefile size to eliminate excess processor and I/O demands.

6. Your Windows NT 4.0 Workstation is equipped with 64MB of RAM. What is the recommended total paging file size?
   A. 64MB
   B. 128MB
   C. 76MB
   D. 96MB

7. Which of the following formulas determines the recommended pagefile size for a Windows NT 4.0 system?
   A. Number of megabytes of RAM plus 12MB
   B. Number of megabytes of RAM times 1.5MB
   C. 1/16 the size of the system disk
   D. 1/16 the size of all hard disk space, distributed among each of the available disks

8. Which of the following is a useful method of optimizing hard disk and system performance, enabling I/O to occur simultaneously across all disks?

   A. Creating mirror sets

   B. Creating striped sets

   C. Using the NTFS file system

   D. Windows NT does this automatically.

9. Windows NT 4.0 applications can be started at different priority levels. Which of the following are legitimate priority levels in Windows NT? (Choose all that apply.)

   A. REALTIME

   B. HIGH

   C. NORMAL

   D. LOW

10. You want to start the program analyze.exe with the highest possible priority. Which of the following commands do you type at the command line?

    A. run analyze.exe /highest

    B. start analyze.exe /high

    C. start /realtime analyze.exe

    D. analyze.exe /high

11. In order to start a process using the /realtime switch, the user must have:

    A. Enough virtual memory to handle background applications.

    B. NTFS file system on the drive containing the program.

    C. Administrator privileges.

    D. All other applications set to low priority.

12. Which are valid methods of recovering from configuration changes? (Choose all that apply.)

    A. Using emergency repair disk

    B. Using Windows NT's Backup to store the Registry

    C. Using the Last Known Good Configuration

    D. Using hardware profiles

13. Which are valid settings for the Server service configuration? (Choose all that apply.)

    A. Minimize Memory Used.

    B. Maximize Throughput for File Sharing.

    C. Minimize Throughput for Network Applications.

    D. Windows NT Workstation does not support the Server service.

14. You have decided to optimize your Windows NT 4.0 Workstation computer. How can you safely make the changes?

    A. Record a log on the system. You can use the log to reconstruct the system at a later time.

    B. Use the hardware profiles feature to make a test configuration. If a failure occurs, you can restart the system using the Original Configuration.

    C. Document all changes in the WinMSD utility. The system will recover automatically.

    D. Make sure the user profiles are enabled. Changes made to the system affect only the current user.

15. When creating a new hardware profile:

    A. All device-related information is reconfigured from scratch to provide a fresh profile.

    B. The entire Registry is copied over to the new profile.

    C. The profile begins as an identical copy of the current configuration, and changes are made as needed.

    D. Device drivers must be reinstalled.

16. You have just created a new hardware profile. When you reboot and choose your new profile, the profile fails and the system crashes. What should you do first to allow you to access your Windows NT 4.0 Workstation again?

    A. You must use the emergency repair disk to repair your Windows NT installation.

    B. You must restore the Registry.

    C. You must reboot the computer and choose the Original Configuration.

    D. You must reinstall Windows NT 4.0 Workstation.

17. What is stored in a hardware profile?

    A. Security information from the Registry.

    B. Device and device-related items.

    C. A copy of the Registry.

    D. A copy of the HKEY_LOCAL_MACHINE Registry key.

18. You want to modify the current hardware profile in use. Which tools are recommended for this task? (Choose two.)

    A. Registry Editor

    B. The Device applet in Control Panel

    C. The Services applet in Control Panel

    D. The System Policy Editor

19. The Last Known Good Configuration is updated after:

    A. The user logs off the Windows NT computer successfully.

    B. The user logs on using the Ctrl+Alt+Del logon sequence.

    C. The Windows NT computer boots and the logon screen appears.

    D. The Windows NT computer has been properly shut down.

20. You want to test several new settings for your experimental graphics devices on your Windows NT 4.0 graphics workstation. You are unsure if your new hardware settings will work properly. What is the best option for safely testing the new settings?

    A. Backup the Registry before attempting to change the settings.

    B. Create an emergency repair disk, make the changes to the settings, and use the ERD if necessary.

    C. Create a new hardware profile for experimenting with the new settings.

    D. Make any necessary changes and rely on the Last Known Good Configuration if the settings damage the system.

21. What is the highest thread priority Windows NT 4.0 can assign to a process?

    A. 14

    B. 15

    C. 24

    D. 31

22. The normal thread priority level for applications in Windows NT 4.0 is:

    A. 4

    B. 8

    C. 13

    D. 24

23. What is the recommended buffer size between minimum and maximum pagefile sizes?

    A. 11MB

    B. 12MB

    C. 24MB

    D. 50MB

24. Which scenario makes the least-efficient use of Windows NT 4.0 optimization and disk storage?

    A. The boot partition, system partition, programs, data, and pagefile all on one hard disk.

    B. An often-used pagefile on a different partition from the operating system.

    C. Multiple pagefiles distributed among multiple hard disks.

    D. Program files and their data stored on the same hard disk.

Answers and Explanations: Practice Problems

1. **B** The System applet in Control Panel enables you to alter the size of or create a pagefile.
2. **A** Only one pagefile can be created on a physical disk. Multiple pagefiles can be created on multiple disks.
3. **C** Some threads (such as certain services) cannot be immediately changed by the user, whereas some threads (such as application processes) can be changed in order to change the performance of the overall system and applications.
4. **B** NTFS uses smaller cluster sizes and is more efficient in volumes over 512MB. Volumes less than 512MB may actually have less available disk space when formatted with NTFS. This assumes that file security is not an issue.
5. **A** The Performance Boost sliding control in the System applet allows you to boost the foreground application's responsiveness.
6. **C** Although 75MB (65MB plus 11MB) is technically correct, Microsoft certification exams will always use 12MB as the number to add to physical memory.
7. **A** Again, 12MB is added to the physical memory (RAM) size.
8. **B** Striped sets enable multiple reads and writes across a number of disks, which may all have their own controllers. This can significantly increase speed and efficiency.
9. **A, B, C, D** All of these are valid switches.
10. **C** You type **start /*switch program*** at the command line.
11. **C** Only administrators can start a process in realtime mode.
12. **A, B, C, D** All of these are valid recovery methods.
13. **B, C** Throughput can be maximized for either file sharing or network applications.
14. **B** Hardware profiles are recommended whenever you're making changes to the system that you might need to roll back.
15. **C** A copy of an existing configuration is made first, and then the copy is changed.
16. **C** Choosing the Original Configuration after booting returns you to the normal state of the system.
17. **B** Device and device-related items are stored in a hardware profile.
18. **B, C** The Device and Services applets in Control Panel should be used to modify the hardware profile. The Registry Editor should not be used.
19. **B** Remember that you can reboot the computer before logging on and can still preserve the previous Last Known Good Configuration.

20. **C** Create a new hardware profile. Although creating an ERD can be helpful and is recommended, creating a new hardware profile is ideal for this situation.
21. **D** Although 24 is realtime, 31 can be set by the operating system.
22. **B** Eight (8) is normal thread priority.
23. **D** 50MB is the recommended buffer between minimum and maximum pagefile sizes. For example, 32MB RAM, 44MB–94MB pagefile.
24. **A** When possible, the boot partition, system partition, programs, data, and pagefile should not all be on the same hard disk. This causes excessive disk access for a single drive.

18.3 Key Words

emergency repair disk (ERD)

hardware profile

Last Known Good Configuration

cluster

fragmentation

Practice Exam: Monitoring and Optimization

Use this practice exam to test your mastery of Monitoring and Optimization. This practice exam is 17 questions long. The passing Microsoft score is 70.4 percent (12 questions correct). Questions are in multiple-choice format.

1. You want to print a chart of your processor performance from Performance Monitor to give to your administrative staff. How do you go about this?
   A. Print the chart from the File menu in Performance Monitor.
   B. Save the chart information as a .CSV or .TSV file, and then print it from an application that can view these files.
   C. Save the log and print it from the command prompt.
   D. Export the chart to plain text format and print it from any word processor.

2. Which of the following result from configuring Performance Monitor's log file with a longer period of time between logging intervals? (Choose two.)
   A. Larger log files
   B. Smaller log files
   C. More precise detail
   D. Less precise detail

3. To view a specific section in the Performance Monitor log file, you:
   A. Copy and save the selection to a new log file.
   B. Use the Time Window option in Performance Monitor.
   C. Double-click a selected time period in the log.
   D. Must have third-party administrative tools or the Windows NT 4.0 Resource Kit.

4. You are running a graphics program and are concerned that it is consuming more memory than a comparable program. What tool can you use to quickly gauge how much memory the application is using?
   A. Performance Monitor
   B. MEM.EXE
   C. Task Manager
   D. WinMSD

5. Which is not a type of counter in Performance Monitor?
   A. Averaging
   B. Remote
   C. Instantaneous
   D. Difference

6. Disk performance counters show up in Performance Monitor only if:
   A. The DiskPerf tool has been used to enable disk performance monitoring.
   B. The Disk Administrator has been run since Windows NT 4.0 Workstation was installed.
   C. The disk is formatted NTFS.
   D. You are running Windows NT 4.0 Server.

7. Your % Processor Time counter indicates that your processor normally operates above the threshold for efficiency. Is your processor causing a bottleneck?
   A. Yes. Processor activity consistently above the 80% threshold indicates the processor is causing a bottleneck.
   B. No. The bottleneck is probably caused by an application with excessive resource demands.

C. You cannot determine whether the processor is the actual cause of the bottleneck by monitoring this resource only.

D. Operation above the threshold of efficiency does not indicate a bottleneck.

8. The Performance Monitor should be used to create a baseline log file:

A. During greatest performance trouble.

B. Before any network connections are established.

C. During periods of normal and efficient operation.

D. During emergency periods when the computer is experiencing the most difficulty from bottlenecks.

9. You have identified a definite processor bottleneck while several necessary business applications are running on the workstation. Should you replace the processor immediately? Why or why not?

A. Yes, because the problem has been identified as a processor bottleneck.

B. Yes, because there are few ways to increase processor performance by optimizing other components.

C. No, you should increase virtual memory to accommodate the memory demands of each running application.

D. No, you may want to first determine whether a single application or thread is the cause of the excessive processor load.

10. Which method can be used to start the DiskPerf utility for monitoring disk performance?

A. Starting the Disk Administrator automatically starts DiskPerf.

B. Typing **diskperf –y** at the command prompt.

C. Using the System applet in Control Panel.

D. Performance Monitor automatically starts DiskPerf when disk performance counters are added.

11. You want to use the Event Viewer to look for any and all notifications of a device failure you believe to be impeding system performance. Your logs, however, are very large and require you to scroll through thousands of entries. What can you do to view the data more efficiently?

A. Create a new Event Log and map only the specific error to it.

B. Erase the log regularly so there will be less data to view.

C. Use filtering to filter out all other event information in the view.

D. Save the log and use a third-party utility to analyze it.

12. Fragmentation of hard disks under Windows NT 4.0:

A. Occurs only on FAT partitions.

B. Occurs only on NTFS partitions.

C. Does not occur; Windows NT prevents fragmentation automatically.

D. Occurs on both FAT and NTFS partitions.

13. Using the Applications Performance Boost under the System applet in Control Panel, you set the performance boost to Maximum. What does this do to the foreground application?

A. Increases the foreground application's priority to realtime.

B. Decreases all background applications' priorities by one level.

C. Increases the foreground application's priority by two levels.

D. Increases the foreground application's priority by five levels, bringing Normal priority apps to High priority.

14. How can minimizing a currently unused application help increase efficiency?

A. Minimizing an application reduces its thread priority by 1 level.

B. Minimizing an application reduces its overall memory demand as compared to maximized applications.

C. Minimized applications do not receive Windows messages and require much less processor time.

D. Minimizing an application does not result in an increase in efficiency or a decrease in resource use.

15. You make a change to a hardware setting on your Windows NT 4.0 computer, and then you reboot. After logging back on, you notice a hardware failure error. You shut down Windows NT, reboot the computer, and try the Last Known Good Configuration in order to restore the original settings. Will this work? Why or why not? (Choose one.)

A. Yes. Last Known Good Configuration loads the last configuration in which all system hardware and services worked properly.

B. Yes. Hardware settings are not used to determine a working configuration and thus will not be preserved in the Last Known Good Configuration.

C. No. The Last Known Good Configuration was updated when you logged onto the Windows NT 4.0 Workstation. It will simply bring up Windows NT in the same state.

D. No. The Last Known Good Configuration was updated when you shut down and rebooted the computer to log back on. It will only bring up Windows NT in the same state.

16. An emergency repair disk contains which of the following? (Choose all that apply.)

A. Security account database information

B. All software configuration information

C. All hardware configuration information

D. All devices drivers running on the system at the time the disk is created

17. Which utility is used to create the emergency repair disk?

A. Disk Administrator

B. RDISK.EXE

C. Registry Editor

D. System applet in Control Panel

Answers and Explanations: Practice Exam

1. **B** Unfortunately, Performance Monitor cannot print its views. You can save data to either a comma (.CSV) or tab (.TSV) delimited file and print it from an application (such as a spreadsheet) that can read such a file properly.

2. **B, D** Log files will be smaller because they will not log to a file as often, but the log will be less precise because it will not log as many statistics.

3. **B** The Time Window tool can be used to select and then view a specific time interval in the log.

4. **C** Task Manager's Processes tab shows memory consumption by individual process.

5. **B** Remote is not a valid counter type. However, counters can be used to monitor a remote computer.
6. **A** DISKPERF -Y should be used to enable disk performance monitoring.
7. **C** Although a processor operating above its threshold (80%) indicates a possible bottleneck, it could be the result of other components such as memory or hard disks that may be the actual bottleneck. You should monitor all of these to determine the actual cause of the bottleneck.
8. **C** The baseline log file should be created during periods of normal and efficient operation so it can be used to compare with times of inefficiency and noticeable bottlenecking.
9. **D** In some cases, a single application of thread may cause the processor to run inefficiently, and there are measures to be taken to avoid upgrading to a new processor.
10. **B** The diskperf.exe command with the -y switch enables the disk performance counters.
11. **C** You can use the Event Log to track down specific causes of hardware or application failures, which may aid in optimization troubleshooting. The Filter option enables you to view only specified events in the log, which makes searching easier.
12. **D** Fragmentation occurs on all drives, regardless of the file system.
13. **C** Thread priorities are boosted by two levels.
14. **B** Applications tend to use less memory when minimized.
15. **C** The Last Known Good Configuration is updated at logon, and thus would only return you to the last state because Windows NT booted and allowed logon.
16. **A, B, C** Security account information and hardware and software information are stored on the ERD. These are used to restore the Registry in case of corruption.
17. **B** RDISK.EXE is used to create an emergency repair disk.

CHAPTER 19

Troubleshooting

This chapter helps you prepare for the exam by covering the following objectives:

- Choosing the appropriate course of action to take when the boot process fails.
- Choosing the appropriate course of action to take when a print job fails.
- Choosing the appropriate course of action to take when the installation process fails.
- Choosing the appropriate course of action to take when an application fails.
- Choosing the appropriate course of action to take when a user cannot access a resource.
- Modifying the Registry using the appropriate tool.
- Implementing advanced techniques to resolve various problems.

19.1 Choosing the Appropriate Course of Action to Take When the Boot Process Fails

When you know that your workstation's hardware is correctly functioning, the failure of Windows NT Workstation to start up properly and load the Windows NT shell could be a boot process problem. The key to solving problems of this type is to understand the logical sequence that your workstation uses when starting up. Windows NT shows you various boot sequence errors, the meaning of which should help you determine the problem with your system. You also can diagnose the boot.ini file to determine the nature of any potential problems, and you can apply your emergency repair disks to boot your system and repair common boot process failure problems.

A boot failure is a very obvious error, and one of the most common problems that you will encounter. When you or your client can't start up your computer, you know you have a problem. It's the kind of problem that forces you to stop what you are doing and fix it before you can go on to further work.

A. The Boot Sequence

Your computer begins the operating system boot sequence after the *Power On Self Test (POST)* completes itself. The first series of messages that you see when you turn the power on to your computer are hardware related, and are not associated with the boot process. Your memory is tested, for example, and then your bus structure is tested. Your computer runs a series of tests. These tests signal to peripheral devices and sense their replies to check for successful I/O performance. You might see a series of messages verifying that your mouse and keyboard are detected, the appearance of an IDE drive, whether a SCSI adapter is detected, response from any devices on that SCSI chain, and so forth. Failure at this stage isn't a boot sequence problem.

The boot sequence initiates when the hard drive *Master Boot Record (MBR)* is read into memory and begins to load the different portions of the Windows NT operating system. Windows NT Workstation runs on different microprocessor architectures. The exact boot sequence depends on the type of microprocessor on which you have installed Windows NT Workstation.

Windows NT loads on an Intel x86 computer by reading a file called the *NTLDR*, or *NT Loader*, into memory from the boot sector of the startup or active partition on your boot drive. The NTLDR is a hidden system file set to be read-only. NTLDR is located in the root folder of your system partition, and can be viewed in the Windows NT Explorer when you set the View All File Types option. NTLDR performs the following actions:

- Turns on the 32-bit flat memory model required by the Windows NT kernel to address RAM.
- Turns on the minifile system driver to access the system and boot partitions.
- Displays the Boot Loader menu system that provides the operating system to use. These selections are contained in the boot.ini file in your systemroot directory.

You can install Windows NT Workstation over a previous installation of MS-DOS or Windows 95. These operating systems will appear in the menu and call the bootsect.dos file when they are loaded and executed. Bootsect.dos loads and then at the end of the boot process hands off to the operating system component responsible for I/O communication. In Windows 95, that file is the io.sys file. The following steps round out the boot process:

1. After you select an operating system, a hardware detection routine is initiated. For Windows NT, the NTDETECT.COM program is responsible for this routine and creates a hardware list passed to the NTLDR program.
2. The operating system kernel is then loaded. The ntoskrnl.exe file located in the %systemroot%\System32 folder is called to load the kernel of Windows NT. The menu is replaced by the OS Loader V4.00 screen.
3. A blue screen appears that indicates the loading of the *Hardware Abstraction Layer (HAL)*. To execute this, the hal.dll is called with a set of routines that isolates operating system functions from I/O.
4. The HKEY_LOCAL_MACHINE\System hive of the Registry is read and the system is loaded. Registry hives are stored as files in the %systemroot%\System32\Config folder.
5. The boot time drivers HKEY_LOCAL_MACHINE\System\CurrentControlSet\Control \ServiceGroupOrder are loaded. For each driver loaded, a dot is added to the OS Loader screen.

> **If you enter the /SOS switch in the boot.ini file, Windows NT will list the driver's name in the OS Loader screen as Windows NT Workstation starts up.**

6. The list of supported hardware devices is handed off from ntdetect.com to ntoskrnl.exe.
7. After ntoskrnl.exe executes, the computer's boot phase finishes and the software you have installed begins to be loaded.

1. RISC-Based Boot Sequence

A *RISC computer* contains the NTLDR software as part of its BIOS. Therefore, the boot phase of a RISC-based computer is both simpler and faster than the boot phase of an Intel x86 computer. A RISC computer keeps its hardware configuration in its BIOS, which obviates the need for the ntdetect.com file. Another item kept in firmware is the list of any valid operating systems and how to access them. This means that a RISC computer also doesn't use a boot.ini file.

A RISC computer boots by loading a file called the osloader.exe file. After reading the hardware configuration from the BIOS and executing, osloader.exe hands off the boot process to the ntoskrnl.exe. Then the hal.dll is loaded, followed by the system file, which ends the RISC Windows NT boot process.

Because the boot.ini file is a text file, you can edit this file to control aspects of the boot process. Open the Windows NT Explorer and remove the read-only attribute from this file (which is located in the %systemroot% top-level folder) before you begin. There are two sections to the boot.ini: [boot loader] and [operating systems].

19

You will see parameters that control the amount of time a user has to decide on an operating system (timeout) as well as the default location in an ARC- (Advanced RISC-) compliant path nomenclature. Although you can change the default operating system and the timeout by editing the boot.ini file, you will probably find it easier to change these parameters on the Startup/ Shutdown tab of the Systems Properties dialog box.

To change system startup parameters, complete the following steps:

1. Right-click on the My Computer icon and choose the Properties command from the Shortcut menu.
2. Click on the Startup/Shutdown tab of the Systems Properties dialog box if necessary.
3. Enter the operating system desired in the Startup list box.
4. Change the timeout parameter in the Show List for … Seconds spinner.
5. Click OK.

Making changes in the Systems Properties dialog box offers a distinct advantage to editing in the boot.ini file; any mistake you make while entering information into the boot.ini file can cause your system to fail at boot up.

2. Creating a Memory Dump

When you encounter a blue screen error, you may need to take a memory dump of your system for diagnostic purposes. A *memory dump* is a copy of the data held in RAM. To save that file, you need free disk space equal to that of your installed RAM plus an additional MB of space.

To take a memory dump, check the Write Debugging Information To and Overwrite Any Existing Files check boxes in the Startup/Shutdown tab of System Control Panel. Close that Control Panel and confirm any alerts about page file size should they occur. Then reboot your computer. The memory dump file is written to the location displayed in the Startup/Shutdown tab text box.

C. The Load Process

After the boot portion of the operating system loads, your device drivers load and the boot process is handed off to the operating system kernel. In Windows NT, this portion of the startup occurs when the screen turns a blue color and the text shrinks. At that point, the kernel is initializing and the operating system begins to read various hives in the Windows NT Registry. One of the first hives read is the CurrentControlSet, which is copied to the CloneControlSet and from which a HARDWARE key is written to RAM. The System hive is read to determine whether additional drivers need to be loaded into RAM and initialized. This ends the kernel initialization phase.

The Session Manager reads the System hive in the Registry to determine which programs are required prior to Windows NT itself being loaded. Commonly the AUTOCHK.EXE program (a stripped down version of CHKDSK.EXE) runs and reads the file system. Other programs defined in the HKEY_LOCAL_MACHINE\SYSTEM\CurrentControlSet\Control\Session Manager\BootExecute key are run, and a page file is then created in the location stored in the HKEY_LOCAL_MACHINE\SYSTEM\CurrentControlSet\Control\Session Manager\Memory Management key.

The Software hive is read and the Session Manager loads other required subsystems as defined in the HKEY_LOCAL_MACHINE\SYSTEM\CurrentControlSet\Control\Session Manager\Subsystems\Required key. This ends the portion of the boot process in which services are loaded into RAM.

After services are loaded, the Windows WIN32 Subsystem starts to load. This is where Windows NT Workstation switches into a Graphics (GUI) mode. The WINLOGON module runs and the Welcome dialog box appears. The Windows operating system is still loading at this point, but the user can enter the user name, domain, and password to initiate the logon process. After the Service Controller (SERVICES.EXE) loads and initializes the Computer Browser, Workstation, Server, Spooler, and so on, the request for logon is passed to the domain controller for service.

The SERVICES.EXE program is a central program in the Windows NT operating system. It initializes various system DLL files. Should this file be damaged, you must reinstall Windows NT Workstation. The following DLLs provide operating system services:

- *Alerter (alrsvc.dll).* Provides messaging services and event alerts.
- *Computer Browser (browser.dll).* Provides a way for locating resources on the network.
- *EventLog (eventlog.dll).* Notes and enters events into the three log files.
- *Messenger (msgsvc.dll).* Provides interapplication communications that enable one application to communicate with another.
- *Net Logon (netlogon.dll).* Has the code required to request resource validation from domain servers.
- *NT LM Security Support Provider (ntmssos.dll).* Provides security support.
- *Server (srvsvc.dll).* Enables Windows NT Workstation to provide limited network services to other computers.
- *TCP/IP NetBIOS Helper (lmhsvc.dll).* Handles IP address resolution.
- *Workstation (wkssvc.dll).* Enables a Windows NT Workstation computer to access resources on the network. Workstation includes services that enable the computer to log on to a domain, connect to shared resources such as printers and directories, and participate in client/server applications running over the network.

A successful logon is considered the completion of the boot process. To mark the event, Windows NT Workstation updates the LastKnownGood control set key in the Registry with information about what was loaded and the current system configuration at startup.

19

D. Last Known Good Recovery

The *Last Known Good configuration* provides a method for recovering to your preceding system setup. When you create a specific configuration for Windows NT, that information is stored in a particular control set. The LastKnownGood control set enables you to recover from a boot process error—provided that you use this method immediately after discovering the error on the first boot up attempt and do not log on a second time. Subsequent boots (if they proceed and you log on to the system again) remove this option as a recovery method.

The information contained in the Last Known Good configuration is stored in the Registry in the HKEY_LOCAL_MACHINE\SYSTEM\CurrentControlSet key. To boot to the Last Known Good configuration, follow these steps:

1. Reboot your system.
2. Press the spacebar when a message appears asking you whether you want to boot the Last Known Good configuration.
3. When the Hardware Profile/Configuration Recovery menu appears, select a hardware profile and press the L key for the Last Known Good configuration.

In instances in which a critical system error was encountered, Windows NT Workstation defaults to the Last Known Good configuration on its own accord. This defaulting doesn't always occur, but is a frequent occurrence. Should basic operating system files be damaged, you must boot up using a boot floppy and recover your system as described in the next few sections.

E. Boot Sequence Errors

The most common boot sequence errors occur when the operating system components required for the boot process cannot be found or are corrupted. Often a modification of the boot.ini file leads to a failure to boot properly. If you or your client have recently made a modification to the startup files, you should suspect that problem first.

Catastrophic hardware failure is not a common problem, but it is encountered—particularly in older equipment. If a hard drive stops operating, it will be obvious because your computer makes different sounds when no disk is being accessed. Also, when you open the case of the computer and listen to it, you won't hear the hard drive spin up and achieve its operating speed.

Much less obvious are hardware errors that damage the capability of your system to start up without appearing to alter the performance of your system noticeably. If your hard drive develops a bad disk sector, which contains the operating system components responsible for booting your computer, for example, the computer appears to function correctly. This problem is solved by re-establishing the boot files on another portion of your hard drive.

1. BOOT.INI Error Messages

The following error messages appear when there is a problem with the boot.ini file. If you get one of these error messages and the Windows shell doesn't load, you should suspect the boot.ini file and use a boot disk or an *emergency repair disk (ERD)* to repair the boot.ini file. Later in this chapter, you learn how to create an ERD. This message indicates that the Windows NT Loader file is either damaged or corrupted:

```
BOOT: Couldn't find NTLDR
Please insert another disk
```

Typically, the error with the NTLDR file occurs early on in the boot process. When you see a repeated sequence of error messages indicating that Windows NT Workstation is checking hardware, the error is a problem with the ntdetect.com file. These messages appear as follows:

```
NTDETECT V1.0 Checking Hardware…
NTDETECT V1.0 Checking Hardware…
NTDETECT V1.0 Checking Hardware…
```

It is possible for Windows NT to load even if the boot.ini file is missing. If that is the case, the NTLDR starts Windows NT loading files it finds in the <default>\WINNT folder. If the operating system was installed in another location, an error message appears indicating that the ntoskrnl.exe file is missing or corrupt. The following error message appears when the boot.ini file is damaged or when it points to a location that no longer contains the Windows NT Workstation operating system files:

```
Windows NT could not start because the following file is missing or corrupt:
\<winnt root>\system32\ntoskrnl.exe
Please re-install a copy of the above file.
```

This message indicates that the Windows NT operating system kernel has failed to load. The problem most often occurs when someone inadvertently renames the folder containing the operating system files without realizing the consequences of that action. The solution is to use your boot disk to gain access to the system and to rename the folder with the location contained in the boot.ini file. It is less common to see a change in the boot.ini file giving rise to this problem because that requires a knowledgeable user's action.

Another potential explanation for the inability of the kernel to load could be that you used the Disk Administrator to create a partition with free space. If you changed the partition number that contains your Windows NT operating system files, the pointer in the boot.ini file no longer points to the correct location. To fix this problem, you need to edit the pointer to the partition to correct the partition number so that it correctly locates your Windows NT operating system files.

When there is a problem with the boot sector, the following error message appears during startup:

```
I/O Error accessing boot sector file
Multi(0)disk(0)rdisk(0)partition(1):\bootsect.dos
```

This error message could indicate a problem with your hard drive. You should boot from a boot disk and run the RDISK utility.

Windows NT Workstation also posts a more specific message when it can determine that the error in locating the boot sector is hardware related. The operating system checks hardware (as you have just seen) by testing it during startup. Failure to respond to one of these tests generates the following message:

```
OS Loader V4.00
Windows NT could not start because of a computer disk hardware configuration
problem.
Could not read from the selected boot disk. Check boot path and disk hard-
ware.
Please check the Windows NT™ documentation about hardware disk configuration
and your hardware reference manuals for additional information.
```

The preceding message indicates that the pointer in the boot.ini file that locates the Windows NT operating system references a damaged or non-existing device, or a partition that doesn't contain a file system that Windows NT can access with the boot loader.

Finally, you may see a STOP error when the Windows NT Loader cannot resolve the appropriate partition that contains your operating system files. This error takes the following form:

```
STOP: 0x000007E: Inaccessible Boot Device
```

This error appears when the hard disk controller has difficulty determining which device is the boot device— for example, if your computer contains an Adaptec SCSI disk controller, and there is an ID number conflict. Another instance in which this error occurs is when the Master Boot Record (MBR) is corrupted by a virus or a disk error.

If you have an internal IDE drive on the workstation and a SCSI disk drive with an ID number set to 0, you will see the inaccessible boot device problem appear. The 0 ID number is used to specify which disk is the internal disk, and this drive conflicts with a boot partition on the IDE drive. Any bootable SCSI disks can also be booted in preference to your internal IDE drive, so you might want to make all SCSI drives non-bootable to prevent the SCSI disk controller from booting a SCSI drive. (Some disk adapters dynamically assign SCSI device numbers, but these adapters aren't particularly common.) If the Windows NT DETECT program in the boot loader assigns the number 0 to the SCSI bus adapter, this too makes the reference in the boot.ini file to your internal IDE drive inaccurate.

As a general rule, SCSI drives are faster than IDE drives and preferred by the operating system. Don't mix and match these two different drive types. If you have a SCSI disk controller and SCSI drives, locate your boot partition on those.

If your system proceeds through the load phase and boots correctly but still seems to be malfunctioning, you should check the System Event Log to see whether any system messages were written to the log.

???Is it System Event Log (as above) or System Log (as below)? Same thing? Should be referred to consistently if alternate term is not introduced?

The *System Log* can display errors, warnings, or informational events that explain the conditions leading to an anomaly due to an error in the boot sequence. Use the Event Viewer program in the Administrative Tools folder on the Program submenu of the Start menu to view the System Log. Choose the System Log command on the Log menu to open the System Log.

F. Boot Disk Recovery

If your hard disk boot partition fails, you can start up from a floppy disk, provided you've created a Windows NT boot disk prior to the occurrence of the error condition. If you have installed a multipartition system and your boot partition contains Windows NT, you can also use your boot disk to start up. After you have started your system using the floppy disk, you can perform procedures to test and repair any errors that exist.

Most computers are started up from their floppy disk drives—commonly given the volume label A. If your computer is configured to start up from your hard drive, you must change this in your computer's BIOS setup. Press the keystroke displayed in the startup sequence to open your computer's setup. Then change the boot sequence to start up from the floppy disk drive prior to attempting to boot from a floppy boot disk.

To create a floppy boot disk, do the following:

1. Insert a blank 1.44MB floppy disk in your floppy disk drive.
2. Double-click My Computer on your Desktop.
3. Right-click the icon for your floppy disk drive, and then select the Format command from the shortcut menu.
4. Click OK to begin the formatting, and then click OK to confirm that formatting occurred.
5. Select the Windows NT Explorer command from the Programs submenu of the Start menu.

6. Select the boot.ini, NTLDR, ntbootdd.sys, and ntdetect.com files in the root directory of your hard drive in the Windows NT Explorer. This directory is commonly called the C:\ drive.
7. Right-click on any of the selected files and drag them to the icon for your floppy disk drive.
8. Choose the Copy Here command from the shortcut menu.
9. Restart your computer with the boot floppy disk in the floppy disk drive to test the disk.

G. The Emergency Repair Disk (ERD)

When a portion of the Windows NT Registry becomes corrupted, your workstation can become unstable and crash. In some instances, these errors even prevent you from starting your computer up and booting the Windows NT operating system itself. You can repair the Windows NT Registry if you have created an ERD that contains the important system Registry information.

An ERD contains backup information about your workstation's security account manager (SAM) database, your system configuration, and important system configuration parameters. Also copied to the ERD are the two files required to create a virtual DOS machine (NTVDM): autoexec.nt and config.nt.

You are prompted to create an ERD when you install Windows NT Workstation. If you prefer, you can create an ERD at a later time. Regardless of whether you choose to create an ERD, the appropriate files are copied to the %systemroot%\Repair directory.

If you search for the topic of the Emergency Repair Disk in the online Help system, Windows NT Workstation's Help system steps you through the process of either creating or updating your ERD. You can also open a Command Prompt window and create or update your ERD by using the rdisk.exe command. RDISK copies the following files:

- Tthe Registry default hive (HKEY_USERS\DEFAULT)
- The Registry security hive (HKEY_LOCAL_MACHINE\Security)
- The Registry software hive (HKEY_LOCAL_MACHINE\Software)
- The Registry system hive (HKEY_LOCAL_MACHINE\System)
- The workstation SAM
- The Registry autoexec.nt file
- The config.nt file

These files are copied into the %systemroot%\REPAIR folder, after which, the RDISK utility prompts you for a floppy disk on which to create an ERD. The information in the REPAIR folder is copied onto this disk.

The ERD is useful only if you update it on a regular basis. You should consider updating the ERD before performing any major software installations or upgrades, making any changes to your security policy, or changing the hardware configuration of your workstation.

If this information is not current on your ERD, the restoration you can perform using the ERD is of limited value. The ERD doesn't take the place of a full volume backup—it saves only data that can help re-establish your system configuration based on information contained in the Registry.

1. Creating the ERD

To create an ERD, follow these steps:

1. Open the Start menu and choose Programs, Command Prompt.
2. Enter **RDISK /S** at the command prompt, and then press Enter.
3. Click on the Create Repair Disk button in the Repair Disk Utility dialog box.
4. Insert a formatted floppy disk, and then click OK.
5. After Windows NT Workstation creates the ERD, remove the floppy disk, write-protect the disk, and store it away.
6. Click Exit to close RDSIK.
7. Click Close. The information copied to the ERD is in compressed format. To restore a Registry key by using the Registry Editor and the ERD data, expand the files by using the Windows NT Expand program. The following list of files are found on an ERD:

   - *autoexec.nt* and *config.nt.* The two files responsible for a Virtual DOS Machine. They correspond to the autoexec.bat and config.sys files on MS-DOS. The first file runs a batch file; the second sets an environment.
   - *default._.* The compressed copy of the System's default profile.
   - *ntuser.da_.* The compressed copy of the ntuser.dat file, which stores user profiles.
   - *sam._.* The compressed copy of the SAM hive of the Registry with a copy of the Windows NT accounts database. A workstation SAM doesn't contain as much information as a server (especially a domain server) SAM does. Missing is information about other machine and user accounts that the workstation doesn't know about.
   - *security._.* The compressed copy of the Security hive with SAM and security policy information for your workstation's users.
   - *setup.log.* A text file with the names of the Windows setup and installation files, and checksums for each file. The file is used to determine whether essential system files are either missing or corrupt. If so, it replaces them in a recovery operation.
   - *software._.* A compressed copy of the Software hive with information about installed programs and associated files and configuration information for those programs.
   - *system._.* A compressed copy of the System hive of the Registry. This hive contains the Windows NT control set.

To update the ERD, run the RDISK program and select the Update Repair Info button. Confirm that you want to overwrite the current repair information.

The importance of using the /S switch for the RDISK program is worth noting. This switch updates the DEFAULT,_ SECURITY, and SAM changes without requiring that you go through the Create Repair Disk? dialog box first. Without the /S switch, changes to your account information are not noted. If you have a lot of accounts, updating this information can take some time. Also, your ERD will likely expand beyond the single floppy disk limit. In that case, the RDISK program asks you for additional disks, as needed.

2. Restoring Your System Using the ERD

When you use the ERD to repair a damaged Windows NT Workstation, the procedure essentially reinstalls the sections of the operating system that are required for your particular setup. The data that you copied to the ERD contained in the Windows NT Registry determines which files need to be replaced, and how the configuration should be re-established. Among the things that the ERD does are the following:

- Runs CHKDSK to determine the validity of the partition containing your Windows NT system files.
- Determines whether the individual files on a system partition are valid, as determined by the use of a checksum.
- Restores missing or corrupt files from your Windows NT installation disks.
- Replaces your default system and security Registry hives.
- Replaces the Security Account Manager hives.
- Reinstalls the files responsible for booting your system in the Boot Loader: boot.ini, NTLDR, ntbootdd.sys, and ntdetect.com.

Before you begin to restore your system, make sure you have your Windows NT Setup floppy disks handy. If you can't find those disks, you can create them from the installation CD by using the WINNT /O or the /OX switch. You can find online documentation for the WINNT.EXE program in the Help system. To restore Windows NT Workstation on an Intel x386 system, complete the following steps:

19

1. Insert the Windows NT Workstation Setup boot disk into your floppy disk drive. (Make sure your system boots from a floppy disk first.)
2. Turn on your system, and then insert Setup Disk 2 when asked. Press the Enter key.
3. Press the R key to perform a repair.
4. Press Enter to mark any options that you want to restore, press Tab to move to the Continue button, and press Enter again.
5. Press Enter to detect devices.
6. Insert the Setup Disk 3 into your floppy disk when requested.
7. Insert additional disks with device drives when the Other Disk option appears, and then replace that (those) disk(s) with Setup Disk 3 again.
8. Press Enter and insert your ERD when requested, and then press Enter again.
9. Press Enter to select each Registry hive you want to restore, and then move to the Continue button and press Enter again.
10. Press the A key to replace all modified system files.

11. Insert any required device driver files requested.
12. Press Esc to have Setup ignore the Windows NT Workstation DRVLIB disk, if you want.
13. When the program is complete, reboot your computer.

You can choose the following four main options to repair in the recovery process:

- *Inspect Registry Files.* By using your ERD, you can repair corrupt portions of the Registry. You can select to repair any or all of the following hives: Default, Security/SAM, Software, and/or System. Changes to the Registry do not require the use of the Windows NT installation CDs.
- *Inspect Startup Environment.* Any boot files are inspected, dissected, and potentially rejected. Because all default boot files are equivalent, you can use any ERD to replace startup files.
- *Verify Windows NT System Files.* This option compares any system file (with the system attribute) in the Windows NT directory and any subdirectories and verifies them using the checksum values in the setup.log file. You need your installation disks to perform this repair.
- *Inspect Boot Sector.* Often the boot sector becomes invalid when youupgrade MS-DOS, or Windows 95 by using the SYS command. Use an ERD (any ERD) and the installation disks to repair this problem.

Each ERD that you create is specific to the type of computer (vendor and CPU type) on which it is created. An ERD that you create on one system does not work on another system. The process of restoring a RISC system containing the Windows NT Workstation as its operating system is similar in concept to the procedure previously described. The individual sequence differs, however, depending on the specific manufacturer for your system. To restore a RISC-based Windows NT system, complete the following steps:

1. Start the Windows NT Setup program as your computer's manual instructs you to.
2. Insert the ERD, and then follow the instructions that appear on your monitor.

After the repair is complete, remove the ERD and reboot your system. Creating and maintaining an ERD is one of the most effective troubleshooting tools that you have in your arsenal. It cures a host of ills. It is only effective, however, if you remain diligent in updating it whenever a workstation's configuration changes.

19.1.1 Exercise: Creating a Boot Floppy Disk and Emergency Repair Disks

Objective: Create a set of disks that enable you to start your workstation in case of boot failure, and to repair a workstation that doesn't boot properly.

Time Estimate: 20 minutes

To create the boot floppy, follow these steps:

1. Insert a blank floppy disk in the disk drive and format that disk.
2. Open the Windows NT Explorer and select the boot.ini, NTLDR, and ntdetect.com.

3. Copy these four files to the floppy disk to create the Windows NT boot floppy disk.
4. Restart your computer without removing the floppy disk from the drive. If disk is valid, it boots your computer.
5. Label the disk and store it in a secure location.

To create a set of emergency repair disks, follow these steps:

1. Choose the Command Prompt command from the Programs submenu of the Start menu.
2. Type **RDISK /S** and press Enter.
3. Click the Create Repair Disk button in the Repair Disk Utility dialog box.
4. Insert a formatted floppy disk, and then click OK.
5. After Windows NT Workstation creates the ERD, remove the floppy disk, write-protect the disk, and store it away.
6. Click Exit to close RDISK.
7. Click on the Close box.

19.1.1 Answers and Explanations: Exercise

You should update your boot floppy whenever you make a significant hardware installation. You should update your ERDs whenever you make any significant change that is recorded in your Registry. Without regular update (of your ERDs in particular), these disks are of limited use to you.

19.1.2 Exercise: Displaying Device Drivers at Startup

Objective: Modify the boot.ini file to enumerate your drivers when the kernel is loading.

Time Estimate: 15 minutes

To display the device drivers, follow these steps:

1. Choose the Notepad command from the Accessories folder on the Programs submenu of the Start menu.
2. Select the Open command from the File menu.
3. Select All Files in the File of Type list box and select the boot.ini file in the root directory.
4. Find the line in the boot.ini file that reads `Windows NT Server Version 4.00 [VGA]` followed by /basevideo and /sos switches. If your system uses a VGA driver, skip to Step 6.
5. Choose the Save As command from the File menu and save the boot.ini file to a different name, such as boot.bak.
6. Delete the /basevideo switch and leave the /sos switch intact. Modify the bracket text to read **Windows NT Server Version 4.00 [SOS]**.
7. Select the Save As command on the File menu and save the file as the boot.ini file in the root directory. (Note that the file boot.ini is read-only, system, and hidden. You will probably have to change the attributes to be able to save the file.)

8. Exit Notepad and reboot your system.
9. Select the SOS option from the boot menu when it appears. Your device drivers appear listed on-screen as they load in ARC format.
10. Log on to Windows NT Workstation.
11. Restore the original boot.ini file with the VGA configuration and /basevideo switch; then reboot to test your system.

19.1.2 Answers and Explanations: Exercise

If your system hangs when a device loads, that device is the last one listed in the sequence. Don't forget to restore your VGA setting, as you may need it in the future should you experience a video problem.

19.1 Practice Problems

1. Which of the following files are not on the emergency repair disk?

   A. SETUP.LOG

   B. NTUSER.DA_

   C. CONFIG.NT

   D. NTSYSTEM.DA_

2. Which of the following is a collection of configuration information used during boot by Windows NT?

   A. LastKnownGood

   B. Control set

   C. BOOT.INI

   D. NTLDR

3. Which of the following is a collection of configuration information used in troubleshooting Windows NT boot problems?

   A. LastKnownGood

   B. Control set

   C. BOOT.INI

   D. NTLDR

4. The user screen switches into GUI mode after which phase of startup?

   A. Kernel Initialization

   B. Services Load

   C. Windows Start

   D. Win32 subsystem

5. Before editing the BOOT.INI file, which of the following should you do? (Choose two.)

   A. Back up the existing file.

   B. Turn off the system attribute.

   C. Turn off the read-only attribute.

   D. Rename the file with a .TXT extension.

6. With which of the following can you change the BOOT.INI file? (Choose all that apply.)

   A. EDIT.COM

   B. NOTEPAD.EXE

   C. The Environment tab of the Control Panel System application

   D. The Startup/Shutdown tab of the Control Panel System application

7. Which of the following is the preferred method of changing the BOOT.INI file?

   A. EDIT.COM

   B. NOTEPAD.EXE

   C. The Environment tab of the Control Panel System application

   D. The Startup/Shutdown tab of the Control Panel System application

8. Which of the following choices is not available from the Emergency Repair Process menu?

   A. Inspect Registry Files

   B. Event Viewer

   C. Inspect Startup Environment

   D. Verify Windows NT System Files

9. In the Registry, under which of the following is LastKnownGood boot information stored?

   A. HKEY_LOCAL_MACHINE

   B. HKEY_LOCAL_MACHINE\SYSTEM

   C. HKEY_LOCAL_MACHINE\SYSTEM\CurrentControlSet

   D. HKEY_LOCAL_MACHINE\SYSTEM\CurrentControlSet\LastKnownGood

10. Which two of the following are files needed during an Intel-based boot that are not needed for a RISC boot operation?

    A. NTDETECT.COM

    B. NTLDR

    C. OSLOADER.EXE

    D. NTOSKRNL.EXE

11. To update the SAM information on the emergency repair disk, which switch must you use with RDISK?

    A. /SAM

    B. /S

    C. /OX

    D. SYSTEM

12. Which of the following items will RDISK not update, by default, in the Emergency Repair directory?

    A. SAM

    B. SETUP.LOG

    C. DEFAULT._

    D. SYSTEM._

13. Which of the following items will RDISK update, by default, in the Emergency Repair directory?

    A. SAM

    B. SETUP.LOG

    C. DEFAULT._

    D. SYSTEM._

14. Which of the following is responsible for building the hardware list during boot operations?

    A. HAL.DLL

    B. NTLDR

    C. NTOSKRNL.EXE

    D. NTDETECT.COM

15. Which two files are common to RISC-based boots as well as Intel-based boots?

    A. OSLOADER.EXE

    B. HAL.DLL

    C. NTDETECT.COM

    D. NTOSKRNL.EXE

16. Which of the following is a system file that is read-only and hidden in the root of your system partition?

    A. HAL.DLL

    B. NTLDR

    C. NTOSKRNL.EXE

    D. NTDETECT.EXE

17. Which of the following is a system file that is in the <winnt_root>\SYSTEM32 directory of your system?

    A. HAL.DLL

    B. NTLDR

    C. NTOSKRNL.EXE

    D. NTDETECT.COM

18. Which of the following should you do to boot with the LastKnownGood configuration?

    A. Start WINNT with the /L switch.

    B. Select the option from the Boot Loader menu.

    C. Use the /lastknowngood switch in the BOOT.INI file.

    D. Press the spacebar, when prompted, during the boot process.

19. Which utility is used to update the emergency repair information?

    A. RDISK.EXE

    B. REPAIR.EXE

    C. DISKPERF

    D. Server Manager

20. Which two items are updated by running the RDISK utility?

    A. The Emergency Repair directory

    B. The emergency repair disk

    C. The LastKnownGood control set

    D. HKEY_LOCAL_USER

21. On Intel x86-based computers, what is the name of the file loaded by the boot sector of the active partition?

    A. NTLDR

    B. IO.SYS

    C. BOOT.INI

    D. MSDOS.SYS

22. Selecting VGA mode during boot uses which settings? (Choose all that apply.)

    A. 16 color

    B. 256 color

    C. 640 × 480

    D. 800 × 600

23. Which BOOT.INI file switch tells Windows NT to load the standard VGA driver rather than the optimized driver written for your video card?

    A. /basevideo

    B. /sos

    C. /crashdebug

    D. /nodebug

24. Which of the following are two ways to turn on the Automatic Recovery and Restart capability?

    A. The /crashdebug switch in the BOOT.INI file

    B. The /recovery switch in the BOOT.INI file

    C. The System application in the Control Panel

    D. Server Manager

25. Which BOOT.INI file switch turns on the Automatic Recovery and Restart capability?

    A. /basevideo

    B. /sos

    C. /crashdebug

    D. /nodebug

26. Which BOOT.INI file switch limits the amount of usable memory to a specified amount?

    A. /basevideo

    B. /maxmem

    C. /noserialmice

    D. /nodebug

27. Which BOOT.INI file switch turns off the tracking of each piece of executing code during the loading of Windows NT?

    A. /basevideo

    B. /sos

    C. /crashdebug

    D. /nodebug

28. Which BOOT.INI file switch tells NTDETECT.COM to not look for the presence of serial mice?

    A. /basevideo

    B. /sos

    C. /noserialmice

    D. /nodebug

29. If you need to recreate the Setup Boot disks, which command should be used?

    A. WINNT32

    B. WINNT

    C. WINNT /OX

    D. REPAIR

30. Which BOOT.INI file switch is useful in differentiating between multiple SCSI controllers in a system?

    A. /scsiordinal

    B. /scsi

    C. /nononscsi

    D. /nodebug

31. If Windows NT hangs during the loading of system drivers, which switch should be added to the BOOT.INI file to assist with troubleshooting?

    A. /nodebug

    B. /crashdebug

    C. /sos

    D. /drivers

32. Which BOOT.INI file switch lists every driver to the screen as it loads during the kernel load phase?

    A. /basevideo

    B. /sos

    C. /crashdebug

    D. /nodebug

33. On an x86-based Windows NT Server, what is the default location of the NTOSKRNL.EXE file?

    A. <winnt_root>

    B. <winnt_root>\SYSTEM32

    C. <winnt_root>\SYSTEM32 \CONFIG

    D. <winn_root>\SYSTEM

34. Which of the following choices is not available from the Emergency Repair Process menu?

    A. Inspect Security Environment

    B. Inspect Boot Sector

    C. Inspect Startup Environment

    D. Verify Windows NT System Files

35. If Windows NT is installed in a location other than the default directory and an error message indicating that NTOSKRNL.EXE is missing or corrupt occurs, what is the most likely cause of the error?

    A. The BOOT.INI file is missing or corrupt.

    B. The Registry has not saved the new location.

    C. The NTOSKRNL.EXE has been moved.

    D. The LastKnownGood was automatically invoked.

36. What section of the BOOT.INI file contains a reference for every OS on the Boot Loader menu?

    A. [initialize]

    B. [common]

    C. [boot loader]

    D. [operating systems]

37. What section of the BOOT.INI file defines the default operating system that will be loaded if a choice is not made on the Boot Loader menu?

    A. [initialize]

    B. [common]

    C. [boot loader]

    D. [operating systems]

38. The BOOT.INI file includes which sections? (Choose all correct answers.)

    A. [initialize]

    B. [common]

    C. [boot loader]

    D. [operating systems]

39. Which of the following files are not the emergency repair disk?

    A. DEFAULT._

    B. NTUSER.DA_

    C. BOOT.INI

    D. SYSTEM._

40. Which of the following is a hidden, read-only, system file in the root of the system partition and contains information that was present in the boot sector prior to the installation of Windows NT?

    A. NTBOOT.INI

    B. NTLDR

    C. BOOT.INI

    D. BOOTSECT.DOS

41. Windows NT installation always creates an Emergency Repair directory. Where is this directory located?

    A. <winnt_root>

    B. <winnt_root>\SYSTEM

    C. <winnt_root>\REPAIR

    D. <winnt_root>\SYSTEM\REPAIR

42. If you upgrade to a new version of DOS and find that you suddenly cannot boot to Windows NT anymore, what is a possible cause?

    A. Your boot sector has been replaced.

    B. The BOOT.INI file has been deleted.

    C. NTOSKRNL.EXE has been moved.

    D. The two operating systems are not compatible.

43. What single file contains the code necessary to mask interrupts and exceptions from the kernel?

    A. HAL.DLL

    B. NTLDR

    C. NTOSKRNL.EXE

    D. NTDETECT.COM

44. Which of the following is an editable text file that controls the Boot Loader menu?

    A. NTBOOT.INI

    B. NTLDR

    C. BOOT.INI

    D. BOOTSECT.DOS

45. Which file is responsible for starting the minifile system driver necessary for accessing the system and boot partitions on an Windows NT system?

    A. NTLDR

    B. IO.SYS

    C. BOOT.INI

    D. MSDOS.SYS

46. Which of the following files is not on the emergency repair disk?

    A. NTLDR

    B. NTUSER.DA_

    C. CONFIG.NT

    D. SYSTEM._

47. The Verify Windows NT System Files option available during the emergency repair process relies upon information contained in what file?

    A. SOFTWARE._

    B. CONFIG.NT

    C. SAM

    D. SETUP.LOG

48. Which file of those on the emergency repair disk contains the names of all Windows NT installation files?

    A. AUTOEXEC.NT

    B. SETUP.LOG

C. NTLDR

D. WINNT.LOG

49. On an x86-based Windows NT Server, what is the default location of the HKEY_LOCAL_MACHINE\SYSTEM file?

    A. <winnt_root>

    B. <winnt_root>\SYSTEM32

    C. <winnt_root>\SYSTEM32\CONFIG

    D. <winn_root>\SYSTEM

50. The BOOT.INI file allows for the use of several troubleshooting switches. Those switches are added to which section of the file?

    A. [initialize]

    B. [common]

    C. [boot loader]

    D. [operating systems]

51. Which of the following is not a valid BOOT.INI switch?

    A. /maxmem

    B. /msgsvc

    C. /noserialmice

    D. /nodebug

52. Which of the following is not a valid BOOT.INI switch?

    A. /maxmem

    B. /readonly

    C. /noserialmice

    D. /nodebug

53. Under which of the following are Boot-time drivers stored in the Registry?

    A. HKEY_LOCAL_MACHINE

    B. HKEY_LOCAL_MACHINE\SYSTEM

    C. HKEY_LOCAL_MACHINE\SYSTEM32

    D. HKEY_LOCAL_MACHINE\SYSTEM\CurrentControlSet\Control\ServiceGroupOrder

19.1 Answers and Explanations: Practice Problems

1. **D** A compressed copy of the Registry's SYSTEM hive is stored as SYSTEM._ instead of NTSYSTEM.DA_.

2. **B** A control set is a collection of configuration information used during boot, whereas LastKnownGood is a special single control set used for troubleshooting.

3. **A** A control set is a collection of configuration information used during boot, whereas LastKnownGood is a special single control set used for troubleshooting.

4. **D** After the Win32 subsystem starts, the screen switches into GUI mode.

5. **A, C** Always back up the file because an error can cause serious harm. Also, take off the default read-only attribute to save your changes.

6. **A, B, D** An editable text file, BOOT.INI can be changed with any text editor, but doing so from the Startup/Shutdown tab is preferred because one typographical error in the BOOT.INI file can cause serious boot problems.

7. **D** An editable text file, BOOT.INI can be changed with any text editor, but doing so from the Startup/Shutdown tab is preferred because one typographical error in the BOOT.INI file can cause serious boot problems.

8. **B** Event Viewer is a stand-alone utility and not a part of the emergency repair process.

9. **C** HKEY_LOCAL_MACHINE\SYSTEM\CurrentControlSet houses the LastKnownGood information.

10. **A, B** Much of the work of NTDETECT.COM and NTLDR are performed by the firmware on the RISC platform.

11. **B** None of the DEFAULT._, SAM, or SECURITY._ items are updated with RDISK unless the /S option is used.

12. **A, C** None of the DEFAULT._, SAM, or SECURITY._ items are updated with RDISK unless the /S option is used.

13. **B, D** None of the DEFAULT._, SAM, or SECURITY._ items are updated with RDISK unless the /S option is used.

14. **D** NTDETECT.COM builds the hardware list and returns the information to NTLDR.

15. **B, D** NTDETECT.COM is used only on Intel boots, whereas OSLOADER.EXE is used only on RISC boots. HAL.DLL and NTOSKRNL.EXE are common to both boot operations.

16. **B** NTDLR is the system file responsible for the majority of the early boot operations.

17. **C** NTOSKRNL.EXE is the kernel file and it is loaded during boot by the NTLDR.

18. **D** Pressing the spacebar during the boot process presents you with the Hardware Profile/Configuration Recovery menu. Select a hardware profile and enter **L** for LastKnownGood configuration.

19. **A** RDISK will update the Emergency Repair directory and the emergency repair disk.

20. **A, B** RDISK will update the Emergency Repair directory and the emergency repair disk.

21. **A** Similar to the IO.SYS file in MS-DOS environments, the NTLDR file is a hidden, read-only, system file in the root of the system partition.

22. **A, C** Standard VGA consists of 16 colors displayed at 640 × 480.

23. **A** The /basevideo switch performs this operation.

24. **A, C** The /crashdebug switch enables this, as does the System application in the Control Panel.

25. **C** The /crashdebug switch performs this operation.

26. **B** The /maxmem switch performs this operation.

27. **D** The /nodebug switch performs this operation.

28. **C** The /noserialmice switch performs this operation. At times, other devices connected to the serial port can be falsely identified as mice. After boot, the serial port is unavailable because the system expects a mouse to be there.

29. **C** The /OX switch, used with WINNT, will recreate the Setup Boot disks.

30. **A** The /scsiordinal switch performs this operation.

31. **C** The /sos switch causes all drivers to be displayed on the screen as they are loaded.

32. **B** The /sos switch performs this operation.

33. **B** The <winnt_root>\SYSTEM32 directory holds the NTOSKRNL.EXE file.

34. **A** The Boot Sector, Startup Environment, and Windows NT System files can all be inspected and verified during the emergency repair process.

35. **B** The BOOT.INI file contains a pointer to the NTOSKRNL.EXE location.

36. **D** The BOOT.INI file contains only two sections: [boot loader] and [operating systems]. The first defines the default operating system, whereas the second contains a reference for each OS on the menu.

37. **C** The BOOT.INI file contains only two sections: [boot loader] and [operating systems]. The first defines the default operating system, whereas the second contains a reference for each OS on the menu.

38. **C, D** The BOOT.INI file contains only two sections: [boot loader] and [operating systems]. The first defines the default operating system, whereas the second contains a reference for each OS on the menu.

39. **C** The BOOT.INI file is not on the emergency repair disk.

40. **D** The BOOTSECT.DOS file contains information about previous operating systems and calls the correct files if a choice other than Windows NT is made from the Boot Loader menu.

41. **C** The directory on which the Emergency Repair directory resides is <winnt_root>\REPAIR.

42. **A** The DOS and Windows 95 SYS commands will often overwrite the boot sector, which can be restored from the emergency repair disk.

43. **A** The HAL.DLL file contains the code necessary to mask interrupts and exceptions from the kernel.

44. **C** The NTLDR calls the Boot Loader menu, but it is the BOOT.INI file that controls it and its choices.

45. **A** The NTLDR file is responsible for carrying out the vast majority of the early initialization operations, including starting the minifile system driver.

46. **A** The NTLDR is not on the emergency repair disk.

47. **D** The SETUP.LOG file contains names and checksum values of files used during Windows NT installation.

48. **B** The SETUP.LOG file has the name and checksums of all Windows NT installation files. It can find corrupted files and report which ones need to be fixed.

49. **C** The SYSTEM component of the Registry is stored in <winnt_root>\SYSTEM32\CONFIG.

50. **D** The [operating systems] section contains information about each operating system offered on the menu, whereas the [boot loader] lists only the default operating system if one is not chosen from the Boot Loader menu.

51. **B** There is not a /msgsvc switch for the BOOT.INI file.

52. **B** There is not a /readonly switch for the BOOT.INI file.

53. **D** This is the hive of the Registry responsible for boot-time driver information.

19.1 Key Words

boot

Master Boot Record (MBR)

NTLDR

Advanced RISC Computer (ARC)

19.2 Choosing the Appropriate Course of Action to Take When a Print Job Fails

One of the benefits of Windows printing is that the operating system handles all print job output in a standardized manner, regardless of the application from which you are printing. Windows NT, being a network operating system, enables you to define network printers that are available as shared resources for other Windows NT Workstations to print to. Any client or server on a network can serve as the print server to a network printer. Additionally, you can have local printers that are not shared resources to other network computers, but that need to be managed and troubleshot.

The centralization of printing services is a beautiful thing; you must admit. A single standardized print model under Windows replaces the individual print models of applications under MS-DOS and is more easily understood. The down side is that when problems do arise they affect your entire application suite and maybe an entire workgroup.

Keep in mind that Windows still retains the older model for printing for MS-DOS applications that run in Windows NT Workstation from the command prompt. These applications require their own printer drivers to print anything other than ASCII output. If you are using WordPerfect 5.1, for example, you require that both a WordPerfect and printer driver be installed. Some MS-DOS applications can require that you turn on the printer port by using a command such as the following prior to printing:

```
NET USE LPT1: \\servername\printername
```

19

A. Understanding the Windows Print Subsystem

The Windows printing subsystem is modular and works hand-in-hand with other subsystems to provide printing services. When a printer is local and a print job is specified by an application, data is sent to the *Graphics Device Interface (GDI)* to be rendered into a print job in the printer language of the print device. The GDI is a module between the printing subsystem and the application requesting the printing services. This print job is passed to the *spooler*, which is a .DLL. The print job is written to disk as a temporary file so that it can survive a power outage or your computer's reboot. Print jobs can be spooled using either the RAW or EMF printer languages.

The client side of the print spooler is winspool.drv, and that driver makes a *Remote Procedure Call (RPC)* to the spoolss.exe server side of the spooler. When the printer is attached to the same computer as the spooler, both files are located on the same computer. When the printer is attached to a Windows NT Workstation in a peer-to-peer relationship, those files are located on different computers.

Spoolss.exe calls an API that sends the print job to a route (spoolss.dll). Spoolss.dll then sends the print job to the computer with the local printer. Finally, the localspl.dll library writes the file to disk as a spooled file. At this point, the printer is polled by localspl.dll to determine whether the spooled print job is capable of being processed by the printer, and is altered if required.

The print job is then turned over to a separator page processor and despooled to the print monitor. The print device receives the print job and raster image processes it to a bitmap file that is then sent to the print engine to output.

1. Network Printer Process

For network printers the process is very much the same, but client requests and server services are more clearly defined and separate. The routers found in the spooler modules—winspool.drv, spoolss.exe, and spoolss.dll—are identical to the ones used for a local printer. A local print provider on the client localspl.dll is matched to a remote print provider (win32sp.dll for Windows print servers or nwprovau.dll for NetWare print servers) on the server side. In a network printer process, the print processors and print monitors may use several different server DLLs, each one required by a supported operating system.

2. Multiple Virtual Printer Setup

You generally install a printer by using the Add Printer Wizard that you find in the Printer folder accessed from the Settings submenu of the Start menu. After you step through the wizard you create a virtual printer with a name that you provide. You can create any number of virtual (or logical, if you will) printers that use the same physical printer for a number of purposes. If you want to print to a different printer, have different security schemes, or provide different access times, having multiple virtual printers provides a means to do this. You can manipulate printers by any of the following means:

- Double-click on the printer to see any spooled jobs, provided you have the privilege to do so.
- Right-click on a printer to view a shortcut menu that provides several actions. You can use this menu to delete a printer that no longer exists, for example. You can use the Default Printer command to set the default printer for a Windows NT Workstation from the shortcut menu.
- Right-click on a printer and select the Properties command from the shortcut menu to access the Printer Properties and control any number of settings.

B. Using a Basic Error Checklist

Any number of things can go wrong when you attempt to print to a printer. In many cases, Windows NT simply alerts you to an error, and in some cases Windows NT actually tells you what the error type is. Here is a standard checklist of the most common solutions to print problems. If your print job spools, but it will not print, first eliminate the following potential problems:

- Your printer is turned off, or a connection is loose.
- The paper tray is empty.
- A piece of paper is jammed in the printer.
- The printer has an error condition that prevents print processing.

The preceding problems are so simple that its easy to waste time by overlooking them. Also, the percentage of printer problems that disappear when you restart your printer is amazing. If restarting your printer fails to work, restart Windows NT Workstation—that is, if your printer worked before you specified the print job. If none of these solutions seems to work, try the following:

- Verify that the printer you think you printed to is either the default printer or was selected within the application from which the print job comes.
- Print a simple text file from Notepad. This often verifies whether the print problem is application specific. Try printing from DOS to test the DOS subsystem, if that is the problem environment.
- Print to a different printer, or substitute another printer on the same printer port. This helps determine whether the printer is malfunctioning.
- Check the amount of available hard disk space on your system partition to see whether there was room to create the temporary spooled print file.
- Print to a file, and then copy that file to the printer port in question. If you can print in this manner, you should suspect the spooler or a data-transmission error. Otherwise, you are probably dealing with a hardware, device driver, or application error.

At the very worst, you can try reinstalling the printer and providing a new or updated printer driver. These are the usual sources of printer drivers:

- The Windows NT operating system distribution disks.
- The setup disks that come with your printer.
- The printer manufacturer's BBS or web site.
- Microsoft's technical support line. You can contact Microsoft at 206-882-8080. Microsoft's current printer driver library is on the Windows NT Driver Library disk.
- The Microsoft web site. Use the Search button to search for the keyword "NT driver," or search for the name of your particular model of printer.
- CompuServe. Enter **GO WINNT** or **GO WDL** (Windows Driver Library) to go to that area of the service.

If the problem printing to a printer is observed after you have installed a new printer, you should probably suspect a configuration issue. Check that you assigned to the correct serial port in the Configure Port dialog box of the Add Printer Wizard. You can open a printer's Properties sheet to check port settings after the fact. Make sure that you have assigned the appropriate communication settings: baud rate, data bits, parity, start and stop bit, and flow control that your printer requires. These settings should be listed in your printer's manual. Failure to configure these settings properly may result in your printer operating too slowly, improperly processing print jobs, or not working at all.

C. Printers as Shared Resources

Network printers are shared resources. You must either own the printer (have created or installed it), be an administrator, or be assigned the rights to use a printer in some way to be able to view, modify, and use a printer. Different levels of rights can be assigned by an owner or an administrator. You assign shared rights by using the Sharing command on a printer's shortcut menu, which brings up the Sharing tab of the Printer Properties dialog box.

Creating additional printer shares for the same physical printer proves useful for the following reasons:

- Each share can have different printer setups.
- You can assign different access privileges to groups of users.
- Each group can have different printing priorities.
- You can control access to the printer at different times for each group.
- You can use one share name for a network printer, and another share name for a local printer.

> **The control of a network printer is likely to be of focus on the exam because this ability is one of the essential functions that a system administrator is expected to manage in a Windows NT network.**

If users cannot see a printer, they may not have been given the right to access that printer. An administrator should be able to view and modify printers on any Windows NT Workstation.

If you have MS-DOS clients on the network and you want them to see a printer share, you must use a file-naming convention that DOS recognizes. Names can be up to 12 characters long, but cannot use spaces or any of the following characters:

```
? * # ¦ \ / = > < %
```

To hide a printer share, add a dollar sign character to the end of the share name, as in *sharename*$. Any printer with that kind of a name will not show up in the Connect To Printer dialog box, which is one of the steps in the Add a Printer Wizard. A user must know that this printer share exists and be able to enter both the correct name and path to the printer share name to connect to that printer.

D. Solving Print Spooler Problems

Any print job spooled to a printer is written as a temporary file to the %systemroot%\System32\Spool\Printers folder. The file is deleted after the printer indicates that the job has been printed. The primary print spool problem encountered is a lack of available disk space. If you print high-resolution graphics, you might have print jobs as large as 20MB to 80MB per file for a 32-bit image at standard page size. Not surprisingly, it doesn't take many print jobs to overwhelm the typical Windows NT Workstation configuration.

When you print to the spooler, you create two files for each print job. The .SPL file is the actual print job spool file. You also create a shadow file, given the .SHD extension. The *shadow* file contains additional information about the print job that is not part of the print job itself, such as owner, priority, and so forth. If your computer crashes, .SPL and .SHD files remain in the default spool file until the service restarts and they are processed and printed. After being printed, these files are deleted from disk. Should your spooled files become corrupted, they will be orphaned and remain in the spool folder, taking up valuable space.

You can print directly to a printer from your application by turning off the print spooling feature. Before you print, open the Scheduling tab of the Printer Properties dialog box and select the Print Directly to the Printer option button. When the printer next becomes available, your document prints. Until that point, you cannot use the application that originates the print job. You can, however, switch to another application and continue working until your printing application becomes available.

1. Spooler Performance Problems

You also can relieve spooler performance problems by increasing the priority that Windows NT Workstation assigns to the Spooler service. By default, Windows NT assigns this service a rating of 7, which is consistent with other background processes that run. Increase the rating to 9 to improve the performance of the spooler to the level of a foreground operation. Only consider doing this as a temporary measure to print a large print job, or if your workstation is used heavily as a print server. Changing this rating on a permanent basis degrades the performance of other services and applications on that workstation.

To change the priority of the Spooler service, open the RegEdit32 application and change the value of the PriorityClass of type REG_DWORD in the following key:

```
HKEY_LOCAL_MACHINE\System\CurrentControlSet\Control\Print
```

Set that value to the priority class required. A value of 0, or no value entered, is substituted with the default value of a background process of 7 for Windows NT Workstation. (For Windows NT Server background processes, assign a value of 9.)

One very simple and effective procedure that improves printer performance is to defragment your hard drive on a regular basis.

19

2. Changing the Default Spool Folder

Should you run out of room on your system partition for spooled print jobs, you can specify a different default spool folder. To do so, make the change in the Advanced tab of the Server Properties dialog box. Open that dialog box by double-clicking on the Server Control Panel. To change the location of spooled documents, complete the following steps:

1. Create a new spool directory.
2. Choose the Printers command from the Settings menu of the Start menu.
3. Choose the Server Properties command from the File menu.
4. Click on the Advanced tab, and then enter the location of the spool file directory
5. Click OK.

You may want to create the spool folder on an NTFS volume and set security for this folder. You can also edit the Registry to change the value of the DefaultSpoolDirectory of type REG_SZ. The path is entered into the following key of the Registry:

```
HKEY_LOCAL_MACHINE\System\CurrentControlSet\Control\Print\Printers
```

After you enter the new folder and its path, save the change and restart your machine for the change to take effect. Any spooled job in the original location will be lost, but will not be deleted. You need to delete the TEMP file manually.

If you want to have individual spooled folders for each virtual printer, you can assign them. Find your printers in the following key:

```
HKEY_LOCAL_MACHINE\System\CurrentControlSet\Control\Print\~Printers\printername
```

Enter the folder and its path as the data in the SpoolDirectory value for that key. Again, you need to restart the workstation to effect the change.

3. Enabling Printer Logging

You can enable event logging to your spooler by adding a check mark to the Log spooler error events, Log spooler warning events, or Log spooler information events check boxes on the Advanced tab.

To turn on auditing of a printer share, complete the following steps:

1. Enable file and object access auditing in the User Manager.
2. Enable printer auditing for a specific printer share. Open the Security tab of the Printer Properties dialog box and click the Auditing button.
3. In the Printer Auditing dialog box click the Add button.
4. In the Add Users and Groups dialog box, select a group or user to be audited.
5. Click OK to return to the Printer Auditing dialog box.
6. Select a user or group and click the check boxes in the Events to Audit section to track events you want to log for that user and group.
7. Click OK.

Use the Event Viewer utility in the Administrative Tools folder to view logged events.

4. Installing Print Pooling

If you have adequate printer resources and want to distribute the print queue load, you may want to install printer pooling. Printer *pooling* enables you to take two or more identical printers and print to them as if they were a single printer. The print job goes to the first available printer and is managed as if it were a single print queue.

To use printer pooling, complete the following steps:

1. Choose the Printers command from the Settings submenu of the Start menu.
2. Right-click on a printer icon and select the Properties command.
3. Click the Ports tab and select the logical printer to which you want to print.
4. Click the Enable Print Pooling check box, and then close the Printer Properties dialog box.

To set up a logical printer you can use the Add Printer Wizard to add a printer to a port and use the same share name. Although the printers must be identical, the ports do not. You can mix and match local, serial, and parallel ports in the same logical printer.

5. Scheduling a Print Job

You cannot specify when a particular job will print on a printer within the current Windows NT Workstation architecture. You can control when a printer is available for printing, however, as part of a printer share's definition. Use two differently named printer shares for the same printer, and have one printer always be available. Restrict the availability of the second printer and use that printer share to schedule your print job.

To set availability times, complete the following steps:

1. Click the printer icon in the Printers folder and press Alt + Enter to open the Printer Properties dialog box.
2. Click the Scheduling tab of the Printer Properties dialog box.
3. Click the From option button in the Available section, and then enter the starting and ending times for which the printer is available.

Any print job printed off-hours is left in the print queue until the printer becomes available.

E. Using the Print Troubleshooter

To aid in solving printer problems, Windows NT comes with an interactive print troubleshooting aid as part of the online Help system. To access the Print Troubleshooter, complete the following steps:

1. Choose the Help command from the Start menu.
2. Click the Index tab and enter the keyword **troubleshooting** into the 1 Type the First Few Letters text box.
3. Double-click on the problem type and follow the instructions in the Help system.

Printers are one of the most important network resources in many organizations. Therefore, you will be called on often to solve problems that crop up with printer shares and printer hardware, as discussed in this section.

19.2.1 Exercise: Enabling Printer Auditing

Objective: Turn on printer auditing of a share.

Estimated Time: 5 minutes.

To turn on auditing of a printer share, complete the following steps:

1. Enable file and object access auditing in the User Manager.
2. Enable printer auditing for a specific printer share. Open the Security tab of the Printer Properties dialog box and click the Auditing button.

3. In the Printer Auditing dialog box, click the Add button.
4. In the Add Users and Groups dialog box, select a group or user to be audited.
5. Click OK to return to the Printer Auditing dialog box.
6. Select a user or group and click the check boxes in the Events to Audit section to track events you want to log for that user and group.
7. Click OK.

19.2.1 Answers and Explanations: Exercise

By turning on printer auditing, you can see what jobs are sent to the printer and track its usage. The problem, too often, is that too much data builds up and you do not have the time or resources to evaluate what you have collected.

19.2 Practice Problems

1. If you cannot print to a printer, what should be one of the first things you try?

   A. Change print drivers.

   B. Reconfigure the print spool.

   C. Try a different printer to see if the problem appears there.

   D. Stop and restart the printing services.

2. By default, where do spooled print jobs reside?

   A. \<winnt_root>

   B. \<winnt_root>\SYSTEM32

   C. \<winnt_root>\SYSTEM32\SPOOL

   D. \<winnt_root>\SYSTEM32\SPOOL\PRINTERS

3. If a Windows NT-based computer is to function as a print server for the network, what is one of the most critical components?

   A. Free disk space

   B. Frequent backups

   C. A fast processor

   D. Accelerated PCI local bus video

4. What priority level is assigned to the print spooler service by Windows NT Workstation?

   A. 1

   B. 3

   C. 7

   D. 15

5. How can you change the location of the spool directory?

   A. Change the entry in the Spool tab of the Control Panel\Printers option.

   B. In the Registry, add a value called DefaultSpoolDirectory to HKEY_LOCAL_MACHINE\System\CurrentControlSet\Control\Print\Printers.

   C. Map a drive to the new location.

   D. Change port settings at the printer.

6. Which of the following is a potential solution to problems with printing from non-Windows-based applications to a printer that works fine in Windows?

   A. Install additional printer drivers.

   B. Elect to use RAW data instead of EMF.

   C. Stop spooling services and send data directly to the printer.

   D. Configure the printer on a different port.

7. If DOS-based applications will not print, what command should you first try?

   A. PRINT

   B. NET PRINT

   C. NET PRINT LPT1: _ HYPERLINK \\\\servername\\printername __\\servername\printername_

   D. NET USE LPT1: \\servername\printername

8. Files in the printer spool should have which two of the following extensions?

   A. TXT

   B. SHD

   C. SHT

   D. SPL

9. How long do files remain in the printer spool?

   A. Until there is a clean boot of the system

   B. Until the system is shut down

   C. Until the job finishes printing

   D. Until the administrator empties the spool

10. What becomes of spooled print jobs in the event of a computer crash?

    A. When the system restarts, the printer should process these files immediately.

    B. They wait until the administrator restarts them before continuing.

    C. They do not restart.

    D. They perform a checksum operation to identify corruption that may have occurred.

11. If a print job appears stuck in the printer after recovering from a system crash and you cannot delete it, what should you do?

    A. Continue rebooting the computer until the problem goes away.

    B. Stop the spooler service in Control Panel Services and delete the files for that job in the spool directory.

    C. Invest in a more industrial printer.

    D. Use Regedit to change stuck job parameters.

12. What priority level is assigned to the print spooler service by Windows NT Server?

    A. 15

    B. 9

    C. 7

    D. 1

13. If a Windows NT-based workstation moonlighting as a print server appears to print too slowly, what action should be done on the priority level of the print service?

    A. Raise the priority by one or two classes.

    B. Raise the priority by three to four classes.

    C. Lower the priority by one or two classes.

    D. Make no change—the priority level does not affect this service.

14. To change the priority class of a print service, which component of the Registry should you edit?

    A. HKEY_LOCAL_MACHINE\System\CurrentControlSet

    B. HKEY_LOCAL_MACHINE\System\CurrentControlSet\Control

    C. HKEY_LOCAL_MACHINE\System\CurrentControlSet\Control\Print

    D. HKEY_LOCAL_MACHINE\System\CurrentControlSet\Control\Printers

19.2 Answers and Explanations: Practice Problems

1. **C** Always try to isolate the problem as much as possible before taking other actions.

2. **D** By default, print jobs are in \<winnt_root>\SYSTEM32\SPOOL\PRINTERS until they are completely printed.

3. **A** If a Windows NT-based computer is acting as a print server for the network, make sure plenty of free disk space is available on the partition that contains the default spool directory. Spooled print jobs can be quite large and can eat up disk space more quickly than you might think, especially during peak printing periods.

4. **C** Windows NT Workstation assigns a default priority level of 7 to the print spooler service.

5. **B** You can change the spool directory in the Registry by adding a value called DefaultSpoolDirectory of type REG_SZ to HKEY_LOCAL_MACHINE\System\CurrentControlSet\Control\Print\Printers and entering the path to the new spool directory.

6. **A** Non-Windows-based applications—for example, MS-DOS-based applications—require their own printer drivers if the application requires any kind of formatted output other than plain ASCII text.

7. **D** You may need to use the NET USE LPT1: \\servername\printername command to enable the DOS-based application to print.

8. **B, D** When a document prints, two files are created for the print job in the spool directory (by default, <winnt_root>\SYSTEM32\SPOOL\PRINTERS). One of the files, which has an .SPL extension, is the actual print job spool file. The other file, which has an .SHD extension, is a shadow file that contains information about the job, including its owner and priority.

9. **C** When a document prints, two files are created for the print job in the spool directory (by default, <winnt_root>\SYSTEM32\SPOOL\PRINTERS). One of the files, which has an .SPL extension, is the actual print job spool file. The other file, which has an .SHD extension, is a shadow file that contains information about the job, including its owner and priority. These files remain in the spool directory until the jobs finish printing, at which point they are deleted.

10. **A** In the event of a system crash, some spool and shadow files may be left over from jobs that were waiting to be printed. When the spooler service restarts (along with the rest of the system), the printer should process these files immediately.

11. **B** If a print job appears stuck in the printer and you cannot delete it, stop the spooler service in Control Panel Services and delete the SPL and/or SHD file for that job from the spool directory (match the date/time stamp on the files and in Print Manager to determine which files are causing the problem).

12. **C** Windows NT Server assigns a default priority level of 7 to the print spooler service.

13. **A** If a Windows NT-based workstation moonlighting as a print server appears to print too slowly, consider raising the priority by one or two classes. If the workstation is responding sluggishly to the user while printing, consider lowering the priority by a class or two.

14. **C** To change the priority class for the Spooler service, add a value called PriorityClass of type REG_DWORD to HKEY_LOCAL_MACHINE\System\CurrentControlSet\Control\Print and set it equal to the priority class desired.

19.2 Key Words

Printer

Graphics Device Interface

RAW data

EMF data

19.3 Choosing the Appropriate Course of Action to Take When the Installation Process Fails

The Windows NT Setup program makes installation errors much less common than they use to be. Several categories of errors may still occur after an installation has been made, but they are also easier to track down and eliminate.

A. Installation Disk Errors and Upgrades

In rare cases, there may be a problem with the CD that you have obtained to perform the Windows NT Workstation installation. Typically a read error is posted, but less frequently the installation may not complete itself and you may not be able to determine why this is so.

To obtain a replacement disk, contact Microsoft at 800-426-9400. Have your registration number handy; the sales and support staff requires this to process your request. New media requests under the warranty are generally sent without cost. If the upgrade is a slipstream upgrade, you may be charged postage.

A note about slipstream upgrades and service packs is also in order. Many small problems are often repaired as part of a minor version change in the operating system. If you have a problem related to an installation, either get the latest version of the operating system from Microsoft or download any available service packs from the Microsoft web site.

A *service pack* is a self-running program that modifies your operating system. It isn't uncommon within the lifetime of an operating system to have two or three service packs. Windows NT Server 4.0 prior to the release of beta for Windows NT Server 5 had Service Pack 3 available, for example. You should try to install the latest service pack because it generally solves a lot more problems than it creates. (It is not unknown, however, for a service pack to create error conditions that didn't previously exist in your workstation's configuration.)

B. Inadequate Disk Space

The Windows NT Setup program examines the partition you specified for the amount of free space it contains. If there isn't adequate free space, the installation stops and fails. You need to take corrective action to proceed with the installation.

In some respects the Setup program is both smart and stupid. Although it protects your files in the Recycle Bin by not deleting them, which is wise, it also leaves any number of TEMP files that could be safely deleted scattered about your disk.

To free up some room on your disk, consider doing any of the following:

- Empty your Recycle Bin.
- Delete any TEMP files that you find in the various locations that they are stored in (for example, the Print Cache folder).
- Delete any files that you find in your Internet browser's cache folder or any other cache folder that you have.

- Uninstall any programs that you no longer need.
- Compress any files that you use on an infrequent basis.
- Go into the Disk Administrator and change the size of the system partition that you want to use for your installation.
- Create a new partition with adequate room for the installation.
- Compress your NTFS partition to make more room.

Several other methods enable you to reclaim or recover lost disk space, and it's possible to get really creative in this area. Those mentioned previously, however, are often sufficient to help you get over the crunch.

C. Disk Configuration Errors

The best way to ensure that you are using hardware compatible with Windows NT Workstation is to check the *Hardware Compatibility List (HCL)* to see whether the device is approved for use and supported.

If you have inherited a configuration with a non-supported SCSI device adapter, you might not be able to boot your newly installed Windows NT Workstation operating system. In that instance, boot to a different operating system and try starting WINNT on the installation CD. You can also use a network installation to try and rectify the problem. Short of these solutions you may be forced to replace the adapter with one recommended on the Hardware Compatibility List.

D. Cannot Connect to a Domain Controller Error

The error message Cannot Connect to a Domain Controller is one of the more common error messages that you see when you install Windows NT Workstation, change your hardware configuration, or change network settings. There are a number of explanations for this problem.

Carefully verify that you are entering the correct user name and password and that the Caps Lock key is not on. The next thing you should check is that the account name that you are using is listed in the User Manager for Domains on the primary domain controller. An incorrect password generates a different error message than the lack of the user account.

Because the inability of a user to connect to a domain controller is one of the most common problems that a user encounters, this topic and its variety of causes are likely to be on the exam.

You should also check to see whether the machine account has been added to the User Manager for the primary domain controller. Next, open the Network Control Panel and check that the network bindings are properly installed on the Bindings tab. Some bindings such as TCP/IP require not only computer names but IP addresses and subnet masks as well. If there is a conflict on the network with two machines having the same IP address, you get an error condition.

Failure to enter the subnet mask (or entering an incorrect subnet mask) also leads to your workstation being unable to find and connect to a domain controller and get its network identity properly verified.

The failure to connect to a domain controller is such a common problem that it is really unfortunate that the message isn't more descriptive of the problem.

E. Domain Name Error

If you make a mistake selecting the domain name, you get an error message when you attempt to log on. The solution is obvious when you realize what the problem is. Just reselect the correct domain name.

19.3 Practice Problems

1. Which of the following should be one of the first steps taken to resolve a dependency service that fails to start after a Windows NT installation?

   A. Boot to a different operating system and run WINNT from there.

   B. Compress NTFS partitions.

   C. Verify the local computer has a unique name from the Control Panel.

   D. Call Microsoft Sales to replace the disks.

2. Which of the following should be one of the first steps taken to resolve an error caused by a non-supported SCSI adapter during a Windows NT installation?

   A. Boot to a different operating system and run WINNT from there.

   B. Compress NTFS partitions.

   C. Verify the local computer has a unique name from the Control Panel.

   D. Call Microsoft Sales to replace the disks.

3. Which of the following should be one of the first steps taken to resolve an error of insufficient disk space during a Windows NT installation?

   A. Boot to a different operating system and run WINNT from there.

   B. Compress NTFS partitions.

   C. Verify the local computer has a unique name from the Control Panel.

   D. Call Microsoft Sales to replace the disks.

4. Which of the following should be one of the first steps taken to resolve an error with the installation CD during a Windows NT installation?

   A. Boot to a different operating system and run WINNT from there.

   B. Compress NTFS partitions.

   C. Verify the local computer has a unique name from the Control Panel.

   D. Call Microsoft Sales to replace the disks.

5. From which media can Windows NT 4.0 be installed?

   A. CD-ROM

   B. 5.25" floppies

   C. 3.5" disks

   D. A network share point

6. To install Windows NT 4.0 on a previous version of Windows NT, and keep all settings, what should you do?

   A. Install in the same directory the old version was in.

   B. Install in a new directory.

   C. Do nothing—it will automatically find and install over the old version.

   D. Run the MIGRATE utility.

7. How do you create a dual-boot machine with a previous version of Windows NT?

   A. Install in the same directory the old version was in.

   B. Install in a new directory.

   C. Do nothing—it will automatically find and install over the old version.

   D. Run the MIGRATE utility.

8. How do you upgrade Windows 95 to Windows NT?

   A. Install in the same directory the old version was in.

   B. Install in a new directory.

   C. Do nothing—it will automatically find and install over the old version.

   D. Run the MIGRATE utility.

9. If you lose the startup disks made during Windows NT's install, how can you remake them?

   A. WINNT32

   B. WINNT

   C. WINNT /OX

   D. WINNT /STARTUP

19.3 Answers and Explanations: Practice Problems

1. **C** A duplicate computer name on the domain can prevent all services from starting. Make certain the computer has a unique name.

2. **A** Booting to an operating system that can use the SCSI adapter can enable you to use the CD and try a network installation.

3. **B** Compressing the partition can free up more disk space, enabling the installation to successfully execute.

4. **D** Microsoft Sales can replace the faulty media. The phone number is 800-426-9400.

5. **A, D** Windows NT can be installed from a network share point, or CD-ROM. 3.5" floppies are needed to start the CD install, but Windows NT cannot be installed strictly from disks or floppies.

6. **A** To install 4.0 on a previous version of Windows NT and keep all settings, install it in the same directory the old version was in. If you install into any other directory, you have not upgraded, but created a dual-boot machine.

7. **B** To install 4.0 on a previous version of Windows NT and keep all settings, install it in the same directory the old version was in. If you install into any other directory, you have not upgraded, but created a dual-boot machine.

8. **B** Windows 95 cannot be upgraded to Windows NT because there are incompatibilities in the Registries, drivers, and so on. You must install Windows NT in a separate directory from Windows 95 and reinstall all applications.

9. **C** Three startup disks are made at the time of install. If you lose these disks, you can recreate them by running WINNT /OX.

19.3 Key Words

NTFS partitions

FAT

Startup disks

Domain Controller

Domain Name

19.4 Choosing the Appropriate Course of Action to Take When an Application Fails

Unlike MS-DOS and earlier versions of Windows, an application failure won't bring your system to a complete halt. Most application failures are recoverable, and in many cases you won't even need to reboot your computer to re-establish a working configuration. That is not to say that a system crash is impossible. It happens very infrequently, however.

Most often the worst culprits are applications written for MS-DOS or 16-bit Windows applications. These programs tend to crash more frequently than 32-bit Windows applications—a good reason to upgrade.

If you have a malfunctioning application, bring up the Task Manager and close the process. You can access the Task Manager by using either your mouse or your keyboard (useful in case one or the other is hung up by a malfunction). To use your keyboard to close an application, complete the following steps:

1. Press Ctrl + Alt + Delete to open the Windows NT Security dialog box.
2. Click on the Task Manager button there to open the Task Manager.
3. Click on the Applications tab.
4. Select the offending application and click on the End Task button.
5. Close the Task Manager.

You can also open the Task Manager by moving the cursor over the Status bar area and right-clicking, and then selecting the Task Manager command.

If you need to end a 16-bit Windows or an MS-DOS application, you must close the entire session. When you close a 32-bit Windows application, only the process or thread must be closed.

A. Using the Application Log

Many errors are logged into the Application log for native Windows NT applications. The developer of the application determines the events that are logged, their codes, and meanings. Often an application's manual or online Help system documents the events you see in the Application log, as well as your ability to control the events that are noted.

B. Service Failures

Many applications run as *services* on Windows NT Workstation. Internet Information Server's three applications (WWW, FTP, and Gopher), for example, all are services. Services are started, stopped, and paused from within either their central administrative tool (for IIS, that tool is the Internet Service Manager), or the Services Control Panel. If you want to configure a service so that it runs automatically when your workstation boots, more often than not you will set this behavior in the Services Control Panel.

Sooner or later, you will see this infamous error message and instruction when your Windows NT Workstation starts up after the load phase:

```
One or more services failed to start.
Please see the Event Viewer for details.
```

Although the error message doesn't tell you anything useful, the Event Viewer does. Open the System log using the Event heading in the Event Viewer and look for the Event code that has a value of 6005. That event is an informational message that indicates that the EventLog service has started up. Any event prior to that is a boot event and should be resolved. Double-click on the event message to view an Event Detail dialog box.

19.4 Practice Problems

1. Which type of application is least likely to crash on Windows NT Workstation?
   A. MS-DOS-based
   B. Windows 16-bit
   C. Windows 32-bit
   D. Real-mode

2. How can the Task Manager be opened?
   A. Click on the Task Manager button in the Windows NT Security dialog box.
   B. Right-click on the status bar.
   C. Select Task Manager from the control panel.
   D. Right-click on the desktop and choose Task Manager from the menu.

3. Which services does Internet Information Server run?
   A. HTTP (WWW)
   B. FTP
   C. Gopher
   D. VRML

4. Which type of application is most prone to crash on a Windows NT Workstation?
   A. MS-DOS-based
   B. Windows 16-bit
   C. Windows 32-bit
   D. Real mode

5. What utility can be used to shut down a malfunctioning application?
   A. Performance Monitor
   B. Network Monitor
   C. Task Manager
   D. Event Viewer

6. Closing a 32-bit runaway application can involve closing which one of the following?
   A. That application
   B. The entire session
   C. The errant process or thread
   D. Windows NT Workstation

7. Closing a 16-bit runaway application can involve closing which one of the following?
   A. That application
   B. The entire session
   C. The errant process or thread
   D. Windows NT Workstation

8. Joe has a bet going with Bill, who heard from Sue that errors are kept in the Error log. Joe says this is incorrect, and they are really kept in a separate file. Where are the errors from most applications written?
   A. Event log
   B. Error Log
   C. System Log
   D. Application Log

9. Alex is attempting to set a service to start automatically when his Workstation starts. He calls the system administrator who tells him this can be accomplished from where?
   A. Control Panel, Network
   B. Control Panel, Services
   C. Control Panel, System
   D. Control Panel, Devices

10. The System log can be viewed with which of the following?
    A. Any ASCII text viewer
    B. Event Viewer
    C. Performance Monitor
    D. The Windows NT Diagnostic Utility

19.4 Answers and Explanations: Practice Problems

1. **C** Windows 32-bit applications are least likely to crash on Windows NT Workstation.
2. **A, B** Task Manager can be opened from the status bar or the Windows NT Security dialog box.
3. **A, B, C** IIS runs HTTP, FTP, and Gopher applications as services.
4. **A, B** MS-DOS-based and Windows 16-bit applications are more prone than Windows 32-bit applications to crash on Windows NT Workstation.
5. **C** Task Manager is used to shut down malfunctioning applications.
6. **C** You can close either the errant process or thread with a runaway 32-bit application.
7. **B** You must close the entire session with a runaway 16-bit application.
8. **D** Errors from applications are logged in the Application log.
9. **B** The Services applet of Control Panel enables you to configure a service to automatically start when Workstation does.
10. **B** Event Viewer is used to view the System log.

19.4 Key Words

Task Manager

Windows 16-bit applications

Windows 32-bit applications

19.5 Choosing the Appropriate Course of Action to Take When a User Cannot Access a Resource

Windows NT's security system controls access network resources through user and machine accounts. Your logon to a particular domain is validated by a domain controller and provides you with certain privileges and rights that are registered in the *Security Accounts Manager (SAM)* database.

When you log on to Windows NT, the system provides a *Security Access Token (SAT)* based on your user name and password. This SAT is a key that enables you to access objects that Windows NT manages by maintaining a *Security Descriptor (SD)* file. That SD file contains the *access control list (ACL)* for each resource.

Two types of accounts are created and managed in Windows NT: machine accounts and user accounts. Both of these accounts are stored in the SAM database stored on the *primary domain controller (PDC)* and are replicated to any *backup domain controllers (BDC)* on the system. Accounts are assigned an internally held *System Identification number (SID).*

You create and manage accounts in the User Manager for Domains. Log on as an administrator so that you can fully access accounts for machines and different users. Other levels of users also have privileges, but what they can do is limited. An account is specified by the machine and user name, as in <computername>\<username>.

A *group* is an account that contains other accounts. Every computer contains a Users group to which all user accounts belong. There is also a Guest group that allows limited privileges to users who log in without a password (if you allow it).

The logon provides the definition of your group membership and other properties assigned to you. Groups are sets of users as well as other groups that are given the same access rights to resources. Access privileges are cumulative. Local groups can be created to provide control over resource access. Windows NT also comes with some prebuilt global groups that are available system wide, and you can define additional global groups. Users, groups, and domains offer a flexible system for managing resource access through security settings that you make either in the file system or on your desktop for various system objects.

A. Password Issues

Passwords enable you to log on to a particular user account. To log on successfully, you must know both the user name and the exact password. The important thing to know about passwords is that they are *case-sensitive.* Therefore, one of the most commonly encountered errors is when the Caps Lock key is pressed accidentally. Users can enter the correct password and still be denied because the password is entered in uppercase letters.

Because the control of user passwords is the key to making network resources available through the challenge/response mechanism, this topic likely to be on the exam.

To protect passwords, Windows NT has an option that enables you to retire a password after a certain period. You can also set an option that requires that Windows NT Workstation users change the assigned password the first time they log on to the system. Users logging on after that time are required to change their passwords. Windows NT also allows a "no password" password for anonymous access, which provides limited access to system resources. This password is used for a web server running an FTP service, which enables a user to access a PUB folder, for example. To change your USSR's password options, complete the following steps:

1. Select the User Manager for Domains from the Administrative Tools folder on the Programs submenu of the Start menu.
2. Select the account name in the Username panel of the User Manager for Domains.
3. Choose the Account command from the Policies menu.
4. In the Account Policy dialog box, select the options you want, and then click OK.

The options of interest are as follows:

- Minimum and maximum password age before a password expires
- The minimum length of a password
- Whether blank or no character passwords are permitted
- Whether a password list is maintained for an account and enables the user to cycle between passwords
- How many failed attempts to log on with a user name results in an Account Lockout

If you use the Account Lockout feature, it is important to enter a Lockout Duration. After that duration, the account can be used again after a set of failed logons invalidates the account.

It is important not to have a very large number of workstation passwords expire at the same time in a domain. The changing of 2,000 passwords at a time will require that the entire SAM be desynchronized across the domain—a time-consuming procedure.

By the way, the common method used to change your own password is to press Ctrl + Alt + Delete, and then click on the Change Password button in the Windows NT Security dialog box. The use of the Ctrl + Alt + Delete keystroke to initiate a logon or password change is meant to prevent the posting of a spoofed Password Change dialog box and theft of a user account and associated password.

B. Troubleshooting Profiles and System Policies

A user profile is created when a user logs on to Windows NT Workstation the first time. User profiles can be created that provide a specific configuration of the desktop, programs, accessories, printers, taskbar and Start menu configuration, Help system bookmarks, and options in the Windows NT Explorer. This enables an administrator to provide a default profile that is used by a standard user in a domain.

Profiles offer a method for creating an environment based on the user account. To set this option, or to check whether a problem with the environment can be corrected, select the user account in the User Manager for Domains, and then click on the Profile button. Check the User Environment Profile dialog box for the startup script that modifies the environment at logon. Scripts can be BAT (batch), CMD (OS/2), or EXE (program or executable) files. You can also create a new script and specify its location.

> **Because profiles and system policies are an efficient way of managing user access to network resources, this topic is likely to be on the exam.**

Profiles can be stored on the server and retrieved as a cached copy on a local machine when a user logs on. A stored local profile can be used when a problem occurs with a network connection or with a logon. To enable users to have their profiles and configurations travel with them regardless of which workstation that they log on to in the domain, you can create *roaming profiles*.

You can find user profile settings in the Windows NT Registry in the HKEY_CURRENT_USER key. To modify a user profile, complete the following steps:

1. Log on to the system with the user name whose profile you want to modify.
2. Open the Registry Editor (regedit32.exe).
3. Choose the Read Only Mode command on the Options menu if you don't intend to make changes (optional).
4. Click on the HKEY_CURRENT_USER key to expand the settings; then alter the setting you desire.
5. Close the Registry Editor.

Close the Registry Editor to have your new settings take effect. The actual information that the Registry reads for a user profile is contained in the ntuser.dat file of the User Profile folder. This file is cached on a local computer when the user profile is read.

If you want to modify your user profiles, you can find them stored in the C:\WINNT\Profiles folder. The default profile is in the Default User folder, with other user accounts contained in folders with the same name as the user account. Each user profile folder contains a directory of shortcuts or link (.LNK) files to desktop items and the ntuser.dat file. The following shortcuts are contained in these folders:

- *Application Data.* Any application data or settings are stored in this folder.
- *Desktop.* Shortcuts to files or folders are contained in the Desktop folder.
- *Favorites.* Any shortcuts to programs, folders, or favorite locations on the web can be stored in this folder.
- *NetHood.* This folder stores shortcuts to Network Neighborhood objects. This is a hidden folder.
- *Personal.* This folder contains program items.
- *PrintHood.* Any network printer connections and settings are stored in this folder. This is a hidden folder.

- *Recent.* The list of files that appear on the Documents menu are stored as shortcuts in this folder. This is a hidden folder.
- *SendTo.* This contains shortcuts to document items.
- *Start Menu.* Any items that appear on the Start menu are stored in this folder.
- *Templates.* Any template items stored to disk by a user are contained in this folder. This is a hidden folder.

A user profile can be opened and read in any text editor, because a .DAT file is a simple text file. The information contained in the<USERNAME>\NTUSER.DAT file is stored in the following subkeys of the HKEY_CURRENT_USER:

- AppEvents (sounds)
- Console (command prompt and installed applications)
- Control Panel (accessible Control Panels and their settings)
- Environment (system configuration)
- Printers (printer connections)
- Software (available software programs and their settings)

C. Working with System Policies

To enforce a set of rules on a computer, a network administrator can create a system policy that applies to a single user, a group of users, or all users in a domain. You create a specific policy with custom options in the System Policy Editor. This utility enables you to edit portions of the Windows NT Registry or edit system policy. Policies that you see in the System Policy Editor are contained in the winnt.adm and common.adm system policy template files. *Template files* are a set of stored Registry entries. You can modify a template file in the System Policy Editor or create new template files.

System policy settings are stored in the Windows NT Registry in the HKEY_CURRENT_USER and HKEY_LOCAL_MACHINE keys. When you open the System Policy Editor in the Registry mode, you expose various keys in this area of the Registry.

System policy can restrict network logon or access, customize the desktop, or limit access to settings in the Control Panel. A system policy can be applied to a single user, a group of users, or all the users in a domain. Windows NT comes with two standard policies, *Default Computer* and *Default User*, both of which control options applied to all computers and users in a domain. You can create and enforce additional system policies. To create a system policy, do the following:

1. Log on to the computer as an administrator.
2. Select the System Policy Editor from the Administrative Tools folder on the Programs submenu of the Start menu.
3. Choose the New Policy command from the File menu. Two icons appear in the System Policy Editor window: Default Computer and Default User.

4. Select the Add User, Add Computer, or Add Group commands to add a policy.
5. Enter a name for the user, computer, or group in the Add User, Add Computer, or Add Group dialog box; then click OK.
6. Select the Exit command on the File menu to close the System Policy Editor.

With the System Policy Editor in Policy File mode, you can create or modify system policy files (.POL) for the domain. Any modifications you make for a user, group, or computer in the system policy is written as an entry into the ntconfig.pol file. To be enforced, you must save this file in the NETLOGON share on the *primary domain controller (PDC).*

To have more than one system policy in a domain, you need to change the Remote Update setting from automatic to manual in the computer policy section of the system policy. Then the local policy is enforced instead of the default action of Windows NT searching the ntconfig.pol file on the domain controller to validate a user logon.

When a lot of users log on to the network at the same time, there can be long delays when a large number of different policies are contained in the netlogon.pol file. To improve performance on Windows NT Workstation, enable manual updating and create system policy files on workstations other than the domain controllers to balance the load.

When a user presses Ctrl + Alt + Delete, the Logon Information dialog box shows the name of the person who last logged on to the system in the User Name text box. To suppress this default action, change the DontDisplayLastUserName in the \Microsoft\Windows NT\Current Version\Winlogon key of the HKEY_LOCAL_MACHINE\SOFTWARE to off. The value should be set to 1, and the key is of the REG_SZ type. This setting suppresses the display of the last user name.

D. Accessing Shared Resources

Files, shared folders (or simply shares), printer shares, and other shared resources require resource permissions. To create a share for an object, typically you right-click on the object and select the Sharing command. In many instances, the Sharing tab of the object appears and enables you to specify users, groups, and access privileges that are allowed.

The person who creates the resource "owns" the resource and has full privileges to it. The administrator also has full access to resources and can take ownership of them. When an administrator takes ownership of a resource, the original owner's access to the resource is denied. This is a safety mechanism to make it obvious that ownership has be removed and that the resource has been fully taken over.

When users can't access a shared resource, they might not have the privileges required to do so. Try logging on under a different account to attempt to access that resource. If the resource has been accessed in the past under a particular user account, make sure that the resource is spelled correctly, and that it has been located properly.

Because the management of shared resources is one of the central tasks that an administrator is expected to be responsible for, this topic is likely to be on the exam. Failure to access a share is one of the most common problems requiring resolution by an administrator.

If there is a general problem accessing shared resources, open the Control Panel folder and check the Services Control Panel to see whether the various services responsible for validation services are running properly. These services are the following:

- NetLogon service
- Server service
- Workstation service

You should also check the Network Control Panel to ascertain whether the network bindings are correctly bound. These binding are contained on the Bindings tab, and individual binding settings are determined by selecting that binding and clicking on the Properties button.

Inadvertent, or even purposeful, changes to a user's group memberships in the User Manager for Domains or a change in System Policy can also lead to denied access to resources that were previously permitted.

19.5.1 Exercise Changing Password Options

Objective: Change the password options for users.

Estimated Time: Five minutes.

To change your users' password options, complete the following steps:

1. Select the User Manager for Domains from the Administrative Tools folder on the Programs submenu of the Start menu.
2. Select the account name in the Username panel of the User Manager for Domains.
3. Choose the Account command from the Policies menu.
4. In the Account Policy dialog box, select the options you want, and then click OK.

Answers and Explanations: Exercise

Changing the password options affects all newly created user accounts.

19.5.2 Exercise Create a System Policy

Objective: Create a system policy.

Estimated Time: 10 minutes.

To create a system policy, do the following:

1. Log on to the computer as an administrator.
2. Select the System Policy Editor from the Administrative Tools folder on the Programs submenu of the Start menu.
3. Choose the New Policy command from the File menu. Two icons appear in the System Policy Editor window: Default Computer and Default User.
4. Select the Add User, Add Computer, or Add Group commands to add a policy.
5. Enter a name for the user, computer, or group in the Add User, Add Computer, or Add Group dialog box; then click OK.
6. Select the Exit command on the File menu to close the System Policy Editor.

Answers and Explanations: Exercise

Creating a system policy affects the way the workstation will be used by those users for whom the policy is in effect.

19.5 Practice Problems

1. What are two likely possibilities for failure to log on to a network from a workstation you have used in the past?

   A. Incorrect password

   B. Incorrect username

   C. Incorrect media

   D. Incorrect frame type

2. If you cannot log on to a server from a workstation you were using earlier, and are certain that the username and password are correct, what should you check next?

   A. Verify that you are logging on to the correct domain or workgroup.

   B. Check the media.

   C. Verify frame types.

   D. Look for CRC errors.

3. If you cannot log on to the network from a workstation you have used earlier, and are certain that username, password, and domain name are correct, what is the next logical step to try?

   A. Down the network and begin an emergency repair procedure.

   B. Verify that the proper permissions are on the SAM database.

   C. Attempt to log on using another account.

   D. Look for CRC errors.

4. If you cannot log on to a workstation using any account, what is the next logical step in solving the problem?

   A. Repair the accounts database by using the emergency repair process.

   B. Verify the proper permissions are on the SAM database.

   C. Look for CRC errors.

   D. Verify frame types.

5. Which of the following is one of the most common logon problems?

   A. Programmable keyboards

   B. Hashing table errors

   C. Duplicate SIDs

   D. The Caps Lock key

6. If a user can't access a file, a share, a printer, or some other resource, what should you check first?

   A. The resource permissions

   B. The Global groups

   C. The Local groups

   D. TechNet

7. If there is a suspected logon problem from a workstation, check the Control Panel Services application to ensure that which of the following services are running properly?

   A. The NetLogon service

   B. The Server service

   C. The Workstation service

   D. The Bindings service

8. Checking the Bindings tab in the Control Panel Network application verifies which of the following? (Choose two.)

   A. Services are bound to applications.

   B. Correct frame types have been selected.

   C. Dirty RAM is not causing a failure to update SAM.

   D. Services are bound to adapters.

9. Which tool should you use to find restrictions on the user's access to computers?

   A. Network Monitor

   B. User Manager

   C. User Manager for Domains

   D. System Policy Editor

10. Karen calls to report that she cannot log on to the system. She is getting a message that says, "NT cannot log you on. Check your userid and password information and try again." As an administrator, what should you check first?

    A. Make sure that Karen types in the correct password and userid combination. Also check that Karen has entered the password in the correct case and is specifying the correct domain name.

    B. Nothing. It's a normal message that the user would get when the server is down for maintenance.

    C. Log on as administrator and restart the domain controller to clear out any unused connections. When the server comes back up, Karen should be able to log on.

    D. Check the System log in Event Viewer.

19.5 Answers and Explanations: Practice Problems

1. **A, B** If you can't log on, you could be using an incorrect username or password.
2. **A** Enable the check box beneath the password to make certain that you are logging on to the correct domain or workgroup (or the local machine).
3. **C** Try logging on using another account. If other accounts are working normally, check the settings for your account.
4. **A** If you can't log on from any account, repair the accounts database by using the emergency repair process.
5. **D** One of the worst culprits for logon problems is the Caps Lock key. Make certain that the user isn't typing the password in all caps.
6. **A** If a user can't access a file, a share, a printer, or some other resource, check the resource permissions.
7. **A, B, C** Check the Control Panel Services application to ensure that the NetLogon service, the Server service, and the Workstation service are running properly.
8. **A, D** Check the Bindings tab in the Control Panel Network application to verify that the services are bound to applications and adapters.
9. **D** Check the System Policy Editor for restrictions on the user's access to computers or other resources.
10. **A** If users can't log on, they could be using incorrect usernames or passwords.

19.5 Key Words

Shared Resources

System Policy

19

19.6 Modifying the Registry Using the Appropriate Tool

Windows NT 4.0 introduced the Registry database to this operating system, building on an early version in Windows NT 3.1 that stored OLE location information on object servers. The first complete Registry appeared in Windows 95, although each version is different. The Registry is a database of settings and parameters. Among the features set by the Registry are the nature of the interface, operating system hardware and software settings, user preferences, and other settings. Prior to Windows NT Workstation 4.0 and Server 4.0, these settings appeared as sections and lines in various .INI files.

The Registry is hierarchical and each branch is referred to as a *hive*. Individual sub-branches are called *keys*, which is a binary file. The top or first key of a hive is the *primary key*, with each key composed of subkeys that take value entries. Most Registry entries are permanent, although some are session dependent, transient, and never written to disk. An example of a *transient key* is the HKEY_LOCAL_MACHINE\Hardware as generated by automatic hardware detection by the Hardware Recognizer (ntdetect.com for Intel computers). The *Hardware key* is an example of a session value. Another transient value is the information written as part of a logon for a session, including security tokens.

When you install software, either a program or a part of the operating system such as a device driver or service, new subkeys and value entries are written to the Registry. Uninstall these components to remove the information. Subkeys and value entries store information about hardware settings, driver files, environmental variables that need to be restored, and anything the application developer requires reference to.

Because many troubleshooting operations require access to the Windows NT Registry, this topic is likely to be on the exam.

Only members of the Administrators or Power Users group can access the Registry by default. You can assign other users rights to modify all or part of the Registry by hives, but you should think long and hard before doing so. The potential to compromise security or corrupt an installation is high. By default, any user can see the Registry files, but cannot edit, delete, or copy Registry files without specific permission to do so.

A. Modifying the Registry

You use the Registry Editor to view and modify the Windows NT Registry. Of the two versions of the Registry Editor, regedt32.exe and regedit.exe, the former is more generally useful and offers more options.

These programs are not listed on the Start menu and are not found in the Administrative Tools folder where you might expect to find them; this is to discourage their casual use. Their programs are located in the WINNT folder, and you can add them to your Start menu, if you want.

Whenever you change a setting in a Control Panel or alter your desktop, you are writing changes to the Registry associated with the user account profile with which you logged on. If you want to view and modify Registry information relating to services, resources, drivers, memory, displays, or network components, you can use the Windows NT Diagnostic program (WINMSD). This utility is found in the <System Root>\System32 folder, or in the Administrative Tools folder on the Programs submenu of the Start menu. When you make a change in WINMSD, you are limited in what you can alter, and prevented from making destructive changes.

When you alter a value in the Registry using the Registry Editor, the changes you can make are unlimited and can be hazardous to your computer's health. If you delete or modify a required key, you can cause your computer to malfunction. The only recovery method that you can count on in that instance is to reinstall Windows NT or use the Repair disk. Proceed with caution when working in the Registry, and consider wandering around with the files opened as read-only (use the Read Only menu command in the Registry Editor to achieve this) to begin with.

The six root keys and their subtrees are as follows:

- *HKEY_CLASSES_ROOT.* This subtree stores OLE, file, class, and other associations that enable a program to launch when a data file is opened. Although the HKEY_CLASSES_ROOT is displayed as a root key, it is actually a subkey of HKEY_LOCAL_MACHINE\Software.
- *HKEY_CURRENT_USER.* All user settings, profiles, environment variables, interface settings, program groups, printer connections, application preferences, and network connections for each user are stored in the subkeys of this root key.
- *HKEY_LOCAL_MACHINE.* This subkey contains information that identifies the computer on which the Registry is stored. Information in this key includes settings for hardware such as memory, disk drives, network adapters, and peripheral devices. Any software that supports hardware—device drivers, system services, system boot parameters, and other data—also is contained in this subkey.
- *HKEY_USERS.* All data on individual user profiles is contained in this subkey. Windows NT stores local profiles in the Registry, and the values are maintained in this subkey.
- *HKEY_CURRENT_CONFIG.* The current configuration for software and any machine values are contained in this key. Among the settings stored in this root key are display device setup and control values required to restore the configuration when the program launches or your computer starts up.
- *HKEY_DYN_DATA.* Transient or dynamic data is stored in this last key in the Windows NT Registry. This root key cannot be modified by the user.

When the system loads the Registry, most of the data is contained in the HKEY_LOCAL_MACHINE and HKEY_USERS keys. As an example of the kinds of changes you can make, individual settings that you make in the Control Panels are written back to different keys in the Registry. You can modify those settings directly. Table 19.6.1 shows you the location of the different Control Panel settings. When you install a program using the Add/Remove Programs Control Panel, the data isn't written directly to the Registry, but the installer creates Registry entries in the Software hive.

Table 19.6.1 Control Panel Relations to Registry Keys

Control Panel	Registry Data Location
Accessibility	HEKY_CURRENT_USER\Control Panel\Accessibility Options
Add/Remove	HEKY_CURRENT_USER\Console\Application Console Software
Date/Time	HKEY_LOCAL_MACHINE\System\CurrentControlSet\Control\TimeZoneInformation
Devices	HKEY_LOCAL_MACHINE\System\CurrentControlSet\Services
Display	HKEY_LOCAL_MACHINE\Hardware\ResourceMap\Video (Machine settings)
Display	HKEY_CURRENT_USER\Control Panel\Desktop (User settings)
Fast Find	HKEY_LOCAL_MACHINE\Software\Microsoft\Shared Tools\Fast Find
Fonts	HKEY_LOCAL_MACHINE\Software\Microsoft\Windows NT\CurrentVersion\Fonts
Internet	HKEY_LOCAL_MACHINE\Software\Microsoft\Windows\CurrentVersion\Internet Settings
Keyboard	HKEY_CURRENT_USER\Control Panel\Desktop
Mail	Several places
Modems	HKEY_LOCAL_MACHINE\Software\Microsoft\Windows\CurrentVersion\Unimodem
Mouse	HKEY_CURRENT_USER\Control Panel\Mouse
Multimedia	HKEY_LOCAL_MACHINE\Software\Microsoft\Windows\Multimedia
Network	Several locations
PC Card	HKEY_LOCAL_MACHINE\Hardware\Description\System\PCMCIA PCCARDs
Ports	HKEY_LOCAL_MACHINE\Hardware\ResourceMap
Printers	HKEY_CURRENT_USER\Printers
Regional Settings	HKEY_CURRENT_USER\Control Panel\International
SCSI Adapters	HKEY_LOCAL_MACHINE\Hardware\ResourceMap\ScsiAdapter
Server	Several locations
Services	HKEY_LOCAL_MACHINE\System\CurrentControlSet\Services
Sounds	HKEY_CURRENT_USER\AppEvent\Schemes\Apps\ Default
System	Several locations

Control Panel	Registry Data Location
Tape Devices	HKEY_LOCAL_MACHINE\Hardware\ResourceMap\OtherDrivers\TapeDevices
Telephony	HKEY_LOCAL_MACHINE\Software\Microsoft\Windows\CurrentVersion\Telephony
UPS	HKEY_LOCAL_MACHINE\System\CurrentControlSet\Services\UPS

When you make a mistake and delete a key or value in the Registry Editor, you cannot use an Undo command to recover from this error. The Confirm On Delete command on the Options menu offers a limited safeguard. As everyone knows, it is easy to confirm a deletion and repent the mistake later. To correct a critical deletion, complete the following steps:

1. Close the Registry Editor.
2. Immediately restart your computer.
3. Hold down the spacebar as Windows NT loads and select the Last Known Good option.

When Windows NT boots your system, it uses the backup copy of the Windows NT Registry. Any changes you made to your system since your last startup are discarded. The Last Known Good configuration, however, enables you to recover from any critical deletion in the Registry that you made—provided that you recognize the error before logging on to your computer successfully again.

B. Backing Up the Registry

The most important thing you can do to protect your investment in your system's configuration is to back up the Registry files. When you create an ERD, as described earlier in this chapter, you back up only specific hives of the Registry. You should keep a full backup of the Registry on hand.

You find the Registry file in the %system root%\System32\Config folder. For most installations the %system root% is typically C:\WINNT. An individual user's Registry data is written to the ntuser.dat file contained in that user's folder at the location C:\WINNT\Profiles\<username>\NTUSER.DAT. When a user logs on to the workstation, a Profile folder is created for the user with an ntuser.dat file to hold the user's profile. Roaming profiles for a domain are stored as the original copy of the ntuser.dat file on the domain controller. The following CONFIG folder files store direct information on Registry hives:

- DEFAULT
- NTUSER.DAT
- SAM
- SECURITY
- SOFTWARE
- SYSTEM

- USERDIFF
- USERDIFR

Several files are associated with each Registry hive in the CONFIG folder. The first and primary file takes no extension. The CONFIG directory also contains auxiliary files for the Registry, which are the backup, log, and event files. These files have the same names as those listed previously, but take the .LOG, .EVT, or .SAV extension. The System file also has a system.alt file associated with it. The .EVT, or event, files are viewable in the Event Viewer, and contain audited events. Log files store changes that can be rolled back. The .SAV files are part of the Last Known Good boot configuration that enables you to restore your Registry based on your last booted session. The Last Known Good option was described earlier in this chapter.

The LOG file is a backup file that enables changes to be rolled back. It is a fault-tolerance feature; changes are written to the LOG file first. When the data is completely written in the LOG file, updating of the matching Registry hive begins. The data section to be changed is marked, and the data is transferred. When the data transfer is completed, the update flag is reset to indicate successful transfer. Should there be a problem or should your computer malfunction during the transfer, the update is begun again from scratch.

The SYSTEM file is updated in a somewhat different manner because your computer relies on that key to start up. The duplicate system.alt file is used and operates as the replacement for a .LOG file. The entire file is mirrored and replicated. Then, in the event of a crash, the backup file is used and the entire file is replaced.

It is unnecessary to back up the entire Registry. Much of the information is transitory and session dependent. Only specific portions of the Registry need be protected. The files of greatest importance are the SYSTEM and SOFTWARE files. They are generally small and can be fit on a single floppy disk. You should also note that the SAM and SECURITY files can't be modified and cannot be copied or backed up.

To back up the Registry, use the RDISK program described earlier in this chapter and set that option. Do not try to copy the files directly to a disk. You can also back up individual hive files from within the Registry Editor by saving a branch by using the Save Key command on the Registry menu. You can use the Restore Key command to load those backup files.

The hives of the Registry are locked and cannot be accessed to be copied directly. In a dual-boot system, or if you boot your system using MS-DOS or some other operating system, these files are not locked and may be copied directly to another drive or volume.

You can view Registry files on a FAT volume from any other operating system. If the file system is an NTFS volume, only a Windows NT or Linux system running a disk access utility can view the files, read them, and copy them. On Windows NT, one program that can do this is NTFSDOS.EXE.

For a temporary copy of a key, use the Restore Volatile command rather than the Restore Key command. This command loads the key in the Registry Editor, but it does not load that key again in a future session after your computer reboots.

C. Changing the Registry Size

The default size of the Windows NT Workstation Registry is sufficient for most configurations. If you have a large organization and store a lot of user profiles and application data configurations, however, you may find that the Registry runs out of room. You might need to alter the allowed size of the Registry. To change the maximum Registry size, complete the following steps:

1. Double-click the System icon in the Control Panel folder.
2. Click the Performance tab, and then click the Change button in the Virtual Memory section to view the Virtual Memory dialog box.
3. Enter a size in the Maximum Registry Size (MB) text box, and then click OK.

The Registry size can be somewhat larger than the value entered in the System Control Panel. It is related to the size of your paging file, which is related to the amount of installed RAM in your system. When the Registry exceeds the size you set, it brings your system to a halt with a STOP error. This problem is very rarely encountered unless you attempt to reduce the size of the Registry artificially. Keep a maximum Registry size about 2MB larger than the current size in the Virtual Memory dialog box.

D. Troubleshooting the Registry

Several problems can be directly related to Registry errors. The most common categories of problems are the following:

- Your computer won't boot properly or at all.
- Your computer looks or works differently than it once did.
- Your computer won't shut down correctly.
- You receive the "Blue Screen of Death" resulting from a STOP error.
- A software or hardware component that operated correctly stops working without any physical changes being made to the files or to the device.
- Something stops working after you add new software or hardware, and the two are not known to be incompatible with one another.

Most of these error conditions are at least correctable from backup. The one really frightening error is the STOP error because you can't access your machine. To correct the Blue Screen of Death, try booting from your boot disk and running the Check Disk program to repair these type of errors associated with disk and file problems. The CHDSK.EXE program is located in the <SYSTEM ROOT>\SYSTEM32 directory.

19.6 Practice Problems

1. The System Tab in the Windows NT Diagnostics box displays information stored in the Registry under which hive?

   A. HKEY_LOCAL_MACHINE\SOFTWARE

   B. HKEY_LOCAL_MACHINE\HARDWARE

   C. HKEY_LOCAL_MACHINE\SOFTWARE\MICROSOFT\WINDOWS NT\CurrentVersion

   D. HKEY_LOCAL_MACHINE\SYSTEM

2. Version information is stored in the Windows NT Registry under which hive?

   A. HKEY_LOCAL_MACHINE\SOFTWARE

   B. HKEY_LOCAL_MACHINE\SOFTWARE\MICROSOFT\WINDOWS NT

   C. HKEY_LOCAL_MACHINE\SOFTWARE\MICROSOFT\WINDOWS NT\CurrentVersion

   D. HKEY_LOCAL_MACHINE\SYSTEM

3. Service information is stored in the Windows NT Registry under which hive?

   A. HKEY_LOCAL_MACHINE\SOFTWARE

   B. HKEY_LOCAL_MACHINE\SOFTWARE\MICROSOFT\WINDOWS NT

   C. HKEY_LOCAL_MACHINE\SOFTWARE\MICROSOFT\WINDOWS NT\CurrentVersion

   D. HKEY_LOCAL_MACHINE\SYSTEM

4. Members of which groups can access the Registry, by default?

   A. Administrators

   B. Power Users

   C. Users

   D. Replicator

5. Which two utilities can be used to edit entries in the Registry?

   A. Task Manager

   B. Regedit

   C. User Manager

   D. Regedt32

6. Where is the Registry Editor started?

   A. From the Control Panel

   B. Under Administrative Utilities

   C. From the Run command

   D. As a choice on the menu that Ctrl + Alt + Del displays

7. A graphical—and limiting—version of the Registry Editor that is found on the Administrative Tools folder is which of the following?

   A. Windows NT Diagnostic program

   B. Performance Monitor

   C. Network Monitor

   D. Task Manager

8. The graphical tool referred to in question number 7 can be called from the command line with what command?

   A. Watson

   B. MSD

   C. WINMSD

   D. TSKMGR

9. Spencer has made a critical deletion in the Registry while playing around with regedit.exe. He calls Kristin, the administrator, for help. Kristin tells him that his best course of action is to do what?

A. Select the Undo command.

B. Press Ctrl + Alt + Del.

C. Correct the problem with Regedt32.exe.

D. Shut down, restart, and choose the Last Known Good option.

10. The registry file, on most systems by default, is located where?

A. C:\

B. C:\WINNT

C. C:\WINNT\SYSTEM32

D. C:\WINNT\SYSTEM32\DRIVERS

19.6 Answers and Explanations: Practice Problems

1. **B** HKEY_LOCAL_MACHINE\HARDWARE stores information about what is available on the machine.
2. **C** HKEY_LOCAL_MACHINE\SOFTWARE\MICROSOFT\WINDOWS NT\CurrentVersion stores information about the current version of Windows NT on the machine.
3. **D** HKEY_LOCAL_MACHINE\SYSTEM\ CurrentControlSet\Services stores information about the current services available to Windows NT on the machine.
4. **A, B** Power Users and Administrators, by default, are the only groups that can access the Registry.
5. **B, D** Regedit and Regedt32 are the two versions of the Registry Editor included with Windows NT Workstation.
6. **C** Either of the two Registry Editors can be started by typing the command on the Run line.
7. **A** The Windows NT Diagnostic program is a graphical—and limited in feature—version of the Registry Editor.
8. **C** The Windows NT Diagnostic program can be called from the command line with WINMSD.
9. **D** There is no method in place to correct a deletion in the registry editor. To correct the situation, you must reboot with the Last Known Good option.
10. **B** By default, the registry goes in the root directory. Unless otherwise changed, that defaults to C:\WINNT.

19.6 Key Words

Registry

Regedit.exe

Regedt32.exe

19

19.7 Implementing Advanced Techniques to Resolve Various Problems

Windows NT comes with several diagnostic tools to help you optimize and tune the system and to correct error conditions. In many ways, the operating system is meant to be *self-tuning* and to require relatively few settings be altered to make the computer run well. To track errors, Windows has a system of events that are recorded in log files. These events can be tracked and controlled, and they prove very useful in troubleshooting. The following subsections delve into the Event logs in some detail.

To aid in solving network problems, Windows NT also offers you the Network Monitor. This utility enables you to examine and analyze network performance and utilization. Common network issues are also discussed in the upcoming subsections.

A. Working with the Event Logs and Event Viewer

Events are actions that occur on your system. The system itself generates events and records them in the System and Security log files. Applications record their events in the Application log. There are standard events that you see, and you can audit resources to add additional events. Many application developers use the event system to aid in analysis of their application. The Event Viewer enables you to view the Event logs and analyze them.

The Event logs can be viewed by anyone who cares to see the information. You can also remote view an Event log, if you have the permission to do so, from another machine. An administrator may want to restrict access to these logs so that the information is secure and can't be erased.

Because careful analysis of a systems Event log enables you to diagnose many problems this topic is likely to be on the exam.

To restrict who can open the System or Application logs, you can set the following key:

```
HKEY_LOCAL_MACHINE\System\CurrentControlSet\Services\EventLog\-<log_name>
```

The RestrictGuestAccess value of type REG_DWORD is set to 1. When the RestrictGuestAccess is set to 0 or doesn't exist, the default condition is for anyone to access these two logs.

The log files are a *first-in, first-out (FIFO)* system. When the ultimate limit of a log file is reached, the oldest events are deleted to make room for new events. The default size is 512KB, and the oldest event stored is up to one week old. You can modify these settings from within the Event Viewer.

1. Changing Settings of Event Logs

To change the settings of the Event logs, complete the following steps:

1. Open the Event Viewer.
2. Choose the Log Settings command on the Log menu.

3. Select the log type in the Change Settings for ... Log list box of the Event Log Settings dialog box.
4. Set the size of the log in the Maximum Log Size spinner.
5. Select one of the option buttons in the Event Log Wrapping section to determine what happens to old events.
6. Close first the Event Log Settings dialog box, and then the Event Viewer.

A prudent administrator makes a habit of checking the Event logs on a regular basis. Many events occur so frequently that they can overwhelm the Event logs and make it difficult to determine what other error conditions or trends exist. By analyzing the Event logs, you can determine what event types are worth keeping, and how often they should be noted.

Another useful option that the Event Viewer enables is the export of Event logs to data files. Several different output formats are offered to enable you to more easily analyze the data in the logs. You can export your log data out to text file (.TXT), Event log file (.EVT), spreadsheet file (.SYLK), and database data file (.DBF) formats, among others. Numerous third-party tools help analyze Windows NT Workstation log files.

The Event Viewer (like the Performance Monitor) is one of the Windows NT operating system's central diagnostic tools. Learning how to use this tool well will reward the administrator with a smoothly running workstation, a limited occurrence of errors, and a low stress level.

2. The Event Detail Dialog Box

If you want additional information about an event, double-click on that event to view the Event Detail dialog box. You find the following information generated for an event:

- Date of the event
- Time of the event
- User account that generated the event, information that is recorded in the Security log, when applicable
- Computer on which the event occurred
- Event ID (the actual Event Code)
- Source or the component that recorded the error
- Type of error: Error, Information, or Warning
- Category of the event
- Description of the event
- Data describing the event in hexadecimal form

You can find many of the error messages in the documentation and resource kits for Windows NT Workstation. Microsoft also keeps a technical database that contains many of the sources of error messages. You can search the Knowledge Base on the Microsoft web site (as a premium service) or on The Microsoft Network (MSN) to obtain error information stored in the logs.

Another database is delivered on CD-ROM to programmers as part of their subscription to the Microsoft Developer Network program. This database contains information about not only error conditions, but internal error codes of interest to programmers. All levels of participation in MSDN result in your receiving this database.

The Event log is very flexible. You can turn event logging on and off for a number of resources by specifying the auditing properties for that resource. Many developers use the event logs to record information specific to their applications.

3. Find and Search Function

The Event log is almost an embarrassment of riches. To help you find the particular event you need, the Event Viewer has a find and search function. You can use any of the following filters to limit the search of the Event log derived from your own computer by using the View menu:

- Computer
- Event date and time
- Event ID
- Event type
- User
- Source of the event

B. Network Diagnostics

Numerous network problems arise relating to both hardware and software configuration. Some of these problems require that you experiment with cabling and couplings, while others can be solved with software that comes with Windows NT Workstation.

If you have a complex network installation, you could need diagnostic equipment to test your hardware. Often you can test individual components by rearranging their positions in the network (swapping cables or boards) and isolating the offending piece of hardware.

1. Using Network Monitor

Windows NT comes with a utility called the *Network Monitor*, which can be very useful in diagnosing network activity. This Administrative Tools utility collects and filters network packets and can analyze network activity. This utility diagnoses only the computer that it is running on.

The Network Monitor is a supplementary component of the Windows NT Workstation installation. To install this program, open the Network Control Panel's Service tab and click the Add button. After Windows NT Workstation builds its list of services, you can select the Network Monitor from the list.

Network Monitor is both statistical and graphical. In the four panes of the Network Monitor, the current activity in real time appears. The Graph pane at the upper left shows the following bar graphs:

- % Network Utilization
- Broadcasts Per Second
- Bytes Per Second
- Frames Per Second
- Multicasts Per Second

These parameters show you the level of activity that your network is experiencing, and how saturated your network bandwidth is. The Session Stats pane shows you which nodes are communicating, and the number of frames (of the first 128 measured) sent and received from each. The Total Stats pane (on the right half of the Network Monitor) shows complete network statistics in the following categories:

- Captured Statistics
- Network Card (Mac) Error Statistics
- Network Card (Mac) Statistics
- Network Statistics
- Per Second Statistics

You must scroll to see each of the panels in the pane for these different categories. The last pane at the bottom of the window is the Station Stats pane. Information here displays what your workstation is communicating to the network. Click on a column head to sort by that category. The following categories appear:

- Broadcasts Sent
- Bytes Rcvd
- Bytes Sent
- Directed Frames Sent
- Frames Rcvd
- Frames Sent
- Multicasts Sent
- Network Address

2. Diagnosing TCP/IP Problems

An amazing number of network problems are related to TCP/IP protocol addressing. Ensure that your workstation has a unique address, or uses a DHCP (Dynamic Host Configuration Protocol) service for its TCP/IP assignment. Also check that the subnet address you entered into the TCP/IP Properties dialog box is correct. To view TCP/IP settings, complete the following steps:

1. Double-click on the Network Control Panel.
2. Click on the Protocols tab of the Network dialog box.

3. Select the TCP/IP protocol, and then click on the Properties dialog box.
4. Examine the settings to see whether they are correct.

The *PING utility* is also included in Windows NT Workstation. You can "ping" other computers on the network to determine whether they are active, your own workstation with the specific address, the default gateway, and any computer on the Internet or your intranet. Use the PING command in a Command Prompt session without any other parameters to see an informational screen detailing its use.

C. Resource Conflicts

Many configuration errors are resource conflicts. These take the form of duplicate interrupts or I/O assignments, or SCSI devices with duplicate or improper assignments. You might see these problems when you first boot your system, or they might show up later, when a device doesn't work properly.

Check the Event log to see what error events are listed. Also run the Windows diagnostic program WINMSD (in the Administrative Tools folder) to examine your resource settings. Errors in software can be rolled back using the Last Known Good Configuration.

D. Using the Windows NT Diagnostics Program

The *Windows NT Diagnostics program* is the worthy successor to the MSD program found in Windows 3.1. This dialog box shows you information on many of the Registry items found in the HKEY_LOCAL_MACHINE subtree. Using WINMSD, you can obtain detailed information and reports on the state and configuration of your workstation. You cannot use this diagnostic tool to change any configuration settings, but you can use it to determine what conditions exist so that you can fix a problem.

This dialog box contains the following tabs:

- *Display.* Information about your video adapter, its firmware, and any adapter settings are found on this tab.
- *Drives.* A list of drives and volumes is contained in a hierarchical display. Drives include floppy disk drives, hard disk drives, CD-ROM drives, optical drives, and mapped drives through any network connections. If you double-click on a drive letter, the Drive Properties dialog box appears. The Drive Properties dialog box shows you the cluster size, bytes per sector, the current status of the use of the disk, and the file system in use.
- *Environment.* Any environmental variables in use for a Command Prompt session appear on this tab.
- *Memory.* The installed memory, virtual memory, and usage of both is shown on this tab.
- *Network.* The network tab shows any installed logons, transports (protocols and bindings), settings, and statistics.

- *Resources.* If you open this tab, the listing of device assignments appears. Shown here is the IRQ, port numbers, DMA channels, and UMB locations being used by each device. If you suspect a device conflict, this is the place to go to attempt to locate the suspect.
- *Services.* The information stored in the HKEY_LOCAL_MACHINE\System\CurrentControlSet\Services key is displayed on this tab. If you select a service and click on the Devices button, the information stored in the HKEY_LOCAL_MACHINE\System\CurrentControlSet\Control key appears, along with the status of that control.
- *System.* The information stored in the HKEY_LOCAL_MACHINE\Hardware key shows the CPU type and information on other installed devices.
- *Version.* The information stored in the HKEY_LOCAL_MACHINE\Software\Microsoft\Windows\NT\CurrentVersion key is shown on this tab. You will find the operating system version, build number, Service Pack update, and the registered owner of the software.

Windows NT ships with several utilities for evaluating a workstation's configuration and performance. A thoughtful administrator, by being proficient at the use of these tools, can solve many problems, and prevent others from occurring.

19.7.1 Exercise Changing Event Log Settings

Objective: Change the settings governing the Event log.

Estimated time: Five minutes.

To change the settings of the Event logs, complete the following steps:

1. Open the Event Viewer.
2. Choose the Log Settings command on the Log menu.
3. Select the log type in the Change Settings for … Log list box of the Event Log Settings dialog box.
4. Set the size of the log in the Maximum Log Size spinner.
5. Select one of the option buttons in the Event Log Wrapping section to determine what happens to old events.
6. Close first the Event Log Settings dialog box, and then the Event Viewer.

Answers and Explanations: Exercise

This lab exercise provided practice at troubleshooting Windows NT workstation Event log settings. You saw how to bring up the Event log and look at the information written in it.

19

19.7 Practice Problems

1. By default, who can view Event Log information?
   - A. Administrators
   - B. Members of Domain Users
   - C. Guests
   - D. Anyone

2. There is only one restriction you can place on who can see Event Log information. That restriction applies to whom?
   - A. Administrators
   - B. Members of Domain Users
   - C. Guests
   - D. Anyone

3. The Save As option in the Event Viewer log menu will enable you to save the files as comma-delimited fields. When you choose to do so, what extension is used on the files?
   - A. TXT
   - B. EVT
   - C. DAT
   - D. CHK

4. The Save As option in the Event Viewer log menu, by default, saves the event log file with what extension?
   - A. TXT
   - B. EVT
   - C. DAT
   - D. CHK

5. What program creates EVT extension hex files?
   - A. Event Viewer
   - B. Performance Monitor
   - C. DiskPerf
   - D. System

6. Which extension indicates hex files that were saved from the Event Viewer?
   - A. TXT
   - B. EVT
   - C. DAT
   - D. CHK

7. To see information about DMA channels and VMB locations in the Windows NT Diagnostics tool, which tab should you select?
   - A. Services
   - B. Memory
   - C. Resources
   - D. Network

8. Which three log files can Event Viewer view?
   - A. System
   - B. Application
   - C. Security
   - D. Netlogon

9. If a Windows NT service fails to start, what tool should you use?
   - A. Performance Monitor
   - B. Event Viewer
   - C. Tracert
   - D. System Recovery

10. Which of the following tabs does the Windows NT Diagnostics dialog box not include?
    - A. Memory
    - B. Network
    - C. Global
    - D. Resources

11. What would be a common cause of warning events in the System log?

    A. Browser elections

    B. Failure of a service to start

    C. Low disk space on a hard drive partition

    D. Configuration errors

12. To see information about network component configuration in the Windows NT Diagnostics tool, which tab should you select?

    A. Services

    B. Memory

    C. Resources

    D. Network

13. What is a common cause of error events in the System log?

    A. Browser elections

    B. PCMCIA cards not present on a notebook computer

    C. Low disk space on a hard drive partition

    D. Configuration errors

14. Which of the following tools cannot be used for looking at configuration errors?

    A. Event Viewer

    B. Performance Monitor

    C. Windows NT Diagnostics

    D. System Recovery

15. Which of the following tabs does not appear on the Windows NT Diagnostics dialog box?

    A. Services

    B. Resources

    C. Environment

    D. Profiles

16. What are two common causes of device problems?

    A. Interrupt conflicts

    B. Installation of graphic-intensive game packages

    C. Installation of new software

    D. SCSI problems

17. To see information stored in HKEY_LOCAL_MACHINE\SYSTEM\CurrentControlSet\Services in the Windows NT Diagnostics tool, which tab should you select?

    A. Services

    B. Memory

    C. Resources

    D. Network

18. When viewed with Event Viewer, how is a Failure Audit displayed in the Security log?

    A. A stop sign

    B. A key

    C. An exclamation mark

    D. A padlock

19. When viewed with Event Viewer, how is a Success Audit displayed in the Security log?

    A. A stop sign

    B. A key

    C. An exclamation mark

    D. A padlock

20. Which two symbols are displayed in the Security log—when viewed with Event Viewer?

    A. A stop sign

    B. A key

    C. An exclamation mark

    D. A padlock

21. By default, on a busy system with large event log files that reach their maximum default sizes, you can choose how much information should be maintained in terms of which of the following?

    A. Hours

    B. Days

    C. Weeks

    D. Months

22. If you are not using any Win32 applications on a system, what are the contents of the Application log?

    A. The log is empty.

    B. Only the Win16 application information.

    C. The Application log mirrors the System log.

    D. Only events for those applications manually selected.

23. Recovery options are configured by which of the following:

    A. Using Regedit to change parameters

    B. Running the SYSTEM command-line utility

    C. Changing values in the bottom frame of the Startup/Shutdown tab

    D. Running Server Manager

24. By default, on a busy system with large event log files that reach their maximum default sizes, how many days' worth of information are kept before the information is overwritten?

    A. 1 days

    B. 7 days

    C. 14 days

    D. 21 days

25. The Event Viewer is found on a Windows NT Server in which program group?

    A. User Manager

    B. System

    C. Administrative Tool

    D. Diagnostics

26. What are two common reasons for configuration errors?

    A. Installation of a new device

    B. Failing hard drives

    C. Installation of new software

    D. Incorrect SCSI settings

27. Until an administrator enables auditing, what are the contents of the Security log?

    A. Only configuration errors.

    B. The log is empty.

    C. The Security log mirrors the System log.

    D. Only share permission errors.

28. Which two types of events does the Security log track?

    A. Success Audits

    B. Failure Audits

    C. Permission Audits

    D. Registry Audits

29. If your Windows NT-based computer manages to boot successfully, yet still is not performing correctly, what is the first thing to check?

    A. The system event log

    B. The Performance Monitor

    C. Server Manager

    D. BOOT.INI

30. Which of the following logs is the default log displayed in Event Viewer?

    A. System

    B. Application

    C. Security

    D. Netlogon

31. In a series of stop errors in a System log, what is the most likely source of all the errors?

    A. The stop error at the top of the list.

    B. The stop error at the bottom of the list.

    C. Each error stands alone.

    D. The error most replicated.

32. The System log, which can be viewed with Event Viewer, tracks which three kinds of events?

    A. Warnings

    B. Information

    C. Configuration

    D. Errors

33. Which of the following events is not tracked in the System log?

    A. Warnings

    B. Information

    C. Configuration

    D. Errors

34. Windows Diagnostics is a front end to information contained where?

    A. HKEY_LOCAL_MACHINE

    B. HKEY_LOCAL_USER

    C. USER

    D. SYSTEM

35. To see information about virtual memory statistics in the Windows NT Diagnostics tool, which tab should you select?

    A. Services

    B. Memory

    C. Resources

    D. Network

36. Error events are symbolized in the System log—as displayed in Event Viewer—by which of the following symbols?

    A. Stop sign

    B. Exclamation mark

    C. Question mark

    D. An "I" in a blue circle

37. Information events are symbolized in the System log—as displayed in Event Viewer—by which of the following symbols?

    A. Stop sign

    B. Exclamation mark

    C. Question mark

    D. An "I" in a blue circle

38. Warning events are symbolized in the System log—as displayed in Event Viewer—by which of the following symbols?

    A. Stop sign

    B. Exclamation mark

    C. Question mark

    D. An "I" in a blue circle

39. Which of the following is not a symbol found in the System log—as displayed by Event Viewer?

    A. Stop sign

    B. Exclamation mark

    C. Question mark

    D. An "I" in a blue circle

40. Which of the following tabs does not appear on the Windows NT Diagnostics dialog box?

    A. Version

    B. Connections

    C. System

    D. Display

19.7 Answers and Explanations: Practice Problems

1. **D** By default, anyone can view Event Log information. By editing the Registry, you can prevent Guests from seeing the log information, but that is the only restriction available.

2. **C** By default, anyone can view Event Log information. By editing the Registry, you can prevent Guests from seeing the log information, but that is the only restriction available.

3. **A** By default, the files are saved as EVT hex files, but can also be saved as comma-delimited TXT files for importing into spreadsheets or databases.

4. **B** By default, the files are saved as EVT hex files, but can also be saved as comma-delimited TXT files for importing into spreadsheets or databases.

5. **A** By default, the files are saved as EVT hex files, but can also be saved as comma-delimited TXT files for importing into spreadsheets or databases.

6. **B** By default, the files are saved as EVT hex files, but can also be saved as comma-delimited TXT files for importing into spreadsheets or databases.

7. **C** DMA channel and VMB location information is displayed under the Resources tab.

8. **A, B, C** Event Viewer shows the contents of the System, Application, and Security log files.

9. **B** Event Viewer shows the System log, which indicates what services have started and which ones have failed.

10. **C** Global is a type of group, a function of the user and User Manager for Domains rather than Windows NT Diagnostics.

11. **C** Low disk space in a partition is a common cause of warning events in the System log.

12. **D** Network component configuration information is displayed under the Network tab of the Windows NT Diagnostics tool.

13. **B** On notebook computers, the absence of a PCMCIA card is a common cause of an error event in the System log.

14. **B** Performance Monitor is used to gather statistics on running services and processes—not to diagnose configuration errors.

15. **D** Profiles are a function of the user and User Manager for Domains rather than Windows NT Diagnostics.

16. **A, D** SCSI problems and interrupt conflicts are common causes of device problems.

17. **A** Services information in the Registry is displayed under the Services tab of the Windows NT Diagnostics tool.

18. **D** Success Audits are displayed as a key; Failure Audits are displayed as a padlock.

19. **B** Success Audits are displayed as a key; Failure Audits are displayed as a padlock.

20. **B, D** Success Audits are displayed as a key; Failure Audits are displayed as a padlock.

21. **B** The default on a busy system is for the event log files to be overwritten every seven days. This can be changed to any other day value.

22. **A** The Application log stores information only about Win32 applications.

23. **C** The bottom frame of the Startup/ Shutdown tab contains configuration information for the Recovery options.

24. **B** The default on a busy system is for the event log files to be overwritten every seven days. This can be changed to any other day value.

25. **C** The Event Viewer is located in the Administrative Tool program group.

26. **A, C** The most common cause of configuration errors is the installation of new software or devices.

27. **B** The Security log remains empty until auditing is enabled.

28. **A, B** The Security log tracks only success and failure audits.

29. **A** The system event log will show all services that have started, or attempted to start, and the results of that operation.

30. **A** The System log is the default log displayed when Event Viewer is started.

31. **B** The System log lists entries in sequential order, with new entries at the top. The error most likely to be causing others would be the first one written to the file—the entry at the bottom of the list.

32. **A, B, D** The System log tracks warnings, errors, and information events.

33. **C** The System log tracks warnings, errors, and information events.

34. **A** The Windows Diagnostic tool is a front end to the Registry information stored in HKEY_LOCAL_MACHINE.

35. **B** Virtual memory statistics are displayed under the Memory tab of the Windows NT Diagnostics tool.

36. **A** Warning events are identified by an exclamation mark, errors by a stop sign, and information by an "I" in a blue circle.

37. **D** Warning events are identified by an exclamation mark, errors by a stop sign, and information by an "I" in a blue circle.

38. **B** Warning events are identified by an exclamation mark, errors by a stop sign, and information by an "I" in a blue circle.

39. **C** Warning events are identifiedby an exclamation mark, errors by a stop sign, and information by an "I" in a blue circle.

40. **B** Windows NT Diagnostics contains information about Windows NT, which would not include current connections.

19.7 Key Words

errors

warnings

information events

hive

stop error

Practice Exam: Troubleshooting

Use this practice exam to test your mastery of Troubleshooting. This practice exam is 20 questions long. The passing Microsoft score is 70.4 percent (14 questions correct). Questions are in multiple-choice format.

1. When is the Last Known Good Configuration overwritten?

   A. When you indicate an update in the Startup/Shutdown tab of the Services Control Panel

   B. When you start up your computer

   C. When you shut down your computer

   D. When you log on successfully to your workstation

2. An error message appears that a service failed to load. Where would you determine the nature of the problem?

   A. The Network Control Panel's Services tab

   B. The User Manager for Domains

   C. The System log in the Event Viewer application

   D. The Services Control Panel

3. Which SCSI addresses for an external hard drive are valid?

   A. 4

   B. 10

   C. 8

   D. 1

4. Which file is not required on a boot disk for an x86 Windows NT Workstation?

   A. BOOT.INI

   B. NTLDR

   C. ntdetect.com

   D. ntbootdd.bat

5. Which program creates an ERD?

   A. FORMAT

   B. RDISK

   C. RECOVER

   D. ERD

6. Your print job spools, but does not print. Which of the following could not be the cause?

   A. The printer is turned off.

   B. The paper tray is empty.

   C. The printer's memory is full.

   D. Your hard drive is full.

7. How do you hide a printer share?

   A. Move the file to your system WINNT folder.

   B. Add a dollar sign after the share name.

   C. Set an option in the Printer Properties dialog box.

   D. Create a hidden spool folder.

8. What happens when you don't have adequate space for an installation?

   A. The Setup program detects this and stops, canceling the operation.

   B. The space available is used to overwrite as many files as possible.

   C. Your installation is corrupted.

   D. You are given the choice of installing MS-DOS as a temporary measure.

9. Which one of the following should you not do to reclaim space on your disk?

   A. Delete any TEMP files that you find in the various locations that they are stored in (for example, the print cache folder).

   B. Empty your Recycle Bin.

C. Uninstall any programs that you no longer need.

D. Change your file system.

10. Which methods can you use to open the Task Manager?

A. Select the Task Manager from the Administrative Tools folder.

B. Click on the Task Manager button in the Windows NT Security dialog box.

C. Select the Task Manager command from the Start menu's Status bar shortcut menu.

D. Press Ctrl+Esc.

11. Which user profile does not exist?

A. Default user profile

B. User account profile

C. Anonymous user profile

D. Roaming profiles

12. How do you control what action to take when your workstation encounters a STOP error?

A. Use the System Control Panel to specify the action.

B. No action is possible. The computer logs an error and reboots.

C. Use the Network Control Panel to specify the action.

D. Reboot to MS-DOS and enter the RECOVER command.

13. When is the LastKnownGood control set updated?

A. After a user successfully logs on to a system

B. After the Win32 subsystem starts

C. During shutdown

D. During the Kernel Initialization phase

14. What is the system of choice to recreate the Setup Boot disks with the WINNT command?

A. A DOS machine with a CD-ROM drive and floppy drive

B. A Windows NT Workstation machine with a CD-ROM drive and floppy drive

C. A Windows NT Server machine with a CD-ROM drive and floppy drive

D. Any RISC-based machine with a CD-ROM drive and floppy drive

15. On an Intel-x86 computer, which set of files is required to boot Windows NT?

A. NTLDR; BOOT.INI; NTDETECT.COM; NTOSKRNL.EXE; NTBOOTDD.SYS

B. NTLDR; BOOT.MNU; NTDETECT.EXE; OSLOADER; NTBOOTDD.SYS

C. OSLOADER; NTOSKRNL.EXE; NTDETECT.COM; NTBOOTDD.SYS

D. NTLDR; HAL.DLL; BOOT.INI; NTDETECT.COM; NTOSKRNL.EXE

16. Evan wants to know if you can reduce the amount of time his computer takes to boot. He also wants to change the default operating system from MS-DOS to Windows NT Workstation. Which utility should be used?

A. Control Panel, Boot

B. Control Panel, System

C. Server Manager

D. Configure on a user-by-user basis in the users' profiles

17. Spencer calls to say that he was playing around and accidentally changed the SCSI controller card driver and now the computer won't boot Windows NT. It stops at the blue screen and gives him a system error. What should Spencer do?

    A. Boot into DOS and rerun the Windows NT Setup program.

    B. Purchase and install the SCSI device that he selected.

    C. Reinstall Windows NT.

    D. Select the LastKnownGood configuration during Windows NT booting, and then remove the incorrect driver.

18. Annie works in the South building. She calls to say that the message I/O Error accessing boot sector file multi(0)disk(0)rdisk(0)partition(1):\bootsect.dos, is showing up on her screen. Which one of the critical boot files is really missing?

    A. NTLDR

    B. NTDETECT.COM

    C. BOOTSECT.DOS

    D. MSDOS.SYS

19. What information does the BOOTSECT.DOS file contain?

    A. A copy of the information that was originally on the boot sector of the drive before Windows NT was installed. You use it to boot an operating system other than Windows NT.

    B. A copy of the information needed to boot a RISC-based computer.

    C. The file that detects the hardware installed on a PC with a Plug-and-Play BIOS.

    D. The file that contains the boot menu selections.

20. If BOOTSECT.DOS becomes corrupted on one machine, can you copy it from another machine?

    A. Yes; the file is standard on every machine.

    B. Only if the other machine is identical to the corrupted one in every way.

    C. Only with the RDISK utility.

    D. No; the file is machine specific.

Answers and Explanations: Practice Exam

1. **D** A successful logon overwrites changes in the Registry for the Last Known Good Configuration.

2. **C** Any system failure is written as an event in the System log.

3. **A, D** SCSI addresses of 1 and 4 are legitimate addresses.

4. **D** Choice D is fictitious. All the other choices are essential files that get copied to a floppy boot disk.

5. **B** RDISK creates and updates emergency repair disks.

6. **D** A full hard drive has no effect on a previously spooled print file because that file has already been written to disk.

7. **B** When you add a dollar prefix to a sharename, you are hiding that share from view.

8. **A** One of the first things that SETUP does is to examine the file system and disk size, and assess the amount of free space that you have. If you don't have the required amount of free space, the installation is aborted. This is true even if you are overwriting enough files to free up sufficient disk space for the installation.

9. **D** Changing the file system permanently deletes all the data on your disk. In almost all instances, this is neither necessary nor required.

10. **B, C** **A** is incorrect because there is no command for the Task Manager on the Start menu. **D** is incorrect because the keystroke used to open the Task Manager is Ctrl + Shift + Esc.

11. **C** **A, B,** and **D** all exist and support both local and remote users on a networkTthere is no "guest" or anonymous user profile—only the default profile.

12. **A** The System Control Panel contains a setting for the action to be taken when a STOP error is encountered.

13. **A** When a user successfully logs on to a system, the LastKnownGood control set is updated.

14. **A** WINNT works on DOS machines, whereas WINNT32 is used on all other choices.

15. **A** The files needed to load Windows NT on an Intel-x86 platform are NTLDR, BOOT.INI, NTDETECT.COM, NTOSKRNL.EXE, and NTBOOTDD.SYS

16. **B** The System utility enables you to choose a default operating system and reduce boot time.

17. **D** Booting with LastKnownGood boot gets around recent driver change problems.

18. **C** Never try to make a problem harder than it is. If the error message says BOOTSECT.DOS is missing, it is probably BOOTSECT.DOS that is missing.

19. **A** BOOTSECT.DOS is a copy of the information that was originally on the boot sector of the drive before Windows NT was installed. You use it to boot an operating system other than Windows NT.

20. **B** BOOTSECT.DOS can be borrowed from another machine if the two machines are identical in every way.

Part IV

MCSE TestPrep

Networking Essentials

CHAPTER 20

Standards and Terminology

20.1 Define Common Networking Terms for LANs and WANs

A. Definition of a Network

A *network* is a group of interconnected computers that share information and resources. Connected computers sharing resources is referred to as *networking*. The physical pathway in which computers are connected is the *transmission medium*. When a computer is not connected to a network, it is referred to as a *stand-alone* system. The simplest network consists of two computers communicating over a single cable.

B. The Local Area Network

The most common form of networks is the *local area network* (LAN). The LAN is a group of computers interconnected within a building or campus setting. The most common network topology is Ethernet. Ethernet comes in many types.

C. Network Topologies

The physical layout of a network is the *network topology*. The three common topologies are:

Bus

Star

Ring

1. Bus Topology

The *bus topology* or *linear bus* is the simplest form of networking, making it the least expensive to implement. This topology consists of a single cable that connects all computers of the network in a single line, without any active electronics to amplify or modify the signal. This bus must be terminated at each end. Without *termination*, the signals on the bus reflect back upon reaching each end of the bus. This reflection causes serious network errors.

The most common form of the bus topology is *10Base2*. 10Base2 is also referred to as *Thinnet*. 10Base2 employs *RG58* type cable, which has a 50-ohm impedance. This bus must be terminated with a 50-ohm terminator on each end. The maximum segment distance on a 10Base2 network is 185 meters (607 feet).

Another bus topology is *10Base5* or *Thicknet*. 10Base5 networks use RG6 cable, which is much thicker and harder to work with than RG58.

The bus network is a *passive topology* because each computer only monitors the signals on the bus. The signals do not pass through the NIC board in the computer. As the distance between these signals increases, their level decreases. This is referred to as *attenuation*. One way to increase the distance for this bus is to add *repeaters*. Repeaters are active devices that regenerate incoming signals. Signals are boosted as they pass through the repeater.

2. Star Topology

In a star topology, all devices on the network are connected directly to a hub. This type of network is usually easy to troubleshoot because each device can be individually unplugged from the hub. The first star network was *ArcNet,* invented by Datapoint Corporation in 1977. This *token-passing* network used RG62 cable, which is about the same size as RG58 but with a higher impedance.

The most common star topology in use today is 10Base-T. 10Base-T is an Ethernet network running over *category 3 unshielded twisted pair* (UTP). On 10Base-T, the data rate is 10 Mbits per second. Logically, the star topology sends data like the bus topology.

A newcomer to the star topology is 100Base-T, which has a data rate of 100 Mbits per second. This network requires *category 5* UTP cable.

A variation of the star topology is the *star bus* topology. In the star bus topology, hubs are interconnected with linear bus trunks. This enables networks to grow beyond the number of ports on a single hub.

3. Ring Topology

In a ring network, all computers are connected by segments of cable in a ring fashion, with no ends to the network. The signal passes through each computer on the network and is reconditioned before being retransmitted. If any network adapter fails then the entire network goes down.

This network was invented by IBM and is referred to as *Token Ring*.

D. Bus Arbitration

Network Interface Cards (NICs) must implement a standard signaling methodology to gain access to the network bus. There are three popular access methods in use today.

CSMA/CD (Carrier Sense Multiple Access with Collision Detection)

CSMA/CA (Carrier Sense Multiple Access with Collision Avoidance)

Token passing

1. CSMA/CD

Ethernet employs CSMA/CD, which is the most popular access method today. When a computer wants to send data, the following sequence of events occurs:

1. The computer *senses* the cable to make sure there is no traffic on the cable. If this is the case, then the computer can access the cable. If not, the computer must wait until the cable is free of traffic.
2. When the cable is free, the computer can transmit a signal onto the cable.
3. If two or more computers transmit at the same time, they each detect that a collision has occurred. Each computer backs off for a random amount of time, then tries the entire sequence again until the message is transmitted.

In CSMA/CD networks, as the number of computers communicating on the network increases, so does the number of collisions. It is best to break up large networks into segments with switching hubs or bridges.

2. CSMA/CA

CSMA/CA is slower than token passing and CSMA/CD; thus, it is not as popular. In this access method, a computer wanting to transmit waits a random amount of time after the last transmission on the cable. When this timer has expired, the computer transmits data. The transmitting computer does not detect collisions; instead, it waits for a response from the destination computer. If a response is not received in a certain amount of time, the computer waits for the cable to be idle and tries again. *LocalTalk,* which is the transmission medium for AppleTalk, uses CSMA/CA.

3. Token Passing

Datapoint developed the first token-passing network in 1977. ArcNet computers do not transmit data onto the medium until they own a token. The token is passed sequentially to each computer on the network based upon the NIC ID. ArcNet networks require the system administrator to set the NIC ID between 1 and 255. Duplicate IDs can be a real problem in ArcNet networks. If a computer has no data to transmit, that computer simply passes the token along. ArcNet supports both active and passive hubs.

E. The Wide Area Network

When computers must share information over long distances, the *wide area network* (WAN) is used. WANs are typically much slower than LANs but can span distances from a few miles to around the world. WANs are typically created using telephone lines, but they are also created with fiber links, microwave radio, leased lines, and satellite links.

Several telephone line technologies are in use today:

- *PSTN* (Public Switched Telephone Network) is in use in most homes.
- *ISDN* (Integrated Services Digital Network)is divided into three channels—two for data and one for control. These channels are referred to as 2B+D. Each of the B channels moves data at 64 Kbps while the D channel is 16 Kbps. If both B channels are utilized, 128-Kbps data transfers can be achieved.
- *T1* lines are used by many businesses to achieve transfer rates of 1.544 Mbps.

F. Protocols

For computers to successfully communicate, they must follow a common set of communication rules (*protocols*). Thousands of communication protocols are in use today, each with its own acronym.

1. Internet Protocols

One of the most popular protocols in use today is the Internet suite of protocols. The Department of Defense funded development of this suite of protocols along with the Internet in the 1970s. The original name for the Internet was *ARPAnet* (Advanced Research Projects Agency Network).

Included in the Internet suite are two of the best known protocols, *TCP* (Transmission Control Protocol) and *IP* (Internet Protocol). This suite is often referred to as *TCP/IP.* The Internet protocols are routable.

When a corporation uses the Internet suite of protocols on a local LAN, the term *intranet* is used. Some other Internet protocols are:

FTP (File Transfer Protocol)

SMTP (Simple Mail Transfer Protocol)

SNMP (Simple Network Management Protocol)

NFS (Network File System)

ARP (Address Resolution Protocol)

DNS (Domain Naming Service)

Telnet

UDP (User Datagram Protocol)

2. NetWare Networks

NetWare networks have their own suite of protocols, the most popular being *Internetwork Packet Exchange* (IPX) and *Sequenced Packed Exchange* (SPX). These protocols are referred to as *IPX/SPX.* These protocols are routable.

3. NetBEUI

NetBEUI (NetBIOS Extended User Interface) is an extension to NetBIOS (Network Basic Input/Output System). NetBEUI was developed by IBM and is targeted toward small workgroups; thus, it is not routable.

4. The World Wide Web

The protocol to transfer web pages to browsers is Hypertext Transport Protocol (HTTP), which has become very popular in the last few years.

20.1.1 Exercise

1. Your company wants to set up a temporary classroom that will be used once per month for Windows NT training classes. The room must be set up the night before each class begins, it is used for 3 days, then it is torn down. The class is designed for 15 workstations and must be configured as inexpensively as possible. Choose a network topology and explain the reasons for choosing this topology.

2. You work for a brokerage firm in which uptime is of utmost importance. Thus, the time required to isolate and fix network problems must be minimized. This firm employs over 300 brokers, each with their own computer. Choose a network topology and explain the reasons for choosing this topology.

20.1.1 Exercise Explanation

1. Because the network is contained in one room, distance between computers is not an issue with any available topology. The entire network contains only 15 workstations, which could be easily handled by all topologies.

   Ease of setup and cost are the driving factors for determining the best topology.

   > A ring network can be used, but the NICs for ring networks typically cost more than NICs for other topologies.
   >
   > A 10Base-T–type network can be used. However, a 15-port hub significantly adds to the cost.
   >
   > ArcNet is a low-cost alternative. However, 15 ports are too many for inexpensive ArcNet passive hubs.

   In this case, the bus topology 10Base2 is the best choice. Because no hubs are required, cost is reduced. Installation is simple because a T connector on the back of each computer is all that is required to wire the network.

2. Reliability is the issue here. This immediately disqualifies the ring topology because any individual computer can bring down the entire network.

   An ArcNet implementation would be complicated by the fact that there are more than 255 computers in the network. ArcNet IDs only allow for 255 computers.

   10Base2 or 10Base5 could be implemented, but the time required to diagnose a problem can be quite long. A bad connector can require testing at least half the segments in the network.

   10Base-T is probably the best choice because diagnosing problems does not require much time. One problem with 10Base-T is that, if the hub fails, all connected computers lose their networking capability. Purchasing backup hubs can solve this.

20.1 Practice Problems

1. CSMA of CSMA/CD stands for:

   A. Copper System Media Access

   B. Collision Sense Media Access

   C. Collision Sense Multiple Access

2. Which media access network tries to detect collisions instead of avoiding collisions?

   A. Token Ring

   B. CSMA/CD

   C. AppleTalk

   D. ArcNet

   E. CSMA/CA

3. Which is a media?

   A. Twisted-pair wire

   B. Television

   C. Radio waves

   D. Microwave signals

   E. Disk drive

   F. Tape backup

   G. All

   H. None

4. Which company invented ArcNet?

   A. DEC

   B. XEROX

   C. Datapoint

   D. Apple

   E. Standard Microsystems Corporation

5. Token Ring networks use CSMA/CA network arbitration.

   A. True

   B. False

6. 10Base5 is also called:

   A. Thinnet

   B. Ethernet

   C. AppleTalk

   D. Thicknet

   E. None of the above

7. 10Base2 uses which type of cable?

   A. RG59

   B. RG62

   C. RG58

   D. UTP

8. When using 10Base2, you:

   A. Must terminate each end with 50-ohm terminators

   B. Must terminate each end with 75-ohm terminators

   C. Don't need to terminate UTP

9. 10Base-T is often referred to as:

   A. Thinnet

   B. Thicknet

   C. Twisted Pair (UTP)

   D. Ethernet

10. Which is not a protocol?

    A. TCP/IP

    B. NetBEUI

    C. AppleTalk

    D. ARP

    E. NFS

    F. Ethernet

11. Star topologies always require a hub, which means they:

    A. Use more wire than bus topologies

    B. Are easier to troubleshoot than ring topologies

C. Can bring the entire network down if the hub fails

D. Are easy to add new computers

E. All of the above

12. SMP means:

A. Simultaneous Multi-Processing

B. Symmetric Multi-Processing

C. Simple Mail Protocol

13. FDDI is a fiber-optic network based on which topology?

A. Star

B. Ring

C. Bus

14. A gigabyte is:

A. $1x10^9$

B. $10x10^9$

C. $10x10^6$

D. 1,073,741,824 bytes

15. Web browsers communicate using:

A. HTML

B. FTP

C. HDLC

D. HTTP

16. Which networking topology would be easiest to configure for a 10-workstation Windows peer-to-peer network.

A. NetBEUI

B. IPX/SPX

C. TCP/IP

17. The OSI reference model has how many layers?

A. 2

B. 4

C. 10

D. 7

E. 5

18. RAID 0 is also known as:

A. Striping

B. Mirror set

C. Striping with parity

D. None of the above

19. Which type of cable will operate at 100 Mbs?

A. Category 3 cable

B. Category 5 cable

C. Category 2 cable

D. 10BASE2

20. SQL is used to:

A. Access remote mail servers

B. Perform fast searches on web sites

C. Access databases

D. Program mainframes

21. T1 service is:

A. 64 Kbps

B. 56 Kbps

C. 1 Mbps

D. 1.544 Mbps

E. 1.024 Mbps

22. UTP is:

A. Universal Transaction Protocol

B. TCP/IP protocol

C. A type of wiring

D. A signaling method over Ethernet

23. Why do bridges provide better network performance than repeaters?

    A. Because they analyze packets and only forward them on required ports.

    B. They use faster hardware than repeaters.

    C. They ignore bad input signals.

24. Which channel is data carried on over ISDN?

    A. The A channel

    B. The B channel

    C. The C channel

    D. The D channel

25. Which network access method does LocalTalk use?

    A. CSMA/CD

    B. CSMA/CA

    C. Token passing

    D. AppleTalk

26. Which network access method does ArcNet use?

    A. CSMA/CD

    B. CSMA/CA

    C. Token passing

    D. AppleTalk

27. Which network access method does Ethernet use?

    A. CSMA/CD

    B. CSMA/CA

    C. Token passing

    D. AppleTalk

28. CSMA/CA networks are typically slower than CSMA/CD networks because:

    A. There are more collisions on CSMA/CA networks.

    B. CSMA/CA networks must wait a random amount of time before transmitting on the media.

    C. CSMA/CA networks must wait for a token before transmitting on the cable.

    D. CSMA/CA networks use twisted-pair cable and CSMA/CD networks use coaxial cable.

29. NetWare networks use which protocols?

    A. IPX/SPX

    B. NetBEUI

    C. TCP/IP

    D. None of the above

30. Which is not a routable protocol?

    A. IP

    B. IPX

    C. AppleTalk

    D. NetBEUI

    E. None of the above

31. ATM networks can easily switch and route packets because:

    A. All packets are a fixed size.

    B. Packets are variable in size, making switching more effective for small packets.

    C. ATM packets do not have headers that require decoding.

32. Token Ring networks determine who gets the token based on:

    A. Who is ready to transmit data

    B. Synchronized network timers

    C. Random back-off timers

    D. NIC address

33. WANs are typically slower than LANs because:

A. WANs have more hops than LANs, thus the network signal must be processed by each hop.

B. WANs typically use public switching networks to cover great distances.

C. WAN hardware technology is years behind LAN technology.

34. Which topology is easiest to troubleshoot?

A. Star topology

B. Ring topology

C. Bus topology

35. NetBEUI was invented by IBM to be used:

A. In small workgroup-type networks

B. In large networks containing mainframes

C. In OS/2 networks to compete with Windows NT

36. A star network is more expensive to set up than a bus network because:

A. Star hubs are very expensive.

B. Star networks require expensive connectors at the end of each cable.

C. Star-based NICs are more expensive than bus-based NICs.

D. Star networks require much more cable than bus networks.

37. When several hubs are interconnected in the star network, it is referred to as:

A. Star bus topology

B. An intranet

C. Switched network

38. Which topology is a passive topology?

A. Star

B. Ring

C. Bus

39. As signals travel over long distances, they become weaker. This is referred to as:

A. Signal to noise ratio

B. Attenuation

C. 3db point

40. A device that regenerates signals, allowing for greater distances between devices in a LAN without regard to packet information, is a:

A. Bridge

B. Router

C. Switching hub

D. Repeater

41. Logically, the star topology sends data like which topology?

A. Bus

B. Mesh

C. ArcNet

D. Ring

42. In a correctly terminated 10Base2 network, if you remove a T connector from any computer on the network and measure the resistance of the bus between the center conductor and the shield, you should measure about:

A. 50 ohms

B. 75 ohms

C. 100 ohms

D. 25 ohms

43. In a bus network, if one computer is not able to communicate with any other computer on the network, but all other computers communicate fine, what is the most likely cause of the problem?

A. The terminator closest to the computer is not communicating.

B. The segment of cable that connects the noncommunicating computer to its nearest neighbor is defective.

C. The NIC board in the computer is not communicating

D. The length of cable for the network exceeds maximum length.

44. One computer in an ArcNet network is having problems communicating with other computers on the network. You have changed the NIC card, the cable connecting to the hub, and the port on the hub. What is the most likely cause of the problem?

A. The length of cable to the hub.

B. The type of cable is wrong. ArcNet uses RG62.

C. The connector on the computer motherboard where the NIC is plugged in.

D. The network address of the NIC is a duplicate address.

45. You are the network administrator for a small company that has grown steadily over the years. You have a 10Base-T network; with each new employee, you add a new connection. Your network currently has 150 computers connected to it, and you are getting complaints about how slow the network is at certain times of the day. You test the network at lunch and find no problems. What is the most likely cause of the network slowdown?

A. The network servers are overloaded.

B. You have exceeded the maximum cable length for your 10Base-T network, which causes intermittent problems.

C. You have too many hubs on the network, which causes delays.

D. Your large network is susceptible to network traffic.

20.1 Answers and Explanations: Practice Problems

1. **C** Collision Sense Multiple Access, a type of access method.
2. **B** CSMA/CD, the CD stands for collision detect.
3. **G** All of the above items are forms of media.
4. **C** DataPoint Corporation of San Antonio, Texas invented ArcNet in 1977.
5. **B** False. Token ring networks use tokens for media access.
6. **D** 10Base5 is also called thicknet. An easy way to remember this is thicknet can carry signals about 500 meters, while thinnet can carry signals about 200 meters. Thus 10Base5 and 10Base2.
7. **C** 10Base2 uses 50-ohm RG58 coaxial cable.
8. **A** You must terminate each end of a 10Base2 bus with 50-ohm terminators.
9. **C** 10Base-T uses standard twisted pair, and the T stands for twisted pair.
10. **F** Ethernet is a physical network not a protocol.
11. **E** All the statements are characteristics of the star topology.
12. **B** Symmetric Multi-Processing. This is the type of multi-processing employed by Windows NT when more than one processor is present.
13. **B** FDDI employs the ring technology. The signal passes through each computer in the ring.
14. **D** This is 2 raised to the 20th power. Another standard for a gigabyte is 1024×1024×1000 = 1,058,576,000.
15. **D** HTTP, or Hypertext Transfer Protocol, is the method in which web pages are transmitted.

16. **A** NetBEUI was designed for small networks, thus configuration is automatic. TCP/IP requires assigning an IP address to each computer on the network. IPX/SPX is designed for Novell networks.

17. **D** The Open Systems Interconnection (OSI) reference model has seven layers.

18. **A** Raid level 0 refers to disk striping. Other popular implementations are Raid level 1, called disk mirroring, and Raid level 5, called disk striping with parity.

19. **B** Category 5. Remember that as the number gets larger, the cable can support higher data rates and the expense also rises.

20. **C** Structured Query Language (SQL) is used to communicate with databases.

21. **D** T1 service operates at 1.544 Mbps.

22. **C** UTP stands for Unshielded Twisted Pair.

23. **A** Bridges can intelligently look at packets and only retransmit them on required ports. Repeaters do not look at incoming data, so they must retransmit on all ports.

24. **B** ISDN has three channels: 2B+D. Data is carried on the B channels.

25. **B** LocalTalk employs collision-avoidance access.

26. **C** ArcNet was the first commercial token-passing network.

27. **A** Ethernet employs collision-detection access.

28. **B** CSMA/CA networks are typically slower than CSMA/CD because CSMA/CA network must wait a random amount of time before transmitting on the media.

29. **A** NetWare uses the IPX/SPX suite of protocols.

30. **D** NetBEUI, invented by IBM, is not a routable protocol.

31. **A** All packets in an ATM network are 53 bytes and are called cells. Fixed-size packets are easier to design hardware and allocate buffers for.

32. **D** Network Interface Card IDs determine the order of token passing.

33. **B** A WAN is typically slower than a LAN due to the cost of high-speed transmission equipment required for long distances. Phone lines are typically used for WANs.

34. **A** The star is easiest to troubleshoot because the bad connection can be found by unplugging links from the hub.

35. **A** NetBEUI, an extension to NetBIOS, was invented by IBM for small workgroup networks.

36. **D** Every connection in a star network must run back to the hub, which usually results in more wiring.

37. **A** Star bus topology.

38. **C** The bus topology is a passive topology.

39. **B** Attenuation.

40. **D** A repeater simply retransmits any incoming signals on any port to all other ports. Bridges, routers, and switching hubs analyze each packet at different levels of the OSI model to determine what to do.

41. **A** Logically, a star network is like a bus because each computer transmits to all computers.

42. **D** 25 ohms. This is because each end of the bus is terminated with 50 ohms between the center conductor and the shield. These 50-ohm terminators are parallel, which results in a resistance of 25 ohms.

43. **C** If there are any cable problems in a bus network then typically the entire network is down. Therefore, if a terminator is missing or the cable is too long or defective, the entire network would fail. The only choice left is the NIC board.

44. **D** In ArcNet networks, it is up to the system administrator to set the NIC ID. If duplicate IDs exist, one of the duplicated computers will not be able to access the network.

45. **D** Your 10Base-T network is a CSMA/CD-type network. As you add connections, you add network traffic. This traffic varies during the day. It can be heavy in the morning as all the computers log on and idle at lunch when most employees are not using the network. As traffic increases, so does the number of collisions causing the network to slow down. It is time to break this network into segments.

20.1 Key Words

Attenuation

Local Area Network (LAN)

Network

Network topology

Passive topology

Repeater

Stand-alone system

Thicknet

Thinnet

Transmission medium

Wide Area Network (WAN)

20.2 Compare File and Print Servers with Application Servers

A. Server-Based Networking

After a network is wired, there are several methods to effectively share network resources. A *peer-to-peer network* is the simplest network configuration that enables users to access each other's resources. As the network grows, it becomes necessary to dedicate computers specifically for resource sharing. A peer-to-peer network cannot handle the volume of requests that a large network generates.

When a network contains computers designated for management and sharing of resources, this is termed a *server-based network.* In many cases, these computers may have specialized hardware to perform that task, such as RAID controllers or Open PrePress Interface (OPI) spoolers.

1. Clients

In a server-based network, the users of the shared resources are termed *clients.* Client computers are typically less powerful computers than the network servers to which they are attached. Two types of client architecture are in use today, *thin clients* and *thick clients.*

- **Thin**—The thin client has very little hardware in the computer and typically consists of software, such as browsers, to access network servers. This type of client is receiving much press as the NetPC.
- **Thick**—The thick client, such as Windows 95 and Windows NT Workstation, is in wider use today. These computers execute programs in their own RAM and have local disks to store files.

2. File Servers

File servers are computers whose main task is to provide file sharing to computers on the network. These computers must handle multiple and simultaneous requests for file resources. These computers may also employ specialized hardware to increase reliability, speed, and capacity. Typically, this is accomplished with the help of *Redundant Arrays of Inexpensive Disks* (RAID).

There are six levels of RAID.

Level 0 Striping

Level 1 Disk mirroring

Level 2 Disk striping with ECC

Level 3 ECC stored as parity

Level 4 Disk striping with large blocks

Level 5 Disk striping with parity

Only three of the preceding levels are common today—levels 0, 1, and 5. All levels except level 0 (Striping) provide varying levels of fault tolerance.

- **Level 0 (Disk striping without parity)**—Employed for systems that require the fastest access without regard to redundancy. In this configuration, the disks are arranged to provide parallel access. If a file contains 4 sectors worth of data, then sectors 1 and 3 are stored on one disk while sectors 2 and 4 are on the other.
- **Level 1 (Disk mirroring)**—Employed when data redundancy and downtime is critical. In this method, when a write is issued to one disk, the other disk also receives the write. If one disk becomes defective, the other disk can take over without shutting down the computer.
- **Level 5 (Disk striping with parity)**—Provides faster access and better utilization of disks than level 1 as the number of disks increases. A parity sector is maintained across all disks and can be rebuilt if one disk fails.

Raid controllers contain specialized hardware to communicate with the disk arrays, thus offloading the main CPU.

The file sever must also provide security for all the files on the server. A common file server is Windows NT Server. Security is provided by limiting access to the shares and to the files.

When a disk or directory is shared, the administrator decides who can access the share. With Windows NT *New Technology File System* (NTFS), the administrator can grant or reject file and directory access to any user or group of users on the network.

File backup and maintenance are easier in a server-based network because only the file servers must be backed up.

3. Print Servers

Print servers are used to maintain a single printer or a group of printers across the network. A print server manages access to a shared printer, making it accessible to users at other network machines.

The print server usually incorporates a *spooler* that can accept jobs from clients much faster than the printer can print them. This quickly frees up the client machine because the client machine believes printing is complete. The spooler writes the job to the disk and sends the job to print when the printer is available. A *non-blocking spooler* can accept jobs from many clients in parallel.

Print servers can range from the spooler built into Windows NT to high-end Cluster Printing Systems, such as the MicroPress from T/R Systems. *High-end spoolers* provide high-speed image storage and management (OPI) that enables the clients to work with low-resolution representations of the actual images.

4. Application Servers

An *application server* runs all or part of an application on behalf of the client, then transmits the result to the client for further processing.

A common application server is a SQL database server. The client asks the SQL server to find a record, and the SQL server does all the work in locating the information, returning the desired record to the client.

B. Comparison Between File, Print, and Application Servers

Application servers run part or all of an application for clients, thus requiring a lot of CPU horsepower. File and print servers do not offload processing of client computers. They must service many requests from many computers in parallel, however, requiring large amounts of RAM and disk space.

20.2.1 Exercise

When you joined your company, there were 10 employees and a simple peer-to-peer network, which worked well. Your company has received a new contract and has just added 30 employees, all using email, word processing, printing capability, and access to the corporate database that is stored on your computer.

You must convince your boss to migrate from the peer-to-peer network to a client/server network. List the advantages of the server-based network and the equipment required for the migration.

20.2.1 Exercise Explanation

In this environment, you could install one server computer that acts as an application server as well as a file server and print server. The database stored on your local machine should be moved to the new file server and be maintained by a SQL application. You should show your boss the advantages of the security and speed of server applications, data reliability through server backups, and reduced administrative costs because only a single server needs to be maintained. Each user no longer needs to be concerned with sharing resources and setting security on the shared resources. Also show how easy it is to grow a server-based network versus a peer-to-peer network.

20.2 Practice Problems

1. Select the most appropriate configuration for a SQL server with 100,000 records.

    A. Pentium 100 processor, 64 MB RAM, RAID controller with 5 disks (4.3 GB 7200 rpm)

    B. Pentium 200 with MMX, 128 MB of RAM, 2 IDE disks (3.1 GB 5400 rpm)

    C. Pentium II 266 processor, 64 MB of RAM, 2 IDE disks (3.1 GB 5400 rpm)

    D. Pentium 100 processor, 128 MB RAM, 2 IDE disks (3.1 GB 5400 rpm)

2. Select the most appropriate configuration for a file server accessed by 200 computers.

    A. Pentium 100 processor, 64 B RAM, Raid controller with 5 disks (4.3 GB 7200 rpm)

    B. Pentium 200 with MMX, 128 MB of RAM, 2 IDE disks (3.1 GB 5400 rpm)

    C. Pentium II 266 processor, 64 MB of RAM, 2 IDE disks (3.1 GB 5400 rpm)

    D. Pentium 100 processor, 128 MB RAM, 2 IDE disks (3.1 GB 5400 rpm)

3. Select the most appropriate configuration for a print server accessed by 200 computers.

    A. Pentium 100 processor, 64 MB RAM, RAID controller with 5 disks (4.3 GB 7200 rpm)

    B. Pentium 200 with MMX, 128 MB of RAM, 2 IDE disks (3.1 GB 5400 rpm)

    C. Pentium II 266 processor, 64 MB of RAM, 2 IDE disks (3.1 GB 5400 rpm)

    D. Pentium 100 processor, 128 MB RAM, 2 IDE disks (3.1 GB 5400 rpm)

4. Your corporation has 10 executives that access the corporate web site for company news and stock prices only. What is the best type of client to service these executives?

    A. A thin client architecture

    B. A thick client architecture

    C. Windows 3.11

    D. Windows 95

5. A print server:

    A. Will make your printers run faster

    B. Will free up client computers faster when the client is printing

    C. Requires a lot of CPU horsepower to keep up with laser printers

6. A file server:

    A. Is more difficult to back up because the volume of data is much greater

    B. Requires the fastest available CPU to handle the large amount of file accesses

    C. Requires fast disks because the disk I/O is typically the bottleneck in file servers

7. Network administrators employ RAID to:

    A. Provide reliable storage for important information

    B. Make backups easier

    C. Help programmers eliminate bugs

8. The simplest method of protecting a single disk from failure is:

    A. RAID Level 0

    B. RAID Level 1

    C. RAID Level 5

9. Your company provides video streaming applications in which the data can easily be regenerated from CD-ROM. Which RAID level is best suited for this application?

   A. RAID Level 1

   B. RAID Level 0

   C. RAID Level 5

10. Your large network has five 24-ppm laser printers. Which is the best implementation to share the printers?

   A. Plug each printer into a separate parallel port on a print server.

   B. Simply provide a network connection for each printer.

   C. Install two network cards in your print server and put the five printers in a separate network along with the print server.

11. Which is not an example of client/server computing?

   A. A workstation application accessing a SQL database on a server

   B. A workstation application accessing the corporate mail server to find an address

   C. A terminal accessing a mainframe database

12. A database system utilizing SQL is an example of:

   A. A file server

   B. A print server

   C. An application server in a client/server architecture

13. Which is not true about a client/sever application?

   A. The client must have some processing power to take the load off the server.

   B. The server processes the database request and only sends the results across the network.

   C. The client must have as much processing power as the server to handle the responses from the server quickly, and not slow the server down.

14. The most common use of client/server networking is:

   A. Database servers

   B. Mail servers

   C. GroupWare

15. In a server-based network, what component of the operating system intercepts file and print requests and sends them out the network to the server?

   A. The interceptor

   B. The NDIS driver

   C. The redirector

   D. The OSI model

16. Which is not an advantage of storing applications on network servers instead of on the client's computer?

   A. Lower licensing cost

   B. Easier to upgrade

   C. Greater uptime because application is on the server

   D. Requires less disk space because the application is only installed on the server

17. Spooling a job means:

   A. Employing a special spool driver that transmits the print job to the network spooler

   B. Storing the job in memory or on disk until the physical printer is ready to accept the job

   C. Sending a print job across the network instead of printing on a local printer

18. Every time an employee of your company prints a job the output contains funny characters and numbers instead of what was intended. What is the most likely cause of this problem?

    A. The network card on the employee's computer is causing error, which accounts for the weird characters.

    B. The employee does not have the correct access to the printer.

    C. The print driver does not match the printer.

19. When setting up a client/server network, the server computer should be:

    A. More powerful than the client computers

    B. Less powerful than the client computers

    C. The same as the client computers

20. Clustering refers to:

    A. Installing servers in the same location forming clusters

    B. All the computers connected to a multi-port hub are considered a cluster

    C. Technology that enables a group of computers to appear as one high-speed computer to users on the network

21. SMP would be more important to which of the following?

    A. An application server running SQL

    B. A file server with hundreds of clients

    C. A print server controlling 30 printers

22. Network-aware applications:

    A. Provide file locking to prevent data from being corrupted by multiple users

    B. Must know the type of NIC installed to access the network

    C. Can only run over a network

23. PostScript is:

    A. A database-scripting language

    B. A method of writing efficient web pages

    C. A printer-description language

24. Windows NT Server has what levels of RAID built in?

    A. RAID level 0

    B. RAID level 1

    C. RAID level 2

    D. RAID level 5

    E. All of the above

25. A hot-swappable disk is:

    A. A disk that exactly mirrors another disk and can be exchanged with the other disk

    B. A disk that can be plugged or unplugged with power applied

    C. A disk that can be moved or tilted when spinning

20.2 Answers and Explanations: Practice Problems

1. **C** This is an application server that requires processing power more than anything else. Searching large databases is processor intensive. The most powerful processor in this group is the Pentium II 266.

2. **A** This is a large file server. Access speed and redundancy are the two most important aspects of a large file server. Here, a RAID controller is used to provide redundancy and to offload the system CPU to speed access.

3. **D** Print servers are not demanding on CPUs, so a less expensive Pentium 100

will do fine. The extra RAM and hard disks are used to spool files.

4. **A** For simple dedicated tasks, a thin client is the choice. The executives will not be required to learn how to get around in the operating system of a thin client.

5. **B** Print servers are non-blocking, which means they are always ready to accept data. If the printer is busy, the print server spools the incoming data to RAM or to the hard disk. This frees up the client computer faster because the client is not required to wait for the printer.

6. **C** The bottleneck on file servers is usually the disk, so increasing the bandwidth to the disks is of utmost importance.

7. **A** RAID provides reliable storage because the system can tolerate and recover from single disk failures.

8. **B** RAID level 1 provides disk mirroring, in which one disk exactly mirrors the other disk. If a disk fails, the other disk takes over.

9. **B** RAID level 0, striping with no parity, is the fastest of all RAID levels. Here the disks are accessed in parallel, and no parity calculations are required.

10. **C** The fastest method of supplying a printer with data is the network connection. However, if you plug the printers into the same network as the server and clients, the job must traverse the network twice—once from the client computer to the server and again from the server to the printer. This adds network traffic. If the printers are installed on their own network, then traffic is reduced and data is supplied to the printers in the fastest possible manner.

11. **C** In client/sever computing, both the client and the server share the task of processing. Terminals do not process data; they simply display data from the mainframe.

12. **C** This is the classic example of client/server computing in which the server is an application server.

13. **C** Clients usually do not require as much processing power as servers because the server must handle many requests from many clients.

14. **A** SQL database servers are the largest use of the client/server architecture in use today.

15. **C** It is the job of the redirector to redirect disk and print requests from the local machine to a server on the network.

16. **C** This is not true. If the server goes down, then all users of the application stored on the server cannot run the application.

17. **B** Spooling a job simply means storing the job somewhere until the printer is ready to accept the job. Spooling can occur locally or at the print server if one is used.

18. **C** This is a common problem when PostScript jobs are sent to PCL printers. If your printer is a PCL printer, then all users must have the correct PCL driver installed.

19. **A** The server computer must be more powerful than the clients because the server is performing most of the processing and handling multiple request from different clients.

20. **C** Clustering technology enables groups of computers to present themselves as one computer to the network. Clustering also refers to fault-tolerant computers—if one computer in a cluster fails, the other computer takes over without affecting any network connections.

21. **A** Having multiple processors is a big plus in SQL configurations. This enables the SQL server to handle requests in parallel.

22. **A** Network-aware applications must provide a mechanism to prevent data corruption when several users access data.

File locking is usually the method chosen by these applications.

23. **C** PostScript, invented by Adobe Systems, is a very powerful Page Description Language (PDL) used for printing.

24. **A, B, D** The three levels of RAID built into Windows NT are 0, 1, and 5—Striping without parity, mirroring, and striping with parity.

25. **B** The term "hot swappable" refers to a component's capability to be swapped with power applied. This is a bonus in a RAID system. If a disk fails, another disk is hot swapped and the RAID controller rebuilds the new disk.

20.2 Key Words

Application server

Clients

File server

New Technology File System (NTFS)

Peer-to-peer network

Print server

Redundant Arrays of Inexpensive Disks (RAID)

Server-based network

Spooler

20.3 Compare User-Level Security with Access Permission Assigned to a Shared Directory on a Server

Two basic network security models are in use today, *password-protected shares* and *access permissions.* These two models are often referred to as *share-level security* and *user-level security.*

A. Password-Protected Shares

In the password-protected shares network security model, also referred to as *share-level security,* each shared resource is assigned a password. To access the resource, the user enters the correct password and is granted access to the resource. This method does not require user authentication.

The type of access can be controlled by the operating system; however, you cannot grant different levels of access to different users. Different operating systems expose different types of access to shares. Windows 95 is a good example of an operating system that implements share-level security.

B. Access Permissions

Access-permissions security (user-level access) is more advanced and flexible than password-protected shares. Rights are assigned on a user-by-user basis and authentication is employed. A user logs on to the network by supplying a user name and a password associated with the user name. The server validates the user name and password before access to any network resource is granted. The server or domain controller in this architecture must maintain a database of users and passwords.

Each resource in the network has permissions associated with it. After the user is validated, access to resources is granted based on permissions granted to that user. In user-level access configurations, it is easy to think of passwords being associated with users and permissions being associated with resources.

Windows NT employs *discretionary access control.* This is the capability to assign permissions at the discretion of the owner (or other authorized person).

Windows NT incorporates access-permissions security in two different models, the *workgroup model* and the *domain model.*

1. Workgroup Model

In the workgroup model, every server in the network maintains its own set of users and passwords in the Security Account Manager (SAM) database. Each time a user logs on, the Local Security Authority (LSA) validates the user name and password against the SAM database. Each server in a workgroup maintains its own SAM.

After a user is authenticated, an access token is created for that user. This token is used to determine the level of access to network resources for that user.

Each resource has an Access Control List (ACL) associated with it. This list identifies which groups or users have access to the object the ACL represents. The ACL consists of Access Control Entries (ACEs), which specify the permissions for a particular user or group.

Each ACE has an access mask, which defines all possible permissions for a particular user to that object. When a user attempts to access a network resource, Windows NT compares the security information in the user's access token with the ACE, and permission is either granted or denied.

This model is appropriate for workgroups consisting of few servers. As the number of servers grows, the amount of work to keep all the SAM databases up-to-date also grows.

2. Domain Model

The domain model maintains a single SAM database for the entire network. This database is maintained on a computer designated as the domain controller. All security validation works basically the same as the workgroup model, with the difference that the LSA must communicate with the domain controller to validate the user against the domain's SAM database.

3. Windows NT Groups and Permissions

As the number of users increases, the difficulty in maintaining permissions for these users also increases. Windows NT enables the system administrator to create groups of users and to apply permissions to the entire group.

The security of a network resource varies depending on the type of resource. For example, a Windows NT printer has four categories of security:

Full Control	Gives the user administrative control of the printer
Manage Documents	Allows a user to change the status of print jobs but not of printers
Print	Allows a user to print and to change the status of only his jobs
No Access	Means the user has no access to the printer

Permissions on NTFS directories under Windows NT are as follows:

Full Control	Gives all access to the directory including changing permissions
Read	Allows the user to read or to execute programs from the subdirectory
List	Allows viewing of file names and subdirectories under the current subdirectory
Add	Allows adding files or subdirectories
No Access	Denies all access to the subdirectory
Change	Allows reading, writing, deleting, and creating files and subdirectories
Add and read	Allows reading and creating files and subdirectories

The preceding directory permissions are only supported under the NTFS file system. If the disk is formatted with the FAT file system, directory permissions are not available. When a share is created under Windows NT, the following permissions are available:

Full Control	Gives all access to the directory including changing permissions
Read	Allows the user to read or to execute programs from the share or any subdirectory under the share
Change	Allows reading, writing, deleting, and creating files and subdirectories under the share
No Access	Denies all access to the share

The share permissions are available regardless of the type of file system on the disk (such as FAT or NTFS).

20.3.1 Exercise

You are a systems administrator for a small company that has one Windows NT file server. On this file server, there is a series of database files all under the same directory. Certain users in the company update the database, and other users only access the database. How can you allow certain users to modify the database while at the same time allow other users only read access to the database?

20.3.1 Exercise Explanation

There are two methods to accomplish this goal. The first method is to grant all users full control to the subdirectories and files on the disk. After this is done, a share is set up and access permissions to the share are set on a user-by-user basis. The other method is just the opposite, in which all users are granted access to the share, but subdirectory and file access is determined on a user-by-user basis. The most common approach today is the first approach.

20.3 Practice Problems

1. Windows for Workgroups employs which type of resource sharing architecture?
   A. User-level security
   B. Share-level security
   C. Password-protected shares
   D. Access permissions

2. User-level security is good for:
   A. Large networks with more than 50 computers
   B. Peer-to-peer networks with less than 10 computers
   C. Networks that have many servers but few users

3. Which file system allows specific permissions for files and directories on Windows NT?
   A. HPFS
   B. NTFS
   C. FAT
   D. FAST FAT32

4. Which file system allows setting of permissions on disk shares?
   A. NTFS
   B. FAT
   C. HPFS
   D. All of the above

5. Discretionary access control means:
   A. The operating systems employs ACLs.
   B. The administrator decides who can or cannot log on to the server.
   C. The owner of a resource decides who has access and the type of access to the resource.

6. Which operating system(s) implements discretionary control?
   A. Windows 95
   B. DOS
   C. Windows NT

7. How many different modes of network operation does Windows NT server support?
   A. 1
   B. 2
   C. 3
   D. 4

8. In a Windows NT workgroup network, there are five Windows NT servers. How many SAM databases are there?
   A. 1
   B. 2
   C. 10
   D. 5

9. In a Windows NT domain network with five Windows NT servers, how many SAM databases are there?
   A. 1
   B. 2
   C. 10
   D. 5

10. In a Windows NT network with one server and nine clients, which networking model is easier to implement?
    A. Windows NT workgroup
    B. Windows NT domain
    C. Windows NT trusted domain

11. The Windows NT SAM database is where:
    A. User names and passwords are stored

B. Disk-sharing information is stored

C. Printer-sharing information is stored

12. In a peer-to-peer network, which network security model is used?

A. User-level security

B. Share-level security

C. Password-protected shares

D. Access permissions

13. ACE is an acronym for:

A. Access control entity

B. Access control entry

C. Access control enabled

14. ACLs:

A. Contain users' passwords

B. Contain resource passwords

C. Contain ACEs

15. In user-level access, network resources:

A. Only have one password associated with them

B. Have multiple passwords associated with them

C. Have no passwords but have permissions associated with them

16. When a user logs on to Windows NT, who is responsible for authentication?

A. The LSA

B. The ACL administrator

C. The SAM process

D. The ACE generator

17. When a print server grants a user print access:

A. That user can delete his own job

B. That user can pause other jobs to allow clearing of paper jams

C. That user can change the priority of other jobs from the console to allow his job to print sooner

18. Which type of access is not associated with directory shares?

A. Read

B. Change

C. Add

D. No Access

19. Which access is not associated with FAT directories?

A. List

B. Read

C. Write

D. Full Control

E. No Access

F. All the above

20. Which access is not associated with NTFS directories?

A. List

B. Read

C. Write

D. Full Control

E. No Access

F. None of the above

21. How many Primary Domain Controllers can exist in a Windows NT Domain?

A. 1

B. 2

C. As many as the administrator wants, although each domain controller must run on a separate computer

22. In a Windows NT domain, the Local Security Authority must verify logins with:

    A. The local SAM database

    B. The ACL manager on the domain controller

    C. The remote SAM database on the domain controller

    D. The local LSA security database

23. One reason domains are easier to manage than workgroups with a large network is:

    A. Users can be combined into groups to minimize the number of changes required when security changes.

    B. There is only one SAM database for the entire network, requiring only one database to be updated.

    C. ACLs are automatically updated when users are added to the domain.

24. When a user attempts to print a job on a shared Windows NT printer, the user's access is verified:

    A. By checking the user's credentials against the SAM

    B. By checking the user's credentials in the local ACL

    C. By using the user's token and ACL for the share

25. In Windows NT, if you delete a user then add the user back in with the exact name and rights:

    A. His security is automatically recognized because the name is the same and all resources are updated.

    B. All security information is lost because each time a new user is created a unique security ID is created for that user.

26. You are a systems administrator. A user complains he gets access denied each time he attempts to read a shared NTFS directory. You look at the shares, and the user has Change access to the share. What is the most likely cause of this problem?

    A. The user's network card is defective.

    B. The user logged on to the network with the wrong password.

    C. You gave the user correct share permissions but forgot to give the user access to the NTFS directory.

    D. The server was in the process of coming up and was not ready to handle user requests.

27. To create a new subdirectory under an NTFS volume, what is the minimum level of access required?

    A. Full Control

    B. Write

    C. Read

    D. Change

    E. Add

20.3 Answers and Explanations: Practice Problems

1. **B, C** Windows for Workgroups supports only the password-protected shares model, also called share-level security.

2. **A** As a network grows larger, it is easier to manage user-level security than share-level security.

3. **B** NTFS, New Technology File System, enables the user to apply permissions on files and directories on the Windows NT platform.

4. **D** All disk architectures allow setting of permissions on shares.

5. **C** In discretionary access control systems, the owner (usually the creator) of

an object decides the type of access granted to users of the object.

6. **C** Windows NT employs discretionary access control to all objects in the system.

7. **B** Windows NT supports the workgroup model and the domain model of server networking.

8. **D** In the Windows NT workgroup model, each computer maintains its own SAM database.

9. **A** The Windows NT domain model has only one SAM database for the entire domain. This database is located on the Primary Domain Controller (PDC) and is replicated on any Backup Domain Controllers.

10. **A** The Window NT workgroup model is easier to set up than the domain model. In small networks, the Windows NT workgroup model is easy to maintain because the number of users is small.

11. **A** The Security Account Manager (SAM) database is where user names and passwords are stored.

12. **B** Peer-to-peer networks implement share-level security. There is not a database of users in the peer-to-peer network architecture.

13. **B** An ACE is simply an entry in the access control list (ACL) for an object under Windows NT. The ACE contains access information about a user or group for this object.

14. **C** The access control list (ACL) is a collection of ACEs.

15. **C** In user-level access, network users have passwords and resources have permissions.

16. **A** The Local Security Authority (LSA) is responsible for logon authentication in the Windows NT operating system.

17. **A** Print access only allows the user to modify his job.

18. **C** Add access is not associated with directory shares. Add access is a security attribute for disk files and directories under NTFS.

19. **F** Directory permissions cannot be individually set on FAT directories or files.

20. **C** There is no such permission as Write access under Windows NT.

21. **A** In a Windows NT domain, there is only one domain controller; however, there may be several backup domain controllers.

22. **C** In the domain model, the LSA communicates with the PDC to verify logons against the PDC SAM database.

23. **B** Updating one database each time a change occurs is much easier than updating every server on the network.

24. **C** Each time a user logs on, the user is given a token. This token is used each time the user attempts to access any resources. The token is used to identify the user's entry in the ACL for the share.

25. **B** Each time a user or group is created, a unique Security Identifier (SID) is assigned. If you delete a user and then add the user back, a different SID is created for the user; thus, the rights the original user had are lost.

26. **C** Under NTFS, if you grant a user access to a share, it does not guarantee that the user can access directories or files. The user must also have permissions to gain file and directory access under NTFS.

27. **E** Add. This enables the user to create the subdirectories but does not grant access to any files.

20.3 Key Words

Access Control Entry (ACE)
Access Control List (ACL)
Access mask
Access permission security
Discretionary access control
Domain model
Share-level security
User-level security
Workgroup model

20.4 Compare a Client/Server Network with a Peer-to-Peer Network

All networks share some common elements, including:

Resources	Disks, printers, faxes, and other resources used by clients on the network
Servers	Machines that share local resources on the network
Clients	Machines that request and use shared resources
Media	The interconnection between networked computers

PC networks generally fall into one of these two categories:

- **Server-based network.** Consists of groups of user-oriented PCs (*clients*) that request and receive network resources from network servers.

  Included in these resources are file services, print services, e-mail, fax services, and application services.

- **Peer-to-peer network.** Consists of groups of user-oriented PCs that operate as equals (*peers*), sharing and using each other as resources.

  In a peer-to-peer network, each computer is responsible for its own security. A peer that shares and uses resources is essentially a server and a client. These networks work well with 10 or fewer computers.

When deciding which type of network to implement, several factors must be considered, including:

Number of computers

Cost

Security requirements

Administrative requirements

20

A. Peer-to-Peer Implementations

Peer-to-peer networks have several advantages over server-based networks:

Lower Cost

Easy to set up and install

Usually no dedicated network administrator is required

Users have control over their own resources and manage their own security

Simple cabling schemes are possible

Along with the advantages of the peer-to-peer network, there are several disadvantages:

Limited growth

No central organization

Weak security

Additional load on computers acting as clients and servers

B. Server-Based Implementations

Server-based networks include specialized high-performance computers dedicated to certain tasks, such as file servers, print servers, or application servers.

Advantages of the server-based network include:

Centralized management of a large number of users

Strong security that is centralized

Capability to grow

Capability to create redundant systems

Some disadvantages of the server-based architecture include:

More expensive to set up due to dedicated server hardware

More difficult to initially set up due to centralized management of users and resources

Usually requires a network administrator to manage the network

C. Windows Implementations

Windows operating systems implement both types of networking. Windows 95 and Windows NT Workstation implement peer-to-peer networks, while Windows NT Server is used to implement a server-based network that is scalable to thousands of computers and users.

20.4.1 Exercise

A small accounting firm consisting of 10 computer stations wants to install networking. The company is not large enough to justify the cost of a dedicated network administrator, but it keeps very sensitive accounting information about its clients, so security is very important. The computer operators are experienced at accounting software but not at other aspects of networking or computer support.

List the reasons for installing a peer-to-peer network. List the inadequacies of a peer-to-peer network in this scenario.

List the reasons for installing a server-based network. List the inadequacies of a server-based network in this scenario.

20.4.1 Exercise Explanation

Because there are only 10 computers and no network administrator, a peer-to-peer network is very attractive. A peer-to-peer network is cheaper to implement in this firm because no dedicated server is required. The peer-to-peer network is weak in providing adequate security for the client's information. A server-based network is an excellent choice for providing security. However, a dedicated server adds expense to the network.

20.4 Practice Problems

1. Windows 95 implements which type of networking?

   A. User-level security

   B. Peer-to-peer

   C. Server-based

2. Peer-to-peer networks are best for:

   A. Large networks with more than 50 computers

   B. Peer-to-peer networks with less than 10 computers

   C. Networks that have many servers but few users

3. Security in a peer-to-peer network:

   A. Is weak and centrally managed

   B. Is the responsibility of each user sharing resources

   C. Does not exist

   D. Requires a systems administrator to implement

4. Security in a server-based network:

   A. Is strong and centrally managed

   B. Is the responsibility of each user sharing resources

   C. Is easy to manage and does not require a system administrator

   D. None of the above

5. A Windows NT workgroup model in which each computer has a user is a:

   A. Peer-to-peer network

   B. Server-based network

   C. Application server

6. Windows NT domain model is a:

   A. Peer-to-peer network

   B. Server-based network

   C. Application server

7. If cost is the most important issue in deciding network architecture, which statement is correct?

   A. A peer-to-peer network it the best choice.

   B. A server-based network is the best choice.

   C. It depends on the number of computers and how they are to be used.

   D. The NT domain model is the best choice.

8. In a network with 20 users, one file server, and no network administrator, which is the best choice for the network?

   A. Windows NT Server domain model with Windows 95 clients

   B. Windows NT Server workgroup model with Windows 95 clients

   C. Windows 95 peer-to-peer network

   D. Window NT Workstation peer-to-peer network

9. What is the largest file size on a Windows NT Server disk?

   A. 1 gigabyte

   B. 4 gigabytes

   C. 1 exabyte

   D. 100 megabytes

10. What is the maximum number of characters in a Window NT Server file name?

    A. 8

    B. 12

    C. 64

    D. 128

    E. 255

11. How big is an exabyte?

    A. One million gigabytes

    B. $1x10^9$ bytes

    C. $1x10^{32}$ bytes

    D. $1x10^{64}$ bytes

12. NT Server can distribute processing across several processors utilizing SMP. How many processors can be used effectively in a Windows NT 4.0 SMP system?

    A. 2

    B. 4

    C. 8

    D. 32

13. Your company has purchased 100 Pentium-based computers with 8 megabytes of RAM to serve as client computers in a Windows NT Server domain. Which is the best choice of client operating system for these computers?

    A. Window NT Workstation

    B. Windows NT Server for Workgroups

    C. Windows 95

    D. Windows 3.1

14. In which type of network does the computer act as a client and as a server?

    A. A Windows NT domain server network

    B. A peer-to-peer network

    C. A server-based network

15. In user-level access, network resources:

    A. Only have one password associated with them

    B. Have multiple passwords associated with them

    C. Have no passwords but have permissions associated with them

16. Which server-based operating system supports the MIPs platform?

    A. Windows 95

    B. Windows NT Server 4.0

    C. Windows NT Server 3.51

17. Windows NT Server can support how many incoming RAS connections?

    A. 4

    B. 16

    C. 32

    D. 256

    E. 128

18. Minimum RAM requirements for servers are typically?

    A. 8 megabytes

    B. 16 megabytes

    C. 32 megabytes

    D. 128 megabytes

20.4 Answers and Explanations: Practice Problems

1. **B** Windows 95 implements a peer-to-peer networking scheme.

2. **B** Peer-to-peer is intended for networks consisting of 10 or fewer computers. As the number of computers increases, the demands placed on a peer-to-peer network make it difficult to use.

3. **B** Security in a peer-to-peer network is set by each user sharing his resources. There is no central security authority in a peer-to-peer network.

4. **A** Security in a server-based network such as the Windows NT domain is centrally managed. Here, there is one user database for the entire network.

5. **A** In Windows NT workgroup, each computer is responsible for its own resources. There are no dedicated servers, so this is the peer-to-peer model.

6. **B** The Windows NT domain model is a server-based networking architecture that is centrally managed by the Primary Domain Controller (PDC).

7. **A** Peer-to-peer networks are less expensive than server-based networks. There are not dedicated servers, and the operating systems are simpler and less expensive.

8. **B** Windows NT Server would manage the file server, and the clients would use Windows 95. With a dedicated server, this architecture is better than a simple peer-to-peer network.

9. **C** Windows NT uses 64-bit addressing for the file system. This allows a file as large as 1 raised to the power of 64 bytes, or 1 exabyte.

10. **E** Windows NT allows up to 255 characters in a file name.

11. **D** An exabyte is 1 raised to the power of 64 bytes.

12. **B** Windows NT 4.0 is optimized for up to four processors in the same system.

13. **C** Windows NT will not function with only 8 megabytes of memory, and Windows 3.1 is not a good client for network operating systems. Windows 95 was designed to be a networking client and will run with 8 megabytes of RAM.

14. **B** In a peer-to-peer network, each computer that shares resources is a server. It is also a client if it uses resources shared by other computers.

15. **C** User-level access networks have passwords for users and permissions for resources.

16. **C** Windows NT is the only multi-platform operating systems from Microsoft. Support for the MIPs platform was dropped from Windows NT 4.0, so the only operating system on the list is Windows NT 3.51.

17. **D** Windows NT Server can support up to 256 RAS connections.

18. **C** Having adequate RAM in a server is very important and can increase performance significantly. The minimum amount of RAM for servers is 32 megabytes.

20.4 Key Words

Peer-to-peer networking

Server-based networking

Peer

Client

20.5 Compare the Implications of Using Connection-Oriented Versus Connectionless Communications

The Network Layer of the OSI model determines the route a packet travels as it passes through routers from source to destination.

Communications between computers can be set up in two different manners:

- **Connection-Oriented**—These systems assume there will be communication errors between computers. With this in mind, these protocols are designed to make sure data is delivered in sequential order, error-free to its destination. TCP/IP is an example of connection-oriented protocol.
- **Connectionless-Oriented**—These systems assume data will reach its destination with no errors; thus, there is no protocol overhead associated with these systems. Without this overhead, these systems are typically very fast. User Datagram protocol is an example of connectionless-oriented protocol.

Connectionless-mode protocols work well in LAN environments in which the number of transmission errors is kept to a minimum. In a WAN environment in which the data must pass through multiple routers and errors are more frequent, these protocols do not perform as well. Sequential-packet delivery is not guaranteed in connectionless systems, so it is up to the higher-level protocols to assemble packets in the correct order as well as to handle errors.

A. Connection-Oriented Mode

In connection-oriented mode, the path from source PC to destination PC is predetermined. This path can contain several links, which form a logical pathway called a *connection.* The nodes forwarding the data packet have the capability to track which packet is part of which connection. This enables the internal nodes to provide flow control as the data moves along the connection. If a node detects a transmission error, it requests the preceding node to retransmit the bad packet. 20

The nodes keep track of which packets belong to which connection, allowing several concurrent connections through the node.

B. Connectionless-Oriented Mode

Connectionless-oriented mode does not incorporate all the internal control mechanisms found in connection-oriented mode. Error recovery is delegated to the source and destination nodes. These nodes acknowledge receipt of packets and retransmission of bad or lost packets. Connectionless-oriented mode is faster than connection-oriented mode because internal nodes only forward packets without tracking connections and handling errors.

In an error-prone environment with many links, the connectionless-oriented mode can actually be slower because the packet must be retransmitted from the source node instead of from internal nodes.

20.5 Practice Problems

1. What ISO layer determines the route a packet will take through a network?
   - A. Data Link Layer
   - B. Presentation Layer
   - C. Network Layer
   - D. Physical Layer
2. Which connection mode is faster when there are little or no errors?
   - A. Connectionless-oriented mode
   - B. Connection-oriented mode
3. In a LAN, which mode is most appropriate?
   - A. Connectionless-oriented mode
   - B. Connection-oriented mode
4. Which Internet protocol is connection-oriented?
   - A. NetBEUI
   - B. TCP/IP
   - C. UDP/IP
   - D. None of the above
5. Which Internet protocol is connectionless-oriented?
   - A. NetBEUI
   - B. TCP/IP
   - C. UDP/IP
   - D. None of the above
6. Which OSI layer facilitates transmission of data across a single link between nodes?
   - A. Network Layer
   - B. Physical Layer
   - C. Application Layer
   - D. Data Link Layer
7. Which mode puts the responsibility of reliable data delivery on the two end nodes?
   - A. Connection-oriented
   - B. Connectionless-oriented
   - C. None of the above
8. Which mode is used in the global Internet?
   - A. Connection-oriented mode
   - B. Connectionless-oriented mode
   - C. All of the above
9. Which mode guarantees packets will be delivered in sequence?
   - A. Connection-oriented mode
   - B. Connectionless-oriented mode
   - C. None of the above
10. A connection is:
    - A. A physical link between two computers on a LAN
    - B. A remote dial-up link between a client and server
    - C. A logical pathway between source and destination nodes
    - D. A physical link between any two nodes in a link
11. Which mode enables concurrent connections through nodes in a network?
    - A. Connection-oriented mode
    - B. Connectionless-oriented mode
12. Which description is associated with connection-oriented mode protocols?
    - A. Guaranteed delivery of packets
    - B. Fast but unreliable
    - C. Used for microwave communication links
    - D. Used in wireless systems

13. Which description is associated with connectionless-oriented mode protocols?

    A. Fast but unreliable

    B. Used for microwave communication links

    C. Guaranteed delivery of packets

    D. Used in wireless systems

20.5 Answers and Explanations: Practice Problems

1. **C** The Network Layer describes the process of routing a packet through a series of nodes to a destination elsewhere on the network.

2. **A** Connectionless-oriented mode is faster because there is no overhead for error handling.

3. **A** In a LAN there are very few errors so a connectionless-oriented mode is most appropriate.

4. **B** TCP/IP is a connection-oriented protocol. NetBEUI is not a member of the Internet protocol suite, and UDP/IP is connectionless-oriented.

5. **C** UDP/IP is a connectionless-oriented protocol. NetBEUI is not a member of the Internet protocol suite, and TCP/IP is a connection-oriented protocol.

6. **D** The Data Link Layer facilitates the transmission of data across a single link between two nodes.

7. **B** Connectionless-oriented mode does no error checking so the responsibility is up to the two end nodes communicating through the network.

8. **A** The global Internet is very complicated and very error-prone, thus connection-oriented protocols are used.

9. **A** Connection-oriented mode not only handles error recovery but also guarantees packets will be delivered in sequence.

10. **C** A connection is a logical pathway between source and destination nodes.

11. **A** Connection-oriented mode enables concurrent connections through nodes because this mode tracks each connection and examines all packets passing through the node.

12. **A** Connection-oriented mode guarantees all packets arrive error-free in correct sequence.

13. **A** Connectionless-oriented communications are not responsible for error detection or delivering packets in correct sequence. Without this overhead, this mode is faster but not reliable.

20.5 Key Words

Connectionless-oriented mode

Connection-oriented mode

20.6 Distinguish Whether SLIP or PPP Is Used as the Communications Protocol for Various Situations

These two protocols are used primarily for dial-up access. Serial Line Internet Protocol (SLIP) operates at the OSI Physical Layer while Point-to-Point Protocol (PPP) provides Physical Layer and Data Link Layer functionality. There are three protocols that can be used to access the Internet: SLIP, PPP, and CSLIP. CSLIP is a compressed form of SLIP. PPP is becoming the protocol of choice because it is faster and more reliable than SLIP or CSLIP. SLIP is still used on older systems that dial up to SLIP-supported hosts.

A. Serial Line Internet Protocol (SLIP)

When using SLIP to connect to the Internet, the user must know the IP address assigned by the Internet Service Provider (ISP). SLIP does not provide any automated fashion to register IP addresses. If the address is dynamically assigned via Dynamic Host Configuration Protocol (DHCP), the user must assign the address manually or run a logon script. SLIP was originally implemented in 1984.

The simplicity of SLIP leads to the following disadvantages:

Operator intervention is required during connection because SLIP cannot register IP addresses automatically.

SLIP can only support one protocol at a time over a serial link.

SLIP does not perform any error-checking for bad frames.

Windows NT supports the client end of SLIP; however, the server component of Remote Access Service (RAS) does not provide SLIP support.

B. Point-to-Point Protocol (PPP)

The design goal of PPP, as referenced in RFC 1171, has three major components:

A method for encapsulating datagrams over serial links

An extensible Link Control Protocol (LCP)

A family of Network Control Protocols (NCPs) for establishing and configuring different network layer protocols

A goal of PPP was to address the shortcomings of SLIP. The improvements implemented to achieve this goal include:

The capability to dynamically negotiate IP addresses

The addition of checksum error-checking for each frame

The capability to support multiple protocols over a single serial connection

The addition of NCPs to negotiate choices of network layer protocols

The addition of LCP to establish link options

PPP is a bit-oriented protocol that identifies the beginning and end of a packet with bit patterns referred to as flags. This characteristic of PPP was derived from the High Data Link Control (HDLC) protocol.

Including the beginning and end flag, the PPP packet can be as large as 1508 bytes with a maximum of 1500 data bytes.

20.6 Practice Problems

1. Your computer has remote access dial-up utilizing TCP/IP; however, automatic IP addressing is not supported. What dial-up protocol are you using?
   A. TCP/IP
   B. UDP/IP
   C. SLIP
   D. PPP

2. You want to run several protocols across your remote access communication link. Which dial-up protocol should you use?
   A. TCP/IP
   B. PPP
   C. SLIP
   D. UDP/IP

3. Which protocol was partially derived from HDLC?
   A. SLDC
   B. PPP
   C. SMB
   D. SLIP

4. PPP is which type of protocol?
   A. Bit-oriented protocol
   B. Byte-oriented protocol
   C. Character-oriented protocol
   D. Count-oriented protocol

5. Which part of PPP enables it to verify whether the line has a good enough quality connection to reliably support the connection?
   A. SLIP
   B. LCP
   C. NCP
   D. HDLC

6. Which dial-up protocol has a 2-byte CRC associated with each frame?
   A. SLIP
   B. PPP
   C. HDLC
   D. TCP/IP

7. PPPTP is:
   A. A higher-speed version of PPP
   B. A tunneling protocol that that uses PPP to establish a secure link to a remote LAN over the Internet
   C. An Internet protocol that used PPP for secure transactions such as banking and credit card usage
   D. A version of PPP that can employ multiple phone lines for a higher-speed connection

8. Which protocol operates only at the Physical Layer?
   A. PPP
   B. SLIP
   C. TCP/IP
   D. UDP/IP

9. Which dial-up protocol provides Data Link Layer functionality?
   A. PPP
   B. SLIP
   C. TCP/IP
   D. UDP/IP

10. Which protocol is typically found in older dial-up systems?
    A. SLIP
    B. PPP
    C. TCP

11. What is the most popular serial-link protocol?
    A. SLIP
    B. HDLC
    C. PPP

12. Which dial-up protocol does not support NetBEUI?
    A. SLIP
    B. PPP
    C. HDLC

13. Which dial-up protocol supports IPX?
    A. SLIP
    B. PPP
    C. SDLC

14. What is the purpose of DHCP?
    A. To allow easy access to web pages
    B. To assign standard addresses to web pages
    C. To enable users to share IP addresses so that a relatively small number of IP addresses can support many users

15. Which dial-up protocol is not used with DHCP?
    A. SLIP
    B. PPP
    C. HDLC
    D. TCP/IP

16. Multi-Link under Windows NT allows:
    A. SLIP connections utilizing multiple communications links in parallel
    B. PPP connections utilizing multiple communications links in parallel
    C. Multiple Internet protocols running across the same communications link

17. The CSLIP communication protocol is:
    A. A new form of SLIP to support faster modems
    B. A new form of SLIP to support features that are in PPP
    C. SLIP with compression

18. Which dial-up protocol employs the Logical Link Control (LLC) level error control?
    A. PPP
    B. SLIP
    C. CSLIP

19. LLC is a sublayer to which OSI level?
    A. Physical Layer
    B. Data Link Layer
    C. Network Layer

20. Which protocol provides physical device addressing at the Media Access Control (MAC) sublayer?
    A. PPP
    B. SLIP
    C. CSLIP

21. MAC is a sublayer to which OSI level?
    A. Physical Layer
    B. Data Link Layer
    C. Network Layer

22. Most ISDN links use which serial-link protocol?
    A. PPP
    B. CSLIP
    C. SLIP
    D. HDLC

23. AppleTalk is supported over which dial-up protocol?

    A. Ethertalk

    B. PPP

    C. SLIP

    D. CLSIP

24. How many information data bytes can be contained in a PPP packet?

    A. 256

    B. 1024

    C. 2048

    D. 1500

25. The first implementation of SLIP appeared in:

    A. 1984

    B. 1992

    C. 1970

    D. 1990

20.6 Answers and Explanations: Practice Problems

1. **C** SLIP does not support automatic IP addressing. This must be accomplished manually or via a script.

2. **B** One improvement of PPP over SLIP is the capability to transport multiple protocols over a single serial connection.

3. **B** PPP is one of many derivative protocols of High Level Data Link Control.

4. **A** Being a derivative of HDLC makes PPP a bit-oriented protocol with each frame beginning and ending with a flag character of 0x7e which is 6 "1" bits in a row.

5. **B** PPP uses an extensible Line Control Protocol (LCP) that establishes the link after it has determined the quality of the connection is sufficient to support a reliable connection.

6. **B** Because SLIP does not support error detection, and HDLC and TCP/IP are not dial-up protocols, PPP is the only choice left. The Frame Check Sequence field (FCS) or CRC consists of 16 bits prior to the ending flag character.

7. **B** Point-to-point tunneling protocol is a feature of NT enabling secure connections to remote LANs to be established across the Internet.

8. **B** SLIP operates only at the Physical Layer of the OSI model. This is one of the limitations addressed in designing the PPP protocol.

9. **A** PPP operates at the Data Link Layer as well as the Physical Layer of the OSI model.

10. **A** SLIP was developed before PPP; thus, it is found on older dial-up systems.

11. **C** With its added capabilities, PPP has overtaken SLIP as the most used dial-up protocol.

12. **A** SLIP only supports a single IP connection. HDLC is not a dial-up protocol and PPP supports NetBEUI.

13. **B** PPP supports IPX; SLIP does not. SDLC is not a dial-up protocol.

14. **C** Dynamic Host Configuration Protocol (DHCP) dynamically assigns IP addresses, enabling a few IP addresses to support a larger number of users than fixed IP addressing.

15. **A** SLIP does not support automatic IP addressing; PPP does.

16. **B** Multi-Link is a feature of Windows NT that enables pooling of serial communication links to achieve higher bandwidth connections utilizing PPP.

17. **C** Compressed Serial Line Internet Protocol (CSLIP) is a compressed version of the SLIP protocol.

18. **A** SLIP and CSLIP do not support error detection. PPP utilizes LLC for error control.

19. **B** LLC is one of two sublayers to the Data Link Layer of the OSI model.

20. **A** Because SLIP and CSLIP only implement the Physical Layer of the OSI model and MAC is a sublayer to the Data Link Layer, the only choice is PPP.

21. **B** MAC is a sublayer to the Data Link Layer of the OSI model.

22. **A** ISDN lines are popular for connecting LANs to the Internet. When connecting a LAN, multiple protocols must share the same dial-up link. PPP is the only dial-up protocol with this capability.

23. **B** PPP is the only dial-up protocol that supports multiple protocols across the same serial connection. AppleTalk is one of the protocols supported.

24. **D** There can be up to 1500 information bytes in a PPP packet. The total length of a PPP packet is 1508 if all information bytes are used.

25. **A** The first implementation of SLIP appeared in 1984, based on standards set forth by the Internet Engineering Task Force (IETF).

20.6 Key Words

Bit-oriented protocol

Flag

Remote Access Service (RAS)

Serial Line Internet Protocol (SLIP)

Point-to-Point Protocol (PPP)

CSLIP

20.7 Define the Communication Devices That Communicate at Each Level of the OSI Model

A. The OSI Model

The Open Systems Interconnection (OSI) model was developed by the International Standards Organization (ISO) to establish global standards for information exchange across networks. The model consists of seven layers.

- **Layer 1, the Physical Layer**—Consists of protocols that define communication on the network media.
- **Layer 2, the Data Link Layer**—Receives data frames from the Network Layer and packages these frames for the Physical Layer. The Data Link Layer packages raw data bits from the Physical into frames for the Network Layer. The Data Link Layer was improved by the IEEE 802 project to include two sublayers: Media Access Control (MAC) and Logical Link Control (LLC).
- **Layer 3, the Network Layer**—Determines the route packets take to reach their destination. It is the Network Layer that translates logical network addresses into physical addresses. If packets are too large to traverse a link in the route to the destination, it is the job of the Network Layer to break these packets into smaller ones.
- **Layer 4, the Transport Layer**—Ensures that packets are delivered in sequence error-free. The Transport Layer breaks large messages from the Session Layer into manageable packets to be sent out to the network.
- **Layer 5, the Session Layer**—Creates a virtual connection between two applications on separate computers. This virtual connection is called a *session*. The Session Layer maintains synchronization between applications by placing checkpoints in the data stream. It is this layer that performs the name recognition and security that enable the applications to communicate.
- **Layer 6, the Presentation Layer**—Defines the format used by applications to exchange data. In this sense, this layer is also called the *translator*. This layer is responsible for protocol conversion, data encryption, and data compression. This is where the redirector service operates.
- **Layer 7, the Application Layer**—The topmost layer of the OSI model. This layer exposes all the network services to the applications. When an application accesses the network, it is through this layer all actions are carried out.

B. Devices at each OSI Layer

1. The Physical Layer

The lowest layer of the OSI is the Physical Layer. Devices at this layer include hubs, transmitters, receivers, cables, connectors, and repeaters.

Repeaters simply regenerate weak incoming signals. Because no packet information is necessary to perform this task, repeaters reside at the Physical Layer. A repeater simply retransmits any frame it receives including frames with errors.

2. The Data Link Layer

The Data Link Layer adds information to each packet coming from the Network Layer. Thus, the Data Link Layer has knowledge of the packet structure and fields. Devices such as intelligent hubs, bridges, and Network Interface Cards (NICs) with associated drivers reside at this layer.

A *bridge* is a step up from repeater; the bridge can intelligently forward incoming packets. A bridge does not simply retransmit each frame out all ports. Instead, it only transmits the frame out the port leading to the next destination segment of the frame. To perform these functions, the bridge must build internal routing tables to determine the correct segment to send a packet.

3. The Network Layer

The Network Layer has the responsibility of determining the route a packet must take to reach its destination. Devices that accomplish this are routers, brouters, and gateways. Included in this layer are circuit, packet, and message switching.

Gateways perform protocol conversion by totally rebuilding the protocol stack between networks. Gateways can reside at the Network Layer OSI model. However, gateways typically reside at the Application Layer.

Routers and *brouters* are a step up from bridges. The router builds routing tables like the bridge, but the information available to the router enables it to pass packets through a chain of other routers and, in many cases, determine the best route. This is a vast improvement over determining the next segment a packet will take.

Brouters are a combination bridge and router that act as a bridge for nonroutable protocols.

4. The Higher Layers

The higher layers (Transport, Session, Presentation, and Application) typically reside in the computers that are communicating with each other across the network. The one exception is the gateway, which can span all layers.

20.7.1 Exercise

You are a systems administrator for a small company that has grown significantly over the years. You have seven 10Base-T hubs, each with 24 ports. You have just added a new 24-port hub and filled all the ports to support new sales and marketing staff. The network seems very sluggish, and you are receiving many complaints about network speeds. Your boss wants to know what is wrong and how you intend to fix the problem. He read an article about 100-megabit Ethernet and thinks this will solve the problem. What is the most likely cause of the problem and the real solution?

20.7.1 Exercise Explanation

Speed is not the problem with your network, and upgrading to 100 megabits may not help the problem. In fact, if the cabling is not at least category 5, upgrading can cause more problems than it solves. Your most likely problem is network traffic. You have over 190 computers on your 10Base-T network, all causing collisions. The simplest solution is to purchase a bridge and put each major department on a segment of the bridge. This will cut down on network traffic and solve your problem.

20.7 Practice Problems

1. The OSI Presentation Layer is named so because:
   - A. It presents data to the user.
   - B. It presents data to the application.
   - C. It presents a uniform data format to the application layer.
   - D. It does all of the above.

2. Which OSI layer includes cable and connectors?
   - A. The Data Link Layer
   - B. The Physical Link Layer
   - C. The Connection Layer
   - D. The Physical Layer

3. Which layer defines network topology?
   - A. The Network Layer
   - B. The Physical Layer
   - C. The Data Link Layer
   - D. The Physical Link Layer

4. Which layer is concerned with bits instead of frames?
   - A. The Network Layer
   - B. The Session Layer
   - C. The Physical Layer
   - D. The Data Link Layer
   - E. None of the above

5. Which layer builds frames from received raw bits?
   - A. The Data Link Layer
   - B. The Physical Layer
   - C. The Session Layer
   - D. The Network Layer

6. IEEE 802 project provided enhancements to which OSI layer?
   - A. The Data Link Layer
   - B. The Application Layer
   - C. The Session Layer
   - D. The Physical Layer
   - E. None of the above

7. The Media Access Control is a sublayer of which OSI layer?
   - A. The Presentation Layer
   - B. The Physical Layer
   - C. The Session Layer
   - D. The Data Link Layer
   - E. The Application Layer

8. Which OSI layer determines the route a packet will take to reach its destination?
   - A. The Route Layer
   - B. The Presentation Layer
   - C. The Data Link Layer
   - D. The Network Layer
   - E. The Physical Layer

9. Network interface cards and their associated drivers reside at which OSI layer?
   - A. The Physical Layer
   - B. The Data Link Layer
   - C. The Network Layer
   - D. None of the above

10. Which device can bridge non-routable protocols?
    - A. Gateway
    - B. Router
    - C. Brouter
    - D. Repeater

11. Which device tears down a frame and rebuilds it to accommodate a different protocol stack?

    A. Gateway

    B. Router

    C. Brouter

    D. Bridge

12. Which device resides at the OSI Network Layer?

    A. Bridge

    B. Router

    C. Gateway

    D. Repeater

13. Which device resides at the OSI Data Link Layer?

    A. Cable

    B. Bridge

    C. Repeater

    D. Router

14. Which device does not reside at the OSI Physical layer?

    A. Repeater

    B. Cable

    C. Connectors

    D. Bridge

15. Which device simply regenerates incoming signals?

    A. Repeater

    B. NIC

    C. Bridge

    D. Gateway

16. Which device does not build routing tables?

    A. Bridge

    B. Router

    C. Brouter

    D. Repeater

17. When a bridge cannot determine to which port to send a frame:

    A. It sends an error message back to the originator.

    B. It sends a request to the next bridge to find the correct port.

    C. It sends the frame out all ports.

18. Which OSI layer translates logical network addresses into physical addresses?

    A. The Network Layer

    B. The Data Link Layer

    C. The Session Layer

    D. The Presentation Layer

    E. The Application Layer

19. In which layer would you find a redirector?

    A. The Application Layer

    B. The Presentation Layer

    C. The Data Link Layer

    D. The Physical Layer

    E. The Network Layer

20. Which type of switching provides a dedicated path with well-defined bandwidth?

    A. Virtual switching

    B. Message switching

    C. Circuit switching

    D. Packet switching

    E. Physical switching

21. Which switching model treats each message as a separate entity?

    A. Virtual switching

    B. Message switching

C. Circuit switching

D. Packet switching

E. Physical switching

22. Which switching model breaks up the message into smaller components and routes the components to the destination address independently?

A. Packet switching

B. Virtual switching

C. Circuit switching

D. Message switching

E. Physical switching

23. Which layer enables two computers to establish, use, and tear down a communication channel?

A. The Session Layer

B. The Application Layer

C. The Data Link Layer

D. The Physical Connection Layer

24. What layer performs compression and encryption?

A. The Presentation Layer

B. The Data Link Layer

C. The Application Layer

25. Which layer inserts checkpoints in the data stream between applications?

A. The Data Link Layer

B. The Physical Layer

C. The Presentation Layer

D. The Network Layer

E. The Session Layer

26. Which layer presents API calls to user programs?

A. The Presentation Layer

B. The Application Layer

C. The Transport Layer

D. The Data Link Layer

27. Which layer is the only layer that can send information directly to its counterpart on another computer?

A. The Network Layer

B. The Application Layer

C. The Data Link Layer

D. The Physical Layer

E. None of the above

28. Which layer adds the Cyclic Redundancy Check (CRC) field to the data frame?

A. The Physical Layer

B. The Data Link Layer

C. The Network Layer

D. The Physical Link Layer

29. Of the two sublayers comprising the Data Link Layer, which is lowest providing access to the NICs hardware?

A. The Media Access Control (MAC) sublayer

B. The Logical Link Control (LLC) sublayer

C. The LAN Interface Control (LIC) sublayer

D. None of the above

30. What type of device is commonly used to interface personal computer networks to mainframes?

A. Bridge

B. Brouter

C. Gateway

D. SMA converter card

31. Which is not a common characteristic of a gateway?

A. They are task-specific.

B. They are expensive.

C. They are fast.

32. What is the device that typically resides at the Application Layer of the OSI model?

A. Application programs

B. Software-based router

C. Brouter

D. Gateway

33. Which communication device can actually use all seven layers of the OSI model?

A. AppleTalk router

B. Gateway

C. Brouter

D. Software-based router

34. Which communication device can be used to prevent broadcast storms?

A. Gateway

B. Bridge

C. Repeater

D. Router

35. Which of the following protocols will not work with routers?

A. IPX

B. IP

C. AppleTalk

D. DECnet

E. NetBEUI

36. Which of the following is not a routing algorithm?

A. Open Shortest Path First (OSPF)

B. Routing Information Protocol (RIP)

C. NetWare Link Services Protocol (NLSP)

D. Microsoft Services Protocol (MSP)

37. There are two basic types of routers. They are:

A. Fast and slow

B. Static and dynamic

C. Frame-based and packet-based

D. Message-based and packet-based

38. Implementation of the OSI model is called:

A. A protocol stack

B. A gateway

C. A communication network

D. A networking protocol

39. Datagrams are associated with which OSI layer?

A. The Network Layer

B. The Presentation Layer

C. The Application Layer

D. The Data Link Layer

E. The Transport Layer

20.7 Answers and Explanations: Practice Problems

1. **C** Many people confuse the Presentation Layer because it seems to present data to the user when in fact it presents a uniform data format to the Application Layer.

2. **B** The Physical Layer of the OSI model includes cables and connectors.

3. **B** The Physical Layer also defines network topology.

4. **C** The Physical Layer only recognizes bits. It transmits and receives bits. Higher layers recognize frames constructed by the Data Link Layer.

5. **A** This is the job of the Data Link Layer. It packages received bits into frames to be passed to the Network Layer.
6. **A** Two sublayers, the Media Access Control (MAC) and Logical Link Control (LLC), were added to the Data Link Layer.
7. **D** As discussed in question 6, the MAC is a sublayer of the Data Link Layer.
8. **D** The Network Layer determines network-wide routing. The Data Link Layer can route packets to the next segment but not across several segments.
9. **B** Network interface cards and drivers operate at the Data Link Layer. They accept frames from higher layers and put the bits on the wire.
10. **C** A brouter can bridge non-routable protocols.
11. **A** The job of the gateway is protocol conversion. This is accomplished by tearing down the received packet and reforming it to match the destination protocol.
12. **B** The router resides at the Network Layer. The router requires network configuration information to build internal network routing tables.
13. **B** The bridge resides at the Data Link Layer and requires address information to pass the frame to the correct next segment.
14. **D** The bridge resides at the Data Link Layer.
15. **A** The repeater simply regenerates incoming signals to all ports without regard for the information in the frame. For this reason, the repeater resides at the Physical Layer.
16. **D** The repeater has no knowledge of segments or routes; thus, it does not build routing tables.
17. **C** If a bridge cannot determine the correct port to send a packet, it will send it out to all ports except the port it came in on.
18. **A** The Network Layer translates logical network addresses into physical addresses.
19. **B** The redirector is found at the Presentation Layer. This is an important component of many operating systems that make remote devices appear to be local.
20. **C** In circuit switching, a dedicated physical path is established and maintained for the length of the communication session.
21. **B** In message switching, also referred to as store and forward switching, each device receives a frame and waits until the next device in the chain is ready to receive it. Each frame is treated as a separate entity.
22. **A** In packet switching, frames are broken down into individual smaller packets, each with source and destination address information. The packets can take separate routes to the destination. This has the advantage of changing routes when bandwidth loads become high on certain links.
23. **A** After a communication channel is established between two computers, this is called a session. It is the job of the Session Layer to establish, use, and tear down sessions.
24. **A** The Presentation Layer performs protocol conversion, data encryption, data translation, data compression, character-set conversion, and graphic-command expansion.
25. **E** The Session Layer can insert checkpoints in the data stream between two computers to maintain synchronization.
26. **B** The Application Layer interfaces to programs by exposing a set of network APIs.

27. **D** The Physical Layer is the only layer that can directly send information to its counterpart on another system. All other layers must pass data down the protocol stack to reach the other computer.

28. **B** The Data Link Layer builds a frame consisting of a header, data, and a trailer. The trailer contains a CRC to guarantee error-free transmissions.

29. **A** The MAC Layer communicates directly with the NIC.

30. **C** Gateways are employed to perform the protocol conversion required for personal computers to communicate with mainframes. One popular gateway is the SNA gateway.

31. **C** Gateways are task-specific, expensive, and usually slow. It requires a lot of CPU horsepower and RAM to provide protocol conversion.

32. **D** Gateways usually reside at the Application Layer but can span all layers of the OSI model.

33. **B** As previously stated, the gateway can span all layers of the OSI model and usually a dedicated server on the network.

34. **B** A bridge can be employed to prevent broadcast storms. This is because a bridge examines all frames and will not forward bad frames.

35. **E** NetBEUI is a non-routable protocol and will not be passed through a router.

36. **D** NetWare RIP and NLSP are routing algorithms used in NetWare networks. Internet RIP and NetWare RIP reside in the Network Layer of the OSI model. OPSF is similar to RIP but is more efficient and supports class of service. OPSF is replacing RIP in an effort to cut down the number of bottlenecks caused by RIP. MSP is not a routing protocol.

37. **B** Static and dynamic are the two types of routers in use today. In static routers, the routing tables must be manually input; in dynamic routers, the routing tables are built automatically.

38. **A** A protocol stack consists of layers of protocols, each communicating with the layer above and below it (thus the term stack).

39. **E** The datagram is associated with the Transport Layer. Datagrams are a component of Datagram Delivery Protocol (DDP) or AppleTalk.

20.7 Key Words

Application Layer
Bridge
Brouter
Data Link Layer
Gateway
Network Layer
Physical Layer
Presentation Layer
Session Layer
Transport Layer
Repeater

20.8 Define the Characteristics and Purpose of Media Used in IEEE 802.3 and IEEE 802.5 Standards

A. The 802 Project

As networks became popular, the IEEE began the 802 project in February 1980 to define certain LAN standards. The name of the project (802) comes from the year and month the project was started. Project 802 focused on the physical aspects of networking relating to cabling and data transmission on the cable. These specifications fall into the bottom two layers (Physical and Data Link) of the OSI mode. There are 12 categories contained in the 802 standards:

802.1	Internetworking
802.2	Logical Link Control (LLC)
802.3	Carrier-Sense Multiple Access with Collision Detection (CSMA/CD) or Ethernet
802.4	Token Bus LAN
802.5	Token Ring LAN
802.6	Metropolitan Area Network (MAN)
802.7	Broadband Technical Advisory Group
802.8	Fiber-Optic Technical Advisory Group
802.9	Integrated Voice/Data Networks
802.10	Network security
802.11	Wireless networks
802.6	Demand Priority Access LAN, 100BaseVG-AnyLAN

B. 802.3 Carrier-Sense Multiple Access with Collision Detection (CSMA/CD) or Ethernet

Xerox Corporation developed Ethernet in late 1970. In 1980, DIX (or DEC), Intel, and Xerox began to jointly publicize this network. The implementation was a baseband network that employed CSMA/CD as the media access control mechanism. In a *baseband system*, a single signal carried on a cable can use all available bandwidth of the cable.

In 1985, version II of the network was released and Project 802 chose this version of Ethernet as the basis for the 802.3 standard. The two versions of Ethernet are for the most part interchangeable, with the main difference being the network packet header.

When computers employ the CSMA/CD or Ethernet signaling method, the following sequence of events occurs:

1. The computer listens to the wire and waits until there is no traffic.
2. The computer transmits its data onto the wire. At this time, no other computer on the network can transmit until the data reaches its destination and the cable is traffic free.
3. If the computer sending the data detects a collision (caused by two computers sending data at the same time), the computer stops transmitting, waits a random amount of time, and retries by returning to step 1.

This method of media access puts several limitations on Ethernet. The main limitations include the total distance of any two nodes on the network, the number of repeaters between any two nodes, and segment lengths between any two nodes.

Different cables have different characteristics. The two important characteristics to Ethernet are *impedance* and *propagation delay.*

Propagation delay is the amount of time it takes a signal to travel through a medium. Propagation delay of RG58 cable is typically .66 times the speed of light, which is about 299,792,458 meters per second. If the time to propagate the signal end-to-end of the network is greater than the amount of time required to transmit a frame, collisions may not be detected. This is called a *late collision.*

The time it takes a repeater to regenerate the signal must also be considered. The propagation and attenuation characteristics of different Ethernet cabling schemes cause the rules to change based on the type of cabling used.

Ethernet cabling comes in the following forms:

10Base2	Segments up to 185 meters (sometimes rounded up to 200) and referred to as thinnet. Uses RG58U cable of 50-ohms, which is about ¼-inch thick.
10Base5	Segments up to 500 meters and referred to as thicknet. Uses RG6, which is about ½-inch thick.
10Base-F	Segments up to 2,000 meters, incorporating fiber optic cable.
10Base-T	Segments up to 100–150 meters are generally accepted; however, the maximum signal loss must not exceed 11.5db. This cabling scheme incorporates Unshielded Twisted Pair (UTP).
10Broad36	Segments up to 3,600 meters in a dual-cable configuration. This is a broadband configuration.

There are also rules governing the number of repeaters and cable segments between any two nodes on the network. This is commonly referred to as the *5-4-3 rule.* There can be no more than five repeated segments, no more than four repeaters, and only three of the five cable segments can be populated.

This can be a problem on 10Base-T networks in which several hubs may be cascaded because hubs count as repeaters.

C. 802.5 Token Ring

The 802.5 token ring network is physically cabled as a star network, but it is logically a ring. Wiring each connection back to a central hub (Multistation Access Unit, or MAU) creates the physical star; however, the logical ring must be maintained when equipment is added or removed from the network. The hub, or MAU, contains a "collapsed ring." If a workstation falls off the network, the MAU immediately bypasses that particular workstation, maintaining the logical ring.

This topology is intended for commercial and light industrial usage. IBM made this commercially possible with the introduction of a 4 Mbit/sec token ring network in the mid-1980s.

Tokens are small frames passed logically around the network from one workstation to another. When a workstation wants to transmit, it must wait for the token. The workstation can acquire the token by changing 1 bit in the token, which changes the token into the start-of-frame field for a data frame. The workstation can then transmit the rest of the frame. No other workstation transmits at this time because only one workstation owns the token. The frame makes the round trip of the network and, when it returns to the transmitting workstation, it is changed back into a token. The token is then passed to the next workstation downstream.

As the number of workstations on the network increases, the efficiency of the token ring topology increases. This is because there are no collisions to contend with. The round-robin architecture gives all workstation equal opportunity to access the media. A priority scheme is implemented, however, that enables a workstation to request future use of the token.

Each workstation has a unique Medium Access Control (MAC) address, and one workstation on the network takes the job of the *active monitor* by transmitting a *claim token.* It is the job of the active monitor to look for errors, bad frames, and workstations that are malfunctioning. If the active monitor fails, the other workstations on the network arbitrate to determine which workstation becomes the next active monitor.

The 802.5 specification does not describe cabling techniques for token ring.

20.8.1 Exercise

A company with 50 workstations has hired you as a consultant to network the computers that have been stand-alone until now. You notice that each office has RG59 coaxial cable and 6-pair UTP cable terminating in a central room. The company wants an easy-to-manage network at the lowest cost. What type of network would you recommend?

20.8.1 Exercise Explanation

At first you might be tempted to use the coaxial cable; however, RG59 is 75 ohms and Ethernet uses RG58, which is 50 ohms. The best choice is 10Base-T because the UTP cable is in place, and the components to implement a 10Base-T solution are inexpensive. A token ring solution would be much more expensive.

20.8 Practice Problems

1. Which company invented Ethernet?

   A. Digital Equipment Corporation (DEC)

   B. Intel

   C. Datapoint

   D. Xerox

2. Which company invented 4 Mbit/sec token ring?

   A. Datapoint

   B. Xerox

   C. IBM

   D. Intel

3. Which 802 protocol describes Ethernet?

   A. 802.1

   B. 802.3

   C. 802.5

   D. 802.2

4. Which 802 protocol describes token ring Media Access Control?

   A. 802.1

   B. 802.3

   C. 802.5

   D. 802.2

   E. None of the above

5. What is the maximum number of segments between any two nodes on an 802.3 network?

   A. 2

   B. 5

   C. 3

   D. 4

6. What is the maximum number of repeaters between any two nodes on an 802.3 network?

   A. 2

   B. 5

   C. 3

   D. 4

   E. None of the above

7. What is a MAC address on an Ethernet network?

   A. A logical address that identifies the workstation

   B. An address assigned by the system administrator

   C. A workstation's logical domain address

   D. A physical address assigned by the system administrator

   E. A physical address assigned by the NIC manufacturer

8. In IBM token ring, how are tokens claimed?

   A. They are not passed on until the transmitting workstation has put its frame on the wire.

   B. They are converted to a start-of-frame for a packet.

   C. They are converted to a claim token.

   D. They are converted to an acknowledge token.

9. CSMA/CD networks have total length restrictions between the furthest nodes on a network because:

   A. Attenuation degrades the signal

   B. Impedance changes as the cable length increases

C. Propagation delays

D. None of the above

10. What is the difference between baseband networks and broadband networks?

    A. Broadband networks are WAN; baseband are LAN.

    B. Broadband networks carry several channels on a single cable; baseband only caries one.

    C. Broadband networks operate at higher bit rates than baseband networks.

    D. All of the above.

11. What is the difference between an Ethernet frame and an 802.3 frame?

    A. The length of the Ethernet frame is much larger than the 802.3 frame.

    B. The length of the 802.3 frame is much larger than the Ethernet frame.

    C. 802.3 uses LLC to distinguish multiple clients and has a length field; Ethernet uses a 2-byte field to distinguish multiple client protocols.

12. What is the size of an 802.3 MAC address?

    A. 16 bits

    B. 8 bits

    C. 64 bits

    D. 48 bits

13. How many bits of the MAC address determine the manufacturer?

    A. 8

    B. 12

    C. 16

    D. 24

14. What is the CRC used for?

    A. To denote the end of frame

    B. To denote the beginning of frame

    C. Address resolution on Ethernet

    D. To detect errors that occurred during transmission

15. Token Ring is a physical:

    A. Bus network

    B. Ring network

    C. Star network

16. As the number of active nodes increases, what network topology is favorable?

    A. Ethernet

    B. Token Ring

    C. 10Base2

    D. 10Base5

17. What is the maximum end-to-end distance between nodes in a 10BASE2 network?

    A. 200 meters

    B. 2,000 meters

    C. 185 meters

    D. 200 feet

18. What is the maximum end-to-end distance between nodes in a 10Base5 network?

    A. 250 meters

    B. 5,000 meters

    C. 500 meters

    D. 500 feet

19. What is the maximum bit rate in 10Base-F network?

    A. 10 Mbits/sec

    B. 100 Mbits/sec

C. 2.4 Mbits/sec

D. 4 Mbits/sec

20. What is the hub called in a token ring network?

 A. Multi-station access unit

 B. Hub

 C. Central hub

 D. Bridge

 E. Router

21. To increase the distance of a 10Base2 network to more than 2.5 kilometers, which device should be used?

 A. Repeater

 B. Bridge

 C. Passive HUB

 D. Active HUB

22. Which topology employs RG58 coaxial cable?

 A. Token Ring

 B. 10Base2 Ethernet

 C. 10Base5 Ethernet

 D. 10Base-T Ethernet

 E. None of the above

23. Which cable is used in thicknet?

 A. RG58U coaxial cable

 B. RG6 coaxial cable

 C. RG59 coaxial cable

 D. UTP cable

24. How many tokens can exist on a token ring topology at the same time?

 A. 1

 B. 2

 C. Number of workstations/2

25. How many active monitors are on a token ring network?

 A. 1

 B. 2

 C. Up to 8

26. The speed electronic signals travel through cable is:

 A. Faster than the speed of light

 B. Same as the speed of light

 C. Slower than the speed of light

27. Propagation delay is:

 A. Signal attenuation due to long cable lengths

 B. The amount of time it takes a signal to travel through a medium

 C. Reflections caused by poorly terminated systems

20.8 Answers and Explanations: Practice Problems

1. **D** Xerox invented Ethernet in 1970.

2. **C** IBM invented 4 Mbit/sec token ring in the mid-1980s.

3. **B** IEEE 802.3 describes the Ethernet protocol.

4. **C** IEEE 802.5 describes token ring media access.

5. **B** Remember the 5-4-3 rule, in which 5 is the maximum number of repeated segments, 4 is the maximum number of repeaters, and 3 is the maximum number of segments of the 5 that can be populated.

6. **D** Four, as in the 5-4-3 rule.

7. **E** The MAC address is a permanent address assigned by the manufacturer to each NIC separately.

8. **B** A single bit is changed in the token, and it becomes the start-of-frame sequence.

9. **C** Propagation delays are the finite amount of time it takes an electronic signal to travel through cabling. This delay must be less than the amount of time it takes to put a frame on the wire or collisions could be missed.

10. **B** Broadband systems assign carrier frequencies to different channels allowing multiple channels to use the same medium. In baseband systems, a single signal has full use of the medium.

11. **C** There are very minor differences between the Ethernet frame and the 802.3 frame. The differences are the method used to distinguish protocols.

12. **D** A MAC address consists of six bytes, which make 48 bits.

13. **D** Of the six bytes, three are used to define the manufacturer.

14. **D** The Cyclic Redundancy Check, or CRC, is used to verify the integrity of each frame.

15. **C** Token Ring is a physical star because each workstation is connected to a central hub.

16. **B** As the number of active nodes increases, the number of collisions increases in an Ethernet topology. Token ring does not suffer from this problem; thus, it is favored as the number of active nodes increases.

17. **C** 10Base2 specifies the maximum distance between endpoints as 185 meters.

18. **C** 10Base5 specifies the maximum distance between endpoints as 500 meters.

19. **A** Even though fiber can handle much higher bit rates, this version of Ethernet is 10 Mbits/sec.

20. **A** In token ring, the hub is called the Multi-station Access Unit, or MAU.

21. **B** A bridge must be used to segment the network. This is because 2.5 kilometers is the maximum end-to-end distance for the network. A repeater will not help.

22. **B** 10Base2 uses 50-ohm RG58 cable.

23. **B** RG6 coaxial cable is used in thicknet. The cable is so named because it is ½-inch thick.

24. **A** Only one token can exist on a token ring network.

25. **A** Only one active monitor can exist on a token ring network. The active monitor is usually the workstation with the lowest MAC address.

26. **C** Electronic signals are always slower than the speed of light. Cables have propagation delay specifications. RG58 is .66, which means signals travel .66 times the speed of light.

27. **B** Propagation delay is the amount of time it takes a signal to travel through a medium.

20.8 Key Words

5-4-3 rule

10Base2

10Base5

10Base-F

10Base-T

10Broad36

Active monitor

Hub

Impedance

Late collision

Medium Access Control address

Propogation delay

20.9 Explain the Purpose of NDIS and Novell ODI Network Standards

A. Reason for Low-Level Standards

In the late 1980s, as the number of companies manufacturing Network Interface Cards increased, so did the complexity of developing protocol stacks to support these cards. The capability to bind several protocol stacks to one NIC also became important.

Before the late 1980s, layers 3 and 4 of the OSI model were tightly coupled with proprietary implementations of the Media Access Control (MAC) interface sublayer. This made it very difficult for multiple vendors to support all the operating systems on the market.

NDIS and ODI accomplished these goals by allowing the higher levels of the protocol stack to be independent of the NIC. This was accomplished by providing a standard interface.

B. NDIS

Microsoft and 3Com jointly developed Network Device Interface Specification (NDIS) in 1989. This standard defined an interface between the MAC sublayer and higher layers of the OSI model. The two goals of NDIS are:

- To provide a vendor-neutral boundary between the transport protocols and the NIC driver. This enables the protocol stack to function with any NDIS-compliant adapter driver.
- To define a binding methodology, enabling multiple protocols to share the same NIC. In addition, NDIS allows binding one protocol to multiple NICs.

Non-Windows NT implementations of NDIS include a "protocol manager" (PROTMAN), which binds the different protocols with the MAC layer. It is the job of the protocol manager to route incoming packets from the MAC layer to the correct protocol stack. Under Windows NT, the PROTMAN is not required. Binding is accomplished through information in the Registry and a small wrapper around the NDIS code.

C. ODI

Open Data-Link Interface (ODI) was jointly developed by Novell and Apple Computer Corporation and was released in 1989. The goals of ODI are similar to the goals of NDIS in providing a seamless integration between the Data Link Layer and the Transport Layers of the protocol stack. Before ODI there was dedicated IPX, which only allowed one protocol IPX to utilize a NIC. This became a major limitation as the number of different protocol stacks increased.

ODI consists of three main components:

Protocol Stacks

Multiple Link Interface Drivers (MLIDs)

Link Support Layer (LSL)

1. Protocol Stacks

The *protocol stack* component consists of the Transport and Network Layer of the OSI model. It is the protocol stack that acts as the interface to the Application Layers.

The protocol stacks package data from the Presentation and Application Layers, then provides network functionality by routing the packets to their destination. Multiple ODI protocol stacks can coexist on a single system. To distinguish media frames, two IDs are used—the stack ID and the protocol ID.

2. Multiple Link Interface Drivers (MLID)

The MLID has two basic functions: to build and strip media headers off of packets, and to send and receive packets at the Physical Layer. To accomplish these tasks the MLID consists of three modules:

- **Media Support Module (MSM)**—Performs initialization functions independent of the media. This module also builds the configuration table (information about the hardware and driver) based on information obtained from the Hardware Specific Module (HSM). It is the MSM that handles I/O requests such as reset, enabling and disabling promiscuous mode, and shutdown.
- **Topology Specific Module (TSM)**—Provides support for specific media types. This module builds the MAC headers, collects statistics depending on the type of media, and manages the Event Control Block. The Event Control Block is a mechanism for passing data between OSI modules.
- **Hardware Specific Module (HSM)**—Directly controls the hardware. This module resets the hardware and is responsible for moving packets on and off the NIC. This is the module developed by vendors.

The only part of the MLID that vendors must develop is the HSM, which requires less effort than developing the entire protocol stack.

3. Link Support Layer (LSL)

The LSL is the packet router in the ODI protocol. It is instrumental in keeping the other layers independent of each other. It routes incoming and outgoing packets.

20.9.1 Exercise

You work for a small company that has slowly migrated from Novell to Windows NT. There is a Novell server on the network, but it is not used by anyone because the newer Windows NT servers are faster and larger. One user wants to copy an old file off of the Novell server but cannot see the server from his machine. What is the most likely cause of the problem?

20.9.1 Exercise Explanation

You probably have one of two situations. Either there is no IPX driver installed on the Windows NT machine, or the IPX protocol stack is not bound to the NIC.

20.9 Practice Problems

1. Which companies developed NDIS?
    - A. Microsoft and Digital Equipment Corporation (DEC)
    - B. Microsoft Intel
    - C. Microsoft and 3Com
    - D. Novell and Apple
2. Which companies developed ODI?
    - A. Apple and Novell
    - B. Microsoft and Novell
    - C. Novell and 3Com
    - D. Apple and Microsoft
3. ODI is a replacement for which protocol?
    - A. Dedicated IPX
    - B. 802.3
    - C. 802.5
    - D. NDIS 2.0
4. What is the name of the module that manages bindings in NDIS systems?
    - A. The binder
    - B. The binding manager
    - C. The protocol manager
    - D. The NDIS binding layer (NBL)
    - E. None of the above
5. Which Microsoft operating system does not incorporate the binding module?
    - A. Windows for Workgroups
    - B. Windows 95
    - C. Windows NT 3.51
    - D. All of the above
6. The NDIS specification includes which layer(s) of the OSI model?
    - A. 1
    - B. 1 and 2
    - C. 2
    - D. 2 and 3
    - E. All of the above
7. How many protocols can dedicated IPX support on a NIC?
    - A. 1
    - B. 2
    - C. 4
    - D. One per installed NIC
8. MLIDs are a component of which protocol?
    - A. NDIS
    - B. ODI
    - C. Neither
9. The PROTMAN is used by which protocol?
    - A. NDIS
    - B. ODI
    - C. Neither
10. Which protocol routes packets in a round-robin fashion to determine the correct protocol stack?
    - A. NDIS
    - B. ODI
    - C. Neither
11. Which protocol supports 802.3 frames?
    - A. NDIS
    - B. ODI
    - C. Both
12. Which is not a difference between NDIS 2.0 and NDIS 3.0?
    - A. NDIS 3.0 implements a C-call interface.
    - B. NDIS 3.0 is multi-processor safe.

C. NDIS 3.0 drivers are 32-bit drivers.

D. NDIS 3.0 supports quality of service.

13. Under Windows NT, where is protocol binding information maintained?

A. By the protocol manager

B. In the file ndis.ini

C. In the file sys.ini

D. In the Registry

14. Which is not a goal for NDIS and ODI?

A. To support multiple protocols on same NIC

B. To define common interface to make driver development easier

C. To define a common set of lower-level protocols that both Microsoft and Novell would jointly support

20.9 Answers and Explanations: Practice Problems

1. **C** Microsoft and 3Com in 1989.
2. **A** Apple and Novell developed ODI and released it in 1989.
3. **A** Novell replaced dedicated IPX with ODI in release 4.0 of NetWare.
4. **C** NDIS systems use the protocol manager to bind protocol stacks.
5. **C** Windows NT 3.51 maintains binding information in the Registry and does not use the protocol manager.
6. **C** NDIS includes the Data Link Layer of the OSI module, specifically the MAC sublayer.
7. **A** A limitation of dedicated IPX is the capability to support only 1 protocol.
8. **B** MLIDs are the interface drivers that build and strip media headers in the ODI protocol.
9. **A** PROTMAN is the protocol manager under NDIS in Windows systems.
10. **A** NDIS routes packets in a round-robin fashion. This is why it is important to have the most-used protocol first in the binding order.
11. **C** Both protocols support Ethernet.
12. **D** NDIS 3.0 does not support quality of service.
13. **D** Windows NT maintains the protocol binding information in the Registry.
14. **C** Microsoft and Novell developed separate low-level protocols working with other companies, not each other.

20.9 Key Words

Hardware Specific Module (HSM)

Link Support Layer (LSL)

Media Support Module (MSM)

Multiple Link Interface Drivers (MLID)

Network Device Interface Specification (NDIS)

Open Data-Link Interface (ODI)

Protocol manager (PROTMAN)

Practice Exam: Standards and Terminology

1. CSMA of CSMA/CD is:
   A. Collision Sense Media Access
   B. Copper System Media Access
   C. Collision Sense Multiple Access
   D. Complete Signal Media Access
2. Which media access network tries to detect collisions instead of avoiding collisions.
   A. AppleTalk
   B. ArcNet
   C. CSMA/CD
   D. CSMA/CA
3. 10Base5 is also called:
   A. Thinnet
   B. Ethernet
   C. AppleTalk
   D. Thicknet
4. When using 10Base2, you
   A. Must terminate each end with 50-ohm terminators
   B. Must terminate each end with 75-ohm terminators
   C. Don't need to terminate UTP
   D. Must terminate each connection with 75-ohm terminators
5. The OSI reference model has how many layers?
   A. 2
   B. 8
   C. 7
   D. 4
6. Which type of cable will operate at 100 Mbs?
   A. 10Base2
   B. Category 2 cable
   C. Category 5 cable
   D. Category 3 cable
7. Why do bridges provide better network performance than repeaters?
   A. They analyze packets and only forward them on required ports.
   B. They use faster hardware than repeaters.
   C. They simply regenerate the signal.
   D. They are active versus passive devices.
8. Which network access method does Ethernet use?
   A. CSMA/CD
   B. CSMA/CA
   C. Token passing
   D. AppleTalk
9. NetWare networks use which protocols?
   A. NetBEUI
   B. IPX/SPX
   C. TCP/IP
   D. NDIS
10. How many levels of RAID are there?
    A. 1
    B. 5
    C. 6
    D. 4

11. Which is not an example of client/server computing?
    A. A workstation application accessing a SQL database on a server
    B. A workstation application accessing the corporate mail server to find an address
    C. A terminal accessing a mainframe database
    D. A workstation using a proxy server to access the Internet

12. User-level security is good for:
    A. Large networks with more than 50 computers
    B. Peer-to-peer networks with less than 10 computers
    C. Networks that have many servers but few users
    D. Systems that are not networked

13. In a peer-to-peer network, which network security model is used?
    A. User-level security
    B. Share-level security
    C. Password-protected shares
    D. Access permissions

14. In user-level access, network resources
    A. Only have one password associated with them
    B. Have multiple passwords associated with them
    C. Have different passwords based upon desired access
    D. Have no passwords but have permissions associated with them

15. Which connection mode is faster when there are little or no errors?
    A. Connectionless-oriented mode
    B. Connection-oriented mode

16. You want to run several protocols across your remote access communication link. Which dial-up protocol should you use?
    A. TCP/IP
    B. PPP
    C. SLIP
    D. UDP/IP

17. Which dial-up protocol is typically found in older dial-up systems?
    A. SLIP
    B. PPP
    C. TCP
    D. UDP

18. What is the purpose of DHCP?
    A. To allow easy access to web pages
    B. To assign standard addresses to web pages
    C. To enable users to share IP addresses so that a relatively small number of IP addresses can support many users
    D. To allow first time users access to the Internet without an IP address

19. The OSI Presentation Layer is named so because:
    A. It presents data to the user.
    B. It presents data to the application.
    C. It presents a uniform data format to the Application layer.
    D. It presents packets to the Data Link Layer.

20. Which OSI layer is the only layer that can send information directly to its counterpart on another computer?
    A. The Network Layer
    B. The Application Layer
    C. The Data Link Layer
    D. The Physical Layer

21. What type of device is commonly used to interface personal computer networks to mainframes?

    A. Bridge

    B. Brouter

    C. Gateway

    D. SMA converter card

22. Which 802 protocol describes Ethernet?

    A. 802.1

    B. 802.3

    C. 802.5

    D. 802.2

23. Which 802 protocol describes Token Ring media access control?

    A. 802.1

    B. 802.3

    C. 802.5

    D. 802.2

24. What is a MAC address on an Ethernet network?

    A. A logical address that identifies the workstation

    B. A physical address assigned by the NIC manufacturer

    C. A workstation's logical domain address

    D. A physical address assigned by the system administrator

25. CSMA/CD networks have total length restrictions between the furthest nodes on a network because:

    A. Attenuation degrades the signal.

    B. Impedance changes as the cable length increases.

    C. Propagation delays.

    D. Emissions from signals cause interference.

Answers and Explanations: Practice Exam

1. **C** Collision Sense Multiple Access. A type of media access method.

2. **C** CSMA/CD. The CD stands for collision detect.

3. **D** Thicknet, because the coaxial cable (RG6) used to implement 10Base5 is about ½-inch in diameter.

4. **A** You must terminate each end of a 10Base2 bus with 50-ohm terminators.

5. **C** The OSI model has seven layers.

6. **C** Category 5 cable will operate at 100Mbs. As the number increases, so does the quality of the cable.

7. **A** A bridge has the capability to read the destination address of a frame and only forward the frame to the required ports, thus cutting down on traffic and collisions. This increases network performance.

8. **A** Ethernet employs collision detection access.

9. **B** Novell, along with Apple, invented IPX/SPX in 1989; these protocols are used in Novell NetWare networks.

10. **C** There are six levels of RAID, commonly referred to as RAID Level 0–RAID Level 5.

11. **C** In client/sever computing, both the client and the server share the task of processing. Terminals do not process data; they simply display data from the mainframe.

12. **A** As a network grows larger, it is easier to manage user-level security than share-level security.

13. **B** Peer-to-peer networks implement share-level security. There is not a database of users in the peer-to-peer network architecture.

14. **D** In user-level access, network users have passwords and resources have permissions.

15. **A** Connectionless-oriented mode is faster because there is no overhead for error handling.

16. **B** One improvement of PPP over SLIP is the capability to transport multiple protocols over a single serial connection.

17. **A** SLIP was developed before PPP; thus, it is found on older dial-up systems.

18. **C** Dynamic Host Configuration Protocol (DHCP) dynamically assigns IP addresses, enabling a few IP addresses to support a larger number of users than fixed IP addressing.

19. **C** Many people confuse the Presentation Layer because it seems to present data to the user when, in fact, it presents a uniform data format to the Application Layer.

20. **D** The Physical Layer is the only layer that can directly send information to its counterpart on another system. All other layers must pass data down the protocol stack to reach the other computer. Other layers have virtual connections.

21. **C** Gateways. This is because protocol conversion is usually required to communicate with mainframe computers.

22. **B** IEEE 802.3 describes the Ethernet protocol.

23. **C** IEEE 802.5 describes token ring media access.

24. **B** The MAC address is a permanent address assigned by the manufacturer to each NIC separately.

25. **C** For detection methods to work correctly, the propagation delay must be less than the amount of time it takes to put a packet on the wire.

CHAPTER 21

Planning

21.1 Selecting the Appropriate Media for Various Situations

Media choices include:

- Coaxial cable
- Twisted-pair cable
- Fiber-optic cable
- Wireless communications

Situational elements include:

- Cost
- Distance limitations
- Number of nodes

On any network, the various entities must communicate through some form of media; this includes cables, light, and radio waves. Transmission media enable computers to send and receive messages but do not guarantee the messages will be understood—that function is left to the upper-layer protocols.

A. Transmission Media Types

The most common type of LAN media is *copper cable—twisted-pair* and *coaxial.* The next most popular type of LAN connection media is *fiber-optic cable,* which has two major types—*single mode* and *multimode.* Wireless media (which is, in a sense, no media at all) is also gaining popularity.

Cable Type	Description
Twisted-pair	Similar to the cabling used to connect your telephone to the wall outlet
Network coaxial	Similar to the cable used to connect your television set to the cable TV outlet
Fiber-optic	Consists of a number of glass or high-grade plastic optical strands surrounded by a tough outer wrapping
Wireless transmissions	Uses radio waves or light to transmit data

B. Characteristics of Transmission Media

Each type of transmission media has special characteristics that make it suitable for a specific type of service:

Cost

Installation requirements

Bandwidth

Band usage (baseband or broadband)

Attenuation

Electromagnetic interference

1. Bandwidth

Bandwidth refers to the measure of the capacity of a medium to transmit data.

Data transmission rates frequently are stated in terms of the bits that can be transmitted per second. An Ethernet LAN theoretically can transmit 10 million bits per second (bps) and has a bandwidth of 10 megabits per second (Mbps).

The bandwidth that a cable can accommodate is determined in part by the cable's length. A short cable generally can accommodate greater bandwidth than a longer cable, which is one reason all cable designs specify maximum lengths for cable runs. Beyond those limits, the highest-frequency signals can deteriorate, and errors begin to occur in data signals.

2. Band Usage

Two ways to allocate the capacity of transmission media are:

- **Baseband:** Devotes the entire capacity of the medium to one communication channel. Most LANs function in baseband mode.
- **Broadband:** Enables two or more communication channels to share the bandwidth of the communications medium.

These are both illustrated in Figure 21.1.1.

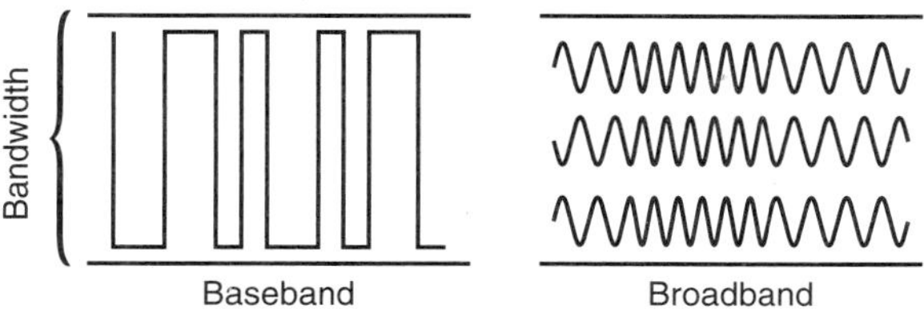

Figure 21.1.1 Baseband and broadband transmission modes.

Multiplexing enables broadband media to support multiple data channels. Multiplexing makes sense under a number of circumstances:

- **When media bandwidth is costly:** High-speed leased lines are expensive. If a leased line has sufficient bandwidth, multiplexing can enable the same line to carry mainframe, LAN, voice, video conferencing, and other data types.
- **When bandwidth is idle:** Many organizations have installed fiber-optic cable that is used only to partial capacity. With proper equipment, a single fiber can support hundreds of megabits—or even a gigabit or more—of mixed voice, video, and data.
- **When large amounts of data must be transmitted through low-capacity channels:** Multiplexing techniques can divide the original data stream into several lower-bandwidth channels, each of which can be transmitted through a lower-capacity medium. The signals then can be recombined at the receiving end.

Demultiplexing refers to recovering the original separate channels from a multiplexed signal. Multiplexing and demultiplexing are performed by a *multiplexor* (also called a *MUX*), which usually has both capabilities.

3. Attenuation

Attenuation is a measure of how much a transmission medium weakens a signal. Attenuation measurements always specify the frequency used to make the measurement because attenuation varies with frequency. As a rule, the higher the frequency, the greater the attenuation. Attenuation is one of the major factors limiting cable lengths that can be used in networks. Too much attenuation weakens a signal to the point where a station might not be able to distinguish it from background electrical noise.

4. Electromagnetic Interference

Electromagnetic interference (EMI) is electrical background noise that distorts a signal carried by a transmission medium. EMI makes it harder for a station listening to a medium to detect valid data signals on it. Some network media are more susceptible to EMI than others. Fiber-optic cable is generally considered immune to all forms of EMI.

Crosstalk is a special kind of EMI caused by having wires next to each other carrying data and "leaking" some of their data signals as EMI. Crosstalk is of particular concern in high-speed networks that use copper cables because there are typically many individual cables in close proximity to each other.

C. Cable Media

You need to know how to make decisions about network transmission media. The following sections discuss three types of network cabling media: coaxial cable, twisted-pair cable, and fiber-optic cable.

1. Coaxial Cable

Coaxial cable, the first cable type used in LANs, gets its name because two conductors share a common axis. It is most frequently referred to as *coax.* Figure 21.1.2 shows what this looks like.

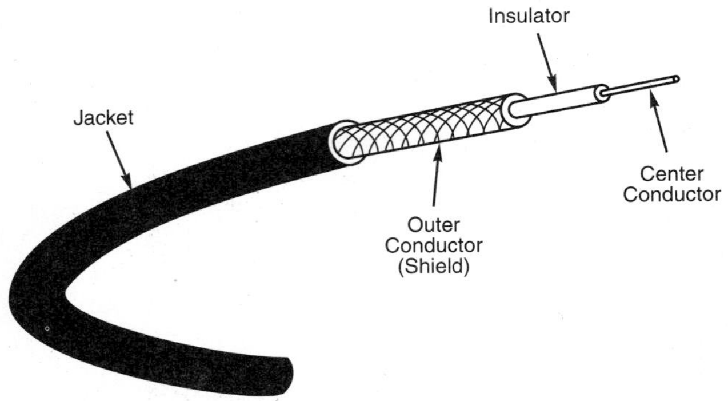

Figure 21.1.2 The structure of coaxial cable consists of four main components.

The components of a coaxial cable are:

- **Center conductor:** Usually solid copper wire, although it is sometimes made of stranded wire.
- **Outer conductor (shield):** Forms a tube surrounding the center conductor. It can consist of braided wires, metallic foil, or both. The outer conductor serves as a ground and also protects the inner conductor from EMI.
- **Insulator:** Keeps the outer conductor spaced evenly with the inner conductor.
- **Jacket:** Non-conductive encasement that protects the cable from damage.

All copper cables have a characteristic measurement called *impedance,* which is measured in ohms. Impedance is a measure of the apparent resistance to an alternating current. You must use a cable that has the proper impedance in any given situation.

There are two types of coaxial cable:

- **Thinnet:** A light and flexible cabling medium that is inexpensive and easy to install. Thinnet is similar enough to some members of the RG-58 family of cables, which also have a 50-ohm impedance, that one is sometimes substituted for the other. Thinnet is approximately .25 inches (6 mm) in thickness. Thinnet cable can reliably transmit an Ethernet signal for 185 meters (about 610 feet).
- **Thicknet:** Thicknet is thicker than Thinnet and is approximately 0.5 inches (13 mm) in diameter. Because it is thicker and does not bend as readily as Thinnet, Thicknet cable is harder to work with. A thicker center core and better shielding means that Thicknet can carry signals a longer distance than Thinnet. Thicknet can transmit an Ethernet signal approximately 500 meters (1,650 feet).

Thicknet cable is sometimes called *Standard Ethernet*. Thicknet can be used to connect two or more small Thinnet LANs into a larger network.

Thicknet is also more expensive than Thinnet. Some Thicknet cabling is durable enough that it can be installed outside, running from building to building—although doing so can create ground loops and act as a conduit for lightning damage. Electrical surge protectors should be used when a Thicknet segment is used to connect buildings.

a. Coaxial Characteristics

You should be familiar with the installation, cost, bandwidth, and EMI resistance characteristics of coaxial cable:

- **Installation:** Coaxial cable is reasonably easy to install because the cable is robust and difficult to damage. In addition, connectors can be installed with inexpensive tools and a bit of practice. The device-to-device cabling approach that coax uses can be difficult to reconfigure when new devices cannot be installed near an existing cable.

  Coaxial cable can be installed in either of two configurations: daisy-chain (from device to device—Ethernet) and star (ARCnet). Both of these are shown in figure 21.1.3.

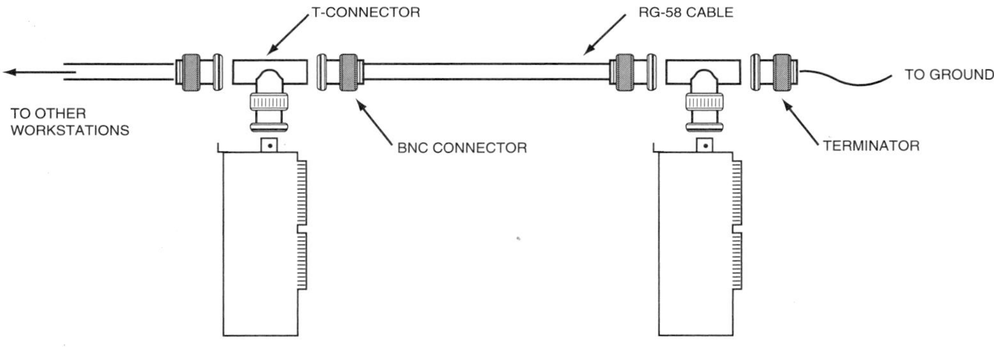

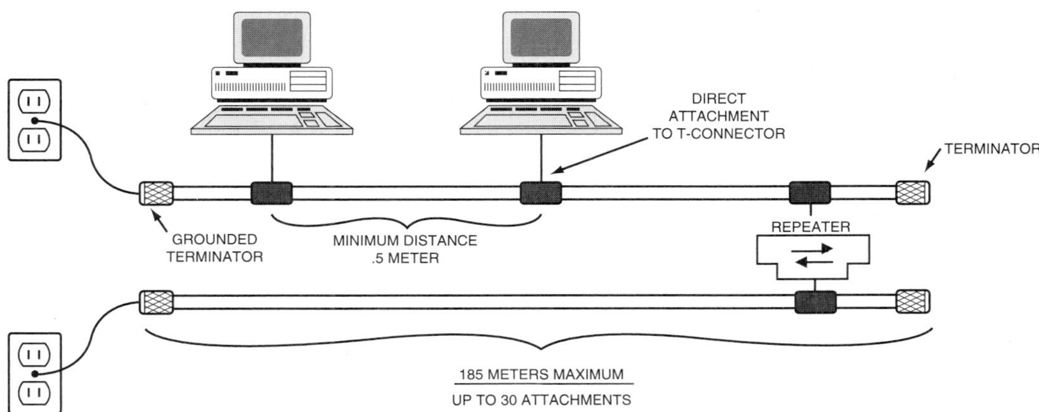

Figure 21.1.3 Coaxial cable wiring configurations—the top illustration is the daisy-chain configuration and the bottom illustration is the star configuration.

- **Cost:** The coaxial cable used for Thinnet falls toward the low end of the cost spectrum, whereas Thicknet is among the more costly options.
- **Bandwidth:** LANs that employ coaxial cable typically have a bandwidth between 2.5 Mbps (ARCnet) and 10 Mbps (Ethernet).
- **EMI Characteristics:** All copper media are sensitive to EMI, although the shield in coax makes them fairly resistant. Coaxial cables, like other copper cables, radiate a portion of their signal, and electronic eavesdropping equipment can detect this radiated signal.

b. Connectors for Coaxial Cable

The most common connector used with coaxial is the *Bayonet-Neill-Concelman* (BNC). BNC connectors and Thinnet cabling have the following characteristics:

- A BNC T-connector must be used to connect the network interface card in the PC to the network. The T-connector attaches directly to the network board. (See figure 21.1.3 to see an illustration of a BNC T-connector.)
- BNC cable connectors attach cable segments to the T-connectors.
- A BNC barrel connector connects two Thinnet cables.
- Both ends of the cable must be terminated. A BNC terminator is a special connector that includes a resistor that is carefully matched to the characteristics of the cable system. This is necessary to arrest signal reflections.
- One of the terminators must be grounded. A wire from the terminator is attached to a grounded point, such as the center screw of a grounded electrical outlet.

Thicknet uses N-connectors, which screw on instead of requiring crimping or a twist-lock. As with Thinnet, both ends of the cable must be terminated, and one end must be grounded (see fig. 21.1.4).

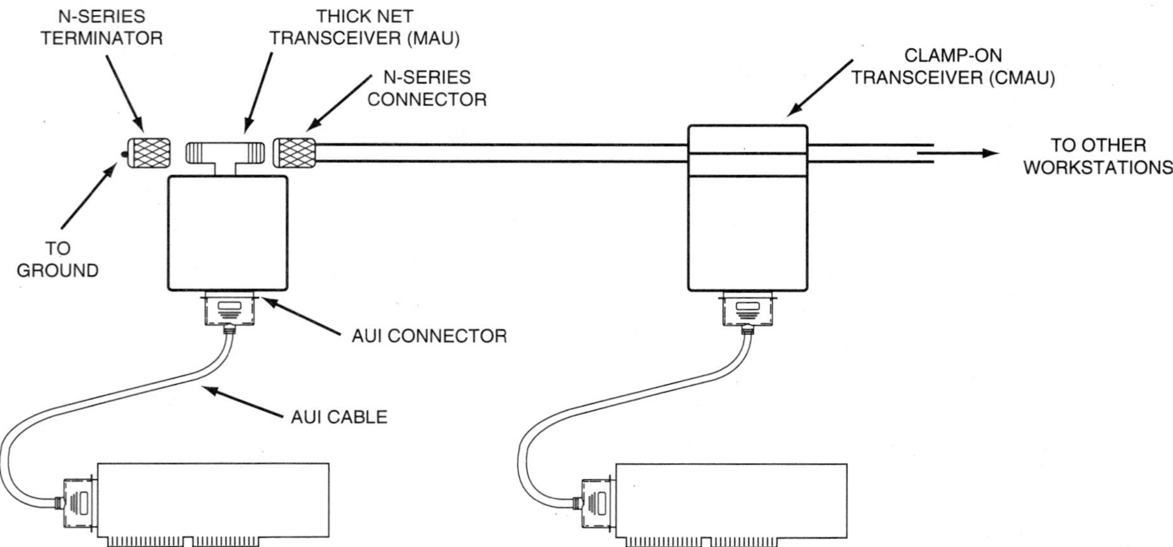

Figure 21.1.4 Connectors and cabling for Thicknet.

Workstations don't connect directly to the cable with Thicknet. Instead, a *transceiver* is attached to the Thicknet cable. This transceiver has a port for an *Attachment Unit Interface,* or *AUI connector*; an *AUI cable* (also called a *transceiver cable* or a *drop cable*) connects the workstation to the Thicknet medium. Transceivers can connect to Thicknet cables in two ways:

- Transceivers can be connected if you cut the cable and use N-connectors and a T-connector on the transceiver.
- The more common approach is to use a clamp-on transceiver, which has pins that penetrate the cable without the need for cutting it. These are frequently referred to as *vampire taps*.

2. Twisted-Pair Cable

Twisted-pair cable has become the dominant cable type for all new network designs that employ copper cable. Twisted-pair cable is inexpensive to install and offers the lowest cost-per-foot of any cable type.

A basic twisted-pair in a cable consists of two strands of copper wire that are twisted together and used to carry a single signal (see fig. 21.1.5). This twisting reduces the sensitivity of the cable to EMI and also reduces the tendency of the cable to radiate radio frequency noise that interferes with nearby cables and electronic components. This is because the radiated signals from the twisted wires tend to cancel each other out.

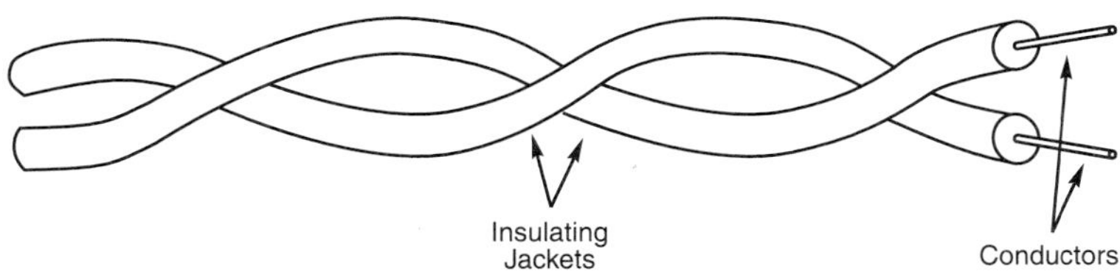

Figure 21.1.5 Twisted-pair cable.

Twisting also controls the tendency of the wires in the pair to cause EMI in each other. Whenever two wires are in close proximity, the signals in each wire tend to produce noise, called *crosstalk,* in the other. Twisting the wires in the pair reduces crosstalk in much the same way that twisting reduces the tendency of the wires to radiate EMI.

21

a. Shielded Twisted-Pair (STP) Cable

Shielded twisted-pair cabling consists of one or more twisted pairs of wire enclosed in a foil wrap and woven-copper shielding. Figure 21.1.6 shows IBM Type 1 cabling, the first cable type used with IBM Token Ring. Early LAN designers used shielded twisted-pair cable because the shield reduces the tendency of the cable to radiate EMI and thus reduces the cable's sensitivity to outside interference.

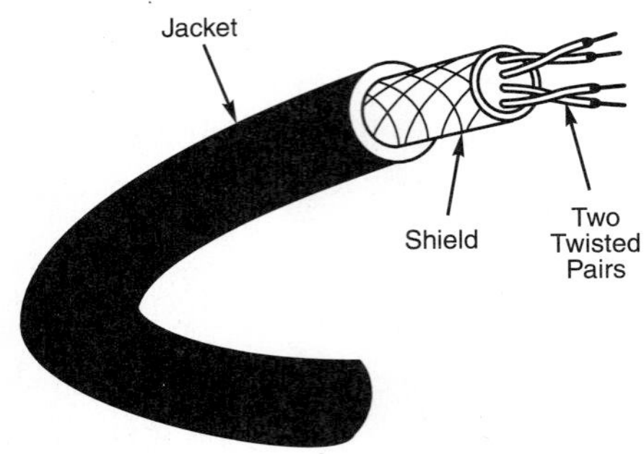

Figure 21.1.6 A shielded twisted-pair cable.

The shield is connected to the ground portion of the electronic device to which the cable is connected. A *ground* is a portion of the device that serves as an electrical reference point, and it usually is connected to a metal stake driven into the ground. A properly grounded shield minimizes signals getting into or out of the cable.

Various types of STP cable exist; some shield each pair individually and others shield several pairs. Each cable type is appropriate for a given kind of installation.

Because so many different types of STP cable exist, stating precise characteristics for STP is difficult. The following list offers some general guidelines:

- **Cost:** STP cable costs more than thin coaxial or unshielded twisted-pair cables. STP is less costly, however, than thick coax or fiber-optic cable.
- **Installation:** Different network types have different installation requirements. One major difference is the connector used. IBM Token Ring uses a unisex data connector (the connectors are both male and female), which can be installed with such common tools as a knife, a wire stripper, and large pliers.

  STP cable tends to be rather bulky. IBM Type 1 cable is approximately 1/2-inch (13 mm) in diameter. Therefore, cable paths fill up quickly when using STP cables.
- **Capacity:** STP cable has a theoretical capacity of over 500 Mbps, although no common technologies exceed 155 Mbps with 100-meter cable runs. The most common data rates for STP cable are 4 and 16 Mbps, which are the data rates for token ring networks.
- **Attenuation:** All varieties of twisted-pair cable have attenuation characteristics that limit the length of cable runs. Different STP cable types have different attenuation characteristics.
- **EMI Characteristics:** The shield in STP cable results in good EMI characteristics for copper cable, compared to coaxial cable. This is one reason STP might be preferred to unshielded twisted-pair cable. As with all copper cables, STP is sensitive to interference and vulnerable to electronic eavesdropping.
- **Connectors for STP:** AppleTalk and token ring networks can be cabled using UTP cable and RJ-45 connectors (see fig. 21.1.7), but both networks originated as STP cabling systems. For STP cable, AppleTalk employs a DIN-type connector. IBM Token Ring networks use the IBM Data Connector (see fig. 21.1.8).

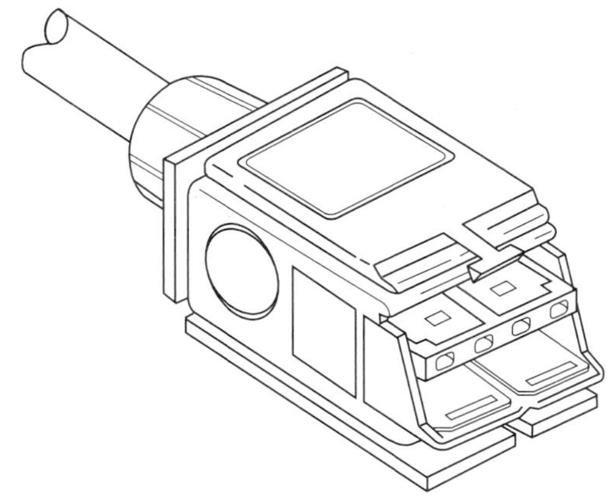

Figure 21.1.7 Connectors used with STP cable.

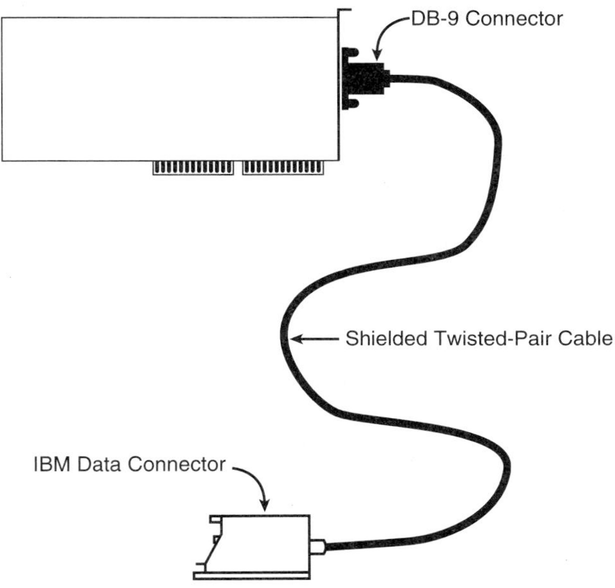

Figure 21.1.8 A PC ready to connect to a token ring network.

b. Unshielded Twisted-Pair (UTP) Cable

Unshielded twisted-pair cable doesn't incorporate a braided shield into its structure (see fig. 21.1.9). The characteristics of UTP are similar in many ways to STP, however, differing primarily in attenuation and EMI. Several twisted pairs can be bundled together in a single cable. These pairs typically are color coded.

Telephone systems typically use UTP cabling. Network engineers can sometimes use existing UTP telephone cabling (if it is of a high enough quality to support network communications) for network cabling.

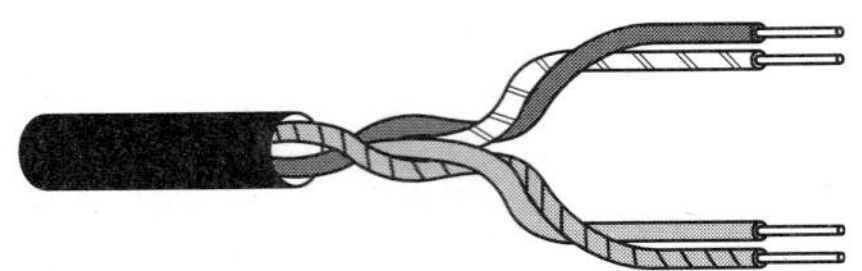

Figure 21.1.9 A multipair UTP cable.

UTP cable is a latecomer to high-performance LANs because engineers only recently solved the problems of managing radiated noise and susceptibility to EMI. Now all new copper-based cabling schemes are based on UTP.

UTP cable is available in five standardized grades, or categories:

- **Category 1 and 2:** These voice-grade cables are suitable only for voice and for low data rates (below 4 Mbps). The growing need for data-ready cabling systems has caused Category 1 and 2 cable to be supplanted by Category 3 for new installations.
- **Category 3:** The lowest data-grade cable, this is generally suited for data rates up to 10 Mbps. Some encoding schemes enable the cable to support data rates up to 100 Mbps. Category 3, which uses four twisted-pairs with three twists per foot, is now the standard cable used for most telephone installations. It is also the minimum type of UTP cable that supports 10Base-T.
- **Category 4:** This data-grade cable, which consists of four twisted pairs, is suitable for data rates up to 16 Mbps but isn't widely used.
- **Category 5:** This data-grade cable, which also consists of four twisted pairs, is suitable for data rates up to 100 Mbps. Most new cabling systems for 100 Mbps or faster data rates are designed around Category 5 cable.

UTP cable offers an excellent balance of cost and performance characteristics:

- **Cost:** UTP cable is the least costly of any cable type, although properly installed Category 5 tends to be fairly expensive. In some cases, existing cable in buildings can be used for LANs, but you need to verify the category of the cable and know the length of the cable in the walls. Distance limits for voice cabling are much less stringent than for data-grade cabling.
- **Installation:** UTP cable is easy to install. Some specialized equipment might be required, but the equipment is low in cost and can be mastered with very little practice. Properly designed UTP cabling systems can be reconfigured to meet changing requirements easily.

  Category 5 cable has stricter installation requirements than lower categories of UTP. Special training is recommended for dealing with Category 5 UTP.
- **Capacity:** The data rates possible with UTP have pushed up from 1 Mbps, past 4 and 16 Mbps, to the point where 100-Mbps data rates are now common.
- **Attenuation:** UTP cable shares similar attenuation characteristics with other copper cables. UTP cable runs are limited to a few hundred meters, with 100 meters as the most frequent limit.
- **EMI Characteristics:** Because UTP cable lacks a shield, it is more sensitive to EMI than coaxial or STP cables. The latest technologies make it possible to use UTP in the vast majority of situations, provided that reasonable care is taken to avoid electrically noisy devices such as motors and fluorescent lights. UTP usually is not suitable for electrically noisy environments such as factories, where very high-powered tools and equipment can radiate EMI significant distances.

- **Connectors for UTP:** The most common connector used with UTP cables is the *8-pin modular plug/jack* (commonly called an *RJ-45 connector*). These connectors are easy to install on cables and are also extremely easy to connect and disconnect. They have eight pins and look like a common RJ-11 telephone jack (see fig. 21.1.10). They are slightly different sizes and don't work together because of the different pin-outs.

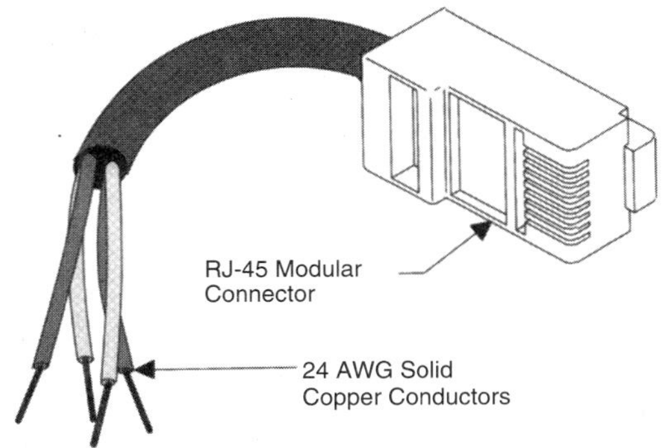

Figure 21.1.10 An 8-pin modular connector.

3. Fiber-Optic Cable

Fiber-optic cable is the ideal cable for data transmission. This type of cable accommodates extremely high bandwidths, presents no problems with EMI, and supports durable cables and cable runs as long as several kilometers. Two disadvantages of fiber optic cables are cost and installation difficulty.

The center conductor of a fiber-optic cable is a fiber that consists of highly refined glass or plastic designed to transmit light signals. The fiber is coated with a cladding that reflects signals back into the fiber to reduce signal loss. A plastic sheath protects the fiber (see fig. 21.1.11).

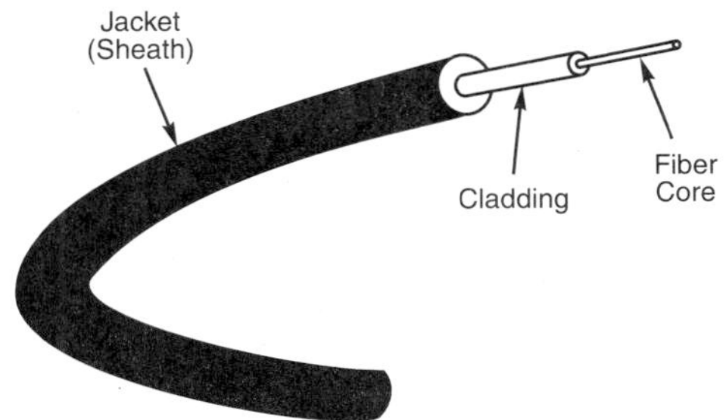

Figure 21.1.11 A fiber-optic cable.

A fiber-optic network cable consists of two strands that are enclosed in plastic sheaths—one strand sends and the other receives. Two types of cable configurations are available:

- **Loose:** Incorporates a space between the fiber sheath and the outer plastic encasement; this space is filled with a gel or other material.
- **Tight:** Contains strength wires between the conductor and the outer plastic encasement.

In both cases, the plastic encasement must supply the strength of the cable, while the gel layer or strength wires protect the delicate fiber from mechanical damage.

Optical fiber cables don't transmit electrical signals. Instead, the data signals must be converted into light signals. Light sources include:

- **Laser:** The purity of laser light makes lasers ideally suited to data transmissions because they can work at long distances and high bandwidths. Lasers are expensive light sources and are used only when their special characteristics are required.
- **Light-emitting diode (LED):** LEDs are inexpensive and produce a relatively poorer quality of light than lasers. LEDs are suitable for less-stringent applications, such as 100 Mbps or slower LAN connections that extend less than two kilometers.

The end of the cable that receives the light signal must convert the signal back to an electrical form. Several types of solid-state components can perform this service.

As with all cable types, fiber-optic cables have their share of advantages and disadvantages.

- **Cost:** The cost of the cable and connectors has fallen significantly in recent years, but fiber-optic cable is still the most expensive cable type to install. The electronic devices required to use it are significantly more expensive than comparable devices for copper cable.
- **Installation:** Greater skill is required to install fiber-optic cable than to install most copper cables. Improved tools and techniques have reduced the training required. Still, fiber-optic cable requires greater care because the cables must be treated fairly gently during installation.
- **Capacity:** Fiber-optic cable can support very high data rates (into the terabits per second) even with long cable runs. Although UTP cable runs are limited to less than 100 meters with 100-Mbps data rates, certain types of fiber-optic cables may be able to carry a 100 Mbps signal for 20 kilometers.
- **Attenuation:** Attenuation in fiber-optic cables is much lower than in copper cables. Multimode fiber-optic cables are capable of carrying most signals for two kilometers, while single-mode fiber-optic cables may carry the same signal for as far as 20 kilometers.
- **EMI Characteristics:** Because fiber-optic cables don't use electrical signals to transmit data, they are totally immune to electromagnetic interference. The cables also are immune to a variety of electrical effects that must be taken into account when designing copper cabling systems.

> **When electrical cables are connected between two buildings, the ground potentials (voltages) between the two buildings can differ. When a difference exists, current flows through the grounding conductor of the cable—even though the ground is supposed to be electrically neutral and no current should flow.**
>
> **When current flows through the ground conductor of a cable, the condition is called a *ground loop.* Ground loops can result in electrical instability and various other types of anomalies.**
>
> **Because it is immune to electrical effects, fiber-optic cable is the best cable to use when connecting networks in different buildings.**

Because the signals in fiber-optic cable are not electrical in nature, they cannot be detected by the electronic eavesdropping equipment that detects electromagnetic radiation. Therefore, fiber-optic cable is the best choice for high-security networks.

4. IBM Cabling

IBM uses its own separate names, standards, and specifications for network cabling and cabling components. These IBM cabling types roughly parallel standard forms used elsewhere in the industry.

IBM uses a unique, unisex connector—any two of these connectors can be connected together.

Table 21.1.1 IBM Cabling Types

Cable Type	Description	Comment
Type 1	Shielded twisted-pair (STP)	Two twisted-pairs of 22 AWG[1] wire in braided shield
Type 2	Voice and data	Two twisted-pairs of 22 AWG wire for data and braided shield, and two twisted-pairs of 26 AWG for voice
Type 3	Voice	Four solid UTP pairs; 22 or 24 AWG wire
Type 4	Not defined	
Type 5	Fiber-optic	Two 62.5/125-micron multimode fibers
Type 6	Data patch cable	Two twisted pairs of 26 AWG wire, dual foil, and braided shield
Type 7	Not defined	
Type 8	Carpet grade	Two twisted pairs of 26 AWG wire with shield for use under carpets
Type 9	Plenum grade	Two twisted pairs, shielded (see previous discussion of plenum-grade cabling)

1. The AWG designation in this table stands for the American Wire Gauge standard, a specification for wire gauges. The higher the gauge, the thinner the wire.

21

5. Comparison of Cable Media

When comparing cabling types, remember that the characteristics you observe depend highly on the implementations.

Some comparisons between cable types are fairly involved. Although fiber-optic cable is costly on a per-foot basis, for example, you can construct a fiber-optic cable that is many kilometers in length. To build a copper cable many kilometers in length, you would need to install repeaters and/or bridges at several points along the cable to amplify the signal. These repeaters could easily exceed the cost of a fiber-optic cable run.

Table 21.1.2 Comparison of Cable Media

Cable Type	Cost	Installation	Capacity	Range	EMI
Coaxial Thinnet	<STP	Inexpensive/ easy	10 Mbps typical	185 m	<sensitive than UTP
Coaxial Thicknet	>STP <Fiber	Easy	10 Mbps typical	500 m	<sensitive than UTP
Shielded Twisted-Pair (STP)	>UTP <Thicknet	Fairly easy	16 Mbps typical, up to 500 Mbps	100 m typical	<sensitive than UTP
Unshielded Twisted-Pair (UTP)	Lowest	Inexpensive/ easy	10 Mbps typical, up to 100 Mbps	100 m typical	Most sensitive
Fiber Optic	Highest	Expensive/ difficult	100 Mbps typical	10s of kilo-meters	Insensitive

D. Wireless Media

All signals transmitted between computers consist of some form of electromagnetic (EM) waveform, ranging from radio frequencies up through infrared light and microwave.

You can subdivide wireless networking technology into three basic types, corresponding to three basic networking scenarios:

- **Local Area Networks (LANs):** Occasionally, you will see a fully wireless LAN; more typically, however, one or more wireless machines will function as members of a cable-based LAN. A LAN with both wireless and cable-based components is called a *hybrid.*
- **Extended local networks:** A wireless connection serves as a backbone between two LANs. For instance, a company with office networks in two nearby but separate buildings could connect those networks using a wireless bridge.
- **Mobile computing:** A mobile machine connects to the home network using cellular or satellite technology.

1. Reasons for Wireless Networks

Wireless networks are especially useful for the following situations:

- **Spaces where cabling would be impossible or inconvenient:** These include open lobbies, inaccessible parts of buildings, older buildings, historical buildings where renovation is prohibited, and outdoor installations.
- **People who move around a lot within their work environment:** Network administrators, for instance, must troubleshoot a large office network. Nurses and doctors need to make rounds at a hospital.

- **Temporary installations:** These situations include any temporary department set up for a specific purpose that soon will be torn down or relocated.
- **People who travel:** Many employees now travel outside the work environment and need instantaneous access to network resources.

2. Wireless Communications with LANs

It is often advantageous for a network to include some wireless nodes. Typically, though, the wireless nodes will be part of what is otherwise a traditional, cable-based network.

An *access point* is a stationary transceiver connected to the cable-based LAN that enables the cordless PC to communicate with the network. The access point acts as a conduit for the wireless PC.

You can classify wireless LAN communications according to transmission method. The four most common LAN wireless transmission methods are:

- **Infrared transmission:** Similar to a television with a remote control that transmits pulses of infrared light carrying coded instructions to a receiver on the TV, this technology has also been adapted to network communication. Four varieties of infrared communications are:

  Broadband optical telepoint: This method uses broadband technology. Data transfer rates in this high-end option are competitive with those for a cable-based network.

  Line-of-sight infrared: Transmissions must occur over a clear, line-of-sight path between transmitter and receiver.

  Reflective infrared: Wireless PCs transmit toward a common central unit, which then directs communication to each of the nodes.

  Scatter infrared: Transmissions reflect off floors, walls, and ceilings until (theoretically) they finally reach the receiver. Because of the imprecise trajectory, data transfer rates are slow. The maximum reliable distance is around 100 feet.

  Infrared transmissions typically are limited to within 100 feet. Within this range, however, infrared is relatively fast. Infrared's high bandwidth supports transmission speeds of up to 10 Mbps.

  Infrared devices are insensitive to radio-frequency interference, but reception can be degraded by bright light. Because transmissions are tightly focused, they are fairly immune to electronic eavesdropping.

- **Laser transmission**: High-powered laser transmitters can transmit data for several thousand yards when line-of-sight communication is possible. Lasers can be used in many of the same situations as microwave links without requiring an FCC license. For indoor LANs, laser light technology is rarely used, but it is similar to infrared technology.
- **Narrow-band radio transmission:** In narrow-band radio communications (also called *single-frequency radio*), the range is better than infrared, effectively enabling mobile computing over a limited area. Neither the receiver nor the transmitter is required to be in a direct line of sight. The signal can bounce off walls, buildings, and even the atmosphere; but heavy walls, such as steel or concrete enclosures, can block the signal.

- **Spread-spectrum radio transmission:** Spread-spectrum radio transmission is a technique originally developed by the military to solve several communication problems. Spread-spectrum improves reliability, reduces sensitivity to interference and jamming, and is less vulnerable to eavesdropping than single-frequency radio.

  As its name suggests, spread-spectrum transmission uses multiple frequencies to transmit messages. Two techniques employed are *frequency hopping* and *direct-sequence modulation*.

  Frequency hopping switches (*hops*) between several available frequencies (see fig. 21.1.12), staying on each frequency for a specified interval of time. The transmitter and receiver must remain synchronized during a process called a *hopping sequence* in order for this technique to work. The range for this type of transmission is up to two miles outdoors and 400 feet indoors. Frequency hopping typically transmits at up to 250 Kbps, although some versions can reach as high as 2 Mbps.

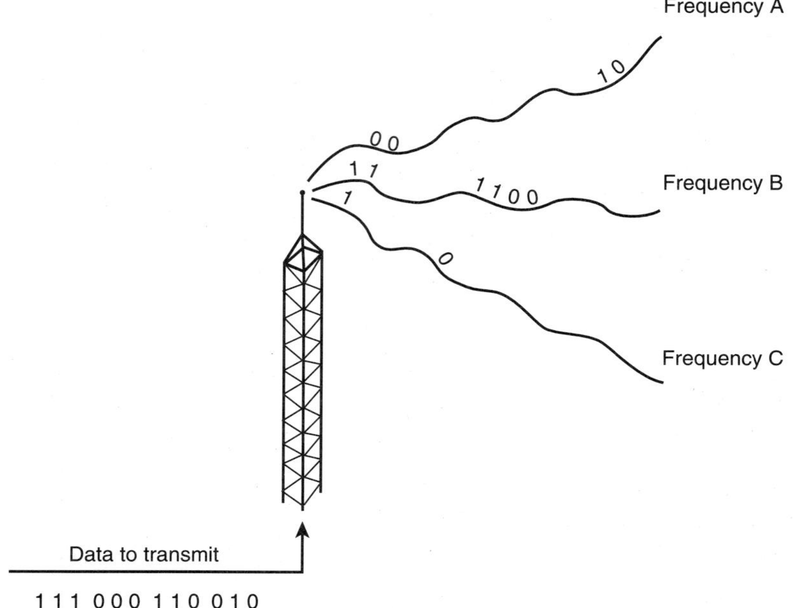

Figure 21.1.12 Frequency hopping employs various frequencies for a specific time period.

  Direct-sequence modulation breaks original messages into parts called *chips* (see fig. 21.1.13), which are transmitted on separate frequencies. To confuse eavesdroppers, decoy data also can be transmitted on other frequencies. The intended receiver knows which frequencies are valid and can isolate the chips and reassemble the message. Eavesdropping is difficult because the correct frequencies are not known, and the eavesdropper cannot isolate the frequencies carrying true data. Because different sets of frequencies can be selected, this technique can operate in environments that support other transmission activity. Direct sequence modulation systems operating at 900 MHz support bandwidths of 2–6 Mbps.

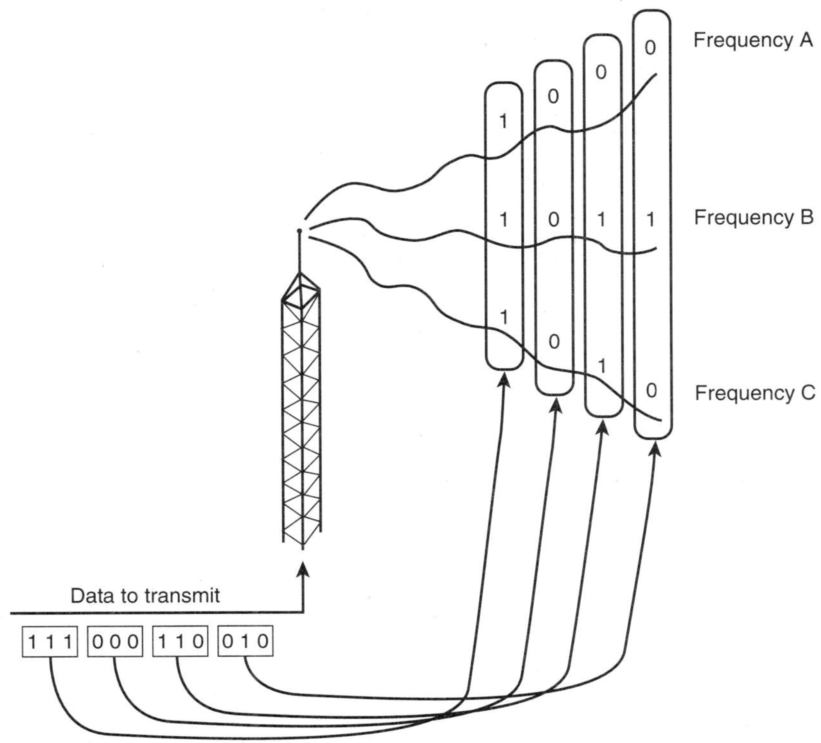

Figure 21.1.13 Direct-sequence modulation.

3. Wireless Bridging

Wireless technology can connect LANs in two different buildings into an extended LAN. This capability is, of course, also available through other technologies (such as a T1 line or a leased line from a telephone provider), but depending on the conditions, a wireless solution is sometimes more cost effective. A wireless connection between two buildings also provides a solution to the ground-potential problem.

A *wireless bridge* acts as a network bridge, merging two local LANs over a wireless connection. Wireless bridges typically use spread-spectrum radio technology to transmit data for up to three miles. (Antennae at each end of the bridge should be placed in an appropriate location, such as a rooftop.) A device called a *long-range wireless bridge* has a range of up to 25 miles.

4. Mobile Computing

Mobile computing is a growing technology that provides almost unlimited range for traveling computers by using satellite and cellular phone networks to relay the signal to a home network. Mobile computing typically is used with portable PCs or personal digital assistant (PDA) devices.

Three forms of mobile computing are:

- **Packet-radio networking:** The mobile device sends and receives network-style packets via satellite. Packets contain a source and destination address, and only the destination device can receive and read the packet.

- **Cellular networking:** The mobile device sends and receives cellular digital packet data (CDPD) using cellular phone technology and the cellular phone network. Cellular networking provides very fast communications.
- **Satellite station networking:** Satellite mobile networking stations use satellite microwave technology, which is described later in this chapter.

5. Microwave Technology

Microwave technology has applications in all three of the wireless networking scenarios: LAN, extended LAN, and mobile networking. Microwave communication can take two forms: terrestrial (ground links) and satellite links.

- **Terrestrial microwave:** Employs Earth-based transmitters and receivers. Uses low-gigahertz range frequencies, which limits all communications to line-of-sight. These typically use a parabolic antenna that produces a narrow, highly directional signal. A similar antenna at the receiving site is sensitive to signals only within a narrow focus. The highly focused antennas require careful adjustment.

  Costs are highly variable depending on requirements. Long-distance microwave systems can be quite expensive but might be less costly than alternatives with their recurring monthly expenses. When line-of-sight transmission is possible, a microwave link is a one-time expense that can offer greater bandwidth than a leased circuit.

  Attenuation characteristics are determined by transmitter power, frequency, and antenna size. Properly designed systems are not affected by attenuation under normal operational conditions. Rain and fog, however, can cause attenuation of higher frequencies.

  Because microwave signals are vulnerable to electronic eavesdropping, signals transmitted through microwave are frequently encrypted.

- **Satellite microwave:** Relay transmissions through communication satellites that operate in geosynchronous orbits 22,300 miles above the earth. Satellites orbiting at this distance remain located above a fixed point on earth.

  Earth stations use parabolic antennas (satellite dishes) to communicate with satellites. These satellites then can retransmit signals in broad or narrow beams, depending on the locations intended to receive the signals.

  Because no cables are required, satellite microwave communication is possible with most remote sites and with mobile devices. This enables transmission with ships at sea and motor vehicles.

  The distances involved in satellite communication result in an interesting phenomenon: Because all signals must travel 22,300 miles to the satellite and 22,300 miles when returning to a receiver, the time required to transmit a signal is independent of distance. It takes as long to transmit a signal to a receiver in the same state as it does to a receiver a third of the way around the world. The time required for a signal to arrive at its destination is called *propagation delay.* The delays commonly encountered with satellite transmissions range from 0.5 to 5 seconds.

  Attenuation characteristics depend on frequency, power, and atmospheric conditions. Microwave signals are sensitive to electronic eavesdropping, so signals transmitted through microwave frequently are encrypted.

21.1.1 Exercise

Go to a local computer store that sells networking equipment and ask to see their selection of network cards and cables. Write down their prices for each of the different major technologies offered, and pay attention to any recommendations they make about material selection.

Use this information to calculate the materials cost of installing transmission media to support a 40-computer office with 10Base-T versus 100Base-T. Assume average cable length to a hub is 50 feet, and make sure you get category ratings (Category 3 for 10 Mbps, Category 5 for 100 Mbps) for all equipment.

Next, assume that you have been directed to install IBM type 1 cabling because this will be a token ring network. Calculate the materials cost of installing type 1 STP for this 40-station network and using IBM data connectors to terminate it.

21.1.1 Exercise Explanation

Sample calculation (fictitious pricing):

Average cable length = 50 feet
Cost per foot of cable = $0.20
Number of cables = 40
Connectors = $0.90

Total materials cost = cable + connectors

Cable = (number of cables × average cable length × cost per foot)
= (40 × 50 ft. × 0.2)
= $40

Connectors = 2 × number of cables
= 2 × 40
= $80

Total materials cost = $40 + $80

Total materials cost = $120

Note that the cost of tools and skilled labor is extremely variable. It's not uncommon for a cabling company to charge in excess of $100 per cable installed.

21.1 Practice Problems

1. When installing a network, you must heed the distance limitations on the cable because the primary limiting factor for data transmission in a very long cable is:

   A. Crosstalk

   B. Collisions

   C. Attenuation

   D. EMI

2. *Baseband* is:

   A. A method for transmitting one signal at a time through the network medium

   B. The lowest (base) frequency a signal requires for transmission

   C. The network adapter requirement for wireless networks

   D. A method for transmitting multiple signals at a time through the network medium

3. When would you consider the use of multiplexing on your network?

   A. With typical 56k, T-1, or T-3 leased lines

   B. When a station has more than one network adapter installed

   C. In order to overcome cable length limitations

   D. When the server receives two signals simultaneously

4. The bandwidth presented to a device when using time-division multiplexing (TDM) is determined by:

   A. The network utilization

   B. The protocol

   C. The channel capacity

   D. The programmed configuration in the MUX

5. The use of fixed-time divisions to multiplex a given channel is known as:

   A. Synchronous TDM

   B. FDM

   C. Channel multiplexing

   D. ATM

6. In a multiplexing environment in which efficient line utilization is most important, what is used?

   A. Repeaters

   B. A transmission control MUX

   C. Capacity sensitive allocation units

   D. Stat-TDM

7. Typical LAN cable is made of:

   A. Aluminum

   B. Plenum

   C. Platinum

   D. Copper

8. Due to extreme signaling requirements, the data transmissions to your space probe operate very slowly. This application can be classified as:

   A. Time Division Multiplexing (TDM)

   B. High bandwidth

   C. Low bandwidth

   D. Baseband

9. Most common LANs operate in:

   A. Baseband mode

   B. Frequency transmission mode

   C. Multiplex mode

   D. Broadband mode

10. You are experiencing some transmission troubles on your network and suspect crosstalk. Crosstalk occurs:
    A. From such interferences as lightning
    B. When the network cables are installed to close to telephone wires
    C. When the multiplex time slots are not synchronized
    D. From adjacent wires

11. You will use BNC-style connectors to connect:
    A. Transceivers to AUI ports
    B. 10Base-T cable segments
    C. Thick coax cable segments
    D. Thin coax segments

12. The thickness of Thicknet cabling is due to:
    A. Increased shielding around the wires
    B. The superior insulation
    C. The number of outer conductors
    D. A thicker core cable

13. In deciding which type of network to install, you consider that one of the benefits of Thicknet over Thinnet is:
    A. Lower cost
    B. Easier to use
    C. Increased bandwidth for Ethernet
    D. Longer transmission distances

14. You are experiencing signaling problems on your coax-based LAN. A protocol analyzer indicates that signals keep bouncing back. What did you forget to install?
    A. A T connector
    B. An impedance reducer
    C. A terminator
    D. An RJ-45 type jack

15. Which type of connectors will you need with Thicknet?
    A. T-connectors
    B. RJ-45 type jacks
    C. RJ-11 type jacks
    D. N-connectors

16. Vampire taps are:
    A. Used to connect Thinnet networks to a Thicknet cable
    B. A type of transceiver
    C. Used to connect a transceiver to the cable in Thicknet networks
    D. All of the above

17. Coax cable consists of two conductors. The outer conductor:
    A. Transmits data
    B. Insulates the inner conductor from damage
    C. Serves as the ground or shield
    D. Is for voice communication

18. You are troubleshooting a Thinnet LAN. Which of the following cable lengths that you found is/are legal?
    A. 150 meters
    B. 200 meters
    C. 500 meters
    D. All of the above

19. You are troubleshooting a Thicknet LAN. Which of the following cable lengths that you found is/are legal?
    A. 150 meters
    B. 200 meters
    C. 500 meters
    D. All of the above

20. You are designing an Ethernet LAN. Which of the following is true of Thicknet?

    A. It has higher bandwidth than Thinnet.

    B. It has lower bandwidth than Thinnet.

    C. It has the same bandwidth as Thinnet.

    D. It can only transmit as 2.5 Mbps.

21. You are designing an Ethernet network wired with Category 5 twisted-pair copper cable:

    A. The cables used consist of only two wires.

    B. The cables used consist of two pairs of wires.

    C. The cables used consist of four pairs of wires.

    D. The cables used don't need to connect to a hub.

22. UTP cables should not run over or next to fluorescent lights due to:

    A. Crosstalk

    B. EMI

    C. Transmission resonance

    D. Luminary distortion

23. The twisting feature of twisted-pair copper cable is important for:

    A. Amplifying the transmission

    B. Reducing cable diameter

    C. Strengthening the cable

    D. Canceling crosstalk

24. The shielding in shielded twisted-pair (STP) cable:

    A. Is necessary to meet fire code regulations

    B. Is for grounding and shielding purposes

    C. Is to prevent crosstalk

    D. Is to keep out dust

25. Transmission speed is important to your particular network needs, and you need to choose the appropriate cable. The highest standard data rate for UTP is:

    A. 4 Mbps

    B. 10 Mbps

    C. 16 Mbps

    D. 100 Mbps

26. Twisted-pair cable is the most common LAN cable due to:

    A. Its low cost

    B. Ease of installation

    C. High availability of compatible network components

    D. All of the above

27. The most common STP cable used in networks is:

    A. IBM type 1

    B. IBM type 2

    C. TP-PMD

    D. Category 5

28. One of the disadvantages in STP:

    A. Is the short cable limitations

    B. Is that data transmission is limited to 16 Mbps

    C. Is its thickness

    D. Is the poor EMI characteristics

29. While wiring a LAN, you must limit your UTP cable length to:

    A. 100 meters

    B. 150 meters

    C. 200 meters

    D. 250 meters

30. EMI characteristics are not as good for UTP as they are for STP because:

    A. UTP uses a thinner cable wire.

    B. UTP has no outer shielding.

    C. UTP has four pairs of wire; STP only has two pairs.

    D. UTP connectors cause resonance interference.

31. The two strands in fiber-optic cabling are necessary for:

    A. Redundancy

    B. Crosstalk elimination

    C. Multiplexing signal strength

    D. Transmission and reception

32. Signal loss in fiber-optic cable is mostly a problem with which of the following?

    A. Data-to-light translation devices

    B. Cable-to-cable connections

    C. Lasers

    D. Light-emitting diodes

33. Fiber-optic cables provide which of the following?

    A. The least expensive network cable

    B. The highest transmission rates

    C. The most simple to install

    D. The most damage resistant

34. In order for electronic data to be transmitted via fiber optic cable:

    A. The data must be converted to light signals.

    B. A laser must be used.

    C. Special network couplers must be used.

    D. Manchester encoding must be used.

35. One benefit of fiber-optic cable is:

    A. Lower installation cost

    B. Error recovery features

    C. Better security

    D. Lower network equipment costs

36. An allowable cable length for multimode fiber-optic cable carrying a full duplex 10 Mbps Ethernet signal would be:

    A. 2 km

    B. 5 km

    C. 10 km

    D. 20 km

37. Two disadvantages of fiber-optic cable are:

    A. Limited capacity and EMI interference

    B. Short cable limits and cost

    C. Installation and degradation over time

    D. Cost and installation

38. Fiber-optic cables come in two types. They are:

    A. Full duplex and half duplex

    B. Single mode and asynchronous

    C. Laser and LED

    D. Single mode and multimode

39. In using fiber-optic cable, a faster transmission is achieved with:
    A. LEDs
    B. Radio frequency beams
    C. Lasers
    D. Electrical transmissions

40. A disadvantage of fiber-optic cable over copper cable is that:
    A. Fiber-optic cables are more durable.
    B. Fiber-optic cables don't work with the most common type of network, Ethernet.
    C. Fiber-optic cables can work over much longer distances than copper cables.
    D. Fiber-optic cables are more expensive than copper cables.

41. A standard, cabled LAN that includes some wireless components is known as:
    A. A hybrid LAN
    B. A point-to-point LAN
    C. A wireless LAN
    D. A spread-spectrum LAN

42. Wireless computers typically connect through:
    A. The frequency transmission conduit
    B. Infrared radio frequencies
    C. An access point cabled to a regular LAN
    D. Mobile computing

43. Laser, infrared, and radio transmissions are used:
    A. In fiber-optic cables
    B. In wireless networks
    C. In most small LANs
    D. Only in very large networks

44. Scatter infrared transmission:
    A. Doesn't need a transceiver
    B. Has shorter transmission distances than other forms of infrared
    C. Has longer transmission distances than other forms of infrared
    D. Works best out of doors

45. Radio, laser, and _______are the most common means of wireless LAN transmission.
    A. Satellite
    B. Infrared
    C. LEDs
    D. Transmission beam

46. Wireless laser transmission has an advantage over other wireless technologies in that:
    A. It doesn't require an FCC license.
    B. It doesn't require line-of-sight.
    C. It requires a line-of-sight between the transmitter and the receiver.
    D. It is much less expensive to install.

47. A technical obstacle to using satellites for data traffic is:
    A. The expense
    B. The long latency
    C. The speed limitations
    D. Unavailable from remote areas

48. Satellite communications are done via:
    A. Laser
    B. Infrared
    C. Radio
    D. Microwave

49. You need to build a wireless network, and security is your dominant concerns. Which of the following transmission methods is the most secure?

    A. Infrared

    B. Laser

    C. Radio

    D. Spread spectrum

50. When planning a line-of-sight wireless connection between adjacent buildings, important considerations are (select three):

    A. Resistance to weather conditions

    B. Data throughput, or speed

    C. Technology used

    D. Monthly line costs

21.1 Answers and Explanations: Practice Problems

1. **C** Attenuation is the limiting factor for data transmission in very long cables. The longer the cable, the weaker the signal at the end.

2. **A** Baseband signaling only allows for transmitting one signal at a time through the same physical network medium.

3. **A** Multiplexing is used with typical 56k, T-1, or T-3 leased lines. A T-1 carries 24 multiplexed DS-0s, while a T-3 carries 24 multiplexed T-1s.

4. **D** The bandwidth presented by a Time Division MUX (TDM) is controlled by the MUX's configuration.

5. **A** Synchronous TDM is another name for using fixed-time divisions to multiplex a given channel.

6. **D** Stat-TDM can use a line more efficiently than a fixed TDM configuration.

7. **D** Most network cables are made of copper. Less frequently, plastic or glass is also used for fiber-optic cables.

8. **C** Low bandwidth is a descriptive term used for low-speed transmissions. The line between high and low bandwidth varies depending on the context in which it is used.

9. **A** Most common LANs, including token ring, FDDI, and Ethernet over 10Base-T, 10Base2, and 10Base5, all use baseband signaling.

10. **D** Crosstalk is the electromagnetic interference from adjacent wires in a pair or bundle of cables.

11. **D** BNC connectors are only used with thin coax (10Base2) segments

12. **D** The thicker core contributes most of the thickness of Thicknet (10Base5) cable

13. **D** A single Thicknet cable segment supports Ethernet data transmission over 500 meters, or more than twice the distance of Thinnet cabling. Thicknet is more expensive and harder to work with than Thinnet, and they both run at the same speed of 10 Mbps.

14. **C** A terminator is used with coax cabling to match the cable's impedance, which has the effect of keeping signals from being reflected and bouncing back.

15. **D** N-connectors are used with Thicknet.

16. **C** Vampire taps are used to connect a station to the cable in Thicknet networks. They are a way of connecting to the Thicknet without cutting it.

17. **C** The outer conductor in a coaxial cable serves as the ground or shield.

18. **A** Thinnet cable can support cable segments of up to 185 meters, so the only correct choice in this example is 150 meters.

19. **D** Thicknet cable can support cable segments of up to 500 meters, so all the choices listed are correct.

20. **C** Both Thicknet and Thinnet are used with the 10 Mbps variety of Ethernet, so they can be said to have the same bandwidth in that context.

21. **C** Category 5 cables by always consist of four pairs of wires.

22. **B** The ballast in fluorescent lights can generate enough EMI to distort data signals, so installers of network cables need to avoid them.

23. **D** Twisting the cables of each pair together has the effect of canceling crosstalk between them.

24. **B** The shield used in STP is used for grounding and shielding purposes.

25. **D** 100 Mbps is the speed Category 5 cabling is tested at, and it is the highest standard data rate for UTP.

26. **D** Twisted-pair cable is the most common LAN cable installed today due to its low cost, its ease of installation, and the high availability of compatible network components.

27. **A** IBM type 1 cabling is the most common type of STP used in data networks. It is only commonly used for token ring networks.

28. **C** STP is one of the thickest types of network cabling, which makes it more expensive and harder to work with.

29. **A** 100 meters is the maximum allowed length for standard UTP cables.

30. **B** UTP is more susceptible to EMI because it has no outer shielding like STP (or coaxial cable) does.

31. **D** In a fiber-optic data cable, one strand is used for transmitting and the other strand is used for receiving.

32. **B** The most dramatic signal loss in a fiber optic environment happens at the connectors.

33. **B** Fiber-optic cables support the highest data transmission rates available, with theoretical bandwidth of many gigabits per second.

34. **A** Before transmitting any data through a fiber-optic cable, the data must be converted to light.

35. **C** Fiber-optic cable is very difficult to eavesdrop on compared to copper cables, and so it is more secure.

36. **A** Multimode fiber can generally carry a 10 Mbps signal for 2 km before attenuation becomes a problem.

37. **D** The two major drawbacks of fiber-optic cable are its relatively expensive cost and the requirement for skilled installers to polish the cable ends and to make the connections.

38. **D** The two different types of fiber-optic cables are single mode and multimode. The transmitters used on single mode cables are usually lasers, while the transmitters on multimode cables are typically LEDs.

39. **C** Although both lasers and LEDs are used for different types of fiber-optic transmissions, lasers can turn on and off much more rapidly and so are used for high-speed data transmissions.

40. **D** Fiber-optic cables are typically more expensive than copper cables, although they work over longer distances and potentially higher speeds than copper cables.

41. **A** A LAN that has both wireless and standard cabled components is called a hybrid LAN.

42. **C** Most wireless devices connect to the rest of the network through an access point cabled to a regular LAN.

43. **B** Laser, infrared, and radio frequency transmissions are all commonly used in wireless networks.

44. **B** Scatter infrared technologies have shorter transmission distances than other forms of infrared.
45. **B** Infrared is one of the most common types of wireless communication.
46. **A** Laser-based wireless communications don't require an FCC license, but radio and microwave may require one.
47. **B** Because the signal has to travel over 44,000 miles, the long latency (half a second or more) can be unbearable for interactive traffic like Telnet, and it will seriously limit the throughput of non-interactive traffic.
48. **D** Satellite transmissions are done via microwave, in which each earth station uses a small parabolic antenna.
49. **D** Spread spectrum is the most secure of the options presented because its frequency-hopping makes it hard to eavesdrop on.
50. **A, B, C** The only choice that should not be a consideration is the monthly line charge, because in a wireless environment there are no line charges.

21.1 Key Words

Access point
Attenuation
AUI
Bandwidth
Baseband
Broadband
Category 5
Coaxial cable
Crosstalk
Data transmission rate
Direct sequence modulation
EMI (Electromagnetic interference)
FDM
Fiber-optic
Frequency hopping
Impedance
Infrared
Laser
Laser transmission
LED (Light-emitting diode)
Microwave transmission
Mobile computing
Multiplexing
Mux: multiplexor
N-connector
Narrow-band radio transmission
Plenum-grade cable
Propagation delay
PVC cable
RG-58
RJ-45
Shield
Spread-spectrum radio transmission
STP
T-connector
TDM
Terminator
Terrestrial microwave
Thicknet
Thinnet
Transceiver
Transmission media
UTP
Vampire tap
Wireless
Wireless bridging

21.2 Selecting the Appropriate Topology for Various Token Ring and Ethernet Networks

A. Access Methods

An *access method* is a set of rules governing how the network nodes share the transmission medium. The rules for sharing among computers are similar to the rules for sharing among humans—they both boil down to a pair of fundamental philosophies: *first come, first serve* and *take turns*. These two philosophies define the two most important types of media access methods:

Access Method	Description
Contention	*Contention* means that the computers are contending for use of the transmission medium. Any computer in the network can transmit at any time (*first come, first serve*).
Token passing	The computers take turns using the transmission medium (*take turns*).

1. Contention

On contention-based networks, the nodes have equal transmission priority. Any computer can transmit at any time. When several computers attempt to transmit at the same time, a collision occurs. When a network gets extremely busy, most attempts to transmit result in collisions and little effective communication can take place.

Characteristics of Contention

The characteristics of contention are:

- **It is the most popular media access control method on LANs (used in Ethernet).**
- **It is a simple protocol that can operate with inexpensive network software and hardware.**
- **Unless traffic levels consistently exceed about 30 percent of bandwidth, contention works well.**
- **It provides good performance at low cost.**
- ***Probabilistic*: A computer's chance of being permitted to transmit cannot be predicted.**
- **Collisions occur at unpredictable intervals, and no computer is guaranteed the capability to transmit at any given time.**
- **Collisions increase in frequency as more computers use the network. When too many computers use the network, collisions dominate network traffic, and relatively few frames are transmitted on the first try.**

Mechanisms such as Ethernet's random back-off are usually put into place to minimize the effects of collisions.

- **Carrier sensing:** Each computer listens to the network before attempting to transmit. If the network is busy, the computer refrains from transmitting until the network quiets down.
- **Collision detection:** Computers continue to listen to the network as they transmit. If a computer detects another signal that interferes with the signal it's sending, it stops transmitting. Both computers then wait a random amount of time and attempt to retransmit.

Carrier detection and carrier sensing used together form the protocol used in all types of Ethernet: *Carrier Sense Multiple Access with Collision Detection (CSMA/CD).* CSMA/CD limits the size of the network to the round-trip time of its smallest data frame (2,500 meters for thicknet). At longer distances, the collision detection mechanisms don't work—a node at one end can't sense when a node at the other end is sending data until too late in the transmission for the datalink to handle the back-off and retransmission.

Apple's LocalTalk network uses the protocol *Carrier Sense Multiple Access with Collision Avoidance (CSMA/CA).* Collision avoidance uses additional techniques to further reduce the likelihood of collisions. In CSMA/CA, each computer signals a warning that says it is *about* to transmit data, and then the other computers wait for the broadcast. This increases order and reduces collisions, but it also increases the network traffic and system load.

Demand Priority

Demand priority **is an access method used with the 100-Mbps 100VG-AnyLAN standard. Although demand priority is officially considered a contention-based access method, demand priority is considerably different from the basic CSMA/CD Ethernet. In demand priority, network nodes are connected to hubs, and those hubs are connected to other hubs. Contention, therefore, occurs at the hub. (100VG-AnyLAN cables can actually send and receive data at the same time. 100VG-AnyLAN cabling uses four twisted pairs in a scheme called** ***quartet signaling.*****) Demand priority provides a mechanism for prioritizing data types.**

2. Token Passing

Token passing utilizes a frame called a *token*, which circulates around the network. A computer that needs to transmit must wait until it receives the token. When the computer is finished transmitting, it passes the token frame to the next station on the network.

Token-passing methods can use station priorities and other methods to prevent any one station from monopolizing the network. Because each computer has a chance to transmit each time the token travels around the network, each station is guaranteed a chance to transmit at some minimum time interval.

Networks That Employ Token Passing Access Control

Token Ring	The most common token-passing standard, embodied in IEEE standard 802.5
IEEE standard 802.4	Implemented infrequently; defines a bus network that also employs token passing
FDDI	A 100-Mbps fiber-optic network standard that uses token passing and rings in much the same manner as 802.5 token ring

3. Comparing Contention and Token Passing

Token passing is more appropriate than contention under the following conditions:

- **When the network is carrying time-critical data:** Because token passing results in more predictable delivery, token passing is called *deterministic.*
- **When the network experiences heavy utilization:** Token-passing networks cannot become gridlocked due to excessive numbers of collisions.
- **When some stations should have higher priority than others:** Some token-passing schemes support priority assignments.

As an access-control mechanism, token passing appears to be clearly superior to contention. You find, however, that Ethernet—by far the dominant LAN standard—has achieved its prominence while firmly wedded to contention access control.

Token passing requires a variety of complex control mechanisms for it to work well. The necessary hardware is considerably more expensive than the hardware required to implement the much simpler contention mechanisms. The higher cost of token passing networks is difficult to justify unless special features are required.

Because token-passing networks are designed for high reliability, building network diagnostics and troubleshooting capabilities into the network hardware is common. These capabilities increase the cost of token-passing networks.

Conversely, although token-passing networks perform better than contention-based networks when traffic levels are high, contention networks exhibit superior performance under lighter loading conditions. Passing the token around (and other maintenance operations) eats into the available bandwidth.

B. Physical and Logical Topologies

A topology defines the arrangement of nodes, cables, and connectivity devices that make up the network. Two basic categories form the basis for all discussions of topologies:

Physical topology	Describes the actual layout of the network transmission media
Logical topology	Describes the logical pathway a signal follows as it passes among the network nodes

The term *topology*, as used in Microsoft's test objectives for the Networking Essentials exam, applies not to the physical and logical topology archetypes describe in this section but to the complete network specifications (such as 10BASE-T or 10BASE5) described in the "Ethernet" and "Token Ring" sections of this chapter.

1. Bus Topologies

A *bus physical topology* is one in which all devices connect to a common, shared cable (sometimes called the *backbone*). This is shown in figure 21.2.1.

Figure 21.2.1 A bus physical topology.

The bus topology is ideally suited for networks that use contention-based access methods. Ethernet, the most common contention-based network architecture, typically uses a bus as its physical topology. Bus networks send all signals throughout the entire cable plant immediately.

2. Ring Topologies

Ring topologies are wired in a circle. Each device incorporates a receiver and a transmitter and serves as a repeater that passes the signal on to the next device in the ring in one direction only (see fig. 21.2.2). Because the signal is regenerated at each device, signal degeneration is low and longer distances are generally supported.

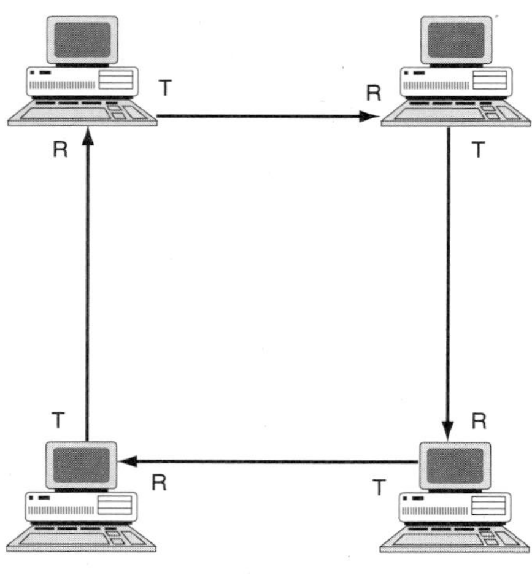

Figure 21.2.2 A ring topology.

Ring topologies are ideally suited for token-passing access methods. The token passes around the ring, and only the node that holds the token can transmit data.

Ring physical topologies are quite rare. The ring topology is almost always implemented as a logical topology. Token ring, for example—the most widespread token-passing network—always arranges the nodes in a physical star (with all nodes connecting to a central hub) but passes data in a logical ring (see fig. 21.2.3).

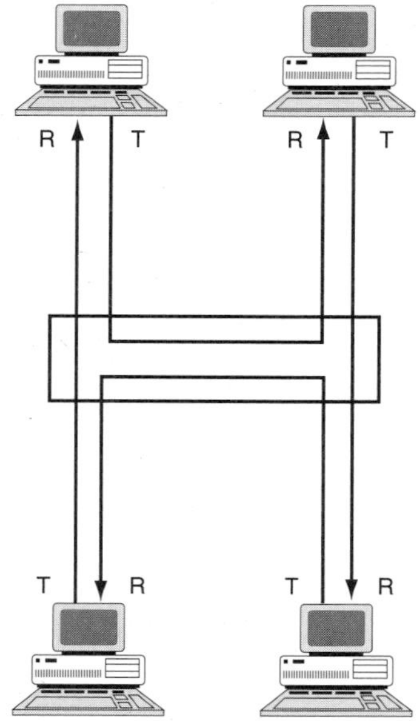

Figure 21.2.3 A logical ring configured in a physical star.

3. Star Topologies

Star topologies require that all devices connect to a central hub. The hub receives signals from other network devices and routes the signals to the proper destinations. Star hubs can be interconnected to form *tree* or *hierarchical* network topologies.

A *star physical topology* is often used to implement a bus or ring logical topology. A *star physical topology* means that the nodes are all connected to a central hub (see fig. 21.2.4). The path the data takes among the nodes and through that hub (the logical topology) depends on:

The design of the hub

The design of the cabling

The hardware and software configuration of the nodes

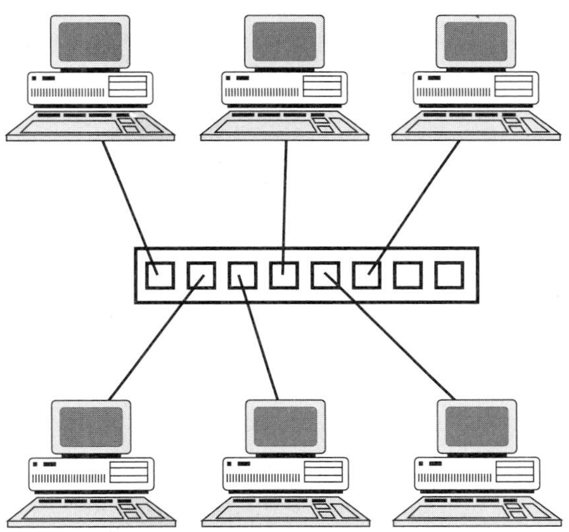

STAR

Figure 21.2.4 A star topology.

C. Ethernet Topologies

Ethernet is a very popular local area network architecture based on the CSMA/CD access method. In common usage, the term *Ethernet* refers to original Ethernet (or Ethernet II, the latest version) as well as the earlier IEEE 802.3 standards.

Ethernet networks, depending on the particular variety, typically operate at 10, 100, or 1000 Mbps using baseband transmission. Each of the IEEE 802.3 specifications specifies which cable types it supports.

The name of each Ethernet topology begins with a number (10 or 100). That number specifies the transmission speed for the network. For instance, 10Base5 is designed to operate at 10 Mbps, and 100Base-X operates at 100 Mbps.

Ethernet networks transmit data in small units called *frames*. The size of an Ethernet frame can be anywhere between 64 and 1,518 bytes. Eighteen bytes of the total size are taken up by frame overhead, such as the source and destination addresses, protocol information, and error-checking information.

Sections in a Typical Ethernet II Frame

Preamble	A field that signifies the beginning of the frame
Addresses	Source and destination addresses for the frame
Type	A field that designates the network layer protocol
Data	The data being transmitted
CRC	Cyclical Redundancy Check for error checking

Ethernet generally is used on light-to-medium traffic networks and performs best when a network's data traffic transmits in short bursts. Ethernet is the most commonly used network standard.

The 5-4-3 Rule of Thumb

The 5-4-3 rule states that the following can appear between any two nodes in the Ethernet network:

- **Up to 5 cable segments in a series**
- **Up to 4 concentrators or repeaters**
- **Up to 3 segments of cables that contain nodes (This really only applies to coaxial cables because UTP and fiber are always implemented in a point-to-point fashion.)**

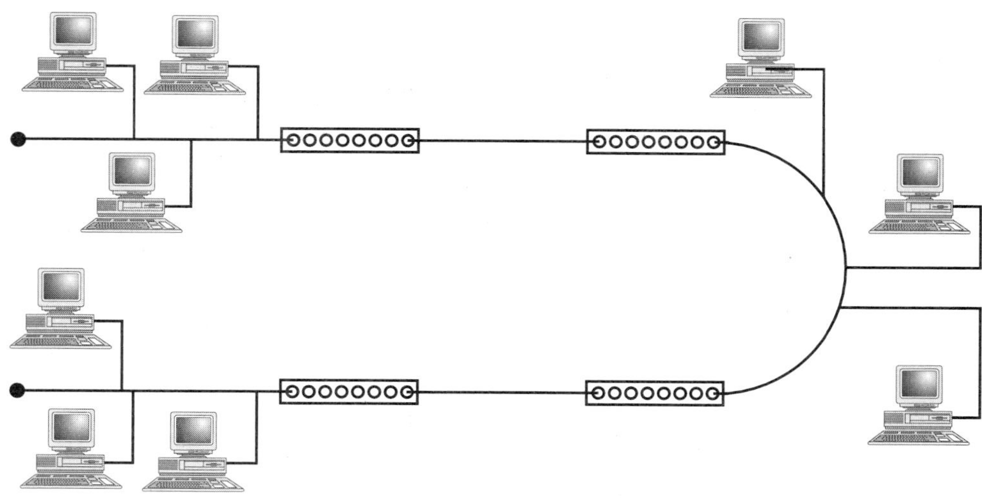

Figure 21.2.5 The 5-4-3 rule: 5 segments on a LAN, 4 repeaters, and 3 segments that contain nodes.

1. 10Base2

The 10Base2 cabling topology (Thinnet) uses the network interface card's on-board transceiver to translate the signals to and from the rest of the network (see fig. 21.2.6). Thinnet cabling uses BNC T-connectors that directly attach to the network adapter. Each end of the cable should have a terminator, and you must use a grounded terminator on one end.

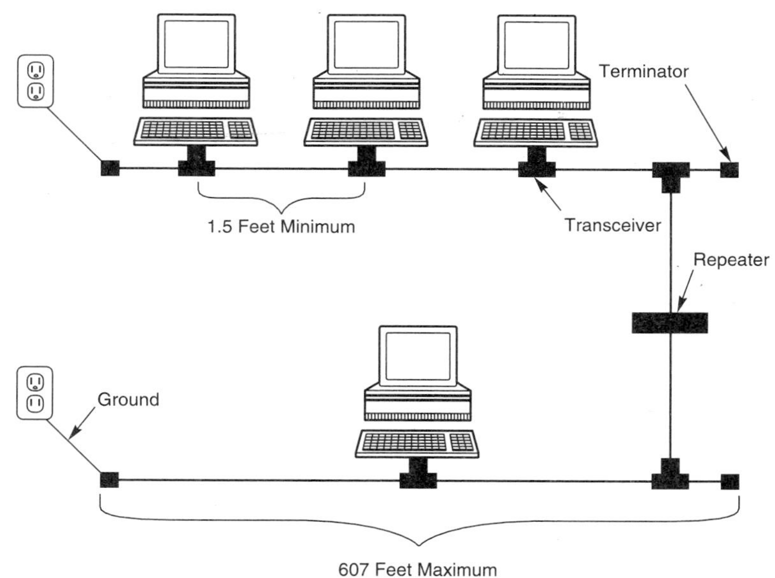

Figure 21.2.6 Two segments using 10Base2 cabling.

Reasons to use Thinnet:

- **Cost:** When any given cable segment on the network doesn't have to be run further than 185 meters (607 feet), 10Base2 is often the cheapest network cabling option.
- **Ease of installation:** 10Base2 is relatively simple to connect. Each network node connects directly to the network cable by using a T-connector attached to the network adapter.

Requirements in 10Base2 Ethernet Environments

For a successful installation, you must adhere to several rules in 10Base2 Ethernet environments:

- **The minimum cable distance between clients must be 0.5 meters (1.5 feet).**
- ***Pig tails*, also known as *drop cables*, from T-connectors shouldn't be used to connect to the BNC connector on the network adapter. The T-connector must be connected directly to the network adapter.**
- **You cannot exceed the maximum network segment limitation of 185 meters (607 feet).**
- **The entire network cabling scheme cannot exceed 925 meters (3,035 feet) in its longest path.**
- **The maximum number of nodes per network segment is 30 (this includes clients and repeaters).**
- **A 50-ohm terminator must be used on each end of the bus with only one of the terminators having either a grounding strap or a grounding wire that attaches it to the screw holding an electrical outlet cover in place.**
- **You cannot have more than five segments on a network. These segments can be connected with a maximum of four repeaters, and only three of the five segments can have network nodes. This is called the 5-4-3 rule.**

2. 10Base5

The 10Base5 cabling topology (Thicknet) uses an external transceiver to attach to the network adapter card (see fig. 21.2.7). The external transceiver clamps to the Thicknet cable. An Attachment Universal Interface (AUI) cable runs from the transceiver to a DIX connector on the back of the network adapter card. As with Thinnet, each network segment must be terminated at both ends, with one end using a grounded terminator (see fig. 21.2.8).

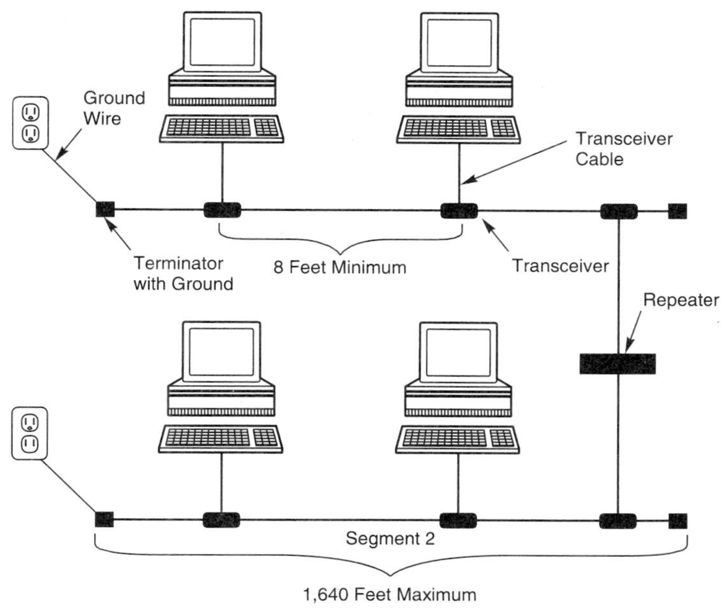

Figure 21.2.7 Two segments using 10Base5 cabling.

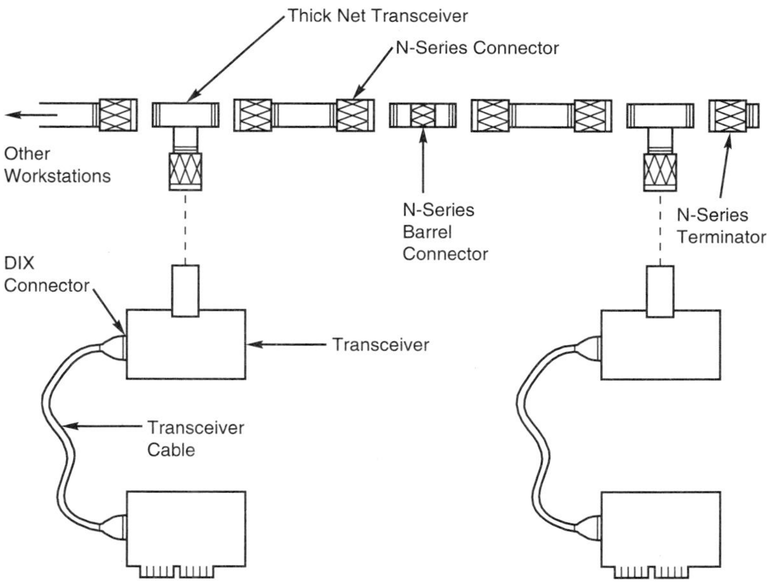

Figure 21.2.8 Components of a Thicknet network.

The primary advantage of 10Base5 is its capability to exceed the cable restrictions that apply to 10Base2. 10Base5 does pose restrictions of its own, however, which you should consider when installing or troubleshooting a 10Base5 network.

Requirements in 10Base5 Networks

As with 10Base2 networks, the first consideration when troubleshooting a 10Base5 network should be the established cabling rules and guidelines. Along with the 5-4-3 rule, you must follow several additional guidelines when configuring Thicknet networks, such as:

- **The minimum cable distance between transceivers is 2.5 meters (8 feet).**
- **Transceivers must be installed only at multiples of 2.5 meters. (Thicknet has marks on it every 2.5 meters to make compliance with this easy.)**
- **You cannot go beyond the maximum network segment length of 500 meters (1,640 feet).**
- **The entire network cabling scheme cannot exceed 2,500 meters (8,200 feet).**
- **One end of the terminated network segment must be grounded.**
- **Drop cables (transceiver cables) can be as short as required but cannot be longer than 50 meters from transceiver to computer.**
- **The maximum number of nodes per network segment is 100. (This includes all repeaters.)**

The length of the drop cables (from the transceiver to the computer) is not included in measurements of the network segment length and total network length.

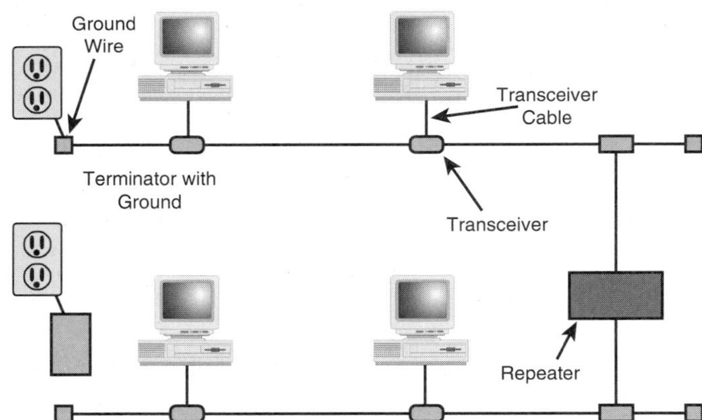

Figure 21.2.9 Two segments using Thicknet and the appropriate hardware.

3. 10Base-T

The trend in wiring Ethernet networks is to use unshielded twisted-pair (UTP) cable. 10Base-T, which uses UTP cable, is one of the most popular implementations for Ethernet. It is based on the IEEE 802.3 standard. 10Base-T supports a data rate of 10 Mbps using baseband transmission.

10Base-T cabling is wired in a star topology (see fig. 21.2.10). The nodes are wired to a central hub, which serves as a multiport repeater. A 10Base-T network functions logically as a linear bus. The hub repeats the signal to all nodes, and the nodes contend for access to the transmission medium as if they were connected along a linear bus. The cable uses 8 pin modular (RJ-45 type) connectors, and network adapter cards often have an RJ-45 type jack built into the back of the card.

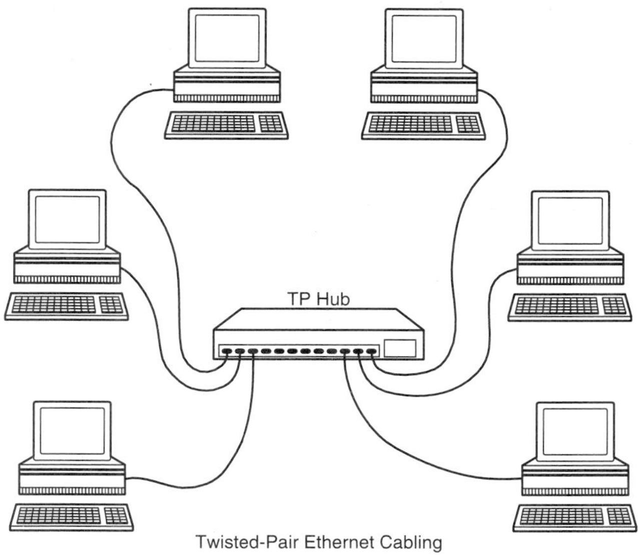

Figure 21.2.10 A 10Base-T network.

10Base-T segments can be connected by using coaxial or fiber-optic backbone segments. Some hubs provide connectors for Thinnet and Thicknet cables (in addition to 10Base-T UTP-type connectors).

By attaching a 10Base-T transceiver to the AUI port of the network adapter, you can use a computer setup for Thicknet on a 10Base-T network.

The star wiring of 10Base-T provides several advantages, particularly in larger networks:

- **The network is more reliable and easier to manage:** 10Base-T networks use a *concentrator* (a centralized wiring hub). These hubs are "intelligent" in that they can detect defective cable segments and shut them down.
- **You can design and build your LAN one segment at a time:** This capability makes 10Base-T more flexible than other LAN cabling options.
- **10Base-T is also relatively inexpensive to use:** In some cases, existing data-grade phone cable can be used for the LAN.
- **Star-based networks are significantly easier to troubleshoot and repair than bus-wired networks:** With a star network, a problem node can be easily isolated from the rest of the network.

Requirements for a 10Base-T Network

The requirements for a 10Base-T network are:

- **The maximum number of computers on a single collision domain is 1,024. (Practical considerations such as traffic volume usually keep it to a much smaller number.)**
- **The cabling should be UTP Category 3, 4, or 5.**
- **The maximum unshielded cable segment length (hub to transceiver) is 100 meters (328 feet).**

4. 10Base-FL

10Base-FL is a specification for Ethernet over fiber-optic cables. The 10Base-FL specification calls for a 10 Mbps data rate using baseband.

The most important advantages of 10Base-FL are:

Long cabling runs (10Base-FL supports a maximum cabling distance of about 2,000 meters)

The elimination of any potential electrical complications

5. 100VG-AnyLAN

100VG-AnyLAN is defined in the IEEE 802.12 standard. *IEEE 802.12* is a standard for transmitting Ethernet and token ring packets (IEEE 802.3 and 802.5) at 100 Mbps. 100VG-AnyLAN is sometimes called 100Base-VG. The "VG" in the name stands for voice grade.

100VG-AnyLAN's demand priority access method provides for two priority levels when resolving media access conflicts.

100VG-AnyLAN uses a *cascaded star* topology, which calls for a hierarchy of hubs (see fig. 21.2.11). Computers are attached to *child hubs*, and the child hubs are connected to higher-level hubs called *parent hubs*.

The maximum length for the two longest cables attached to a 100VG-AnyLAN hub is 250 meters (820 ft). The specified cabling is Category 3,4, or 5 twisted pair or fiber optic. 100VG-AnyLAN is compatible with 10Base-T cabling.

Both 100VG-AnyLAN and 100Base-X can be installed as a plug-and-play upgrade to a 10Base-T system.

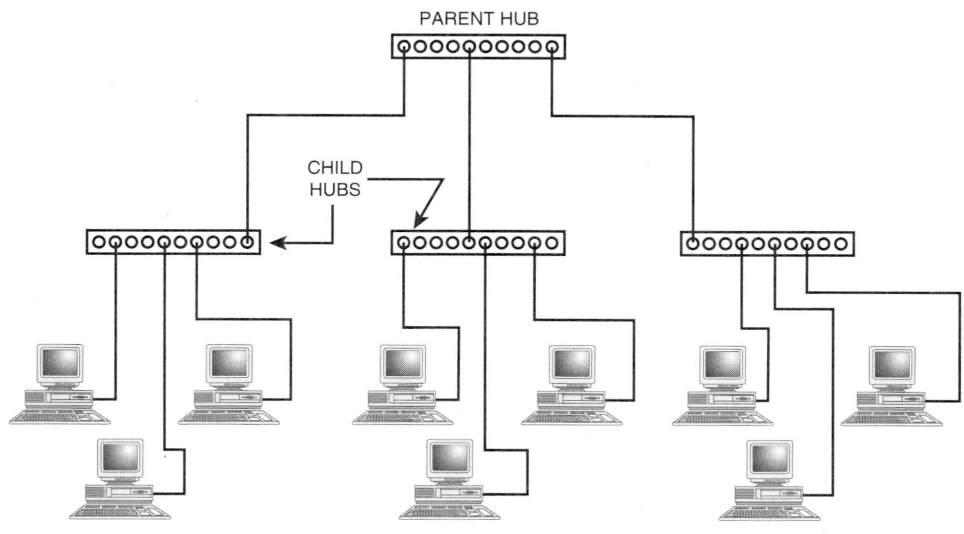

Figure 21.2.11 A cascaded star topology.

6. 100Base-X

100Base-X uses a star bus topology similar to 10Base-T's. 100Base-X provides a data transmission speed of 100 Mbps using baseband.

Cabling Specifications for the 100Base-X Standard

100Base-TX	Two twisted pairs of Category 5 UTP or STP
100Base-FX	Fiber-optic cabling using 2-strand cable
100Base-T4	Four twisted pairs of Category 3, 4, or 5 UTP

100Base-X is sometimes referred to as *Fast Ethernet.* Like 100VG-AnyLAN, 100Base-X provides compatibility with existing 10Base-T systems (that were properly cabled) and thus enables plug-and-play upgrades from 10Base-T.

D. Token Ring

Token ring uses a token-passing architecture that adheres to the IEEE 802.5 standard. The topology is always physically a star, but token ring uses a logical ring to pass the token from station to station. Each node must be attached to a concentrator called a *multistation access unit (MSAU or MAU).* The MSAU is used to bypass token ring stations that are not active.

Although 4-Mbps token ring network interface cards can run only at that data rate, 16-Mbps cards can be configured to run at 4 or 16 Mbps. All cards on a given ring must run at the same rate.

Each node acts as a repeater that receives tokens and data frames from its *Nearest Active Upstream Neighbor* (NAUN). After the node processes a frame, the frame transmits it downstream to the next attached node (see fig. 21.2.12). Each frame makes one trip around the entire ring and then returns to the originating node, which removes it from the ring and releases the token. Workstations that detect problems send a *beacon* to identify the fault domain of the potential failure.

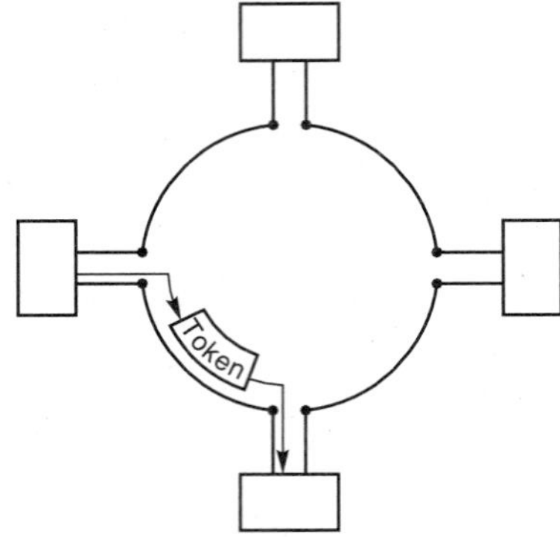

Figure 21.2.12 Operation of a token ring.

1. Token Ring Cabling

Traditional token ring networks use twisted-pair cable. The following is a list of standard components and cables used in token ring networks:

- **Type 1**

  A braided shield surrounds two twisted pairs of solid copper wire.

  Type 1 is used to connect terminals and distribution panels or to connect between different wiring closets that are located in the same building.

  It uses two STPs of solid-core 22 AWG wire for long, high data-grade transmissions within the building's walls.

  It is the most popular transmission medium for token ring.

  A token ring network using Type 1 STP cabling can support up to 260 computers.

- **Type 2**

  Type 2 uses a total of six twisted pairs: two are STPs (for networking) and four are UTPs (for telephone systems).

  It is used for the same purposes as Type 1, but enables both voice and data cables to be included in a single cable run.

- **Type 3**

  Type 3 is used as an alternative to Type 1 and Type 2 cable because of its reduced cost.

  It has unshielded twisted-pair copper with a minimum of two twists per inch.

It has four UTPs of 22 or 24 AWG solid-core wire for networks or telephone systems.

It cannot be used for 16-Mbps token ring networks.

Type 3 is used primarily for long, low data-grade transmissions within walls. Signals don't travel as fast as with Type 1 cable because of the lack of shielding.

The maximum cabling distance (according to IBM) is 45 meters (about 148 feet). Some vendors specify cabling distances of up to 150 meters (500 feet).

Type 3 uses RJ-11 or RJ-45 connectors. (Media filters, if necessary, can convert the network adapter to RJ-11 or RJ-45 format.)

- **Patch cable**

  Patch cable connects MSAUs.

  Typically IBM Type 6 cables come in standard lengths of 8, 30, 75, or 150 feet. (A Type 6 cable consists of two shielded 26-AWG twisted-pairs.) You can also get patch cables in custom lengths.

  It is used to extend the length of Type 3 cables or to connect computers to MSAUs.

  You need to have an IBM connector at each end.

- **Adapter cable**

  You should have an IBM data connector at one end and a nine-pin connector at the other end.

  You can connect client and server network adapters to other network components that use IBM data connectors.

- **MSAU**

  MSAU is a central cabling component for IBM Token Ring networks.

- **8228 MSAU**

  This is the original wiring hub developed by IBM for Token Ring networks.

  Each 8228 has 10 connectors, eight of which accept cables to clients or servers.

  RI (ring in) and RO (ring out) connectors are used to connect multiple 8228s to form larger networks.

  It has mechanical devices that consist of relays and connectors. Their purpose is to switch clients in and out of the network.

  Each port is controlled by a relay powered by a voltage sent to the MSAU from the client.

  When an 8228 is first set up, each of these relays must be initialized with the setup tool that is shipped with the unit.

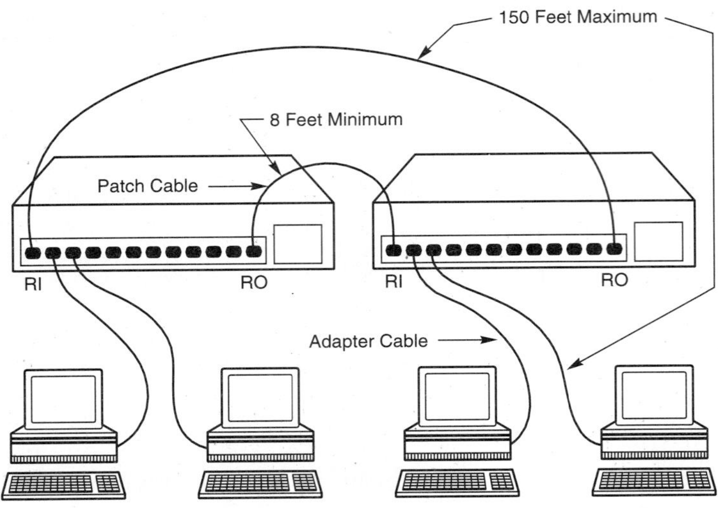

Figure 21.2.13 An example of a network cabling several clients and MSAUs. The distances noted are based on the rules for the small movable cabling system.

> **When you connect a token ring network, make sure you:**
>
> 1. **Initialize each port in the 8228 MSAU by using the setup tool shipped with the MSAU.**
> 2. **If you're using more than one MSAU, connect the RO port of each MSAU with the RI port of the next MSAU in the loop. Complete the loop so that the MSAUs form a circle or ring.**

2. Passing Data on Token Rings

A frame called a *token* perpetually circulates around a token ring. The computer that holds the token has control of the transmission medium.

The actual process of passing data on a token ring is as follows:

1. The Active Monitor generates the token.
2. A computer in the ring captures the token.
3. If the computer has data to transmit, it holds the token and transmits a data frame. A token ring data frame contains the fields listed in table 21.2.1.
4. Each computer in the ring checks to see if it is the intended recipient of the frame.
5. When the frame reaches the destination address, the destination PC copies the frame to a receive buffer, updates the frame status field of the data frame (see step 2), and puts the frame back on the ring.
6. When the computer that originally sent the frame receives it from the ring, it acknowledges a successful transmission, takes the frame off the ring, and places the token back on the ring.

Table 21.2.1 Token Ring Data Frame Fields

Field	Description
Start delimiter	Marks the start of the frame
Access control	Specifies the priority of the frame; also specifies whether the frame is a token or a data frame
Frame control	Media Access Control information
Destination address	Address of receiving computer
Source address	Address of sending computer
Data	Data being transmitted
Frame check sequence	Error-checking information (CRC)
End delimiter	Marks the end of the frame
Frame status	Tells whether the destination address was located and whether the frame was recognized

3. The Beaconing Process

Beaconing is the strategy token ring networks use to auto-configure themselves and to resolve soft errors (ones that don't require administrator intervention).

The first station that is powered-up on a token ring network automatically becomes what is called the *active monitor station.* The primary responsibility of the active monitor station is to generate the token and to detect if the token gets lost. Any time the token is lost, the active monitor generates a new token.

The active monitor also sends out an Active Monitor Present frame every seven seconds, which starts the *Neighbor Notification process.* The Neighbor Notification process tells each station its Nearest Active Upstream Neighbor (NAUN). After each station announces itself to its next active downstream neighbor, the announcing station becomes the nearest active upstream neighbor (NAUN) to the downstream station (see fig. 21.2.14).

21

If a station detects a ring configuration change or an error, or doesn't receive one of its expected seven-second announcements from its upstream neighbor, it attempts to notify the network of the lack of contact from the upstream neighbor. It sends a message out onto the network ring, which includes:

The sending station's network address

The receiving NAUN's network address

The beacon type

From this information, the stations on the ring can determine which station might be having a problem and then can attempt to fix the problem without disrupting the entire network. This process is known as *autoreconfiguration*. If autoreconfiguration proves unsuccessful, manual correction becomes necessary.

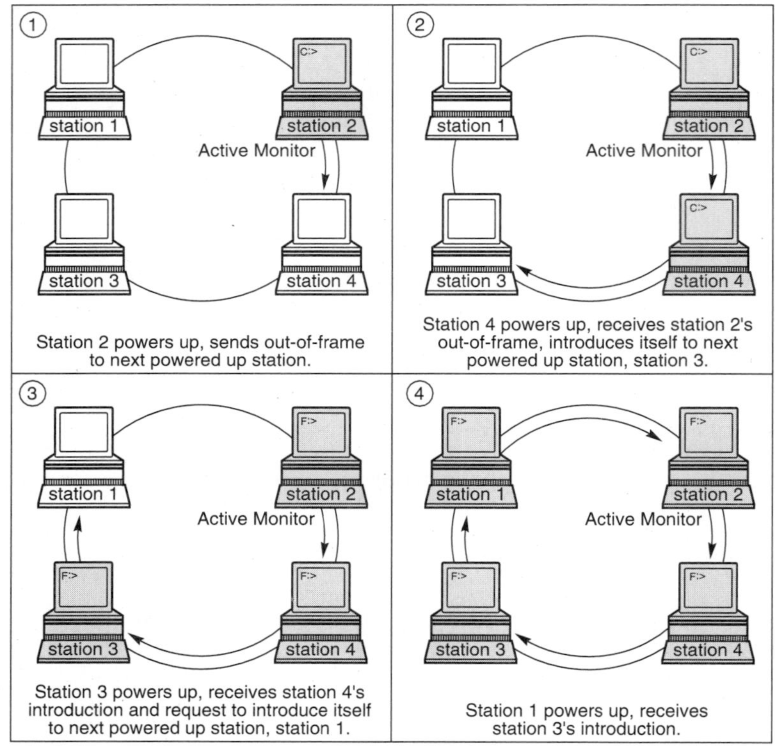

Figure 21.2.14 A token ring network utilizing the beaconing process.

21.2.1 Exercise

Go online and use a web browser to read through the Ethernet Home Page maintained by Charles Spurgeon at http://wwwhost.ots.utexas.edu/ethernet/ethernet-home.html and the Token Ring Design Rules from South Hills Datacom at http://jmazza.shillsdata.com/tech/tr/design_rules.

21.2 Practice Problems

1. In a CSMA/CD network, access to the transmission medium is:

   A. Deterministic

   B. Unlikely

   C. Always available to all stations

   D. Probabilistic

2. A difference between the contention-based and the token-passing access methods is that:

   A. Contention-based networks can run efficiently at very high utilization.

   B. Token-passing networks can run efficiently at very high utilization.

   C. A station can begin transmitting at any time on a contention based network.

   D. Token-passing networks are always faster than contention based networks.

3. The most common access method used is:

   A. Contention based

   B. Token passing

   C. Logical bus

   D. Physical star

4. Token passing is a _______ access method.

   A. CSMA/CD

   B. Simple to implement

   C. Primitive

   D. Deterministic

5. Under light loads, contention-based networks:

   A. Are more efficient than token passing networks

   B. Are less efficient than token passing networks

   C. Have many collisions

   D. Perform poorly with typical office applications

6. Under heavy traffic loads, token passing networks:

   A. Perform worse than contention based networks

   B. Perform better than contention based networks

   C. Have many collisions

   D. Stop exhibiting deterministic behavior

7. Ring topologies are usually implemented:

   A. As a star-wired physical bus

   B. As a physical ring, with one end station directly connected to other end stations

   C. As a physical star, but a logical ring

   D. As a logical bus, but wired as a physical star

8. Star topologies can be used with (choose two):

   A. Logical busses

   B. Physical busses

   C. Logical rings

   D. Physical rings

9. A central hub is required when using:
   A. A contention-based access method
   B. A token-passing access method
   C. A physical ring
   D. A physical star

10. Wiring your building in a physical star enables you to support (select all correct answers):
    A. networks that use a logical bus
    B. networks that use a logical ring
    C. networks that use CSMA/CD
    D. networks that use token passing

11. In an Ethernet network, access to the transmission medium is:
    A. Deterministic
    B. Unlikely
    C. Always available to all stations
    D. Probabilistic

12. You have a small office with four computers you want to connect together. None of the computers are more than 50 feet from the others. What type of network will be least expensive to install?
    A. Ethernet using 100Base-TX
    B. Ethernet using 10Base5
    C. Ethernet using 10Base2
    D. Ethernet using 10Base-T

13. You need to connect two Ethernet repeaters that are 200 meters apart. An appropriate cable choice would be:
    A. Thinnet
    B. Thicknet
    C. 10Base-T
    D. Unshielded Twisted Pair (UTP)

14. You are designing the Ethernet network for a new office building that will hold several hundred computer users on several floors. What type of Ethernet should you use to minimize your total cost of ownership?
    A. 10Base5 (Thicknet)
    B. 10Base2 (Thinnet)
    C. 10Base-F (fiber-optic)
    D. 10Base-T (UTP)

15. Your office is very dynamic, with existing users needing to move their computers frequently. Which type of Ethernet best accommodates this environment?
    A. 10Base5 (Thicknet)
    B. 10Base2 (Thinnet)
    C. 10Base-F (fiber-optic)
    D. 10Base-T (UTP)

16. You are moving into a new building, where the previous tenant had used Category 3 data-grade wiring for the telephone system. What type of Ethernet enables you to reuse that cabling for your network?
    A. 10Base5 (Thicknet)
    B. 10Base2 (Thinnet)
    C. 10Base-F (fiber-optic)
    D. 10Base-T (UTP)

17. You need to design a new network for a client who is concerned that they might need to upgrade from a 10 Mbps network to a 100 Mbps network. What type of Ethernet would you recommend they install?
    A. 10Base5 (Thicknet)
    B. 10Base2 (Thinnet)
    C. 10Base-F (fiber-optic)
    D. 10Base-T (UTP)

18. You need to connect offices on both sides of a very large manufacturing facility to an Ethernet network. The cable will have to pass some very electrically noisy devices, and will have to be over 500 meters long. What type of Ethernet would you recommend be installed for the connection between the two offices?

    A. 10Base5 (Thicknet)

    B. 10Base2 (Thinnet)

    C. 10Base-F (fiber-optic)

    D. 10Base-T (UTP)

19. What type of Ethernet is an easy upgrade from 10Base-T if you have Category 5 wiring installed?

    A. 10Base5

    B. 100Base-TX

    C. 100Base-T4

    D. 100Base-FX

20. You are called in to troubleshoot a coax-based Ethernet network. You see that they have four repeaters in the network data path between some stations. This:

    A. Will always create problems

    B. Always breaks the 5-4-3 rule

    C. May break the 5-4-3 rule if there are computers on more than three segments

    D. Is never a problem

21. All token ring networks must use which of the following physical topology layouts?

    A. Bus

    B. Hybrid

    C. Star

    D. Ring

22. The MAU serves what purpose?

    A. A means of generating a token

    B. Letting stations join and leave the network

    C. Initiating NIC tests when no one claims the token

    D. All of the above

23. Standard token ring speeds are:

    A. 10 and 100 Mbps

    B. 1 and 4 Mbps

    C. 4 and 16 Mbps

    D. 16 and 32 Mbps

24. A signal on a token ring network indicating a problem is called:

    A. A beacon

    B. A warning

    C. A network failure frame

    D. A broadcast frame

25. What port of a token ring MAU is connected to what port on a second MAU?

    A. RO to RI

    B. RO to RO

    C. RI to RI

    D. Master to slave

26. How many computers can be used on the same ring when using IBM type 1 cabling and 8228 MSAUs?

    A. None, this is an illegal configuration

    B. 72

    C. 128

    D. 260

27. How many computers can be used on the same ring when using IBM type 1 cabling and 8228 MSAUs?

    A. None, this is an illegal configuration

    B. 72

    C. 128

    D. 260

28. What is the primary duty of the Active Monitor in a token ring network?

    A. To monitor the (T_ANYTOKEN) timer

    B. To generate the token for the ring

    C. To notify each station when it is that station's turn to transmit

    D. To remove faulty computers from the network

29. On token rings, beacons happen:

    A. Whenever a station sends a frame

    B. Every seven seconds

    C. When a station joins or leaves a ring

    D. Only when there is a hard error requiring administrator intervention

30. Token ring uses an access arbitration method that can be considered:

    A. Deterministic

    B. Stochastic

    C. Probabilistic

    D. Simple

21.2 Answers and Explanations: Practice Problems

1. **D** In a CSMA/CD network, access to the network is probabilistic because any station can transmit any time, and overlapping transmissions are handled by making the stations perform a random back-off before retransmitting.

2. **B** Token-passing networks can run much more efficiently at very high utilization because the access method they use doesn't degrade under heavy loads the way contention based networks do.

3. **A** The most common network access method is Ethernet, which is contention-based (CSMA/CD).

4. **D** Token passing is a deterministic network access method because each station is guaranteed an opportunity to transmit in its turn.

5. **A** Under light network traffic loads, contention-based networks are more efficient than token-passing networks because the contention-based networks don't have all the overhead associated with token passing and maintenance.

6. **B** Under heavy traffic loads, token-passing networks typically perform better than contention-based networks because they do not use any more bandwidth arbitrating access with a heavy load than they do with a light load.

7. **C** Most ring topologies are implemented as a physical star, but as a logical ring. Token ring is the best example of this.

8. **A, C** Both logical bus topologies and logical ring topologies are frequently implemented using a physical star topology.

9. **D** A hub is required when using a physical star topology, in which all the cables in the star connect to the hub.

10. **A, B, C, D** Star wiring (with high-grade UTP) is generally the preferred way of cabling buildings for networks because it offers the most flexibility.

11. **A** Ethernet networks guarantee access to the transmission medium via a probabilistic scheme. Stations do not always have access to begin transmitting because they may sense another station is already transmitting (the Carrier Sense part of CSMA/CD).

12. **C** Ethernet using 10Base2 is the least expensive cabling option to install for small networks (in which the total cable length is under 185 meters) because it only needs one relatively inexpensive cable and no repeaters or hubs.

13. **B** Thicknet is the only choice listed that would work for Ethernet at 200 meters. STP is not standardized for Ethernet, and both Thinnet and 10Base-T are limited to less than 200 meters.

14. **D** The star wiring that 10Base-T uses is inexpensive and much easier to troubleshoot and maintain than coaxial wiring like Thicknet or Thinnet.

15. **D** 10Base-T (UTP) is the best choice when computers move frequently because a single cable can be moved without affecting other users.

16. **D** 10Base-T is compatible with Categories 3, 4, and 5 of unshielded twisted-pair (UTP) wiring.

17. **D** 10Base-T is clearly the best choice here because the same cable plant can be used if they need to migrate to 100Base-T, 10Base-T is much less expensive than 10Base-F, and many newer networking devices can support both 10 Mbps and 100 Mbps speeds.

18. **C** 10Base-F using fiber-optic cable supports distances of up to 2,000 meters and is completely resistant to electrical noise.

19. **B** 100Base-TX and 10BASE-T can both use Category 5 copper wiring, and 100Base-TX is 10 times faster than 10Base-T.

20. **C** The 5-4-3 rule only allows four repeaters in the path if there are computers on no more than three of the cable segments.

21. **C** All token ring networks use a star physical topology even though they have a ring logical topology.

22. **B** The MSAU enables stations to join and leave the network dynamically. The stations themselves are responsible for the token.

23. **C** Standard token ring networks operate at either 4 Mbps or 16 Mbps. All stations on the same ring must be configured for the same speed.

24. **A** Stations begin to beacon when they detect a problem or certain types of changes in the network.

25. **A** When connecting two token ring MSAUs, the Ring Out (RO) of one always goes to the Ring In (RI) of the other.

26. **D** The classic IBM design using model 8228 MSAUs and type 1 STP cabling supports up to 260 computers on a ring.

27. **B** The classic IBM design using model 8228 MSAUs and type 3 UTP cabling supports up to 72 computers on a ring.

28. **B** The primary job of the active monitor is to generate the token for the ring.

29. **C** One of the common causes for self-correcting beacons is a station joining or leaving the ring.

30. **A** Because each station gets a turn to transmit when the token arrives, token rings are considered deterministic.

21.2 Key Words

Beacon	MAU
Bus	MSAU
Carrier detection	Patch cable
Carrier sensing	Physical topology
Contention	Repeater
CRC	RI
CSMA/CA	Ring
CSMA/CD	RO
Ethernet	Star
Frame	Token
IEEE standard	Token ring
Logical topology	Topology

21.3 Selecting the Appropriate Network and Transport Protocols for Various Token Ring and Ethernet Networks

Protocols include:

- DLC
- AppleTalk
- IPX
- TCP/IP
- NFS
- SMB

A. Transport Protocols

The *OSI reference model* is a standard describing the activities at each level of a protocol stack. The OSI reference model is useful primarily as a conceptual tool for understanding protocol layering. Although some protocols have been designed in strict conformance with the OSI reference model, full OSI compliance hasn't become popular.

Protocols are real implementations of the conceptual rules defined in the OSI reference model. Some protocols and protocol suites existed before the OSI reference model was published and can be matched only very loosely to the seven-layer model.

1. Packets and Protocols

Protocols describe the way in which network data is encapsulated in packets on the source end, sent via the network to a destination and then reconstructed at the destination into the appropriate file, instruction, or request. Breaking network data into packet-sized chunks provides smoother throughput because the small packets don't tie up the transmission medium as a larger unit of data might. Also, packets simplify the task of error detection and correction. Each file is checked separately for errors, and if an error is discovered, only that packet (instead of a whole file) must be retransmitted.

Table 21.3.1 Parts of a Packet[1]

Part	Function
Header	The header signifies the start of the packet and contains a bundle of important parameters, such as the source and destination address and time/synchronization information.
Data	This portion of the packet contains the original data being transmitted.
Trailer	The trailer marks the end of the packet and typically contains error-checking (Cyclical Redundancy Check, or CRC) information.

1. The exact composition of a network packet depends on the protocols you're using.

As the data passes down through the protocol layers, each layer performs its prescribed function, such as interfacing with an application, converting the data format, or adding addressing and error-checking parameters. Actual protocol stacks don't often comply exactly with the OSI model—some, in fact, predate the OSI model—but the concepts and terminology used in the OSI model are nevertheless useful for describing protocol functions.

When the packet reaches the transmission medium, the network adapter cards of all computers on the network segment examine the packet, checking the packet's destination address (see fig. 21.3.1). If the destination address matches the computer's hardware address, the network adapter interrupts the processor, and the protocol layers of the destination system process the incoming packet.

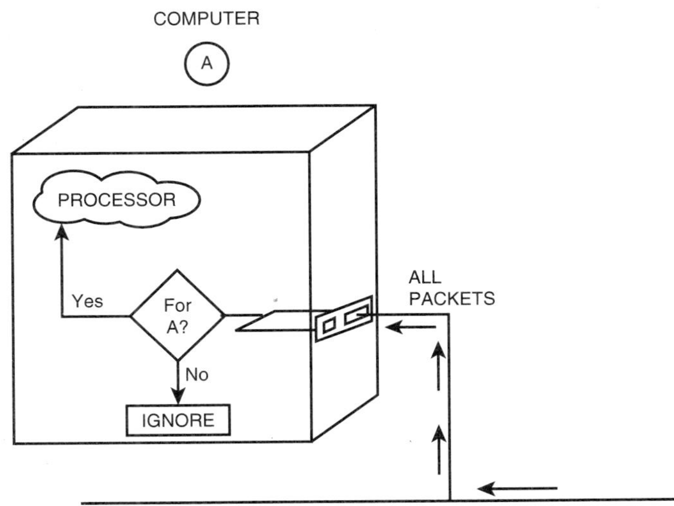

Figure 21.3.1 The network adapter card checks whether the packet's destination address matches the PC's address.

2. Protocols and Protocol Layers

Many of the addressing, error-checking, retransmission, and acknowledgment services most commonly associated with networking take place at the Network and Transport OSI layers. Protocol suites are often referred to by the suite's Transport and Network protocols. In TCP/IP, for instance, TCP is a Transport Layer protocol and IP is a Network Layer protocol. (Note, however, that TCP/IP predates OSI and diverges from OSI in a number of ways.)

IPX/SPX is another protocol suite known by its Transport and Network Layer protocols, but the order of the protocols is backward from the way the protocols are listed in TCP/IP. IPX is the Network Layer protocol; SPX is the Transport Layer protocol.

The lower Data Link and Physical Layers provide a hardware-specific foundation, addressing items such as the network adapter driver, the media access method, and the transmission medium. Transport and Network Layer protocols, such as TCP/IP and IPX/SPX, rest on that

Physical and Data Link Layer foundation. With the help of the NDIS and ODI standards, multiple protocol stacks can operate simultaneously through a single network adapter.

Upper-level protocols provide compatibility with a particular networking environment. For instance, *NetBIOS over TCP/IP* (sometimes called NBT) provides Microsoft clients with full connectivity over TCP/IP.

Table 21.3.2 Common Transport and Network Layer Protocols

TCP/IP	A standards-based networking protocol defined by the IETF in a series of RFCs. It is the protocol used on the Internet and the one that everything seems to be moving toward.
IPX/SPX	A protocol defined by Novell for use with its NetWare servers, but now used by other devices and companies. It is less popular than TCP/IP and is derived from Xerox's XNS.
NWLink	Microsoft's version of the IPX/SPX protocol essentially spans the Transport and Network Layers.
NetBEUI	Designed for Microsoft networks, NetBEUI includes functions at the Network and Transport Layers. NetBEUI isn't routable and therefore doesn't make full use of Network Layer capabilities.
AppleTalk Transaction Protocol (ATP) and Name Binding Protocol (NBP)	ATP and NBP are AppleTalk Transport Layer protocols.
Datagram Delivery Protocol (DDP)	DDP is the AppleTalk Network Layer protocol.

B. Windows NT Networking

In the Windows NT networking structure, it is the NDIS interface, NDIS wrapper, and NDIS-compatible drivers that enable the TCP/IP, NWLink, NetBEUI, AppleTalk, and DLC protocols to interact simultaneously with the lower layers (see fig. 21.3.2).

The Transport Driver Interface (TDI) is an interface that enables the server, redirector, and file system drivers to remain independent of the transport protocol.

Windows NT (like other Microsoft operating systems such as Windows for Workgroups and Windows 95) services client requests by using the Server Message Block (SMB) protocol. *SMB* is an Application Layer protocol primarily used for file and print sharing.

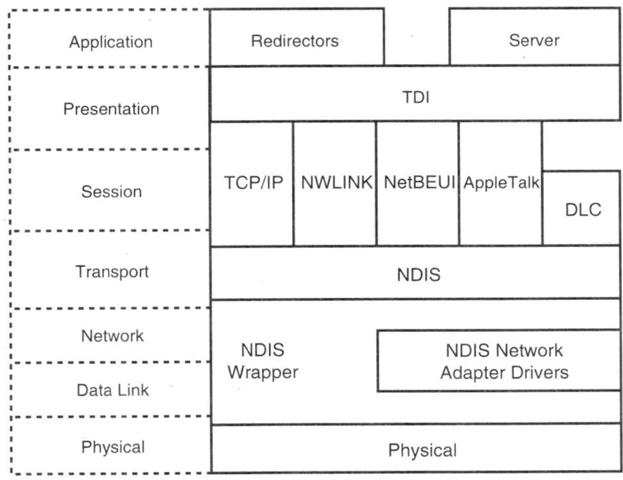

Figure 21.3.2 Microsoft Windows NT networking architecture.

Three stages must take place before a protocol is useful:

1. **A model describes the general function of the protocol.**
2. **The protocol is defined in complete detail.**
3. **The protocol must be realized by software and hardware designers in real products.**

Consider the process of designing a building. The architect first produces sketches that describe the general nature of the building. Then the architect, possibly working with a specialist in particular building trades, develops blueprints that describe every detail of the building. Finally, an actual building is constructed.

C. Internet Protocols (TCP/IP)

The Internet protocol suite (also commonly called the TCP/IP protocol suite) was originally developed by the United States Department of Defense to provide robust service on large internetworks that incorporate a variety of computer types.

In recent years, the Internet protocols have become increasingly popular and constitute the most popular network protocols. Two reasons for this popularity are:

- **No one vendor owns TCP/IP:** TCP/IP evolved in response to input from a wide variety of industry sources. Consequently, TCP/IP is the most open of the protocol suites and is supported by the widest variety of vendors. Virtually every brand of computing equipment now supports TCP/IP.
- **Early availability on Unix:** The protocols were built into the Berkeley Standard Distribution (BSD) Unix implementation. Since then, TCP/IP has achieved universal acceptance in the Unix community and is a standard feature on all versions of Unix.

TCP/IP doesn't include protocols for the Data Link or Physical Layers (see fig.21.3.3). It was designed to work over established standards such as Ethernet. Over time, TCP/IP has been interfaced to the majority of Data Link and Physical Layer technologies.

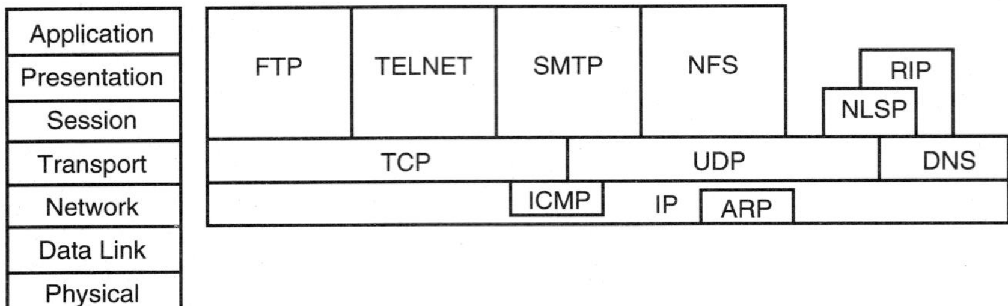

Figure 21.3.3 The relationship of the protocols in the Internet suite to the layers of the OSI reference model.

Table 21.3.3 The Relationship Between Layers of Department of Defense Model and OSI Model

Department of Defense	OSI	Significance
Network Access	Data Link, Physical	Enables the DoD protocols to coexist with existing Data Link and Physical Layer standards
Internet	Network	Moves data between devices on networks
Host-to-Host	Transport	Enables peer communication between hosts on the internetwork
Process/ Application	Session, Presentation, and Application	Provides network services

One huge advantage of TCP/IP is that TCP/IP is required for communication over the Internet. The biggest disadvantage is that it is usually considered harder to manage because the network administrator has to manage network addresses carefully and beware of the possibility of conflicts.

Table 21.3.4 Protocols Associated with TCP/IP Relevant to Microsoft's Networking Essentials Test

Protocol	Description
Internet Protocol (IP)	A connectionless protocol that provides datagram service at the OSI Network Layer. IP is primarily responsible for addressing.
Routing Information Protocol (RIP)	Not the same protocol as RIP in the NetWare suite, although the two serve similar functions and operate in basically the same way. IP RIP performs route discovery by using a distance-vector method, calculating the number of hops that must be crossed to route a packet by a particular path. Each router running RIP broadcasts all the routes it knows about and the hop count it uses for each one to all of its neighbors.

Protocol	Description
Open Shortest Path First (OSPF)	A link-state routing protocol that is designed to overcome the limitations of RIP. OSPF's primary advantages over RIP are that it learns about changes in the network much faster and that it consumes less bandwidth for overhead.
Transmission Control Protocol (TCP)	An internetwork protocol that corresponds to the OSI Transport Layer. TCP provides a reliable Transport Layer for connections. TCP and UDP operate at the same layer.
User Datagram Protocol (UDP)	A connectionless Transport (host-to-host) Layer protocol. UDP does not provide message acknowledgments or error correction; rather, it simply transports datagrams.
Address Resolution Protocol (ARP)	Given an IP address, the Address Resolution Protocol (ARP) can determine the data link address (MAC layer address) to use for packets destined to that station.
Domain Name System (DNS)	Provides name and address resolution as a service to client applications. DNS servers enable humans to use logical node names instead of IP addresses to access network resources.
File Transfer TCP/IP hosts	Enables users to transfer files between Protocol (FTP) by supporting a request/response structure that is independent of specific operating systems.
Simple Mail Transfer Protocol (SMTP)	Used for transferring electronic mail through TCP/IP internetworks. SMTP doesn't provide a mail interface for the user, just one between systems.
Telnet	A terminal emulation application and protocol. Telnet enables PCs and workstations to function as dumb terminals in sessions with host systems on internetworks.
Network File System (NFS)	A family of file-sharing protocols for TCP/IP developed by Sun Microsystems. These protocols enable an NFS client to access disk space on an NFS server as if the drives were directly attached. NFS is the traditional file-sharing protocol in Unix networks.

21

Table 21.3.5 Address Information Used on TCP/IP Internetworks

Type of Address	How it is Used
Physical addresses	Used by the Data Link Layer
IP addresses	Provide logical network numbers and host IDs. IP addresses consist of 32 bits typically expressed in dotted-decimal form. An example of an IP address is 134.135.100.13.
Logical node names	Identify specific hosts with alphanumeric identifiers, which are easier for users to recall than the numeric IP addresses. An example of a logical node name is MYHOST.MYCOMPANY.COM.

D. NetWare IPX/SPX

The NetWare protocols have been designed with a high degree of modularity, which makes them adaptable to different hardware and simplifies the task of incorporating other protocols into the suite. Windows NT uses a Microsoft implementation of the IPX/SPX suite, the *NWLink IPX/SPX Compatible Transport,* to communicate with NetWare resources. NWLink IPX/SPX is generally smaller and faster than Microsoft's TCP/IP and, like TCP/IP, it is routable. Because of these advantages, NWLink IPX/SPX is the best choice for modern small networks that don't require Internet connectivity. The NetWare protocol architecture is shown in relation to the OSI model in figure 21.3.4, and its components are described in table 21.3.6.

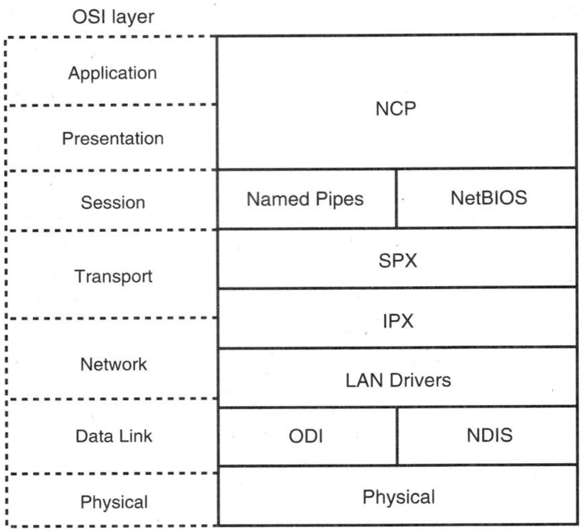

OSI layer
Application
Presentation
Session
Transport
Network
Data Link
Physical
NCP
Named Pipes
NetBIOS
SPX
IPX
LAN Drivers
ODI
NDIS
Physical

Figure 21.3.4 The NetWare protocol architecture.

Table 21.3.6 Components of NWLink IPX/SPX

Protocol	Description
Internetwork Packet Exchange Protocol (IPX)	A Network layer protocol that provides connectionless (datagram) service. Responsible for internetwork routing and maintaining network logical addresses. Relies on hardware physical addresses found at lower layers to provide network device addressing, which makes it much easier to manage than TCP/IP.
Sequenced Packet Exchange (SPX)	A Transport Layer protocol that provides connection-oriented services with reliable delivery. Reliable delivery is ensured by retransmitting packets in the event of an error. SPX is used in situations in which reliable transmission of data is needed.

Protocol	Description
NetWare Core Protocol (NCP)	Provides remote function calls that support network services, such as file sharing, printing, name management, file locking, and synchronization. NetWare client software uses NCP to access NetWare services. NCP covers aspects of the Session, Presentation, and Application Layers of the OSI reference model.

E. NetBEUI

NetBEUI is a transport protocol that serves as an extension to Microsoft's Network Basic Input/Output System (NetBIOS). Because NetBEUI was developed for an earlier generation of DOS-based PCs, it is small, easy to implement, and relatively fast. Because it was built for small isolated LANs, however, NetBEUI is non-routable, making it somewhat anachronistic in today's diverse and interconnected networking environment. In general, one shouldn't design new LAN's to use NetBEUI.

Fortunately, the NDIS standard enables NetBEUI to coexist with other, routable protocols. For instance, you could configure a network to use NetBEUI for communications on the LAN segment and to use TCP/IP for communications that require routing. Because NetBEUI cannot be routed, you have to use a switch, bridge, or brouter if you need to introduce some isolation on network segments that use it.

F. AppleTalk

AppleTalk is the network computing architecture developed by Apple Computer for the Macintosh family of personal computers (see fig. 21.3.5).

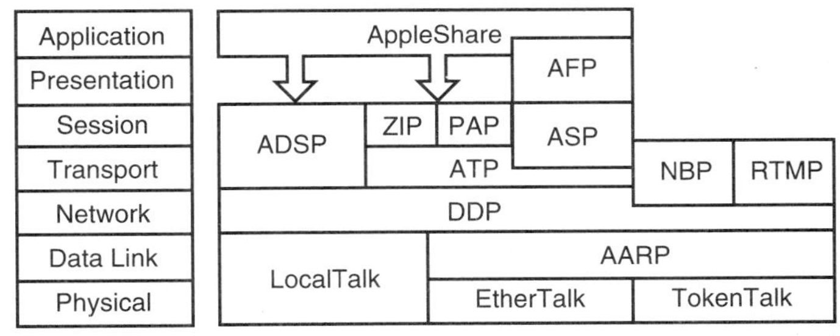

Figure 21.3.5 A layered perspective of the AppleTalk protocol suite.

Table 21.3.7 The AppleTalk Protocol Family

Protocol	Description
Datagram Delivery Protocol (DDP)	A Network Layer protocol that provides connectionless service between two AppleTalk systems.
AppleTalk Transaction Protocol (ATP)	A connectionless Transport Layer protocol that provides reliable service through a system of acknowledgments and retransmissions.

continues

21

Table 21.3.7 Continued

Protocol	Description
AppleTalk File Protocol (AFP)	Provides remote file services. Responsible for enforcing file system security. Verifies and encrypts logon names and passwords during connection setup.
AppleShare	A client/server system for Macintosh. Provides file and print sharing services.

G. Data Link Control (DLC)

In a Windows networking environment, the Data Link Control (DLC) protocol is most commonly used to access Hewlett-Packard JetDirect network printers. DLC's more traditional use has been for connectivity to IBM mainframes via 802.2 LLC Type 2.

Summary of Protocol Characteristics

The Microsoft Networking Essentials Test is intended to ensure that you are able to select the appropriate network and transport protocols for various Ethernet and token ring networks. The table below provides you with a quick summary of the most important points of these protocols.

Protocol	Routable	Primary Use	Should Be Used
DLC	No	Communicate with mainframes and printers	Only when required
AppleTalk	Yes	Communicates with Apple Macintosh computers	For Apple Macintosh computers only
IPX	Yes	Novell NetWare networks	For small to moderate-sized networks
TCP/IP	Yes	Internet	For large networks, WAN communications, and Internet access
NetBEUI	No	Small LANs	Only when required for backward compatibility
NFS	Yes[1]	Unix file sharing	For Unix file sharing
SMB	Yes/No[2]	Windows file and print sharing	Windows file and print sharing

1. NFS uses TCP/IP

2. Depends on network layer protocol used

21.3.1 Exercise

Compare and contrast TCP/IP, IPX/SPX, and NetBEUI.

21.3.1 Exercise Explanation

NetBEUI is only well-suited for small networks because it is not routable. Because it is not routable, the entire network must be in a single broadcast domain. This does not scale well because excessive broadcasts cause network performance problems.

IPX/SPX is easy to configure because workstations always learn their addresses automatically. It is both fast and routable, and therefore is well-suited to use in large networks. Because networks that use IPX are not joined by a global IPX network, there are no restrictions on IPX network addressing other than network numbers must be unique within an area with IPX connectivity. IPX also must be used for any connections to NetWare servers.

TCP/IP is the language of the Internet and has always been the primary protocol on Unix-based computers. TCP/IP is routable and scales extremely well. It is the protocol of choice on both very large networks and networks that need to connect to the Internet. TCP/IP has historically been considered difficult to configure because network addresses had to be allocated by a central registry to ensure global uniqueness and host addresses had to be configured manually. Although the requirement for global network number uniqueness still exists so that the Internet can function, host configuration has largely been automated in recent years.

21.3 Practice Problems

1. Your network includes over 40,000 users at a total of 200 sites connected by WAN circuits. What protocol is most suitable for use with this environment?

   A. DLC

   B. AppleTalk

   C. NWLink IPX

   D. TCP/IP

2. What protocol should you configure if your network needs access to the Internet?

   A. DLC

   B. AppleTalk

   C. NWLink IPX

   D. TCP/IP

3. Your company's new CEO asks you to reconfigure the network file server so that he can access it from his Macintosh computer. What protocol do you need to configure on the server?

   A. DLC

   B. AppleTalk

   C. NWLink IPX

   D. TCP/IP

4. One of the advantages of TCP over UDP is:

   A. TCP uses very small packets.

   B. TCP uses link-state route discovery.

   C. TCP provides error correction.

   D. TCP is faster than any other protocol for small networks.

5. What native TCP/IP protocol would allow file sharing on a Unix system?

   A. TCP/IP

   B. NWLink IPX

   C. SMB

   D. NFS

6. What protocol is used for file sharing on a Windows NT Server?

   A. TCP/IP

   B. NWLink IPX

   C. SMB

   D. NFS

7. You have a Hewlett-Packard JetDirect-family printer to install for shared network use on the same LAN segment as the Windows NT Server. What is the easiest protocol to install for it?

   A. DLC

   B. AppleTalk

   C. NWLink IPX

   D. TCP/IP

8. You need to use the Simple Network Management Protocol (SNMP) to monitor the health of some Unix database servers at a remote site. What protocol does your network need to support?

   A. DLC

   B. AppleTalk

   C. NWLink IPX

   D. TCP/IP

9. ARP involves which two types of information?

   A. Network number and host ID

   B. Network address and data link address

   C. Logical node names and IP address

   D. Protocol type and frame number

10. NFS is functionally most similar to which of the following protocols?

    A. NWLink IPX

    B. TCP/IP

    C. SMB

    D. OSPF

11. Which of the following is true of the IPX/SPX protocol suite used by NetWare?

    A. It requires specialized hardware and configurations.

    B. It is incompatable with other protocols.

    C. Host number allocations must be carefully managed.

    D. It is routable.

12. A consultant is getting ready to configure a new Unix server on your network, and he asks you if it should support file sharing. If you say yes, which protocol will he probably add to the system configuration?

    A. TCP/IP

    B. NWLink IPX

    C. SMB

    D. NFS

13. You have 200 Windows 95 workstations configured with a mixture of TCP/IP and NetBEUI on your office network. The network performance is beginning to degrade because of frequent broadcast storms. What device can you install to reduce this problem while still retaining full connectivity for all the workstations?

    A. Repeater

    B. Bridge

    C. Brouter

    D. Router

14. You have 200 Windows 95 workstations all configured to use TCP/IP on your office network. You need to add another 100 workstations, but frequent broadcast storms are causing performance problems. What device should you add to reduce the broadcasts while still retaining full connectivity for all the workstations?

    A. Repeater

    B. Bridge

    C. Brouter

    D. Router

15. You have to design a large WAN. What protocol should that WAN use?

    A. TCP/IP

    B. NWLink IPX

    C. NetBEUI

    D. AppleTalk

16. You need to design a small network for a software company that is focused on Internet-related products. What protocol should you use?

    A. DLC

    B. TCP/IP

    C. AppleTalk

    D. NWLink IPX

17. What file and print sharing protocol do Windows networks use?

    A. TCP/IP

    B. NWLink IPX

    C. NFS

    D. SMB

18. You have been directed to configure some Windows NT Workstations to use LLC Type 2 connections to communicate with the company's mainframe through an IBM 3745 FEP. Which protocol do you need to install on the Windows NT Workstations?

    A. DLC

    B. TCP/IP

    C. AppleTalk

    D. NWLink IPX

19. You need to configure a Windows NT Server so that a Unix system can use one

of its printers. Which protocol will the Windows NT Server need to use?

A. DLC

B. TCP/IP

C. AppleTalk

D. NWLink IPX

20. You have to decide which protocol to use for your Windows networking. One requirement is that all workstations must be able to access NetWare servers. Which of the following protocols does this suggest that you should use?

A. DLC

B. TCP/IP

C. AppleTalk

D. NWLink IPX

21. Which of the following are standards that enable multiple network-layer protocols to coexist on the same computer without having to be aware of the datalink protocol in use?

A. NDIS

B. NDS

C. ODI

D. DLC

22. TCP uses port numbers:

A. To identify which virtual circuit the data stream belongs to

B. To identify the protocol in use

C. To identify which data streams need to be passed to UDP

D. For additional speed

23. Which of the following are generally parts of network data packets?

A. Preamble

B. Header

C. Data

D. Trailer

24. You need to subnet your TCP/IP network. Which of the following protocols might your routers use to communicate routes to each other?

A. RIP

B. SNMP

C. ICMP

D. OSPF

25. You have a large network with many redundant paths in it. When there is a problem in the network, it takes a long time before the routers all know how to direct the traffic around the problem. What is a reasonable way to alleviate this problem?

A. Adjust the RIP timers so that route updates happen 10 times as often.

B. Adjust the RIP timers so that route updates happen 10 times less often.

C. Convert the routers to use only static routes.

D. Convert the routers to OSPF.

26. Which part of the IPX family of protocols is most similar to Microsoft's SMB protocol?

A. IPX

B. SPX

C. NCP

D. ODI

27. Which IP-based protocol should an application use if it requires a reliable transport protocol with automatic error detection and recovery?

A. TCP

B. UDP

C. SNMP

D. SMTP

28. Which IP-based protocol should an application use if it cannot tolerate the overhead of a reliable transport protocol?

    A. TCP

    B. UDP

    C. SNMP

    D. SMTP

29. Which Novell protocol is most like TCP?

    A. IPX

    B. SPX

    C. NCP

    D. ODI

30. What protocol should you configure if you need to connect to Novell NetWare servers?

    A. NWLink IPX

    B. TCP/IP

    C. DLC

    D. AppleTalk

31. Which Novell protocol is most like UDP?

    A. IPX

    B. SPX

    C. NCP

    D. ODI

32. Which of the following is an advantage of distance vector routing protocols?

    A. They converge faster than link-state protocols.

    B. They use more bandwidth than link-state protocols.

    C. They use more reliable routing metrics than link-state protocols.

    D. They are easier to configure than link-state protocols.

33. Which of the following is a disadvantage of link-state routing protocols?

    A. They converge faster than distance vector protocols.

    B. They use more bandwidth than distance vector protocols.

    C. They are less likely to create loops.

    D. They are harder to configure than distance vector protocols.

34. Using a web browser to connect with www.microsoft.com uses which protocols?

    A. NWLink, NetBIOS, and NetBEUI

    B. TCP, OSPF, and DLC

    C. NWLink, RIP and SMB

    D. TCP, ARP, and DNS

35. It is taking your routers too long to respond to changes in the network. Which protocol change might help them?

    A. NetBIOS to NetBEUI

    B. RIP to OSPF

    C. AppleTalk to NWLink

    D. SMB to TCP/IP

36. Microsoft provides updates and patches to some of its programs on the Internet. Which protocol might you use to download the necessary files?

    A. FTP

    B. UDP

    C. IP

    D. DNS

37. On your network, you have PCs running Windows 95 that access both NetWare and NT Servers. The MIS department needs access to the Internet. Which of the following protocols do you not need at all?

    A. IPX/SPX

    B. TCP/IP

C. NCP

D. DLC

38. In order to check the configuration of your routers from off-site, you use which protocol?

    A. Telnet

    B. DLC

    C. RIP

    D. NFS

39. Which protocol should you configure on an NT Server if Mac computers need to access it for file sharing or printing?

    A. NWLink IPX

    B. TCP/IP

    C. DLC

    D. AppleTalk

40. You have to design a WAN to support 20,000 users and 200 NT Servers.

    Required Result:
    Efficient use of expensive WAN bandwidth

    Desired Results:
    Capbility to triple in size without changing protocol

    Good Internet connectivity

    Proposed solution:
    Use NetBEUI to minimize addressing problems

    Configure regional NT Servers as gateways to TCP/IP for Internet access

    A. This solution meets the required result and both the desired results.

    B. This solution meets the required result and one of the desired results.

    C. This solution meets the required result but neither of the desired results.

    D. This solution does not meet the required result.

21.3 Answers and Explanations: Practice Problems

1. **D** TCP/IP makes the most efficient use of WAN circuits.

2. **D** TCP/IP is the protocol used on the Internet.

3. **B** Macintosh computers use AppleTalk.

4. **C** TCP is a reliable protocol and, as such, provides error correction that unreliable protocols, such as UDP, do not.

5. **D** NFS is the native way of file sharing on most Unix systems.

6. **C** SMB is the protocol that Windows NT uses for file and print sharing. SMB can be transported inside of other protocols, including TCP/IP, NetBEUI, and NWLink IPX.

7. **A** DLC is often considered the easiest protocol to configure because it has so few options.

8. **D** Although SNMP *can* be carried inside of other protocols, it is almost always used with TCP/IP. The fact that the devices you are monitoring run Unix makes this an easy question because Unix devices almost exclusively support TCP/IP.

9. **B** ARP finds the data link address by asking all stations whether they have the network layer address being looked for.

10. **C** NFS is functionally most similar to SMB because they are both used for file sharing.

11. **D** The IPX/SPX protocol suite popularized by NetWare is routable.

12. **D** NFS is the traditional file-sharing protocol on Unix systems.

13. **C** You have to use a brouter to maintain full connectivity for both the routed TCP/IP and the bridged NetBEUI.

14. **D** Routers are used to contain broadcasts and to reduce broadcast storms.

15. **A** TCP/IP is considered the best protocol for a WAN.

16. **B** TCP/IP is the protocol used on the Internet, so it would be the best fit for this company.

17. **D** Windows networks use SMB as their file and print sharing protocol.

18. **A** DLC is used for LLC Type 2 connections, which are most commonly used to access mainframes and HP JetDirect printers.

19. **B** To interoperate with Unix systems, you'll need to configure TCP/IP.

20. **D** NWLink IPX is used to access NetWare servers.

21. **A, C** NDIS and ODI both define programmatic interfaces that enable upper-layer protocols to share the same network card seamlessly.

22. **A** TCP uses port numbers to identify which virtual circuit the data stream belongs to.

23. **B, C, D** Headers, data, and trailers are all generally parts of network data packets. Only Ethernet frames use a preamble.

24. **A, D** RIP and OSPF are both routing protocols that you might use.

25. **D** Converting the routers to OSPF enables them to learn about network changes faster.

26. **C** Novell's NCP protocol is similar in functionality to Microsoft's SMB protocol.

27. **A** TCP is a reliable transport protocol with automatic error detection and recovery.

28. **B** UDP is an IP-based protocol sometimes used to avoid the overhead of a reliable transport protocol.

29. **B** SPX is the Novell protocol most like TCP.

30. **A** NWLink IPX is used to connect to Novell NetWare servers.

31. **A** IPX is the Novell protocol most like UDP.

32. **D** Distance vector routing protocols are easier to configure than link-state protocols.

33. **D** Link-state routing protocols are harder to configure than distance vector protocols.

34. **D** TCP, ARP, & DNS are all used. DNS resolves the name into an address, ARP finds the hardware address of your default router, and TCP is used for the actual connection.

35. **B** Changing from RIP to OSPF can help routers learn about changes in the network faster.

36. **A** FTP is sometimes used to download files over the Internet.

37. **D** There was no connectivity requirement described for DLC.

38. **A** Telnet is a convenient way of providing a virtual terminal connection to devices like routers.

39. **D** Mac computers use AppleTalk for file sharing or printing.

40. **D** This solution does not meet the requirement because NetBEUI does not use WAN bandwidth efficiently.

21.3 Key Words

AppleTalk
ARP
Data
Datagram
DLC
DNS
FTP
Header
Internet Protocol (IP)
IP address
IPX
IPX/SPX
Logical node names
NetBEUI
NetBIOS
NFS
NWLink
OSI model
OSPF
Packet
RIP
SMB
SMTP
SNMP
SPX
TCP
TCP/IP
TELNET
Trailer
Transport protocol
UDP

21.4 Selecting the Appropriate Connectivity Devices for Various Token Ring and Ethernet Networks

Connectivity devices include repeaters, bridges, switches, routers, brouters, and gateways.

An *internetwork* consists of multiple independent networks that are connected and can share remote resources. These networks can be dissimilar in type. The device that connects the independent networks might need to determine when packets stay on the local network and when they are forwarded to a remote network.

A. Repeaters

Repeaters work at the Physical Layer of the OSI model. Each media type has a maximum distance that it can carry data reliably. The purpose of a *repeater* is to regenerate the data signal and thereby extend this maximum distance (see fig. 21.4.1).

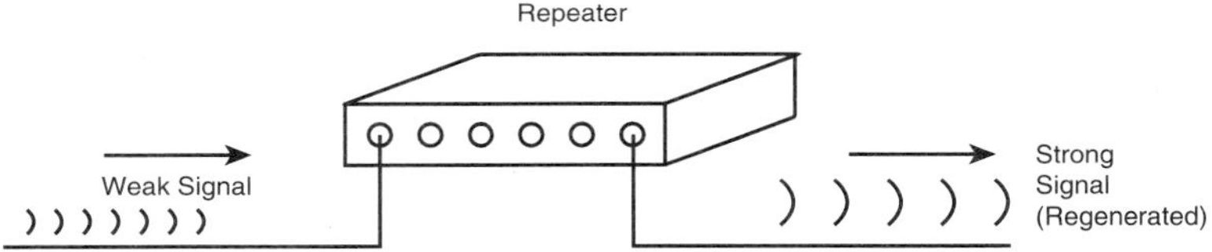

Figure 21.4.1 A repeater regenerates a weak signal.

Characteristics of Repeaters

The characteristics of repeaters are:

- Repeaters regenerate a signal that comes in on one port and transmit it out through the other repeater ports.
- They operate mostly in the OSI Physical Layer.
- They do not filter or interpret—merely repeat (regenerate) a signal, passing all network traffic (even errors) in all directions.
- Repeaters do not require any addressing information from the data frame because they merely repeat bits of data. This means that if data is corrupt, a repeater repeats it anyway. A repeater even repeats a broadcast storm caused by a malfunctioning adapter.
- They are inexpensive.
- They are simple.
- Although they cannot connect networks with dissimilar data frames (such as a token ring network and an Ethernet network), some repeaters can connect segments with similar frame types but dissimilar cabling.

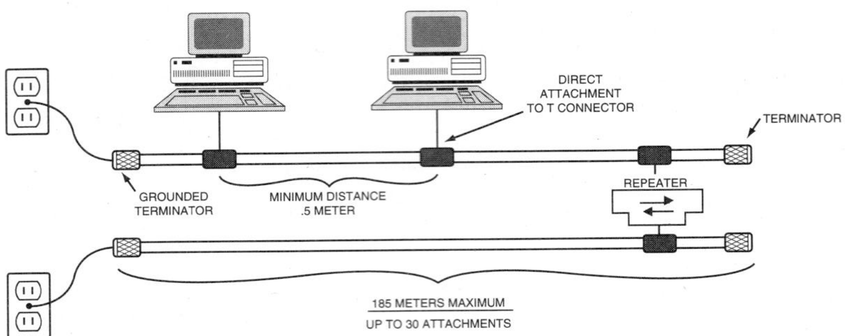

Figure 21.4.2 Using a repeater to extend an Ethernet LAN. Connecting two Ethernet cable segments results in doubling the potential length of the network.

All network designs limit the size of the network. The most important reason for this limitation is *signal propagation.* Networks must work within reasonable expectations about the maximum time a signal might be in transit. This is known as *propagation delay*—the time it takes for a signal to reach the farthest point on the network and return. If this maximum propagation delay interval expires and no signals are encountered, a network error condition is assumed. Given the maximum propagation delay allowed, it is possible to calculate the maximum permissible cable length for the network. Even though repeaters enable signals to travel farther, the maximum propagation delay still sets a limit to the maximum size of the network.

Most vendors of repeaters call those repeaters *hubs*. If you are asked questions about hubs, remember to think of them as repeaters.

B. Bridges

Bridges work at the Data Link Layer of the OSI model. Bridges can extend the maximum size of a network (see fig 21.4.3). Although the bridged network in figure 21.4.3 looks much like the earlier example of a network with a repeater, the bridge is a much more flexible device. Bridges operate at the MAC sublayer of the OSI Data Link Layer.

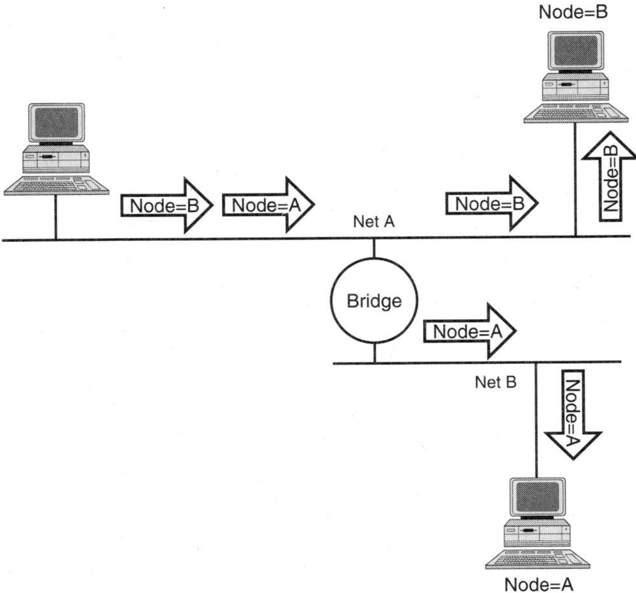

Figure 21.4.3 Extending a network with a bridge.

A repeater passes on all signals that it receives. A bridge is more selective and passes only those signals targeted for a computer on the other side. A bridge can make this determination because each device on the network is identified by a unique address. Each packet that is transmitted bears the address of the device to which it should be delivered. The process works as follows:

1. The bridge receives every packet on LAN A and LAN B.
2. The bridge learns from the packets which device addresses are located on LAN A and which are on LAN B. The bridge then builds a table with this information.
3. Packets on LAN A that are addressed to devices on LAN A are discarded, as are packets on LAN B that are addressed to devices on LAN B. These packets can be delivered without the help of the bridge.
4. Packets on LAN A addressed to devices on LAN B are retransmitted to LAN B for delivery. Similarly, the appropriate packets on LAN B are retransmitted to LAN A.

On truly ancient bridges, the network administrator had to manually configure the address tables. Modern bridges are called *learning bridges.* Learning bridges function as described in step 2, automatically updating their address tables as devices are added to or removed from the network.

Bridges accomplish two major things:

- **Divide busy networks into smaller segments:** If the network is designed so that most packets can be delivered without crossing a bridge, traffic on the individual network segments can be reduced. If the Accounting and Sales departments are overloading the LAN, for example, you might divide the network so that Accounting is on one segment and Sales on another. Only when Accounting and Sales must exchange packets does a packet need to cross the bridge between the segments.
- **Extend the physical size of a network:** Although the individual segments (made up of the cable and repeaters) still are restricted by the maximum size imposed by the network design limits, bridges enable network designers to stretch the distances between segments and extend the overall size of the network.

Bridges have certain limitations that become more significant in complex network situations:

- A network with bridges generally cannot make use of redundant paths.
- Bridges cannot analyze the network to determine the fastest route over which to forward a packet. When multiple routes exist, this is a desirable capability, particularly in wide area networks (WANs) where some routes are often considerably slower than others.
- Bridges do not filter broadcast packets, so they are of no help in avoiding broadcast storms.
- Bridges cannot join dissimilar types of LANs because bridges depend on the physical addresses of devices. Physical device addresses are functions of the Data Link Layer, and different Data Link Layer protocols are used for each type of network. A bridge, therefore, cannot be used to join an Ethernet segment to a token ring segment.

C. Switches

A relatively recent addition to the networking scene has been the advent of *switches.* Switches operate at the Data Link Layer of the OSI model. A switch performs the same function as a learning bridge, but typically with many more ports and at higher throughput rates.

Switches do not block broadcast packets. The primary reason people use switches is to improve network performance by reducing network contention. A switch filters out traffic that isn't destined for a station on a given port, so that the station sees less network traffic and can perform better.

It has become common practice in the network industry to replace repeaters (often called *hubs*) with switches to increase the network's performance without requiring any changes to computers on the network.

D. Routers

Routers work at the Network Layer of the OSI model. Because each network in an internetwork is assigned an address, each network can be considered logically separate; that is, each network functions independently of other networks on the internetwork. Internetwork connectivity devices, such as routers, use network address information to assist in the efficient delivery of messages. Using network address information to deliver messages is called *routing*. The common feature that unites internetwork connectivity devices (routers and brouters) is that these devices can perform routing.

Routers organize the large network in terms of logical network segments (see fig. 21.4.4). Each network segment is assigned an address so that every packet has both a destination network address and a destination device address.

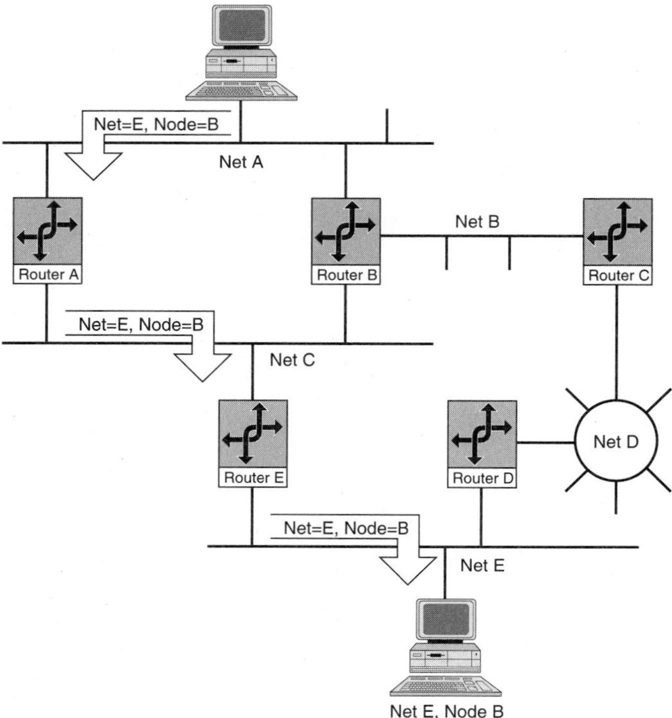

Figure 21.4.4 A complex network based on routers. Router A knows that the most efficient step is to send the packet to Router E, not Router B.

Routers are more intelligent than bridges. Not only do routers build tables of network locations, they also use algorithms to determine the most efficient path for sending a packet to any given network. Even if a particular network segment isn't directly attached to the router, the router knows the best way to send a packet to a device on that network.

Notice in figure 21.4.4 that Router B presents a redundant path to the path Router A provides. Routers can cope with this situation because they exchange routing information to ensure that packet loops don't persist. If Router A fails, Router B provides a backup message path.

You can use routers to divide large, busy LANs into smaller segments, much as you can use bridges. Routers, however, also can connect different network types. Notice that the network in figure 21.4.4 includes a token ring segment with the Ethernet segments. On such networks, a router is the device of choice.

Routers come in two types:

- **Static Routers:** These routers do not determine paths dynamically. Instead, you must configure the routing table, specifying potential routes for packets. If the network connections change, a router using statically configured routes must be manually reconfigured. These preprogrammed routers cannot adjust to changing network conditions.
- **Dynamic Routers:** These routers have the capability to determine routes dynamically (and to find the optimum path among redundant routes) based on information obtained from other routers via a routing protocol or routing algorithm.

After route costs are established, routers can select routes—either statically or dynamically—as follows:

- **Static route selection:** This selection method uses only routes that have been programmed by the network administrator. Static routers can use this method and no other.
- **Dynamic route selection:** Under this selection method, routing cost information is used to select the best route for a given packet. As network conditions change and are reflected in routing tables, the router selects different paths to continue using the lowest cost path.

Two common methods that dynamic routers use to discover routes are *distance vector routing* and *link-state routing*.

Remember that routers are always used to connect different networks that run the same protocol. Also, if a question asks about subnetting (the process of subdividing a network into smaller pieces), it is implying that you must use either a router or a brouter.

Table 21.4.1 Generic Routing Protocol Comparison

	Distance Vector	Link State
How often routing information is sent	Repeated broadcasts	Only when a route changes
Which routes are transmitted	All routes, even those learned second-hand	Only routes for directly connected networks or subnets
How long until all routers know about route changes	At least several minutes, possibly many minutes	Seconds to tens of seconds
Ease of configuration	Simple and easy	More complex
Bandwidth overhead	Substantial in large networks	Small even in large networks (unless unstable)

Characteristics of Routers

The characteristics of routers are:

- **Routers connect different types of LANs (different media types).**
- **They connect different networks (different network numbers).**
- **They isolate broadcasts to within their originating network, reducing and containing broadcast storms.**
- **Protocols used to send data through a router must be specifically designed to support routing functions. IP, IPX, and AppleTalk are routable protocols. NetBEUI and DLC are nonroutable protocols.**
- **Routers usually are employed to connect a LAN to a wide area network (WAN). WANs often are designed with multiple paths, and routers can ensure that the various paths are used most efficiently.**
- **There are two types: static and dynamic.**

E. Brouters

A *brouter* is a router that also can act as a bridge. A brouter attempts to deliver packets based on network protocol information, but if a particular Network Layer protocol isn't supported, the brouter bridges the packet using device addresses.

If you need to connect networks that are using both a routable protocol such as TCP/IP and a non-routable protocol such as NetBEUI, you need to use a brouter. This gives you the subnetting advantages of a router, while maintaining the full connectivity of a bridge.

Almost all dedicated hardware routers (including those from 3Com, Cisco, and Bay Networks, for example) include an option to support bridging and can be considered brouters. *Brouter* is becoming an obsolete term in the networking industry, but it is still used on Microsoft's tests because it emphasizes the combination of bridging and routing functionality.

F. Gateways

Gateways function at the Application Layer of the OSI model. The term *gateway* originally was used in the Internet protocol suite to refer to a router. Today, the term *gateway* more commonly refers to a system functioning at the top levels of the OSI model that enables communication between dissimilar protocol systems. A gateway generally is dedicated to a specific conversion, and the exact functioning of the gateway depends on the protocol translations it must perform. Gateways commonly function at the OSI Application Layer.

Gateways connect dissimilar environments by removing the layered protocol information of incoming packets and replacing it with the packet information necessary for the dissimilar environment (see fig. 21.4.5).

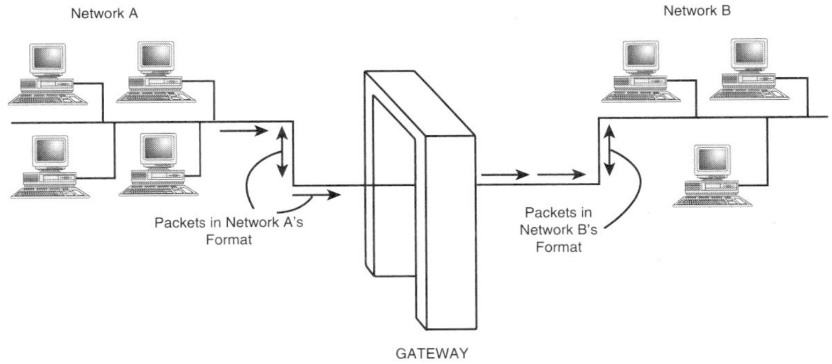

Figure 21.4.5 Gateways convert packet protocol information to connect dissimilar environments.

Gateways can be implemented as software, hardware, or a combination of both.

The NetBIOS Gateway

Windows NT 4.0 RAS can act as an IP or an IPX router, but RAS's NetBIOS gateway is an even more powerful feature. Not only does the NetBIOS gateway forward remote packets to the LAN, it also acts as a gateway, providing NetBEUI clients with access to the LAN even if the LAN uses only TCP/IP or IPX/SPX (see fig. 21.4.6).

The NetBIOS gateway is very much like the gateways described in this section. The NetBIOS gateway accepts a packet from the remote computer using one protocol (NetBEUI) and converts the packet, stripping incompatible protocol headers and replacing them with the headers the packet needs to circulate under a different protocol.

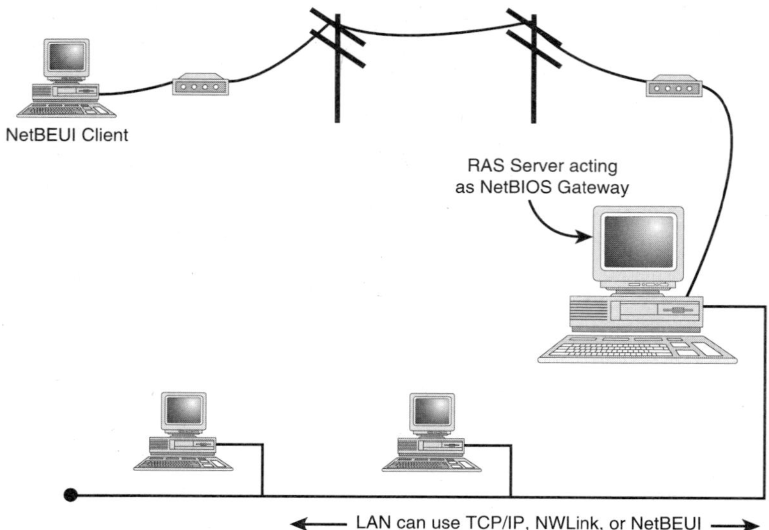

Figure 21.4.6 The Windows NT NetBIOS gateway.

21.4.1 Exercise

Name the OSI layer in which the primary function of each of the following connectivity devices occurs.

Application
Presentation
Session
Transport
Network
Data Link
Physical

1. Router
2. Concentrator
3. Bridge
4. Gateway
5. Hub
6. Switch
7. Repeater
8. Brouter

21.4.1 Exercise Explanation

1. Router: Network
2. Concentrator: Physical
3. Bridge: Data Link
4. Gateway: Application
5. Hub: Physical
6. Switch: Data Link
7. Repeater: Repeater
8. Brouter: Data Link and Network

21.4 Practice Problems

1. You need to connect an Ethernet network with a token ring network. Which device should you use?

   A. Repeater

   B. Bridge

   C. Router

   D. Gateway

2. You need to use 10Base-T to connect two computers that are 180 meters apart. What is the least expensive device you could use?

   A. Repeater

   B. Bridge

   C. Router

   D. Gateway

3. A multiport repeater:

   A. Is used to monitor network traffic

   B. Is a more technical name for a hub

   C. Must filter network traffic

   D. Provides ports for different networks such as token ring and Ethernet to connect

4. One simple, inexpensive way to connect or to extend two sections of the same network without any packet filtering is to install:

   A. A gateway

   B. A router

   C. A repeater

   D. A switch

5. A network is encountering a large number of Ethernet errors after installing yet another repeater. This problem is likely due to:

   A. Exceeding the network size limitations

   B. A need for a transceiver

   C. Using the wrong network number

   D. An incorrectly configured repeater

6. Due to the size of your network, you can't add any more repeaters to extend it. You should instead consider:

   A. A gateway

   B. A multiport repeater

   C. Rewiring with Category 5

   D. A bridge

7. What device is used to connect different networks?

   A. A gateway

   B. A bridge

   C. A repeater

   D. A router

8. In order to connect your token ring segment to your Ethernet segment you need a:

   A. Repeater

   B. Router

   C. Bridge

   D. Gateway

9. Network reliability is crucial for your company, and you have included redundancy in many components of your network design. In order to make efficient use of your network's redundant paths, you need to use:

   A. Bridges

   B. Repeaters

   C. Gateways

   D. Routers

10. Which connectivity device chooses to use the most efficient path between two networks?

    A. A repeater

    B. A bridge

C. A router

D. A gateway

11. The least expensive device that can connect two segments of coaxial cable is:

A. A repeater

B. A bridge

C. A router

D. All of the above

12. The retiming function of a repeater is necessary to:

A. Allow data to cross time zones without corruption

B. Keep network devices synchronized

C. Prevent time outs

D. Remove electrical noise from the signal

13. You need to use 10Base-T to connect two computers that are 180 meters apart. What is the fastest device you could use?

A. Repeater

B. Bridge

C. Router

D. Gateway

14. Your network has 150 stations all running NetBEUI, and traffic levels are becoming a problem. What device can help alleviate the problem without reconfiguring any workstations?

A. Repeater

B. Bridge

C. Router

D. Gateway

15. In token ring, subnets are connected via which of the following?

A. Repeaters

B. Bridges

C. Routers

D. Gateways

16. According to the OSI model, bridges work at the _____ and _____ layers of the network, connecting segments using the same LLC protocols.

A. Data Link and Physical

B. Data Link and Network

C. Network and Transport

D. Physical and Transport

17. Which device do you need for a station that uses only TCP/IP to communicate with another station on the network that uses only NetBEUI?

A. Switch

B. Router

C. RPC

D. Gateway

18. You need to connect many 10Base-T network segments. Which network device gives you the highest overall performance?

A. Repeater

B. Switch

C. Router

D. Gateway

19. You have PCs running only NWLink IPX. They need to communicate with a mainframe that expects LLC Type 2 connections. What device do you need to install?

A. Repeater

B. Switch

C. Router

D. Gateway

20. Your network has grown to 200 PCs and is beginning to experience severe broadcast storms. Which device is used to contain broadcasts?

    A. Repeater

    B. Switch

    C. Router

    D. Gateway

21. You need to configure a device to do protocol translation. What device fits this description?

    A. Repeater

    B. Switch

    C. Router

    D. Gateway

22. You need to extend a network farther than repeater limits will allow. Which device should you use?

    A. Repeater

    B. Bridge

    C. Router

    D. Gateway

23. You have a WAN. Which device uses the bandwidth most efficiently?

    A. Repeater

    B. Switch

    C. Router

    D. Bridge

24. You have redundant paths in your network. Which device uses the paths most efficiently?

    A. Repeater

    B. Switch

    C. Router

    D. Gateway

25. You have two networks that use different protocols. Which device must you use to connect them?

    A. Repeater

    B. Switch

    C. Router

    D. Gateway

26. Which network device removes electrical noise from a signal, but otherwise passes it without modification?

    A. Repeater

    B. Switch

    C. Router

    D. Gateway

27. **Scenario:**
    You have a 200- PC network running a mixture of NWLink IPX and NetBEUI. Broadcast storms are already a frequent problem, and you need to add 100 more PCs.

    Required:
    You need to implement a strategy to minimize broadcasts while allowing for continued growth.

    Desirable:
    1. Minimal reconfiguration
    2. Minimum expense

    Proposed solution:
    Replace the cabling with Category 5 and implement 100Base-TX switching to the desktop.

    A. Meets the requirement and both desirable goals

    B. Meets the requirement and one of the desirable goals

    C. Meets the requirement but neither of the desirable goals

    D. Does not meet the requirement

28. **Scenario:**
You have a 200-PC network running a mixture of NWLink IPX and NetBEUI. Broadcast storms are already a frequent problem, and you need to add 100 more PCs.

Required:
You need to implement a strategy to minimize broadcasts while allowing for continued growth.

Desirable:
1. Minimal reconfiguration
2. Minimum expense

Proposed solution:
Configure the stations running NetBEUI to use NWLink IPX instead and install an IPX router.

A. Meets the requirement and both desirable goals

B. Meets the requirement and one of the desirable goals

C. Meets the requirement but neither of the desirable goals

D. Does not meet the requirement

29. What is the least expensive device that connects different Ethernet media types?

A. Repeater

B. Bridge

C. Router

D. Gateway

30. You have a network that includes Ethernet, token ring, and FDDI. What device can join all of these?

A. Repeater

B. Bridge

C. Router

D. Gateway

31. Which device decides whether to forward a data frame based on the hardware address in the frame?

A. Repeater

B. Bridge

C. Router

D. Gateway

32. Which device decides whether to forward a data frame based on the logical address in the frame?

A. Repeater

B. Bridge

C. Router

D. Gateway

33. You have decided to subnet your network to reduce the broadcast levels. Which device do you use?

A. Repeater

B. Bridge

C. Router

D. Gateway

34. You have to connect to the Internet. Which device do you use?

A. Repeater

B. Bridge

C. Router

D. Gateway

35. The Windows NT servers your predecessor had configured for routing don't reroute traffic when a LAN segment goes down. What could be the problem?

A. They are configured for Open Shortest Path First, and they always try to use the first path they learned.

B. They are configured for RIP, which is a distance vector protocol.

C. They are configured for static routing.

D. They are using a link-state protocol.

36. The function of a traditional switch is:

A. To switch between network types such as Ethernet and token ring

B. To switch between network protocols such as NetBEUI and TCP

C. To bridge network segments

D. To block out broadcast packets for improved network efficiency

37. As a security measure, your Internet firewall isn't allowed to learn routes dynamically. This is a good reason for using:

A. Network address translation (NAT)

B. Proxies

C. Firewalls

D. Static routes

38. Which routing algorithm generates more traffic in a stable network?

A. Distance vector

B. Link state

C. TPC/IP

D. DNS

39. Gateways require

A. Specialized configurable hardware

B. An intelligent hub

C. Identical protocol environments

D. Different protocols

40. Your network utilization is high because of too much broadcast traffic. One way of improving this situation isto install:

A. A network filter

B. A router

C. A switch

D. A gateway

21.4 Answers and Explanations: Practice Problems

1. **C** Routers are the networking device that can connect different types of data links.

2. **A** A repeater is the least expensive device listed, and it would allow each 10Base-T cable to be up to 100 meters.

3. **B** A multiport repeater is a more technical name for an hub.

4. **C** Using a repeater is a simple, inexpensive way to connect or to extend two sections of the same network without any packet filtering.

5. **A** Exceeding the network size limitations generates a lot of Ethernet errors in the form of late collisions.

6. **D** Using a bridge starts the network size limits over at each port.

7. **D** A router is used to connect different networks or subnets.

8. **B** You need a router to connect a token ring segment to an Ethernet segment.

9. **D** Routers are able to take advantage of multiple redundant paths.

10. **C** A router can be configured to choose to use the most efficient path between two networks.

11. **A** A repeater is the least expensive device listed that can connect two segments of coaxial cable.

12. **D** The retiming function of a repeater is necessary to remove electrical noise from the signal.

13. **A** This distance is within the limits supported by a repeater, and because repeaters operate at the lowest layers of the OSI model, they have the least overhead.

14. **B** Because NetBEUI is not routable, you have to use a bridge or switch to filter this traffic.

15. **C** Routers are always used to connect subnets.

16. A Bridges work at the Data Link and Physical Layers of the network. All devices that work at one layer must also include components of the lower layers.

17. D Gateways must be used any time there is a translation from one protocol to another.

18. B A switch is the highest performance device listed because it has lower latency than a router and it hides network traffic from ports that don't need to see that traffic.

19. D You have to use a gateway any time there is a translation from one protocol to another.

20. C Routers are used to contain broadcasts.

21. D Gateways are the only devices that do protocol translation.

22. B Bridges allow you to extend the same network farther than repeater limits allow. You can't use a routers because they divide networks.

23. C Routers use the bandwidth on a WAN most efficiently.

24. C Routers can calculate how to use redundant paths most efficiently.

25. D Gateways must be used between networks that use different protocols.

26. A Repeaters remove electrical noise from a signal but otherwise pass it without modification.

27. D Replacing the cabling with Category 5 and implementing 100Base-TX switching to the desktop does not meet the requirement because it does nothing to change the broadcast levels.

28. A Configuring the stations running NetBEUI to use NWLink IPX instead and installing an IPX router reduces broadcasts while requiring minimal reconfiguration and expense. You might even be able to use an existing NT Server or NetWare server for the IPX router if you really have no budget.

29. A A repeater is the least expensive device listed that connects different Ethernet media types.

30. C Routers must be used to join networks with different data links.

31. B A bridge decides whether to forward a data frame based on the hardware address in the frame.

32. C A router decides whether to forward a data frame based on the logical address in the frame.

33. C Routers are the only type of device that can divide a network into subnets.

34. C Routers are used to connect to the Internet.

35. C It is still common to configure Windows NT servers for static routing, in which an administrator has to reconfigure the routing table to reflect network changes.

36. C A classical switch is just an high-performance bridge with a lot of ports.

37. D If the firewall can't learn routes dynamically, the only alternative is to use static routes.

38. A Distance vector routing protocols produce much more traffic than link-state protocols in a stable environment because they have to rebroadcast their entire routing table periodically.

39. D Gateways are only used to convert between different protocols.

40. B Routers are used, among other things, to filter broadcasts.

21.4 Key Words

Bridge

Brouter

Gateway

Hub

Internetwork

Repeater

Router

21.5 Learning the Characteristics, Requirements, and Appropriate Situations for WAN Connection Services

WAN connection services include: T1, X.25, ISDN, Frame Relay, and ATM.

A. Digital and Analog Signaling

Signaling amounts to communicating information. The information being communicated can take one of two forms:

Analog — Changes continuously and can take on many different values. Music is a good example.

Analog signals constantly vary in one or more values, and these changes in values can be used to represent data (see fig. 21.5.1). Analog waveforms frequently take the form of sine waves that have these characteristics: frequency, amplitude, and phase. These characteristics can be used either in combination or individually to encode data.

Digital — Characterized by discrete states, typically "on" and "off" or "one" and "zero." Computer data is a good example.

Because computer data is inherently digital, most WANs use some form of digital signaling.

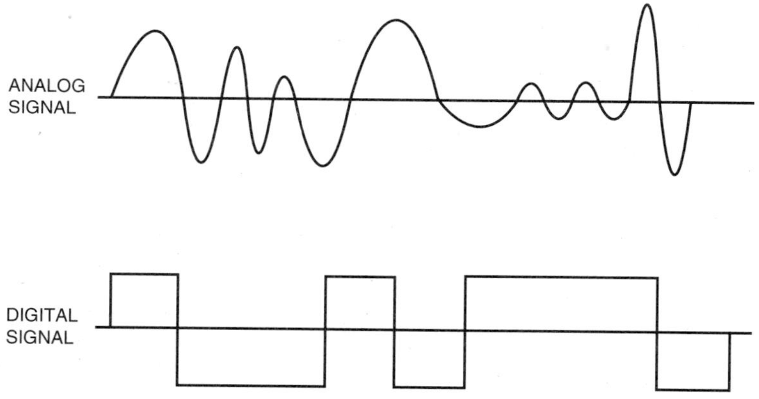

Figure 21.5.1 Analog signals constantly change and take on values throughout the range of possible values. Digital signals take on only two (or a few) specific states.

Frequently, information existing as one form must be converted to the other. This conversion involves the use of an encoding scheme that enables the original information to be recovered from a signal after the signal has been received. When an analog or a digital signal is altered so that it contains information, the process is called *modulation* or *encoding.*

A *modem* is the most common computer connectivity device that transmits an analog signal. Modems transmit digital computer signals over telephone lines by converting them to analog form. Modems are wonderfully handy for PC-to-PC communications or for accessing a LAN from a remote location, but modems are generally too slow and too unreliable for linking LAN segments into a WAN.

B. The Public Switched Telephone Network (PSTN)

Public telephone networks offer two general types of service:

- **Dial-up services:** The customer pays on a per-use basis. Subscribers don't have exclusive access to a particular data path.
- **Leased dedicated services:** The customer is granted exclusive access to some amount of bandwidth.

Table 21.5.1 Types of Leased Dedicated Services

Type	Description
T1	A very popular digital line, *T1,* provides point-to-point connections and transmits a total of 24 channels across two wire pairs—one pair for sending and one for receiving—for a transmission rate of 1.544 Mbps in each direction. *DS-1* service is a full T1 line.[1]
T3	T3 is similar to T1, but T3 has an even higher capacity. In fact, a T3 line can transmit data at up to 45 Mbps.
Fractional and multiple T1 or T3	Subdivided channels of a T1 or T3 line or combined channels of a T1 or T3 line, respectively. Each channel of a T1's 24-channel bandwidth can transmit at 64 Kbps. This single-channel service is called *DS-0,* and it is one of the most popular service types.
Digital data service (DDS)	Usually implies a relatively low-speed digital service used for SNA connectivity. DDS circuits usually transmit data point-to-point at 2.4, 4.8, 9.6, or 56 Kbps.
Switched 56	A full-duplex, wide area, digital data line offering 56-kbits/s service on a dial-up basis.

1. DS-2 is four T1 lines. This is uncommon. You typically have to order as a fractional T3.

C. Packet Services

Many organizations must communicate between several points. Leasing a line between each pair of points can prove too costly. Many telecommunications services are now available to route packets between different sites. Packet-routing services include:

X.25

Frame Relay

ISDN

ATM

These services are available on a leased basis from service providers. An organization that must communicate between many sites simply pays to connect each site to the service, and the service assumes the responsibility of routing packets. The expense of operating the network is then shared among all network subscribers. Because the exact switching process is concealed from the subscriber, these networks frequently are depicted as a communication cloud. This sort of WAN architecture can be vastly more cost effective than leasing enough lines to provide equivalent connectivity.

1. Virtual Circuits

Packet-switching networks use virtual circuits to route data from the source to the destination. A *virtual circuit* is a specific path through the network—a chain of communication links leading from the source to the destination (as opposed to a scheme in which each packet finds its own path). Virtual circuits enable the network to provide better error checking and flow control.

Types of Virtual Circuits	Description
Switched Virtual Circuit (SVC)	Is created for a specific communication session and then disappears after the session. The next time the computers communicate, a different virtual circuit might be used.
Permanent Virtual Circuit (PVC)	A permanent route through the network that is always available to the customer. With a PVC, charges may or may not be billed on a per-use basis.

2. X.25

X.25 is a packet-switching network standard, referred to as *Recommendation X.25*, implemented most commonly in old or international WANs.

X.25 is one level of a three-level stack that spans the Network, Data Link, and Physical Layers (see fig. 21.5.2). The middle layer, *Link Access Procedures-Balanced (LAPB),* is a bit-oriented, full-duplex, synchronous Data Link Layer LLC protocol. Physical Layer connectivity is provided by a variety of standards, including X.21, X.21bis, and V.32.

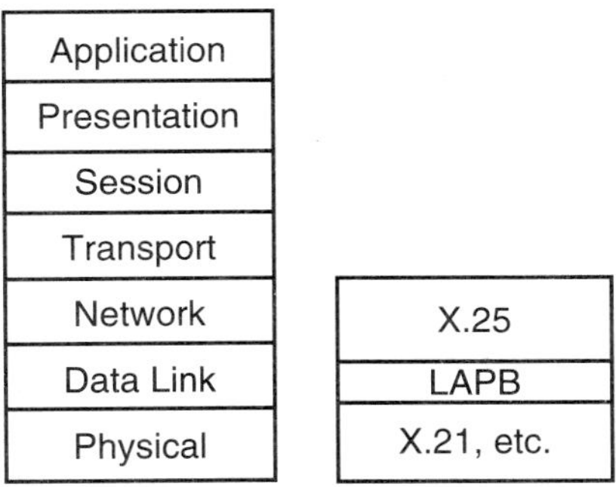

Figure 21.5.2 The relationship of X.25 to the OSI reference model.

X.25 packet-switching networks provide the options of permanent or switched virtual circuits. X.25 is required to provide reliable service and end-to-end flow control. Because each device on a network can operate more than one virtual circuit, X.25 must provide error and flow control for each virtual circuit.

The error checking and flow control slow down X.25. Generally, X.25 networks are implemented with line speeds up to 64 Kbps. These speeds are suitable for the mainframe terminal activity that comprised the bulk of network traffic when X.25 was defined. Such speeds, however, are inadequate to provide LAN-speed services, which typically require speeds of 1 Mbps or better. X.25 networks, therefore, are poor choices for providing LAN application services in a WAN environment.

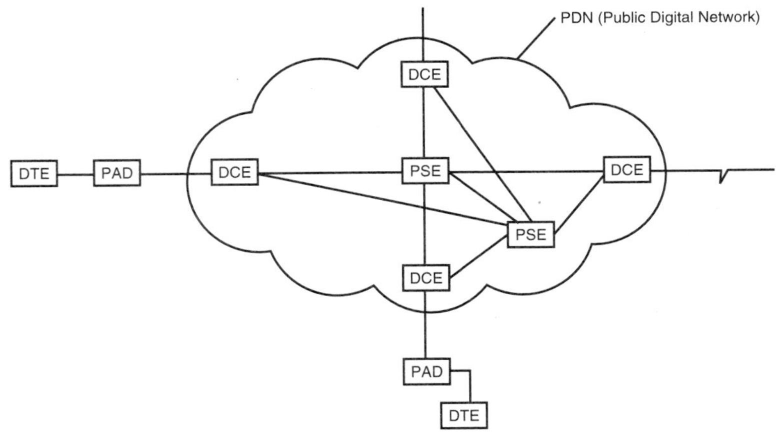

Figure 21.5.3 A typical X.25 network.

In X.25 parlance, a computer or terminal is called *data terminal equipment (DTE)*. A DTE could also be a gateway providing access to a local network. *Data communications equipment (DCE)* provides access to the *public switched telephone network* (*PSTN*). A PSE is a packet-switching exchange, also called a *switch* or *switching node.*

The X.25 protocol defines the communication between the DTE and the DCE. A device called a *packet assembler/disassembler (PAD)* translates asynchronous input from the DTE into packets suitable for the PDN.

21

X.25 should be used for international data circuits in which other, higher-speed technologies are either not available or not cost-effective.

3. Frame Relay

Frame relay was designed to support the *Broadband Integrated Services Digital Network (B-ISDN)*. The specifications for frame relay address some of the limitations of X.25. Frame relay is a packet-switching network service like X.25, but frame relay was designed around newer, faster fiber-optic networks.

Unlike X.25, frame relay assumes a reliable network. This enables frame relay to eliminate much of the X.25 overhead required to provide reliable service on less reliable networks. Frame relay networks rely on higher-level protocol layers to provide error control.

Frame relay typically is implemented as a public data network and, therefore, is regarded as a WAN protocol.

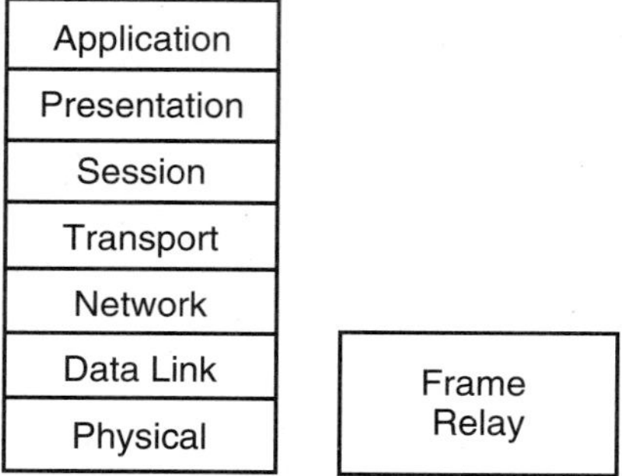

Figure 21.5.4 The relationship of frame relay to the OSI reference model. Notice that the scope of frame relay is limited to the Physical and Data Link Layers.

Frame relay provides permanent virtual circuits, which supply permanent virtual pathways for WAN connections. Frame relay services typically are implemented at line speeds from 56 Kbps up to 1.544 Mbps (T1).

Customers typically purchase access to a specific amount of bandwidth on a frame-relay service. This bandwidth is called the *committed information rate (CIR)*, a data rate for which the customer has guaranteed delivery for its data. Customers are usually also permitted to access data rates faster than their CIR by incurring the risk that their additional data might be discarded by the network if it becomes congested. Many people feel that this is an acceptable risk because most applications can tolerate some amount of packet loss.

Frame relay circuits generally should be used when they are less expensive than equivalent point-to-point circuits, and the data being transported can tolerate the additional delay that packet switching introduces.

Frame relay has less overhead than other packet- or cell-switching technologies such as ATM and X.25.

4. ISDN and B-ISDN

Integrated Services Digital Network (ISDN) is a term used for a group of ITU (CCITT) standards designed to provide full-featured, next-generation services via digital telephone networks.

The original idea behind ISDN was to enable existing phone lines to carry digital communications. Thus, ISDN is more like traditional telephone service than some of the other WAN services discussed in this chapter. ISDN is intended as a dial-up service and not as a permanent, 24-hour connection. Like other dial-up services, it often includes a per-use fee.

ISDN Types	Description
Basic Rate ISDN (BRI)	The most common type, originally intended to replace standard analog telephone lines. Uses three channels. Two channels (called *B channels*) carry the digital data at 64 Kbps. A third channel (called the *D channel*) provides link and signaling information at 16 Kbps. Commonly described as *2B+D*. A single PC transmitting through ISDN can sometimes use both B channels simultaneously, providing a maximum data rate of 128 Kbps (or higher with compression).
Primary Rate ISDN (PRI)	Larger scale, supports 23 B channels at 64 Kbps and one 64-Kbps D channel. Sometimes used in place of a T1.
Broadband ISDN (B-ISDN)	A refinement of ISDN that is defined to support higher-bandwidth applications. Physical Layer support for B-ISDN is provided by *Asynchronous Transfer Mode (ATM)* and the *Synchronous Optical Network (SONET)*. Some typical B-ISDN data rates are 51 Mbps, 155 Mbps, and 622 Mbps.

ISDN BRI circuits should be used for places that don't need full-time connectivity or high speeds. If you have many dial-in connections using BRIs, it is most cost effective to have them dial in to different channels on a PRI.

5. Asynchronous Transfer Mode (ATM)

Asynchronous Transfer Mode (ATM) is considered the best choice for mixing voice, video, and data. It is a high-bandwidth switching technology developed by the ITU Telecommunications Standards Sector (ITU-TSS). An organization called the ATM Forum is responsible for defining ATM implementation characteristics. ATM can be layered on other Physical Layer technologies, such as SONET or SDH (see fig. 21.5.5).

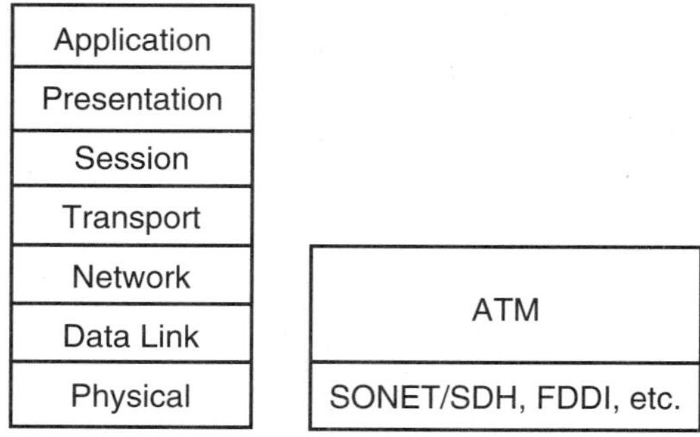

Figure 21.5.5 The relationship of ATM to the OSI reference model.

ATM is based on fixed-length, 53-byte cells (with 5 bytes of header and 48 bytes of data), whereas other technologies employ frames that can vary in length to accommodate different amounts of data. Because ATM cells are uniform in length, switching mechanisms can be easily implemented in hardware to operate with a high level of efficiency. This high efficiency results in very high data-transfer rates. Some ATM systems can operate at several gigabits per second, but the most common two speeds for ATM are 155 Mbps and 622 Mbps.

Asynchronous delivery refers to the characteristic of ATM in which transmission time slots don't occur periodically (as in the traditional telecommunications TDM environment) but are granted at irregular intervals as needed. Traffic that is time-critical, such as voice or video, can be given priority over data traffic that can be delayed slightly with no ill effect. A high-priority transmission need not be held until its next time slot allocation. Instead, it might be required to wait only until the current 53-byte cell has been transmitted.

As in other switched WAN services, devices communicate on ATM networks by establishing a virtual circuit.

ATM is relatively new technology, and only a few suppliers provide the equipment necessary to support it. (ATM networks must use ATM-compatible switches, routers, and other connectivity devices.)

An interesting advantage of ATM is that ATM makes it possible to use the same technology for both LANs and WANs. Some disadvantages, however, include the cost, the limited availability of the equipment, and the present lack of expertise regarding ATM due to its recent arrival.

The most compelling reason to use ATM is that you require WAN speeds of over 100 Mbps. Relatively few networks have this very expensive requirement.

21.5.1 Exercise

Given that a single channel of a T1 is a DS-0 that provides you with 64 kbps, and that a T1 is made up of 24 DS-0 circuits, calculate the speed of a T1. Next, given that a T3 is made up of 28 T1s (672 DS-0 channels), calculate the speed of a T3. Compare these speeds to typical LAN speeds.

21.5.1 Exercise Explanation

Sample T1 calculation:

```
 64000
 ×24
 ———
 256000
1280000
 ———
1536000 bits per second*
```

* The actual speed of a T1 is 1.544 Mbps, but 8000 bps of that is used for line overhead and cannot be used for other purposes.

A T1 transmits data at about 15 percent of the speed a standard Ethernet does. T1s, however, always operate in full-duplex mode, whereas Ethernet is usually in half-duplex. T1s are much slower than regular LANs.

Sample T3 calculation:

```
 1536000
   ×28
 ————
12288000
30720000
 ————
43008000 bits per second*
```

* The actual speed of a T3 is 44.736 Mbps, but 1.728 Mbps of that is used for line overhead and cannot be used for other purposes.

A T3 is fast compared to a standard Ethernet, running at almost 4.5 times the standard LAN speed and in full-duplex. It would be a huge waste of money and resources to hook a single Ethernet to a T3 because the Ethernet wouldn't be able to keep up. A T3 runs at close to half the theoretical speed of a full-duplex 100Base-T or FDDI LAN.

21.5 Practice Problems

1. *Analog* signals:
   - A. Can take on many values
   - B. Can take on only two values
   - C. Cannot be transmitted over long distances
   - D. Are primarily used with asynchronous services like ATM

2. *Digital* signals:
   - A. Can take on many values
   - B. Can take on only two values
   - C. Cannot be transmitted over long distances
   - D. Are primarily used by dial-up modems

3. You require LAN connectivity between two sites at 1 Mbps or faster. What type of leased line most cost-effectively meets this requirement?
   - A. DS-0
   - B. T1
   - C. T2
   - D. T3

4. Your company already uses several T1 lines to provide Internet access and is considering ordering a faster line. What is the next commonly available standard leased line speed?
   - A. 56 kbps
   - B. 1.544 Mbps
   - C. 10 Mbps
   - D. 45 Mbps

5. How many T1s are in a T3?
   - A. None—a T1 is faster than a T3.
   - B. One—they are different names for the same speed.
   - C. 3 T1s are in a T3.
   - D. 28 T1s are in a T3.

6. Which of the following is fastest?
   - A. DS-0
   - B. DS-1
   - C. DS-2
   - D. DS-3

7. You need high-speed (minimum of 1.5 Mbps guaranteed) connectivity between two LANs in distant cities. Which type of WAN connection is probably most cost effective?
   - A. Leased T1
   - B. X.25
   - C. ATM
   - D. SMDS

8. You need to build an international WAN that supports mostly terminal emulation traffic. What WAN type should you use?
   - A. Leased T1
   - B. X.25
   - C. ATM
   - D. Frame relay

9. You require several LANs to have any-to-any communication at 1 Mbps or greater, but you want to minimize cost. What WAN type should you use?
   - A. Leased T1
   - B. X.25
   - C. ATM
   - D. Frame relay

10. A switched virtual circuit:
    - A. is always active
    - B. becomes active only where there is data to transfer

C. is another name for a PVC

D. is typically used with point-to-point leased lines

11. Which WAN connection service can use a PAD to packetize asynchronous data?

A. Leased T1

B. X.25

C. ATM

D. Frame relay

12. Which WAN connection service has the most overhead?

A. Leased T1

B. X.25

C. ATM

D. Frame relay

13. Which WAN connection service has the least overhead?

A. Leased T1

B. X.25

C. ATM

D. Frame relay

14. You require a WAN connection with throughput of at least 100 Mbps. Which WAN connection service meets this requirement?

A. Leased T1

B. X.25

C. ATM

D. Frame relay

15. You require a reliable, error-correcting WAN protocol. Which WAN connection service meets this requirement?

A. Leased T1

B. X.25

C. ATM

D. Frame relay

16. You need to configure a dial-backup for use when there is a problem with your leased T1 to headquarters. Which WAN connection service is well-suited for dial-up?

A. Leased T1

B. X.25

C. ISDN BRI

D. Frame relay

17. Which of the following technologies are usually limited to 64 kbps and below?

A. Leased T1

B. X.25

C. ATM

D. Frame relay

18. Which of the following WAN connection services is sometimes described as 2B+D?

A. Leased T1

B. X.25

C. ISDN BRI

D. Frame relay

19. You determine that you need a low-overhead packet-switching WAN connection service. Which one of the following best fits this description?

A. Leased T1

B. X.25

C. ATM

D. Frame relay

20. You have some remote offices that only need occasional connectivity to the main office. Which WAN connection service is best suited to on-demand connections?

A. Leased T1

B. X.25

C. ISDN BRI

D. Frame relay

21. Which of the following is NOT a disadvantage of ATM?
    A. There are relatively few suppliers.
    B. It is expensive.
    C. It supports very high speeds.
    D. It is difficult to work with.

22. You need to build a WAN that connects offices in China, France, and Australia. What WAN connection type is best suited for this type of requirement?
    A. Leased T1
    B. X.25
    C. ISDN BRI
    D. Frame relay

23. Your new CEO decides that the company must use the same technology on both the LAN and on the WAN. What WAN connection type enables him to do this?
    A. Leased T1
    B. X.25
    C. ATM
    D. Frame relay

24. Which WAN connection type is typically the most expensive?
    A. Leased T1
    B. X.25
    C. ATM
    D. Frame relay

25. Which WAN connection type is typically the least expensive?
    A. Leased T1
    B. X.25
    C. ISDN BRI
    D. Frame relay

26. You need a WAN connection that can simultaneously carry voice, video, and data traffic to allow your company to realize a cost savings from consolidating these existing WAN circuits. Which WAN connection service meets this requirement?
    A. Leased T1
    B. X.25
    C. ATM
    D. Frame relay

27. You want to take advantage of a WAN cloud for communications between your offices. Which type of WAN cloud commonly provides speeds of around 1 Mbps?
    A. Leased T1
    B. X.25
    C. ATM
    D. Frame relay

28. Which of the following uses a cell-based architecture?
    A. Leased T1
    B. X.25
    C. ATM
    D. Frame relay

29. Which of the following uses data frames that can vary in size?
    A. Leased T1
    B. X.25
    C. ATM
    D. Frame relay

30. Select all of the following technologies that can be used with a router:
    A. Leased T1
    B. X.25

C. ATM

D. Frame relay

31. You determine that your WAN traffic is very bursty. What WAN connection service has a feature that can let you send data above the speed at which delivery is guaranteed?

A. Leased T1

B. X.25

C. ATM

D. Frame relay

32. What WAN connection service is sold with a Committed Information Rate (CIR) guaranteeing a certain throughput?

A. Leased T1

B. X.25

C. ATM

D. Frame relay

33. If your headquarters needs to accept up to 20 ISDN dial-up calls on individual B channels, what would be the best way to deliver those calls?

A. On B-ISDN

B. ATM

C. SONET

D. PRI

34. What assumption does frame relay make that X.25 didn't?

A. That the speed of light will be the limiting factor in data transmission

B. That the underlying network media may be error prone

C. That larger packets are always better packets

D. That there will be very few errors introduced

35. How do devices on ATM networks communicate?

A. They establish a session with the router, which forwards all their traffic to the correct ATM host.

B. They use broadcasts for most ATM-related communications.

C. They establish virtual circuits between the devices that need to communicate.

D. They use IP addresses for all communications.

36. One of the advantages of ATM's using such small cells is that:

A. It means there is less overhead than larger cells would have.

B. Each cell can contain complete, end-to-end addressing.

C. Time-sensitive data can be safely multiplexed with non-time-sensitive data.

D. Software-based cell switching is much faster.

37. Which WAN connection services can run at high enough speeds to require delivery on fiber optic cables?

A. ATM

B. Frame Relay

C. T3

D. X.25

38. You need to transport high-quality video across a WAN that normally carries only data traffic. Which WAN connection service should you choose?

A. X.25

B. Frame relay

C. ISDN

D. ATM

39. You have to design a WAN that connects three offices. One is in Boston, another is in Minneapolis, and another is in San Diego.

    Required outcome:
    Each site must be able to communicate with the other sites.

    Desired outcome:
    Connection speed must be 1 Mbps or greater.

    Communications between all sites must continue even if one WAN line fails.

    Your solution:

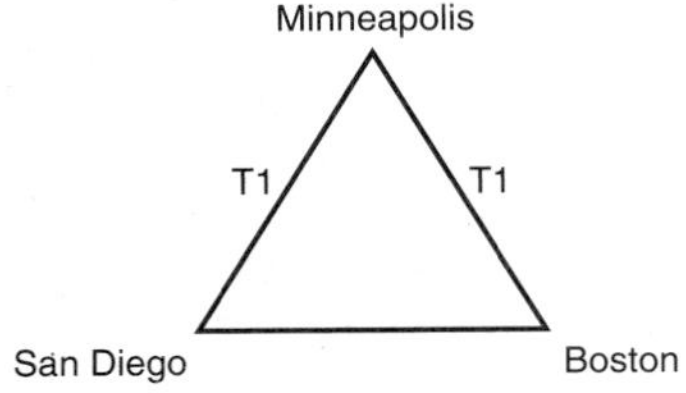

    A. This solution meets the required outcome and both of the desired outcomes.
    B. This solution meets the required outcome and one of the desired outcomes.
    C. This solution meets the required outcome but neither of the desired outcomes.
    D. This solution does not meet the required outcome.

40. You have to design a WAN that connects three offices. One is in Boston, another in is Minneapolis, and another is in San Diego.

    Required outcome:
    Each site must be able to communicate with the other sites.

    Desired outcome:
    Connection speed must be 1 Mbps or greater.

    Communications between all sites must continue even if one WAN line fails.

    Your solution:

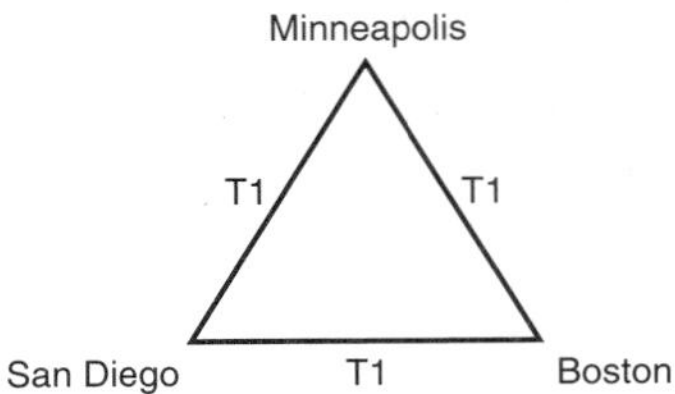

    A. This solution meets the required outcome and both of the desired outcomes.
    B. This solution meets the required outcome and one of the desired outcomes.
    C. This solution meets the required outcome but neither of the desired outcomes.
    D. This solution does not meet the required outcome.

21.5 Answers and Explanations: Practice Problems

1. **A** Analog signals can take on many values.
2. **B** Digital signals can take on only two values, one or zero.
3. **B** A T1 transmits data at 1.544 Mbps, the closest choice to 1 Mbps presented.
4. **D** A T3 is the next commonly available leased line speed, and it runs at 45 Mbps.
5. **D** There are 28 T1s in a T3.
6. **D** A DS-3, which runs at 45 Mbps, is the fastest choice presented.
7. **A** Leased T1s are usually most cost effective of the choices presented when there is a point-to-point full-time connectivity requirement.
8. **B** X.25 is best suited for international use because of its wide availability.
9. **D** Frame relay is the most cost-effective way to provide any-to-any connectivity for LANs because it runs at over 1 Mbps and only requires one line at each site.

10. **B** A switched virtual circuit becomes active only when there is data to transfer.

11. **B** An X.25 service can use a PAD to packetize asynchronous data.

12. **B** X.25 has the most overhead of the choices presented.

13. **A** A leased T1 network has the least overhead because it is point-to-point and therefore doesn't require the additional header information that packet switching networks do.

14. **C** ATM is the only WAN connection service that runs at speeds of at least 100 Mbps.

15. **B** X.25 is the only reliable, error-correcting WAN protocol listed.

16. **C** ISDN BRI circuits were originally envisioned as replacing analog dial-up lines, and they remain well-suited for dial-up applications.

17. **B** X.25 is usually limited to 64 kbps and below because of its high overhead.

18. **C** ISDN BRI circuits are sometimes described as 2B+D because they have two B channels and one D channel.

19. **D** Frame relay is a low-overhead packet-switching WAN connection service.

20. **C** ISDN BRI circuits are best suited to on-demand connections.

21. **C** Being able to go very fast is not a disadvantage.

22. **B** X.25 is best suited to international WANs.

23. **C** ATM has the potential of being used both on the WAN and on the LAN.

24. **C** ATM is typically the most expensive because it usually is only used for very high speeds.

25. **C** ISDN BRIs are typically the least expensive WAN connection service because they are used for dial-on-demand applications in which full-time connectivity isn't required.

26. **C** ATM was designed to carry voice, video, and data traffic simultaneously.

27. **D** A frame relay WAN cloud commonly provides speeds of around 1 Mbps.

28. **C** ATM uses a cell-based architecture.

29. **A, B, D** Leased T1, X.25, and frame relay all use data frames that can vary in size.

30. **A, B, C, D** Leased T1, X.25, ATM, and frame relay can all be used with a router.

31. **D** Frame relay has a feature that can let you send data above the speed at which delivery is guaranteed.

32. **D** Frame relay is sold with a Committed Information Rate (CIR) guaranteeing a certain throughput.

33. **D** A PRI circuit delivers 23 ISDN B channels.

34. **D** Frame relay assumes there will be very few errors introduced, so it doesn't do any error recovery, unlike X.25 which assumes that it will need to correct errors.

35. **C** Devices on ATM networks have to establish at least one virtual circuit between the devices that need to communicate.

36. **C** Because ATM cells are so small, time-sensitive data can be safely multiplexed with non-time-sensitive data.

37. **A** ATM can run at high enough speeds to require delivery on fiber-optic cable.

38. **D** ATM can support the efficient mixing of data and video.

39. **B** This solution meets the required outcome and one of the desired outcomes. The connectivity requirement is met, and the speed goal is met. There is, however, no redundancy.

40. **A** This solution meets the required outcome and both of the desired outcomes.

21.5 Key Words

Amplitude

Analog

ATM

Digital

Frame relay

ISDN

T1

T3

X.25

Practice Exam: Planning

1. You need to design a 100-Mbps backbone network connecting five heavily used LANs. You should use:
   A. Fiber
   B. Coaxial cable
   C. 10Base-T
   D. Token ring

2. You need to design a LAN to run at 100 Mbps. What kind of cabling should you use?
   A. Category 3 UTP
   B. Category 5 UTP
   C. Fiber
   D. Coaxial

3. A device used to penetrate the cable in a thicknet connection is:
   A. An AUI connector
   B. A T-connector
   C. A vampire tap
   D. An N-connector

4. The best network cable in terms of transmission characteristics is which of the following?
   A. STP
   B. Cat 5 UTP
   C. Fiber
   D. Thinnet

5. Cable length limitations of 100 meters are fairly standard for which type of cable
   A. Fiber
   B. Thicknet
   C. Thinnet
   D. Twisted pair

6. You are getting ready to move to a new building that already has network cables installed. You require 100 Mbps support, and the building is already wired. You have the cabling tested and find that it passes all Category 3 tests. The best course of action is to:
   A. Replace all the cable with Category 5
   B. Use the cable as it is
   C. Install fiber cable
   D. Explore wireless options

7. In which topology is a single cable failure a serious problem?
   A. Star
   B. Bus
   C. Ring
   D. Mesh

8. To increase bandwidth in an existing network, you need to ______.
   A. Segment the network
   B. Re-cable the network
   C. Add RAM to the server
   D. Upgrade the Network Interface Cards

9. Which type of network topology requires a connection from every device to every other device?
   A. Bus
   B. Star
   C. Ring
   D. Mesh

10. In an Ethernet network, collisions:
    A. Indicate network overload
    B. Are caused by synchronization problems with the server
    C. Are normal events
    D. Are errors

11. According to the OSI model, what is responsible for making sure data is delivered reliably?
    A. The Physical Layer
    B. The Data Link Layer
    C. The Network Layer
    D. The Transport Layer

12. In an Ethernet network, a network interface card accepts a frame if:
    A. The destination Data Link address matches the NIC
    B. The destination Network Layer address matches the NIC
    C. The source Data Link address matches the NIC
    D. The source Network Layer address matches the NIC

13. Token rings are similar to Ethernet LANs in that they both:
    A. Can support multiple protocols
    B. Use source route bridging
    C. Rely on a token
    D. Can experience collisions

14. You determine that there are too many collisions on your network. The best solution is to:
    A. Change to a token ring network
    B. Add an Ethernet switch
    C. Install a NetBEUI to TCP/IP gateway
    D. Upgrade the network cable to Category 5

15. You determine that there are too many broadcasts on your network. The best solution is:
    A. To install a router to subnet the network
    B. To install a repeater to block the broadcasts
    C. To install a bridge to divide the network in two
    D. To install an Ethernet switch because it will reduce the broadcasts by filtering them at ports that don't need to see them

16. You are using a mixture of NetBEUI and TCP/IP, and the network performance is poor because of the broadcast levels. What device can be installed to minimize the problem while maintaining full connectivity?
    A. A repeater
    B. A bridge
    C. A router
    D. A brouter

Answers and Explanations: Practice Exam

1. **A** Fiber is the best choice for backbone networks that may have to run under high loads or be upgraded to higher speeds.
2. **B** Category 5 UTP is the best choice for most 100 Mbps LANs.
3. **C** A vampire tap is used to penetrate the cable in a thicknet environment.
4. **C** Fiber network cables have the best transmission characteristics.
5. **D** Twisted-pair cables are commonly limited to 100 meters.
6. **A** If you need 100 Mbps support, you should replace all the cable with Category 5.
7. **B** In a bus topology, a single cable failure can cripple the entire network.
8. **A** Segmenting the network is a common way to increase bandwidth.
9. **D** A mesh network topology requires a connection from every device to every other device.

10. **C** In an Ethernet network, collisions are normal events.

11. **D** The Transport Layer is responsible for making sure data is delivered reliably.

12. **A** In an Ethernet network, a network interface card accepts a frame if the destination data link address matches the NIC's address.

13. **A** Token rings are similar to Ethernet LANs in that they both can support multiple protocols.

14. **B** Ethernet switches are the most effective way to reduce collisions on a network without making other changes.

15. **A** A router is the only device listed that can block broadcast traffic.

16. **D** You have to use a brouter because one of the protocols is routable and the other one is not routable.

CHAPTER 22

Implementation

22.1 Choose an Administrative Plan to Meet Specified Needs, Including Performance Management, Account Management, and Security

The Networking Essentials test focuses heavily on elements of Microsoft networking. Other network architectures, such as Novell NetWare and AppleTalk, are not as important.

In order to choose an administrative plan, it is important that you understand the scope of what you are managing.

We list users last, because the core of the network is actually the *network resources,* made available via the concept of *sharing,* which in turn is modified through *permissions.* Only then are users, as defined by your user administrative plan, able to access network resources.

The core elements of your management plan will incorporate the following:

- **Resources:** These are typically disk drives or printers. However, a mail or mainframe gateway, a shared modem or fax device, or a shared tape drive can all be resources.

  A disk drive or printer is not a network resource simply by virtue of being part of a networked PC, though. It must be *shared* (as defined next) or otherwise accessible from the network. If the disk or printer in question is accessible only from the one computer to which it is attached, it is not a network resource.

  As network technology advances, more and more device types can be shared across a network. Because of this, the list of possible resources is constantly changing. Simply remember this: If it can be accessed from another computer on the network, it is a network resource. Any computer sharing a resource can be called a "server." This includes Windows for Workgroups and Windows NT workstation.

- **Sharing:** This is how a particular device becomes a network resource. Your hard drive or printer must be given a *share name.* This share name is how the resource is accessed by other computers on the network. For example, I might share my printer using the name \\workstation\inkjet. (This format is often referred to as *\\servername\sharename.* "Servername" does not refer to the domain controller or network name, but the name of the computer sharing the resource.)

- **Permissions:** *Permissions* refers specifically to the security access a user or group has to a resource. Permissions can be managed in two ways: with share-level security or user-level security.

  Share-Level Security

  Share-level security is a simple security implementation. The share can be made either read-only or full access, either or both of which can be protected with a password. The user supplies the appropriate password to access the share for read- only or full access.

  Owing to the minimal security offered by share level, this security scheme is typically not recommended. However, share-level security is the only level of security available if you do not have an NT server, NT workstation, Novell server, or other OS/2 LAN server. If you have a network of only Windows for Workgroups and Windows 95 workstations, you cannot implement user-level security.

  The administrative burden with share-level security is considerably less than with user-level security. For this reason, Microsoft will recommend it in cases where some security is required but the administrative burden must be reduced.

  User-Level Security

  User-level security is far more secure than share-level security. To implement user-level security, the network must contain a database of users, typically on a Windows NT or Novell NetWare server. If a user management tool such as *User Manager for Domains* is used, access permissions can be granted to individual users or groups of users. An access control list is maintained for each network resource.

  When a user attempts to connect to or "use" a server share, the server first checks to see if the user's name exists in the user accounts database. If so, the user's password is checked. If both of these security checks pass, the server completes the connection, and the user is allowed access to the shared resource according to the permissions in the resource's Access Control List.

- **Users:** A *user* is any entity that requests network resources. Some user accounts, such as *Administrator* or *guest*, are built-in, but most users are added. You assign a unique username and password to each individual on your network. Users can be created on a number of operating systems, including Windows NT, NetWare, and UNIX.

- **Groups:** Users can be placed into *groups* to simplify user management. Resources can then be made available to groups. A system administrator might create a group called "marketing," which could be given access to the marketing files and printers. Because users can be added or removed, this is far easier than modifying the rights of each user.

- **Rights:** *Rights* refer to specific abilities a user or group might possess. Unlike permissions, rights focus on the user or group instead of the resource. Typical rights include the ability to perform the following actions:

  Create accounts

  Log on to a particular computer

  Log on as a service

Take ownership of files or other objects

Back up and restore files

Basically, rights modify the abilities of a particular user or group, enabling that person or group to carry out administrative functions.

A. Managing User Accounts and Groups

One of the most important items in user management is the interaction of user accounts and group membership. Windows NT includes Global groups and Local groups.

Most user accounts are typically created for a single user. Exceptions to this are special accounts created for a network service. User accounts contain:

- **Username:** This must be unique. No two users can have the same username.
- **Password:** This secures the account and prohibits one user from logging on as another user. Individual passwords should be kept private to avoid unauthorized access.
- **Group membership:** If resource permissions have been appropriately granted to groups, group membership determines the user's rights and permissions on the network.

A number of other optional components exist, such as a home directory (a place where a user can store personal files on the network) or specific information about the user (such as his full name or description).

The simplest way to manage user accounts is through groups. The Microsoft definition of *groups* is a tool for simplifying user management. Windows networks contain two types of groups:

- **Global groups:** Domain-level groups that can contain only users. These groups may be exported to other domains via trust relationships.
- **Local groups:** Groups that can contain users and global groups. Local groups are given certain rights to network resources.

Using groups simplifies user management. Remember this phrase:

> Users go into global groups; global groups go into local groups; local groups get the resources.

Windows NT comes ready-made with a set of groups that are adequate for most security needs. Here is a list of those groups and a brief description of each: 22

Domain Users: A group that contains all users in the domain. User rights and resources granted to this group are usually severely limited. For example, the Domain Users group does not have the right to access parts of the control panel on a Windows NT workstation.

Domain Admins: A very powerful *global* group. This group is able to create and delete users, take control of files and other resources, and act as part of the operating system. Only authorized persons should be in this group.

Administrators: A *local* group. The global group Domain Admins typically is placed in this local group on each server in the domain.

Power users: A group that is given greater rights over their own workstations than domain users are given.

Everyone: A special group that contains all users in local or trusted domains, as well as unrecognized users. It is impossible to add or delete users to this special group.

Other groups are defined with the rights necessary to perform particular tasks. These built-in groups are adequate for most network needs.

A system administrator must balance the concerns of security, user-access, and administrative ease when defining security. If the network requires little security or requires a minimum of administration, use an easy password policy and perhaps only share-level security.

B. Implementing Security on Windows NT

After you assign an account to a user in a group, you can assign that group access to resources. This follows the use pattern explained above: Place users into global groups, place global groups into local groups, grant resources to local groups. You must set permissions on each resource. Setting permissions is a time-consuming process that should be undertaken with care. If not, the process can become confusing.

Basically, network security can take three forms:

- **Access permissions applied to a shared resource**

  Access permissions refer to the simple password-protection schemes applied to network shares. A resource is shared with two passwords, one for full access and one for read-only access. The user supplies the correct password for access.

- **User-level security applied to a shared resource**

  This is more robust than simply applying access-level protection using a password. In this method, the network administrator shares a certain resource and adds user groups from the user database to have access. This type of access is the most common.

- **File-level security applied to a shared resource**

  This is the highest level of network security, and it requires the shared drive to be formatted NTFS (the native file system of Windows NT). In addition to the share-level security, the network administrator can grant (or deny) individual users and groups the ability to read specific files or directories individually.

C. Creating and Assigning Permissions to a Shared Folder on Windows NT

In exercise 22.1.2, you create and share a directory called Public. You will:

- Grant the group Everyone Read access.
- Grant the group Local Training Full Control.

All security in this example is assuming no NTFS file-level security, so security is granted at the share level.

You can also give rights and permissions directly to user accounts themselves, but such security is cumbersome and difficult to administer. For ease of use and administration, remember: Place users into global groups, place global groups into local groups, and grant resources to local groups.

D. Assigning File-Level Permissions on an NTFS Partition

Exercise 22.1.3 assumes that your network partition is formatted with NTFS. NTFS is superior because it allows the administrator to implement a very sophisticated security policy. Also, NTFS provides local security. Local users are unaffected by share-level security options but are stymied by NTFS file-level security.

In the Public folder shared in exercise 22.1.2, you see that two share-level permissions exist for this directory:

Everyone: Read

Administrators: Full Control

In exercise 22.1.3, you assign a new permission to the directory, this time through NTFS security. The permission to be assigned will be:

Everyone: Change

Use a dedicated server such as Windows NT or NetWare to provide resource access on your network. In some situations, though, you might need to implement a workgroup sharing model or use a Windows 95 machine as a server. This is more common in situations where the sensitivity of data is relatively low, or where the administrative cost of managing a large user database is high.

E. Implementing Access-Level Security

Windows 95 also can act as a server, but it does not support user-level security unless there is a server on your network. Under Windows 95's security model, passwords are assigned to permit access to each directory or printer share. To access the share, a user must supply the correct password. When creating a shared directory using share-level security, you can grant one of three types of access:

- **Read-only access:** Users can access files and subdirectories in a directory but cannot delete or save files to that share.
- **Full access:** Users can read, write, and delete files in the directory.
- **Depends on password:** Two different passwords can be created, one that allows read-only access and one that allows full access. The type of access granted to a user depends on the password that user supplies.

If no password is entered, all users have full or read-only access to the directory, depending on which option was specified when the shared directory was created.

Table 22.1.1 outlines both the advantages and disadvantages of using Windows 95's model of access-level security.

Table 22.1.1 Advantages and Disadvantages of Access-Level Security

Disadvantages	Advantages
To access different shares, a network user must know numerous passwords.	Very simple to administer.
Passwords can easily be forgotten.	Flexible, as a user can be granted new permission with a new password.
Nothing prevents a user from disclosing the password to unauthorized users.	

F. User-Level Security on Windows 95

Windows 95 cannot manage user accounts by itself. Instead, it requires a Windows NT or NetWare server to authenticate the user trying to access the resource.

When a directory is shared with user-level security, the users or groups to be granted access to the share are assigned privileges. You can grant each user or group one of the following privileges:

- **Read-only:** Users can access files and subdirectories in a directory but cannot delete or save files to that share.
- **Full access:** Users can read, write, and delete files in the directory.
- **Custom:** Any number of the following privileges can be granted: Read Files, Write to Files, Create Files, List Files, Delete Files, Change File Attributes, Change Permissions.

G. Security for Printer Resources

To connect to a network printer, you first must install and configure the printer on a server. Both Windows NT and NetWare support printing directly to print devices, such as HP JetDirect cards.

To use either a Windows NT or Windows 95 printer as a network print server, you simply share a printer directly connected to the computer. The printer must then be shared to allow other users to access it. To share a printer in Windows 95 installation, the File and Print Sharing component must be enabled. This feature is on by default in Windows NT.

When the printer has been configured and shared on the network print server, users from Windows 95, Windows for Workgroups, Windows NT, or Novell's DOS requester can be configured to connect to the print server and print to the printer over the network.

H. Monitoring the Security Policy

The typical systems administrator has the following security responsibilities:

- **Auditing:** The Windows NT Event Viewer can be used to view system events that affect security. In *User Manager for Domains*, the system security policy can be set to audit security events.

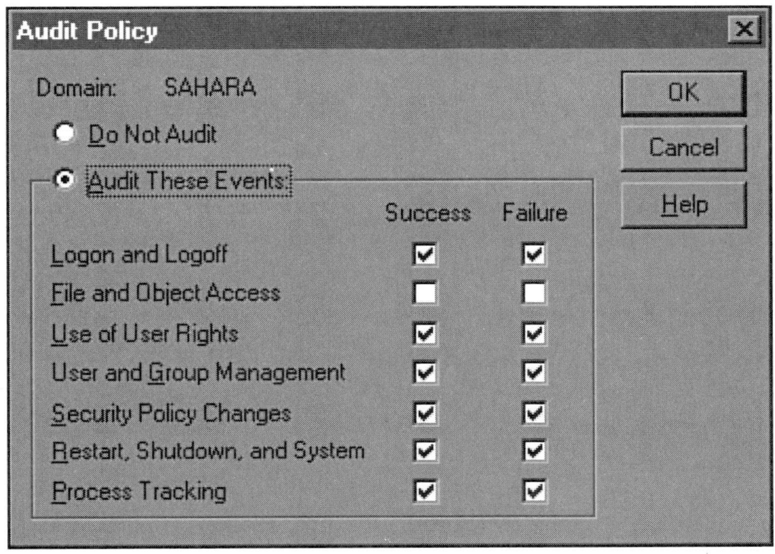

Figure 22.1.1 This window is used to create a security audit. System Administrators can view events that could become security threats.

Event Viewer - Security Log on \\NERDNET

Log View Options Help

Date	Time	Source	Category	Event	User	Computer
8/15/97	8:26:36 PM	Security	Privilege Use	576	Rob	NERDNET
8/15/97	8:26:36 PM	Security	Logon/Logoff	528	Rob	NERDNET
8/15/97	8:26:36 PM	Security	Privilege Use	576	Rob	NERDNET
8/15/97	8:26:36 PM	Security	Logon/Logoff	528	Rob	NERDNET
8/15/97	8:26:28 PM	Security	Logon/Logoff	538	Administrator	NERDNET
8/15/97	8:26:27 PM	Security	Detailed Tracking	593	Administrator	NERDNET
8/15/97	8:26:26 PM	Security	Detailed Tracking	593	Administrator	NERDNET
8/15/97	8:26:26 PM	Security	Detailed Tracking	593	Administrator	NERDNET
8/15/97	8:26:25 PM	Security	Detailed Tracking	593	Administrator	NERDNET
8/15/97	8:26:24 PM	Security	Detailed Tracking	593	Administrator	NERDNET
8/15/97	8:26:21 PM	Security	Privilege Use	578	Administrator	NERDNET
8/15/97	8:26:18 PM	Security	Detailed Tracking	593	Administrator	NERDNET
8/15/97	8:25:38 PM	Security	Detailed Tracking	592	Administrator	NERDNET

Figure 22.1.2 Here is a sample audit trail created using the auditing functions selected in Figure 22.1.1. Events in this window can easily be viewed and analyzed as potential security threats. Note the logon, access, and logoff functions.

- **Virus protection:** Computers are susceptible to virus programs. A new type of virus can spread through word-processing macros. Networked computers are particularly susceptible to viruses due to the extraordinary rate of interaction.

  In order to detect viruses, your antivirus software must search for every specific virus that exists. Most antivirus programs maintain these definitions in a data file. You *must* periodically update this definition file. Most antivirus manufacturers have mailing lists or Web sites that list their latest virus definition files.

- **Physical security:** If your data is sensitive, you will need to consider physical security of your network servers. If your server is not secure, no amount of backups, RAID, share security, and NTFS permissions will protect your data from prying eyes.

  As with all security issues, you need to weight the needs of security against the costs of administration and ease of use.

Section Goals

Be able to create users and groups.

Be able to configure sharing and security for Microsoft resources.

Be able to connect to either Windows NT or Windows 95 machines to gain access to their shared files and printers.

Have knowledge of optional security measures available for sensitive data.

Know how to create network resources through sharing.

Experiment with permissions and user rights and have a clear understanding of the relationship between groups and users.

22.1 Exercises

1. Creating a User Account in Windows NT

Objective: Create a new Windows NT user account.

Estimated time: 10 minutes

1. Click Start, Programs, Administrative Tools. Choose either User Manager (Windows NT Workstation) or User Manager for Domains (Windows NT Server). User Manager opens. The Guest account is disabled by default and should remain that way unless your security policy dictates otherwise.

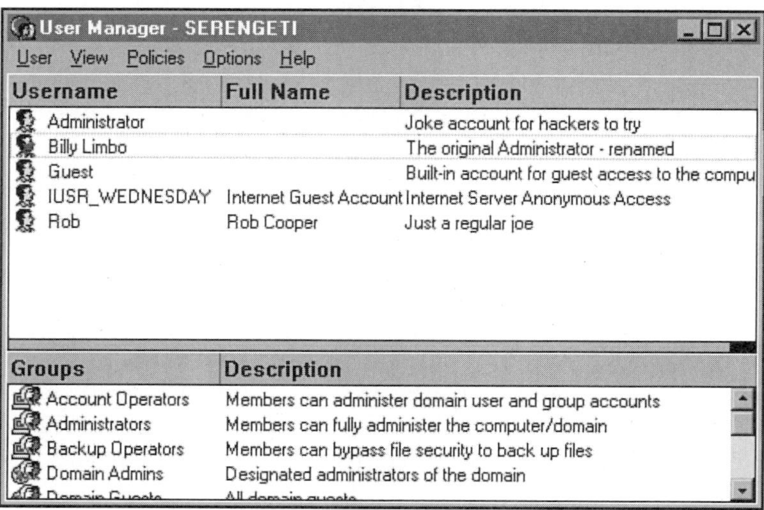

Figure 22.1.3 Account administration is done through the Windows NT User Manager for Domains program.

2. Click File, New User. The New User dialog box appears.

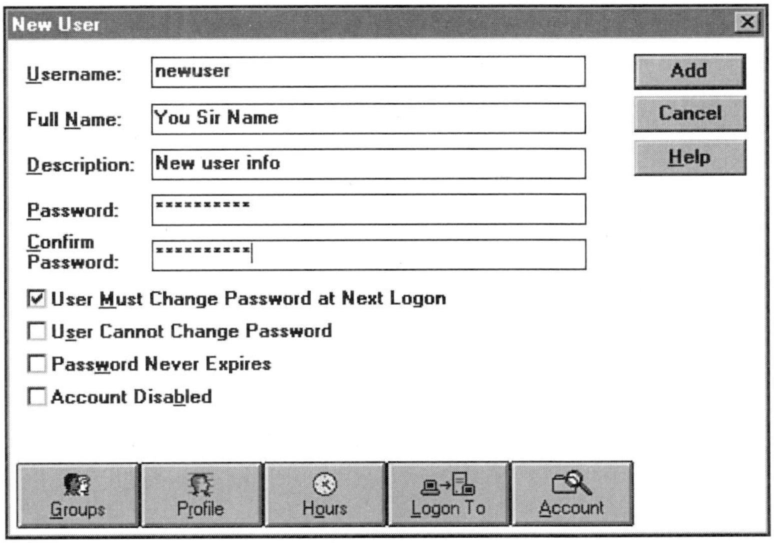

Figure 22.1.4 The Windows NT New User dialog box enables you to record information about a new user.

3. In the top field, type a unique username (in this case, **newuser**) for the new account. This name can be between 1 and 20 characters and cannot include spaces or any of the following characters:

   " / \ [ ] : ; | = , + * ? < >

4. Fill in the two text fields in order to identify the user for whom the account is being created.
5. In the password field, enter any combination of 1 to 14 characters of your choice, with the same exceptions that apply to the creation of usernames. The password will not be displayed. All passwords are case-sensitive.
6. Examine the check boxes below the Confirm Password field. By default, the User Must Change Password at Next Logon field should be checked. The first time that new user logs on, he is asked to provide a new password.
7. The User Cannot Change Password option generally is used only for guest or multi-user accounts to prevent one guest from changing the password and locking all other guest users out. Leave this box unchecked.
8. The Account Disabled field enables you to disable an account temporarily while a user is on vacation or when he is no longer allowed network access. Leave this box unchecked.
9. Click the Add button.
10. Click Close to return to User Manager. Your new user will appear with the others. You can delete the new user if you want.

2. Sharing a Directory and Implementing Share-Level Security

Objective: Share a Windows NT directory and assign share-level security to it.

Estimated time: 15 minutes

1. Click Start, Programs. Then click the Windows NT Explorer icon to bring up the Explorer window.
2. Select the root of the C: drive, and then right-click it to display a context-sensitive menu.
3. Select New, Folder. A folder appears under C:, and you are prompted to enter a name for the folder. Type **Public** and press Enter.
4. Click the new Public folder (in the left window). The folder is highlighted, and the right window is now empty.
5. Select the Public folder again. Click File, Properties (or use the quick menu and select Sharing from there) to open the Properties dialog box.
6. Click the Sharing tab. Note that the directory currently is not shared.
7. Click the Shared As option button. "Public" appears in the Share Name box. You can change or leave this initial name. In this case, change the share. Replace Public with **My Share** to illustrate the difference between a directory name and a share name.
8. Observe the Maximum Connections option. Leave the default setting, which enables unlimited concurrent connections to the share.
9. Click the Permissions button to call the Access Through Share Permissions dialog box. Observe that, by default, Everyone has Full Control over the new share.

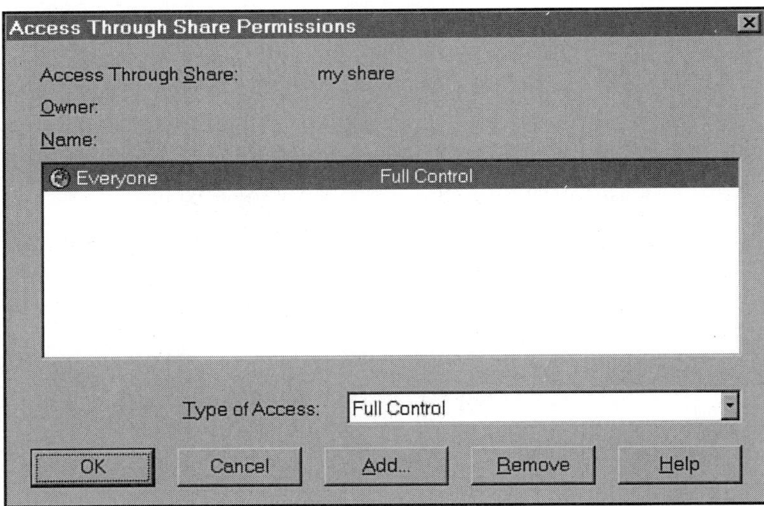

Figure 22.1.5 The Access Through Share Permissions dialog box enables you to determine the type of access for a particular group.

10. Select the Everyone group and click the Type of Access drop-down arrow. The following four selections appear:

    No Access: A member of any group with this permission is banned from the shared resource.

    Read: Members can list, read, and execute files but cannot modify or delete them.

Change: Members can read, list, execute, and delete files but are not able to change file permissions or assume ownership of the files.

Full Control: Members have complete control of the resources, assuming that they have sufficient rights to match their permissions.

3. Setting NTFS Permissions on a Shared Folder

Objective: Add NTFS security to the Public share.

Estimated time: 15 minutes

1. Click Start, Programs. Select Windows NT Explorer to open the Explorer window. Choose a directory on an NTFS partition. If you do not have an NTFS partition, you cannot complete this lab.
2. Create a directory called TestNTFS, and then right-click it. Select the Properties option from the menu to open the TestNTFS Properties window.
3. In the TestNTFS Properties window, click the Security tab, and then click the Permissions button to open the Directory Permissions dialog box.
4. Observe that the directory has only one permission set: Everyone: Full Control.
5. Select Everyone. Click the Type of Access drop-down arrow and choose Read.

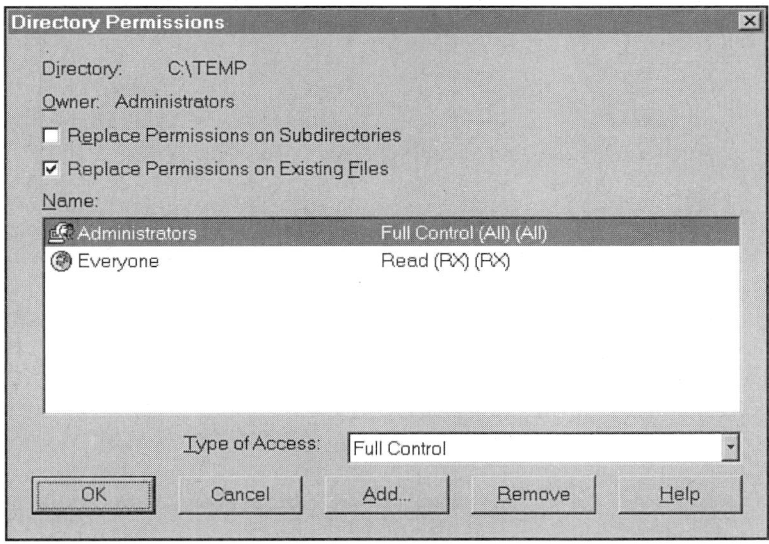

Figure 22.1.6 The Directory Permissions dialog box enables you to update or replace permissions for a group.

6. Take note of the check boxes near the top of the window. The Replace Permissions on Files option is checked, while the Replace Permissions on Subdirectories option is not checked. Because no subdirectories exist in this instance, leave the defaults as they are.
7. If you need to enter additional groups into the list, you can do so by using the Add button. Click this button, and then observe the Add Users and Groups window. Give Administrators Full Control permissions.

22

8. Click OK to return to the Directory Permissions window. Then click OK to set the new permissions and return to Explorer.
9. Click File, Exit to close Explorer.
10. Share the TestNTFS directory with Everyone—Full Control permissions and log on to the share from a remote machine. You should be able to modify, create, and delete files across the share if you are logged on as an Administrator, but you should only be able to read and execute while logged on as a TestUser.

4. Sharing a Directory Using Share-Level Security

Objective: Share a Windows 95 directory using share-level security.

Estimated time: 10 minutes

1. From the Start menu, choose Settings, Control Panel to display the Control Panel.
2. Double-click the Network icon to display the Network dialog box.
3. Choose the Access Control tab, and then choose share-level access control.
4. Select the Configuration tab and choose File, Print Sharing to display the File and Print Sharing dialog box.
5. Select both the I Want to be Able to Give Others Access to My Files check box and the I Want to be Able to Allow Others to Print to My Printer(s) check box to enable others to access your printers and files. Then choose OK to automatically install File and Printer Sharing for Microsoft Networks.
6. Choose OK and restart the computer.
7. After Windows 95 restarts, click Start, Windows Explorer and make a new folder on your C: drive named Password. Then choose the Password directory and make a text file within it called Password Test.
8. Right-click the Password directory to display the context-sensitive menu.
9. Choose Sharing from the context-sensitive menu to open the Sharing dialog box.
10. Accept Password as the share name and choose Access Type: Read-Only. Enter the password **read** for read-only access, and then choose OK. The sharing hand symbol replaces the folder symbol for the shared directory.
11. If you have another computer on the network, browse the first computer in Network Neighborhood to display the share name. The share name Password is displayed under the appropriate computer name.
12. Double-click the share name Password, and you are prompted for the password.
13. Enter **read** at the password prompt and choose OK to display the directory contents.
14. Copy the Password Test file from the share to your local hard drive. The file read will be successful.
15. Modify the file and try to copy it back. Then try to delete the original from the shared directory. Neither the file write nor the file delete will be allowed.

5. Creating a Local Printer with Windows NT

Objective: Create a locally installed printer on Windows NT

Estimated time: 20 minutes

1. Click Start, Settings. Then choose Printers to open the Printers window.
2. Click Add Printer to display the Add Printer Wizard. As with many other administrative tasks, the process of creating and sharing a printer has been streamlined and simplified by the use of a *wizard*, a small program that leads you through a particular task. Choose My Computer and click Next.
3. The wizard asks you to specify the port or ports to which the new printer should print. Choose LPT1: and click Next.
4. The wizard now asks you to specify the type of physical device to which you are printing or the device type that your printer emulates. Click HP in the left pane, and then find and select Color LaserJet. Then click Next.
5. Now you are asked to name your new printer. Remember that each printer on your machine must have a unique name and that the name should be descriptive of its type or function. Type **Color Printer** and click Next.
6. Now you are asked whether the printer will be shared and, if so, what other operating systems will access it. Click Shared, call the new share **MyLaser,** and select Windows 95 from the list of additional operating systems. Note that each supported Windows NT platform requires a different driver. Click Next.
7. The wizard now has all the information it needs. Leave the Print Test Page option on and click Finish. You will need the source files for both your Windows NT Server or Workstation and for Windows 95. You are prompted for the location of the source files, and the necessary drivers are loaded.
8. The Printer icon for Color Printer is created in the Printers window. Select it, and the queue appears. Print a document to the new printer and check the queue again. The document should be waiting to print.

22.1 Practice Problems

1. An overall administrative plan must consider:
   - A. Users, resources, sharing, and permissions.
   - B. Security, resources, permissions, and files.
   - C. Files, printers, and network adapters.
   - D. Users, files, documents, and resources.
2. Which of the following can be a *network resource*?
   - A. Disk drives
   - B. Printers
   - C. A modem
   - D. All of the above
3. In order to restrict access to a network resource, you modify:
   - A. User rights.
   - B. File locations.
   - C. Permissions.
   - D. Passwords.
4. True or False: Only a limited number of items can be *network resources.*
   - A. True
   - B. False
5. A *networked printer* is:
   - A. Any printer attached to a networked computer.
   - B. A printer shared using network server software.
   - C. A printer attached to a shared networked PC.
   - D. A printer attached or connected to a dedicated network server.
6. *Sharing* refers to:
   - A. Users in a workgroup accessing common documents.
   - B. Software-enabling access across the network.
   - C. Passwords used by multiple users.
   - D. None of the above.
7. A share name:
   - A. Is used to access the resource and should indicate its characteristics.
   - B. Must include department or workgroup information about the device.
   - C. Is required by the UNC naming convention to include the two-slash "\\" server name.
   - D. Must be mapped to a drive letter before it can be used.
8. The UNC naming system uses the following syntax:
   - A. \\username\servername
   - B. net use d: \\vol1\sys
   - C. \\servername\sharename
   - D. \\sharename\username

The next five questions use the following scenario.

Network type:

Windows NT server with Windows 3.11 workstations

Protocols used:

TCP/IP, NetBEUI

Network size:

1 server, 10 workstations

You are the administrator of a small network, in addition to your primary job of law clerk. Most of the users know each other very well, yet there is some data on the network that is not appropriate for all users. In addition, most of the users are computer literate and can be considered "power users." Your department has been awarded a large grant, so cost is no object for your network.

You want to implement a security plan.

Required goals:

- The plan must protect the sensitive data.
- The plan cannot adversely impact the current business practices.

Desired goals:

- You want the plan to be exceedingly simple and easy to administer.
- You would like to track user access to the sensitive data.

9. You decide to implement Windows NT workstation and convert to NTFS on the workstations with auditing enabled. This plan will:

   A. Perform both of the required goals and both of the desired goals.

   B. Perform both of the required goals and one of the desired goals.

   C. Perform both of the required goals and none of the desired goals.

   D. Not perform the required goals.

10. You implement Windows NT workstation, and you use user-level access permissions on the sensitive network resources to protect them. This plan will:

    A. Perform both of the required goals and both of the desired goals.

    B. Perform both of the required goals and one of the desired goals.

    C. Perform both of the required goals and none of the desired goals.

    D. Not perform the required goals.

11. You leave the workstations at Windows 3.11 and create user accounts for each user. You then assign them into groups and control access to network resources. This plan will:

    A. Perform both of the required goals and both of the desired goals.

    B. Perform both of the required goals and one of the desired goals.

    C. Perform both of the required goals and none of the desired goals.

    D. Not perform the required goals.

12. You leave the workstations at Windows 3.11 and convert the Windows NT server's disk to NTFS. You enable auditing for the shared resources, and you use a shared password to protect the sensitive data. This plan will:

    A. Perform both of the required goals and both of the desired goals.

    B. Perform both of the required goals and one of the desired goals.

    C. Perform both of the required goals and none of the desired goals.

    D. Not perform the required goals.

13. You leave the workstations at Windows 3.11 and create user accounts for each user. You convert the Windows NT server's disk to NTFS and enable file-level auditing. You enable user-level access to control access to network resources. This plan will:

    A. Perform both of the required goals and both of the desired goals.

    B. Perform both of the required goals and one of the desired goals.

    C. Perform both of the required goals and none of the desired goals.

    D. Not perform the required goals.

14. Which of the following groups of operating systems natively support user-level share access?

    A. Windows for Workgroups 3.11, Windows 95, Windows NT Workstation, Windows NT Server

    B. Windows 95, Windows NT Workstation, Windows NT Server

    C. Windows NT Server, Windows NT Workstation

    D. Windows 95, Windows NT Workstation

15. When using a network share,

    A. The password in the user account is checked against the password in the network resource. If they match, the user is authenticated.

    B. The network resource is checked in the Access Control List (ACL) to see if that user is granted access. If the resource is listed, the user is granted access.

    C. The username is checked against the user accounts database. If the user exists, the user's password is checked. Then the user is granted access.

    D. Because the user is authenticated by the domain controller during login, there is no need to check the user database. The server checks the user's password. Then the user is granted access.

16. A user is:

    A. Placed into groups to be given access to resources.

    B. Granted *permissions* to use resources.

    C. An entity that requests access to network resources.

    D. All of the above.

17. Windows 95 security

    A. Uses the same 32-bit engine as Windows NT and is, therefore, secure.

    B. Uses only passwords to enforce security and is, therefore, easier to administer.

    C. Can use Windows NT Workstation database to control access to resources.

    D. Cannot access NTFS partitions over a network.

18. Global groups

    A. Add a layer of complexity on user management and are, therefore, difficult to administer.

    B. Are available across platforms to Windows NT, Novell NetWare, and UNIX.

    C. Must contain users before they can be given access.

    D. Can contain users, local groups, or global groups.

19. User rights include:

    A. The ability to access printers and files.

    B. The ability to create printers and files.

    C. The ability to create users or other accounts.

    D. Focus on network resources.

20. Windows NT user accounts are:

    A. Created as part of the installation process and can be created later.

    B. Created with a tool such as *User Manager for Domains* and can be created during the installation process.

C. Transferable to a Windows 95 workstation.

D. Used via the Access Control List to manage resources.

21. Share-level security:

A. Uses passwords to restrict access to Full Access or Read-Only.

B. Cannot be used with NTFS file-level security.

C. Is not adequate security for protecting data.

D. Cannot be used to restrict a *network user*.

22. On Windows NT, the Administrator account

A. Cannot be renamed but can be deleted.

B. Is very powerful but can be protected with NTFS file-level security.

C. Cannot be deleted but can be renamed.

D. Is created during installation, but like *guest*, it is disabled.

23. User accounts:

A. Are typically shared among people on small networks.

B. Can be placed into groups to ease administrative burdens.

C. Are saved in the Access Control List (ACL).

D. Are managed using the Administrative Tools program in Windows NT Server.

24. Usernames on a network server:

A. Can appear to use the same name because the SID (Security ID) is different for each user.

B. Must be unique.

C. Must contain information about that user.

D. Are saved in the global ACL.

25. Passwords should be:

A. Case sensitive (to avoid being compromised by hackers).

B. Written down and stored in a very safe place to keep them private.

C. Used to restrict access to user accounts.

D. Generated by the system administrator to ensure that hard-to-guess passwords are used.

26. A *user profile*

A. Contains security information about a user to ensure sensitive data is not shared.

B. Can contain optional user information, such as a home directory or desktop settings.

C. Is a database of access rights for each user.

D. Can be copied from one user to another, creating duplicates.

27. When permissions are granted to groups:

A. Permissions cannot be granted to users.

B. Users should be added to groups.

C. Users should be granted group permissions.

D. Groups are added to the Access Control List (ACL).

28. Which of the following is an example of a special user account?

A. A system account to log in as a service

B. A user account to log in as a service

C. The Administrator and Guest accounts created during installation

D. All of the above

29. Which of the following is a tool used to simplify user management?

A. Groups

B. *User Manager for Domains*

C. *Syscon*

D. The ACL (Access Control List)

30. True or False: In order to manage your user database properly, you will most likely need to modify or add to the default groups provided in *User Manager for Domains*.

A. True

B. False

31. Which of the following is true about Windows NT groups?

A. Local groups can be added together and exported into global groups.

B. Global groups can be added to other global groups.

C. Global groups can be added to local groups.

D. Local groups can be exported into other trusted domains.

32. A system administrator:

A. Must consider security above all else when determining network configuration.

B. Must balance ease-of-use, user convenience, and security when determining network configuration.

C. Must affix a dollar value to each resource to determine if security is appropriate for that resource.

D. Must never let mere economics be a driving force in determining network configuration.

33. Which of the following is not true? Passwords should:

A. Be set to expire frequently to expose stolen or misused passwords.

B. Use upper- and lowercase letters to stymie password-cracking programs.

C. Be set in *User Manager for Domains* to require a mixture of characters and numbers to stymie password-cracking programs.

D. Be set in *User Manager for Domains* to ensure that they meet minimum length requirements.

34. In order for the *Backup* group to back up files, it must:

A. Have the appropriate user right.

B. Be a member of the local Administrators group.

C. Be in the global ACL (Access Control List) for that resource.

D. Be modified from the default group created during installation.

35. The *Everyone* group:

A. Like the *guest* account, should be disabled to avoid unauthorized access.

B. Is a global group.

C. Is a special group that cannot be modified.

D. Is a special group that contains the global ACL (Access Control List).

36. Most network operating systems:

A. Manage groups through a dedicated tool such as *Group Manager for Domains.*

B. Do not use groups the way an advanced operating system such as Microsoft Windows NT Server does.

C. Use groups and users interchangeably.

D. Manage groups through the user management tool.

37. Which is the phrase you should have memorized to simplify user and resource management?

A. Users go into local groups, local groups go into global groups, global groups are shared across domains.

B. Users are grouped together into a local group, local groups are grouped together into a domain group, global groups are grouped together into a domain group.

C. Users go into global groups, global groups go into local groups, local groups get resources.

D. Local groups are placed into workgroups, workgroups are placed into domain groups, domain groups are placed into global groups, global groups go into the group *Everyone*, which cannot be modified.

38. To set user permissions,

A. You must first select a group for that user to be placed in.

B. You must create a user account and should place the user in a group.

C. You must first place the user in a local group.

D. You must add the user to the ACL (Access Control List).

39. Setting permissions:

A. Can be a time-consuming process that should be undertaken with care.

B. Is necessary for users to have access to files and printers.

C. Is a simple process eased by the use of user accounts and groups.

D. Cannot be performed on a Windows 95 machine.

40. Access permissions applied to a shared resource

A. Describes sharing an item with two passwords, one for read-only and one for full access.

B. Must be enabled to grant access to the network resource.

C. Is the act of adding users to a shared resource.

D. Requires a Windows NT or Novell NetWare server.

41. Access permissions applied to a shared resource

A. Is the easiest method of network security to administer.

B. Requires that a user be added to a group before he or she can be authenticated.

C. Enables workgroups to share data.

D. Happens automatically when you connect a PC to the network.

42. User-level security applied to a shared resource:

A. Cannot be performed on a Windows 95 workstation.

B. Requires a Windows NT Server.

C. Uses the ACL (Access Control List) to authenticate users.

D. Requires that a user be placed in a local or global group.

43. A shared resource using user-level security on a Windows 95 workstation

A. Requires a Windows NT computer for the user database.

B. Can use a Novell NetWare server for user authentication.

C. Is the easiest secure way to manage access control.

D. Can use NTFS-level security if a Windows NT server is used for authentication.

44. File-level security

A. Is easy and fast to administer.

B. Requires NTFS on the partition to be secured.

C. Cannot be used with users belonging to the *Everyone* user group.

D. Should only be used for C-2 level security.

45. Rights and permissions can be granted to users directly to:

A. Make things easier in the long run instead of dealing with users and groups.

B. Streamline system performance.

C. Avoid security breaches by separating users and not keeping them in the same group.

D. Implement a quick-fix, but it will be more cumbersome in the long run.

46. NTFS file-level security

A. Allows the administrator to implement a very sophisticated security policy.

B. Is self-configuring, using the built-in groups and permissions created during the Windows NT installation process.

C. Can be used on a FAT volume.

D. Does not use the ACL (Access Control List).

47. NTFS file-level security

A. Does not work over the network because all network shares are equal.

B. Works over the network but can be overridden by an administrator with physical access to the server.

C. Allows for advanced auditing functions and will lock out a user logging in at the server as well as over the network.

D. Removes the need for physical security of your server.

48. If your NTFS-level security volume can be accessed by the *Everyone* group,

A. Your file system is secure because *Everyone* is a special built-in group creating during the Windows NT installation process.

B. You can remove users from the *Everyone* group to secure the volume.

C. You cannot secure this volume because the *Everyone* group cannot be modified.

D. You can remove the *Everyone* group's access.

49. A relatively weak password policy

A. Is a bad idea.

B. Might be appropriate if security needs are light.

C. Can be overridden by effective NTFS file-level security.

D. Would use numbers and letters as part of the password.

50. Which of the following is not contained in a Windows NT profile?

A. Password

B. Home directory

C. Login script

D. None of the above: All of these are contained in the profile

51. Windows 95's level of security gives the sharing PC these choices:

    A. Login, print, read-only, full access

    B. Full access, read-only, execute

    C. Full, read-only, depends on password

    D. User, group, domain user

52. If no password is used on Windows 95's access control,

    A. All users have read-only access.

    B. All users have full access.

    C. The administrator can still choose read-only or full access.

    D. Windows 95 requires a password.

53. Which of the following is a disadvantage of Windows 95's access control implementation?

    A. It is a relatively insecure security implementation.

    B. It becomes difficult to administer because you have to remember so many passwords.

    C. The system administrator must change the access control when the passwords expire.

    D. They will not work over a network connection.

54. Which of the following is an advantages of Windows 95's access control implementation?

    A. It uses a smaller ACL (Access Control List).

    B. It works with NTFS partitions.

    C. It is very easy to grant full access to a new user (by giving him or her the new password).

    D. Passwords can be made case-sensitive to improve security.

22.1 Answers and Explanations: Practice Problems

1. **A** Files, network adapters, and documents are not core aspects of an administrative plan.
2. **D** If an item can be accessed using the network, it is a network resource.
3. **C** Permissions are used to modify access to resources.
4. **A** The scope of network resources is limited only by the skill and imagination of programmers and engineers.
5. **B** The printer must be shared in order to be used across the network. The software enabling this does not have to be on a dedicated server, as any software creating a network resource is called server software.
6. **C** A network resource is made available by sharing.
7. **A** The UNC name can be used instead of a drive letter. In addition, there is no requirement that it be a meaningful name, although network administrators should use meaningful names when possible. In addition, the share only refers to the resource name, not the full UNC in \\servername\sharename construction.
8. **D** \\servername\sharename
9. **D** This result will not track any activity on the server, nor will it protect sensitive data.
10. **D** Windows NT workstation would involved a major network overhaul that could upset the business flow. This plan is not easy to administer, nor will it track sensitive data.
11. **C** This plan will not be easy to administer, as you must create and manage user accounts. In addition, it will not track access to files.

12. **D** This plan will not function. Windows NT Server does not support a shared password to protect resources. In this scenario, item 11 is the best alternative, even though it does not meet all the required and desired goals.

13. **B** This plan, though not perfect, is the best available option for this network. Because it involves the management of user accounts, it will involve some administrative burden.

14. **C** Windows 95 does not natively support user-level security. It must use the database in Windows NT or Novell NetWare.

15. **C** This level of redundancy may seem unnecessary, but it is the core of Windows NT security.

16. **C** Users can be given access directly; groups are merely used to make administration easier. Permissions are applied to resources, not users.

17. **B** A partition that is NTFS is viewed the same as any partition when shared over a network. Windows 95 uses passwords only to handle security; it must authenticate users to a Windows NT Server (not workstation) to enforce security.

18. **D** Global groups are a Windows NT group that make administration easier and can be exported to other Windows NT domains.

19. **C** User rights focus on abilities, not resources. Therefore, the ability to create files and printers is associated with permissions.

20. **A** Two user accounts, Administrator and Guest, are always created during the installation process.

21. **A** Share-level access works great with NTFS file security. Also, it is perfectly acceptable to restrict access to data, depending on your specific security needs. Also, if any network user does not have the correct password, that network user will not have access.

22. **C** You should rename your Administrator account to protect it from intrusion.

23. **B** User accounts should never be shared by people. If they are, security is at risk.

24. **B** Usernames must always be unique.

25. **C** Never write down passwords. Only the user should know his or her password.

26. **B** A user profile can contain a home directory and desktop settings, and it can be mandatory or user-generated. It can be copied, but not to create duplicates.

27. **B** Groups are not added to the ACL; the users in the groups are added to the ACL. Add users to groups to grant them permissions.

28. **D** All of the above. A user account or a system account can log in as a service.

29. **A** Groups are used to simplify user management.

30. **B** False. Microsoft has provided a large number of groups, most of which are adequate for user and resource management.

31. **C** Remember this for user management: Place users into global groups, place global groups into local groups, grant resources to local groups.

32. **B** All of the business needs, including economics and user satisfaction, must be considered when determining network security configuration.

33. **C** Setting the minimum length for a password is reasonable and is supported in User Manager for Domains.

34. **A** The group should have the appropriate user right. Adding the Backup Operators group to the Administrators group defeats the purpose of having a group that is capable of backing up and restoring files.

35. **C** The Everyone group contains all defined and undefined users and cannot be modified. No users can be added to or removed from this group.

36. **D** There is no tool called Group Manager for Domains.

37. **C** Remember this phrase: Users go into global groups, global groups go into local groups, local groups get resources.

38. **B** You may assign resources directly to a user, but you will save yourself many administrative headaches by placing users in groups and assigning rights on a group basis.

39. **A** It is not necessary to set permissions to give users access.

40. **A** This method of access is called Access Permissions applied to a shared resource.

41. **A** Although it's not very secure, it is the easiest to administer.

42. **C** The ACL is the list of users that have access to the resource.

43. **B** A Novell NetWare server will authenticate users, and although access-control is not as secure as user-level control, it is secure enough for some networks.

44. **B** File-level security requires that your server be formatted NTFS on the drive to be secured.

45. **D** If you eschew placing users into groups for management, it will come back to haunt you at a later date. A good administrator always uses groups.

46. **A** Setting up permissions on an NTFS volume can be time-consuming, but it's very secure. It will not function on a FAT volume.

47. **C** Although NTFS can keep a user with physical access from logging in, there is never a substitute for physical security.

48. **D** Simply remove the Everyone group's access, as shown in exercise 3.1.3.

49. **B** Even the most stringent security in the world can be broken if passwords are not secure. However, some organizations do not require a high degree of security.

50. **A** The password is the user account. The profile contains only additional information.

51. **C** Windows 95 only allows share-level security set by a password. You may set a password for read-only, full access, or both.

52. **C** If no password is used, the "depends on password" box is grayed out and the administrator has to choose between read-only and full-access.

53 **A** This level of access is the least secure of all Microsoft implementations. Windows 95 passwords do not expire.

54. **C** It's very quick and easy to administer.

22.1 Key Words

Server
User
Resource
Authenticate
Groups
Print Server
User-level security
Share-level security
Read-only
Depends on password

22.2 Choose a Disaster Recovery Plan for Various Situations

One of the major issues that a network administrator must address is the possibility of system failure and associated downtime. The administrator must handle two major issues to guard against the danger of a failed server:

Protecting data

Reducing downtime

A. Protecting Data

Natural disasters, equipment failures, power surges, and deliberate vandalism can all damage your network. Microsoft focuses on these strategies for preventing data loss:

Backup (technical, procedural)

Uninterruptible Power Supply (UPS)

1. Backup

A backup schedule is an essential part of any data-protection strategy. You should design a backup system that is right for your situation and the data on your network. A comprehensive backup policy will fall into one of the following categories:

Single backup server

Individual tape units on each server

Independent, redundant backup network

The old method of simply copying data from one drive to another is not effective for a network. Many companies choose to rotate multiple copies of tape and store the additional copies off-site. Storing the backups off-site is a critical part of any backup policy, as it guards against physical calamity.

- **Single backup server:** This strategy uses a centralized backup server with a very large tape drive or an array of multiple tape drives. Each server is connected to the backup server over the network. If you have a large amount of data to back up, you may need a large array of multigigabyte tape drives to store all the data. This can get very expensive.

  If your servers are spread out over multiple floors, you can administer and monitor all the backup activity from a central location.

- **Individual tape units:** This system involves a smaller tape unit installed on each server. Individual units may cost less than the larger array required to back up an entire network. However, this can be more difficult to administer, and you must manage a larger number of individual tapes. For a network spread across several buildings, this may present an attractive alternative if management of the units can be delegated to on-site personnel.

- **Independent, redundant backup network:** If you have chosen a centralized backup server, you should be aware that huge amounts of data are transferred during a backup. This enormous amount of data can seriously degrade system performance. For that reason, you may want to connect your servers to the central backup server using a second network card in each data server.

Any backup plan should include a combination of full and incremental backups. A *full* backup is used to create a complete backup, whereas an *incremental* backup is used to backup all files modified since the last full backup.

If your network is capable, you should attempt to perform full backups nightly. Most likely, this is an option for only the smallest servers. Because full backups can be so lengthy, most administrators perform full backups weekly and perform incremental backups each night during the week.

A log of backups can be important. Also, a strategy that uses tape names and dates create a self-organizing log that can assist in managing tapes. Don't rely on your server as the tape log!! If it crashes and you need to restore from tape, you won't be able to get to the log. Microsoft recommends that you make two copies of the backup log: Store one with the backup tapes, and keep one at the computer site.

You should simulate a disaster recovery plan before you rely on your system. Never experiment with crucial data. Only test with items you can afford to lose.

2. Uninterruptible Power Supply

An Uninterruptible Power Supply (UPS) is a special device that continues to supply electricity after a power failure. UPSs commonly are used with network servers to prevent a disorderly shutdown that could damage data on the server.

The UPS can communicate with the server via software. In the event of a power failure, you can configure the server to:

- Shut down the server gracefully to avoid data loss.
- Send a broadcast message to all users about the power failure and notify them that the server will shut down.
- Send an administrative alert to the system administrator about power loss.
- Page the administrator using a regular phone pager (not all systems support this).

Most UPSs provide roughly fifteen minutes within which the server will be shut down gracefully.

Backups mainly provide a quick method for system recovery. They require a long and tedious restore process that can cost your company dearly in lost revenue and productivity.

B. Recovering from System Failure

In order for a network to be secure, it must perform as expected. If the network is not kept up and running on a daily basis, the users will be unable to rely on it. Therefore, procedures for preventing downtime from a hardware failure should be implemented.

1. Implementing a Fault-Tolerant Design

Any fault-tolerant design needs to balance the concerns of cost versus the loss to be avoided. If your network absolutely must function 24 hours a day, 7 days a week, 365 days a year (as in a medical environment, for example), a more-expensive design that provides advanced levels of redundancy is more appropriate. The severity of a projected loss must be balanced against the likelihood of the disaster occurring.

2. Using RAID

A vital tool for protecting a network's data is the use of a Redundant Array of Inexpensive Disks (RAID). A RAID system combines two or more disks to create a virtual disk structure that can continue functioning even if one of the disks fails.

RAID 1 and RAID 5 are the only fault-tolerant RAID levels currently in use. RAID 2 through 4 were attempts to perfect what later became RAID 5. RAID 1 refers to *disk mirroring*, in which a complete duplicate of the mirrored disk is created. If one disk fails, the array continues to function. If you split your RAID 1 array across multiple disk controllers, this is called *duplexing* instead of *mirroring*. RAID 5 uses three or more disks to create a *stripe set with parity*. RAID 0 is used, but is not fault-tolerant.

Disk mirroring is defined as two hard drives—one primary, one secondary—that use the same disk channel (controller cards and cable). Disk mirroring is most commonly configured by using disk drives contained in the server. Duplexing is a form of mirroring that enables you to configure a more robust hardware environment.

Both RAID 1 and RAID 5 require that you have disks of approximately the same size. Both Windows NT and Novell NetWare will build RAID arrays using software only. A number of different vendors also offer hardware RAID systems, which tend to be faster and more expensive. Hardware RAID will operate with any operating system, including Windows 95.

Most network administrators prefer the RAID 5 solution. However, mirroring tends to be the favorite on smaller, non-dedicated servers.

A fault-tolerant disk scheme is used only to speed recovery time from a hardware fault. None of these RAID levels is intended to be a replacement for regular tape backups. If you damage your data, the RAID array will faithfully duplicate your mistake.

Table 22.2.1 provides a comparison of the two types of RAID.

Table 22.2.1 RAID 1 versus RAID 5

RAID 1	RAID 5
Costs less initially, as it requires only two disks.	Costs more initially because it requires at least three disks.
Costs more per megabyte because the array gives you only 50% of the usable space. The other 50% is used as the mirror.	Costs less per megabyte. This advantage grows as you add additional disks. The usable space is drivesize * n–1.
Is the only software RAID type available for the Windows NT system partition.	A software RAID 5 array cannot be used for the Windows NT system volume.

RAID 1	RAID 5
Drives are paired or mirrored, with each byte of information being written to each identical drive. You can duplex these devices by adding a separate drive controller for each drive.	A Windows NT server using software RAID can combine a maximum of 32 disks. Assuming a 20G disk, this would be a 640G array. As the saying goes, 640G should be more space than anyone should ever need.
	Uses striping with parity information written across multiple drives to enable fault-tolerance with a minimum of wasted disk space. This level also offers the advantage of enabling relatively efficient performance on writes to the drives, as well as excellent read performance. RAID 5 requires at least three drives because it writes data across two of them and then calculates parity block on the third disk.

22.2 Exercise: Exploring Windows NT's Disk Administrator

Remember that changes made to your disk configuration can have a serious effect on the system. Do not make any changes in Disk Administrator unless you have carefully planned them previously!

Objective: Explore the options available through Disk Administrator, such as establishing and breaking mirrored drives and creating or regenerating stripe sets with parity.

To complete this exercise, log on to a Windows NT 4.0 server or workstation with an account that has administrative authority. The server or workstation used can be a production machine; no changes will actually be made to the computer's configuration during this exercise.

1. Click Start, Programs, Administrative Tools. Then choose Disk Administrator.
2. Observe the Disk Administrator window and maximize it if it is not already in this state. The configuration of the disk or disks on your machine appears.
3. Click one of the partitions on your screen. A dark black line appears around the partition, indicating that the partition is selected. Right-click the partition to open the context-sensitive menu. Note that you can format the partition, change its logical drive letter, or examine its properties. If the disk is removable, the Eject option is also available.
4. Click Partition in the menu bar and examine the choices. Most of the choices are unavailable, but they include Create Volume Set and Create Stripe Set. You also can change your active partition in this menu.
5. Click Fault Tolerance on the menu bar (Windows NT Server only) and observe that this menu enables you to establish and break mirrored drives, as well as to create or regenerate stripe sets with parity.
6. Feel free to explore further. When you are finished examining the menus and options, close the Disk Administrator by clicking Partition, Exit.

22.2 Practice Problems

1. The possibility of catastrophic system failure:

   A. Is reduced through the robust architecture of Windows NT Server.

   B. Is a very real possibility that must be planned for to minimize its negative impact.

   C. Can be prevented through the use of tape backups.

   D. Requires that you use a rotating schedule of tape backups.

2. Disaster recovery should include

   A. Antivirus software and a tape backup.

   B. A backup system or, if necessary, a fully redundant backup network.

   C. A copy of the user database and user passwords.

   D. A plan for protecting crucial data and reducing downtime.

3. A UPS is crucial for a backup plan because

   A. It can deliver new equipment faster than the US post office.

   B. A UPS can allow your system to shut down gracefully in a power outage.

   C. A UPS allows your tape units to restore the software even while the power is out.

   D. A UPS will act as a central tape library.

The following four questions use this situation as a scenario.

Network type:

Windows NT servers, NetWare servers

Protocols:

NetBEUI, IPX

Workstations:

30 Windows NT workstations

Servers:

7 servers, NetWare and Windows NT

Your network contains some mission-critical data. If a disaster caused the data to be permanently lost, the company would have no choice but to go out of business. However, it is acceptable to roll back to the previous day's work. Traffic and network performance are operating within normal baseline parameters. The office has three locations, connected via a WAN.

You want to implement a backup plan.

Required objectives:

- The network must have no more than eight hours of downtime.
- If one site goes down, the others must be able to function.

Desired objectives:

- Network performance should not be adversely impacted by the strategy.
- Cost should be kept to reasonable levels.

4. You decide to implement a fully redundant backup network. You use an isolated network segment and a centralized tape backup server. You also keep a spare server in reserve. This plan will:

   A. Perform both of the required objectives and both of the desired objectives.

   B. Perform both of the required objectives and one of the desired objectives.

C. Perform both of the required objectives and none of the desired objectives.

D. Not perform the required objectives.

5. You decide to use single tape units on each server. You maintain a spare server just in case. In addition, you do daily full backups and move the tapes to each of the other locations. This plan will:

   A. Perform both of the required objectives and both of the desired objectives.

   B. Perform both of the required objectives and one of the desired objectives.

   C. Perform both of the required objectives and none of the desired objectives.

   D. Not perform the required objectives.

6. You decide to implement a redundant-heartbeat server for each server so that if a catastrophe occurs, the new server will simply take over for the failed unit. You augment this with tape units on each server. This plan will:

   A. Perform both of the required objectives and both of the desired objectives.

   B. Perform both of the required objectives and one of the desired objectives.

   C. Perform both of the required objectives and none of the desired objectives.

   D. Not perform the required objectives.

7. You implement full RAID 1 mirroring for each disk drive on your servers. In this way, you determine that you can recover from a failure quickly, and you no longer have to rely on tapes. This plan will:

   A. Perform both of the required objectives and both of the desired objectives.

   B. Perform both of the required objectives and one of the desired objectives.

   C. Perform both of the required objectives and none of the desired objectives.

   D. Not perform the required objectives.

8. A single centralized backup server can:

   A. Reduce network traffic.

   B. Back up all servers at once.

   C. Remove tapes to remote sites.

   D. Help in the event of network cable failure.

9. With a central backup server, the tape unit

   A. Can be more expensive, because it tends to have more capacity than a standalone unit.

   B. Is always cost-effective because it can do more work per tape unit.

   C. Is more useful in larger networks.

   D. Is faster than a directly connected unit.

10. Which of the following is an advantage of using centralized tape servers?

   A. Larger tape drives

   B. Shorter access times

   C. Self-rotating tapes

   D. Centralized administration

11. If your network is spread across multiple buildings, your backup strategy could include:

    A. A separate, redundant backup network.

    B. Single tape units on each server.

    C. Both A and B.

    D. Neither A nor B.

12. An *incremental backup*:

    A. Is a backup of only the important data.

    B. Always uses the DOS *archive* attribute to mark files.

    C. Is a backup of the data that has changed since the last full backup.

    D. Is always much smaller than a full backup.

13. A satisfactory backup plan should use

    A. A combination of full, incremental, and differential backups.

    B. A full backup every night if possible and incremental nightly backups if the capacity for daily full backups is unavailable.

    C. Your existing supply of tapes over and over again.

    D. A combination of tape and disks to back up all crucial files.

14. *Differential* backups are used to

    A. Back up more data than an incremental backup.

    B. Reset the DOS *archive* attribute.

    C. Measure the difference in tape speed between a full and incremental backup.

    D. Create backups between full backups.

15. Your network tapes should be

    A. Kept in a central, safe location.

    B. Kept in separate locations. That way, if a physical disaster strikes, the data will survive.

    C. Secured with passwords to prevent infiltration from hackers.

    D. Kept near the server in case they are needed during an emergency.

16. A written log of your tape backups

    A. Is a security risk.

    B. Will be very helpful if you need to piece your network back together from tapes.

    C. Is redundant; that data is all on the server and is backed up on the tapes.

    D. Might be destroyed in a fire.

17. Disaster recovery planning should:

    A. Be taken very seriously. Don't joke around by having a simulated disaster. No one likes a comedian!

    B. Be practiced by having a complete simulated disaster drill. This will uncover holes in your recovery plan.

    C. Use your actual server for testing purposes. What good is a test unless it's on your real server?

    D. Be done without the rest of your department or company's knowledge. After all, how could it be a legitimate test?

18. An independent, redundant backup network

    A. Uses separate protocols over your existing network to minimize traffic and provide a secure path for data to travel.

    B. Uses routers and bridges to create a separate path to your backup server.

C. Uses an additional NIC and cabling to provide a redundant isolated network segment for backups.

D. Uses separate global groups and local groups and keeps a backup copy of the domain controller database.

19. Full backups

A. Should be reserved only for the times when you need to perform a complete backup.

B. Should be performed weekly or, if you can manage it, daily.

C. Should contain all the data that has *fully* changed since the last backup.

D. Are created by combining all the *incremental* backups.

20. When managing tapes, you should

A. Overwrite your tapes nightly (there's no reason to keep old data around anyway).

B. Lock them in a safe in the server room so they're available during an emergency.

C. Have a regular plan that moves tapes off-site, so if a disaster strikes the building, your data will be safe.

D. Password protect them to keep them safe from hackers.

21. If you decide to keep a log of your tape backups,

A. A date-oriented log would be nearly self-organizing (and ease-of-use helps in an emergency).

B. You should use a secret code to organize the tapes so hackers cannot uncover your organizational plan.

C. Simply save it on the server; no reason to duplicate data.

D. You must use a rigid plan that balances cost, secrecy, and economic impact.

22. Which of the following statements is Microsoft's recommendation for a tape backup log?

A. Create duplicates so you can keep one with the off-site backups and one on-site near the server.

B. Keep it safely secured in a safe place.

C. Keep it off-site with the off-site backup tapes. After all, you won't need it on-site if the server is still functioning.

D. Keep the log on a Microsoft Windows NT NTFS file-level secured partition.

23. A UPS can do which of the following?

A. Shut the server down gracefully.

B. Send a broadcast message to the users.

C. Send a telephone pager message to the system administrator.

D. All of the above.

24. An *uninterruptible power supply* is used to

A. Provide uninterrupted power during a power outage.

B. Move your server from one building to the next without unplugging it.

C. Shut the server down gracefully, providing roughly fifteen minutes of power during an outage.

D. Replace the standard fuse box in a server room.

25. Which of the following is the most common type of hardware failure?

A. Power failure

B. Drive failure

C. Server failure

D. User failure

26. A system that is able to function despite a hardware failure is:

    A. Using a UPS to provide power.

    B. Called *fault-tolerant.*

    C. Called *hardware-resistant.*

    D. Not yet a possibility; however, advanced operating systems like Microsoft Windows NT Server help a system continue to function.

27. A fault-tolerant design must

    A. Not be concerned with price and performance. Fault-tolerance defines only its ability to function.

    B. Use a *redundant array* of servers and disks.

    C. Use an advanced operating system, such as Microsoft Windows NT or Novell NetWare.

    D. Balance the concerns of downtime versus cost and performance. No one solution is best for all users.

28. A good plan for balancing the needs of a fault-tolerant system would

    A. Consider the cost of the operating system, the time needed to reinstall, and the likelihood of disaster.

    B. Balance price of the fault-tolerant array with the performance of no array.

    C. Balance the severity of a projected loss with the likelihood of the loss occurring.

    D. Use meetings to talk to each department in your company.

29. A fully redundant network array with duplicate hubs, wiring, routers, and switches would

    A. Not be justified because you need to weigh the cost against the severity of a projected loss.

    B. Be justified if the severity of the projected loss were high enough.

    C. Not be required if you back up your data with tapes and move the tapes to off-site locations.

    D. Keep the primary network from being overburdened during back-ups.

30. Hardware RAID

    A. Kills software bugs dead.

    B. Is slower than software RAID.

    C. Groups disks into a fault-tolerant design.

    D. Can be used in place of tape backups.

31. Which is true of RAID?

    A. RAID 2 should always be used instead of RAID 1.

    B. RAID 1 is disk mirroring; RAID 2 is duplexing with two controllers.

    C. RAID 1 and RAID 5 are the only fault-tolerant RAID designs being used.

    D. The RAID number refers to the number of disks in your array, so the higher the number, the more fault-tolerant your array. That's why RAID 0 is not fault-tolerant.

32. RAID 1 is called

    A. Disk mirroring or disk duplexing.

    B. Disk mirroring or disk striping.

    C. Disk mirroring with parity.

    D. Disk parity with striping.

33. Which is not true of RAID 1?

    A. You can split your disk mirror across multiple controllers.

    B. You can split your disk stripe across multiple controllers.

C. RAID 1 is preferred over RAID 2.

D. You can rebuild a disk array if one disk completely fails and crashes.

34. RAID mirroring:

A. Creates a complete duplicate of the primary drive.

B. Uses parity information stored on the mirrored disk to rebuild lost information.

C. Can be used instead of a tape backup.

D. Can be used with three or more disks.

35. RAID 5

A. Can be used with 2 to 32 disks.

B. Duplexes data across multiple controllers.

C. Includes disks, tapes, and a UPS.

D. Requires at least three disks.

36. All fault-tolerant RAID arrays

A. Can use disks of different sizes if RAID is implemented in software.

B. Should use disks of approximately the same size.

C. Can continue running during a power failure if properly configured.

D. Require special *software drivers* to function.

37. RAID can be

A. Implemented in hardware only.

B. Implemented in hardware and software.

C. Implemented in software only.

D. Replaced by a redundant backup network.

38. Software RAID

A. Must be used if you use Windows 95, because Windows 95 does not support hardware RAID.

B. Requires an advanced operating system such as Windows NT or Novell NetWare.

C. Is faster than hardware RAID.

D. Uses the HMA (High Memory Area) to store buffers and data.

39. Which of the following statements about the cost of a RAID array is true?

A. RAID 1 cost more in larger arrays.

B. RAID 1 costs the same as RAID 5; the difference is software.

C. RAID 1 costs less in larger arrays.

D. RAID 5 costs more in larger arrays.

40. Which is NOT true of RAID 1?

A. It is the only software RAID level available for Windows NT Workstation.

B. It is the only software RAID level available for the Windows NT system partition.

C. It stores a parity checksum on a duplicate drive.

D. It is available in Novell NetWare.

41. RAID 5

A. Can use an infinite number of disks to create large arrays.

B. Uses half of the space to store parity checksum data.

C. Can use up to 32 disks in a Windows NT array.

D. Costs less than RAID 1 to start.

42. A hardware RAID 5 array
    A. Is slower than a more advanced Windows NT software array.
    B. Is faster than a Windows NT or Novell NetWare software array.
    C. Does not support "hot swapping" of disks.
    D. Creates a duplicate disk for each disk in the array.

43. A truly fault-tolerant disk array and plan
    A. Does not replace your tape drive; the RAID array will faithfully recreate all your mistakes in disk management.
    B. Allows you to move away from slow, cumbersome tape drives.
    C. Includes a log of each disk, kept off-site to guard against physical calamity.
    D. Will page the administrator and send a broadcast alert to users.

44. Which is true of RAID arrays?
    A. Disk mirroring is a form of disk duplexing.
    B. Disk duplexing is a form of disk striping.
    C. Disk duplexing is a form of disk mirroring.
    D. Disk striping is a form of disk duplexing.

45. The purpose of a fault-tolerant RAID array is to
    A. Speed recovery in the event of a hardware failure.
    B. Replace cumbersome tape devices and procedures.
    C. Duplicate data across servers and WAN networks.
    D. Keep the server functioning in the event of a power failure.

46. The term *fault tolerance* actually refers to
    A. Only RAID levels 1 through 5.
    B. The ability of a system to continue functioning despite a hardware failure.
    C. A RAID array or a UPS device.
    D. The prevention of downtime.

22.2 Answers and Explanations: Practice Problems

1. **B** Count on it. If you plan for it, it won't hurt as bad.
2. **D** The core components of a disaster recovery are safeguarding data and getting the network back up and running quickly.
3. **B** An uninterruptible power supply is crucial for server integrity.
4. **D** If the centralized tape server fails, the entire network is without a backup.
5. **A** Network performance will not suffer because the tape units are directly connected to each server.
6. **C** This is not a cost-effective solution.
7. **D** A RAID unit will not save you in the event of data loss. It will faithfully replicate your mistake across all drives in the array.
8. **B** A centralized server can increase network traffic.
9. **A** The costs can vary, but centralized tape servers tend to be more expensive per tape unit. Because of this, they tend to be more effective in small to mid-sized networks.

10. **D** A large tape unit could be used in a standalone tape unit. The key benefit is centralized administration.

11. **C** Both of these plans would work in a multibuilding WAN.

12. **C** Some incremental backups can be huge, and some file systems do not use the DOS *archive* attribute.

13. **B** Smaller networks can use a full backup daily. If you use a large number of tapes, you can still restore data that dates back a week, a month, or as long as you have tapes for.

14. **A** An *incremental* backup can be used instead, but it will take longer to restore.

15. **B** If you kept the tapes in a separate location, you would be able to rebuild the entire network with all new equipment.

16. **B** A written log is not an appreciable risk, but it can save volumes of time during an emergency.

17. **B** You should have a drill, but don't keep it a secret. And don't use your company's production network either. Sensitive data is at stake.

18. **C** The backup network is completely separate from the primary network.

19. **B** If you can manage, do a full backup daily.

20. **C** Keep the tapes off-site.

21. **A** A log can be very useful. If it's based on date and time, it's practically self-organizing!

22. **A** Microsoft recommends duplicating the tape log and keeping one on-site and one with the off-site backups.

23. **D** UPSs can typically do all of these things.

24. **C** A UPS is designed to bring the server down gracefully.

25. **B** Hard disk drive failure is the most common type of hardware failure.

26. **B** This system would be called *fault tolerant.*

27. **D** All system plans should be concerned the cost of downtime versus the cost of a fault-tolerant system.

28. **C** You should balance the severity against the likelihood of a projected loss.

29. **B** If the severity of the projected loss is high enough, an expensive solution might be justified.

30. **C** RAID is the acronym for redundant disk arrays.

31. **C** RAID 1 and RAID 5 are the only fault-tolerant RAID types currently in use. RAID 0 is not fault-tolerant, and RAID 2 through RAID 4 were precursors to RAID 5.

32. **A** Disk mirroring uses one controller; disk duplexing is just like mirroring, but it uses two controllers.

33. **B** RAID 1 does not use disk striping.

34. **A** RAID 1 uses only two disks; parity information is how RAID 5 stores data.

35. **D** RAID 5 cannot be used with fewer than three disks.

36. **B** All fault-tolerant RAID arrays should use disks of approximately the same size.

37. **B** RAID can be implemented in hardware and software.

38. **B** NetWare and Windows NT support software RAID.

39. **A** RAID 1 costs more in larger arrays because you must double the disk size to be mirrored.

40. **C** RAID 1 stores a copy of the data, not a checksum. RAID 5 stores a checksum.

41. **C** Windows NT can create an array with up to 32 disks.

42. **B** Hardware RAID is faster than software RAID.

43. **A** RAID does not replace tape. RAID guards against hardware failure.

44. **C** Duplexing and mirroring both create drive duplicates, but duplexing simply uses an additional disk controller.

45. **A** The primary purpose of RAID is to get the system back up quickly or to continue running if a drive fails.

46. **B** Fault tolerance means the system will tolerate a fault or hardware failure.

22.2 Key Words

Disk mirroring

Disk duplexing

RAID 1

RAID 0

Fault tolerant

RAID 5

UPS

Antivirus software

22.3 Given the Manufacturer's Documentation for the Network Adapter, Install, Configure, and Resolve Hardware Conflicts for Multiple Network Adapters in a Token-Ring or Ethernet Network

A *network adapter card* is required for network communications. Ethernet and token-ring are two types of network adapter cards. You should be able to install and configure your network adapter cards, and you should be able to troubleshoot problems associated with them.

A Network Interface Card (NIC) links a PC with the network cabling system. The card has one or more user-accessible ports to which the network cabling medium is connected. Typical connections include RJ-45 and BNC. It is the job of the NIC to prepare the data for transmission over the network.

All NICs require a *driver*, (software that manages the device). The driver activates the NIC and *binds* it to the network protocols being used. If you were to view the OSI 7-layer model, you'd see the NIC near the Data Link Layer at the bottom. The Data Link Layer is right above the physical layer and has been split into two sublayers: the Media Access Control and the Logical Link Control. The driver is found in the Media Access Control sublayer, from which we derive the MAC address, the unique burned-in address of the NIC.

Functions of the NIC include:

- **Preparing data for the transmission medium**

  This role is where the data from higher layers is placed into an Ethernet frame or token-ring frame. On the receiving card, the data packet is removed from the frame and passed to higher layers.

- **Sending data**

  This refers to the physical communications of the network. For example, on a 10-Base 2 network, this refers to the card creating the pulses of electricity and sending them over the coaxial cable. On a token-ring network, this would refer to the card inserting into the ring and generating a token, if necessary.

- **Controlling the flow of data from the PC to the transmission medium**

  On an Ethernet network, the card is responsible for collision-detection and avoidance. If the card detects a collision, it will wait a random interval before retransmitting. On a token-ring network, the card will generate a token or receive a token before communicating.

A. Installing Network Adapter Cards

The details of how to install a network adapter card depend on the card. You should check the manufacturer's documentation. On the *Networking Essentials* test, some questions will state that you have followed the manufacturer's instructions; some will not. Also, the installation steps will vary depending on the operating system. Common steps will be something like this:

1. Physically plug the card into the expansion slot, configuring jumpers and DIP switches as required, or configure the card using the manufacturer's software utility.

2. Install the network adapter card driver.
3. Configure the card so that the network adapter card won't conflict with other devices.
4. Add the appropriate network protocols for your network.
5. Add the appropriate client software for your network.
6. Attach the network cable to the card.

Depending on the hardware and operating system, some of these steps might happen automatically when you plug a card into the slot and start your system.

If the NIC will not physically fit in your system, you have probably purchased the incorrect *data bus* type. PCs currently support four data bus types:

- **ISA:** This is the standard data bus architecture, originally developed for the IBM AT.
- **VESA Local Bus:** This is one enhancement to the ISA bus. An additional slot continues after the ISA slot for VESA Local Bus devices. VESA Local Bus cards *can* be installed in ISA slots, but they will then function only in ISA mode.
- **EISA:** These slots will accept either EISA cards or ISA cards. However, EISA cards cannot be placed into an ISA slot.
- **MicroChannel:** This standard was proposed by IBM to replace the ISA bus. It was not widely accepted and has fallen into disuse.
- **PCI:** This is the most popular bus today. Most Pentium and above systems include both ISA and PCI slots. PCI slots are shorter and more offset than ISA slots.

If you can't physically install your card into the slot, you have probably purchased the incorrect data bus type for your computer.

In addition, certain network cards support only some types of cabling. In general, three types of cabling connections are used:

- **RJ-45** is used to connect to Category 5 or Category 3 twisted-pair cable.
- **RG-56** is used to connect to coaxial cable used for 10-Base 2 networks.
- **AUI connectors** are used to connect to Category 5 or Category 3 twisted-pair cables through a *media filter*, which converts the 9-pin AUI interface to the RJ-45 style interface.

If you cannot physically connect your NIC to the network cable, you have probably purchased a NIC with the wrong connector type for your network.

B. Configuring Network Adapter Cards

You must configure your card to communicate with the operating system. In many cases, you must manually configure the adapter card (through jumper or DIP switch settings) so that it can communicate with the operating system. In other cases, you may use a software utility provided by the manufacturer to configure the card.

There are several settings that must be properly set in order to prevent conflict with other devices on your system. These are some of the resource settings for a network adapter that you have to be concerned with:

IRQ

Base I/O port address

Base memory address

Table 22.3.1 contains a list of IRQs, including those that should *not* be used for a NIC and those that *might* be used for a NIC.

Table 22.3.1

IRQ	Reserved By	Might Be Used By
1	Keyboard	
2	IRQ9	
3		COM2 (modem, mouse)
4		COM1
5		LPT2
6	Floppy controller	
7	LPT1	
8	System Clock	
9		
10		
11		
12		PS/2 Mouse
13	Math processor	
14	Hard drive controller	
15	Additional IDE controller	

Those items reserved by a device cannot be used by the NIC. The possible exception is IRQ 2, which is linked to IRQ9. Other IRQs might be used by some devices but might not be used for others. For example, IRQ 3 is a popular choice for NIC cards, but it will not function on a computer that has a modem or mouse operating on COM2.

The base I/O port address defines a memory address through which data flows to and from the adapter. The base I/O port address functions more like a port, defining a channel to the adapter.

The *base memory address* is a place in the computer's memory that marks the beginning of a buffer area reserved for the network adapter. Not all network adapter cards use the computer's RAM, and therefore, not all adapters require a base memory address setting. Typical regions are C800 through CFFF or D800 through DFFF. If you are using a DOS memory manager such as EMM386.exe, you must exclude this region from use by EMM386.exe.

C. Resolving Hardware Conflicts

Hardware conflicts occur when the devices on the system compete for the same system resources, such as interrupt request lines, base I/O port addresses, and base memory addresses.

In Windows NT, a hardware conflict might invoke a warning message from the system or an entry in the Event Log. If you experience a hardware conflict, use Windows NT Diagnostics to check resource settings for system devices. Then change the resource settings of any conflicting devices.

In Windows 95, use Device Manager (see the following note) to spot hardware conflicts and track resource settings.

If the NIC won't initialize correctly, the problem may be one of three things:

- IRQ conflict with another device
- I/O base address conflict with another device
- The NIC has a physical problem and should be replaced

An adapter RAM conflict will typically not show as a physical problem. The symptoms associated with a RAM conflict are more subtle. The adapter will appear to initialize correctly, but it will not be able to view any resources on the network. In some cases, the configuration lights on the back of the NIC will fail to light.

D. Resolving Software Conflicts

Many questions on the *Networking Essentials* exam will assume your NIC is functioning properly. When this is the case, you may rule out IRQ conflicts, base address conflicts, and adapter RAM conflicts. You must then turn your attention to software issues.

There are several problems associated with software problems and their common symptoms. Memorize this list:

- **Protocol mismatch:** Many networks will use multiple protocols. This is because different server types traditionally use different protocols. For example, Novell NetWare servers typically use IPX to communicate. UNIX servers might use TCP/IP, whereas older Microsoft servers might use NetBEUI.

  If your client can connect to only some network resources but not others, and all other workstations can connect to all network resources, your workstation probably is suffering from a protocol mismatch. You must load the correct protocol to connect to the appropriate resource.

- **Client misconfiguration:** In addition to protocols, each server type requires that client PCs are using the correct client software. For example, both Windows NT and Novell NetWare can use the IPX protocol, but they use different client software. Windows 95 and Windows NT have a specific client for NetWare networks that must be loaded before the client PC can connect to a NetWare server.

For a DOS workstation, the NetWare requester must be loaded before that workstation can connect to a NetWare server. The Microsoft MS-DOS networking client must also be loaded before the workstation can connect to a Windows NT server.

If all your servers and workstations run the IPX protocol only, but your workstations can only see some of the servers, you likely have a client misconfiguration issue.

- **Protocol misconfiguration:** Finally, you may suffer from a protocol misconfiguration issue. The IPX protocol may use different frame types. Most modern implementations use the more advanced 802.2 frame type, while older implementations use 802.3.

  A Microsoft workstation will attempt to auto-detect the appropriate frame type. If it is unable to correctly detect the frame type, it will default to 802.2. If this is not correct, you will not be able to communicate with the server. If this occurs, you must manually set the frame type to 802.3.

This section examined the network adapter card—an essential component in Ethernet and token-ring networks. The network adapter card performs several functions, including preparing, sending, and controlling the flow of data to the network transmission medium. This chapter also discussed how to install and configure network adapters. Configuration tasks for a network adapter card include setting jumpers or DIP switches on the card itself, as well as configuring resource settings (such as IRQ, Base I/O port address, and base memory address) that the operating system must use to communicate with the card.

22.3 Exercises

1. Network Adapter Resource Settings

Objective: Become familiar with the process of configuring network adapter resource settings in Windows NT

Estimated time: 10 minutes

Earlier in this chapter, you learned how to install a network adapter card driver by using Windows NT's Network application. You also can use the Network application to check or change the resource settings for an adapter that is already installed.

1. Click the Start button and choose Settings/Control Panel. Double-click the Windows NT Control Panel Network application.
2. In the Network application, click the Adapters tab.
3. Select the network adapter that is currently installed on your system.
4. Click the Properties button, and the Network Card Setup dialog box appears on your screen.

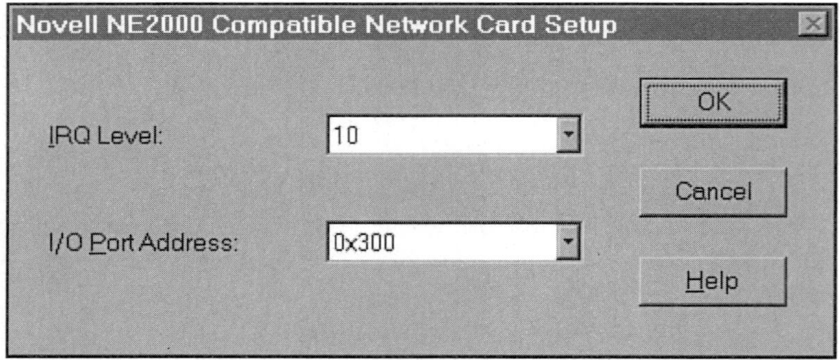

Figure 22.3.1 A Network Card Setup dialog box.

5. In the Network Card Setup dialog box, you can change the resource settings as required. Don't change the settings unless you're experiencing problems, though, because you could introduce a hardware conflict with another device.
6. Click Cancel to leave the Network Card Setup dialog box, and then click Cancel again to leave the Network application.

2. Windows NT Diagnostics

Objective: Learn to check resource settings through Windows NT Diagnostics

Estimated time: 10 minutes

Windows NT Diagnostics tabulates a number of important system parameters. You can use Windows NT Diagnostics to help resolve resource conflicts for network adapters.

1. Click the Start button and choose Programs/Administrative Tools. Choose Windows NT Diagnostics from the Administrative Tools menu.
2. Windows NT Diagnostics provides several tabs with information on different aspects of the system. Choose the Resources tab.
3. Figure 22.3.2 displays the IRQ settings for system devices. (Note that the network adapter card for which the resource settings were displayed in Figure 22.3.2 is listed here beside IRQ10.) The buttons at the bottom of the screen invoke views of other resource settings. Click a button to see the associated list, such as the I/O ports. Don't be alarmed if the list looks complex.

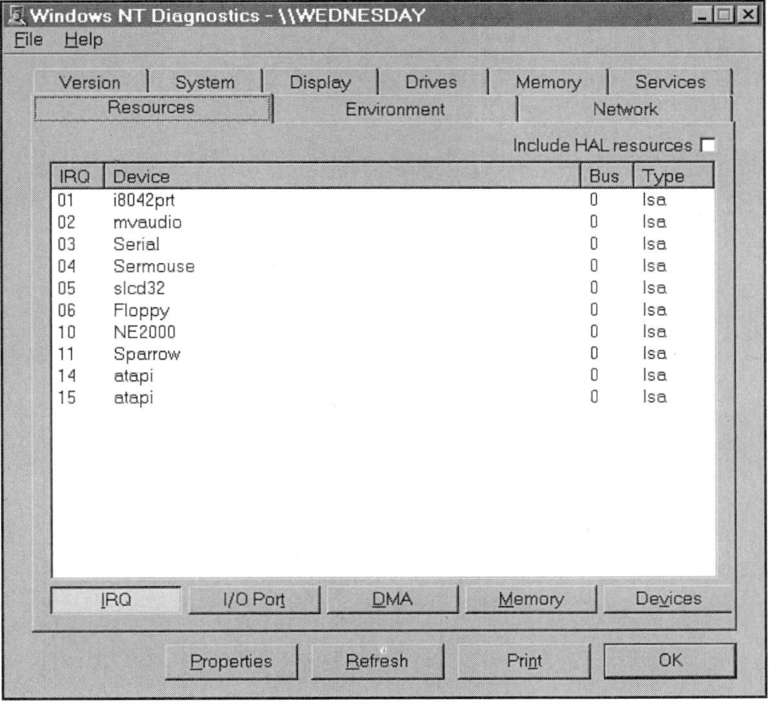

Figure 22.3.2 The Windows NT Diagnostics Resources tab showing IRQ settings.

22.3 Practice Problems

1. The Network Card *driver* is responsible for

   A. Enabling the hardware and binding the software.

   B. Managing the network path of the protocol software.

   C. Pushing the data across the network.

   D. Beaconing to the other adapter cards to limit network traffic.

2. NIC is shorthand for:

   A. Network International Committee for standards and practices.

   B. Network Interface Card.

   C. Networking Intelligent Card management software.

   D. New International Conference for networking.

3. If your network card cannot be physically connected to the cable,

   A. You don't have enough cable.

   B. Your network adapter uses the wrong connector type.

   C. You need a converter to connect the cable.

   D. You must re-read the manufacturer's instructions.

4. Once the network driver is loaded,

   A. You can communicate to all devices on your network.

   B. You can communicate to all devices that use a compatible protocol.

   C. You can communicate using the selected protocols.

   D. You can communicate to all devices that use a compatible client.

5. The network driver is located where in the 7-layer OSI model?

   A. Near the bottom, to interface between the physical layer and the protocol stack.

   B. Near the top, so it can direct and control action further down in the protocol stack.

   C. Near the session and transport layers in the protocol stack.

   D. The 7-layer OSI model does not include the network driver.

6. Once the network driver is loaded:

   A. It takes over all functions of the OSI 7-layer model.

   B. The OSI 7-layer load sequence is complete.

   C. Frames can be transmitted across the network.

   D. Protocols and higher levels of the OSI 7-layer model can be loaded.

7. The Network Interface Card is responsible for which actions?

   A. Only a small part of communications; preparing data for the transmission medium, sending data, and controlling the flow of data from the PC to the transmission medium

   B. Binding protocols and clients to lower-level processes

   C. Inserting the ring-token into the Ethernet

   D. Managing communications between each level of the OSI 7–layer network model

8. When installing a Windows NT-compatible NIC,

   A. The process is the same for all Windows NT-compliant cards.

B. You can use Plug-n-Play to configure the card.

C. You should consult the manufacturer's installation instructions.

D. You always need to use NetBEUI to communicate to Windows NT.

9. When configuring your NIC,

   A. You must decide between the available protocols and load the one you need for your network.

   B. You can decide to load all protocols to your NIC and use as many of them as you want.

   C. You must explicitly bind each protocol to the network card after loading that protocol.

   D. You can decide to load all network drivers to your NIC and use as many of them as you want.

10. The manufacturer's instructions for a NIC should be

   A. Stored in a safe place away from the server in case a physical disaster occurs.

   B. Usd during the installation of the card.

   C. Used during the installation of the protocol.

   D. Checked only as a last resort; advanced operating systems such as Microsoft Windows NT Server and Novell NetWare are too complicated for them.

11. When configuring the NIC, it is most important to

   A. Avoid conflicts with other devices.

   B. Avoid conflicts with other protocols.

   C. Configure the NIC to use the correct protocol type.

   D. Configure the 10-Base 2 NIC to use an RJ-45 connector.

12. Once the NIC is installed and is not conflicting with other devices, it is important to:

   A. Load the token and insert it into the frame.

   B. Load the frame type into the protocol stack.

   C. Create a unique token based on the MAC address.

   D. Load the driver, protocols, and clients and attach the network cable.

13. If you suspect that your NIC is not compatible with Windows NT,

   A. Check the H.A.L.

   B. Check the H.C.L.

   C. Check the A.C.L.

   D. Check the manufacturer's instructions.

14. Some network adapters will not fit in all systems. If yours doesn't fit:

   A. Push really hard; new computer slots are often very tight.

   B. Make sure you have the correct data bus architecture.

   C. Make sure you have the correct CPU processor type.

   D. Check the H.C.L.

15. Which of the following is not true?

   A. MCA cards can be used in a VESA LB slot.

   B. VESA LB cards can be used in an ISA slot.

C. EISA cards cannot be used in a PCI slot.

D. ISA cards can be used in an EISA slot.

16. Which of the following describes the PCI bus slot?

A. It was invented by IBM to work on their MicroChannel™ PCs.

B. It was invented by Intel for the Pentium™ line of computers.

C. It was an industry reaction against the MicroChannel™ architecture, and it can accommodate ISA cards.

D. It was invented for the original AT™ line of computers.

17. If your NIC supports 10-Base 2 networks:

A. You can connect it to twisted-pair wire using RJ-45.

B. You can connect it using BNC connectors.

C. You must insert it into your token-ring before enabling communications.

D. It will support token-ring but not Ethernet.

18. To configure your NIC,

A. You must set DIP switches and jumpers.

B. You must consult the manufacturer's documentation.

C. You can configure it using software.

D. You must insert it into the computer.

19. Plug and Play

A. Works with Windows NT to configure network adapters.

B. Works with Windows 95 to configure network protocols.

C. Works with Windows 95 to configure hardware devices.

D. Works with Windows 95 or Windows NT to configure hardware devices.

20. When configuring your network adapter, typical settings you must configure are:

A. IRQ, I/O port, and RAM address.

B. IRQ, I/O port, and interrupt.

C. Slot number, protocol, and IRQ.

D. I/O port, DMA channel, and adapter ROM.

21. Which of the following is a good IRQ to use for your NIC?

A. 7

B. 4

C. 3

D. 14

22. Which of the following typically uses IRQ 7?

A. COM1

B. LPT1

C. A Sound Blaster™

D. IRQ 9

23. Which of the following typically shares with IRQ 2?

A. IRQ 9

B. A Sound Blaster™

C. LPT2

D. COM1

24. If your computer uses a serial mouse and an external modem, which of these should you configure the NIC to use?

A. IRQ 4

B. IRQ 3

C. IRQ 10

D. IRQ 1

25. What tool would you use in Windows NT to see if resources are available?

A. System Administrator

B. NT Diagnostics

C. Resource Administrator

D. Right-click Resources and double-click Availability.

26. If you configure your NIC and the software fails to load properly,

A. You probably have a conflict with the shared RAM address.

B. You are using the incorrect protocol stack.

C. You probably have a conflict with the I/O port or IRQ.

D. Your I/O port and IRQ are conflicting with one another.

27. If you configure your NIC and the software loads properly but the NIC is not functioning at all,

A. You have loaded the incorrect network driver.

B. Your protocol stack is incompatible with the network driver.

C. Your adapter is not connected to the network.

D. Your memory manager may be conflicting with your RAM address.

28. Hardware conflicts occur:

A. When you have the incorrect data bus architecture.

B. When two components compete for the same resource.

C. When two protocols compete for the same network card.

D. With incompatible software.

29. In Windows NT, where should you check if you suspect a hardware conflict?

A. The Event Viewer

B. The Hardware Manager

C. The Resource Viewer

D. The Windows NT System Manager

30. In Windows 95, where should you check if you suspect a hardware conflict?

A. The Event Viewer

B. The Device Manager

C. The Resource Viewer

D. The Windows 95 System Manager

31. Base Memory Address:

A. Is the central area used by all applications for memory.

B. Is the area of a network card shared with the PC's main memory.

C. Is the memory area the network uses in 10-Base T and 10-Base 2 baseband communication.

D. Is the hardware location of the NIC's resources.

32. A hardware conflict is usually apparent because

A. The adapter fails to initialize or the software does not load.

B. The yellow exclamation point in Windows 95's Device Manager shows up.

C. The Hardware Conflict Wizard (in the Control Panel) shows the conflict.

D. The adapter's software loads fine but the card fails to function.

33. The lights on the back of the network card
    A. Are used only during the boot-up phase to isolate hardware conflicts.
    B. Always flash regularly when the adapter is functioning properly.
    C. Indicate the adapter status.
    D. Are used to illuminate the PC when you are working under a dark desk or cabinet.

The following four questions use this situation as a scenario.

Network type:

Windows NT servers, NetWare servers, UNIX servers

Protocols:

NetBEUI, IPX, TCP/IP

Workstations:

Windows NT workstations, Unix workstations, Windows 95 workstations

NIC cards:

Ethernet 10-base T using twisted pair

34. You recently installed several new Windows 95 workstations on your network. Although you installed all the default software, you cannot see all of the servers. Others on your segment can see all of the servers, and you can see all the computers on your segment and some of the computers on other segments.

    Your network software appears to have loaded properly. The most likely reason you cannot see the servers is:
    A. A hardware conflict with other PCs on your segment.
    B. An inappropriate TCP/IP address or subnet mask.
    C. A protocol mismatch between your workstations and the servers.
    D. You are using 10-base 2 NICs on your 10-base T network.

35. One user cannot access the file and print servers, but he can access all the Internet applications. What is the most likely source of the problem?
    A. Your client software is misconfigured.
    B. You are using the incorrect frame type for your NetBEUI servers.
    C. The networking software has not been loaded, and the Internet software has been loaded in its place.
    D. The user has not installed any file or printer drivers.

36. One client cannot access the NetWare servers, but he can access the Windows NT and Unix servers just fine. Your troubleshooting has determined that the correct client software and protocols are loaded. The most likely problem is:
    A. An incorrect Ethernet link.
    B. An incorrect BNC to 9-pin media filter.
    C. An incorrect token-ring link.
    D. An incorrect frame type.

37. You decide that you need to access only the Novell NetWare servers. For your Windows 95 workstation, you install and configure all the protocols correctly. You recall that you were able to connect to the Windows NT servers before removing the other protocols.
    A. You need to load the Microsoft Client for Windows 95.
    B. You need to load the Novell NetWare client.

C. You need to load the Novell Client for Windows NT servers.

D. You need to configure the IPX protocol.

38. DOS workstations

A. Must load a redirector or requester before attaching to a network.

B. Must load special memory-management software before attaching to a network.

C. Must redirect memory to the requester before attaching to the network.

D. Are not capable of attaching to the network.

39. If your network contains NT servers,

A. MS-DOS workstations must "break the 640K" barrier before attaching to the server.

B. MS-DOS workstations cannot participate in domain networking.

C. MS-DOS workstations must request their network traffic through a NetWare redirector before attaching to the servers.

D. MS-DOS workstations must load the Microsoft MS-DOS network client before attaching to the servers.

40. Suppose your network contains Novell NetWare servers and you add Windows NT or Windows 95 clients to your network. If the clients you added can view one another but not the servers, you should

A. Let Windows 95 autodetect the frame type.

B. Manually choose 802.3 because it is more advanced.

C. Manually choose 802.2 because it is more advanced.

D. Calculate the 802.2 and 802.3 to 802.5 *parity checksum*.

41. Which is not true about frame types?

A. 802.3 can connect to 802.2, but not vice-versa.

B. 802.2 can connect to 802.3 because it is more advanced.

C. Windows 95 workstations can request the appropriate frame type from a DCHP server.

D. All of the above.

The following four questions use this situation as a scenario.

Network type:

Windows NT servers using NetBEUI, NetWare servers using IPX, Unix servers using TCP/IP

Workstations:

Windows NT workstations, Unix workstations, Windows 95 workstations

NIC cards:

Ethernet 10-base T using twisted pair

42. You have a large network with multiple routers. You limit access to certain servers by loading only those protocols necessary for communication. You find that you cannot connect to your Windows NT servers across your router. The most likely problem is:

A. Your routers are using frame type 802.2, but the Windows NT servers have defaulted to 802.3.

B. You have a protocol misconfiguration issue.

C. Your TCP/IP address is invalid.

D. NetBEUI is not a routable protocol.

22

43. You trace the trouble to the NetBEUI protocol. The most likely trouble you are having with it is:

    A. NetBEUI has defaulted to frame type 802.3.

    B. You must configure NetBEUI to use the router broadcast address.

    C. NetBEUI is not a routable protocol.

    D. NetBEUI is causing a software conflict with IPX.

44. You decide to abandon your plans to use protocols to secure the network. However, for Microsoft networking you will need to use NetBIOS. Because of this, you *must* use which protocol:

    A. IPX

    B. TCP/IP

    C. NetBEUI

    D. You may use any of the above protocols.

45. Which is true about NetBIOS and NetBEUI?

    A. NetBIOS (basic-input-output-system) is an interface, while NetBEUI (basic-enhanced-user-interface) is a protocol.

    B. NetBIOS (basic-input-output-system) is a protocol, while NetBEUI (basic-enhanced-user-interface) is an interface.

    C. NetBEUI can be used with any protocol, even TCP/IP.

    D. NetBEUI is required to connect to a Windows NT server.

46. When installing network components:

    A. Always install the software and drivers before you install the network adapter, in order to enable Plug and Play.

    B. Always install the network adapter before you install the software and drivers.

    C. Never install the adapter software while the PC is on.

    D. Always connect to a network location to install the software and drivers for the network adapter.

47. If you are unsure about a certain network adapter:

    A. Install all the network driver software, because one of them will work.

    B. Consult the manufacturer's documentation.

    C. Install the generic IBM-compatible networking software.

    D. Use the Windows NT Plug and Play utility.

48. If you are unsure which protocols your network uses:

    A. Install all the protocols, because one of them will work.

    B. Consult the manufacturer's documentation.

    C. Install the generic Ethernet-compatible networking software.

    D. Use the Windows NT Plug and Play utility.

49. Networking protocols

    A. Must be loaded separately to avoid causing a conflict.

    B. Do not conflict and can be loaded one after the other.

    C. Can conflict if they are not on the Windows NT HCL list.

    D. Require a unique IRQ address.

50. Multiple networking client software in Windows NT and Windows 95:

    A. Usually conflict if they are from different network cards.

    B. Can be run simultaneously.

    C. Are not necessary; they're built-in to the operating system.

    D. Use the Windows 95 Plug and Play model.

51. Network adapter drivers

    A. Can only be used one at a time. You cannot load two adapter drivers for one card.

    B. Do not conflict and can be loaded one after the other.

    C. Must be on the HCL to be used by Windows NT.

    D. Use the protocol stack to communicate with the network card.

52. A Microsoft Windows NT or 95 workstation will do what with the frame type?

    A. Set it to 802.2

    B. Set it to 802.3

    C. Attempt to detect it

    D. Insert the frame type into the token-ring

53. The purpose of the NDIS standard is:

    A. To replace the older and more cumbersome ODI standard.

    B. Like the MLID standard, to provide an API for developers.

    C. Like the ODI standard, to provide an API for developers.

    D. To create a meaningful transition to the OSI 7-layer model.

54. If the network adapter loads the software but nothing happens,

    A. There is probably a hardware conflict preventing the software from functioning.

    B. The software is empty and must have protocols installed in it.

    C. There is probably a protocol or client misconfiguration issue.

    D. There is probably a software error preventing the hardware from functioning.

55. In Windows NT, hardware errors usually show up in which of the following?

    A. Hardware Manager

    B. Conflict Viewer

    C. Device Manager

    D. Event Viewer

56. Typical devices that may conflict with your network adapter include

    A. Video adapters, sound cards, and game ports.

    B. Mice, modems, and other network adapters.

    C. Joysticks, video accelerators, and game ports.

    D. Sound cards, video accelerators, and game software.

57. Software that tends to conflict with DOS networking software includes:

    A. TSRs and mouse drivers.

    B. DOS games and sound programs.

    C. Memory-management software.

    D. Modem and mouse software.

58. If your network adapter is not functioning and you suspect a hardware conflict, you should

    A. Remove all cards except the video card and see if the problem persists.

    B. Unload all software and reboot the system from scratch.

    C. Re-read the manufacturer's instructions.

    D. Use the manufacturer's configuration utility.

59. The IRQs can be:

    A. Shared among several devices because they can "interrupt" one another.

    B. A major source of conflict.

    C. Moved from any device to another using Windows NT diagnostics or the Windows 95 device manager.

    D. Hidden system files.

60. A *reserved* IRQ means:

    A. It is available for use because it is "reserved" by the operating system.

    B. Proceed cautiously before using.

    C. It does not conform to the OSI 7-layer networking model, nor is it on the HCL.

    D. It is used by a built-in component, such as the hard drive controller.

61. An I/O port

    A. Is used by a device to communicate to the computer.

    B. Is used by a communication device to connect to the Internet via a modem.

    C. Uses an IRQ to connect to a hardware device.

    D. Uses an *expanded memory manager* to manage resources.

22.3 Answers and Explanations: Practice Problems

1. **A** Without a *driver*, or software, the NIC will fail to function. In addition to enabling the NIC, the driver also binds the protocols to the adapter.

2. **B** NIC is short for Network Interface Card.

3. **B** NICs can use a variety of connectors and cable types. If your card doesn't match your cable, you won't be able to connect the two.

4. **C** The NIC binds the protocols to the adapter. At that point, the protocols are available for use.

5. **A** The driver is located in layer 2, the Data Link Layer.

6. **D** Protocols cannot be loaded until the NIC driver has enabled the card. Without the NIC driver, the card will not function.

7. **A** The card itself actually plays a relatively small role in network communications. It is, however, a crucial role.

8. **B** NT installation can be more difficult. The manufacturer's instructions may indicate whether or not the card is compatible with Windows NT and where software updates can be obtained.

9. **B** You cannot load multiple drivers per card, but there is often no limit to how many protocols you can bind to a card.

10. **B** Instructions are seldom used after installation and often needed during installation.

11. **A** Hardware conflicts can cause the NIC (or the rest of your system) to stop functioning.

12. **D** Installation of the NIC is only a small step.

13. **B** The HCL is the Hardware Compatibility List.

14. **B** Varying bus types are common. As bus types advance, this problem will continue.

15. **A** The EISA slot will accept both EISA and ISA slots. Technically, you can fit a VESA LB card into an ISA slot, but the VESA connector will not be connected, and the card will not function in VESA LB mode.

16. **B** The PCI standard was developed to work with the Pentium.

17. **B** 10 Base-2 is defined as using BNC connectors and coaxial cable. RJ-45, by contrast, uses Category 5 twisted-pair.

18. **C** Not all cards use jumpers, and you cannot use the instructions if you want. If your card does use jumpers, you can even configure it outside the PC. The only correct answer is that you can configure it using software.

19. **C** Plug and Play is not supported by the current versions of Windows NT.

20. **A** B is incorrect: The IRQ and interrupt are the same thing. C is incorrect: The slot number is not required. D is incorrect: NICs don't use a DMA channel. A is correct.

21. **C** IRQ 7 is used by LPT1, the printer. IRQ 14 is used by the hard disk controller. IRQ 4 might work, but almost all PCs have COM1.

22. **B** Even though a Sound Blaster™ can be configured to use IRQ 7, as it uses by default, LPT1 is the most typical device using LPT1.

23. **A** IRQ 2 and IRQ 9 are the links between the two IRQ controllers. For this reason, Windows 95 lists IRQ 2 as "programmable interrupt controller." Because of this, you cannot use both IRQ 2 and IRQ 9.

24. **C** IRQ 1 is reserved, and IRQ 3 and 4 are used by COM2 and COM1, respectively. If you have a serial mouse and external modem, you are most likely using both COM ports. This leaves IRQ 10.

25. **B** NT Diagnostics is the only choice that exists. All the others are not NT components.

26. **C** If the software fails to load, it is because it cannot allocate one or more of the resources, such as IRQ or I/O port.

27. **D** A and B are not possible options. Once the software loads, the card will function unless overwritten. This can happen with memory managers that allocate memory after the network drivers have loaded.

28. **B** This is the dictionary definition of a hardware conflict.

29. **A** There are no such items as the Hardware Manager, the Resource Viewer, or the Windows NT System Manager.

30. **B** Windows 95 does not have an event viewer. You must use the Device Manager found in the SYSTEM applet of the control panel.

31. **B** This is different than the I/O port. This is an area of memory the NIC can use to store card information or other items needed. It executes much faster than ROM memory.

32. **A** It is true the yellow exclamation point will show up in Windows 95's Device Manager, but this doesn't work in other operating systems, and you must open several windows before viewing the Device Manager. It is better to rely on the behavior of the device—in this case, the software not loading.

33. **C** The behavior of the light varies from adapter to adapter. The only common behavior is that the lights are used to indicate the status of the adapter (another name for NIC).

34. **C** If some servers use TCP/IP and you have loaded only NetBEUI or IPX/SPX,

you will not be able to connect to the TCP/IP-enabled servers. This is a *protocol mismatch*.

35. **A** This is akin to a protocol mismatch. However, even if different server types use the same protocols, they may still require different client software, such as the Client for Microsoft Networks.

36. **D** IPX can use more than one frame type. The frame types cannot be used with one another.

37. **B** Because the protocols have been installed and configured correctly, no configuration of IPX is necessary. This is a client misconfiguration issue. You need to load the client for NetWare networks.

38. **A** All operating systems must load a redirector or requester before attaching to a network, or they must have one built into the operating system.

39. **D** The MS-DOS network client is the DOS-mode redirector for Microsoft networks.

40. **C** 802.2 is more advanced. Unfortunately, Windows 95's autodetect function works like this: It checks for 802.3; if it finds another PC using 802.3, it uses it. If it doesn't, it checks for 802.2 the same way. Occasionally Windows 95 machines checking for 802.3 will find one another and default to that frame type.

41. **D** None of the answers are true. The frame types cannot read one another, and DHCP is not for IPX, but only TCP/IP.

42. **D** In the situation described, the resources that can't be seen are running NetBEUI from the other side of a router. If they were running a routable protocol, the workstations could connect to the servers.

43. **C** Once again, NetBEUI cannot be routed. All the other answers in this question are gibberish.

44. **D** NetBIOS is an interface, not a protocol. It can be bound to any protocol.

45. **A** Unfortunately, NetBIOS is the interface, and NetBEUI is the protocol. This is confusing because NetBEUI stands for Network Basic Enhanced User Interface. The important point is that Microsoft Networking, which requires NetBIOS, can use any protocol, including TCP/IP only.

46. **B** A is incorrect because Plug and Play will load the software and drivers. C is incorrect because it is impossible to install software of any kind while the PC is off. D is incorrect because you will be unable to load anything from the network until you have connected to the network. With no software or drivers, it would be difficult to connect to the network.

47. **B** Network adapters are not easy to configure without the manufacturer's documentation.

48. **A** Although this seems like an inelegant solution, it will allow you to connect to the network resources. Multiple protocols can be used simultaneously. This might cause additional network traffic if all PCs were configured this way, but it is an excellent troubleshooting tool.

49. **B** Protocols do not use an IRQ, nor would they appear on the Windows NT hardware-compatibility list. You can load as many protocols as you want.

50. **B** Like protocols, you can run multiple network clients.

51. **A** Only one driver can be loaded for a particular NIC. D is incorrect because the protocol stack uses the driver to communicate with the card, not the other way around.

52. **C** Windows workstations attempt to detect the frame type currently in use on the network.

53. **C** The NDIS standard for networking was developed differently from Novell's

ODI standard, but both were designed to allow a more flexible interface for networking programmers and device driver manufacturers. They both segment the networking layers, but not as cleanly as the OSI theoretical model did.

54. **C** If the NIC is functioning properly but the user cannot access anything, it usually means the network resources and the networking client on the user's workstation are using different protocols.

55. **D** The only valid choice here is the Event Viewer. None of the other items exist.

56. **B** Typically, IRQ conflicts are the most frequent conflicts in network adapters, with COM2 and COM1 using IRQ3 and 4, respectively. Next, additional network cards typically take the last remaining bit of resources.

57. **C** Memory management software has a special problem with networking software. During installation, memory management software, such as QEMM or EMM386.EXE will scan the upper memory area for available areas. While sound cards, serial cards, and other devices will register their functionality without a driver, network cards do not do so until the driver is loaded. But the memory management scan occurs before the network driver is loaded. Because memory management operations occur after the NIC driver is loaded, the memory manager simply overwrites the RAM address of the NIC.

58. **A** The only way to completely isolate the network card is to remove all the expansion boards, including the I/O (serial and parallel) card on some older systems. If you take out the video card, you won't be able to see anything. This is an excellent way to isolate compatibility problems, which are often with other peripherals, not the system itself.

59. **B** The IRQ channels must be properly set. 75% or more of your problems in using a new NIC or a new configuration will likely be traced to an IRQ conflict. For this reason, always use the same manufacturer and, if possible, the model of NIC across your enterprise.

60. **D** The reserved IRQs cannot be used by a NIC or any other expansion device, with the exception of IRQ2, which cascades to IRQ 9. You cannot use both IRQ 2 and IRQ 9. Often times you can freely choose one or the other for your device.

61. **A** The I/O channel is where the device sends data when communicating with the computer. The IRQ, by contrast, alerts the CPU to impending communication.

22.3 Key Words

IRQ

I/O port

Memory management software

Frame type

Protocol

Client software

Server software

IPX/SPX, TCP/IP, NetBEUI

Redirector/requester

22.4 Implement a NetBIOS Naming Scheme for all Computers on a Given Network

NetBIOS is an interface that provides applications with access to network resources. It is *not* a protocol. Every computer on a Windows NT network must have a unique name for it to be accessible through the NetBIOS interface. This unique name is called a computer name or a NetBIOS name.

NetBIOS (Network Basic Input/Output System) is an application interface that provides PC-based applications with uniform access to lower protocol layers. NetBIOS was once most closely associated with the NetBEUI protocol (a poor performer). *NetBEUI*, in fact, is an abbreviation for NetBIOS Extended User Interface. This is confusing when you realize that NetBIOS is actually the interface, and NetBEUI is the protocol. Today, the NetBIOS interface can be carried over IPX and TCP/IP, as well as NetBEUI. NetBIOS over IPX can cause routing problems if not properly configured, but NetBIOS over TCP/IP avoids all these issues.

On a NetBIOS network, every computer must have a unique name. The computer name must be no more than 15 characters long. A NetBIOS name can include alphanumeric characters and any of the following special characters:

! @ # $ % ^ & ( ) - _ ' { } . ~

Note that you cannot use a space or an asterisk in a NetBIOS name. Also, NetBIOS names are not case-sensitive.

Within these character limitations, you can choose any name for a PC. The rule of thumb is to choose a name that helps you identify the computer. Names such as PC1, PC2, and PC3 are difficult to visualize and easy to confuse. Likewise, an ad-hoc naming convention, such as SNEEZY, DOC, and BASHFUL does not tell you enough about the PC, especially if you have many computers on your network. The name should include information about the PC's location, department, and primary user.

A list that uses a unique hexadecimal address to identify each PC would satisfy the technical requirements of a NetBIOS naming scheme, but it would be difficult, if not impossible, to administer. It would be better to have a naming system that includes several characters for location or department, several characters for a sub-department (or floor, perhaps), and the remaining characters to identify the primary user, perhaps using an e-mail address.

Consider this naming system:

ADMIN-013-SALLY

ADMIN-014-BETTY

MRKTG-001-KARL

This naming system uses a department (ADMIN for Administration and MRKTG for Marketing) to identify the location of the computer. Also, the floor of the building was used to pinpoint the location. Finally, the user's e-mail name was used to identify each PC. You can change the name of a Windows 95 or Windows NT computer using the control panel.

A NetBIOS computer name must:

- **Be unique.**
- **Consist of no more than 15 characters.**
- **Consist of a combination of alphanumeric characters and these characters:**
  ! @ # $ % ^ & ( ) - _ ' { } . ~

The Universal Naming Convention is a standard for identifying resources on Microsoft networks. A UNC path consists of the following components:

- A NetBIOS computer name preceded by two backslashes (left-leaning slashes)
- The share name of a shared resource located on the given PC (optional)
- The MS-DOS-style path of a file or a directory located on the given share (optional)

Elements of the UNC path are separated with single backslashes. The following list shows examples of legal UNC names:

\\ADMIN-113-BETTY\CDRIVE

\\MRKTNG-001-KARL\DOCUMENTS

\\PET_DEPT\CATS\SIAMESE.TXT

Various Windows NT commands use UNC paths to designate network resources. For instance, the command

net view \\PET_DEPT

enables you to view the shared resources on the computer with the NetBIOS name PET_DEPT. Like wise, the command

net use G: \\PET_DEPT\CATS

maps the shared directory CATS on the computer PET_DEPT to the drive letter G:.

A computer on a NetBIOS network must have a NetBIOS computer name. The NetBIOS name is configured at installation and, in Windows NT or Windows 95, can be changed later through the Control Panel Network application. Computers use the NetBIOS name (sometimes combined with a share name or a path name) to locate resources on the network.

22.4 Practice Problems

1. A NetBIOS name can have how many characters?

    A. 14

    B. 15

    C. 11

    D. 8 plus a three-character extension

2. Which character cannot be used in a NetBIOS name?

    A. \

    B. !

    C. $

    D. @

3. Using the character limitations, you

    A. Must choose a meaningful name for your computer.

    B. Must choose a name that includes the computer's role.

    C. Must choose a name of 15 characters or less.

    D. Must choose a combination of upper- and lowercase letters.

The following four questions use this situation as a scenario:

Network type:

Windows NT servers, multiple domains

Protocols:

NetBEUI, IPX, TCP/IP

Your workstations:

30 Windows NT workstations

You decide to implement a NetBIOS naming scheme for your network. You are currently part of a standalone network with one server, but you are scheduled to be connected to the multidomain corporate WAN in several months. Your users have e-mail accounts on the corporate WAN mail hub.

Required objectives:

- The naming scheme must contain unique names.
- The naming scheme must continue to function after the WAN integration.

Desired objectives:

- The naming scheme should help streamline user administration.
- The naming scheme should be informative about the computer's role.

4. You decide to generate a unique hexadecimal number for your workstations. You will keep a list of each number on a list and carefully control which numbers are available. You will submit your list to corporate HQ to guarantee they are not using your unique hexadecimal names. This plan will:

    A. Perform both of the required objectives and both of the desired objectives.

    B. Perform both of the required objectives and one of the desired objectives.

    C. Perform both of the required objectives and none of the desired objectives.

    D. Not perform the required objectives.

5. You decide to use the burned-in MAC address of the Ethernet cards in each system as the NetBIOS name. Because the first several characters of the MAC address indicate the manufacturer, you feel this will help indicate the role of the PC. This plan will:

    A. Perform both of the required objectives and both of the desired objectives.

B. Perform both of the required objectives and one of the desired objectives.

C. Perform both of the required objectives and none of the desired objectives.

D. Not perform the required objectives.

6. You decide to use the user's e-mail address as the computer's name. This plan will:

   A. Perform both of the required objectives and both of the desired objectives.

   B. Perform both of the required objectives and one of the desired objectives.

   C. Perform both of the required objectives and none of the desired objectives.

   D. Not perform the required objectives.

7. You create a naming convention that uses a three-character building code, followed by a four-character floor code, followed by the user's e-mail address. This plan will:

   A. Perform both of the required objectives and both of the desired objectives.

   B. Perform both of the required objectives and one of the desired objectives.

   C. Perform both of the required objectives and none of the desired objectives.

   D. Not perform the required objectives.

8. The UNC convention

   A. Uses the NetBIOS name followed by the drive name.

   B. Includes the NetBIOS name for Microsoft computers.

   C. Allows use of any alphanumeric character, plus ! @ # $ % ^ & ( ) - _ ' { } . ~, but never slashes because they are reserved.

   D. Allows use of no fewer than 15 characters.

9. When using resources with the UNC naming convention, you must

   A. Use the MAP ROOT command for NetWare networks.

   B. Precede the statement with a username and password.

   C. Precede the share name with two slashes and the NetBIOS name.

   D. Always use *net use* and use a drive letter.

10. Elements within the UNC name are separated:

    A. By servers with NTFS file-level security.

    B. By single slashes.

    C. By preceding double-slashes.

    D. By a hard return on multiple lines.

11. On a Windows 95 workstation,

    A. UNC names must be mapped to a drive letter to be used.

    B. UNC names are supported via the 32-bit Windows NT kernel.

    C. UNC names are built into the Microsoft NetWare Requester.

    D. UNC names can be used instead of drive letters.

12. A computer on a NetBIOS network:

    A. Must have a NetBIOS name only if it wants to share resources.

    B. Must have a unique hexadecimal address.

C. Must have a NetBIOS name to participate in networking.

D. Must have a NetBIOS name of no fewer than 15 characters.

13. Computers use the NetBIOS name:

A. To manage the protocols and network drivers.

B. To view and share resources on the network.

C. To attach to remote printers and files.

D. To populate the ACL (Access Control List).

14. Once the NetBIOS name is created,

A. It cannot be changed because it uniquely identifies that computer on the network

B. It can be used to secure resources.

C. It can be used to select a password.

D. It can be changed easily.

15. Which is the correct NetBIOS statement?

A. net use * \\ago-ncls1\ntw

B. net view g: \\Wednesday\system

C. net use root g: \\server\drive

D. net delete g:

16. The NetBIOS share name

A. Is hidden using the ACL (Access Control List).

B. Is used to access a resource.

C. Cannot be made hidden by using a '$' as the last character.

D. Allows access to users in the local share group only.

17. A computer on a NetBIOS network:

A. Must have a NetBIOS name only if it wants to share resources.

B. Must have a unique hexadecimal address.

C. Must have a NetBIOS name only if it wants to use resources.

D. Must have a NetBIOS name of no more than 15 characters.

18. The statement net use d: \\server\share

A. Is incorrect.

B. May prompt the user for a password.

C. Will not function on Windows 95. Instead, it requires the advanced networking built into Windows NT.

D. Will share the user's d: drive over the network.

19. The statement copy \\cats\docs\burmese.txt

A. Is illegal.

B. Must be mapped to a drive letter to be used.

C. Can be used instead of mapping \\cats\docs to a drive letter.

D. Will not function unless the share name \docs is unique.

20. A UNC name consists of the following components:

A. Server name, share name, MS-DOS style path

B. Server name, NetBIOS name, and drive letter

C. "net use" or "net view" followed by a server name

D. The ACL (Access Control List), the user's SID (Security ID), and the file name

21. Finding resources on a Microsoft NetBIOS network
    A. Uses the User Manager for Domains.
    B. Uses the Windows NT Server Manager.
    C. Is as simple as typing "net view."
    D. Can degrade network performance.

22. NetBIOS names on Windows NT
    A. Are case-sensitive.
    B. Are case-insensitive.
    C. Are maintained in the ACL.
    D. Break the 15-character limitation imposed by Windows for Workgroups.

23. On a NetBIOS network,
    A. Each computer must have a unique name.
    B. Each server must have a unique name, but workstations can be named more leniently.
    C. Servers and workstations create a security-token based on the NetBIOS name and its uniqueness.
    D. The protocol must use NetBEUI.

24. If all NetBIOS names are unique,
    A. The usernames can be shared.
    B. The usernames are case-sensitive.
    C. The users can be connected using "net use \\servername\username."
    D. The usernames must be unique.

22.4 Answers and Explanations: Practice Problems

1. **B** A NetBIOS name can no more than 15 characters.
2. **A** The slash (\ ) is reserved for directory names and UNC entries.
3. **C** You are not required to use a meaningful name or a name that satisfies any other role. The name cannot be more than 15 characters, though.
4. **C** The hexadecimal naming scheme will make it difficult to administer and will indicate nothing about the computer's role. The carefully controlled list will also be difficult and cumbersome to administer.
5. **C** The MAC address will only indicate the manufacturer of the NIC. But the numbers would be unique.
6. **B** This is a great naming scheme, as it is easier to administer and is also unique. In this case, it fails to indicate the computer's role.
7. **A** This plan will work perfectly, but the e-mail address portion can contain only eight characters or less, because you will have used seven characters on the building and floor codes.
8. **B** It is true that slashes are reserved for NetBIOS names, but this is not a requirement for the UNC naming convention. However, in a Microsoft network, the NetBIOS name is the computer or server name.
9. **C** A username is required only if the currently authenticated user does not have access to the network share. The map root command is not necessary for mapping using UNC names. The NetWare MAP command does support UNC naming. It's much easier to use than map root j: server/vol1:dirame\otherdir.

10. **B** Single slashes separate the elements.
11. **D** UNC names can be used instead of drive letters for COPY, XCOPY, DIR, and a host of other commands. Batch files can behave erratically when executed from a UNC name, but executables do not suffer from this.
12. **C** A NetBIOS name is required to be a server *and* a client.
13. **B** NetBIOS names are also used to access resources on the network, but C is incorrect because files are not attached across the network.
14. **D** The NetBIOS name can be changed easily in the Control Panel.
15. **A** B is incorrect: You would not include a drive letter in this manner in a NET VIEW statement. C is incorrect: Only because the drive letter (in \\SERVER\DRIVE is not used.).
16. **B** A, C, and D are all false statements.
17. **D** A NetBIOS name is used for sharing and using resources. The name need not be a hexadecimal address. It must, however, not have more than 15 characters.
18. **B** If the currently logged in user does not have access to the network resource, the statement will generate a password or username prompt.
19. **C** COPY can be used with UNC names, and a drive letter is not required. Many applications also support this.
20. **A** A full UNC file name would include the MS-DOS path in addition to the share name. This MS-DOS path refers to the directories beneath the share.
21. **C** The NET VIEW command shows all computers within the specified domain or workgroup that are sharing resources.
22. **B** NetBIOS names are never case-sensitive.
23. **A** NetBIOS names do not have a lot of requirements, but one is that they must all be unique. If not, users in the conflicting workstations or servers will not be able to access resources.
24. **D** There can be no duplicate of user names.

22.4 Key Words

UNC

NetBIOS name

Naming scheme

MAC address

NET commands

Resources

Sharing

Accessing

Username

NetBIOS name

22.5 Select the Appropriate Hardware and Software Tools to Monitor Trends in the Network

A. Tools to Use to Document Network Activities

An important part of network management involves monitoring trends on the network. By effectively monitoring network behavior, you can anticipate problems and correct them before they disrupt the network. Monitoring the network also provides you with a *baseline*, a sampling of how the network functions in its equilibrium state. This baseline is beneficial because if you experience a problem later, the changes in certain related parameters could lead you to a possible cause.

Monitoring the network is an ongoing task that requires data from several different areas. The following list details some tools you can use to document network activities:

- A performance-monitoring tool, such as Windows NT's Performance Monitor
- A network-monitoring and protocol-analysis program—such as Windows NT's Network Monitor or the more powerful Network Monitor tool included with Microsoft's BackOffice System Management Server (SMS) package—or a hardware-based protocol analyzer
- A system event log, such as the Windows NT event log, which you can access through Windows NT's Event Viewer application.

B. Keeping Network Records

A detailed history of changes to the network is critical for accurate troubleshooting. When a problem occurs, simply cross-reference the problem's occurrence with the network changes or modifications carried out at the same time.

Your initial configuration records should include descriptions of all hardware, including installation dates, repair histories, configuration details (such as interrupts and addresses), and backup records for each server. In addition, you should maintain a running log that contains the following details:

- A list of all software modifications, version updates, and service packs
- A map of the network showing locations of hardware and cabling details
- Current copies of workstation configuration files, such as CONFIG.SYS and AUTOEXEC.BAT files
- Service agreements and important telephone numbers, such as the numbers of vendors, contractors, and software support lines
- Software licenses to ensure that your network operates within the bounds of the license terms
- A history of past problems and related solutions

C. Monitoring Performance

Windows NT's Performance Monitor tool lets you monitor important system parameters for the computers on your network. Performance Monitor can keep an eye on a large number of system parameters, providing a graphical or tabular profile of system and network trends. You can use Performance Monitor to track statistical measurements for components such as these:

Network segment

Server

Server work queues

Protocol-related objects, such as NetBEUI, NWLink, and NetBIOS

Service-related objects, such as Browser and Gateway Services for NetWare

D. Baseline Measurement

You should use Performance Monitor when your network is first upgraded or installed. By identifying acceptable performance standards and relating them to the Performance Monitor, you can establish a *baseline* set of statistics.

A baseline is critical for measuring network performance using the Performance Monitor. Without a baseline, the measurements viewed by Performance Monitor will be basically meaningless. When you experience problems, you can compare the current readings with the readings listed in your baseline. To establish a baseline, follow these steps:

1. Use Performance Monitor to view the statistics you are concerned with.
2. View Performance Monitor over a period of several days to observe where the utilization of each statistic tends to cluster.
3. Associate current spikes in each statistic to correlate these activity spikes with events and performance degradation.

After you establish a baseline, you can refer back to your baseline to monitor against problems you may experience. For example, during your baseline period, you may have observed that a large database query caused a performance spike in server utilization. You would consider this a normal part of your network's performance. If, however, the statistic in question had an abnormal spike duration or spiked much higher than usual, this would indicate a problem. Without your baseline to refer to, such problems would be difficult to distinguish.

E. Monitoring Network Traffic

Protocol analysis tools monitor network traffic by intercepting and decoding frames. Software-based tools, such as Windows NT Server's Network Monitor, analyze frames coming and going from the computer on which they run.

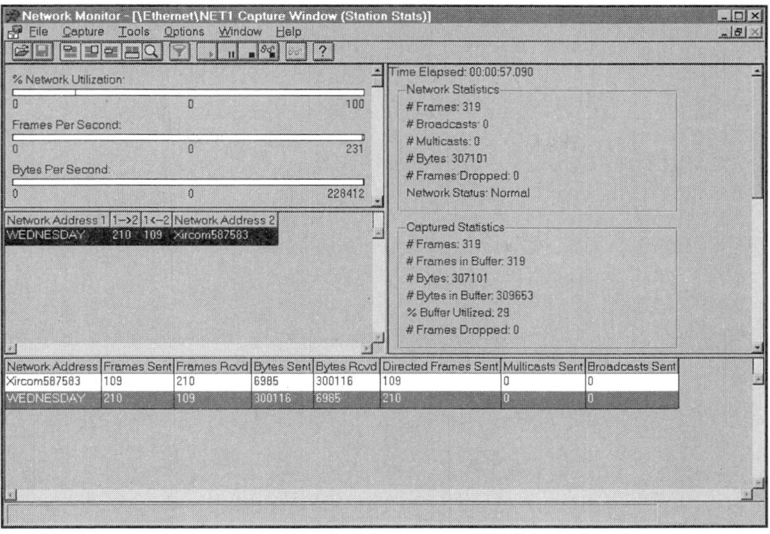

Figure 22.5.1 Windows NT Server's Network Monitor main screen.

An enhanced version of Network Monitor, which is included with the Microsoft BackOffice System Management Server (SMS) package, monitors traffic not just at the local system, but also at other computers on the network.

Other protocol analyzers are more sophisticated. HP Lanalyzer™ and Network Sniffer™ are two examples of dedicated protocol analyzers. For larger networks, you should consider a dedicated network analysis tool.

In addition to keeping network traffic statistics, protocol analyzers can capture bad frames and often isolate which PC is causing the problem. A dedicated protocol analyzer is often a good investment for a large network because it concentrates a considerable amount of monitoring and troubleshooting power into a single, portable unit. Depending on your network, you will want to choose between a dedicated hardware-based or a specific software-based protocol analysis tool.

F. Logging Events

Some operating systems, such as Windows NT, have the ability to keep a running log of system events. That log serves as a record of previous errors, warnings, and other messages from the system. Studying the event log can help you find reccurring errors and discover when a problem first appeared.

Windows NT's Event Viewer application provides you with access to the event log. You can use Event Viewer to monitor the following types of events:

- **System events:** Warnings, error messages, and other notices describing significant system events. Examples of system log entries include browser elections, service failures, and network connection failures.
- **Security events:** Events tracked through Windows NT's auditing features.
- **Application events:** Messages from applications. If you're having a problem with an application, you can check the application log for an application-related error or warning messages.

Event Viewer - System Log on \\WEDNESDAY

Log View Options Help

Date	Time	Source	Category	Event	User
8/16/97	2:02:15 PM	Wins	None	4097	N/A
8/16/97	2:02:02 PM	DhcpServer	None	1024	N/A
8/16/97	2:01:49 PM	Dns	None	2	N/A
8/16/97	2:01:47 PM	Dns	None	1	N/A
8/16/97	2:01:46 PM	SNMP	None	1001	N/A
8/16/97	2:01:45 PM	SNMP	None	1106	N/A
8/16/97	2:01:36 PM	SLnet	None	1006	N/A
8/16/97	2:01:29 PM	BROWSER	None	8015	N/A
8/16/97	2:00:17 PM	EventLog	None	6005	N/A
8/16/97	1:57:50 PM	BROWSER	None	8033	N/A
8/16/97	1:54:34 PM	SLnet	None	1006	N/A
8/16/97	1:53:22 PM	SLnet	None	1006	N/A
8/16/97	11:41:31 AM	Print	None	10	Rob
8/16/97	11:40:29 AM	Print	None	10	Rob
8/16/97	11:38:58 AM	Print	None	10	Rob
8/16/97	11:30:04 AM	Print	None	10	Rob

Figure 22.5.2 The Event Viewer main screen.

If you double-click a log entry in Event Viewer, a dialog box called an Event Detail appears on your screen. An Event Detail provides a detailed description of the event.

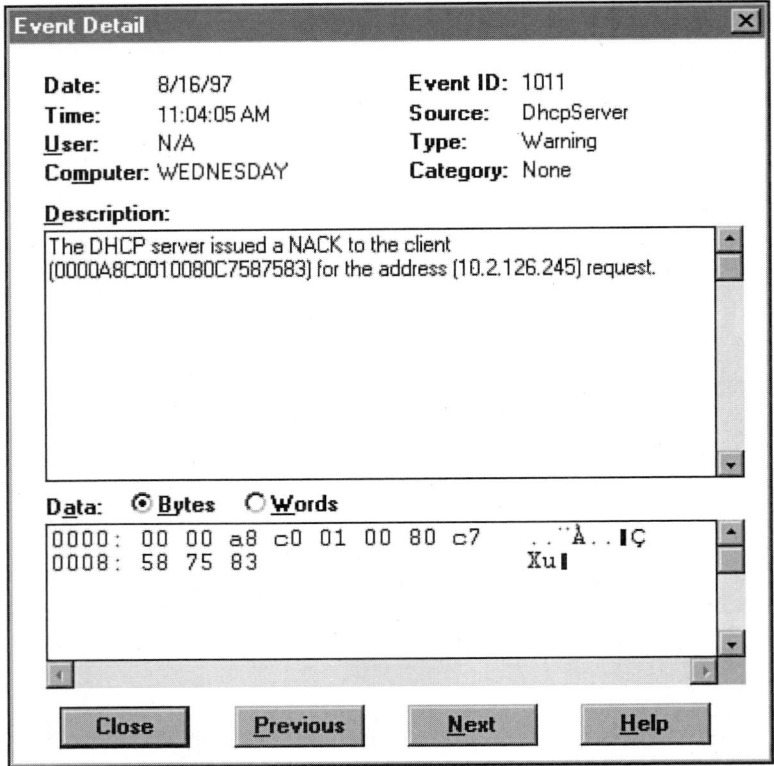

Figure 22.5.3 Event detail describing a system event.

22.5 Exercises

1. Using Network Monitor

Objective: Examine the main window display of Windows NT Server 4.0's Network Monitor application

Estimated time: 15 minutes

1. If Network Monitor has been installed on your system, click the Start menu and choose Programs/Administrative Tools. Then choose the Network Monitor application from the Administrative Tools group and proceed to step 4.
2. If Network Monitor hasn't been installed on your system, you must install it, along with a component called the Network Monitor Agent. Network Monitor and the Network Monitor Agent can be installed together by using the Control Panel Network application. Click the Start menu and choose Settings/Control Panel. Double-click the Network application and choose the Services tab.
3. In the Network application Services tab, click the Add button. Choose Network Monitor and Agent from the Network Service list and click OK. Windows NT prompts you for the Windows NT installation disk. When the installation is complete, click OK to shut down your system and restart Windows NT. Then start the Network Monitor application, as described in step 1.
4. Examine the four panes of the Network Monitor main screen (refer to Figure 3.5.1). The following list describes the four panes:
   - The Graph pane is located in the upper-left corner of the display. The Graph section includes five bar graphs describing network activity. Only two of the graphs are visible; use the scroll bar to view the other three graphs.
   - The Session Statistics pane, which appears below the Graph pane, tracks network activity by session, showing the two computers in the session and the frames sent each way.
   - The Total Statistics pane, which appears to the right of the Graph pane, lists such important statistics as the number of frames and the number of broadcasts. You can use the scroll bar to reach other entries that are not visible.
   - The Station Statistics pane, which sits at the bottom of the window, shows statistics for frames listed by network address.
5. Pull down the Capture menu and choose Start. Network Monitor then starts monitoring the network.
6. Ping the Network Monitor PC from another computer on the network. (Go to the command prompt and type **Ping**, followed by the IP address on the Network Monitor computer—for example, ping 111.121.131.141.) Watch the Station Statistics pane at the bottom of the screen to see if any new information appears.
7. Experiment with sending files or other requests to or from the Network Monitor PC. Study the effect of network activity on the values displayed in the four panes of the Network Monitor main window.
8. When you are finished, pull down the Capture menu and click Stop to stop capturing data. Then exit Network Monitor.

2. Creating a Chart in Performance Monitor

Objectives: Become familiar with the process of creating and reading a Performance Monitor chart. Understand the basic components of the Performance Monitor main window and the Add to Chart dialog box. Learn how to turn on disk performance counters using the *diskperf* command.

Estimated time: 25 minutes

1. From the Start menu, select Programs. Choose the Administrative Tools group and click Performance Monitor. The Performance Monitor main window appears on your screen.
2. Pull down the Edit menu and choose Add to Chart. The Add to Chart dialog box appears. You can also open the Add to Chart dialog box by clicking the plus sign in the toolbar of the Performance Monitor main window.

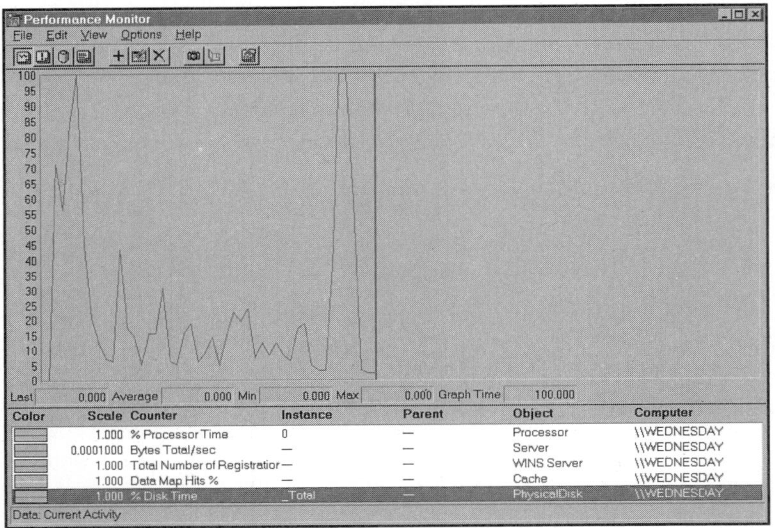

Figure 22.5.4 The Performance Monitor main window.

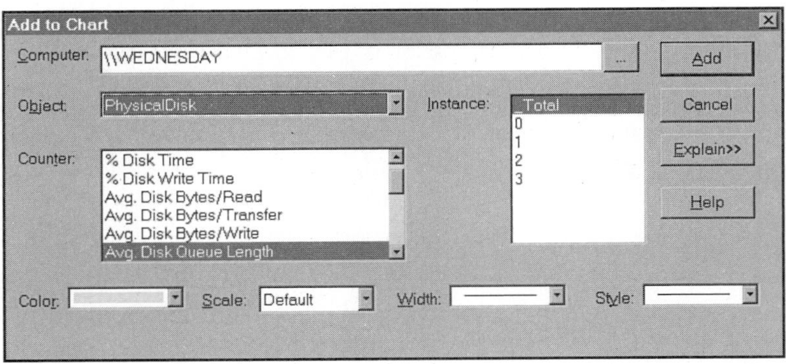

Figure 22.5.5 The Add to Chart dialog box.

3.a. The box labeled Computer at the top of the Add to Chart dialog box tells Performance Monitor which computer you want to monitor. The default is the local system. Click the ellipsis button to the right of the box for a list of computers on the network.

3.b. The box labeled Object tells Performance Monitor which object you want to monitor. As you learned earlier in this chapter, an object is a hardware or software component of your system. You can think of an object as a *category* of system statistics. Pull down the Object menu. Scroll through the list of objects and look for the Processor, Memory, PhysicalDisk, LogicalDisk, Server, and Network Segment objects described earlier in this chapter. Choose the PhysicalDisk object. If you have more than one physical disk on your system, a list of your physical disks will appear in the Instances box to the right of the Object box. The Instance box lists all instances of the object selected in the Object box. If necessary, choose a physical disk instance.

3.c. The box labeled Counter displays the counters (the statistical measurements) that are available for the object displayed in the Object box. Scroll through the list of counters for the PhysicalDisk object. If you feel like experimenting, select a different object in the Object box. Notice that the new object is accompanied by a different set of counters. Switch back to the PhysicalDisk object and choose the %Disk Time counter. Click the Explain button on the right side of the Add to Chart dialog box, and a description of the %Disk Time counter appears at the bottom of the dialog box.

3.d. Click the Done button in the Add to Chart dialog box. The dialog box disappears, and you see the Performance Monitor main window.

4. In the Performance Monitor main window, a vertical line sweeps across the chart from left to right. You may also see a faint colored line at the bottom of the chart recording a %Disk Time value of 0. If so, you haven't enabled the disk performance counters for your system. (If the disk performance monitors are enabled on your system, you should see a spikey line that looks like the readout from an electrocardiogram. You're done with this step. Go on to step 5.)

   If you need to enable the disk performance counters, click the Start button and go to the command prompt. Enter this command: **diskperf -y**. Then reboot your system and repeat steps 1 through 4. (You don't have to browse through the object and counter menus this time.)

5. You should now see a spikey line representing the percentage of time that the physical disk is busy reading or writing. Select Add to Chart from the Edit menu. Select the PhysicalDisk object and choose the counter Avg. Disk Queue Length. Click the Add button. Then choose the counter Avg. Disk Bytes/Read. Click the Add button and then click the Done button.

6. Examine the Performance Monitor main window. All three of the counters you selected should be tracing out spikey lines on the chart. Each line is a different color. At the bottom of the window is a table showing which counter goes with which color. The table also gives the scale of the output, the instance, the object, and the computer.

7. Below the chart (but above the table of counters) is a row of statistical parameters labeled Last, Average, Min, Max, and Graph Time. These parameters pertain to the counter that is selected in the table at the bottom of the window. Select a different counter, and you see that some of these values change. The Last value is the counter value over the last second. Graph time is the time it takes (in seconds) for the vertical line that draws the chart to sweep across the window.

8. Start Windows Explorer. Select a file (a graphics file or a word processing document) and choose Copy from Explorer's Edit menu. (This copies the file you selected to the clipboard.) Go to another directory and select Paste from the Edit menu. (This creates a copy of the file in the second directory.) Then minimize Explorer and return to the Performance Monitor main screen. The disk activity caused by your Explorer session is now reflected in the spikes of the counter lines.

9. Pull down the Options menu and select Chart. The Chart Options dialog box appears on your screen. The Chart Options dialog box provides a number of options governing the chart display. The Update Time section enables you to choose an update interval. The update interval tells

Performance Monitor how frequently it should update the chart with new values. (If you choose the Manual Update option, the chart will update only when you press Ctrl+U or click Update Now in the Options menu.) Experiment with the Chart Options or click the Cancel button to return to the main window.

10. Pull down the File menu and choose Exit to exit Performance Monitor. Note that the Save Chart Settings and Save Chart Settings As options in the File menu enable you to save the collection of objects and counters you're using now so you can monitor the same counters later and avoid setting them up again. The Export Chart option enables you to export the data to a file that you can then open with a spreadsheet or database application. The Save Workspace option saves the settings for your chart, as well as any settings for alerts, logs, or reports specified in this session.

3. Performance Monitor Alerts, Logs, and Reports

Objectives: Become familiar with the alternative views (Alert view, Log view, and Report view) available through the Performance Monitor View menu and log performance data to a log file

Estimated time: 25 minutes

1. Click Programs in the Start menu and choose Performance Monitor from the Administrative Tools group. The Performance Monitor main window appears on-screen (refer to Figure 3.5.4).
2. Pull down the View menu. You'll see the following four options:
    - The Chart option plots the counters you select in a continuous chart.
    - The Alert option automatically alerts a network official if the predetermined counter threshold is surpassed.
    - The Log option saves your system performance data to a log file.
    - The Report option displays system performance data in a report format.

    The setup is similar for each of these view formats. All use some form of the Add to Chart dialog box. All have options that are configured through the first command at the top of the Options menu. (The first command at the top of the Options menu changes its name depending on the active view.)

3.a. Click the Alert option in the View menu.

3.b. Click the plus sign in the toolbar or choose Add to Alert from the Edit menu. The Add to Alert dialog box is similar to the Add to Chart dialog box except for two additional items at the bottom of the screen. The Alert If box enables you to enter a threshold for the counter. The Over/Under option buttons specify whether you want to receive an alert if the counter value is over or under the threshold value. The Run Program on Alert box lets you specify a command line that will execute if the counter value reaches the threshold you specify in the Alert If box. You can ask Performance Monitor to send a message to your beeper, to send you an e-mail message, or to notify your paging service.

> **Don't specify a batch file in the Run Program on Alert box. Performance Monitor uses Unicode format, which can confuse the command-prompt interpreter. (The < and > symbols, which are used in Unicode format, are interpreted as a redirection of input or output.)**

3.c. The default object in the Add to Alert dialog box should be the Processor object. The default counter should be %Processor Time. Enter the value **5%** in the Alert If box and make sure the Alert If option button is set to Over. In the Run Program on Alert box, type **SOL**. Set the Run Program on Alert option button to First Time. This configuration tells Performance Monitor to execute Windows NT's Solitaire program when the %Processor Time exceeds 5%.

> **If the Run Program on Alert option button is not set to First Time, Performance Monitor will execute a new instance of Solitaire every time the %Processor Time exceeds 5%, which happens every time it executes a new instance of Solitaire. You'll probably have to close Performance Monitor using the Close (X) button or reboot to stop the incessant shuffling and dealing.**

3.d. Click the Add button and then click the Done button. The Alert legend at the bottom of the Alert window describes the active alert parameters. The Alert Log shows every instance of an alert.

3.e. Make some change to your desktop. (Hide or reveal the taskbar, or change the size of the Performance Monitor window, for example—anything that will cause a 5% utilization of the processor.) The Solitaire program should miraculously appear on your screen. In a real alert situation, Performance Monitor would execute an alert application instead of starting a card game.

3.f. Pull down the Edit menu and select Delete Alert.

4.a. Pull down the View menu and select Log. Performance Monitor's Log view saves performance data to a log file instead of displaying it on the screen.

4.b. Pull down the Edit menu and select Add to Log. Notice that only the objects appear in the Add to Log dialog box. The counters and instances boxes don't appear because Performance Monitor automatically logs all counters and all instances of the object to the log file. Select the Memory Object and click Add. If you want, you can select another object, such as the Paging File object, and click Add again. When you are finished adding objects, click Done.

4.c. Pull down the Options menu and select Log. The Log Options dialog box appears on your screen. The Log Options dialog box enables you to designate a log file that Performance Monitor will use to log the data. In the File Name box, enter the name **exer2**. You also can specify an update interval. The update interval is the interval at which Performance Monitor records performance data to the log. The Manual Update option button specifies that the file won't be updated unless you press Ctrl+U or select Update Now from the Options menu. Click the Start Log button to start saving data to the log. Wait a few minutes, and then return to the Log Options dialog box and click the Stop Log button.

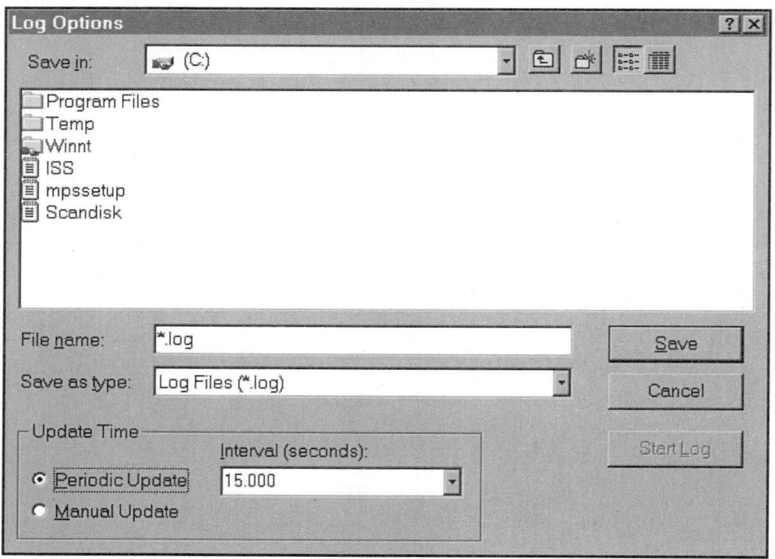

Figure 22.5.6 The Log Options dialog box.

4.d. Pull down the View menu and switch to Chart view.

4.e. Pull down the Options menu and select Data From. The Data From dialog box enables you to specify a source for the performance data that appears in the Chart. Note that the default source is Current Activity. (That is why the chart you created in the previous exercise took its data from current system activity.) The alternative to using the Current Activity option is to use data from a log file. Click the Log File option button. Click the ellipsis button to the right of the log file window and select the exer2 file you created in step 4.c. Click OK.

4.f. Pull down the Edit menu and click Add to Chart. Click the down arrow to the right of the Object menu. Notice that your only object choices are the Memory object and any other objects you selected in step 4.b. Select the Memory object. Browse through the counter list and select Pages/sec. Click the Add button. Select any other memory counters you want to display and click the Add button. Click Done.

4.g. The log file's record of the counters you selected in 4.f appears in the chart in the Performance Monitor's main window. Notice that, unlike the chart you created in the previous exercise, this chart does not continuously sweep out new data. That is because this chart represents static data from a previous, finite monitoring session.

5.a. Pull down the View menu and switch to Report view. Pull down the Options menu and select Data From. Switch the Data From setting back to Current Activity. Report view displays the performance data in a report instead of in a graphics format.

5.b. Select Add to Report from the Edit menu. Select the processor object and choose the %Processor Time, %Interrupt Time, and Interrupts/sec counters. (Hold down the Ctrl key to select all three, and then click Add.) Select the PhysicalDisk object and choose the %Disk Time, Avg. Disk Queue Length, and Current Disk Queue Length counters. Click the Add button. Select the Memory object and choose the Pages/sec, Page Faults/sec, and Available Bytes counters. Click the Add button. Then click Done.

5.c. Examine the main report window. Performance Monitor displays a report of the performance data you specified in a hierarchical format, with counters listed under the appropriate object.

6. Select Exit in the File menu to exit Performance Monitor.

22.5 Practice Problems

1. By monitoring the network, you can:
   - A. Get a "hands-on" view of problems as they occur.
   - B. Anticipate problems before they disrupt network performance.
   - C. Keep a permanent record of just how bad performance becomes.
   - D. Use a baseline to keep a list of the maximum and minimum performance.

2. A "baseline" set of readings
   - A. Is provided by the hardware manufacturer to help tune your network.
   - B. Is developed over time and can be used later to compare performance spikes.
   - C. Is the foundation based on which network performance can be improved upon.
   - D. Can be used by a Microsoft Certified System Engineer to help troubleshoot network performance issues.

3. Tools that you can use to monitor network performance include:
   - A. A time-domain reflectometer.
   - B. An ohmmeter and cable tester.
   - C. Windows NT's *Performance Monitor* and *Network Monitor.*
   - D. A NIC set to *promiscuous* mode.

4. Two good tools to create records of network performance are:
   - A. Windows NT's Event Viewer and Performance Monitor.
   - B. Windows NT's Network Monitor and NetWatcher™.
   - C. Windows NT's disk administrator and system monitor.
   - D. The MLID and ODI network drivers.

5. You should keep detailed records of your network changes, because
   - A. Technical Support won't help you unless you have good records.
   - B. A physical disaster could destroy your system, and you must be able to rebuild it.
   - C. You can compare your records with performance changes to see if your changes impacted the network.
   - D. You may be unable to comprehend your network without them.

6. Your records of the network should include:
   - A. Hardware settings, service pack installations, and service agreements.
   - B. A detailed map showing cabling layouts and so on.
   - C. Current copies of workstation files and other workstation information.
   - D. All of the above.

7. Windows NT's Performance Monitor:
   - A. Follows the NT security model and, therefore, can be run on only one PC.
   - B. Can connect to any Windows NT computer on the network.
   - C. Can be used only by the Domain Admins.
   - D. Is accessed using the NetBIOS *servername**sharename* convention.

8. Once you develop your system baseline:
   - A. Never modify it; you will be unable to make meaningful comparisons unless it stays put.

22

B. Modify and alter your baseline statistics as your network grows.

C. Keep two copies: one that stays with the server and another that stays with the backup tapes.

D. It should be kept safe to prevent intrusion from hackers.

9. You can use *Performance Monitor* to track such items as:

A. Protocol use, drive use, and processor use.

B. A user's performance while using certain applications.

C. How long a computer takes to boot up.

D. Whether the user is suffering from a protocol mismanagement issue.

10. You should take your first baseline reading:

A. When your system is finally stable and functioning normally.

B. As soon as you have installed the operating system.

C. Before installing the NetBIOS networking and unique name.

D. Early in the morning, when there are no users present.

11. To establish your baseline readings:

A. Choose your desired settings and check the minimum levels; this is your baseline.

B. Choose common items such as processor utilization and drive usage and check the minimum levels; this is your baseline.

C. Choose your favorite settings and check where the use tends to cluster; this is your baseline reading.

D. Choose common items such as processor utilization and drive usage and check where they tend to cluster; this is your baseline reading.

12. The time to establish a baseline is:

A. During the morning hours, when users are not there. This will be an accurate benchmark.

B. During peak hours. This is when usage is most critical.

C. During off hours, which you will compare against peak hours.

D. Before you decide which protocol to use.

13. Protocol analysis tools measure performance by:

A. Decoding frames.

B. Filtering packets through NetBEUI, IPX, and TCP/IP.

C. Must use a *gateway*.

D. Checking current network performance against a *baseline*.

14. Windows NT's Network Monitor is:

A. An example of a protocol analyzer.

B. An example of a network analysis tool.

C. The most advanced network utility to date.

D. Required in order to run Systems Management Server.

15. Windows NT's Event Viewer is useful because it records what type of events?

A. Warnings, errors, and events created by the system

B. Messages from applications

C. Events tracked through the auditing features of Windows NT

D. All of the above

16. The Windows NT Event Viewer

    A. Can be opened to provide a great amount of detail for each event.

    B. Is enhanced with the Event Viewer that ships with Systems Management Server.

    C. Views events created in the Performance Monitor.

    D. All of the above.

17. Protocol analyzers

    A. Are advanced software tools used to view the performance of each protocol.

    B. Are hardware or software tools used to view inside network packets.

    C. Analyze protocols for bottlenecks and lost frames.

    D. Can replace the need for detailed paper-based notes.

18. A Performance Monitor chart:

    A. Immediately indicates bottlenecks and performance problems.

    B. Must be analyzed by a seasoned network professional to be understood.

    C. Should be compared with your baseline to get meaningful results.

    D. Should be printed out and hung near the server.

19. Performance Monitor

    A. Is used to view the major portions of the operating system.

    B. Can be configured to use a very high degree of detail to match your particular needs.

    C. Only displays line-charts.

    D. Must be installed separately in Windows 95.

20. Performance Monitor reports

    A. Must be checked diligently if it is to be used.

    B. Should be printed and stored at regular intervals.

    C. Must be viewed using the *Event Viewer.*

    D. Can be used to send an alert if you prefer, to your pager.

22.5 Answers and Explanations: Practice Problems

1. **B** The overriding reason to keep records is to help you maintain the stability of the network by anticipating and avoiding problems.
2. **B** Although answer C can be correct in a limited set of circumstances, the baseline is to reflect the ordinary usage of your network.
3. **C** The other items mentioned will help troubleshoot faults, but not monitor performance.
4. **A** In addition to Network Monitor, the Event Viewer can be used to track performance-related events, including performance spikes in Network Monitor.
5. **C** Without detailed records of what you've modified on the network, it will be difficult over time to correlate network changes with performance changes.
6. **D** All of these items will be most useful in the event of a catastrophe.
7. **B** The Event Viewer can be connected to any NT computer on the network. This makes it very flexible. The Performance Monitor can also be used this way.
8. **B** The baseline should be continually changed to reflect the current state of your network.
9. **A** The Performance Monitor has a very high level of detail.

10. **B** If you wait until your network is finally stable, you may never take a baseline reading. Because it will be modified continually, take the initial reading after the operating system has been installed, and be prepared to update it.

11. **D** You will want to choose critical system items such as processor and disk activity. Look at where the use tends to cluster. Take note of spikes, but spikes are not as important as the average utilization of the items.

12. **B** A baseline is not meant to measure hardware in the absence of users, it is meant to view how your network performs within the organization. So establish your baseline during peak hours. Then compare it to other times and adjust your baseline accordingly.

13. **A** Protocol analysis tools decode frames in order to determine such items as packet source, packet destination, packet size, and data.

14. **B** Network Monitor is not a protocol analyzer; it is a network analysis tool.

15. **D** By default, the Event Viewer does not capture all of these items, but they can be activated in the User Manager for Domains (in the Audit item).

16. **A** Each event can be viewed in detail, down to the hexadecimal level.

17. **B** There are hardware protocol analyzers and software protocol analyzers.

18. **C** Without comparing the chart to your baseline, it is difficult to spot trends or abnormalities.

19. **B** You can use Performance Monitor to view extremely detailed items.

20. **D** The Performance Monitor can be set to trigger an alert if a component reaches a critical level. This alert can be sent to the Event Viewer, to an e-mail account, or to a pager.

22.5 Key Words

Protocol analyzer

Event Viewer

Event

Frame

Baseline

Systems Management Server

Practice Exam: Implementation

1. A network resource can only be:
   A. A file, printer, disk drive, or fax modem.
   B. A gateway, a modem, or a network share or device.
   C. A network-attached scanner.
   D. Any of the above devices and more.

2. Network resources must be shared before they can be
   A. Secured.
   B. Accessed.
   C. Seen.
   D. Placed in the ACL.

3. When using a network share:
   A. The password in the user account is checked against the password in the network resource. If they match, the user is authenticated.
   B. The network resource is checked in the Access Control List (ACL) to see if that user is granted access. If so, the user is granted access.
   C. The username is checked against the user accounts database. If the user exists, the user's password is checked. Then the user is granted access.
   D. There is no need to check the user database because the user is authenticated by the domain controller during login. The server checks the user's password. Then the user is granted access.

4. Global groups
   A. Add a layer of complexity on user management and are, therefore, difficult to administer.
   B. Are available across platforms to Windows NT, Novell NetWare, and Unix.
   C. Must contain users before they can be given access.
   D. Can contain users, local groups, or global groups.

5. Windows NT user accounts are:
   A. Created as part of the installation process and can be created later.
   B. Created with a tool such as *User Manager for Domains* and can be created during the installation process.
   C. Transferable to a Windows 95 workstation.
   D. Used via the Access Control List to manage resources.

6. The primary purpose of a disaster recovery plan is to
   A. Reduce downtime and protect data.
   B. Protect the system from hardware faults and infiltration from hackers.
   C. Avoid monetary losses from lost data.
   D. Keep heads cool during an emergency.

7. A "backup" refers to
   A. A tape backup unit.
   B. A procedural or data backup.
   C. A fully redundant backup network.
   D. A procedure used during an emergency.

8. With a central backup server, the tape unit
   A. Can be more expensive, because they tend to have more capacity than standalone units.
   B. Is always cost-effective because it can do more work per tape unit.

C. Is more useful in larger networks.

D. Is faster than directly connected units.

9. Your network tapes should be

A. Kept in a central safe location.

B. Kept in separate locations. That way if a physical disaster strikes, the data will survive.

C. Secured with passwords to prevent infiltration from hackers.

D. Kept near the server in case they are needed during an emergency.

10. A fault-tolerant design must

A. Not be concerned with price and performance. Fault-tolerance defines only its ability to function.

B. Use a *redundant array* of servers and disks.

C. Use an advanced operating system, such as Microsoft Windows NT or Novell NetWare.

D. Balance the concerns of downtime versus cost and performance. No one solution is best for all users.

11. A fully equipped Network Adapter Card

A. Requires a driver to run.

B. Can be used immediately once it is installed.

C. Will be listed in the manufacturer's HCL.

D. Is used to avoid hardware conflicts with reserved devices.

12. The primary job of the network card is to:

A. Bind the protocols to all layers of the OSI 7-layer model.

B. Bind the clients to the network protocols.

C. Prepare data for transmission over the medium.

D. Avoid collisions on the network.

13. If your NIC supports 10-Base 2 networks:

A. You can connect it to twisted-pair wire using RJ-45.

B. You can connect it using BNC connectors.

C. You must insert it into your token-ring before enabling communications.

D. It will support token-ring but not Ethernet.

14. Plug and Play

A. Works with Windows NT to configure network adapters.

B. Works with Windows 95 to configure network protocols.

C. Works with Windows 95 to configure hardware devices.

D. Works with Windows 95 or Windows NT to configure hardware devices.

15. When configuring your network adapter, typical settings you must configure are:

A. IRQ, I/O port, and RAM address.

B. IRQ, I/O port, and interrupt.

C. Slot number, protocol, and IRQ.

D. I/O port, DMA channel, and adapter ROM.

16. NetBIOS names

A. Can include spaces and are case-sensitive.

B. Include the two slash (\\ ) prefix.

C. Must have 15 or fewer characters.

D. Cannot use the reserved %% variable identifier.

17. One popular NetBIOS naming scheme

    A. Uses randomly generated hexadecimal addressing to retain uniqueness.

    B. Allows users to assign their own names and relies on security for uniqueness.

    C. Combines a location code with a portion of the username.

    D. Avoids the unnecessary slashes (\\ ) of the UNC naming convention.

18. Which of the following is true about this statement: net use d: \\server\share

    A. It is incorrect.

    B. It might prompt the user for a password.

    C. It will not function on Windows 95. Instead, it requires the advanced networking built into Windows NT.

    D. It will share the user's d: drive over the network.

19. Which of the following is true about this statement: copy \\cats\docs\burmese.txt

    A. It is illegal.

    B. It must be mapped to a drive letter to be used.

    C. It can be used instead of mapping \\cats\docs to a drive letter.

    D. It will not function unless the share name \docs is unique.

20. A UNC name consists of the following components:

    A. Server name, share name, MS-DOS style path.

    B. Server name, NetBIOS name, and drive letter.

    C. "net use" or "net view" followed by a server name.

    D. The ACL (Access Control List), the user's SID (Security ID), and the file name.

21. A network baseline:

    A. Becomes the yardstick to measure system performance.

    B. Must be somewhat flexible to grow with the network.

    C. Should be generated during peak times rather than off-times.

    D. All of the above.

22. To establish your baseline readings:

    A. Choose your desired settings and check the minimum levels; this is your baseline.

    B. Choose common items such as processor utilization and drive usage and check the minimum levels; this is your baseline.

    C. Choose your favorite settings and check where the use tends to cluster; this is your baseline reading.

    D. Choose common items such as processor utilization and drive usage and check where they tend to cluster; this is your baseline reading.

23. Windows NT's Event Viewer is useful because it records what type of events?

    A. Warnings, errors, and events created by the system.

    B. Messages from applications.

    C. Events tracked through the auditing features of Windows NT.

    D. All of the above.

24. Performance Monitor reports
    A. Must be checked diligently if it is to be used.
    B. Should be printed and stored at regular intervals.
    C. Must be viewed using the *Event Viewer.*
    D. Can be used to send an alert, if you prefer, to your pager.

25. Your initial and ongoing configuration records and baseline reports should *not* include:
    A. A list of the service packs and software installed.
    B. A list of licensing agreements.
    C. The original system administrator password.
    D. A history of past problems and useful solutions.

Answers and Explanations: Practice Exam

1. **D** If a device can be shared over the network, it is a network resource.
2. **B** Some network shares are invisible.
3. **C** This level of redundancy may seem unnecessary, but it is the core of Windows NT security.
4. **D** A global group is a Windows NT group that makes administration easier and can be exported to other Windows NT domains.
5. **A** Two user accounts, ADMINISTRATOR and GUEST are always created during the installation process.
6. **A** The most effective job a system admin can perform during disaster recovery is to get the network back up as quickly as possible.
7. **B** A backup includes more than simply data backups.
8. **A** The costs can vary, but centralized tape servers tend to be more expensive per tape unit. Because of this, they tend to be more effective in small to mid-sized networks.
9. **B** If you keep the tapes in a separate location, you would be able to rebuild the entire network with all new equipment.
10. **D** All system plans should be concerned with the cost of downtime versus the cost of a fault-tolerant system.
11. **A** A network card requires a driver to run. Not all compatible adapters are listed on the Hardware Compatibility List, but it is a good place to start.
12. **C** The network card's job is small but important. It prepares data for transmission over the physical network.
13. **B** 10 Base-2 is defined as using BNC connectors and coaxial cable. RJ-45, by contrast, uses Category 5 twisted-pair.
14. **C** Plug and Play is not supported by the current versions of Windows NT.
15. **A** B is incorrect: The IRQ and interrupt are the same thing. C is incorrect: The slot number is not required. D is incorrect because NICs don't use a DMA channel. A is correct.
16. **C** The NetBIOS name cannot use spaces. Some operating systems, such as Windows 95, allow you to create a name with spaces and may appear to function. But this will cause problems.
17. **C** This is the most useful naming scheme in a large organization, but an e-mail address as the PC name also works very well.
18. **B** If the currently logged in user does not have access to the network resource, the statement will generate a password or username prompt.

19. **C** COPY can be used with UNC names, and a drive letter is not required. Many applications also support this.

20. **A** A full UNC file name would include the MS-DOS path in addition to the share name. This MS-DOS path refers to the directories beneath the share.

21. **D** Each of these elements comprise a baseline.

22. **D** You will want to choose critical system items such as processor and disk activity. Look at where the use tends to cluster. Take note of spikes, but spikes are not as important as the average utilization of the items.

23. **D** By default, the Event Viewer does not capture all of these items, but they can be activated in the User Manager for Domains (in the Audit item).

24. **D** The Performance Monitor can be set to trigger an alert if a component reaches a critical level. This alert can be sent to the Event Viewer, to an e-mail account, or to a pager.

25. **C** Never write down the Administrator password—ever.

Chapter 23

Troubleshooting

Troubleshooting is the art of seeking out the cause of a problem and then eliminating the problem by managing or eliminating the cause. With something as complex as a computer network, the list of possible problems and causes is nearly endless. Almost anything can go wrong, and for that reason, you must use all your networking knowledge to troubleshoot network problems.

The troubleshooting questions on the Networking Essentials exam draw from the concepts discussed in all chapters of this book. To solve a specific network problem, for instance, you may need to know that the NetBEUI protocol is non-routable (see Chapter 20) or that only the NTFS file system supports local file-level security (see Chapter 22). Therefore, an essential part of preparing for the troubleshooting section is to study the other sections and be prepared to apply the networking concepts you learned in previous chapters to real-life situations.

Microsoft targets four specific troubleshooting objectives for the Networking Essentials exam. Those objectives center around the following topics:

- Communication problems
- Connectivity problems with cards, cables, and related hardware
- Broadcast storms
- Network performance problems

This chapter focuses on each of these important troubleshooting topics. But keep in mind that almost any problem within the broad subject of networking could fit somewhere in the preceding bulleted list. The distinguishing characteristic of a troubleshooting problem is not its subject but its viewpoint: You are working backwards from a symptom to a cause.

The Troubleshooting Process

Microsoft recommends the following five-step approach to network troubleshooting:

1. Set the problem's priority. Ask yourself a few questions: How serious is this problem? Will the network still function if I attend to other matters first? Can I quantify the loss of work time or productivity the problem is causing?
2. Collect information to identify the symptoms. Ask users to describe the problem. A user's description can lead to further questions, which can lead to a deeper description. Compare the present behavior of the network with the baseline behavior. Search logs and journals for previous occurrences of the problem.
3. Develop a list of possible causes. Is the problem related to connectivity devices? Cabling? Protocols? A faltering workstation? What do past occurrences have in common with the present occurrence?
4. Test to isolate the cause. Develop tests that will prove or disprove each of the possible causes. A test could be as simple as checking a setup parameter or as complicated as studying network traffic with a protocol analyzer.
5. Study the results of the test to identify a solution. Your tests will (ideally) point you to the real problem. After you know the problem, you can determine a solution.

These five steps are sufficient to guide you through a myriad of network problems, and similar approaches appear in the documentation of other network vendors. Part of the challenge of network troubleshooting is to determine how you can apply these five troubleshooting steps to your own situation.

In many cases, network troubleshooting is really a matter of common sense. Few troubleshooting tips will bring you more success than the following:

- Make sure that all cables and connectors are securely plugged in and that all electrical devices are turned on.
- Step through the logical and physical pathways of the connection in your mind. Verify that each hardware and software component along the path of the connection is functioning properly. Check cables and adapters; check protocol bindings and system settings; verify that all required services are running.
- Test and experiment to isolate the problem. Remove and replace suspected components one at a time to isolate the defective component. (Keep extra hard drives, cables, jumpers, and network adapters around in case of emergency.)

Most of the troubleshooting techniques in this chapter are refinements of these simple rules.

23.1 Identify Common Errors Associated with Components Required for Communications

Without communication, there would be no networking, so the components required for communication are essential features for any networking environment. These components were all covered in previous chapters, but they are worthy of second notice here in a troubleshooting context. In particular, this section focuses on the following networking components, which must function properly if communication is to succeed.

- Protocols
- NetBIOS names
- Network services
- Permissions and rights
- Modems

The components discussed in section 23.2 (cables, cards, and cable-related network hardware) are also communication components. In a sense, sections 23.1 and 23.2 belong together. Together they encompass the hardware and software components that pass a message from one computer across the network to another computer.

This section begins with a discussion of some important troubleshooting tools.

A. Troubleshooting Tools

Network administrators use a number of tools to search out network problems. Section 23.2 discusses some of the tools that pertain specifically to network cabling problems. These are a few of the more general-purpose tools:

- **Protocol analyzers.** These hardware or combined hardware and software products are used to monitor network traffic, track network performance, and analyze packets. Protocol analyzers can identify bottlenecks, protocol problems, and malfunctioning network components.
- **Network monitors.** These software-based tools monitor network traffic, displaying packet information and keeping statistics on network usage. Windows NT's Network Monitor is an example of a network monitoring tool. See Chapter 22 (and the discussion later in this section) for more on Network Monitor.
- **Event Log.** Windows NT's Event Log is a log of important system events. If a service or device fails, check the event log for information on the failure and clues about possible causes. See Chapter 22 for a discussion of Windows NT's Event Log and the Event Viewer tool. The Event Log is also an important historical record. You can look for past occurrences of similar failures and compare them with your present situation.

B. Protocol Troubleshooting

Network protocols are at the heart of any networking system, and misused or misconfigured protocols are a common source of network problems. Chapters 20 and 21 discuss network protocols. You should be familiar with when to use which protocol: A common troubleshooting scenario is that a given protocol is implemented in the wrong situation.

After installing and configuring a protocol, you must also *bind* the protocol to the appropriate hardware and services. (See section 20.9 for more on network bindings.) If network bindings are not configured properly, the protocol will not function.

Two computers must be using compatible protocols in order to communicate. If one workstation is using TCP/IP and a second workstation is using only the NetBEUI protocol, the workstations can't establish a connection. Other troubleshooting issues apply to specific protocols:

- **NetBEUI.** NetBEUI is not a routable protocol. Workstations on opposite sides of routers cannot establish communications.
- **DLC.** DLC is used exclusively for network printers and mainframe traffic. Windows NT doesn't use DLC to establish workstation or server sessions.
- **TCP/IP.** Each node on a TCP/IP network must have a unique IP address. Nodes on the same subnet should have the same network ID, which usually means they should have the same subnet mask. Some TCP/IP networks may require additional addressing parameters, such as DNS names, default gateways, and addresses for WINS servers, DNS servers, and DHCP servers.
- **NWLink/IPX.** Each NWLink or IPX node should have a unique network number. Sometimes it is also important to make sure that network nodes are using compatible frame types.
- **SLIP.** The serial line protocol SLIP is not as versatile as its newer counterpart PPP. A typical troubleshooting scenario occurs when the SLIP protocol is applied to a situation for which it was not intended. Specifically, SLIP supports only the TCP/IP protocol and requires a static IP address. See section 1.6 for more on PPP and SLIP.

Sections 20.1, 20.9, and 21.3 discuss network protocols and when to use which protocol.

Windows NT Server's Network Monitor enables you to monitor, filter, and analyze network data frames or packets transmitted and received by the local Windows NT machine. You can use Network Monitor to unravel certain problems with protocols. Each frame of data contains a header that encapsulates information including:

- Protocol type
- Source address
- Destination address
- Data

Network Monitor permits you to investigate intricate details of data frames, including certain types of errors that may be affecting network traffic. If your network is plagued with bad frames or with an overabundance of frames from an unknown source, Network Monitor can help you find the culprit. You can dissect the incoming frames and look for a source address. This strategy is useful if you're trying to find the source of a broadcast storm (discussed later in this chapter).

Network Monitor includes individual modules called *protocol parsers.* Each protocol parser examines a specific protocol. Network Monitor includes more than 60 protocol parsers that cover most of the protocols used in Windows NT network environments.

See section 22.5 for more on Windows NT's Network Monitor tool.

C. NetBIOS Names

Each computer on a Microsoft network must have a unique NetBIOS name (also called a computer name). See section 22.4 for a complete description of NetBIOS names and how to configure them. For a quick summary, NetBIOS names must follow these guidelines:

- They must be unique.
- They can consist of 15 characters or fewer.
- They can contain alphanumeric characters and these characters: ! @ # $ % ^ & ( ) - _ ' { } . ~

A computer cannot participate in the network if its computer name doesn't follow these rules. From the standpoint of troubleshooting, uniqueness is the biggest issue. In most circumstances, a Windows computer won't let you give it a name with too many characters or with illegal characters. If you're trying to connect to a computer and you're using a name that doesn't follow these rules, the name you're using is probably incorrect.

D. Network Services

Network services are processes that enable the network to function. Windows NT includes numerous network services that provide a wide range of capabilities. (Examples include the Browser service, the Replicator service, and the DNS Server service.) The details of these network services are, for the most part, beyond the scope of the Networking Essentials exam, but there are two important services that you should know about:

- **Server service.** The Server service enables a Windows NT system to share resources on the network. In other words, the Server service lets the Windows NT computer offer (serve) its resources to the network. If the Server service on Computer A is stopped or if it isn't bound to the necessary protocols (see section 20.9), other computers will not be able to connect to Computer A.
- **Workstation service (redirector).** The Workstation service enables a Windows NT computer to act as a client. If the Workstation service is stopped or if it isn't bound to the necessary protocols, the computer will not be able to access network resources. The Workstation service is actually what is called a *redirector*. A redirector is a software entity (often a file system driver) that redirects I/O calls to the network. Network client software packages typically include a redirector. If a network client can't connect, make sure the redirector is running properly on the client.

E. Permission and Rights

Security is important on all networks, and Windows NT in particular is a security-conscious operating system. If a user can't make a network connection, it may be because the user doesn't have the necessary rights or permissions to access the resource. See section 22.1 for a discussion of security in Windows NT and Windows 95.

F. Modems

A modem presents all the potential problems you find with any other device. You must make sure that the modem is properly installed, that the driver is properly installed, and that the resource settings are consistent and do not conflict with other devices. Modems also pose some unique problems because they must connect directly to the phone system, because they operate using analog communications, and because they must make a point-to-point connection with a remote machine.

The online help files for both Windows NT and Windows 95 include a topic called Modem Troubleshooter. The Modem Troubleshooter leads you to possible solutions to modem problems by asking questions about the symptoms. As you answer the questions (by clicking the gray box beside your answers), the Modem Troubleshooter zeroes in on more specific questions until (ideally) it leads you to a solution.

Some common modem problems (in addition to the basic device problems such as connectivity and resource settings) include:

- **Dialing problems.** The dialing feature is configured improperly. For instance, the modem isn't dialing 9 to bypass your office switchboard, or it *is* dialing 9 when you're away from your office. The computer also could be dialing an area code or an international code when it shouldn't. Check the dialing properties for the connection.
- **Connection problems.** You can't connect to another modem. Your modem and the other modem might be operating at different speeds. Verify that the maximum speed setting for your modem is the highest speed that both your modem and the other modem can use. Also make sure the Data Bits, Parity, and Stop Bits settings are consistent with those of the remote computer.
- **Protocol problems.** The communicating devices are using incompatible line protocols. Verify that the devices are configured for the same or compatible protocols. If one computer initiates a connection using PPP, the other computer must be capable of using PPP.

G. Troubleshooting RAS

Windows NT Remote Access Service (RAS) is a source of much troubleshooting. Possible problems include faulty user modems and bad lines. As an administrator, you should frequently consult the event log. By investigating the audit and error messages created by RAS, you can often track down problems. The event log might even reveal a bad serial port or driver, indicating a hardware-level problem. Such clues can be vital when intermittent errors occur. You can use the Remote Access Administration tool (in Windows NT Server's Administrative Tools group) to monitor users' logon attempts and to view port usage.

Other problems associated with RAS include:

- Invalid permissions to the resources the user is trying to access
- Invalid user accounts
- Incompatible modems
- Invalid telephone numbers
- Incorrect external modem cables
- Phone system issues (such as dialing 9 for an outside line)
- Phone system has call waiting (dial *70 or get instructions from the local phone company)
- Poor line causing static or noise (In some cases, lowering the baud rate on the modems may create a steady connection.)
- The NT server is down or offline

- User account logon hours violation
- Damaged or faulty modem (Was the user recently operating in an electrical storm?)
- Encryption Authentication level that's set too high or does not match both the server and client

23.1.1 Exercise: Modem Troubleshooter

This exercise describes how to access Windows NT's or Windows 95's Modem Troubleshooter.

Modem Troubleshooter is part of Windows NT's online help system. The easiest way to access it is to start Help and search for "modems" in the index. Follow these steps:

1. Click the Start button and choose Help.
2. In the Help Topics dialog box, click the Index tab. Enter **modem** in the search box at the top of the screen.
3. Look for the "troubleshooting" subtopic under the "modems" topic in the index. Double-click troubleshooting, and the Modem Troubleshooter appears.
4. Browse through the Modem Troubleshooter's topics. Click the gray box to the left of each symptom for a look at possible causes and/or more diagnostic questions.
5. When you're finished, close the Help window.

23.1 Practice Problems

1. If a modem's dial-up phone number is improperly configured (for example, if it's not configured to dial 9 to bypass your office switchboard), the modem has a __________ problem.
   - A. Broadcast
   - B. Protocol
   - C. Connection
   - D. Dialing
2. Suppose you start your Windows NT system and receive a message saying the network adapter was not found. Where should you look first for information on what happened?
   - A. Performance Monitor
   - B. Network Monitor
   - C. Windows NT Diagnostics
   - D. The event log
3. Your LAN has two Thicknet Ethernet segments, one in the engineering wing and one in the marketing wing. The segments are separated by a router. The distance between the segments is approximately 70 meters. The marketing segment uses the NetBEUI protocol. The engineering segment uses NetBEUI and also TCP/IP. You are unable to make a connection from the engineering segment to the marketing segment. The first thing you should do is:
   - A. Make sure all computer names are unique.
   - B. Make sure that the router is properly configured and all cables are fastened securely.
   - C. Implement TCP/IP on the marketing segment.
   - D. Move NetBEUI to a higher priority on the engineering segment.
4. Suppose Computer A can't seem to ping computer B on a TCP/IP network. You know that TCP/IP is installed on both PCs. The next thing you should check is:
   - A. The network utilization.
   - B. The protocol binding.
   - C. To see whether a competing protocol has control of the adapter.
   - D. To see whether the Server service is running on Computer A.
5. Which of the following enables a Windows NT computer to act as a client?
   - A. Workstation
   - B. Server
   - C. Browser
   - D. NTClient

23.1 Answers and Explanations: Practice Problems

1. **D** A problem related to dialing information is a Dialing problem. (Forgetting to bypass the office switchboard is a very common dialing problem.)
2. **D** The event log tracks system events, such as the failure of devices. Windows NT Diagnostics might help you determine the cause of the failure, but you're better off starting with the event log so you know exactly what happened.
3. **C** NetBEUI is a nonroutable protocol. You'll need to install a different protocol on the marketing segment if you want packets to pass through the router.
4. **B** You must bind a protocol to a specific adapter in order to use it. The NDIS and ODI standards ensure that you don't have "competing protocols" fighting for control of the adapter. The Server service enables you to share resources, but it isn't required for a simple diagnostic check such as a ping.

5. **A** The Workstation service is Windows NT's redirector. It routes I/O requests to the network and enables the Windows NT machine to act as a client.

23.1 Key Words

Protocol analyzer

Network Monitor

Event log

Protocol binding

Data frame

Packet

Network service

Server service

Workstation service

Redirector

Remote Access Service (RAS)

23.2 Diagnose and Resolve Common Connectivity Problems with Cards, Cables, and Related Hardware

Most network problems occur out on the wires. The components that connect PCs and enable them to communicate are susceptible to many kinds of problems. The following subsections (listed here) discuss these important connectivity and communication components and some of the problems associated with them.

- Cables and connectors
- Network adapter cards
- Hubs and MSAUs
- Connectivity devices (bridges, routers, repeaters, and other network devices)

This section also discusses some cable-related troubleshooting tools.

A. Troubleshooting Cables and Connectors

Most network problems occur at the OSI Physical layer, and cabling is one of the most common causes. A cable might have a short or a break, or it might be attached to a faulty connector. Tools such as DVMs and TDRs (discussed later in this section) help search out cabling problems.

If a workstation cannot access the network and you think the problem might be the cabling, try disconnecting the network cables and attaching them to a portable PC. If the portable reaches the network, cabling probably isn't your problem.

When troubleshooting any network, begin with the more obvious physical problems. For example, make sure that all connectors are tight and properly connected, that ground wires and terminators are used when required, and that manufacturer's specifications (such as cable grade, cable lengths, and maximum number of nodes) are met and are consistent with the specifications for the transmission medium.

Chapter 21 discusses the various network cabling standards and some of their requirements and limitations. Be aware of the capacity and range limitations for the various transmission media. Typical troubleshooting scenarios include situations in which the cabling distance exceeds the range of the transmission medium or the required throughput exceeds the capacity of the transmission medium. Table 21.1.2 summarizes the requirements and characteristics of the various media standards. One of the best things you can do for yourself as you prepare for the Networking Essentials exam is to memorize the information in Table 21.1.2.

Here are some other guidelines to follow when troubleshooting cable-related network problems:

- With 10baseT, make sure the cable that's used has the correct number of twists to meet the data-grade specifications.
- Look for electrical interference. Electrical interference can result from tying the network cable together with monitor and power cords. Outdoor fluorescent lights, electric motors, and other electrical devices can cause interference.

- Make sure that connectors are pinned properly and crimped tightly.
- If excess shielding on coaxial cable is exposed, make sure it doesn't ground out the connector.
- Make sure that coaxial cables are not coiled tightly together.
- On coaxial Ethernet LANs, look for missing terminators or terminators with improper impedance ratings.
- Watch out for malfunctioning transceivers, concentrators, or T-connectors. Make sure that connectors have not been mixed up (for example, ARCnet connectors cannot be used on an Ethernet network).
- Test the continuity of the cable by using the various physical testing devices discussed in the following section or by using a software-based cable testing utility.
- Make sure that all the component cables in a segment are connected. A user who moves his client and removes the T-connector incorrectly can break a segment.
- Examine cable connectors for bent or broken pins.
- On token-ring networks, inspect the attachment of patch cables and adapter cables. Remember, patch cables connect MSAUs, and adapter cables connect the network adapter to the MSAU.

One benefit of a token-ring network is its built-in capability to monitor itself. Token-ring networks provide electronic troubleshooting and, when possible, actually make repairs. When the token-ring network can't make its own repairs, a process called *beaconing* narrows down the search for the portion of the ring in which the problem is most likely to exist.

Because cabling problems are so prevalent and, often, so difficult to trace, network administrators use some special tools to seek out damaged wires. Those tools include the following:

- **Digital Volt Meter (DVM).** This hand-held electronic measuring tool enables you to check the voltage and resistance of network cables. You can use a DVM to find a break or a short in a network cable.
- **Time-Domain Reflectometer (TDR).** TDRs send sonar-like pulses along a cable to look for imperfections that might be caused by a break or a short in the line. A good TDR can pinpoint breaks to within feet.
- **Oscilloscope.** This device measures fluctuations in signal voltage and can help find faulty or damaged cabling.

B. Troubleshooting Network Adapter Cards

Network problems often result from malfunctioning network adapter cards. The process of troubleshooting the network adapter works like any other kind of troubleshooting process: You start with the simple. The following list details some things you can check if you think your network adapter card might be malfunctioning:

- Make sure the cable is connected to the card properly.
- Confirm that you have the correct network adapter card driver and that the driver is installed properly. Be sure the card is properly bound to the appropriate transport protocol.
- Verify that the network card matches your network's topology (for instance, 10baseT versus 100baseT.

- Make sure the network adapter card and the network adapter card driver are compatible with your operating system. If you use Windows NT, consult the Windows NT hardware compatibility list. If you use Windows 95 or another operating system, rely on the adapter card vendor specifications.
- Test for resource conflicts. Make sure another device isn't attempting to use the same resources. (See section 22.3 for more on resolving resource conflicts for network adapter cards.) If you think a resource conflict might be the problem but you can't pinpoint the conflict using Windows NT Diagnostics, Windows 95's Device Manager, or some other diagnostic program, try removing all the cards except the network adapter and then replacing the cards one by one. Check the network with each addition to determine which device is causing the conflict.
- Run the network adapter card's diagnostic software.
- If necessary, remove the card and clean the connector fingers (don't use an eraser because it leaves grit on the card).
- Examine the jumper and DIP switch settings on the card. Make sure the resource settings are consistent with the settings configured through the operating system.
- Make sure the card fits properly in the slot.
- Replace the card with one that you know works. If the connection works with a different card, you know the card is the problem.

Token-ring network adapters with failure rates that exceed a preset tolerance level might actually remove themselves from the network. Some token-ring networks experience problems if a 16 Mbps card is inserted into a 4 Mbps ring. (Other 16 Mbps cards can adjust to a 4 Mbps network.)

Broadcast storms (discussed later in this chapter) are often caused by faulty network adapters.

Review your event log on a regular basis. The event log may reveal a network adapter that experiences intermittent problems.

C. Troubleshooting Hubs and MSAUs

If you experience problems with a hub-based LAN, such as a 10baseT network, you often can isolate the problem by disconnecting the attached workstations one at a time. If removing one of the workstations eliminates the problem, the trouble may be caused by that workstation or its associated cable length. If removing each of the workstations doesn't solve the problem, the fault may lie with the hub. Check the easy components first, such as ports, switches, and connectors. Then use a different hub (if you have it) and see if the problem persists. If your hub doesn't work properly, call the manufacturer.

If you're troubleshooting a token-ring network, make sure the cables are connected properly to the MSAUs, with ring-out ports connecting to the ring-in ports throughout the ring. If you suspect the MSAU, isolate it by changing the ring-in and ring-out cables to bypass the MSAU. If that makes the ring functional again, consider replacing the MSAU. In addition, if your network has MSAUs from more than one manufacturer, you might find that they are not wholly compatible. Impedance and other electrical characteristics can show slight differences between manufacturers, causing intermittent network problems. Some MSAUs (other than the 8228) are active and require a power supply. These MSAUs fail if they have a blown fuse or a bad power source. Your problem also might result from a misconfigured MSAU port. MSAU ports might need to be reinitialized with the setup tool. Removing drop cables and reinitializing each MSAU port is a quick fix that is useful on relatively small token-ring networks.

Isolating problems with patch cables, adapter cables, and MSAUs is easier to do if you have a current log of your network's physical design. After you pinpoint the problem, you can isolate potential problem areas from the rest of the network and then use a cable tester to find the actual problem.

D. Connectivity Devices (Bridges, Routers, Repeaters, and Other Network Devices)

If you are experiencing problems with a bridge, router, or repeater, your troubleshooting effort should begin where it begins for other network hardware: Make sure that the unit is plugged in and turned on and that all cables and connectors are fastened securely. Your problem might also be that you are deploying the unit in an inappropriate situation. Each of these connectivity devices is designed for a specific role, and if you deploy the device in the wrong situation, you may not get the results you expect. Section 21.4 outlines the roles of bridges, routers, repeaters, switches, brouters, and gateways.

The following list offers some important troubleshooting considerations:

- If you are extending your network using repeaters, remember the 5-4-3 rule (see section 20.8.B). Use a maximum of five repeated segments, with no more than four repeaters, and only three of the five segments should be populated.
- A repeater can extend the length of a LAN segment, but the maximum distance is still limited by the propagation delay (see section 21.4.A).
- Bridges and repeaters do not filter broadcast traffic and thus do not prevent or contain broadcast storms (see section 21.4.B).
- Bridges and repeaters cannot connect dissimilar LAN types (such as an Ethernet segment and a token-ring segment). See sections 21.4.A and 21.4.B.
- A router can route only routable protocols. (Routable protocols include TCP/IP, NWLink, IPX/SPX, and AppleTalk; Nonroutable protocols include NetBEUI and DLC.) See section 21.4.D.
- A router can connect dissimilar LAN types (such as Ethernet and token-ring), but it cannot connect dissimilar protocol systems (such as a TCP/IP network and an IPX network). Use a gateway to connect dissimilar protocol systems (see section 21.4.F).

23.2.1 Exercise: Using the Event Log to Diagnose Trace Problems

Exercise 23.2 shows you how you can trace problems quickly using the event log and Windows NT's Event Viewer application. The problem with an exercise in network problems is that you must induce a problem in order to perform the exercise. In this case, you'll simulate a network problem by disabling your network adapter. Here's how:

1. On a Windows NT system, start Control Panel and double-click the Devices application icon.
2. Look for your network adapter card driver in the list of devices. Select your network adapter card and click the Startup button.

3. Write down your current startup type setting so you'll remember what it is. Then, under Startup Type, click Disabled and select OK.
4. Close the Devices application and shut down your system.
5. Reboot Windows NT and log on.
6. Click the Start button and choose Programs, Administrative Tools, Event Viewer.
7. In the Event Viewer main window, make sure the System log is active. If it isn't, pull down the Log menu and select System.
8. Look for red error icons in the left column of Event Viewer. On most systems, the absence of a network adapter causes some services (such as the Remote Procedure Call (RPC) service and protocol-related services) to fail. Double-click a line with a red error icon for an *event detail*—a description of the event. In a real-life failure situation, the event detail gives you clues about the cause of the failure.
9. (Very important!) When you finish inspecting the event log, start the Control Panel Devices application, find your network adapter card in the devices list, click the Startup button, and restore the startup type to its original setting (most likely Automatic). Then reboot. (You can start your adapter directly from the Devices application, but starting your adapter might not automatically resurrect all the failed services.)

23.2 Practice Problems

1. Which of the following can you use to look for breaks in network cables by measuring cable voltage?
   - A. Protocol analyzer
   - B. DVM
   - C. TDR
   - D. MSDL

2. Which of the following sends sonar-like pulses down the cable to look for imperfections?
   - A. DVM
   - B. Oscilloscope
   - C. TDR
   - D. None of the above

3. Of the following possible problems, which two relate to token-ring network adapters?
   - A. Broadcast messages from the card are not timed properly.
   - B. The card is not bound to a network service.
   - C. The card removed itself from the network.
   - D. A 16Mbps card exists on a 4Mbps ring.

4. Most network problems occur at which layer of the OSI model?
   - A. Physical
   - B. Data Link
   - C. Network
   - D. Session

5. Which of the following suggestions offers a means of isolating a network problem on a hub-based 10baseT network?
   - A. You can disconnect the attached workstations one at a time to isolate a bad cable, a bad network card, or a bad workstation.
   - B. You can isolate a bad hub by bypassing it.
   - C. By changing port assignments of all the workstations, you can isolate a potential network problem.
   - D. By disconnecting all of the attached workstations simultaneously, you can isolate a bad cable, a bad network card, or a bad workstation.

23.2 Answers and Explanations: Practice Problems

1. **B** A DVM (Digital Voltage Meter) measures cable voltage.
2. **C** TDRs (Time-Domain Reflectometers) send sonar-like pulses.
3. **C, D** A token-ring card can remove itself from the network. A disparity between the speed of the card and the speed of the other cards in the ring can cause problems. A network adapter is not bound directly to a service; it is bound to a protocol.
4. **A** Most network problems occur at the Physical layer.
5. **A** Of the choices given, the easiest way to isolate a network problem on a hub-based network is to disconnect workstations from the hub one at a time.

23.2 Key Words

Electrical interference

Beaconing

Digital Volt Meter (DVM)

Time-Domain Reflectometer (TDR)

Oscilloscope

Resource conflict

Jumper

DIP switch

Broadcast storm

Connectivity device

Multistation Access Unit(MSAU)

23.3 Resolve Broadcast Storms

A *broadcast storm* is a sudden flood of broadcast messages that clogs the transmission medium, approaching 100 percent of the bandwidth. Broadcast storms cause performance to decline and, in the worst case, computers cannot even access the network. The cause of a broadcast storm is often a malfunctioning network adapter, but a broadcast storm also can occur when a device on the network attempts to contact another device that either doesn't exist or for some reason doesn't respond to the broadcast.

If the broadcast messages are viable packets (or even error-filled but partially legible packets), a network-monitoring or protocol-analysis tool often can determine the source of the storm. If the broadcast storm results from a malfunctioning adapter throwing illegible packets onto the line, and a network monitor or protocol analyzer can't find the source, try to isolate the offending PC by removing computers from the network one at a time until the line returns to normal. (For more information, see "Troubleshooting Network Adapter Cards," earlier in this chapter.)

The Windows NT Network Monitor tool, discussed earlier in this chapter and in Chapter 22, can help you find the source of a broadcast storm.

23.3 Practice Problems

1. A broadcast storm is

   A. A network broadcast that begins properly but doesn't terminate.

   B. An infinite loop caused by a faulty redirector.

   C. A sudden deluge of network traffic.

   D. A hard drive consecutively outputting all its bits to the network.

2. Which two of the following problems are the most common causes of network broadcast storms?

   A. A malfunctioning network adapter card.

   B. A short in a section of the transmission medium.

   C. Incorrect transport protocol assignments.

   D. A device on the network that is unable to contact another device because the other device either does not exist or, for some reason, does not respond.

3. Which is the best tool to locate the source of a broadcast storm?

   A. TDR

   B. DVM

   C. Performance Monitor

   D. Network Monitor

4. If the broadcast storm contains illegible packets, a good way to find the source is to

   A. Use an analysis tool to decode the packets.

   B. Isolate the offending PC by removing computers from the network one at a time.

   C. Disable the current default protocol and then test the network using a different protocol with the same adapter.

   D. All of the above.

23.3 Answers and Explanations: Practice Problems

1. **C** A broadcast storm is a large, sudden increase in network traffic.

2. **A, D** The most common causes of broadcast storms are a malfunctioning adapter and a device looking for a missing network node.

3. **D** TDRs and VDMs find cabling problems. Performance Monitor can help you discover that there is a broadcast storm, but it cannot directly discover the source. Network Monitor is the best candidate for finding the source of an incoming packet.

4. **B** An analysis tool can't decode the packets if they're illegible. If the broadcast storm is caused by a malfunctioning adapter, it won't help to use a different protocol with the same adapter. The fastest way to find the offending computer is to remove the computers from the network one at a time.

23.3 Key Words

Broadcast storm

Protocol analyzer

Network monitor

Network adapter

23.4 Identify and Resolve Network Performance Problems

If your network runs slower than it used to run (or slower than it ought to run), the problem might be that the present network traffic exceeds the level at which the network can operate efficiently. Some possible causes for increased traffic are new hardware (such as a new workstation) or new software (such as a network computer game or some other network application). A generator or another mechanical device operating near the network could cause a degradation of network performance. In addition, a malfunctioning network device could act as a bottleneck. To determine which is true, ask yourself what has changed since the last time the network operated efficiently, and begin there with your troubleshooting efforts.

The increased traffic could be the result of increased usage. If usage exceeds the capacity of the network, you might want to consider expanding or redesigning your network. You also might want to divide the network into smaller segments using a router or a bridge. A protocol analyzer can help you measure and monitor the traffic at various points on your network. If your Ethernet network is using more than 20–25 percent bandwidth utilization, this would be a good time to either break the network into segments or use a router. This also applies to a token-ring network that has more than 50 percent bandwidth utilization.

Underdesigned networking components can sometimes cause performance problems for an entire network. A busy server, for instance, should use a high-end bus mastering 32-bit or 64-bit network adapter card. A 16-bit network adapter can cause performance degradation.

If you suspect that a particular component is slowing down your network, you can use Windows NT's Performance Monitor to look for the bottleneck. Performance Monitor is an essential tool for troubleshooting network performance problems. Performance Monitor collects performance-related statistics and enables you to graph, log, or tabulate those statistics. See section 22.5 for a discussion of Windows NT's Performance Monitor tool.

If possible, spend some time with Performance Monitor so you can become familiar with the kinds of statistics it measures. If you see an exam question on network performance, look for clues in the question that point toward a particular measurement. Even if you aren't an expert on Performance Monitor, you can usually find the appropriate counter if you think through the problem logically and you have a good understanding of the PC's components (processor, hard drive, protocols, network adapters, and so forth).

Performance Monitor has a vast selection of counters relating to both hardware and software components: processors, adapters, protocols, disks, services. This means you can monitor several suspected bottleneck candidates simultaneously to determine problems and possible solutions. You may discover, for instance, that a protocol is rarely used, indicating that you could increase your network's bandwidth by disabling or removing that protocol.

Section 22.5 describes some other strategies for record keeping and discusses the importance of maintaining a baseline of performance data. A baseline helps you troubleshoot network performance by providing you with a reference point from which you can measure later fluctuations in performance.

A. Handling Other Network Problems

The following list details some other common problems that could affect your network:

- **Operating system conflicts.** Operating system upgrades sometimes cause older programs to become incompatible with the operating system itself. This problem is compounded in network environments because, during the transition to a new network operating system, some servers run the new version for a period of time while others are still running the previous version. Microsoft recommends that you perform a test upgrade on an isolated part of the network to ensure that all hardware and software systems function properly when the upgrade is made.
- **Server crashes.** A server disk crash can be disastrous if you aren't adequately prepared for it. You should devise a system of regular backups and, depending on the nature of your data, explore other safeguards such as a RAID fault-tolerant system.
- **Power fluctuations.** A small fluctuation in the power supply can make the network misbehave. If the power goes off completely—even for a moment—the whole network could shut down, causing users to lose their work in progress. A disorderly shutdown also can cause problems with file servers. The best solution is to prepare for a power outage before it happens. Connect each server to an Uninterruptible Power Supply (UPS), and encourage your users to perform occasional saves as they work.

If you implement all the measures discussed so far and you still experience problems, your next step may be to consult the experts. Or, even before you start your own troubleshooting, you may want to consult the available information to learn more about the problem. The next section discusses some online and offline sources of help.

B. Getting Support

You are rarely alone when you are troubleshooting network problems. An important aspect of troubleshooting is knowing where to turn for critical information about your network environment. Many online and offline sources can provide troubleshooting information. Some of these sources (in addition to the online help provided with your operating system), include the following:

- **Vendor documentation and help lines.** Hardware and software vendors often provide troubleshooting tips with the documentation. Vendors also often provide technical assistance by phone.
- **Bulletin board services.** A number of electronic bulletin boards supply networking information. You can download information on Microsoft network products from the Microsoft Download Library (MSDL), which you can reach by dialing 206-936-6735. Other vendors also have active bulletin board systems, such as Novell's NetWire BBS. See vendor documentation for more information on how to reach a particular vendor's official BBS.
- **The Internet.** The major network vendors all sponsor active forums and newsgroups on the Internet, CompuServe, and other online services. See your vendor's documentation.
- **CD-ROMs.** Several vendors now market CD-ROMs with network and PC hardware information. These are some examples:

  Windows NT Server's Books Online (located on the Windows NT Installation CD-ROM) provides an additional source of documentation that isn't available with online help.

Microsoft's TechNet contains product information, technical information, articles, and announcements. TechNet is available on a subscription basis through Microsoft (call 800-344-2121).

Novell's NSEPro CD-ROM is a NetWare-oriented encyclopedia of network information.

The Micro House Technical Library (MHTL) is another impressive database of technical information. The MHTL addresses such items as BIOS settings for IDE drives and jumper settings for popular peripheral boards. The MHTL comes with a rich collection of informative illustrations.

23.4 Practice Problems

1. Which three of the following could degrade network performance?

   A. A generator or mechanical device near the network

   B. A computer game

   C. A sudden disorderly shutdown of a workstation

   D. New hardware

2. Which one of the following devices is a solution for power fluctuation problems?

   A. Uninterruptible Power Supply (UPS)

   B. NT Clustering

   C. RAID

   D. Grounded circuit

3. To avoid potential operating system conflicts, what course of action does Microsoft recommend when upgrading?

   A. Do not upgrade any servers or nodes on any network, unless absolutely necessary.

   B. Upgrade the entire network simultaneously.

   C. Perform a test upgrade on an isolated part of the network to ensure that all hardware and software systems function properly when the upgrade is made.

   D. Use only Microsoft products to ensure complete compatibility.

4. Suppose there appears to be some interference on network cables installed over an acoustic tile ceiling. What is a possible (probable) cause for the interference?

   A. Fluorescent lights

   B. Adverse weather

   C. Electrical motors and devices

   D. Network cables tied together with monitor wires

5. You should consider subdividing your Ethernet network if the bandwidth utilization exceeds

   A. 25%.

   B. 50%.

   C. 90%.

   D. 95%.

23.4 Answers and Explanations: Practice Problems

1. **A, B, D** A shutdown of a workstation typically won't affect network performance. A mechanical device could cause electrical interference. A computer game or a faulty new device could disrupt or slow down the network.

2. **A** A UPS protects the network from power fluctuations.

3. **C** Microsoft recommends that you test a part of the network first to ensure that all systems are compatible.

4. **A** If you are experiencing interference in network cables installed over an acoustic tile ceiling, fluorescent lights are a logical first guess for the cause.

5. **A** Ethernet networks use a contention-based access control method, and performance can start to degrade a seemingly low network utilization of 25%.

23.4 Key Words

Bandwidth utilization

Performance Monitor

Baseline

Operating system conflict

Power fluctuation

TechNet

Practice Exam: Troubleshooting

1. Which of the following services enables a Windows NT computer to share its resources?

    A. Workstation

    B. Server

    C. Browser

    D. NTClient

2. Suppose you are not able to establish a SLIP connection to an IPX/SPX network. The most likely cause is:

    A. You are using an incompatible frame type.

    B. Your network number is not unique.

    C. Your modem speed is different from the speed of the modem to which you're connecting.

    D. SLIP won't work with IPX/SPX.

3. Your network is a small workgroup of Windows 95 machines. You want to switch from share-level to user-level security. You go to the Access Control tab in the Control Panel Network application, select the option button for user-level access control, and enter the name of your workgroup. You receive an error message. A likely cause for this is:

    A. Windows 95 machines do not have an account database that supports user-level access.

    B. The other machines in the workgroup are all set for share-level access.

    C. You must cancel all network shares before you switch to user-level access.

    D. All of the above.

4. The PPP protocol requires:

    A. TCP/IP.

    B. A static IP address.

    C. A point-to-point connection.

    D. All of the above.

5. You access a directory on an NTFS partition through a network share. You then discover that you can't access a file on the NTFS partition. Which of the following might be the cause?

    A. The share permissions do not provide access to the file.

    B. Your user rights specifically exclude access to that file.

    C. The file-level permissions for the file exclude you from accessing the file.

    D. All of the above.

6. Which troubleshooting tool can you use to verify that a network card does not have a resource conflict?

    A. Windows NT Diagnostics

    B. Windows 95 Device Manager

    C. Network adapter card's diagnostic software

    D. A third-party diagnostic utility

    E. All of the above

7. From the following list, which two devices can be used to monitor network traffic, track network performance, and analyze packet frames?

    A. Oscilloscopes

    B. Network monitors

    C. Protocol analyzers

    D. Time-Domain Reflectometers

8. On a Windows NT system, which tool would you use to change a conflicting IRQ setting for a network adapter card?

    A. Windows NT Diagnostics

    B. Control Panel Devices Application

    C. Control Panel Network Application

    D. Device Manager

9. Your 10Base5 network is not behaving reliably. Which three of the following things do you need to verify?

   A. The maximum length for the entire network is 2500 meters.

   B. The maximum network segment length is 500 meters.

   C. The minimum drop cable length is 2.5 meters.

   D. The maximum drop cable length is 50 meters.

10. Your laptop communicates with the internal network using scatter infrared, and you are experiencing reliability problems. Your office contains a large quantity of high-voltage electrical equipment. You typically roam around the office within a range of approximately 150 feet from the access point, and your path takes you around corners where you are not always in a direct line of sight to the access point. Which of the following is a likely source of the problems?

    A. You are not always in direct line of sight to the access point.

    B. You exceed the reliable distance to the access point.

    C. The electrical equipment is causing interference that disrupts the signal.

    D. All of the above.

11. You should consider subdividing your token-ring network if the bandwidth utilization exceeds

    A. 25%.

    B. 50%.

    C. 90%.

    D. 95%.

12. Using Performance Monitor, you have discovered that the frequency with which your Windows NT Server system accesses the paging file (Pages/sec) is unusually high. This could indicate that you should:

    A. Increase the size of the paging file.

    B. Spread the paging file over multiple disks.

    C. Upgrade memory.

    D. Upgrade your processor.

13. The number of interrupts per second processed by your PC recently increased drastically. A possible cause is:

    A. The processor is overloaded.

    B. A network adapter is malfunctioning.

    C. The operating system is searching for a missing hardware component.

    D. An application is incompatible with the operating system.

14. Which tool would you use to determine whether a network slowdown is caused by a slow hard disk?

    A. Disk Administrator

    B. Task Manager

    C. Server Manager

    D. None of the above

15. Of the following possible solutions, which two are most likely to improve the performance of a Windows NT Server system acting as a file server?

    A. Replace the hard disk to add capacity.

    B. Replace the hard disk for better I/O performance.

    C. Replace the 16-bit network adapter with a 32-bit adapter.

    D. Implement disk mirroring.

Answers and Explanations: Practice Exam

1. **B** The Server service enables a computer to share resources.
2. **D** SLIP works only with TCP/IP; you can't use it with IPX/SPX.
3. **A** A Windows 95 machine cannot access user information on a Windows NT or NetWare machine in order to support user-level security. Because the workgroup contains only Windows 95 machines, user-level security is not an option.
4. **A** PPP (Point-to-Point Protocol) is designed for point-to-point connections. Unlike its forerunner, SLIP, it does not require TCP/IP or a static IP address.
5. **C** The file permissions for the file may exclude you from accessing the file. Share permissions apply to a directory, and you have already accessed the directory, so you know share permissions are not a problem. A user right applies to a type of activity, not to a specific resource such as a file.
6. **E** All of the choices could help you verify the resource settings for a network adapter card.
7. **B, C** Protocol analyzers and network monitors perform sophisticated network analysis functions. Oscilloscopes and TDRs diagnose only network cabling problems.
8. **C** The Network application lets you change the IRQ settings. Windows NT Diagnostics lets you view the setting, but not change it. Device Manager is a Windows 95 tool. The Devices application lets you start and stop devices, but not reconfigure them.
9. **A, B, D** There is no minimum length for drop cables. The other choices are limits included in the 10Base5 specification (see section 21.2.C.2).
10. **B** Infrared broadcasts are reliable up to 100 feet. Scatter infrared does not require a line-of-sight connection, and infrared is not affected by electrical interference.
11. **B** Token-rings can support more utilization than Ethernet networks, but they still operate more efficiently at >50% bandwidth utilization.
12. **C** If you increase the RAM memory, you'll reduce the need for paging.
13. **B** A device such as a network adapter card uses interrupts to contact the processor. A malfunctioning adapter may be flooding the system with interrupt requests.
14. **D** None of the options listed will give you any direct statistics on the performance of the hard disk. Your best choice is Performance Monitor.
15. **B, C** A faster hard disk will spend less time reading and writing to files. The network adapter is often the bottleneck for a busy server. Disk mirroring doesn't improve, and could actually slow down, I/O performance. Adding capacity could have a secondary effect on performance in some situations, but B and C still are the best answers.

Part V

MCSE TestPrep

Practice Exams

Practice Exam 1

Implementing and Supporting Microsoft Windows NT Server 4.0

NT Server exam instructions:

You have 90 minutes to complete 67 questions. There will be two types of questions:

- Multiple Choice—Select the correct answer.
- Multiple Multiple Choice—Select all answers that are correct.

We suggest that you set a timer to track your progress while taking the practice exam, since the time-constraint on the tests is often a big obstacle to overcome.

Begin after you set your timer.

Practice Exam Begins

1. In the Control Panel, the Virtual Memory settings are controlled by which applet?
   A. Devices icon
   B. Server icon
   C. Services icon
   D. System icon
   E. None of the above
2. Windows NT Server will automatically load which of the following services? Select all that apply:
   A. Computer Browser
   B. Schedule
   C. RPC Locator
   D. Server
   E. Workstation
3. Which permissions can be assigned to a given directory (folder) under Windows NT Server (using NTFS partition)?
   A. No Access
   B. Deny
   C. Change
   D. Full Control
   E. Share Folder
   F. Scan

4. When copying files from a Windows NT NTFS partition to a Windows NT FAT partition, what will happen to the file-level permissions for the file that is copied?
   A. They are retained.
   B. The new file permissions granted will be Full Control rights.
   C. FAT permissions override NTFS permissions.
   D. All NTFS permissions are dropped.
5. What is the best reason for the creation of a user's home directory on a Windows NT PDC?
   A. So that there is a centralized location to back up all the data from the user.
   B. To allow other users to gain access of that user's data.
   C. So that data can be shared with all users from other trusted domains.
   D. Increased performance.
6. Printing priorities that can be assigned to a printer are in a range from:
   A. 1 through 255
   B. 1 through 100
   C. 1 through 64
   D. 1 through 99
   E. 1 through 10
   F. Printer priorities cannot be changed.
7. You want to ensure that your backup procedures and restore processes are fully completed and accurate. Which of the following options would you select to make sure a backup/restore was successful?
   A. Perform a backup on a single file to a tape device; and verify that the file exists on the tape. Next, restore the file on the hard drive to verify the backup and restore process.
   B. Select Verify when performing a complete backup.
   C. Select Verify when performing a complete restore.
   D. Restore files to a different path option from your backup procedure and compare the restore files with the original files.
   E. Perform a backup once a month.
8. You are the administrator of your Windows NT Domain and decide to delegate the responsibilities to perform auditing to other users on your team. By default, which members of the following groups can perform auditing?
   A. Backup Operator's group
   B. Server Operator's group
   C. Everyone's group
   D. Administrator's group
   E. None of the above

9. You are working on your Windows NT Workstation using the User Manager for Domains utility from the Server Tools option on the CD-ROM. You are about to create new users for the domain you are in. Where is the user account information being stored?
   A. On the Windows NT Workstation on which you are currently working
   B. Windows NT Backup Domain Controller
   C. Windows NT Member Server
   D. Windows NT Primary Domain Controller
   E. Windows NT Primary Domain Controller from the other Domain
10. You are in charge of your MIS team. You noticed that users are complaining about missing files. You want to be able to track files and directory accesses. Which of the following must be selected to achieve this, assuming NTFS partitions?
    A. Logon and Logoff
    B. Process Tracking
    C. Use of User Rights
    D. User and Group Management
    E. File and Object Access
11. You are working at night in a high-volume manufacturing plant. Your network consists of 150 Member Servers, four Backup Domain Controllers, 355 Windows NT Workstations, and 56 Windows 95 clients. An alarm goes off, indicating that your Primary Domain Controller has gone down. What will be your first reaction to this situation?
    A. Install a new Primary Domain Controller.
    B. Upgrade one of the Backup Domain Controllers to Primary.
    C. Do nothing, one of the four Backup Domain Controllers will promote itself to Primary.
    D. Upgrade any one of the Windows NT Workstations to Primary Domain Controller.
    E. Select the closest physical Backup Domain Controller and promote it to Primary Domain Controller.
    F. Do nothing.
12. How does a member of the Domain Administrator's Group receive the proper rights to administrate every computer with the domain design?
    A. Domain administrators automatically have full access to all computers in the domain.
    B. The Domain Administrator's Global Group content is automatically added to the Local Group Power Users when the computer is joined to the domain.
    C. The Domain Administrator's Local Group contents are automatically added to the Local Group Administrator's Group by default.
    D. The Domain Administrator's Global Group is added to the Local Group Administrators automatically when the computer joins the domain.
13. Windows NT Server 4.0 DS (Directory Services) provides which of the following features? Select all that apply:
    A. Single-user logon
    B. Automated backup operations
    C. Decentralized administration
    D. Centralized administration
    E. Universal access to resources
    F. Single access to a resource

14. In which situation would a Windows NT Domain configuration be used in preference to a workgroup model?
    A. When no security is required.
    B. When the maximum number of users for a workgroup model has exceeded 100 users.
    C. When there is no clearly defined system administrator and everyone must share administrative responsibilities.
    D. When security is required.
15. Which of the following files on a Windows NT Application server under NTFS should be backed up on a daily basis? Select all that apply:
    A. User data on the server
    B. Directories
    C. Operating system files
    D. MS-DOS boot files
    E. System Registry
    F. SQL database
16. You are working in the network communication room and need to send a message to all users that the Windows NT Server will be off-line for six hours. How do you send the message to the connected users in your domain?
    A. Use the SEND option in the Network Client Admin Utility.
    B. Use the SEND option in User Manager for Domains.
    C. Use the SEND option in Events Manager.
    D. Use the SEND option in Server Manager.
    E. There is no such option.
17. Which of the following administrative utilities is used to manage administrative alerts?
    A. User Profile Manager
    B. System Policy Editor
    C. WinMSD
    D. Server Manager
    E. Disk Administrator
    F. Alert Monitor
18. You have just created a printer on your Windows NT Print Server and then shared the printer. What must a client do when he is connecting to that shared printer so that the print driver will make the client's workstation print to the shared printer?
    A. Copy the print driver to the client's memory as the client logs on the NT Domain.
    B. Share the print driver with the printer.
    C. Make sure that the print driver is compatible with ALPHA, MIPS, INTEL chipsets.
    D. The client does nothing. This procedure is automatic when the client prints the document to that shared printer.
19. Which application would you use on your Primary Domain Controller to view the roles of all the computers in your network?
    A. Explorer
    B. Server Manager
    C. User Manager for Domains
    D. Network Administrator
    E. Control Panel, System
    F. None of the above

20. Your network uses three protocols—TCP/IP, NetBEUI, and NWLink. The binding order of these protocols on your Windows NT Server and Windows NT Workstation is the following: NetBEUI, NWLink, and TCP/IP. The users on your network are accessing resources using NWLink. Where must the binding order sequence of your three protocols be changed to increase the performance of your network?
    A. On the Windows NT Server only.
    B. On the Windows NT Workstation only.
    C. On the PDC only.
    D. On the BDC only.
    E. On the PDC, BDC, and Windows NT Workstations.

21. Susan is installing TCP/IP protocol on a Windows NT server that is a member in the domain. Susan manually assigns a TCP/IP address to the member server. What other parameters must she specify to install TCP/IP protocol on her Windows NT server?
    A. The DHCP server IP address scheme
    B. The WINS server IP address scheme
    C. The default gateway address
    D. The subnet mask

22. There are several WFW 3.11 Workstations that are part of your Windows NT domain that need access to resources that are located on a NetWare 3.12 server. How can you set up the WFW 3.11 Workstations so that they can access the NetWare 3.12 server without adding additional client software to their workstations?
    A. By installing NWLink protocol on the Windows NT Server.
    B. By installing IPX/SPX protocol on the Windows NT Server.
    C. By installing IPX/SPX protocol on the WFW 3.11 Workstations.
    D. By installing Gateway Services for NetWare on the WFW 3.11 clients.
    E. By installing Gateway Services for NetWare on the Windows NT Server.
    F. By doing nothing.

23. There are 75 Windows NT Workstations running NT 4.0 on your network. These workstations print to a Windows NT member server that is acting as a print server. You just downloaded from the Internet an updated print driver that must be implemented. What is the best way to update the new print driver to all 75 Windows NT Workstations?
    A. Go to all 75 Windows NT Workstations and update the driver.
    B. Update the driver on the Windows NT PDC.
    C. Update the driver on the Windows print server.
    D. Update the driver on the Windows NT print server, and when the workstations connect, the driver will install on each workstation.

24. You have 200 MS-DOS computers on your network. You decided to install Windows NT 4.0 Workstation on all 200 computers. How would you install Windows NT Workstation 4.0 on all 200 MS-DOS computers?
    A. Connect to a network share directory that contains the

Windows NT 4.0 CD-ROM and run SETUP.EXE from the \i386 directory.

B. From a MS-DOS prompt, type WINNT32.EXE from the \i386 directory.

C. You cannot install Windows NT 4.0 OS with MS-DOS already installed.

D. Connect to a network share directory that contains the Windows NT 4.0 CD-ROM and run WINNT.EXE from the \i386 directory.

E. FDISK.EXE and slice the disk.

25. You have RAS services running on your Windows NT Server. You have a RAS problem occurs and you want to troubleshoot this problem. You have enabled the RAS log file called device.log. In your Windows NT RAS Server, where is device.log located?

A. WINNT directory

B. WINNT\SYSTEM directory

C. C:\

D. WINNT\SYSTEM32\REPL directory

E. WINNT\SYSTEM32\RAS directory

26. Which of the following is an example of RAID 0 on Windows NT Server?

A. Four disk drives

B. Two logical partitions

C. Two disk drives mirrored

D. Two disk drives duplexed

E. Two hard drives

27. You have been notified by management that you will receive a new tape device to be installed in your Windows NT Server. You already have a spare SCSI controller in your lab. You installed the tape device and controller in your server. What should you do to enable these devices? Select all that apply:

A. Install the driver for the tape device.

B. Install the driver for SCSI.

C. Install the driver for the controller.

D. Do nothing.

E. Reboot.

F. Install the driver for the first controller again.

28. You have a Primary Domain Controller installed on your new network. You installed Visual FoxPro application on your PDC. How would you tune your server for clients to access this server to query the FoxPro Database?

A. Minimum memory used

B. Balance

C. Maximize throughput for file sharing

D. Maximize throughput for network applications

E. It's dynamic

29. Mike wants to design a fault-tolerance solution to his SQL NT server. He has a UPS connected to the server, but this unit has a very limited battery supply time. Which fault-tolerance solution should Mike design? Select all that apply:

A. Volume sets

B. Stripe sets without parity

C. Stripe sets with parity

D. Mirror sets

E. Duplex sets

F. Both A and B

G. Both D and B

H. None of the above

30. You have received a piece of hardware and installed it in your Windows NT server. You have installed the driver for the hardware device, and the Windows NT server cannot boot anymore. What is the easiest way to troubleshoot this boot problem for your Windows NT Server?
    A. FDISK.
    B. Reinstall Windows NT Server.
    C. Boot to the Emergency Repair Disk—restore the registry.
    D. Select Windows NT VGA Boot Mode.
    E. Select Last Known Good.
    F. Boot to MS-DOS, and then run WINNT /B switch for repair.
31. You are running Windows NT Workstation 4.0 and have one partition, C drive. The file format is FAT and you have one page file on the local drive. How would you convert this format to NTFS?
    A. Format C: /NTFS
    B. Convert C:/FAT /NTFS
    C. NTFS C:
    D. Convert C: /NTFS /FAT /Y
    E. Cannot convert FAT to NTFS on only one partition
    F. Convert C: /FS:NTFS /V
    G. None of the above
32. You want to use a Null Modem. Which of the following are valid statements for a Null Modem? Select all that apply:
    A. To test and evaluate a Remote Access Server locally
    B. To enable subnet routing from location x to location y over Frame Relay
    C. To have a Windows NT Workstation attached to two different networks that are not physically attached by a 10BaseT cable
    D. To have Windows NT Workstation log into a DOMAIN A without a network interface card installed and protocol binded
    E. Cannot use NULL MODEM cable under Windows NT
33. What is the minimum amount of hardware configurations for disk duplexing?
    A. One drive and two controllers
    B. Two drives and one controller
    C. Two drives and four controllers
    D. Disk duplexing is not supported under Windows NT
    F. Two drives and three controllers
    G. Two drives and two controllers with the same controller architecture
    H. Two drives and two controllers without the same controller architecture
34. You have a UNIX network and want to introduce Windows NT Server. What is the best protocol to use to connect to a UNIX environment?
    A. NetBEIU
    B. IPX/SPX
    C. NWLink
    D. DLC
    E. TCP/IP
    F. None of the above
35. You have created a printer pool under Windows NT Server 4.0. You have configured 10 print devices. Which condition must be met to have all 10 print devices communicate in the printer pool?
    A. All 10 devices must have the same protocol.

B. All 10 devices must be located on the same physical floor.

C. You cannot create a printer pool in NT 4.0.

D. All print devices must use COM2 port.

E. All print devices must use LPT1 port.

F. All devices must be connected to the same Print Server destination.

36. Frank is a design graphics artist in his art department. He is running on Windows NT 4.0 Workstation with 1.5GB SCSI disk on a Pentium 166 Mhz system. His default spooler folder is on the 1.5GB hard drive known as C:. He is running out of space, so he added another drive with a 4 GB capacity. How can Frank move his default spooler folder to the new hard drive known as D:?

A. Modify the print driver.

B. Reinstall Windows NT Workstation.

C. Modify Printer Control Option in Settings, Control Panel.

D. Modify the Registry by using the command \HKEYLocalMachine\System\Microsoft\Printers.

E. Modify the Registry by using the command HKEYLocalMachine\System\CurrentControlSet\Control\Print\Printers.

F. None of the above.

37. You have field sales representatives moving around the country on a weekly basis. They want to gain access to the company's network over the Internet by a RAS service. What method would you use to provide access to network over the Internet and provide security?

A. TCP/IP

B. PPP (Point to Point Protocol)

D. ISDN connection

E. X.25 connection

F. SLIP connection

G. PPTP connection

38. In which configuration can a Windows NT system partition and boot information be supported?

A. RAID 0

B. RAID 5

C. RAID 1

D. RAID 10 (Software)

E. Volume sets

F. Stripe sets without parity

G. Windows NT does not support the above options

39. John has access to the Disk Administrator program, and he tried to delete the Windows NT System Partition. What results would you expect from the system?

A. Continue with Deletion (YES) or (NO)

B. System Partition Deleted

C. Dialog Box appears and prompts you to "Commit Changes Now"

D. System Reboots Automatically

E. Error message appears

40. Sam misplaced his three Windows NT Server 4.0 setup disks. He needs to re-create them. How can Same accomplished this task?

A. Call Microsoft Support.

B. Run WINNT32.EXE /B.

C. Run WINNT32.EXE /R.

D. Run SETUP.EXE.

E. Run WINNT.EXE.

41. Susan is a domain administrator for the Sales domain. She constantly is updating the logon scripts for her 350-user database. What is the best method she can use to ensure that the logon scripts are replicated correctly?
    A. Store the logon scripts in the following directory: WINNT\SYSTEM32\REPL\EXPORTS and replicate to all domain controllers.
    B. Store the logon scripts in the following directory: WINNT\SYSTEM32\REPL\EXPORTS and replicate to all Windows NT Workstations.
    C. Store the logon scripts in the following directory: WINNT\SYSTEM32\REPL\IMPORTS and replicate to all Windows NT Workstations.
    D. Store the logon scripts in the following directory: WINNT\SYSTEM32\REPL\EXPORTS and replicate to all Windows NT PDC Domain Controllers.
    E. Store the logon scripts in the following directory: WINNT\SYSTEM32\REPL\EXPORTS, create a subdirectory under EXPORTS, and replicate to all Backup Domain Controllers.

42. How can Lucy convert from NTFS back to FAT?
    A. Run CONVERT.EXE NTFS FAT.
    B. Run CONVERT.EXE NTFS C:\FS:FAT.
    C. Run CONVERT.EXE /FAT.
    D. Cannot be converted.
    E. Lucy must format the disk, choose FAT, and then reinstall the operating system, applications, and data.

43. You just installed a new printer on your Windows NT 4.0 Print Server. You go to a Windows NT Workstation and submit a print job for testing by right-clicking on the new printer object and then selecting properties and pressing the Print Test Page button. When the job prints, it comes out as garbage. What is the most likely cause of the problem?
    A. DLC protocol is not installed.
    B. Ran out of disk space.
    C. The Print Spooler is corrupted.
    D. The Print Router is corrupted.
    E. Incorrect print driver is installed.

44. By default, the initial paging file is determined by which of the following formulas?
    A. 24 + initial memory
    B. 16 + initial memory
    C. 12 + initial memory
    D. 32 + initial memory
    E. Random number
    F. None of the above

45. Which of the following protocols can be used as a dial-out protocol for Windows NT Server?
    A. TCP/IP only.
    B. NWLink only.
    C. NetBEUI, NWLink.
    D. NWLink, NetBEUI, and TCP/IP.
    E. None of the above can be used as a dial-out protocol.

46. Mike wants to set up Directory Replication in his network. Which of the following configurations would accomplish this goal? Select all that apply:
    A. Windows NT Member Server.
    B. Windows NT Primary Domain Controller.

C. Windows NT Backup Domain Controller.

D. Windows NT Workstation.

E. Directory Replication is not supported.

47. You're running Windows NT Server 4.0 and you launched 3GL Screen Saver. You noticed that the system is running SQL queries extremely slowly. Which counters would you use from Performance Monitor to determine whether the CPU is being hit hard? Select all that apply:

A. %USAGE PEAK

B. %MEMORY PAGES/SEC

C. %PROCESS

D. %PROCESSOR TIME

E. System Object Processor Queue Length

F. %Interrupt Time

G. %DPC

48. You wanted to use a null modem cable in Windows NT Server 4.0. Which of the following ways are true tests? Select all that apply:

A. Subnet routing

B. Testing another Windows NT RAS Server locally in your test lab

C. Using Windows 95 Workstation to access the domain of which they are a member without any hardware network interface cards

D. None of the above

49. You have a UNIX system across the campus in your college network. You have just installed Windows NT Workstation on your local network. To be able to use the router from building A to building B, what protocol must you install on Windows NT Workstation?

A. DLC

B. SNA

C. NetBEUI

D. NWLink

E. TCP/IP

F. X.25

G. Frame Relay

50. You hire Stacy to work in your IS dept. Stacy's responsibility for the first two weeks is to create user accounts in your Windows NT domain. You do not want to give Stacy full administrative rights. You created her account, and by default she belongs to the Domain User Account. In which group would you place Stacy to enable her to create accounts?

A. Domain Administrator group

B. Backup Operator group

C. Server Operator group

D. Account Operator group

E. None of the above

F. All of the above

51. Mike just purchased a laptop to work both at the office and at home. When he comes to work in the morning, he inserts his laptop into the docking station, which contains an external CD-ROM writer. Later, Mike leaves the office and goes home to work on a spreadsheet document. When he boots his laptop running Windows NT Workstation, an error message appears: "One or more services failed to start. See the Event Viewer for details." Mike does not want the device drivers to load on his CD-ROM unit that is attached to his docking station while he works at home. How can Mike accomplish this without any errors appearing when he's booting at home?

A. Reinstall Windows NT at home.

B. Create a separate user account for home.

C. Create a separate user account for work.

D. Boot with the emergency repair disk.

E. Create a roaming account for home.

F. Create a separate hardware profile.

52. You have an MS-DOS application that does not support UNC redirection to a remote printer. Which of the following options makes it possible to print out to a remote printer from your MS-DOS application under Windows NT Workstation 4.0?

A. NT does not support MS-DOS printing.

B. Map LPT1 \\print server name\printer name.

C. Install MS-DOS Printing Services from your Windows NT Server CD-ROM.

D. Download redirection program from `http://www.microsoft.com/support/printing`.

E. Map a physical port to the network printer in your network.

F. None of the above.

53. You just installed seven Windows NT Version 4.0 Workstations in your network. They are installed with NWLink protocol only and you can see all seven NT Workstations. You go home over the weekend and come in on Monday morning to add another Windows NT Workstation. After you installed the NT Workstation Version 3.51, you could not see the original seven. What is most likely the cause of this problem?

A. The protocol is corrupted.

B. Reboot NT Workstation again.

C. There is a mismatch in Windows NT Workstation Build Numbers.

D. Windows NT Version 4.0 is not compatible with Windows NT Version 3.51.

E. There is a frame mismatch.

54. You have 10 workstations connected to your local Windows NT Server. Which of the following optimization methods would be the best choice in this situation?

A. Maximize throughput for Network Applications

B. Maximize throughput for File Sharing

C. Minimize memory used

D. Balance

E. None

55. You discovered that you could use Windows NT Server as a router. You purchase two network adapter cards and physically install them in your server. The two networks that you must connect have the following IP addresses assigned to each segment: Segment # 1—150.50.0.0 and Segment #2—150.51.0.0. You must configure the IP addresses of the two network cards in your NT Server. Which of the following addresses would you choose?

A. 150.50.0.99, 150.50.0.100

B. 150.50.0.0, 150.50.0.1

C. 150.50.0.1, 150.51.0.1

D. 150.50.0.50, 150.51.50.1

E. None of the above

56. Chris wants to use LFN on both Windows 95 and Windows NT 4.0 Workstation products on one machine. Which of the following file system structures would satisfy Chris' requirements?

A. HPFS
B. NTFS
C. FAT32
D. FAT
E. CDFS
F. FAT8

57. You executed the Windows NT registry by REGEDT32.EXE from a command prompt. You edited an entry in the network section and then rebooted the Windows NT server. Your Windows NT Server comes up with a blue screen. What is the best way to get the server back to the original state?
    A. Boot to ERD.
    B. Reinstall.
    C. Boot to MS-DOS, and then execute NTOSKRNL.EXE.
    D. Boot to MS-DOS, and then execute NTLDR.EXE /B.
    E. Press the spacebar, select Last Known Good by selecting L, and then press Enter.

58. You installed a Windows NT Server running DHCP. You created a scope of addresses with an IP expiration of 20 days. You changed a Windows NT Workstation from static address to DHCP to get an IP address from the server. The next day your DHCP Server crashes. How long will it take for the NT Workstation to request for a renewal of the IP address?
    A. 20 days
    B. 1 day
    C. 5 days
    D. 15 days
    E. Infinity
    F. 0 days
    G. 10.5 days
    H. 17.5 days

59. You have installed a color laser printer and want your users to use it, but it will not be available off-hours. What will happen to all the print jobs that are queued to the new color laser printer during the regular peak hours during the day, but are not printed at that time?
    A. The print jobs must be printed no matter what.
    B. The print jobs must be redirected to another printer.
    C. The print jobs will be removed automatically if no printer is available.
    D. The print jobs will be stored in a temp. directory.
    E. The print jobs will be stored in the print spooler.

60. You have TCP/IP installed on your network. You want to gather some performance analysis remotely from a Windows NT Server in your local domain. On your Windows NT Workstation, you invoke perfmon.exe from the command prompt. What must you do before tracking the TCP/IP performance counters on your network from your local Windows NT Workstation?
    A. Install SNMP Service on all systems.
    B. Install SNMP Service on your workstation.
    C. Install SNMP Service on all BDCs.
    D. Install SNMP Service on your PDC.
    E. Install SNMP Service on the server.

61. What is the most likely cause of the following error message when booting up Windows NT Server or Workstation Product: "Can't find NTLDR."
    A. The disk is corrupt.
    B. You are using IDE only.
    C. Mirroring is corrupted.
    D. Raid 5 is corrupted.
    E. There is a floppy in the disk drive.
62. Tim has an account in the Newriders Domain. Tim is currently set up to log into the Newriders Domain. What must Tim do if he wants to use a resource in the Sams Domain?
    A. Set up a two-way trust relationship by using User Manager for Domains.
    B. Set up a one-way trust relationship from Newriders Domain to trust Sams Domain.
    C. Set up a one-way trust relationship from Sams Domain to Trust Newriders Domain.
    D. Do nothing.
63. You have an SCSI drive in your Windows NT Server environment. The boot partition is located by the following path: c:\winnt, which is SCSI. Jumpers on the board disable the BIOS for the SCSI adapter card. You want to create a recovery disk. Which of the following files need to be placed on the recovery disk? Select all that apply:
    A. SCSI.DRV
    B. SCSI.SYS
    C. OSLOADER.EXE
    D. BOOTSCSI.DOS
    E. BOOT.INI
    F. NTLDR
    G. NTDETECT.COM
    H. FAT.SYS
    I. NTBOOTDD.SYS
    J. All of the above
64. Which of the following is required in order for a Windows NT Workstation 4.0 running CSNW to access a NetWare 3.12 server? Select all that apply:
    A. NWLink Protocol
    B. TCP/IP Protocol
    C. GSNW
    D. User Account on Windows NT
    E. User Account on NetWare Server 3.12
65. You have just installed RAS on your Windows NT server. Which of the following encrypted authorization methods provides the most secure environment for RAS connections in this network?
    A. PAP
    B. SPAP
    C. CHAP
    D. LDAP
    E. MS-CHAP
66. You have installed Windows NT 3.51 Server. What will be the best way to upgrade the server to Windows NT 4.0?
    A. Run WINNT.EXE from the NT 4.0 CD-ROM \i386.
    B. Run WINNT32.EXE from the NT 4.0 CD-ROM \i386.
    C. Run WINNT32.EXE from the NT 3.51 directory.
    D. Run WINNT.EXE from the NT 3.51 directory.
    E. Run WINNT32.EXE /NEW from the NT 4.0 CD-ROM \i386.
67. You have a Windows NT RAS server and WINS running on your network. You have Windows NT Workstation clients connecting to your RAS Server

(using TCP/IP). Where should the LMHOSTS and HOST files be placed for the best performance on your network to your RAS clients?

A. In the LMHOST file on the RAS Server only.

B. In the LMHOST and HOST file on the RAS Server only.

C. In the LMHOST and HOST file on all remote clients.

D. In the LMHOST and HOST file on only one remote client.

E. It is not necessary to have LMHOST and HOST files on Windows NT RAS clients.

Answers and Explanations

1. **D** The System icon contains the Virtual Memory setting. By default, Windows NT uses the formula, 12 MB + physical memory, as the base start for Virtual Memory. To change the Virtual Memory, go to the Performance Property Page, select Change Button, and then select the drive for the Virtual Memory value. Performance is the best when the paging file is off the operating system drive.

2. **A, C, D, E** The Schedule service is used to work the with AT utility. The Task Scheduler starts each time Windows NT boots if this service is set to automatic. The `at` command schedules commands and programs to run on a computer at a specified time and date. The Schedule service must be running to use the `at` command. Note that in Control Panel, Services there are three options for startup: Disabled, Manual, and Automatic.

   The `at` command runs the command on every specified day(s) of the week or month (for example, every Thursday, or the third day of every month). Specify date as one or more days of the week (M,T,W,Th,F,S,Su) or one or more days of the month (using numbers 1 through 31). Separate multiple date entries with commas. If the date is omitted, the current day of the month is assumed.

   A. /next:date[,...]

   Runs the specified command on the next occurrence of the day (for example, next Thursday). Specify date as one or more days of the week (M,T,W,Th,F,S,Su) or one or more days of the month (using numbers 1 through 31). Separate multiple date entries with commas. If date is omitted, the current day of the month is assumed.

3. **D** By default under Windows NTFS, creating a new folder will assign the group Everyone full control access to that folder created. You must then reset the permissions for that folder if you want to reassign rights. You can view the properties content of the folder by right-clicking on it.

4. **D** When moving a file from NTFS (security based on Folder/File structure), the FAT file structure does not support advanced security indexes on each file/folder format. So, for example, if a file contained Change permissions, it will lose that file right attribute when copied to a FAT partition.

5. **A** The Home Directory is a place where users can save their data on the NT Server. Because the server is backed up from proper backup procedures, all the users' data are saved and organized.

6. **D** You can change the order of documents in the print queue only if you have Full Control access permissions. Members of the Administrators, Server Operators, Print Operators, or Power Users groups have Full Control permission by default. Priority 1 is the lowest, and priority 99 is the highest; you can control the priority by moving the slide bar from the property sheet of any print object by right-clicking on it.
7. **D** Backing up files to a device media, such as DAT system, and then restoring those files to a different path, verifies complete backup and restores functionality.
8. **D** Auditing is turned off by default under Windows NT. Only the Administrators (members of the Administrator group) can turn on Auditing. Auditing is activated through the User Manager for Domains, Policies menu. Auditing Events are placed in the Event Viewer, which is located in the Administrator Tools Group. With Event Viewer, you can troubleshoot various hardware and software problems. You can also use Event Viewer to monitor Windows NT Server security events, which are significant system or program problems about which users should be notified.
9. **D** Windows NT Primary Domain Controller contains the master database for all users groups. A read-only copy of the directory services database is replicated to all Backup Domain Controllers in the domain model. User Manager for Domains enables you to manage security for domains and computers. This includes creating and managing user accounts and groups, and managing the domain's security policies such as accounts (passwords), user rights, auditing, and trust relationships.
10. **E** You must select File and Object Access. This way you can track user access to a directory or a file on an NTFS partition that is set for directory or file auditing, and you can monitor files that are sent to printers when the printers are set for printer auditing.

    Audit Policy

    Selected activities of users can be tracked by auditing security events and then placing the entries in a computer's security log. Use the Audit policy to determine the types of security events that will be logged.

    When administering domains, the Audit policy affects the security logs of the domain controller and of all servers in the domain, because they share the same Audit policy.

    When administering a computer running Windows NT Workstation or a Windows NT Server that is not a domain controller (a member server), this policy affects only the security log of that computer.

    Because the security log is limited in size, carefully click on events to be logged. The maximum size of each computer's security log is defined in Event Viewer. Entries in a security log can be reviewed using Event Viewer. Managing your computer's security with User Manager for Domains enables you to manage security for domains and computers. This includes creating and managing user accounts and groups, and managing the domain's security policies such as accounts (passwords), user rights, auditing, and trust relationships.

11. **E** Windows NT BDC will not automatically promote itself to PDC status. You must go to the closest BDC and promote it to PDC in Server Manager Utility. You can use Server Manager to administer domains and computers. With Server Manager, you can display the member computers of a domain, manage server properties and services for a selected computer, share directories, and send messages to connected users.

    You can also use Server Manager to reassign a backup domain controller as the primary domain controller, synchronize computers with the primary domain controller, and add or remove computers in a domain.

12. **D** Global groups can cross trusted domains. A Global group can be imported to a Local group. By default, members of the Global group domain will be added to the Administrator Local group when the computer joins the Domain.

13. **A, D, E** With Directory Services, users can have a single logon to the domain model and have access to all resources assigned to them if the users are placed into groups. Directory Services also provides full centralized administration—up to 40,000 users.

14. **B** Using a domain model provides centralized security by requiring the users to be checked against a security system before being allowed into the Domain. If the user is not a member of the Domain, the user does not have access to resources. User Manager for Domains enables you to manage security for domains and computers. This includes creating and managing user accounts and groups, and managing the domain's security policies such as accounts (passwords), user rights, auditing, and trust relationships.

15. **A, E, F** User data is one of the most important pieces of data that should be backed up routinely, because workstations in an environment usually do not have backup devices attached. The SQL database is the heart of most businesses today. It usually contains the financial, accounting, payroll, and mission-critical data that must be backed up on a consistent basis. The Windows NT Registry database is the most important data in the operating system. The registry defines security, applications installed on your server, and users defined in the master database. The System Registry is the mission-critical system file of the Windows NT operating system.

16. **D** To send a message to all attached to a Windows NT Server, the Server Manager utility located in the Administrator Tools is the best method. You can use Server Manager to administer domains and computers. With Server Manager, you can display the member computers of a domain, manage server properties and services for a selected computer, share directories, and send messages to connected users.

    You can also use Server Manager to reassign a backup domain controller as the primary domain controller, synchronize computers with the primary domain controller, and add or remove computers in a domain.

17. **D** You can use Server Manager to administer domains and computers. With Server Manager, you can display the member computers of a domain,

manage server properties and services for a selected computer, share directories, and send messages to connected users.

18. **D** The driver is downloaded automatically when the user accesses the shared printer on the network (only if you specify all platforms the Print Server supports at the time you create the printer).

19. **B** Server Manager is used to administer domains and computers on your network. Server Manager can display the member computers of a domain, manage server properties and services for a selected computer, share directories, and send messages to connected users. You can also use Server Manager to reassign a backup domain controller as the primary domain controller, synchronize computers with the primary domain controller, and add or remove computers in a domain.

20. **B** The protocol that is used the most frequently on your network, in this case NWLink, should be bound first. The Windows NT Server can accept any protocol directed to it, but the Windows NT Workstation network performance is controlled by the Windows NT Workstation only.

21. **D** When installing the protocol TCP/IP, the IP address and the subnet mask parameters must be specified on the server.

22. **E** The Gateway Service for NetWare provides access to the NetWare 3.12 server for Workstations that are part of the Microsoft Network. Because these workstations do not have any NetWare client loaded, the Windows NT Server will automatically load NWLink protocol by default when Gateway Service for NetWare Service is loaded. Essentially, the NT Server mounts the Novel volume.

23. **D** When the workstation connects to the print server, the new updated driver will be copied automatically to each workstation without the user having to do an installation procedure.

24. **D** When you are in Real Mode (MS-DOS), you can run the WINNT.EXE command. This will start the installation process. If you are running the Windows NT 3.51 release, you can use the WINNT32.EXE command for an upgrade. (Installation and Configuration.)

25. **E** The DEVICE.LOG file is located in the WINNT\SYSTEM32\RAS directory. This log traps sessions between the Modem and RAS services.

26. **E** RAID 0 is disk striping without parity. This serves as a performance gain by moving data across two drives at the same time. In this case, RAID 0 does not offer fault tolerance. By defining the two separate physical drives with Disk Administrator, such as Device 0 and Device 1, each drive is striped.

27. **A, C, E** You must install the drivers for all new hardware to be recognized in Windows NT. After the drivers are loaded into memory, you must reboot the server to update the HKEY_LOCAL_MACHINE registry database.

28. **C** Maximize throughput for network applications is used for databases that use memory-caching in their programs.

29. **C, D, E** Fault tolerance is supported by disk mirroring (two separate physical drives); disk duplexing (two separate physical drives and two separate controllers); and RAID 5, which is disk striping with parity (at least three physical drives).
30. **E** After installing the new device driver, select Last Known Good by pressing the spacebar at boot up. This will load the original Current Control Set Registry Driver database and recover the system.
31. **F** You can convert FAT into NTFS format by going to a CMD prompt and typing **Convert C: /FS:NTFS /V**. (/FS represents File System; NTFS represents NTFS file format; and /V represents Verbose Mode.)
32. **A, B, C** You can use a Null Modem cable to test and stimulate a RAS server locally by using RS232 signaling. Null Modem cable can attach two workstations on two different networks by using the COM ports as the medium of transfer. Frame relay is a packet switch service that does not provide for error detection and correction, which results in minimal routing delays.
33. **G** You must have two drives and any combination of two controllers that support different technologies; for example, drive one can be attached to IDE controller, whereas drive two can be attached to a SCSI controller. It is recommended to have both controllers of the same technology.
34. **E** TCP/IP is the protocol that is routable and is the de facto protocol used on the Internet.
35. **F** To have a printer pool, all devices must be connected to the same Windows NT print server
36. **E** Modify the spooler folder to the new hard drive by editing the key entry DefaultSpoolDirectory from C:\winnt\system32\spool\printers to D:\winnt\system32\spool\printers.
37. **G** PPTP is Point to Point Tunneling Protocol that provides security over the Internet into Windows NT RAS server.
38. **C** Disk Mirroring (RAID 1) supports both system partition and boot partition information.
39. **E** You cannot delete the system partition that contains Windows NT files. You can, however, delete other partitions—this should be done with extreme caution.
40. **E** WINNT.EXE is the format used to make the SETUP disks. This format is used in REAL MODE—MS-DOS, Windows 3.x, or Windows 95, for example. When used with the /ox switch, you can create all three boot disks without installing any other Windows NT source files. You can also create boot disks while running Windows NT by using the WINNT32 /ox switch.
41. **E** When scripts are located in a subdirectory under the Exports directory all files are replicated to all Import Servers, such as Backup Domain Controllers. In the case of a failed PDC, the BDC will authenticate and process any logon scripts to the users due to the replication that takes place from PDC to BDC.
42. **D** You can convert from FAT to NTFS, but you cannot convert from NTFS to FAT without reformatting the disk. This is a one-way process only.

43. **E** With a incorrect print driver installed, the document spooling to the print device can be distorted. This is especially true for Post Script drivers that are installed incorrectly.

44. **C** The initial page file is 12 plus the amount of physical memory that is installed on the server. For example, if the Windows NT Server has 64 MB of RAM, the initial page file is 64 MB plus 12, which equals 76 MB.

45. **D** All three protocols are supported by both dial-in and dial-out services under Windows NT RAS.

46. **B** and **C** The configurations that enable user authentication are a PDC and a BDC controller.

47. **D, E** The percentage of elapsed time a processor spends executing a non-idle thread is measured by the %Processor Time Counter. The number of processors contributing to the processor's usage can be found by evaluating the System Object Queue Length counter. If the processor is over 80% and the System Object Queue Length is greater than the value of 2, a much faster CPU would be recommended. Windows 95 can use dialup networking to be authenticated by a Domain Controller just like NT RAS for a Windows NT Workstation, by asynchronous connection, but without NIC cards.

48. **B, C** Just remember that a null modem cable is really RS232C cable. You can test a Windows NT Workstation connection to the Windows NT RAS Server without any modems involved by using the null modem cable assembly.

49. **E** TCP/IP is a routable protocol that can pass through the routers by configuring TCP/IP to route. All UNIX systems use TCP/IP protocol as a de facto because it is the primary protocol used in the Internet.

50. **D** You can create user accounts when you are a member of the Account Operator Local group, but more importantly, you cannot assign user rights.

51. **F** When you create a separate hardware profile using Control Panel, System Properties, and choosing Hardware Profiles Property page, you can set what drivers can be loaded from mobile (home) to permanent (docking station at work). After the Windows NT Workstation boots, you must select the spacebar to invoke a different hardware profile.

52. **E** Map the physical port using the following syntax: net use LPTx: \\server \name\print_share name.

53. **E** Frame mismatches can cause this error. For example, if the frame is set to 802.2 and you have another workstation configured to use frame 802.3, the frame type structure headers are different. This mismatching means you can't see the frame from the Data Link Layer or the Data Packet.

54. **C** When you have 10 network connections or fewer, the best optimization would be set to Minimize Memory Used.

55. **C** You must manually add IP addresses to a router because it is static, not dynamic, such as DHCP. The address range from segment #1 matches 150.50.0.x and segment #2 matches 150.51.0.x on the other segment. This will bridge the two segments together.

56. **D** FAT supports both Windows 95 and Windows NT 4.0 Workstation

for LFN support. FAT32 is not supported by the Windows NT 4.0 product line.

57. **E** Last Known Good selects the last configuration database from the registry database (a copy of the most recent registry that successfully booted Windows NT).

58. **H** The Windows NT Workstation will broadcast a request to any DHCP server when 87.5% of the lease time has expired (or again at reboot).

59. **E** Any print jobs that are delayed will be stored in the print spooler.

60. **E** The TCP/IP performance counters become available for monitoring when the SNMP Service is installed on the machine you're monitoring.

61. **E** When you leave a floppy disk in the floppy drive system, most computers look into the drive first before booting to the C drive, by default. When Windows NT reboots, the NTLDR file cannot be located from the master boot device (usually the C drive), by default.

62. **B** As long there is an account setup in the domain, a user can join that domain from his workstation by using the settings in Network option and changing the Domain setting within the Control Panel environment.

63. **E, F, G, I** When SCSI is used and the BIOS are disabled, remember to include BOOTSECT.DOS driver.

64. **A, E** When running CSNW, NWLink protocol must be configured to talk IPX to the NetWare server. To gain access inside the NetWare server, a user account also must be created.

65. **E** MS-CHAP, which is RSA Message Digest 4 or RSA MD4, uses the RC4 algorithm and supports the DOD DES encryption. It will encrypt all data structures (including passwords) that are processed during a RAS session connection.

66. **B** When running Windows NT 3.51, you must execute the WINNT32 executable because it runs a 32-bit run code for the upgrade. The best choice is to run it unattended by WINNT32.EXE /U from the NT 4.0 CD-ROM \i386.

67. **C** For the best performance in static name resolution for a Windows NT RAS Server and Windows NT RAS Clients, place both files on the RAS Clients' local cache hard drives. This eliminates traffic by name resolution requests with the WINS server. The LMHOST file is a local text file that maps IP addresses to the computer names of Windows NT networking computers outside the local subnet. In Windows NT, this file is stored in the \systemroot \System32\Drivers\Etc directory.

Practice Exam 2

Implementing and Supporting Microsoft Windows NT Server 4.0

NT Server exam instructions:

You have 90 minutes to complete 55 questions. There will be two types of questions:

- Multiple Choice—Select the correct answer.
- Multiple Multiple Choice—Select all answers that are correct.

The answers and explanations follow the actual test and include the objective covered in the question. We suggest that you set a timer to track your progress while taking the practice exam, as the time-constraint on the tests is often a big obstacle to overcome. Begin after you set your time.

Practice Exam Begins

1. Jeff is logged in as the local administrator on his NT workstation computer. He needs to have his computer joined to the domain Developers. How can Jeff join his computer to the Developers Domain? Choose all that apply:
   A. The domain administrator for Developers can add Jeff's workstation on the PDC. Then, Jeff can join the domain in the Network option of Control Panel.
   B. Jeff can add his computer to the domain using Server Manager and his administrator password.
   C. The domain administrator can add Jeff to the domain Developers by using the Network option on the PDC.
   D. The administrator of the Developers domain can add Jeff's machine to the domain by using the Network option in Control Panel on Jeff's machine after supplying the domain administrator username and password.

2. You want to change a member server on your domain to a BDC. What is the correct procedure to do so? Choose one:
   A. Promote the member server to a BDC.
   B. Copy the user accounts database to the member server so that it can validate users.
   C. Reinstall the member server as a BDC.
   D. Use the services option in Control Panel to start the BDC service for the member server.
3. Increasing the Pulse registry entry on the PDC does what? Choose one:
   A. Frees memory on the PDC for use by other processes.
   B. Decreases the frequency that BDCs are synchronized, freeing processor time on the PDC.
   C. Increases communication with the BDCs, causing domain information to be updated more frequently.
   D. Increases the number of BDCs allowed on the Domain.
4. The developers department has hired a new user named Mary. You would like to add a user account for Mary with the same attributes as an existing worker in the department. Using User Manager for Domains, what procedure would you follow? Choose one:
   A. Select the existing user and choose New User from the user pulldown.
   B. Create a new user for Mary, and then copy the existing user's profile to Mary's account.
   C. Create a new user, and then use Edit, Copy Permissions to copy the existing user's permissions.
   D. Select the existing user's account and choose User, Copy.
5. You have created roaming profiles for users in your domain. Your coworkers suggest that you rename the NTUser.dat to NTUser.man. What will this accomplish? Choose one:
   A. This enables users to choose whether or not to run the profile at login.
   B. This has no affect on the profile.
   C. This enables the user to change the profile.
   D. This keeps the user from saving any changes to the profile.
6. The users in your domain would like to be able to log in at any workstation while retaining desktop attributes specific to each user. How would you implement this? Choose one:
   A. As long as the users are logging onto the domain at each workstation, their individual profiles will be used by default.
   B. Use the User Manager for Domains to specify the full UNC profile path for each user.
   C. A copy of each user's profile must be placed on the NETLOGON share.
   D. Set up replication to copy all user profiles to each machine.
7. Where would you look to find out why RAS connections from many different users to your NT Server are being dropped after users have been connected for various amounts of time? Choose one:
   A. The device.log.
   B. Use the administrative tools Event Viewer on the RAS Server.
   C. The ras.log.
   D. The remote machine's Event Viewer.

8. Which of the following statements are true of PPP (Point-to-Point Protocol)? Choose all that apply:
   A. Built-in error correction
   B. Built-in password encryption
   C. Used by RAS clients only
   D. Supports secure authentication
9. The development department in your company will share a single new server with one large capacity hard drive. This department is divided into five groups. The managers of these groups have asked you to create separate locations on the hard drive that will have controlled access for each group. Which of the following methods can you use? Choose one:
   A. Create a single primary partition with directories for each group. Share the directories with appropriate permissions for each group.
   B. Create five separate Extended partitions, one for each group. Share each partition with the appropriate permissions.
   C. Create five separate primary partitions shared with the appropriate permissions for each group. Additionally, create one primary partition for the operating system.
   D. Create a single primary partition and subdivide it into five smaller logical drives.
10. Which statements are true of a FAT file system under Windows NT? Choose all that apply:
   A. You can use filenames up to 255 characters.
   B. FAT is generally slower than NTFS.
   C. The maximum file, directory, or partition size under FAT is 2 GB.
   D. FAT does not offer the security features offered by NTFS.
11. Your company needs to implement a fault-tolerance method for the PDC that currently contains one 4 GB hard drive. You have decided that 8 GB of data storage is necessary. Your co-worker suggests that you implement RAID Level 5 (Disk Stripping.) Select the true statements regarding this plan. Choose all that apply:
   A. This will be more efficient than disk mirroring (RAID Level 1).
   B. The more disks you use, the more efficient RAID Level 5 becomes.
   C. A minimum of three partitions will be needed to implement this plan.
   D. In the case of a disk failure, this plan will recover lost data faster than RAID Level 1.
12. Which of the following is not true of TCP/IP? Choose all that apply:
   A. It is routable.
   B. It is a widely accepted standard.
   C. It provides compatibility with Novel NetWare IPX/SPX networks.
   D. It was designed for Microsoft Networks.
13. Which of the following are not one of the eight default Windows NT domain local groups? Choose all that apply:
   A. Administrators
   B. Users
   C. Backup Operators
   D. Power Users
   E. Replicator

14. Which of the following are true of the Guest account? Choose all that apply:
    A. It is permanent.
    B. Its group memberships can be changed.
    C. It can be disabled.
    D. It inherently has restricted permissions.
15. Your company has hired some temporary employees. You would like to allow them some access to the domain, yet you want them to be able to log on only at a single machine. How would you accomplish this? Choose one:
    A. Using User Manager for Domains, add a new user. Use the Logon To option to specify the computer.
    B. Add the user locally to the workstation that you want them to be able to log on to.
    C. Under user manager for domains, add a new user, and then use the permission pulldown to restrict access to a single machine.
    D. Add the user locally to the workstation you would like them to be able to log on to. Then add this user to the domain's Guest group.
16. Which of the following statements are not true about ACLs (Access Control Lists) in an NTFS file or folder? Choose all that apply:
    A. They are retained after backup/restore to any NTFS volume.
    B. They are retained when moved to the same volume.
    C. They are retained when copied to any other NTFS folder or volume.
    D. They are retained when moved to another NTFS volume.
17. Martha would like to know if she can access the share "info" from your Server. Martha is a member of the global Software group and the global Software Engineers group. Software is a member of your local Reviewers group. Software Engineers group is a member of your local Testers group.

    The "info" share on your server grants the Reviewers group Read and the Testers group Change access. The NTFS permissions in this share grant the Testers group Read and the Reviewers group Full Control access. What access will Martha have to this share? Choose one:
    A. Read and Change
    B. Read and Full Control
    C. Read
    D. Full Control
    E. Change
18. Which of the following can be configured through Scope Options of DHCP? Choose all that apply:
    A. Default gateway
    B. WINS server address
    C. WINS node type
    D. DNS server address
    E. DNS domain name
19. What attributes are true for NetBEUI? Choose all that apply:
    A. Fast for small networks
    B. Easy to administer
    C. Routable
    D. Frequent Broadcasts

20. You have a group of NT Workstations that need to be able to access files on a NetWare server. You would like to set up a gateway via an NTServer. Which of the following steps are necessary on the NetWare Server? Choose all that apply:

    A. Create a user account for the NT Server's gateway service.

    B. Put the user account in a group called NTGateway on the NetWare Server.

    C. Assign Trustee Rights to the previously mentioned accounts.

    D. Put the Gateway Service Account in a group called NWLINK.

21. Your company's support department has 10 users. They have a computer running NT Server that has been optimized for its current workload. The department is adding 15 users over the next month. What server setting should you configure to keep the machine optimized for the new number of users? Choose one:

    A. Virtual Memory

    B. Foreground and Background Task Balance

    C. Workstation service

    D. Server service

22. What is true of a hardware-based security host? Choose all that apply:

    A. It sits between the RAS server and modem.

    B. It provides encryption.

    C. It adds a layer of password protection.

    D. It requires two or more data lines.

23. You have a RAS Server that will be used by employees using a PPP client. This client supports CHAP encryption for logon authentication only. You want to provide the highest level of security possible. What type of authentication should you use? Choose one:

    A. Clear text

    B. Microsoft Encrypted Authentication

    C. Data Encryption

    D. PAP encryption

24. You would like to use DHCP to configure TCP/IP settings on your remote clients. Which of the following configuration settings cannot be set on your remote clients that are using RAS to connect? Choose all that apply:

    A. DNS Server address

    B. Default Gateway address

    C. WINS server address

    D. IP address

    E. Default WWW server address

25. What location should you place your system policy, config.pol, and logon scripts on your Windows NT workstation to have them replicated to your Window NT Server machine? Choose one:

    A. NT workstation cannot be used as an export replication machine.

    B. The files must be placed in the Replication share on your NT Workstation computer.

    C. The files should be placed in the %systemroot%\system32\repl\export directory.

    D. The files should be placed in the %systemrrot%\system32\repl\exports\scripts directory.

26. Your Software department has just purchased a new computer that they would like to use to store source code. They would like to make the computer fault-tolerant. What are the minimum disk requirements? Choose one:
    A. Two disk drives with one controller
    B. Two disk drives with two controllers
    C. Three disk drives with one controller
    D. Three disk drives with three controllers
27. What fault-tolerant levels of RAID are standard with Windows NT Server? Choose all that apply:
    A. 5
    B. 4
    C. 3
    D. 2
    E. 1
28. Your company has four servers (one PDC and three BDCs). You also have NT Workstation 3.51, NT Workstation 4.0, and Windows 95 clients. You will configure one of the servers as a print server. On which machines will you need to load the appropriate drivers? Choose one:
    A. The Print Server and the Windows 95 clients
    B. The PDC only
    C. The Print server only
    D. The PDCs and the BDCs
    E. The PDC and the Print Server (if they are not the same machine)
29. In order to establish a printer pool, you must do what? Choose all that apply:
    A. Configure the printers with the appropriate driver.
    B. Select "Enable Print Pooling."
    C. Configure all printers in the pool with the same name.
    D. Add a "Pooled" port.
    E. Connect all the printers to the same port.
30. Which of the following clients cannot download print drivers from an NT 4.0 print server? Choose all that apply:
    A. Windows for Workgroups
    B. Windows 95
    C. Windows NT 3.51 Server
    D. Windows NT 4.0 Workstation
    E. Windows NT 4.0 Server
31. Your support department has just purchased a new machine to use as an application server. They will use the hard drive from the old server for the system and boot drive, plus they have budgeted to purchase some additional hardware. How would you suggest they spend their money and configure the server for maximum performance in disk I/O? Choose one:
    A. Buy as many drives as needed to support their needs and set up a Stripe set.
    B. Set up as many mirrored sets (with one controller per set) as needed to meet their requirements.
    C. Buy as many drives as needed and set up a Stripe set with parity.
    D. Purchase multiple drives, each with its own controller, to set up a Stripe set.

32. Which of the following are true for point-to-point Tunneling Protocol? Choose all that apply:
    A. It uses the Internet for connections.
    B. It has lower hardware costs than other network solutions.
    C. It provides security.
    D. It has high transmission costs.
    E. It has higher administration costs compared to other protocols.
33. Which statements about NTFS are true? Choose all that apply:
    A. NTFS is the only file system for NT that can support filenames over 8.3.
    B. NTFS can easily be converted to FAT.
    C. NTFS is the most commonly supported file system.
    D. NTFS has less overhead than FAT.
    E. None of the above.
34. Which protocols can be used by Windows NT Server for Remote Access Service? Choose all that apply:
    A. TCP/IP
    B. NetBEUI
    C. IPX
    D. SNMP
35. Jim, who is currently a member of the support group, calls to request access to the Accounting Group share. You add him to the Accounting Group, which currently has Change access to this share. Jim calls back an hour later complaining that he still cannot access the Accounting share. Which option might fix the problem? Choose one:
    A. Wait until synchronization has occurred.
    B. Have Jim log off and then log back on.
    C. The next time the PDC is rebooted, the access permission will be correct.
    D. Wait until directory replication occurs.
36. Your company has purchased several 4 GB drives for setting up servers throughout your building. The Marketing department needs fault-tolerant data storage of at least 12 GB. Excluding space for Boot and System partitions, what is the minimum number of drives the Marketing department must have in its server in order to set up RAID 5 and still meet the 12 GB minimum requirement? Choose one:
    A. 2
    B. 3
    C. 4
    D. 5
    E. 6
37. By creating a paging file on each physical disk, you will:
    A. Improve overall performance, because more than one disk I/O can be performed simultaneously.
    B. Be able to use less disk space for the paging file.
    C. Make it easier to convert to RAID 5 if you need to do so later.
    D. Degrade overall performance.
38. Which of the following cannot be implemented using a DHCP server? Choose all that apply:
    A. IP addresses
    B. DNS server address
    C. WINS server address
    D. Profile path
    E. NetBios name resolution type

39. The administrator of the domain XYZ has noticed problems with the application server's performance. The administrator suspects that the processor needs to be upgraded. Using Performance Monitor, which counter values would prove the suspicions about the processor activity being too high? Choose two:
    A. System Object processor Queue length < 2
    B. System Object processor Queue length > 2
    C. % Processor Time = 1%
    D. % Processor Time = 99%
40. You have a NetWare 4.X network to which you would like to add a Windows NT server to utilize as an application server. In order to do this, you must install what to enable your NetWare Clients to access applications on your server? Choose one:
    A. TCP/IP protocol
    B. The NWLink protocol
    C. IPX Service
    D. Gateway Services for NetWare
41. You are considering converting all of your existing NetWare clients to NT. If you decide not to convert them, what must be done to each NetWare client PC so that they can connect to the NT Servers? Choose one:
    A. Install Gateway Services for NetWare on the NT Server.
    B. Install Gateway and Client Services for NetWare on the NT Server.
    C. Install file and print services for NetWare on each client.
    D. Install a Microsoft Redirector on each client.
42. You would like to have DHCP broadcast across two subnets. Which service is required on an NT Server in order to accomplish this? Choose one:
    A. Gateway Services for DHCP
    B. DHCP relay agent
    C. RIP for TCP/IP
    D. BOOTP
43. You would like to migrate all of your NetWare Clients to Windows NT by using the Migration Tool for NetWare. What needs to be loaded on the NT Server in order to complete the migration? Choose one:
    A. File and print services for NetWare
    B. Directory Replicator for NetWare
    C. Gateway Services for NetWare
    D. RIP for NetWare
44. You would like to upgrade NT Server from 3.51 to 4.0 from a distribution share on the network. Which command line would you execute in order to perform a floppyless upgrade while running NT 3.51? Choose one:
    A. winnt.exe /F
    B. setup.exe
    C. winnt32.exe /F
    D. winnt32.exe /B
45. You currently have 1,000 domain users that are complaining about logons being too slow. You notice that the Logons/sec counter in performance monitor is high. What can be done to speed up the time it takes to log on to the Domain? Choose one:
    A. Add another PDC.
    B. Increase the Logon Concurrency entry in the registry.

C. Increase the Pulse Concurrency entry in the registry.

D. Add another BDC.

46. You have an NT Server with two physical drives. Currently, the system and boot files are on the first drive and the page file is on the second. By splitting the page file between the two drives, what benefits will you receive? Choose all that apply:

A. You will get better performance.

B. You will get a crash dump file if the system fails.

C. You will get fault tolerance.

D. You will decrease page swapping.

47. You are attempting to figure out the best time to schedule your weekly backups for the NT Servers on your network. How can you gather this information? Choose one:

A. Review the Event Log.

B. Use the Chart option Performance Monitor.

C. Use the Log option in Performance Monitor.

D. Review the System Load log.

48. When repairing a damaged Windows NT installation, the repair option "Verify Windows NT System files" does what? Choose one:

A. It prompts for replacement of each Registry file.

B. It verifies that NT is an option in boot.ini.

C. It replaces files such as NTLDR and NTOSKRNL.EXE.

D. It verifies and/or fixes boot sector and NTLDR.

49. Using the NTBackup utility, which of the following options must be selected in order to perform a successful backup of the local registry on an NT Server? Choose all that apply:

A. Select the local drive to backup.

B. Select the "Backup Local Registry" check box.

C. Select the "Registry" check box.

D. Select the directory that contains the registry.

50. You currently have an NT server running virus scan software that automatically detects and cleans viruses. You accidentally left a floppy in the server while rebooting it. After the server comes back up, a virus alert pops up notifying you that,the server was infected with a boot sector virus and the contents of the boot sector have been cleaned to remove the virus. The next time the server is restarted, the server will not boot successfully because it cannot find the operating system. What steps need to be taken in order to fix the problem? Choose one:

A. Boot from the emergency repair disk and restore the boot partition.

B. Boot the server with the Windows NT installation disks and use Server Manager to restore the boot partition.

C. Boot the server with the Windows NT installation disks and use the emergency repair disks to restore the boot partition.

D. Boot the system using an NT boot disk and use the emergency repair disk to restore the boot partition.

51. You have a total of five hard disks in your NT Server. The first disk contains the boot and system partitions. The remaining four disks are configured as a stripe set with parity containing user data files. The first disk fails and needs to be replaced. What step must you take in order to recover from this failure? Choose one:

    A. Re-install NT Server to disk one.

    B. You need to recover all five disks from tape backup.

    C. Re-install NT Server to disk one, and then restore the other four disks from tape backup.

    D. Re-install NT Server to disk one and then restore the registry information tape backup.

52. You have installed a new video card in your NT Server because the old one has failed. The new video card is from a different vendor. What must be done to get the NT Server working with the new video card? Choose one:

    A. Boot with the three NT Installation disks and then load the driver for the new video card.

    B. Boot with the three NT Installation disks and then perform an emergency repair to change the video driver to Standard VGA.

    C. Choose the VGA option for Windows NT Server during the boot process. After the system comes up, install the driver for the new video card.

    D. Install the new driver.

53. The system partition in your server has just failed. Fortunately, the system partition was part of a mirror set. So, now all you have to do is create a fault-tolerant boot disk so that you can boot the system into Windows NT from the mirrored partition. Both the physical disks are SCSI without the SCSI BIOS enabled. They are both connected to the same SCSI controller card. Which ARC name should be used in the boot.ini file on the boot disk to ensure that the disk boots the server successfully into Windows NT? Choose one:

    A. scsi(0)disk(0)rdisk(0)partition(1)

    B. multi(0)disk(1)
    rdisk(0)partition(1)

    C. scsi(0)disk(1)rdisk(0)partition(1)

    D. multi(0)disk(0)
    rdisk(0)partition(1)

54. Which of the following statements are true of disk striping with parity? Choose all that apply:

    A. Striping requires less disk overhead than mirroring.

    B. Striping has better read performance than mirroring.

    C. Striping supports up to 32 hard disks.

    D. Striping requires two hard disks.

55. You have the memory.dmp file that your NT Server created after a system failure. What utility can you use to decode the data in that file? Choose one:

    A. dumpexam.exe

    B. rdisk.exe

    C. dumpflop.exe

    D. dumpchk.exe

Answers and Explanations

1. **A, D** Only domain administrators have the ability to add a computer to a domain. After this has been done, a local administrator can join a machine to the domain, as in answer A. In answer D, the machine is added and joined in a single step. (Installation and Configuration.)

2. **C** The only way to create a BDC is during installation of NT server. A member server can never be promoted to a BDC. (Installation and Configuration.)
3. **B** The Pulse registry entry controls the amount of time between synchronization of the BDCs and the PDC on the domain. Increasing this time decreases the workload on the PDC. (Monitoring and Optimization.)
4. **D** Copying an existing account enables the creation of a new user with identical attributes. (Managing Resources.)
5. **D** The .man extension on a profile makes it unchangeable by the user. (Managing Resources.)
6. **B** The profile path can be set only in the User Manager for Domains, and it must be a full UNC path in order to be accessed from any machine. (Managing Resources.)
7. **A** Device errors, such as modem errors, are written to the device.log file. Because multiple users are having the same problem, the problem is likely to be on the server end. (Troubleshooting.)
8. **A, B, D** PPP can be used by RAS Clients and Servers. (Connectivity.)
9. **A** B is incorrect because only one extended partition can reside on a hard drive. C is incorrect because a hard drive can contain only four primary partitions. B is incorrect because primary partitions cannot be divided into logical drives. (Planning.)
10. **A, B, D** The maximum file, directory, or partition size under FAT is 4 GB. (Planning.)
11. **A, B, C** is incorrect because you need to have at least one additional partition for the boot and system partition. D is incorrect because RAID Level 5 needs to regenerate missing data, whereas RAID Level 1 has a complete copy of missing data. (Planning.)
12. **A, B** NWLink is required for Novel compatibility, and NetBEUI was designed for Microsoft Networks. (Connectivity.)
13. **D** Default NT domain local groups are Administrators, Users, Guests, Backup Operators, Replicator, Print Operators, Server Operators. (Managing Resources.)
14. **A, B, C** The Guest account has no inherent power or lack of power. Group membership for the account establishes its scope. (Managing Resources.)
15. **A** By default, a domain user has the capability to log on to all domain machines. The Logon To option in User Manager for Domains gives you the ability to restrict user accounts to certain machines. (Managing Resources.)
16. **C, D** In both cases, the ACLs are inherited from the destination folder. (Planning.)
17. **E** The files have Full Control privilege on NTFS because multiple privileges will result in the least restrictive privileges. The share will have Change privileges for the same reason. When calculating the result between the share and the file privileges, the most restrictive privilege is used, which in this case is Change. (Managing Resources.)

18. **A, B, C, D, E** All these options are configurable under the Scope option of DHCP. (Connectivity.)
19. **A, B, D** NetBEUI is not routable. (Connectivity.)
20. **A, B, C** These three are the only steps that need to be performed on the NetWare server in order to set up a gateway via an NT Server. (Connectivity.)
21. **D** The Server services can be set to Balance, which is optimal for up to 64 connections.(Monitoring and Optimization.)
22. **A, C** A hardware-based security host requires only the normal communication lines set up for RAS communication, and it does not supply encryption. (Connectivity.)
23. **B** This is the most secure encryption and it supports CHAP. (Connectivity.)
24. **E** The following addresses can be assigned through DHCP to RAS clients: IP Address, Default Gateway Address, WINS Server Address, WINS Node Type, DNS Server Address, and DNS Domain Names. (Connectivity.)
25. **A** Only NT server can be used as an export replication machine. (Installation and Configuration.)
26. **A** Disk mirroring (RAID 1) requires only two drives and a single controller. (Planning.)
27. **A, E** The following levels of RAID are options under NT: RAID 0 (Striping), RAID 1 (Mirroring/ Duplexing), and RAID 5 (Striping with Parity). (Planning.)
28. **C** Each machine will load the appropriate drivers from the print server as needed. (Installation and Configuration.)
29. **A, B** All printers in a Printer Pool must be able to utilize the same printer driver. "Enable Print Pooling" must be selected on the print server. (Installation and Configuration.)
30. **A** All Microsoft clients except for WFW clients can download drivers from 4.0 print servers. (Installation and Configuration.)
31. **D** Stripe sets with multiple controllers allow concurrent I/O request, dramatically improving performance. (Planning.)
32. **A, B, C** PPP uses the Internet for connections, is less expensive when compared to other network solutions, and requires higher administrative costs. (Connectivity.)
33. **E** FAT file systems under NT can support long filenames. NTFS can not be converted to FAT. NTFS is only usable by Windows NT, and it uses more overhead than FAT. (Planning.)
34. **A, B, C** The following protocols can be used with RAS: Netbeui, TCP/IP, and IPX. (Connectivity.)
35. **B** Permissions are contained in the user's access token. This token is generated when the user logs on. Jim will have access to the Accounting share the next time he logs on. (Troubleshooting.)
36. **C** The formula for % of disk space available is *(no. of disks –1)/no. of disks × 100%.* In this case, (4–1)/4 ×100% = 75%. 75% of the total disk space, 16 GB (4 disks × 4 GB), is 12 GB. (Planning.)
37. **A** When a page file is split between physical disks, performance is improved because disk I/O is shared between the separate disks. (Monitoring and Optimization.)

38. **D** These options can be configured using the Defaults, Global, and Scope options on the DHCP server. (Connectivity.)

39. **B, D** The System Object processor Queue length should always be two or less, and the 99% Processor time shows that the processor is loaded so much that it has no free time while tasks are waiting. (Monitoring and Optimization.)

40. **B** NWLink protocol must be loaded on any NT server for NetWare Clients to access it. (Connectivity.)

41. **D** Microsoft Redirector is all that the client PCs need in order to communicate with the NT Server. (Connectivity.)

42. **B** DHCP Relay Agent allows DHCP to broadcast over multiple subnets. (Installation and Configuration.)

43. **C** Gateway Services for NetWare enable workstations connected to your NT Server to also access NetWare drives. (Connectivity.)

44. **D** Winnt32.exe is the 32-bit installation program for NT. The /B parameter invokes a floppyless install. (Installation and Configuration.)

45. **D** One way to speed up the logon process is to add another BDC. When the PDC is busy, the logons will be validated by any available BDC. (*Note* Another method is to make sure that the PDC Server service is optimized for Network Applications. This increases logons from 6-7 per second to around 20 per second.) (Monitoring and Optimization.)

46. **A, B** You will get some performance increase because you will be able to do concurrent reads from the page file. When any part of the page file exists on the system drive, a system failure will generate a crash dump file. (Monitoring and Optimization.)

47. **C** The logging option of the performance monitor will save information over long periods of time that can reviewed later. (Monitoring and Optimization.)

48. **C** All the other answers are tasks performed by other valid installation repair options, but C is the task performed for "Verify Windows NT System files" for repairing the NT system boot files. (Troubleshooting.)

49. **A, B, D** The local drive and directory that contains the registry must be selected along with the "backup local registry" check box. If you do not choose any one of those options, the registry backup will fail. (Installation and Configuration.)

50. **C** The windows NT installation disks must be loaded first in order to repair anything from the emergency repair disk. (Troubleshooting.)

51. **D** NT server will need to be installed to disk one and the registry will need to be recovered in order to recover the shares on the user data files that reside on the remaining four disks. (Troubleshooting.)

52. **C** The VGA option for Windows NT is added by default to the boot.ini file during the installation of NT. This option is used for troubleshooting video problems with NT. (Troubleshooting.)

53. **C** SCSI represents a disk on which SCSI BIOS is not enabled, and MULTI represents a disk other than SCSI or a SCSI accessed by the SCSI BIOS. DISK indicates the hard drive of the controller that you are using. RDISK is ignored for SCSI controllers and represents the ordinal number of the disk you are using. PARTITION refers to the partition number and is always assigned beginning with the number 1. SCSI/MULTI, DISK, and RDISK all begin with the number 0. (Troubleshooting.)
54. **A, B, C** If you have four hard drives, mirroring utilizes only 50% of disk space and striping would utilize 75%. With disk striping, data is split over multiple drives and can be read simultaneously. Disk striping supports from three to 32 harddisks. (Planning.)
55. **A** DUMPEXAM.EXE writes information from the dump file to a text file so that you can find out what caused the system failure. (Troubleshooting.)

Practice Exam 3

Implementing and Supporting Windows NT Server 4.0 in the Enterprise

The Windows NT Server Enterprise exam is an adaptive test—meaning that the number of questions you must answer is indeterminate. The following describes how an adaptive test works:

- The test covers six categories: Planning, Installation and Configuration, Managing Resources, Connectivity, Monitoring and Optimization, and Troubleshooting. Test questions are associated with these categories.
- The testing system asks an extremely difficult question for one of the five test categories. If you answer correctly, the testing system asks you a few easier questions to pass the category.

  If you answer incorrectly, the testing system presents you with at least one less difficult question for the category. If you continue to incorrectly answer questions for the category, the questions become increasingly less difficult until the testing system determines that you do not have sufficient knowledge to pass the category.

  If you finally answer a question correctly, the testing system asks increasingly difficult questions for the category until you correctly answer a certain number of questions (the number is unknown to you or me).

You are not asked the questions in order. The testing system presents questions for all six categories in a seemingly random order. The following are the two types of questions in the test:

- Multiple-choice questions—Select the correct answer.
- Scenario-based questions—Select the response or best scenario from the scenario description.

It is suggested that you set a timer to track your progress while taking the practice exam, because the time restrictions on the tests are often the biggest obstacles to overcome. Begin the following practice exam after you set your time.

Practice Exam Begins

Questions 1 and 2 are based on the following scenario:

Your company has chosen to replace its current network platform with Windows NT. The current network has 1600 users—21 file servers located at four wide-area sites.

Day-to-day business requires a substantial amount of file sharing and remote printing among sites.

To date, each site has its own information systems department that manages and supports all users and resources at the respective site. Your company has decided to maintain this network management structure.

1. What directory services architecture is the best choice for the new Windows NT network?
   A. Double domain
   B. Single master domain
   C. Single domain
   D. Complete trust domains

2. In addition to the 1600 users, it is estimated that the new Windows NT network requires 200 global groups, 55 local groups on domain controllers, and 1150 computer accounts. The average global group has 35 members and the average local group has five members. If all this information were installed in a single SAM database, approximately how large would the database be?
   A. 1 megabyte
   B. 2.45 megabytes
   C. 4.4 megabytes
   D. 700 kilobytes

3. A large number of your company's employees work at more than one of the wide-area sites that comprise the network. Generally, what directory services architecture is best suited for "traveling" users?
   A. Full-trust domains so that the traveling users can have a logon ID for each site and still access resources at other sites.
   B. Single domain so that each user has one logon ID, and all resources on the network are accessible.
   C. Full-trust domains so that the user has one logon ID and can use any local domain controller for the logon process.
   D. None of the above.

4. The Widget company network consists of three domains, DM_Sales, DM_Mfg, and DM_Admin. At present, the three domains do not share resources. Users in the DM_Sales domain need to access some resources that belong to the DM_Mfg domain. How would you enable access to the resources in DM_Mfg for users in DM_Sales?
   A. Establish a two-way trust relationship between DM_Mfg and DM_Sales.
   B. Configure DM_Mfg to trust DM_Sales.
   C. Configure DM_Mfg to trust DM_Sales and DM_Sales to allow DM_Mfg to trust DM_Sales.
   D. Set up user accounts in the DM_Mfg domain with the same username and password as the corresponding accounts in DM_Sales.

5. When a trust relationship is broken by a failed network connection, you can easily reestablish the trust relationship (after the network connection is restored) by which method?

   A. Rebooting the domain controllers.

   B. Reestablishing the network connection restores the trust relationship.

   C. Reestablishing the network connection and rebooting the Primary Domain Controller for each domain.

   D. Reestablishing the network connection, deleting the trust relationship in both domains, and creating a new trust relationship.

6. What are the limitations of local user accounts?

   A. They cannot be used to access resources across domains.

   B. Their passwords cannot be synchronized.

   C. They do not support the interactive logon process.

   D. All of the above.

7. Which of the following statements is true about the local Administrator account on a Windows NT domain controller?

   A. It cannot be deleted.

   B. It is by default a member of the local Server Operators group.

   C. It cannot be renamed.

   D. None of the above.

8. After a trust relationship has been established between two domains, users may access resources across domains because:

   A. Establishing the trust relationship merges the user account databases from the two domains.

   B. The logon services from the trusted domain pass the resource access request to the trusting domain's logon services, where the resource access permissions are authenticated.

   C. Duplicate logon IDs are created in the trusting domain's account database when you assign permissions.

   D. The trust relationship allows logon services from the trusting domain to access the trusted domain's account database.

9. Which RAID fault-tolerance levels are built in to Windows NT Server?

   A. Levels 1, 2, and 3

   B. Levels 1, 2, and 5

   C. Levels 0, 1, and 5

   D. All levels of RAID fault-tolerance

10. What is the maximum number of physical disks that Windows NT Server RAID fault-tolerance supports?

   A. There is no limit.

   B. 16

   C. 32

   D. 128

11. Which is the best Windows NT disk fault-tolerance configuration for read performance?
    A. RAID Level 1
    B. Disk mirroring
    C. Disk striping
    D. Disk striping with parity

12. What is the method by which Windows NT Server protects against writing data to a bad sector on its fault-tolerant volume of a hard disk?
    A. RAID Level 5
    B. Hot swapping
    C. Sector sparing
    D. Hot fixing

13. What is one reason why TCP/IP is the protocol of choice for most networks?
    A. It allows connectivity between dissimilar networks and devices.
    B. TCP/IP is more easily installed and configured than other protocols.
    C. It is a *self-encrypting* protocol that provides secure communications.
    D. All the above.

14. If you shut down a Windows NT Server that is a master browser, you must:
    A. Do nothing; the network will elect a new master browser when the time limit on the downed browser expires.
    B. Promote a domain controller to master browser.
    C. Manually trigger a WINS replication for the entire network.
    D. None of the above.

15. What switch is used with the Windows NT Server installation program to suppress the creation of floppy startup disks?
    A. /B
    B. /N
    C. /NOBOOT
    D. /SI

16. To promote a member Windows NT Server to domain controller, you must:
    A. Select the Domain Controller option from Add/Remove software in the Control Panel.
    B. Run the Windows NT installation program using the /DC switch.
    C. Reinstall the server and configure it as a domain controller during installation.
    D. Promote the server to domain controller using Server Manager.

17. You are the network administrator for a small network that consists of 12 workstations and a single Windows NT Server. Your boss asks you to set up an intranet web site. What is required to install Internet Information Server?
    A. Purchase Internet Information Server and install it on the current server.
    B. Install Internet Information Server from the Windows NT Server CD-ROM if you did not install it during the initial installation of the Windows NT Server software.

C. Install Internet Information Server from the Windows NT Server CD-ROM only if the Windows NT Server is a domain controller.

D. Activate Internet Information Server, which is automatically included in the Windows NT Server installation process.

18. The NETLOGON service is used to:

A. Facilitate SAM database synchronization.

B. Process logon requests.

C. Facilitate pass-through authentication.

D. All the above.

19. To promote a Backup Domain Controller to a Primary Domain Controller, you must:

A. Reinstall Windows NT Server and specify the server as a PDC during installation.

B. Choose the Primary Domain Controller option from the Networks applet in the Control Panel.

C. Choose Promote to Primary Domain Controller in the File menu for Server Manager.

D. Backup Domain Controllers cannot be manually promoted. This is handled automatically by Windows NT.

20. A Windows NT Server that has more than one network adapter installed is called:

A. A routable server.

B. A multihomed server.

C. A proxy server.

D. None of the above. A Windows NT Server is limited to a single network interface card.

21. DHCP can be used on a Windows NT Network to:

A. Set the default gateway for DHCP clients.

B. Assign IP addresses to DHCP clients.

C. Set the WINS server addresses for DHCP clients.

D. All the above.

22. The TCP/IP subnet mask 255.255.255.0 is:

A. Class A

B. Class B

C. Class C

D. Class A or Class B, depending on the value of the first octet.

23. What happens when duplicate IP addresses are assigned to two Windows NT Workstations on the same network?

A. All network communications stop.

B. When the second workstation is started, a warning message is issued, and it does not connect to the network.

C. DHCP automatically assigns a new, unique address to the second workstation that starts.

D. WINS automatically translates communications to and from the second workstation started.

24. Your Microsoft network is a single domain network to the Internet via an ISDN router. You use Windows NT DNS service to provide access to your web server. How do you configure the DNS service to *know* your web server name and IP address?
    A. The web server automatically registers its name and IP address with any DNS services running in its domain.
    B. The web server registers its name and IP address with WINS and WINS automatically updates the DNS server.
    C. The web server name and IP address must be added to the DNS service's database manually.
    D. The web server automatically registers its name and IP address with WINS. When the DNS service cannot find the name request, it interrogates WINS and finds the web server IP address.

25. The purpose of a DHCP relay agent is:
    A. To facilitate communication between WINS servers across routers.
    B. To forward DHCP broadcasts to DHCP servers across routers.
    C. To redirect NetBIOS broadcasts to the domain master browser.
    D. To provide communication between WINS-enabled hosts and WINS servers across routers.

26. A multihomed Windows NT Server can be used in which capacities?
    A. As a NetBEUI router
    B. As an IPX router
    C. As an IP router
    D. As either an IPX router, an IP router, or both

27. When configuring a Windows NT Server to connect to a NetWare 3.11 Server using Ethernet, it is very likely that the correct frame type will be:
    A. 802.5
    B. Ethernet_SNAP
    C. 802.2
    D. 802.3

28. For development purposes, a Windows NT Server is installed on your network to use both as a workstation and a test server for no more than three programmers. What server service optimization option should be selected for this server?
    A. Minimize Memory Used
    B. Balance
    C. Maximize Throughput for File Sharing
    D. Maximize Throughput for Network Applications

29. You can edit the Windows NT Server Registry using:
    A. Any text editor
    B. NOTEPAD.EXE
    C. REGEDT32.EXE
    D. REDIT.EXE

30. To better manage traffic on your network, you manually configure one of the Windows NT Servers to be the master browser. What should you know about manually configured master browsers?

A. The Windows NT Server configured to be the master browser will remain the master browser until it is manually reconfigured.

B. The Windows NT Server cannot be manually configured to act as a master browser.

C. The Windows NT Server may loose its status as a master browser if it is downed or disconnected from the network.

D. The Windows NT Server must be a domain controller to be a master browser.

31. The users on your company's network require different configurations. As a result, many users require a special logon script. You have just installed the second Windows NT Server on your network and configured it as a Backup Domain Controller. Because users will now be logging on to one of two domain controllers, how are the special logon scripts best managed?

A. Place all logon scripts in the default logon script location, configure user profiles to use the default location for logon scripts, and configure the Windows NT directory replication service to replicate the logon script directory between the domain controllers.

B. Leave all logon scripts on one domain controller, and then modify the profile for each user to access the logon script from only the domain controller that contains the scripts.

C. Create a logon script for each user and place it in their respective home directories; change all user profiles to access logon scripts in home directories.

D. Place all logon scripts in the default logon script directory on the Primary Domain Controller. Logon scripts are automatically replicated to all domain controllers in the domain.

32. Configure the Directory Replication service using what utility?

A. Server Manager.

B. The Services applet in Control Panel.

C. Directory Replication service must be configured when Windows NT Server is installed.

D. Directory Replication Manager.

33. Which of the following volume formatting types support volume extension?

A. FAT

B. VFAT

C. NTFS

D. CDFS

34. What utility can you use to convert a FAT file system to NTFS format?

A. NTDETECT.COM

B. SCANDISK.EXE

C. CONVERT.EXE

D. NTFS.EXE

35. Which of the following are required to configure a mirrored drive set on a Windows NT Server? Choose all that apply.
    A. A minimum of four gigabytes storage space.
    B. At least two physical disk drives.
    C. Disk volumes must use NTFS file formatting.
    D. None of the above.

36. What Windows NT Server utility is used for disk fault-tolerance configuration?
    A. Server Manager
    B. Disk Manager
    C. Server Administrator
    D. Disk Administrator

37. One way to configure a printer on a Windows NT Server is:
    A. Using the Printers applet in Control Panel.
    B. Using Printer Manager.
    C. Using Printer Administrator.
    D. None of the above.

38. One possible disadvantage to printer pooling is:
    A. If one printer is taken offline, the pooled print queue is disabled.
    B. All printers must use the same print driver.
    C. The print queue assigned to the pooled printers can only be written to by one user at a time.
    D. A print driver must be installed for each printer in the pool.

39. What Windows NT Server utility is used to share client-based Windows NT administration tools?
    A. Network Client Administrator
    B. Disk Administrator
    C. Server Manager
    D. User Manager for Domains

40. Which of the following workstation platforms can join a Windows NT domain?
    A. Windows NT Servers and Windows NT Workstations
    B. Windows NT Servers only
    C. Windows NT Workstations and Windows 95 Workstations
    D. Windows NT Servers, Windows NT Workstations, Windows 95 Workstations

41. Which of the following Windows NT Server programs can you use to create user accounts? Select all correct answers.
    A. Network Client Administrator
    B. NET.EXE
    C. Server Manager
    D. User Manager for Domains

42. Which of the following groups can lock out global user accounts in a Windows NT domain?
    A. Domain Admins
    B. Administrators
    C. Account Operators
    D. System

43. A Windows NT logon script can be of which types? Select all that apply.
    A. *.BAT
    B. *.CMD
    C. *.EXE
    D. *.SYS
    E. All the above.

44. Windows NT passwords must include which of the following character types? Choose all that apply.
    A. At least one non-alphanumeric character.
    B. At least one numeric character.
    C. At least one uppercase alpha character.
    D. None of the above.

45. Which of the following statements about global groups is true? Choose all the correct answers.
    A. Global groups can have local groups as members.
    B. Global groups can be accessed across domains.
    C. Global groups can be members of local groups.
    D. Members of local groups inherit file rights assigned to global groups.

46. What Windows NT tool is used to create global groups?
    A. Domain Administrator
    B. User Manager
    C. Server Manager
    D. User Manager for Domains

47. What are the global groups created when you create a Windows NT domain?
    A. Domain Admins, Domain Controllers, Domain Guests
    B. Domain Admins, Domain Guests, Domain Users
    C. Domain Administrators, Domain Users, Everyone
    D. Domain Admins, Domain Guests, Everyone

48. Which built-in local group is found only on domain controllers? Choose all that apply.
    A. Everyone
    B. Administrators
    C. Domain Admins
    D. Account Operators

49. A user needs sufficient file access to a Windows NT member server to administer file backups. As a member of the Power Users group on that server, how would you grant the appropriate rights to the user?
    A. Make the user a member of the local group Backup Operators on the member server.
    B. Make the user a member of the local group Administrators on the member server.
    C. Explicitly assign the appropriate rights for the user to all files and directories on the server.
    D. None of the above.

50. After adding a Windows NT Workstation or Server to a domain, what must you do to allow Domain Admins to manage this workstation?
    A. Add the global group Domain Admins to the workstation's local Administrators group.

B. No additional configuration is required. The global group Domain Admins is automatically added to the local group Administrators when a Windows NT workstation successfully joins a domain.

C. Add the local group Administrators to the global group Domain Admins.

D. Set the local user Administrator's password to be the same as the local group Administrator's password on the Primary Domain Controller.

51. A user must have what right in order to create a page file on Windows NT Server?

A. The Create Permanent Shared Objects right

B. The Log On as a Service right

C. The Create Token Object right

D. The Create a Pagefile right

52. Where is the user profile for Windows NT Workstations stored?

A. On the workstation's local hard drive.

B. In the same directory as the Windows NT Registry.

C. In the user's home directory as defined in the user account properties.

D. In the directory specified by the Profile Path in the user account properties (the local hard drive if the Profile Path field is blank).

53. What Windows NT utility do you use to set system policies for users?

A. Domain Administrator

B. User Manager for Domains

C. System Policy Editor

D. Policy Editor for Domains

54. Which of the following restrictions can you assign to users on a Windows NT network? Choose all that apply.

A. Disallow creation of drive mappings.

B. Disable booting from the A drive.

C. Lock out access to the C: prompt (DOS command line).

D. All the above.

55. When a Windows NT Workstation reads a machine policy file, how does the workstation store the information?

A. The information is merged into the HKEY_CURRENT_MACHINE subtree of the Workstation Registry.

B. It is stored in the home directory of the current user.

C. It is merged into the HKEY_LOCAL_MACHINE subtree of the Windows NT Workstation Registry.

D. It replaces the HKEY_CURRENT_MACHINE subtree of the Windows NT Workstation registration.

56. A user requires which permissions on a file share in order to change directories within that share? Choose all that apply.

A. Change

B. Read & Add

C. Full Control

D. Modify

E. None of the above.

57. What implicit file share permission do you assign to all users that do not have explicit permission to a give file share?

   A. Read Only.

   B. Read and Execute.

   C. Access Denied.

   D. Users not assigned explicit rights to a file share have no rights assigned.

58. A user belongs to a local group on a domain controller that is assigned No Access rights to a file share on that server. This user also belongs to another local group that is assigned Change permissions to the same file share. What is this user's effective permission to the file share?

   A. No Access

   B. Change

   C. Change and No Access

   D. Access Denied

59. Why might the FAT file format be used on a Windows NT volume?

   A. The FAT file structure offers a greater degree of flexibility in assigning permissions to directories than NTFS.

   B. FAT may be needed to provide filename compatibility with Windows for Workgroups workstations connected to the network.

   C. Due to hardware resource limitations, your only option for disk fault-tolerance is disk mirroring, and you want to mirror the boot sector.

   D. None of the above.

60. What NTFS directory permission is minimally required to change the current NTFS permissions?

   A. Change Permission

   B. Change

   C. Full Control

   D. List

61. What NTFS file permission is minimally required to view the contents of a file?

   A. Read

   B. Read and Execute

   C. Execute

   D. Full Control

62. You have just added a new disk drive to your Windows NT Server, formatted it (NTFS), and configured the new drive as a volume. Several local groups will store data on the new volume in separate directories. How should you configure the directory permissions?

   A. You should assign Full Control to the root directory for the group Everyone, create the required directories, and assign appropriate permissions to the subdirectories.

   B. You should assign the No Access permission to the group Everyone in the root directory, create the required directories, and add the appropriate permissions to the directories.

   C. You should assign permissions to the root directory for all groups that will access the volume.

   D. The group Everyone is automatically assigned Full Control to the root directory. You remove the group Everyone from the root directory permissions list, create the required directories, and assign appropriate rights to groups for the directories.

63. Some data files are stored on a Windows NT Server in the (NTFS) directory `C:\INVENTORY\DATA`. You assign Read permission for the Accounting local group and Change permission for the Management local group. They are copied to (NTFS) directory `C:\INVENTORY\SECRET`, which is located on the same server volume. The target directory for these files has Read permission for both Accounting and Management. What access permissions will Management have to these files after they are copied to the target directory?
    A. Read
    B. Change
    C. Access Denied
    D. List

64. Some data files are stored on a Windows NT Server in the (NTFS) directory `C:\INVENTORY\DATA`. You assign Read permission for the Accounting local group and Change permission for the Management local group. They are moved to the (NTFS) directory `C:\INVENTORY\SECRET` on the same server. The target directory for these files has Read permission for both Accounting and Management. What access permissions will Management have to these files after they are moved to the target directory?
    A. Read
    B. Change
    C. Access Denied
    D. List

65. Directory `C:\TEST\DATA` is shared with Read permissions for the group Users. The NTFS permissions for `C:\TEST\DATA` is set to Change for the group Domain Users. What permission does Domain Users have for directory `C:\TEST\DATA`?
    A. Change
    B. Read
    C. Change and Read
    D. None of the above.

66. DomainA and DomainB have a one-way trust relationship: DomainA trusts DomainB. What can you do in terms of adding users from one domain to groups in the other?
    A. You can add users in DomainA to global groups in DomainB.
    B. You can add users in DomainB to global groups in DomainA.
    C. You can add users from DomainA to local groups in DomainB.
    D. You can add users from DomainB to local groups in DomainA.
    E. None of the above. Domains must have a full-trust relationship to add users from one domain to a group in the other.

67. The marketing department has some files stored in a directory on an NTFS volume. All users on the network need read access to some of these files and write access to others. The Mktg group requires read and write access to all the files. How would you configure the file share and NTFS permissions to satisfy the requirements?
    A. You should assign Read permission for Everyone to the file share and Change permission to the NTFS directory for the Mktg group.

B. You should assign Full Control permission for Everyone to the file share, Change permission to the Mktg group, and the appropriate Change or Read permissions to each file in the directory for Everyone.

C. You should assign Change permission for Everyone in the file share, assign the NTFS Read permission to Everyone for all files in the directory, and assign the NTFS Change permission to all files for the Mktg group.

D. You should assign Change permission for Everyone in the file share, for each file in the directory assign the appropriate NTFS Change or Read permission for Everyone, and assign the NTFS Change permission for the Mktg group to all files in the directory.

68. John requires access to a Windows NT resource. He is assigned to a local group that has permission to access the resource. John attempts to access the resource, but is greeted with an `Access Denied` message. What is the most likely reason that John cannot access the resource?

A. John has not logged in since he was added to the local group.

B. Another group that John belongs to has the default Access Denied permission assigned for that resource.

C. John is not a member of the domain to which the local group belongs.

D. Users can be added only to global groups.

69. You suspect that an unauthorized person attempted to log on to your network. What audit policy could you activate to check for attempted unauthorized logons?

A. Process Tracking: Look for excessive failed logon processes.

B. Use of User Rights: Look for excessive failed logon attempts.

C. Lockout Tracking: Track the user lockout count.

D. Logon and Logoff: Look for excessive failed logon attempts.

70. To use file-level auditing on a given Windows NT Server, you must first do what?

A. Enable File and Object Access Auditing on the target file server.

B. Assign Full Control NTFS permission for the built-in group, System, to all volumes that you will audit.

C. Rebuild the file tables on the target volume by using NTFSCVT.EXE.

D. Add Change permission for the built-in group, Administrators, to the target volume using CACLS.EXE.

71. You are required to audit an NTFS directory, `C:\DATA\ACCTG`, on your Windows NT Server for changes to all files in that directory. You are asked to move `C:\DATA\ACCTG` to a new location under directory `C:\COMMON` on the same Windows NT Server. What must you do to continue to audit the ACCTG directory?

A. You should do nothing. The audit information in the ACCTG directory will not change.

B. You should reestablish the auditing configuration using Windows NT Explorer.

C. You should not move the directory because all auditing information to date will be lost.

D. You should maintain the auditing configuration on the ACCTG directory by first copying the directory to the new location and then deleting the original directory.

72. Which of the following IP addresses is a valid Class C address?

A. 222.18.22.4

B. 191.255.255.1

C. 127.34.56.199

D. 225.275.8.44

73. Your IP network is assigned the Class B address range of 129.48.0.0–129.48.255.255. You are using a subnet mask of 255.255.192.0. How many subnets can you have on your network using this subnet mask?

A. 8

B. 5

C. 4

D. 64

74. Using the IP address information from the previous question, which of the following IP addresses does not belong to the subnet 129.48.128.0? Choose all that apply.

A. 129.48.128.8

B. 129.48.191.123

C. 129.48.127.17

D. 129.48.132.255

75. What service is used to facilitate bi-directional print services between Windows NT Server and UNIX (IP) hosts?

A. LPR

B. TCP/IP Printing Support

C. LPD

D. UNIX Gateway for Windows NT

76. What service does Windows NT Server use to connect to NetWare servers?

A. IPX

B. Gateway Service for NetWare

C. SPX

D. NWLink

77. What utility do you use to manage and configure DHCP on a Windows NT network?

A. DHCP Administrator

B. Server Manager

C. DHCP Manager

D. Protocol Manager

78. What utility do you use to migrate Novell directories and files to a Windows NT domain controller?

A. NTFSCVT.EXE

B. NWCONV.EXE

C. NET.EXT

D. NW2NT.EXE

79. Which of the following protocols are network protocols supported by Windows NT Remote Access Service? Choose all that apply.

A. SLIP

B. NetBIOS

C. IPX

D. TCP/IP

80. Although you can substantially improve system performance on a Windows NT Server by moving the paging file from the default location on the system partition to another partition, what is one disadvantage?
    A. The paging file uses more disk space.
    B. The CRASHDUMP utility is disabled.
    C. Physical stress increases on the partition to where you moved the paging file.
    D. There are no disadvantages.

81. In terms of network protocols on a Windows NT network, what is the simplest way to optimize network performance?
    A. Always use TCP/IP.
    B. Use NetBEUI on segmented networks.
    C. Match the network size and load requirements to the protocol.
    D. Use compressed network packets.

82. What tool would you typically use to view processes running on a Windows NT Server or Workstation?
    A. Server Manager
    B. Windows Diagnostics
    C. MSD.EXE
    D. Task Manager

83. What Windows NT utility is used to monitor network activity?
    A. Performance Monitor
    B. Network Monitor
    C. Network Manager
    D. Windows Diagnostics

84. Which of the following are counter types used by Performance Monitor? Choose all that apply.
    A. Averaging
    B. Instantaneous
    C. Delayed
    D. Difference

85. What might a high rate of hard page faults on a Windows NT Server indicate?
    A. Not enough disk space in the system partition.
    B. Not enough physical memory.
    C. The paging file is not large enough.
    D. Memory errors.

86. The hardware address of a device on an Ethernet network is called the:
    A. IP address
    B. Socket number
    C. Port number
    D. MAC address

87. How might a Windows NT Workstation client locate a domain controller to log on? Choose all the correct answers.
    A. The address of the domain controller is in the client's Registry.
    B. The client sends out a broadcast looking for a NETLOGON mail slot.
    C. The client sends a request for a NETLOGON address to a WINS Server.
    D. The client uses a browse list to locate the domain controller.

88. How do you change the update interval time on master and backup Windows NT browsers?

   A. Run WINS Manager, select the browser, choose Configuration from the File menu.

   B. Modify the browser's Registry.

   C. Run Server Manager, select the browser, choose the Browser option from the File menu.

   D. None of the above. The interval time for browsers cannot be changed from their default 12 minutes.

89. What is the purpose of the `%systemroot%\System32\Autoexec.nt` file?

   A. It runs as a batch command file when the Windows NT Server is initialized.

   B. It is used as the AUTOEXEC. BAT file for DOS sessions.

   C. The boot process uses this file to locate the system partition.

   D. None of the above.

90. You perform an emergency repair to a Windows NT computer using what utility?

   A. SETUP.EXE

   B. RDISK.EXE

   C. WINNT.EXE or WINNT32.EXE

   D. WINREP.EXE

   E. None of the above.

91. You are installing Windows NT Server on a computer that has multiple SCSI adapters. For Windows NT to install correctly on this computer, what must you do?

   A. You must enable the BIOS on all SCSI adapters.

   B. You must enable the BIOS on only the first physical SCSI adapter.

   C. You must disable the BIOS for all the SCSI adapters.

   D. Windows NT automatically configures for multiple SCSI adapters regardless of their BIOS configuration.

92. Which program provides hardware detection when an Intel-based Windows NT Server boots?

   A. NVRAM

   B. NTLDR

   C. NTDETECT

   D. NTMENU

93. What Windows NT utility do you use to view log files created by the Remote Access Service?

   A. Any text editor

   B. Event Viewer

   C. Server Manager

   D. Windows NT Diagnostics

94. What utility do you use to monitor RAS connections from the Windows NT Server console?

   A. RAS Admin

   B. Windows Diagnostics

   C. Network Monitor

   D. RAS Monitor

95. Assuming that all workstations on the network are Windows NT or Windows 95, how do you know that there is a duplicate workstation (NetBIOS) name on a Windows NT network?

A. A warning message displays on all domain controllers on the network.

B. A warning message displays on the offending workstation during initialization, and the workstation will not connect to the network.

C. A warning message sends to any Domain Admins that are logged on to the network.

D. The offending workstation issues a warning, and then automatically renames itself at startup time.

96. Which of the following is a utility that you can use to discover the IP address and subnet mask assigned to a Windows NT computer?

A. PING

B. CONFIG

C. INETD

D. IPCONFIG

97. Which of the following is a utility that you can use to test the connectivity between two IP hosts?

A. PING

B. IPFIND

C. SEARCHIP

D. GROPE

98. The protocol you use to translate Ethernet MAC addresses to IP addresses on a TCP/IP network is:

A. RARP

B. ARP

C. WINS

D. DNS

99. The Windows NT utility you use to view the current NetBIOS names registered by the client, as well as to view the cache of NetBIOS names to IP addresses that have been resolved by a Windows NT client, is:

A. NETSTAT.EXE

B. NBTSTAT.EXE

C. ROUTE.EXE

D. NET.EXE

100. How does a differential backup data set differ from an incremental backup data set?

A. An incremental backup data set contains files that have been modified since the last incremental backup was performed; a differential backup data set contains files that have been modified since the last full backup was performed.

B. An incremental backup data set contains files that have been modified since the last full backup was performed; a differential backup data set contains files that have been modified since the last differential backup was performed.

C. An incremental backup data set contains files that have been modified since the last incremental or full backup was performed; a differential backup data set contains files that have been modified since the last full or differential backup was performed.

D. An incremental backup data set contains files that have been modified since the last differential backup was performed; a differential backup data set contains files that have been modified since the last full backup was performed.

Answers and Explanations

1. **D** Complete trust domains is the best choice because management wants to retain distributed administration of users. (Planning.)
2. **B** The SAM database size is calculated as follows:
   - Add 1024 (1 KB) bytes per user in the account.
   - Add 512 (0.5 KB) bytes per local group on domain controllers plus 36 bytes per member for each group.
   - Add 512 (0.5 KB) bytes per global group plus 12 bytes per member for each group.
   - Add 512 (0.5 KB) bytes per computer account.

   Using this information, you can calculate as follows:

   1600 users * 1024 bytes = 1638400 bytes + 200 global groups * 512 bytes = 102400 bytes + 200 global groups * 35 members * 12 bytes = 84000 bytes + 55 local groups * 512 bytes = 28160 bytes + 55 local groups * 5 members * 36 bytes = 9900 bytes + 1150 computer accounts * 512 bytes = 588800 bytes + = 2451660 bytes = 2.45 MB. (Planning.)
3. **B** Single domain directory services are best suited for *traveling* users so that each user has one logon ID, all resources on the network are accessible, and logon authentication is performed at the nearest domain controller. The single domain directory services architecture may not work best for networks that have few traveling users, but it is the best choice of the options offered when only traveling users are considered. (Installation and Configuration.)
4. **C** To enable access to the resources in DM_Mfg for users in DM_Sales, use the User Manager for Domains utility to configure DM_Mfg to trust DM_Sales and to configure DM_Sales to allow DM_Mfg to trust DM_Sales. (Managing Resources.)
5. **A** When a trust relationship breaks, it is easily reestablished by rebooting the domain controllers. (Managing Resources.)
6. **D** All the listed issues are limitations of local user accounts. (Managing Resources.)
7. **A** You cannot delete the local Administrator account on a Windows NT domain controller. (Managing Resources.)
8. **B** After a trust relationship is established between two domains, users may access resources across domains because the trust relationship allows logon services from the trusted domain to pass through access requests to the trusting domain. (Managing Resources.)
9. **C** RAID fault-tolerance levels 0, 1, and 5 are built in to Windows NT Server. (Installation and Configuration.)
10. **C** Windows NT Server RAID fault-tolerance supports at maximum 32 disks. (Installation and Configuration.)
11. **D** The best Windows NT disk fault-tolerance configuration for read performance is disk striping with parity. (Installation and Configuration.)

12. **C** Sector sparing is the method by which Windows NT Server protects against writing data to a bad sector on its hard disk drive(s). (Installation and Configuration.)
13. **A** TCP/IP is the protocol of choice for most networks because it is the network industry standard and allows connectivity between dissimilar networks and devices. (Connectivity.)
14. **A** If you shut down a Windows NT Server that is a master browser, you do nothing; the network elects a new master browser when the time limit on the downed browser expires. (Managing Resources.)
15. **A** Use the /B switch with the Windows NT Server installation program to suppress the creation of floppy startup disks. (Installation and Configuration.)
16. **C** You must configure a Windows NT Server as a domain controller at installation time. To promote a member server to domain controller, you must reinstall Windows NT Server. (Installation and Configuration.)
17. **B** Internet Information Server ships with Windows NT Server. You may install IIS on any Windows NT Server (domain controller or not), and you have the option of installing IIS when you install Windows NT Server. (Installation and Configuration.)
18. **D** The NETLOGON service facilitates SAM database synchronization, processes logon requests, and processes authentications for trusted domains (pass-through authentication). (Troubleshooting)
19. **C** You can promote a Backup Domain Controller to a Primary Domain Controller by starting Server Manager, selecting the target Backup Domain Controller, and choosing the Promote to Primary Domain Controller option in Server Manager's File menu. (Managing Resources.)
20. **B** A multihomed server is a Windows NT Server that has more than one network adapter installed. (Connectivity.)
21. **D** DHCP can set a number of configuration parameters on a DHCP client, including setting the default gateway, assigning an IP address to the client, and setting the IP address for the (usually nearest) WINS server. (Connectivity.)
22. **C** By definition, a TCP/IP address that uses the first three octets for the network address is a Class B IP address. Note that any valid subnet mask may be used for any Class IP network address: the subnet mask in this question is the standard Class C subnet mask. (Installation and Configuration.)
23. **B** When a Windows NT Workstation starts up, it looks for a duplicate of its IP address on the network before connecting to the network. If the Windows NT Workstation finds a duplicate IP address, it issues a warning message, and it does not connect to the network. (Connectivity.)
24. **C** The DNS database is static. You must add addresses manually. (Connectivity.)
25. **B** DHCP relay agents are configured with the IP address(es) of one or more DHCP servers that are connected to another network segment.

The agents capture client DHCP broadcasts and send them to the DHCP server. (Connectivity.)

26. **D** NetBEUI is not routable. You can configure Windows NT Server to be both an IPX router and an IP router. Windows NT Server can also route both protocols simultaneously. Note that answers B and C are correct answers, but D is the most correct answer. (Installation and Configuration.)
27. **D** 802.3 is the default frame type for NetWare 3.11. (Installation and Configuration.)
28. **A** Minimize Memory Used is the server optimization option that you should select for this server. Minimize Memory Used is the setting when fewer than 10 connections are guaranteed as the maximum. (Installation and Configuration.)
29. **C** You can also use REGEDIT.EXE. (Troubleshooting.)
30. **C** The Registry setting can change if the computer is rebooted, or if it is disconnected from the network long enough for the other browsers on the network to hold a master browser election. (Connectivity.)
31. **A** Answers A, B, and C all work; however, A provides the best way to manage a messy situation. If logon scripts are replicated among domain controllers, any additional logon scripts or edits to existing logon scripts are replicated to other domain controllers. The logon scripts run regardless of which domain controller processes the logon. (Managing Resources.)
32. **A** Configure the Directory Replication service using Server Manager. (Installation and Configuration.)
33. **C** VFAT is a non-existent file format, CDFS is a CD-ROM file format. Of FAT and NTFS, only NTFS supports volume extension. (Installation and Configuration.)
34. **C** CONVERT.EXE is used to convert a FAT file system to NTFS format. (Installation and Configuration.)
35. **D** You can mirror any size disk; you can use a single physical drive to mirror a volume. The boot partition cannot be mirrored, but you can mirror FAT file format disks. (Installation and Configuration.)
36. **D** Use Disk Administrator to configure disk fault-tolerance. (Installation and Configuration.)
37. **A** One way to configure a printer on a Windows NT Server is to use the Printers applet in Control Panel. (Managing Resources.)
38. **B** Because printer pooling sends jobs to a single print queue, all printers that belong to a given printer pool must use the same print driver. (Managing Resources.)
39. **A** Use Network Client Administrator to share client-based Windows NT administration tools. (Managing Resources.)
40. **A** Windows 95 computers cannot join the domain. (Managing Resources.)
41. **B, D** User Manager for Domains is normally the tool you use to create new user accounts. NET.EXE is a command-line utility that is useful for batch processing of new user accounts. The Windows NT Server Resource kit also comes with a tool, ADDUSER.EXE, for batch processing of user accounts. (Managing Resources.)

42. **D** Only System can lock out accounts. Note that users with the appropriate permissions can disable user accounts. (Installation and Configuration.)

43. **A, B, C** A Windows NT logon script can be either a batch file (*.BAT, *.CMD) or an executable (*.EXE). (Managing Resources.)

44. **D** Although you can configure Windows NT password security to require any or all the character types listed, none are required by default. The Windows NT Server Resource Kit includes a toolset that can enable the character types feature, as well as other password security enhancement features. (Installation and Configuration.)

45. **B,C** Global groups may be accessed across domains, and they can be members of local groups. (Managing Resources.)

46. **D** User Manager for Domains is one tool you use to create global groups. (Managing Resources.)

47. **B** When you create a Windows NT domain, the global groups Domain Admins, Domain Guests, and Domain Users are automatically created. Domain Controllers is not a standard group, and Everyone is a special group. (Installation and Configuration.)

48. **D** The built-in group Account Operators is created automatically on Windows NT Servers only when you configure the server as a domain controller. (Installation and Configuration.)

49. **D** As a member of the Power User group, you do not have the necessary rights to perform A, B, or C. Only members of the local group Administrators may add or delete members from the local group Backup Operators. (Installation and Configuration.)

50. **B** The global group Domain Admins is automatically added to the local Administrators group when a Windows NT computer joins a domain. (Managing Resources.)

51. **D** Users must have the Create a Pagefile right to create a page file on a Windows NT Server. The right is assigned by default to the local groups Administrators and Power Users. (Managing Resources.)

52. **D** The user profile for a Windows NT Workstation is stored in the directory specified by the Profile Path in the user account properties. If you do not specify the profile path in the user account, the user profile is stored on the local hard drive of the Windows NT Workstation. Although a user profile is stored somewhere other than the Windows NT Workstation hard drive, a copy of the profile is also stored on the Windows NT Workstation hard drive as a backup in case the system cannot locate the server-stored copy of the profile at boot time. (Installation and Configuration.)

53. **B** You use the User Manager for Domains to set system policies for users. (Managing Resources)

54. **D** You can assign all the listed restrictions to users. The best source of information on this subject is the Windows NT Server Resource Kit. (Managing Resources.)

55. **C** When a Windows NT Workstation reads a machine policy file, the information merges into the HKEY_LOCAL_MACHINE subtree of the workstation's registry. Machine policy files are one method of updating network and workstation security. (Managing Resources.)

56. **A, C** The Change and the Full Control permissions are the only two valid file share permissions listed. The three file share permissions that enable any access to a shared directory are Read, Change, and Full Control. These three permissions enable the user to change directories. (Managing Resources.)

57. **C** Users and groups for which you do not assign explicit rights to a file share have an implied Access Denied right. (Managing Resources.)

58. **A** In this case, the user's effective permission to the file share is No Access because when an access request to a file share is authenticated, the system uses the most restrictive right assigned to the user. (Managing Resources.)

59. **D** The FAT file structure is less flexible than NTFS in terms of file and directory permissions. The FAT file structure on a Windows NT Server employs the same long names and associated shorthand 8.3 format short names as NTFS. On mirrored drives, the boot partition is mirrored for both FAT file systems and NTFS. (Planning.)

60. **A** Change Permissions is the minimally required right for changing file permissions. You can explicitly set or clear this right for a user or group by using the Special file permissions option when you assign file and directory permissions. (Managing Resources.)

61. **A** The NTFS file permission of Read is minimally required to view the contents of a file. (Managing Resources.)

62. **D** By default, the group Everyone is granted Full Control rights to the root directory of a newly created volume. You should delete this group from the permissions list for the root directory, so that the directories you subsequently create do not inherit the permissions. Removing Everyone also blocks any users from creating new directories and changing permissions on existing directories. After removing Everyone from the root directory permission list, you should create the required directories and assign appropriate permissions. (Managing Resources.)

63. **A** When files are copied from one NTFS directory to another, the files inherit the permissions of the target directory. (Managing Resources.)

64. **B** Management will have Change permissions after the files move to the target directory. Files that are moved within the same NTFS volume retain their original permissions. (Managing Resources.)

65. **B** After you share an NTFS directory, the most restrictive permissions. (Managing Resources.)

66. **B** You can add users from a trusted domain to global groups in the trusting domain. You cannot add users to local groups across domain lines. (Managing Resources.)

67. **D** When Windows NT determines file access permissions for a shared NTFS directory, the system compares NTFS permissions and the file share permissions, and the most restrictive permissions of the two are the effective permissions. Conversely, when a user is a member of two groups that are both assigned permissions to an NTFS file or directory, the least restrictive permissions are the effective permissions. (Managing Resources.)

68. **A** After permissions change, users must re-log on to a Windows NT network to rebuild their access tokens. (Troubleshooting.)

69. **D** Logon and Logoff is the correct audit category where you set the audit flag for failed logon attempts. (Managing Resources.)

70. **A** To use file-level auditing on a Windows NT Server, you must first enable File and Object Access Auditing on the target file server. (Managing Resources.)

71. **A** Audit policies associated with files operate under the same copy/move rules as NTFS permissions. (Managing Resources.)

72. **A** 222.18.22.4 is a valid Class C address because the first octet of the address is within the range of Class C IP addresses (192–224). (Planning.)

73. **C** The four subnets are defined by the third octet in the subnet mask, 192 (binary 11000000). This is referred to as a two-bit subnet mask. The possible values for these two bits are: 00, 01, 10, and 11. The four subnet address ranges are:

    (a) 129.48.0.0 to 129.48.63.255,

    (b) 129.48.64.0 to 129.48.127.255,

    (c) 129.48.128.0 to 129.48.191.255, and

    (d) 129.48.192.0 to 129.48.255.255. (Planning.)

74. **C** Refer to the listing of IP address ranges in the answer to question 73. (Planning.)

75. **B** TCP/IP Printing Support is the service you use to facilitate bidirectional printing between Windows NT networks and UNIX hosts. Note that LPD and LPR are components of TCP/IP Printing Support. (Installation and Configuration.)

76. **B** Use Gateway Service for NetWare with the NWLink protocol to connect Windows NT networks to Novell servers. (Connectivity.)

77. **C** You use DHCP Manager to configure DHCP. (Installation and Configuration.)

78. **B** Use NWCONV.EXE to migrate Novell directories and files to a Windows NT domain controller. (Installation and Configuration.)

79. **C, D** RAS does not support NetBIOS, and SLIP is a line protocol. (Connectivity.)

80. **B** When the paging file is located on any partition other than the system partition, the CRASHDUMP utility is disabled. (Monitoring and Optimization.)

81. **C** The overall network requirements and size are important factors to consider when you select the appropriate protocol for a new Microsoft network. Although TCP/IP is the de facto standard for network protocols, NWLink or NetBEUI is a better choice in some cases. (Planning.)

82. **D** You use Task Manager on Windows NT Workstations to view running processes on that workstation. (Troubleshooting.)

83. **B** You can use Network Monitor to view network activity on a Windows NT network. (Monitoring and Optimization.)

84. **A, B, D** The three types of counters used by Performance Monitor are: Averaging, Instantaneous, and Difference. (Monitoring and Optimization.)

85. **B** Insufficient physical memory on a Windows NT Server or Workstation usually causes excessive hard-page faults. (Troubleshooting.)

86. **D** MAC (Media Access Control) address is the hardware address of a device on an Ethernet network. (Monitoring and Optimization.)

87. **B, C** After a Windows NT Workstation attempts to find a domain controller by sending a request to a WINS Server (if the Windows NT Workstation has been assigned at least a primary WINS Server), and the WINS Server fails to respond, the Windows NT Workstation sends out a broadcast request for a NETLOGON service mailbox. (Troubleshooting.)
88. **B** The only way to change the update interval time for browsers is to manually modify the Registry. (Monitoring and Optimization.)
89. **B** The `%systemroot%\system32\Autoexec.nt` runs at the start of a Windows NT DOS session. (Monitoring and Optimization.)
90. **E** To perform an emergency repair, you boot the Windows NT Server using the original installation diskettes. The system prompts you to repair the file server. (Troubleshooting.)
91. **B** You must enable the BIOS on only the first physical SCSI adapter (generally the SCSI adapter located in the lowest slot number). (Connectivity.)
92. **C** NTDETECT provides hardware detection when an Intel-based Windows NT Server boots. (Troubleshooting.)
93. **A** Remote Access Service log files are ordinary ASCII text files. You can use any text editor to view them. (Troubleshooting.)
94. **A** RAS Admin is the tool you use to monitor RAS connections from the Windows NT Server console. (Troubleshooting.)
95. **B** As with duplicate TCP/IP addresses, when a Windows 95 or Windows NT workstation boots, it checks the network for a duplicate NetBIOS name. If the system finds a duplicate NetBIOS name, the workstation issues a warning message and does not connect to the network. (Troubleshooting.)
96. **D** The command-line utility IPCONFIG displays, as well as other information, such as the IP address and subnet mask assigned to the workstation. (Troubleshooting.)
97. **A** PING is a utility that you can use to test the connectivity between two IP hosts. (Troubleshooting.)
98. **A** The protocol used to translate Ethernet MAC addresses to IP addresses on a TCP/IP network is RARP (Reverse Address Resolution Protocol). (Troubleshooting.)
99. **B** Use NBTSTAT.EXE to view the current NetBIOS names registered by the client and view the cache of NetBIOS names to IP addresses that a Windows NT client resolved. (Troubleshooting)
100. **C** Remember that both incremental and differential backup processes are based on file archive flags. Full backups clear the archive flag when a file successfully saves. Incremental backups save only files with the archive flag set and then clear the archive flag. Differential backups save only files with the archive flag set and leave the archive flag set. (Installation and Configuration.)

Practice Exam 4

Implementing and Supporting Windows NT Server 4.0 in the Enterprise

The Windows NT Server Enterprise exam is an adaptive test—meaning that the number of questions you must answer is indeterminate. The following describes how an adaptive test works:

- The test covers six categories: Planning, Installation and Configuration, Managing Resources, Connectivity, Monitoring and Optimization, and Troubleshooting. Test questions are associated with these categories.
- The testing system asks an extremely difficult question for one of the five test categories. If you answer correctly, the testing system asks you a few easier questions to pass the category.

  If you answer incorrectly, the testing system presents you with at least one less difficult question for the category. If you continue to incorrectly answer questions for the category, the questions become increasingly less difficult until the testing system determines that you do not have sufficient knowledge to pass the category.

  If you finally answer a question correctly, the testing system asks increasingly difficult questions for that category until you correctly answer a certain number of questions (the number is unknown to you or me).

You are not asked the questions in order. The testing system presents questions for all six categories in a seemingly random order. The following are the two types of questions in the test:

- Multiple-choice questions—Select the correct answer.
- Scenario-based questions—Select the response or best scenario from the scenario description.

It is suggested that you set a timer to track your progress while taking the practice exam, because the time restrictions on the tests are often the biggest obstacles to overcome. Begin the following practice exam after you set your time.

Practice Exam Begins

1. A user on your Windows NT network requires full access to all services, files, and directories on a Windows NT applications server. Which of the following actions is the best solution?
   A. Assign the user to the Domain Admins group.
   B. Create a global group, add the user to the global group, and add the global group to the local Administrators group for the target file server.
   C. Grant the user full access to all files and directories on the target server.
   D. A and C.
   E. B and C.

2. A large number of your company's employees work at more than one of the wide-area sites that comprise the network. Generally, what directory services architecture is best suited for *traveling* users?
   A. Full trust domains so that the traveling users can have a logon ID for each site and still access resources at other sites.
   B. Single domain so that each user has one logon ID, and all resources on the network are accessible.
   C. Full trust domains so that the user has one logon ID and can use any local domain controller for the logon process.
   D. None of the above.

3. DomainA trusts DomainB. DomainB trusts DomainC. Which of the following statements is true? Choose all correct answers.
   A. DomainA trusts DomainC.
   B. DomainC trusts DomainA.
   C. Domains A, B, and C have a full-trust relationship.
   D. None of the above.

4. When establishing a trust relationship between two domains, which of the following is true?
   A. The Administrator password is used to establish the communications link between the domains.
   B. After the trust relationship is established, the domain controllers generate a password to secure their communications link.
   C. After the trust relationship is established, it can break only if both domain controllers agree to break the trust relationship.
   D. None of the above.

5. To assign administrative control to the global group Domain Admins when adding domain controllers to an existing domain, what should you do?
   A. You should do nothing. Domain Admins is automatically added to the local group Administrators.
   B. You should add Domain Admins to the local group Administrators, and then delete the local (built-in) user Administrator.

C. You should assign full permissions to Domain Admins and to all volumes on the server, and then add Domain Admins to the local (built-in) group Administrators.

D. You should add Domain Admins to the local (built-in) group Users, and then assign the Administrate This Computer permissions to Users.

6. To assign permissions across a trust relationship, you should:

A. Directly assign permissions to a local user account belonging to the trusted domain.

B. Create a local group in the trusting domain, assign permissions to a local group in the trusting domain, add a global group from the trusted domain to the local group, and add users to the global group from the trusted domain.

C. Assign permissions to a global group from the trusting domain.

D. Assign permissions to a local group from the trusting domain.

7. A complete-trust directory services model is effective on large networks because:

A. You manage all users in one domain.

B. Any user can use resources on any of the trusted domains.

C. It is the best way to configure a *one user, one account* network.

D. None of the above.

8. Of the disk fault-tolerance methods supported by Windows NT Server, which method offers the best protection for data recovery?

A. Disk striping

B. Disk striping with parity

C. Disk compression

D. Sector swapping

E. None of the above

9. What is the name of disk mirroring in combination with independent disk controller cards for each physical disk drive?

A. Disk balancing

B. Disk duplexing

C. RAID Level 0

D. Parallel disks

10. Disk striping with parity offers better data recovery characteristics than disk striping without parity because:

A. The assumption is false. Disk striping without parity offers better data recovery characteristics than disk striping with parity.

B. Exact copies of all data are stored on different disk volumes. If one volume fails, you can replace the volume and restore the data from the other parity volume. Disk striping without parity stores blocks of data across at least two physical drives. If one of the drives fails, you have no way to recover the data.

C. Data is stored in blocks across at least three physical disk drives along with parity information. Because parity information is stored, you can regenerate data on any one drive if the drive fails. Without parity information, you cannot recover any data from the striped set.

D. Disk striping with parity employs *hot swapping* technology, which enables you to replace a failed physical disk drive without downing the server and without data loss. Disk striping without parity does not support the *hot swapping* feature.

11. The NetBEUI protocol is best suited for large, segmented networks because:

 A. It is efficient and easily routed.

 B. NetBEUI is the Internet standard protocol.

 C. It offers scalability.

 D. None of the above. NetBEUI is not well-suited for large, segmented networks.

12. How do you exclude a Windows NT Server from functioning as a master browser?

 A. Disable the Master Browser setting on the Browsing tab in Network Neighborhood properties.

 B. Set the Registry entry MaintainServerList to False.

 C. Set the IsBrowser setting in WIN.INI to 0.

 D. Do not use the NetBEUI protocol.

13. What program do you use to install Windows NT Server? Choose all correct responses.

 A. WINNT.EXE

 B. WINNT32.EXE

 C. SETUP.EXE

 D. SETUP32.EXE

14. What is the default installation directory for Windows NT Server?

 A. \WINDOWS

 B. \WINNT on the system partition

 C. \WINNT on the first available NTFS volume

 D. \SYSTEM32

15. After installing and configuring a Primary Domain Controller, it is a good idea to: Choose all that apply.

 A. Delete the local Administrator account.

 B. Delete the local group Administrators.

 C. Add the global group Domain Admins to the local group Administrators.

 D. None of the above.

16. Windows NT network logon requests are processed by:

 A. Primary Domain Controllers

 B. Backup Domain Controllers

 C. Both Primary and Backup Domain Controllers

 D. Any Windows NT Server that has an account on the domain

17. What is the software interface that communicates between system hardware and Windows NT?
    A. Hardware Interface Layer
    B. Hardware Abstraction Layer
    C. Windows Hardware Interface
    D. MPR

18. How many browsers are on a Windows NT network?
    A. There is a master browser and a backup browser.
    B. At least one master browser for each network segment and a domain master browser.
    C. One browser for each Windows NT Server on the network.
    D. One browser for each network segment.

19. A TCP/IP subnet mask is used to:
    A. Define the host and network portions of an IP address.
    B. Hide the IP address from non-domain resources.
    C. Determine which DHCP clients must be renewed.
    D. None of the above.

20. One difference between WINS and DNS is:
    A. WINS is completely dynamic; DNS is a static service.
    B. WINS services Internet Names; DNS handles NetBIOS names.
    C. DNS services Internet Names; WINS handles NetBIOS names.
    D. DNS is a dynamic service; WINS is a static service.

21. The DNS domain name must be the same as the Windows NT domain name on a Windows NT network because:
    A. WINS and DNS exchange information to translate NetBIOS names to Internet Names.
    B. The Windows NT domain name and the DNS name are not required to be the same on a Windows NT network.
    C. Microsoft Network clients use their assigned WINS servers to locate the nearest DNS server.
    D. Microsoft Network clients use their assigned DNS servers to locate the nearest WINS server.

22. You just installed a Windows NT member server on your multisegment TCP/IP network. You configure this new server as the first DHCP server on your network and configure workstations on several different segments as DHCP clients. Workstations not connected on the same segment as the DHCP server are unable to obtain an IP address from the DHCP server. Which of the following describes the possible reason that the workstations cannot connect to the DHCP server and the solution? Choose all that apply.
    A. The DHCP clients must be members of the same domain as the DHCP server. Add the workstations to the appropriate domain.
    B. The routers that connect the network segments are configured with BOOTP broadcasts disabled. Enable BOOTP broadcasts on the routers that connect the DHCP server's segment.

C. The workstations do not know the IP address of the DHCP server. You must add the IP address of the DHCP server to the LMHOSTS file on each workstation.

D. The workstations do not know the IP address of the DHCP server. You must configure the workstation to query its assigned WINS server for the IP address of the DHCP server.

23. You are the network administrator for a small (20-user) single-segment Windows NT network using NWLink protocol. Your boss asks you to create an additional segment on the network for a special development project. Four new Windows NT Workstations will connect to the additional segment. All network cabling is in place for the new segment. You have been instructed to create this new segment as inexpensively as possible. Which of the following offers the best solution?

    A. Add a network adapter to one of the new workstations and configure the workstation as a router.

    B. Add a network adapter to the Windows NT Server and configure the server as a router.

    C. Change the network protocol to TCP/IP, add a network adapter to the Windows NT Server, and configure the server as a router.

    D. Purchase an inexpensive network bridge and connect the bridge between the two physical segments.

24. What is the primary purpose of NWLink?

    A. To guarantee connectivity between domain controllers.

    B. NWLink is used only for communication between Windows NT and Windows 95 workstations.

    C. To facilitate communications with Novell NetWare hosts.

    D. None of the above.

25. The binding order of network services on a Windows NT Server can be important to network and server performance because the binding order determines which of the following?

    A. The order in which Windows NT services network requests.

    B. The order in which Windows NT services network clients.

    C. The amount of memory used by protocol drivers.

    D. The number of broadcasts that the server must issue.

26. The best server service optimization setting for a Windows NT Server running Microsoft Exchange is:

    A. Minimize Memory Used

    B. Balance

    C. Maximize Throughput for File Sharing

    D. Maximize Throughput for Network Applications

27. Select all statements that are true:

    A. Unless specifically excluded, all Windows NT Servers act as browsers.

    B. Browsers maintain a list of workstations and their IP addresses.

C. All the domain controllers on the network elect master browsers.

D. Browsers maintain information only about the domain to which they belong.

28. The criteria used to elect a browser are:

A. Operating system type

B. Operating system version

C. Whether the computer is currently a browser, master browser, or able to become a browser

D. All the above

29. Directory replication requires which of the following user accounts?

A. A service account.

B. A user account assigned to the global group Domain Admins.

C. A user account that belongs to the local group Administrators on each server that is a replication partner.

D. None of the above.

30. You configure import and export servers to use with Directory Replication service using what utility?

A. Server Manager

B. The Services applet in Control Panel

C. You must configure Directory Replication service when Windows NT Server is installed

D. Directory Replication Manager

31. Your Windows NT Server has 64 MB of RAM and a single 4 GB hard drive. The hard drive is configured as a single FAT partition that serves as the system partition. You are installing another 4 GB hard drive. After installing and partitioning the new disk drive, what must you do to add the additional disk space to the existing partition?

A. You must extend the existing volume.

B. You must format the new disk drive as FAT, and then extend the existing volume.

C. You must convert the existing disk partition to NTFS file format, configure the new partition to NTFS file format, and then add the new partition to the existing volume as an extended volume.

D. You must reinstall Windows NT, defining both physical disk drives as a single volume.

32. What utility do you use to extend a volume set?

A. Server Manager

B. Disk Manager

C. Server Administrator

D. Disk Administrator

33. The most secure disk fault-tolerance supported by Windows NT Server is:

A. Disk duplexing

B. Disk striping with parity

C. Disk striping

D. Sector swapping

34. Assigning multiple printers to a single print queue is called:
    A. Printer sharing
    B. Printer pooling
    C. Printer polling
    D. Printer integration

35. What Windows NT Server utility do you use to create client startup disks?
    A. Network Client Administrator
    B. Disk Administrator
    C. Server Manager
    D. User Manager for Domains

36. What utility do you use to create a domain account for a Windows NT client system?
    A. Server Administrator
    B. User Manager for Domains
    C. Server Manager
    D. Server Manager for Domains

37. How do you install Network Services for Macintosh on a Windows NT Server?
    A. Use the Services tab in the Network applet in Control Panel
    B. Use Server Manager
    C. Use the Windows NT Server installation program
    D. None of the above

38. Which of the following Windows NT programs are used to create local user accounts, but not global accounts? Choose all correct answers.
    A. User Manager
    B. Disk Administrator
    C. Server Manager
    D. User Manager for Domains

39. Which of the following statements is true about the Primary Group property of a user account?
    A. It is used by Services for Macintosh.
    B. It is used to assign default user account permissions.
    C. You assign a primary group only to users that use Macintosh services.
    D. All the above.

40. Your new company's home office has a new computer training facility. You are asked to create user accounts for each of the eight training workstations that can log on to the domain at the home office. What can you do to limit the use of these user accounts to their intended role as training tools?
    A. Remove the training account from the Domain Users group.
    B. Limit account access to the training workstations.
    C. Set logon times to office hours at the home office.
    D. Both B and C.

41. A user at your office succumbs to marital bliss and takes her husband's last name. You must change her logon ID and the full name field in her user account. Using User Manager for Domains, what is the best way to make these changes?
    A. You must create a new account from scratch that reflects the user's new name and adds this account to the appropriate groups.
    B. You can create a new account by copying the old account and assigning the new logon ID, Full Name. This preserves the

original user account group membership and user profile.

C. You can change the logon ID name and edit the Full Name field in the existing account.

D. You can create a new account from scratch, and then use the CACLS command-line utility to copy security information from the original user account to the newly created user account.

42. What Windows NT utility do you use to set user account policies for domain user accounts?

A. User Manager

B. Server Manager

C. User Manager for Domains

D. Domain Administrator

43. To increase logon security on a Windows NT Server, which of the following can you do? Choose all that apply.

A. Reduce the lockout duration for user accounts.

B. Increase the lockout duration for user accounts.

C. Decrease the minimum length of passwords.

D. Configure Windows NT auditing to track failed logon attempts.

44. Some users belonging to (trusted) domain DM_Sales need access to files on a member Windows NT Server that belongs to (trusting) domain DM_Mktg. How can you facilitate access for the global group belonging to DM_Sales to the member server belonging to DM_Mktg?

A. Create a local group in DM_Sales, add the required user accounts, and assign the appropriate rights to the server in DM_Mktg.

B. Create a global group in DM_Sales, add the required user accounts, create a local group in the local account database on the server in DM_Mktg, assign the appropriate rights to the local group, and add the global group from DM_Sales to the local group on the target server.

C. Create a global group in DM_Sales, add the required user accounts, create a local group on a domain controller in DM_Mktg, assign the appropriate rights to the local group, and add the global group from DM_Sales to the local group on the target server.

D. Create a local group on a domain controller in DM_Mktg, assign the appropriate rights to the group, and add the required users from DM_Sales to the local group.

45. To how many global groups can a single user account belong on a Windows NT network?

A. 32

B. 16

C. 8

D. None of the above.

46. What Windows NT Server tool creates local groups?

A. User Manager

B. User Manager for Domains

C. NET.EXE

D. All the above

47. User accounts that you use to back up disk drives on domain controllers should be members of what group?
    A. Domain Admins.
    B. Server Operators.
    C. Administrators.
    D. Backup Operators.
    E. None of the above. These users should simply be granted Full Control rights to all volumes on the domain controller.

48. What functions are members of the local group Print Operators able to perform on a Windows NT member server? Choose all that apply.
    A. Manage print jobs
    B. Create new printers
    C. Create print shares
    D. All the above

49. Your company's human resources department wants to place several documents on the network and make them available to users only on your single domain Windows NT network. These documents should be read/write access for the local group HRDept and read only access for all other users. How should you set the NTFS permissions for these files?
    A. You should assign Change permission for the local group HRDept and Read permission for the special group Everyone.
    B. You should assign Change permission for the local group HRDept and Read permission for the global group Domain Users.
    C. You should assign Full Control permission for the local group HRDept and Read permission for the Global group Domain Users.
    D. You should create a local group on the target server, add the global group Domain Users to that local group, assign Read permission to the local group, and then assign Change permission to the local group HRDept.

50. What special attribute does a user account known as a service account have?
    A. A service account is a user account that is assigned the right to logon as a service.
    B. A service account is a Windows NT service that emulates a user account.
    C. A service account is a user account that is a member of the built-in local group Service Admins.
    D. Service accounts are system-level objects used by the special group System and are not accessible by any user accounts.

51. You configured your Windows NT network so that all user profiles for Windows NT Workstations are stored on a shared network drive. A user modifies her desktop and then logs off the Windows NT Workstation. After logging off, she realizes that she was not connected to the network when she modified her desktop. Has she lost the changes that she made to her desktop?
    A. No. A copy of the modified profile is saved on the Windows

NT Workstation's local hard drive. When the Windows NT Workstation boots, the system automatically uses the newest user profile.

B. Yes. If a Windows NT Workstation is configured to store profiles on a shared network drive, any changes made while the workstation is not connected to the network are lost.

C. No. A copy of the modified profile is saved on the Windows NT Workstation's local hard drive. When the Windows NT Workstation boots, the system prompts the user to update the profile stored on the shared network drive.

D. No. A copy of the modified profile saves to the shared network drive whether or not the user is logged on.

52. By default, where is the policy file NTCONFIG.POL stored in a Windows NT network?

   A. On the local hard drive of the workstation.

   B. In the NETLOGON share directory.

   C. In the user's home directory.

   D. None of the above.

53. Which of the following Windows NT Workstation actions can you control using system policies? Choose all correct answers.

   A. The boot sequence of the workstation.

   B. Customized logon screen.

   C. Remove the last logged on name from the logon dialog box.

   D. Standard Startup menu.

54. What is the name of the file in which Windows 95 policies are stored on a Windows NT network?

   A. POLICY.CFG

   B. NTCONFIG.POL

   C. CONFIG.POL

   D. WIN95.POL

55. When a Windows NT Workstation reads a user policy file, how does it store the information?

   A. The policy file is stored in a policy file on the local hard drive.

   B. The Windows NT Workstation does not store the information, but the workstation reads the policy file from the network each time Windows NT starts.

   C. It is stored in the Default User directory.

   D. The information merges into the HKEY_CURRENT_USER subtree of the Windows NT Workstation Registry.

56. What are the four explicit share permissions available in Windows NT file share security?

   A. Read, Execute, Full Control, No Access

   B. Read, Change, Full Control, No Access

   C. Read, Change, File Scan, Full Control

   D. Read, Write, Execute, File Scan

57. A user belongs to two groups that have permissions assigned to a file share. One group is assigned No Access permission, the other group is assigned Full Control permission.

Which of the following file-related functions can the user perform within the share?

A. Can change the share permissions.

B. Can read, write, and create files and directories.

C. Can only view files and directories.

D. Has no permission to perform any file access functions within the share.

58. A user belongs to a local group that is assigned Read rights to a file share on a domain controller. The user also belongs to another local group on the domain controller that is assigned Change rights to the same file share. What is this user's effective right(s) to the file share?

A. Read

B. Change

C. Change and Read

D. Full Control

59. What is the maximum number of users that can connect simultaneously to a file share on a Windows NT Workstation?

A. 32

B. 16

C. 8

D. 10

60. What NTFS directory permissions are required to view only directory contents and navigate only subdirectories?

A. View and Execute (VX)

B. List (RX)

C. Read

D. All the above.

61. Assuming NTFS, which of the following file permissions can be assigned under the Special permission? Choose all correct answers.

A. Read

B. Take Ownership

C. File Scan

D. Add

62. NTFS file permissions are:

A. Mutually exclusive

B. Hierarchically exclusive

C. Cumulative

D. Collective

63. Some data files are stored on a Windows NT Server in the (NTFS) directory `C:\INVENTORY\DATA`. These files are assigned Read permission for local group Accounting and Change permission for local group Management. They are moved to (NTFS) directory `C:\INVENTORY\SECRET`, which is located on a different server. The target directory for these files has Read permission for both Accounting and Management. What access permissions will Management have to these files after they move to the target directory?

A. Read

B. Change

C. Access Denied

D. List

64. Some data files are stored on a Windows NT Server in the (NTFS) directory `C:\INVENTORY\DATA`. These files are assigned Read permission for local group Accounting and Change permission for local group Management. They are moved to (NTFS) directory `C:\INVENTORY\SECRET`, which is located on the same server. The target directory for the files has Read permission for both Accounting and Management. What access permissions will Management have to these files after they move to the target directory?
   A. Read
   B. Change
   C. Access Denied
   D. List

65. Bryan has been asked to create a local group named Sales on a Windows NT Server named ACCTG and to assign Change permission for Sales to a large, complex directory on ACCTG. Several different NTFS permissions already are assigned for other local groups to numerous subdirectories within this directory. How can Bryan add the NTFS permissions Sales without disturbing the existing permissions?
   A. Bryan has to work through the entire directory manually with Windows NT Explorer to add the new permissions.
   B. Using the Add feature of Windows NT Explorer.
   C. Using the NET.EXE utility.
   D. Using the CACLS.EXE utility.

66. When calculating effective permissions for a file share on an NTFS directory, Windows NT compares the file share permissions and the NTFS permissions. As a result of this comparison, what is the effective access permission?
   A. The least restrictive permission is the effective permission.
   B. The most restrictive permission is the effective permission.
   C. The permissions are cumulative.
   D. The least restrictive permission is the effective permission except when No Access is assigned to either the share or the NTFS directory.

67. To assign a user NTFS permissions to a volume in a trusting domain, you should:
   A. Directly assign permissions to the user with Windows NT Explorer.
   B. Create a local group in the trusted domain, add the user to the local group, and make the local group a member of a global group that has the appropriate NTFS permissions for the target volume.
   C. Add the user to a global group in the trusted domain, and add the global group to a local group in the trusting domain that has appropriate NTFS permissions.
   D. None of the above solutions works because the domains do not have a full-trust relationship.

68. A user's *credentials* that facilitate access to resources on a Windows NT network are called:
    A. Access Control Lists (ACL)
    B. Access Control Entries (ACEs)
    C. Security IDs (SIDs)
    D. Access tokens

69. What utility do you use to set auditing policies for domain controllers on a Windows NT network?
    A. User Manager for Domains
    B. Server Manager
    C. Server Manager for Domains
    D. User Administrator

70. You suspect that one or more of the users on your Windows NT network are attempting to hack into unauthorized resources. What audit policy do you use to look for these users?
    A. File and Object Access: Look for failed attempts to access unauthorized resources.
    B. Process Tracking: Look for attempts to access unauthorized resources.
    C. Logon and Logoff: Look for excessive failed logon attempts.
    D. Use of User Rights: Look for failed attempts to perform a task.

71. What Windows NT utility do you use to view the log file where audit information is stored? Choose all correct answers.
    A. Event Viewer
    B. User Manager for Domains
    C. Server Manager
    D. NotePad

72. You configure auditing for all files stored in directory `C:\DATA\SENSITIVE` on a Windows NT Server. Files from directory `C:\DATA\SENSITIVE` are moved to directory `D:\SENSITIVE`. Auditing is disabled for directory `D:\SENSITIVE`. What is true about the auditing configuration for these moved files?
    A. The audit settings for the files does not change.
    B. The audit settings for the files does not change; however, you must change audit settings in Event Viewer for audit information to be logged correctly.
    C. Auditing is disabled for these files; however, you can restore their original audit settings with the Windows NT command-line utility NTAUDIT.EXE.
    D. Auditing is disabled for these files.

73. What is the purpose of a print spooler?
    A. A print spooler is responsible for receiving, distributing, and processing print jobs.
    B. A print spooler formats print jobs before they are sent to the printer.
    C. A print spooler queues jobs for distribution to Print Manager.
    D. A print spooler is responsible for managing printer shares.

74. To monitor disk drive activity using Performance Monitor, you must first:
    A. Create a service account that has full access to the physical drive you want to monitor, and then

assign the service account to Performance Monitor.

B. Configure the target drive(s) as striped sets.

C. Start the Disk Monitor service.

D. Run the command-line utility DISKPERF.EXE.

75. Which of the following is a valid Class B address?

A. 197.18.87.114

B. 131.255.25.10

C. 255.255.15.67

D. 127.19.181.78

76. What service do you use to provide printer access to Windows NT network printers for UNIX (IP) print requests?

A. TCP/IP printing support

B. LPD

C. LPR

D. UNIX Gateway for Windows NT

77. What utility do you use to manage and configure WINS on a Windows NT network?

A. Server Manager

B. WINS Manager

C. WINS Administrator

D. Protocol Manager

78. What command do you use to add routes to a multihomed Windows NT Server?

A. ARP

B. ROUTE

C. RARP

D. NET

79. What line protocols does Windows NT Remote Access Service support? Choose all correct answers.

A. PPP

B. PPTP

C. SLIP

D. TCP/IP

80. When analyzing the performance of a Windows NT Server, what are the two types of memory you should monitor? Choose two answers.

A. Virtual Memory

B. Chip cache memory

C. Memory with parity

D. Physical memory

81. A multihomed Windows NT Server can provide improved performance over a single-homed Windows NT server because:

A. It can serve as a router between networks, eliminating the need for an additional hop between networks (in the form of a router).

B. It can simultaneously process network requests.

C. It can run more protocols on a single network.

D. There is no performance advantage to a multihomed server.

82. What tool would you use to view user connections on a Windows NT Server?

A. User Manager

B. Server Manager

C. NET.EXE

D. Windows Diagnostics

83. What Windows NT utility do you use to log system resource utilization?
    A. Performance Monitor
    B. Resource Manager
    C. Windows Diagnostics
    D. Task Manager

84. Which of the following Windows NT Server objects is not an object that you can monitor using Performance Monitor?
    A. Paging file
    B. Memory
    C. Network adapter
    D. Redirector

85. What Windows NT program do you use to initialize the physical disk counters for use with Performance Monitor?
    A. NTFSCVT.EXE
    B. DISKPERF.EXE
    C. FDISK.EXE
    D. NET.EXE

86. What might a steady increase in Pool Nonpaged memory usage without an increase in server activity indicate?
    A. Not enough physical memory on the server.
    B. Memory errors.
    C. A *leaky* process or thread.
    D. Excessive network traffic.

87. What is the maximum length of a NetBIOS name?
    A. 16 characters.
    B. 15 characters.
    C. 32 characters.
    D. Unlimited, but you use only the first 15 characters.

88. Under what circumstances does a browser election take place?
    A. When a master browser announces that it is being shut down.
    B. When a client cannot find a master browser.
    C. When a domain controller is being initialized.
    D. All the above.

89. What Windows NT utility do you use to create an emergency repair disk?
    A. RDISK.EXE
    B. FDISK.EXE
    C. ERD.EXE
    D. NET.EXE

90. How can you create a Windows NT boot diskette?
    A. Format a diskette from within Windows NT, copy NTLDR, BOOT.INI, NTDETECT.COM, and NTBOOTDD.SYS (if required) to the diskette.
    B. Run the FORMAT /S command from a DOS session.
    C. Run RDISK, and then delete the non-system files from the emergency repair disk.
    D. Copy all the files (including hidden and system files) from the root directory of the Windows NT system partition to a formatted floppy diskette.

91. Which of the following statements are true about performing an emergency repair on a Windows NT Server? Choose all correct answers.
    A. RISC systems do not require a boot disk.

B. Intel systems with FAT system partitions boot with an MS-DOS diskette.

C. RISC systems can boot with an MS-DOS diskette.

D. Intel system with NTFS system partitions can boot with an MS-DOS diskette.

92. You installed Windows NT Server on a new computer and configured it as a Backup Domain Controller. When the new server boots, it fails to connect to the Primary Domain Controller. You confirm that all hardware, protocol drivers, and configurations are correct. Why might the Backup Domain Controller not connect to the Primary Domain Controller?

A. You failed to assign the same password to the local user Administrator on the new BDC as the password of the local administrator on the PDC. The two computers, therefore, fail to make a valid RPC connection.

B. You did not create the share IPC$ on the new PDC before attempting to join the domain.

C. You installed the BDC while it was not connected to the network or while the PDC was not available to the new BDC.

D. You did not enable the Server service on the new BDC.

93. Hardware detection is not required when Windows NT boots on a RISC computer because:

A. All RISC computers have exactly the same hardware configuration, and Windows NT for RISC-based computers is already configured for RISC.

B. Hardware information is stored in non-volatile memory on RISC computers.

C. RISC computer manufacturers provide a machine-specific Hardware Abstraction Layer (HAL) with each computer.

D. None of the above. Hardware detection is required on RISC computers.

94. Which of the following statements are true concerning TCP/IP? Choose all that apply.

A. TCP/IP is a connectionless protocol.

B. FTP uses TCP/IP to transfer files over a TCP/IP network.

C. TCP/IP transmits and receives data in frame format.

D. TCP/IP transmits and receives data as byte streams.

95. What utility do you use to monitor RAS connections from the Windows NT or Windows 95 RAS client side?

A. RAS Admin

B. Network Monitor

C. Dial-Up Networking Monitoring

D. Windows Diagnostics

96. Which of the following are RAS security features? Choose all that apply.

A. PPTP filtering

B. Callback security

C. Encryption

D. All the above

97. Which of the following is a utility that you can use to change a DHCP-assigned IP address on a Windows NT Workstation or Server?
    A. CONFIG
    B. RELEASE
    C. IPCONFIG
    D. RARP

98. You are the network engineer for a single-segment Windows NT network that uses the TCP/IP protocol. You are asked to break the network into two segments by adding another network adapter to one of the Windows NT Servers, and then configuring the server as a router. For the two network segments to communicate correctly, which of the following statements are true? Choose all that apply.
    A. The IP address range for both segments must be the same.
    B. The server that is used as a router must be a domain controller.
    C. The subnet masks on both segments must be the same.
    D. You must define the IP address on each card in the router/server on hosts as the default gateway for the respective segments.

99. The protocol used to translate MAC addresses to IP addresses on a TCP/IP network is:
    A. RARP
    B. ARP
    C. FTP
    D. DNS

100. The backup schedule used on your Windows NT Server is as follows:

     Sunday night through Friday night:
     Incremental backup

     Saturday night:
     Full backup

     Your server has a volume named ACCTDATA. Data is modified every day on this volume. If all data on ACCTDATA is lost after the Wednesday backup completes, how many backup data sets must you restore to recover the volume?
     A. 2
     B. 4
     C. 1
     D. 5

Answers and Explanations

1. **B** Members of the Administrators local group have full access to the server's resources. (Managing Resources.)
2. **B** The rationale for the other two answers is incorrect. When operating in a full-trust domain environment, the user does not automatically have a logon ID for each site (site is synonymous with domain in this example), and logon requests are processed by the nearest domain controller that belongs to the user's domain, not simply the nearest domain controller. (Managing Resources.)
3. **D** Domain trust relationships are nontransitive. (Planning.)
4. **B** The two domains involved in a trust relationship establish a password-secured communication link. You must have administrative rights to set up a trust relationship, but you don't

use the Administrator password. Either domain in a trust relationship may break the trust. (Managing Resources.)

5. **A** The global group is automatically added to the local group Administrators after a Windows NT Server or Workstation joins a domain. (Installation and Configuration.)
6. **B** The standard for assigning permissions is AGLP: Account to Global group to Local group to Permissions. (Managing Resources.)
7. **D** A complete-trust domain is not the ideal directory service structure for a large network. (Planning.)
8. **B** Disk striping with parity enables you to regenerate lost data, if a physical disk drive fails. (Installation and Configuration.)
9. **B** Disk duplexing is disk mirroring in combination with independent disk controller cards for each physical disk drive. (Installation and Configuration.)
10. **C** Data, along with parity information, is stored in blocks across at least three physical disk drives. Because parity information is stored, data on any one drive can be regenerated, if the drive fails. Without parity information, you cannot recover any data from the striped set. (Installation and Configuration.)
11. **D** NetBEUI is not routable—TCP/IP is the Internet standard—and NetBEUI offers only limited scalability. (Connectivity.)
12. **B** You exclude a Windows NT Server from functioning as a master browser by setting the Registry entry MaintainServerList to False. (Installation and Configuration.)
13. **A, B** Use both WINNT.EXE and WINNT32.EXE to install Windows NT Server. (Installation and Configuration.)
14. **B** The default installation directory for Windows NT Server is \WINNT on the system partition. (Troubleshooting.)
15. **D** Neither the built-in Administrator nor the local group Administrators can be deleted. The global group Domain Admins is automatically added to the local group Administrators when you install a domain controller. (Installation and Configuration.)
16. **C** Both Primary and Backup Domain Controllers handle Windows NT network logon requests. (Troubleshooting.)
17. **B** The software interface that communicates between system hardware and Windows NT is called the Hardware Abstraction Layer (HAL). (Troubleshooting.)
18. **B** "At least" is the key phrase. You can have more than one browser per network segment, depending on the number of hosts on the segment. (Installation and Configuration.)
19. **A** Use a TCP/IP subnet mask to define the host and network portions of an IP address. (Connectivity.)
20. **C** You might answer A; however, remember that you can add static addresses to a WINS database. (Installation and Configuration.)
21. **B** The Windows NT domain name and the DNS name do not have to be the same on a Windows NT network. (Installation and Configuration.)
22. **B** DHCP clients look for a DHCP server via BOOTP broadcasts. (Installation and Configuration.)

23. **B** Although C will work, B is the best solution because it requires only a single network adapter and a very limited configuration. Answer D seems to be a viable option except the bridges do not route; therefore, the network still is a single segment. (Connectivity.)
24. **C** NWLink is an implementation of the Novell IPS/SPX protocol. It is used to facilitate communication between Windows NT and NetWare hosts. (Connectivity.)
25. **A** The binding order of network services on a Windows NT Server determines the order in which the system services network requests. (Monitoring and Optimization.)
26. **D** The best server service optimization setting for a Windows NT Server running Microsoft Exchange is the Maximize Throughput for Network Applications setting. (Monitoring and Optimization.)
27. **A, D** By default, Windows NT Servers act as browsers; browsers maintain information only about the domain to which they belong. (Managing Resources.)
28. **D** The criteria used to elect a browser are: the operating system type, the operating system version, and whether the computer is currently a browser, master browser, or able to become a browser. (Managing Resources.)
29. **A** To facilitate directory replication, you must assign a user account permission to log on as a service (service account). (Installation and Configuration.)
30. **A** Use Server Manager to configure import and export servers to be used with Directory Replication service. (Installation and Configuration.)
31. **D** The system partition on a Windows NT Server is not extendible. To increase the size of the system partition, you must reinstall Windows NT defining both physical drives as a single volume. (Installation and Configuration.)
32. **D** Use Disk Administrator to extend a volume set. (Installation and Configuration.)
33. **B** Disk striping with parity is the most secure disk fault-tolerance supported by Windows NT Server. (Installation and Configuration.)
34. **B** Assigning multiple printers to a single print queue is called printer pooling. (Managing Resources.)
35. **A** Network Client Administrator creates client startup disks. (Managing Resources.)
36. **C** Server Manager creates a domain account for a Windows NT client system. (Managing Resources.)
37. **A** You install Network Services for Macintosh by selecting the Services tab in the Network applet in Control Panel. (Managing Resources.)
38. **A** User Manager is used to create local user accounts. User Manager for Domains can create either local or global user accounts. (Managing Resources.)
39. **A** Services for Macintosh uses the Primary Group property of a user account. (Managing Resources.)
40. **D** To limit the use of the user accounts to their intended role as training tools, limit account access to the training workstations and set logon times to office hours at the home office. (Managing Resources.)
41. **C** The Rename option is on the User menu in User Manager and User

Manager for Domains. (Managing Resources.)

42. **C** Use User Manager for Domains to set user account policies for domain user accounts. (Managing Resources.)

43. **B, D** Increasing the lockout duration for failed logon attempts and tracking failed logon attempts can enhance network logon security. (Monitoring and Optimization.)

44. **B** The recommended AGLP standard applies here: Account to Global group to Local group to Permissions. (Managing Resources.)

45. **D** A user account can belong to an unlimited number of global and/or local groups. (Managing Resources.)

46. **B, C** User Manager is not a Windows NT Server tool. (Managing Resources.)

47. **D** User accounts that you use to back up disk drives on domain controllers should be members of the local group Backup Operators. (Managing Resources.)

48. **D** Print operators can manage print jobs, create new printers, and create print shares. (Managing Resources.)

49. **D** Following the AGLP rule, you should create a local group on the target server, add the global group Domain Users (actual users that belong to the domain) to the local account, and then assign Read permission for the target files. Remembering that NTFS permissions are cumulative (except for No Access), when you assign Change permissions to the local group HRDept, users have Read/Write permissions to the target files. (Managing Resources.)

50. **A** A service account is a user account that you assign the right to logon as a service. (Installation and Configuration.)

51. **C** A copy of the modified profile is saved on the Windows NT Workstation's local hard drive. When the Windows NT Workstation boots, the system prompts the user to update the profile stored on the shared network drive. (Installation and Configuration.)

52. **B** The Windows NT policy file is stored in the NETLOGON share directory because all clients connect to the NETLOGON share during authentication to check for a system policy. (Installation and Configuration.)

53. **B, C, D** You can control whether or not a workstation can boot from the A drive, but the boot sequence is set in the workstations CMOS configuration. (Installation and Configuration.)

54. **C** Windows 95 policies are stored as CONFIG.POL. (Installation and Configuration.)

55. **D** After a Windows NT Workstation reads a user policy file, the information merges into the HKEY_CURRENT_USER subtree of the Windows NT Workstation Registry. (Installation and Configuration.)

56. **B** Read, Change, Full Control, and No Access are the four explicit share permissions available in Windows NT file share security. (Managing Resources.)

57. **D** The No Access permission on a file share overrides any other assigned permissions. (Managing Resources.)

58. **B** Change includes the Read permission, so the effective permission is Change. (Managing Resources.)

59. **D** The maximum number of users that can connect simultaneously to a

file share on a Windows NT Workstation is ten. (Installation and Configuration.)

60. **B** List (RX) directory permissions are required to view only directory contents and navigate only subdirectories. (Installation and Configuration.)
61. **A, B** File Scan and Add are not valid NTFS permissions for creating Special Permissions. (Managing Resources.)
62. **C** NTFS file permissions are cumulative. (Managing Resources.)
63. **A** If a file is moved from one directory to another across NTFS volumes, the files inherit the permissions from the target directory. (Managing Resources.)
64. **A** The files are moved to a directory on the same volume. When files move to a new location on the same NTFS volume, they retain their original permissions. (Managing Resources.)
65. **D** CACLS.EXE is a Windows NT command-line utility that can edit (rather than replace) permissions on files and directories. (Managing Resources.)
66. **B** The most restrictive permission between NTFS and file share permissions is the effective permission. (Managing Resources.)
67. **C** Answer C follows the AGLP rule. (Managing Resources.)
68. **D** Access tokens are a user's *credentials* that facilitate access to resources on a Windows NT network. (Managing Resources.)
69. **A** Use User Manager for Domains to set auditing policies for domain controllers on a Windows NT network. (Managing Resources.)
70. **A** File and Object Access: By looking for failed attempts to access unauthorized resources, you can identify attempts to access unauthorized resources. (Monitoring and Optimization.)
71. **A** Use Event Viewer to view the log file in which audit information is stored. (Monitoring and Optimization.)
72. **D** Auditing information associated with files and directories works the same as NTFS permissions; when the files are moved from one NTFS volume (C:) to another (D:), the files inherit the auditing information from the target directory. (Managing Resources.)
73. **A** A print spooler is responsible for receiving, distributing, and processing print jobs. (Managing Resources.)
74. **D** To monitor disk drive activity using performance monitor, you must first run the command-line utility DISKPERF.EXE. (Monitoring and Optimization.)
75. **B** The first octet in answer A is a Class C number, the first octet in C is an invalid number, the first octet values in D are reserved for local loopbacks. (Connectivity.)
76. **B** LPD (Line Printer Daemon) enables UNIX to access Windows NT printers; LPR enables the Windows NT network to access UNIX printers; and TCP/IP printing support is the LPD and LPR services. (Connectivity.)
77. **B** Use WINS Manager to manage and configure WINS on a Windows NT network. (Installation and Configuration.)
78. **B** You use the ROUTE command to add routes to a multihomed Windows NT Server. (Installation and Configuration.)

79. **A, B, C** RAS supports TCP/IP, but TCP/IP is a network protocol, not a line protocol. (Connectivity.)

80. **A, D** You should monitor virtual and physical memory when analyzing the performance of a Windows NT Server. (Monitoring and Optimization.)

81. **B** Answer A is true, but B is the better answer. (Connectivity.)

82. **B** You use Server Manager to view user connections on a Windows NT Server. (Monitoring and Optimization.)

83. **A** Use Performance Monitor to log system resource utilization. (Monitoring and Optimization.)

84. **C** You cannot directly monitor network adapters by Performance Monitor. (Monitoring and Optimization.)

85. **B** Use DISKPERF.EXE to initialize the physical disk counters for use with Performance Monitor. (Monitoring and Optimization.)

86. **C** A steady increase in Pool Nonpaged memory usage without an increase in server activity often indicates a *leaky* process or thread. (Monitoring and Optimization; Troubleshooting.)

87. **A** You are limited to 15 characters by Windows NT because the system internally uses the 16th character. (Managing Resources.)

88. **D** A browser election takes place when a master browser announces that it is being shut down, when a client cannot find a master browser, and when a domain controller is being installed. A browser election can also take place when a master browser fails to respond to other hosts on the network for a predetermined period of time (the default is 12 minutes). (Troubleshooting.)

89. **A** You use RDISK.EXE to create an emergency repair disk. (Troubleshooting.)

90. **A** To create a Windows NT boot diskette, format a diskette from within Windows NT, and then copy NTLDR, BOOT.INI, NTDETECT.COM, and NTBOOTDD.SYS (if required) to the diskette. (Installation and Configuration.)

91. **A, B** When performing an emergency repair on a Windows NT Server, RISC computers do not require a boot disk. You can boot Intel computers FAT system partitions with an MS-DOS diskette. (Troubleshooting.)

92. **C** The successful installation of a Backup Domain Controller requires that a PDC is already installed and available over the network to the new BDC. (Installation and Configuration.)

93. **B** Hardware detection is not required when Windows NT boots on a RISC computer because hardware information is stored in non-volatile memory on RISC computers. (Troubleshooting.)

94. **B, D** TCP is a connection-oriented protocol that utilities, such as FTP, use. TCP transmits and receives data as byte streams. (Connectivity.)

95. **C** Use Dial-Up Networking Monitoring to monitor RAS connections from the Windows NT or Windows 95 RAS client side. (Troubleshooting.)

96. **D** PPTP filtering, callback security, and encryption are all RAS security features. (Monitoring and Optimization.)

97. **C** You can use IPCONFIG to change a DHCP-assigned IP address on a Windows NT Workstation or Server. (Connectivity.)

98. **C, D** Subnet masks on a Windows NT Server that you configure to route must all be the same; in this example the Windows NT Server serves as the default gateway for both network segments. (Installation and Configuration.)

99. **B** ARP (Address Resolution Protocol) is used to translate MAC addresses to IP addresses on a TCP/IP network. (Connectivity.)

100. **D** Because both incremental and full backups reset the file archive bit, you must restore all data sets beginning with the last full backup. (Troubleshooting.)

Practice Exam 5

Windows NT Workstation Exam

You are tested in seven categories: Planning, Installation and Configuration, Managing Resources, Connectivity, Running Applications, Monitoring and Optimization, and Troubleshooting. Test questions are associated with these categories.

You are not asked these questions in order. Questions for all seven categories are presented in a seemingly random order. There are two types of questions:

- **Multiple-choice questions**—Select the correct answer.
- **Scenario-based questions**—Select the response or best scenario from the scenario description.

We suggest that you set a timer to track your progress while taking the practice exam, as the time constraint on the tests is often a big obstacle to overcome. Begin after you set your time.

Practice Exam Begins

1. You are a LAN administrator tasked with configuring 100 workstations with Windows NT Workstation 4.0 and three additional applications. Each workstation will be configured for a specific user. All machines have identical hardware configurations. Select all of the following tools that will assist you with this task.

   A. Windiff.exe

   B. Uniqueness database file

   C. Syscon.exe

   D. Unattend.txt

   E. Network boot disk

2. You need to complete an unattended upgrade of 25 workstations from Windows NT Workstation 3.51 to Windows NT Workstation 4.0. You established a directory named Workstation on a Novell NetWare distribution server named SERVER1. You then created a network share for this folder named WORKSTATION. Within the Workstation folder, you created a subfolder named \i386, and you copied all the source files from the Windows NT Workstation CD into the folder. You also placed the unattended text file called answers.txt in the Workstation folder. You will use a single account to log on to both the Windows NT domain and the NetWare server. This account will execute a script to map the local Z:\ drive to the share //SERVER1/WORKSTATION. What is the proper command to begin the installation?

   A. Z:\winnt32.exe /s:Z:\i386 /b /UDF:Z:\i386 /u:z:\answers.txt

B. Z:\i386\winnt.exe /s:Z:\i386 /ox /b /u:z:\answers.txt

C. You cannot use Novell Servers as the share point for a network installation of Windows NT.

D. Z:\i386\winnt32.exe /s::Z:\i386 /b /u:z:\answers.txt

3. Mary has been using Windows NT Workstation for three days and realizes a certain mission critical application will run only under MS-DOS. She has become frustrated and has asked if you could restore her operating system to Windows 95. Luckily, you installed Windows NT Workstation in a separate directory and did not delete her old Windows 95 files. What is the best way to restore Mary's previous environment?

   A. You cannot. The only way to uninstall Windows NT is to reformat the hard disk.

   B. Run sys.com from a bootable Windows 95 floppy, delete the Windows NT root directory, and reboot her machine.

   C. Execute the file uninstall.exe in the root directory of the Windows NT installation.

   D. Run sys.com from a bootable Windows 95 floppy, remove the hidden system files installed by Windows NT, delete the Windows NT root directory, and then reboot the machine.

4. You want to add Windows NT Workstation 4.0 to a system with existing OS/2 and DOS installations. You successfully install Workstation, but when the system boots, you no longer have the option of loading OS/2. What is the problem?

   A. You cannot dual boot a system with Windows NT 4.0 and OS/2.

   B. Windows NT automatically detects and deletes OS/2 installations.

   C. You must manually re-enable OS/2 Boot Manager by marking the Boot Manager partition as active with Windows NT's Disk Administrator program.

   D. OS/2 Boot Manager can support only bootable operating systems.

5. What is the proper sequence of activities for installing a SCSI tape backup device?

   A. From Control Panel, start the Tape Devices applet, load the drivers through the Drivers tab, and select Detect from the Devices tab.

   B. From Control Panel, start the Detect New Hardware applet.

   C. From Control Panel, start the Devices applet and set the startup properties for the SCSIBKUP device to Automatic.

   D. From Control Panel, start the Services applet and start the NT Backup service.

6. What is the proper sequence of events for installing a sound card in a Windows NT 4.0 Workstation?

   A. All sound cards on the Hardware Compatibility List (HCL) are automatically detected and installed.

   B. In Control Panel, select Add New Hardware and let the operating system detect the new hardware.

   C. In Control Panel, start the Sound applet, open the Tools menu, and select Install New Hardware.

   D. In Control Panel, select Devices, select the soundsys device, and enable the Start on Boot option.

   E. In Control Panel, select the Multimedia applet, click the Devices tab, choose Audio Devices, and then install the correct driver.

7. John calls you with a question about why his machine fails to restart after the Text portion of Setup is complete during the installation of Windows NT Workstation 4.0. He reports that he received the following message: "Windows NT could not start because the following file is missing or corrupt: \winnt root\system32\ntoskernl.exe. Please reinstall a copy of the above file." Upon further questioning, you determine that he is installing Windows NT to the first partition on the second disk drive in the machine. What is the first thing you should do to assist John?
   A. Tell him he needs to restart the installation and complete the Text portion of the installation routine again.
   B. Inform him that Windows NT must install on the first partition of the first physical disk.
   C. Check the hidden boot.ini file with a text editor to ensure the ARC path is correct.
   D. Boot to DOS and copy ntoskernl.exe from the \i386 directory on the CD-ROM to the directory where he installed Windows NT.

8. Heidi, a member of the Users group, has a shared folder she created with default permissions on her hard disk. For everyone except herself, she would like to place the strictest access permission possible on the folder. She is running Windows NT Workstation 4.0, and the disk is formatted with FAT. What should she do?
   A. Right-click the folder, select Properties, select Security, set the permissions for the Everyone group to No Access, and add her account with Full Control Privileges.
   B. Right-click the folder, select Properties, select Security, and set the permissions for the Everyone group to No Access.
   C. Right-click the folder, select Sharing, select Permissions, set the permissions for the Everyone group to No Access, and add her account with Full Control Privileges.
   D. Nothing. There is no way for Heidi to limit access to this folder.

9. From the following, select all file systems supported by Windows NT 4.0 Workstation.
   A. HPFS
   B. FAT 32
   C. FAT
   D. NTFS

10. You have successfully completed the Text portion of Windows NT Workstation 4.0 Setup. After you reboot, the Windows NT Setup Wizard will complete which of the following three phases during the GUI phase of Setup?
   A. Gathering Information About your Computer
   B. Installing Windows NT Networking
   C. Display Properties
   D. Finishing Setup
   E. Security Setup

11. A remote user needs to configure a Dial-Up Networking connection to dial using a credit card. Which Control Panel applet would he or she use to configure the modem to use a calling card when dialing?
   A. Modems
   B. Regional
   C. System
   D. Ports

12. A remote user needs to establish a Dial-Up Networking connection to a local ISP (Internet service provider) for access to the corporate Web site. Which type of Dial-Up Networking connection should the user set up?

A. PPP

B. Internet Direct

C. NetWare Connect

D. Universal Serial Connection

13. In the following scenario, you are presented with a situation, a primary result, two secondary results, and a solution. Based on the solution presented for the situation, determine which, if any, of the desired results were achieved.

    Situation: Three Windows 16-bit applications exchange information through shared memory. One application becomes unstable and crashes from time to time.

    Primary Desired Result: Maximize system stability.

    Secondary Desired Result #1: Maximize data exchange between the applications.

    Secondary Desired Result #2: Maintain efficient utilization of memory resources.

    Solution: You start each application in its own NTVDM.

    Which results were achieved?

    A. The primary result and both secondary results

    B. Only one secondary result

    C. The primary result and one secondary result

    D. Only the primary result

14. You want to install Peer Web Services. What system configurations should you check prior to beginning the installation?

    A. TCP/IP is installed and functioning properly.

    B. A default gateway is installed and functional.

    C. Microsoft Internet Services is installed.

    D. Internet Explorer is installed and configured as the default browser.

15. From the following, select all of the methods Windows NT offers for creating an emergency repair disk.

    A. During the Finishing Setup phase of the GUI portion of Setup.

    B. During the Gathering Information phase of the GUI portion of Setup.

    C. Starting the application ERU.EXE from the command prompt.

    D. Using Disk Administrator.

    E. Running RDISK.EXE from the command prompt.

16. What are the minimum requirements for successfully installing TCP/IP services on a Windows NT workstation?

    A. Subnet mask

    B. Default gateway

    C. Unique IP address

    D. Correctly installed network adapter

17. You suspect that Windows NT Workstation 4.0 is not properly detecting a SCSI card that causes the Text portion of Setup to lock up your system. You have already verified that the SCSI card is supported on the Hardware Compatibility List (HCL). What can you do to confirm your suspicions?

    A. Run MSD.EXE (Microsoft Diagnostics) from the DOS command prompt.

    B. Use the NTHQ utility located in the \SUPPORT\HQTOOL directory of the Workstation CD-ROM.

    C. Run SYSCHECK.EXE, a utility available from the Microsoft Web site.

    D. Install Windows 95. If Windows 95 supports the SCSI card, use the Windows 95 drivers when installing Windows NT.

18. Windows NT installs the boot files on which partition (a) and the system files on which partition (b)?

A. (a) SYSTEM, (b) BOOT
B. (a) BOOT, (b) SYSTEM
C. (a) BOOT, (b) RUN-TIME
D. (a) SYSTEM, (b) MAIN

19. A user has Windows NT Workstation 3.51 installed on the only partition on her computer. The partition is formatted with HPFS. She wants to upgrade to Windows NT Workstation 4.0 and convert the partition to NTFS. What is the proper method for completing the upgrade?
    A. Use the convert utility by typing **convert c: /FS:HPFS** at the command prompt before performing the Windows NT Workstation 4.0 upgrade.
    B. Although Windows NT 4.0 does not support HPFS, you have the option of automatically converting the partition without data loss during Windows NT Workstation 4.0 Setup.
    C. Install Windows NT Workstation 4.0 and run the convert utility from the command prompt by typing **convert c: /FS:HPFS**.
    D. Use the convert utility by typing **convert c: /FS:NTFS** at the command prompt, and then complete the Windows NT Workstation 4.0 upgrade.

20. A user has four 230MB partitions on his workstation. What is the most efficient file system for a new installation of Windows NT Workstation 4.0?
    A. HPFS
    B. FAT
    C. FAT32
    D. NTFS
    E. NFS

21. Heidi currently has a 1-gigabyte volume set created from two 500MB partitions formatted with FAT. She installs an additional hard disk with a 550MB partition and a 600MB partition. What is the largest volume set that she can create?
    A. 2,150MB
    B. 1,150MB
    C. 1,100MB
    D. 1,500MB

22. Don has a network printer installed on his Windows NT Workstation 4.0 computer. When he tries to print from a DOS application, nothing happens. However, other documents seem to print fine. What advice do you have for Don?
    A. He should install a local printer and connect to it directly through the serial port on his computer.
    B. He should install the print drivers included with his application, as some MS-DOS and Windows 3.1 applications require their own printer drivers in order to print successfully.
    C. His print spooler is hung. He needs to restart his local print spooler through the Services applet in the Control Panel.
    D. His network connection is down. He should reboot and log on to the network again.

23. What is the responsibility of the print spooler in Windows NT Workstation?
    A. To track the location of the print job and ensure the print job reaches the appropriate destination
    B. To assign appropriate print priorities
    C. To track the status of the print job
    D. To release the port when the job is complete

24. Installing the Client Services for NetWare in Windows NT Workstation 4.0 accomplishes which of the following tasks? Select all answers that apply.
    A. Authentication to an NDS tree.
    B. Browses NetWare servers in Network Neighborhood.

C. Connection to NetWare servers in Bindery Mode.

D. Sets up print options such as default printer, notification when the print job is complete, and use of a banner page to be included with each print job.

25. Kathy has been granted No Access to a folder named Cards. Cards has a network share with Everyone assigned Read permission. Kathy is also a member of the global group Sales. The group Sales has Full Control on the Cards folder. What is Kathy's access level to the Cards folder through a network share?

A. No Access

B. Read

C. Full Control

D. Change

26. Which of the following is the only Windows NT Registry key not written to disk at shutdown?

A. KEY_LOCAL_MACHINE\HARDWARE

B. HKEY_LOCAL_MACHINE\SYSTEM

C. HKEY_CURRENT_USER\Environment

D. HKEY_CURRENT_CONFIG\System

27. The "Last Known Good" configuration is loaded from what Registry key during startup?

A. HKEY_LOCAL_MACHINE\HARDWARE

B. HKEY_LOCAL_MACHINE\SYSTEM

C. HKEY_CURRENT_CONFIG\System

D. HKEY_CURRENT_USER\Environment

28. If you select Copy from the User menu in the User Manager utility, what items are required for the new account? Select all answers that apply.

A. Account name

B. Description

C. Password

D. Full name

29. From the following list, select all the local groups that have the authority to create network shares.

A. Power Users

B. Backup Operators

C. Users

D. Guests

30. In the following scenario, you are presented with a situation, a primary result, two secondary results, and a solution. Based on the solution presented for the situation, determine which, if any, of the desired results were achieved.

Situation: You need to install a workstation with network connectivity to other Windows NT Workstation computers running both NetBEUI and TCP/IP on the local subnet, as well a remote subnet connected through a router to the corporate WAN.

Desired Result: Network connectivity with workstations on both the local and remote subnets.

Secondary Result #1: Minimize setup requirements.

Secondary Result #2: Minimize additional network traffic.

Solution: Install the NetBEUI protocol on the new workstation.

Which results were achieved?

A. The primary and both secondary results

B. Only one secondary result

C. The primary result and one secondary result

D. None of the desired results

31. You want to see whether you should add memory to enhance system performance. Which counter or counters should you monitor with the Performance Monitor application? Select all correct answers.

A. Processor Object—%Processor Time

B. Memory Object—Pages/Sec

C. Logical Disk—Avg. Disk sec/Transfer

D. Physical Disk—Disk Queue Length

32. In the following scenario, you are presented with a situation, a primary result, two secondary results, and a solution. Based on the solution presented for the situation, determine which, if any, of the desired results were achieved.

Situation: You install Windows NT Workstation 4.0 on a graphics workstation for a new user. The machine has four 1-gigabyte SCSI drives. The typical file size is 35MB.

Primary Result: Maximize system performance.

Secondary Result #1: Maximize disk capacity.

Secondary Result #2: Maximize data integrity and recoverability.

Solution: You format all drives with NTFS. Then you install the system files on the first drive, and you create a stripe set with the remaining three drives. Finally, you place the paging file on the stripe set.

Which results were achieved?

A. The primary and both secondary results

B. Only one secondary result

C. The primary result and one secondary result

D. None of the desired results

33. Jane tries to connect to a local resource on your machine through a network share to open a document she needs to update. She calls and states that she cannot save the document in the shared folder even though she entered the correct password for the share. You check and see that her account permission for folder is set to Change, her permission for the share is Execute, and her permission for the file is No Access. Because there is nothing sensitive in the document, you change her access permission to Write. She attempts the save again, but nothing happens. What's the problem?

A. Because you changed her permission, her password is no longer valid.

B. She must disconnect from all resources on your workstation and reconnect before she can gain access.

C. Execute permissions on network shares do not allow users to save documents in the shared folder.

D. Her network connection must be down. She should reboot and try again.

34. Jane tries to connect to a local resource on your machine through a network share to open a document she needs to update. She calls and states that she cannot save the document in the shared folder even though she entered the correct password. You check and see that her account permission for folder is set to Read, her access level for the share is Read, and her permission for the file is set to Read. You change her permission levels for both the folder and file to Execute. She disconnects from the resource and reconnects, but still cannot gain access. What went wrong?

A. You should have changed the permission for the file to Change.

B. You should have changed the permission for the folder to Change.

C. You should have changed the permission for the share to Change.

D. You did the right thing, but Jane needs to reboot her machine to properly connect.

35. Select all of the files that a dual boot Windows NT Workstation 4.0 installation uses during the system boot sequence when booting to Windows NT.

A. BOOT.INI

B. NTLDR

C. NTOSKRNL.EXE

D. BOOTSECT.DOS

E. COMMAND.COM

36. During what part of the Windows NT boot sequence is the kernel loaded?

A. Boot phase

B. Initialization phase

C. Services Load phase

D. Subsystem Startup

37. Select all of the following statements that are true of a Windows NT boot disk.

A. It is formatted with NTFS for security purposes.

B. It has a boot sector that references the NTLDR.

C. It contains a copy of the boot files.

D. It can also boot to Windows 95.

38. Hardware profiles are created through which of the following methods?

A. The System applet in Control Panel

B. The Services applet in Control Panel

C. The Devices applet in Control Panel

D. User Manager

39. How can you modify a standalone Windows NT Workstation installation so it does not display the name of the last user to log in?

A. Use the System Policy Editor

B. Use the System applet in Control Panel

C. Edit the HKEY_LOCAL_MACHINE\SOFTWARE\MICROSOFT\WINDOWS NT\CURRENTVERSION\WINLOGON\DONTDISPLAYLAST-USERNAME Registry key.

D. Use the User Manager utility

40. Dale, a member of the Local Users group, realizes that the system time on his Windows NT workstation is incorrect. He calls you and states that he is unable to change the time on his workstation. What can you do to fix this problem, yet still limit Dale's ability to modify the operating system on his local workstation?

A. Remotely edit the Registry on his machine to change the time.

B. Add his account to the Local Administrators group.

C. Grant the user right "Change the system time" to Dale's account.

D. Reinstall the Control Panel application on Dale's computer.

41. You notice a particular application, app.exe, seems sluggish. You want to try starting the particular application with a higher than normal priority to see if this helps performance. How do you accomplish this?

A. At the command line, type **START /REALTIME app.exe**.

B. At the command line, type **EXECUTE /NORMAL app.exe**.

C. At the command line, type **RUN /HIGH app.exe**.

D. At the command line, type **START /HIGH app.exe**.

42. Bill frequently needs to have multiple instances of spreadsheet calculations running in the background. However, he complains that when the applications are minimized, they seem to take an excessive time to complete. He asks if there is anything he can do. What would you tell him?
    A. Leave the applications maximized when performing the calculations.
    B. On the Performance tab of the System applet, set the foreground application responsiveness to None.
    C. Start the spreadsheet calculations immediately before logging out and leaving for the day.
    D. Increase the hard disk size to improve memory paging operations.

43. You start the Performance Monitor application to analyze the amount of time servicing disk I/O requests to see if you need to upgrade the hard disk controller in your workstation. When you select the %Disk Time counter for monitoring, you notice the counter does not move. What is wrong?
    A. The resources required to monitor disks are so demanding that they would skew the data on the local machine. You can monitor disk activity only for remote computers.
    B. The lack of movement in the counters indicates there is no problem with the amount of time spent servicing the disk I/O requests.
    C. You must initialize the resources to monitor the disks through the Services applet in Control Panel.
    D. You must initialize the disk performance counters by typing **DISKPERF –Y** at the command prompt.

44. An accounting firm needs to set up a local area network for file and print sharing. They currently have 10 standalone workstations. The workstations are a mix of 486DXs (66MHz) and Pentiums (100MHz). All have 16MB of RAM and 1-gigabyte hard disks. They have spent their hardware budget for the year on purchasing network cards and hubs, so they cannot upgrade any machines. They have prioritized their objectives for the new local area network as follows:
    1. File and print sharing
    2. Security on files and network shares
    3. Operating System stability
    4. Minimal network management
    5. Preemptive multitasking with all applications

    They have requested that you assist in selecting an operating system prior to installing the network. Which of the following is the best operating system choice in this scenario? (Select only one.)
    A. Windows 3.1
    B. Windows for Workgroups
    C. Windows 95
    D. Windows NT Workstation

45. You want to use the Multilink Protocol on your analog dial-up connection to the central office. The Remote Access Server is configured for dial-back security. How should you configure Dial-Up Networking on your workstation?
    A. Multilink Protocol cannot be used when the server is configured for dial-back security.
    B. The RAS server will call back both telephone numbers sequentially.
    C. Check the Multilink Dial option on the Advanced Properties tab of the Phone Book entry for the Dial-Up Networking connection.

D. Do nothing. Windows NT Workstation 4.0 detects two modems and automatically activates the Multilink Protocol.

46. You want to add an additional network adapter to an existing installation of Windows NT Workstation 4.0 to perform IP routing. What is the proper sequence of events to install the new adapter?

    A. From Control Panel, start the Add New Hardware applet and allow the operating system to detect the new adapter.

    B. From Control Panel, select the Network applet, choose the Adapter tab, and click Add.

    C. Windows NT Workstation cannot perform IP routing; this is a feature found only in Windows NT Server.

    D. Reinstall Windows NT Workstation to add the second adapter.

47. You install a new video adapter that is listed in the HCL in a Windows NT Workstation. When you boot the machine, the screen remains black. How should you fix the problem?

    A. The adapter must be faulty. Exchange the adapter for a functional unit.

    B. Turn the machine off and restart it. When the boot menu appears, select the VGA option and use the Display applet in the Control Panel to update the video drivers.

    C. Reboot the machine with a DOS disk and edit the HKEY_LOACL_MACHINE\System\Video Registry entry.

    D. Reboot to DOS and run the VideoUpdate.exe located in the \i386 directory on the Windows NT Workstation CD-ROM.

48. You have three DOS applications that users need to run concurrently. One application often becomes unstable and hangs the system. How can you ensure that each application is started in its own NTVDM?

    A. Start the System applet in Control Panel. On the Applications tab, check the Start all DOS Applications in Separate Memory Space option.

    B. From the Start menu, choose Run. Make sure the Run in Separate Memory Space box is checked for each application.

    C. Do nothing. When Windows NT detects that an application has become unstable, the remaining applications in that NTVDM are moved to a separate memory space automatically.

    D. In the HKEY_LOCAL_MACHINE\ Software Registry key, set the value of StartinSeperate-NTVDM to **0x001** for the appropriate applications.

49. Bill needs to take ownership of a file created by Mindy. What permission must Mindy set for the file in order for Bill to take ownership?

    A. Execute

    B. Change

    C. Full Control

    D. Take Ownership

50. You want to have all user profiles on a workstation stored on the D:\ drive in a directory called \USERS\<*username*> (where <*username*> is the Windows NT account name). How would you accomplish this?

    A. For each account, start the System applet from Control Panel, select the Profiles tab, select the user account, and then click the Path button. Enter the correct path to the directory in the resulting dialog box.

B. Create a template account and click the Profile button. In the Profile text box, enter D:\USERS\%USERNAME%. Then use the Copy command in the User Manager utility to copy the template account, renaming the account for the correct user.

C. Create a template account and click the Profile button. In the Profile text box, enter D:\USERS\%USER_NAME%. Then use the Copy command in the User Manager utility to copy the template account, renaming the account for the correct user.

D. For each user, create a login script that maps the user profile to the appropriate directory using the NET USE PROFILE command.

51. In which of the following situations is it prudent to delete the user account?

A. The user has taken an extended leave of absence.

B. The user was a temporary employee, and a replacement will not be hired.

C. The user has been fired, and a replacement will be hired next week.

D. The user will be on vacation for the next month.

52. You determine that a user's print jobs are stuck in the print queue. How do you restore the print queue to a functional status?

A. Reboot the print server.

B. Launch the Services applet from Control Panel. Select the Print Spooler Service, choose Stop, and then choose Start.

C. Right-click the appropriate printer in the Printer folder and select Properties from the shortcut menu. Then select the Spooler tab, click Stop, and click Start.

D. Launch the Devices applet from Control Panel. Select the appropriate printer, click Stop, and then click Start.

53. Which of the following subsystems run in the Kernel mode of Windows NT Workstation 4.0?

A. GDI (Graphics Device Interface)

B. WIN32 USER (Windows Manager)

C. CSR (Client Service Subsystem)

D. POSIX Subsystem

54. Jill is running three 16-bit applications in a single NTVDM. When one application crashes, all other applications become unresponsive. She calls and asks why, if Windows NT provides preemptive multitasking, do all the other applications hang? What do you tell her?

A. Windows NT starts all 16-bit applications in the same NTVDM unless the Run Application in Separate Memory Space option is checked in the Run dialog box.

B. She must enable multitasking for 16-bit applications through the System applet in Control Panel.

C. Windows NT can provide true preemptive multitasking only for native 32-bit applications.

D. Windows NT can provide true preemptive multitasking only for applications that run in the Kernel mode.

55. Your Windows NT Workstation computer must connect to an enterprise-wide network running servers with all versions of NetWare. You notice that you can connect to only some of the servers. What is the proper course of action to fix this problem? Select all answers that apply.

A. You must load multiple instances of Client Services for NetWare to create connections to different versions of NetWare.

B. From the CSNW applet in Control Panel, select the General tab and enable auto detection for each of the appropriate frame types.

C. Edit the parameters in the Registry key HKEY_LOCAL_MACHINE\System\CurrentControlSet\Services\Nwlinklpx\NetConfig*network adapter card1*, where *network adapter card1* is the entry for your adapter card.

D. Client Services for NetWare can connect to only one NetWare version during a session.

56. If Ellen pauses the Workstation Service on her computer, what effect will it have on her machine?

A. All connected network shares currently connected to her workstation will be disconnected.

B. All her network connections to other workstation resources will be disconnected.

C. All network shares currently connected to her workstation will remain connected, but no new connections can be made to her workstation.

D. All her current connections to other workstation resources will remain connected, but she will not be able to create any new connections.

Answers and Explanations

1. **B, D, E** The Uniqueness Database File extends the functionality of the answer file. Unattend.txt is the default name of the answer file that automates the Text and GUI portions of the Windows NT Setup process. The network boot disk provides network connectivity to the server share containing the Windows NT Workstation setup files.

2. **D** The setup program used to upgrade existing Windows NT installations is winnt32.exe. This program resides in the \i386 directory. To complete an unattended installation, you need to use the /s, /b, and /u switches. The /s switch specifies the path to the installation source files, the /b indicates that boot disks should not be created, and the /u indicates the location of the automated answer file.

3. **D** You must remove the hidden system files installed by Windows NT as well as the Windows NT root directory to complete the removal of the Windows NT installation. You must run the DOS command sys.com to ensure that the hard disk will boot to DOS/Windows 95.

4. **C** Windows NT automatically disables the OS/2 Boot Manager during installation. You must manually re-enable it after completing the Windows NT installation.

5. **A** Tape devices and drivers must be loaded through the Control Panel applet Tape Devices.

6. **E** Windows NT Workstation 4.0 does not currently support Plug-and-Play; sound hardware drivers must be manually installed through the Multimedia applet in Control Panel.

7. **C** This message typically occurs when Windows NT does not correctly set the ARC boot path in BOOT.INI file. This file can be edited with any DOS text editor.

8. **D** Members of the Users group cannot modify the permissions on network shares. Because the file system is FAT, there is no way Heidi can modify the permissions on the folder itself.

9. **C, D** Windows NT no longer supports HPFS. Only Windows 95 supports FAT 32.

10. **A, B, D** Display properties are configured during the Finishing Setup phase; Security Setup is not a phase of Windows NT Setup.

11. **A** Dialing properties for all modem connections are set through the Modem applet in the Control Panel.
12. **A** PPP is the only type of valid Dial-Up Networking connection listed.
13. **D** Only the primary result was achieved. Starting each application in its own NTVDM ensures that application crashes affect only that NTVDM; the remaining applications are unaffected. Because the applications use shared memory to exchange information, starting each application in a separate NTVDM does not allow the applications to exchange information. Therefore, Secondary Desired Result #1 is not achieved. Starting each application in a separate NTVDM requires separate, additional memory resources for each application. Therefore, Secondary Desired Result #2 is not achieved.
14. **A** A default gateway is not required for Peer Web Services; there is no Microsoft Internet Service; and Peer Web Services does not require a specific browser.
15. **B, E** Windows NT Setup prompts for the creation of an emergency repair disk during the Gathering Information Phase. After installation, an emergency repair disk can be created or updated with the RDISK.EXE utility.
16. **A, C, D** A default gateway is not required for successful completion of TCP/IP installation. A network card is required for protocol binding. A subnet mask and IP address are required for machine identification on the network.
17. **B** Of all the options presented, only NTHQ has the capability of identifying the hardware Windows NT Setup detects.
18. **A** Windows NT installs the boot files on the system partition and the system files on the boot partition.
19. **D** Because Windows NT no longer supports HPFS, the conversion must be completed prior to performing the upgrade. Currently, the convert utility only supports conversions to NTFS; therefore, the correct command line would be convert c:/FS:NTFS.
20. **B** For partitions less than 400MB, FAT is considered the most efficient file system for file access.
21. **B** The existing volume set could not be extended because it is formatted with FAT; only NTFS formatted volume sets can be extended. Therefore, a new volume set could be created with the two new partitions with a total size of 550 + 600 megabytes, or 1,150 megabytes.
22. **B** Because other documents are printing successfully, the problem must reside with the DOS application. Some DOS and 16-bit Windows applications require their own print drivers in order to print successfully.
23. **A, B** The print spooler is responsible for tracking the location of the print job, ensuring the print job is sent to the correct port, and assigning print priorities. The print monitor is responsible for tracking the status of the print job and releasing the port when a print job is complete.
24. **A, B, C** Client Services for NetWare does not allow the user to select the default printer. This is a function of the Windows NT operating system and Windows NT Explorer.
25. **A** The No Access permission takes precedence over all other file, folder, and share permissions.
26. **A** Because the Hardware key is built during startup, it is the only Registry key that is not saved to disk.
27. **B** The "Last Known Good" control set is in the HKEY_LOCAL_MACHINE\SYSTEM Registry key.
28. **A, C** The Description and Full Name are not needed to create a new account.
29. **A** Of the built-in local groups listed, Power Users is the only local group that can create network shares.

30. **B** Minimize setup requirements was the only result achieved by installing NetBEUI because it is a self-configuring protocol. Because NetBEUI is not routable, the workstation cannot connect with workstations on a different subnet. NetBEUI is a "chatty" protocol, resulting in more network traffic than TCP/IP.

31. **B, C** Microsoft recommends multiplying the average Pages/Sec (memory object) by the average value of the Avg. Disk sec/ Transfer (Logical Disk object) to determine the percentage of disk I/O used by paging. If this value exceeds 10 percent, additional physical memory should be installed.

32. **C** Placing the paging file on a disk other than the boot partition will enhance system performance. Formatting disks larger than 400MB with NTFS will also maximize disk I/O, increasing overall system performance. Therefore, the primary objective has been met. By creating a stripe set, you maximize the amount of disk space available, achieving Secondary Desired Result #1. However, creating a stripe set decreases recoverability because the failure of one disk will destroy the stripe set, including all data. Therefore, Secondary Desired Result #2 is not achieved.

33. **B** Changes to user accounts will not take effect until the user access token is refreshed. This is accomplished by disconnecting from the resource and reconnecting to refresh the token.

34. **C** The security reference monitor determines access to folders across shares by determining the most restrictive permissions between the folder/files and the network share. In this case, because the share permission is still Read, you need to change the share permission to Write to allow Jane to save the document. Because the reference monitor determines file access by applying the least-restrictive permissions between the file and folder, the file access does not need to be changed.

35. **A, B, C** Windows NT uses BOOT.INI, NTLDR, and NTOSKERNL.EXE when the system is booted to Windows NT. BOOTSECT.DOS and COMMAND.COM are used when booting to DOS.

36. **A** Windows NT loads the kernel during the Kernel Load phase, which occurs during the Boot phase. The kernel is initialized during the Initialization phase.

37. **B, C** The NTFS file system is too large to fit on a formatted floppy. In order to boot to Windows 95, the disk must contain the Windows 95 boot files.

38. **A** Hardware profiles are created with the System applet. Hardware profiles are defined using the Services and Device applets.

39. **C** The best way to remove the last user to log in is with the system policy editor. However, this is a Windows NT Server utility only; it is not available with a standalone Windows NT Workstation installation. Therefore, the only other available means is a direct Registry edit.

40. **C** Granting the Change System Time right to Dale's account will allow Dale to change the time, while ensuring that he cannot modify other parameters of the local operating system.

41. **D** To launch an application with a priority other than the default, use the command START /PRIORITY. The REALTIME priority should never be used for applications; it is typically reserved for operating system components.

42. **B** The foreground application responsiveness control is the only way to modify the responsiveness of all background applications.

43. **D** Because the resources required to monitor disk activity are rather demanding, they are not started by default. The resources must be started prior to monitoring the disk object counters.

44. **D** Windows NT is the operating system that will meet the most objectives set forth by the accounting firm.
45. **A** The Multilink Protocol cannot be used with analog connections when the server is configured to provide call-back security.
46. **B** Network adapters must be installed through the Network applet in Control Panel.
47. **B** When Windows NT will not boot correctly due to video problems, the machine should be restarted in the VGA mode so proper modifications can be made to the video drivers.
48. **B** The preferred way for users to launch applications in separate NTVDMs is by enabling the Run in Separate Memory Space option from the Run command on the Start menu.
49. **C** The only file permission that allows accounts other than those included in the Administrators group to take ownership is Full Control.
50. **B** The proper way to create similar user accounts is to create a template and use the Copy command in User Manager to create the new accounts. The %USERNAME% macro will substitute the account name when creating profiles and home directories.
51. **B** Once deleted, user accounts cannot be recalled; the account should be disabled or renamed if the account will need to be reactivated or reused. Of all the options listed, the only situation in which the account will no longer be needed is the case of retirement with no replacement being hired.
52. **B** The print spooler runs as a service in Windows NT 4.0 and must be controlled from the Services applet in Control Panel.
53. **A, B** Both the GDI and WIN32 USER portions of the operating system have been moved into the Kernel with Windows NT 4.0 for increased system performance.
54. **A** Windows NT launches all 16-bit applications in the same NTVDM to conserve memory unless the user specifies that the applications should be run in separate NTVDMs when the applications are started.
55. **C** The only way to configure Windows NT Workstation to recognize multiple frame types is to edit the Registry. Only Windows NT Server can be configured through the CSNW applet in the Control Panel.
56. **D** Because the workstation service is responsible for creating network connections to other workstation resources, Ellen will not be able to create any new connections. Because the service is paused, existing connections remain active.

Practice Exam 6

Windows NT Workstation Exam

You are tested in seven categories: Planning, Installation and Configuration, Managing Resources, Connectivity, Running Applications, Monitoring and Optimization, and Troubleshooting. Test questions are associated with these categories.

You are not asked these questions in order. Questions for all seven categories are presented in a seemingly random order. There are two types of questions:

- **Multiple-choice questions**—Select the correct answer.
- **Scenario-based questions**—Select the response or best scenario from the scenario description.

We suggest that you set a timer to track your progress while taking the practice exam, as the time-constraint on the tests is often a big obstacle to overcome. Begin after you set your time.

Practice Exam Begins

1. Bill and Susan use the same computer. Bill needs Windows NT and Susan needs Windows 95. Which kind of partition type should you use on this computer?

   A. HPFS

   B. NTFS

   C. FAT (FAT 16)

   D. FAT32

2. You work for a government contractor working on top secret files. Obviously, security is very important to your company. You need to make sure that the documents you store on your local hard drive cannot be accessed by others via the network or locally. Which partition type should you use?

   A. FAT

   B. NTFS

   C. HPFS

   D. NFS

3. You want to install Windows NT and Windows 95 on the same system. Identify the series of steps that will result in a working dual boot scenario. (Choose all that apply.)

   A. Install Windows 95, and then upgrade to Windows NT in the same directory.

   B. Install Windows 95, and then install Windows NT in another directory.

   C. Install Windows NT, and then install Windows 95 in the same directory.

D. Install Windows NT, install Windows 95 in a different directory, and then use the boot disks to repair the Windows NT installation.

4. Bill has decided to add a new IDE CD-ROM to his Windows NT workstation installation. Which Control Panel applet does Bill need to use to allow Windows NT to see the CD-ROM?
   A. CDROMs
   B. Multimedia
   C. Devices
   D. SCSI Adapters

5. You've installed a new Microsoft IntelliPoint Mouse. Which Control Panel applet enables you to install the correct drivers?
   A. Devices
   B. Mouse
   C. Keyboard
   D. System

6. You just attached a new SCSI tape drive because the old tape drive went out. The old drive was 4MM, and the new drive is a DLT. Which Control Panel applet do you use to set up the tape drive?
   A. Devices
   B. SCSI Adapters
   C. Tape Devices
   D. Multimedia

7. You've copied the Windows NT Workstation files from the CD onto an NT Server to be used to update Windows 3.1 computers to Windows NT Workstation 4.0. Which commands upgrade a Windows 3.11 workstation from the server?
   A. WINNT /OX
   B. WINNT /B
   C. WINNT32 /OX
   D. WINNT32 /B

8. You have a Windows NT workstation that is shared by five users. Two of them are third-shift maintenance workers who enter the maintenance schedules for the machines in the plant. One is the office receptionist who creates monthly calendars for the employees, showing birthdays, parties, and other events. The final two employees use the workstation to track production information relating to when jobs were completed and how much money the company made. Which of the following structures is the most desirable in this situation?
   A. Create user accounts for each user, and then assign each user access to the resources he or she needs.
   B. Create three user accounts: one for the two maintenance workers, one for the receptionist, and one for the employees tracking production information.
   C. Allow everyone to use the Administrator account.
   D. Create a user account for each user. Create three groups: maintenance, general office, and production. Assign the users to the appropriate groups, and then assign each group access to the appropriate resources.

9. You're an administrator of a medium-sized network and want to have easy access to installable copies of applications available to you no matter who is logged in at a particular workstation. However, you don't want the users to be able to browse and see these applications. How can you name the share so that others can't browse it?
   A. ~INSTAPPS
   B. $INSTAPPS
   C. INSTAPPS~
   D. INSTAPPS$

10. You want everyone to be able to modify files in the DATA directory while logged in locally to a Windows NT workstation, but

you don't want anyone to be able to modify the data when they are not logged into the workstation locally. How should the file permissions and share permissions be set up?

A. Share: Everyone with Full Permissions
Directory: Everyone with Read Only Permission

B. Share: Everyone with Read Permission
Directory: Everyone with Full Permission

C. Share: Everyone with Change Permission
Directory: Everyone with Change Permission

D. Share: Power Users with Change permission
Directory: Everyone with Full Permission

11. You're installing Windows NT Workstation on a network that's running TCP/IP without a DHCP server. You're in a routed environment and use routers that can pass BOOTP packets. Which of the following are required?

A. IP address

B. DNS address

C. WINS address

D. Subnet mask

12. You're installing Windows NT Workstation on a network that's running TCP/IP, NWLink IPX/SPX, and NetBEUI with a DHCP server. Which of the following are required for TCP/IP to work?

A. DHCP server hardware address

B. IP address

C. Subnet mask

D. A local DHCP server, or a DHCP server connected via a router set to pass BOOTP packets

13. You're running Windows NT Workstation at home and need to access NetWare servers at work via Dial-Up Networking. You also occasionally log into the company intranet to review management reports and enter orders. Which network protocols must you use?

A. NetBEUI

B. SLIP

C. PPP

D. NWLink IPX/SPX

E. TCP/IP

14. You want to run a processor-intensive application, but you don't want to slow down your other work. How can you start this application so that it will not interfere with your other work?

A. Click the Start button and select Run. Then check the Run in a Separate Memory Space option.

B. Click the Start button and select Run. Then uncheck the Run in a Separate Memory Space option.

C. From the Task Manager, select File and then Run.

D. Use the Start command from a command prompt.

15. Your boss just came in asking for a financial projection, and he needs it in five minutes for a board meeting. The program normally takes 10 minutes to run. How do you start an application to run quickly?

A. START /HIGH MYAPP.EXE

B. START MYAPP.EXE /HIGH

C. START /REALTIME MYAPP.EXE

D. START /QUICK MYAPP.EXE

16. You are running Windows NT on a Digital Alpha-based computer, and you receive a 32-bit program that a friend wrote on her Windows 95 system. It won't run on your computer. What is the problem?

A. It isn't compiled for Windows NT.

B. It isn't compiled for Alpha-based systems.

C. The Multiplatform flag wasn't turned on when the program was compiled.

D. The program must be compiled under Windows NT.

17. Your computer is performing slowly. You've noticed that when you're running certain applications, things take longer than they should to complete. You use Performance Monitor to monitor various objects, but none of the disk counters show any activity. What course of action should you take?

A. Replace the hard disk controller with one supported by Windows NT.

B. Replace the hard disks in question.

C. Turn on disk performance counters.

D. Turn off disk performance counters.

18. Your computer is slow accessing a SQL database and the Internet. You know that the slow Internet access isn't a result of your connection speed because Bill, the network administrator, isn't having the same Internet access problem. You want to determine where the bottleneck is. Which is the best tool to start with?

A. Performance Monitor

B. Task Manager

C. Network Monitor

D. SQL Trace

19. Because you installed the XYZ system, your computer is constantly accessing the disk drive. You are unsure what the cause of the disk activity is and whether the disk needs to be upgraded. Calls to XYZ technical support aren't any help. Which objects should be watched? (Choose all that apply.)

A. Paging File

B. Memory

C. Physical Disk

D. Server

20. Your Windows NT workstation is sluggish immediately after a reboot, but it seems to work fine after it has been on for a while. You're starting quite a few services when you first start up, including Peer Web Services. What might you suspect the problem is?

A. Windows NT is searching for new Plug and Play devices.

B. Windows NT is initializing file allocation tables in memory for all of the connected disks.

C. The paging file initial size is too small.

D. Windows NT is backing up configuration files.

21. Printing has stopped on a printer connected to your computer. No matter what jobs you submit to the printer, they aren't printing. How do you reset the printer subsystem without rebooting?

A. You can't; rebooting is the only way to reset the printer subsystem.

B. Type **PRINTER RESET SYSTEM** at the command line.

C. Stop and restart the printer service.

D. Stop and restart the spooler service.

22. Sam calls you to tell you he can't read a file in a shared folder on your hard drive. Other people are using the same file without problems. What might be the problem?

A. Sam isn't using the right password.

B. Sam doesn't have access to the share.

C. Sam doesn't have access to the file.

D. The Workstation service on your computer is corrupted.

23. You contacted Microsoft technical support with a problem, and they suggested you add a multistring Registry entry to fix the problem. Which utility should you use to edit the Registry?

A. REGEDIT

B. REGEDT32

C. Control Panel

D. EDITREG

24. Your computer has three 4GB drives connected to a SCSI controller. You want to maximize the performance of your system so you can get more work done. Which of the following disk configurations is the fastest?

 A. One 12GB volume set across all drives

 B. One 12GB stripe set across all drives

 C. One 4GB system partition and an 8GB volume set

 D. One 4GB system partition and an 8GB stripe set

25. Your computer has four 4GB drives connected to a SCSI controller. You want to get the maximum space available and have fault tolerance. What is the best way to accomplish this?

 A. Create a 4GB system partition and an 8GB stripe set with parity partition.

 B. Create a 4GB system partition and a 12GB stripe set partition.

 C. This cannot be done.

 D. Create a 4GB mirrored system partition and a 4GB mirrored data partition.

26. The chief financial officer of your company approaches you to report that the company projections that are written inside of Excel aren't running fast enough on her Windows NT-based computer. You run Performance Monitor and notice two things: There is a lot of disk activity, and the processor utilization is about 50% while the projections are running. What is the most likely cause of the performance bottleneck?

 A. The network card

 B. The CPU

 C. The amount of memory

 D. The disk drive

27. The chief financial officer of your company approaches you to report that the company projections that are written inside of Excel aren't running fast enough on his Windows NT-based computer. You run Performance Monitor and notice two things: There is very little disk activity, and the processor utilization is almost 100% while the projections are running. What is the most likely cause of the performance bottleneck?

 A. The network card

 B. The CPU

 C. The amount of memory

 D. The disk drive

28. You've discovered that the company's projections are suffering from a CPU bottleneck. They are prepared using a single-threaded Visual Basic application that the IS staff wrote for you. Which upgrade is likely to have the greatest benefit?

 A. Another processor

 B. A faster processor

 C. More memory

 D. A faster network card

29. You're getting a message that one or more services failed during startup. You don't notice any problems, but you want to check just to be sure. Where should you go to find out more about this message?

 A. Event Viewer

 B. Control Panel, System applet

 C. User Manager

 D. Backup

30. You've installed Windows NT Workstation on a partition formatted with FAT because you used to have Windows 95 installed. You're now ready to move to using Windows NT exclusively on this machine.

Which command-line program should you use to change this partition to NTFS?

A. This cannot be done.

B. MAKENTFS

C. CHANGEFS

D. CONVERT

31. You've installed Windows NT Workstation on a partition formatted with NTFS. Now you want to install Windows 95 so you can dual boot between the two operating systems. Which command-line program should you use to change this partition to FAT?

A. This cannot be done.

B. MAKEFAT

C. CHANGEFS

D. CONVERT

32. When running Windows NT, you notice some strange things on the file system. There doesn't seem to be as much space as there should be, and some directory entries have strange characters in them. Which command can you run to have Windows NT run a diagnostic on the drives?

A. DIAGNOSE

B. SCANDISK

C. CHKDSK

D. CHKDSK /F

33. Which of the following files is used to install Windows NT without user intervention?

A. USRRESP.TXT

B. NOPROMPT.TXT

C. UNATTEND.TXT

D. SYSDIFF.EXE

34. Which of the following programs is used to create an image that can later be used by SYSDIFF to replicate an installation?

A. SYSIMG.EXE

B. UNATTEND.TXT

C. SYSDIFF.EXE

D. IMAGE.EXE

35. You want to install Windows NT on a machine that isn't on the Hardware Compatibility List. Which of these utilities can you use to determine which drivers might work for the hardware?

A. MSD

B. NTHQ

C. NTHWANZ

D. HDWANLZR

36. It's Christmas, and instead of getting a Sony Playstation, you decided to buy a new sound card for your Windows NT Workstation. So now you have a new sound card that you want to install in Windows NT Workstation. Which Control Panel applet do you use to set up this new hardware?

A. Add new hardware

B. Sound Cards

C. Multimedia

D. Devices

37. It's Christmas again, and you decided the sound card wasn't enough, so you bought a new faster video card. Which of the following are valid steps for replacing the video card?

A. Power down the system, replace the video card, run Windows NT, and then go to the Display applet in the Control Panel.

B. Power down the system, replace the video card, run Windows NT in VGA mode, and then go to the Display applet in the Control Panel.

C. Go to the Control Panel, change the Display Driver to VGA, power down the system, replace the video card, and then run Windows NT and go to the Display applet in the Control Panel.

D. Go to the Control Panel, change the Display Driver to the new video card, shut down NT, and then replace the video card.

38. You're a pioneering soul and have decided that you want to use Windows NT Workstation despite the fact that the rest of the network uses Windows 95. Which pieces of information do you need from the NetWare administrator to make your Windows NT workstation work?

A. The login server name

B. The IPX network number

C. The version of IPX being used

D. The frame type of the network

39. While installing your Windows NT workstation on your Novell network, you notice that Windows NT didn't detect the correct frame type. Instead of asking the network administrator, you decide to figure out what frame types are valid for ethernet. Which of the following are valid ethernet frame types?

A. 802.5

B. 802.2

C. 802.3

D. Ethernet_II

E. Ethernet_Snap

40. Despite the resistance of your IS department, you are installing Windows NT on a NetWare network that uses NetWare 4.0. What must be done in order for the Windows NT workstation to access the NetWare 4.0 server?

A. Nothing; Windows NT can't access NetWare 4.0 servers.

B. Nothing; Windows NT will automatically detect the server's presence and connect to it.

C. Enter the name of the NDS tree into Windows NT's Client Services for NetWare when prompted.

D. Set Bindery emulation context on the Windows NT server.

41. Because it's the end of the year, your boss allowed you to spend the money that was left in the budget on a new printer for yourself. So now you want to install a new printer on a Windows NT workstation. Which utility do you use?

A. Server Manager

B. Print Manager

C. The Add New Printer applet

D. NET USE

42. You have HP JetDirect cards installed in several HP printers on the network. What protocols can be used to connect to these printer cards?

A. SNA

B. DLC

C. IPX

D. TCP/IP

43. You have HP JetDirect cards on your network, and you have TCP/IP with manually assigned IP addresses. No UNIX systems are installed on your network. Which protocol should you use to connect to the HP JetDirect cards?

A. SNA

B. DLC

C. IPX

D. TCP/IP

44. Your company has switched to a cellular manufacturing structure, which means that each worker will log in to different Windows NT workstations as they move from computer to computer. You want users to have roaming profiles for their logins. How do you accomplish this in Windows NT Workstation?

A. Enter a Mandatory profile in the profile path of the user's properties in User Manager.

B. Enter a directory in the profile path of the user's properties in User Manager.

C. You can't. This requires a Windows NT Server.

D. Establish a login script with the command PROFILE in it.

45. You're having security problems at work. People seem to be getting information that they shouldn't have access to. You want to review which people have access to a specific file. How do you do this?

A. Press Alt+Enter to get the file's properties. Then select the Security tab.

B. Press Alt+Esc to get the file's properties. Then select the Security tab.

C. Press Alt+Enter to get the file's properties. Then choose the General tab and click the Permissions button.

D. Press Alt+Enter to get the file's properties. Then choose the Security tab and click the Permissions button.

46. You're having trouble with one of the modems in your modem pool, so you want to take it out of service. You need to reconfigure RAS. Which utility or process do you use?

A. Control Panel, Network, Services tab, Remote Access Server properties

B. Remote Access Admin utility

C. Control Panel, Network, Protocols tab, Remote Access Server properties

D. Remote Access Configurator utility

47. You're installing Windows NT on a network with only Windows NT workstations and Windows 95 machines. Your network type is called:

A. A domain

B. A collective

C. A tree

D. A workgroup

48. Network administration is getting to be too much for you. Too many people join and leave the company. You've decided that you want to establish only one user account on a manufacturing floor computer, but many people will use the computer. What user options should be set for this account?

A. User must change password at next login

B. Password never expires

C. User cannot change password

D. Account Disabled

E. Account Locked out

49. You're running Windows NT, and suddenly performance becomes sluggish. You're running Excel, Word, Access, PowerPoint, and Visio. If you have limited access to Windows NT to get diagnostic tools running, which diagnostic tool should you use first to determine what the problem is?

A. Performance Monitor

B. Network Monitor

C. Task Manager

D. NT Diagnostics

50. You just changed offices and installed a new CD-ROM drive in your computer. Now your Windows NT Workstation continually gets a "blue screen of death." You can't determine why, but you want to resolve the issue as soon as possible. How do you get the diagnostic information you need to resolve this problem?

A. Write an Event to the system log.

B. Send an administrative alert.

C. Write the debugging information to a MEMORY.DMP file.

D. Automatically reboot.

51. When doing your weekly maintenance on the system, you notice that CHKDSK /f keeps giving you a message that the drive can't be locked for exclusive use. You don't want to have to reboot to check this drive. What are the likely causes of the problem?

A. The drive is the system drive.

B. The drive has a paging file on it.

C. Remote users are browsing the shares on the server.

D. Windows NT system files are corrupted and need to be restored.

52. To automate a process for your developers, you're writing a batch file. You want to run applications, but you don't want to wait for them to finish. Which command do you use?

A. LAUNCH

B. RUN

C. START

D. LOAD

53. You do complex Finite Element Analysis with your workstation and want to protect it from power failures. You purchase a Standby Power Supply for the computer and want to connect it to Windows NT so that it will shut down when the power starts to run low in the device. Which utility or applet do you use to configure this feature?

A. None. No connectivity exists for the Standby Power Supply.

B. Control Panel, UPS applet

C. Control Panel, Devices

D. Control Panel, Power

54. Which Control Panel applet is used to set up communications devices such as modems?

A. Devices

B. Modems

C. Telephony

D. System

55. You run two 16-bit programs: The first is a graphics application that is somewhat buggy, and the second is a payroll application that has important data you don't want to lose. Which option protects the Payroll application?

A. Run At Ring 0

B. Run in a Separate Memory Space

C. Run on a Separate Processor

D. Run in Exclusive Mode

56. You need to search the Registry keys, values, and data for a particular string. Which Registry editor should you use?

A. REGEDIT

B. REGEDT32

C. SEARCHREG

D. FINDREG

Answers and Explanations

1. **C** Windows NT doesn't understand FAT32 or HPFS, and Windows 95 doesn't understand HPFS or NTFS. The only common partition type is FAT.

2. **B** NTFS is the only partition type supported by Windows NT with security. FAT is also supported by Windows NT, but it doesn't support security. HPFS support was dropped in Windows NT 4.0, and NFS support is not native to Windows NT.

3. **B, D** Either Windows 95 must be installed first, or Windows NT must be repaired after the Windows 95 installation. Windows 95 and Windows NT must be in separate directories to be able to dual boot.

4. **D** Although the CD-ROM isn't a SCSI CD-ROM, all drives, both hard disk and CD, are handled via SCSI. CDROMs isn't a Control Panel applet.

5. **B** Mouse drivers are controlled through the Mouse applet. Devices is used for some miscellaneous devices; keyboard handles only keyboards; and system doesn't handle any devices—but it does control hardware profiles.

6. **C** Tape devices are configured through the Tape Devices applet. However, the SCSI controller must already be set up. Devices can be used to remove the tape device if you know the specific driver, but it's not recommended. Multimedia has nothing to do with tape drives.
7. **B** Because the workstations are currently running Windows 3.11, WINNT must be used—not WINNT32. WINNT32 is used only when installing over previous versions of Windows NT. Additionally, the /B specifies to copy the boot files locally, so even if the network doesn't come up in Windows NT, the installation can continue. /OX is used to create boot floppies.
8. **D** Each user should have his own account with his own password. This prevents some users from being locked out because they don't know what the latest password is and allows auditing of activities on a per-user basis. This eliminates options B and C. Resources should always be assigned to groups so that, when more users are added, it's easy to give them the same access to the same resources as the rest of the group. This eliminates A, leaving D as the only possible correct answer.
9. **D** The dollar sign ($) following the share name prevents it from being browsed. You must specifically enter the name of the share to use it.
10. **B** To be able to modify the file locally, you must have at least Change permissions. This rules out option A. Because you don't want remote users to be able to change documents, the share permission must be set to Read Only, which eliminates C and D.
11. **A, D** When IP is used, the IP address and subnet mask are required. Default gateway is also required if the TCP/IP is used in a routed environment. Both DNS and WINS are optional TCP/IP parameters used for name resolution. They are not required to run Windows NT Workstation on a TCP/IP network.
12. **D** When DHCP is used, the workstation automatically discovers the address of the DHCP server, thus it doesn't have to know the server's hardware address. The IP address, subnet mask, and default gateway are all required for TCP/IP in a routed environment; however, DHCP will provide all of these parameters. But in order to do so, the DHCP server must be accessible by being connected either to the local subnet or via a router that forwards BOOTP packets.
13. **D, E** The question asks for network protocols, which SLIP and PPP are not. This eliminates B and C as possibilities. NetWare uses IPX/SPX, and intranets use TCP/IP. NetBEUI isn't needed in this scenario, which eliminates option A. Answers D and E are correct because they are required for communication with the two systems indicated.
14. **D** None of the options except using the Start command from a command prompt allow you to specify the priority at which to run an application. It is necessary to run the application at a low priority to prevent it from interfering with other work.
15. **A** /QUICK isn't a valid option for the Start command, which eliminates option D. Option B has an incorrect ordering of options. Once the Start command encounters the application to run, the rest of the options are considered options for the application. This eliminates option B. Option C is a bit trickier. It's not recommended that applications be run in the realtime priority mode unless they're specifically designed to run at that priority. This is because in realtime priority, the application actually runs at a higher priority than some parts of the operating system. As a result, option A is the only valid option for running a general-purpose application so it will finish quickly.
16. **B** Although Windows NT supports multiple processors, applications are not binary compatible between platforms—meaning that they must be recompiled for

each platform. There is no such thing as a multiplatform flag, and there's no difference between compiling under Windows 95 versus Windows NT, thus eliminating options A, C, and D.

17. **C** In Windows NT, disk performance counters are turned off by default to improve performance. Before monitoring disk objects, you must turn on the counters with DISKPERF -Y.

18. **C** Both the SQL database and the Internet are accessed via the network. The best place to start is to review the data from Network Monitor, watching specifically to see how long it takes for the Internet server or the SQL server to respond to the request from your computer. Network congestion is implied by this question. None of the other utilities can show how long it takes to get a response from the remote server. Note, however, that performance monitor is a close second because it can show the performance of the local network segment.

19. **A, B, C** The key in determining if a faster disk or additional disks are needed is to determine how much disk activity is caused by paging. By watching the Paging file and Memory objects, you can determine how much paging is happening, and how often the paging file is being extended. If paging is excessive, more memory—rather than a disk—is needed. If the paging file keeps growing, the virtual memory settings should be changed. You should watch physical disk time as well to determine how much of the disk drive is actually in use. If the drive, active or not, doesn't use more than 50% of disk time on average, it probably doesn't need to be replaced. Server doesn't provide any useful statistics for determining if the system is memory starved or if it needs a new disk.

20. **C** Windows NT doesn't support Plug and Play devices unless a special add-in is loaded. This eliminates answer A. Windows NT doesn't keep file allocation tables in memory (like NetWare does), ruling out answer B. Although Windows NT does back up configuration files during bootup, this happens very quickly and isn't likely to be noticed by the user, ruling out D. Answer C is correct because Windows NT will be forced to extend the paging file several times during startup (as all of the services, drivers, and applications start requesting memory) instead of allocating the paging file once.

21. **D** In Windows NT, the printing subsystem is controlled by the spooler service that can be stopped either from the command line or from the Services applet in the Control Panel. Answer B isn't valid because there is no Printer command in Windows NT. Answer C is incorrect because the name of the service isn't printer.

22. **B, C** If Sam doesn't enter the correct password to access your computer, he'll get an error message about his user ID or password, not a file error, so option A cannot be correct. Option D isn't a possible answer because the Workstation service on your computer isn't involved with sharing files.

23. **B** Although REGEDIT will work in Windows NT, it doesn't support multistring entries, so option A isn't a valid answer. The Control Panel applets do edit some Registry settings; however, Microsoft would have told you specifically how to change the entry via the Control Panel if that was an option. EDITREG isn't a valid command. Thus REGEDT32 must be used to edit the Registry.

24. **D** Striping gives better performance over volume sets; this eliminates options A and C. Stripe sets may not exist for the system partition; this eliminates answer B. Answer D is the best configuration given this situation.

25. **C** Windows NT workstation doesn't support fault tolerant disk options, such as mirroring or striping with parity. This eliminates options A and D. A standard stripe set, as specified in option B, isn't fault tolerant.

26. **C** High disk activity while running a memory-intensive application indicates that paging is occurring. Add memory to reduce the amount of paging and increase performance.

27. **B** Because the CPU is running at 100 percent most of the time the projections are running, the processor is the most likely cause of the bottleneck.

28. **B** It's true that Windows NT supports multiple processors; however, the application that is running (Excel) is single-threaded (or at least the calculation portion is). Therefore, adding a second processor probably won't help much because it won't be fully utilized. A faster processor is the best answer.

29. **A** All logged events are stored in the System, Application, and Security logs, which are accessible only via Event Viewer.

30. **D** CONVERT is used to convert file systems from FAT to NTFS. Neither option B or option C is a valid command.

31. **A** CONVERT can be used to convert FAT to NTFS but not to convert NTFS to FAT. MAKEFAT and CHANGEFS are not valid commands.

32. **D** DIAGNOSE and SCANDISK are not valid Windows NT commands. CHKDSK performs extensive testing on the drive only if the /F option is specified. Without the /F, CHKDSK provides basic statistics on the drive.

33. **C** The UNATTEND.TXT file is used to tell Windows NT how to respond to normal prompts without user intervention.

34. **C** SYSDIFF makes the image file and installs it. It is controlled via command line options.

35. **B** The NTHQ utility performs a hardware detection on Windows NT-based computers that is similar to the hardware detection phase that Windows NT itself runs. It can be used to identify system components and suggested compatabilities.

36. **C** Multimedia devices, including video capture and sound cards, are controlled via the Multimedia applet. The Devices applet isn't used to control Multimedia devices, although some devices are controlled there. Add New Hardware exists only in Windows 95, not in Windows NT. There is not a Sound Cards Control Panel applet in Windows NT.

37. **B, C** When you're installing a new video card, Windows NT needs to boot in VGA mode so that you can see and run the display applet to change to the specific driver. Option A doesn't work because it doesn't reboot Windows NT in VGA mode. Option D doesn't work for two reasons. 1) The installation for the driver may try to query the card to install the appropriate driver for the BIOS level and so on, and the card isn't present for it to query. 2) Changing the display prompts for a soft reboot, and it won't allow you to shut down the computer unless you cancel the dialog box and then separately shut down the computer.

38. **A** The only piece of information that is needed is the login server name. Windows NT will get the IPX network number from the NetWare servers when it boots, and it will autodetect the frame type. There is only one version of the IPX protocol.

39. **B, C, D, E** The IEEE 802.5 is a token ring standard. 802.2 and 802.3 are ethernet standards, and Ethernet_II and Ethernet_Snap are other NetWare supported frame types.

40. **C** Windows NT can see NetWare 4.0 servers, but it needs to know which server, or NDS tree, to log into. This invalidates options A and B. Answer D isn't valid because bindery emulation context is set on the NetWare server, not the Windows NT Workstation, and Windows NT would still need the server name in the login server field of Client Services for NetWare.

41. **C** The Server manager is used to control servers and membership in a domain. Print Manager doesn't exist in Windows NT 4.0.

NET USE cannot be used to create a printer; it can be used only to map a local printer port to a remote print queue.

42. **B, D** SNA isn't a valid protocol option, it's a networking architecture. IPX/SPX is supported in Windows NT and on the JetDirect cards; however, JetDirect cards require the use of NetWare in order to use IPX/SPX.

43. **B** Although your network is already running TCP/IP, there is no way for you to set the IP address of the JetDirect card. JetDirect cards require a special RARP procedure (which Windows NT doesn't support) or BOOTP to get an IP address. BOOTP is now available through the DHCP server in Windows NT Server, but the question specifies that IP addresses are manually assigned—which means that DHCP isn't running.

44. **C** Windows NT Workstation does not support roaming profiles without the use of a Windows NT server.

45. **D** You display a file's properties by pressing Alt+Enter. The Permissions button, which reveals those users and groups with permissions, is available on the Security tab.

46. **A** The Remote Access Admin utility enables you to monitor RAS as well as start and stop it, but it can't be used to configure RAS. The Remote Access Configurator utility doesn't exist. Finally, the Remote Access Server is on the Services tab, not the Protocols tab.

47. **D** In Microsoft networking, there are two structures: A domain, which requires a Windows NT server, and a workgroup, which doesn't require any server.

48. **B, C** To allow multiple users to use the same account, it's important that the user not be able to change the password and that the password not expire so that it will be consistent. This way, a single upset user can't lock other users out of the system; however, they could potentially still destroy the login or lock out the account.

49. **C** Although some of the other tools can be useful for determining what is causing a system to perform badly, Task Manager is integrated into the interface and can be accessed via the Security dialog box, which makes it the best choice for a diagnostic tool.

50. **A, B, C, D** All of these things will help determine what the problem is. Writing an event to the system log ensures that you know the exact time the error occurred, which may or may not be important. Sending an administrative alert ensures that you're aware the reboot occurred, even if you're not logged into your computer. You can also send the alert to the network administrator's workstation, or the network administrator's user login.

51. **A, B** Windows NT will not allow you to run a CHKDSK/F on the system drive while it's running. Nor will it run on any drive with any open file. Any drive with a paging file on it always has an open file—the paging file.

52. **C** The START command starts another process. None of the other commands are valid in Windows NT.

53. **B** Standby Power Supplies are UPSs (or rather the close cousin that most people use). Windows NT provides the UPS applet to allow Windows NT to communicate with a UPS and gracefully shut down when the power is about to fail.

54. **B** Modems and other communications devices are set up through the Modems applet. The Devices applet controls devices that don't fall into any other category. Telephony specifies the local telephone number and other characteristics of the telephone line, but not modems. System contains configuration options, but not options for Modems.

55. **B** Running a 16-bit Windows application in its own memory space protects it from other 16-bit applications that don't behave. None of the other options are valid Windows NT options.

56. **A** Only REGEDIT supports searching Keys, Values, and Data for a string. REGEDT32 supports limited searching. Answers C and D are not valid Windows NT commands.

Practice Exam 7

Networking Essentials Exam

The exam consists of 58 questions that cover four major topics. You have 75 minutes to complete this test. Remember that time is a factor. You should be around question 19 after 33 minutes and question 37 after 60 minutes.

Before the actual exam begins, the exam program will give you the option of taking a sample orientation exam to familiarize yourself with the way the exam operates. You should take that orientation exam. If you are unsure about how to use the testing equipment or software, or if you have any questions about the rules for the exam, ask the exam administrator before the exam begins.

Practice Exam Begins

1. An infrared network can transmit at what speed?
   A. 10 Mbps
   B. 100 Mbps
   C. 1 Mbps
   D. 1.544 Mbps
   E. 2 Mbps
   F. 4 Mbps
   G. 100 Kbps
   H. None of the above

2. Thicknet is used as a backbone in some installations to connect a number of Thinnet-based networks. Why would it be an advantage to use Thicknet cabling as a backbone solution?
   A. Thicknet can transfer data much faster than Thinnet cable can.
   B. Thicknet can carry data over greater distances than Thinnet cable can.
   C. You cannot mix Thicknet and Thinnet cable.
   D. Thicknet is less expensive and easier to install than Thinnet.
   E. Thicknet is the most common type of cable used in most networks.
   F. You cannot use Thicknet as a backbone cable; it is used only for cable TV transmissions.

3. Which of the following are used for Infrared Networks (choose all that apply):
   A. Reflective
   B. Line-of-sight
   C. Scatter transmissions
   D. Spread-spectrum

E. Broadband optical

F. Narrow-band

G. RF

H. AF

4. Which method is used in TCP/IP protocol to isolate the host ID from the network ID in a 32-bit address?

   A. Network Address

   B. Node Address

   C. Class A

   D. Class B

   E. Class C

   F. Default gateway

   G. Subnet mask

   H. None of the above

5. Which utility under the Windows NT operating system is used to create accounts on the PDC?

   A. User Profile Editor

   B. User Manager for Domains

   C. Server Manager

   D. Client Administrator

   E. Registry Editor

6. You have a Thinnet cable in your network. How far can the cable transmit correct data frames before it degrades (attenuates) the data signal?

   A. 500 Meters

   B. 250 Meters

   C. 100 Meters

   D. 75 Meters

   E. 50 Meters

   F. 10 Meters

   G. 185 Meters

7. In a primary rate ISDN system, what is the D channel used for?

   A. 16 Kbps

   B. 32 Kbps

   C. 64 Kbps

   D. Voice, Data, and Images

   E. Signaling and link management data

   F. Handshaking only

8. What is the definition of *attenuation*?

   A. The signal crossover in wires

   B. The signal overflow from an adjacent wire

   C. The loss of a signal strength in a wire as the data signal travels further

   D. The signal increase in a data packet in a long distance cable run

9. In Windows NT, a redirector is used for which of these two things?

   A. To assign a logical drive letter to a share resource on the network.

   B. To divide the hard disk into multiple sectors.

   C. To intercept requests in the computer.

   D. To determine if the specific resource is on the local computer, or is on a remote computer on the network.

   E. To determine the degree of sharing of resources on the network.

   F. To redirect SMB blocks into NetWare NCP blocks.

   G. There is no such thing as a redirector.

10. Your service provider just installed ISDN service in your home. What are the 64Kbps channels known as?
    A. Z Channel
    B. Y Channel
    C. D Channel
    D. C Channel
    E. A Channel
    F. B Channel

11. What is the most common type of digital line used in most networks today?
    A. 56 Kbps
    B. T1
    C. T3
    D. E1
    E. Asynchronous modems

12. The RJ-45 connector used in networking has how many connections?
    A. Eleven
    B. Seven
    C. Four
    D. Six
    E. Eight
    F. Sixteen

13. Which of the following statements is true of Time Domain-Reflectometers (TDR)?
    A. TDR is an advanced cable tester used for WANs.
    B. TDR sends light to locate breaks or shorts in a cable run.
    C. TDR sends sonar-like pulses to locate breaks or shorts in a cable run.
    D. TDR sends a laser signal to locate breaks or shorts in a cable run.

14. Which level of RAID divides data into 64K blocks and spreads it equally in a fixed organized order under a fault-tolerance setup with parity?
    A. RAID 0
    B. RAID 1
    C. RAID 2
    D. RAID 3
    E. RAID 4
    F. RAID 5
    G. RAID 10

15. Which of the following techniques enables you to reduce network traffic by backing up several Unix servers across the network?
    A. Back up only once a year.
    B. Schedule backups after business hours.
    C. Back up only the operating system.
    D. Back up only files and directories.
    E. Place the backup computer on an isolated network.
    F. Back up during business hours only.

16. In which layer of the OSI model does packet assembly begin?
    A. Network
    B. Presentation
    C. Session
    D. Physical
    E. Data Link
    F. Application
    G. Transport
    H. ATM
    I. FDDI

17. Which type of cable does a 10BaseT network used?
    A. Thicknet
    B. Thinnnet
    C. RJ-11
    D. Fiber
    E. Unshielded Twisted-Pair (UTP)
    F. RJ-56

18. Your company purchased 100BaseTX cable. Which category of UTP cable is required?
    A. CAT 1
    B. CAT 2
    C. CAT 3
    D. CAT 4
    E. CAT 5
    F. CAT 10
    G. CAT 100

19. Which of the following categories supports transmission for 10BaseT?
    A. 1
    B. 2
    C. 3
    D. 4
    E. 5
    F. 10
    G. 50

20. Which of the techniques listed below does broadband transmission use?
    A. Digital signaling
    B. Analog signaling
    C. Bidirectional signal flow
    D. Unidirectional signal flow
    E. Repeaters to amplify signals
    F. Repeaters to regenerate signals
    G. Hon/Hoff signaling

21. You installed DHCP service in your Windows NT network. Which of the following statements is true of DHCP?
    A. It serves as an Internet server service.
    B. It serves as a gateway service.
    C. It serves as a NIC card address service.
    D. It serves as a TCP/IP service to automatically issue TCP/IP addresses.

22. Which of the following is contained inside a packet header frame?
    A. Data
    B. CRC
    C. TTL
    D. SA (source address)
    E. DA (destination address)
    F. Alert signal
    G. None of the above

23. Which of the following cables would you think is the least expensive?
    A. Fiber
    B. 10Base5 – Thicknet
    C. 10Base2 – Thinnet
    D. 10BaseT – UTP
    E. IBM TYPE 2

24. Which of the following describes the 10Base5 cable type?
    A. CAT 5 UTP
    B. CAT 3 UTP
    C. Thin coaxial (Thinnet)
    D. Thick coaxial (Thicknet)
    E. None of the above

25. Which of the following wireless transmission techniques is the slowest method of transmitting a data packet from location A to location B?
    A. Infrared
    B. Laser
    C. Narrow-band radio
    D. Spread-spectrum radio
    E. 10BaseT

26. You're a consultant. You are asked what is the maximum distance for 10BaseT (UTP) cabling for a proposal. Which of the following is the correct answer?
    A. 100 meters (328 feet)
    B. 500 meters (1,640 feet)
    C. 25 meters (82 feet)
    D. 185 meters (607 feet)
    E. 50 meters (164 feet)
    F. 1 meter (3 feet) without a repeater

27. You installed a Windows 95 client in your network, and you're running a Novell Network with version 3.12. What is needed to gain access to the application GAMES on the Novell NetWare server?
    A. NDS
    B. NCP
    C. NWLink with GSNW
    D. NWLink with CSNW
    E. IPX/SPX with Microsoft Client for NetWare

28. What is the function of CSMA/CD?
    A. It's part of token-ring algorithm.
    B. It breaks data into smaller formats.
    C. It's an Ethernet tool for finding wiring faults.
    D. It regulates traffic on the segment.
    E. It is a cable repeater system.
    F. It's a 1000BaseT protocol only.

29. *Impedance* is defined as:
    A. The opposite of resistance.
    B. Signal overflow errors.
    C. Resistance to DC.
    D. Resistance to AC.
    E. The CAT 5 standard.

30. To avoid data loss and reduce downtime, which is the best method of fault tolerance?
    A. UPS system
    B. RAID 5
    C. RAID 0
    D. Tape backup

31. What type of hardware connector assembly is used by 10Base2 for connection to a standard Network Adapter Card?
    A. A BNC barrel connector assembly.
    B. A BNC T connector assembly.
    C. An RJ-11 connector assembly.
    D. An RJ-45 connector assembly.
    E. An AUI connector assembly.

32. Which media access method is used commonly by IEEE 802.3 standards?
    A. CDMS/CA
    B. Ethernet Passing
    C. Token Passing
    D. Demand priority
    E. CSMA/CD

33. Which of the following is a non-routable transport protocol?
    A. NetBEUI
    B. DLC
    C. IPX
    D. IP
    E. AppleTalk

34. 10Base5 cable has another name. Which of the following is the correct term?
    A. CAT 2
    B. CAT 4
    C. Thinnet
    D. Outernet
    E. Thicknet
    F. None of the above

35. Raw data bits that convert into data frames are handled by which layer of the OSI model?
    A. Transport
    B. Session
    C. Physical
    D. Presentation
    E. Data Link

36. Which of the following is true of a star topology design?
    A. An opening in the cable segment cannot take down the entire network infrastructure.
    B. It is more difficult to configure than a ring design.
    C. It provides centralized monitoring and management control.
    D. It requires less cable than a bus design.

37. Translating the data format is the responsibility of which layer of the OSI model?
    A. Application
    B. Physical
    C. Data Link
    D. Communication
    E. Presentation

38. Which type of connector assembly is responsible for twisted-pair?
    A. AUI
    B. BNC
    C. BBC
    D. RJ-55
    E. RJ-45

39. Which of the following protocols is an NDIS x.x-compliant version of the Internetwork Packet Exchange protocol?
    A. IP
    B. SMB
    C. NCP
    D. NWLink
    E. NetBEUI

40. Which sublayer of the Data Link layer directly communicates with the Network Adapter Card assembly?
    A. LLC
    B. LAC
    C. MAC
    D. DAC
    E. None of the above

41. Which system parameter determines whether a file request is intended for the local computer or for a remote computer on the network?
    A. The frame type
    B. The networking protocol
    C. The redirector
    D. The transceiver
    E. The TDI

42. Which of the following statements is true of NetBEUI?
    A. NetBEUI is routable.
    B. NetBEUI is slow in a LAN design.
    C. NetBEUI is a NetWare protocol only.
    D. NetBEUI is a small, very fast, and efficient transport layer protocol used primarily with Microsoft networks.

43. Which of the following devices can use all seven layers of the OSI model?
    A. Bridges
    B. Routers
    C. Repeaters
    D. Mux
    E. Modems
    F. Gateways

44. Which of the following networks typically use a design with star bus topology?
    A. 10BaseT
    B. 10Base5
    C. 100Base5
    D. 100BaseX
    E. 100BaseVG-AnyLAN
    F. None of the above

45. Which of the following are dial-up data communications protocols?
    A. FTP
    B. TCP
    C. SLIP
    D. PPP
    E. ATM

46. Which of the following devices can perform protocol conversions in an infrastructure setup?
    A. Gateways
    B. Routers
    C. Bridges
    D. Brouters
    E. Repeaters
    F. None of the above

47. Which of the following cable types can be used for 100 Mbps networks?
    A. RG-58 A/U
    B. RG-58 U
    C. CAT 3
    D. CAT 5
    E. CAT 1

48. Which of the following types of cable can transmit 1,000 meters without a repeater working at the Physical layer of the OSI model?
    A. CAT 3
    B. CAT 5
    C. CAT 1
    D. 10Base 5
    E. Fiber optic

49. Which of the following tasks can a bridge accomplish?
    A. Connecting a 10BaseT segment with a 10Base5 segment.
    B. Translating network protocols.

C. Segmenting a network traffic load.

D. Connecting a token-ring segment with an Ethernet segment.

50. If your goal is to increase the strength of a baseband signal (10Base2) over a long cable length, which device would solve this problem in your design?

A. Repeaters

B. Oscilloscopes

C. Amplifiers

D. Multiplexers

E. Switches

51. Which of the following is an implementation of packet switching technology?

A. ISDN

B. Modem

C. ATM

D. Switched 56

E. T1

52. You have just finish a design that connects Unix and Windows NT operating systems. Which protocol is used in your design to enable communication between the two systems?

A. NetBEUI

B. DLC

C. NWLink

D. TCP/IP

E. FDDI

53. You want to change the parallel data stream used on the computer's PCI bus into a serial data stream. Which device in your system is responsible for this conversion?

A. Hub

B. Terminator

C. Bridge

D. Multiplexer

E. Transceiver

54. Which of the following protocols uses a distance-vector algorithm to determine routes?

A. RIP

B. NFS

C. SNA

D. DLC

E. XNS

F. AAP

55. You want to implement sector sparing on your network. Which of the following devices can perform sector sparing?

A. IDE

B. ESDI

C. AT

D. AT Advanced

E. SCSI

F. PCI

G. ISA

56. Which of the following is a TCP/IP protocol for monitoring networks?

A. SMP

B. NCP

C. SMTP

D. SNMP

E. FTAM

57. You are setting up a network in your new office for the first time, and there is no preinstalled wiring. Which type of cabling should you consider first?

    A. Thicknet
    B. Thinnet
    C. STP
    D. UTP
    E. Flatnet

58. You want to allow users to access network resources freely, but you also want to protect a few resources with special passwords. Which of the following security models should you implement?

    A. Domain-level security
    B. Share-level security
    C. User-level security
    D. Server-level security
    E. None of the above

Answers and Explanations

1. **A** 10 Mbps is the current specification for infrared network.
2. **B** It can support the same data over longer distances that Thinnet can, which is 10Base2 cabling.
3. **A, B, E, F** Reflective, line-of-sight, broadband optical, and narrow-band are used in the transmission of infrared data.
4. **G** Subnet Mask is used to separate the host ID from the network ID.
5. **B** User Manager for Domains is the utility used to create accounts and groups.
6. **G** The specification is 185 meters for 10Base2 (Thinnet cable).
7. **E** It is used only for signaling (handshaking) and Link Data Management at 16 Kbps speed.
8. **C** As the length increases beyond IEEE specifications, attenuation takes place and degrades the signal.
9. **A, E** It assigns a logical drive letter to a share resource on the network. (A *logical drive letter* is a drive letter outside the local drive assignments, such as the floppy drive, local hard disk drive, and CD-ROM in the computer.) It also determines the degree of sharing of resources on the network.
10. **F** B Channel is described as 64 Kbps. When two channels are used, the total combination is 128 Kbps, which is two B Channels.
11. **B** T1 is the most common type at 1.544 Mbps.
12. **E** RJ-45 cable has eight connections, four pairs of wire assembly.
13. **C** TDR sends sonar-like pulses signal to locate breaks or shorts in a cable run. It is an excellent tool for the network professional.
14. **F** RAID 5 divides the data into 64K blocks of equal increments across disks. These disks must be three physical drives and greater in order for RAID 5 to function.
15. **E** By placing the server on an isolated network, you can reduce the amount of traffic on the network. This is also called *segmentation network traffic*.
16. **F** The Application layer is number seven in the OSI model, and that is where the packet assembly begins and transcends to the lowest layer (the Physical layer—number one).
17. **E** UTP is a four pair cable that 10BaseT topology uses.
18. **E** CAT 5 cabling will use 10BaseT, 100BaseTX, and 100BaseT.
19. **C, D, E** CAT 3 cable, CAT 4 cable, CAT 5 cable.
20. **A, B, E, F** Digital signaling, analog signaling, repeaters to amplify signals, and repeaters to regenerate signals.
21. **D** DHCP assigns TCP/IP addresses automatically when the client computer comes on-line and issues a DHCP LEASE IP ADDRESS from the DHCP server.
22. **D, E** The source address and destination address are required fields in a packet header frame.
23. **D** Unshielded Twisted-Pair is the cheapest per foot in comparison to coaxial (Thicknet and Thinnet), fiber cable, and IBM TYPE 2 (which is used for token-ring signaling).

24. **D** Thick coaxial or Thicknet is used only for 10Base5 cabling. The disadvantages of using 10Base5 are its handling for installations, its difficulty to install, and the cost per foot. It serves as a backbone for Thinnet networks interconnecting to Thicknet.

25. **D** Spread-spectrum radio has a maximum output between 2 Mbps and 10 Mbps, whereas infrared can scale over 10 Mbps, and laser can scale at the speed of light.

26. **A** 100 meters or 328 feet is the exact IEEE specification for CAT 5 cable with 10BaseT cable.

27. **E** You must load IPX/SPX protocol with a Windows 95 client. You must also load Microsoft Client for NetWare, which is a service under Windows 95. GSNW is Gateway Services for NetWare and is part of the Windows NT server service. CSNW (Client Services for NetWare) is used in the Windows NT workstation product.

28. **D** CSMA/CD (which stands for Carrier Sense Multiple Access with Collision Detection) regulates traffic on the segment.

29. **D** Impedance is the opposite of conduction. In signals flowing in a network cable, impedance is the resistance factor to AC (alternating current). AC is the type of voltage that is sent in network cabling topologies.

30. **B** RAID 5 will provide the ability to reconstruct your data when a disk failure occurs.

31. **B** For 10Base2, which is termed Thinnet, a BNC T connector is used to join the network interface card in the local computer to the cable assembly, which is in the form of a coaxial cable.

32. **E** CSMA/CD is a standard called Carrier Sense Multiple Access with Collision Detection and is a media access method used in Ethernet networks. With CSMA/CD, a computer "listens" to the physical medium to determine whether another computer is transmitting the data frame.

33. **A** NetBEUI is a popular transport protocol that is used in a small non-routable network and is very fast.

34. **E** 10Base5 cabling is Thicknet. This coaxial cable is very rigid in material and serves as an excellent backbone for signals up to 500 meters in length.

35. **E** At the Data Link layer, the conversion of data frames from raw bits takes place. This layer is also responsible for transferring frames from one computer to another. After the Data Link layer sends a frame, it waits for ACK, which is an acknowledgment from the receiving computer.

36. **A** In a star design, cable segments to a centralized component device called a *hub* that connects the computers. Signals transmitted by a computer on the star pass through the hub to all computers on the network.

37. **E** The Presentation layer is responsible for translating data from the Application layer into an intermediary format. The Presentation layer is also responsible for security issues and the compression of data.

38. **E** The RJ-45 connector assembly is an eight-wire modular connector used by twisted-pair cables.

39. **D** NWLINK is an NDIS-compliant version of the IPX protocol that is used with Microsoft products.

40. **C** The MAC (Media Access Control) layer communicates directly with the network adapter card and is responsible for delivering error-free data between two computers on the network.

41. **C** The redirector is a small section of the code in the NOS that intercepts requests in the computer and determines if the requests should be local to be redirected out to the network computer.

42. **D** NetBEUI is a small, efficient, and fast Transport layer protocol. It is very dynamic in the way it can be optimized for very high performance when used in mostly departmental LANs that are not routable.

43. **F** Gateways are used to connect networks using different protocols so that information can be passed from one system to another. For example, Microsoft SNA Server for Windows NT is a gateway product that connects one form of protocol to another for connectivity to a mainframe system.

44. **A, D** 100BaseX Ethernet uses the CSMA/CD in a star wired bus design, similar to 10BaseT where all cables are attached to a hub. Also, 10BaseT and 100BaseX are configured in a star pattern, but internally they use a bus signaling system like other Ethernet configurations.

45. **C, D** The two protocols have been adopted by the Internet community to transmit Internet Protocol (IP) datagram over serial point-to-point lines.

46. **A** A gateway can perform protocol conversions that act as a translator between two systems that do not use the same communication protocols, data formatting structures, languages, or architecture.

47. **D** CAT 5 supports speeds up to and including 100 Mbps in an unshielded twisted-pair design. CAT 3 and RG-58U will support signal speeds up to 10Mbps in both unshielded twisted-pair and coaxial cable designs.

48. **E** Fiber optics can transmit speeds in excess of 100 Mbps in a distance of 1,000 to 2,000 meters without any special fiber repeaters.

49. **A, C** Bridges can perform the same functions as repeaters, but they can also reduce traffic by segmenting the network. Bridges can join dissimilar physical media such as twisted-pair and coaxial networks.

50. **A** A repeater is an amplifier that increases the power factor of the electrical signal so that it can travel beyond the specification of the cable length depending on the type of cable. A repeater strengthens baseband signals in LANs.

51. **C** ATM, which stands for Asynchronous Transfer Mode, is a packet-switch technology that provides high-speed data transmission rates for sending fixed-size cells over broadband LANs or WANs.

52. **D** TCP/IP is a standard routable protocol and is the most complete and accepted protocol available that is used to connect dissimilar systems such as Unix and Windows NT.

53. **E** A transceiver is a device that connects a computer to the network. A transceiver is basically a device that receives data and transmits the signal.

54. **A** Routing Information Protocol uses a distance-vector algorithm to determine routes. With RIP, routers

transfer information among other routers to update their internal routing tables, and they use that information to determine the best routes.

55. **E** SCSI devices do perform *sector sparing*, which is a fault-tolerance system that automatically adds sector-recovery capabilities to the file system during operating. All other devices (other than SCSI) do not perform sector sparing at all.

56. **D** SNMP (Simple Network Management Protocol) is a TCP/IP protocol for monitoring networks.

57. **C** CAT 5 cable design would be appropriate because it can support transmission speeds of 100 Mbps, and because all new installations have CAT 5 cable as a de facto standard in cable designs. CAT 5 can support video, multimedia, and imaging at higher data-transfer speeds than other categories of cable.

58. **B** Implementation of share-level security involves assigning a password to each shared resource. Access to a shared resource is granted when a user enters the appropriate password.

Practice Exam 8

Networking Essentials Exam

The exam consists of 58 questions that cover four major topics. You have 75 minutes to complete this test. Remember that time is a factor. You should be around question 19 after 33 minutes and question 37 after 60 minutes.

Before the actual exam begins, the exam program will give you the option of taking a sample orientation exam to familiarize yourself with the way the exam operates. You should take that orientation exam. If you are unsure about how to use the testing equipment or software, or if you have any questions about the rules for the exam, ask the exam administrator before the exam begins.

The first three questions use the following scenario.

Situation

You have to design a simple network given the following parameters:

- You have five users located in offices on the same floor less than 100 meters apart.
- These users do not have dedicated network cabling.
- These users do have additional open pairs with their telephone wiring (CAT 3).
- They want to share each other's files and printers.
- They do not want to have their applications file served.
- All users use Windows 95 in a standalone environment.
- The owner does not have a large budget for this project.

Practice Exam Begins

1. Which network cabling scheme would you choose to implement?
   A. Coaxial
   B. Twisted-pair
   C. Wireless
   D. Infrared

2. Which operating system would you choose to use?
   A. Windows NT
   B. Novell
   C. Windows 95 Peer to Peer
   D. Lantastic Peer to Peer

3. Based on your answer to question number 1, which type of networking equipment would support your cable solution?
   A. A repeater
   B. A hub

   C. A transmitter
   D. A router

4. From the types of cable listed below, which can be used for a LAN with a maximum distance of 370 feet between network devices?
   A. Thicknet coaxial
   B. Thinnet coaxial
   C. Twisted-pair
   D. Fiber optic

5. Which wireless LAN transmission method typically has the slowest response time?
   A. Laser
   B. Narrow-band radio
   C. Spread-spectrum radio
   D. Infrared

6. Which categories of Unshielded Twisted-Pair cable are certified to carry data transmissions faster than 10Mbps?
   A. 1
   B. 4
   C. 2
   D. 5
   E. 3

The next two questions use the following scenario.

Situation

You have a small office with three users who are located six feet apart and are separated by half-wall cubicles.

You do not have an existing network, and there are no additional free pairs in the phone cable.

You want to share files and printers, but you do not want to serve applications.

All of your users are using Windows 95.

You have a very, very limited budget.

7. Based on the information above, which network cabling scheme makes sense?
   A. Coaxial
   B. Twisted-pair
   C. Fiber
   D. Microwave

8. Which network operating system would work best?
   A. Windows 95 (Peer to Peer)
   B. Windows NT
   C. Novell
   D. Appleshare

9. Select three attributes of a server-based network:
   A. Individual users are responsible for the security of their resources.
   B. It has a dedicated server.
   C. Files are stored on a central file server.
   D. Applications are centrally managed on a central file server.
   E. System managers are responsible for the security and protection of resources.

10. What are two functions of a network operating system's redirector?
   A. To determine the level of sharing between network resources.
   B. To segment the hard disk into different areas.

C. To intercept requests and forward them to the computer.

D. To assign a letter to a shared resource.

E. To determine if a task should be left on a local computer or sent to another server on the network.

11. In which layer of the OSI model does the packet creation begin?

A. Physical

B. Network

C. Transport

D. Session

E. Application

F. Presentation

12. Choose the parts of a packet header:

A. Source address

B. Destination address

C. Alert signal

D. Actual address

13. In a ring topology, how many computing devices can transmit at one time?

A. 10

B. 2

C. All computing devices

D. 1

E. Only the computing device with the assigned token

The next two questions use the following scenario.

Situation

You have an office with 20 people who have an open CAT 5 cable next to their phone connections. This open CAT 5 cable runs into a central wiring closet.

Your users currently use Windows 95.

You want to serve applications to save on concurrent application usage.

You want to have centrally managed IP addresses for your users.

The person identified as the Network Administrator is very proficient in Windows 95.

You are willing to spend a reasonable amount of money to implement this solution.

You are concerned about how reliable your power source is.

14. Which type of network cabling scheme would work best?

A. Fiber

B. Coaxial

C. Twisted-pair

D. Microwave

15. Your supervisor has requested that you centrally manage the IP addresses in your network. Which protocol could you use to perform this task?

A. ARP

B. HTTP

C. SLIP

D. PPP

E. DHCP

Question 16 uses the following scenario.

Situation

You're planning an addition to your current network, and you want to connect two networks that are on different floors of a multifloor building. Your main objective with this design is to reduce the risk of someone tapping into your network.

16. Which media would work best in this scenario?
    A. Coaxial cable
    B. UTP cable
    C. Wireless
    D. Fiber optic cable

The next four questions use the following scenario.

Situation

You are assigned the task of designing a network for a lab at a local school. Listed below are your operating conditions:

- You will network 10 workstations together (all PCs).
- The workstations are currently standalone, so they cannot be networked.
- The workstations are all in a row on four tables.
- You do not have enough money to have a dedicated file server.
- You want to run applications locally but share printers and files.
- You will be connected to an Internet provider and given the IP addresses 134.93.4.10 through 134.93.4.25.
- This design should be built to expand in the future to include other network cabling schemes where appropriate.
- You will be hired to install this system, but the librarian (who is Windows 95 literate) will manage it after installation.

17. Suppose you were contracted to install this network. Of the following questions and statements, which three represent major concerns you will face?
    A. What type of experience does the librarian have?
    B. How old is the school?
    C. A security plan needs to be addressed.
    D. Identify the existing hardware to ensure a minimum platform for your solution.

18. What type of network cabling would be the simplest to install and the most cost-effective?
    A. Fiber
    B. Coax
    C. Twisted-pair
    D. Wireless

19. Based on the requirement for future expansion, what type of network card would be appropriate?
    A. Combo card with coax and twisted-pair
    B. Combo card with fiber and twisted-pair
    C. Twisted-pair only

20. Which operating system would be a good choice here?
    A. Lantastic
    B. Windows NT
    C. Windows 95
    D. Novell Lite

21. How far can a signal be reliable when transmitted over a Thinnet cable?
    A. 100 meters
    B. 50 meters
    C. 250 meters
    D. 185 meters

22. What is the theoretical capacity of STP cable?
    A. 200Mbps
    B. 400Mbps

C. 500Mbps
D. 100Mbps

23. Which of the three statements below are true characteristics of Category 3 cables?
    A. These cables are suitable for 100Mbps data rates.
    B. These cables are suitable for 4Mbps data rates.
    C. This cable is considered to be the lowest data-grade cable.
    D. This cable uses four twisted pairs with three twists per foot.

24. What is the most common type of connector used with twisted-pair cabling?
    A. RJ-11
    B. RJ-24
    C. RJ-45
    D. RJ-8

25. Select three valid reasons for implementing wireless networking:
    A. For people who move around a lot within their work environments.
    B. For temporary installations within your network.
    C. For spaces where cabling would be impossible or inconvenient to implement.
    D. For people who want to use their cell phones to contact their resources at work.

26. What is the typical maximum transmission distance for infrared signals?
    A. 50 feet
    B. 10 feet
    C. 100 feet
    D. 150 feet

27. What is the outdoor operating range of a frequency-hopping scheme under a spread-spectrum radio transmission?
    A. 100 feet
    B. 500 feet
    C. 1 mile
    D. 2 miles

28. What is the transmission rate of a frequency-hopping transmission scheme?
    A. 10Mbps
    B. 100Mbps
    C. 250Kbs
    D. 4Mbs

Question 29 uses the following scenario.

Situation

Suppose you are implementing a network with the following requirements:

Servers: 6 that run Microsoft Windows NT; 3 that run Novell 3.12

Client computers: 800 that run Windows 95

Hubs: 40

Routers: 6

29. Which protocols should you configure on each router in order for traffic to pass freely across your network?
    A. NetBEUI, TCP/IP
    B. AppleTalk, TCP/IP
    C. IPX, TCP/IP
    D. TCP/IP, AppleTalk

30. Your existing 10Base2 Ethernet cable is 185 meters long. You are planning to extend your network by adding another 100 meters of cable. Therefore, the total length of the cable will be 285 meters. If the network uses NetBEUI, which of the following devices should you use?
    A. Gateway
    B. Hub
    C. Repeater
    D. Router

31. Of the statements below, which three describe 10Base5?
    A. 10Mbs data rate
    B. Signal range of 500 meters per cable segment
    C. Uses thin coaxial cable
    D. Referred to as Thicknet

32. From the list below, select the four Windows NT special groups created during the installation of Windows NT.
    A. Active user
    B. Everyone
    C. Network
    D. Interactive
    E. Creator-owner

33. At which layer of the OSI model does a repeater operate?
    A. Physical
    B. Network
    C. Session
    D. Transport
    E. Presentation

34. Select three types of backups identified by Microsoft.
    A. Full backup
    B. Semi-contingent backup
    C. Incremental backup
    D. Differential backup

35. From the list below, select three network standards that employ token-passing access control.
    A. FDDI
    B. IEEE Standard 802.3
    C. IEEE Standard 802.4
    D. Token-ring

36. Of the following statements, which four describe benefits of using a dedicated file server?
    A. Files are in a specific place where they can be reliably archived.
    B. Central file servers can be managed more efficiently, with user and security data located in a single database.
    C. Dedicated file servers have a single point of failure.
    D. Dedicated file servers allow data backups to be implemented more easily.
    E. The cost of specialized file server technology is shared by a large number of users.

37. What is *disk mirroring*?
    A. The function of simultaneously writing data to separate disks using one channel on one disk controller.
    B. The function of simultaneously writing data to separate disks on different servers.

C. The function of simultaneously writing data to disks using separate channels.

38. What is the minimum number of disks needed to configure a stripe set with parity on a Windows NT server?

A. Seven

B. Two

C. Three

D. Four

39. From the list below, select three duties of a network adapter.

A. To format and prepare data

B. To control the flow of data in and out of the computer

C. To send the data

D. To identify network cabling issues within the network

40. A characteristic of Ethernet networks is that data flows from the network adapter card to the transmission medium in which of the following forms?

A. Serial

B. Parallel

C. Both serial and parallel

D. Neither parallel or serial

41. Select four basic data-bus architectures in use today.

A. ICI

B. EISA

C. PCI

D. Micro Channel

E. ISA

42. From the options below, identify three typical resource settings.

A. IRQ

B. SQA

C. Base I/O port addresses

D. Base memory address

43. Suppose you're designing a network and you need to install network adapters in 10 ISA computers. Which rule must you follow when installing the NICs?

A. All network adapters in all computers on the same network must be set to different IRQs.

B. All adapters in a computer, including the network adapter, must be set to the same IRQ.

C. All network adapters in all computers on the same network must be set to the same IRQ.

D. All adapters in a computer, including the network adapter, must be set to different IRQs.

44. What tool helps a network administrator view operations in real-time and record time for processors, hard disks, memory, network utilization, and the network as a whole on a Windows NT server?

A. Network management tools for software vendors

B. Problem device

C. Performance Monitor

D. Systems Management Server

45. Which tool would you use to check the physical condition of the cable including excess collisions and congestion errors?

A. DV

B. Protocol analyzer

C. Advanced cable tester

D. TDR

46. What is the set of message-handling standards developed by the CCITT?

 A. X.400

 B. MHS

 C. SMTP

 D. X.500

47. What service would you need to install on Windows NT Server to allow Macintoshes in a Windows NT environment?

 A. Gateway

 B. GSNW

 C. Services for Macintosh

 D. Redirector

48. What tool does Microsoft have that provides a broader scope on network systems management with centralized administration of all computers in a WAN?

 A. Performance Monitor

 B. TraceRoute

 C. Ping

 D. SMS

49. What happens in the Network layer if the network adapter on the router cannot transmit a data chunk as large as the source computer sends?

 A. It causes network activity failure.

 B. It retransmits the data chunk.

 C. It breaks the data into smaller units.

 D. It organizes the data frame.

50. A terminal sends a request for information to a mainframe. The mainframe retrieves the information and displays it on the terminal. What type of computing is this ?

 A. Client-server

 B. Peer to peer

 C. Centralized

 D. Decentralized

The next three questions use the following scenario.

Situation

You are in charge of installing cables for an Ethernet network in your office. Your building has limited workspace, and the cable will have to share an existing conduit with the phone system cable. The maximum length of a cable segment is 320 feet.

51. Which type of cable should you install in this situation?

 A. Fiber optic

 B. Thicknet coax

 C. CAT 3 UTP

 D. CAT 1 UTP

52. Based on the situation above, how many pairs are needed to connect to a 10BaseT network?

 A. 1 pair

 B. 2 pairs

 C. 3 pairs

 D. 4 pairs

53. If you choose to use Ethernet and use 10BaseT, what type of cable connector should you use?

 A. RJ-11

 B. RJ-45

 C. RJ-6

 D. RJ-12

54. Your company has a corporate-wide Windows NT network using TCP/IP protocol. You have been receiving a lot of complaints that client computers are getting IP address conflicts. What is Microsoft's preferred solution to this problem?
    A. Increase the TCP window size.
    B. Implement a DHCP server.
    C. Change the MAC address for each network.
    D. Manually configure IP addresses on each computer.

55. Which two layers of the OSI model define how multiple computers can simultaneously use the network without interfering with one another?
    A. Media Access Control and Logical Link Control
    B. Session and Transport
    C. Physical and Data Link
    D. Transport and Network

56. What blocks out a portion of the IP address so TCP/IP can distinguish the network ID from the host ID?
    A. Node number
    B. Subnet mask
    C. Default gateway
    D. Network address

57. Of the Internet tools listed below, which two assist in validating hosts that are active on the Internet?
    A. PING
    B. FTP
    C. TraceRoute
    D. Multi-homing

58. Which e-mail standard is used on the Internet and is part of the TCP/IP protocol?
    A. MHS
    B. SNMP
    C. X.400
    D. SMTP

Answers and Explanations

1. **B** Because there are open Category 3 pairs from the phone system, the fastest and most cost-effective approach would be to implement a twisted-pair network solution. Another important piece of information here is that the users are fewer than 100 meters apart, which means a twisted-pair solution would work fine.
2. **C** Because each of the users currently uses Windows 95 and their only requirement is to share one another's files and printers, Windows 95 Peer to Peer is the clear choice. Choosing Windows 95 is the most cost-effective solution. Another advantage here is that the learning curve for the end user is smaller because they currently are using the Windows 95 interface.
3. **B** In a twisted-pair network, hubs are a requirement for connectivity.
4. **A, B, D** All of these cables have been tested and approved to operate at or above the 370 foot requirement. Twisted-pair cabling is guaranteed to work reliably at 362 feet. With newer technology in twisted pair cabling (CAT 5), vendors are hyping longer distances for twisted-pair; however, the IEEE recommendation for twisted-pair is still 362 feet.
5. **C** Spread-spectrum radio transmission speeds are typically 1.54Mb or slower.

6. **B, D** To date, Category 4 and 5 cables are the only cables rated that are certified to operate faster than 10Mbps.
7. **A** Because the users are close together and their cubicles are half-walled, it makes sense to choose a coaxial solution. Other major factors in this decision are that there are no available twisted-pair cables in the phone cable, and that this network needs to be installed at minimum cost.
8. **A** Because each of the users currently uses Windows 95 and their only requirement for networking is to share one another's files and printers, the logical solution here is to implement Windows 95 Peer to Peer networking.
9. **B, C, E** Server-based networks consist of dedicated servers, centrally located files on one or many servers, and centrally managed applications. Server-based networks also put more responsibility on systems managers for the security and protection of system resources and files.
10. **C, E** A network operating system's redirector intercepts requests and forwards them to the computer. The redirector also determines if a task should be left on a local computer or sent to another server on the network.
11. **E** The Application layer is the first layer where the raw data is housed. In layers under the Application layer, the major focus is shaking hands both electronically and physically.
12. **A, B** A packet header consists of a source address and a destination address.
13. **D** In a bus topology, only the computing device with the assigned token can communicate at one time.
14. **C** Because there is an available twisted-pair cable in each office and it is home run to a central wiring closet, the most logical choice here is twisted-pair cabling.
15. **E** Windows NT's DHCP enables you to distribute and manage your IP addresses centrally.
16. **D** Fiber would be the best choice here because tapping into fiber is virtually impossible. Fiber connectivity requires a high level of expertise; the other media types are easier to connect to.
17. **A, C, D** When planning a network such as the one described here, you must first diagnose your existing hardware to make sure you understand the current operating environment. This information establishes a base from which to plan. You also need to be concerned with the level of knowledge the librarian has to ensure that he will be able to manage your solution at his level of expertise without having to rely on you. The issue of security should always be discussed.
18. **B** In this situation, coax seems to be appropriate because the workstations are all lined up in a row in the same room. This would be the simplest and most cost-effective approach.
19. **A** Because the CPUs are together in a line, coax would be the current cable of choice. To plan for future expansion, a combo card with coax and twisted-pair would be the best choice because a combo of fiber and twisted-pair card is not available.
20. **C** Because the librarian is familiar with Windows 95 and because Peer to Peer networking will solve all of the networking issues, the best choice for this situation is Windows 95.

21. D A signal transmitted over Thinnet can reliably run 185 meters.

22. C The theoretical capacity of STP cable is 500Mbps.

23. A, C, D Category 3 cabling is the lowest data-grade cable. This type of cable is generally suited for data rates up to 10Mbps, although some innovative schemes enable the cable to support data rates up to 100Mbps. Category 3 cabling uses four twisted pairs with three twists per foot and is now considered to be the standard cable for most telephone systems.

24. C RJ-45 connectors are the most common type of connector used with UTP cables.

25. A, B, C Wireless networks are great solutions for people who move around a lot within their environments and for temporary installations within networks. Wireless networks are also great solutions where cabling would be impossible or inconvenient to implement.

26. C The maximum transmission distance for infrared signals is 100 feet.

27. D The outdoor operating range of a frequency-hopping scheme under a spread-spectrum radio transmission is two miles.

28. C Frequency-hopping typically transmits at up to 250Kbps.

29. C In order to get access to NetWare servers, IPX must be able to be routed across routers. Windows NT can be accessed by TCP/IP, IPX, and NetBEUI. Therefore, the only answer that works in this situation is C because of the IPX for NetWare resources.

30. C Because the maximum signal distance of a 10base2 segment is 185 meters, you would want to add a repeater in this scenario to regenerate the signal.

31. A, B, D 10Base5 has a data rate of 10Mbs with a signal range of 500 meters per cable segment. This type of cable is also referred to as Thicknet.

32. B, C, D, E Windows NT creates four special groups, each of which has special uses and access privileges. These groups are Everyone, Creator-owner, Interactive, and Network.

33. A Repeaters operate at the Physical layer of the OSI model.

34. A, C, D Microsoft identifies the following backup types: full, incremental, and differential.

35. A, C, D Three network standards that employ token-passing access control are FDDI, IEEE Standard 802.4, and token-ring.

36. A, B, D, E Benefits of using dedicated file servers include:

    Files are stored in a specific place where they can be reliably archived.

    Central file servers can be managed more efficiently with user and security data located in a single database.

    Dedicated file servers enable data backup to be implemented more easily.

    The cost of specialized file server technology can be shared by a larger number of users.

37. A Disk mirroring is the function of simultaneously writing data to separate disks using one channel on one disk controller.

38. C Three disks is the minimum number needed to configure a stripe set with parity on a Windows NT server.
39. A, B, C Network adapters format and prepare data, control the flow of data in and out of the computer, and send data to other resources.
40. A Data travels on the network in serial form, one bit at a time.
41. B, C, D, E In today's networking environments, EISA, PCI, Micro Channel, and ISA data-bus architectures are used most often.
42. A, C, D Typical resource settings are IRQs, base I/O port addresses, and base memory addresses.
43. D The rule for IRQs is that no two components can use an IRQ at the same time. Therefore, option D is the only viable answer.
44. C Windows NT uses Performance Monitor to track these resources.
45. C An advanced cable tester will provide more information, including collisions and congestion errors, than a TDR.
46. A The CCITT standards committee is responsible for developing and maintaining the X.400 set of message-handling standards.
47. C After loading Services for Macintosh on a Windows NT server, you have to define Macshare files so that Macs can access the files.
48. D Microsoft uses its SMS product to monitor Windows NT networks.
49. C When a router is sent a data stream that is larger than it can handle in one session, it breaks the data into smaller units and transmits them in smaller units.
50. C In a centralized network model, terminals send requests for data to a mainframe. The mainframe then retrieves the data and displays it on the requesting terminal.
51. C The length of the maximum cable run meets the requirement of CAT 3, and 95 percent of all existing phone systems use CAT 3 cabling. Therefore, CAT 3 UTPis the best choice for this situation.
52. B Because the logical choice for cabling here is twisted-pair, you will need 2 pairs (4 wires) to comply with 10BaseT connectivity.
53. B RJ-45s are required connectors for 10BaseT specifications.
54. B By implementing a DHCP server, you will be guaranteed that no duplicate addresses will ever be served.
55. C In the OSI model, the Physical and Data Link layers are responsible for allowing multiple computers to simultaneously access the network without interfering with one another.
56. B A subnet mask is used to block out a portion of the IP address so TCP/IP can distinguish the network ID from the host ID.
57. A, C These two tools enable a user or network administrator to validate host machines that are active.
58. D SMTP is the e-mail standard used on the Internet. SMTP is also part of the TCP/IP protocol.

Part VI

MCSE TestPrep

Appendixes

Appendix 

Glossary

$ character—Character used to create a hidden share.

10base2—Also called *Thinnet*. Ethernet implemented in a bus topology using coaxial cable.

10base5—Also called *Thicknet*. Ethernet implemented with thick coaxial cable.

10baseF—Ethernet implemented over fiber optic cable.

10baseT—Ethernet implemented with Unshielded Twisted-Pair (UTP) cabling.

10broad36—Ethernet implemented over a broadband system.

5-4-3 rule—5 is the maximum number of repeated segments, 4 is the maximum number of repeaters, and 3 is the maximum number of segments of the five that can be populated.

Access Control Entry (ACE)—An ACE is an entry in an Access Control List for any type of object under Windows NT. The ACE contains access information about a user or group for each object. Each object under Windows NT contains an ACL.

Access Control List (ACL)—The list of user and group permissions maintained by a resource for access to that resource.

access mask—Each ACE has an access mask. The access mask defines all possible permissions for a particular user to that object. Permissions include read, write, and change.

access permission security—Another phrase for *user-level access*. Rights to network resources are assigned on a user-by-user basis.

access point—A stationary transceiver connected to the cable-based LAN that enables the cordless PC to communicate with the network.

Accessibility Options—Windows NT interface options for aiding the physically impaired in performing computing tasks.

account lockout—You can specify to lock out an account after a given number of unsuccessful logon attempts.

Account Operators group—Group that holds the right to administer user accounts.

account policies—Specific information that applies to all global accounts, such as password age and length, as well as account lockout policies.

account rights—Windows NT uses account rights to determine what users and groups are allowed to do while logged on to the workstation.

ACL—See *Access Control List*.

active monitor—Used in 802.5 token-ring networks to monitor the health of the network and correct problems.

Address Resolution Protocol (ARP)—Determines the MAC layer address associated with a logical network address.

Administrators group—Group that holds the right to administer the local server; members of this group have complete control over the workstation.

Advanced RISC Computer (ARC)—A non-Intel x86-based computer. Windows NT support includes MIPS, PPC, and Alpha only.

AGLP—Stands for Accounts, Global Groups, Local Groups, Permissions. It is the methodology used for assigning permissions in a multidomain environment.

alert—An indication by Performance Monitor that a specific performance counter instance has exceeded a predetermined "safe" value.

All Users folder—This folder stores desktop settings for every user that will log on to the local workstation.

amplitude—The difference between the highest and lowest points of a signal, often measured by voltage.

analog—Type of signal that changes continuously and can take on many different values.

antivirus software—Software that locates and eliminates computer viruses.

AppleTalk—Protocol family used by Apple computers.

Application Event Log—The Application event log contains error messages specific to applications installed on a Windows NT system. These include services such as the DHCP service and BackOffice applications such as Microsoft Exchange Server.

Application layer—Layer 7 or the topmost layer of the OSI model. This layer exposes all the network services to the applications. When an application accesses the network, all actions are carried out through this layer.

application server—An application server runs all or part of an application on behalf of the client and then transmits the result to the client for further processing.

ARP—See *Address Resolution Protocol.*

Asynchronous Transfer Mode (ATM)—A cell-based networking technology that scales to tremendous speeds.

at.exe—An executable used to schedule batch files to run at a given time. This can be used to start or stop services, as well as to start other executables such as ntbackup.exe.

ATM—See *Asynchronous Transfer Mode.*

Attachment Unit Interface (AUI)—The connector used with Thicknet.

attenuation—A measure of how much a signal weakens as it travels through a medium.

auditing—Logs accesses to files and directories and helps to track object usage and security credentials. It is generally used to determine successes and failures of use of rights, object access, process tracking, logons and logoffs, shutting down the server, and so on.

AUI—See *Attachment Unit Interface.*

AutoDial—A Windows NT feature that automatically associates network connections with Phonebook entries. If a resource is needed that is accessible only via a dial-up connection, Windows NT will attempt to make the connection automatically.

BackOffice support—The MS BackOffice application most often requires Windows NT Server as the underlying operating system to operate.

backup browsers—The backup browser gets a copy of the browse list from the Browse Master (on the subnet) and distributes the browse list to subnet clients who request it.

backup domain controller—Added as a "load-balancing" mechanism to validate users to the domain. This can also serve as a file, print, and application server. It receives regular updates from the PDC of the domain accounts database so that it may also validate users logging onto the domain.

Backup Operators group—Group that holds rights to back up and restore servers. This gives members the capability to back up and restore files as needed. Members can access files only for archiving and restoring purposes.

bandwidth—The measure of the capacity of a medium to transmit data.

bandwidth utilization—The percent of total network capacity that is actually used by the network.

baseband—The entire capacity of the medium is used for one communication channel.

baseline—A collection of performance statistics depicting the average (typical) behavior of the network. Later fluctuations in network performance can be measured against the baseline.

batch file—An ASCII text file that contains Windows NT commands that are run sequentially when the program runs.

BDC—See *Backup Domain Controller*.

beacon—A message sent in a token-ring network to indicate a problem and start the auto-reconfiguration process. Beaconing is a process used by token-ring networks to narrow down the portion of the ring in which a problem is most likely to exist.

Bindings—Network Bindings are software interfaces between network cards, protocols, and services. The Bindings tab enables you to tweak the arrangement of bindings to increase performance on your Windows NT machine. It also allows you to configure in which order protocols will be used when attempting to negotiate connections with the server and workstation services.

bit-oriented protocol—A protocol that identifies the beginning and end of a packet with bit patterns referred to as flags.

boot—The process of initializing the operating system.

boot partition—Partition that contains the Windows NT operating system files.

BOOT.INI—On Intel-based Windows NT systems, the menu of selectable operating systems is stored in this text file.

bottleneck—A resource snag that limits the rate at which a task can be completed. This can also refer to a resource operating at or near 100% capacity, causing most inefficiency and performance problems on a system.

bound applications—Term used to describe OS/2 applications that can run under either OS/2 or DOS.

bridge—Links networks and is commonly used to overcome node per-segment limitations. Passes only frames targeted for a computer on the other side of the bridge (and all broadcast frames).

broadband—Two or more communication channels can share the bandwidth of the communications medium.

broadcast storm—A sudden deluge of network traffic often caused by a faulty network adapter.

brouter—A device that can simultaneously perform both routing and bridging.

browse list—List of available resources for a workstation.

Browse Master—The browser keeping the current list of available resources.

built-in accounts—When Windows NT Workstation is installed, two built-in accounts are created: Administrator and Guest. Neither can be deleted, but both can be renamed.

built-in groups—When Windows NT Workstation is installed, six default account groups are created: Administrator, Power Users, Users, Guests, Backup Operators, and Replicators.

bus—A topology in which all devices connect to a common shared cable.

Bytes total/sec—Performance Monitor counter that measures the number of bytes sent to and received from the network.

Cache—A temporary storage area in memory where data is stored while awaiting transfer from one location to another.

callback—A security feature incorporated into RAS that disconnects the incoming caller and calls back at a predetermined number (can also be a user-defined callback number).

carrier detection—Transmission method in which computers continue to listen to the network as they transmit in order to detect whether another signal interferes with their signal.

Carrier Sense Multiple Access with Collision Avoidance (CSMA/CA)—Each computer signals a warning that says it is *about* to transmit data. The other computers then wait for the transmission.

Carrier Sense Multiple Access with Collision Detection (CSMA/CD)—Carrier detection and carrier sensing used together form the protocol used in all types of Ethernet.

carrier sensing—Transmission method in which computers listen to see if the network is busy before they attempt to transmit.

Category 5—Data-grade cable, which consists of four twisted pairs and can support data rates of 100Mbps.

CDFS—CD File System. A system implemented on CD-ROMs.

centralized user management—A format in which user information (such as logon information) is stored in a central location.

Change permissions—A shared folder permission that allows any group or account attempting to access a resource to change the contents of the folder.

characterization file—Contains all the printer-specific information, such as memory, page protection, soft fonts, graphics resolution, paper orientation and size, and so on; it's used by the two dynamic link libraries whenever they need to gather printer-specific information.

clients—The computers that use the shared resources in a server-based network.

Client Services for NetWare (CSNW)—Enables Windows NT Workstation to access file and print resources on a NetWare server. Used in conjunction with NWLink with IPX/SPX protocol.

cluster—Smallest storage unit on a hard drive.

coaxial cable—Two conductors in the cable share a common axis.

compact.exe—Utility to compress files from the command prompt on NTFS partitions.

Complete trust domain model—A trust model with two or more domains. Each domain has a mixture of accounts and resources. All the domains trust the other domains with two-way trusts. These trusts allow the users in any domain to access resources in any of the other domains.

compression—Used to minimize the storage space needed for files on NTFS partitions.

connectionless mode—These systems assume that data will reach its destination with no errors; thus there is no protocol overhead associated with these systems. Without this overhead, these systems are typically very fast. User datagram protocol is an example of connectionless-oriented protocol.

connection-oriented mode—Assuming that communication errors will occur between computers, these protocols are designed to make sure data is delivered in sequential order and error-free to its destination. TCP/IP is an example of connection-oriented protocol.

connectivity device—A device used to extend or subdivide a network or to connect a network to a larger network.

contention—Computers are contending for use of the transmission medium.

control set—A set of controls used to determine configuration.

counters—Statistical measurements used to track levels of performance on system and hardware components in Performance Monitor.

CRC—See *Cyclical Redundancy Check.*

creating groups—Task of creating new groups, either local or global.

creating users—Task of adding new user accounts to an account database.

Creator Owner group—Special group representing the owner of a resource.

crosstalk—Interference caused by adjacent wires.

CSLIP—A compressed version of SLIP.

CSMA/CA—See *Carrier Sense Multiple Access with Collision Avoidance.*

CSMA/CD—See *Carrier Sense Multiple Access with Collision Detection.*

CSNW—See *Client Services for NetWare.*

Cyclical Redundancy Check (CRC)—A procedure used on disk drives to verify that data written to a sector is read correctly later and to check for errors in data transmission. This is known as a redundancy check because each data transmission includes extra (redundant) error-checking values in addition to data. The sending device generates a number based on the data to be transmitted and sends its result along with the data to the receiving device. The receiving device repeats the calculation after transmission. If both devices obtain the same result, it is assumed that the transmission is error-free.

data—The content of a network packet.

data frame—A unit of network data; the term "frame" is typically used with Ethernet and token-ring (see also *packet*).

Data Link Control (DLC)—Protocol most commonly used to access mainframes and Hewlett-Packard JetDirect network printers.

Data Link layer—The Data Link layer of the OSI model adds information to each packet coming from the Network layer. Thus the Data Link layer has knowledge of the packet structure and fields.

data transmission rate—The speed at which information is sent over network media.

datagram—An independent data packet being transported by a stateless protocol.

decentralized user management—A format in which user information is spread across different machines; changes have to be made to all machines when a user account is being changed.

Default User—The Default User is a template profile for users that do not have an existing profile assigned.

deleting groups—Task of deleting a group. You cannot delete built-in groups.

deleting users—Task of deleting user accounts from a server.

Devices—Control Panel applet used to start, stop, or disable device drivers.

Dynamic Host Configuration Protocol (DHCP)—A service that works with TCP/IP to automatically assign IP addresses to clients, relieving administrators from the burden of manually configuring IP addresses on all the clients on the network.

DHCP Server Service—Service that facilitates the assignment of IP addresses to clients.

Dial-Up Networking—Connecting to the network through phone lines. This is the client version of the software used to connect to a RAS server.

difference file—File developed for use with sysdiff.exe. It records the directory and Registry changes that were made between the baseline system and the system with the desired applications installed.

digital—A signal that can take only one of two discrete states.

Digital Audio Tape (DAT)—A reliable and fast tape media.

Digital Volt Meter (DVM)—A hand-held electronic measuring tool that checks the voltage of network cables.

DIP switch—A small switch on a circuit board (typically in a group) that enables you to physically configure a resource setting for the board.

directory replication—A facility that enables you to configure Windows NT Servers to automatically transmit updated versions of important directories to other computers on the network. This is commonly the NETLOGON share. It maintains the identical version of the directory contents on all import servers based on contents at the export server.

Directory Services—The Windows NT components that enable users to log on with an account in the SAM database and then use that account to access resources throughout the enterprise.

Directory Synchronization—Any changes to the SAM database are copied from the PDC to all the BDCs at regular intervals. (See also *Security Account Manager (SAM)*.)

direct sequence modulation—Breaks original messages into parts, which are transmitted on separate frequencies.

disabling users—Task of disabling a user account that doesn't delete the account but prevents the use of it.

discretionary access control—The owner of an object is allowed to assign permissions to the object.

Disk Administrator—A graphical utility used in Windows NT Server to manage all aspects of drives.

disk duplexing—Disk duplication using a separate controller for each disk.

Disk Manager—Graphical utility provided by Windows NT to manage disk resources.

disk mirroring—Duplication of data across multiple disks, which means that any failed disk can simply be replaced.

Disk striping—Known as RAID 0. Combines equal areas from several physical disks into one logical drive. Data can be written to or read from the disks simultaneously. This provides both faster reads and writes. This scheme does not provide fault-tolerance, so if one drive fails, the data on all the drives is lost. It supports disk sets of 2 to 32 disks.

Disk striping with parity—Known as RAID 5. Combines equal areas from several physical disks into one logical drive. Data can be written to or read from the disks simultaneously. This can improve read and write performance. Data on one disk is devoted to redundant information, so if one disk fails, the data on the array can still be recovered. Supports disk sets of 3 to 32 disks.

DLC—See *Data Link Control.*

DNS—See *Domain Name Service.*

domain—A network model in which user management is handled in central locations. Also refers to a collection of computer accounts. Only Windows NT workstations and servers can be true members of a domain.

Domain Admins group—Global group of users who will administer a domain. Initially contains the Administrator account.

domain controller—The primary server on a network used for authentication. The domain controller maintains a copy of the account database for the domain, providing central management of all accounts and resources.

Domain Guests group—Global group of guests.

Domain Master Browser—The Domain Master Browser requests subnet browse lists from the Master Browsers and merges the subnet browse lists into a master browse list for the entire domain. The computer functioning as the Domain Master Browser is always the Primary Domain Controller.

domain model—In a domain model, one Security Account Manager (SAM) database is maintained for all members of the domain in a network.

domain name—The name of the networking entity.

Domain Name Service (DNS)—Used to map computer names to IP addresses and vice versa.

Domain Users group—Global group of users that includes all users except the Guest account. All new users are automatically made members of this group.

dual boot— A dual-boot system allows users to select between operating systems, such as Windows 95 or Windows NT Workstation, when the machine is booted.

DUMPCHK—Used to verify that the contents of a memory dump file are valid and not corrupted.

DUMPEXAM—Used to write the key contents of a memory dump file to a text file named memory.txt. It can only be used with STOP 0x0000000A and STOP 0x0000001E errors.

DUMPFLOP—Used to copy the contents of a memory dump file to a series of floppy disks. It copies the file in a compressed format.

Dynamic Host Configuration Protocol (DHCP)—A service installed on Windows NT Server that facilitates the assignment of IP addresses to clients.

ElectroMagnetic Interference (EMI)—Outside noise that distorts the signal in a medium.

emergency repair disk (ERD)—A disk that can be used to return a Windows NT computer to its original operating state since its last ERD backup. The ERD contains important Registry information used to repair damaged Windows NT installations.

EMF data—Data that is compiled on the processor and then sent to the printer.

EMI—See *ElectroMagnetic Interference.*

encryption—Masking values sent to avoid capture by unwanted third parties.

Enhanced Integrated Drive Electronics (EIDE)—Common hard drives found in computer systems. When multiple EIDE drives are installed on a computer, ensure that the proper MASTER/SLAVE settings have been configured on the drives.

errors—Problems that create Windows NT Server conditions about which the user should be concerned.

Ethernet—The most popular OSI layer-two networking technology.

event log—A log of system events. Windows NT's event log includes a system log, a security log, and an application log. You can view the event log using Windows NT's Event Viewer tool.

Event Viewer—The Windows NT tool used to view operating system warnings, errors, and general information. For performance monitoring, the System and Application event logs are of primary interest.

Everyone group—Special group of which every user is automatically member. Includes all people who can connect to the network and have been defined as a security issue.

Exclusive OR function—Function used in disk striping with parity to calculate the parity information.

Export server—The machine that makes information available to be replicated.

extended partition—A partition that can be subdivided into logical drives. There can only be one extended partition on a drive. Extended partitions may contain data and applications.

FAT (File Allocation Table)—FAT is a file system named for the way the directory structure is stored. It was originally designed for DOS and is supported by DOS, Windows 3.x, Windows 95, and Windows NT. It is the alternative format for media to NTFS.

FAT32—Enhanced FAT introduced with Windows 95b.

fault-tolerance—Capability to recover from hardware errors, such as a failing drive. The ability of a system to withstand a failure and continue to function.

FDISK—The MS-DOS utility that creates and deletes disk partitions.

FDM—See *Frequency-Division Multiplexing.*

File and Print Services for NetWare—This service makes a Windows NT Server emulate a NetWare 3.12 server. Using this service enables Novell NetWare clients to use file and print services on the NetWare server without installing Microsoft Networking client software.

File and Print sharing—The services for defining how resources are shared. Enables other users to connect to resources on your computer.

fiber optic—Cable that consists of a highly refined glass or plastic core designed to transmit light signals.

file copies—When you copy files between folders on the same or different partitions, the file inherits the permissions of the target folder.

File Delete Child—Special security option available for POSIX compliance. If a user has been given the NTFS No Access permission to a particular file but has Full Control of the directory that contains the file, the user can actually delete the file even though he doesn't even have the ability to read the file.

file moves—When you move a file between folders on the same partition, the NTFS permissions do not change. However, when you move a file between folders on different partitions, the file is actually copied and will, therefore, assume the permissions of the new folder.

file server—A computers whose main task is to provide file sharing to computers on a network.

File Transfer Protocol (FTP)—Enables users to transfer files between diverse host types.

filter—A specific set of options that determine which Event Viewer events will be displayed; this is useful in finding specific events when thousands are displayed by default.

flag—A distinct sequence of ones and zeroes used to delineate packets.

fragmentation—A condition in which data is stored in non-continuous blocks of clusters and becomes increasingly inefficient to access.

frame—The minimum unit of data at OSI layer two.

frame relay—A type of WAN packet service that is especially well-suited for data traffic.

Frame types—NWLink uses varying frame types to transport information across the network. For communication to be successful, the client and server must be using the same frame type.

Frequency-Division Multiplexing (FDM)—Dividing bandwidth into frequency bands on broadband media.

frequency hopping—Switching among several available frequencies, yet staying on each frequency for a specified interval of time.

FTP—See *File Transfer Protocol.*

Full Control permission—A shared folder permission that allows any group or account attempting to access a resource to change the file permissions, to take ownership of files, and to perform all tasks allowed by the Change permission.

Fully Qualified Domain Name (FQDN)—The common name used to refer to locations on the Internet (such as **www.mcp.com**).

gateway—A device or program that enables communication between systems that use dissimilar protocols.

Gateway Services for NetWare (GSNW)—Enables Windows NT Server systems to access NetWare file and print resources directly and to act as a gateway to NetWare resources. Non-NetWare clients on a Windows NT network can access NetWare resources through the gateway as if they were accessing Windows NT resources without any need for NetWare client licensing.

global groups—Groups defined on the domain controller and available to all servers. Used to group accounts together (must be from the same domain).

Gopher—A means to create a set of hierarchical links to other computers. An Internet protocol that provides hierarchical links to Telnet and FTP sites.

Graphics Device Interface—The interface used by all graphic devices.

group—Logical grouping of user accounts that perform similar tasks and need the same rights and permissions.

GSNW—See *Gateway Services for NetWare.*

GuardTime—A REG_WORD value that defines how long a directory must be stable before its files can be replicated. The range of acceptable values is 0 to one half of the interval value.

Guests group—Local group of guests that can log on to the server. Allows members to log on to the workstation but limits their ability to use workstation and network resources.

Hardware Compatibility List (HCL)—Specifies all the computer systems and peripheral devices that have been tested for operation with Microsoft Windows NT 4.0. Devices not listed on the HCL can cause intermittent failures or, in extreme cases, system crashes.

hardware profile—A method of configuring which devices and services should be started upon startup, depending on the location of the hardware or the tasks to be completed. This method allows a user to configure which devices will be available for use when starting up the computer. You can create multiple HW profiles so that if you're using a docking station, you can have a network-enabled or network-disabled profile.

Hardware Quantifier Tool—On Intel systems, this utility can be used to identify all installed hardware on a system. It is found in the \Support\HQTool directory on your Windows NT installation CD-ROM.

hardware requirements—The requirements your computer must meet to run specific software or hardware components.

Hardware Specific Module (HSM)—In the ODI model, the HSM directly communicates with the hardware.

header—Signifies the start of the packet and contains important parameters.

High Performance File System (HPFS)—The primary file system used by OS/2. Earlier versions of Windows NT such as 3.1, 3.5, and 3.51, offered HPFS support; however, support for HPFS has been dropped in Windows NT 4.0.

hive—A subkey structure and component of the Windows NT Registry.

HOSTS—A local file for host name resolution.

hot fixing—Automatic error correction implemented in NTFS for moving data from bad sectors on a hard disk and permanently marking the bad sectors as unusable.

HPFS—See *High Performance File System.*

HSM—See *Hardware Specific Module.*

HTML—Hypertext Markup Language. The language of HTTP documents.

HTTP (Hypertext Transfer Protocol)—A client/server protocol used on the World Wide Web for the transmission of web documents.

hub—A central connection point where all workstations are physically connected. A multiport repeater.

IEEE standard—A standard endorsed by the IEEE.

impedance—A measure of a medium's resistance to an alternating current.

Import server—A machine configured to receive information from export servers.

information events—Informational messages or problems of non-critical nature of which you should be aware. In the Event Viewer these are marked by blue "I" icons.

infrared—A low-frequency light used in some wireless LANs.

Integrated Services Digital Network (ISDN)—A digital media provided by telephone companies that provides faster communication and higher bandwidth than traditional phone lines.

Interactive group—Special group that everyone becomes a member of when logged on locally.

Internet—International Wide Area Network using the TCP/IP protocol.

Internet Information Server (IIS)—Installed on an NT server, runs with TCP/IP. Provides web server, FTP server, and Gopher server capabilities.

Internet Service Manager—The main utility for administering and configuring IIS.

Internet Protocol (IP)—A connectionless protocol that provides datagram service.

Internetwork—A set of connected networks.

Internetwork Packet eXchange protocol (IPX)—A network layer protocol that is primarily used in NetWare networks.

Internetwork Packet eXchange protocol/Sequenced Packet eXchange (IPX/SPX)—A protocol suite used by NetWare and Microsoft's NWLink stack.

Interrupts/sec—Performance Monitor counter that measures the amount of interrupts the processor handles per second.

Interval—A REG_WORD value that defines how often an export server checks for updates. The range is from one to 60 minutes, and the default is five minutes.

IP—See *Internet Protocol.*

IP address—A logical network and host ID that consists of a 32-bit number. It's typically represented in a four octet dotted-decimal form.

IPCONFIG—The command used to retrieve current IP configuration information about a host in Windows NT.

IPX—See *Internetwork Packet eXchange protocol.*

IPX/SPX—See *Internetwork Packet eXchange protocol/Sequenced Packet eXchange.*

IRQ conflicts—A situation that occurs when the hardware interrupt request lines for two or more hardware devices are identical and create conflicts in addressing the processor.

ISDN—See *Integrated Services Digital Network.*

jumper—A small connector on a circuit board that enables you to physically configure a resource setting for the board.

Kernel debugger—Enables a system technician to investigate the state of a system after a STOP error has occurred. It enables the technician to perform stack traces and investigate what drivers were in use at the time of the STOP error. The kernel debugger can also be invoked when there is no STOP error.

Keyboard Input Locale—Specifies the international keyboard layout preferred for your keyboard; this helps foreign users tailor the keyboard layout appropriately.

LAN—See *Local Area Network.*

laser—A light source that produces an especially pure light that is monochromatic and coherent.

laser transmission—Sending a data signal using a laser, typically on fiber optic cable.

Last Known Good Configuration—The last working configuration since a user has logged on, updated at successful logon.

late collision—When a collision is missed on an 802.3 network due to propagation delay.

LED—See *Light-Emitting Diode.*

Light-Emitting Diode (LED)—A low-powered light source used with multimode fiber optic cable.

Link Support Layer (LSL)—In the ODI model, the LSL is the packet router.

LIP (Large Internet Protocol)—Used to determine the largest possible frame size that can be used to communicate with NetWare servers.

LMHOSTS—A local file for computer name resolution.

Local Area Network (LAN)—A group of computers interconnected within a building or campus setting.

local groups—Windows NT provides the administrator with local groups to manage users' rights and permissions by group. By adding users to local groups, those users inherit the rights and permissions of the group.

local security—The ability to restrict access to a file or directory to someone who is sitting at the keyboard of that particular machine.

Local User profiles—Local User profiles are the default type of profile assigned to users by Windows NT. They reside on the local machine (in the file ntuser.dat) and are available only when the user logs on to that machine. Includes users' Start menu entries and desktop settings.

Log—Documentation of what has occurred. In the case of Performance Monitor, a log file is used to record objects and counters on a server.

Logical disk—A means of dividing a physical disk into multiple partitions that appear to be separate disk drives.

logical node names—Human-readable names for computer devices that can be mapped to a protocol-specific address.

logical topology—The logical pathway a signal follows as it passes among the network nodes.

logon scripts—Scripts that run when users log on to a Windows NT computer.

LPD (Line Printer Daemon) service—Enables a Windows NT Print Server to control a TCP/IP Network Interface Printer. It also enables UNIX clients to send print jobs to a Windows NT Printer using the LPR command.

LPQ (Line Printer Query) tool—Enables a UNIX host or Windows NT client to check where a job is in the queue for a printer controlled by the LPD Service. The Windows NT client must install the TCP/IP Print Services to have access to the LPQ command.

LPR—Command that enables Windows NT computers to print to printers managed by UNIX hosts. It also is used by UNIX hosts to print to a Windows NT printer controlled by the LPD service.

LSL—See *Link Support Layer.*

MAC address—See *Medium Access Control address.*

managing shares—A task usually done with Server Manager that enables you to fine-tune shares (involves setting permissions and connection limits to the shares).

Mandatory User profile—A Mandatory User profile can be assigned by administrators when the user must not be able to permanently change the profile. They must be server-based. They are created by renaming the ntuser.dat file ntuser.man.

Master Boot Record (MBR)—The primary boot record used at each boot.

MAU—See *Multistation Access Unit.*

Media Access Unit (MAU)—The central wiring center for a token-ring network.

Media Support Module (MSM)—In the ODI model, the MSM manages the hardware configuration tables and performs initialization functions independent of the media.

Medium Access Control address (MAC address)—The NIC address on an 802.5 network. Each workstation has a unique MAC address.

member server—A Windows NT server computer that plays no part in maintaining the domain's account database and does not authenticate users' logons to the domain. It does not act as a domain controller. May exist in a domain or workgroup environment.

Memory Dump file—An option that can be configured to dump the contents of memory at the time of a STOP event. The contents of memory are initially stored into the page file and then are copied into the configure memory dump file when the system is restarted.

MEMORY:PAGES/SEC—Performance Monitor counter that measures the number of times that a memory page had to be paged into memory or out to disk.

microwave transmission—Sending a signal using microwave frequencies. Typically requires line-of-sight connectivity.

Migration Tool for NetWare—A relatively simple method of transferring file and directory data, along with user and group account data and directory rights, from a NetWare server to a Windows NT domain controller.

mirrored set-fault tolerance RAID Level 1—Requires two hard drives in Windows NT Server. Data written to a mirrored partition on Disk 0 will be "mirrored" to a partition that's equal in size on Disk 1.

MLID—See *Multiple Link Interface Driver.*

mobile computing—Uses portable PCs or PDA devices and connects to the network via some form of telephone.

Monitoring shares—Auditing turned on for shares.

MSAU—See *Multistation Access Unit.*

MSM—See *Media Support Module.*

multilink—Combines multiple physical links into a single logical link to increase bandwidth when using Dial-Up Networking. Can be used for bundling multiple ISDN channels or two or more standard modems.

Multiple Link Interface Driver (MLID)—The MLID has two basic functions: to build up and strip media headers off packets and to send and receive packets at the Physical layer.

Multiple master domain model—A trust model with two or more domains containing user accounts and one or more domains with resources. In this model, all resource domains trust each of the master domains with one-way trusts. The master domains also trust each other with two-way trusts.

multiplexing—Enables a medium to support multiple data channels.

multiprocessor—Term relating to the capability of an operating system to use more than one processor.

Multiprotocol routing—Using more than one protocol and routing them across the network.

Multistation Access Unit (MAU or MSAU)—A concentrator used in token-ring networks.

mux—A device that has the capability of acting as a multiplexer and a demultiplexer.

narrow band radio transmission—Transmissions that occur at a single radio frequency.

NBTSTAT—A TCP/IP utility that can be used to determine what NetBIOS names your computer has registered. It also can be used to list all NetBIOS names that your client has resolved to IP addresses and stored in the NetBIOS name cache.

N connector—Used in Thicknet, a connector that screws on.

NDIS—See *Network Device Interface Specification.*

NetBEUI—A non-routable protocol used to carry NetBIOS information on a local LAN only.

NetBIOS—The Network Basic Input/Output System, which extends all the way to the Session layer and is used to handle naming and file services. Defines a software interface and a naming convention, not a protocol.

NetBIOS name—Each computer in Microsoft Networking must have a unique name. This name is used to identify the computer and its services that are offered on the network.

Net share—Command to share a directory from the command prompt.

NETSTAT—A TCP/IP utility is used to determine what ports are in use during a TCP/IP session.

NetWare—Novell's network operating system.

NetWare Directory Service (NDS)—A distributed database of network resources primarily associated with NetWare 4.x systems.

network—A group of interconnected computers that share information and resources.

network adapter—A device that provides physical access to a network. The term network adapter is typically used for an internal card that connects a PC to an Ethernet or token-ring network.

Network Client Administrator—Utility that creates the Windows NT client-based administration tools setup directory. Allows for the configuration of a network installation point for the installation of client software. Client software that can be installed includes MS_DOS, LANMAN DOS, LANMAN OS/2, and so on.

Network Device Interface Specification (NDIS)—Microsoft and 3Com jointly developed Network Device Interface Specification in 1989. This standard defined an interface between the MAC sublayer and higher layers of the OSI model.

network distribution server—Used to install software across the network. The easiest and fastest way to do this is to copy installation files from the CD-ROM to a hard disk and then create a share to the directory.

Network File System (NFS)—A family of file sharing protocols for TCP/IP.

Network group—Special group of which everyone becomes member when connected to a network share on a server.

Network layer—The Network layer of the OSI model determines the route a packet must take to reach its destination.

Network Monitor—A software-based tool that monitors network traffic, displaying packet information and keeping statistics on network usage. Windows NT's Network Monitor is an example of a network monitoring tool.

network service—A process (running on a PC) that facilitates networking. Windows NT includes numerous network services.

network topology—The physical layout of a network.

New Technology File System (NTFS)—This is the transaction-based file system native to Windows NT. Provides better security, better disaster recovery, better performance on larger partitions, and better fault tolerance than FAT.

NFS—See *Network File System.*

No Access permission—A shared folder permission that will deny access to the contents of the resource for any group or account that is trying to access the resource. This permission overrides all other permissions.

Non-paged memory—Data that is written to a specific location without being written to or read from a physical disk first.

Non-transitive trusts—Trusts do not flow from one domain to another through a middle domain. A trust always involves only two domains. (See also *trust relationships.*)

Novell NetWare—Server software from Novell.

NT Backup Manager—Windows NT utility provided to create and manage data backup and recovery.

NTFS—See *New Technology File System.*

NTFS file permissions—Those permissions that can be set at the file level on NTFS formatted partitions. Unlike share permissions, NTFS permissions apply to local resource access.

NTFS folder permissions—Those permissions that can be set at the folder level on NTFS formatted partitions. Unlike share permissions, NTFS permissions apply to local resource access.

NTFS partitions—Disk partitions formatted with NTFS rather than FAT.

NTFS permissions—Permissions of files and directories on an NTFS volume.

NTLDR—The load program\routine for the Windows NT operating system on the Intel architecture.

NTVDM—NT Virtual DOS Machine. Used for every DOS application and each copy of Windows being used. There will be a separate NTVDM for each Win16 application running in a separate memory space, plus one for the base Win16 box.

NWLink—Microsoft's version of the IPX/SPX protocol. The NWLink IPX/SPX-compatible transport provides support for IPX/SPX sockets and NetBIOS APIs.

objects—System and hardware components tracked by counters in Performance Monitor.

ODI—See *Open Data-Link Interface.*

One-way trust—A trust relationship with a single trusted domain and a single trusting domain. (See also *trust relationships.*)

Open Data-Link Interface (ODI)—Open Data-Link Interface was jointly developed by Novell and Apple Computer Corporation and released in 1989. The goals of ODI are similar to the goals of NDIS: to provide a seamless integration between the Data-Link layer and the Transport layer of the protocol stack.

Open Shortest Path First (OSPF)—A link-state routing protocol.

operating system—The software required to run any other programs, such as word processors or spreadsheet applications.

operating system conflict—A situation in which an application is not fully compatible with the operating system.

optimal performance—Getting the best performance from the software and hardware currently in place.

orphan—A remaining disk from a broken mirror set.

oscilloscope—The device that measures fluctuations in signal voltage.

OSI model—A seven-layer model used primarily as a reference model.

OSPF—See *Open Shortest Path First.*

packet—A unit of network data transmitted from a sending PC to a receiving PC; sometimes called a *Protocol Data Unit* (*PDU*).

Paged memory—Virtual memory that all applications use when the applications believe that they have the full memory range available.

page fault—A situation in which information cannot be retrieved from physical memory and often must be retrieved from the pagefile.

pagefile—This is where pages are stored when they are not active in RAM. Windows NT, by default, controls the size of the paging file.

Pages/sec—Performance Monitor counter that measures the number of times that a memory page had to be paged into memory or out to disk.

paging—The action of moving information between the pagefile and physical memory.

Parity—Redundant information, such as a checksum. If a piece of data is lost, parity can be used to recalculate the original piece of data.

partition—A section on a hard disk that has been created to act as a separate disk.

partitioning—The method of dividing a physical hard disk into smaller units.

passive topology—The interconnection of passive systems using no power or electronics.

patch cable—Relatively short, flexible cable used to connect two network devices.

PC Cards (PCMCIA)—Control Panel applet used to add and configure PCMCIA device drivers. Also used to identify cards that Windows NT does not support.

PDC—Primary Domain Controller. The first Windows NT Server online in a domain. Maintains a master database of all user account information in the domain.

per-seat licensing—Each computer that accesses a Windows NT Server requires a separate client access license. Clients are free to connect to any server, and there are unlimited connections to the server. Each client participating in the network must have a per-seat license.

per-server licensing—For each per-server license you purchase, one concurrent network connection is allowed access to the server. When the maximum specified number of concurrent connections is reached, Windows NT returns an error to a connecting user and prohibits access. An administrator, however, can still connect to the server to increase the number of per-server licenses.

Performance Monitor—Used to monitor and analyze Windows NT resources and gauge your computer's efficiency.

Phonebook entries—Phonebook entries, in essence, make up the address book for all established telephone links assigned in the Dial-Up Networking dialog box.

Physical layer—The lowest layer of the OSI model.

physical topology—The actual physical layout of the network.

PING—Packet Internet Groper. A tool used to test the connectivity between two systems.

platform independence—Windows NT is platform-independent as it exists in versions for Intel, Alpha, and others.

Plenum-grade cable—Cabling specially designed to be used without conduit in areas where fire codes prohibit PVC cabling.

Point-to-Point Protocol (PPP)—A very popular dial-up protocol that allows dynamic negotiation of IP addresses and multiple protocols over a single serial connection.

Point-to-Point Tunneling Protocol (PPTP)—A protocol similar to PPP, but it encapsulates enhanced security through encryption. Provides secure connections to a network attached to a public network by encapsulating information with PPP packets.

policy file mode—Mode of operation for System Policy Editor; edits the system policy file that is used for different users and computers for your domain.

policy templates—Template files used for System Policy Editor when creating system policies.

Ports—Control Panel applet that lists the available serial ports. Also used to add a port under Windows NT.

power fluctuation—A fluctuation in the power supply that can cause the network to misbehave.

Power Users group—Nearly as powerful as Administrators, this group allows members to perform certain system tasks without gaining complete administrative control of the workstation.

PPP—See *Point-to-Point Protocol.*

PPTP—See *Point to Point Tunneling Protocol.*

Preferred Server—A NetWare (3.x) server selected from a list of available NetWare servers in conjunction with GSNW and CSNW during the Windows NT logon process. The Preferred Server indicates which NetWare server you want to validate your NetWare Logon process.

Presentation layer—The Presentation layer defines the format used by applications to exchange data. This layer is also called the *translator*. This layer is responsible for protocol conversion, data encryption, and data compression, and it is where the redirector service operates.

Primary Domain Controller—The first server installed in a Domain. The PDC maintains the master copy of the directory database and provides logon validation for users.

primary partition—Partition that cannot be subdivided, It holds the files used to start the operating system. Windows NT supports up to four primary partitions on a single drive or three primary partitions and one extended partition.

print device—The hardware device that places the marks on the paper.

print driver—The software that enables applications to communicate properly with the print device.

Print job—Data destined for a print device.

Print Operators group—Group that holds rights to administer printers.

print processor—Responsible for completing the rendering process. The tasks performed by the print processor differ depending on the print data's data type.

print router—The print router receives the print job from the spooler and routes it to the appropriate print processor.

print server—A print server maintains a single printer or group of printers across the network. It manages access to a shared printer, making it accessible to users at other network machines.

print spooler—A collection of DLLs (Dynamic Link Libraries) that accept, process, schedule, and distribute the print jobs.

printer—Software between the operating system and the physical printing device.

printer graphics driver DLL—This dynamic link library consists of the rendering or managing portion of the driver; it's always called by the Graphics Device Interface.

printer interface driver—This dynamic link library consists of the user interface or configuration management portion of the printer driver; it's used by an administrator to configure a printer.

printer pool—A collection of identical printing devices configured as one printer. Using a printer pool increases printing productivity because each job is printed on the first available printing device.

priority—An arbitrary ranking that places one process ahead of or behind another in processing order.

process—A program or application that can contain one or more threads of execution (generally an .EXE file).

profiles—Stored information about a user's settings for desktop, Network Neighborhood, program files, and more. Profiles can be local or roaming.

propagation delay—A delay resulting from the amount of time it takes an electrical signal to travel through cable and associated electronics before arriving at its destination.

Promiscuous—A program that is not limited to just monitoring the network traffic going in and out of one computer, but all the traffic on the network.

protocol analyzer—A hardware or combined hardware and software product that monitors network traffic, tracks network performance, and analyzes packets.

protocol binding—A potential logical pathway from a network/transport protocol (such as TCP/IP) to a specific adapter. In Windows NT, you must also bind the protocol to certain higher-level network services, such as the server and workstation services.

Protocol Manager (PROTMAN)—The protocol manager routes packets from the MAC layer to the correct protocol stack in the NDIS model.

PROTMAN—See *Protocol Manager.*

PVC cable—Cable that is covered with polyvinyl chloride.

Queue—A series of print jobs waiting to be printed.

RAID—See *Redundant Array of Inexpensive Disks.*

RAID 0—A non-fault tolerant method of speeding disk access.

RAID 1—Disk duplexing and disk mirroring.

RAID 5—Disk striping with parity. The ability for an array of multiple disks to have one disk fail and continue to function.

RAS—See *Remote Access Service.*

RAW data—Data that is sent to the printer for compilation there.

RDISK—The RDISK utility is used to back up all hives in the Registry except the SAM and SECURITY hives. These hives can be backed up using this utility if the /S parameter is used.

Read permission—A shared folder permission that allows any group or account attempting to access a resource to display files or folders within the folder as well as to execute any programs contained within the folder.

REALTIME—The highest priority in Windows NT. This priority can be specified only by administrators. A program must be specifically written to run at this priority because it is higher than some system threads.

redirector—A software module (typically implemented as a file system driver) that redirects I/O requests to the network and thus allows a networked computer to act as a client.

Redundant Array of Inexpensive Disks—A system used for fault tolerance. A method of paralleling many disks to make them appear as one large disk with the option of fault tolerance. Windows NT Server provides software implementations of RAID 1 (disk mirroring) and RAID 5 (stripe sets with parity).

REGEDIT—The Windows 95 Registry Editor is also included with Windows NT. It provides greater search capabilities than REGEDT32 but cannot edit the REG_MULTI_SZ data type.

REGEDT32—The native Windows NT Registry Editor. It contains native editors for all supported data types in the Windows NT Registry.

Registry mode—Mode of operation for System Policy Editor that edits the local Registry.

Remote Access Service (RAS)—Windows NT RAS extends the power of Windows NT networking to a remote user via dial-up connectivity. RAS provides dial-up connectivity to remote users over phone lines, X.25, or ISDN links.

remote monitoring—Using Performance Monitor or other tools to connect to remote computers on the network and monitor their performance from a local computer.

Remote server—A server remotely connecting to the network.

renaming users—Task of renaming a user account. This doesn't affect the SID assigned to the account.

repeater—Repeaters regenerate weak incoming signals. Because no packet information is necessary to perform this task, repeaters reside at the Physical layer. A repeater simply retransmits any frame it receives, including frames with errors.

Replication service—The service that performs replication for export and import servers.

Replicator group—A system group used by Windows NT Workstation when replicating directory content with Windows NT servers.

resource conflict—A situation in which two or more devices simultaneously attempt to use the same system resource (such as interrupts, base I/O port address, or base memory address).

RG-58—A type of coax commonly used interchangeably with Thinnet.

RI—See *Ring In.*

ring—A descriptive term used for the logical path used in a token-ring network.

Ring In (RI)—Type of port on a token-ring MSAU.

Ring Out (RO)—Type of port on a token-ring MSAU.

RIP—See *Routing Information Protocol.*

RIP for IP—A routing protocol available for NT.

RIP packets—Data transferred across routers.

RJ-45—Common term for the 8-pin modular connector or jack used in most networks today.

RO—See *Ring Out.*

Roaming User profile—Administrators may assign a roaming profile to a user when that user will log on to the network from multiple machines. Roaming profiles must be server-based.

router—Internetwork connectivity device that connects different networks or subnetworks. A router helps LANs and WANs achieve interoperability and connectivity and can link LANs that have different network topologies (such as ethernet and token ring). Especially useful for containing broadcasts.

Routing Information Protocol (RIP)—Distance-vector routing protocol.

Scope—A series of IP addresses available for distribution by the DHCP server. Options can be set in DHCP Manager on a scope-by-scope basis.

SCSI Adapters—Control Panel applet used to install SCSI adapter drivers and IDE drivers.

secondary cache—(Also called a Level 2 or L2 cache.) The internal cache is called a Level 1 (L1) cache and can generally outperform an L2 cache. The real factor with cache is the cache controller and system design.

Sector sparing—Data in a fault-tolerant array is automatically written to a good sector if NT detects a bad sector as the data is written to the drive.

Security Account Manager (SAM)—The database in which user accounts, group accounts, and computer accounts are stored. The read/write copy is stored on the Primary Domain Controller, whereas a read-only copy is stored on all the Backup Domain Controllers in the domain.

Security Event Log—Contains error messages related to auditing. This event contains success and failure events based on the audit setting policy set in the User Manager for Domains.

Security log—One of the major NT logs that tracks security-related events.

Security Reference Monitor—This is the component of Windows NT that checks a user's rights and privileges prior to granting access to a resource.

Sequenced Packet eXchange (SPX)—Extends IPX to provide connection-oriented service with reliable delivery.

Serial Line Internet Protocol (SLIP)—A protocol that carries IP over an asynchronous serial communications line. An older dial-up protocol that is being replaced by PPP.

server-based network—A network that contains computers designated for management and sharing of resources.

Server Manager—Utility to manage a server on the network.

Server Message Block (SMB)—A file-sharing protocol jointly developed by Microsoft, Intel, and IBM. SMB specifies a series of commands used to pass information between computers using the following four message types: file, printer, session control, and message.

Server Operators group—Group that holds rights to administer a server.

Server service—A Windows NT service that enables a Windows NT machine to act as a server (provide resources to the network).

Server tool—An administrative tool used to monitor remote users and the resources they are using. The Server tool allows you to disconnect users from shares and other resources.

Service Advertising Protocol (SAP)—A NetWare protocol that enables servers to advertise their services to the network.

Services for Macintosh—A service that enables the system administrator to create shares for Macintosh users, as well as to create printer queues for Macintosh.

Session layer—The Session layer creates a virtual connection between two applications on separate computers. This virtual connection is called a *session*. The Session layer maintains synchronization between applications by placing checkpoints in the data stream. It is this layer that performs name recognition and security that allows the applications to communicate.

SETUP.LOG—This file is a listing of all files and their CRC values installed by the Windows NT installation process.

Setup Manager—The Setup Manager is a utility supplied with the Windows NT Workstation Resource Kit. The Setup Manager allows you to programmatically create answer files for an unattended installation.

Share permissions—Permissions that are applicable to share points; they include Full Control, Change, Read, and No Access.

shared folder—A folder and its contents that are available from the local machine as well as from remote machines connected by a network.

sharing—Creating a share point on a server that can be accessed from the network.

share-level security—Security level in which each shared resource on the network has an associated password. To access the resource, the user must simply enter the correct password. No user authentication is required in share-level security models.

shield—The outer conductor that serves as a ground and protects the inner conductor.

Shielded Twisted-Pair (STP)—Cable that consists of one or more twisted pairs of cables enclosed in a foil wrap and woven copper shielding.

SID—The security account identifier is a unique identifier used by Windows NT to manage users and groups. All permissions and rights are assigned to the account or group SID. When a SID is deleted, it can never be re-created.

Simple Mail Transfer Protocol (SMTP)—A protocol used to transport electronic mail through internetworks.

Simple Network Management Protocol (SNMP)—Network management protocol used with TCP/IP networks.

Single domain model—A trust model with only one domain. All accounts and resources are in one domain.

Single master domain model—A trust model with one domain containing user accounts and one or more domains with resources. All the resource domains trust the account (master) domain with one-way trusts, which enables users in the master domain to access resources in any of the resource domains.

SLIP—See *Serial Line Internet Protocol.*

SMB—See *Server Message Block.*

SMP—Symmetric MultiProcessing. A system that has more than one processor, but where no processor is dedicated to the system or scheduling.

SMTP—See *Simple Mail Transfer Protocol.*

SNMP—See *Simple Network Management Protocol.*

Small Computer System Interface (**SCSI**)—High performance hard disks commonly found in high-end server computers. SCSI enable larger quantities of hard disks to be installed into a system.

special groups—Groups that cannot be administered but are used by Windows NT for local or remote users. These groups are based on the task being performed or where the task is being performed (Network versus Interactive).

spool—Temporary holding place for jobs waiting to print; operates in the background to manage the printing process.

spool directory—The directory in which the Windows NT printer server stores all the print jobs for a particular printer during spooling.

spooler—Accepts print jobs and spools the jobs to disk until the printer is ready to accept data.

spread-spectrum radio transmission—Type of radio transmission that changes frequencies regularly.

SPX—See *Sequenced Packet eXchange.*

standalone system—A computer that isn't connected to a network.

star—Descriptive term for the physical layout of certain network types, such as 10Base-T.

START—The primary utility for starting applications at another priority. START creates another process for the applications started with it.

Stop error—The most critical type of error possible in Windows NT.

STP—See *Shielded Twisted-Pair.*

stripe set—A hardware solution that increases performance by writing data to multiple drives (2–32 drives in Windows NT Server and Workstation) in 64KB segments. Stripe sets may enhance performance because data is written across multiple disks concurrently. However, stripe sets offer no fault tolerance; if a single disk were to break down, all data would be lost. (See also *stripe set with parity.*)

stripe set with parity—RAID Level 5 hardware and software solution that increases performance by writing data to multiple drives (3–32 drives in Windows NT Server) in 64KB segments. Information is written across the disk set in a 64KB stripe. For each stripe, parity data is written to one of the disks so that if a single disk were to cease working, the missing information could be rebuilt using the remaining data and the parity information for the stripe. Stripe sets with parity offer fault-tolerance support because parity information is written to each disk in the stripe set in rotation.

Striping—Combining equal areas from several disks into one logical drive. When the data is written to these disks, it is striped in 64K units and written to each disk simultaneously. The data can also be read simultaneously from the disks. This scheme improves read/write performance.

subnet—A division of a network into sub-networks. Subnets are used to break up a larger pool of IP addresses into smaller pools—most often due to performance or physical separation of the network.

subnet mask—Used to mask a portion of the 32-bit IP address so that the TCP/IP protocol can distinguish the host portion of the IP address from the network portion.

Sysdiff—A Microsoft-supplied application that allows you to set up additional applications that do not support scripted setup when completing an automated Windows NT Workstation setup.

System Event Log—Contains all error messages related to the Windows NT operating system. This includes startup errors that may occur.

system partition—Partition that contains the files necessary to boot the Windows NT operating system.

system policies—Templates of the Registry that are merged with the user's existing Registry. These can be implemented as a computer, user, or group policy and are stored in the file ntconfig.pol for Windows NT and config.pol for Windows 95.

System Policy Editor—Program that enables you to edit system policies via a user interface.

T1—Digital line that provides point-to-point connections and transmits 1.544Mbps in a total of 24 DS-0 channels. Also called a *DS-1*.

T3—Digital line that can transmit data at up to 45Mbps. Made up of 28 MUXed T1 circuits.

Take Ownership—Permission allowing a user of the network to take ownership of a file or directory.

Target computer—The computer that is suffering from the STOP errors. This computer has its boot.ini edited to enable a kernel debugger to investigate its memory space after a STOP error has occurred.

Task Manager—Used to control the applications and processes running on your computer and to monitor memory and CPU performance at a glance.

TCP—The Internet's reliable Transport layer protocol.

TCP/IP—Transmission Control Protocol/Internet Protocol. A suite of protocols used to connect dissimilar hosts on a network. This is the primary protocol used on the Internet.

T connector—Used in Thinnet-based LANs, this connects the network interface card to the cable.

TDM—See *Time-Division Multiplexing.*

TDR—See *Time-Domain Reflectometer.*

TechNet—A CD-ROM-based repository of technical information available from Microsoft.

Telephony Application Program Interface (TAPI)—A device driver for the PC's phone system. It provides a standard interface with telephony applications. TAPI manages communications between the computer and the phone system.

Telnet—A protocol that enables PCs and workstations to function as dumb terminals in sessions with host systems on internetworks.

template account—A template account allows the administrator to specify a user's environment, group memberships, and rights for a single account and copy that account when creating new users.

terminator—A special connector that includes a resistor.

terrestrial microwave—Land-based microwave.

Thicknet—Also known as *10Base5,* the Thicknet topology employs RG6 cable, which is much thicker and harder to work with than RG58. It is the oldest standard for coax-based Ethernet.

Thinnet—Also known as *10Base2,* Thinnet is the most common bus topology. This topology employs RG58 cable, which has a 50ohm impedance. It is the newest standard for coax-based Ethernet.

thread—The smallest execution unit. A thread is a string of code execution that cannot run on more than one processor at one time.

Time-Division Multiplexing (TDM)—Supports digital signals.

Time-Domain Reflectometer (TDR)—A device that sends sonar-like pulses along a cable and looks for imperfections that might be caused by a break or a short in the line.

token—A special network frame passed around some networks to control which station has permission to transmit.

Token-ring—A type of network that uses token-passing.

topology—Defines the arrangement of nodes, cables, and connectivity devices that make up the network.

TRACERT—A TCP/IP utility that can be used to determine the route that packets take when being transferred to a remote network.

trailer—Marks the end of the packet and contains error-checking information.

transceiver—Used with Thicknet as part of the network-host connection.

transmission media—The network medium used to send data signals.

transmission medium—The physical pathway in which computers are connected.

Transport layer—The Transport layer ensures that packets are delivered in sequence and error free. The Transport layer breaks large messages from the Session layer into manageable packets to be sent out to the network.

Transport protocol—Protocol that operates at the Transport layer of the OSI model and is responsible for reliable packet delivery.

Trust relationships—A secured communication link between two domains implemented as a Remote Procedure Call, or RPC. One of the domains acts as the trusted domain, and the other is the trusting domain. The trusting domain permits users from the trusted domain to access its resources.

Twisted-pair—See *10Base-T*.

Two-way trust—Two one-way trusts. In a two-way trust, both domains are trusted domains and trusting domains. (See also *trust relationships.*)

UDF (Uniqueness Database File)—A text file that allows you to supply answers to an automated Windows NT unattended setup file for machine-specific information (such as network address, machine name, and user name). It must be used in conjunction with an unattended text file.

UDP—See *User Datagram Protocol.*

unattended answer files (unattend.txt)—The unattended answer file supplies specific answers for the Setup routine in order to automate selective portions of or the complete Windows NT Setup routine.

Uninterruptible Power Supply (UPS)—Uninterruptible power supply. An online backup battery that enables your system to keep running for a short period of time in the event of a power outage.

Universal Naming Convention (UNC)—A method of referring to resources in a standardized way.

Universal Resource Access—Users can access all resources with a single account, regardless of physical location.

Unshielded Twisted-Pair (UTP)—Cable that doesn't incorporate a shield into its structure.

UPS—See *Uninterruptible Power Supply.*

User—Account representing a person who is allowed to log on to a domain.

User Datagram Protocol (UDP)—Unreliable, connectionless Transport protocol.

user-level security—Security level in which rights are assigned on a user-by-user basis and authentication is employed.

User Manager—Program for managing users and groups, as well as user rights, account policy, and trust relationships.

User Manager for Domains—The main utility for user account administration on an NT Server. It is used to maintain the domain's account database making any updates to the copy on the PDC. A member server runs only User Manager.

User policies—Rules governing users that are merged with the HKEY_CURRENT_USER registry and stored in the file NTCONFIG.pol.

user profiles—A means by which the administrator can create and maintain settings for an individual user's working environment. User profiles can be local (stored only on the system that they are working at) or roaming.

user rights—Specific rights to which users have been assigned.

Users group—A built-in Windows NT Workstation group that allows members to effectively use the operating system on a daily basis while limiting their ability to configure advance system parameters that may cause system instabilities and crashes.

UTP—See *Unshielded Twisted-Pair.*

vampire tap—A clamp-on transceiver that forces sharp teeth into the Thicknet cable.

Virtual Memory Manager—The Virtual Memory Manager is responsible for keeping track of each application's address space, the real list of physical memory, and the pagefile memory used to store the information.

Virtual Private Network—A wide area network existing through virtual connections. Makes use of existing network connections to create secure tunnels enabling a secure, wide-area network to be implemented over an existing network such as the Internet.

volume sets—Areas of free space combined into a single logical drive. Provided by Windows NT to allow 2–32 areas of free space to be combined into one logical disk partition.

WAN—See *Wide Area Network.*

warnings—Problems that create Windows NT Server conditions about which the user should be alerted. In the Windows NT Event Viewer, warnings are indicated by yellow exclamation marks.

Web Administration Tools—Tools used to administer your network through the web.

Wide Area Network (WAN)—A group of computers connected over long distances. These are typically created using telephone lines, but they can also be created with fiber links, microwave radio, leased lines, and satellite links.

Windows 16-bit applications—Those applications originally written for Windows 3.x.

Windows 32-bit applications—Those applications written in 32-bit code for Windows 95 or Windows NT.

Windows 95—Operating system created as a successor to Windows 3.1.

Windows 95 clients—Computers running Windows 95 in a network environment.

Windows NT clients—Computers running Windows NT in a network environment.

Windows NT Hardware Qualifier Tool (NTHQ.EXE)—A simple tool on the Windows NT CD-ROM that creates a boot disk capable of detecting installed hardware for comparison with the Hardware Compatibility List.

Windows NT Server—The server operating system version of Windows NT, optimized for file-sharing and server applications.

Windows NT Setup—When referring to the tab in the Add/Remove Programs applet, the set of categories presented in Custom setup that allow you to install standard Windows NT components after installation has already occurred.

Windows NT Workstation—The workstation version of Windows NT, optimized for single users.

WinMSD utility—A tool that shows an exhaustive amount of system information, ranging from device driver to memory information; the WinMSD diagnostic utility can be used to print out a detailed summary of the current state of the computer and Windows NT installation.

winnt.exe—The 16-bit version of the Windows NT Setup program, used to install under MS-DOS, Windows 3.x, and Windows 95.

winnt32.exe—The 32-bit version of the Windows NT Setup program, used to upgrade from a previous version of Windows NT.

WINS—Windows Internet Naming Service. A service installed on Windows NT that dynamically registers and records NetBIOS names and the IP addresses associated with them.

wireless—A type of network that doesn't rely on physical network cabling.

wireless bridging—A bridge that uses something such as satellite or radio frequency instead of standard network cabling to connect two segments of a network.

workgroup—A network in which each computer manages its own resources (including user accounts).

workgroup model—The model in which each server within the network maintains its own SAM database for its shared resources.

Workstation service—Windows NT's redirector. (See also *redirector*.)

X.25—A packet-switching network standard best suited for low-speed use. (This is fading from use.)

Appendix B

All About the Exam

The exam incorporates a variety of questions from a question bank intended to determine if you have mastered the subject. Here are some tips to keep in mind as you prepare for your exam:

- Make sure you understand the material thoroughly.
- Go through all of the practice problems. Reread those sections that you were having trouble with.
- Make sure you are comfortable with the style of the scenario questions. These will probably be the most challenging part of the exam.
- Review the exam objectives.

The Microsoft Certification Process

Microsoft has a variety of certifications available for their products. You can find out more about their certifications on the WWW page: `http://www.microsoft.com/train_cert/`.

How to Become a Microsoft Certified Professional (MCP)

Becoming an MCP requires you to pass one operating system exam. The following list shows the names and exam numbers of all the operating systems from which you can choose to get your MCP certification:

- Implementing and Supporting Microsoft Windows 95 #70-064 (formerly #70-063)
- Implementing and Supporting Microsoft Windows NT Workstation 4.0 #70-073
- Implementing and Supporting Microsoft Windows NT Workstation 3.51 #70-042
- Implementing and Supporting Microsoft Windows NT Server 4.0 #70-067
- Implementing and Supporting Microsoft Windows NT Server 3.51 #70-043
- Microsoft Windows for Workgroups 3.11-Desktop #70-048
- Microsoft Windows 3.1 #70-030
- Microsoft Windows Architecture I #70-160
- Microsoft Windows Architecture II #70-161

How to Become a Microsoft Certified Professional—Specialist: Internet (MCP-Specialist: Internet)

Becoming an MCP with a specialist in Internet technology requires you to pass three exams. The following list shows the names and exam numbers of the three exams you must pass in order for you to get your MCP certification:

- Internetworking Microsoft TCP/IP on Microsoft Windows NT 4.0 #70-059
- Implementing and Supporting Microsoft Windows NT Server 4.0 #70-067
- Implementing and Supporting Microsoft Internet Information Server 3.0 and Microsoft Index Server 1.1 #70-077

How to Become a Microsoft Certified Systems Engineer (MCSE)

MCSE candidates need to pass four operating system exams and two elective exams. The MCSE certification path is divided into two tracks: the Windows NT 3.51 track and the Windows NT 4.0 track. The exams included in this software product span the core requirements for the Windows NT 4.0 track.

Table B.1 shows the core requirements (four operating system exams) and the elective courses (two exams) for the Windows NT 3.51 and 4.0 tracks.

Table B.1 MCSE Tracks

Windows NT 3.51 Track Core Requirements
1. Implementing and Supporting Microsoft Windows NT Server 3.51 #70-043
2. Implementing and Supporting Microsoft Windows NT Workstation 3.51 #70-042
3. Networking Essentials #70-058
4. Microsoft Windows 3.1 #70-030
OR Microsoft Windows for Workgroups 3.11 #70-048
OR Implementing and Supporting Microsoft Windows 95 #70-063
OR Implementing and Supporting Microsoft Windows 95 #70-064
Windows NT 4.0 Track Core Requirements
1. Implementing and Supporting Microsoft Windows NT Server 4.0 #70-067
2. Implementing and Supporting Microsoft Windows NT Server 4.0 in the Enterprise #70-068
3. Networking Essentials #70-058
4. Microsoft Windows 3.1 #70-030
OR Microsoft Windows for Workgroups 3.11 #70-048
OR Implementing and Supporting Microsoft Windows 95 #70-063
OR Implementing and Supporting Microsoft Windows 95 #70-064
OR Implementing and Supporting Microsoft Windows NT Workstation 4.0 #70-073

Electives (choose two)

1. Implementing and Supporting Microsoft SNA Server 3.0 #70-013

   OR Implementing and Supporting SNA Server 4.0 #70-085
2. Implementing and Supporting Microsoft Systems Management Server 1.0 #70-014

   OR Implementing and Supporting Microsoft Systems Management Server 1.2 #70-018
3. Microsoft SQL Server 4.2 Database Implementation #70-021

   OR Implementing a Database Design on Microsoft SQL Server 6.5 #70-027
4. Microsoft SQL Server 4.2 Database Administration for Microsoft Windows NT #70-022

   OR System Administration for Microsoft SQL Server 6.5 #70-026
5. Microsoft Mail for PC Networks 3.2-Enterprise #70-037
6. Internetworking Microsoft TCP/IP on Microsoft Windows NT (3.5-3.51) #70-053

   OR Internetworking with Microsoft TCP/IP on Microsoft Windows NT 4.0 #70-059
7. Implementing and Supporting Microsoft Exchange Server 4.0 #70-075

   OR Implementing and Supporting Microsoft Exchange Server 5 #70-076
8. Implementing and Supporting Microsoft Internet Information Server 3.0 and Microsoft Index Server 1.1 #70-077

   OR Implementing and Supporting Microsoft Internet Information Server 4.0 #70-087
9. Implementing and Supporting Microsoft Proxy Server 1.0 #70-078

   OR Implementing and Supporting Microsoft Proxy Server 2.0 #70-088
10. Implementing and Supporting Microsoft Internet Explorer 4.0 by Using the Internet Explorer Resource Kit #70-079

How to Become a Microsoft Certified Solution Developer (MCSD)

MCSD candidates need to pass two core technology exams and two elective exams. Table B.2 shows the required technology exams, plus the elective exams that apply toward obtaining the MCSD.

Table B.2 MCSD Requirements

Core Technology Requirements

1. Microsoft Windows Architecture I #70-160
2. Microsoft Windows Architecture II #70-161

Electives (choose two)

1. Microsoft SQL Server 4.2 Database Implementation #70-021

   OR Implementing a Database Design on Microsoft SQL Server 6.5 #70-027
2. Developing Applications with C++ Using the Microsoft Foundation Class Library #70-024

continues

Table B.2 Continued

Electives (choose two)

3. Microsoft Visual Basic 3.0 for Windows-Application Development #70-050

   OR Programming with Microsoft Visual Basic 4.0 #70-065

   OR Developing Applications with Microsoft Visual Basic 5.0 #70-165
4. Microsoft Access 2.0 for Windows-Application Development #70-051

   OR Microsoft Access for Windows 95 and the Microsoft Access Development Toolkit #70-069
5. Developing Applications with Microsoft Excel 5.0 Using Visual Basic for Applications #70-052
6. Programming in Microsoft Visual FoxPro 3.0 for Windows #70-054
7. Implementing OLE in Microsoft Foundation Class Applications #70-025

Becoming a Microsoft Certified Trainer (MCT)

To understand the requirements and process for becoming a Microsoft Certified Trainer (MCT), you need to obtain the Microsoft Certified Trainer Guide document (MCTGUIDE.DOC) from the following WWW site:

```
http://www.microsoft.com/train_cert/download.htm
```

On this page, click on the hyperlink MCT GUIDE (mctguide.doc) (117k). If your WWW browser can display DOC files (Word for Windows native file format), the MCT Guide displays in the browser window. Otherwise, you need to download it and open it in Word for Windows or Windows 95 WordPad. The MCT Guide explains the four-step process to becoming an MCT. The general steps for the MCT certification are as follows:

1. Complete and mail a Microsoft Certified Trainer application to Microsoft. You must include proof of your skills for presenting instructional material. The options for doing so are described in the MCT Guide.
2. Obtain and study the Microsoft Trainer Kit for the Microsoft Official Curricula (MOC) course(s) for which you want to be certified. Microsoft Trainer Kits can be ordered by calling 800-688-0496 in North America. Other regions should review the MCT Guide for information on how to order a Trainer Kit.
3. Pass the Microsoft certification exam for the product for which you want to be certified to teach.
4. Attend the Microsoft Official Curriculum (MOC) course for the course for which you want to be certified. This is done so you can understand how the course is structured, how labs are completed, and how the course flows.

You should use the preceding steps as a general overview of the MCT certification process. The actual steps you need to take are described in detail in the MCTGUIDE.DOC file on the WWW site mentioned earlier. Do not misconstrue the preceding steps as the actual process you need to take.

If you are interested in becoming an MCT, you can receive more information by visiting the Microsoft Certified Training (MCT) WWW site at `http://www.microsoft.com/train_cert/mctint.htm`; or call 800-688-0496.

Registering and Taking the Exam

When you are ready to schedule your exam, contact the Sylvan Prometric test Registration Center that will be most convenient for you from the following table:

Sylvan Prometric Test Registration Centers

Country	Telephone Number
Australia	1-800-808-657
Austria	0660-8582
Belgium	0800-1-7414
Canada	800-755-3926
China	10800-3538
France	1-4289-8749
Germany	0130-83-9708
Guam	001-61-800-277583
Hong Kong	800-6375
Indonesia	001-800-61571
Ireland	1-800-626-104
Italy	1-6787-8441
Japan	0120-347737
Korea	007-8611-3095
Malaysia	800-2122
Netherlands	06-022-7584
New Zealand	0800-044-1603
Philippines	1-800-1-611-0126
Puerto Rico	800-755-3926
Singapore	800-616-1120
Switzerland	155-6966
Taiwan	008-061-1142
Thailand	001-800-611-2283
UK	0800-592-873

continues

Sylvan Prometric Test Registration Centers Continued

Country	Telephone Number
United States	800-755-3926
Vietnam	61-2-9414-3666

If this is your first time registering for a Sylvan Prometric exam, Sylvan will assign you an identification number. They will ask to use your Social Security or Social Insurance number as your identification number, which works well for most people because it's relatively easy for them to remember. You also have the option of having them assign you a Sylvan ID number if you prefer not to disclose your private information.

If this is not your first exam, be prepared to give Sylvan your identification number. It's very important that you use the same identification number for all of your tests—if you don't, the exams won't be credited to your certification appropriately. You have to provide Sylvan Prometric with the following additional information: mailing address and phone number, e-mail address, organization or company name, and method of payment (credit card number or check).

Sylvan requires that you pay in advance. Microsoft certification exam prices are related to the currency exchange rates between countries. Exams are U.S. $100, but certification exam prices are subject to change, and in some countries, additional taxes might apply. Please verify the price with your local Sylvan Registration Center when registering. You can generally schedule exams up to six weeks in advance, or as late as the day before.

You can always cancel or reschedule your exam if you contact Sylvan Prometric at least two working days before the exam, or by Friday if your test is scheduled on Monday. If you cancel, exams must be taken within one year of payment.

Same-day registration is available in some locations if space is available. You must register at least 30 minutes before test time. The day of the test, plan to arrive a few minutes early so that you can sign in and begin on time. You will be provided with something to write notes to yourself on during the test, but you are not allowed to take these notes with you after the test.

You are not allowed to take in books, notes, a pager, or anything else that might contain answers to any of the questions.

Hints and Tips for Doing Your Best on the Tests

The Microsoft Certification exams are all between 75 and 90 minutes long. The more familiar you are with the test material and the actual test's style, the easier it is for you to concentrate on the questions during the exam.

You can divide your time between the questions however you like. There are 55 questions on this exam. If there are any questions you don't know the answers to, mark them to come back to later if you have time. You will have 75 minutes for the actual exam, but you will be scheduled for 90 minutes so that you can spend up to 15 minutes on a practice pre-test (on unrelated subjects) to get familiar with how the test engine works. Make sure that you think about whether you want to try out the practice test before you sit down to take it—some people find that the additional familiarity helps them, but others find that it increases their stress level.

Things to Watch For

Make sure that you read each question and all of its possible answers thoroughly. This is especially important for the scenario questions. Many people lose points because they select the first answer that looks right to them when there is a better answer following on their screens.

After you've made sure that you understand the question, eliminate those answers you know to be wrong. If you still have two or three choices, consider which of them would be the *best* answer and select it.

Marking Answers for Return

In the event that you aren't quite sure of an answer, you have the option of marking it by selecting a box in the upper-left and returning to the question at the end when you are given the option of reviewing your answers. Pay particular attention to related questions you find later in the test in case you can learn enough from them to figure out the answer to the question you were unsure of before.

If you pay close attention, you will probably find that some of the other questions help to clarify questions of which you were uncertain. You should practice marking questions during your CD-ROM practice exams because doing so may be very helpful during the certification exam.

Attaching Notes to Test Questions

When you finish a Microsoft exam, you are allowed to enter comments on the individual questions as well as on the entire test. This feature enables you to give the team that reviews Microsoft exams some feedback. If you find a question that is poorly worded or seems ambiguous, this is the place to let them know about it.

REGISTRATION CARD

MCSE TestPrep Core Exams

Name ______________________________ Title ______________________

Company ____________________________ Type of business ____________

Address ____

City/State/ZIP ____

Have you used these types of books before? ☐ yes ☐ no

If yes, which ones? ____

____

How many computer books do you purchase each year? ☐ 1–5 ☐ 6 or more

How did you learn about this book? _____________________________

Where did you purchase this book? ______________________________

Which applications do you currently use? ________________________

____

Which computer magazines do you subscribe to? ___________________

____

What trade shows do you attend? ________________________________

____

Comments: ____

____

____

Would you like to be placed on our preferred mailing list? ☐ yes ☐ no

☐ **I would like to see my name in print!** You may use my name and quote me in future New Riders products and promotions. My daytime phone number is: ______________________

New Riders Publishing 201 West 103rd Street ◆ Indianapolis, Indiana 46290 USA

Fax to **317-817-7448**

Fold Here

NO POSTAGE
NECESSARY
IF MAILED
IN THE
UNITED STATES

BUSINESS REPLY MAIL

FIRST-CLASS MAIL PERMIT NO. 9918 INDIANAPOLIS IN

POSTAGE WILL BE PAID BY THE ADDRESSEE

NEW RIDERS PUBLISHING
201 W 103RD ST
INDIANAPOLIS IN 46290-9058